2019 Medicare Handbook

Judith A. Stein and Alfred J. Chiplin, Jr., Editors-in-Chief*

Challenging improper denials of Medicare for necessary health services remains essential to obtaining coverage. This is particularly important in light of the settlement agreement in *Jimmo v. Sebelius* and the resulting Medicare policy changes clarifying that improvement is not a prerequisite for coverage for most nursing and therapy services. The *2019 Medicare Handbook* continues to provide key coverage information and practical advocacy tips for all care settings with new and updated information. As with previous editions, the *2019 Medicare Handbook* provides ready access to relevant Medicare law and regulations, case law developments, agency policies, and other program-implementing materials. Armed with this information, beneficiary advocates can formulate effective strategies to secure necessary Medicare-covered services.

2019 EDITION HIGHLIGHTS

The future of the Affordable Care Act (ACA), Medicaid, and the expansion of Medicare Advantage have been an ongoing focus as this *Handbook* was updated, particularly in matters concerning quality of care, program transitions, and cost-containment. The integrity of the Medicare program as a unified public program is also in play, even as we strive to address the health care needs of an increasingly diverse Medicare population, many of whom are dually eligible for Medicare and Medicaid.

We also note a surge in problems related to the interaction of the Medicare program and the Consolidated Omnibus Budget Reconciliation Act of 1985, commonly referred to as COBRA, as more people continue to work beyond age 65. COBRA extends the opportunity to stay on one's employer's health plan and pay the insurance premiums privately for a period of time, but only if the employer is of a certain size and if the employer offers health insurance to its active employees and their families. Because COBRA coverage is not considered coverage due to current employment, an individual is not entitled to a special enrollment period (SEP) for Medicare when COBRA coverage ends. In addition, the former employee is not permitted to enroll in Medicare until the next general enrollment period, which runs January through March of the year, with coverage beginning July 1.

---

* Mr. Chiplin passed away on July 10, 2017.

Wolters Kluwer

The *2019 Medicare Handbook* continues the authors' efforts to help advocates contest limited oversight of and access to coverage under private Medicare Advantage (MA) plans (Part C). Other developments discussed in the *2019 Medicare Handbook* include:

- Discussion of the Bipartisan Budget Act of 2018 and its impact on the Medicare home health benefit.
- Analysis of the Patient-Driven Payment Model, the new prospective payment system.
- Discussion of the expansion of Medicare Advantage and its complex changes and choices.
- The Medicare home health and hospice benefits, and the increasing problems accessing necessary Medicare-covered home care.
- Hospital outpatient "observation status" as opposed to inpatient admission and the impact on accessing Medicare coverage for necessary skilled nursing facility care.
- Appropriate coverage and services for persons with long-term and chronic conditions.

12/18

For questions concerning this shipment, billing, or other customer service matters, call our Customer Service Department at 1-800-234-1660.

For toll-free ordering, please call 1-800-638-8437.

2019 MEDICARE HANDBOOK

Center for Medicare Advocacy

Editors-in-Chief

Judith A. Stein, Esq.

and

Alfred J. Chiplin, Jr., Esq.

Contributing Authors

Mary A. Ashkar

Alfred J. Chiplin, Jr.

Toby S. Edelman

Paul R. Grabowski

Kathleen Holt

Kata M. Kertesz

Wey-Wey Kwok

David A. Lipschutz

Judith A. Stein

Wolters Kluwer

Published by Wolters Kluwer in New York.

Wolters Kluwer Legal & Regulatory U.S. serves customers worldwide with CCH, Aspen Publishers and Kluwer Law International products.

Printed in the United States of America

1 2 3 4 5 6 7 8 9 0

ISBN 978-1-5438-0045-6

ISSN 1530-8979

SUSTAINABLE FORESTRY INITIATIVE Certified Sourcing
www.sfiprogram.org
SFI-00756

About Wolters Kluwer Legal & Regulatory U.S.

Wolters Kluwer Legal & Regulatory U.S. delivers expert content and solutions in the areas of law, corporate compliance, health compliance, reimbursement, and legal education. Its practical solutions help customers successfully navigate the demands of a changing environment to drive their daily activities, enhance decision quality and inspire confident outcomes.

Serving customers worldwide, its legal and regulatory portfolio includes products under the Aspen Publishers, CCH Incorporated, Kluwer Law International, ftwilliam.com and MediRegs names. They are regarded as exceptional and trusted resources for general legal and practice-specific knowledge, compliance and risk management, dynamic workflow solutions, and expert commentary.

WOLTERS KLUWER SUPPLEMENT NOTICE

This product is updated on a periodic basis with supplements and/or new editions to reflect important changes in the subject matter.

If you would like information about enrolling this product in the update service, or wish to receive updates billed separately with a 30-day examination review, please contact our Customer Service Department at 1-800-234-1660 or email us at: *customer.service@wolterskluwer.com*. You can also contact us at:

Wolters Kluwer
Distribution Center
7201 McKinney Circle
Frederick, MD 21704

Important Contact Information

- To order any title, go to *www.WoltersKluwerLR.com* or call 1-800-638-8437.
- To reinstate your manual update service, call 1-800-638-8437.
- To contact Customer Service, e-mail *customer.service@wolterskluwer.com*, call 1-800-234-1660, fax 1-800-901-9075, or mail correspondence to: Order Department—Wolters Kluwer, PO Box 990, Frederick, MD 21705.
- To review your account history or pay an invoice online, visit *www.WoltersKluwerLR.com/payinvoices.*

Wolters Kluwer

CONTENTS

A complete table of contents for each chapter is included at the beginning of the chapter.

Chapter 2
HOSPITAL COVERAGE

Chapter 3
SKILLED NURSING FACILITY COVERAGE

Chapter 4
HOME HEALTH COVERAGE

Chapter 5
HOSPICE COVERAGE

PREFACE

While the Medicare program continues to provide reliable, defined health care benefits for most older and disabled people, improper denials of coverage continue with surprising frequency, especially for services needed by people with long-term and chronic conditions. Challenges to improper denials remain essential to ensure fair access to coverage and necessary care—for individual beneficiaries, for all those who rely on Medicare for their health insurance coverage, and for the integrity of the Medicare program itself. The *2019 Medicare Handbook* serves as a foundation for this work.

Intended as a guide for attorneys and other advocates, the *Medicare Handbook* provides comprehensive, up-to-date information about Medicare coverage and appeals. Its goal is to provide important information and assist advocates with practical tips. The *2019 Medicare Handbook* continues this work and pays particular attention to the issues that face Medicare beneficiaries with chronic conditions.

Knowledgeable advocates, working in concert with physicians and other health care providers, can help ensure access to necessary Medicare-covered services. This is one of the reasons a standard set of benefits and coverage rules is so important, particularly as the original Medicare program has been fragmented into numerous private plan options. Armed with the *Handbook's* information, practical tools, and primary source materials, attorneys and advocates will be better able to protect the rights of Medicare beneficiaries.

The Editor also hopes the *2019 Medicare Handbook* will continue to illuminate the importance of preserving Medicare as a broad and universal health insurance program.

Judith A. Stein
Executive Director/Attorney
Center for Medicare Advocacy
November 2018

ABOUT THE CENTER FOR MEDICARE ADVOCACY

The Center for Medicare Advocacy (the Center), is a national, nonprofit, nonpartisan law organization. The Center provides education, advocacy, and analysis to help older people and people with disabilities obtain Medicare and quality health care. Established in 1986, the Center focuses on the needs of Medicare beneficiaries, people with chronic conditions, and those in need of long-term care. Our work includes writing, consulting, and legal assistance regarding issues of importance to Medicare beneficiaries and their families nationwide.

The Center's primary offices are in Connecticut and Washington, D.C., with additional attorneys in Massachusetts, New Jersey, and California. The Center is staffed by attorneys, a nurse, legal assistants, and information management specialists, and includes staff members who are fluent in Spanish. In addition, a translation service is available to help people in other languages. We also have TDD equipment to assist people who are deaf. Substantive material and examples of the Center's publications, products, and services are available upon request and on Center's website at *www.MedicareAdvocacy.org*.

The Center's policy work (and this *Medicare Handbook*) are driven by the concerns and stories of the real people with whom we speak daily. Annually, we respond to approximately 7,000 telephone and email inquiries and appeal thousands of Medicare denials. Center staff write and speak extensively about Medicare and related topics; produce a wide array of electronic and hard copy periodicals and educational materials; advocate in administrative and legislative forums; pursue class action litigation on behalf of individuals and groups improperly denied access to Medicare and health care; provide webinars, seminars, and support nationally, including serving as the primary training source for Connecticut's State Health Insurance and Assistance Program (SHIP, known as CHOICES in Connecticut).

When necessary, the Center pursues strategic litigation to ensure fair access to coverage, health care, and due process for Medicare beneficiaries. In October 2012, the Center and U.S. Centers for Medicare & Medicaid Services (CMS) settled the national class action law suit, *Jimmo v. Sebelius*, which promises to remove the improvement standard as a barrier to Medicare coverage. *Jimmo* clarifies that coverage is available for skilled nursing and therapy to maintain a patients' condition.

The organization sponsors an annual conference in Washington, D.C., the *National Voices of Medicare Summit and Senator Jay Rockefeller Lecture*. This event connects advocates, scholars, and policy-makers to advance the interests of older and disabled people, their families, and caregivers.

ACKNOWLEDGMENTS

The Editor gratefully acknowledges the staff members of the Center for Medicare Advocacy, for their many contributions to the development and maintenance of this book. In particular, she thanks Kata Kertesz and Toby Edelman for their patient and varied supervision of this edition of the *Handbook*. She also thanks writers of significant portions of earlier versions of this *Handbook*: Alfred J. Chiplin, Jr., Brad Plebani, Patricia Nemore, Vicki Gottlich, Sally Hart, Mary T. Bethelot, Margaret Murphy, and Pam Meliso.

The Center for Medicare Advocacy also recognizes and thanks Legal Counsel for the Elderly, Inc., of AARP, which published the original version of this book, then the *Medicare Practice Manual,* written in 1990 by the Center for Medicare Advocacy. It was the genesis of the current publication. Legal Counsel for the Elderly graciously released its copyright control over the *Medicare Practice Manual* and encouraged the Center for Medicare Advocacy to update and expand the earlier material as the Medicare program evolves.

Finally, she acknowledges Alfred J. Chiplin, Jr., who was the lead coordinator of this project for the Center for Medicare Advocacy. Mr. Chiplin led this project for over a decade and kept everyone on track and reasonably on time with his special blend of intelligence, decency, and good humor. He is dearly missed.

The Editor
November 2018

CHAPTER 1

AN INTRODUCTION TO MEDICARE COVERAGE AND APPEALS

§ 1.01 HISTORY AND OVERVIEW

Medicare is the country's flagship national health insurance program for older people and people with disabilities. Individuals entitled to Social Security retirement benefits who are 65 years of age or older and individuals entitled to Social Security disability benefits for not less than 24 months are eligible to participate in Medicare. Individuals entitled to Railroad Retirement benefits or Railroad Retirement disability benefits and individuals with end-stage renal disease (ESRD) and amyotrophic lateral sclerosis (ALS, also known as Lou Gehrig's disease), are also entitled to participate.[1] In addition, individuals who are not otherwise eligible for Medicare, but who are over age 65, can purchase coverage by paying a monthly premium.[2] Since January 1, 1983, most federal employees can count their government work toward eligibility for the Medicare hospital insurance program, Medicare Part A.[3]

Medicare is a health insurance program, based on a private health insurance model. Passed in 1965 as Title 18 of the Social Security Act,[4] the program was intended to pay some of the cost of some health care in order to ensure access to a basic level of health care for older people.[5] Medicare requires deductibles and copayments and pays only a portion of the cost of certain services for certain patients. Claims are submitted to an insurance company or other entity that acts as an agent for the federal government for the approval of coverage and payment of claims for health care services.[6]

---

[1] 42 U.S.C. § 1395c. *See* 42 C.F.R. §§ 406.12 and 406.13, regarding qualifying due to disability or end-stage renal disease (ESRD). Persons with ALS can qualify for Medicare without the 24-month waiting period, effective July 1, 2001. *See* the Benefits Improvement and Protection Act (BIPA), Pub. L. No. 106-554 (Dec. 21, 2000), §§ 115.

[2] 42 U.S.C. § 1395i-2. The individual must be a U.S. citizen or a permanent resident for five years.

[3] 42 U.S.C. § 426(a)(2)(c), (b)(2)(c); 42 C.F.R. § 406.15.

[4] 42 U.S.C. §§ 1395 *et seq., available at* https://www.ssa.gov/OP_Home/ssact/title18/1800.htm (site visited Aug. 6, 2018); *see also* Center for Medicare Advocacy (CMA), "Basic Introduction to Medicare," *available at* http://www.medicareadvocacy.org/medicare-info/medicare-basics-2/ (site visited Aug. 6, 2018).

[5] Whitman v. Weinberger, 382 F. Supp. 256, 262 (E.D. Va. 1974). Coverage for certain individuals deemed permanently disabled for 24 months was added in 1972. Social Security Amendments of 1972, Pub. L. No. 92-603 (Oct. 30, 1972), § 201(a). Medicare celebrated its 50th anniversary in 2015. *See* CMS, "Medicare and Medicaid 50th Anniversary Count Down," (June 10, 2015), *available at* https://www.cms.gov/newsroom/press-releases/medicare-and-medicaid-50th-anniversary-count-down (site visited Aug. 6, 2018).

[6] For beneficiaries in traditional Medicare, doctors and suppliers are required by law to file Medicare claims for covered services and supplies a beneficiary receives. *See* CMS, "How Do I File a Claim?" *available at* https://www.medicare.gov/claims-and-appeals/file-a-claim/file-a-claim.html (site visited Aug. 6, 2018). For information on filing a claim, *see* CMS, "Patient's Request for Medical Payment Form," *available at* http://www.medicare.gov/claims-and-appeals/file-a-claim/file-a-

Unlike Medicaid, Title 19 of the Social Security Act,[7] neither Medicare eligibility nor coverage is predicated on the income or assets of the beneficiary.[8] Medicaid is a shared state-federal program, paid in part by both entities and administered by state agencies with federal oversight. Medicare, on the other hand, is entirely a federal program. Its benefits are paid from entirely federal sources. Both programs are overseen by the Centers for Medicare & Medicaid Services (CMS), formerly known as the Health Care Financing Administration (HCFA),[9] a component of the United States Department of Health and Human Services (HHS).

Because Medicare is a national program, Medicare procedures and qualifying criteria should not vary significantly from state to state. When they do, advocates should be certain that there are valid reasons for the discrepancies and assure that such discrepancies do not inappropriately result in a denial of coverage for necessary services.

[A] The Medicare Program in Transition

Over the past decades, Congress has added new features and limitations to the Medicare program. The Balanced Budget Act of 1997 (BBA '97)[10] created Medicare Part C, then known as the Medicare+Choice program and now known as Medicare Advantage (MA).[11] Medicare Part C added a variety of managed care plans, including Health Maintenance Organizations (HMOs) and other private delivery options for Medicare-covered services, while retaining the original (or traditional) Medicare program.

Medicare Part C authorizes private Medicare plans, including HMOs, Provider Service Organizations (PSOs), Special Needs Plans (SNPs), and both local and regional Preferred Provider Organizations (PPOs), as options for

claim.html (site visited Aug. 6, 2018). Note that beneficiaries in a Medicare Advantage Plan (Part C) do not have to file claims because Medicare pays these private insurance companies a set amount each month.

[7] 42 U.S.C. §§ 1396 *et seq.*, *available at* https://www.gpo.gov/fdsys/pkg/USCODE-2011-title42/pdf/USCODE-2011-title42-chap7-subchapXIX-sec1396a.pdf (site visited Aug. 6, 2018).

[8] Starting in January 2007, however, individuals and couples with incomes over $85,000 for individuals and $170,000 for couples pay more for the Part B premium and, starting in January 2011, more for the Part D premium. Additionally, individuals with incomes *below* a certain threshold may receive a subsidy to help pay premiums and cost-sharing under Part D. *See* **Chapter 6** of this Handbook for Part B details and **Chapter 11** for Part D details.

[9] *See* Federal Register, "Health Care Finance Administration," *available at* https://www.federalregister.gov/agencies/health-care-finance-administration (site visited Aug. 6, 2018).

[10] The Balanced Budget Act of 1997 (BBA '97), Pub. L. No. 105-33 (Aug. 5, 1997).

[11] Medicare Part C, *see* BBA '97 § 4001 (enacting Social Security Act §§ 1851–1859). As discussed later, Medicare+Choice was renamed "Medicare Advantage" (MA) in December 2003. *See* the Medicare Prescription Drug, Improvement, and Modernization Act of 2003 (MMA), Pub. L. No. 108-173 (Dec. 8, 2003), § 201, *available at* https://www.congress.gov/bill/108th-congress/house-bill/1 (site visited Aug. 6, 2018).

receiving coverage. Other options include Medical Savings Accounts (MSAs),[12] Health Savings Accounts (HSAs) under the Internal Revenue Code (I.R.C.),[13] Private Fee-for-Service (PFFS) plans,[14] and Private Religious-Fraternal Order plans.[15] While these options were allowed commencing January 1999, in most areas of the country only managed care plans, including HMOs and PPOs, are available for enrollment.

BBA '97 also created, outside the MA program, an option for "private contracts between physicians and their Medicare patients for the receipt of Medicare-covered services for which no Medicare payment will be made." Any physicians entering into such contracts must agree not to accept Medicare reimbursement for any Medicare-covered service for two years.[16]

In December 2000, Congress passed legislation that made significant adjustments to the Medicare program through the Medicare, Medicaid, and SCHIP Benefits Improvement & Protection Act of 2000 (BIPA),[17] which returned some of the funds to providers and HMOs that were reduced by BBA '97 and made minor enhancements for beneficiaries. More changes occurred at the end of 2003 with the enactment of the Medicare Prescription Drug, Improvement, and Modernization Act of 2003 (MMA),[18] including providing Medicare beneficiaries with assistance to pay for prescription drugs through a new Medicare Part D. The law also changed the name of private plans offered under Medicare Part C, from "Medicare+Choice" (M+C) to "Medicare Advantage (MA)."

The 2003 MMA also began a major restructuring of the Medicare program, relying heavily on private insurance to deliver benefits through increased payments to Part C plans and increased beneficiary cost-sharing responsibilities. The Medicare Improvements for Patients and Providers Act of 2008 (MIPPA),[19] primarily designed to address problems with the way Medicare pays physicians, also made modest improvements for beneficiaries, including reducing the cost-sharing for mental health services and increasing the asset limits for eligibility for programs that assist with Part B premiums and cost-sharing.

---

[12] MSA plans were made available for the first time in January 2006.

[13] Medicare Prescription Drug, Improvement, and Modernization Act of 2003 (MMA), Pub. L. No. 108-173 (Dec. 8, 2003), § 1201 (amending Internal Revenue Code [I.R.C.] of 1986 by redesignating § 223 as § 224 and by inserting new I.R.C. § 223 after § 222).

[14] *See* CMS, "Private Fee-for-Service Plans," *available at* http://www.cms.gov/Medicare/Health-Plans/PrivateFeeforServicePlans/index.html (site visited Aug. 6, 2018).

[15] *See* CMS, Medicare Managed Care (MMC) Manual, Ch. 1, *available at* https://www.cms.gov/Regulations-and-Guidance/Guidance/Manuals/downloads/mc86c01.pdf (site visited Aug. 6, 2018).

[16] BBA '97 § 4507 (amending § 1802 of the Social Security Act, 42 U.S.C. § 1395a(b)(3)(B)(ii)). *See also* **§ 6.04[E]** of this Handbook.

[17] Pub. L. No. 106-554 (Dec. 21, 2000).

[18] Pub. L. No. 108-173 (Dec. 8, 2003).

[19] Pub. L. No. 110-275 (July 15, 2008). *See also* CMA, "Weekly Alerts," (describing MIPPA provisions of importance to beneficiaries and their advocates), *available at* www.medicareadvocacy.org (site visited Aug. 6, 2018).

The Patient Protection and Affordable Care Act of 2010 (PPACA)[20] and the Health Care and Education Reconciliation Act of 2010 (HCERA),[21] together known as the Affordable Care Act (ACA, also referred to as Obamacare), contain significant changes to the Medicare program, particularly with regard to reimbursement for Medicare Advantage plans and to providers. The ACA also provides for system delivery mechanisms and demonstrations and pilot projects to improve coordination of care; other initiatives to improve quality of care; and initiatives to reduce unnecessary hospital readmissions. The law adds coverage for an annual wellness visit, eliminates cost-sharing for most preventive services, adds some consumer protections to Medicare Advantage, and phases out the Part D coverage gap for prescription drugs known as the "Donut Hole."[22]

The Medicare Access and CHIP Reauthorization Act of 2015 (MACRA) made several changes to the Medicare program, including revamping the way the Medicare pays physicians, further means testing premiums for higher income beneficiaries, and changes to those who will be eligible for certain Medigap policies starting in 2020.[23] The 21st Century Cures Act, signed into law in December 2016, made further changes, including removing the barrier for people with ESRD to enroll in MA plans, beginning in 2021, and, effective 2019, reinstates Medicare Part C and D enrollment periods as they existed prior to the ACA.[24] The Bipartisan Budget Act of 2018 (BBA '18) made additional changes, including removing the annual dollar cap on outpatient therapy, and permanently fixing restrictions in the law that limited Medicare coverage and access for Speech Generating Devices (SGDs) – which are a crucial means of communicating for people with ALS and other degenerative diseases.[25]

[B] A Historical Perspective

BBA '97, BIPA, MMA, MIPPA, BBA'18 and the Affordable Care Act are not the only alterations of the Medicare program.[26] Since its enactment in 1965, Medicare has been revised several times by Congress, often to increase coverage.

---

[20] Pub. L. No. 111-148, 111th Congress (Mar. 23, 2010), *available at* http://www.gpo.gov/fdsys/pkg/PLAW-111publ148/pdf/PLAW-111publ148.pdf (site visited Aug. 6, 2018). The ACA is also known as Obamacare.

[21] Pub. L. No. 111-152, 111th Congress (Mar. 30, 2010), *available at* http://www.gpo.gov/fdsys/pkg/PLAW-111publ152/pdf/PLAW-111publ152.pdf (site visited Aug. 6, 2018).

[22] *See* CMS, "Costs in the Coverage Gap," *available at* https://www.medicare.gov/part-d/costs/coverage-gap/part-d-coverage-gap.html (site visited Aug. 6, 2018).

[23] MACRA.

[24] The 21st Century Cures Act.

[25] Balanced Budget Act of 2018 (BBA '18), Pub. L. No. 115-123 (Feb. 9, 2018), *available at* https://www.congress.gov/bill/115th-congress/house-bill/1892/text (site visited Aug. 6, 2018).

[26] In 2017, Congress attempted to repeal the ACA, multiple times. This would have had significant consequences for Medicare and Medicaid. As of the time this Handbook went to print, ACA was still the law of the land.

In 1972, for example, coverage was extended to people with disabilities.[27] Also in 1972, coverage was extended to skilled nursing facility (SNF) patients needing skilled rehabilitation rather than only to those in need of skilled nursing.[28] In 1980, Congress removed the requirement that home health patients have a prior hospitalization in order to receive Medicare home health coverage; Congress also removed the 100-visit limitation on home health coverage.[29] Despite this apparent congressional intent to increase coverage, Medicare coverage criteria are often strictly interpreted by those who administer the program, with denials for many types of care being the norm rather than the exception.

A significant exception to the movement by Congress to enlarge Medicare coverage occurred in 1989, with the repeal of the Medicare Catastrophic Coverage Act of 1988 (MCCA).[30] Signed into law in July 1988, MCCA was the most significant revision and enhancement of the Medicare program since its inception. The law increased the amount of coverage available in all care settings, established some limits on beneficiary cost-sharing responsibilities, and added new benefits. The law also altered the manner in which Medicare was financed by looking only to those eligible for the program to pay for the new benefits. MCCA increased the monthly Part B premium and required a payment of a set amount for every $150 of tax liability, not to exceed a certain limit each year. This payment, which quickly became known as the Medicare surtax, was mandatory for all those eligible for Medicare, even if they did not participate in the program or did not need the new benefits. This payment mechanism proved to be the death knell of MCCA; almost all the Medicare components of MCCA were repealed in December 1989.[31]

As discussed above, Congress altered the Medicare program again in the BBA '97. This Act created a variety of private options for receiving Medicare

---

[27] Social Security Amendments of 1972 § 201(a).

[28] Social Security Amendments of 1972 § 238(a), Social Security Act § 1814, 42 U.S.C. § 1395f, *available at* https://www.law.cornell.edu/uscode/text/42/1395f (site visited Aug. 6, 2018).

[29] Omnibus Budget Reconciliation Act of 1980 (OBRA '80), Pub. L. No. 96-499 (Dec. 5, 1980), § 930(b), (g); 94 Stat. 2599, 2631 (1980). Note that BBA '97 § 4611 established a prior institutionalization requirement for payment of home health services and a 100-visit limit on post-institutional home health services for payment under Part A for persons entitled to benefits under Parts A and B. Other home health care for these individuals is paid under Part B. See discussion of the Medicare home health benefit at **§ 1.05[A][3]** of this Handbook. For a discussion of plan costs, *see also* Kaiser Family Foundation, "How ACA Marketplace Premiums Measure Up to Expectations," (Aug. 1, 2016), *available at* http://kff.org/health-reform/perspective/how-aca-marketplace-premiums-measure-up-to-expectations/ (site visited Aug. 6, 2018).

[30] Pub. L. No. 100-360 (July 1, 1988).

[31] Medicare Catastrophic Coverage Repeal Act of 1989, Pub. L. No. 101-234 (Dec. 13, 1989). Note that the Qualified Medicare Beneficiary program and the Medicaid spousal impoverishment provisions were not repealed.

coverage. It also made other significant changes, which have had the effect of limiting some payments and services.[32]

In 2003, the MMA greatly expanded the role of private health insurance providers in Medicare.[33] For example, prescription drug benefits under Part D are available only through private insurance companies and not through Medicare itself.[34] In an effort to increase enrollment in managed care and other private insurance plans, Congress also created new private options under Part C. Congress also further increased funding to private plans, paying them an average of 14 percent more per enrollee than Medicare would pay if the enrollee had remained in the traditional program. In addition, in the MMA, Congress changed the way actuaries calculate the solvency of the Medicare program, which raised concerns about the security of Medicare and the possibility of benefit reductions and increased cost-sharing in future years.

The Affordable Care Act (ACA) addressed many of the payment and solvency issues created in 2003 by the MMA. The health care reform law changes the payment structure for private Medicare Advantage plans to reduce the overpayments and create greater payment equity with the traditional Medicare program. These and other changes actually increased the number of years that the Medicare Part A trust fund is projected to remain solvent by about 10 years. Instead of changing the way that actuaries calculate Medicare solvency, however, the Affordable Care Act created a new entity, the Independent Payment Advisory Board (IPAB), to make recommendations to limit cost growth in Medicare beginning in 2014. Spending levels required to trigger IPAB recommendations were not met, however, before IPAB was repealed by the Bipartisan Budget Act of 2018.[35]

§ 1.02 FINANCING

Part A of the Medicare program is financed largely through federal payroll taxes paid by employers and employees into Social Security's Federal Hospital Insurance Trust Fund. Parts B and D are financed by monthly premiums paid by Medicare beneficiaries and by general revenues from the federal government. In

---

[32] *See* BBA '97 § 4611 *et seq.* (amending Social Security Act § 1812, 42 U.S.C. §§ 1395d *et seq.*) *See also* BBA '97 home health care discussion at **§ 1.05[A][3]** of this Handbook.

[33] *See* CMS, "Health Plans - General Information," *available at* http://www.cms.gov/Medicare/Health-Plans/HealthPlansGenInfo/index.html (site visited Aug. 6, 2018).

[34] *See* Kaiser Family Foundation, "The Medicare Part D Prescription Drug Benefit," (Oct. 2, 2017) *available at* http://kff.org/medicare/fact-sheet/the-medicare-prescription-drug-benefit-fact-sheet/ (site visited Aug. 6, 2018).

[35] Section 52001 of the BBA '2018.

addition, Medicare beneficiaries share the cost of the program through copayments and deductibles that are required for many of the services covered under Parts A, B, and D.[36]

Medicare beneficiaries also share in the costs of the Medicare Advantage program (Medicare Part C). In these plans the beneficiary's cost-sharing may be modest for some services; however, cost-sharing may exceed that of traditional Medicare for other, more expensive services.[37] The beneficiary share is permitted to increase under the law as long as overall the increases do not exceed the actuarial value of the cost-sharing that would be applicable, on average, to individuals who are in traditional Medicare.[38] Since January 2011, however, MA plans cannot impose cost-sharing for chemotherapy administration services, renal dialysis services, and skilled nursing care services that exceed the cost-sharing for those services under traditional Medicare.[39]

§ 1.03 ADMINISTRATION

The Medicare program is administered by CMS, under the direction of the Secretary of HHS. It has 10 regional offices throughout the country that both oversee certain program operations in their areas and serve as program-wide focal points for certain "consortia" or business lines of agency oversight.[40] CMS contracts with private organizations, usually insurance companies, to review claims and make payments. These entities were known as fiscal intermediaries for Part A hospital, SNF, home health, and hospice cases and as carriers for all Part B cases, but they are now all known as Medicare Administrative Contractors (MACs), most of which process claims under *both* Part A and Part B.[41] Quality Improvement Organizations (QIOs), are responsible for "quality oversight in all traditional Medicare settings, provider-requested higher-weighed DRG [diagnosis-related group] reviews, EMTALA [Emergency Medical Treatment and Active Labor Act] reviews, provider education regarding quality of care issues, and expedited determinations."[42]

---

[36] *See, e.g.*, Kaiser Family Foundation, "The Facts on Medicare Spending and Financing" (June 22, 2018), *available at* http://www.kff.org/medicare/issue-brief/the-facts-on-medicare-spending-and-financing/ (site visited Aug. 6, 2018).

[37] *See* "Medicare Advantage Fact Sheet," (Oct. 17, 2017), *available at* http://kff.org/medicare/fact-sheet/medicare-advantage-fact-sheet/ (site visited Aug. 6, 2018).

[38] 42 U.S.C. § 1395w-24(e).

[39] ACA § 3203; Health Care and Education Reconciliation Act (HCERA) § 1102.

[40] *See* CMS, "CMS Consortia," *available at* https://www.cms.gov/About-CMS/Agency-Information/Consortia/index.html (site visited Aug. 6, 2018).

[41] *See* CMS, "Medicare Administrative Contractors," *available at* http://www.cms.gov/Medicare/Medicare-Contracting/Medicare-Administrative-Contractors/MedicareAdministrativeContractors.html (site visited Aug. 6, 2018).

[42] CMS, "Inpatient Prospective Payment System Hospital and Long-Term Care Hospital Review and Measurement Fact Sheet," *available at* www.cms.hhs.gov/AcuteInpatientPPS/downloads/Inpa

In 2012, CMS issued Transmittal 17, which revised and created new procedures for the review of quality of care concerns[43] by QIOs.[44] The new procedures apply to QIO review of the quality of services "among different cases and settings

---

tientReviewFactSheet.pdf (site visited Aug. 6, 2018). For a full description of the QIO function, *see* Social Security Act, § 1154(a), 42 U.S.C. § 1320c-3. The language of § 1154(a)(1) gives the Secretary broad authority to limit or expand QIO functions by contract.

[43] For purposes of Transmittal 17, quality of care concerns relate to a range of matters from how a beneficiary is or was treated by provider staff, whether the beneficiary is receiving or received the treatment or services requested or expected, and/or whether the services in question are or were provided in a way that meets accepted standards of care. *See* 42 U.S.C § 1320c-3. Matters of premature discharge from a Medicare-covered care setting may often start with a QIO complaint. Even so, with respect to matters of premature discharge or where there has been a denial of a continuing stay in a Medicare-participating hospital, skilled nursing facility, home health agency, or hospice, advocates should use the standard or expedited appeals process. *See* 42 U.S.C. § 1395ff, 42 C.F.R. §§ 405.900 *et seq.* (Traditional Medicare) and §§ 422.560 *et seq.* (Medicare Advantage).

[44] CMS, Transmittal 17, QIO Manual Ch. 5 (Apr. 6, 2012), *available at* http://www.cms.gov/Regulations-and-Guidance/Guidance/Transmittals/Downloads/R17QIO.pdf (site visited Aug. 6, 2018). On May 9, 2014, the Centers for Medicare & Medicaid Services (CMS) announced the first phase of its restructuring of the QIO functions. In the first phase, CMS has contracted with Livanta LLC (for geographic areas 1 and 5), located in Annapolis Junction, Maryland, and KePRO (for geographic areas 2, 3, and 4), located in Seven Hills, Ohio. These contractors will be responsible for ensuring consistency in the review process with respect to beneficiary complaints. CMS describes these two contractors as its Beneficiary and Family-Centered Care (BFCC) QIO contractors. The states in the designated geographic areas are Area 1: Connecticut, Maine, Massachusetts, New Hampshire, New Jersey, New York, Pennsylvania, Puerto Rico, Rhode Island, Vermont, Virgin Islands; Area 2: District of Columbia, Delaware, Florida, Georgia, Maryland, North Carolina, South Carolina, Virginia, West Virginia; Area 3: Alabama, Arkansas, Colorado, Kentucky, Louisiana, Mississippi, Montana, North Dakota, New Mexico, Oklahoma, South Dakota, Tennessee, Texas, Utah, Wyoming; Area 4: Iowa, Illinois, Indiana, Kansas, Michigan, Minnesota, Missouri, Nebraska, Ohio, Wisconsin; and Area 5: Alaska, Arizona, California, Hawaii, Idaho, Nevada, Oregon, Washington. The CMS announcement is *available at* https://www.cms.gov/Newsroom/Newsroom-Center.html (site visited Aug. 6, 2018). For more details, *see* CMS, "All Fee-For-Service Providers," *available at* http://www.cms.gov/Center/Provider-Type/All-Fee-For-Service-Providers-Center.html (site visited Aug. 6, 2018) & CMA, "CMS Restructures Quality Improvement Organization (QIO) Program," *available at* http://www.medicareadvocacy.org/cms-restructures-quality-improvement-organization-qio-program/ (site visited Aug. 6, 2018).

On July 18, 2014, as part of the restructuring of the QIO program—separating the beneficiary quality of care complaint review process from provider quality improvement functions—CMS awarded additional contracts to assist providers with quality improvement matters. The new contracts represent the second phase of QIO restructuring. These QIOs will be known as Quality Innovation Network (QIN)-QIOs. *See* CMS, "CMS launches next phase of new Quality Improvement Program," *available at* https://www.cms.gov/newsroom/press-releases/cms-launches-next-phase-new-quality-improvement-program (site visited Aug. 6, 2018). Each QIN-QIO will work on strategic quality improvement initiatives. *See also* CMS, Quality Improvement Organization (QIO) Manual, Ch. 1, *available at* http://www.cms.gov/Regulations-and-Guidance/Guidance/Manuals/Downloads/qio110c01.pdf (site visited Aug. 6, 2018).

(including post-acute-care settings, ambulatory settings, and health maintenance organizations)."[45]

Qualified Independent Contractors (QICs) began reviewing Part A reconsiderations in 2005; they began reviewing Part B reconsiderations in 2006. MA determinations are made by the private insurance companies that offer the plans and then by a private entity under contract with CMS.[46] Under the traditional Medicare program, MACs review coverage decisions issued by providers and issue notices known as initial determinations from which a beneficiary can appeal. These entities make initial determinations and issue payments when Medicare coverage is available.

Initial coverage determinations for beneficiaries enrolled in MA plans are made by the plan itself. The MA plan is required to apply CMS policy and coverage rules when making coverage decisions. Reviews of unfavorable plan decisions are handled by the private contractor. CMS guides the claim review, decision, and payment process by issuing health insurance coverage manuals as well as various mailings, bulletins, "guidance," and memoranda. These CMS instructions purport to interpret the statute and regulations, but they sometimes go beyond interpretation and create criteria that are more restrictive than the Medicare Act. Practically, the manuals and other guidance and informal directives from CMS form the basis for the coverage decisions that affect most beneficiaries.

Advocates should be alert to discrepancies between standards established by CMS and those established by the Medicare Act and regulations.[47] Where detrimental discrepancies exist, they may be the grounds for appeals or federal court challenges. Importantly, Administrative Law Judges (ALJs) and federal judges rely on the Medicare statute and regulations, not on CMS's guidelines, although regulatory changes require ALJs to give greater deference to CMS guidelines than was given in the past. Still, many cases are won on appeal to an ALJ that were denied initially and through reconsideration based on CMS rules. Furthermore, successful challenges to CMS's restrictive criteria have been brought in United

[45] *See* Social Security Act, § 1154(a)(4)(A), *available at* https://www.ssa.gov/OP_Home/ssact/title11/1154.htm (site visited Aug. 6, 2018); 42 U.S.C. § 1320c–3(a)(4)(A); Transmittal 17, § 5020. *See* CMS, "New Procedures for Review of Quality of Care Complaints," *available at* http://www.medicareadvocacy.org/new-procedures-for-review-of-quality-of-care-complaints/ (site visited Aug. 6, 2018). QIOs are entities comprising health care professionals—physicians, nurses, and other clinical professionals—who contract with the Medicare agency to review quality of care concerns, including beneficiary-generated complaints. *See also* CMS, "CMS launches improved Quality Improvement Program," *available at* https://www.cms.gov/Newsroom/Newsroom-Center.html (site visited Aug. 6, 2018).

[46] The MMA also included changes to the administration of Medicare. As of 2011, all claims are reviewed by MACs chosen by CMS through a competitive bidding process, replacing the current structure of intermediaries and carriers.

[47] Medicare appeals regulations require Administrative Law Judges (ALJs) to give deference to CMS program guidance. 42 C.F.R. §§ 405.1062 and 405.1063.

States district court as violating the due process clause of the Fifth Amendment to the United States Constitution, the Medicare Act and regulations, and the Administrative Procedure Act.[48]

Advocates should also watch for discrepancies that may exist between standards enforced by CMS's regional offices and MACs. Since Medicare is a federal program, beneficiaries should not be subject to more restrictive criteria in one region of the country than in another. If regional policy is promulgated in a Local Coverage Determination that infringes on an individual's coverage, check to ensure it does not conflict with federal law.

§ 1.04 ENROLLMENT AND ELIGIBILITY

Generally, individuals who are 65 and are entitled to and receiving Social Security or Railroad Retirement benefits are automatically entitled to and enrolled in Medicare Part A and will be deemed to have also enrolled in Part B unless they opt out.[49] Persons who are not yet receiving Social Security or Railroad Retirement benefits must enroll in Part A during an initial enrollment period, which begins in the third month before the person reaches age 65 (or reaches age 65 and becomes a U.S. citizen, or a permanent resident who has lived continually in the United States for the five years immediately preceding application for Medicare). The initial enrollment period extends for the next seven months. In addition, note that married individuals may be able to qualify for Medicare under their spouse's account. Since 2013, this includes spouses in legally recognized same-sex marriages.[50]

---

[48] *See* Grijalva v. Shalala, 152 F.3d 1115 (9th Cir. 1998), *vacated and remanded*, 526 U.S. 1096, 119 S. Ct. 1573, 143 L. Ed. 2d 669 (1999); Healey v. Shalala, Civ. Action No. 3:98 CV 418 (DJS) (Mar. 2000); Linoz v. Heckler, Medicare & Medicaid Guide (CCH) 35,876 (9th Cir. 1986); Duggan v. Bowen, 691 F. Supp. 1487 (D.D.C. 1988); Fox v. Bowen, 656 F. Supp. 1236 (D. Conn. 1987); Hooper v. Sullivan, Medicare & Medicaid Guide (CCH) 37,985 (D. Conn. 1989); Sarrassat v. Bowen, No. C88-20161 (N.D. Cal. 1989).

[49] Social Security Act, § 206, 42 U.S.C. § 1395p(f). *See* **Appendix 1-1** of this Handbook for a summary of the traditional Medicare program (Parts A & B).

[50] 42 U.S.C. § 1395i-2(a); 42 C.F.R. § 406.21(b). On June 26, 2015, the Supreme Court ruled favorably in Obergefell v. Hodges, Dir., Ohio Dep't of Health, Nos. 14-556, 14-562, 14-571, and 14-574, 576 U. S. ___ (2015), *available at* http://www.supremecourt.gov/opinions/14pdf/14-556_3204.pdf (site visited Aug. 6, 2018). The Court found that the failure to grant same-sex couples a marriage license is a violation of equal protection under the United States Constitution. Advocates should pay close attention to implementation issues as they arise.

For background on the tortuous history of the recognition of same-sex marriages at the federal level and access to benefits, *see* United States v. Windsor, 570 U.S. ___ (2013), 133 S. Ct. 2675, *available at* http://www.supremecourt.gov/opinions/12pdf/12-307_6j37.pdf (site visited Aug. 6, 2018). The *Windsor* decision holds Section 3 of the Defense of Marriage Act (DOMA) unconstitutional because DOMA limited a valid marriage to being only between a man and a woman. With respect to *Windsor*, persons in state-recognized same-sex marriages (and equivalent relationships as defined in states) should consider filing for spousal benefits as appropriate.

An application for Social Security or Railroad Retirement will also suffice for Medicare. A separate application is not necessary. Individuals who take early retirement under Social Security will be automatically enrolled in Medicare when they attain age 65.

Individuals who are receiving Social Security benefits cannot waive their entitlement to Medicare Part A. In order to waive Part A, they must withdraw their Social Security application and return any retirement or disability benefits they have received.[51] Because Part B is voluntary, an individual may always decline Part B.

Those who are 65 years of age and are not receiving Social Security benefits may still enroll in Medicare but must file an application.[52] As the full retirement age for Social Security is gradually increasing to 67, this is an important point. Every year more people reaching age 65 must apply for Medicare because they are not yet eligible for Social Security. Individuals who have been entitled to Social Security or Railroad Retirement disability benefits for 24 months are entitled to Medicare but also must apply to enroll in the program. Applications may be made with Social Security after receiving disability benefits for 21 months.[53] Effective July 1, 2001, the 24-month waiting period is eliminated for

---

Same-sex spouses of Medicare beneficiaries who are in valid marriages may be eligible for benefits as a spouse and should apply for benefits as appropriate. *See* CMA, "Demise of DOMA: Implementing Federal Benefits for Same-Sex Spouses," *available at* http://www.medicareadvocacy.org/demise-of-doma-implementing-federal-benefits-for-same-sex-spouses/ (site visited Aug. 6, 2018); *see also* Attorney General Holder's Memorandum to the President, "Implementation of *United States v. Windsor* (June 20, 2014)," *available at* http://www.justice.gov/iso/opa/resources/9722014620103930904785.pdf (site visited Aug. 6, 2018). In addition, the Social Security Administration (SSA), on August 23, 2013, added two Program Operation Manual Systems (POMS) provisions: SSA, GN 00210.005, Holding Claims, Appeals, and Post-Entitlement Actions Involving Same-Sex Marriages or Legal Same-Sex Relationships other than Marriage, *available at* https://secure.ssa.gov/apps10/poms.nsf/lnx/0200210005 (site visited Aug. 6, 2018) & SSA, GN 00210.010, Interviewing Individuals with Claims Involving Same-Sex Relationships, *available at* https://secure.ssa.gov/apps10/poms.nsf/lnx/0200210010 (site visited Aug. 6, 2018). *See also* Dept. Health & Human Servs. (HHS), LGBT Protections In Affordable Care Act Section 1557, 81 Fed. Reg. 31,375 (May 18, 2016), *available at* https://www.federalregister.gov/articles/2016/05/18/2016-11458/nondiscrimination-in-health-programs-and-activities?utm_campaign=subscription+mailing+list&utm_medium=email&utm_source=federalregister.gov (site visited Aug. 6, 2018); *see* Health Affairs, "LGBT Protections In Affordable Care Act Section 1557," *available at* http://healthaffairs.org/blog/2016/06/06/lgbt-protections-in-affordable-care-act-section-1557/ (site visited Aug. 6, 2018). *See also* HHS, Nondiscrimination in Health Programs and Activities, 81 Fed. Reg. 31,376 (May 16, 2016), *available at* https://www.gpo.gov/fdsys/pkg/FR-2016-05-18/pdf/2016-11458.pdf (site visited Aug. 6, 2018).

[51] SSA, Program Operations Manual System (POMS), § HI 000801.002; Hall v. Sebelius, 2011 WL 891818 (D.D.C. Mar. 16, 2011).

[52] The Social Security Administration (SSA) began accepting on-line Medicare applications in March 2010. *See* SSA, "How to Apply Online for Medicare Only," *available at* https://www.ssa.gov/pubs/EN-05-10531.pdf (site visited Aug. 6, 2018).

[53] 42 U.S.C. § 1395p(g).

disabled persons diagnosed with ALS.[54] Persons under age 65 and entitled, for more than 24 months, to monthly Social Security or Railroad Retirement benefits based on disability do not need to file an application for hospital insurance.[55]

Medicare coverage can be extended up to 93 months after disability benefits are terminated if the beneficiary is engaged in an approved nine-month trial work period (TWP) after a period of disability.[56] The previous period of disability benefits will count toward the 24-month eligibility requirement, should the beneficiary seek to reestablish Medicare eligibility.[57]

Individuals who miss their initial enrollment period must wait for a general enrollment period to enter Medicare Part B. The general enrollment period is the first three months of each calendar year (January 1 through March 31). Medicare Part B benefits do not begin until July of that year.[58]

The Part D prescription drug benefit, which became effective January 1, 2006, requires individuals who want drug coverage to affirmatively enroll in a prescription drug plan (PDP) or a Part C MA plan with prescription drug coverage (MA-PD). The initial enrollment period for Part D corresponds to the individual's initial enrollment period for Part B.[59] Individuals who do not enroll during their initial enrollment period or who want to change the plan in which they have enrolled may do so during the annual coordinated enrollment period (ACEP), October 15 through December 7 of each year.[60]

Penalties apply for late enrollment under Part A, Part B, and Part D. Under Part A, a 10 percent penalty, based on the monthly Part A premium price, is imposed for every month of late enrollment up to twice the number of months for which the beneficiary has failed to enroll.[61] Under Part B, a 10 percent penalty is also imposed. The Part B penalty is for each full year (12-month gap) of late

[54] BIPA, § 115.

[55] 42 C.F.R. § 406.6.

[56] 42 C.F.R. § 406.12(e)(2).

[57] Note that most people with disabilities who choose to work will continue to receive at least 93 consecutive months of hospital and supplemental medical insurance under Medicare Parts A and B after completing a trial work period (TWP). *See* CMA, "Medicare Coverage for People with Disabilities," *available at* http://www.medicareadvocacy.org/medicare-info/medicare-coverage-for-people-with-disabilities/# (site visited Aug. 6, 2018). Additional discussion is available in Vol. VII, No. 4 of the Center's "Healthcare Rights Review" (Winter 2007). *See* the Medicare statute at 42 U.S.C. § 422(c) & implementing regulations at 20 C.F.R. § 404.1592; 42 C.F.R. § 406.12(e) (individual under age 65 who is entitled to social security or railroad retirement disability benefits); 20 C.F.R. § 220.170 (the trial work period). *See also* SSA, "Trial Work Period," *available at* http://www.ssa.gov/oact/cola/twp.html (site visited Aug. 6, 2018) & SSA, "SSDI only employment Supports," *available at* http://www.ssa.gov/redbook/eng/ssdi-only-employment-supports.htm#1 (site visited Aug. 6, 2018).

[58] 42 C.F.R. §§ 406.21(c) and 407.12(a)(2).

[59] 42 C.F.R. § 423.38(a).

[60] 42 U.S.C. § 1395w-101(b).

[61] 42 U.S.C. § 1395i-2(c)(6).

enrollment.[62] Unlike Part A, there is no end point to the penalty under Part B. Under Part D, the penalty is the greater of an amount that is actuarially sound for each uncovered month or 1 percent of the national average monthly beneficiary base premium for each uncovered month, whichever is greater. As with Part B, there is no end point to the penalty.[63]

Individuals who receive Medicare based on disability have a new initial enrollment period when they become eligible for Medicare based on age. Any late enrollment penalty they are paying because of delayed enrollment in Part B and/ or Part D when they became eligible based on disability will be eliminated during the enrollment period based on age.[64]

Medicare has established a special enrollment period (SEP) for persons who do not purchase Medicare Part B at age 65 because they (or their spouse) are covered under an employer's group health plan based on current, active employment.[65] The SEP is generally defined to include each month in which a person is enrolled in a group health plan as described in Sections 1862(b)(1)(A)(v) and 1862(b)(1)(B)(iv) of the Social Security Act and to end with the last day of the eighth consecutive month after the person is no longer enrolled.[66]

Individuals who delay enrolling in a Part D plan because they have creditable drug coverage, that is, drug coverage that is as good as Medicare, through another source also have a SEP if that drug coverage ends. There are additional SEPs that allow individuals to change drug plans at times other than the annual enrollment period, under limited circumstances.[67]

[A] Medicare Advantage (HMO, PPO, SNP, and PFFS) Eligibility and Enrollment

Beneficiaries have the option to receive their Medicare coverage through a participating private Medicare Advantage (MA) plan. In order to do so, beneficiaries must be enrolled in both Part A *and* Part B.[68] The beneficiary must live within the service area served by the MA plan[69] and must not be enrolled in any other Medicare-participating plan.[70]

---

[62] 42 U.S.C. § 1395r (b); 42 C.F.R. § 408.22.

[63] 42 U.S.C. § 1395w-113(b).

[64] 42 U.S.C. § 1395w-113(b).

[65] 42 U.S.C. § 1395p(i); 42 C.F.R. § 406.24.

[66] 42 U.S.C. § 1395p(i)(3)(A), (B).

[67] Medicare Prescription Drug (MPD) Manual, Ch. 3: § 30.3, *et seq.*, *available at* https://www.cms.gov/Medicare/Eligibility-and-Enrollment/MedicarePresDrugEligEnrol/Downloads/CY_2018_PDP_Enrollment_and_Disenrollment_Guidance_6-15-17.pdf (site visited Aug. 6, 2018).

[68] 42 C.F.R. § 422.50(a).

[69] Medicare Advantage (MA) plans receive a capitated payment from Medicare for each enrollee in return for providing all Medicare covered services.

[70] 42 C.F.R. §§ 422.2 and 422.50(a)(2)(iii)(3)(i). The service area, as defined by CMS, is the geographic area for which CMS grants its approval for the plan to enroll eligible individuals. A

MA plans must cover the services currently available under Medicare Parts A and B, except hospice. Plans must pass on to beneficiaries cost savings achieved through efficient plan administration in the form of additional benefits, including a reduction in the Part B premium. MA plans may offer supplemental benefits for which a separate premium is charged, but the separate premium may not vary among individuals within the plan and must not exceed certain actuarial and community rating requirements.

To enroll, a beneficiary must file an application with a participating MA plan. Filing an application does not guarantee enrollment. To ensure fairness in the enrollment process, each application must be dated when it is received by the MA plan and processed in chronological order by date of receipt. Under Medicare regulations, the MA plan is required to provide prompt notification to the applicant in writing of acceptance or denial.[71]

The MA plan may deny enrollment only if acceptance of the individual (1) would require the plan to exceed its overall enrollment capacity; (2) would cause the enrollment to become substantially non-representative of the general population in the plan's geographic area; or (3) would prevent the plan from complying with the terms of its contract with CMS.[72] MA plans may choose to close enrollment. However, unless MA plans receive a "capacity waiver" from CMS, they must accept applications from certain beneficiaries, such as those who move into the geographic area.

Generally, application decisions may not be based on the health of the applicant.[73] However, until 2021, ESRD patients may only enroll as new enrollees in an MA SNP that serves people with chronic conditions or those dually eligible for Medicare and Medicaid.[74] Individuals who develop ESRD while already enrolled in an MA plan may remain in the plan. If the plan requires periodic re-enrollment, they must also be permitted to re-enroll.[75] Enrollment in the MA plan continues until such time as the enrollee is disenrolled voluntarily or involuntarily.[76]

---

service area generally consists of a full county or counties. In 2006, regional Preferred Provider Organizations (PPOs) serving multiple states became available in some areas of the country. *See* Academy Health, Regional PPOs in Medicare: What Are the Prospects?, *available at* http://hcfo.org/files/hcfo/ppo_1.pdf (site visited Aug. 6, 2018); Avalere Health LLC, "Regional and Local Preferred Provider Organizations (PPOs) Achieved Sizeable Enrollment Gains in 2008," *available at* http://avalere.com/research/docs/PPO_Growth_20080609.pdf (site visited Aug. 6, 2018).

[71] 42 C.F.R. § 422.60.

[72] 42 C.F.R. § 422.60.

[73] 42 C.F.R. § 422.110.

[74] The 21st Century Cures Act, Pub. L. No. 114-255 (Dec. 13, 2016) (removing the barrier for people with ESRD to enroll in MA plans, beginning in 2021).

[75] 42 C.F.R. § 422.50(a)(2). For additional exceptions to the general rule that individuals with ESRD are barred, including those converting from an employer plan offered by the MA company, *see also* MMC Manual, Ch. 2: §§ 20.2.2 & 20.2.3.

[76] 42 C.F.R. § 422.74.

MA involuntary disenrollment

Issues of disenrollment are a critical concern, particularly when costly care and services are involved. Medicare has established specific regulatory requirements defining the circumstances for involuntary disenrollment. They include the failure to pay premiums or deductibles as required, a permanent move outside the MA plan's service area, fraudulent statements on behalf of the enrollee leading to enrollment, and disruptive behavior that impairs the plan's ability to provide services. Beneficiaries must be provided notice and appeal rights information before disenrollment.[77]

[B] Process for Exercising Choice of Medicare Advantage Plan

Beneficiaries can elect to enroll or disenroll from an MA plan only in accord with certain limitations.[78]

1. If there are one or more MA plans offered in an individual's service area at the time the individual first becomes entitled to benefits under Part A and enrolled under Part B, the individual may make an election during an initial election period. Coverage under the MA plan becomes effective as of the first date on which the individual may receive coverage, that is, the month in which the individual becomes entitled to Medicare Parts A and B.
2. "Lock-in" rules, so called because beneficiaries become "locked in" to the choices they made during the previous fall's annual enrollment period, became effective on January 1, 2006.[79] Starting in 2019, the Open Enrollment Period (OEP) that was in effect before 2011 has been reinstated.[80] The OEP allows an additional period of MA enrollment and disenrollment for the first three months of the calendar year.
3. All beneficiaries may make an election during an "annual, coordinated open enrollment period." This annual election permits beneficiaries to enroll or disenroll from the various offerings during the period from October 15 through December 7.
4. Certain "special election periods" apply only in certain situations, including if (a) the MA plan was terminated; (b) the beneficiary ceased to be eligible for enrollment in such plan; (c) the beneficiary demonstrated that the plan violated its contract with Medicare, including marketing requirements; or (d) some other exceptional circumstance exists. Beneficiaries who reside in a nursing home have a SEP that allows them

---

[77] 42 C.F.R. § 422.74.

[78] 42 U.S.C. § 1395w-21(e).

[79] 42 U.S.C. § 1395w-21(e)(2).

[80] Section 17005, 21st Century Cures Act.

to enroll and disenroll at any time. There is also an SEP for individuals with Medicare who receive any type of assistance from the Medicaid program, including through one of the Medicare Savings Programs (QMB, SLMB, or QI) and/or the Part D low-income subsidy (LIS).[81] Eligible individuals may enroll in an MA SNP for people with chronic conditions at any time; however, they may only disenroll during the annual enrollment period or the open enrollment period. A new SEP allows beneficiaries to enroll in, but not to disenroll from, an MA plan with a five-star quality rating at any time.[82]

5. Beneficiaries in the traditional Medicare program who do not make a plan election during the annual election period remain in the original program. If an individual does not make an election and is in an MA plan, that individual will remain in the MA plan. Elections made during the annual election period become effective January 1 of the following year. However, a beneficiary who was previously covered by traditional Medicare and who elected an MA plan will, if hospitalized as of the effective date of the election, have that hospitalization covered by original Medicare until discharge. Note that this special rule applies only to hospital stays; all other ongoing Medicare-covered services should be covered by the MA plan.

6. CMS must conduct a special educational and publicity campaign every fall to inform beneficiaries about MA election procedures.[83] At the time of enrollment and every year thereafter, MA plans must disclose to enrollees in their service area the number and mix of participating doctors, emergency service options, out-of-service coverage, procedures for obtaining emergency services, optional supplemental coverage and costs, prior authorization rules, grievance and appeals procedures, quality assurance mechanisms, number of grievances and appeals and their disposition, and a summary of the method of compensating doctors.

§ 1.05 COVERAGE

The Medicare Act authorizes coverage for services that are "reasonable and necessary for the diagnosis or treatment of illness or injury or to improve the functioning of a malformed body member." Coverage *is* available for skilled nursing facility, home health and outpatient therapy for beneficiaries who need skilled

[81] A final rule issued in 2018 revised this SEP from an open-ended monthly SEP to one that may be used only once per calendar quarter during the first nine months of the year (January through September). For final rule, *see* 82 Fed. Reg. 16,440 (Apr. 16, 2018) (amending 42 C.F.R. § 423.38(c)).

[82] CMS, MMC Manual, Ch. 2: §§ 30.3, 30.4.

[83] 42 C.F.R. §§ 422.50–422.80.

nursing or therapy to *maintain* their condition or slow deterioration, to the same extent as they are to improve an individual's condition.[84] Medicare coverage is *excluded* by statute for custodial care, except in the case of hospice services.[85] These requirements, that the care be medically reasonable and necessary for treatment or diagnosis and that the care be "skilled," are often strictly interpreted by those who administer the Medicare program; they create the most frequent obstacles to coverage.

Medicare has four parts: Part A, Part B, Part C, and Part D. Part A covers inpatient hospital care, inpatient care in a skilled nursing facility (SNF), home health care services, and hospice care.[86] Part B covers medical care and services provided by physicians and other medical practitioners, durable medical equipment (DME), a variety of outpatient care services, and home health services not otherwise covered under Part A.[87] Medicare Part C, or Medicare Advantage (MA), includes a variety of private plan options for the *financing* of Medicare-covered health services. These MA options must offer the core package of benefits available under Parts A and B, plus additional benefits.[88] In 2006, Medicare Part D added a prescription drug benefit offered through private insurance plans. Part D only specifies the deductible, copayment, and out-of-pocket limits for the drug benefits. Within certain statutory requirements, Part D plans set their own drug formularies and premiums and may vary the cost-sharing as long as the overall cost-sharing is the "actuarial equivalent" of the statutory standard benefit.[89]

---

[84] 42 U.S.C. § 1395y(a)(1)(A). Obtaining Medicare coverage when a patient is not improving, but needs skilled care to maintain or slow deterioration, has long been a major problem for beneficiaries with longer-term, chronic and progressive conditions. As a result of a national class action lawsuit, *Jimmo v. Sebelius*, CMS clarified that medical improvement should *not* be the basis for Medicare coverage determinations for skilled nursing facility, home health, and outpatient therapy care. *See* http://www.medicareadvocacy.org/medicare-info/improvement-standard/ (site visited Aug. 6, 2018). *See also* CMA, Jimmo v. Sebelius Settlement Agreement: Fact Sheet, *available at* http://www.medicareadvocacy.org/wp-content/uploads/2013/04/Jimmo-FactSheet.pdf (site visited Aug. 6, 2018). Clarifying language has been added to various CMS manuals. *See* CMS, MLN Matters MM8458, "Manual Updates to Clarify Skilled Nursing Facility (SNF), Inpatient Rehabilitation Facility (IRF), Home Health (HH), and Outpatient (OPT) Coverage Pursuant to *Jimmo v. Sebelius*" (Jan. 14, 2014), *available at* http://www.cms.gov/Outreach-and-Education/Medicare-Learning-Network-MLN/MLNMattersArticles/Downloads/MM8458.pdf (site visited Aug. 6, 2018) & CMS, Pub. 100-02, Medicare Benefit Policy (MBP) Manual, *available at* http://cms.gov/Regulations-and-Guidance/Guidance/Manuals/Internet-Only-Manuals-IOMs-Items/CMS012673.html (site visited Aug. 6, 2018). *See also* CMS, *Jimmo* Settlement, *available at* https://www.CMS.gov/Center/Special-Topic/Jimmo-Center.html (site visited Aug. 6, 2018). *See also* **Appendix 1-9** of this Handbook.

[85] 42 U.S.C. § 1395y(a)(9).

[86] 42 U.S.C. §§ 1395c and 1395d.

[87] 42 U.S.C. §§ 1395j and 1395k.

[88] 42 U.S.C. §§ 1395w-21 *et seq.*

[89] *See* MMA, adding §§ 1860D-1–1860D-42 of the Social Security Act, 42 U.S.C. §§ 1395w-101–1395w-151.

[A] Part A

[1] Hospital Coverage

A beneficiary is entitled to 90 days of Medicare coverage for hospital care as an inpatient during each benefit period, or "spell of illness," after the beneficiary meets the deductible ($1,364 in 2019).[90] If the patient remains in the hospital beyond the 60th day, he or she is responsible for a daily coinsurance amount for days 61 to 90 ($341 in 2019). A spell of illness begins when a beneficiary receives Medicare-covered inpatient hospital care and ends when the patient has spent 60 consecutive days outside the hospital (or SNF) or remains in a health care institution but does not receive Medicare-covered services for 60 consecutive days.[91] In addition, the beneficiary is entitled to 60 days of hospital care as a "lifetime reserve." Once exhausted, lifetime reserve days are not replenished.[92] The coinsurance for lifetime reserve days is even heftier ($670 per day in 2018).

In 1983, Congress established a prospective payment system (PPS) for Medicare reimbursement of inpatient acute care hospital services.[93] Care in Medicare-certified rehabilitation and psychiatric hospitals and hospital units is

[90] Defining when a beneficiary is an inpatient has become increasingly difficult. Moreover, inpatient status is critical to meeting the required three-day inpatient hospitalization requirement for skilled nursing facility care. For a discussion of this issue, *see e.g.* CMA, "Outpatient Observation Status," *available at* http://www.medicareadvocacy.org/medicare-info/observation-status/ (site visited Aug. 6, 2018). *See also* CMA, "CMS Issues Instructions Regarding the Medicare Outpatient Observation Notice (MOON)" *available at* http://www.medicareadvocacy.org/cms-issues-instructions-regarding-the-medicare-outpatient-observation-notice-moon/ (site visited Aug. 6, 2018). The latter piece discusses the Medicare Outpatient Observation Notice (MOON) required by the Notice of Observation Treatment and Implication for Care Eligibility Act (NOTICE Act). Pub. L. No. 114-42, 42 U.S.C. § 1395cc(a)(1)(Y). Effective August 6, 2016, the NOTICE Act requires that hospitals provide written and oral notice, within 36 hours, to patients who are in observation or other outpatient status for more than 24 hours. The notice must explain the reason that the patient is an outpatient and describe the implications of that status both for cost-sharing in the hospital and for subsequent "eligibility for coverage" in a skilled nursing facility (SNF). However, in effect, CMS did not require hospitals to issue the MOON notice until March 8, 2017, when the notice was finalized.

[91] 42 U.S.C. § 1395x(b) and 42 C.F.R. §§ 409.10–409.18 (inpatient hospital services covered); 42 U.S.C. § 1395d(a) and 42 C.F.R. § 409.61 (scope of benefit); 42 C.F.R. § 409.82 (hospital deductible); 42 C.F.R. § 409.83 (hospital coinsurance); 42 C.F.R. § 409.60 (benefit period rules). *See* **Appendix 1-1** and **Appendix 1-3** of this Handbook for a summary of premiums, deductibles, and coinsurance payments. *See* CMS, 2018 Medicare Costs, *available at* http://www.medicare.gov/Pubs/pdf/11579-Medicare-Costs.pdf (site visited Aug. 6, 2018).

[92] For a discussion of lifetime reserve days, *see* MBP Manual, Ch. 5 (site visited Aug. 6, 2018).

[93] 42 U.S.C. § 1395ww(d).

exempt from the diagnosis-related group (DRG) system.[94] Under PPS, Medicare payment is made at a predetermined, specific rate for each discharge.[95] All discharges are classified according to a list of DRGs. The list contains hundreds of specific DRGs. Each DRG is assigned a dollar amount based on the average cost of caring for patients with similar diagnoses in the past, regardless of whether the patient's care actually cost the hospital less, or more, to deliver.

[2] Skilled Nursing Facility Care

Medicare Part A provides payment for post-hospital care in SNFs for up to 100 days during each spell of illness.[96] If Medicare coverage requirements are met, the patient is eligible for full coverage of the first 20 days of SNF care. From day 21 through day 100, Medicare pays for all covered services except for a daily coinsurance amount ($170.50 per day in 2019). Individuals are not eligible for any Medicare coverage unless he or she was hospitalized as an *inpatient* for at least three days prior to the SNF admission and was admitted to the SNF within 30 days of the hospital discharge involving an inpatient stay of three days (generally spanning three midnights).[97]

SNF coverage includes the services generally available in a SNF: nursing care provided by registered professional nurses, bed and board, physical therapy, occupational therapy, speech therapy, social services, medications, supplies, equipment, and other services necessary for the patient to attain or maintain the highest practicable level of functioning. However, "convenience" items, such as a telephone, are not covered by Medicare.

There are certain requirements that must be met in order for a patient to receive Medicare coverage. These requirements include:[98]

1. A physician must certify that the patient needs SNF care;

---

[94] *See* definitions at 42 C.F.R. § 412.29, Classification criteria for payment under the inpatient rehabilitation facility prospective payment system, *available at* http://www.gpo.gov/fdsys/pkg/CFR-2014-title42-vol2/xml/CFR-2014-title42-vol2-part412.xml#seqnum412.20 (site visited Aug. 6, 2018).

[95] *See* CMS, Medicare Learning Network (MLN), Acute Care Hospital Inpatient Prospective Payment System (Apr. 2013), *available at* http://www.cms.gov/Outreach-and-Education/Medicare-Learning-Network-MLN/MLNProducts/downloads/AcutePaymtSysfctsht.pdf (site visited Aug. 6, 2018).

[96] *See* CMS, "Skilled Nursing Facility (SNF) Facilities," *available at* https://www.medicare.gov/coverage/skilled-nursing-facility-care.html (site visited Aug. 6, 2018).

[97] 42 U.S.C. § 1395x(h) and 42 C.F.R. § 409.20 (SNF services); 42 U.S.C. § 1395d(a)(2)(A) and 42 C.F.R. § 409.60 (scope of benefit); 42 U.S.C. § 1395f(a)(2)(b) (physician certification requirement); 42 C.F.R. § 409.35 (practical matter rule); 42 U.S.C. § 1395x(i) (three-day qualifying hospital stay); 42 U.S.C. § 1395x(i) (30-day rule); 42 C.F.R. §§ 409.30–409.34 (daily skilled care requirement).

[98] 42 U.S.C. § 1395x(h) and 42 C.F.R. § 409.20 (SNF services); 42 U.S.C. § 1395d(a)(2)(A) and 42 C.F.R. § 409.60 (scope of benefit); 42 U.S.C. § 1395f(a)(2)(b) (physician certification

2. The beneficiary must generally be admitted to the SNF within 30 days of a three-day inpatient hospital stay;[99]
3. The beneficiary must require daily skilled nursing or rehabilitation; and
4. The care needed by the patient must, as a practical matter, be available only in a SNF on an inpatient basis.

---

requirement); 42 C.F.R. § 409.35 (practical matter rule); 42 U.S.C. § 1395x(i) (three-day qualifying hospital stay); 42 U.S.C. § 1395x(i) (30-day rule); 42 C.F.R. §§ 409.30–409.34 (daily skilled care requirement).

[99] Defining when a beneficiary is a hospital inpatient has become very difficult. Increasingly, patients are classified as "outpatients" in observation status, even when they remain in the hospital receiving medical care for many days. Since "inpatient" status is necessary to meet the required three-day inpatient hospitalization requirement for skilled nursing facility care, these so-called outpatients are not eligible for any SNF coverage. The final rule is codified at 78 Fed. Reg. 50,495, 50,906–954 (Aug. 19, 2013). For a discussion of the final rule, *see* CMA, "Observation Status: 'Morphed into Madness,'" *available at* http://www.medicareadvocacy.org/observation-status-morphed-into-madness/ (site visited Aug. 6, 2018). *See also* CMS, "CMS-1632-F and IFC, CMS-1632-CN2 and Changes due to The Consolidated Appropriations Act of 2016," *available at* https://www.cms.gov/Medicare/Medicare-Fee-for-Service-Payment/AcuteInpatientPPS/FY2016-IPPS-Final-Rule-Home-Page-Items/FY2016-IPPS-Final-Rule-Regulations.html?DLPage=1&DLEntries=10&DLSort=0&DLSortDir=ascending (site visited Aug. 6, 2018); *see also* CMS, FY 2014 IPPS Rule Outreach (CMS 1599-F)–8-12-13, *available at* https://www.cms.gov/medicare/medicare-fee-for-service-payment/acuteinpatientpps/downloads/fy-2014-ipps-rule-outreach.pdf (site visited Aug. 6, 2018). The final rule is codified at 78 Fed. Reg. 50,495–51,040, 50,950 (Aug. 19, 2013). For a discussion of the final rule, *see* CMA, "Observation Status: New Final Rules from CMS Do Not Help Medicare Beneficiaries," *available at* http://www.medicareadvocacy.org/observation-status-new-final-rules-from-cms-do-not-help-medicare-beneficiaries/ (site visited Aug. 6, 2018). In addition, the decision in Alexander v. Azar, Civ. No. 3:11-CV-1703 (MPS) (D. Conn., Memorandum of Decision, 9/23/2013) doc. # 106, deferred to the Secretary's position that a patient must be admitted as an inpatient in order for inpatient rights to pertain; that persons who are in outpatient status do not have the rights and protections of inpatients. For a discussion of *Barrows* and the need for legislation, *see also* CMA, "Disappointing Decision from Court in Challenge to 'Observation Status' Highlights Need to Pass Legislation," *available at* http://www.medicareadvocacy.org/disappointing-decision-from-court-in-challenge-to-observation-status-highlights-need-to-pass-legislation/ (site visited Aug. 6, 2018). However, the Barrows court allowed the case to go forward to determine if beneficiaries have a right to appeal their Observation Status (vs. inpatient admission); the court also certified a national class. For commentary on the recent favorable decision, *see also* CMA, "Court Allows Medicare 'Rubber Stamp' Case to Go Forward and Certifies Nationwide Class," *available at* http://www.medicareadvocacy.org/court-allows-medicare-rubber-stamp-case-to-go-forward-and-certifies-nationwide-class/ (site visited Aug. 6, 2018). In its holding, the court found that on August 8, 2016, a federal judge in Connecticut largely denied the government's motion to dismiss and granted plaintiff's motion for certification of a nationwide class. Sherman v. Burwell, No. 3:15-cv-1468 (JAM) (D. Conn. 2016). The case challenges the fact that, for the last several years, decisions at the earliest two levels of appeal in the Medicare administrative process (Redetermination and Reconsideration) have overwhelmingly resulted in upholding denials of coverage for home health care services. The judge referred to the decisions in the original named plaintiff's case (who was replaced by his wife when he died) as "unnerving." This is especially true since over 60 percent are granted if people are able to continue to the third level of appeal, the ALJ level of review).

[3] Home Health Care

Medicare covers home health services in full, with no deductible or copayments from the beneficiary. Services must be medically necessary and reasonable, and the following criteria must be met to qualify for ("trigger") coverage:[100]

1. A physician has signed or will sign a plan of care.
2. A physician must have a face-to-face encounter with the beneficiary within 90 days prior to the start of the home health care or within 30 days of the actual start of care.
3. The patient is "confined to home," often known as "homebound." This criterion is met if leaving home requires a considerable and taxing effort, which may be shown by the patient's needing personal assistance, or the help of a wheelchair or crutches, etc. Homebound does not mean "bedbound." Absences for medical purposes and for other non-medical, but infrequent and short outings, are allowable.
4. The patient needs or will need physical or speech therapy, *or* intermittent skilled nursing (from once a day for periods of 21 days at a time if there is a predictable end to the need for daily nursing care, to once every 60 days).
5. The home health care is provided by, or under arrangement with, a Medicare-certified provider.

If the triggering conditions described above are met, the beneficiary is eligible for Medicare coverage for home health services.[101] Home health services include:[102]

---

[100] *See* 75 Fed. Reg. 70,372–486 (Nov. 17, 2010) (amending 42 C.F.R. § 424.22).

[101] 42 U.S.C. § 1395x(m) and 42 C.F.R. §§ 409.40 *et seq.* (home health coverage and coverage criteria); 42 U.S.C. §§ 1395x(f)(a)(8) and 1395n(a)(2)(f) (homebound criteria). Note that BIPA amended the "homebound" definition to clarify that an individual who attends adult day centers or religious services should not be disqualified from Medicare home health coverage on grounds that he or she has violated the homebound definition.

[102] Good discharge planning is an important tool in obtaining proper home health and other post-hospital services, including SNF services and rehabilitation services. It is significantly underused as an advocacy tool. Discharge planning is available to Medicare beneficiaries and others as a condition of a hospital's participation in the Medicare program. Services should be more than a rudimentary search for the next nursing home bed or home health agency opening. *See* 42 U.S.C. § 1395x(ee) (added to the Medicare statute in OBRA '87); 42 C.F.R. §§ 482.43 *et seq.*, effective January 12, 1995. Interpretive guidelines and survey procedures for hospital discharge planning are available in the Medicare State Operations Manual (SOM), CMS Pub. No. 100–07, Appendix A, § 482.43, *available at* http://www.cms.gov/Regulations-and-Guidance/Guidance/Manuals/downloads/som107ap_a_hospitals.pdf (site visited Aug. 6, 2018). *See also* CMA, "Discharge Planning: Tips for Evaluating a Hospital's Skilled Nursing Facility Placement Choices," *available at* http://www.me

- Part-time or intermittent nursing care provided by or under the supervision of a registered professional nurse;
- Physical, occupational, or speech therapy;
- Medical social services under the direction of a physician; and
- To the extent permitted in regulations, part-time or intermittent services of a home health aide.[103]

In addition to the coverage criteria described above the following points are also important:[104]

1. The qualifying term "part time and intermittent," for purposes of defining the nursing services that will trigger coverage, is defined as nursing care that is provided as little as once every 60 days and as much as daily for predictable periods of 21 days at a time, with extensions in exceptional circumstances when the need for additional care is finite and predictable.
2. Part-time <u>or</u> intermittent services, for purposes of coverage, are defined as skilled nursing and home health aide services furnished any number of days per week so long as they are furnished fewer than eight hours each day and 28 or fewer hours each week combined (or, on a case-by-case basis, up to 35 hours per week combined).

---

dicareadvocacy.org/discharge-planning-tips-for-evaluating-a-hospitals-skilled-nursing-facility-placement-choices/ (site visited Aug. 6, 2018).

On May 17, 2013, CMS released an update of Appendix A of the State Operations Manual (SOM) revising its interpretive guidelines for hospital discharge planning. *See* CMS's memorandum to State Survey Agency Directors about the revised discharge planning guidance, Ref: S&C: 13-32-Hospital (May 17, 2013), *available at* http://www.cms.gov/Medicare/Provider-Enrollment-and-Certification/SurveyCertificationGenInfo/Downloads/Survey-and-Cert-Letter-13-32.pdf (site visited Aug. 6, 2018). For regulatory guidance, *see* Medicare SOMS, Transmittals for Appendix A, *available at* http://www.cms.gov/Regulations-and-Guidance/Guidance/Manuals/downloads/som107ap_a_hospitals.pdf (site visited Aug. 6, 2018); *see also* Alfred J. Chiplin, Jr., *Breathing Life into Discharge Planning*, 13 Elder L.J. 1, 1–83 (2005). CMS, CMS Pub. No. 11376 (revised June 2015), Discharge Planning Checklist, *available at* https://www.medicare.gov/pubs/pdf/11376-discharge-planning-checklist.pdf (site visited Aug. 6, 2018). Note also that the ACA adds provisions to help with transitions from the hospital to other care settings and to prevent unnecessary re-hospitalizations.

[103] 42 C.F.R. 405(b) importantly sets out the details of what are Medicare's coverable home health services, including "hands on personal care," which includes far more care than commonly understood.

[104] The regulations are effective January 1, 2011; however, since they clarify rather than change coverage rules, they are also applicable to services prior to that time. *See* 75 Fed. Reg. 70,461 (Nov. 17, 2010) (amending 42 C.F.R. § 409.44(c), effective January 1, 2011).

3. Individuals who attend adult day centers or religious services should *not* be disqualified from Medicare home health coverage on grounds that they violate the homebound definition.[105]

4. The Medicare capitated payment system for home health care includes incentives and disincentives provisions that have led to reductions and terminations of care for some patients, particularly those with chronic or long-term conditions.[106]

CMS issued regulations on November 17, 2010, regarding coverage for home health services. One of the most important aspects of the home health coverage regulations is a detailed explanation clarifying when Medicare covers establishment or *performance* of therapy to maintain an individual's condition. The regulation states:

> The unique clinical condition of a patient may require the specialized skills of a qualified therapist to perform a safe and effective maintenance program required in connection with the patient's specific illness or injury. When the clinical condition of the patient is such that the complexity of the therapy services required to maintain function involve the use of complex and sophisticated therapy procedures . . . by the therapist . . . **or** the clinical condition of the patient is such that the complexity of the therapy services required to maintain function must be delivered by the therapist . . . to ensure the patient's safety and to provide an effective maintenance program, then those reasonable and necessary services shall be covered.[107]

For therapy services to be covered, the patient's clinical record must include a plan of care established by a qualified therapist, in conjunction with the physician, which describes a course of therapy treatment and goals that are consistent with the patient's functional evaluation.[108] Documentation in the clinical record

---

[105] *See* BIPA.

[106] Obtaining and continuing home health care is an increasing problem, especially for people with longer-term needs. While the Medicare Act does not limit the time a qualified patient can obtain coverage, it is often difficult to continue services for more than a few 60-day episodes of care. Further, the care available during an episode is generally far less that authorized under the law. For more details and advocacy tips pertaining to home health, *see* CMA, "Home Health Care," *available at* http://www.medicareadvocacy.org/medicare-info/home-health-care/ (site visited Aug. 6, 2018). Note that the Bipartisan Budget Act of 2018 (Pub. L. No. 115-123) includes a number of provisions relating to the home health benefit that, among other things, will implement a payment model that may further reduce access to Medicare-covered home care. One of these provisions will reduce home health episodes of payment from 60 days to 30 days. For further discussion and the Center's analysis, *see e.g.* CMA, "Center for Medicare Advocacy Statement on the Health Extenders in the Budget Agreement," (Feb. 9, 2018), *available at* http://www.medicareadvocacy.org/statement-on-the-health-extenders-in-the-budget-agreement/ (site visited Aug. 6, 2018).

[107] 42 C.F.R. § 409.44(c)(2)(iii)(C).

[108] 42 C.F.R. § 409.44(c)(1)(i).

must describe the goals of the treatment plan,[109] be measurable,[110] and demonstrate that the method used to assess the patient's function, including activities of daily living (ADLs), is in accordance with acceptable practice standards.[111]

[4] Hospice Care

Medicare has provided coverage for hospice care since 1982. Hospice care is intended to provide palliative and supportive care for terminally ill people and their families rather than treatment for the underlying condition. Medicare covers two 90-day periods of hospice care and an unlimited number of additional periods of 60 days each.[112]

On March 10, 2014, CMS issued a memorandum entitled "Part D Payment for Drugs for Beneficiaries Enrolled in Hospice—Final 2014 Guidance."[113] The Guidance directs Part D Plan Sponsors to "place beneficiary-level prior authorization (PA) requirements on all drugs for beneficiaries who have elected hospice. . . ." As a result of advocacy, on July 18, 2014, CMS issued a memorandum to Part D Plan Sponsors and Medicare hospice providers replacing its March 10, 2014 Guidance. Pursuant to the replacement guidance, the only Part D medications requiring a "hospice prior authorization" are analgesics (medications used to treat pain), antiemetic drugs (medications used to treat nausea), laxatives, and anxiolytics (medications used to treat anxiety).[114] This means that when Medicare beneficiaries elect hospice, they should not have difficulty accessing medically necessary medications that are not related to their terminal condition through their Part D plans.

To receive Medicare hospice coverage, a patient must elect affirmatively to hospice services and, as a consequence, forego most other Medicare coverage for treatment of the underlying terminal condition. The hospice care must generally be provided by, or under arrangement with, one Medicare-certified hospice program during each period.

---

[109] 42 C.F.R. § 409.44(c)(1)(ii).

[110] 42 C.F.R. § 409.44(c)(1)(iii).

[111] 42 C.F.R. § 409.44(c)(1)(iv). *See also* CMS, Transmittal 17, QIO Manual, Ch. 5 (Apr. 6, 2012), *available at* http://www.cms.gov/Regulations-and-Guidance/Guidance/Transmittals/Downloads/R17QIO.pdf (site visited Aug. 6, 2018).

[112] *See* **Chapter 5** of this Handbook for a discussion of recent revisions to the Medicare conditions of participation for hospices.

[113] *See* CMS, Part D Payment for Drugs for Beneficiaries Enrolled in Hospice—Final 2014 Guidance, (Mar. 10, 2014), *available at* http://www.cms.gov/Medicare/Medicare-Fee-for-Service-Payment/Hospice/Downloads/Part-D-Payment-Hospice-Final-2014-Guidance.pdf (site visited Aug. 6, 2018).

[114] *See* CMA, "Hospice and Access to Medications Update: CMS Replacement Guidance," *available at* http://www.medicareadvocacy.org/hospice-and-access-to-medications-update-cms-replacement-guidance/ (site visited Aug. 6, 2018).

To receive Medicare coverage for hospice care, the patient must be certified as terminally ill by the patient's physician and/or the hospice staff physician,[115] and the hospice care must be part of a written plan of treatment established by the attending physician and hospice medical professionals. The hospice medical records should have clinical documentation supporting the physician's certification.

If coverage conditions are met, Medicare is available for an array of services, including:[116]

- Nursing care;
- Physician services;
- Counseling services for the patient and the family or other caretakers;
- Medical social services;
- Short-term inpatient care;
- Home health aides;
- Homemaker services;
- Medical supplies, equipment, appliances, and biologicals (including pain medication); and
- Physical, occupational, and speech therapy.

[B] Part B

Part B of Medicare provides coverage for a host of services, generally for beneficiaries who are in non-institutionalized settings. Part B is optional. It is financed by premiums paid by individuals enrolled in the program and by general revenues from the federal government. Since 1973, individuals receiving Social Security retirement benefits, individuals receiving Social Security disability benefits for 24 months, and individuals otherwise entitled to Medicare Part A are

---

[115] Both the hospice physician and the patient's attending physician (if the patient has an attending physician) must certify that the patient is terminally ill for the first 90-day election period. For subsequent election periods, only a hospice physician can recertify the patient as terminally ill. 42 C.F.R. § 418.22(c). Starting January 1, 2011, prior to the 180th day recertification and for subsequent recertification, a hospice physician or nurse practitioner must have a "face-to-face encounter" with the hospice patient to determine continued eligibility for hospice coverage. ACA § 3132, HCERA § 3004, amending 42 U.S.C. § 1395f(i). *See* CMA, "New Hospice Regulations Are a Mixed Bag for Beneficiaries Seeking High Quality End of Life Care," *available at* http://www.medicareadvocacy.org/new-hospice-regulations-are-a-mixed-bag-for-beneficiaries-seeking-high-quality-end-of-life-care/ (site visited Aug. 6, 2018).

[116] 42 U.S.C. § 1395x(dd) and 42 C.F.R. Pt. 418 (hospice benefit); 42 C.F.R. § 418.22 (physician certification); 42 U.S.C. § 1395d(d) (benefit periods); 42 C.F.R. § 418.24(a) (hospice election rules).

automatically enrolled in Part B unless they decline coverage. Others must enroll in Part B by filing a request with Social Security during certain designated periods.

All Medicare beneficiaries enrolled in Part B owe a monthly premium. Most participants have their premium automatically deducted from their Social Security check. Beneficiaries with low incomes and resources may be eligible for assistance in paying the Part B premium through one of the Medicare Savings Programs (MSPs).[117] The premium has been income-related for beneficiaries with higher incomes since January 2007. Individuals with incomes of $85,000 or more and couples with incomes of $170,000 or more pay higher Part B premiums than those below these income levels. The standard Part B premium for 2019 is $135.50. See **Appendix 1-3** for the premium for individuals who are not "held harmless."

Part B also has an annual deductible ($185 in 2019). Each year, before Medicare pays anything, the patient must incur medical expenses sufficient to meet the deductible, based on Medicare's approved "reasonable charge," not on the provider's actual charge.[118]

After the beneficiary meets the deductible, Part B will pay 80 percent of the reasonable charge for covered services, the reimbursement rate determined by Medicare; the beneficiary is responsible for the remaining 20 percent as coinsurance.[119] Unfortunately, the reasonable charge is often less than the provider's actual charge. If the provider agrees to "accept assignment," the provider agrees to accept Medicare's reasonable charge rate as payment in full, and the patient is responsible for only the remaining 20 percent.

If the provider does not accept assignment, the patient can be billed for a balance beyond the 20 percent coinsurance payment. There is, however, a ceiling on charges to Medicare beneficiaries even for providers who do not accept assignment. This ceiling is known as the "Limiting Charge," which is often higher than the Medicare reasonable charge but often less than the provider's actual charge, but it can be no more than 115 percent of the Medicare reasonable charge.[120]

---

[117] *See* **§ 1.06** of this Handbook.

[118] As a result of the MMA, the Part B deductible will increase yearly based on the yearly percentage increase in the monthly actuarial value of benefits paid out of the Part B trust fund. MMA, § 629 (amending 42 U.S.C. §§ 1395l(b), 1395r, and 1395w).

[119] Previously, Part B paid only 50 percent (62.5 percent of the approved amount times 80 percent) of the reasonable charge for outpatient mental health treatment. As a result of MIPPA, Medicare paid 60 percent of the reasonable charge in 2012 (the beneficiary paid 50 percent). The cost-sharing slowly phased down so that, by 2014, Medicare paid 80 percent of the reasonable charge. Note, however, that diagnostic services such as psychological testing to establish a diagnosis, brief office visits to monitor or change prescriptions, and medical management furnished to someone with Alzheimer's disease or a related disorder are not subject to the additional payment limitation. 42 C.F.R. § 410.155.

[120] 42 U.S.C. § 1395w-4(g); *see* Garelick v. Sullivan, 987 F.2d 913 (2d Cir. 1993) (constitutionality of provision upheld), *cert. denied*, 510 U.S. 821, 114 S. Ct. 78, 126 L. Ed. 2d 47 (1993); *see also* A. Chiplin, *The Medicare Limiting Charge: An Issue of Implementation and Enforcement*, 26

The major benefit under Part B is payment for physicians' services. In addition, DME, outpatient therapy, diagnostic X-rays, and laboratory tests are covered. Congress has also mandated an increase in the home health services covered under Part B and added additional preventive benefits.[121] Medicare is also requiring a face-to-face interview with the patient for certain services and equipment as a fraud protection measure.[122]

The following is a partial list of items and services that can be covered under Part B:[123]

- Annual "Wellness Visit"
- Physicians' services;
- Home health services;
- Services and supplies, including drugs and biologicals that cannot be self-administered, furnished incidental to physicians' services;
- Diagnostic X-ray tests, diagnostic laboratory tests, and other diagnostic tests;
- X-ray therapy, radium therapy, and radioactive isotope therapy;
- Surgical dressings and splints, casts, and other devices used for fractures and dislocations;
- DME;
- Prosthetic devices;
- Braces, trusses, artificial limbs, and eyes;

Clearinghouse Rev. 167 (1992), *available at* http://heinonline.org/HOL/LandingPage?handle=hein.journals/clear26&div=28&id=&page= (site visited Aug. 6, 2018); *see* further limiting charge discussion at **§ 1.05[B][2]**.

[121] 42 U.S.C. §§ 1395k and 1395x. For a list of Medicare's coverage of preventive services, *see* CMS, "Your Medicare Coverage: Preventive & Screening Services," *available at* https://www.medicare.gov/coverage/preventive-and-screening-services.html (site visited Aug. 6, 2018).

[122] *See* ACA § 6407 (amending 42 U.S.C. § 1395m(a)(11)(2)(B)). *See* CMS, "Face to Face Encounter Requirement for Certain Durable Medical Equipment" (Sept. 9, 2013), *available at* http://www.cms.gov/Research-Statistics-Data-and-Systems/Monitoring-Programs/Medicare-FFS-Compliance-Programs/Medical-Review/FacetoFaceEncounterRequirementforCertainDurableMedicalEquipment.html (site visited Aug. 6, 2018).

[123] *See* CMS, "What Part B Covers," *available at* http://www.medicare.gov/what-medicare-covers/part-b/what-medicare-part-b-covers.html (site visited Aug. 6, 2018).

With respect to non-emergency ambulance providers, *see* CMS, Announcement of the Extension of Temporary Moratoria on Enrollment of Part B Non-Emergency Ground Ambulance Suppliers and Home Health Agencies in Designated Geographic Locations, 82 Fed. Reg. 2363 (Jan. 1, 2017) (CMS's moratorium on new non-emergency ground ambulance providers), *available at* https://www.federalregister.gov/documents/2017/01/09/2016-32007/medicare-medicaid-and-childrens-health-insurance-programs-announcement-of-the-extension-of-temporary (site visited Aug. 6, 2018).

- Ambulance services;
- Some outpatient and ambulatory surgical services;
- Some outpatient hospital services;
- Some physical therapy services;[124]
- Some occupational therapy (see footnote 122);
- Some outpatient speech therapy (see footnote 122);
- Comprehensive outpatient rehabilitation facility (CORF) services;
- Rural health clinic services;
- Institutional and home dialysis services, supplies, and equipment;
- Ambulatory surgical center services;
- Antigens and blood-clotting factors;
- Influenza, pneumococcal, and hepatitis B vaccines;
- Some Pap smear screenings;
- Some mammography screenings;
- Some diabetes tests;
- Some other preventive services including colorectal, prostate cancer, and glaucoma screening, smoking cessation services, and some medical nutrition therapy;
- Qualified psychologist services;
- Therapeutic shoes for patients with severe diabetic foot disease;
- Screening for depression in adults; and
- Screening and counseling to reduce alcohol misuse.

[124] Note that the Bipartisan Budget Act of 2018 (Pub. L. No. 115-123) repealed the outpatient cap on annual outpatient therapy services covered by Medicare. Since the Balanced Budget Act of 1997, outpatient therapy under Medicare Part B *had* been subject to annual dollar limits, or caps. During most of these 20 years, an "exceptions" process has allowed beneficiaries and providers to seek coverage above the caps. The exceptions process expired December 31, 2017. The BBA of 2018 permanently repeals the caps. However, it continues to require providers to attach a modifier code to claims above the current cap level to indicate the services are medically necessary, and claims above a higher limit ($3,000) may be subject to a targeted manual medical review.

After the beneficiary satisfies the annual Part B deductible ($183 in 2018), Medicare pays 80 percent of the therapy costs. *See* CMS, Medicare Claims Processing (MCP) Manual, CMS Pub. No. 100-04, *available at* https://www.cms.gov/Regulations-and-Guidance/Guidance/Transmittals/downloads/R2073CP.pdf (site visited Aug. 6, 2018). *See also* CMS, "Therapy Services," *available at* http://www.cms.gov/TherapyServices (site visited Aug. 6, 2018).

Medicare Part B is fairly comprehensive but far from complete. Certain items and services are *excluded* from coverage. They include:

- Services that are not medically reasonable or necessary;
- Custodial care;
- Personal comfort items and services;
- Care that does not meaningfully contribute to the treatment of illness, injury, or a malformed body member;
- Prescription drugs that do not require administration by a physician;
- Routine physical checkups (except for one "Welcome to Medicare" checkup when an individual first enrolls in Medicare);
- Eyeglasses or contact lenses in most cases;
- Eye examinations for the purpose of prescribing, fitting, or changing eyeglasses or contact lenses;
- Hearing aids and examinations for hearing aids;
- Orthopedic shoes and other supportive devices for the foot unless intended as an instrumental part of a leg brace;
- Cosmetic surgery;
- Routine dental services;[125] and
- Routine foot care.

[1] Preventive Services

Historically, Medicare coverage did not include much preventive care, checkups, comfort items, or respite care. However, since the late 1990s Congress has been adding preventive services to those few that already existed in the Medicare program (which included influenza, pneumococcal, and hepatitis B vaccines).[126] The Affordable Care Act removed additional barriers to accessing

[125] The law *does* provide authority for coverage of *medically necessary* oral health care, the exclusion is for routine care, but CMS interprets the coverage narrowly. For more information on oral health care, *see* CMA, "Dental/Oral Health Care," *available at* http://www.MedicareAdvocacy.org.

[126] MIPPA § 101 provides that, effective January 1, 2009, CMS may use its national coverage determination (NCD) process to add coverage for additional preventive services that have been recommended by the U.S. Preventive Services Task Force that are reasonable and necessary for the prevention or early detection of an illness or a disability and that are appropriate for individuals entitled to benefits under Medicare Part A and enrolled in Medicare Part B. Also effective January 1, 2009, MIPPA extended eligibility for the Welcome to Medicare physical from the initial six months of Part B eligibility to the initial year, eliminated application of the Part B deductible to the

preventive services, adding coverage for an annual wellness visit that includes development of a personalized prevention plan[127] and removing cost-sharing for most preventive services that receive an A or B rating by the United States Preventive Services Task Force.[128] Preventive services covered under Medicare include:[129]

- Annual wellness visit.
- Annual mammogram for women age 40 and over.
- Annual Pap smears and pelvic exams for beneficiaries considered at high risk for cervical cancer or following an abnormal Pap smear. For women not in these groups, coverage is for Pap smears and pelvic exams once every two years.
- Prostate cancer screening on an annual basis for men over age 50.
- Colorectal cancer screening tests for beneficiaries age 50 and older. Frequency and payment limits are to be determined by the Secretary.
- Outpatient diabetes self-management training services, blood testing strips, and monitors.
- Bone mass measurement tests.
- Telehealth services when a beneficiary resides in a rural county designated as a health professional shortage area and where other criteria are met.
- Coverage of screening colonoscopy once every 10 years or within four years of a screening flexible sigmoidoscopy for all persons who are *not* at high risk.
- Coverage of medical nutrition therapy services for patients with diabetes or kidney disease.
- Coverage for routine glaucoma screening for persons at risk for glaucoma.

---

initial physical, and added services to be included in the examination. The ACA also gives the Secretary discretion to modify or eliminate coverage of preventive services to the extent that the modification is consistent with recommendations of the U.S. Preventive Services Task Force ACA § 4105. *See* U.S. Preventive Services Task Force, "Home," *available at* http://www.uspreventiveservicestaskforce.org/ (site visited Aug. 6, 2018).

[127] ACA § 4103. *See also* CMA, "Making Sense of Medicare's Preventive Service Benefits" (Sept. 20, 2012), *available at* http://www.medicareadvocacy.org/making-sense-of-medicares-preventive-service-benefits/ (site visited Aug. 6, 2018).

[128] ACA § 4104. *See also* CMS, Pub 100-20, Transmittal 864, *available at* https://www.cms.gov/Regulations-and-Guidance/Guidance/Transmittals/downloads/r864otn.pdf (site visited Aug. 6, 2018).

[129] *See* CMS, "Your Medicare Coverage: Preventive & Screening Services."

- Coverage of an initial physical examination performed within the first year of an individual's initial coverage under Part B.
- Coverage of a blood test for early detection of cardiovascular disease including tests for cholesterol levels and other lipid or triglyceride levels for individuals determined to be at risk.
- Coverage of diabetes screening tests for the purpose of early detection in individuals who are considered to be at risk for diabetes.
- Coverage of intravenous immune globulin for the treatment of primary immune deficiency diseases in the home.

[2] Limits on Physician Charges

As discussed above, when an item or a service is determined to be coverable under Medicare Part B, it is reimbursed at 80 percent of a payment rate approved by Medicare known as the "approved charge;" the patient is responsible for the remaining 20 percent. Unfortunately, the approved (or "reasonable") charge is often substantially less than the *actual* charge. The obvious result of this reimbursement system is that Medicare payment, even for items and services covered by Part B, is often inadequate. The patient is left with out-of-pocket expenses. When a physician accepts assignment, he or she agrees to accept the Medicare-approved charge as full payment for the services provided. Medicare pays 80 percent of the approved charge. Either the patient or supplemental insurance pays the remaining 20 percent copayment. No further payment is due to the physician.

Often local senior centers, area agencies on aging, and Social Security offices have lists of physicians, other providers, and medical equipment suppliers who accept Medicare assignment.[130] Also, a few states require physicians and other Part B providers who serve Medicare patients to accept assignment via their own balanced billing statutes. Massachusetts, for example, requires physicians to accept assignment for all Medicare patients; Connecticut requires the acceptance of assignment for low- and moderate-income Medicare patients. New York, Pennsylvania, Vermont, Minnesota, and Ohio also limit what physicians can charge Medicare patients.

When a physician does not accept assignment, he or she may "balance bill" the patient above the Medicare-approved charge. "Balance bill" refers to the physician's charge above the Medicare-approved rate. Federal law sets a limit known as the "limiting charge" on the amount a physician may balance bill. Since 1991

[130] For more information about the Medicare assignment program and lists of participating physicians and suppliers, *see* at CMS, "Home," *available at* www.medicare.gov (site visited Aug. 6, 2018).

the limiting charge has been based on a percentage of the Medicare approved charge for physician services.

Generally, a doctor who does not accept assignment may not charge a total of more than 115 percent of the Medicare-approved amount. The patient's Medicare Summary Notice (MSN),[131] the written notice that is sent to patients after a Medicare claim is processed, will state the approved charge for the doctor's services. Usually, the patient can calculate the physician's limiting charge for the services described in the MSN by multiplying the Medicare-approved charge by 115 percent. Medicare's calculation of the limiting charge will be stated on the MSN.

For example, assume the patient goes to a doctor who does not accept assignment. The doctor's actual charge is $600, but the Medicare approved charge allows only $349.37. The doctor's total bill may not exceed $401.78 (115 percent × $349.37); this is the limiting charge. Medicare will pay $279.50 (80 percent of the $349.37 approved charge). The physician cannot charge the patient more than $122.28 ($401.78 minus Medicare payment of $279.50). If the doctor bills more than $401.78, he or she is billing above the limiting charge and is violating federal law.

In some instances, the limiting charge will be more or less than 115 percent of the approved charge. If this seems to be the case, or if other questions arise, you can obtain specific limiting charge information by calling the provider's Medicare carrier.

§ 1.06 MEDICARE SAVINGS PROGRAMS

The Qualified Medicare Beneficiary (QMB) program, the Specified Low-Income Medicare Beneficiary (SLMB) program, and the Qualified Individual (QI) program, collectively referred to as the Medicare Savings Programs (MSPs), provide varying levels of assistance to Medicare beneficiaries with low incomes.[132]

---

[131] Medicare has made revisions to the layout of its MSNs in an effort to make them more user-friendly. *See* CMS, What is New on Your Redesigned 'Medicare Summary Notice?'(Part A), *available at* https://www.medicare.gov/pubs/pdf/SummaryNoticeA.pdf (site visited Aug. 6, 2018); CMS, What is New on Your Redesigned 'Medicare Summary Notice?'(Part B), *available at* http://www.medicare.gov/pubs/pdf/SummaryNoticeB.pdf (site visited Aug. 6, 2018); *see also* CMS, MLN Matters Number MM7676, Redesign of the Medicare Summary Notice (MSN)—Final Implementation—and Major Update to Chapter 21 of the Claims Process Manual, *available at* http://www.cms.gov/Outreach-and-Education/Medicare-Learning-Network-MLN/MLNMattersArticles/downloads/MM7676.pdf (site visited Aug. 6, 2018).

[132] *See also* **Appendix 1-8** of this Handbook for more information on programs targeted to low-income beneficiaries.

[A] Qualified Medicare Beneficiary Program

States are required to pay the deductibles, coinsurance, and premiums for Medicare Parts A and B for certain low-income Medicare beneficiaries, under the QMB program.[133] These individuals can have incomes up to the federal poverty level (FPL), which was $1,032 per month for an individual and $1,392 per month for a couple (for 2018), indexed each year according to the Consumer Price Index.[134] States may also liberalize the income and resource criteria; advocates should check with their state for specific information about how income and resources are calculated. States that liberalized income and/or resource criteria for the QMB program generally must also do so for other MSPs.

BBA '97 made modifications to the states' payment and cost-sharing obligations under the QMB program. It also allowed states to pay no more in deductibles, coinsurance, or copayments for Medicare cost-sharing than its Medicaid program would have paid for services for its Medicaid recipients who are not eligible for QMB. These modifications were effective on August 5, 1997.[135] Since the BBA '97, many states have implemented legislation that limits these Medicare cost-sharing payments to Medicaid levels. This has created access problems for some QMB patients whose physicians do not accept Medicaid and will not accept the lower payment rate.

[B] Specified Low-Income Beneficiary Program and Qualified Individual Program

Under the SLMB program, states cover Medicare Part B premiums for persons of somewhat greater means than those who qualify <u>just</u> for the QMB. These are persons with incomes up to 120 percent of the FPL, or $1,234 for an individual per month in 2018, and resources at the same level as QMB[136] and $1,666 for a married couple per month.

Effective for premiums payable from January 1998 to December 2002, the BBA '97 also established a block grant to states for payment of Part B premiums for individuals with income of at least 120 percent but less than 135 percent of the FPL ($1,386/month in 2018) (the QI program).

Persons in the QI group cannot be otherwise eligible for Medicaid; the resource limit for QI is the same as for QMB. Note that the SLMB program

---

[133] 42 U.S.C. § 1395d(p).

[134] MIPPA § 112 (amending 42 U.S.C. § 1396d(p)(1)). *See* Dept. of Health & Human Servs. (HHS), "HHS Poverty Guidelines for 2018," *available at* https://aspe.hhs.gov/poverty-guidelines (site visited Aug. 6, 2018). The 2019 poverty level guidelines were not available at the time of publication.

[135] BBA '97 § 4714 (amending 42 U.S.C. § 1396a(n)).

[136] 42 U.S.C. § 1396a(a)(10)(E)(iii); HHS, Annual Update of the HHS Poverty Guidelines, 74 Fed. Reg. 4199 (Jan. 23, 2009), *available at* https://www.gpo.gov/fdsys/pkg/FR-2009-01-23/pdf/E9-1510.pdf (site visited Aug. 6, 2018).

remains an entitlement, while the BBA '97 block grant for QI is to be allotted on a first-come, first-serve basis with the number of eligible individuals who can participate in the program being limited by each state's block grant allocation for the fiscal year. Individuals must apply each year, and enrollment is redetermined annually.[137]

§ 1.07 THE MEDICARE APPEALS PROCESS

Because of the size and complexity of the Medicare program and because of the desire to contain costs, Medicare coverage is often denied when it should be granted. Sometimes these denials are a result of errors; sometimes they are a result of policy that places cost containment concerns over the needs of individual beneficiaries. Whatever the underlying reasons for the denial, the Medicare program includes an appeals system that is designed, at least in theory, to reverse erroneous denials and to correct mistakes.[138] If the patient's attending physician feels the care in question is medically necessary and the care is not simply excluded from Medicare coverage (e.g., hearing aids, routine dental care), the beneficiary should appeal. Unfortunately, changes to the appeals process enacted as part of BIPA and the MMA made the appeals process less friendly to beneficiaries.

BIPA unified the appeals process for claims arising under Parts A and B, other than for claims for hospital services. The Medicare statute establishes different processes for claims arising under Part C and Part D through the reconsideration level of review. For the most part, once a claim reaches the ALJ level of review and beyond, the process is the same regardless of whether the claim arises under Medicare Part A, B, C, or D.

---

[137] BBA '97 § 4732 (amending Social Security Act § 1902(a)(10) (42 U.S.C. § 1396(a)(10)) and enacting Social Security Act § 1933); *see also* BBA '97 § 4732(c). On December 9, 2009, CMS issued final rules to implement BIPA § 521, and MMA Title IX. *See* CMS, Changes to the Medicare Claims Appeal Procedures, 74 Fed. Reg. 65,296 *et seq.* (Dec. 9, 2009), *available at* https://www.gpo.gov/fdsys/pkg/FR-2009-12-09/pdf/E9-28707.pdf (site visited Aug. 6, 2018).

[138] *See* 42 U.S.C. §§ 1395ff *et seq.*; 42 C.F.R. §§ 405.904 *et seq.*, modified by final regulations at 74 Fed. Reg. 65,296 *et seq.* (Dec. 9, 2009); *see* http://edocket.access.gpo.gov/2009/pdf/E9-28707.pdf (site visited Aug. 6, 2018) (Subpart I–Determinations, Redeterminations, Reconsiderations, and Appeals under Original Medicare (Parts A and B combined process)). The final rule clarifies that when the regulations refer to "day" that a "calendar day" is intended. This final rule also includes changes that are of a more substantive nature. *See also* CMS, Medicare Parts A & B Appeals Process, (June 2017), *available at* https://www.cms.gov/Outreach-and-Education/Medicare-Learning-Network-MLN/MLNProducts/Downloads/MedicareAppealsProcess.pdf (site visited Aug. 6, 2018).

[A] Traditional Medicare

[1] Notice of Medicare Payment

Generally, official notice from Medicare must be obtained before a beneficiary has a right to appeal. The Medicare Summary Notice (MSN) constitutes the "initial determination," or written notice that briefly explains what Medicare will pay on a claim. The MSN is prepared by the Medicare contractor that reviews the claim.[139] CMS issues MSNs quarterly, rather than monthly, unless a reimbursement check is due the beneficiary.[140] Many claims are denied in whole or in part on the MSN due to insufficient information and mistakes. Determinations that find that the medical service was not medically necessary and is, therefore, not covered under Medicare should be closely examined. Errors are often made. If the claimant does not think Medicare is allowing a sufficient reimbursement amount, the claimant should also question the MSN.

It may be useful to telephone the contractor to question why Medicare benefits were denied. Sometimes the claimant will discover that inadequate information or documentation was mailed to the contractor and that the coverage denial can be resolved by providing better documentation.

It is important to note that, for all Part A claims, the first notice Medicare beneficiaries should receive informing them that care will not be covered by Medicare is from the health care provider. This is also the case for most Part B services. Before they can charge a beneficiary, providers who participate in the Medicare program must first issue a written notice to patients informing them that Medicare coverage will not be available. Providers have a financial incentive to issue denial notices because they may have to absorb the cost of the care they provide if they erroneously inform beneficiaries that the care will be covered but not if they erroneously deny coverage.

While a doorway to the next steps to contest a denial, provider notices do not form the basis for an appeal. The beneficiary must seek a Medicare coverage determination or initial determination from the appropriate Medicare contractor to proceed into the appeal system.[141] Patients who receive denial notices from their provider must, therefore, request that a claim for payment be submitted to Medicare if they want to obtain an initial determination that can then be appealed. In addition, the initial determination does sometimes grant coverage that was

---

[139] Claims are reviewed by contractors known as Medicare Administrative Contractors (MACs). Previously, contractors known as fiscal intermediaries reviewed Part A claims, and contractors known as carriers reviewed Part B claims.

[140] CMS, Trans. 1347 (Sept. 28, 2007) (implementation date: Oct. 29, 2007), Change Request No. 5722, *available at* https://www.cms.hhs.gov/transmittals/downloads/R1347CP.pdf (site visited Aug. 6, 2018).

[141] Medicare Claims Processing (MCP) Manual, CMS Pub. No. 100-04, Ch. 29, §§ 10, 30.2, and 30.3, *available at* https://www.cms.gov/Regulations-and-Guidance/Guidance/Manuals/downloads/clm104c29.pdf (site visited Aug. 6, 2018).

denied by the provider. Note that if the beneficiary or representative requests a provider to submit a claim to Medicare, the provider is required to do so.[142]

[2] Redeterminations

If the claimant remains dissatisfied with the initial determination, a redetermination may be requested. The redetermination is the first formal level of appeal for Medicare Part A and Part B claims.[143] The request for redetermination must be filed within 120 days of receipt of the MSN. The redetermination is performed by the entity that issued the initial determination denying benefits: the MAC for Part A SNF, home health, and hospice claims; the QIO for hospital claims,[144] and Part B claims. Generally, these appeals simply entail submitting a written request (forms are available on the Medicare.gov website at "Medicare forms")."[145] If at all possible, the claimant should attach to the redetermination request a copy of the denial notice issued by the health care provider and a supporting letter and/or documentation from the treating physician.[146]

Assistance from the attending physician is always key to a successful appeal. Claimants should include a written statement from the physician explaining the need for the service if possible and be sure to keep copies of all appeal requests and all supporting data.

Although current regulations require that redetermination decisions be issued within 60 calendar days of receipt of the redetermination request,[147] it is

---

[142] MCP Manual, Ch. 1: § 50.1.5. (CMS implementation of this provision has been spotty.)

[143] *See* **Appendix 1-2** for a summary of the traditional Medicare appeals process and **Appendix 1-4** for a chart outlining the process.

[144] Note, too, that QIOs are tasked with reviewing quality of care concerns. *See* 42 U.S.C. § 1320c-3. Quality of care concerns relate to a range of matters from, among others, how one is or was treated by provider staff to whether one is receiving or received the treatment or services requested or expected to whether the services in question are or were provided in a way that meets accepted standards of care. *See* 42 U.S.C § 1320c-3. Matters of premature discharge from a Medicare-covered care setting may often start with a QIO complaint. Even so, with respect to matters of premature discharge or where there has been a denial of a continuing stay in a Medicare-participating hospital, SNF, home health agency, or hospice, advocates should use the standard or expedited appeals process. *See* 42 U.S.C. § 1395ff; 42 C.F.R. §§ 405.942 *et seq.* (Traditional Medicare) and 422.580–422.596 *et seq.* (Medicare Advantage). *See also* CMA, "New Procedures for Review of Quality of Care Complaints," *available at* http://www.medicareadvocacy.org/new-procedures-for-review-of-quality-of-care-complaints/ (site visited Aug. 6, 2018).

[145] *See* CMS, "Medicare Forms," *available at* http://www.medicare.gov/forms-help-and-resources/forms/medicare-forms.html (site visited Aug. 6, 2018). *See also* CMS, "How to file a complaint (grievance)," *available at* http://www.medicare.gov/claims-and-appeals/file-a-complaint/complaint.html (site visited Aug. 6, 2018).

[146] *See* CMS, MLN, "Medicare Parts A & B Appeals Process."

[147] 42 C.F.R. § 405.950(a) (2009). Note that the regulations extend this time frame if the provider or supplier, as well as the beneficiary, files an appeal. However, adherence to this time frame is not enforceable by the beneficiary.

not unusual to wait many months for a decision from this first appeal stage. Unfortunately, it is also not unusual for meritorious claims to be denied at the redetermination stage. However, some of these decisions do result in additional benefits, and this step is a prerequisite to move forward to the next steps in the appeal process.[148]

[3] Reconsideration

Beneficiaries dissatisfied with their redetermination decision can appeal to the next stage of the process: reconsideration. Individuals must complete the "reconsideration" step before receiving a hearing.[149] Reconsiderations are a paper review conducted by a review entity that is under contract with CMS, the QIC. A beneficiary has 180 days after receipt of an unfavorable redetermination to request a QIC reconsideration. The QIC must issue a decision within 60 days, with certain exceptions. If the QIC does not issue the decision in a timely manner, the beneficiary may request to escalate the case to an ALJ hearing. Regulations implementing the reconsideration review impose limitations on the submission of evidence on providers and suppliers, but not beneficiaries, who appeal to this level.[150] Beneficiaries may appeal an unfavorable reconsideration decision to an ALJ.

[4] Where to File an Appeal Request

Beneficiaries and their advocates must file a request for an appeal to the next level of review with the entity identified in the initial determination, redetermination, reconsideration, or ALJ decision.[151] In addition, the regulations set forth specific requirements for advocates who want to serve as appointed representatives and/or collect fees for their advocacy at the ALJ level and above.[152]

---

[148] 42 C.F.R. §§ 405.702–405.710 and 466.83 (2009) (reconsideration and appeals).

[149] 42 C.F.R. § 405.974.

[150] 42 C.F.R. §§ 405.950–405.978 (2009). Note that §§ 405.962(a) and 409.972(b)(3)(2009) now provide for a 60 calendar day filing time frame to request a reconsideration of a contractor's redetermination dismissal action, as an exception to the 180 calendar day time frame for filing a request for reconsideration of a contractor's redetermination decision. Note, too, that § 405.972(e) (2009) has been amended to clarify that a Qualified Independent Contractor's (QIC's) dismissal of a request for reconsideration of a contractor's dismissal action is binding and not subject to further review unless vacated under paragraph (d) of the section, which provides that if good and sufficient cause is established, a QIC may vacate its dismissal of a request for reconsideration within six months of the date of the notice of dismissal.

[151] 42 C.F.R. §§ 405.944 (2005); 405.964 (2009); and 405.1014 (2009). Before 2005, many beneficiaries and their advocates filed appeals through the Social Security office.

[152] 42 C.F.R. § 405.910 (2009).

[5] Summary of Expedited Appeals Process

Beneficiaries may seek expedited review of a SNF, home health, hospice, or CORF services discharge or termination.[153] The provider must give the beneficiary a general, standardized notice at least two days in advance of the proposed end of the service. If the service is fewer than two days, or if the time between services is more than two days, then notice must be given by the next to last service.[154] The notice must describe the service, the date coverage will end, the beneficiary's financial liability for continued services, and how to file an appeal.[155]

A beneficiary must request expedited review, orally or in writing, by noon of the next calendar day after receiving notice. At that time, the beneficiary is given a more specific notice that includes a detailed explanation of why services are being terminated, a description of any applicable Medicare coverage rules and information on how to obtain them, and other facts specific to the beneficiary's case. The beneficiary is not financially liable for continued services until the later of two days after receiving the notice or the termination date specified on the notice.[156]

Expedited review is available in cases involving a discharge from the provider of services, or a termination of services where "a physician certifies that failure to continue the provision of such services is likely to place the individual's health at risk."[157] Services furnished by a residential provider, such as a hospital, SNF, or hospice, are discharges for which a doctor's certificate is not required. Services furnished by a "non-residential provider," such as home health services, are treated as a termination of services for which a doctor's certificate of significant health risk must be provided.[158] A reduction in service is not considered a termination or discharge for purposes of triggering expedited review.[159]

A beneficiary who wishes to exercise the right to an expedited determination must submit a request for a determination with the QIO in the state in which the beneficiary is receiving the services at issue. The request may be made in writing or by telephone, but it must be made no later than noon of the calendar day following receipt of the provider's notice of termination. If the QIO is unavailable to accept the beneficiary's request, the beneficiary must submit the request by noon of the next day the QIO is available.[160]

---

[153] 42 U.S.C. § 1395ff(b)(1)(F), 42 C.F.R. §§ 405.1200–405.1204 (2009).

[154] 42 C.F.R. § 405.1200(b)(1).

[155] 42 C.F.R. § 405.1200(b)(2).

[156] 42 C.F.R. § 405.1202(c).

[157] 42 U.S.C. § 1395ff (b)(1)(F).

[158] 42 C.F.R. § 405.1202(a).

[159] 42 C.F.R. § 405.1200(a)(2).

[160] 42 C.F.R. § 405.1202(b). See also **§ 1.03** of this Handbook describing the QIO restructuring. The restructuring does not change the rules of the program with respect to time periods or decisional criteria. *See* CMS, "All Fee-for-Service Providers," *available at* http://www.cms.gov/Center/Provider-Type/All-Fee-For-Service-Providers-Center.html (site visited Aug. 6, 2018); CMA, "CMS

Coverage for the services at issue will continue until the date and time designated on the termination notice, unless the QIO reverses the provider's service termination decision. If the QIO's decision is delayed because the provider did not timely supply necessary information or records, the provider may be liable for the costs of any additional coverage, as determined by the QIO.[161] If the QIO finds that the beneficiary did not receive valid notice, coverage of the provider services continues until at least two days after valid notice has been received. Continuation of coverage is not required if the QIO determines that coverage could pose a threat to the beneficiary's health or safety.[162]

If the QIO affirms the decision to terminate services or discharge the beneficiary, the beneficiary may request an expedited reconsideration, orally or in writing, by noon of the calendar day following initial notification. The reconsideration will be conducted by the QIC, which must issue a decision within 72 hours of the request. If the QIC does not comply with the time frame, the beneficiary may escalate the case to the ALJ level.[163]

Beneficiaries retain the right to utilize the standard appeals process rather than the expedited process in all situations. A QIO may review an appeal from a beneficiary, whose request is not timely filed, but the QIO does not have to adhere to the time frame for issuing a decision, and the limitation on liability does not apply.

[6] Special Rules for Hospital Claims

Hospitals must deliver a revised version of the *Important Message from Medicare* (IM) (CMS-R-193) and the *Detailed Notice of Discharge* (CMS 10066).[164] Under 42 C.F.R. § 405.1205 (for traditional Medicare) and 42 C.F.R. § 422.620 (for MA), Medicare participating hospitals must deliver the written IM notice with information about an individual's rights as a hospital patient. The information must include discharge and appeal rights and must be delivered within two calendar days of admission. A follow-up copy of the signed IM is to be given again as far as possible in advance of discharge but, in any case, no more than two calendar days prior to discharge.[165] The follow-up notice is not required if the admission IM was issued to the individual within two calendar days of discharge.[166]

Restructures Quality Improvement Organization (QIO) Program"; CMS, "CMS Launches Next Phase of New Quality Improvement Program."

[161] 42 C.F.R. § 405.1202(c).

[162] 42 C.F.R. § 405.1202(c).

[163] *See* 42 C.F.R. § 405.1204.

[164] 72 Fed. Reg. 17,169 (Apr. 6, 2007).

[165] 72 Fed. Reg. 17,169 (Apr. 6, 2007).

[166] 72 Fed. Reg. 17,169 (Apr. 6, 2007).

For a hospital stay, a beneficiary must make a timely request for expedited review, orally or in writing, no later than the day of discharge. CMS, in its policy manual, interprets a "timely" request as no later than midnight of the day of discharge.[167] The beneficiary (or his or her authorized representative), upon request by the QIO, must be prepared to discuss the case with the QIO.[168] On the date that the QIO receives the beneficiary's request, the QIO must notify the hospital that the beneficiary has filed a request for intermediate review.[169] The hospital must supply any information, including medical records, that the QIO requires to conduct its review and must make it available, by phone or in writing, by the close of business of the first full working day after the day the beneficiary receives notice of the planned discharge.[170] When the beneficiary requests an expedited determination in accordance with Section 405.1206(d)(1), the QIO must make a determination and notify the beneficiary, the hospital, and the physician of its determination by close of business of the first working day after it receives all requested pertinent information.[171]

[7] Outpatient Observation Notice

Until 2016, CMS required hospitals to inform patients of their outpatient status only if the hospitals' utilization review committee reversed the patient's status from inpatient to outpatient under Condition Code 44. However, effective August 6, 2016, the Notice of Observation Treatment and Implication for Care Eligibility Act (NOTICE Act) requires all hospitals to notify all patients of their outpatient status if they are in observation or other outpatient status for more than 2 hours.[172] CMS mandates use of a notice called the Medicare Outpatient Observation Notice (MOON).[173] Although final regulations implementing the NOTICE Act became effective October 1, 2016,[174] full implementation of the Act did not occur until March 8, 2017, when hospitals were first required to issue the MOON.[175]

---

[167] 71 Fed. Reg. 68,721 (Nov. 27, 2007) (adding a new 42 C.F.R. § 405.1205 and revising 42 C.F.R. § 405.1206). *See* revised 42 C.F.R. § 405.1206(b)(1). *See also* MCP Manual, Ch. 30: § 200.4.1.

[168] *See* revised 42 C.F.R. § 405.1206(b)(2).

[169] *See* revised 42 C.F.R. § 405.1206(e)(1).

[170] *See* revised 42 C.F.R. § 405.1206(e)(2).

[171] *See* revised 42 C.F.R. § 405.1206(d)(6).

[172] 42 U.S.C. § 1395cc(a)(1)(Y).

[173] For a draft MOON notice, *see* CMA, Medicare Outpatient Observation Notice, *available at* https://www.medicareadvocacy.org/wp-content/uploads/2017/09/CMS-10611-MOON_v508.pdf (site visited Aug. 6, 2018).

[174] 81 Fed. Reg. 56,761 (Aug. 22, 2016), *available at* https://www.gpo.gov/fdsys/pkg/FR-2016-08-22/pdf/2016-18476.pdf (site visited Aug. 6, 2018).

[175] For more information about the MOON, *see, e.g.*, CMA "CMS Issues Instructions Regarding the Medicare Outpatient Observation Notice (MOON)" (Feb. 15, 2017), *available at* http://www.

[B] Appeal and Grievance Procedures in Medicare Part C Plans

[1] Medicare Advantage Claims

Medicare Part C establishes a different appeals process for MA cases, including those from HMOs, PPOs, SNPs, and PFFS plans.[176] In MA cases, initial determinations are known as "organization determinations." Organization and reconsideration determinations are made by the MA plan. If a reconsidered decision is denied in whole or in part, it is sent automatically to MAXIMUS Federal Services (MAXIMUS), an external review organization hired by CMS to review Medicare HMO reconsidered decisions.[177]

In addition, MA plans are required to have internal grievance procedures.[178] They must provide information to members regarding this grievance process in the plan's written membership rules, along with timetables and information about the steps necessary to utilize the grievance process.[179] The grievance procedures are to be used in all cases that do not involve an organization determination. For example, controversies about hours of service, location of facilities, or courtesy of personnel would go through the grievance process.[180]

MA plans must also inform enrollees of the appeals process in writing.[181] They are required to provide access to QIO review on issues of hospital non-coverage;[182] to provide pre-termination review of home health, SNF, and CORF services;[183] to make expedited determinations with respect to emergency or urgently needed services;[184] to provide reconsideration review;[185] and to provide

---

medicareadvocacy.org/cms-issues-instructions-regarding-the-medicare-outpatient-observation-notice-moon/ (site visited Aug. 6, 2018).

[176] *See* **Appendix 1-6** of this Handbook for a chart summarizing the Part C appeals process.

[177] 42 U.S.C. § 1395w-22(f)-(g); 42 C.F.R. §§ 422.560–422.626. Note that the MMA requires private insurance companies that offer a prescription drug plan under Part D to have grievance and appeals mechanisms that accord with the grievance and appeals mechanisms under Part C. *See also* CMS, "Medicare Managed Care Appeals & Grievances," *available at* https://www.cms.gov/Medicare/Appeals-and-Grievances/MMCAG/ (site visited Aug. 6, 2018). *See also* CMS, "Medicare Managed Care Appeals," *available at* http://www.medicareappeals.com/ (site visited Aug. 6, 2018); SSA, "Medicare Benefits," *available at* https://www.medicare.gov/claims-and-appeals/ (site visited Aug. 6, 2018).

[178] 42 C.F.R. §§ 422.560 and 422.564.

[179] 42 C.F.R. § 422.111(b)(8).

[180] 42 C.F.R. § 422.564(b).

[181] 42 C.F.R. §§ 422.111(b)(8) and 422.562(a)(2). (Issues for appeal include coverage of emergency or urgently needed services, and denial or termination of other medical service, including specialist care and/or referrals.).

[182] 42 C.F.R. § 422.622.

[183] 42 C.F.R. § 422.624.

[184] 42 C.F.R. § 422.570.

[185] 42 C.F.R. §§ 422.578 and 422.580.

access to independent review outside the plan by an entity under contract with CMS for such review.[186]

If an unfavorable reconsideration determination is issued, whether through the expedited review process or within ordinary time frames, and the amount in controversy is $160 or more (in 2019), the enrollee has a right to a hearing before an ALJ.

The written request for a hearing must be filed within 60 days of the date of the notice of the reconsideration determination. In MA cases, the plan must be made a party to the hearing and subsequent levels of review.[187]

The following is a summary of the due process and grievance procedures required of MA plans:

1. Grievance Mechanism

   Each MA organization/plan must provide meaningful procedures for hearing and resolving grievances between the organization (including any entity or individual through which the organization/plan provides health care services) and its enrollees.[188]

2. Non-Expedited Appeals Process[189]

   An MA organization must have a procedure for making determinations regarding whether an individual enrolled with the plan is entitled to receive coverage for a health service under Medicare and the amount (if any) that the individual is required to pay with respect to the service. Decisions must be made on a timely basis.

   Determinations that deny coverage, in whole or in part, must be in writing, and must include a statement in understandable language of the reasons for the denial and a description of the reconsideration and appeals process.

   If the organization makes a decision that is completely favorable to the beneficiary, the organization must issue the determination as expeditiously as the enrollee's health condition requires, but no later than 30 calendar days from the date it receives the request for a standard reconsideration.[190]

---

[186] 42 C.F.R. § 422.592 (currently provided by MAXIMUS Federal Services); *see* HHS, "Home," *available at* https://www.externalappeal.com/ferpportal/#/home (site visited Aug. 6, 2018).

[187] *See* 42 C.F.R. § 422.602(b)-(c).

[188] 42 C.F.R. § 422.564.

[189] 42 C.F.R. § 422.568 (standard time frames and notice requirements for organization determinations). The MA organization must notify the enrollee of its determination as expeditiously as the enrollee's health conditions require, but no later than 14 calendar days after the date the organization receives the request for a standard organization determination. This time period can be extended for a period of 14 days upon justification by the organization.

[190] 42 C.F.R. § 422.590(a).

The organization must provide for reconsideration of an adverse determination upon request by the enrollee involved. The reconsideration decision must be made within 30 days after the date of the receipt of the request for reconsideration.[191] A reconsideration relating to a determination to deny coverage based on a lack of medical necessity must be made only by a physician with appropriate expertise in the field of medicine at issue and by other than a physician involved in the initial determination.

3. Expedited Appeals Process[192]

The MA plan must maintain procedures for expediting organization determinations and reconsiderations when, upon request of an enrollee, the organization determines that the application of the normal time frame for making determinations or reconsiderations could seriously jeopardize the life or health of the enrollee or the enrollee's ability to regain maximum function. An enrollee or a physician may request expedited consideration orally or in writing. If the physician requests an expedited determination or reconsideration, the expedited review is mandatory and commences right away.[193]

If the request is not made by or supported by a physician, it is within the discretion of the MA organization to grant the request for expedited determination or reconsideration.[194] If the MA organization denies a request for expedited determination or reconsideration, it must automatically transfer the request to the standard time frame and make the reconsideration determination within standard time frames.

If the organization expedites a request for reconsideration, it must complete its reconsideration and give the enrollee (and the physician involved, as appropriate) notice of its decision as expeditiously as the enrollee's health condition requires, but no later than 72 hours after receiving the request.[195]

4. Fast Track Review[196]

An MA organization must provide an enrollee with notice at least two days in advance of termination of home health services, SNF services, and therapy services in CORFs. The enrollee may request review by the QIO by noon of the day following receipt of the notice. The QIO

---

[191] The MA organization must make its reconsidered determination as expeditiously as the enrollee's health condition requires, but no later than 30 calendar days from the date it receives the request for a standard reconsideration. 42 C.F.R. § 422.590(a)(1).

[192] 42 C.F.R. §§ 422.570–422.572.

[193] 42 C.F.R. § 422.584.

[194] 42 C.F.R. § 422.584(c)(2)(i).

[195] 42 C.F.R. § 422.590(d).

[196] 42 C.F.R. §§ 422.624, 422.626.

then must request information from the plan, solicit the view of the enrollee, and issue a decision by close of business of the day after it receives the necessary information.

5. Independent Review[197]

   The Secretary contracts with an independent, outside entity, MAXIMUS, to review and resolve in a timely manner reconsiderations that affirm the denial or coverage, in whole or in part. When the independent entity makes the reconsidered determination, it is responsible for mailing a notice of its reconsidered determination to the parties and for sending a copy to CMS.[198]

6. Appeal to ALJ and Federal District Court[199]

   An enrollee in an MA plan who is dissatisfied with a MAXIMUS determination may appeal to an ALJ using the same process as is used in traditional Medicare.

7. QIO Review: An Alternative Means of Appealing Hospital Denials[200]

   An enrollee who wishes to appeal a determination by an MA plan or hospital that inpatient hospital care is no longer necessary may request immediate QIO review and may remain in the hospital without additional financial liability according to the following procedures:

   - The enrollee must submit the request for immediate review to the QIO, in writing or by telephone, by noon of the first working day after receipt of written notice that the MA plan or hospital has determined that the hospital stay is no longer necessary;
   - On the date of receipt of the request, the QIO must notify the MA plan that the enrollee has filed a request for immediate review; the organization must supply any information that the QIO requires to conduct its review, including medical records and other pertinent information; information is to be provided by telephone or in writing by the close of business of the first full working day immediately following the day the organization makes its request; the QIO must solicit the views of the enrollee with respect to the denial at issue.

Where the MA plan has authorized inpatient coverage of admission directly or by delegation, the organization continues to be financially responsible for the costs of the hospital stay when a timely appeal is filed until noon of the calendar day following the day the QIO notifies the enrollee of its review determination.

---

[197] 42 C.F.R. § 422.592.

[198] 42 C.F.R. §§ 422.600–422.616.

[199] 42 C.F.R. § 422.622.

[200] *Id.*

If coverage of the hospital admission was never approved by the MA plan, the MA plan is liable for the hospital costs only if it is determined on appeal that the hospital stay should have been covered under the MA plan.

[C] Appeal and Grievance Procedures in Medicare Part D Plans

[1] Coverage Determination Process

As directed by Congress, the coverage determination and appeals process for Part D PDPs[201] mirrors closely the process utilized for Medicare Part C, the MA program. The process begins when the PDP or MA-PD issues a coverage determination.[202] The plan enrollee may request a redetermination by the drug plan of an unfavorable coverage determination and then a reconsideration decision by the Independent Review Entity (IRE) of an unfavorable redetermination. Following IRE review, the enrollee may appeal to an ALJ, to the Medicare Appeals Council (Council), and then to federal court. Expedited review is available if the Part C standards are met.

Plans must notify enrollees and the prescribing physician involved, as appropriate, of initial coverage determinations as expeditiously as the enrollee's health condition requires, but no later than 72 hours after receipt of the request. Plans must act on requests for expedited coverage determinations no later than 24 hours after receiving the request, and on expedited redeterminations within 72 hours. When a coverage determination involves a request for payment, a plan has 14 days to notify the beneficiary of its decision and to make payment, where applicable, to the beneficiary.[203] A plan may provide oral notice of an unfavorable coverage determination as long as it also provides written notice.[204]

---

[201] The coverage determinations and exceptions process for Medicare Part D, the prescription drug benefit, is authorized in the Medicare statute at 42 U.S.C. § 1395w-104(f)-(h). Implementing regulations are located at 42 C.F.R. §§ 423.560 *et seq. See* **Appendix 1-7** of this Handbook for a chart summarizing the Part D appeals process.

[202] The final regulations create a new heading for subpart M. It is now called "Grievances, Coverage Determinations, Redeterminations, and Reconsiderations." *See* 42 C.F.R. Pt. 423, subpt. M. (2009). The scope of the renamed subpart M is set out in new § 423.558 (2009) as follows: Requirements of Part D plan sponsors with respect to grievances, coverage determinations, and redeterminations are set forth in § 423.558(a)(1)(2009). The requirements of the Part D Independent Review Entity (IRE) with respect to reconsiderations are set forth in § 423.558(a)(2)(2009), and the rights of Part D enrollees with respect to grievances, coverage determinations, redeterminations, and reconsiderations are set forth in § 423.558(a)(3) (2009). The final rules also provide, in § 423.558(b) (2009), that requirements regarding reopenings, ALJ hearings, Council review, and judicial review are set forth in subpart M.

[203] 75 Fed. Reg. 19,677 (amending 42 C.F.R. § 423.568(c)). CMS in the preamble to the regulations encourages plan sponsors to issue unfavorable payment determinations sooner than 14 days, though the regulatory language does not include such a requirement. 75 Fed. Reg. at 19,677, 19,779.

[204] CMS, Changes to the Medicare Advantage and the Medicare Prescription Drug Benefit Programs for Contract Year 2012 and Other Changes, 76 Fed. Reg. 21,431 (Apr. 15, 2011), (amending

Coverage determinations that trigger appeal rights include a decision not to pay for or provide a Part D drug because the drug is not on the formulary, is not medically necessary, is furnished by an out-of-network pharmacy, or is not a drug for which Medicare will pay under Part D. A denial of a request for prior authorization by the plan (i.e., the plan does not approve a physician's request to pay for a formulary drug for which the plan must first grant approval) is also a coverage determination. A coverage determination also includes the failure to provide a coverage determination in a timely manner when that delay would adversely affect the health of the enrollee, a decision concerning an exception request, and a decision on the amount of cost-sharing for a drug. Affected beneficiaries may seek a coverage determination of a dispute involving the availability and amount of manufacturer discount applicable to brand name drugs provided in the coverage gap.

[2] Exceptions Process

PDPs and MA-PDs must have an exceptions process in which enrollees can ask that a formulary drug be provided at a lower tier for cost-sharing or that a non-formulary drug be covered by the plan. A beneficiary may also request an exception to a prior authorization requirement. Because exception requests are coverage determinations and governed by the rules for coverage determinations, the plan must act within the time frame for standard coverage determinations (72 hours) and expedited coverage determinations (24 hours).

The plan may grant an exception request to change the cost-sharing tier (i.e., the amount the beneficiary pays as a copayment or as coinsurance) if it determines that the non-preferred drug is medically necessary, consistent with the physician's statement in support of the exception that the preferred drug would not be as effective or would have adverse consequences. In addition, the exceptions process must address situations where a formulary's tiered structure changes during the year and an enrollee is using a drug affected by the change.. If the plan maintains a formulary tier in which it places very high cost and unique items, such as genomic and biotech products, it may exclude the very high cost or unique drugs from its tiered exception process.

The plan may grant an exception request to cover a non-formulary drug whenever it determines that the drug is medically necessary, consistent with the physician's statement that formulary drugs would not be as effective or would have adverse consequences, and that the drug would be covered but for the fact

42 U.S.C. § 423.568(f)), *available at* https://www.gpo.gov/fdsys/pkg/FR-2011-04-15/pdf/2011-8274.pdf (site visited Aug. 6, 2018). *See also* CMA, "Medicare Part D Grievances, Appeals, and Exceptions," *available at* http://www.medicareadvocacy.org/old-site/Projects/AdvocatesAlliance/Issue Briefs/10_04.12.PartDGrievancesAndAppeals.pdf (site visited Aug. 6, 2018)

that it is an off-formulary drug. Formulary use includes the application of cost utilization tools, such as a dose restriction, including the dosage form, that causes a particular Part D drug not to be covered for the number of doses prescribed, or a step therapy requirement that causes a particular Part D drug not to be covered until the requirements of the plan's coverage policy are met, or a therapeutic substitution requirement.

Although the regulations include some criteria for plans to consider when evaluating an exception request to change the tiered cost-sharing or to pay for a non-formulary drug, each plan has the flexibility to establish its own criteria and to develop its own exception process. In addition, the regulations leave to a plan's discretion whether, after an exception has been granted, it will continue coverage into subsequent plan years.

[3] Appeals

The first level of appeal from an unfavorable coverage determination, *including* an unfavorable exception request, is a redetermination by the drug plan. The enrollee must file a request for a redetermination with the drug plan. Drug plans have seven days in which to notify their enrollees of a standard redetermination decision. They have 72 hours to notify the enrollee of an expedited redetermination request.

An enrollee may request a reconsideration by the IRE of an unfavorable drug plan redetermination. The reconsideration request is filed with the IRE. The Part D regulations require the IRE to issue its reconsideration decision within the time frames for issuing a redetermination. Note that pursuant to a final rule issued in 2018, CMS has lengthened existing timeframes for adjudicating enrollee payment appeal requests at the redetermination and IRE reconsideration levels from a maximum of seven calendar days to a maximum of 14 calendar days.[205] Note that the regulations provide for an automatic reconsideration review by the IRE if the Part D plan fails to issue either a timely coverage determination or redetermination. The regulations require drug plans to forward the enrollee's request to the IRE within 24 hours if they do not act timely on the coverage determination or redetermination.[206] Advocates report, however, that drug plans that do not meet the regulatory time frames also do not comply with the requirement to send those cases to the IRE.

---

[205] For final rule for Parts C & D (CMS-4182-F), *see* 82 Fed. Reg. 16,440 (Apr. 16, 2018).

[206] 42 C.F.R. §§ 423.568(e) (2005) and 423.590(c) (2005). Reopenings, ALJ hearings, MAC review, and judicial review are available pursuant to the regulations of new subpart U. *See* 42 C.F.R. §§ 423.1968–423.2140 (2009).

[4] Notice

Plans must send written notice of a formulary change, including a change in cost-sharing tier placement, *only to those enrollees who use an affected drug*, at least 60 days in advance of the change. Notice must also be provided to CMS, state pharmacy assistance programs, pharmacies, and prescribing providers. The notice must include the name of the affected drug, whether the drug is being removed from the formulary or moved to another cost-sharing tier, the reason for the change, what alternative drugs in the same class are available to enrollees, and the right to request an exception. Alternatively, the plan may give the enrollee a 60-day supply of the drug and the 60-day notice at the time the enrollee presents a prescription for an affected drug.

The PDP or MA-PD must provide notice of appeal rights for other coverage determinations.[207] CMS does not consider the transaction at the pharmacy to be a coverage determination; thus, pharmacies have no obligation to provide individualized notice at the point of sale when coverage for a prescription is denied. However, effective January 1, 2012, plans are required to arrange with their network pharmacies to distribute general notices instructing enrollees how to contact their plan to obtain a coverage determination or to request an exception. The notices must comply with standards set by CMS, notices must be written: oral notice may only be given if the PDP mails a written notice not more than three days later.[208]

[D] Administrative Law Judge Hearings

As described above, a beneficiary who has received an unfavorable reconsideration decision for a claim under any part of Medicare may request an ALJ hearing. For all claims *except* hospital claims, in 2019 there must be at least $160 in controversy to proceed to an ALJ hearing; this amount may increase yearly.[209] Hospital claims may be appealed to an ALJ if $200 or more remains at issue. The request for hearing must be filed within 60 days of receipt of the reconsideration determination. For claims under Parts A and B, the ALJ must issue a decision within 90 days of receipt of the appeal request, with certain exceptions. The

---

[207] A plan sponsor may provide oral notice of a coverage determination or redetermination (either standard or expedited) provided that the plan sends written notice within three calendar days. 75 Fed. Reg. 19,677 (amending 42 C.F.R. §§ 423.568, 423.572, and 423.590).

[208] 76 Fed. Reg. 21,431 (Apr. 15, 2011) (amending 42 C.F.R. § 423.562(a)(3)).

[209] Section 1869(b)(1)(E) of the Social Security Act requires that the amount in controversy for ALJ hearings and for judicial review be adjusted annually. For the new number, *see* CMS, Medicare Appeals; Adjustment to the Amount in Controversy Threshold Amounts for Calendar Year 2019 83 Fed. Reg. 47,619 (Sept. 20, 2018) *available at* www.federalregister.gov/documents/2018/09/20/2018-20506/medicare-program-medicare-appeals-adjustment-to-the-amount-in-controversey-threshold-amount-for (site visited Nov. 9, 2018).

90-day time frame applies to Part D claims other than claims in which the beneficiary's prescriber indicates, or the ALJ determines, that applying the standard time frame may seriously jeopardize the beneficiary's life, health, or ability to regain maximum functioning. The ALJ must decide a request for expedited consideration within five days of receiving the request and must issue a decision as expeditiously as the beneficiary's health requires, but no later than 10 days from the date the request for the hearing is received.[210]

The ALJ hearing has traditionally been the beneficiary's best chance to win Medicare coverage previously denied. ALJs have considered the beneficiary's right to Medicare coverage in accordance with the Medicare statute and regulations (in contrast to the less formal and more restrictive guidelines and directives used by Medicare Administrative Contractors (QIOs and IREs) at their decision levels).[211] Thus, it makes sense for advocates to spend the greatest time and energy on the ALJ hearing stage where vigorous representation will often lead to satisfying results.

The Office of Medicare Hearings and Appeals (OMHA) in HHS was created in 2005, and all Medicare ALJ hearings are conducted by OMHA's corps of Medicare ALJs. Instead of being located throughout the country, Medicare ALJs are housed in four offices, in Arlington, Virginia; Cleveland, Ohio; Irvine, California; and Miami, Florida.

On January 17, 2017, CMS published a final rule that revised the procedures HHS follows for Medicare Appeals.[212] These changes became effective on March 20, 2017. The revised regulations, in part, authorize "Attorney Adjudicators," rather than ALJs to perform a portion of OMHA's workload that does not require a hearing.[213] Attorney adjudicators can issue decisions when a decision can be issued without an ALJ conducting a hearing under the regulations, dismissals when an appellant withdraws his or her request for an ALJ hearing, certain remands, and reviews of QIC and IRE dismissals. The revised regulations also make telephone hearings the default hearing method for individuals other than unrepresented beneficiaries.[214] Video-teleconferencing (VTC) were retained as the default method of conducting hearings for unrepresented beneficiaries,

---

[210] 74 Fed. Reg. 65,340 *et seq.* (Dec. 9, 2009) (adding 42 C.F.R. § 423.2016(b)).

[211] Although ALJs are not bound by CMS policy and directives, they are required to give them deference. If an ALJ decides not to follow a policy, the ALJ must explain in the decision why the policy is not being followed.

[212] CMS, Changes to the Medicare Claims and Entitlement, Medicare Advantage Organization Determination, and Medicare Prescription Drug Coverage Determination Appeals Procedures, 82 Fed. Reg. 4974 (Jan. 17, 2017), *available at* https://www.gpo.gov/fdsys/pkg/FR-2017-01-17/pdf/2016-32058.pdf (site visited Aug. 6, 2018). For a discussion of some of these changes, *see, e.g.*, CMA, "Issue Brief: CMS Issues New Rules Governing Medicare Appeals" (Feb. 8, 2017), *available at* http://www.medicareadvocacy.org/issue-brief-cms-issues-new-rules-governing-medicare-appeals/ (site visited Aug. 6, 2018).

[213] 42 C.F.R. § 405.902.

[214] 42 C.F.R. § 405.1020(b).

unless good cause for an in-person appearance is shown or the beneficiary requests a phone hearing.[215]

In Part A and Part B appeals, CMS may participate in an ALJ hearing as a party, with the right to submit evidence and cross-examine witnesses; CMS cannot examine and cross-examine witnesses if the beneficiary is unrepresented.

[E] Beyond ALJ: Medicare Appeals Council and United States District Court

If the ALJ decision is unsatisfactory[216] and at least $160[217] in 2019 ($200 in hospital cases)[218] remains in controversy, the case may be further appealed to the Medicare Appeals Council (Council). The Council is the final administrative level of appeal for all Medicare cases under Part A, Part B, Part C, and Part D. There is one Council for all Medicare cases. Cases are almost always decided on the record; the Council may grant oral argument if it decides that the case raises important questions of policy or law or questions of fact that cannot be decided on the record. A request for Appeals Council review must be filed within 60 days of receipt of the ALJ decision. Cases are sometimes won or remanded for new hearings. The Council traditionally has taken a long time to issue decisions, although rules require decisions in Part A and Part B appeals to be issued within 90 days of receipt of the appeal, with some exceptions. As with ALJ decisions, the Council must issue a written decision within 10 days after receipt of a request for review in Part D cases involving expedited consideration.

Generally, a Council decision is a prerequisite for proceeding with an individual Medicare appeal in federal court. The required amount in controversy for federal court appeals is $1,630 in 2019 ($2,000 for hospital cases).[219] Again, other than for hospital cases, these jurisdictional amounts will increase yearly. The complaint appealing a Medicare denial must be filed in federal court within 60 days of receipt of the Council decision and must name the Secretary of HHS, in his or her official capacity, as defendant.[220]

---

[215] *Id.*

[216] 42 C.F.R. § 478.44

[217] *See* **Appendix 1-5** of this Handbook. For an update for the amount in controversy (AIC) requirement for 2018 (for ALJ and federal court review), *see* CMS, Medicare Appeals; Adjustment to the Amount in Controversy Threshold Amounts for Calendar Year 2019, 83 Fed. Reg. 47,619 (Sept. 20, 2018), *available at* www.federalregister.gov/documents/2018/09/20/2018-20506/medicare-program-medicare-appeals-adjustment-to-the-amount-in-controversey-threshold-amount-for (site visited Nov. 9, 2018).

[218] 42 C.F.R. § 478.46 (amount in controversy for review of unfavorable ALJ decisions in hospital cases).

[219] 81 Fed. Reg. 65,653.

[220] If the defendant is not properly named, the plaintiff will be given 60 days to amend the complaint. 42 C.F.R. § 405.1136(d).

[F] Expedited Access to Judicial Review

A party may request expedited access to judicial review (EAJR) in place of an ALJ hearing or Council review. To do so, the party must show that there are no material facts in dispute. The party must also challenge the constitutionality of a statutory provision or the constitutionality or validity of a regulation or of a national coverage determination. After the party files a request for an ALJ hearing, the party may file a request for EAJR with the ALJ office. A determination on the request is made by a review entity consisting of up to three ALJs or members of the Appeals Council. If the review entity certifies the request, the party may file an appeal with federal district court within 60 days. If the request is denied, the case is returned to the ALJ hearing or Council if a hearing has already been held.[221]

[G] Challenges to Coverage Policies

A separate appeals process exists for beneficiaries who want to challenge the validity of a local coverage determination (LCD) or a national coverage determination (NCD) which sets rules concerning Medicare payment for a particular item or service.[222] Unlike the coverage appeals process described above, a beneficiary does not have to receive a service or procedure before challenging the LCD or NCD governing the procedure as long as the beneficiary needs the service.

A beneficiary who needs, but has not yet received the service, may file an appeal with the Appeals Council within 6 months of the treating physician's written statement indicating that the service is needed. A beneficiary who has received the service must file an appeal with the DAB within 120 days of receipt of the initial determination. Someone who has received the service may appeal the claims denial at the same time as challenging the validity of the LCD or NCD used to deny the service. It is critical in both situations to include a statement from the doctor concerning the necessity of the service and other medical information to document why the LCD or NCD is no longer valid.

If the appeal involves a challenge to an LCD, it is conducted by an ALJ. The Council conducts the review if the challenge involves an NCD. If the ALJ or the Council upholds the appeal, the ALJ or the Council may order the contractor to reconsider any claim filed by the beneficiary without application of the LCD or NCD in question.

---

[221] 42 C.F.R. §§ 405.990 and 423.1990.

[222] 42 C.F.R. §§ 426.100–426.587.

§ 1.08 CONCLUSION

Unfair denials of Medicare coverage occur with surprising frequency. Because Medicare administrators and providers often use rules and procedures that improperly restrict coverage, patients are sometimes required to pay for care that should be covered by Medicare. In addition, the Medicare law is very complicated and errors are frequently made.

The appeal system was designed to find and correct mistakes. No matter what the service at issue, assistance from the patient's *attending physician is the key* to convincing those who make coverage decisions initially, and on appeal, that the care is in fact medically necessary and/or skilled and should be covered.

APPENDIX 1-1 2019 MEDICARE SUMMARY (TRADITIONAL PROGRAM)

Care Setting[223]	*Coverage*	*Premium*	*Deductible*	*Coinsurance*	*Appeals*
PART A		For Voluntary Enrollees Only $437/mo in 2019 if 29 or fewer quarters Soc. Sec. $240/mo in 2019 if 30 to 39 quarters Soc. Sec.			
HOSPITAL	90 days/spell of illness+60 lifetime reserve days after deductible if medically necessary and reasonable		$1,364 per spell of illness in 2019	61st-90th day: $341/day 91st-150th day: $682/day	Redetermination by QIC Hearing by ALJ (if at least $200) HHS Medicare Appeals Council Federal Court (if at least $2,000)
SKILLED NURSING FACILITY	100 days if daily skilled care and if within 30 days of 3-day hospital stay			21st-100th day: $170.50/day in 2019	Reconsideration by QIC Hearing by ALJ (if at least $160) HHS Medicare Appeals Council Federal Court (if at least $1,630 in 2019)

continues

[223] On January 1, 2006, the Medicare prescription drug program began. MA (formerly Medicare+Choice and also known as Medicare Part D) is a set of financing systems including managed care plans.

APPENDIX 1-1 continued

Care Setting	*Coverage*	*Premium*	*Deductible*	*Coinsurance*	*Appeals*
HOME HEALTH (For individuals who *also* have Part B)	100 visits if homebound and need skilled care within 14 days of 3-day hospital stay or SNF stay of any duration				Reconsideration by QIC Hearing by ALJ (if at least $160) HHS Medicare Appeals Council Federal Court (if at least $1,560 in 2017)
HOME HEALTH (For individuals who *only* have Part A)	Full coverage for undefined number of visits if homebound and need skilled care				Reconsideration by QIC Hearing by ALJ (if at least $160) HHS Medicare Appeals Council Federal Court (if at least $1,560 in 2017)
HOSPICE	Two 90-day periods+ unlimited 60-day periods if physician certifies and recertifies that patient is terminally ill and if elect palliative care only				Reconsideration by QIC Hearing by ALJ (if at least $150) HHS Medicare Appeals Council Federal Court (if at least $1,560 in 2017)

PART B		$135.50 in 2019* for individuals with incomes below $85,000	Part B Deductible in 2018 ($185 in 2019)		
HOME HEALTH (If *only* have Part B *or* have used 100 Part A visits or did not meet institutionalization rules)	Full coverage for undefined number of visits if homebound and need skilled care		Deductible does *not* apply		Reconsideration by QIC Hearing by ALJ (if at least $160) HHS Medicare Appeals Council Federal Court (if at least $1,630 in 2019)
Physician Services Outpatient Services Therapy Services Durable Medical Equipment Prosthetic Devices Ambulance Services	80% of Medicare approved rate for covered services			*Assigned Claims:* 20% of Medicare approved rate *Unassigned Claims:* 20% of approved rate balance of actual charge up to an additional 15% of the approved charge	Reconsideration by QIC ALJ Hearing (if at least $160) HHS Medicare Appeals Council Federal Court (if at least $1,630 in 2019)

continues

* See **Appendix 1-3** for the premium for individuals who are not "held harmless."

APPENDIX 1-1 continued

Care Setting	*Coverage*	*Premium*	*Deductible*	*Coinsurance*	*Appeals*
Some Preventive Benefits (Including Flu Shots, Some Mammograms and Pap Smears, Bone Mass Tests, Prostate Screening, Diabetes Tests, etc.)	Some paid at 100%		Deductible waived for *some* preventive services		Reconsideration by QIC ALJ Hearing (if at least $160), HHS Medicare Appeals Council Federal Court (if at least $1,630 in 2019)

APPENDIX 1-2 TRADITIONAL MEDICARE APPEALS PROCESS

Level[224]	*Decision Maker*	*Time Frame for Issuing Decision*	*Extension of Time Frame for Issuing Decision Availability*	*Time Frame for Requesting Next Level of Appeal*	*Escalation*
INITIAL	FI	Within 30 days of receiving "clean" claim. § 405.922		Within 120 days of receipt of initial determination to request redetermination. § 405.942(a)	No right to escalation
REDETERMINATION	FI	Within 60 calendar days of receipt of request. § 405.95(a)	If redetermination request filed untimely, time frame commences w/granting of "good cause." § 405.942(b) If multiple timely requests filed, time frame is w/in 60 days of receipt of last request.	Within 180 days of receipt of redetermination to request reconsideration. § 405.962(a)	No right to escalation

continues

[224] *See* 42 C.F.R. 405, Pt. 900, subpt. I—"Determinations, Redeterminations, Reconsiderations, and Appeals Under Original Medicare" (Part A and Part B).

APPENDIX 1-2 continued

Level[224]	*Decision Maker*	*Time Frame for Issuing Decision*	*Extension of Time Frame for Issuing Decision Availability*	*Time Frame for Requesting Next Level of Appeal*	*Escalation*
			§ 405.950(b)(l)& (2) If additional evidence submitted by party, time frame extended for 14 calendar day for each submission. § 405.9500(3)		
RECONSIDERATION	QIC NCDs binding on QIC. § 405.968(a)(4) LCDs not binding on QIC but must give "substantial deference" to them in making decision. § 405.968	Within 60 days of receipt of request. § 405.970(a)	Same as for redeterminations § 405.970(b)	Within 60 days of receipt of reconsideration to request ALJ. § 405.1002(a)(l)	If time frame not met, have right to escalation. Must notify QIC in writing. § 405.970(d) QIC has 5 days from receipt of escalation request to issue a decision or forward to ALJ. § 405.970(d)(2)

ALJ	HHS ALJ NCDs binding on ALJ; LCDs not binding on ALJ but must give "substantial deference" to them in making decision. § 405.968 (CMS may "participate" or be "party," unless appellant is unrepresented beneficiary) § 405.1000 § 405.1010 § 405.1012	Within 90 days of timely filing of ALJ request. § 405.1016 (but requesting party may—by motion or stipulation—waive this time frame)	If ALJ request filed untimely, but "good cause" granted, time frame commences w/granting of "good cause." § 405.1016(b) If ALJ request is escalated to ALJ from QIC, time frame for issuing decision is 180 days of timely filing of request. § 405.1016(c) If CMS is a party and a party requests discovery, time frame for issuing decision is tolled. § 405.1016(d) If additional evidence	Within 60 days of receipt of ALJ decision to request MAC appeal. § 405.1102(a) [copy of request for MAC review must be sent by requestor to all parties]. § 405.1105(a)	If time frame not met, have right to escalation to MAC Must file request to escalate with ALJ in writing. § 405.1104(a)(l) ALJ has 5 days from receipt of escalation request to issue a decision or forward to ALJ. Must file escalation request w/both ALJ and MAC and copy all parties. § 405.1104(a)(2) escalation request to issue a decision or forward to ALJ. Must file escalation request w/both ALJ and MAC and copy all parties. § 405.1104(a)(2)

continues

APPENDIX 1-2 continued

Level[224]	*Decision Maker*	*Time Frame for Issuing Decision*	*Extension of Time Frame for Issuing Decision Availability*	*Time Frame for Requesting Next Level of Appeal*	*Escalation*
			submitted later than 10 days after receiving notice of hearing, period between when it should have been submitted and when received by ALJ is not counted toward adjudication deadline. § 405.1018(b) If hearing is postponed at request of appellant, time between original hearing date and new hearing date not counted toward adjudication deadline. § 405.1020(h)		

Council	Medicare Appeals Council (Council) (de novo review) § 405.1108(a) (CMS may "participate" or be "party," unless appellant is unrepresented beneficiary)	Within 90 days of timely filing of Council request (Council may issue decision or remand to ALJ). § 405.1100(c)	If appellant fails to send copy of request to escalate from ALJ or request for Council review to all parties, deadline tolls until all parties receive notice of the request for Council review. § 405.1106(b) Time frame tolled, if party asks to review evidence from the Council and an opportunity to comment, beginning w/date Council received request to review evidence through date comment received. § 405.1118 Time frame tolled, if party requests to file brief, beginning w/date request to brief received through date brief filed. § 405.1120	Within 60 days of receipt of Council decision, can request judicial review. § 405.1102(a) (Also, can file w/in 60 days of receipt of Council's notice that it cannot issue timely final action & cannot appeal ALJ dismissal to federal court, which, according to regs., is not available. § 405.1116)	If time frame not met, have right to escalation to federal court.§ 405.1132(a) Must file civil action w/in 60 days of receipt of Council's notice that it cannot issue timely final action Cannot obtain Judicial review of a dismissal of a claim. § 405.1116

APPENDIX 1-3 2019 MEDICARE DEDUCTIBLE, COINSURANCE, AND PREMIUM AMOUNTS

Hospital

Deductible: $1,364

Coinsurance:

1st through 60th day: $0
61st through 90th day: $341/day
91st through 150th day: $682/day

Skilled Nursing Facility

Coinsurance:

1st through 20th day: $0
21st through 100th day: $170.50/day

Part A Premium (for voluntary enrollees only):

$437/month (if individual has 29 or fewer quarters of Social Security coverage) (an increase from 2017)

$240/month (if individual has 30 to 39 quarters of Social Security coverage) (an increase from 2017)

If uncertain of quarters, please call your local Social Security office.

Part B Deductible: $185.00/year

Part B Standard Premium: $135.50/month for those not held harmless*

* The standard monthly premium for Medicare Part B enrollees will be $135.50 for 2019. However, some people with Part B in 2019 will be partially protected from premium increases by a statutory "hold harmless" provision, which prevents Medicare beneficiaries from having their monthly Social Security payment decrease as a result of an increase in Part B premiums. *See* 42 U.S.C. § 1395r(f).

APPENDIX 1-4 2019 PART B INCOME-RELATED PREMIUMS AND PART D INCOME-RELATED PREMIUM ADJUSTMENTS

Beneficiaries who file an individual tax return with income:	*Beneficiaries who file a joint tax return with income:*	*Part B income-related monthly adjustment amount:*	*Total monthly Part B premium amount:*	*Part D income-related monthly adjustment amount paid to Medicare:*
Less than or equal to $85,000	Less than or equal to $170,000	$0.00	$135.50	$0.00
Greater than $85,000 and less than or equal to $107,000	Greater than $170,000 and less than or equal to $214,000	$54.10	$189.60	$12.40
Greater than $107,000 and less than or equal to $133,500	Greater than $214,000 and less than or equal to $267,000	$135.40	$270.90	$31.90
Greater than $133,500 and less than or equal to $160,000	Greater than $267,000 and less than or equal to $320,000	$216.70	$352.20	$51.40
Greater than $160,000 and less than $500,000	Greater than $320,000 and less than $750,000	$297.90	$433.40	$70.90

continues

Beneficiaries who file an individual tax return with income:	*Beneficiaries who file a joint tax return with income:*	*Part B income-related monthly adjustment amount:*	*Total monthly Part B premium amount:*	*Part D income-related monthly adjustment amount paid to Medicare:*
Greater than or equal to $500,000	Greater than or equal to $750,000	$325	$460.50	$77.40

Enrollees in Medicare Part D prescription drug plans pay premiums that vary from plan to plan. Beginning in 2011, Part D enrollees whose income exceeds the same thresholds that apply to higher income Part B enrollees must also pay a monthly adjustment amount. The regular plan premium will be paid to their Part D plan, and the income-related adjustment will be paid to Medicare.

The Affordable Care Act established income-related premiums (IRPs) for Part D beginning in 2011, and it froze through 2019 the income thresholds at which IRPs begin for both Parts B and D—at $85,000 for single beneficiaries and $170,000 for married couples who file joint tax returns. Under current law, the income thresholds will revert in 2020 to the levels they would have reached had they been indexed for inflation since 2007.[225] Adjustments for Parts B and D: (a) § 1839(i)(3)(C)(i) of the Social Security Act (42 U.S.C. § 1395r(1)(3)(C)(i)) for years before 2018, and by adding at the end the following: § 402 (a) (2)(II) Subject to paragraph 5 for years beginning with 2018, and corresponding modified adjusted gross income table; and (b) conforming amendments, § (b)—Section 1839(i) of the Social Security Act (42 U.S.C. § 1395r(i)).

[225] *See* Congressional Budget Office, "Increase Premiums for Parts B and D of Medicare," (Nov. 13, 2013), *available at* http://www.cbo.gov/budget-options/2013/44897 (site visited Aug.6, 2018). *See also* Medicare Access and CHIP Reauthorization Act, Pub. L. No. 114-10 (Apr. 16, 2015), and § 402. Income Related Premium, *available at* https://www.congress.gov/114/plaws/publ10/PLAW-114publ10.pdf (site visited Aug. 6, 2018).

See www.cms.gov/newsroom/press-release/cms-announces-2019-medicare-parts-b-premiums-and-deductibles.

APPENDIX 1-5 ORIGINAL MEDICARE (PARTS A & B) APPEALS PROCESS

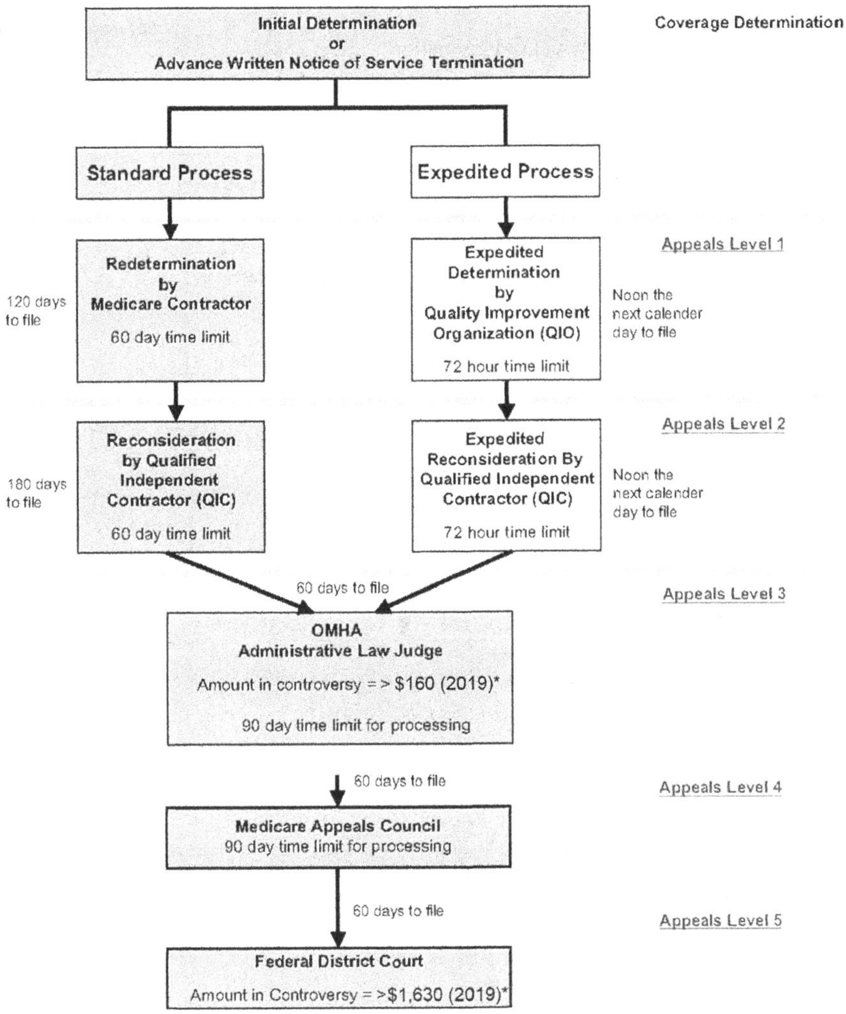

*The AIC requirements for an ALJ hearing and federal District Court are adjusted annually in accordance with the medical care component of the Consumer Price Index.

APPENDIX 1-6 MEDICARE ADVANTAGE (PART C) APPEALS PROCESS

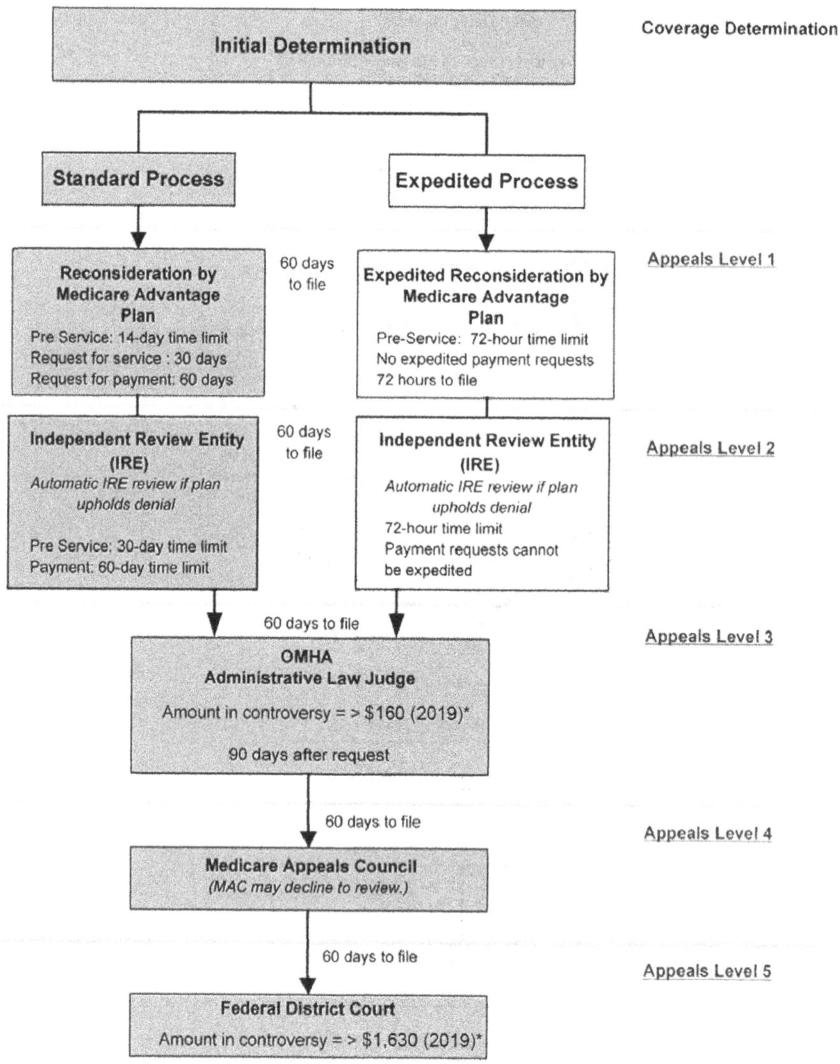

*The AIC requirements for an ALJ hearing and Federal District Court are adjusted annually in accordance with the medical care component of the Consumer Price Index.

APPENDIX 1-7 MEDICARE PRESCRIPTION DRUG PLAN (PART D) APPEALS PROCESS

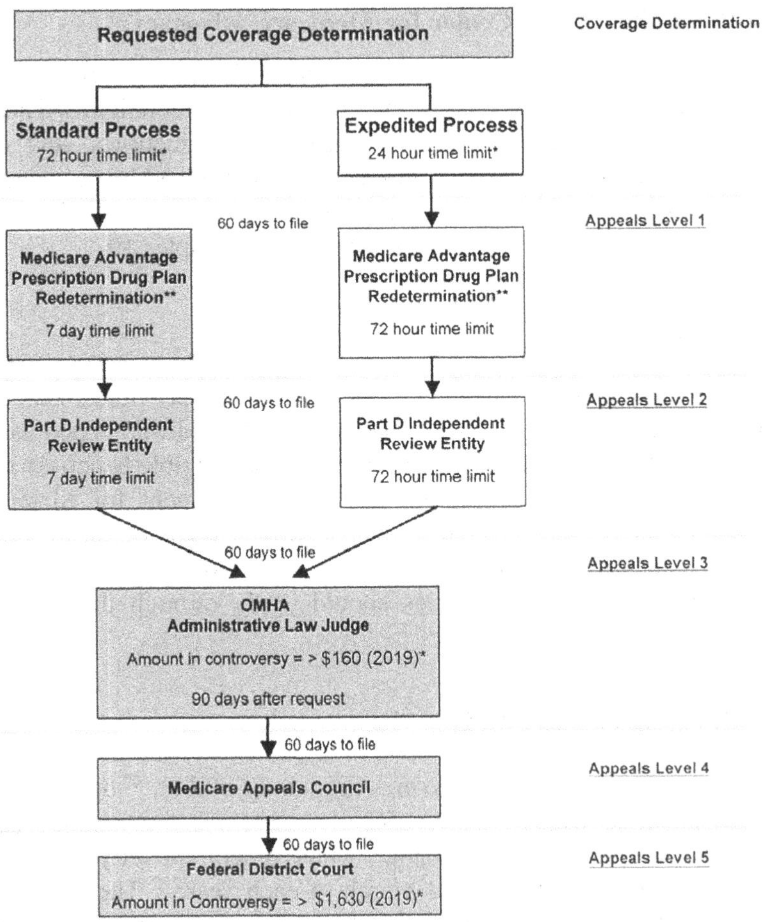

* The adjudication timeframes generally begin when the request is received by the plan sponsor. However, if the request involves an exception request, the adjudication timeframe begins when the plan sponsor receives the physician's supporting statement.

** A request for a coverage determination includes a request for a tiering exception or a formulary exception. A request for a coverage determination may be filed by the enrollee, the enrollee's appointed representative, or the enrollee's physician.

*** Starting in 2005, the AIC requirements for an ALJ hearing and Federal District Court are adjusted in accordance with the medical care component of the consumer price index.

APPENDIX 1-8 PROGRAMS TO ASSIST LOW-INCOME MEDICARE BENEFICIARIES

(Compiled by the Center for Medicare Advocacy)

A variety of programs exist to provide assistance to low-income Medicare beneficiaries or beneficiaries meeting other specified conditions. These programs provide beneficiaries with reduced premiums, deductibles, and copayments. Unfortunately, many of these programs are underutilized by the populations they are intended to serve. Below, we have briefly outlined some of the most important programs. More information is available in Chapter 10.

MEDICAID

The combined federal-state Medicaid program provides medical assistance to persons based on income and/or medical need. Medicaid beneficiaries who are also eligible for Medicare are referred to as "dual eligible beneficiaries." For this population, state Medicaid programs provide payment for Medicaid-covered drugs and services not covered by Medicare and for some or all of Medicare's premiums, deductibles, and co-insurance costs. Medicaid eligibility and coverage rules vary by state. Beneficiaries should apply through their State Medicaid Agency (SMA).

MEDICARE SAVINGS PROGRAMS

The collective Medicare Savings Programs (MSPs),[226] described below, provide financial assistance to beneficiaries meeting the income and resource requirements. Income levels change when federal poverty levels (FPLs) are announced between January and March of each year.[227] The resource (or asset) levels are aligned with those of the Part D full low-income subsidy and are indexed annually. The rules used to count income and resource levels must be at least as liberal as those for the Supplemental Security Income (SSI) program (see below), but states may use more liberal rules. Beneficiaries should apply through

---

[226] For ongoing information on the QI and other programs, *see* CMS, "Medicare Savings Programs," *available at* http://www.medicare.gov/your-medicare-costs/help-paying-costs/medicare-savings-program/medicare-savings-programs.html (site visited Aug. 6, 2018) and CMS. CMS, "Get Help With Your Medicare Costs," *available at* https://www.medicare.gov/Pubs/pdf/10126-Getting-Help-With-Your-Medicare-Costs.pdf (site visited Aug. 6, 2018).

[227] For the 2018 poverty guidelines, *see available at* HHS, "HHS Poverty Guidelines for 2018," *available at* https://aspe.hhs.gov/poverty-guidelines (site visited Aug. 6, 2018). The 2019 poverty guidelines were not available at the time of publication.

their SMA.[228] The chart below indicates the requirements for eligibility for each program and the assistance that each program provides.

LOW-INCOME SUBSIDY

The Low-Income Subsidy (LIS) was created when the Part D prescription drug benefit was added to Medicare, and the program provides assistance specifically for beneficiaries' prescription drug costs. Like the MSPs, the income levels for LIS change when new FPLs are announced between January and March of each year (the changes are effective retroactive to January 1 of that year). Like the MSPs, the resource levels for LIS change each year based on the Consumer Price Index (CPI). The rules used to count income and resources are generally the same as those of the SSI program. Beneficiaries who receive full Medicaid (dual eligible beneficiaries), SSI, or any of the MSPs are deemed eligible for the LIS and do not have to apply for it. Other beneficiaries may apply through the Social Security Administration (SSA) or through their SMA (where the state must also screen for MSP eligibility and other Medicaid benefits). The chart below indicates the requirements for eligibility for each LIS group and the assistance that each group receives as compared with the standard Part D benefit. Note that individuals in the four LIS groups do not have the "donut hole" gap in coverage.

STATE PHARMACEUTICAL ASSISTANCE PROGRAMS

Some states provide cost-sharing and supplemental drug coverage for special populations and low-income residents through their State Pharmaceutical Assistance Programs (SPAPs). Any payments made by an SPAP on behalf of a Part D enrollee will count toward the enrollee's true out-of-pocket costs, which count toward meeting the catastrophic threshold which leads to reduced or eliminated enrollee cost-sharing. Income and resource levels vary from state to state and not all states operate an SPAP.[229] Beneficiaries should contact their state to find out how to apply.

---

[228] *See* CMS, "Report of the Study Panel on Medicare/Medicaid Dual Eligibles: Improving the Medicare Savings Programs" (June 2006), *available at* www.nasi.org/usr_doc/Improving_the_Medicare_Savings_Programs.pdf (site visited Aug. 6, 2018); *see also* CMS, "Dual Eligible Beneficiaries Under Medicare and Medicaid" (May 2018), *available at* https://www.cms.gov/Outreach-and-Education/Medicare-Learning-Network-MLN/MLNProducts/downloads/Medicare_Beneficiaries_Dual_Eligibles_At_a_Glance.pdf (site visited Aug. 6, 2018).

[229] For a recent list of operating SPAPs, *see* CMS, http://www.medicare.gov/pharmaceutical-assistance-program/state-programs.aspx (site visited Aug. 6, 2018).

AIDS DRUG ASSISTANCE PROGRAMS

AIDS Drug Assistance Programs (ADAPs) provide crucial prescription drug coverage to patients with HIV/AIDS who have low incomes or are uninsured or underinsured. Income and resource levels vary from state to state. For more information, see the Kaiser Family Foundation's AIDS Drug Assistance Programs (ADAPs).[230]

PHARMACY PRESCRIPTION DRUG DISCOUNT PROGRAMS

Discount drug cards offered through chain pharmacies (such as CVS and Eckerd) for a small monthly premium provide discounts on a number of services, including prescription drugs. Those with a Part D plan may use a discount card, but the two drug programs operate independently of one another. That is, drug card discounts cannot be applied to Part D prices or to Part D copayments, nor can the cost of drugs purchased using a discount card be applied toward Part D out-of-pocket costs. Discount cards may be useful for those whose drugs are excluded by Part D or for those who have reached the donut hole but will not have enough drug costs to reach catastrophic coverage. Discount cards also provide discounts on services not covered by Medicare, such as vision and dental. The utility of these cards depends on each individual's situation and will likely require detailed calculations of costs and savings. Beneficiaries and advocates should contact the pharmacy directly.

PATIENT ASSISTANCE PROGRAMS

Many pharmaceutical manufacturing companies offer Patient Assistance Programs (PAPs) to provide free or reduced-cost prescriptions to persons with low incomes and/or no insurance.[231] Some companies may be able to provide this assistance to Part D enrollees. Beneficiaries and advocates should contact the individual pharmaceutical manufacturer.

PROGRAM OF ALL-INCLUSIVE CARE FOR THE ELDERLY

The Program of All-Inclusive Care for the Elderly (PACE) provides a unique opportunity for beneficiaries with complex needs to receive their care completely from an interdisciplinary team funded by a capitated payment financed by Medicare

---

[230] Kaiser Family Foundation, "AIDS Drug Assistance Programs (ADAPs)," (Apr. 8, 2014), *available at* http://kff.org/hivaids/fact-sheet/aids-drug-assistance-programs/ (site visited Aug. 6, 2018).

[231] For a directory of programs available, see http://www.medicare.gov/pharmaceutical-assistance-program/ (site visited Aug. 6, 2018).

and Medicaid. To be eligible, beneficiaries must be older than 55 years old, "meet a Nursing Facility level of care," and live in the service area of a local PACE.[232]

MEDICARE ADVANTAGE SPECIAL NEEDS PLANS

Certain Medicare Advantage plans are authorized by law to serve specified populations, each of which includes many low-income Medicare beneficiaries. The populations are persons dually eligible for Medicare and Medicaid, people in institutions or those in the community who need an institutional level of care, and people with severe and disabling conditions.[233] These SNPs are required to serve the designated population either exclusively or disproportionately.[234] Also, they must be "coordinated care" plans and they must offer the Part D prescription drug benefit.

SUPPLEMENTAL SECURITY INCOME

The SSI program makes payments to people with very low incomes and resources, and who are age 65 or older, blind, or have a disability.[235] Resources must be less than $2,000 for an individual or $3,000 for a couple. Items that are not counted as resources include the home the person lives in and the land it is on, life insurance policies with a face value of $1,500 or less, a car, burial plots, and up to $1,500 in burial funds per person. Beneficiaries may apply for SSI through the SSA.

---

[232] *See* CMS, "PACE Fact Sheet," *available at* https://www.cms.gov/Medicare/Health-Plans/pace/downloads/pacefactsheet.pdf (site visited Aug. 6, 2018). More information on the PACE program can be found at https://www.medicare.gov/your-medicare-costs/get-help-paying-costs/pace (site visited Sept. 19, 2018).

[233] Special Needs Plans, *see* http://www.cms.gov/Medicare/Health-Plans/SpecialNeedsPlans/index.html (site visited Aug. 6, 2018).

[234] SNP models of care summaries, *available at* http://www.cms.gov/Medicare/Health-Plans/SpecialNeedsPlans/SNP-Model-Of-Care-Summaries.html (site visited Sept. 19, 2018).

[235] *See* Social Security, Supplemental Security Income (SSI), *available at* http://www.ssa.gov/pubs/EN-05-11000.pdf (site visited Sept. 19, 2018); www.socialsecurity.gov (site visited Sept. 19, 2018), or call toll-free at 1-800-772-1213; *see also* What You Need to Know When You Get Supplemental Security Income (SSI) (Publication No. 05-11011), *available at* http://www.ssa.gov/pubs/EN-05-11011.pdf (site visited Sept. 19, 2018).

APPENDIX 1-9 CMS'S *JIMMO V. SEBELIUS* SETTLEMENT INFORMATION

Important Message About the Jimmo Settlement[236]

The CMS reminds the Medicare community of the *Jimmo* Settlement Agreement (January 2013), which clarified that the Medicare program covers skilled nursing care and skilled therapy services under Medicare's skilled nursing facility, home health, and outpatient therapy benefits when a beneficiary needs skilled care in order to maintain function or to prevent or slow decline or deterioration (provided all other coverage criteria are met). Specifically, the *Jimmo* Settlement Agreement required manual revisions to restate a "maintenance coverage standard" for both skilled nursing and therapy services under these benefits:

Skilled nursing services would be covered where such skilled nursing services are necessary to maintain the patient's current condition or prevent or slow further deterioration so long as the beneficiary requires skilled care for the services to be safely and effectively provided.

Skilled therapy services are covered when an individualized assessment of the patient's clinical condition demonstrates that the specialized judgment, knowledge, and skills of a qualified therapist ("skilled care") are necessary for the performance of a safe and effective maintenance program. Such a maintenance program to maintain the patient's current condition or to prevent or slow further deterioration is covered so long as the beneficiary requires skilled care for the safe and effective performance of the program.

The *Jimmo* Settlement Agreement may reflect a change in practice for those providers, adjudicators, and contractors who may have erroneously believed that the Medicare program covers nursing and therapy services under these benefits only when a beneficiary is expected to improve. The *Jimmo* Settlement Agreement is consistent with the Medicare program's regulations governing maintenance nursing and therapy in skilled nursing facilities, home health services, and outpatient therapy (physical, occupational, and speech) and nursing and therapy in inpatient rehabilitation hospitals for beneficiaries who need the level of care that such hospitals provide.

Important Links

Additional Information

In essence, the *Jimmo* Settlement Agreement clarifies Medicare's longstanding policy that coverage of skilled nursing and skilled therapy services in the Skilled

[236] *See* CMS, "*Jimmo* Settlement," *available at* https://www.cms.gov/Center/Special-Topic/Jimmo-Center.html (site visited Aug. 6, 2018).

Nursing Facility (SNF), Home Health (HH), and Outpatient Therapy (OPT) settings does not turn on the presence or absence of a beneficiary's potential for improvement, but rather on the beneficiary's need for skilled care.

For ready reference, this CMS web page serves to provide access, in one location, to various public documents related to the *Jimmo* Settlement Agreement. Included in those public documents is an FAQ document for easy access. We note that the *Jimmo* Settlement Agreement does not represent an expansion of coverage, but rather, it provides clarifications that are intended to help ensure that claims are adjudicated accurately and appropriately in accordance with the existing Medicare policy. Similarly, the *Jimmo* Settlement Agreement does not alter or supersede any other applicable coverage requirements beyond those involving the need for skilled care, such as Medicare's overall requirement that covered services must be reasonable and necessary to diagnose or treat the beneficiary's condition, or existing statutory limitations on the amount or duration of Medicare benefits.

Resources

Jimmo Settlement Agreement approved by the court on January 24, 2013 (https://www.cms.gov/Medicare/Medicare-Fee-for-Service-Payment/SNFPPS/Downloads/Jimmo-Settlement-Agreement.pdf)

Jimmo v. Sebelius Settlement Agreement – Program Manual Clarifications (Fact Sheet) - Updated 2/3/2014 (https://www.cms.gov/Medicare/Medicare-Fee-for-Service-Payment/SNFPPS/Downloads/jimmo_fact_sheet2_022014_final.pdf)

Jimmo v. Sebelius Settlement Agreement (Fact Sheet) - 4/4/2013 (https://www.cms.gov/Medicare/Medicare-Fee-for-Service-Payment/SNFPPS/Downloads/Jimmo-FactSheet.pdf)

MLN Matters® Article MM8458: Manual Updates to Clarify SNF, HH, and OPT Coverage Pursuant to Jimmo v. Sebelius Settlement Agreement (https://www.cms.gov/Outreach-and-Education/Medicare-Learning-Network-MLN/MLNMattersArticles/Downloads/MM8458.pdf)

CR 8458 (https://www.cms.gov/Regulations-and-Guidance/Guidance/Transmittals/Downloads/R179BP.pdf): Manual Updates to Clarify SNF, HH, and OPT Coverage Pursuant to Jimmo v. Sebelius Settlement Agreement

CR 8644 (https://www.cms.gov/Regulations-and-Guidance/Guidance/Transmittals/Downloads/R2911CP.pdf): Manual Updates to Clarify Skilled Nursing Facility Advanced Beneficiary Notice (SNF ABN) Requirements Pursuant to Jimmo v. Sebelius Settlement Agreement

MLN Connects® Call materials - December 2013 (https://www.cms.gov/Outreach-and-Education/Outreach/NPC/National-Provider-Calls-and-Events-Items/2013-12-19-Jimmo-vs-Sebelius.html)

Medicare Benefit Policy Manual - Chapters 1, 7, 8, 15 (https://www.cms.gov/Regulations-and-Guidance/Guidance/Manuals/Internet-Only-Manuals-Ioms-Items/Cms012673.html)

Frequently Asked Questions

FAQs (August 2017) (https://www.cms.gov/Center/Special-Topic/Jimmo-Settlement/FAQs.html)

Additional Questions

Providers and Suppliers: Contact your Medicare Administrative Contractor (https://www.cms.gov/Research-Statistics-Data-and-Systems/Monitoring-Programs/Medicare-FFS-Compliance-Programs/Review-Contractor-Directory-Interactive-Map/)

Beneficiaries: Please call 1-800-Medicare

Chapter 2

HOSPITAL COVERAGE

§ 2.01 INTRODUCTION TO HOSPITAL COVERAGE

[A] Access to Covered Services

Access to Medicare hospital coverage is essential to the financial and physical well-being of millions of aged and disabled Americans. Part A of the Medicare program is financed by the Hospital Insurance Trust Fund, which in turn is funded through a mandatory Social Security payroll tax imposed on all wage earners.[1]

Although Medicare Part A is sometimes known as "hospital insurance," coverage is available under Part A for much more than services provided by a hospital. Of course, inpatient hospital services are covered under Part A, but Medicare Part A also provides coverage for skilled nursing facility (SNF) care, home health care, and hospice care.[2] This chapter addresses eligibility for Medicare Part A as well as Medicare coverage for inpatient hospital care, including long-term care hospitals (LTCHs) and rehabilitation hospitals.

[B] Medicare Administration

Section 1874A of the Social Security Act authorizes the Secretary of the Department of Health and Human Services (HHS) to contract with entities to serve as "Medicare Administrative Contractors" to perform certain functions including determination of payment amounts and making payments; the development of local coverage determinations; beneficiary education and assistance; provider consultation, communication, education, and technical assistance; and other necessary functions, including functions concerning the Medicare Integrity Program.[3] These functions were previously performed by entities known as "fiscal intermediaries" and "carriers." Section 1874A defines the appropriate Medicare Administrative Contractor (MAC) as an entity that has a contract to perform one or more of the described functions in relation to an individual entitled to benefits under Part A or enrolled under Part B, or to a provider, supplier, or class of providers or suppliers. In addition, 42 U.S.C. §§ 1395h and 1395u specifically

---

[1] Social Security Act § 1817, *available at* https://www.ssa.gov/OP_Home/ssact/title18/1817.htm (site visited Aug. 6, 2018), 42 U.S.C. § 1395i(a).

[2] 42 C.F.R. § 406.2 (Scope).

[3] 42 U.S.C. § 1395kk-1, with respect to payment functions (including the function of developing local coverage determinations, as defined in § 1869(f)(2)(B)), provider services functions, and functions relating to services furnished to individuals entitled to benefits under part A or enrolled under part B, or both.

remove references to fiscal intermediaries and carriers, which, as noted, are now referred to as "contractors."[4]

§ 2.02 ELIGIBILITY FOR MEDICARE HOSPITAL INSURANCE (PART A)

Medicare Part A provides basic protections against certain medical costs to persons age 65 or over who are eligible for retirement benefits under Title II of the Social Security Act (or would be eligible for such benefits if certain government employment were covered employment under Title II, or under the Railroad Retirement system); individuals under age 65 who have been entitled for not less than 24 months to benefits under Title II of the Social Security Act (or would have been so entitled if certain government employment were covered employment under Title II) or under the Railroad Retirement system on the basis of a disability;[5] and certain individuals who do not meet the requirements set out above but are medically determined to have end-stage renal disease (ESRD).[6] For people with amyotrophic lateral sclerosis (ALS) Medicare Part A begins with the first month of Social Security disability payments.[7]

Under the Medicare program, eligibility begins the first month in which an individual meets all the requirements, including application and enrollment.[8] The first month of entitlement is the first month for which the individual meets all the

---

[4] This provision was added by Sections 911 and 912 of the Medicare Prescription Drug, Improvement, and Modernization Act of 2003 (MMA), Pub. L. No. 108-173 (Dec. 8, 2003), amending § 1874A of the Social Security Act. For a list of the Medicare Administrative Contractor (MAC) geographic jurisdictions, *see* Centers for Medicare & Medicaid Services (CMS), "Who are the MACs," https://www.cms.gov/Medicare/Medicare-Contracting/Medicare-Administrative-Contractors/Who-are-the-MACs.html (site visited Aug. 6, 2018).

[5] 42 C.F.R. § 406.12.

[6] Social Security Act § 1811, 42 U.S.C. § 1395c; 42 C.F.R. § 406.13 (individual who has ESRD). A three-month waiting period is provided. 42 C.F.R. § 406.13(e).

[7] CMS, "Medicare Basics: A Guide for Families and Friends of People with Medicare," at 4, *available at* https://dfwbgh.org/documents/MedicareBasics.pdf (site visited Aug. 6, 2018).

[8] 42 C.F.R. § 406.3. *See also* Social Security Act § 226(c)(1)(B),42 U.S.C. § 426(c)(1)(B), which states:

> (c) For purposes of subsection (a)—
>
> (1) entitlement of an individual to hospital insurance benefits for a month shall consist of entitlement to have payment made under, and subject to the limitations in, part A of title XVIII on his behalf for inpatient hospital services, post-hospital extended care services, and home health services (as such terms are defined in part C of title XVIII) furnished him in the United States (or outside the United States in the case of inpatient hospital services furnished under the conditions described in section 1814(f)) during such month; except that (A) no such payment may be made for post-hospital extended care services furnished before January 1967, and (B) no such payment may be made for post-hospital extended care services unless the discharge from the hospital required to qualify such services for payment under part A of title XVIII occurred (i) after June 30, 1966, or on or after the first day of the month in which he attains age 65, whichever is later, or (ii) if he was entitled to hospital insurance benefits pursuant to subsection (b), at a time when he was so entitled.

requirements for entitlement to Part A benefits.[9] An insured is an individual who has the number of quarters of coverage required for monthly Social Security benefits.[10] A quarter of coverage is a calendar quarter that is counted toward the number of covered quarters required for eligibility for monthly Social Security benefits; a quarter is counted if during that quarter (or that calendar year) the individual earned a required minimum amount of money.[11]

Persons who are age 65 or over and certain persons under age 65, who do not meet the requirements for premium-free benefits, may obtain benefits by paying a premium.[12] Monthly premium amounts are usually promulgated in October of each year, effective for the succeeding calendar year.[13]

§ 2.03 APPLICATION OR ENROLLMENT FOR MEDICARE PART A

[A] Who Must File

Most Medicare beneficiaries are eligible for Medicare Part A as a result of being age 65 or older and entitled to monthly Social Security or Railroad Retirement cash benefits.[14] Persons eligible for benefits on this basis, as well as those eligible based on disability, do not need to file an application for hospital insurance (Medicare Part A).[15]

---

[9] 42 C.F.R. § 406.3.

[10] 42 C.F.R. § 406.3.

[11] 42 C.F.R. § 406.3. *See also* 20 C.F.R. Pt. 404, subpt. B (determining quarters of coverage and minimum amounts necessary).

[12] 42 C.F.R. § 406.5. For the requirements for premium hospital insurance, *see* 42 C.F.R. § 406.20. Most people do not pay a monthly Part A premium if either they or their spouse have 40 or more quarters of Medicare-covered employment. The Part A premium is $240/month in 2019 for enrollees who have 30–39 quarters of Medicare-covered employment. The Part A premium is $437/month in 2019 for those who are not otherwise eligible for premium-free hospital insurance and have fewer than 30 quarters of Medicare-covered employment.

[13] 42 C.F.R. § 406.32(a). The procedure for determining the monthly premium amount is found at 42 C.F.R. § 406.32(b)–(d); for collection of payments and payments due, *see* 42 C.F.R. § 406.32(e), (f); and for group payment option, see 42 C.F.R. § 406.32(g). Other premium rules are defined at § 406.33 (determination of months to be counted for premium increase: enrollment) and § 406.34 (determination of months to be counted for premium increase: reenrollment).

[14] 42 C.F.R. § 406.6. Note, however, that since the age of eligibility for Social Security benefits is floating upward depending on one's birth year, the alignment of who must file is no longer accurate. For example, for persons born between 1943 and 1954, the age of retirement for Social Security purposes is 66. For the retirement age calculator, *see* Social Security Administration (SSA), "Benefits Planner: Retirement - If you were born between 1943 and 1954," *available at* http://www.socialsecurity.gov/retirement/1943.html (site visited Aug. 6, 2018). Persons in this circumstance must file an application for Medicare at age 65 and may do so online. *See* SSA, "Medicare Benefits," *available at* https://www.ssa.gov/benefits/medicare/ (site visited Aug. 6, 2018).

[15] 42 C.F.R. § 406.6(b).

An individual must file an application for Medicare Part A if he or she seeks entitlement on the basis of:

- Transition benefits;[16]
- Deemed entitlement to disabled widow's or widower's benefits;[17]

---

[16] 42 C.F.R. § 406.6(c)(1). *See* 42 C.F.R. § 406.11 for discussion of transition benefits.

[17] 42 C.F.R. § 406.6(c)(2). *See* 42 C.F.R. § 406.12 for discussion of widow's and widower's benefits. With the June 26, 2015, favorable Supreme Court ruling in Obergefell v. Hodges, Dir., Ohio Dep't of Health, Nos. 14-556, 576 U. S. ____ (2015), same-sex spouses of Medicare beneficiaries in all states who have valid same-sex marriages may be eligible for benefits as a spouse and should apply for benefits as appropriate. *See* http://www.supremecourt.gov/opinions/14pdf/14-556_3204.pdf (site visited Aug. 6, 2018). *Obergefell* holds that denying same-sex couples the right to marry is an improper denial of equal protection under the United States Constitution. Advocates should pay close attention to implementation issues in *Obergefell* as they arise.

For background on the tortuous history of and the recognition of same sex-marriage, see United States v. Windsor, 70 U. S. ____ (2013), *available at* http://www.supremecourt.gov/opinions/12pdf/12-307_6j37.pdf (site visited Aug. 6, 2018). The Supreme Court in *Windsor* found unconstitutional Section 3 of the Defense of Marriage Act (DOMA). *See also* Center for Medicare Advocacy (CMA), "Demise of DOMA: Implementing Federal Benefits for Same-Sex Spouses," *available at* http://www.medicareadvocacy.org/demise-of-doma-implementing-federal-benefits-for-same-sex-spouses/ (site visited Aug. 6, 2018).

For other useful information, *see* SSA, Program Operation Manual Systems (POMS) provisions, GN 00210.005, "Holding Claims, Appeals, and Post-Entitlement Actions Involving Same-Sex Marriages or Legal Same-Sex Relationships Other than Marriage," *available at* https://secure.ssa.gov/apps10/poms.nsf/lnx/0200210005 (site visited Aug. 6, 2018) & GN 00210.010, "Interviewing Individuals with Claims Involving Same-Sex Relationships," *available at* https://secure.ssa.gov/apps10/poms.nsf/lnx/0200210010 (site visited Aug. 6, 2018). Medicare has updated its information on determining who is a same-sex spouse. *See e.g.*, SSA, POMS, GN 00210.002, "Same-Sex Marriage—Determining Marital Status for Title II and Medicare Benefits," *available at* https://secure.ssa.gov/poms.nsf/lnx/0200210002 (site visited Aug. 6, 2018).

In addition, on June 20, 2014, Attorney General Holder published a Memorandum to the President entitled "Implementation of *United States v. Windsor*." The Holder Memorandum can be found at http://www.justice.gov/iso/opa/resources/9722014620103930904785.pdf (site visited Aug. 6, 2018). The memorandum states that most federal agencies recognize a marriage as valid based on where the married couple currently resides (the place of domicile). Further, the memorandum states that for purposes of "processing surviving spouses' claims and appeals involving same-sex marriages, including Medicare-only claims," the SSA uses the place of domicile rule. *See also* SSA, POMS, GN 00210.400, "Same-Sex Marriage—Benefits for Surviving Spouses," *available at* https://secure.ssa.gov/poms.nsf/lnx/0200210400 (site visited Aug. 6, 2018).

In a separate writing, the Medicare agency is requiring skilled nursing facilities (SNFs) in the Medicare Advantage program (managed care) to allow all married Medicare beneficiaries to receive care where their spouse resides, regardless of whether they are a same- or opposite-sex couple. *See* CMS, "Impact of United States v. Windsor on Skilled Nursing Facility Benefits for Medicare Advantage Enrollees – IMMEDIATE ACTION REQUIRED " (Aug. 29, 2013), *available at* http://www.cms.gov/Medicare/Health-Plans/HealthPlansGenInfo/Downloads/SNF_Benefits_Post_Windsor.pdf (site visited Aug. 6, 2018), & CMS, "HHS announces important Medicare information for people in same-sex marriages," (Apr. 3, 2014), *available at* http://www.medicare.gov/sign-up-change-plans/same-sex-marriage.html (site visited Aug.6, 2018). *See also* Center for Medicare

- A diagnosis of ESRD;[18]
- Eligibility for Social Security cash benefits if the individual has attained age 65 without applying for these benefits;[19] and
- Special provisions applicable to government employment.[20]

[B] Time Periods for Filing Application

An application is deemed filed, based on the transition periods or on ESRD as described above, in the first month of eligibility if it is filed not more than three months before the first month of eligibility and is retroactive to the first month of eligibility if filed within 12 months after the first month of eligibility.[21] Similarly, an application filed more than 12 months after the first month of eligibility is retroactive to the twelfth month before the month it is filed.[22]

A valid application based on entitlement to widow's or widower's benefits is deemed filed if, before the first month in which the individual meets the conditions of eligibility, the conditions of eligibility are met before an initial determination, reconsideration, or hearing decision is made on the application.[23] An application, if validly filed within 12 months after the first month of eligibility, is deemed retroactive to that first month. If filed more than 12 months after the first month of eligibility, it is retroactive to the twelfth month before the month of filing.[24] A similar rule applies for persons eligible for Social Security benefits at or after age 65 for an application that is filed before the first month in which the individual meets all the eligibility conditions for that benefit.[25]

Advocacy (CMA), "LGBT (Lesbian, Gay, Bisexual, and Transgender) People: Available Resources," *available at* http://www.medicareadvocacy.org/medicare-info/lesbian-gay-bisexual-and-transgender-lgbt-seniors/ (site visited Aug.6, 2018).

[18] 42 C.F.R. § 406.6(c)(3). *See* 42 C.F.R. § 406.13 for discussion of end-stage renal disease (ESRD).

[19] 42 C.F.R. § 406.6(c)(4). *See* 42 C.F.R. § 406.10(a)(3) for discussion of eligibility based on this status.

[20] 42 C.F.R. § 406.6(c)(5). *See* 42 C.F.R. § 406.15 for discussion of provisions applicable to eligibility based on government employment.

[21] 42 C.F.R. § 406.6(d)(1). *See* 42 C.F.R. § 406.21 (individual enrollment), § 406.22 (effect of month of enrollment on entitlement). *See also* 42 C.F.R. § 406.24 for a discussion of special enrollment periods (SEPs) applicable to group health plan (GHP) and large group health plan (LGHP) individuals; and *see* 42 C.F.R. § 406.26 (enrollment under state buy-in).

[22] 42 C.F.R. § 406.6(d)(1).

[23] 42 C.F.R. § 406.6(d)(2).

[24] 42 C.F.R. § 406.6(d)(2).

[25] 42 C.F.R. § 406.6(d)(3).

[C] Forms and Where to File

Forms for applying for Medicare Part A benefits may be obtained online at https://www.ssa.gov/benefits/medicare/ or by mail, free of charge, from the Centers for Medicare & Medicaid Services (CMS) or at any Social Security branch or district office.[26] In the alternative, an individual may use the application for monthly Social Security benefits to apply for Medicare entitlement if eligible for Medicare Part A at that time.[27]

§ 2.04 SCOPE OF BENEFITS—INPATIENT HOSPITAL COVERAGE BENEFIT PERIODS

[A] In General

An individual insured under Medicare Part A is entitled to inpatient hospital or critical access hospital (CAH) services for up to 150 days during any spell of illness (or "benefit period"), minus one day for each day of such services in excess of 90 days, which were previously used during a prior spell of illness or benefit period.[28] (These days in excess of 90 days are known as "lifetime reserve

[26] 42 C.F.R. § 406.7. For online forms, *see* http://www.gpo.gov/fdsys/pkg/CFR-2011-title42-vol2/pdf/CFR-2011-title42-vol2-sec406-7.pdf (site visited Aug. 6, 2018).

[27] 42 C.F.R. § 406.7.

[28] Social Security Act § 1812(a), 42 U.S.C. § 1395d(a); 42 C.F.R. § 409.61 (general limitations on amount of benefits), § 409.82 (inpatient hospital deductible), § 409.83 (inpatient hospital coinsurance). Inpatient hospital status is a critical component of accessing Medicare-covered hospital services as well as post-hospitalization services such as the skilled nursing facility benefit. Defining inpatient status has become increasingly challenging as Medicare has increased its use of "observation status" for the provision of observation services. For many patients in observation status, the care received is indistinguishable from that of persons in inpatient status, but for the status designation itself. Nonetheless, the status designation has enormous consequences in terms of the benefits and services that are available. Persons in observation status receive observation services as an outpatient (Medicare Part B). Moreover, inpatient status is critical to meeting the required three-day inpatient hospitalization requirement for skilled nursing facility care. For a discussion of this issue, *see e.g.* CMA, "Outpatient Observation Status," *available at* http://www.medicareadvocacy.org/medicare-info/observation-status/ (site visited Aug. 6, 2018). *See also* CMA, "CMS Issues Instructions Regarding the Medicare Outpatient Observation Notice (MOON)" *available at* http://www.medicareadvocacy.org/cms-issues-instructions-regarding-the-medicare-outpatient-observation-notice-moon/ (site visited Aug. 6, 2018). The latter piece discusses the Medicare Outpatient Observation Notice (MOON) required by the Notice of Observation Treatment and Implication for Care Eligibility Act (NOTICE Act), Pub. L. No. 114-42, 42 U.S.C. § 1395cc(a)(1)(Y). Effective August 6, 2016, the NOTICE Act requires that hospitals provide written and oral notice, within 36 hours, to patients who are in observation or other outpatient status for more than 24 hours. The notice must explain the reason that the patient is an outpatient and describe the implications of that status both for cost-sharing in the hospital and for subsequent "eligibility for coverage" in a skilled nursing facility (SNF). However, in effect, CMS did not require hospitals to issue the MOON notice until March 8, 2017, when the notice became finalized.

days"). This inpatient hospital coverage is available to inpatients in an acute hospital or in a rehabilitation hospital. Coverage for inpatient psychiatric hospitals is somewhat different.[29]

In any benefit period, a Medicare beneficiary is entitled to 60 fully paid days of hospital care, subject only to an initial deductible amount per benefit period; after 60 days, a beneficiary must pay a daily coinsurance amount equal to one-fourth of the initial deductible; and after 90 days, the beneficiary is entitled to 60 "lifetime reserve" days, which may be used only once during the beneficiary's lifetime.[30] The initial deductible is $1,364 in 2019 ($1,340 in 2018); the daily coinsurance amount is $341 in 2019 ($335 in 2018) for days 61 to 90 of a hospital stay; and the lifetime reserve day coinsurance amount is $682 in 2019 ($670 in 2018) for days 91 to 150.[31] The deductible and coinsurance amounts and lifetime reserve day coinsurance amount are adjusted each calendar year. Each adjustment is announced in the *Federal Register*, usually in October or early November prior to the new calendar year.

[B] Benefit Period Explained

A benefit period (or "spell of illness") generally begins when a beneficiary enters a hospital and is admitted as an inpatient and has not received a hospital or SNF level of care within the prior 60 consecutive days.[32] A hospital or SNF level of care is coverable by the Medicare program.

■ **EXAMPLE:** Imagine that Mrs. Brown entered the hospital on January 1, 2019, and stayed for 200 days. Mrs. Brown returns home for 30 days before she is re-hospitalized. The Medicare hospital coverage available to Mrs. Brown may be described as follows: Mrs. Brown first is responsible for the $1,364 deductible before any Medicare coverage is available. She then receives 60 days of hospital coverage without coinsurance. Mrs. Brown is next responsible for $341 of coinsurance per day between days 61 and 90. On day 91 Mrs. Brown begins to use her lifetime reserve days

---

See Bagnall v. Sebelius, No. 3:11cv1703 (MPS) (D. Conn. filed Nov. 3, 2011), Memorandum of Decision dated September 23, 2013. For a discussion of *Bagnall*, *see* CMA, "Disappointing Decision from Court in Challenge to 'Observation Status' Highlights Need to Pass Legislation," *available at* http://www.medicareadvocacy.org/disappointing-decision-from-court-in-challenge-to-observation-status-highlights-need-to-pass-legislation/ (site visited Aug. 6, 2018).

[29] *See* § **2.04[C]** of this Handbook.

[30] 42 C.F.R. § 409.83 (inpatient hospital coinsurance) and § 409.60 (benefit period defined).

[31] *See* CMS, "2018 Medicare Costs," *available at* https://www.medicare.gov/Pubs/pdf/11579-Medicare-Costs.pdf (site visited Aug. 6, 2018).

[32] *See* CMS, Medicare General Information, Eligibility, and Entitlement (MGIEE), Ch. 3, §§ 10.4-10.4.4., *available at* https://www.cms.gov/Regulations-and-Guidance/Guidance/Manuals/downloads/ge101c03.pdf (site visited Aug. 6, 2018).

(assuming that she has not used any of these days in prior hospital stays). The lifetime reserve days require a daily coinsurance payment of $682. After the lifetime reserve days are exhausted on the 150th day, Mrs. Brown will have exhausted her Medicare coverage for her current benefit period. When Mrs. Brown returns to the hospital after 30 days at home, she will be entitled to no additional Medicare coverage. As stated above, a beneficiary is entitled to a maximum of 150 days of hospital coverage in any one "spell of illness."[33] A spell of illness ends and a new spell of illness (with additional hospital coverage) becomes available only after the beneficiary has gone 60 consecutive days without receiving either an inpatient hospital level of care or a SNF level of care.[34] A hospital or SNF level of care is one coverable by the Medicare program. Because Mrs. Brown was at home for only 30 days, she continues in the same spell of illness and her benefits remain exhausted.

It should be noted that it is possible to have more than one benefit period in the same calendar year, requiring the payment of a new deductible and additional coinsurance.[35] This circumstance arises when a beneficiary has two separate hospitalizations in a year, and the first hospitalization is followed by a period of 60 consecutive days without receiving an inpatient hospital or SNF level of care.

[C] Inpatient Psychiatric Hospital Services

With respect to inpatient psychiatric hospital services, a beneficiary is entitled to a total of 190 days of inpatient care during his or her lifetime.[36] Although an individual is entitled to 190 days of such care per lifetime, the individual is permitted to utilize only a maximum of 150 of these days in any given benefit period. Moreover, these 150 days are subject to the same deductible and coinsurance amounts that are applicable to care received in an acute or rehabilitation hospital setting.

■ **EXAMPLE:** If Mr. Jones entered a psychiatric hospital in 2019 with a full 190 lifetime days available, he would be able to use only 150 of those days and would be required to pay the $1,364 deductible. In addition, commencing with the 61st day, he would be required to pay the $341 per day coinsurance and commencing with the 91st day, he would be required to pay the $682 per day coinsurance. Because he is permitted to use only 150 of his 190 lifetime psychiatric inpatient hospital days, the

---

[33] 42 U.S.C. § 1395d.

[34] Social Security Act § 1861(a), 42 U.S.C. § 1395x (a); 42 C.F.R. § 409.60(b).

[35] 42 C.F.R. § 409.80(a).

[36] 42 U.S.C. § 1395d(b)(3); 42 C.F.R. § 409.62. *See also* CMS, "Your Medicare Coverage: Mental Health Care (Inpatient)," *available at* http://www.medicare.gov/coverage/inpatient-mental-health-care.html (site visited Aug. 6, 2018).

remaining 40 days of available coverage can be used only in a new benefit period, that is, only after he has gone 60 consecutive days without receiving an inpatient hospital or SNF level of care.

It should be noted that if the individual was an inpatient in a psychiatric hospital on the first day of Medicare entitlement and for any of the 150 days immediately before the first day of Medicare entitlement, those days are subtracted from the 150 days that would otherwise be available in the initial benefit period for inpatient psychiatric services in a psychiatric or general hospital.[37] These subtracted days are, however, available to the individual in a subsequent benefit period. This reduction applies only if the hospital was participating in Medicare as a psychiatric hospital on the individual's first day of Medicare enrollment,[38] and only to the beneficiary's first benefit period.[39] Days spent in a general hospital before entitlements are not subtracted under this provision even if the stay was for diagnosis or treatment of mental illness.[40]

§ 2.05 MEDICARE-COVERED SERVICES

[A] In General

With respect to the provision of Medicare-covered services, "arrangements" include those arrangements that provide for Medicare payment for services delivered to Medicare beneficiaries; "covered" refers to services authorized for Medicare payment that meet Medicare coverage criteria as defined in the Medicare law and regulations;[41] "nominal charge provider" means a provider that furnishes services free of charge or at a nominal charge and is either a public provider or other provider that demonstrates to CMS's satisfaction that a significant portion of its patients are low income and requests that payment of its services be determined accordingly; "participating" refers to hospitals or other facilities that meet the conditions of participation and have in effect a Medicare provider agreement; a

---

[37] 42 C.F.R. § 409.63(a).

[38] 42 C.F.R. § 409.63(a)(2).

[39] 42 C.F.R. § 409.63(a)(3).

[40] 42 C.F.R. § 409.63(b). *See also* the set of examples explaining the § 409.63 reduction rule found at 42 C.F.R. § 409.63(c); Legion v. Richardson, 354 F. Supp. 456 (S.D.N.Y.), *aff'd*, 414 U.S. 1058 (1973); and Doe v. Colautti, 592 F.2d 704 (1979).

[41] Usually, Medicare coverage results in payment by Medicare for the services or items in question. Some courts, however, have distinguished Medicare coverage from Medicare payment. This is important to a beneficiary, because once Medicare coverage is established, the beneficiary is absolved of full financial responsibility for the items or services in question, regardless of whether the provider receives Medicare payment. *See, e.g.*, New York *ex rel.* Bodnar v. Secretary of HHS, 903 F.2d 122 (2d Cir. 1990), *available at* http://openjurist.org/903/f2d/122/state-of-new-york-bodnar-v-secretary-of-health-and-human-services (site visited Aug. 6, 2018).

"qualified hospital" is one primarily engaged in providing, by or under the supervision of doctors of medicine or osteopathy, inpatient services for the diagnosis, treatment, and care or rehabilitation of persons who are sick, injured, or disabled, is not primarily engaged in providing skilled nursing care or related services, provides 24-hour nursing services, and is licensed in the United States, or in Canada or Mexico, for the purposes of furnishing non-emergency services to U.S. residents.[42]

[B] Covered Benefits

Covered benefits under Part A include the services, except for luxuries (such as a telephone or television), generally provided during a hospital or CAH stay, including use of hospital facilities, room and board in a semiprivate room, nursing and related services, medical social services, operating and recovery room costs, drugs and medical supplies furnished in the hospital, certain diagnostic or therapeutic services, laboratory tests, radiological services billed by the hospital, rehabilitation services, and blood.[43] Inpatient hospital services generally do not include SNF-type care furnished by a hospital or a CAH that has a swing-bed approval, or any nursing-facility-type care that may be furnished as a Medicaid service under the Medicaid program.[44]

§ 2.06 COVERAGE CRITERIA EXPLAINED

[A] Bed and Board

Except for applicable deductibles and coinsurance amounts, Medicare Part A covers the cost of bed and board in semiprivate (two to four beds) or ward (five or more beds) accommodations.[45] Private accommodations are covered only if the patient's treating physician concludes that the patient's condition requires isolation, if the hospital or CAH has no semiprivate or ward accommodations, or if the semiprivate and ward accommodations of the hospital or CAH are fully occupied by other patients.[46] Medicare will continue to pay for private accommodations until the patient's condition no longer requires a private room or until

---

[42] 42 C.F.R. § 409.3.

[43] Social Security Act § 1861(b), *available at* https://www.ssa.gov/OP_Home/ssact/title18/1861.htm (site visited Aug. 6, 2018), 42 U.S.C. § 1395x(b); 42 C.F.R. § 409.10 (included services), § 409.11 (bed and board), § 409.12 (nursing and related services), § 409.13 (drugs and biologicals), § 409.15 (services of interns and residents-in-training), § 409.16 (other diagnostic or therapeutic services), § 409.18 (services related to kidney transplantation), and § 409.14 (services related to cardiac pacemakers and pacemaker leads).

[44] 42 C.F.R. § 409.10(b).

[45] 42 C.F.R. § 409.11(a).

[46] 42 C.F.R. § 409.11(b).

semiprivate or ward accommodations are available.[47] The hospital is free to charge the patient the difference between the private room rate and the semiprivate or ward accommodations rate where the patient requests a private room absent a medical need for such.[48]

[B] Nursing and Related Services

Medicare covers nursing and related services, use of hospital or CAH facilities, and medical social services as inpatient hospital or inpatient CAH services ordinarily furnished by the hospital for the care and treatment of inpatients.[49] Medicare, however, does not pay for private duty nurses or attendants.[50]

[C] Drugs and Biologicals

Medicare pays for drugs and biologicals as inpatient hospital or inpatient CAH services if they represent a cost to the hospital, are ordinarily furnished by the hospital or CAH for the care and treatment of inpatients, and are furnished to an inpatient for use in the hospital or CAH.[51] In addition, Medicare will pay for a limited supply of drugs for use outside the hospital or CAH if it is medically necessary to enable a beneficiary's departure from the hospital or CAH and required until the patient can obtain a continuing supply.[52]

[D] Services Furnished by an Intern or a Resident-in-Training

Inpatient hospital services include the services of medical or surgical interns or residents-in-training.[53] Services must be provided through a teaching program approved by the Council on Medical Education of the American Medical Association or the Bureau of Professional Education of the American Osteopathic Association; a program approved by the Council on Dental Education of the American Dental Association; or a program approved by the Council on Podiatry Education of the American Podiatry Association.[54]

---

[47] 42 C.F.R. § 409.11(b)(2).
[48] 42 C.F.R. § 409.11(b)(3).
[49] 42 C.F.R. § 409.12(a).
[50] 42 C.F.R. § 409.12(b).
[51] 42 C.F.R. § 409.13(a).
[52] 42 C.F.R. § 409.13(b).
[53] 42 C.F.R. § 409.15(a).
[54] 42 C.F.R. § 409.15(b), (c).

[E] Other Diagnostic or Therapeutic Items or Services

Diagnostic or therapeutic items or services are considered inpatient hospital or inpatient CAH services if furnished by the hospital or CAH or others under arrangements made with the hospital or CAH; the billing for such services is performed through the hospital or CAH; and the services are of the kind ordinarily furnished to inpatients either by the hospital or CAH or under arrangements made by the hospital.[55]

In recent years, an increasing trend has been noted in which beneficiaries have been in hospital rooms and beds, not as "admitted" patients, but rather under "observation" status.[56] Hospitals appear to use "observation" status as a cost-savings mechanism to avoid Medicare hospital reimbursement complications related to CMS's Recovery Audit Contractor (RAC) program.[57]

Often, patients are not informed of their observation status. Observation status is not the same as being a hospital inpatient, although the actual services may be the same.[58] When hospital patients are classified as outpatients and are in hospitals on observation status, they may be charged for services that Medicare

---

[55] 42 C.F.R. § 409.16.

[56] For information on observation status and its consequences, *see* CMA, "Observation Status & *Bagnall v. Sebelius*," *available at* http://www.medicareadvocacy.org/medicare-info/observation-status/ (site visited Aug. 6, 2018). For a discussion of this issue, *see e.g.* CMA, "Observation Status." *See also* "CMS Issues Instructions Regarding the Medicare Outpatient Observation Notice (MOON)" *available at* http://www.medicareadvocacy.org/cms-issues-instructions-regarding-the-medicare-outpatient-observation-notice-moon/ (site visited Aug. 6, 2018). The latter piece discusses the Medicare Outpatient Observation Notice (MOON) required by the Notice of Observation Treatment and Implication for Care Eligibility Act (NOTICE Act). Pub. L. No. 114-42, 42 U.S.C. § 1395cc(a)(1)(Y). Effective August 6, 2016, the NOTICE Act requires that hospitals provide written and oral notice, within 36 hours, to patients who are in observation or other outpatient status for more than 24 hours. The notice must explain the reason that the patient is an outpatient and describe the implications of that status both for cost-sharing in the hospital and for subsequent "eligibility for coverage" in a skilled nursing facility (SNF). However, in effect, CMS did not require hospitals to issue the MOON notice until March 8, 2017, when the notice became finalized.

[57] *See* CMS, "Recovery Audit Program," *available at* http://www.cms.gov/Research-Statistics-Data-and-Systems/Monitoring-Programs/Medicare-FFS-Compliance-Programs/Recovery-Audit-Program/Recent_Updates.html (site visited Aug. 6, 2018).

[58] *See* Barrows v. Burwell, No. 3:11-cv-1703 (2d Cir. Jan. 22, 2015), *available at* http://hr.cch.com/hld/BarrowsvBurwell2dCir1-22-2015.pdf (site visited Aug. 6, 2018). *See also* http://www.medicareadvocacy.org and **Chapter 3** of this Handbook. The Center for Medicare Advocacy's litigation to correct this problem was unsuccessful. *See* Bagnall v. Sebelius, No. 3:11cv1703 (MPS) (D. Conn. filed Nov. 3, 2011) (Memorandum of Decision dated Sept. 23, 2013). For a discussion of *Bagnall, see* CMA, "Disappointing Decision from Court in Challenge to 'Observation Status' Highlights Need to Pass Legislation," *available at* http://www.medicareadvocacy.org/disappointing-decision-from-court-in-challenge-to-observation-status-highlights-need-to-pass-legislation/ (site visited Aug. 6, 2018).

would have paid if they were properly admitted as hospital inpatients. Moreover, such patients will not be able to obtain Medicare coverage in SNFs if they need nursing home care after their hospital stay ends.

Medicare Part A covers nursing home care for patients who have a three-day prior inpatient hospital stay, and observation status does not count toward the three-day prior hospital stay.[59] In addition, as a result of retroactive billing practices, beneficiaries have been "admitted" to a hospital but have had that status changed to observation status before the hospital submits the bill to Medicare. The right to notice to beneficiaries in these circumstances is unclear. The Center for Medicare Advocacy continues to pursue strategies to address problems related to observation status.[60]

Beginning August 6, 2016, the Notice of Observation Treatment and Implication for Care Eligibility Act (NOTICE Act)[61] required hospitals to provide written and oral notice, within 36 hours, to patients who are in observation or other outpatient status for more than 24 hours. The notice must explain the reason that the patient is an outpatient (and not an admitted inpatient) and describe the implications of that status both for cost-sharing in the hospital and for subsequent "eligibility for coverage" in a SNF. The NOTICE Act does not give patients appeal rights to challenge their observation status.[62]

In final regulations for inpatient hospital reimbursement that were put on display at the Office of Federal Register on August 2, 2016, CMS announced that the final rules, including rules to implement the NOTICE Act, would be effective October 1, 2016, and that the required written notice to patients—the Medicare Outpatient Observation Notice (MOON)—would not become effective until 90 days following approval of the MOON by the Office of Management and Budget (OMB). CMS did not require hospitals to issue the MOON notice until March 8, 2017, when the notice became finalized. Similarly, diagnostic services of independent clinical laboratories, furnished to Medicare inpatients under arrangements with a Medicare-participating hospital, that are reimbursable under Medicare Part A are affected by observation status.[63] CMS has issued additional

For information on the RACs, *see* CMS, "Recovery Audit Contractor," *available at* http://www.cms.gov/Research-Statistics-Data-and-Systems/Monitoring-Programs/Medicare-FFS-Compliance-Programs/Recovery-Audit-Program/ (site visited Aug. 6, 2018). *See also* Tax Relief and Health Care Act of 2006 § 302, Pub. L. No. 109-432 (Dec. 20, 2006), *available at* www.cms.gov/transmittals/downloads/R139FM.pdf (site visited Aug. 6, 2018).

[59] *See* CMA, "Observation Status & Bagnall v. Sebelius."

[60] CMA, "Observation Status & Bagnall v. Sebelius."

[61] Pub. L. No. 114-42, signed by President Obama on August 6, 2015, 42 U.S.C. § 1395cc(a)(1)(Y).

[62] 42 C.F.R. § 405.926(u); 81 Fed. Reg. 57,267 (Aug. 22, 2016), *available at* https://www.gpo.gov/fdsys/pkg/FR-2016-08-22/pdf/2016-18476.pdf (site visited Aug. 6, 2018).

[63] 42 C.F.R. § 482.27; *see* Medicare Benefit Policy (MBP) Manual, CMS Pub. No. 100-02, Ch. 1, § 50.3, *available at* http://cms.hhs.gov/Regulations-and-Guidance/Guidance/Manuals/Downloads/

guidance through which it attempts to clarify when a person is an inpatient.[64] The CMS guidance is worrisome and confusing. It establishes, for example, a presumption that if a patient is in an inpatient hospital for two midnights, the patient will likely be admitted. The guidance states that claims in which a medically necessary inpatient stay spans at least two midnights after the beneficiary is formally admitted as an inpatient will be presumed appropriate for inpatient admission and inpatient hospital payment and will generally not be subject to medical review of the inpatient admission, absent evidence of systematic gaming, abuse, or delays in the provision of care in an attempt to qualify for the two-midnight presumption.[65]

Nonetheless, an order of admission remains the basis of inpatient hospital status. Furthermore, a physician's intention that his or her patient should be admitted, as expressed in the patient's medical records, is to be given weight but has no presumptive value.[66]

[F] Services Related to Kidney Transplantations

Medicare only pays for kidney transplantations performed in a Medicare-approved renal transplantation center.[67] Provided that the kidney is intended for an individual who has ESRD and is eligible for Medicare, Medicare payment is available for the evaluation or preparation of a potential or actual donor, for the donation of the kidney, or for postoperative recovery services directly related to the kidney donation.[68] The Medicare deductible and coinsurance requirements do not apply to services furnished to an individual in connection with the donation of a kidney for transplant surgery.[69]

[G] Blood Services

With respect to blood, the patient must pay a deductible for the first three units of whole blood or units of packed red cells that a beneficiary receives during

---

bp102c01.pdf (site visited Aug. 6, 2018). *See also* CMS, "Are you a hospital inpatient or outpatient?" *available at* http://www.medicare.gov/Pubs/pdf/11435.pdf (site visited Aug. 6, 2018).

[64] *See* 42 C.F.R. § 412.3(e)(1)-(2), *available at* http://www.ecfr.gov/cgi-bin/text-idx?SID=f907882f7b47ae43d815ee21bd8a9d9e&node=42:2.0.1.2.12.1.47.3&rgn=div8 (site visited Aug. 6, 2018).

[65] 78 Fed. Reg. 50,496, 50,950 (Aug. 19, 2013), *available at* http://www.federalregister.com/Browse/AuxData/DAA2F182-BDD6-482F-8CE4-295DBB108458 (Aug. 6, 2018).

[66] *See* 78 Fed. Reg. 50,496, 50,950 (Aug. 19, 2013). For further discussion of the conundrum of observation status and inpatient status, *see* CMA, "Observation Status: OIG Provides an Analysis and CMS Issues Final Regulations," *available at* http://www.medicareadvocacy.org/observation-status-oig-provides-an-analysis-and-cms-issues-final-regulations/ (site visited Aug. 6, 2018).

[67] 42 C.F.R. § 409.18(a).

[68] 42 C.F.R. § 409.18(b).

[69] 42 C.F.R. § 409.89.

a calendar year as an inpatient of a hospital, CAH, or SNF, or on an outpatient basis under Medicare Part B.[70] A unit of packed red cells is treated as the equivalent of a unit of whole blood.[71] Generally, a provider may charge the patient its customary charge for any of the first three units.[72] The deductible does not apply to other blood components such as platelet, fibrinogen, plasma, gamma globulin, and serum albumin, or to the cost of storing and administering blood.[73] The beneficiary also has the option to arrange for the blood to be replaced rather than paying for it.[74]

The blood deductible is in addition to the inpatient hospital deductible and daily coinsurance.[75] The Part A blood deductible is reduced to the extent that the Part B blood deductible has been applied; for example, the beneficiary has received one unit under Medicare Part B.

The Medicare hospital benefit does not include coverage for physicians' services while in the hospital. Those services are covered under Medicare Part B.[76] The surgeon and anesthesiologist, for example, will bill the patient separately (the cost of physicians' services deemed reasonable and necessary would be covered under Part B of the Medicare program).

§ 2.07 LIMITATIONS ON PAYMENT FOR SERVICES

[A] Physician Certification and Payment Forms

Providers of Medicare services, including hospitals, must submit payment forms indicating that the services provided were medically necessary and appropriate. The forms for submitting a request for payment are promulgated by the Secretary and must be submitted for payment no later than the calendar year following the year in which such services are furnished. Services furnished in the last quarter of a calendar year, however, are deemed to have been delivered in the following calendar year.[77]

■ **EXAMPLE:** If a patient receives services in October 2018, those services will be viewed for billing purposes (but not for deductible purposes) as having been delivered during the calendar year 2019 and, therefore, can properly be billed through the end of 2020. By contrast, services in the calendar year 2018 that were delivered on or before September 2018 could properly be billed only through the end of 2019.

---

[70] 42 U.S.C. § 1395e (a)(2); 42 C.F.R. § 409.87(a)(3).

[71] 42 C.F.R. § 409.87(a)(2).

[72] 42 C.F.R. § 409.87(c).

[73] 42 C.F.R. § 409.87(a)(4).

[74] 42 C.F.R. § 409.87(b).

[75] 42 C.F.R. § 409.87(a)(5).

[76] 42 U.S.C. § 1395d; Social Security Act § 1812(a)(1).

[77] 42 C.F.R. § 424.44.

The physician must certify that the inpatient hospital services provided over a period of time are required to be given on an inpatient basis for such individual's medical treatment, or that inpatient diagnostic study is medically required and such services are necessary for such purposes.[78] This certification must be furnished in such cases, and with such frequency and with supporting material, as appropriate to the case involved and as provided by the Secretary's regulations. The first such certification must be furnished no later than the 20th day of the period in which services are being provided.[79] A similar certification is required for inpatient psychiatric hospital services.[80]

Physicians must also certify that dental services performed in the hospital setting, in connection with the care, treatment, filling, removal, or replacement of teeth or structures that directly support teeth, are such that the services must be performed in the hospital setting.[81] The certification must state that because of the underlying medical condition and clinical status of the patient, or the severity of the dental procedure, hospitalization is required.[82]

[B] Payment for Services Performed Outside the United States

Payment is available for inpatient hospital services furnished to Medicare beneficiaries in a hospital located outside the United States, or under arrangements with it, if such individual is a resident of the United States and only if such hospital is closer to, or substantially more accessible from, the residence of such individual than the nearest United States hospital adequately equipped to deal with and available to treat the beneficiary's illness or injury.[83]

---

[78] 42 U.S.C. § 1395f (a)(2), (a)(3). *See also* 42 U.S.C. § 1395f(a)(6) (physician certification where no utilization review committee findings have been made), § 1395f(a)(8) with respect to inpatient critical access hospital services, requiring physician certification that the patient may reasonably be expected to be transferred to a hospital within 96 hours after admission to the critical access hospital.

[79] 42 U.S.C. § 1395f (a)(3).

[80] 42 U.S.C. § 1395f (a)(2)(A).

[81] 42 U.S.C. § 1395f (a)(2)(D). Access to dental services generally is problematic in Medicare as Medicare does not cover routine dental services. Advocates have found that sustaining coverage for such services is less complicated where the procedures are part of services performed on an inpatient hospital basis. Even so, the setting is not necessarily determinative of coverage. It is whether the non-routine dental services were part of treating a recognized Medicare-covered condition that is determinative. *See also* CMA, "New Report: Expanded Dental Coverage Needed to Confront Health Crisis," *available at* http://www.medicareadvocacy.org/new-report-expanded-dental-coverage-needed-to-confront-health-crisis/ (site visited Aug. 6, 2018).

[82] 42 U.S.C. § 1395f (a)(2)(D).

[83] 42 U.S.C. § 1395f (f).

§ 2.08 THE MEDICAL NECESSITY STANDARD FOR INPATIENT HOSPITAL STAYS

[A] In General

The substantive standard for Medicare coverage for general hospital services (also called acute hospital care) is one of "medical necessity."[84] A physician must certify that hospital "services are required to be given on an inpatient basis for such individual's medical treatment, or that inpatient diagnostic study is medically required. . . ."[85] The regulations provide that inpatient hospital care includes cases where a beneficiary needs a SNF level of care, but under Medicare criteria, a Medicare certified SNF-level bed is not available.[86] The Medicare statute requires that the beneficiary is "entitled to have payment made" for SNF care although remaining in the hospital awaiting an available SNF bed. Therefore, in addition to requiring a SNF level of care, a beneficiary must also have been covered by Medicare for at least three days during the hospital stay in question.[87] A patient must accept the first Medicare-certified bed available[88] or lose continued Medicare inpatient hospital coverage. However, an offer of a non-certified bed may be rejected with no risk to continued inpatient hospital coverage.[89] In addition, the statute explicitly excludes from coverage any expenses incurred for items or services "not reasonable and necessary for the diagnosis or treatment of illness or injury or to improve the functioning of a malformed body member. . . ."[90]

■ **EXAMPLE:** Mrs. Smith sustains a fall and fractures her leg. Surgery is required to repair the fracture, and she is admitted to the hospital in order to receive such treatment. Close monitoring of her post-surgical condition

---

[84] 42 U.S.C. § 1395f (a)(3).

[85] 42 U.S.C. § 1395f (a)(3).

[86] 42 C.F.R. § 412.42(c)(1); *see also* 42 C.F.R. § 424.13(b).

[87] 42 U.S.C. § 1395x(v)(1)(G)(i)(III); *see also* 42 C.F.R. § 409.30.

[88] Occasionally, the question arises as to how geographically distant the SNF bed can be and still be deemed "available" to the patient. For example, can a patient be required to accept a SNF bed that is 300 miles from the patient's home? While there is no unequivocal answer to this question in the Medicare statute or regulations, past Medicare policy stated that this requirement "is not defined to require a patient to be taken away from his family and transported over great distances." *See* CMS, Medicare Intermediary (MI) Manual, CMS Pub. 13, § 3421.1C, *available at* http://www.cms.gov/Regulations-and-Guidance/Guidance/Transmittals/downloads/R420A2.pdf (site visited Aug. 6, 2018). This provision remains in the Paper-Based Manual (but still available on the Internet) as it does not appear to have been transferred to the Internet-Only Manuals, *available at* http://www.cms.gov/Regulations-and-Guidance/Guidance/Manuals/Paper-Based-Manuals.html (site visited Aug. 6, 2018).

[89] 42 C.F.R. § 412.42(c)(1); *see also* 42 C.F.R. § 424.13(b).

[90] Social Security Act § 1862(a)(1)(A), 42 U.S.C. § 1395(a)(1)(A).

is required because she has a history of peripheral vascular disease, venous thrombosis, and leg edema. Her treating physician has prescribed continuous intravenous anticoagulation therapy in order to prevent a stroke and is unable to accurately discern whether the swelling in her leg is attributable to swelling relative to the fracture or to the venous thrombosis. During this entire time, a span of eight days, the services Mrs. Smith is receiving in the hospital could be performed only in a hospital, where 24-hour availability of a physician exists and the requisite close physician monitoring is available. Following resolution of these medical issues, Mrs. Smith's physician orders physical therapy five times per week and includes a statement that Mrs. Smith can be transferred to a SNF. However, no Medicare-certified SNF bed is immediately available. Under these circumstances, Mrs. Smith is still eligible to receive Medicare inpatient hospital coverage, because she needs a SNF level of care, but no Medicare-certified SNF bed is available to her and she has been receiving Medicare covered inpatient hospital care for 3 days or more. The days that Mrs. Smith spends in the hospital waiting for a Medicare-certified SNF bed to become available are covered hospital days, subject to any applicable hospital coinsurance amounts, as well as the 150-day-per-benefit-period inpatient hospital limitation.

[B] Additional Requirements for Rehabilitation Hospitals

Medicare imposes additional coverage requirements for care received in rehabilitation hospitals.[91] Rehabilitation hospital care may be covered when it is provided in a freestanding rehabilitation hospital, or in a distinct rehabilitation unit of an acute care hospital. Effective January 1, 2002, inpatient rehabilitation hospitals and rehabilitation units are paid under a prospective payment system (PPS). Payments are made on the basis of prospectively determined rates and applied on a diagnosis-related group (DRG) basis.[92]

For a rehabilitation hospitalization to be covered, the following requirements must be satisfied:[93]

---

[91] *See* 42 C.F.R. Pt. 482 and all the documentation requirements specified in 42 C.F.R. § 412.622(a)(3), (4), and (5).

[92] 42 C.F.R. §§ 412.600 *et seq.*

[93] 42 C.F.R. § 412.23(b), § 412.29; MBP Manual, Ch. 1: §§ 110.1 *et seq., available at* https://www.cms.gov/Regulations-and-Guidance/Guidance/Manuals/downloads/bp102c01.pdf (site visited Aug. 6, 2018). For many years CMS interpreted "relatively intense" to mean that the patient had to require and receive at least three hours per day of physical and/or occupational therapy in order to qualify for Medicare coverage for hospital-level rehabilitation. This interpretation, found in CMS's Intermediary and Hospital Manuals, was found by the United States District Court to be an arbitrary rule of thumb that could not be used to deny coverage in Hooper v. Sullivan, Medicare & Medicaid Guide (CCH) 37,985 (D. Conn. 1989). *See also* Hooper v. Sullivan, Medicare benefits, *available at* http://www.medicareadvocacy.org/wp-content/uploads/2012/02/RRF-Issue-Brief-14-Medicare-Updates-12-2011-_3_.pdf (site visited Aug. 6, 2018). In *Hooper*, the Secretary was

- The physician must certify that the patient needs inpatient hospital rehabilitation;
- The hospital must be a Medicare-certified facility;
- The patient must require a relatively intense, multidisciplinary rehabilitation program provided by a coordinated team of physical therapists, occupational therapists, speech language pathologists, rehabilitation nurses, and/or training in rehabilitation medicine, which is evidenced by at least bi-weekly team meeting notes;
- The goal of the rehabilitation program must be to upgrade the patient's ability to function as independently as possible;
- The care must be reasonable and necessary, and not actually available at a lower level of care.

It should be noted that the Medicare program pays for rehabilitation services, including physical, speech, and occupational therapies, in different settings and not solely in an inpatient hospital setting. For example, various kinds of rehabilitation can be provided at home through the Medicare home health benefit, in an outpatient therapy facility, in a SNF, in a comprehensive outpatient rehabilitation facility (CORF), in an inpatient rehabilitation facility (IRF),[94] or in a long-term care hospital (LTCH). A patient's medical needs and condition should dictate the setting in which rehabilitation services are provided. In addition, the type and amount of care a person receives varies by setting. Federal regulations published in 2004 began a three-year phase-in of the requirement that to qualify as an IRF, 75 percent of the IRF's patients must have one or more of 13 specified conditions and otherwise require intensive rehabilitation services. However, recent legislation has mandated that the compliance rate be no greater than 60 percent, and CMS has proposed regulations identifying 60 percent as the threshold.[95]

---

ordered to revise the manual provisions to reflect the fact that Medicare determinations are to be made based on an individual assessment of each patient's needs and to prohibit denials based on the three-hour rule or any other rule of thumb. *See also* CMS Ruling 85-2, Medicare & Medicaid Guide (CCH) [1986-1 Transfer Binder] 34,817; and *see* New York *ex rel.* Holland v. Sullivan, 927 F.2d 57 (2d Cir. 1991); New York *ex rel.* Stein v. Secretary, Dep't of Health & Human Servs., 924 F.2d 431 (2d Cir. 1991); Probstein v. Sullivan, Medicare & Medicaid Guide (CCH) 41,423 (D. Conn. 1993).

[94] Hospitals and rehabilitation units must meet the criteria specified in 42 C.F.R. §§ 412.23(b), 412.25, 412.29. Inpatient rehabilitation hospitals and acute care hospital rehabilitation units are collectively referred to as an inpatient rehabilitation facility (IRF) under the IRF Prospective Payment System (IRF PPS). 42 U.S.C. §§ 1395ww (d)(1)(B), 1395ww(d)(1)B)(ii). Note that inpatient rehabilitation hospitals and rehabilitation units are referred to as inpatient rehabilitation facilities (IRFs). *See* CMS, "Inpatient Rehabilitation Facility PPS," *available at* https://www.cms.gov/Medicare/Medicare-Fee-for-Service-Payment/InpatientRehabFacPPS/index.html?redirect=/InpatientRehabFacPPS/ (site visited Aug. 6, 2018).

[95] *See* Medicare, Medicaid, and SCHIP Extension Act of 2007 § 115, Pub. L. No. 110-173 (Dec. 29, 2007). The proposed regulations can be found at 73 Fed. Reg. 22,687–22,688. The 75 percent

There are several proposals for site-neutral payments to IRFs and SNFs. Such proposals persist even when studies indicate that care outcomes are better in IRFs.[96]

[C] Long-Term Care Hospitals

In general, LTCHs are defined in the Medicare law as hospitals that have an average inpatient length of stay greater than 25 days. They typically provide extended medical and rehabilitative care for patients with clinically complex conditions and for those who may suffer from multiple acute or chronic conditions. Services available in such facilities can include comprehensive rehabilitation, respiratory therapy, cancer treatment, head trauma treatment and pain management.[97]

To be eligible to receive payment under the PPS for LTCHs, the facility must meet the criteria to be classified as an LTCH[98] in order to be excluded from hospital inpatient PPS.[99] This condition of payment is subject to special payment provisions,[100] provisions on change in hospital status,[101] provisions related to hospitals within hospitals,[102] and satellite facilities.[103]

---

rule was originally established in 1983 but was suspended by CMS in 2002 after it found inconsistent use of the criteria by inpatient rehabilitation facilities. Government Accountability Office (GAO), GAO-05-366, Medicare: More Specific Criteria Needed to Classify Inpatient Rehabilitation Facilities (Apr. 2005), *available at* www.gao.gov/new.items/d05366.pdf (site Aug. 6, 2018). *See also* CMS, "Inpatient Rehabilitation Facility PPS."

[96] *See* CMA, "Inpatient Rehabilitation Facilities and Skilled Nursing Facilities: Vive la Difference!" *available at* http://www.medicareadvocacy.org/inpatient-rehabilitation-facilities-and-skilled-nursing-facilities-vive-la-difference/ (site visited Aug. 6, 2018).

[97] *See* the Balanced Budget Refinement Act of 1999 (BBRA), Pub. L. No. 106-113, § 123 (Nov. 29, 1999), as amended by § 307 of BIPA. This provision directed the Secretary to develop and implement a per discharge, diagnosis-related group (DRG)–based prospective payment system (PPS) for LTCHs for cost-reporting periods beginning on or after October 1, 2002. The system replaced the reasonable cost-based payment system over a five-year transition period through October 1, 2006. For regulations implementing PPS for LTCHs, *see* 42 C.F.R. §§ 412.500–412.541, *available at* https://www.gpo.gov/fdsys/pkg/CFR-2011-title42-vol2/pdf/CFR-2011-title42-vol2-sec412-500.pdf (site visited Aug. 6, 2018). *See also* CMS, Long-Term Care Hospital PPS," *available at* www.cms.hhs.gov/LongTermCareHospitalPPS/ (site visited Aug. 6, 2018). For links to LTCH PPS federal regulations and notices, *see* CMS, "Long-Term Care Hospital PPS." LTCHs are sometimes referred to as long-term acute care hospitals, although they are referred to by CMS as long-term care hospitals.

[98] 42 C.F.R. §§ 412.505, 412.23(e).

[99] 42 C.F.R. §§ 412.505, 412.1(a)(1).

[100] 42 C.F.R. §§ 412.505, 412.22(c).

[101] 42 C.F.R. §§ 412.505, 412.22(d).

[102] 42 C.F.R. §§ 412.505, 412.22(e).

[103] 42 C.F.R. §§ 412.505, 412.22(h).

LTCHs may not charge beneficiaries for any covered services for which payment is made by Medicare, even if the hospital's costs of furnishing the service are greater than the PPS amount. The facility may charge the beneficiary only for the applicable deductible and coinsurance amounts.[104]

LTCHs must have an agreement with a Quality Improvement Organization (QIO) to provide ongoing review with respect to medical necessity, reasonableness, and appropriateness of hospital admissions and discharges; appropriateness of payments under outlier provisions; the validity of the hospital's diagnostic and procedural information; the completeness, adequacy, and quality of the services furnished by the hospital; and other medical or other practices with respect to beneficiaries or billing for services furnished to beneficiaries.[105]

In 2014, as part of the restructuring of the QIO program—separating the beneficiary quality of care complaint review process from provider quality improvement functions—CMS awarded additional contracts to assist providers with quality improvement matters. The new contracts represent the second phase of QIO restructuring. These QIOs will be known as Quality Innovation Network (QIN)-QIOs.[106]

Also in 2014, CMS announced the first phase of its restructuring of the QIO functions. In the first phase, CMS has contracted with Livanta LLC (for geographic areas 1 and 5), located in Annapolis Junction, Maryland, and KePRO (for geographic areas 2, 3, and 4), located in Seven Hills, Ohio. These contractors will be responsible for ensuring consistency in the review process with respect to beneficiary complaints. CMS describes these two contractors as its Beneficiary and Family-Centered Care (BFCC) QIO contractors.[107] The states in the designated geographic areas are:

- Area 1: Connecticut, Maine, Massachusetts, New Hampshire, New Jersey, New York, Pennsylvania, Puerto Rico, Rhode Island, Vermont, Virgin Islands

---

[104] 42 C.F.R. § 412.507. Applicable deductible and coinsurance amounts are discussed at 42 C.F.R. §§ 409.82, 409.83, and 409.87.

[105] 42 C.F.R. § 412.508. Quality Improvement Organizations (QIOs), formerly known as Peer Review Organizations (PROs), are a creature of the Social Security Act, §§ 1151 *et seq.*, 42 U.S.C. §§ 1320 *et seq.*, and provide certain quality and utilization review oversight with respect to a range of Medicare-covered services.

[106] *See* CMS, "CMS Launches Next Phase of New Quality Improvement Program." Each QIN-QIO will work on strategic quality improvement initiatives. *See also* CMS, "Quality Improvement Organizations," *available at* http://www.cms.gov/Medicare/Quality-Initiatives-Patient-Assessment-Instruments/QualityImprovementOrgs/index.html (site visited Aug. 6, 2018).

[107] For information on Beneficiary and Family-Centered Care (BFCC) QIO contractors, *see also* CMS, "Fact Sheet: Two-Midnight Rule," (Oct. 30, 2015), *available at* https://www.cms.gov/Newsroom/MediaReleaseDatabase/Press-releases/2014-Press-releases-items/2014-05-09.html (site visited Aug. 6, 2018).

- Area 2: District of Columbia, Delaware, Florida, Georgia, Maryland, North Carolina, South Carolina, Virginia, West Virginia
- Area 3: Alabama, Arkansas, Colorado, Kentucky, Louisiana, Mississippi, Montana, North Dakota, New Mexico, Oklahoma, South Dakota, Tennessee, Texas, Utah, Wyoming
- Area 4: Iowa, Illinois, Indiana, Kansas, Michigan, Minnesota, Missouri, Nebraska, Ohio, Wisconsin
- Area 5: Alaska, Arizona, California, Hawaii, Idaho, Nevada, Oregon, Washington.[108]

§ 2.09 HOSPITAL PAYMENT

[A] Prospective Payment

A hospital must meet the conditions of Medicare participation under the Medicare PPS for hospital services furnished to Medicare beneficiaries.[109] If a hospital fails to comply with these conditions, CMS, which administers the Medicare program, may withhold Medicare payment, in full or in part, to the hospital until the hospital provides appropriate assurances of its compliance. Otherwise, CMS may terminate the hospital's provider agreement.[110]

Historically, prior to 1983, the Medicare program paid hospitals on a retrospective basis in an amount equal to the reasonable cost of covered services. In other words, Medicare paid a hospital what it cost the hospital to deliver the service involved. Effective October 1, 1983, however, Congress instituted a new financing structure called the Perspective Payment System (PPS).[111]

[B] Diagnosis-Related Groups

The PPS applies to acute care and rehabilitation hospitals, as well as LTCHs, and to units in acute care hospitals that provide rehabilitation services.[112] Alcohol and drug treatment, psychiatric, and children's hospitals are not included in PPS,

[108] *See* CMS, "CMS Launches Improved Quality Improvement Program."

[109] 42 C.F.R. § 412.40.

[110] 42 C.F.R. § 412.40(b)(1), (2).

[111] 42 U.S.C. § 1395ww(d). Note that, generally, PPSs exist across a range of care settings, including hospitals, SNFs, home health, hospice, and outpatient hospital services. CMS provides updated PPS rates, rules, and data on an ongoing basis. Discussion of PPS is generally incorporated as relevant to a particular care setting.

[112] Regulations establishing a prospective payment system for rehabilitation hospitals were issued by the CMS and became effective on January 1, 2002. 42 C.F.R. §§ 412.600 *et seq.* CMS regularly updates its lists of DRGs and other codes.

nor are units in acute care hospitals that provide alcohol and drug treatment, psychiatric, or pediatric services.[113]

PPS requires the payment of a prospectively determined amount for each Medicare discharge. All patient discharges are classified according to a list of Diagnosis-Related Groups (DRGs). The list includes approximately 490 DRGs. A DRG is assigned a particular value based on the average cost of caring for patients with similar diagnoses in the past.[114]

The DRG for a stroke, for example, might be $6,000. For every patient discharged from a hospital after treatment for a stroke, the hospital would receive, for example, $6,000 in Medicare reimbursement even if the patient's care had actually cost the hospital less, or more, than $6,000 to deliver.

Only when a beneficiary has a medically necessary stay that is much longer or more expensive for the hospital than an average case covered by the appropriate DRG can the hospital receive additional Medicare coverage, called "outlier payments." The outlier payments amount to 60 percent of the average daily cost of caring for a patient with the diagnosis involved.[115] Because the hospital usually receives only the single predetermined DRG amount for a given hospital discharge, the hospital comes under severe pressure to discharge patients at the earliest possible time, thereby maximizing profit or minimizing loss.

[C] Limits on Charges to Beneficiaries

Hospitals may not charge a beneficiary for services that are paid for by Medicare, even if the hospital's cost of furnishing such services to the beneficiary is greater than the amount the hospital is paid under PPS.[116]

Under PPS, a hospital may charge a beneficiary during a covered stay, which includes at least one covered day, only for the following:

---

[113] 42 U.S.C. § 1395ww(d)(1)(B); 42 C.F.R. §§ 412.20–412.32. *See also* 45 C.F.R. Pt. 170 *available at* http://www.gpo.gov/fdsys/pkg/FR-2015-04-30/pdf/2015-09245.pdf (site visited Aug. 6, 2018)

[114] 42 U.S.C. § 1395ww(e). In recent years an increasing trend has been noted in which beneficiaries have been in hospital rooms and beds, not as "admitted" patients, but rather under "observation" status. Hospitals appear to use "observation" status as a cost-saving mechanism and often do not inform beneficiaries of the "observation" status. As a result, more beneficiaries are finding themselves exposed to additional expenses that are not covered by Medicare Part A for observation status. For example, beneficiaries hospitalized under observation status do not meet the three-day prior hospitalization requirement for purposes of accessing the Medicare-covered SNF benefit. In addition, beneficiaries have been "admitted" to a hospital but have had that status changed to observation status before the hospital submits the bill to Medicare. *See also Bagnall,* No. 3:11cv1703(MPS) (D. Conn. filed Nov. 3, 2011) (Memorandum of Decision dated Sept. 23, 2013), *available at* https://casetext.com/case/bagnall-v-sebelius (site visited Aug. 6, 2018).

[115] 42 C.F.R. §§ 412.80–412.84.

[116] 42 C.F.R. § 412.42(a).

- Applicable deductible and coinsurance amounts;[117]
- Custodial care provided that is not part of medically necessary hospital services provided to the patient;[118]
- Items and services that are not medically necessary;[119]
- Non-physician services furnished to hospital inpatients by other than the hospital or a provider or supplier under arrangements made by the hospital;[120]
- Items and services provided when a patient is not entitled to Medicare Part A benefits;[121] and
- Items and services provided after Medicare Part A benefits have been exhausted.[122]

[D] Inpatient Hospitalization No Longer Necessary (Notice to Beneficiaries)

A hospital may charge a beneficiary for items and services provided after the hospital (acting directly or through its utilization review committee) has determined that the beneficiary does not or no longer requires inpatient hospital care;[123] or where the attending physician agrees with the hospital determination

---

[117] *See* 42 C.F.R. §§ 409.82, 409.83, and 409.87.

[118] 42 C.F.R. § 412.42(b)(2)(i). *See also* 42 C.F.R. § 411.15(g).

[119] 42 C.F.R. § 412.42(b)(2)(ii). *See also* 42 C.F.R. § 411.15(k).

[120] 42 C.F.R. § 412.42(b)(2)(iii). *See* http://www.gpo.gov/fdsys/pkg/CFR-2011-title42-vol2/pdf/CFR-2011-title42-vol2-sec412-42.pdf (site visited Aug. 6, 2018). *See also* Electronic Code of Federal Regulations, http://www.ecfr.gov/cgi-bin/text-idx?tpl=/ecfrbrowse/Title42/42tab_02.tpl (site visited Aug. 6, 2018).

[121] 42 C.F.R. § 412.42(b)(2)(iv). *See also* 42 C.F.R. Pt. 408 subpt. A.

[122] 42 C.F.R. § 412.42(b)(2)(v). *See also* 42 C.F.R. § 409.61.

[123] 42 C.F.R. § 412.42(c)(1), (2). Note that inpatient hospital care includes care where a beneficiary needs a SNF level of care and a Medicare-certified SNF bed is not available. 42 C.F.R. § 412.42(b)(2)(v). Occasionally, the question arises as to how distant the SNF bed can be, in order for it to be deemed "available" to the patient. For example, can a patient be required to accept a SNF bed that is 300 miles from the patient's home? The argument from the advocate and patient is that the location of the placement must be reasonable, that it allow family and friends to visit; that options closer by should be explored and used where appropriate. *See* Revision to State Operations Manual (SOM), Ref: S&C:13-32, "Hospital Appendix A–Interpretive Guidelines for 42 CFR 482.43, Discharge Planning," *available at* http://www.cms.gov/Medicare/Provider-Enrollment-and-Certification/SurveyCertificationGenInfo/Downloads/Survey-and-Cert-Letter-13-32.pdf (site visited Aug. 6, 2018). According to § 482.43(c)(6): "The hospital must include in the discharge plan a list of HHAs or SNFs that are available to the patient, that are participating in the Medicare program, and that serve the geographic area (as defined by the HHA) in which the patient resides, or in the case of a SNF, in the geographic area requested by the patient. HHAs must request to be listed

in writing (e.g., by issuing a written discharge order) that inpatient hospital services are no longer necessary.[124] Before a hospital can charge the beneficiary under these circumstances, the hospital must notify the beneficiary (or person acting on his or her behalf) in writing that:

- In the opinion of the hospital, and with the concurrence of the physician or the QIO, customary charges will be made for continued hospital care beyond the second day following the date of the notice.[125]
- The QIO will make a formal determination under the appeals procedures that apply to QIO determinations affecting Medicare Part A payment.[126]
- The charges for continued payment will be invalid and refunded if collected by the hospital, to the extent that a finding is made that the beneficiary required continued care beyond the point indicated by the hospital.[127]

[E] Medically Unnecessary Diagnostic Procedures and Services

A hospital may charge a beneficiary for diagnostic procedures and studies and therapeutic procedures and courses of treatment (such as experimental procedures and treatments) that are excluded from coverage as medically unnecessary items and services.[128] This is true even when the beneficiary receives

---

by the hospital as available." *See also* Alfred J. Chiplin, Jr., *Breathing Life into Discharge Planning*, Elder L.J. (13)1 (2005), *available at* http://publish.illinois.edu/elderlawjournal/files/2015/02/Chiplin.pdf (site visited Aug. 6, 2018).

[124] 42 C.F.R. § 412.42(c)(2). If the hospital believes the patient no longer needs inpatient hospital care and the physician does not concur, the hospital may request immediate review by the appropriate QIO.

[125] *See* 42 C.F.R. § 405.1206(d)(6)(ii).

[126] The QIO or contractor may review any cases in which the hospital advises the beneficiary (or the person acting on the beneficiary's behalf) of the non-coverage of the services. The hospital must identify such cases to the QIO or contractor in accordance with CMS instructions. 42 C.F.R. § 412.42(g); *available at* http://www.ecfr.gov/cgi-bin/text-idx?SID=ba2c595cb77ac7cc63b26ad69e535425&mc=true&node=se42.2.412_142&rgn=div8 (site visited Aug. 6, 2018). A variety of procedural due process issues are raised with respect to when notice is given and the level of detail describing the medical rationale for discharge that is required in the notice (42 C.F.R. § 412.42(c)(1)–(4)); *see also* 42 C.F.R. §§ 412.42–412.48, and time frames (42 C.F.R. § 478.32) for beneficiaries to pursue legal remedies. Advocates should look closely to see that rules on hospital discharge notices are strictly followed.

[127] 42 C.F.R. § 412.42(c)(3)(i)–(v); Revised Advance Beneficiary Notice Forms must be used (mandatory) starting September 4, 2012; *see* http://www.cms.gov/Regulations-and-Guidance/Guidance/Transmittals/Downloads/R2480CP.pdf (site visited Aug. 6, 2018); *see also* CMA, "CMS Clarifies When the Advance Beneficiary Notice of Non-Coverage (ABN) Must be Issued," *available at* http://www.medicareadvocacy.org/cms-clarifies-when-the-advance-beneficiary-notice-of-non-coverage-abn-must-be-issued/ (site visited Aug. 6, 2018).

[128] 42 C.F.R. § 412.42(d).

continued inpatient hospital care, if those services are furnished after the beneficiary (or person acting on his or her behalf) has acknowledged in writing that the hospital has informed him or her that the services are not considered reasonable and necessary under Medicare.[129] The written acknowledgment must state that the services are not considered reasonable and necessary; that customary charges will be made if the services are provided; that if the services are received, a formal determination on the validity of the hospital's finding is made by the Medicare contractor or QIO, as appropriate; and that the determination is appealable by the hospital, the attending physician, or the beneficiary under the appeals procedure that applies to determinations affecting Medicare Part A payment.[130]

[F] Beneficiary Not Entitled to Medicare Part A or Exhaustion of Part A Benefits

A hospital may charge a Medicare beneficiary its usual charges for noncovered items and services furnished on outlier days for which payment is denied because the beneficiary is not entitled to Medicare Part A or has exhausted benefits.[131] If payment is considered for outlier days, the entire stay is reviewed, and days up to the number of days in excess of the outlier threshold may be denied on the basis of the beneficiary's lacking entitlement to Part A or having exhausted benefits.[132] Under this rule, the latest days will be denied first.[133]

In addition, hospitals are required to notify patients who have used or will use 90 days of benefits (lifetime reserve days) in a benefit period, thus exhausting their Part A benefits, that they can elect not to use their reserve days for all or part of a stay. The notice should be given when the beneficiary has five regular coinsurance days left and is expected to be hospitalized beyond that period, or immediately, when fewer days are left. A Medicare beneficiary who is eligible for medical assistance (Medicaid) under a state plan should be advised that such assistance would not be available if the beneficiary elects not to use the lifetime reserve days. The restriction does not apply to cases where the beneficiary is deemed to have elected not to use lifetime reserve days.[134]

[G] Private Rooms and Luxury Services

A hospital may charge a Medicare beneficiary for the differential for a private room or other luxury service that is more expensive than is medically

---

[129] 42 C.F.R. § 412.42(d).

[130] 42 C.F.R. § 412.42(d).

[131] 42 C.F.R. § 412.42(e). Outlier days are defined in 42 C.F.R. §§ 412.82 and 412.84.

[132] 42 C.F.R. § 412.42(e).

[133] 42 C.F.R. § 412.42(e).

[134] *See* MBP Manual, Ch. 5: § 30. Lifetime reserve days are discussed at 42 C.F.R. § 409.65.

required and is furnished for the personal comfort of the beneficiary at his or her request (or the request of the person acting on his or her behalf).[135]

[H] Admission Denials

As described above, if Medicare coverage is granted, the hospital will generally receive a predetermined DRG amount. The QIO, which functions as a watchdog agency seeking to ensure that the hospital does not claim Medicare coverage for medically unnecessary care, will often deny coverage retroactively in certain types of cases. When retroactive denials occur, the hospital loses the entire DRG payment. Moreover, because the hospital had, until the issuance of the QIO denial, considered the case to be covered by Medicare, it has not complied with the required denial notice process and therefore may not charge the patient for the cost of care.[136] This danger of financial penalty is so extreme that hospitals are inhibited from admitting patients whose medical conditions resemble those of patients whose cases have been denied retroactively by the QIO.

■ **EXAMPLE:** Many hospitals have received retroactive QIO denials for hospital care delivered to patients suffering from compression fractures of the spine. Although a substantial proportion of such patients do indeed require a hospital level of care, many QIOs arbitrarily deny such claims on the theory that they constitute "social" admissions for which hospital services are not really necessary. After being intimidated by the QIO, hospitals will often decline to admit spinal compression fracture patients to the hospital unless the patient agrees to accept personal financial liability for the cost of care. In effect, arbitrary denial practices by the QIO can force hospitals to deny access to care for classes of vulnerable and coverage-worthy patients.

[I] Loss of Access to Expensive Care

Even where the DRG amount is paid, the predetermined figure may be inadequate to compensate the hospital for the expense of essential, but expensive, technology, procedure, equipment, and services. Since the advent of PPS, beneficial but cost-increasing medical advances are occasionally assigned to DRGs that do not cover costs. These costs are not to be passed on to beneficiaries but absorbed in the DRG rates.[137] Note, however, Medicare does make provision for

---

[135] 42 C.F.R. § 412.42(f).

[136] Social Security Act § 1879, 42 U.S.C. § 1395pp; 42 C.F.R. §§ 411.400–411.406, *available at* http://www.gpo.gov/fdsys/pkg/CFR-2011-title42-vol2/pdf/CFR-2011-title42-vol2-sec411-400.pdf (site visited Aug. 6, 2018).

[137] *See* 42 C.F.R. §§ 412.80 *et seq.*

additional payment for certain extraordinary high-cost hospital stays and services.[138] Advocates need to remain vigilant about the effects of payment and access to service.

The question of the adequacy of PPS rates for purposes of diagnostic-related groups is ongoing. The focus is on the underlying cost assumptions in setting rates, on geographic variations in costs and wages, and on whether the appropriate national averages have been set for hospital wage levels. In response to these concerns, the Medicare program is continually adjusting and updating these rates.[139]

§ 2.10 UTILIZATION REVIEW AND QUALITY OF SERVICES

[A] Hospital Utilization Review Committees

Each Medicare participating hospital must have a Utilization Review Committee (URC) that reviews services furnished by the hospital and members of its medical staff.

At least two members of the URC must be physicians. URC members are generally hospital medical and administrative staff with medical oversight responsibilities. They work closely with the respective QIOs in their geographic location. Before making a determination that an admission or continued stay is not medically necessary, the URC must consult a practitioner responsible for the care of the patient and afford that practitioner the opportunity to present his or her views. If the URC decides that coverage should be denied, written notification must be given within two days of its decision to the hospital, the patient, and the attending physician.[140] As a practical matter, hospitals tend to notify beneficiaries of the decision that a Medicare admission or continued stay is not medically necessary as soon as possible, usually on the day the determination has been made. The patient's liability for the cost of inpatient hospital care does not begin until the patient has received the required legal notice in writing that Medicare coverage will be denied.[141] Once the beneficiary has been notified of the determination of the URC, the beneficiary may exercise certain appeal rights, described at **§ 2.11**.

[138] *See* 42 C.F.R §§ 412.87–412.88.

[139] *See* CMS, "Acute Inpatient PPS," *available at* www.cms.hhs.gov/AcuteInpatientPPS/ (site visited Aug. 6, 2018).

[140] 42 C.F.R. § 482.30(d).

[141] Social Security Act § 1879, 42 U.S.C. § 1395 pp; 42 C.F.R. §§ 411.400–411.406. *See also* 42 C.F.R. § 412.42.

[B] Recovery Audit Contractors

In Section 302 of the Tax Relief and Health Care Act of 2006, Congress required that its Recovery Audit Contractors (RACs) demonstration be made national and permanent by January 1, 2010.[142] The RAC demonstration focused on overpayments and underpayments by health care providers and suppliers in California, Florida, New York, Massachusetts, South Carolina, and Arizona.[143]

The impact of the RAC program on access to the Medicare hospital benefit is unfolding. As described earlier in this chapter, many beneficiaries are not being admitted as inpatients to Medicare-participating hospitals; and in some cases where they have been admitted, that status has been changed to observation before a payment request has been submitted to Medicare. Some posit that RAC concerns are deterring hospital admissions. Some believe that since the institution of the RAC program, there has been an increase in the number of Medicare beneficiaries being inappropriately classified as outpatients rather than as inpatients. Note that on July 10, 2015, CMS announced that "effective June 4, 2015, CMS has withdrawn the Requests for Quotes for the next round of Recovery Auditor contracts. CMS plans to update the Statement of Work and release new Requests for Proposals shortly. In the meantime, the current Recovery Auditors will continue active recovery auditing through at least December 31, 2015."[144] Patient advocates have argued that the zeal of hospitals to avoid RAC problems has gone too far; that patients would otherwise have been classified as inpatients but for RAC fears; that some patients kept in observation status for multiple days, sometimes weeks, are skewing readmission rates and hospital quality data.

[C] Quality Improvement Organizations

In 1982, as part of the Tax Equity and Fiscal Responsibility Act of 1982, Congress established the Peer Review Organizations (PROs), now called Quality Improvement Organizations (QIOs). This act established a peer review program to perform utilization and quality review of hospital services provided to Medicare beneficiaries.[145] Congress authorized the Secretary of the HHS to contract

---

[142] *See* § 1893 of the Social Security Act (42 U.S.C. § 1395ddd). For CMS's report on the three-year RAC demonstration, *see also* CMS, "Medicare Fee for Service Recovery Audit Program," *available at* http://www.cms.gov/Research-Statistics-Data-and-Systems/Monitoring-Programs/Medicare-FFS-Compliance-Programs/Recovery-Audit-Program/ (site visited Aug. 6, 2018). This site provides comprehensive links to the RAC program and its expansion schedule.

[143] *See* § 1893 of the Social Security Act (42 U.S.C. § 1395ddd). *See also* CMS, "Medicare Fee for Service Recovery Audit Program."

[144] *See* CMS, "Medicare Fee for Service Recovery Audit Program."

[145] 42 U.S.C. §§ 1320c-1–1320c-12. *See* CMS, Pub. 100-10, Medicare Quality Improvement Organizations (QIO) Manual, Ch. 5, *available at* https://www.cms.gov/Regulations-and-Guidance/Guidance/Transmittals/Downloads/R28QIO.pdf (site visited Aug. 6, 2018). QIOs also review the appropriateness of hospital discharge notices. *See* 42 U.S.C. § 1302c-3(e).

with private physician-controlled QIOs by region of the country to carry out such utilization and quality improvement functions.[146]

Each Medicare-participating hospital must have an agreement with a QIO for review of medical appropriateness and utilization of Medicare-covered services on an ongoing basis.[147] The QIO is to review the medical necessity, reasonableness, and appropriateness of hospital admissions and discharges; the appropriateness of inpatient care for which additional payment is sought under the outlier provisions; the validity of the hospital's diagnostic and procedural information; the completeness, adequacy, and quality of the services furnished in the hospital; and other medical or other practices related to beneficiaries or billing for services furnished to them.[148] QIOs have authority to deny Medicare payment for inappropriate or unnecessary services and to recommend that certain providers and physicians be excluded from the Medicare program because of their utilization patterns and practices.[149]

QIOs also have responsibility to monitor hospital performance under PPS. Specifically, QIOs are charged with reviewing and determining for payment purposes "the validity of diagnostic information provided by a hospital, the completeness, adequacy and quality of care provided, and the appropriateness of care for which additional payments are sought."[150] The QIO also has quality of care

---

[146] On July 18, 2014, as part of the restructuring of the QIO program—separating the beneficiary quality of care complaint review process from provider quality improvement functions—CMS awarded additional contracts to assist providers with quality improvement matters. The new contracts represent the second phase of QIO restructuring. These QIOs are known as Quality Innovation Network (QIN)-QIOs. *See* CMS, "CMS Launches Next Phase of New Quality Improvement Program." Each QIN-QIO will work on strategic quality improvement initiatives.

[147] 42 C.F.R. § 412.44.

[148] 42 C.F.R. § 412.44.

[149] 42 U.S.C. § 1320c-5(b)(1); 42 C.F.R. § 412.48. CMS continues to make changes in the functions of the QIO with respect to the scope of the QIO hospital review function. CMS has created a Hospital Payment Monitoring Program (HPMP) as part of its fiscal oversight responsibilities. These entities perform utilization review of randomly selected claims for payment purposes and measure the accuracy of Medicare fee-for-service (FFS) payments to acute inpatient prospective payment (IPPS) hospitals and LTCHs. The QIOs retain responsibility for quality oversight in all Medicare FFS settings, provider requested higher-weighted DRG reviews, reviews under the Emergency Medical Treatment and Active Labor Act (EMTALA), provider education on quality of care issues, and expedited determinations. *See* CMS, Inpatient Prospective Payment System Hospital and Long Term Care Hospital Review and Measurement Fact Sheet, *available at* https://www.cms.gov/AcuteInpatientPPS/downloads/InpatientReviewFactSheet.pdf (site visited Aug. 6, 2018). *See also* Social Security Act § 1154(a), https://www.ssa.gov/OP_Home/ssact/title11/1154.htm (site visited Aug. 6, 2018), 42 U.S.C. § 1320c-3, for a full description of the QIO function. The language of § 1154(a)(1) gives the Secretary broad authority to limit or expand QIO functions by contract. Note, too, that carriers and intermediaries are gradually being re-designated as Medicare Administrative Contractors (MACs) as described in **§ 2.01[B]** of this Handbook.

[150] Social Security Act § 1866(a)(1)(F), 42 U.S.C. § 1395cc(a)(1)(f).

review and oversight responsibility, an area of importance to Medicare beneficiaries who are concerned about the quality of care they have received in the hospital or other care settings.[151]

[D] Hospital Discharge Planning as an Advocacy Tool

Federal law requires a discharge planning process for identifying and planning for the post-hospital care needs of Medicare patients.[152] The Secretary has developed guidelines and standards for the discharge planning process in order to ensure a timely and smooth transition to the most appropriate type of follow-up care for post-hospital or rehabilitative care. The guidelines and standards address the following:[153]

---

[151] *See* 42 U.S.C. § 1320c-3(a)(14), § 1154(a)(14) of the Social Security Act. For the conference findings of the Center for Medicare Advocacy and its citation to relevant documentation of problems with the QIO and its review and oversight of quality of care concerns, *see* CMA, "Quality of Care," *available at* http://www.medicareadvocacy.org/medicare-info/quality-of-care/ (site visited Aug. 6, 2018). *See also* CMS, "Quality Improvement Organizations." *See* Medicare QIO Manual, Ch. 5. The transmittal includes a new oral review option called "Immediate Advocacy" (*see* § 5120). Its approach is much like that of an alternative dispute resolution inquiry. Other features include, among others, a Retrospective Beneficiary Complaint Review, § 5200; Concurrent Beneficiary Complaint Review, § 5300; and Direct Advocacy Review, § 5400. Generally, these new devices are designed to give beneficiaries faster and more complete information about quality of care concerns. *See* CMA, "New Procedures for Review of Quality of Care Complaints," *available at* http://www.medicareadvocacy.org/new-procedures-for-review-of-quality-of-care-complaints/ (site visited Aug. 6, 2018).

[152] 42 U.S.C. § 1395x(ee). On November 3, 2015, CMS published in the *Federal Register*, 80 Fed. Reg. 68,126, proposed revisions to requirements for discharge planning for hospitals, CAHs, and HHAs. *See* National Health Policy Forum, The Basics: Hospital Discharge Planning in Medicare: Current Requirements and Proposed Changes, (Feb, 9. 2016), *available at* https://www.nhpf.org/library/the-basics/Basics_HospitalDischargePlanning_02-09-16.pdf (site visited Aug. 6, 2018); CMS, Revisions to Requirements for Discharge Planning for Hospitals, Critical Access Hospitals, and Home Health Agencies, 80 Fed. Reg. 68,126 (Nov. 3, 2015), *available at* http://www.gpo.gov/fdsys/pkg/FR-2015-11-03/pdf/2015-27840.pdf (site visited Aug. 6, 2018). The rule is designed to reduce avoidable hospital readmissions and improve patient care with a focus on improvements for psychiatric and behavioral health patients, including those with substance abuse disorders. The rule calls for coordination, consultation, and using information from community-based service providers as recognized by the Improving Medicare Post-Acute Care Transformation Act of 2014 (Impact Act) (Pub. L. No. 113-185 (Oct. 6, 2014)); *see* CMA, "October 2014 – The Improving Medicare Post-Acute Care Transformation Act of 2014 (IMPACT Act) & Other Issues," *available at* http://www.medicareadvocacy.org/october-2014-the-improving-medicare-post-acute-care-transformation-act-of-2014-impact-act-other-isues/ (site visited Aug. 6, 2018). The rule fits within the framework of existing discharge planning regulations that are found at 42 C.F.R. § 482.43, applicable to all inpatients. *See also* Social Security Act § 1861(e), 42 U.S.C. § 1395x(ee).

[153] 42 C.F.R. § 482.43 (Condition of Participation: Discharge Planning). For CMS's discharge planning checklist, *see* CMS, "Your Discharge Planning Checklist: For Patients and Their Caregivers Preparing to Leave a Hospital, Nursing Home, or Other Care Setting, *available at* https://www.medicare.gov/pubs/pdf/11376-discharge-planning-checklist.pdf (site visited Aug. 6, 2018). An expanded version of this content, dated December 2014, is *available at* http://www.cms.gov/out

- The hospital must identify, at an early stage of hospitalization, those patients who are likely to suffer adverse health consequences upon discharge in the absence of adequate discharge planning.
- Hospitals must provide a discharge planning evaluation for patients identified under subparagraph (1) and for other patients upon the request of the patient, patient's representative, or patient's physician.
- Any discharge planning evaluation must be made on a timely basis to ensure that appropriate arrangements for post-hospital care will be made before discharge and to avoid unnecessary delays in discharge.
- A discharge planning evaluation must include an evaluation of a patient's likely need for appropriate post-hospital services and the availability of those services.
- The discharge planning evaluation must be included in the patient's medical record for use in establishing an appropriate discharge plan, and the results of the evaluation must be discussed with the patient (or the patient's representative).
- Upon the request of patient's physician, the hospital must arrange for the development and initial implementation of a discharge plan for the patient.
- Any discharge planning evaluation or discharge plan must be developed by, or under the supervision of, a registered professional nurse, social worker, or other appropriately qualified personnel.

Notice about the right to hospital discharge planning is problematic. The only notice provided is a mention of discharge planning in the Medicare-required hospital notice that is given to Medicare patients on admission, a notice entitled

---

reach-and-education/medicare-learning-network-mln/mlnproducts/downloads/discharge-planning-booklet-icn908184.pdf (site visited Aug. 6, 2018). For a discussion of discharge planning issues, *see* CMA, "Medicare and Discharge Planning: Thinking Through Your Needs," *available at* http://www.medicareadvocacy.org/medicare-and-discharge-planning-thinking-through-your-needs/ (site visited Aug. 6, 2018). In addition, CMS has offered further clarification of discharge planning responsibilities of hospitals and others in a survey and certification letter, Ref: S&C: 13-32-Hospital, *available at* http://www.cms.gov/Medicare/Provider-Enrollment-and-Certification/SurveyCertificationGenInfo/Downloads/Survey-and-Cert-Letter-13-32.pdf (site visited Aug. 6, 2018). *See also* CMA, "CMS Updates Guidance for Hospital Discharge Planning," *available at* http://www.medicareadvocacy.org/cms-updates-guidance-for-hospital-discharge-planning/ (site visited Aug. 6, 2018). For more information on discharge planning materials, *see* CMA, "Discharge Planning," *available at* http://www.medicareadvocacy.org/medicare-info/discharge-planning/ (site visited Aug. 6, 2018). *See also* Alfred J. Chiplin, Jr., *Breathing Life into Discharge Planning*, Elder L.J. (13)1 (2005), *available at* http://publish.illinois.edu/elderlawjournal/files/2015/02/Chiplin.pdf (site visited Aug. 6, 2018).

"An Important Message from Medicare."[154] Unfortunately, neither the notice of appeal rights upon hospital discharge (when and if the hospital attempts to charge the patient privately for the cost of care involved)[155] nor the QIO determination notice[156] discusses discharge planning rights other than to say that the "hospital should arrange the services you will need after you leave the hospital."

Thus, it is important that advocates work with discharge planners and physicians to ensure that discharge planning services are requested as discussed above.[157] Advocates may wish to consider approaching the failure to provide discharge planning services as a violation of the Medicare conditions of participation and consider the sanctioning process available there, culminating in the ultimate sanction of a facility's losing its participation agreement.[158]

§ 2.11 APPEALING COVERAGE DENIALS

[A] Overview of an Appeal for Inpatient Hospital Services

[1] Notice and Appeal Rights Generally

Usually, the first notice a Medicare beneficiary receives that care will not be covered by Medicare is from the health care provider, in this case the hospital. As noted,[159] each hospital is required to have as a condition of participation in the Medicare program a Utilization Review Committee (URC), which is charged with making preliminary determinations regarding Medicare coverage for hospital stays.[160] The URC must make such decisions at the time of admission of a patient and, if it determines that Medicare coverage is not warranted, issue a written notice to the beneficiary or someone acting on his/her behalf ("admission denials"). Similarly, the URC must issue a written notice if it decides that Medicare coverage is no longer warranted, after the patient has been admitted and has received some coverage by Medicare ("continued stay denials").[161]

Since July 1, 2007, Medicare-participating hospitals have been required to deliver valid, written notice, the "Important Message from Medicare" (IM), of a

---

[154] Social Security Act § 1866(a)(1)(M), 42 U.S.C. § 1395cc(a)(1)(M); 42 C.F.R. § 476.78(b)(3).

[155] 42 C.F.R. § 476.94 (Notice of QIO Initial Denial Determination and Changes as a Result of a DRG).

[156] 42 C.F.R. §§ 478.40–478.42 (Beneficiary Hearing Rights).

[157] *See* CMA, "Discharge Planning: Tips for Evaluating a Hospital's Skilled Nursing Facility Placement Choices," *available at* http://www.medicareadvocacy.org/discharge-planning-tips-for-evaluating-a-hospitals-skilled-nursing-facility-placement-choices/ (site visited Aug. 6, 2018).

[158] 42 C.F.R. Pt. 488 (Survey, Certification, and Enforcement Procedures).

[159] *See* **§ 2.10[A]** of this Handbook.

[160] 42 C.F.R. § 482.30 (Condition of Participation: Utilization Review).

[161] *See* 42 C.F.R. § 482.30 (Condition of Participation: Utilization Review). *See also* discussion in **§ 2.10[B]** of this Handbook on the impact of the RAC program, as such reviews may have an effect on admission and may frustrate the receipt of a notice of denial.

patient's rights as a hospital patient including discharge appeal rights, within two calendar days of admission. A follow-up copy of the signed IM is given again as far as possible in advance of discharge, but no more than two calendar days prior to discharge. Follow-up notice is not required if the provision of the admission IM falls within two calendar days of discharge.[162]

Hospitals, as with all Medicare Part A providers, have a financial incentive to issue denial notices because they may have to absorb the cost of the care they provide if they erroneously inform the beneficiary that the care will be covered, but not if they erroneously deny coverage.[163]

In issuing a continued stay denial, a hospital must obtain the concurrence of the patient's treating physician before it can issue the written denial notice. If the treating physician does not concur, the hospital cannot issue the written notice, but instead must refer the case to the BFCC-QIO or QIO,[164] which will review the medical records of the patient and decide whether Medicare coverage should continue. If the QIO decides that Medicare coverage should not continue, then the QIO itself issues a notice to the beneficiary. Note that no physician concurrence is required if the URC issues a Medicare denial at the time of the patient's admission to the hospital.

Because of the requirement for physician concurrence, the Medicare patient's treating physician is a key person in the coverage determination. The regulations require that the treating physician be given an opportunity to justify the medical necessity of hospital admissions or continued stays.[165] In practice, however, this often means that the treating physician receives a telephone call informing him or her that a coverage denial is about to be issued in a given case. The treating physician may or may not attempt to convince the URC or QIO reviewer that coverage should be continued. In any event, the written record may not contain any notation beyond a terse statement that "the views of the attending physician were solicited."

As a practical matter, a beneficiary can appeal a denial of coverage of only those services actually received. Therefore, a beneficiary who is being informed

---

[162] *See* 42 C.F.R. § 405.1205 (Traditional Medicare) and 42 C.F.R. § 422.620 (Medicare Advantage); *see also* https://www.cms.gov/Regulations-and-Guidance/Guidance/Transmittals/downloads/R1257CP.pdf (site visited Aug. 6, 2018). *See also* CMS, Important Message from Medicare (IM) and Expedited Determination Procedures for Hospital Discharges, (May 25, 2007), *available at* www.cms.gov/Outreach-and-Education/Medicare-Learning-Network-MLN/MLNMattersArticles/downloads/MM5622.pdf (site visited Aug. 6, 2018).

[163] 42 U.S.C. § 1395pp; *see* https://www.ssa.gov/OP_Home/ssact/title18/1879.htm (site visited Aug. 6, 2018).

[164] *See* **§ 2.11[B]** of this Handbook.

[165] 42 C.F.R. §§ 412.42(c) and 482.30.

that Medicare will not cover his or her stay upon admission must insist on admission anyway.[166] For a continuing hospital stay, the beneficiary must remain in the hospital in order to seek additional Medicare coverage through the appeals process.

When a patient receives a denial notice from the hospital URC at the time of admission, or a continued stay denial notice has been issued with the concurrence of the treating physician, the patient must request that the case be submitted to the Medicare QIO for its review. This patient request will trigger an initial determination that can then be appealed. (In addition, the QIO's initial determination does sometimes grant coverage that was denied by the hospital.) If the beneficiary or the beneficiary's representative requests the hospital to submit a case to the Medicare QIO, the hospital is required to do so.

For a continuing stay denial, actual written concurrence by the attending physician with the denial determination is required before the hospital may issue a Medicare notice of non-coverage.[167] If the attending physician does not concur, the URC may not issue a notice of non-coverage. Instead, it must refer the case to the QIO. The QIO will review the case and, if warranted, will issue a Medicare denial. This denial is the "initial determination."[168]

---

[166] 42 U.S.C. § 1395ff (b) provides for a limited prior determination process regarding physician services determined by the Secretary to be subject to the process. Under the process, a participating physician who has permission from the patient or an individual who has received an advanced beneficiary notice (ABN) may ask the appropriate Medicare contractor for a determination of whether Medicare will pay for a service before actually receiving the service. *See also* Medicare QIO Manual, Ch. 7: §§ 7005 and 7015 (providing for inpatient hospital preadmission review), *available at* https://www.cms.gov/Regulations-and-Guidance/Guidance/Manuals/Downloads/qio110c07.pdf (site visited Aug. 6, 2018).

[167] 42 C.F.R. § 412.42(c)(2). The patient becomes financially responsible for the services provided beyond the second day following the date of the notice. § 412.42(c)(3)(ii). *See also* discussion of § 422.620 in **Chapter 7** of this Handbook and 42 C.F.R. § 489.27 (Beneficiary Notice of Discharge Rights), *see* https://www.gpo.gov/fdsys/pkg/CFR-2010-title42-vol5/pdf/CFR-2010-title42-vol5-sec489-27.pdf (site visited Aug. 6, 2018).

[168] 42 C.F.R. § 412.42(c)(2). Note modified notice requirements discussed above with respect to the use of the Revised Important Message from Medicare (IM), *see* CMS, "Hospital Discharge Appeal Notices," *available at* https://www.cms.gov/Medicare/Medicare-General-Information/BNI/HospitalDischargeAppealNotices.html (site visited Aug. 6, 2018). For QIO details, *see* CMS, "Quality Improvement Organizations Program – Home," *available at* http://www.qioprogram.org/ (site visited Aug. 6, 2018).

On May 9, 2014, CMS announced the first phase of its restructuring of the QIO functions. In the first phase, CMS has contracted with Livanta LLC (for geographic areas 1 and 5), located in Annapolis Junction, Maryland, and KePRO (for geographic areas 2, 3, and 4), located in Seven Hills, Ohio. These contractors will be responsible for ensuring consistency in the review process with respect to beneficiary complaints. CMS describes these two contractors as its Beneficiary and Family-Centered Care (BFCC) QIO contractors, *see* CMS, "CMS Launches Improved Quality Improvement Program."

[2] Expedited Review Requests in Hospital Settings

For a hospital stay, a beneficiary must request expedited review of a discharge decision, orally or in writing, no later than the day of the discharge. A "timely request" is being interpreted by CMS as by midnight of the day of the discharge.[169] The beneficiary (or his or her authorized representative), upon request by the QIO, must be prepared to discuss the case with the QIO.[170] On the date that the QIO receives the beneficiary's request, the QIO must notify the hospital that the beneficiary has filed a request for intermediate review.[171] The hospital must supply any information, including medical records, that the QIO requires to conduct its review and must make the information available, by phone or in writing, by the close of business of the first full working day after the day the beneficiary receives notice of the planned discharge.[172] When the beneficiary requests an expedited determination in accordance with § 405.1206(d)(1), the QIO must make a determination and notify the beneficiary, the hospital, and the physician of its determination by close of business of the first working day after it receives all requested pertinent information.[173]

[3] Expedited Review Requests in Non-Hospital Settings

In addition to expedited reviews in inpatient hospital cases, beneficiaries may seek expedited review of a SNF, home health, hospice or CORF services

---

The states in the designated geographic areas are Area 1: Connecticut, Maine, Massachusetts, New Hampshire, New Jersey, New York, Pennsylvania, Puerto Rico, Rhode Island, Vermont, Virgin Islands; Area 2: District of Columbia, Delaware, Florida, Georgia, Maryland, North Carolina, South Carolina, Virginia, West Virginia; Area 3: Alabama, Arkansas, Colorado, Kentucky, Louisiana, Mississippi, Montana, North Dakota, New Mexico, Oklahoma, South Dakota, Tennessee, Texas, Utah, Wyoming; Area 4: Iowa, Illinois, Indiana, Kansas, Michigan, Minnesota, Missouri, Nebraska, Ohio, Wisconsin; and Area 5: Alaska, Arizona, California, Hawaii, Idaho, Nevada, Oregon, Washington.

On July 18, 2014, as part of the restructuring of the QIO program—separating the beneficiary quality of care complaint review process from provider quality improvement functions—CMS awarded additional contracts to assist providers with quality improvement matters. The new contracts represent the second phase of QIO restructuring. These QIOs will be known as Quality Innovation Network (QIN)-QIOs. *See* CMS, "CMS Launches Next Phase of New Quality Improvement Program." Each QIN-QIO will work on strategic quality improvement initiatives. The restructuring does not alter functions or patient's rights.

[169] *See* 71 Fed. Reg. 68,721 (Nov. 27, 2007), adding a new 42 C.F.R. § 405.1205 and revising 42 C.F.R. § 405.1206. *See also* Medicare Claims Processing (MCP) Manual, CMS Pub. 100-04, Ch. 30, § 200.4.1; 42 C.F.R. § 405.1206(b)(1).

[170] *See* revised 42 C.F.R. § 405.1206(d)(2).

[171] *See* revised 42 C.F.R. § 405.1206(e)(1).

[172] *See* revised 42 C.F.R. § 405.1206(e)(2).

[173] *See* revised 42 C.F.R. § 405.1206(e)(5).

discharge or termination.[174] The provider must give the beneficiary a general, standardized notice at least two days in advance of the proposed end of the service. If the service is fewer than two days, or if the time between services is more than two days, then notice must be given by the next-to-last service.[175] The notice describes the service, the date coverage ends, the beneficiary's financial liability for continued services, and how to file an appeal.[176]

A beneficiary must request expedited review, orally or in writing, by noon of the next calendar day after receiving notice. At that time, the beneficiary is given a more specific notice that includes a detailed explanation of why services are being terminated, a description of any applicable Medicare coverage rules and information on how to obtain them, and other facts specific to the beneficiary's case. The beneficiary is not financially liable for continued services until the later of two days after receiving the notice or the termination date specified on the notice.[177]

Expedited review is available in cases involving a discharge from the provider of services, or a termination of services where "a physician certifies that failure to continue the provision of such services is likely to place the individual's health at risk."[178] Services furnished by a residential provider, such as a hospital, a SNF, or a hospice, are discharges for which a doctor's certificate is not required. Services furnished by a "non-residential provider," such as home health services, are treated as a termination of services for which a doctor's certificate of significant health risk must be provided.[179] A reduction in service is not considered a termination or discharge for purposes of triggering expedited review.[180]

A beneficiary who wishes to exercise the right to an expedited determination must submit a request for a determination of the QIO in the state in which the beneficiary is receiving those provider services, in writing or by telephone, no later than noon of the calendar day following receipt of the provider's notice of termination. If the QIO is unable to accept the beneficiary's request, the beneficiary must submit the request by noon of the next day the QIO is available to accept a request.[181]

Coverage of provider services continues until the date and time designated on the termination notice, unless the QIO reverses the provider's service termination decision. If the QIO's decision is delayed because the provider did not timely supply necessary information or records, the provider may be liable for the

[174] *See* 42 C.F.R. §§ 405.1200–405.1204, to implement 42 U.S.C. § 1395ff (b)(1)(F).
[175] 42 C.F.R. § 405.1200(b)(1).
[176] 42 C.F.R. § 405.1200(b)(2).
[177] 42 C.F.R. § 405.1202(b).
[178] 42 U.S.C. § 1395ff(b)(1).
[179] 42 C.F.R. § 405.1202(a).
[180] 42 C.F.R. § 405.1200(a)(2).
[181] 42 C.F.R. § 405.1202(b).

costs of any additional coverage, as determined by the QIO.[182] If the QIO finds that the beneficiary did not receive valid notice, coverage of the provider services continues until at least 2 days after valid notice has been received. Continuation of coverage is not required if the QIO determines that coverage could pose a threat to the beneficiary's health or safety.[183]

If the QIO sustains the decision to terminate services or discharge the beneficiary, the beneficiary may request expedited reconsideration, orally or in writing, by noon of the calendar day following the notification of the QIO's decision. The reconsideration will be conducted by the Qualified Independent Contractor (QIC), which must issue a decision within 72 hours of the request. If the QIC does not comply with the time frame, the beneficiary may escalate the case to the Administrative Law Judge (ALJ) level.[184]

Beneficiaries retain the right to utilize the standard appeals process rather than the new expedited process in all situations. A QIO may review an appeal from a beneficiary whose request is not timely filed, but the QIO does not have to adhere to the time frame for issuing a decision, and the limitation on liability does not apply.

[B] The QIO Reconsideration and Financial Liability for the Beneficiary

Hospital inpatients denied Medicare during their stay may also request an "expedited reconsideration" of a Medicare denial. These expedited requests must be decided by the QIO within three working days. Under previous regulations, a hospital inpatient who received a denial notice from the hospital and requested review immediately avoided being charged until the QIO issued an initial determination. The expedited appeals regulations protect from liability only those inpatients who did not know or could not reasonably have been expected to know that payment would not be made.[185]

[C] Appeals Arising Under Parts A and B of Medicare

Rules regarding the combined Medicare Parts A and B appeals are found in Subparts H and I of Part 405.[186] These regulations implement statutory changes to the appeals process for Medicare Part A and Part B claims and to the ALJ hearing process for all Medicare claims, including managed care claims and

---

[182] 42 C.F.R. § 405.1202(c).
[183] 42 C.F.R. § 405.1202(c).
[184] *See* 42 C.F.R. § 405.1204.
[185] *See* 42 C.F.R. § 405.1206(f)(2).
[186] *See* 42 C.F.R. §§ 405.800 *et seq.*

prescription drug claims.[187] CMS issued final rules for the combined Part A and B appeals process (non-expedited) that were effective January 8, 2010.[188] CMS has created an additional chart showing appeals processes across Parts A, B, C, and D.[189]

Additionally, CMS recently finalized significant changes affecting Medicare appeals, particularly at the ALJ level of review. These changes apply to appeals of payment and coverage determinations for items and services furnished to Medicare beneficiaries, enrollees in Medicare Advantage (MA) and other Medicare competitive health plans, and enrollees in Medicare prescription drug plans, as well as to appeals of enrollment and entitlement determinations, and certain premium appeals. The final rule was effective on March 20, 2017.[190] The revised regulations, in part, authorize "Attorney Adjudicators," rather than ALJs to perform a portion of Office of Medicare Hearings and Appeals' (OMHA's) workload that does not require a hearing.[191] Attorney adjudicators can issue decisions when a decision can be issued without an ALJ conducting a hearing under the regulations, dismissals when an appellant withdraws his or her request for an ALJ hearing, certain remands, and reviews of QIC and IRE dismissals. The revised regulations also make telephone hearings the default hearing method for individuals other than unrepresented beneficiaries.[192] Video-teleconferencing (VTC) will be retained as the default method of conducting hearings for unrepresented beneficiaries, unless good cause for an in-person appearance is shown or the beneficiary requests a phone hearing.[193]

---

[187] CMS, Changes to the Medicare Claims Appeal Procedures, 70 Fed. Reg. 11,420 (Mar. 8, 2005), *available at* https://www.cms.gov/Regulations-and-Guidance/Regulations-and-Policies/QuarterlyProviderUpdates/downloads/CMS4064ifc.PDF (site visited Aug. 6, 2018). *See* CMS, Medicare Parts A & B Appeals Process (June 2017), *available at* https://www.cms.gov/Outreach-and-Education/Medicare-Learning-Network-MLN/MLNProducts/Downloads/MedicareAppeals Process.pdf (site visited Aug. 6, 2018).

[188] *See* CMS, Changes to the Medicare Claims Appeal Procedures, 74 Fed. Reg. 65,296 (Dec. 9, 2009), *available at* http://www.gpo.gov/fdsys/pkg/FR-2009-12-09/pdf/E9-28707.pdf (site visited Aug. 6, 2018).

[189] *See* CMS, Medicare Appeals, *available at* https://www.medicare.gov/Pubs/pdf/11525.pdf (site visited Aug. 6, 2018).

[190] CMS, Changes to the Medicare Claims and Entitlement, Medicare Advantage Organization Determination, and Medicare Prescription Drug Coverage Determination Appeals Procedures, 82 Fed. Reg. 4974 (Jan. 17, 2017), *available at* https://www.federalregister.gov/documents/2017/01/17/2016-32058/medicare-program-changes-to-the-medicare-claims-and-entitlement-medicare-advantage-organization (site visited Aug. 6, 2018).

[191] 42 C.F.R. § 405.902.

[192] 42 C.F.R. § 405.1020(b).

[193] 42 C.F.R. § 405.1020(b).

[D] Initial Determinations and Redeterminations

The claims process begins when the Medicare contractor issues a Medicare Summary Notice (MSN), which is an initial determination of the claim submitted by the hospital.[194] The regulations make clear that the initial determination goes only to the beneficiary, even when the contractor is aware that the beneficiary has an appointed representative.[195] Someone who wants to appeal from the initial determination must submit a written, signed request for a redetermination within 120 days of receipt of the initial determination. The regulations assume the notice is received 5 days after the actual date of the notice.[196] Requests for redeterminations in this scenario must be filed with the Medicare contractor; beneficiaries can no longer file requests with Social Security offices.[197]

The regulations also allow hospital providers to request appeal of a denial of an initial determination, raising the possibility that both the beneficiary and the hospital will initiate the appeals process.[198] In such a case, the contractor is required to consolidate the appeals.[199] The contractor has 60 days from receipt of the redetermination request to issue a decision.[200] If more than one party files a request, the time period runs from the date the last request is received.[201] For example, if a beneficiary files a redetermination request on day 1, but the hospital files on day 50, the 60-day time period for the contractor to act starts on day 50.

Unlike the initial determination, the notice of the redetermination is sent to a beneficiary's appointed representative.[202] The notice must include an explanation of the facts, policies, and law relied upon in making the redetermination decision; the right to request a reconsideration decision and the process for doing so; and a statement of specific missing documents that must be submitted.[203] The notice must state that the hospital, but not the beneficiary[204] (unless the beneficiary is represented by a provider), must submit all of its evidence by the next level of review in order for the evidence to be considered at any further stage of the appeals process. As a practical matter, the same notice is sent to beneficiaries and hospital providers, with a statement that evidentiary time

---

[194] *See* https://www.cms.gov/medicare/medicare-General-Information/MSN/index.html (site visited Nov. 2, 2018). To obtain various Medicare appeals forms, *see* CMS, "Forms, Help, & Resources," *available at* https://www.medicare.gov/forms-help-and-resources/ (site visited Aug. 6, 2018).

[195] 42 C.F.R. §§ 405.921 and 405.910(i)(1).

[196] 42 C.F.R. § 405.942(a); *see also* 41 C.F.R. § 405.904.

[197] 42 C.F.R. § 405.944(a).

[198] 42 C.F.R. § 405.940.

[199] 42 C.F.R. § 405.944(c).

[200] 42 C.F.R. § 405.950(a).

[201] 42 C.F.R. § 405.950(b)(2).

[202] 42 C.F.R. § 405.910(h)(2).

[203] 42 C.F.R. § 405.956(b), (c); § 405.966(a).

[204] 42 C.F.R. § 405.966(c).

limits do not apply to beneficiaries. However, in some instances the contractors and ALJs have confused this requirement. The advocate should be certain to point out to the adjudicator that a beneficiary is not required to submit all evidence until the ALJ level of appeal.

Contractors are not required to send redetermination notices to multiple beneficiaries in overpayment cases brought by hospital providers if the beneficiary allegedly has no liability for the claim.[205] The regulations create a reopening process to be used instead of the redetermination process to correct minor errors or omissions in initial determinations.[206] This process responds to a section of the Medicare law that allows providers to correct minor mistakes without going through the appeals process. A reopening can also be used at subsequent levels of review. Questions remain concerning the relationship of the new reopening process and the process for deciding remanded cases, as well as the ability of a contractor to reopen a decision in favor of the beneficiary.[207]

[E] The QIC—Reconsideration Determinations

The 2000 law created a third level of review, the reconsideration. Reconsiderations are conducted by a group of Medicare contractors called QICs.[208] Beneficiaries and other parties to the redetermination have 180 days from the date of receipt of the redetermination decision to request a reconsideration by filing a request at the location indicated on the redetermination notice.[209] Again, reconsiderations filed by beneficiaries and the hospital will be consolidated, and the time for issuing a decision runs from receipt of the last-filed appeal.[210] Appeals of redeterminations issued by the QIO in inpatient hospital cases go to the QIC for a requested reconsideration determination.[211]

---

[205] 42 C.F.R. § 405.956(a)(2).

[206] 42 C.F.R. §§ 405.980 *et seq.*

[207] *See, e.g.*, CMS, Transmittal 1069 (Sept. 29, 2006), *available at* http://www.cms.gov/Regulations-and-Guidance/Guidance/Transmittals/downloads/R1069CP.pdf (site visited Aug. 6, 2018).

[208] 42 C.F.R. § 405.960. The jurisdiction of the QICs over reconsideration determinations commenced May 1, 2005, for all Part A determinations and those Part B determinations made by a QIO or Medicare Administrative Contractor (MAC). The jurisdiction of the QIC over Part B reconsideration determinations for all determinations currently made by a Medicare Part B MAC commenced January 1, 2006. 70 Fed. Reg. 11,424–11,426 (Mar. 8, 2005). *See* CMS, Medicare Basics (revised May 2011), *available at* https://www.medicarefaq.com/wp-content/uploads/Medicare-Basics.pdf (site visited Aug. 6, 2018).

[209] 42 C.F.R. § 405.962.

[210] 42 C.F.R. § 405.964(c).

[211] 70 Fed. Reg. 11,424–11,426 (Subpart I—Determinations, Redeterminations, Reconsiderations, and Appeals Under Original Medicare (Part A and Part B)), *available at* http://www.ecfr.gov/cgi-bin/retrieveECFR?gp=&SID=373c3d21e4887af412d9965023l0b8a7&mc=true&n=sp42.2.405.i&r=SUBPART&ty=HTML (site visited Aug. 6, 2018).

The reconsideration level of review is a paper review. The QIC, however, may solicit the views of the beneficiary.[212] As noted above, if hospital providers appeal from the QIO to the QIC, they are required to submit all of the evidence they want considered in the claim to the QIC. Evidence not submitted by the hospital to the QIC may be excluded at subsequent levels of review.[213] However, beneficiaries who appeal (except those who are represented by a provider) may present evidence at further levels of appeal.[214]

The QIC must complete its reconsideration within 60 days of the reconsideration request.[215] The time frame runs from the last request filed if more than one party seeks reconsideration; the QIC must so notify a party who filed an earlier request.[216] The regulations do not indicate how QICs must document receipt of requests or how beneficiaries are to know when the 60-day period ends. Although the statute allows a party to the reconsideration to ask for an extension of not more than 14 days for the QIC to conclude the reconsideration, the regulations add 14 days to the reconsideration time frame each time that additional evidence is submitted.[217]

In making its reconsideration determination, the QIC is bound by national coverage determinations (NCDs) promulgated by Medicare and CMS Rulings, as well as statute and regulations.[218] It is not bound by local coverage determinations made by Medicare contractors, nor by Medicare policy issued by CMS itself, and must give "substantial deference" to these determinations and policy in making its decision.[219] If the QIC declines to apply them, the QIC's decision must state the reason why they were not followed.[220]

[F] Escalation

The Medicare Prescription Drug, Improvement, and Modernization Act of 2003 (MMA) introduced the concept of "escalation" into the Medicare appeals process. Commencing at the reconsideration level of appeal, if a decision is not rendered within a set time frame,[221] a party to the appeal may "escalate" the appeal to the next level. Many possible situations in which extensions of the time

---

[212] 70 Fed. Reg. 11,447–11,478.

[213] 42 C.F.R. § 405.966(a), (c).

[214] 42 C.F.R. § 405.966(c). *See also* CMA, "Hull v. Sebelius," (discussing its recently filed lawsuit challenging inordinately low favorable appeals), *available at* http://www.medicareadvocacy.org/hull-v-sebelius/ (site visited Aug. 6, 2018).

[215] 42 C.F.R. § 405.970(a).

[216] 42 C.F.R. § 405.970(b)(2).

[217] 42 C.F.R. § 405.970(b)(3).

[218] 42 C.F.R. § 405.1050(a)(4).

[219] 42 C.F.R. § 405.968(b)(1) and (2).

[220] 42 C.F.R. § 405.968(b)(3).

[221] The time frames are 60 days for the QIC to render a reconsideration determination; 90 days for an ALJ to issue a hearing decision; 180 days for the Medicare Appeals Council (Council) to issue

frame for the adjudicator to render its decision may occur.[222] Among these situations is the submission of additional evidence to the adjudicator by a party.

Generally, however, if a QIC does not issue a timely reconsideration decision (60 days from the date of its receipt of the request for reconsideration), the statute and regulations allow a party to request that the appeal be escalated to the next level of review, the ALJ level. The regulations give the QIC 5 days to either issue a decision or acknowledge the escalation request and send it to the ALJ level of review. The regulations indicate that an appeal escalated to the ALJ level must be completed within 180 days of receipt, rather than the statutorily mandated 90 days for ALJ decisions. Even at the ALJ level, however, additional extensions of the time frame for issuing a decision can occur.[223]

[G] Administrative Law Judge Appeals

Beneficiaries and other parties have 60 days from receipt of the reconsideration determination to file a request for an ALJ hearing.[224] Amount in controversy requirements apply at the ALJ level of appeal.[225] In addition, a party may escalate to the ALJ hearing from the QIC, when the QIC fails to issue a timely decision.[226] However, if an appeal is escalated to the ALJ, the 90-day time frame for deciding an ALJ appeal is automatically extended to 180 days, with the possibility for additional extensions beyond the 180 days.[227] As noted previously, whether an individual seeking redress from a denial of inpatient hospital coverage pursues an appeal through the QIO process, or pursues an appeal in response to an MSN, the process for the ALJ appeal level (and beyond) is the same.[228]

---

its decision. *See* 42 C.F.R. § 405.970 (Timeframe for making a reconsideration), *available at* http://www.ecfr.gov/cgi-bin/text-idx?SID=1542ce7fdf8a9c88f8d2b85d614172a2&mc=true&node=se42.2.405_1970&rgn=div8 (site visited Aug. 6, 2018).

[222] 42 C.F.R. §§ 405.970(b) and 405.1002(a) (reconsideration level); 42 C.F.R. §§ 405.1016(a)–(d) and 405.1104 (ALJ level); 42 C.F.R. §§ 405.1106(b) and 405.1132 (Council level).

[223] 42 C.F.R. §§ 405.970(b) and 405.1002(a) (reconsideration level); 42 C.F.R. §§ 405.1016(a)–(d) and 405.1104 (ALJ level); 42 C.F.R. §§ 405.1106(b) and 405.1132 (Council level).

[224] Extension of this 60-day time frame may be granted upon a showing of good cause. 42 C.F.R. § 405.1014(c).

[225] 42 C.F.R. § 405.1006. The amount in controversy in 2019 is $160, MCP Manual, Ch. 29, § 330.1. *See* 81 Fed. Reg. 185, P. 65653 (Sept. 28, 2012).

[226] 42 C.F.R. § 405.1002(b)(1)–(3).

[227] 42 C.F.R. § 405.1016(c).

[228] It is important to note that when appealing a termination of service or item the only issue that may be addressed is whether the provider's termination of the service/item was appropriate. A contractor or ALJ may find that they lack jurisdiction to rule on whether Medicare payment should be made for these items/services that the beneficiary *did* continue to receive and pay for, because a claim was never submitted for those items/services. In other words, the scope of review is different for expedited appeals v. regular appeals. By appealing the expedited decision a beneficiary is

The request for hearing must be filed at the address indicated on the reconsideration determination.[229] Currently, ALJs operate out of six field office locations: Miami, Florida; Cleveland, Ohio; Irvine, California; Arlington, Virginia; Kansas City, Missouri; and Seattle, Washington. These are the hearing offices in which Medicare ALJs are currently housed.[230]

HHS recently took administrative actions designed to reduce the number of pending appeals and to encourage resolution of cases earlier in the Medicare appeals process by implementing the regulatory changes in the final rule that became effective on March 20, 2017. The goals of the new/revised regulations were to address "recent workload challenges" as the number of ALJ hearing requests continues to exceed OMHA's adjudication capacity.[231] The changes in the final rule are primarily focused on the ALJ level of review and will do a number of things including the following: permitting designation of Medicare Appeals Council (Council) decisions as precedential; expanding OMHA's available adjudicator pool by allowing attorney adjudicators to decide certain appeals; simplifying proceedings when CMS or CMS contractors are involved; clarifying areas of the regulations; and creating process efficiencies.[232]

The revised regulations authorize "Attorney Adjudicators," rather than ALJs to perform a portion of OMHA's workload that does not require a hearing.[233] Attorney adjudicators can issue decisions when a decision can be issued without an ALJ conducting a hearing under the regulations, dismissals when an appellant withdraws his or her request for an ALJ hearing, certain remands, and reviews of QIC and IRE dismissals. The revised regulations also make telephone hearings the default hearing method for individuals other than unrepresented beneficiaries.[234] VTC will be retained as the default method of conducting hearings for unrepresented beneficiaries, unless good cause for an in-person appearance is shown or the beneficiary requests a phone hearing.[235] A notice of the hearing must be given to all parties, the Medicare contractor and the QIC, advising them of the time and date for the hearing at least 20 days prior to the date of its scheduled date.[236] All of those receiving a notice of hearing are required to acknowledge whether they plan to attend the hearing or object to the proposed time and/or place

only appealing the termination of services decision. In order to obtain an appealable Medicare determination for any services a beneficiary continues to receive they must simultaneously request a demand bill to initiate an appeal for those services.

[229] 42 C.F.R. § 405.1014(c).

[230] *See* the Office of Medicare Hearings and Appeals (OMHA) website: https://www.hhs.gov/about/agencies/omha/contact/index.html (site visited Aug. 6, 2018).

[231] 82 Fed. Reg. 4976.

[232] 82 Fed. Reg. 4974.

[233] 42 C.F.R. § 405.902.

[234] 42 C.F.R. § 405.1020(b).

[235] 42 C.F.R. § 405.1020(b).

[236] 42 C.F.R. §§ 405.1020(c) and 405.1022(a).

of the hearing.[237] An objection to the time and/or place must be in writing and state the reasons for the objection.[238] If a party objects to the issues as stated in the notice of hearing, that party must notify the ALJ in writing no later than five days prior to the hearing of the objections, and send a copy of the objections to all other parties to the appeal.[239] The ALJ will make a decision regarding the objections either in writing, at prehearing conference, or at the hearing.[240]

Any new written evidence that a beneficiary wishes to submit must be submitted with the request for hearing or within 10 days of receiving the notice of hearing.[241] Evidence may be submitted later than 10 days, but the time frame for the ALJ to issue his or her decision is tolled for the period between when the evidence was required to be submitted and when it was actually received.[242] Although providers are generally required to submit all their relevant evidence at the QIC level of appeal, they may submit additional evidence if they establish "good cause" for failing to do so earlier.[243] The ALJ must review the new evidence submitted by the provider and notify all parties whether it is excluded.[244]

Although generally the issues at the hearing will include all issues brought out at any prior level of appeal that were not decided in a party's favor, the ALJ may also include as an issue any portion of any prior determination that was decided favorably.[245] The parties must be notified of all issues before the hearing.[246] New issues may be raised at any time prior to the start of the hearing, if those new issues could have a material impact on the claims that are the subject of the request for hearing.[247]

Discovery at the ALJ level of appeal is permissible only when CMS elects to be made a party to the hearing.[248] Discovery is permissible with respect to any matter that is relevant to the subject matter of the hearing, although the party from

---

[237] 42 C.F.R. § 405.1020(c)(2). On occasion, a party may not receive the notice of hearing. The OMHA is required to attempt to contact the party who has not responded to the notice of hearing to find out why. 42 C.F.R. § 405.1022(c)(1) If the OMHA fails to make such contact, and the ALJ dismisses the appeal for failure of that party to attend the hearing, advocates have found that the OMHA's failure to attempt such contact is grounds for reversal of the dismissal.

[238] 42 C.F.R. § 405.1020(e).

[239] 42 C.F.R. § 405.1024(a), (b).

[240] 42 C.F.R. § 405.1024(c).

[241] 42 C.F.R. § 405.1018(a). Evidence may be submitted beyond this period, but it has the effect of tolling the time frame for the ALJ to render a decision. This provision does not apply to unrepresented beneficiaries. 42 C.F.R. § 405.1018(d).

[242] 42 C.F.R. § 405.1018(b).

[243] 42 C.F.R. § 405.1018(c).

[244] 42 C.F.R. § 405.1028(a)–(d).

[245] 42 C.F.R. § 405.1032(a).

[246] 42 C.F.R. § 405.1032.

[247] 42 C.F.R. § 405.1032(b). Certain limitations apply to this. *See* 42 C.F.R. § 405.980

[248] 42 C.F.R. § 405.1037(a).

whom discovery is sought may raise objections based on the assertion that the material sought is privileged or otherwise protected.[249] Additionally, an ALJ may deny a request for discovery if the ALJ concludes that the discovery request is unreasonable, unduly burdensome or expensive, or otherwise inappropriate.[250] Discovery is limited. A party may request reasonable production of documents for inspection and copying, but depositions may not be taken unless the deponent agrees or the ALJ finds the proposed deposition is appropriate and necessary.[251] Similarly, requests for admissions and interrogatories are generally not permitted.[252]

The ALJ may hold a pre-hearing or a post-hearing conference, either at his or her own initiative or at the request of a party.[253] The ALJ must inform the parties of the time, place, and purpose of the conference at least seven calendar days prior to the conference date.[254] The ALJ may consider matters in addition to those stated on the notice of hearing, if the parties consent in writing.[255] A record of the hearing will be made, and the ALJ must issue an order stating all agreements and actions resulting from the conference.[256]

An administrative record, including marked exhibits, will be made.[257] A party may request and review a copy of the record prior to or at the hearing, or, if a hearing is not held at any time before the notice of decision is issued; however, the party may be asked to pay the costs associated with providing these items.[258]

Once a hearing has been held,[259] the ALJ must issue a written decision that sets out findings of fact, conclusions of law, and the reasons for the decision.[260] The decision must be mailed to each party, the Medicare contractors, and the QIC.[261]

---

[249] 42 C.F.R. § 405.1037(a)(2).

[250] 42 C.F.R. § 405.1037(a)(2).

[251] 42 C.F.R. § 405.1037(b)(1), (2).

[252] 42 C.F.R. § 405.1037(b)(3).

[253] 42 C.F.R. § 405.1040.

[254] 42 C.F.R. § 405.1040(b).

[255] 42 C.F.R. § 405.1040(c).

[256] 42 C.F.R. § 405.1040(c), (d).

[257] 42 C.F.R. § 405.1042. In practice, advocates have found that the exhibit lists are sometimes haphazardly assembled and often insufficiently detailed. If the exhibit list is ambiguous prior to hearing, the advocate should make a written request to the ALJ seeking a copy of the administrative record.

[258] 42 C.F.R. § 405.1042(a)(3), 42 C.F.R. § 405.1042(b)(1).

[259] Parties are free to waive their right to a hearing and have a decision issued solely on the administrative record. 42 C.F.R. §§ 405.1020(d) and 405.1038(b). In addition, an ALJ or Attorney Adjudicator may, without holding a hearing, issue a decision that is fully favorable to the appellant(s) if the hearing record supports such a finding. 42 C.F.R. § 405.1038(a).

[260] 42 C.F.R. § 405.1046(a).

[261] 42 C.F.R. § 405.1046(a).

If an ALJ decision is not rendered within the appropriate time frame for the circumstances of the case, a party may escalate the appeal to the Council.[262] The request for escalation must be filed with the ALJ.[263] Once the request is received, the ALJ has five days to either issue a decision, remand the case to the QIC,[264] or notify the parties that a timely decision cannot be issued.[265] At that point, the QIC decision becomes the decision which the Council will review.[266] In addition, the Council may, on its own initiative, remove a case from the ALJ and assume responsibility for holding a hearing and adjudicating the case itself.[267]

[H] Medicare Appeals Council Review

A party dissatisfied with an ALJ decision may request review by the Council.[268] A written request for Council review must be filed with the Council or the appropriate ALJ office.[269] The request must identify those parts of the ALJ decision (or other determination being appealed, if the case is before the Council due to escalation) to which the party objects, and state the reasons for those objections.[270] Unless the appellant is an unrepresented beneficiary, the Council will limit its review to those parts of the decision below specifically identified as objectionable in the request for review.

If a party has requested review because he or she is dissatisfied with an ALJ decision or has escalated an appeal from the ALJ to the Council, the Council will review *de novo* the decision below.[271] A party seeking Council review does not have a right to a new hearing; however, the Council, in its discretion, may conduct any additional proceedings, including holding a hearing.[272]

Generally, absent good cause,[273] no additional evidence may be introduced at the Council level of appeal, unless the ALJ decision being reviewed decides a new issue that the parties were not afforded an opportunity to address before the

---

[262] 42 C.F.R. § 405.1016(f).

[263] 42 C.F.R. § 405.1016(f)(1).

[264] 42 C.F.R. § 405.1016(f)(2).

[265] 42 C.F.R. § 405.1016(f)(2).

[266] 42 C.F.R. § 405.1016(f)(2)(i).

[267] 42 C.F.R. § 405.1050.

[268] The Council may also exercise its "own motion" review. 42 C.F.R. § 405.1110. This review can occur upon the Council's own initiative or when CMS (or any of its contractors) refers a case to the Council that it thinks has been erroneously decided or the decision presents a broad policy or procedural issue that may affect the public interest. This, of course, we fear, gives CMS the ability to tightly control the decision-making process and its outcomes, even though the MMA requires the independence of ALJs.

[269] 42 C.F.R. § 405.1112(a).

[270] 42 C.F.R. § 405.1112(b).

[271] 42 C.F.R. § 405.1108.

[272] 42 C.F.R. § 405.1108(a), (d)(3).

[273] 42 C.F.R. § 405.1122(c).

ALJ.[274] However, a party to the Council review, which is before the Council because of escalation, may file a request for a subpoena of specified documents within 10 days of the request for escalation.[275]

The parties have the right to file briefs or other written statements with the Council.[276] In addition, the Council may request (but cannot require) CMS or its contractors to file a brief or position paper, if the Council determines that it is necessary to resolve the issues in the case.[277] In some instances, the Council may permit, or seek, oral argument on the appeal.[278]

The Council may dispose of the case in a number of ways: it may remand the case to the ALJ;[279] it may dismiss the request for Council review;[280] or it may issue a decision.[281] If the Council fails to issue its decision within the required 90-day time frame from its receipt of the request for Council review,[282] the appellant may request escalation to federal court.[283] If, upon filing of the escalation request and the lapse of the permissible time plus five additional days, the Council is unable to issue a decision, remand, or dismissal, it must notify the appellant informing him or her that it is not able to do so.[284] A party may file an action in federal district court within 60 days after the date it receives this notification from the Council.[285]

[I] Judicial Review

A party to a Council decision who is dissatisfied with the decision may obtain judicial review if the amount in controversy requirement is met (the amount for ~~2018 is $2,000~~).[286] The civil action must be filed within 60 days after receipt of notice of the Council decision.[287] Provisions exist in the regulations for

274 42 C.F.R. § 405.1122(a).

275 42 C.F.R. § 405.1122(d)(1)–(4).

276 42 C.F.R. § 405.1120.

277 *Id.*

278 42 C.F.R. § 405.1124.

279 42 C.F.R. § 405.1108(d)(3).

280 42 C.F.R. § 405.1108(c), (d)(4)–(5).

281 42 C.F.R. § 405.1108(a), (d)(1).

282 42 C.F.R. § 405.1132. As with the other levels of appeal, the time frame for issuing a determination is subject to various extensions. *See, e.g.*, 42 C.F.R. § 405.1114 (extension when party seeks evidence from the Council); 42 C.F.R. § 405.1120 (extension when briefs are filed); 42 C.F.R. § 405.1122(e)(2)(ii) (stay upon issuance of subpoena).

283 42 C.F.R. § 405.1132.

284 42 C.F.R. § 405.1132(a)(2).

285 42 C.F.R. § 405.1132(b).

286 42 C.F.R. § 405.1136. The amount in controversy required to proceed to federal court in 2018 is $2,000 (81 Fed. Reg. 65,653 (Sept. 27, 2016)), MCP Manual, Ch. 29: § 345.1.

287 42 C.F.R. § 405.1130.

applying to the Council for extension of the filing time.[288] The civil action must be filed in the district court for the judicial district in which the beneficiary resides or, if filed by a provider, in the judicial district where it has its principal place of business.[289] The Secretary of HHS in his or her official capacity is the proper defendant.[290] The standard of review for the court is whether the decision of the Secretary of HHS is supported by substantial evidence.[291]

In addition, Section 932 of the MMA modified 42 U.S.C. § 1395ff(b) to create expedited access to the judicial review process whereby beneficiaries, providers, and suppliers can have expedited access to judicial review in certain appeals of Medicare Part A or Part B claims.[292] The expedited appeals process also applies to provider contract disputes—primarily nursing home enforcement cases.[293] Expedited review is available when it is determined both that the Council lacks authority to decide a question of law or regulation relevant to the case and that there is no material issue of fact in dispute.[294]

A beneficiary may file a request for expedited access to judicial review at the same time as, or after, filing a request for an ALJ hearing.[295] A review entity made up of three reviewers who are ALJs or members of the HHS Departmental Appeals Board (DAB) has 60 days after receipt of the request to issue a written decision.[296] The review entity may request appropriate documents and materials from the beneficiary to support his or her contention that (1) no material issues of fact exist and (2) the Council lacks authority to decide the relevant question of law or regulations.[297] If the review entity agrees with the beneficiary's request for expedited review, or if the review entity fails to act within 60 days of receipt of the request, the beneficiary skips ALJ and DAB review and may go directly to district court.[298] If the review entity finds against the beneficiary, she has no further recourse and may not make another request for expedited review regarding the matter in dispute.[299]

---

[288] 42 C.F.R. § 405.1134.

[289] 42 C.F.R. § 405.1136(b).

[290] 42 C.F.R. § 405.1136(d).

[291] 42 C.F.R. § 405.1136(f).

[292] 42 C.F.R. § 405.990.

[293] 42 C.F.R. §§ 405.906(a)–(c) and 405.990(e).

[294] 42 C.F.R. § 405.990(a)(2).

[295] 42 C.F.R. § 405.990(d)(2).

[296] 42 C.F.R. § 405.990(a)(1).

[297] 42 C.F.R. § 405.990(c).

[298] 42 C.F.R. § 405.990(f)(4).

[299] 42 C.F.R. § 405.990(h)(3)(i).

[J] Appointments of Representatives and Attorneys' Fees

Medicare regulations specify the elements of a proper appointment of representative, its duration, and rules about collection of fees for representing Medicare beneficiaries in an appeal of a Medicare denial.[300]

A valid appointment of representation form must:[301]

- Be in writing and signed and dated by both the beneficiary and the representative.
- Authorize the representative to act on behalf of the beneficiary and authorize the adjudicator to release identifiable health information to the representative.
- Include an explanation of the purpose and scope of the representation.
- Include the name, phone number, and address for the beneficiary and the representative.
- Include the beneficiary's Medicare health insurance claim number.
- Include the representative's professional status or relationship to the beneficiary.
- Be filed with the entity processing the party's initial determination or appeal.

If a form is defective, the representative will be given an opportunity to correct the defect. Otherwise, the representative will not have the authority to act on behalf of the beneficiary or to receive health information.[302]

The regulations limit the duration of the appointment of representation form to one year. A duly appointed representative may file multiple appeals on behalf of an individual beneficiary during the course of that year but must submit a copy of the original appointment form with each additional appeal filed. Once an appointment of representation form has been filed in a case, the appointment lasts for the duration of the appeal unless it is revoked.[303]

The regulations prohibit an appointed representative from delegating the appointment to another person without the beneficiary's consent. Thus, a family member who already serves as an appointed representative cannot delegate that appointment to an advocate for purposes of pursing an appeal unless the beneficiary signs a written notice. A signed statement is not required where both the

---

[300] 42 C.F.R. §§ 405.910 and 405.912.

[301] 42 C.F.R. § 405.910(c). For the appointment of representation form, *see* CMS, Appointment of Representative, *available at* https://www.cms.gov/Medicare/CMS-Forms/CMS-Forms/downloads/cms1696.pdf (site visited Aug. 6, 2018).

[302] 42 C.F.R. § 405.910(d).

[303] 42 C.F.R. §§ 405.910(e) and 405.912(e).

appointed and new representatives are attorneys (but not paralegals) in the same law firm or organization. When a beneficiary lacks the capacity to sign an appointment of representation form or form acknowledging delegation of the appointment, state law determines who has authority to authorize representation on his or her behalf.[304]

Under the regulations, a beneficiary's appointed representative (but not a provider or supplier's representative) who wishes to charge a fee for services at the ALJ and Council levels of review must obtain approval of the fee from the Secretary of HHS. The regulations also say that no award of fees or costs may be made against the Medicare trust fund, and that limitations on the amount of fees that apply in Social Security and SSI disability cases do not apply to Medicare appeals.[305]

The regulations do not contain any standard by which fee requests will be judged. However, the preamble indicates that guidelines for the application of Equal Access to Justice Act (EAJA) claims before HHS may be applicable to Medicare appeals.[306] The preamble further states that HHS will review the guidelines to determine whether they need to be changed in light of the new provision.[307]

The preamble justifies the policy change by saying that a change in the Medicare Act makes provisions concerning approval of fee arrangements from back awards of Social Security disability benefits applicable to Medicare appeals.[308] The preamble goes on to acknowledge, however, that, unlike Social Security cases, there is no back award of benefits from which attorneys can be paid, and that the limitation on Social Security attorneys' fees does not apply.[309]

[K] QIO Appeals for Denial of Hospital Services to Beneficiaries Enrolled in a Medicare Advantage Plan

The appeals system for beneficiaries enrolled in a Medicare Advantage (MA) plan is different, at least through the reconsideration level of appeal. The appeal rules in MA plan cases that reach the ALJ level of appeal or beyond are the same as described above. Beneficiaries who receive Medicare-covered

---

304 42 C.F.R. § 405.400.

305 42 C.F.R. § 405.910(f). *See also* SSA, "Form SSA-1560-Petition For Authorization To Charge And Collect A Fee For Services Before The Social Security Administration," (Petition to obtain approval of a fee for representing a claimant-SSA), *available at* http://www.ssa.gov/forms/ssa-1560.html (site visited Aug. 6, 2018). The appointment of representative in Medicare appeals form refers to the SSA "Petition to Obtain Representative Fee" as the form to use to provide information in support of a petition for fees (no standard form) in Medicare appeals. It should accompany the fee petition.

306 70 Fed. Reg. 11,430 (Mar. 8, 2005).

307 70 Fed. Reg. 11,430 (Mar. 8, 2005).

308 70 Fed. Reg. 11,429 (Mar. 8, 2005).

309 70 Fed. Reg. 11,429 (Mar. 8, 2005).

hospital services through MA plans are entitled to QIO review of denied, reduced, or terminated care. These regulations include the right to a grievance process for non-appealable complaints, specific time frames for each step in the appeals process, and the right to appeal hospital coverage determinations to the QIO, including expedited review.[310]

At the initial stage, MA plans should have a more specific process for addressing grievances, but beneficiaries should be provided, at a minimum level, with the same number of notices as those beneficiaries who receive care under traditional Medicare. The process for higher level appeals for MA plans was originally governed by a different set of provisions; however, CMS changed this to apply the same regulations to both sets of appeals at this level.[311]

Under the MA program, managed care plans are required to provide procedural protections for beneficiaries, including meaningful grievance procedures and appeal rights.[312] These protections include the right to receive notice of an adverse "organization determination" regarding services or payment;[313] the right to an internal plan appeal (called a "reconsideration");[314] a final reconsidered determination by CMS;[315] and further review by an ALJ (if $160.00 or more is in controversy in 2018),[316] by the HHS DAB,[317] and by a federal district court (if $1,630 or more is in dispute in 2019).[318]

[L] Time Frames (Medicare Advantage)

All determinations and reconsiderations must be made "as expeditiously as the enrollee's health condition requires" but not to exceed a stated number of days.[319] Notice of organization determinations (initial decisions regarding the benefits an enrollee is entitled to receive) must be provided no later than 14 days after the initial request,[320] reduced from the previous 60-day limit. Expedited

---

[310] *See also* Weichardt v. Thompson, C.A. No. 03 5490 VRW (N.D. Cal. Settlement Agreement, Oct. 28, 2005). *See* Medicare Program; Notification Procedures for Hospital Discharges, 71 Fed. Reg. 17,052–17,062 (Apr. 5, 2006), 42 C.F.R. §§ 405.1205, 405.1206, 422.620, and 422.622, *inter alia*. *See also* 72 Fed. Reg. 17,169 (Apr. 6, 2007) and discussion at **§ 2.11[N]** of this Handbook.

[311] CMS opted to change this part of the process to reflect exactly the process for appeals for individuals who have traditional Medicare. *See* 42 C.F.R. § 417.600(b)(1) and 70 Fed. Reg. 4588-01 (Jan. 28, 2005).

[312] 42 U.S.C. § 1395(c)(5).

[313] 42 C.F.R. §§ 422.566–422.576.

[314] 42 C.F.R. § 422.578, *available at* http://www.gpo.gov/fdsys/pkg/CFR-2010-title42-vol3/pdf/CFR-2010-title42-vol3-sec422-578.pdf (site visited Sept. 22, 2018).

[315] 42 C.F.R. § 422.592.

[316] 42 C.F.R. § 422.600.

[317] 42 C.F.R. § 422.608.

[318] 42 C.F.R. § 422.612. *See* 81 Fed. Reg. 185, p. 65653 (Sept. 27, 2016).

[319] *See, e.g.*, 42 C.F.R. § 422.568, regarding organization determinations.

[320] 42 C.F.R. § 422.568.

organization determinations must be made within 72 hours.[321] Reconsidered determinations must be issued no later than 30 calendar days from the request for a standard reconsideration,[322] reduced from the previous 60-day time limit. If the reconsideration is expedited, the deadline is 72 hours,[323] with extensions up to 14 days upon enrollee or MA organization requests, and the delay is in the enrollee's interest.[324]

The regulations require CMS to contract with an independent outside entity to conduct a second level of review when the internal reconsideration remains, in whole or in part, adverse to the enrollee.[325] Review must be conducted as expeditiously as the enrollee's health condition requires, but the regulations do not specify a maximum time frame. Contractor deadlines are to be specified in the contract.[326]

[M] Effectuation of Appeal Decisions (Medicare Advantage)

The regulations mandate that if an MA organization reverses its original determination, it must authorize or provide the service under dispute as expeditiously as the enrollee's health requires, but no later than 30 days after the beneficiary requests reconsideration.[327] If the original denial is reversed by the independent outside entity, the MA organization must comply within 60 days.[328]

[N] Non-Coverage of Inpatient Hospital Care (Medicare Advantage)

Notice requirements are slightly different for persons in a hospital that is part of a Health Maintenance Organization (HMO), Preferred Provider Organization (PPO), or Private Fee-for-Service (PFFS) plan sponsored by an MA organization. The MA organization, or the hospital that has been delegated the authority to make the discharge decision, must provide the beneficiary with written notice of non-coverage, but only if and when the beneficiary disagrees with the discharge decision. Notice and appeal rights also arise if the MA organization, or the hospital that has been delegated the authority to make the discharge decision, is not discharging the individual but no longer intends to continue coverage of the inpatient stay.[329]

---

[321] 42 C.F.R. § 422.572.

[322] 42 C.F.R. § 422.590(a)(1).

[323] 42 C.F.R. § 422.590(d)(1).

[324] 42 C.F.R. §§ 422.572(b) and 422.590(d)(2).

[325] 42 C.F.R. § 422.592.

[326] 42 C.F.R. § 422.592(b).

[327] 42 C.F.R. § 422.618(a). Reversals on a request for payment must be acted upon within 60 days. 42 C.F.R. § 422.618(b).

[328] 42 C.F.R. § 422.618(c).

[329] Revised 42 C.F.R. § 422.620(a)(i), (ii).

The "Revised Important Message from Medicare,"[330] a broad, general information notice that is given upon admission, or within two days of admission, is the written notice that an inpatient will receive. Since July 1, 2007, Medicare-participating hospitals, including MA plans, have been required to deliver valid, written notice, in the form of the "Important Message from Medicare" (IM), of a patient's rights as a hospital patient including discharge appeal rights, within two calendar days of admission. A follow-up copy of the signed IM is given again as far as possible in advance of discharge, but no more than two calendar days prior to the proposed date of discharge. Follow-up notice is not required if the provision of the admission IM falls within two calendar days of discharge.[331] If, upon being told that he or she is about to be discharged, the patient disagrees, he or she is to be given a notice of non-coverage with specific information about the basis of the hospital's discharge decision and about appeal rights. Therefore, as a practical matter, an enrollee who wishes to challenge a determination that the hospital stay is no longer necessary may need to remain in the hospital beyond the date on which Medicare non-coverage is slated to commence.

- An enrollee is entitled to coverage until at least noon of the day after the above notice is provided;[332]
- If QIO review is requested under 42 C.F.R § 422.622 (requesting immediate QIO review of non-coverage of inpatient care), coverage is extended, and:

  The enrollee must submit a request for immediate review to the QIO that has an agreement with the hospital;

  The request must be in writing or by telephone;

  The request must be submitted no later than the day of discharge and may be in writing or by telephone; and

  The QIO must make a determination and notify the enrollee, or the hospital and the MA plan by the close of business of the first working day after it receives all necessary information from the hospital, or the organization, or both.

  Before a notice of non-coverage is provided, the entity that makes the non-coverage/discharge determination must obtain the concurrence of the physician who is responsible for the enrollee's inpatient care.[333]

---

[330] *See* CMS, "Hospital Discharge Appeal Notices."

[331] *See* 72 Fed. Reg. 17,169 (Apr. 6, 2007).

[332] 42 C.F.R. § 422.622(f)(2)(i).

[333] 42 C.F.R. § 422.620(b).

The written notice of non-coverage must be issued no later than the day before hospital coverage ends. The written notice must include the following elements[334]

1. The reason inpatient hospital care is no longer needed;
2. The effective date and time of the enrollee's liability for continued inpatient care;
3. The enrollee's appeal rights; and
4. Additional information specified by CMS.

[O] Grievances (Medicare Advantage)

MA organizations must have "meaningful procedures for timely hearing and resolution of grievances," which are complaints or disputes other than those involving organization determinations,[335] expressing dissatisfaction with any aspect of an MA organization or provider's operations, activities, or behaviors, regardless of whether remedial action is requested.

The regulation distinguishes between a grievance and appeal,[336] and requires MA organizations to inform beneficiaries whether their complaint is subject to the grievance procedure or the appeals procedure. It further distinguishes quality of care complaints,[337] and includes a process for expedited grievances,[338] requiring completion in 24 hours.

[P] Identifying Coverable Cases

Medicare claims for inpatient hospital care are suitable for Medicare coverage, and appeal if they have been denied, if they meet the following test:

The patient's condition must have been such that the care he required could only have been provided in a hospital, *or* he required a SNF level of care, and no SNF bed was actually available. (Note: A SNF level of care means that the patient required skilled services—from a physical therapist or a registered nurse, for example—on a daily basis.)[339]

---

334 *See* 42 C.F.R. § 422.622(c).
335 42 C.F.R. § 422.564.
336 42 C.F.R. § 422.561.
337 42 C.F.R. § 422.564.
338 42 C.F.R. § 422.564(d)(1), (2).
339 *See* 42 C.F.R. §§ 409.30 *et seq.*

§ 2.12 DENIAL AND APPEAL PROCESS

Table 2-1 depicts the complex coverage determination and appeals process in Medicare hospital cases. The text that follows the chart describes the various steps in detail.

[A] Medicare Hospital Coverage Determination and Appeals Process

See Table 2-1.

TABLE 2-1
MEDICARE PART A APPEALS
HOSPITAL CARE

Stage of Appeal	*Reconsideration Request*	*Hearing Request*	*Request for Dept. Appeals Board Review*	*Request for Judicial Review*
Time Deadline for Filing Appeal:	60 Days After Receipt of "Notice of Medicare Claim Determination" (or within 3 Days if You Request an "Expedited Appeal")	60 Days After Receipt of "Reconsideration Determination"	60 Days After Receipt of "Hearing Decision"	60 Days After Receipt of "Appeals Board Decision"
Amount of Claim:	No Minimum	$200 Minimum*	$200 Minimum*	$2,000 Minimum
File Appeal Request With:	Quality Improvement Organization (QIO) or Local Social Security Office	Quality Improvement Organization (QIO) or Local Social Security Office (processed & forwarded to Social Security's Office of Hearings & Appeals)	U.S. Dept. of Health and Human Services	United States District Court

continues

TABLE 2-1 continued

Stage of Appeal	*Reconsideration Request*	*Hearing Request*	*Request for Dept. Appeals Board Review*	*Request for Judicial Review*
Appeal Reviewed & Decided By:	Quality Improvement Organization (QIO)	Administrative Law Judge from Social Security Departmental Office of Hearings and Appeals	U.S. Dept. of Health and Human Services Appeals Board	United States District Court
Time Deadline For Decision:	3 Days If Inpatient or Pre-Admission; 30 Days for All Others	None	None	None

* If the appeal is on a question of entitlement to Part A benefits, there is no minimum amount required.

[B] The Appeals Process in Operation

The determination and appeals process depicted in **Table 2-1** is as follows:

1. The patient appears at the hospital seeking admission.

   ■ **EXAMPLE:** Mr. Brown and Mrs. Smith both are driven to the hospital by car. Mr. Brown, whose daughter takes him to the hospital, is having chest pains and has a history of a stroke and severe hypertension that is controlled by oral medications. By contrast, Mrs. Smith was found by a stranger wandering in the middle of a four-lane highway, dressed in a nightgown. Mrs. Smith, who lives alone, was incoherent and had a superficial wound on her leg. The stranger called the police, who took her to the hospital.

2. When confronted by a patient seeking admission, a hospital can choose one of these courses of action:

   a. The hospital may decide that the patient will be covered by Medicare and admit the patient.

   b. The hospital may decide that Medicare coverage is not available but permit the patient to enter the hospital anyway. Under such circumstances, the hospital is required to issue the patient a notice of admission denial, informing the patient that the cost of hospital care will be the patient's responsibility. Written notice of non-coverage to the patient is necessary because the patient is not liable for the cost of care and may not be charged by the hospital until he or she has been given written notice that the services involved are not covered by the Medicare program.[340]

c. Finally, the hospital may deny Medicare coverage and not admit the patient. Often the patient will balk at assuming responsibility for expensive care, or the hospital may simply refuse to allow the patient to enter. Usually no written Medicare denial notice is issued, and the patient has no right to appeal. An exception exists, however, where the QIO has a pre-procedure or preadmission review process in place. Although unusual, involvement of the QIO at the preadmission stage is good news for the advocate because appeal is possible. In such cases the QIO reviews the medical necessity or appropriateness of some or all of the Medicare admissions before they occur. If the QIO determines that Medicare coverage is not available, it issues an appealable initial determination notice to the beneficiary.[341]

■ **EXAMPLE:** Upon arriving at the hospital, Mr. Brown is examined in the emergency room and admitted to the hospital. By contrast, Mrs. Smith is examined and a determination is made that she does not need hospital care, but since she cannot be safely sent home, she will be admitted to the hospital. Mrs. Smith is given a written notice of Medicare non-coverage and placed in one of the hospital's beds.

3. All patients actually admitted to the hospital must be given a special notice entitled "An Important Message from Medicare."[342] The mandatory notice is very explicit about a patient's rights while in the hospital. Most of the information in the "Important Message from Medicare" concerns the procedure to be followed when the hospital issues a continuing care denial of Medicare coverage. A continuing care denial occurs when the patient has been granted Medicare coverage on admission, but the hospital, usually acting through its URC, eventually determines that the patient no longer needs a hospital level of care.

■ **EXAMPLE:** After three days of tests, Mr. Brown is determined to require transfer to a nursing home. The hospital URC determines that

---

340 42 C.F.R. §§ 411.404 and 412.42(c)(3); *see also* Social Security Act § 1879, 42 U.S.C. § 1395pp.

341 MCP Manual, Ch. 30, §§ 240–240.6. *See also* **Appendix 2-2** in this Handbook.

342 Social Security Act § 1866(a)(1)(M), 42 U.S.C. § 1395cc(a)(1)(M); 42 C.F.R § 412.42(c)(3); MCP Manual, Ch. 30: §§ 200–200.6. *See also* **Appendix 2-2** in this Handbook.

he can be terminated from Medicare coverage because he no longer requires inpatient hospital care. A written continuing stay denial is issued to him.

4. Utilization review of a continuing stay often occurs because the stay is longer or more expensive than the average for that DRG. In such instances, the hospital may be motivated to avoid the financial loss represented by the gap between the DRG amount paid and the cost of the patient's care as the stay continues. Before issuing a determination that an admission or a continuing stay is not medically necessary, the URC must consult the attending physician and afford an opportunity to present his or her point of view.[343] Moreover, before a hospital may bill a patient for the cost of services rendered, however, the hospital must comply with a complex coverage determination, notice, and appeals process.

   Federal regulations are quite specific concerning when a hospital may charge a Medicare-eligible patient for hospital services rendered. Generally, a hospital may not charge a beneficiary for any service for which payment is made by Medicare, even if the hospital's cost of furnishing services to the patient is greater than the amount the hospital is paid under PPS.[344] The hospital is always permitted to charge the patient the applicable deductible and coinsurance amounts. The hospital is not permitted to charge the patient for care excluded from Medicare coverage as custodial care or medically unnecessary care[345] unless the following specific steps are followed:

   The hospital must decide that the patient no longer requires inpatient hospital care. Inpatient hospital care includes cases where a beneficiary needs a SNF level of care, but, under Medicare criteria, a SNF level bed is not available.[346]

   ■ **EXAMPLE:** Mr. Brown receives three days of Medicare hospital coverage, following which a determination is made that he can be transferred to a nursing home. Transfer to a nursing home does not necessarily mean that Mr. Brown requires a SNF level of care under Medicare criteria. Therefore, an inquiry into the nature of the care that Mr. Brown requires will have to be made.

   If the attending physician agrees with the hospital's determination in writing, the hospital may immediately issue a continuing care denial to the patient.[347]

---

[343] 42 C.F.R. § 482.30(d)(2).

[344] 42 C.F.R. § 412.42(a).

[345] 42 C.F.R. §§ 411.400, 489.21(d)(1).

[346] 42 C.F.R. § 412.42(c)(1).

[347] 42 C.F.R. § 412.42(c)(2).

■ **EXAMPLE:** Mr. Brown's treating physician, who ordered that Mr. Brown could be discharged to a nursing home, agrees that he no longer requires a hospital level of care. Therefore, the hospital URC issues a denial notice to Mr. Brown.

The continuing care denial notice given the patient must inform the patient that customary charges will be assessed against the patient only *after the second day following the date of the notice.*[348]. For example, if a patient receives a denial notice on Monday, the patient may not be charged for the cost of care until Thursday.

■ **EXAMPLE:** Mr. Brown was admitted to the hospital on Thursday and was determined to be suitable for nursing home placement on Saturday. The hospital URC, therefore, with Mr. Brown's physician's concurrence, issued a denial notice on Saturday. If Mr. Brown does nothing to appeal this denial, he could stay in the hospital, without incurring any financial liability, through Monday. He could be charged for his stay commencing on Tuesday.

For a case where coverage is denied on admission and no covered days whatsoever are granted, the hospital may not charge the patient for hospital care that is not medically necessary until the patient has been notified in writing that Medicare coverage is not available.[349] The notice must also inform the patient concerning the appeal rights described below.

■ **EXAMPLE:** Mrs. Smith was given a denial notice immediately prior to her admission. The hospital would be able to charge her for her stay from the date of admission.

5. The right to appeal for a patient given a continuing care denial differs according to whether the attending physician has concurred with the URC's denial decision or whether the URC was required to obtain QIO approval of the proposed denial determination.[350]

   If the attending physician has agreed with the hospital determination of non-coverage, the QIO has not yet been required to review the case. In this situation the patient is entitled to an expedited QIO review if the patient is still an inpatient in the hospital and requests an expedited review not later than noon of the first working day after the date the patient receives the URC denial notice.[351] The hospital is required to provide the QIO with a copy of the medical records by the close of business of such working day, and the QIO must issue a determination not

[348] This limitation on charges to beneficiaries applies only where Medicare coverage was originally granted on admission, that is, where the patient's stay included at least one covered day. 42 C.F.R. § 412.42(b).

[349] 42 C.F.R. § 411.404(b).

[350] 42 C.F.R. § 412.42(c).

[351] Social Security Act § 1154(e), 42 U.S.C. § 1320c–3(c).

later than one full working day after the date the QIO has received the request for expedited review and the medical records.[352] If the patient is no longer in the hospital, or fails to request an expedited determination by noon of the first working day after the notice of no coverage is received, the QIO is required to issue a review decision within 30 days of the request.

■ **EXAMPLE:** Mr. Brown receives his continuing stay denial notice on Saturday. He must request an expedited review by the QIO by no later than noon on Monday, which he does. The QIO issues, and Mr. Brown receives, a decision that upholds the denial on Tuesday. The hospital may begin charging Mr. Brown for his stay on Tuesday. Under the Medicare regulations, an appeal to the QIO does not result in an extension of the hospital's inability to charge Mr. Brown, beyond two days after the original hospital URC notice was given to him, unless the QIO finds that, in fact, he required continued hospital care.[353] As can be seen, simply by requesting the expedited review, Mr. Brown has received an additional day of Medicare coverage in the hospital.

If the patient's attending physician does not concur with the hospital's determination of non-coverage, the hospital must obtain the QIO's concurrence before it can bill the patient.[354] The QIO must give an opportunity to the provider and to the physician to discuss the merits of the case.[355] If the QIO concurs with the hospital's determination, the hospital is so informed by the QIO, and the hospital will issue a notice to the patient.[356] The QIO's concurrence is binding upon the beneficiary unless the beneficiary is dissatisfied with this determiniation.[357] If still in the hospital, the beneficiary may request reconsideration by asking the QIO to review the case.[358] If the beneficiary is no longer in the hospital, the determination is subject to the general claims appeal process.[359]

It is unclear to what extent a hospital is required to notify the family members or legal representative of ill or incompetent patients. In one case the court found that the hospital had a duty to provide written, not oral, notice of the denial of Medicare coverage to the friend of an incompetent patient, where the hospital knew that the

[352] Social Security Act § 1154(e), 42 U.S.C. § 1320c–3(c).

[353] 42 C.F.R. § 412.42(c)(3)(v).

[354] 42 U.S.C. § 1320c-3(e)(2); 42 C.F.R. § 412.42(c)(2)

[355] 42 C.F.R. § 412.42.

[356] 42 U.S.C. § 1320c-3(e)(2);42 C.F.R. § 412.42(c)(2).

[357] 42 C.F.R. § 405.1208.

[358] 42 C.F.R. § 405.1204.

[359] 42 C.F.R. § 405.1208(e)(2).

friend was acting on the patient's behalf.[360] In practice, hospitals usually attempt to notify both the patient and the relative or representative who has been acting on the patient's behalf.

■ **EXAMPLE:** Mrs. Smith arrived at the hospital in an incoherent state, yet the hospital delivered a denial notice to her. The notice would not be deemed effective if it could be shown that Mrs. Smith's medical condition prevented her from understanding the denial notice. As an alternative, the hospital could try to locate a family member willing and able to act on Mrs. Smith's behalf, and deliver the denial notice to the family member. As a further alternative, if state law permits, the hospital could go to a court of appropriate jurisdiction to petition for appointment of a conservator or guardian for Mrs. Smith. The conservator or guardian could then be given the denial notice.

6. If the QIO reconsideration is unfavorable, the beneficiary may request a hearing before an ALJ of the HHS OMHA. The amount in controversy must be at least $160 in 2019. The administrative hearing will be held by an ALJ of the OMHA. The hearing request must be filed within 60 days of receipt of the notice of the QIO reconsideration determination, unless the time is extended for good cause.[361] The request for reconsideration must be filed with the QIO.[362]

§ 2.13 HOW TO DEVELOP A WINNING APPEAL

While a denial of Medicare inpatient hospital coverage can occur for many reasons, frequently patients are denied coverage (1) in rehabilitation hospitals, (2) when, following at least three days of Medicare coverage in the hospital their condition improves, but they still require a SNF level of care after a hospital stay and no SNF bed is available, or (3) when the hospital determines that the patient requires admission for "social" reasons. The stated reason for denials of rehabilitation hospital care are often based upon the purported lack of intensity of the patient's rehabilitation program; the alleged absence of "sufficient" improvement in the patient's rehabilitation status; or a notion that the overall condition of the patient was such that the rehabilitation services could have been provided in a SNF, instead of a hospital. Denials of hospital coverage when a SNF bed is not available often occur because the hospital is simply unaware of the availability of continued Medicare coverage under such circumstances; or because the hospital improperly believes that, although a patient requires a nursing home placement, the patient's condition does not rise to the level of requiring SNF care. When faced with these

---

[360] Carpenter v. Secretary of HHS, Medicare & Medicaid Guide (CCH) 38,621 (D. Conn. 1990).

[361] 42 C.F.R. § 478.42(b).

[362] Social Security Act § 1861(ee), 42 U.S.C. § 1395x(ee); 42 C.F.R. § 482.43.

bases for denials of Medicare coverage, the advocate must be prepared to analyze thoroughly the facts and the applicable Medicare coverage criteria.

Denial of so-called social admissions (as in the previous example of Mrs. Smith) is often based upon the hospital's assessment that no other support system is available to the patient to assure the patient's overall safety, even though the patient—in the hospital's view—could properly receive medical treatment in some other setting. One argument that has been used successfully in such cases is that Medicare regulations require that care be provided to patients in the most economically feasible manner.[363] "Economically" is defined in the Medicare regulations as "provided at the least expensive, medically appropriate type of setting or care available."[364] Consequently, if it can be established that an inpatient hospital was the only medically appropriate type of setting or care available (and the simple fact that the patient was admitted to the hospital, rather than discharged home or sent to some other, less intensive care setting, is evidence of this fact), then the services received by the patient as a hospital inpatient are medically reasonable and necessary, in the absence of availability of any alternative care.

Of course, in any Medicare inpatient hospital appeal, as is usually the case in other areas of advocacy, effective analysis and factual development will greatly improve your chances of prevailing. Address these areas:

1. Recognize an unfair coverage denial by comparing the facts of the case with the legal criteria of coverage. In acute hospital cases medical necessity is the amorphous standard. This is a two-part standard: (a) Is it medically necessary for the patient to be treated in a hospital[365] and (b) if the patient no longer requires treatment in the hospital and could be treated outside the hospital, does the patient need at least a SNF level of care, and is there no SNF bed available in a participating facility?[366]
2. Build an alliance with the attending physician. The statute and regulations repeatedly require the involvement of the attending physician in the decision-making process. Physicians will typically feel divided loyalties. They do not want to see their hospital lose money, but they also want to protect their patients from unfair charges for care. It is the advocate's job to educate the physician concerning the legitimate rules of Medicare coverage and to encourage the physician to support the patient's claim by expressing an opinion, preferably in writing, that it is medically necessary for the patient to be treated in the hospital, or that the patient requires a SNF level of care and that no SNF bed in a

[363] 42 C.F.R. § 1004.10.
[364] 42 C.F.R. § 1004.1(b).
[365] 42 U.S.C. § 1395f (a)(3).
[366] 42 C.F.R. §§ 412.42(c)(1) and 424.13(b).

participating facility is available. Often an explicit and detailed letter from the attending physician becomes the deciding factor in a successful Medicare appeal.

3. Evaluate the medical record for a hospital level of care. The degree and intensity of skill delivered to a patient is the central factor in determining what level of care the patient requires. If the patient requires a degree of skill and intensity of services available only in a hospital, then it is medically necessary for the patient to be treated in a hospital. One benchmark, although not the exclusive one, is whether the beneficiary required the 24-hour availability of a physician. Such physician availability usually exists only in a hospital. If the patient requires daily skilled care in an institutional setting, then that patient requires a SNF level of care. The details found in the written medical record will often provide the evidence necessary to substantiate the patient's claim.
4. Determine where one is in the process. You will notice that the coverage determination and appeals process is quite complex; your client's rights depend upon where in the process his or her claim happens to be. The advocate must gather all available notices and documentation to determine the present status of the appeal. Generally, it is in the beneficiary's interest for an advocate to take action at the earliest possible time. For example, patients and their families often hear word of an impending continued care denial before a written notice is actually received. By encouraging the attending physician to support the claim at an early stage, an advocate can often delay or even prevent the issuance of the denial notice.

Hospital care is generally the most expensive care that a patient can receive. Because of the expense involved, denials of Medicare inpatient hospital coverage, or the threat of such a denial, can often lead patients to forgo necessary medical care. The result frequently can be a deteriorated and untreated state of health. The availability of advocacy on the patient's behalf, therefore, may mean the difference between the patient receiving needed care or accepting and living with unnecessarily poor health. Hence, an advocate's role where Medicare hospital coverage is concerned is, first, to make sure the patient receives the care he or she requires, and second, to ensure that the patient is not charged for services that should be covered by Medicare.

As observed, economic considerations often override a purely medical perspective when it comes to access to Medicare-covered hospital care. However, a well-prepared advocate who is familiar with the Medicare inpatient hospital coverage criteria and the patient's medical condition and treatment can fight against this tide and ensure that the patient receives appropriate health care. By allying oneself with the patient in this way, the advocate may also influence and inform

Medicare coverage determinations made in general by providers and, so, prevent future improper denials of Medicare coverage.

§ 2.14 LINKING PAYMENT TO QUALITY OUTCOMES UNDER THE MEDICARE PROGRAM

President Obama signed into law the Patient Protection and Affordability Care Act of 2010[367] (PPACA, or the Affordable Care Act, or ACA) on March 23, 2010, and the Health Care and Education Reconciliation Act of 2010[368] (HCERA) on March 30, 2010. Changes in the ACA address measuring the quality of care that is received by Medicare beneficiaries and linking payment to those measures. In the legislation, Congress has placed emphasis on efforts to measure quality and to provide payment for only those services and procedures that meet certain quality of care standards.[369] For an update of CMS activities, review the materials on Medicare Quality Initiatives in the area of Hospital Value Based Purchasing (HVBP).[370] The Secretary is to coordinate the value-based payment modifier with the Physician Feedback Program.[371]

The Secretary must specify an initial performance period for application of the payment modifier for 2015. The Secretary must apply the payment modifier, beginning on January 1, 2015, to specific physicians and groups of physicians the Secretary determines appropriate and, beginning not later than January 1, 2017, to all physicians and groups of physicians.[372]

The Secretary is to create incentives for applicable hospitals to reduce hospital-acquired conditions with respect to discharges occurring during fiscal year 2015 and subsequent fiscal years. The amount of payment for such discharges during the fiscal year must be equal to 99 percent of the amount of payment that would otherwise apply. An applicable hospital is one that is in the top quartile of hospitals (that receive inpatient hospital service payments on the basis of prospective rates as set by the Medicare Geographical Classification Review

---

[367] Pub. L. No. 111-148 (Mar. 23, 2010).

[368] Pub. L. No. 111-152 (Mar. 30, 2010).

[369] For a discussion of quality bonus payments for Medicare Advantage plans, *see* CMA, "Changes to Medicare Advantage Plans And Prescription Drug Plans Under Health Care Reform," (Apr. 8, 2010), *available at* http://www.medicareadvocacy.org/new-rules-for-medicare-advantage-and-part-d-plans/ (site visited Aug. 6, 2018).

[370] *See* CMS, Hospital Value-Based Purchasing, (Sept. 2017) *available at* https://www.cms.gov/Outreach-and-Education/Medicare-Learning-Network-MLN/MLNProducts/downloads/Hospital_VBPurchasing_Fact_Sheet_ICN907664.pdf (site visited Aug. 6, 2018).

[371] *See* CMS, "Value-Based Payment Modifier," *available at* https://www.cms.gov/medicare/medicare-fee-for-service-payment/physicianfeedbackprogram/valuebasedpaymentmodifier.html (site visited Aug. 6, 2018).

[372] *See* CMS, "Value-Based Payment Modifier," *available at* https://www.cms.gov/medicare/medicare-fee-for-service-payment/physicianfeedbackprogram/valuebasedpaymentmodifier.html (site visited Aug. 6, 2018).

Board) relative to the national average of hospital-acquired conditions during the applicable period, as determined by the Secretary. The term "hospital-acquired condition" means a condition identified or determined by the Secretary that an individual acquires during a stay in an applicable hospital. The term "applicable period" means, with respect to a fiscal year, a period specified by the Secretary.[373]

Prior to fiscal year 2015 and in each subsequent fiscal year, the Secretary must provide confidential reports to applicable hospitals with respect to hospital-acquired conditions of the applicable hospital and make information available to the public regarding hospital-acquired conditions of each applicable hospital.[374] Information for the public shall also be posted on the Hospital Compare Internet website.[375]

The Secretary must conduct a study on expanding the health care–acquired conditions policy to payments made to other facilities under the Medicare program. The report, together with recommendations, was to be submitted to Congress not later than January 1, 2012.[376]

[A] National Legislative Strategy to Improve Health Care Quality

- **ACA § 3011. National Strategy.** The Secretary, through a transparent collaborative process, is to establish a national strategy to improve the delivery of health care services, patient health outcomes, and population health. The national strategy must include a comprehensive strategic plan to achieve the priorities described above.[377]

- **ACA § 3012. Interagency Working Group on Health Care Quality.** The President must convene a working group to be known as the Interagency Working Group on Health Care Quality (referred to in this section as the "Working Group"). Not later than December 31, 2010, and annually thereafter, the Working Group must submit to the relevant Committees of Congress and make public on an Internet website a report

[373] *See* CMS, Hospital-Acquired Conditions and Present on Admission Indicator Reporting Provision, (Oct. 2017), *available at* https://www.cms.gov/Outreach-and-Education/Medicare-Learning-Network-MLN/MLNProducts/Downloads/wPOA-Fact-Sheet.pdf (site visited Aug. 6, 2018).

[374] *See* Center for Medicare Advocacy, "Health Reform: Linking Payments to Quality Outcome," *available at* http://www.medicareadvocacy.org/health-reform-linking-medicare-payment-to-quality-outcome/ (site visited Sept. 22, 2018).

[375] *See* https://www.medicare.gov/hospitalcompare/search.html (site visited Sept. 22, 2018).

[376] *See* CMS, Medicare Learning Network, "Hospital-Acquired Conditions Present on Admission Indicator Reporting Provision," *available at* https://www.cms.gov/Outreach-and-Education/Medicare-Learning-Network-MLN/MLNProducts/Downloads/wPOA-Fact-Sheet.pdf (site visited Sept. 22, 2018).

[377] *See* CMS, "Quality Measurement Impact Reports," *available at* http://www.cms.gov/Medicare/Quality-Initiatives-Patient-Assessment-Instruments/QualityMeasures/QualityMeasurementImpactReports.html (site visited Aug. 6, 2018).

describing the progress and recommendations of the Working Group. The goals of the Working Group are to achieve collaboration, cooperation, and consultation between federal departments and agencies with respect to developing and disseminating strategies, goals, models, and timetables that are consistent with the national priorities identified above.[378]

[378] *See* HHS, "National Quality Strategy Annual Reports," *available at* http://www.ahrq.gov/workingforquality/reports/annual-reports/nqs2014annlrpt.htm (site visited Aug. 6, 2018).

APPENDIX 2-1 SELECTED TITLE 42—PUBLIC HEALTH (CODE OF FEDERAL REGULATIONS) PROVISIONS

Below is a list of important provisions related to hospital coverage:

- Title 42—Public Health: Part 405—Federal Health Insurance for the Aged and Disabled (Subpart J—Expedited Determinations and Reconsiderations of Provider Service Terminations and Procedures for Inpatient Hospital Discharges[379]
- Title 42—Public Health: Part 412—Prospective Payment Systems for Inpatient Hospital Services[380]

[379] *See* http://www.gpo.gov/fdsys/pkg/CFR-2007-title42-vol2/pdf/CFR-2007-title42-vol2-part405-subpartJ.pdf (site visited Sept. 22, 2018).

[380] *See* http://www.ecfr.gov/cgi-bin/retrieveECFR?gp=&SID=e07cf54a2d15ed24befdd2ed32aee68f&mc=true&n=pt42.2.412&r=PART&ty=HTML#_top (site visited Sept. 22, 2018).

APPENDIX 2-2 MEDICARE CLAIMS PROCESSING MANUAL, CHAPTER 30

Chapter 30—Financial Liability Protections[381]

[381] *See* https://www.cms.gov/Regulations-and-Guidance/Guidance/Manuals/Downloads/clm104c30.pdf (site visited Sept. 22, 2018).

200—Expedited Review Process for Hospital Inpatients in Original Medicare (Rev. 1257, Issued: 05-25-07; Effective: 07-01-07; Implementation: 07-02-07)

Medicare beneficiaries who are hospital inpatients have a statutory right to appeal to a QIO for an expedited review when a hospital, with physician concurrence, determines that inpatient care is no longer necessary. The instructions that follow stem directly from regulations at 42 CFR 405.1205 and 405.1206 and are effective July 1, 2007. These regulations are also referenced at 42 CFR 489.27 and 412.42 (c)(3). The authority for these instructions stems from Sections 1866(a)(1)(M), 1869(c)(3)(C)(iii)(III), and 1154(e) of the Social Security Act. Instructions for managed care will be located in Chapter 13 of the Medicare Managed Care Manual.

Hospitals must notify Medicare beneficiaries who are hospital inpatients about their hospital discharge appeal rights. Hospitals will use a revised version of the Important Message from Medicare (IM) a statutorily required notice, to explain the beneficiary's rights as a hospital patient, including discharge appeal rights. Hospitals must issue the IM within 2 calendar days of admission, must obtain the signature of the beneficiary or his or her representative and provide a copy at that time. Hospitals will also deliver a copy of the signed notice as far in advance of discharge as possible, but not more than 2 calendar days before discharge.

For those beneficiaries who request a QIO review, hospitals must deliver a Detailed Notice of Discharge as soon as possible, but no later than noon of the day after the QIO's notification. Both the IM and the Detailed Notice must be the standardized notices provided by CMS.

200.1—Scope of the Instructions (Rev. 1257, Issued: 05-25-07; Effective: 07-01-07; Implementation: 07-02-07)

These instructions implement 42 CFR 405.1205 and 405.1206 which require hospitals to inform Medicare beneficiaries who are hospital inpatients of their right to a QIO review. These instructions delineate the expectations of beneficiaries (or their representative, if applicable), responsibilities of hospitals, and the role of the QIOs when the beneficiary requests an expedited review by a QIO of the discharge decision. For purposes of this instruction, the term "beneficiary" means either beneficiary or representative, when a representative is acting for a beneficiary.

Hospitals Affected by These Instructions. The term hospital is defined in the regulation as any facility providing care at the inpatient hospital level, whether that care is short term or long term, acute or non acute, paid through a prospective payment system or other reimbursement basis, limited to specialty care or providing a broader spectrum of services. This definition includes critical access hospitals. This means all hospitals paid under the Inpatient Acute Prospective Payment System (IPPS), sole community hospitals/regional referrals centers or any other type of hospital receiving special consideration under IPPS (for example, Medicare dependent hospitals, Indian Health Service hospitals); hospitals not under IPPS, including, but not limited to: hospitals paid under State or United States territory waiver programs, hospitals paid under certain demonstration projects cited in regulation (§ 489.34), rehabilitation hospitals, long-term care hospitals, psychiatric hospitals, critical access hospitals, children's hospitals, and cancer hospitals. Swing beds in hospitals are excluded, because they are considered a lower level of care. Religious nonmedical health care institutions are also excluded.

Hospital Inpatients Who Are Medicare Beneficiaries. These instructions apply to beneficiaries in original Medicare who are hospital inpatients. Hospital outpatients who are receiving Part B services, such as those in observation stays or in the emergency department, do not receive these notices, unless they subsequently require inpatient care. Medicare beneficiaries in hospital swing beds or custodial care beds do not receive these notices when they are receiving services at a lower level of care.

Definition of Discharge. The term "discharge" is defined as a formal release of a beneficiary from an inpatient hospital. This includes when the beneficiary is physically discharged from the hospital as well as when the beneficiary is discharged "on paper"—meaning that the beneficiary remains in the hospital, but at a lower level of care (for example, the beneficiary is moved to a swing bed or to custodial care).

200.2—Special Considerations
(Rev. 1257, Issued: 05-25-07; Effective: 07-01-07; Implementation: 07-02-07)

Other Insurers. Section 1866(a)(1)(M), delivery of the Important Message from Medicare, applies to each individual who is entitled to benefits under Medicare Part A. Therefore, these requirements apply if a beneficiary is eligible for both Original Medicare and Medicaid (a dual eligible), is eligible for Original Medicare and another insurance program or payer, or has Medicare as a secondary payer. No matter where in the sequence of payers Medicare falls, these requirements still apply.

Inpatient to Inpatient Transfers. Beneficiaries who are being transferred from one inpatient hospital setting to another inpatient hospital setting, do not need to be provided with the follow-up copy of the notice prior to leaving the original hospital, since this is considered to be the same level of care. Beneficiaries always have the right to refuse care and may contact the QIO if they have a quality of care issue. The receiving hospital must deliver the Important Message from Medicare again according to the procedures in these instructions.

Preadmission/Admissions for Services that are not Reasonable and Necessary. When a Medicare beneficiary is planning to be hospitalized for services that Medicare usually pays for, but are not considered to be reasonable and necessary in this particular situation, hospitals must deliver a Preadmission/ Admission Hospital Issued Notice of Non-coverage (HINN). (See Section 240 of this Chapter.) The Important Message from Medicare would be delivered only if the stay became a covered stay.

Admissions for Services that Medicare Never Covers. When a Medicare beneficiary is admitted for hospital services that are never covered by Medicare, hospitals may deliver the Preadmission/Admission HINN. The IM would be delivered only if the stay became a covered stay.

Change of Status from Inpatient to Outpatient. When a hospital utilization review committee determines that an inpatient admission does not meet the hospital's inpatient criteria, the hospital may change the beneficiary's status from inpatient to outpatient. See CR 3444 (Use of Condition Code 44) and MedLearn Matters article, SE0622, published on March 22, 2006, for notification requirements in this situation.

End of Part A days. For purposes of this instruction, the term discharge does not include exhaustion of Part A days, therefore, when a beneficiary exhausts Part A days, these requirements do not apply.

Hospital Requests QIO Review when the Physician does not Concur. There are separate existing requirements under 405.1208 for notifying a beneficiary when the hospital requests a QIO review. Hospitals should deliver the Notice of a Hospital Requested Review (HRR). (See Section 220 of this chapter.)

200.3—Notifying Beneficiaries of their Right to an Expedited Review (Rev. 1257, Issued: 05-25-07; Effective: 07-01-07; Implementation: 07-02-07)

Hospitals must notify Medicare beneficiaries who are hospital inpatients about their hospital discharge appeal rights. Hospitals will use a revised version of the Important Message from Medicare (IM) a statutorily-required notice, to explain the beneficiary's rights as a hospital patient, including discharge appeal rights. Hospitals must issue the IM within 2 calendar days of admission, must obtain the signature of the beneficiary or his or her representative and provide a copy at that time. Hospitals will also deliver a copy of the signed notice as far in advance of discharge as possible, but not more than 2 calendar days before discharge.

200.3.1—Delivery of the Important Message from Medicare (Rev. 1257, Issued: 05-25-07; Effective: 07-01-07; Implementation: 07-02-07)

Hospitals must follow the procedures listed below in delivering the Important Message from Medicare (IM). Valid Notice consists of:

Use of Standardized Notice. Hospitals must use the standardized form (CMS-R-193), see Section 200.6.2. The notices are also available on *www.cms.hhs.gov/bni* at the Link for Hospital Discharge Appeal Notices. Hospitals may not deviate from the content of the form except where indicated (see Section 200.6 on Completing the Notice). The OMB control number must be displayed on the notice.

Delivery Timeframe. Hospitals must deliver the original copy of the IM at or near admission, but no later than 2 calendar days following the date of the beneficiary's admission to the hospital.

Hospitals may deliver the initial copy of the notice if the beneficiary is seen during a preadmission visit, but not more than 7 calendar days in advance of admission. If a beneficiary receives and signs the initial copy of the IM as part of the preadmission process, the follow-up copy of the notice must be delivered if delivery of the initial copy occurred more than 2 calendar days prior.

In-Person Delivery. The IM must be delivered to the beneficiary in person. However, if the beneficiary is not able to comprehend the notice, it must be delivered to and signed by the beneficiary's representative.

Notice Delivery to Representatives. CMS requires that notification of a beneficiary who is not competent be made to a representative of the beneficiary. A representative is an individual who, under State or other applicable law, may make health care decisions on a beneficiary's behalf (e.g., the beneficiary's legal guardian, or someone appointed in accordance with a properly executed "durable medical power of attorney").

Otherwise, a person (typically, a family member or close friend) whom the beneficiary has indicated may act for him or her, but who has not been named in any legally binding document may be a representative for purpose of receiving the notices described in this section. Such representatives should have the beneficiary's best interests at heart and must act in a manner that is protective of the beneficiary and the beneficiary's rights. Therefore, a representative should have no relevant conflict of interest with the beneficiary. A notifier (including the notifier's employees) that has a conflicting interest (such as shifting financial liability to the beneficiary) is not qualified to be a representative. (Note: If the beneficiary wishes to appoint a representative to file an appeal on his/her behalf, a valid Form 1696 or a conforming written instrument must be signed by both the beneficiary and the prospective representative and filed with the appeal request. See Medicare Claims Processing Manual, Publication 100-4, Ch. 29, Section 270 for specific instructions related to the use of Form 1696 and the appointment of representatives).

Notification to the representative may be problematic because that person may not be available in person to acknowledge receipt of the required notification. Hospitals are required to develop procedures to use when the beneficiary is incapable of receiving or incompetent to receive the notice, and the hospital cannot obtain the signature of the beneficiary's representative through direct personal contact.

Regardless of the competency of a beneficiary, if the hospital is unable to personally deliver a notice to a representative, then the hospital should telephone the representative to advise him or her of the beneficiary's rights as a hospital patient, including the right to appeal a discharge decision.

The information provided should include the following at a minimum:

- The name and telephone number of a contact at the hospital;
- The beneficiary's planned discharge date, and the date when the beneficiary's liability begins;
- The beneficiary's rights as a hospital patient, including the right to appeal a discharge decision;
- How to get a copy of a detailed notice describing why the hospital and physician believe the beneficiary is ready to be discharged;
- A description of the steps for filing an appeal;
- When (by what time/date) the appeal must be filed to take advantage of the liability protections;
- The entity required to receive the appeal, including any applicable name, address, telephone number, fax number or other method of communication the entity requires in order to receive the appeal in a timely fashion;
- Direction to the 1-800-MEDICARE number for additional assistance to the representative in further explaining and filing the appeal; and

The date the hospital conveys this information to the representative, whether in writing or by telephone, is the date of receipt of the notice. Confirm the telephone contact by written notice mailed on that same date. Place a dated copy of the notice in the beneficiary's medical file, and document the telephone contact with the beneficiary's representative (as listed above) on either the notice itself, or in a separate entry in the beneficiary's file or attachment to the notice. The documentation should indicate that the staff person told the representative the planned discharge date, the date the beneficiary's financial liability begins, the beneficiary's appeal rights, and how and when to initiate an appeal. The documentation should also include the name of the staff person initiating the contact, the name of the representative contacted by phone, the date and time of the telephone contact, and the telephone number called.

When direct phone contact cannot be made, send the notice to the representative by certified mail, return receipt requested, or other delivery method that requires signed verification of delivery. The date that someone at the representative's address signs (or refuses to sign) the receipt is the date received. Place a copy of the notice in the beneficiary's medical file, and document the attempted telephone contact to the members' representative. The documentation should include: the name of the staff person initiating the contact, the name of the representative you attempted to contact, the date and time of the attempted call, and the telephone number called.

If both the hospital and the representative agree, hospitals may send the notice by fax or email, however, hospitals must meet the HIPAA privacy and security requirements.

Ensuring Beneficiary Comprehension. Hospitals must make every effort to ensure the beneficiary comprehends the contents of the notice before obtaining the beneficiary's signature. This includes explaining the notice to the beneficiary if necessary and providing an opportunity for the beneficiary to ask questions. The hospital should answer all the beneficiary's questions orally to the best of its ability. The beneficiary should be able to understand that he or she may appeal a discharge decision without financial risk, but may have to pay for any services received after the discharge date if he or she stays in the hospital and does not appeal. Notices should not be delivered during an emergency, but should be delivered once the beneficiary is stable.

These instructions do not preclude the use of assistive devices, witnesses, or interpreters for notice delivery. Thus, if a beneficiary is able to comprehend the notice, but either is physically unable to sign it or needs the assistance of an interpreter to translate it or an assistive device to read or sign it, valid delivery may be achieved by documenting use of such assistance.

Beneficiary Signature and Date. The IM must be signed and dated by the beneficiary to indicate that he or she has received the notice and can comprehend its contents, unless an appropriate reason for the lack of signature is recorded on the IM, such as a properly annotated signature refusal (see below).

Refusal to Sign and Annotation. If a beneficiary refuses to sign the notice, hospitals may annotate the notice to indicate the refusal, and the date of refusal is considered the date of receipt of the notice. The annotation may be placed in the unused patient signature line, in the "Additional Information" section on page 2 of the notice or another sheet of paper may be attached to the notice, if necessary.

Any insertions on the notice must be easy for the beneficiary to read in order for the notice to be considered valid. See also Section 200.5.6—Insertions in Blanks.

Notice Delivery and Retention. Hospitals must give the original copy of the signed or annotated notice to the patient. Hospitals must retain a copy of the signed notice and may determine the method of storage that works within their existing processes, for example, storing a copy in the medical record or electronically.

200.3.2—The Follow-Up Copy of the Signed Important Message from Medicare
(Rev. 1257, Issued: 05-25-07; Effective: 07-01-07; Implementation: 07-02-07)

A "follow-up" copy of the signed IM must be delivered to the beneficiary using the following guidelines:

Delivery Timeframe. The follow-up copy must be delivered as far in advance of discharge as possible, but no more than 2 calendar days before the planned date of discharge. Thus, when discharge seems likely within 1-2 calendar days, hospitals should make arrangements to deliver the follow-up copy of the notice, so that the beneficiary has a meaningful opportunity to act on it. However, when discharge cannot be predicted in advance, the follow-up copy may be delivered as late as the day of discharge, if necessary. If the follow-up copy of the notice must be delivered on the day of discharge, hospitals must give beneficiaries who need it at least 4 hours to consider their right to request a QIO review. Beneficiaries may choose to leave prior to that time, however, hospitals must not pressure a beneficiary to leave during that time period. If the hospital delivers the follow-up copy, and the beneficiary status subsequently changes, so that the discharge is beyond the 2-day timeframe, hospitals must deliver another copy of the signed notice again within 2 calendar days of the new planned discharge date. Hospitals may not develop procedures for delivery of the follow up copy routinely on the day of discharge.

Alternative to Delivery of the Signed Copy. A hospital may choose to deliver a new copy of the IM (not a copy of the signed IM) during the required timeframes; however, the hospital must obtain the beneficiary's or representative's signature and date on the notice again at that time.

Exception to Delivery of the Follow-Up Copy. If delivery of the original IM is within 2 calendar days of the date of discharge, no follow-up notice is required. For example, if a beneficiary is admitted on Monday, the IM is delivered on Wednesday and the beneficiary is discharged on Friday, no follow-up notice is required.

If a beneficiary receives and signs the initial copy of the IM as part of the preadmission process, the follow-up copy of the notice must be delivered if delivery of the initial copy occurred more than 2 calendar days prior.

Documentation. Hospitals must document timely delivery of the follow-up copy of the IM in the patient records, when applicable. Hospitals are responsible for demonstrating compliance with this requirement. If hospitals have processes in place to document delivery of other information related to discharge that includes a beneficiary signature and date, hospitals may include the follow-up copy of the notice in those documents. If there are no other existing processes in place, hospitals may use the "Additional Information" section of the IM to document delivery of the follow-up copy, for example, by adding a line for the beneficiary's or representative's initials and date.

200.4—Rules and Responsibilities when a Beneficiary Requests an Expedited Review
(Rev. 1257, Issued: 05-25-07; Effective: 07-01-07; Implementation: 07-02-07)

A beneficiary has a right to request an expedited review by the QIO when a hospital (acting directly or through its utilization review committee), with physician concurrence, determines that inpatient care is no longer necessary.

200.4.1—The Role of the Beneficiary and Liability
(Rev. 1257, Issued: 05-25-07; Effective: 07-01-07; Implementation: 07-02-07)

Submitting a Request: A beneficiary who chooses to exercise the right to an expedited review must submit a request to the QIO that has an agreement with the hospital where the beneficiary is an inpatient. In order to be considered timely, the request must be made no later than midnight of the day of discharge, may be in writing or by telephone, and must be before the beneficiary leaves the hospital. The beneficiary, upon request of the QIO, should be available to discuss the case. The beneficiary may, but is not required to, submit written evidence to be considered by the QIO.

Timely Requests: When the beneficiary makes a timely request for a QIO review—that is, requests a review no later than midnight of the day of discharge—the beneficiary is not financially responsible for inpatient hospital services (except applicable coinsurance and deductibles) furnished before noon of the calendar day after the date the beneficiary receives notification of the expedited determination from the QIO. Liability for further inpatient hospital services depends on the QIO decision:

- **Unfavorable determination:** If the QIO notifies the beneficiary that the QIO did not agree with the beneficiary, liability for continued services begins at noon of the day **after** the QIO notifies the beneficiary that the QIO agreed with the hospital's discharge determination, or as otherwise determined by the QIO.

- **Favorable determination:** If the QIO notifies the beneficiary that the QIO agreed with the beneficiary, the beneficiary is not financially responsible for continued care (other than applicable coinsurance and deductibles) until the hospital once again determines that the beneficiary no longer requires inpatient care, secures the concurrence of the physician responsible for the beneficiary's care or the QIO, and notifies the beneficiary with a follow-up copy of the IM.

Untimely Requests: When the beneficiary fails to make a timely request for an expedited review, and remains in the hospital, he or she still may request an expedited review at any time, but the beneficiary may be held responsible for charges incurred after the day of discharge, or as otherwise stated by the QIO. If the QIO finds that the patient should have remained an inpatient, the hospital will refund the beneficiary any funds that were collected. When the beneficiary fails to make a timely request for an expedited review and is no longer an inpatient at the hospital, he or she may still request a QIO review within 30 calendar days of the date of discharge, or at any time for good cause.

200.4.2—The Responsibilities of the Hospital
(Rev. 1257, Issued: 05-25-07; Effective: 07-01-07; Implementation: 07-02-07)

Provide the Detailed Notice of Discharge: When a QIO notifies the hospital that a beneficiary has requested an expedited review, the hospital must deliver a Detailed Notice of Discharge (the Detailed Notice) to the beneficiary as soon as possible but not later than noon of the day after the QIO's notification. If a beneficiary requests more detailed information prior to requesting a review, hospitals may deliver the detailed notice in advance of the beneficiary requesting a review.

Use of Standardized Notice. Hospitals must use the standardized form (CMS-10066), see Section 200.6.2. This notice is also available on *www.cms.hhs.gov/bni* at the Link for Hospital Discharge Appeal Notices. Hospitals may not deviate from the content of the form except where indicated (see Section 200.6.2 on Completing the Notice). The OMB control number must be displayed on the notice.

The Detailed Notice must be the standardized notice provided by CMS and contain the following:

- A detailed explanation why services are either no longer reasonable and necessary or are otherwise no longer covered.
- A description of any applicable Medicare coverage rule, instruction, or other Medicare policy, including information about how the beneficiary

may obtain a copy of the Medicare policy. (See instructions for the Detailed Notice of Discharge at Section 200.6.3, Exhibit 2)

- Facts specific to the beneficiary and relevant to the coverage determination that are sufficient to advise the beneficiary of the applicability of the coverage rule or policy to the beneficiary's case.
- Any other information required by CMS.

Hospitals must follow requirements in Section 200.5.6 on Insertions in Blanks and Section 200.6. on Completing the Notices.

Provide Information to the QIO. Upon notification by the QIO of the beneficiary's request for an expedited review, the hospital must supply any and all information that the QIO needs to make the expedited determination, including copies of both the IM and the Detailed Notices. The hospital must furnish this information as soon as possible, but no later than noon of the day after the QIO notifies the hospital of the request. At the discretion of the QIO, the hospital may make the information available by telephone or in writing. A written record of any information not transmitted in writing should be sent as soon as possible. If the hospital fails to provide the needed information, the QIO may make a decision based on evidence at hand or defer the decision until it receives the necessary information. If this delay results in extended coverage of an individual's hospital services, the hospital may be held financially liable for those services, as determined by the QIO.

Burden of Proof. The burden of proof lies with the hospital to demonstrate that discharge is the correct decision, either on the basis of medical necessity or based on other Medicare coverage policies.

Provide the Beneficiary with Documentation if Requested. At the request of the beneficiary, the hospital must furnish the beneficiary with a copy of, or access to, any documentation that it sends to the QIO, including written records of any information provided by telephone. The hospital may charge the beneficiary a reasonable amount to cover the costs of duplicating the documentation and/or delivering it to the beneficiary. The hospital must accommodate the request by no later than the first day after the material is requested.

200.4.3—The Role of the QIOs

QIO Availability. The QIO should have methods in place to accept requests for reviews outside of normal business hours, such as an answering machine message. QIOs will issue decisions within one calendar day after it receives all pertinent information.

Notify the hospital of the beneficiary's request for an expedited review. When the QIO receives the request from the beneficiary, the QIO must notify the hospital of the request immediately, or immediately in the morning if the request is received after the QIO's business hours.

Receive and Examine records. The QIO will examine medical and other records that pertain to the services in dispute.

Determine if the hospital delivered valid notice. The QIO will determine whether the hospital delivered valid notice, meaning that the notice is the standardized notice published by CMS, meets the notice delivery timeframes, and has been signed and dated by the beneficiary. If the QIO determines that the hospital did not deliver valid notice, the QIO will instruct the hospital to reissue the notice if necessary, proceed with the review, and educate the hospital retrospectively. If the beneficiary or representative makes an untimely request for a review, and the QIO determines that the beneficiary did not receive valid notice, the QIO will determine the date the beneficiary becomes fully liable for the services.

Solicit the views of the beneficiary. The QIO must solicit views of the beneficiary who requested the expedited review.

Solicit the views of the hospital. The QIO must provide an opportunity for the hospital to explain why the hospital and physician believe discharge is appropriate. The QIO may develop guidelines as to the form and extent of this opportunity.

If needed information is not received. If the QIO does not receive the information from the hospital needed to sustain the discharge decision, it may make its determination based on the evidence at hand or it may defer a decision until it receives the necessary information. If this delay results in extended Medicare coverage of an individual's hospital services, the hospital may be held financially responsible for these services as determined by the QIO.

QIO Determination. QIOs make their determinations based on criteria in § 1154(a) of the Act, which specifies that QIOs will determine whether:

- the services are reasonable and medically necessary,
- the services meet professionally recognized standards of care, and
- the services could be safely be delivered in another setting.

Notification following a timely request. When the beneficiary makes a timely request for an expedited review, the QIO must make its determination and notify the beneficiary, the hospital, and the physician of its determination within one calendar day after it receives all requested pertinent information. When the QIO issues an expedited determination, the QIO must notify the beneficiary, the hospital and the physician of its decision by telephone, followed by a written notice that must include the following information:

- The basis for the determination.
- A detailed rationale for the determination.
- An explanation of the Medicare payment consequences of the determination and the date a beneficiary becomes fully liable for services.
- Information about the beneficiary's right to an reconsideration of the QIO's determination, including how to request the reconsideration and the timeframe for doing so.

Notification following an untimely request. When the beneficiary makes an untimely request for an expedited review, and remains in the hospital, the QIO will make its determination and notify the beneficiary, the hospital, and the physician of its determination within 2 calendar days after it receives all requested pertinent information. When the beneficiary makes an untimely request for an expedited review, and is no longer an inpatient in the hospital, the QIO will make its determination and notify the beneficiary, the hospital, and the physician of its determination within 30 calendar days after it receives all requested pertinent information.

200.4.4—Effect of a QIO Expedited Determination
(Rev. 1257, Issued: 05-25-07; Effective: 07-01-07; Implementation: 07-02-07)

The QIO determination is binding on the beneficiary, the physician, and hospital except in the following circumstances:

Right to pursue a reconsideration. If the beneficiary is still an inpatient in the hospital and is dissatisfied with the determination, he or she may request a reconsideration according to the procedures described in 405.1204.

Right to pursue the general claims appeal process. If the beneficiary is no longer an inpatient in the hospital and is dissatisfied with this determination, the determination is subject to the general claims appeal process (See Chapter 29 of this manual.).

200.5—General Notice Requirements
(Rev. 1257, Issued: 05-25-07; Effective: 07-01-07; Implementation: 07-02-07)

Since the Important Message from Medicare and the Detailed Notice of Discharge are OMB approved, standardized notices, hospitals must comply with the following General Notice Requirements:

200.5.1—Number of Copies
(Rev. 1257, Issued: 05-25-07; Effective: 07-01-07; Implementation: 07-02-07)

The Important Message from Medicare: In most cases, a minimum of three copies of the Important Message from Medicare, including the original, will be needed. The beneficiary keeps the original signed notice and will receive a follow-up copy of the signed notice, except when delivery of the original notice falls within two days of discharge. The hospital must retain a copy of the signed IM and may do so electronically.

The Detailed Notice: A minimum of two copies of the Detailed Notice, including the original, will be needed. The beneficiary keeps the original notice. The hospital must retain a copy of the signed document and may do so electronically.

Providing Copies to the QIO: In addition to the above, if a beneficiary requests a review, hospitals are required to provide copies of both notice described in this section to the QIO.

200.5.2—Reproduction
(Rev. 1257, Issued: 05-25-07; Effective: 07-01-07; Implementation: 07-02-07)

Hospitals may reproduce the notices by using self-carbonizing paper, photocopying the IM, or using another appropriate method. All reproductions must conform to applicable instructions.

200.5.3—Length and Page Size
(Rev.1587, Issued: 09-05-08, Effective: 03-03-08, Implementation: 03-01-09)

The Important Message from Medicare: The IM must NOT exceed two sides of a page in length. The IM is designed as a letter-sized form. If necessary, it may be expanded to a legal-sized page to accommodate information hospitals insert in the notice.

The Detailed Notice: The Detailed Notice must NOT exceed one side of a page in length. The Detailed Notice is designed as a letter-sized form. If necessary, it may be expanded to a legal-sized page to accommodate information hospitals may insert in the notice. Hospitals may attach applicable Medicare policies to the notice.

200.5.4—Contrast of Paper and Print
(Rev. 1257, Issued: 05-25-07; Effective: 07-01-07; Implementation: 07-02-07)

A visually high-contrast combination of dark ink on a pale background must be used. Do not use reversed print (e.g., white on black), or block-shade (highlight) notice text.

200.5.5—Modification
(Rev. 1257, Issued: 05-25-07; Effective: 07-01-07; Implementation: 07-02-07)

The notices described in this section may not be modified, except as specifically allowed by these instructions. In no case may either notice be condensed.

200.5.6—Font
(Rev. 1257, Issued: 05-25-07; Effective: 07-01-07; Implementation: 07-02-07)

The IM and the Detailed Notice must meet the following font requirements in order to facilitate beneficiary understanding:

- **Font Type:** To the greatest extent practicable, the fonts as they appear in the notices on the CMS website should be used. Any changes in the font type should be based solely on software and/or hardware limitations of the notices. Examples of easily readable alternative fonts include: Arial, Arial Narrow, Times New Roman, and Courier.
- **Font Effect/Style:** Any changes to the font, such as italics, embossing, bold, etc., should not be used since they can make the notices more difficult to read.
- **Font Size:** The font size generally should be 12 point. Titles should be 18 point, but handwritten insertions in blanks of the IM can be as small as 10 point if needed.
- **Insertions in Blanks:** Information inserted by hospitals in the blank spaces on the IM and the Detailed Notice may be typed or legibly handwritten using the guidelines above.

200.5.7—Customization
(Rev. 1257, Issued: 05-25-07; Effective: 07-01-07; Implementation: 07-02-07)

Hospitals are permitted to do some customization of IM or the Detailed Notice such as pre-printing agency-related information to promote efficiency and to ensure clarity for beneficiaries. Guidelines for customization are:

- Maintaining underlines in the blank spaces is not required.
- Information in blanks that is constant can be pre-printed, such as the hospital's name, QIO name and telephone number. Note the TTY phone number also needs to be entered.

200.5.8—Retention of the Notices
(Rev. 1257, Issued: 05-25-07; Effective: 07-01-07; Implementation: 07-02-07)

Hospitals are required to retain copies of the signed notices and may do so either in hardcopy or electronically.

200.6—Completing the Notices
(Rev. 1257, Issued: 05-25-07; Effective: 07-01-07; Implementation: 07-02-07)

When completing the Important Message from Medicare and the Detailed Notice of Discharge, hospitals must utilize the following instructions:

200.6.1—Translated Notices
(Rev. 1257, Issued: 05-25-07; Effective: 07-01-07; Implementation: 07-02-07)

Both the "Important Message from Medicare" and the "Detailed Notice of Discharge" are available at http://www.cms.hhs.gov/BNI/ [site visited June 29, 2018]. The notices will be available in English and Spanish, and in PDF and Word formats, under a dedicated link on the left hand margin: "Hospital Discharge Appeal Notices." Hospitals should choose the appropriate version of the Important Message from Medicare and the Detailed Notice of Discharge based on the language the beneficiary best understands. When Spanish-language notices are used, the hospital should make insertions on the notice in Spanish. If this is impossible, additional steps need to be taken to ensure that the beneficiary comprehends the content of the notice.

200.6.2—Exhibit 1—An Important Message from Medicare (CMS-R-193) and Form Instructions
(Rev. 1257, Issued: 05-25-07; Effective: 07-01-07; Implementation: 07-02-07)

Patient Name: DEPARTMENT OF HEALTH & HUMAN SERVICES
Patient ID Number: Centers for Medicare & Medicaid Services
Physician: OMB Approval No. 0938-0692

AN IMPORTANT MESSAGE FROM MEDICARE ABOUT YOUR RIGHTS

AS A HOSPITAL INPATIENT, YOU HAVE THE RIGHT TO:

- Receive Medicare covered services. This includes medically necessary hospital services and services you may need after you are discharged, if ordered by your doctor. You have a right to know about these services, who will pay for them, and where you can get them.
- Be involved in any decisions about your hospital stay, and know who will pay for it.
- Report any concerns you have about the quality of care you receive to the Quality Improvement Organization (QIO) listed here {Insert Name and Telephone Number of the QIO}. [For the QIO Directory, see http://www.qualitynet.org/dcs/ContentServer?cid=1228774346765&pagename=QnetPublic%2FPage%2FQnetTier4&c=Page (site visited June 29, 2018).]

YOUR MEDICARE DISCHARGE RIGHTS

Planning For Your Discharge: During your hospital stay, the hospital staff will be working with you to prepare for your safe discharge and arrange for services you may need after you leave the hospital. When you no longer need inpatient hospital care, your doctor or the hospital staff will inform you of your planned discharge date.

If you think you are being discharged too soon:

- You can talk to the hospital staff, your doctor and your managed care plan (if you belong to one) about your concerns.
- You also have the right to an appeal, that is, a review of your case by a Quality Improvement Organization (QIO). The QIO is an outside reviewer hired by Medicare to look at your case to decide whether you are ready to leave the hospital.
  - **If you want to appeal, you must contact the QIO no later than your planned discharge date and before you leave the hospital.**
  - If you do this, you will not have to pay for the services you receive during the appeal (except for charges like copays and deductibles).
- If you do not appeal, but decide to stay in the hospital past your planned discharge date, you may have to pay for any services you receive after that date.

- **Step by step instructions for calling the QIO and filing an appeal are on page 2.**

To speak with someone at the hospital about this notice, call ______________________

Please sign and date here to show you received this notice and understand your rights.

__________________________ ____________________

Signature of Patient or Representative Date

CMS-R-193 (approved 05/2007)

STEPS TO APPEAL YOUR DISCHARGE

- **STEP 1**: You must contact the QIO no later than your planned discharge date and before you leave the hospital. If you do this, you will not have to pay for the services you receive during the appeal (except for charges like copays and deductibles).
  - Here is the contact information for the QIO:
  - **{insert name of QIO in bold}**
  - **{insert telephone number of QIO}**
  - You can file a request for an appeal any day of the week. **Once you speak to someone or leave a message, your appeal has begun.**
  - Ask the hospital if you need help contacting the QIO.
  - The name of this hospital is __________ {insert the name of the hospital and the provider ID number} __________ .
- **STEP 2**: You will receive a detailed notice from the hospital or your Medicare Advantage or other Medicare managed care plan (if you belong to one) that explains the reasons they think you are ready to be discharged.
- **STEP 3**: The QIO will ask for your opinion. You or your representative need to be available to speak with the QIO, if requested. You or your representative may give the QIO a written statement, but you are not required to do so.
- **STEP 4**: The QIO will review your medical records and other important information about your case.
- **STEP 5**: The QIO will notify you of its decision within **1 day after** it receives all necessary information.
  - If the QIO finds that you are not ready to be discharged, Medicare will continue to cover your hospital services.
  - If the QIO finds you are ready to be discharged, Medicare will continue to cover your services until noon of the day **after** the QIO notifies you of its decision.

IF YOU MISS THE DEADLINE TO APPEAL, YOU HAVE OTHER APPEAL RIGHTS:

- You can still ask the QIO or your plan (if you belong to one) for a review of your case:
  - If you have Original Medicare: Call the QIO listed above.

    - If you belong to a Medicare Advantage Plan or other Medicare managed care plan: Call your plan.
- If you stay in the hospital, the hospital may charge you for any services you receive after your planned discharge date.

For more information, call 1-800-MEDICARE (1-800-633-4227), or TTY: 1-877-486-2048.

Additional Information:

According to the Paperwork Reduction Act of 1995, no persons are required to respond to a collection of information unless it displays a valid OMB control number. The valid OMB control number for this information collection is 0938-0692. The time required to complete this information collection is estimated to average 15 minutes per response, including the time to review instructions, search existing data resources, gather the data needed, and complete and review the information collection. If you have comments concerning the accuracy of the time estimate(s) or suggestions for improving this form, please write to: CMS, 7500 Security Boulevard, Attn: PRA Reports Clearance Officer, Mail Stop C4-26-05, Baltimore, Maryland 21244-1850.

Notice Instructions

The Important Message from Medicare (OMB #0938-0692) (CMS-R-193)

Completing the Notice
PAGE 1 of the Important Message from Medicare

A. Header

Hospitals must display "DEPARTMENT OF HEALTH & HUMAN SERVICES, Centers for Medicare & Medicaid Services" and the OMB number.

The following blanks must be completed by the hospital. Information inserted by hospitals in the blank spaces on the IM may be typed or legibly handwritten in 12-point font or the equivalent. Hospitals may also use a patient label that includes the following information:

Patient Name: Fill in the patient's full name.

Patient ID number: Fill in an ID number that identifies this patient. This number should not be, nor should it contain, the social security number.

Physician: Fill in the name of the patient's physician.

B. Body of the Notice

Bullet # 3 Report any concerns you have about the quality of care you receive to the Quality Improvement Organization (QIO) listed here ___________. Hospitals may preprint or otherwise insert the name and telephone number (including TTY) of the QIO.

To speak with someone at the hospital about this notice call: Fill in a telephone number at the hospital for the patient or representative to call with questions about the notice. Preferably, a contact name should also be included.

Patient or Representative Signature: Have the patient or representative sign the notice to indicate that he or she has received it and understands its contents.

Date: Have the patient or representative place the date he or she signed the notice.

PAGE 2 of the Important Message from Medicare

First sub-bullet—Insert name and telephone number of QIO in BOLD: Insert name and telephone number (including TTY), in bold, of the Quality Improvement Organization that performs reviews for the hospital.

Second sub-bullet—The name of this hospital is: Insert/preprint the name of the hospital, including the Medicare provider ID number (not the telephone number).

Additional Information: Hospitals may use this section for additional documentation, including, for example, obtaining beneficiary initials to document delivery of the follow-up copy of the IM, or documentation of refusals.

200.6.3—Exhibit 2—The Detailed Notice of Discharge (CMS 10066) and Form Instructions
(Rev. 1257, Issued: 05-25-07; Effective: 07-01-07; Implementation: 07-02-07)

Patient Name: OMB Approval No. 0938-1019
Patient ID Number: Date Issued:
Physician:

{Insert Hospital or Plan Logo here}
DETAILED NOTICE OF DISCHARGE

You have asked for a review by the Quality Improvement Organization (QIO), an independent reviewer hired by Medicare to review your case. This notice gives you a detailed explanation about why your hospital and your managed care plan (if you belong to one), in agreement with your doctor, believe that your inpatient hospital services should end on __________ . This is based on Medicare coverage policies listed below and your medical condition.

This is not an official Medicare decision. The decision on your appeal will come from your Quality Improvement Organization (QIO).

- Medicare Coverage Policies:
  __________ Medicare does not cover inpatient hospital services that are not medically necessary or could be safely furnished in another setting. (Refer to 42 Code of Federal Regulations, 411.15 (g) and (k)).
  __________ Medicare Managed Care policies, if applicable: (insert specific managed care policies)
  __________ Other __________ {insert other applicable policies} __________
- Specific information about your current medical condition:
- If you would like a copy of the documents sent to the QIO, or copies of the specific policies or criteria used to make this decision, please call {insert hospital and/or plan telephone number}.

According to the Paperwork Reduction Act of 1995, no persons are required to respond to a collection of information unless it displays a valid OMB control number. The valid OMB control number for this information collection is 0938-1019. The time required to complete this information collection is estimated to average 60 minutes per response, including the time to review instructions, search existing data resources, gather the data needed, and complete and review the information collection. If you have comments concerning the accuracy of the time estimate(s) or suggestions for improving this form, please write to: CMS, 7500 Security Boulevard, Attn: PRA Reports Clearance Officer, Mail Stop C4-26-05, Baltimore, Maryland 21244-1850.

CMS 10066 (approved 5/2007)

Instructions for Completing the Detailed Notice of Discharge (CMS 10066)

This is a standardized notice. Hospitals may not deviate from the content of the form except where indicated. Please note that the OMB control number must be displayed on the notice. Insertions must be typed or legibly hand-written in 12-point font or the equivalent.

Hospitals or plans may modify the following sections to incorporate use of a sticker or label that includes this information:

Patient Name: Fill in the patient's full name.

Patient ID number: Fill in the patient's ID number. This should not be, nor should it contain, the patient's social security or HICN number.

Physician: Fill in the name of the patient's physician.

Date Issued: Fill in the date the notice is delivered to the patient by the hospital/plan.

Insert logo here: Hospitals/plans may elect to place their logo in this space. However, the name, address, and telephone number of the hospital/plan must be immediately under the logo, if not incorporated into the logo. If no logo is used, the name and address and telephone number (including TTY) of the hospital/plan must appear above the title of the form.

BLANK 1: **This notice gives you a detailed explanation of why your hospital and your managed care plan (if you belong to one), in agreement with your doctor, believe that your inpatient hospital services should end on ___________ .** In the space provided, fill in planned date of discharge.

Bullet # 1: **Medicare Coverage Policies:** Place a check next to the applicable Medicare and/or managed care policies. If necessary, hospitals may also use the selection "Other" to list other applicable policies, guidelines or instructions. Hospitals or plans may also preprint frequently used coverage policies or add more space below this line, if necessary. Policies should be written in full sentences and in plain language. In addition, the hospital or plan may attach additional pages or specific policies or discharge criteria to the notice. Any attachments must be included with the copy sent to the QIO as well.

Bullet # 2: **Specific information about your current medical condition"** Fill in detailed and specific information about the patient's current medical condition and the reasons why services are no longer reasonable or necessary for this patient or are no longer covered according to Medicare or Medicare managed care coverage guidelines. Use full sentences and plain language.

Bullet # 3: **If you would like a copy of the documents sent to the QIO, or copies of the specific policies or criteria used to make this decision, please call ___________ .** The hospital/plan should also supply a telephone number for patients to call to get a copy of the relevant documents sent to the QIO. If the hospital/plan has not attached the Medicare policies and/or the Medicare managed care plan policies used to decide the discharge date, the hospital should supply a telephone number for patients to call to obtain copies of this information.

Hospitals or plans may add space below this section to insert a signature line and date, if they so choose.

220—Hospital Requested Expedited Review
(Rev. 1257, Issued: 05-25-07; Effective: 07-01-07; Implementation: 07-02-07)

When a hospital determines that a beneficiary no longer needs inpatient care, but is unable to obtain the agreement of the physician, the hospital may request a QIO review. Hospitals must notify the beneficiary that the review has been requested. These instructions stem directly from Section 1154(e) of the Act and 42 CFR Part 405.1208.

220.1—Responsibilities of the Hospital
(Rev. 1257, Issued: 05-25-07; Effective: 07-01-07; Implementation: 07-02-07)

The hospital must comply with the following procedures when requesting a QIO review:

Notify the Beneficiary. Hospitals must notify the beneficiary that the hospital has requested a review using a model language notice called the Hospital Requested Review (HRR) described in this section. See Section 220.4 for General Notice Requirements.

Supply information to the QIO. Hospitals must supply any pertinent information the QIO needs to conduct its review and must make it available by phone or in writing, by close of business on the first full day immediately following the day the hospital submits the request for review.

220.2—Responsibilities of the QIO
(Rev. 1257, Issued: 05-25-07; Effective: 07-01-07; Implementation: 07-02-07)

The QIO's responsibilities are as follows:

Receive request and examine records. The QIO must notify the hospital that it has received the request for review and must notify the hospital if it has not received pertinent records, examine the pertinent records pertaining to the services, and solicit the views of the beneficiary.

Issue a determination. QIOs make their determinations based on criteria in § 1154(a) of the Act, which specifies that QIOs will determine whether:

- the services are reasonable and medically necessary,
- the services meet professionally recognized standards of care, and
- the services could be safely be delivered in another setting.

The QIO will make a determination and notify the beneficiary, the hospital, and the physician of its decision within 2 days of the hospital's request and receipt of any pertinent information submitted by the hospital.

Notification. When the QIO issues the determination, it must notify the beneficiary, the hospital, and the physician of its decision by telephone and subsequently in writing. The written notice of the expedited initial determination must contain the following:

- The basis for the determination;
- A detailed rationale for the determination;
- A statement explaining the Medicare payment consequences of the expedited determination and the date of liability if any; and
- A statement informing the beneficiary of his or her appeal rights and the timeframe for requesting an appeal.

220.3—Effect of the Hospital Requested Expedited Determination
(Rev. 1257, Issued: 05-25-07; Effective: 07-01-07; Implementation: 07-02-07)

The expedited determination is binding on the beneficiary, physician, and hospital, except in the following circumstances:

When the beneficiary remains in the hospital. When the beneficiary is still an inpatient in the hospital and is dissatisfied with this determination, he or she may request a reconsideration according to the procedures described in Section 300 of this Chapter.

When the beneficiary is no longer an inpatient in the hospital. If the beneficiary is no longer an inpatient in the hospital and is dissatisfied with this determination, this determination is subject to the general claims appeal process (See Chapter 29 of this manual).

220.4—General Notice Requirements
(Rev. 1257, Issued: 05-25-07; Effective: 07-01-07; Implementation: 07-02-07)

Providers should use the HRR to notify a beneficiary that it has requested a QIO review. This notice can be found at *www.cms.hhs.gov/bni*. Since the HRR uses model language, providers have some flexibility in the preparation of this notice. However, it is highly recommended that hospitals use the model language provided in this instruction, or by their QIO, in order to avoid questions of invalid notice. Providers should utilize the General Notice Requirements in Section 200.5 and the Translation requirements in Section 200.6.1 when preparing the notice.

220.5—Exhibit 3—Model Language for Notice of Hospital Requested Review (Rev. 1257, Issued: 05-25-07; Effective: 07-01-07; Implementation: 07-02-07)

Hospital Identifier
Model Notice of Hospital Requested Review (HRR)

Name of Patient:__________ Name of Physician: __________
Patient ID Number: __________ Date Issued: __________

We believe that Medicare will not continue to cover your hospital care because these services are no longer considered medically necessary in your case. Because your doctor disagreed with our finding, the hospital is asking the quality improvement organization (QIO) to review your case. The QIO is an outside reviewer hired by Medicare to look at your case to decide if you are ready to leave the hospital. The name of the QIO is __________ **(insert the name of the QIO)** __________ .

- The QIO will contact you to solicit your views about your case and the care you need.
- You do not need to take any action until you hear from the QIO.

For more information about this notice, call 1-800-MEDICARE (1-800-633-4227), or TTY: 1-877-486-2048.

Please sign your name, the date and time. Your signature does not mean that you agree with this notice, just that you received the notice and understand it.

______________________ __________ __________
Signature of Patient or Representative Date Time

240—Preadmission/Admission Hospital Issued Notice of Non-coverage (HINN)

(Rev. 1257, Issued: 05-25-07; Effective: 07-01-07; Implementation: 07-02-07)

Regulations found at 42 CFR Part 476.71 require QIOs to review the medical necessity of hospital discharges **and admissions**, in addition to other requirements specified in that section of the regulation. Therefore, a beneficiary has a right to request an expedited review by the QIO when a hospital (acting directly or through its utilization review committee) has determined at the time of preadmission or admission, that the beneficiary is facing a non-covered hospital stay because the services are not considered to be reasonable and necessary in this case, the services could be safely provided in another setting, or the care is considered custodial in nature.

The utilization review committee or the hospital may issue a preadmission/admission HINN. QIOs may also issue such notices after having been contacted by a hospital regarding care believed to be medically unnecessary, inappropriate, or custodial. The hospital need not obtain the attending physician's concurrence, or the QIO's, prior to issuing the preadmission/admission HINN. This also applies to direct admissions to swing beds (i.e., the beneficiary is admitted to the swing bed when the hospital determines that the beneficiary does not need hospital-level care, but instead needs only skilled nursing (SNF) or custodial nursing (NF) level services).

240.1—Delivery of the Preadmission/Admission HINN

(Rev. 1257, Issued: 05-25-07; Effective: 07-01-07; Implementation: 07-02-07)

When delivering the Preadmission/Admission HINN, hospitals must follow the notice delivery requirements in Section 200.3.1 regarding:

- In-Person Delivery,
- Notice Delivery to Representatives,
- Ensuring Beneficiary Comprehension.
- Beneficiary Signature and Date.
- Refusal to Sign.
- Notice Delivery and Retention.

240.2—Notice Delivery Timeframes and Liability
(Rev. 1257, Issued: 05-25-07; Effective: 07-01-07; Implementation: 07-02-07)

Preadmission: In preadmission situations, the beneficiary is liable, if admitted, for customary charges for all services furnished during the stay, except for those services for which he or she is eligible to receive payment under Part B.

Admission: If the admission notice is issued at 3 p.m. or earlier on the day of admission, the beneficiary is liable for customary charges for all services furnished after receipt of the notice, except for those services for which the beneficiary is eligible to receive payment under Part B.

If the admission notice is issued after 3 p.m. on the day of admission, the beneficiary is liable for customary charges for all services furnished on the day following the day of receipt of the notice, except for those services for which the beneficiary is eligible to receive payment under Part B.

240.3—Timeframes for Submitting a Request for a QIO Review
(Rev. 1257, Issued: 05-25-07; Effective: 07-01-07; Implementation: 07-02-07)

Preadmission: In preadmission situations, a beneficiary who chooses to exercise the right to a QIO review should request immediately, but no later than 3 calendar days after receipt of the notice, or if admitted, at any point during the stay, an immediate review of the facts related to the admission.

Admission: In admission situations, a beneficiary who chooses to exercise the right to a QIO review should request immediately, or at any point in the stay, an immediate review of the facts related to the admission.

240.4—Results of the QIO Review
(Rev. 1257, Issued: 05-25-07; Effective: 07-01-07; Implementation: 07-02-07)

If the QIO disagrees with the hospital's determination and says the stay is reasonable and necessary, the beneficiary will be refunded any amount collected except applicable coinsurance and deductibles, and convenience items or services not covered by Medicare.

If the QIO agrees with the hospital determination and says the stay is not reasonable and necessary, the beneficiary will be responsible for all services on the date specified by the QIO.

240.5—Effect of the QIO Review
(Rev. 1257, Issued: 05-25-07; Effective: 07-01-07; Implementation: 07-02-07)

The QIO will send the beneficiary a formal determination of the medical necessity and appropriateness of the hospitalization determination is binding on the beneficiary, the physician, and hospital except in the following circumstances:

Right to pursue a reconsideration. If the beneficiary is still an inpatient in the hospital and is dissatisfied with the determination, he or she may request a reconsideration according to the procedures described in § 405.1204 (See Section 300 of this chapter.)

Right to pursue the general claims appeal process. If the beneficiary is no longer an inpatient in the hospital, the determination is subject to the general claims appeal process (See Chapter 29 of this manual.)

240.6—Exhibit 4—Model Language for Preadmission/Admission Hospital Issued Notice of Non-coverage
(Rev. 1257, Issued: 05-25-07; Effective: 07-01-07; Implementation: 07-02-07)

Hospital Identifier
Preadmission or Admission Hospital-Issued Notice of Non-coverage (HINN)
Model Language

Name of Patient: __________ Name of the Physician:__________
Patient ID Number: __________ Date Issued: __________

We believe that Medicare is not likely to pay for your admission for __________ (specify service or condition) __________ because:

__________ it is not considered to be medically necessary
__________ it could be furnished safely in another setting
__________ other ______________________________.

However, this notice is not an official Medicare decision.

If you disagree with our finding:

- You should talk to your doctor about this notice and any further health care you may need.
- You also have the right to an appeal, that is, an immediate review of your case by a Quality Improvement Organization (QIO). The QIO is an outside reviewer hired by Medicare to make a formal decision about whether your admission is covered by Medicare. **See page 2 for instructions on how to request a review and contact the QIO.**
- If you decide to go ahead with the hospitalization, you will have to pay for it. ______________________________[382]

CONTINUED ON PAGE 2

---

[382] *For preadmission notices, insert:* "customary charges for all services furnished during the stay, except for those services for which you are eligible under Part B."

For admission notices issued not later than 3:00 P.M. on the date of admission, insert: "customary charges for all services furnished after receipt of this hospital notice, except for those services for which you are eligible under Part B." *(If these requirements are not met, insert the liability phrase below.)*

For admission notices issued after 3:00 P.M. on the day of admission, insert: "customary charges for all services furnished on the day following the day of receipt of this notice, except for those services for which you are eligible to receive payment under Part B."

If you want an immediate review of your case:

__________ (insert one of the following as appropriate) __________

Preadmission:

- Call the QIO immediately at the number listed below, but no later than 3 calendar days after you receive this notice. If you are admitted, you may call the QIO at any point in the stay.

Admission:

- Call the QIO immediately at the number listed below or you may call the QIO at any point during your stay.
- You may also call the QIO for quality of care issues.

QIO Contact Information: _______ (insert name of QIO in bold) _______

_______ (insert telephone number of QIO) _______

If you do not want an immediate review:

- You may still request a review within 30 calendar days from the date of receipt of this notice by calling the QIO at the number below.

Results of the QIO Review:

- The QIO will send you a formal decision about whether your hospitalization is appropriate according to Medicare's rules, and will tell you about your reconsideration and appeal rights.
    - IF THE QIO FINDS YOUR HOSPITAL CARE IS COVERED, you will be refunded any money you may have paid the hospital except for any applicable copays, deductibles, and convenience items or services normally not covered by Medicare.
    - IF THE QIO FINDS THAT YOUR HOSPITAL CARE IS NOT COVERED, you are responsible for payment for all services beginning on (specify date). (see footnote 1 on page 1).

For more information, call 1-800-MEDICARE (1-800-633-4227), or TTY: 1-877-486-2048.

Please sign your name, the date and time. Your signature does not mean that you agree with this notice, just that you received the notice and understand it.

____________________ __________ __________

Signature of Patient or Representative Date Time

260—Expedited Determination Process for Provider Services Terminations (Rev. 2711, Issued: 05-24-13; Effective: 08-26-13; Implementation: 08-26-13)

260.1—Statutory Authority (Rev. 2711, Issued: 05-24-13; Effective: 08-26-13; Implementation: 08-26-13)

Section 1869(b)(1)(F) of the Social Security Act (the Act), as amended by section 521 of the Medicare, Medicaid, and SCHIP Benefits Improvement and Protection Act of 2000 (BIPA) (Pub. L. 106-554) granted beneficiaries in Original Medicare the right to an expedited determination process to dispute the end of their Medicare covered care in certain provider settings.

This process was implemented through a final rule with comment period, CMS-4004-FC (69 FR 69252, November 26, 2004), effective July 1, 2005. The resulting regulations are located at 42 CFR Part 405, §§ 405.1200-405.1204. There is a parallel process for beneficiaries enrolled in Medicare health plans (See §§ 90.2-90.8 in Chapter 13 of the Medicare Managed Care Manual (CMS Pub. 100-16).)

260.2—Scope (Rev. 2711, Issued: 05-24-13; Effective: 08-26-13; Implementation: 08-26-13)

The expedited determination process is available to beneficiaries in Original Medicare whose covered services are being terminated in the following settings. All beneficiaries receiving services in these settings must receive a Notice of Medicare Non-Coverage (NOMNC) before their services end: For purposes of this instruction, the term "Beneficiary" means either beneficiary or representative, when a representative is acting for a beneficiary.

- Home Health Agencies (HHAs)
- Comprehensive Outpatient Rehabilitation Services (CORFs)
- Hospice
- Skilled Nursing Facilities (SNFs—Includes services covered under a Part A stay, as well as Part B services provided under consolidated billing (i.e., physical therapy, occupational therapy, and speech therapy). A NOMNC must be delivered by the SNF at the end of a Part A stay or when all of Part B therapies are ending. For example, a beneficiary exhausts the SNF Part A 100-day benefit, but remains in the facility under a private pay stay and receives physical and occupational therapy covered under Medicare Part B. A NOMNC must be delivered by the SNF when both Part B therapies are ending.

Skilling Nursing Facilities includes beneficiaries receiving Part A and B services in Swing Beds.

260.2.1—Exceptions
(Rev. 2711, Issued: 05-24-13; Effective: 08-26-13; Implementation: 08-26-13)

The following service terminations, reductions, or changes in care are not eligible for an expedited review. Providers should not deliver a NOMNC in these instances.

When services are being reduced (e.g., an HHA providing physical therapy and occupational therapy discontinues the occupational therapy).

When beneficiaries are moving to a higher level of care (e.g., home health care ends because a beneficiary is admitted to a SNF).

When beneficiaries exhaust their benefits (e.g., a beneficiary reaches 100 days of coverage in a SNF, thus exhausting their Medicare Part A SNF benefit).

When beneficiaries end care on their own initiative (e.g., a beneficiary decides to revoke the hospice benefit and return to standard Medicare coverage).

When a beneficiary transfers to another provider at the same level of care (e.g., a beneficiary transfers from one SNF to another while remaining in a Medicare-covered SNF stay).

When a provider discontinues care for business reasons (e.g., an HHA refuses to continue care at a home with a dangerous animal or because the beneficiary was receiving physical therapy and the provider's physical therapist leaves the HHA for another job).

260.3—Notice of Medicare Non-Coverage
(Rev. 2711, Issued: 05-24-13; Effective: 08-26-13; Implementation: 08-26-13)

The notice is subject to the Paperwork Reduction Act Process and approval by the Office for Management and Budget. OMB-approved notices may only be modified as per their accompanying instructions. Unapproved modifications may invalidate the NOMNC. The notice and accompanying instructions may be found online at *http://www.cms.gov/Medicare/Medicare-General-Information/BNI* [site visited June 28, 2018]

260.3.1—Alterations to the NOMNC

(Rev. 2711, Issued: 05-24-13; Effective: 08-26-13; Implementation: 08-26-13)

The NOMNC must remain two pages. The notice can be two sides of one page or one side of two separate pages, but must not be condensed to one page.

Providers may include their business logo and contact information on the top of the NOMNC. Text may not be shifted from page 1 to page 2 to accommodate large logos, address headers, etc.

Providers may include information in the optional "Additional information" section relevant to the beneficiary's situation.

Note: Including information normally included in the Detailed Explanation of Non-Coverage (DENC) in the "Additional information" section does not satisfy a provider's responsibility to deliver the DENC, if otherwise required.

260.3.2—Completing the NOMNC
(Rev. 2711, Issued: 05-24-13; Effective: 08-26-13; Implementation: 08-26-13)

Providers must use the OMB-approved NOMNC (CMS-10123). Providers must type or write the following information in the corresponding blanks of the NOMNC:

- Patient name
- Medicare patient number
- Type of coverage (SNF, Home Health, CORF, or Hospice)
- Effective date (last day of coverage)

Note: The effective date is always the last day beneficiaries will receive coverage for their services. Beneficiaries have no liability for services received on this date, but may face charges for services received the day following the effective date of the NOMNC for home health, hospice, and CORF services. Because SNFs cannot bill the beneficiary for services furnished on the day of (but before the actual moment of) discharge, beneficiaries may leave a SNF the day after the effective date and not face liability for such services.

260.3.3—Provider Delivery of the NOMNC
(Rev. 2711, Issued: 05-24-13; Effective: 08-26-13; Implementation: 08-26-13)

Providers must deliver the NOMNC to all beneficiaries eligible for the expedited determination process per § 260.2. A NOMNC must be delivered even if the beneficiary agrees with the termination of services.

Medicare providers are responsible for the delivery of the NOMNC. Providers may formally delegate the delivery of the notices to a designated agent such as a courier service; however, all of the requirements of valid notice delivery apply to designated agents.

The provider must ensure that the beneficiary or representative signs and dates the NOMNC to demonstrate that the beneficiary or representative received the notice and understands that the termination decision can be disputed Use of assistive devices may be used to obtain a signature. Electronic issuance of NOMNCs is not prohibited. If a provider elects to issue a NOMNC that is viewed on an electronic screen before signing, the beneficiary must be given the option of requesting paper issuance over electronic if that is what is preferred. Regardless of whether a paper or electronic version is issued and regardless of whether the signature is digitally capture or manually penned, the beneficiary must be given a paper copy of the NOMNC, with the required beneficiary-specific information inserted, at the time of notice delivery.

260.3.4—Required Delivery Timeframes (Rev. 2711, Issued: 05-24-13; Effective: 08-26-13; Implementation: 08-26-13)

The NOMNC should be delivered to the beneficiary at least two calendar days before Medicare covered services end or the second to last day of service if care is not being provided daily. For example, if the last day of covered SNF care is a Friday, the NOMNC should be delivered no later than the preceding Wednesday.

Note: The two day advance requirement is NOT a 48 hour requirement. For example, if a patient's last covered home health service is at 10AM on Wednesday and the notice is delivered at 4PM on the prior Monday, it is considered timely.

If home health services are being provided less frequently than daily, the notice must be delivered no later than the next to last visit before Medicare covered services end. For example, if home health care is provided on Tuesdays and Thursdays, and Tuesday is the last day of Medicare services, the notice must be delivered no later than the preceding Thursday.

The NOMNC may be delivered earlier than two days preceding the end of covered services. However, delivery of the notice should be closely tied to the impending end of coverage so a beneficiary will more likely understand and retain the information regarding the right to an expedited determination.

The notice may not be routinely given at the time services begin. An exception is when the services are expected to last fewer than two days. In these instances, the notice may be given by the provider when services begin.

There is an accepted circumstance when the NOMNC may be delivered sooner than two days or the next to last visit before coverage ends. This exception is limited to cases where a beneficiary receiving home health services is found to be no longer be homebound, and thus ineligible for covered home health care. In this circumstance, the NOMNC should be immediately delivered to the beneficiary upon discovery of the loss of homebound status. We expect that in the vast majority of cases, in all settings, the decision of a physician to end care will be based on medical necessity, and thus, foreseeable by the provider within the required time frames for notice delivery.

260.3.5—Refusal to Sign the NOMNC (Rev. 2711, Issued: 05-24-13; Effective: 08-26-13; Implementation: 08-26-13)

If the beneficiary refuses to sign the NOMNC, the provider should annotate the notice to that effect, and indicate the date of refusal on the notice. The date of refusal is considered to be the date of notice receipt. Beneficiaries who refuse to sign the NOMNC remain entitled to an expedited determination.

260.3.6—Financial Liability for Failure to Deliver a Valid NOMNC (Rev. 2711, Issued: 05-24-13; Effective: 08-26-13; Implementation: 08-26-13)

If a Qualified Independent Contractor (QIO) determines that a provider did not deliver a valid NOMNC to a beneficiary, the provider is financially liable for continued services until two days after the beneficiary receives valid notice, or until the effective date of the valid notice, whichever is later.

260.3.7—Amending the Date of the NOMNC (Rev. 2711, Issued: 05-24-13; Effective: 08-26-13; Implementation: 08-26-13)

If the initial NOMNC was delivered to a beneficiary and the effective date was changed, the provider may amend the notice to reflect the new date. The newer effective date may not be earlier than the effective date of the original notice except in those cases involving the abrupt end of services, as discussed in § 260.3.4.

The beneficiary must be verbally notified as soon as possible after the provider is aware of the change. The amended NOMNC must be delivered or mailed to the beneficiary and a copy retained in the beneficiary's file.

If an expedited determination is already in progress, the provider must immediately notify the QIO of the change and provide an amended notice to the QIO.

260.3.8—NOMNC Delivery to Representatives (Rev. 2711, Issued: 05-24-13; Effective: 08-26-13; Implementation: 08-26-13)

The NOMNC may be delivered to a beneficiary's appointed or authorized representative. Appointed representatives are individuals designated by beneficiaries to act on their behalf during the appeal process. A beneficiary may designate an appointed representative via the "Appointment of Representative" form, the CMS-1696. *http://www.cms.hhs.gov/cmsforms/downloads/cms1696.pdf* [site visited June 29, 2018]. See Chapter 29 of the Medicare Claims Processing Manual, section 270.1, for more information on appointed representatives.

CMS usually requires that notification to a beneficiary who has been deemed legally incompetent be made to an authorized representative of the beneficiary. Generally, an authorized representative is an individual who, under State or other applicable law, may make health care decisions on a beneficiary's behalf (e.g., the beneficiary's legal guardian, or someone appointed in accordance with a properly executed durable medical power of attorney). However, if a beneficiary is temporarily incapacitated, a person (typically, a family member or close friend) whom the provider has determined could reasonably represent the beneficiary, but who has not been named in any legally binding document, may be a representative for the purpose of receiving the notices described in this section. Such a representative should have the beneficiary's best interests at heart and must act in a manner that is protective of the beneficiary and the beneficiary's rights. Therefore, a representative should have no relevant conflict of interest with the beneficiary.

In these instances of delivering a notice to an unnamed representative, the provider should annotate the NOMNC with the name of the staff person initiating the contact, the name of the person contacted, and the date, time, and method (in person or telephone) of the contact. A copy of the NOMNC with this information should be retained in the beneficiary's record.

Note—Exceptions to in-person notice delivery. If the NOMNC must be delivered to a representative not living with the beneficiary, the provider is not required to make off-site in-person notice delivery to the representative. The provider must complete the NOMNC as required and telephone the representative at least two days prior to the end of covered services. The provider should inform the representative of the beneficiary's right to appeal a coverage termination decision.

The information provided should include the following:

- The beneficiary's last day of covered services, and the date when the beneficiary's liability is expected to begin.
- The beneficiary's right to appeal a coverage termination decision.
- A description of how to request an appeal by a QIO.
- The deadline to request a review as well as what to do if the deadline is missed.
- The telephone number of the QIO to request the appeal.

The date the provider communicates this information to the representative, whether by telephone or in writing, is considered the receipt date of the NOMNC.

The NOMNC must be annotated with the following information on the day that the provider makes telephone contact:

- Reflect that all of the information indicated above was communicated to the representative;
- Note the name of the staff person initiating the contact, the name of the representative contacted by phone, the date and time of the telephone contact, and the telephone number called.

A copy of the annotated NOMNC should be mailed to the representative the day telephone contact is made and a dated copy should be placed in the beneficiary's medical file.

If the provider chooses to communicate the information in writing, a hard copy of the NOMNC must be sent to the representative by certified mail, return receipt requested, or any other delivery method that can provide signed verification of delivery (e.g., FedEx, UPS). The burden is on the provider to demonstrate that timely contact was attempted with the representative and that the notice was delivered.

The date that someone at the representative's address signs (or refused to sign) the receipt is considered the date received. Place a copy of the annotated NOMNC in the beneficiary's medical file.

If both the provider and the representative agree, providers may send the notice by fax or e-mail; however, provider's fax and e-mail systems must meet the Health Insurance Portability and Accountability Act of 1996 (HIPAA) privacy and security requirements.

260.3.9—Notice Retention for the NOMNC
(Rev. 2711, Issued: 05-24-13; Effective: 08-26-13; Implementation: 08-26-13)

The provider must retain the original signed NOMNC in the beneficiary's file. The beneficiary should receive a paper copy of the NOMNC that includes all of the required information such as the effective date and covered service at issue. Electronic notice retention is permitted if the NOMNC was delivered electronically.

260.3.10—Hours of NOMNC Delivery
(Rev. 2711, Issued: 05-24-13; Effective: 08-26-13; Implementation: 08-26-13)

Notice delivery should occur within the normal operating hours of the provider. Providers are not expected to extend their hours or days of business solely to meet the requirements of the expedited determination process. However, it is expected that all notices be provided as timely as possible within these constraints.

260.4—Expedited Determination Process
(Rev. 2711, Issued: 05-24-13; Effective: 08-26-13; Implementation: 08-26-13)

260.4.1—Beneficiary Responsibilities
(Rev. 2711, Issued: 05-24-13; Effective: 08-26-13; Implementation: 08-26-13)

260.4.1.1—Timeframe for Requesting an Expedited Determination
(Rev. 2711, Issued: 05-24-13; Effective: 08-26-13; Implementation: 08-26-13)

A beneficiary who receives a NOMNC and disagrees with the termination of services may request an expedited determination by the appropriate QIO for the state where the services were provided. The beneficiary must contact the QIO by noon of the day before the effective date on the NOMNC. The beneficiary may contact the QIO by telephone or in writing. If the QIO is unable to accept the request, the beneficiary must submit the request by noon of the next day the QIO is available.

260.4.1.2—Provide Information to QIO
(Rev. 2711, Issued: 05-24-13; Effective: 08-26-13; Implementation: 08-26-13)

The beneficiary must be available to answer questions or supply information requested by the QIO. The beneficiary may, but is not required to, supply additional information to the QIO that he or she believes is pertinent to the case.

260.4.1.3—Obtain Physician Certification of Risk (Home Health and CORF services only)
(Rev. 2711, Issued: 05-24-13; Effective: 08-26-13; Implementation: 08-26-13)

A beneficiary must obtain a physician certification stating that failure to continue home health or CORF services is likely to place the beneficiary's health at significant risk. Without such a certification statement a QIO may not make a determination for service terminations in these settings.

The physician certification is a written statement from any licensed physician contacted by a beneficiary. This is a special certification required only in this expedited determination process for expedited determinations in home health and CORF settings.

A beneficiary may request an expedited determination from a QIO before obtaining this certification of risk. Once the QIO is aware of a review request, it will instruct the beneficiary on how to obtain the necessary certification from a physician.

260.4.2—Beneficiary Liability During QIO Review
(Rev. 2711, Issued: 05-24-13; Effective: 08-26-13; Implementation: 08-26-13)

A provider may not bill a beneficiary who has timely filed an expedited determination for disputed services until the review process, including a reconsideration by a Qualified Independent Contractor (QIC), if applicable, is complete.

260.4.3—Untimely Requests for Review
(Rev. 2711, Issued: 05-24-13; Effective: 08-26-13; Implementation: 08-26-13)

If the beneficiary makes an untimely request to the QIO, the QIO will accept the request for review, but is not required to complete the review within its usual 72-hour deadline. The QIO will make a determination as soon as possible upon receipt of the request. Beneficiaries have up to 60 days from the effective date of the NOMNC to make an untimely request to a QIO. When the beneficiary is still receiving services, the QIO must make a determination and notify the parties within 7 days of receipt of the request. When the beneficiary is no longer receiving services, the QIO will make a determination within 30 days of the request.

The coverage protections discussed in § 260.4.2 do not apply to a beneficiary who makes an untimely request to the QIO.

260.4.4—Provider Responsibilities
(Rev. 2711, Issued: 05-24-13; Effective: 08-26-13; Implementation: 08-26-13)

When a provider is notified by a QIO of a beneficiary request for an expedited determination, the provider must—

- Deliver the beneficiary a DENC (see § 260.4.5) by close of business the day they are notified;
- Supply the QIO with copies of the NOMNC and DENCs by close of business of the day of the QIO notification;
- Supply all information, including medical records, requested by the QIO. The QIO may allow this required information to be supplied via phone, writing, or electronically. If supplied via phone, the provider must keep a written record of the information it provides within the patient record; and
- Furnish the beneficiary, at their request, with access to or copies of any documentation it provides to the QIO. The provider may charge the beneficiary a reasonable amount to cover the costs of duplicating and delivering the documentation. This documentation must be provided to the beneficiary by close of business of the first day after the material is requested.

260.4.5—The Detailed Explanation of Non-Coverage
(Rev. 2711, Issued: 05-24-13; Effective: 08-26-13; Implementation: 08-26-13)

The DENC is subject to the Paperwork Reduction Act Process and approval by the office of Management and Budget. OMB-approved notices may only be modified as per their accompanying instructions. Unapproved modifications may invalidate the DENC. The notice and accompanying instructions may be found online at *http://www.cms.gov/Medicare/Medicare-General-Information/BNI [*site visited June 29, 2018*]*. Medicare providers are responsible for the delivery of the DENC to beneficiaries who request an expedited determination by the QIO.

The DENC must contain the following information:

- The facts specific to the beneficiary's discharge and provider's determination that coverage should end.

- A specific and detailed explanation of why services are either no longer reasonable and necessary or no longer covered.
- A description of, and citations to, the Medicare coverage rule, instruction, or other policies applicable to the review.

The provider should make insertions on the notice in Spanish, if necessary. If this is impossible, additional steps should be taken to ensure that the beneficiary comprehends the content of the notice. Providers may resource CMS multilingual services provided through the 1-800-MEDICARE help line if needed.

The delivery must occur in person by close of business of the day the QIO notifies the provider that the beneficiary has requested an expedited determination. A provider may also choose to deliver the DENC with the NOMNC.

The DENC does not require a signature but should be annotated in the event of a beneficiary's refusal to accept the notice upon delivery.

Note: An HHA is not required to make a separate trip to the beneficiary's residence solely to deliver a DENC. Upon notification from the QIO of a beneficiary's request for an expedited determination, an HHA may telephone the beneficiary to provide the information contained on the DENC, annotate the DENC with the date and time of telephone contact and file with the beneficiary's records. A hard copy of the DENC should be sent to the beneficiary via tracked mail or other personal courier method by close of business of the day the QIO notifies the provider that the beneficiary has requested an expedited determination. The burden is on the provider to demonstrate that timely contact was attempted with the beneficiary and that the notice was delivered.

DENC delivery to representatives, DENC hours of delivery, and DENC retention requirements are the same as the NOMNC requirements outlined in § 260.3.

Expedited Determination Scenario in a Skilled Nursing Facility—Example

On June 2nd, the SNF delivers a NOMNC to Bob Mills notifying him that his Medicare covered stay will end on June 4th. Bob decides to request an expedited determination.

June 2nd	June 3rd	June 4th	June 4th	June 6th
NOMNC Delivered Bob receives a NOMNC indicating that his coverage is ending June 4th.	**Bob must** request an expedited determination by noon today.	**NOMNC Effective Date** This is the last day of coverage, as stated on the NOMNC.	**If Bob made his request on June 2nd:** The QIO makes its decision and notifies Bob and SNF by COB.	**If Bob made his request on June 3rd:** The QIO makes its decision and notifies Bob and the SNF by COB.
	The QIO must notify the SNF of Bob's request for an expedited determination. **The SNF must deliver the DENC to Bob by COB today.** **The SNF must provide relevant medical records to the QIO by COB today.**	**The beneficiary has no liability for this day as this is the last day of coverage in the SNF.**	**If QIO decision is unfavorable:** Beginning today Bob is liable for his stay if he does not leave the SNF.	

260.5—QIO Responsibilities
(Rev. 2711, Issued: 05-24-13; Effective: 08-26-13; Implementation: 08-26-13)

260.5.1—Receive Beneficiary Requests for Expedited Review
(Rev. 2711, Issued: 05-24-13; Effective: 08-26-13; Implementation: 08-26-13)

QIOs must be available to receive beneficiary requests for review 24 hours a day, 7 days a week.

260.5.2—Notify Providers and Allow Explanation of Why Covered Services Should End
(Rev. 2711, Issued: 05-24-13; Effective: 08-26-13; Implementation: 08-26-13)

When the QIO receives a request from a beneficiary, the QIO must immediately notify the provider of services that a request for an expedited determination was made. If the request is received after normal working hours, the QIO should notify the provider as soon as possible on the morning after the request was made.

260.5.3—Validate Delivery of NOMNC
(Rev. 2711, Issued: 05-24-13; Effective: 08-26-13; Implementation: 08-26-13)

The QIO must validate that the NOMNC included the required elements outlined below:

- Date that coverage of services ends.
- Date that beneficiary's financial liability begins.
- Description of right to an expedited determination (and how to request an expedited determination) and the right to submit relevant information to the QIO.
- Right to detailed information on why the provider believes Medicare will no longer cover services.
- Contact information for QIO in the state where services were delivered.

The QIO should determine that NOMNC delivery was valid of all of the following criteria are met:

- All elements stated above are included.
- The beneficiary signed and dated the notice. If the NOMNC was annotated because the beneficiary refused to sign the notice upon delivery, the QIO may still conduct an expedited determination in these instances.
- Notice was delivered at least two days before services terminate. For a non-residential provider, the notice may be delivered at the next to last visit before services terminate.

Invalidating a NOMNC should be a rare occurrence. The only reasons to invalidate are the lack of one of the criteria stated above or a pattern of minor errors as established by the provider.

If a QIO invalidates a NOMNC, a new NOMNC must be issued to the beneficiary with an effective date at least two days after the beneficiary receives valid notice. If the beneficiary again disagrees with the termination of care, a new request to the QIO must be made.

260.5.4—Solicit the Views of the Beneficiary
(Rev. 2711, Issued: 05-24-13; Effective: 08-26-13; Implementation: 08-26-13)

The QIO must solicit the views of the beneficiary who requested the expedited determination.

260.5.5—Solicit the Views of the Provider
(Rev. 2711, Issued: 05-24-13; Effective: 08-26-13; Implementation: 08-26-13)

The QIO must afford the provider an opportunity to explain why the discharge is appropriate.

260.5.6—Make Determination and Notify Required Parties
(Rev. 2711, Issued: 05-24-13; Effective: 08-26-13; Implementation: 08-26-13)

No later than 72 hours after receipt of the request for an expedited determination, the QIO must make its determination on whether the discharge is appropriate based on medical necessity or other Medicare coverage policies.

Note: If the QIO does not receive supporting information from the provider, it may make its determination based on the evidence at hand, or defer a decision until it receives the necessary information. If this delay results in continued services for the beneficiary, the provider may be held financially liable for these services as determined by the QIO.

The QIO must notify the beneficiary, the beneficiary's physician, and the provider of services of its determination. This notification must include the rationale for the determination and an explanation of Medicare payment consequences and beneficiary liability. QIOs must also inform the beneficiary of the right to an expedited reconsideration by the Qualified Independent Contractor (QIC) and how to request a timely expedited reconsideration. The QIO will make its initial notification via telephone and will follow up with a written determination letter.

260.6—Effect of a QIO Expedited Determination
(Rev. 2711, Issued: 05-24-13; Effective: 08-26-13; Implementation: 08-26-13)

The QIO determination is binding unless the beneficiary pursues an expedited reconsideration per section 270 of this chapter.

260.6.1—Right to Pursue an Expedited Reconsideration
(Rev. 2711, Issued: 05-24-13; Effective: 08-26-13; Implementation: 08-26-13)

If dissatisfied with the expedited determination, the beneficiary may request an expedited reconsideration according to the procedures described in section 270 of this chapter.

260.6.2—Effect of QIO Determination on Continuation of Care (Rev. 2711, Issued: 05-24-13; Effective: 08-26-13; Implementation: 08-26-13)

If the QIO decision extends coverage to a period where a physician's ordered do not exist, either because of the duration of the expedited determination process, or because the physician has already concurred with the termination of care, providers cannot deliver care. In the event of a QIO decision favorable to a beneficiary without physician orders, the ordering physician should be made aware the QIO has ruled coverage should continue, and be given the opportunity to reinstate orders. The beneficiary may also seek other personal physicians to write orders for care as well as find another service provider. The expedited determination process does not override regulatory or State requirements that physician orders are required for a provider to deliver care.

If a QIO decision is favorable to the beneficiary and the beneficiary resumes covered services, a new NOMNC should be delivered if that care is later terminated, per the requirements of this section. If the beneficiary again disagrees with the termination of care, a new request to the QIO must be made.

The QIO decision will affect the necessity of subsequent Advance Beneficiary Notice of Non-coverage (ABN) deliveries.

Example: If covered home health care continues following a favorable QIO decision for the beneficiary, the HHA would resume issuance of Home Health Advanced Beneficiary Notices (HHABNs) as warranted for the remainder of this home health episode. If the QIO decides that Medicare covered care should end and the patient wishes to continue receiving care from the HHA, even though Medicare will not pay, an HHABN with Option Box 1 must be issued to the beneficiary since this would be an initiation of non-covered care.

Example: If covered Skilled Nursing Facility (SNF) care continues following a favorable QIO decision for the beneficiary but later ends due to the end of Medicare coverage, and the patient wishes to continue receiving uncovered care at the SNF, a SNFABN must be issued to the beneficiary.

260.6.3—Right to Pursue the Standard Claims Appeal Process (Rev. 2711, Issued: 05-24-13; Effective: 08-26-13; Implementation: 08-26-13)

If a beneficiary receives services of the type at issue in the expedited determination after the coverage end date, and coverage is denied, the beneficiary may appeal the denial within the standard claims appeal process (see Chapter 29 of this manual).

261—Expedited Determination Notice Association with Advance Beneficiary Notices
(Rev. 2711, Issued: 05-24-13; Effective: 08-26-13; Implementation: 08-26-13)

Delivery of the NOMNC does not replace the required delivery of other mandatory notices, including ABNs. Notice delivery must be determined by the individual NOMNC requirements per this section and ABN delivery requirements per § 1879 of the Act and per guidance in this chapter. Both the NOMNC and an ABN may be required in certain instances.

Only one notice may be required when Medicare covered care is ending.

Example: A beneficiary is receiving CORF services and all covered CORF care is ending. A NOMNC must be delivered at least two days, or two visits, prior to the end of coverage. If the beneficiary does not continue the CORF services, an ABN should not be issued.

Some situations may require two notices at the end of Medicare covered care.

Example: A beneficiary's Part A stay is ending because skilled level care is no longer medically necessary and the beneficiary wishes to remain in the SNF receiving custodial care. The beneficiary must receive the NOMNC two days prior to the end of coverage. A SNFABN must also be delivered before custodial care begins.

It is also possible that no notice is required when Medicare coverage is ending.

Example: A beneficiary exhausts the 100 day benefit in a SNF. In this instance, the NOMNC should not be delivered. The SNFABN is not required in this situation. However, it can be issued voluntarily, as a courtesy to the beneficiary.

300—Expedited Reconsiderations
(Rev. 1257, Issued: 05-25-07; Effective: 07-01-07; Implementation: 07-02-07)

A beneficiary who is dissatisfied with a QIO determination can request a reconsideration by an independent review entity (IRE). Such reconsiderations are codified in regulations effective July 1, 2005 (42 CFR 405.1204) but are familiar to inpatient hospital providers as the process previously available under § 1155 of the Act. This reconsideration process is the same for hospital and non-hospital providers.

300.1—The Role of the Beneficiary and Liability
(Rev. 1257, Issued: 05-25-07; Effective: 07-01-07; Implementation: 07-02-07)

Submitting a Request: A beneficiary who chooses to exercise the right to an expedited reconsideration must submit a request to the appropriate IRE in writing or by telephone no later than noon of the calendar day following the initial notification (whether by telephone or in writing) of the QIO's determination. The beneficiary, upon request of the QIO, should be available to discuss the case or supply information that the IRE may request. The beneficiary may, but is not required to, submit written evidence to be considered by the IRE.

Untimely Requests: When the beneficiary fails to make a timely request for an expedited reconsideration subsequently may request a reconsideration under the standard claims appeal process (See Chapter 29 of this Manual), but the coverage protection described in Section 300.5 would not extend through this reconsideration, nor would the notification timeframes or the escalation process described in Section 300.2 apply.

300.2—The Responsibilities of the IRE
(Rev. 1257, Issued: 05-25-07; Effective: 07-01-07; Implementation: 07-02-07)

Receipt of the Request. On the day the IRE receives the request for an expedited reconsideration, the IRE must immediately notify the QIO that made the expedited determination and the provider of services of the request for the expedited reconsideration.

Examine Records and Other Information. The IRE must offer the beneficiary and the provider an opportunity to provide further information.

Notification. Unless the beneficiary requests an extension (see below), the IRE must notify the QIO, the beneficiary, and the provider of services of its decision no later than 72 hours after receipt of the request for an expedited reconsideration, and any such records needed for the reconsideration. The initial notification may be done by telephone followed by a written notice that includes:

- The rationale for the reconsideration decision,
- An explanation of the Medicare payment consequences of the determination and the beneficiary's date of liability,
- Information about the beneficiary's right to appeal the IRE's reconsideration decision to an ALJ, including how to request an appeal and the time period for doing so.

Escalation. Unless the beneficiary requests an extension, if the IRE does not issue a decision within 72 hours of receipt of the request, the IRE must notify the beneficiary of his or her right to have the case escalated to the ALJ hearing level if the amount remaining in controversy is $100 or more.

Extensions. A beneficiary who requests an expedited reconsideration may request (either in writing or orally) that an IRE grant such additional time as the beneficiary specifies (not to exceed 14 days) for the reconsideration. If an extension is granted, the deadlines described above under notification, do not apply.

300.3—The Responsibilities of the QIO
(Rev. 1257, Issued: 05-25-07; Effective: 07-01-07; Implementation: 07-02-07)

When an IRE notifies the QIO that a beneficiary has requested an expedited reconsideration, the QIO must supply all information that the IRE needs to make its expedited reconsideration as soon as possible, but no later than by close of business of the day that the IRE notifies the QIO of the request for the reconsideration.

At the beneficiary's request, the QIO must furnish the beneficiary with a copy of, or access to, any documentation that it sends to the IRE. The QIO may charge the beneficiary a reasonable amount to cover the costs of duplicating the documentation and/or delivering it to the beneficiary. The QIO must accommodate the request by no later than close of business of the first day after the material is requested.

300.4—The Responsibilities of the Provider
(Rev. 1257, Issued: 05-25-07; Effective: 07-01-07; Implementation: 07-02-07)

The provider may, but is not required to, submit evidence to be considered by an IRE in making its decision. If a provider fails to comply with an IRE's request for additional information beyond that furnished by the QIO for purposes of the expedited determination, the IRE makes its reconsideration decision based on the information available.

300.5—Coverage During an Expedited Reconsideration
(Rev. 1257, Issued: 05-25-07; Effective: 07-01-07; Implementation: 07-02-07)

When a beneficiary makes a timely request for an expedited determination, the provider may not bill the beneficiary for any disputed services until the IRE makes its determination. Beneficiary liability for continued services is based on the QIO's decision.

Transmittals Issued for this Chapter Rev #	*Issue Date*	*Subject*	*Impl Date*	*CR#*
R3187CP	02/06/2015	Language Only Update to Pub 100-04, Chapter 30 for ASC X12 and Claim References	03/06/2015	8992

continues

Transmittals Issued for this Chapter Rev #	*Issue Date*	*Subject*	*Impl Date*	*CR#*
R2911CP	03/14/2014	Manual Updates to Clarify Skilled Nursing Facility Advanced Beneficiary Notice (SNFABN Requirements pursuant to Jimmo vs. Sebelius	03/25/2014	8644
R2872CP	02/21/2014	Correction CR – Advance Beneficiary Notice of Non-coverage (ABN), Form CMS-R-131	05/15/2013	8597
R2782CP	09/06/2013	Advance Beneficiary Notice of Non-coverage (ABN), Form CMS-R-131	12/09/2013	8404
R2781CP	09/06/2013	Home Health Change of Care Notice (HHCCN), Form CMS-10280, Manual Instructions. This CR rescinds and fully preplaces CR 7323.	12/09/2013	8403
R2711CP	05/24/2013	Expedited Determinations for Provider Service Terminations	08/26/2013	7903

continues

Transmittals Issued for this Chapter Rev #	*Issue Date*	*Subject*	*Impl Date*	*CR#*
R2480CP	06/01/2012	Advanced Beneficiary Notice of Non-coverage (ABN, Form CMS-R-131, Updated Manual Instructions	09/04/2012	7821
R2362CP	12/01/2011	Home Health Advance Beneficiary Notice, (HHABN), Form CMS-R-296	02/03/2012	7323
R1983CP	06/11/2010	Clarification on Use of the SNF ABN and Denial Letters	03/01/2010	6987
R1587CP	09/05/2008	Revised Form CMS-R-131 Advance Beneficiary Notice of Non-coverage	03/01/2009	6136
R1257CP	05/25/2007	Important Message From Medicare (IM) and Expedited Determination Procedures for Hospital Discharges	7/02/2007	5622
R1186CP	02/23/2007	Changes to Chapter 30—Updates to Amount in Controversy Requirement and Correction of Appeals Terminology	05/23/2007	5348

continues

Transmittals Issued for this Chapter Rev #	*Issue Date*	*Subject*	*Impl Date*	*CR#*
R1035CP	08/18/2006	Updating Publication 100-04, Chapter 30 Regarding the CD ROM Initiative for the Annual "Dear Doctor" Mailing	09/18/2006	5214
R1025CP	08/11/2006	Revised Home Health Advance Beneficiary Notice	09/01/2006	5009
R994CP	06/30/2006	Special Issues Associated with the Advance Beneficiary Notice (ABN) for Hospice Providers and Comprehensive Outpatient Rehabilitation Facilities (CORFs)	09/29/2006	5117
R594CP	06/24/2005	Preliminary Instructions: Expedited Determinations/ Reviews for Original Medicare	07/01/2005	3903
R577CP	06/03/2005	Preliminary Instructions: Expedited Determinations/ Reviews for Original Medicare	07/01/2005	3903
R001CP	11/01/2003	Initial Publication of Manual	NA	NA

CHAPTER 3

SKILLED NURSING FACILITY COVERAGE

§ 3.01 INTRODUCTION TO SKILLED NURSING FACILITY COVERAGE

The Medicare skilled nursing facility (SNF) benefit provides limited but valuable health care benefits for Medicare beneficiaries. It is, however, one of the most misunderstood areas of Medicare. Many people mistakenly believe that Medicare does not cover nursing home care at all. Others believe that Medicare covers long-term care. Still others realize there is limited coverage, but they do not understand that the level of care received (e.g., skilled versus only custodial care) affects coverage.

Medicare coverage under Part A is available for up to 100 days per benefit period if the patient has had a qualifying three-day hospital stay and requires daily skilled care. If a SNF stay is covered by traditional Medicare, the first 20 days are generally paid in full and the patient must meet a copayment obligation for days 21 through 100. Medicare Advantage plans may have different copayment rules, but they must be actuarially equivalent to copayments under traditional Medicare.

SNF patients who are not in a Part A stay (because, for example, they have used the 100-day benefit or they do not need daily skilled rehabilitation services) may be eligible for Part B coverage (of their less-than-daily skilled rehabilitation services, for example). SNF patients cannot use Parts A and B for their SNF care at the same time.

§ 3.02 COVERAGE

Medicare covers necessary post-hospital extended care services for up to 100 days in a benefit period.[1] Extended care services are defined in the statute as nursing care and rehabilitation provided to a Medicare beneficiary who is an inpatient in a SNF.[2] Such services must be provided daily, and the condition treated in the SNF must be either a condition for which the patient received inpatient hospital services or a condition that arose at the SNF while the individual was being treated for a condition for which the hospital services were received.[3] Traditional Medicare covers the first 20 days in full; however, there is a copayment for the next 80 days. The daily copayment is equal to one-eighth of the hospital deductible amount.[4] Accordingly, for a 100-day stay in 2019, the patient would be responsible for $13,640.00 (80 coinsurance days × $170.50/day). For information about Medicare Advantage, see **Chapter 7**.

This is a significant amount of money, which is either paid out-of-pocket by the patient or covered by a Medigap insurance policy. The copayment obligation

[1] 42 U.S.C. § 1395d(a)(2)(A).

[2] 42 U.S.C. § 1395x(h).

[3] 42 U.S.C. § 1395f(a)(2)(B); 42 C.F.R. § 409.31(b).

[4] 42 C.F.R. § 409.85(a)(2).

can present problems for Medicare patients. Although a patient's Medigap policy may cover the SNF copayment, the patient must pay premiums for private supplemental insurance coverage. Moreover, if Medicare does not cover the stay, neither does a Medigap policy. Long-term care insurance policies are offered in many states, but these policies are generally medically underwritten and may have expensive premiums and limited coverage. Fewer insurance companies are offering new policies.

Regulations promulgated by the Secretary of the Department of Health and Human Services (HHS)[5] define covered skilled *nursing* services, which include overall management and evaluation of a care plan, observation and assessment of a patient's changing condition, and patient education services.[6]

Medicare coverage is also available for *rehabilitation* services for the ongoing assessment of rehabilitation needs and potential, therapeutic exercises or activities, gait evaluation and training, range of motion exercises, *and* maintenance therapy.[7]

Services may be considered skilled, and therefore coverable by Medicare, if they are necessary to *maintain* current status or to prevent further decline or deterioration[8] and if they are provided by, or under the supervision of, a registered nurse or therapist.[9] The regulations explicitly state that in determining whether skilled rehabilitation services are required, the restoration potential of the individual is not dispositive.[10] These are particularly important sections of the regulations since those who administer the Medicare program have regularly denied coverage on the grounds that the care or therapy required is "maintenance only" and that the patient's underlying condition will not improve. The court-approved Settlement in *Jimmo v. Sebelius*[11] ends the myth that Medicare coverage depends solely on the patient's potential for improvement. *Jimmo* confirms that Medicare covers maintenance care and that coverage depends on a patient's need for skilled

---

[5] 42 C.F.R. §§ 409.20 *et seq.* and 409.30 *et seq.*, *available at* https://www.ecfr.gov/cgi-bin/text-idx?SID=fa55df35895f2faa1c0c5a6643164bf9&mc=true&node=pt42.2.409&rgn=div5#sp42.2.409.c (site visited Aug. 6, 2018). *See also* the Medicare Benefit Policy (MBP) Manual, CMS Pub. 100-02, Ch. 8, §§ 10, *et seq.*, *available at* https://www.cms.gov/Regulations-and-Guidance/Guidance/Manuals/Downloads/bp102c08.pdf (site visited Aug. 6 2018).

[6] 42 C.F.R. §§ 409.21 and 409.33(a)(1)–(3). The regulations implementing a prospective payment system, a system based on resource utilization groups (RUGs), deleted these examples. (*See* preamble to May 12, 1998, regulations, 63 Fed. Reg. 26,284–26,285, noting an intent that the RUGs act as proxies for observation, assessment, management, and patient education.) In July 1999, these examples were reinstated into the regulations. 64 Fed. Reg. 41,670 (July 30, 1999); 42 C.F.R. § 409.33(a)(1)–(3).

[7] 42 C.F.R. § 409.33(c).

[8] 42 C.F.R. §§ 409.32(c) and 409.33(c)(5).

[9] 42 C.F.R. §§ 409.32 and 409.33(a), (b).

[10] 42 C.F.R. §§ 409.32(c).

[11] Civil Action No. 5:11-CV-17-CR (D. Vt. Jan. 24, 2013), *available at* http://www.medicareadvocacy.org/wp-content/uploads/2012/12/Jimmo-Settlement-Agreement-00011764.pdf (site visited Aug. 6, 2018).

nursing care or skilled rehabilitation services or both. Implementation of *Jimmo* remains an on-going concern. Plaintiffs returned to court in March 2016 and the court ordered the Secretary to undertake additional actions, including use of a court-mandated Corrective Statement, creation of a dedicated webpage, and additional training.[12] The dedicated *Jimmo* webpage, which includes a court-approved "Important Message About the Jimmo Settlement" and Frequently Asked Questions, was published in August 2017.[13]

§ 3.03 QUALIFYING CRITERIA

[A] Basic Eligibility and Coverage

With respect to the Medicare SNF benefit:[14]

- Only admissions after a three-day inpatient hospital stay are covered;
- Ordinarily, post-hospital transfer to a SNF must be made within 30 days after leaving the hospital;
- The patient must require and receive skilled services on a daily basis—skilled nursing seven days per week or rehabilitation five days per week or a combination of the two for seven days per week—in order to qualify for coverage;
- Skilled care must be related to the condition for which the patient was hospitalized;
- A maximum of 100 days per benefit period (also called spell of illness) may be covered;
- As a practical matter, the care must be required to be provided on an inpatient basis.

[B] Three-Day Test

The Medicare statute limits coverage of SNF stays to:

> extended care services furnished [to] an individual after transfer from a hospital in which he was an inpatient for not less than three consecutive days before his discharge from the hospital in connection with such transfer. For

[12] Opinion and Order Adopting Defendant's Corrective Action Plan and Mandating Two Additional Requirements (Feb. 1, 2017), *available at* http://www.medicareadvocacy.org/wp-content/uploads/2017/02/Jimmo-v.-Sebelius-Corrective-Action-Order.pdf (site visited Aug. 6, 2018).

[13] *See* CMS, "*Jimmo* Settlement," *available at* https://www.cms.gov/Center/Special-Topic/Jimmo-Center.html (site visited Aug. 6, 2018). *See also* **Appendix 1-9**.

[14] See citations in the discussion below.

> purposes of the preceding sentence, items and services shall be deemed to have been furnished to an individual after transfer from a hospital, and he shall be deemed to have been an inpatient in the hospital immediately before transfer there from, if he is admitted to the skilled nursing facility within 30 days after discharge from such hospital. . . .[15]

To qualify for coverage, a Medicare patient first must be an inpatient of a hospital for three consecutive days.[16] The Centers for Medicare & Medicaid Services (CMS) defines "days" as midnights, not 24-hour periods. A patient admitted to the hospital at 11:55 p.m. will have that day counted as the first day of admission. The day of discharge does not count as one of the three qualifying days—hence, the requirement is often referred to as the "three-midnights" rule. If a patient was in the hospital as an inpatient for a time period that crossed three midnights, the patient has satisfied the three-day test.

Language added to the Medicare Benefit Policy (MBP) Manual in 2013 confirms that the three-day test is satisfied when the patient has at least three consecutive days of medically necessary inpatient hospital services, even if the patient's care becomes "less intensive during the latter part of the stay."[17] Similarly, hospital days can be included in the three-day count for a patient whose care needs drop to a SNF level, when no SNF bed is available and the physician certifies that continued stay in the hospital is medically necessary.[18]

A stay in a psychiatric hospital qualifies for the three-day test, although CMS cautions that a patient with "only a psychiatric condition . . . is likely to receive only non-covered care" in a SNF.[19]

Frequently, a patient is first treated in a hospital emergency department. Hospitals may keep patients in the emergency department for lengthy periods of time, even after a decision has been made to admit. Sometimes delays occur because hospital personnel have not had time to do the paperwork for admission. If an inpatient admission is logged in by hospital staff after midnight, the admission date is set as the calendar day when the paperwork is actually completed.

An early case held that if the care in the emergency department constitutes one part of a course of treatment that continues after the formalities of admission are completed, time spent by the patient in the emergency department should

---

[15] 42 U.S.C. § 1395x(i).

[16] *Id.;* MBP Manual, Ch. 8: § 20.1, *available at* https://www.cms.gov/Regulations-and-Guidance/Guidance/Manuals/Downloads/bp102c08.pdf (site visited Aug. 6, 2018).

[17] MBP Manual, Ch. 8: § 20.1, *available at* https://www.cms.gov/Regulations-and-Guidance/Guidance/Manuals/Downloads/bp102c08.pdf (site visited Aug. 6, 2018).

[18] MBP Manual, Ch. 8: § 20.1, *available at* https://www.cms.gov/Regulations-and-Guidance/Guidance/Manuals/Downloads/bp102c08.pdf (site visited Aug. 6, 2018).

[19] MBP Manual, Ch. 8: § 20.1, *available at* https://www.cms.gov/Regulations-and-Guidance/Guidance/Manuals/Downloads/bp102c08.pdf (site visited Aug. 6, 2018).

count toward the required three-day hospital stay.[20] This decision was explicitly overruled by a later case.[21]

Another frequent pattern is that patients move from the emergency department to a bed in the acute care hospital, where they receive "observation services," an outpatient benefit under Medicare Part B. Patients may be formally admitted to inpatient status after receiving observation services. CMS does not count time spent in either the emergency department or observation status in determining whether a patient meets the qualifying three-day hospital stay requirement.[22] A nationwide class action challenging CMS's policy of refusing to count *all* time in the hospital toward meeting the qualifying hospital stay requirement when a patient was, at some point, admitted to inpatient status was not successful.[23]

Increasingly, Medicare beneficiaries are never formally admitted to inpatient status in acute care hospitals. They remain, instead, under observation for their entire hospital stay, or for enough of the stay to prevent a qualifying inpatient stay for SNF coverage. Although the Medicare Manuals provide that observation status should "usually" not continue beyond 24 hours or, at most, 48 hours,[24] many beneficiaries are kept on observation status or are otherwise called outpatients for considerably longer periods. Remaining on observation or outpatient status has significant financial consequences for beneficiaries.[25] They must pay for copayments for Part B services, and for some prescription drugs received in the hospital.[26] In addition, they are denied Medicare coverage for their subsequent SNF stay, with no ability to get the matter before the Medicare agency for an initial determination of whether the beneficiary was "admitted" to the hospital for purposes of SNF coverage. A federal district court dismissed litigation, *Bagnall v. Sebelius*,[27] that challenged observation status as violating the Medicare statute, the Administrative Procedures Act, and the Due Process Clause of the Fifth Amendment.[28] In 2015, a court of appeals reversed and remanded on the due

---

[20] Jenkel v. Shalala, 845 F. Supp. 69 (D. Conn. 1994).

[21] Landers v. Leavitt, 545 F.3d 98 (2d Cir. 2008).

[22] MBP Manual, Ch. 8: § 20.1.

[23] *Landers*, 545 F.3d 98.

[24] MBP Manual, Ch. 6: § 20.6, *available at* https://www.cms.gov/Regulations-and-Guidance/Guidance/Manuals/downloads/bp102c06.pdf (site visited Aug. 6, 2018).

[25] Although the primary consequences of observation services have been financial, the quality of hospital care provided to beneficiaries during observation or outpatient status may become an increasing problem as hospitals establish separate observation units.

[26] People with Medicare Part A only (no Part B) may be responsible for the entire cost of an observation status hospitalization.

[27] Bagnall v. Sebelius, No. 3:11cv1703 (MPS), 2013 WL 5346659, (D. Conn. Sept. 23, 2013).

[28] For additional information about observation status, including the aspects of the *Bagnall* decision that are being appealed, *see* CMA, "Outpatient Observation Status," *available at* http://www.medicareadvocacy.org/medicare-info/observation-status/ (site visited Aug. 6, 2018).

process issues appealed by plaintiffs: notice and opportunity for hearing.[29] The case, known as *Barrows v. Burwell* and now, as *Alexander v. Price*, is currently back in district court. On July 31, 2017, the court certified a nationwide class of Medicare beneficiaries who received "observation services" as an outpatient during a hospitalization, and the class is continuing to seek the establishment of an appeal method for patients placed in observation.[30]

Physicians may order observation services for their patients instead of admitting them as inpatients. Often, however, the decision is made by the hospital in an effort to avoid Medicare audits and denials. Since 2004, CMS has authorized hospitals' utilization review committees to retroactively reverse a physician's inpatient admission of his or her patient, although since 2011, the practitioner responsible for the patient's care must agree to the change in the patient's status.[31]

Regulations published in August 2013[32] defining inpatient hospital status according to time-based factors (i.e., a physician who expects that a patient will remain hospitalized for two midnights should admit the patient as an inpatient, under a *presumption* of inpatient care) are intended, in part, to reduce lengthy observation stays. It is important to note that this "two-midnight rule," which directs providers and Medicare contractors, does not change the coverage requirement of *three* consecutive days as an inpatient for SNF coverage. Preamble language for the two-midnight rule suggests that time spent in the emergency department or in outpatient status (including observation status) is relevant for the two-midnight *benchmark* for inpatient care. That is, CMS auditors should not review inpatient admission decisions if the patient was in the hospital at least two midnights, even if both midnights were not inpatient. Enforcement of the two-midnight rule was stayed for many years by CMS[33] and

---

[29] Barrows v. Burwell, 777 F.3d 106 (2d Cir. 2015).

[30] Alexander v. Price, No. 3:11cv1703 (MPS), 2017 WL 3228119, (D. Conn. July 31, 2017).

[31] Under Condition Code 44, an inpatient admission may be changed retroactively to outpatient when (1) the change in status is made while the patient is still in the hospital; (2) the hospital has not submitted a claim to Medicare for inpatient admission; (3) "the practitioner responsible for the care of the patient" and the utilization review committee "concur with the decision;" and (4) the "the concurrence of the practitioner and UR committee is documented in the patient's medical record." Medicare Claims Processing (MCP) Manual, CMS Pub. 100-04, Ch. 1, § 50.3, originally issued as Inpatient Admission Changed to Outpatient, Transmittal 299 (Sept. 10, 2004), revised by Transmittal 2296 (Sept. 2, 2011) and Transmittal 2386 (Jan. 13, 2012). In 2004, Condition Code 44 allowed a patient's status to be changed from inpatient to outpatient if "a physician," not necessarily the practitioner responsible for the patient's care, agreed to the change.

[32] 78 Fed. Reg. 50,495, 50,938–954 (especially 50,944–949) (Aug. 19, 2013).

[33] Centers for Medicare & Medicaid Services (CMS), Frequently Asked Questions: 2 Midnight Inpatient Admission Guidance & Patient Status Reviews for Admissions on or After October 1, 2013, *available at* https://www.cms.gov/Research-Statistics-Data-and-Systems/Monitoring-Programs/Medical-Review/Downloads/QAsforWebsitePosting_110413-v2-CLEAN.pdf (site visited Aug. 6, 2018); CMS, "Selecting Hospital Claims for Patient Status Reviews: Admissions on or After October 1, 2013, *available at* https://www.cms.gov/Research-Statistics-Data-and-Systems/Monitor

by Congress,[34] but the rule is now fully in effect.[35] Effective January 1, 2016, a minor modification to the two-midnight rule allows physicians to order an inpatient stay for a patient whose expected length of stay is less than two midnights.[36]

Until 2016, CMS required hospitals to inform patients of their outpatient status only if the hospitals' utilization review committee reversed the patient's status from inpatient to outpatient under Condition Code 44. However, the Notice of Observation Treatment and Implication for Care Eligibility Act (NOTICE Act) of 2015 requires all hospitals to notify all Medicare patients of their receipt of "observation services as an outpatient" if they have received those services for more than 24 hours.[37] CMS mandates use of a notice called the Medicare Outpatient Observation Notice (MOON).[38] Although final regulations implementing the NOTICE Act become effective October 1, 2016,[39] full implementation of the Act did not occur until March 8, 2017, when CMS required hospitals to begin using the MOON. CMS also amended the Medicare regulations to state explicitly that patients cannot appeal the MOON.[40]

Medicare Advantage (MA) plans may provide SNF coverage without a prior three-day hospital stay,[41] but they are not required to do so.[42] Most do, but some MA plans charge copayments earlier in a patient's stay. Some Medicare Accountable Care Organizations (ACOs), whose patients remain in traditional Medicare, have also been allowed to waive the prior three-day hospital stay requirement.

---

ing-Programs/Medical-Review/Downloads/SelectingHospitalClaimsforAdmissionsonorafterOctober1st2013forReviewForWebPostingCLEAN.pdf (site visited Aug. 6, 2018); CMS, "Inpatient Hospital Reviews," *available at* https://www.cms.gov/Research-Statistics-Data-and-Systems/Monitoring-Programs/Medicare-FFS-Compliance-Programs/Medical-Review/InpatientHospitalReviews.html (sites visited Aug. 6, 2018).

[34] 42 U.S.C. § 1395ddd note, extending moratorium through March 31, 2015 (added by § 111 of the Protecting Access to Medicare Act of 2014, Pub. L. No. 113-93); 42 U.S.C. § 1395ddd note (as amended), extending moratorium through September 30, 2015 (added by § 521 of the Medicare Access and CHIP Reauthorization Act of 2015, Pub. L. No. 114-10.

[35] 80 Fed. Reg. 70,298, 70538-70549 (Nov. 13, 2015).

[36] 42 C.F.R. § 412.3(d)(3), 80 Fed. Reg. 70,297, 70,538–70,549 (Nov. 13, 2015).

[37] 42 U.S.C. § 1395cc(a)(1)(Y); MCP Manual, Ch. 30: § 400, *available at* https://www.cms.gov/Regulations-and-Guidance/Guidance/Manuals/Downloads/clm104c30.pdf (site visited Aug. 6, 2018).

[38] For an example of a MOON notice (accessible in a zip file), *see* CMS, "Beneficiary Notices Initiative (BNI)," *available at* https://www.cms.gov/Medicare/Medicare-General-Information/BNI/ (site visited Aug. 6, 2018).

[39] 81 Fed. Reg. 56,761 (Aug. 22, 2016),

[40] 42 C.F.R. § 405.926(u); 81 Fed. Reg. 56,761, 57,267 (Aug. 22, 2016).

[41] 42 C.F.R. § 422.101(c).

[42] Rapport v. Leavitt, 564 F. Supp. 2d 186 (W.D.N.Y. 2008).

[C] Thirty-Day Test

Part A coverage requires that a patient be admitted to the SNF within 30 days of discharge from the hospital, not counting the day of discharge.[43] The regulations and Medicare Benefit Policy (MBP) Manual recognize limited exceptions to the 30-day rule. If it is not "medically appropriate" to begin the post-hospital SNF care within the 30-day period and if it is "medically predictable" at the time of discharge from the hospital that the patient will need covered care in a "predeterminable time period," treatment may begin at a later date when it is medically appropriate to begin an active course of treatment or therapy.[44] For example, a patient recovering from a hip fracture will require skilled therapy services. However, the patient may be non-weight-bearing during the 30-day period after discharge from the hospital. In this case, it may not be appropriate to begin therapy until the fracture has had time to heal and the patient achieves a weight-bearing status. The MBP Manual recognizes four to six weeks after hospital discharge as an appropriate and predictable time to begin therapy for a hip fracture. Accordingly, admission to the SNF four to six weeks after discharge from the hospital could be considered timely.[45]

Even if the patient with a hip fracture goes to a SNF, leaves after two days, and returns five weeks later for predictable rehabilitative care, both SNF stays are covered by Medicare.[46] Similarly, a patient who is immediately admitted to a SNF following discharge from a hospital and receives *non-covered care* will get Medicare coverage at a later time if it was "medically predictable that covered SNF care would be required at a predeterminable time interval."[47] The example in the MBP Manual is a patient whose leg is amputated and who, after the stump is healed, requires daily skilled rehabilitative services to learn how to use a prosthesis.[48] The MBP Manual further recognizes that if "complications" prevent initiation of deferred care—for example, the amputee's stump becomes infected—the SNF stay may be covered "even though care is not started within the usual anticipated time frame."[49]

In the "infrequent" situation where a patient goes home following a hospital stay and needs SNF care more than 60 days later, Medicare covers the SNF stay in a new benefit period so long as the need for SNF care was predictable at the time of the hospital discharge.[50]

---

[43] 42 U.S.C. § 1395x(i).

[44] 42 C.F.R. § 409.30(b)(2); MBP Manual, Ch. 8: § 20.2.2.

[45] MBP Manual, Ch. 8: § 20.2.2.1, *available at* https://www.cms.gov/Regulations-and-Guidance/Guidance/Manuals/downloads/bp102c08.pdf (site visited Aug. 6, 2018).

[46] MBP Manual, Ch. 8: § 20.2.2.3, Example 1.

[47] MBP Manual, Ch. 8: § 20.2.2.3, Example 3.

[48] MBP Manual, Ch. 8: § 20.2.2.3, Example 3.

[49] MBP Manual, Ch. 8: § 20.2.2.4.

[50] MBP Manual, Ch. 8: § 20.2.2.5.

However, if a patient's medical needs are *not* predictable at the time of discharge from the hospital, admission to a SNF after 30 days will *not* fall within the exception to the 30-day rule.[51] The MBP Manual's example is a patient who receives covered care for three weeks but, six weeks later, experiences an unexpected change in condition and again requires skilled care. The patient's second need for skilled care is not covered by Medicare.[52]

The 30-day transfer requirement is also considered met if a patient receiving covered SNF care "leaves a SNF and is readmitted to the same or any other participating SNF for further covered care within 30 days of the last covered skilled day."[53] The brief interruption of covered care does not require rehospitalization before Medicare will cover the SNF care. Similarly, a patient whose SNF stay is covered on admission but who subsequently does not require skilled care may resume Medicare coverage as long as the break in covered care does not exceed 30 days.[54] Language added to the MBP Manual in 2015 confirms that coverage under Part A may be resumed "if the beneficiary remains in the SNF to receive custodial care following a covered stay, and subsequently develops a renewed need for covered care there within 30 consecutive days."[55]

[D] Skilled Level-of-Care Requirement

Once a patient has established a qualifying hospital stay, Medicare payment for post-hospital extended care services will be available only when:

> such services are or were required to be given because the individual needs or needed on a daily basis skilled nursing care (provided directly by or requiring the supervision of skilled nursing personnel) or other skilled rehabilitation services, which as a practical matter can only be provided in a skilled nursing facility on an inpatient basis, for any of the conditions with respect to which he was receiving inpatient hospital services . . . prior to transfer to the skilled nursing facility. . . .[56]

The statute requires that (1) the patient needs skilled nursing services or skilled rehabilitation services, which must be performed by or under the supervision of professional or technical personnel and ordered by a physician; (2) the patient needs the services on a daily basis; (3) services can be provided, as a practical

[51] MBP Manual, Ch. 8, § 20.2.2.2.

[52] MBP Manual, Ch. 8: § 20.2.2.3, Example 2.

[53] MBP Manual, Ch. 8: § 20.2.3.

[54] MBP Manual, Ch. 8: § 20.2.

[55] MBP Manual, Ch. 8, § 20.2.3.

[56] 42 U.S.C. § 1395f(a)(2)(B).

matter, only on an inpatient basis in a SNF; and (4) services are reasonable and necessary. Analysis begins with whether the patient needs skilled care.[57]

A patient admitted directly to a SNF after an inpatient hospital stay of three or more days is presumed to meet the level of care for SNF coverage for the first five days if he or she is assigned to one of the upper 52 Resource Utilization Groups (RUG-IV) identified under Medicare's prospective payment system (PPS) for SNFs.[58] A patient assigned to one of the lower 14 RUG-IV categories may receive Medicare-covered care; for such a patient, an individual level of care determination must be made "using existing administrative criteria and procedures."[59] The presumption of coverage for the SNF stay does *not* apply if the patient is discharged from the hospital to another setting and then, within 30 days from the hospital discharge, goes to the SNF.[60] The presumption of coverage applies to a patient who is rehospitalized and returns directly to the SNF for care, although a new Medicare five-day assessment is required.[61]

A patient must receive *skilled*, as opposed to *custodial*, care. Medicare will not reimburse any expenses when the level of care is only custodial.[62] However, custodial services are often provided in addition to skilled care. The key is that the patient must require and receive skilled care, not just custodial care, on a daily basis. If skilled services are provided frequently, but not on a daily basis, Medicare coverage for the stay under Part A will not be available.

[1] Skilled Nursing or Rehabilitation Services

The regulations state that the patient must require skilled nursing or rehabilitation services that are ordered by the attending physician.[63] The skilled services must be provided on a daily basis by, or furnished under the supervision of, skilled personnel.[64] Skilled services may be provided directly by the therapist or under the "general supervision" of the skilled personnel. "'General supervision' requires initial direction and periodic inspection of the actual activity," but "the supervisor need not always be physically present or on the premises when the assistant is performing the services."[65] In addition, the skilled services must be

---

[57] MBP Manual, Ch. 8: § 30.

[58] MBP Manual, Ch. 8: § 30.1.

[59] MBP Manual, Ch. 8: § 30; CMS, Prospective Payment System and Consolidated Billing for Skilled Nursing Facilities (SNF) Final Rule for FY 2019, SNF Value-Based Purchasing Program, and SNF Quality Reporting Program, 83 Fed Reg. 39162, 39179 (Aug. 8, 2018), *available at* https://www.gpo.gov/fdsys/pkg/FR-2018-08-08/pdf/2018-16570.pdf (site visited Aug. 10, 2018).

[60] MBP Manual, Ch. 8: § 30.1, scenario 2.

[61] MBP Manual, Ch. 8: § 30.1 scenario 3.

[62] 42 U.S.C. § 1395y(a)(9).

[63] 42 C.F.R. § 409.31(a)(1).

[64] 42 C.F.R. § 409.31(a)(3) and (b); MBP Manual, Ch. 8: § 30.2.1.

[65] MBP Manual, Ch. 8: § 30.2.1, NOTE.

related to a condition for which the patient received inpatient hospital care or that arose at the SNF while the patient was being treated for such a condition.[66]

The inherent complexity of a service must be evaluated in the context of the patient's need for safe and effective service delivery.[67] Special medical complications may substantiate the need for skilled services that are not ordinarily required.[68] For example, while a qualified physical therapist is not usually required to give whirlpool baths, professional therapy services may be needed for a beneficiary whose condition "is complicated by circulatory deficiency, areas of desensitization, or open wounds."[69] Similarly, skilled management of unskilled services may justify the need for Medicare-covered care.[70] When rehabilitation services are the primary services supporting Medicare coverage, "the key issue is whether the skills of a therapist are needed," not whether the patient has "potential for recovery."[71]

Language added to the MBP Manual in 2014 stresses the importance of thorough and timely documentation of treatment goals and the need for skilled services.[72]

The regulations contain examples of skilled nursing and rehabilitation services.[73] Some of the examples constitute skilled nursing care only if the services of a skilled or professional person are required. Other examples automatically constitute covered skilled nursing services. Skilled rehabilitation services are separately described.

Skilled *nursing* services may include the following activities when the skills of a technical or professional person are needed:[74]

- **Overall management and evaluation of care plan.**[75] Managing and evaluating a care plan constitutes skilled nursing services when skilled nursing personnel are required "to meet the patient's [] needs, promote recovery, and ensure medical safety."[76] Medicare coverage is available for management and evaluation of a care plan "only when, in light of the

---

66 42 U.S.C. §§ 1395f(a)(2)(B) and 1395x(i); 42 C.F.R. §§ 409.31(b)(2)(i)–(ii) and 424.20.

67 42 C.F.R. § 409.32(a).

68 42 C.F.R. § 409.32(b).

69 MBP Manual, Ch. 8: § 30.2.2, Example 2.

70 MBP Manual, Ch. 8: § 30.2.2, Example 3 (describing resident with multiple physical impairments "who is unable to communicate and make her needs known").

71 MBP Manual, Ch. 8: § 30.2.2, Example 1.

72 MBP Manual, Ch. 8: § 30.2.2.1.

73 42 C.F.R. § 409.33. *See also* MBP Manual, Ch. 8: § 30.2.3.

74 42 C.F.R. § 409.33(a). *See also* MBP Manual, Ch. 8: § 30.2.3.

75 42 C.F.R. § 409.33(a)(1); MBP Manual, Ch. 8: § 30.2.3.1.

76 42 C.F.R. § 409.33(a)(1)(i); MBP Manual, Ch. 8: § 30.2.3.1, *available at* https://www.cms.gov/Regulations-and-Guidance/Guidance/Manuals/downloads/bp102c08.pdf (site visited Sept. 22, 2018).

patient's condition, the aggregate of those services requires the involvement of technical or professional personnel."[77] Nonskilled services may require skilled management "when the condition of the beneficiary is such that there is an expectation that a change in condition is likely without that intervention."[78] The regulation's sole example and the MBP Manual's first example find skilled personnel are necessary, based on the patient's condition, age, and immobility, which together create "a high potential for serious complications."[79] The second MBP Manual example also supports a finding of skilled oversight based on the patient's immobility, confusion, and chest congestion, which create "high probability of relapse."[80] If the patient's record "clearly establishes that there was a likely potential for serious complications without skilled management," the Medicare contractor will assume that skilled care was provided even when the patient's clinical record does not "specifically identify 'skilled planning and management activities' as such."[81]

- **Observation and assessment of the patient's changing condition** if treatment may need to be modified, new medical procedures may need to be initiated, or the patient's condition needs to be stabilized.[82] The regulations provide the example of a patient with congestive heart failure who requires close nursing observation "to detect signs of decompensation, abnormal fluid balance, or adverse effects from medications."[83] A patient with acute psychological symptoms in addition to physical problems, such as depression, anxiety, or agitation, may require skilled nursing care to ensure their safety or the safety of others.[84] The examples in the regulations and MBP Manual illustrate the fact-specific nature of the

[77] 42 C.F.R. § 409.33(a)(1).

[78] MBP Manual, Ch. 8: § 30.2.3.1, *available at* https://www.cms.gov/Regulations-and-Guidance/Guidance/Manuals/downloads/bp102c08.pdf (site visited Sept. 22, 2018).

[79] 42 C.F.R. § 409.33(a)(1)(ii); MBP Manual, Ch. 8: § 30.2.3.1 (Example 1), *available at* https://www.cms.gov/Regulations-and-Guidance/Guidance/Manuals/downloads/bp102c08.pdf (site visited Sept. 22, 2018).

[80] MBP Manual, Ch. 8: § 30.2.3.1 (Example 2), *available at* https://www.cms.gov/Regulations-and-Guidance/Guidance/Manuals/downloads/bp102c08.pdf (site visited Sept. 22, 2018).

[81] MBP Manual, Ch. 8: § 30.2.3.1, *available at* https://www.cms.gov/Regulations-and-Guidance/Guidance/Manuals/downloads/bp102c08.pdf (site visited Sept. 22, 2018).

[82] 42 C.F.R. § 409.33(a)(2); MBP Manual, Ch. 8: § 30.2.3.2, *available at* https://www.cms.gov/Regulations-and-Guidance/Guidance/Manuals/downloads/bp102c08.pdf (site visited Sept. 22, 2018).

[83] 42 C.F.R. § 409.33(a)(2)(ii).

[84] 42 C.F.R. § 409.33(a)(2)(ii); MBP Manual, Ch. 8: § 30.2.3.2, *available at* https://www.cms.gov/Regulations-and-Guidance/Guidance/Manuals/downloads/bp102c08.pdf (site visited Sept. 22, 2018).

inquiry.[85] Skilled observation is appropriate if there is a "reasonable probability" of a potential complication or further acute episode, even if the complication or acute episode never develops.[86]

- **Patient education services** to train and teach patients "self-maintenance" and "how to manage their treatment regimen."[87] The regulations provide two examples: a patient with a recent leg amputation who needs skilled personnel to provide gait training and to teach care of the prosthesis and a newly-diagnosed diabetic patient who needs skilled personnel to teach self-administration of insulin and foot-care precautions.[88] Additional examples in the MBP Manual include teaching patients to self-administer medications, insulin injections, or medical gases; to care for a prosthesis, colostomy, or ileostomy; to perform self-catheterization; to self-administer gastrostomy feedings; to use and care for braces, splints, and orthotics and associated skin care; and to care for specialized dressings or skin treatments.[89]

The MBP Manual describes as "questionable situations" those involving patients whose primary need is oral medication or who are "capable of independent ambulation, dressing, feeding, and hygiene."[90]

The regulations provide that the restoration potential of a patient is not the controlling factor in determining whether skilled care is necessary.[91] The maintenance standard of coverage is confirmed by *Jimmo v. Sebelius*.[92] Skilled

[85] 42 C.F.R. § 409.33(1)(2)(ii); MBP Manual, Ch. 8, § 30.2.3.2, *available at* https://www.cms.gov/Regulations-and-Guidance/Guidance/Manuals/downloads/bp102c08.pdf (site visited Sept. 22, 2018).

[86] MBP Manual, Ch. 8: § 30.2.3.2.

[87] 42 C.F.R. § 409.33(a)(3); MBP Manual, Ch. 8: § 30.2.3.3.

[88] 42 C.F.R. § 409.33(a)(3)(ii).

[89] MBP Manual, Ch. 8: § 30.2.3.3.

[90] MBP Manual, Ch. 8: § 30.2.4.

[91] 42 C.F.R. § 409.32(c) ("The restoration potential of a patient is not the deciding factor in determining whether skilled services are needed."); MBP Manual, Ch. 8: § 30.2.2, Example 1 ("When rehabilitation services are the primary services, . . . [t]he deciding factor is not the patient's potential for recovery, but whether the services needed require the skills of a therapist or whether they can be provided by nonskilled personnel."); MBP Manual, Ch. 8: § 30.4 ("Coverage for such skilled therapy services does not turn on the presence or absence of a beneficiary's potential for improvement from therapy services, but rather on the beneficiary's need for skilled care. Therapy services are considered skilled when they are so inherently complex that they can be safely and effectively performed only by, or under the supervision of, a qualified therapist."); Papciak v. Sebelius, 742 F. Supp. 2d 765 (W.D. Pa. 2010) (The Secretary failed to apply the correct legal standard when she considered only the patient's restoration potential, not whether the patient needed SNF care to maintain her level of functioning following hip replacement surgery.).

[92] Civil Action No. 5:11-CV-17-CR (D. Vt. Jan. 24, 2013). *See* CMA, *Jimmo* Settlement Agreement, *available at* http://www.medicareadvocacy.org/wp-content/uploads/2012/12/Jimmo-Settlement-Agreement-00011764.pdf (site visited Aug. 6, 2018). *See also* CMS, *Jimmo v. Sebelius*

care may be necessary to preserve the patient's current status or to slow or prevent further decline or deterioration of the patient's medical condition.[93] Similarly, physical therapy to maintain the patient's present level of functioning may be a covered service when the skills and knowledge of a therapist are needed.[94]

Language added to the MBP Manual in 2014 as a result of *Jimmo* stresses that maintenance nursing services are covered by Medicare.

> Skilled nursing services would be covered where such skilled nursing services are necessary to maintain the patient's current condition or prevent or slow further deterioration so long as the beneficiary requires skilled care for the services to be safely and effectively provided, and all other requirements for coverage under the SNF benefit are met.[95]

The MBP Manual firmly ends the myth of improvement as the sole basis for Medicare coverage: "Coverage does not turn on the presence or absence of an individual's potential for improvement from nursing care, but rather on the beneficiary's need for skilled care."[96]

If a patient is receiving one or more of the following skilled nursing services on a daily basis, the requirement for receiving daily skilled care is met per se:[97]

- "Intravenous/intramuscular injections and intravenous feeding."
- "Enteral feeding that comprises at least 26 percent of daily calorie requirements and provides at least 501 milliliters of fluid per day."
- "Naso-pharyngeal and tracheostomy aspiration."
- "Insertion, sterile irrigation, and replacement of suprapubic catheters."
- "Application of dressings involving prescription medications and aseptic techniques."
- "Treatment of extensive decubitus ulcers" (the MBP Manual says stage 3 or worse) or "other widespread skin disorders."
- "Heat treatments which have been specifically ordered by a physician as part of active treatment and which require observation by skilled nursing personnel to evaluate the patient's progress adequately."

Settlement Agreement: Program Manual Clarifications Fact Sheet, https://www.cms.gov/medicare/medicare-fee-for-service-payment/snfpps/downloads/jimmo_fact_sheet2_022014_final.pdf (site visited Aug. 6, 2018). *See* **Appendix 1-9**.

[93] 42 C.F.R. § 409.32(c).

[94] 42 C.F.R. § 409.33(c)(5) (describing when maintenance therapy qualifies as skilled rehabilitation services).

[95] MBP Manual, Ch. 8: § 30.3.

[96] *Id.*

[97] 42 C.F.R. § 409.33(b). MBP Manual, Ch. 8: § 30.3.

- "Rehabilitation nursing procedures, including the related teaching and adaptive aspects of nursing, that are part of active treatment and require the presence of skilled nursing personnel; e.g., the institution and supervision of bowel and bladder training programs."
- "Initial phases of a regimen involving administration of medical gases."
- "Care of a colostomy during the early post-operative period in the presence of associated complications," which is added by the MBP Manual (justification and documentation in the medical record are required).[98]

Language added to the MBP Manual as a result of *Jimmo* also confirms that maintenance therapy services are covered by Medicare: "Coverage for such skilled therapy services does not turn on the presence or absence of a beneficiary's potential for improvement from therapy services, but rather on the beneficiary's need for skilled care."[99] Skilled therapy services are covered if they are necessary "to improve the patient's current condition, to maintain the patient's current condition, or to prevent or slow further deterioration of the patient's condition."[100]

Skilled physical therapy services must be related to "an active written treatment plan" and must require "the judgment, knowledge, and skills of a qualified physical therapist."[101] The services must be needed either to improve or to establish or perform "a safe and effective maintenance program."[102] The services must also be considered specific and effective treatment for the patient's condition under accepted standards of medical practice, as well as reasonable and necessary for the treatment of the patient's condition.[103] The MBP Manual cautions that many SNF patients require services that may be provided by supportive personnel, without the supervision of a physical therapist, and that these services are not covered by Medicare as skilled physical therapy.[104]

The regulations identify services that qualify as skilled rehabilitation services,[105] with elaboration provided in the MBP Manual:[106]

- "Ongoing assessment of a patient's rehabilitation needs and potential."
- "Therapeutic exercises" that require skilled personnel "due either to the type of exercise employed or to the condition of the patient."

---

[98] MBP Manual, Ch. 8, § 30.3.

[99] MBP Manual, Ch. 8: § 30.4.

[100] MBP Manual, Ch. 8: § 30.4.

[101] MBP Manual, Ch. 8: § 30.4.1.1.

[102] *Id.*

[103] *Id.*

[104] *Id.*

[105] 42 C.F.R. § 409.33(c)(1)–(7).

[106] MBP Manual, Ch. 8: § 30.4.1.2.A-G.

- "Gait evaluation and training furnished to a patient whose ability to walk has been impaired by neurological, muscular, or skeletal abnormality." The MBP Manual elaborates that while gait evaluation and training by a therapist is skilled physical therapy, activities of an aide ("repetitious exercises to improve gait, or to maintain strength and endurance, and assistive walking") are not.
- "Range of motion exercises." The MBP Manual elaborates that range of motion *tests* are skilled physical therapy; range of motion *exercises* generally are not, unless specific circumstances make them skilled for a particular patient. Passive range of motion is not skilled physical therapy.
- "Maintenance therapy" when the services "are so inherently complex that they can be safely and effectively performed only by, or under the supervision of, a qualified therapist." The MBP Manual says, "a maintenance program to maintain the patient's current condition or to prevent or slow further deterioration is covered so long as the beneficiary requires skilled care for the safe and effective performance of the program." It further provides, "If the specialized knowledge and judgment of a qualified therapist are required," the design of the maintenance program, instruction of the patient or appropriate caregiver, and "necessary periodic reevaluations" of the patient and the program are all considered skilled therapy services. As an example of covered maintenance therapy, the MBP Manual describes determining the exercises required to maintain the present level of function for a patient with Parkinson's disease, including conducting an initial evaluation, designing a maintenance program, and instructing the patient or supportive personnel to carry out the maintenance program.
- Ultrasound, shortwave, and microwave diathermy treatments.
- "Hot packs, hydrocollator, infra-red treatments, paraffin baths, and whirlpool baths." The MBP Manual explains that although these treatments do not ordinarily require skilled therapists, skilled therapy services may be necessary "where the patient's condition is complicated by circulatory deficiency, areas of desensitization, open wounds, fractures, or other complications."
- Speech pathologist or audiologist services.[107] The MBP Manual defines speech-language pathology and occupational therapy by reference to Inpatient Hospital Services, Chapter 1 of the MBP Manual.[108]

[107] 42 C.F.R. § 409.33(c); MBP Manual, Ch. 8: § 30.4.2.

[108] MBP Manual, Ch. 8: §§ 30.4.2 and 30.4.3, respectively.

Except in certain circumstances,[109] personal care services do not qualify as skilled services:[110]

- "Administration of routine oral medication, eye drops and ointments." The MBP Manual confirms that these are not skilled services, even if the patient is unable to self-administer these medications or state law requires a nurse to dispense them.
- "General maintenance care of colostomy and ileostomy."
- "Routine services to maintain satisfactory functioning of indwelling bladder catheters."
- "Changes of dressing for uninfected post-operative or chronic conditions."
- "Prophylactic and palliative skin care, including bathing and application of creams, or treatment of minor skin problems."
- Routine incontinence care.
- General maintenance of a plaster cast. The MBP Manual notes that a patient with a preexisting skin or circulatory condition, or who needs adjustment of traction, may require skilled services.
- Routine care of braces and similar devices.
- "Use of heat as a palliative and comfort measure" (e.g., whirlpool or hydrocollator).
- "Routine administration of medical gases after a regimen of therapy has been established."
- "Assistance in dressing, eating, and going to the toilet."
- "Periodic turning and positioning in bed."
- "General supervision of exercises," including carrying out of repetitious exercises in a maintenance program.[111]

[2] Daily Skilled Services

To meet the definition of *daily*, skilled nursing care, or a combination of skilled nursing services and rehabilitation services, must be provided seven days

[109] 42 C.F.R. § 409.32(b) (exceptions allowing services usually viewed as nonskilled to be considered skilled); MBP Manual, Ch. 8: § 30.5.

[110] 42 C.F.R. § 409.33(d)(1)–(13); MBP Manual, Ch. 8: § 30.5.

[111] MBP Manual, Ch. 8: § 30.5.

per week.[112] Skilled rehabilitation services provided five days per week satisfy the daily requirement.[113] The MBP Manual advises that there must be "a valid medical reason" for scheduling therapies on different days and that "arbitrarily staggering the timing of various therapy modalities through the week" to achieve five days of therapy would not qualify a beneficiary for Medicare coverage.[114]

The MBP Manual cautions against applying the "daily" requirement too "strictly," recognizing that the requirement may be met even when therapy is suspended in an "isolated break" for a day or two (e.g., due to a resident's extreme fatigue).[115]

A temporary absence to attend "a special religious service, holiday meal, family occasion, going on a car ride, or for a trial visit home" is not by itself evidence that a beneficiary does not need skilled care.[116] The MBP Manual cautions facilities against taking a "conservative approach" and notifying patients "that leaving the facility will result in denial of coverage."[117] "Frequent or prolonged" absences, however, may suggest that the beneficiary's care needs can be met outside a SNF.[118]

The Medicare Claims Processing (MCP) Manual does not permit SNFs to bill the Medicare program or the beneficiary for care during a beneficiary's brief leave of absence "where the patient is absent, but not discharged, for reasons other than admission to a hospital, other SNF, or distinct part of the same SNF."[119] There is an exception, however. A provision of the MCP Manual authorizes SNFs to bill beneficiaries for bed-hold during a temporary "SNF absence" if the SNF informs patients in advance of both their option to make bed-hold payments and the amount of the charge and if the patients "affirmatively elect" to make bed-hold payments prior to being charged.[120]

[3] "Practical Matter" Test

Even if daily skilled services are medically necessary, Medicare coverage may still be denied unless the services, "as a 'practical matter,' can only be provided in a SNF on an inpatient basis."[121] Whether the "practical matter" test is

---

[112] 42 C.F.R. §§ 409.30 (basic requirements), 409.31 (skilled level of care requirement), and 409.34 (definition of "daily").

[113] 42 C.F.R. § 409.34(a)(2); MBP Manual, Ch. 8: § 30.6.

[114] MBP Manual, Ch. 8: § 30.6.

[115] *Id.*

[116] MBP Manual, Ch. 8: § 30.7.3.

[117] MBP Manual, Ch. 8: § 30.7.3

[118] MBP Manual, Ch. 8: § 30.7.3

[119] MCP Manual, Ch. 6: § 40.3.5.2, *available at* http://www.cms.gov/Regulations-and-Guidance/Guidance/Manuals/Downloads/clm104c06.pdf (site visited Sept. 22, 2018).

[120] MCP Manual, Ch. 1: § 30.1.1.1.

[121] 42 C.F.R. § 409.31(b)(3). *See also* 42 C.F.R. § 409.35; MBP Manual, Ch. 8: § 30.7.

met depends on consideration of "the availability and feasibility of using more economical alternative facilities or services'" specifically, whether more economical services are *actually available* to *this* beneficiary.[122]

If the daily skilled services are not available on an outpatient basis where the patient lives, the "practical matter" test is satisfied and inpatient care in a SNF is covered. However, in evaluating the availability of alternative care, the issue is the feasibility of the alternative care, not whether Medicare will pay for it. As a result, if a physical therapist could provide daily physical therapy to a patient, it is not relevant to the "practical matter" determination that the patient exceeded the outpatient therapy cap[123] or does not participate in Medicare Part B.[124]

If transportation to the outpatient services would pose "an excessive physical hardship" to the patient or would be "less economical" or "less efficient or effective" than inpatient services in the SNF, the practical matter test is satisfied.[125] "Less economical" is determined from the perspective of the health care delivery system. If getting services in a hospital outpatient department would require an ambulance ride and providing care in a SNF would be more economical, the "economy and efficiency" test is met. Similarly, "inordinate travel costs" to a patient's isolated residence also satisfy the "economy and efficiency" test.[126]

The patient's medical condition is critical to the "practical matter" determination. If an alternative care setting would "adversely affect a patient's medical condition," care in a SNF is appropriate.[127] The MBP Manual provides the example of "a 75-year old woman who has suffered a cerebrovascular accident and cannot climb stairs safely."[128] If the patient lives alone in a second-floor apartment, which is accessible only by climbing a flight of stairs, she is eligible for SNF care, even when the physical and occupational therapy she needs is available one mile from her apartment.[129] The MBP Manual concludes, "because of her inability to negotiate the stairs, the daily skilled services she requires cannot, as a practical matter, be provided to the patient outside the SNF."[130]

Goodrich v. Bowen[131] involved Medicare coverage of daily insulin injections for 17 SNF patients. The court appropriately noted that the administration

---

[122] 42 C.F.R. § 409.35(a).

[123] The therapy cap repealed by the Bipartisan Budget Act of 2018, 42 U.S.C. § 1395 l(g).

[124] MBP Manual, Ch. 8: § 30.7.1.

[125] MBP Manual, Ch. 8: § 30.7.

[126] MBP Manual, Ch. 8: § 30.7.2, Examples 1 and 2, respectively.

[127] MBP Manual, Ch. 8: § 30.7.3.

[128] MBP Manual, Ch. 8: § 30.7.3

[129] MBP Manual, Ch. 8: § 30.7.3

[130] MBP Manual, Ch. 8: § 30.7.3, Example.

[131] 1988 WL 235577 (D. Conn. May 31, 1988); *see also* Hoye v. Sebelius, 778 F. Supp. 2d 145 (D. Mass. Mar. 31, 2011).

of subcutaneous injections, at that time, was presumed to be a skilled nursing service pursuant to the Medicare regulations.[132] *Goodrich* addressed the criteria for establishing "practical matter," discussing the availability and feasibility of using alternative services:

> [T]he "practical matter" criteria [sic] requires an individual assessment of each claimant's overall condition and actual investigation into the availability and feasibility of alternatives to inpatient SNF care. It is not sufficient for the Secretary to look at only one aspect of a claimant's care such as the need for daily insulin injections. The Secretary must assess the need for skilled service along with the other services the claimant requires, both skilled and custodial, and then arrive at a determination of the "practical matter" requirement.[133]

As with the skilled care determination, the patient's total condition is important in assessing the practical matter standard. Here, however, the patient's custodial needs may be as important as the need for skilled care.

Finally, home care is not an alternative to SNF care if the patient does not have sufficient assistance at home from "capable and willing family" or others, such as a home health agency.[134] In assessing the practicalities of providing the needed care at home, rather than in a SNF, relevant questions include whether outpatient or home health care services are actually available, whether the patient has access to such services even if they are available, and whether the patient is able to be maintained at home in order to receive the skilled outpatient or home health care services.

[E] The Benefit Period or "Spell of Illness"

Medicare covers a maximum of 100 days of SNF care during a benefit period, also known as the "spell of illness."[135] A benefit period begins the first day a Medicare beneficiary enters a hospital or SNF and ends when he or she has been receiving less than a skilled level of care, or is not receiving care in a hospital or SNF, for 60 consecutive days. It is theoretically possible for a beneficiary to have more than one benefit period during a calendar year. However, the patient must remain outside a hospital or SNF for 60 consecutive days, or, if remaining

---

[132] 42 C.F.R. § 409.33(b)(1). *But see* 63 Fed. Reg. 26,284 (May 12, 1998) (regarding insulin injections and the skilled care concept).

[133] *See also Hoye*, 778 F. Supp. 2d 145 (remand; burden should be on Secretary "to demonstrate the availability and feasibility of outpatient services, and to engage in the practical matter inquiry"); Mazzella v. Heckler, 1985 WL 77596 (D. Conn. Aug. 18, 1985).

[134] MBP Manual, Ch. 8: §§ 30.7, 30.7.1.

[135] 42 U.S.C. §§ 1395d(a)(2)(A) and 1395x(a); 42 C.F.R. § 409.60; *see* Matthews v. Leavitt, 452 F.3d 145 (2d Cir. 2006); Mayburg v. Secretary of HHS, 740 F.2d 100 (1st Cir. 1984); Levi v. Heckler, 736 F.2d 848 (2d Cir. 1984).

in a nursing facility, must receive less than a SNF level of care for 60 consecutive days, in order to end a benefit period and be eligible to begin a new one.[136]

> ■ **EXAMPLE:** Mrs. Jones is admitted to the hospital and, after a four-day inpatient stay, is transferred to the SNF on March 25. Medicare coverage is granted for 100 days, through July 3. Mrs. Jones remains in the SNF through August 28 but does not receive either daily skilled nursing or rehabilitation services. She is then readmitted to the hospital. Following discharge from the hospital, she is readmitted to the SNF.
>
> Mrs. Jones will not be entitled to Medicare coverage for her second SNF admission because she did not have a "break" in her benefit period and has already received 100 days of coverage during this benefit period. (She did not receive daily skilled care in a hospital or SNF for only 58 days, from July 3 to August 28, rather than for the required 60 days.) Mrs. Jones would have to receive a custodial level of care in the SNF for 60 consecutive days and then require inpatient hospital care for at least three days in order to qualify for Medicare SNF coverage under a new benefit period.

[F] Care in a SNF Must Be Related to Condition for Which the Patient Was Hospitalized

To meet Medicare's level of care requirements, a patient must receive services for either a condition for which the patient received inpatient hospital services or a condition that arose while the patient was receiving care in a SNF for a condition for which the patient received inpatient hospital services.[137] In other words, there must be some connection between the patient's condition during the qualifying hospital stay and subsequent SNF admission. A problem that occasionally arises is establishing that the SNF patient is receiving skilled care that is related to the patient's prior hospitalization. The problem most often encountered is a fact-finder's requiring that a SNF patient receive exactly the same services for exactly the same condition as provided in the hospital. Such an interpretation of the law is inappropriate and should be challenged.

In *Sowell v. Richardson*,[138] the court found that hospitalization was due to the patient's general physical condition. In *Hayner v. Weinberger*,[139] the patient's underlying condition was related to the condition subsequently treated at the SNF.

---

[136] 42 C.F.R. § 409.60(b); Medicare General Information, Eligibility, and Entitlement (MGIEE) Manual, CMS Pub. 100-01, Ch. 3: §§ 10.4.3.2 and 10.4.4, *available at* http://www.cms.gov/Regulations-and-Guidance/Guidance/Manuals/Downloads/ge101c03.pdf (site visited Sept. 22, 2018).

[137] 42 U.S.C. § 1395f(a)(2)(B); 42 C.F.R. § 409.31(b)(2)(i)–(ii); MBP Manual, Ch. 8: § 20.1 (New language added in 2013 provides: "In this context, the applicable hospital condition need not have been the principal diagnosis that actually precipitated the beneficiary's admission to the hospital, but could be any one of the conditions present during the qualifying hospital stay.").

[138] 319 F. Supp. 689, 692 (D.S.C. 1970).

[139] 382 F. Supp. 762, 765 (E.D.N.Y. 1974).

Both courts found the patients eligible for Medicare coverage. In *Shepack v. Bowen*,[140] the court noted, "it is critical to ascertain the interrelationship between a claimant's various illnesses in order to determine if the condition for which a claimant received skilled nursing services in a SNF was a condition for which he or she received inpatient hospital services."[141] The court remanded the case to the Administrative Law Judge (ALJ) to obtain further medical documentation. Upon rehearing, the ALJ found the services received at the SNF were for a condition previously treated at the hospital.

A district court liberally construed 42 C.F.R. § 409.31(b)(2) in *Stefanko v. Secretary of HHS*.[142] The patient was treated in the hospital for a primary condition of a fractured knee and secondary conditions of congestive heart failure, diabetes, and kidney failure. The court found that treatment in the SNF of the surgical wound and insulin injections constituted skilled care for conditions that were treated in the hospital.

As a practical matter, it is useful to collect documentation to establish that the SNF stay was for a condition treated or diagnosed, or both, in the hospital. It is important to document all the conditions treated during the hospitalization. Treatment may consist of monitoring a cardiac or pulmonary condition. A person with diabetes experiencing unstable blood sugar levels while in the hospital may require careful monitoring. The patient may be generally weak or may present complexities due to multiple conditions that require skilled management.

§ 3.04 SNF PROSPECTIVE PAYMENT SYSTEM

[A] Prospective Payment System Mandated as of July 1, 1998

The Balanced Budget Act of 1997 mandated a prospective payment system (PPS) for the Medicare SNF benefit.[143] The per diem rates cover all routine service, ancillary, and capital-related costs for Part A-covered stays.

The PPS uses case-mix adjustments to relate payments to resident needs. The system accounts for the relative resource use of different types of patients, based on acuity, as determined by a patient classification system now called Resource Utilization Groups-IV (RUG-IV). Each Medicare-coverable patient is placed into one of ten major classifications and then into one of 66 groups. Originally and until January 1, 2006, the SNF PPS used seven major classifications and

---

[140] No. N-85-157 (JAC) (D. Conn. Mar. 16, 1987).

[141] *Shepack*, No. N-85-157 (JAC), slip. op. at 11.

[142] 1990 U.S. Dist. LEXIS 21041 (D. Conn. Mar. 27, 1990).

[143] The Balanced Budget Act of 1997 (BBA '97), Pub. L. No. 105-33 (Aug. 5, 1997), § 4432(a), amending § 1888 of the Social Security Act, by adding subsection (e), 42 U.S.C. § 1395yy, effective on or after July 1, 1998 (depending on SNF's cost-reporting periods).

44 groups. Effective January 1, 2006, PPS was expanded into 53 groups.[144] In fiscal year 2011, RUG-IV expanded to 66 case-mix groups.[145] The classifications are mutually exclusive; every patient is placed into only one classification at a time.[146]

The process of placing patients into the RUG-IV classifications requires accurate and comprehensive information-gathering about a patient's characteristics and needs. A patient's RUG-IV classification has implications for both reimbursement and Medicare coverage.

[B] Impact on Nursing Home Reimbursement

The RUG classifications are hierarchical, with higher categories providing greater reimbursement. The prospective payment system was phased in over a three-year transition period. Depending upon when a facility's cost-reporting period ends, the phase-in began either October 1, 1998, or January 1, 1999. As discussed below, effective October 1, 2019, CMS has made fundamental changes to the reimbursement system, replacing RUGs with a system called Patient-Driven Payment Model (PDPM).[147]

[C] The Ten Major RUG-IV Categories

The ten major RUG-IV categories, in hierarchical order based upon intensity of resource utilization, are:

1. Rehabilitation Plus Extensive Services
2. Ultra High Rehabilitation

---

[144] 70 Fed. Reg. 45,025, 45,045–46 (Aug. 4, 2005).

[145] CMS announced in August 2009 that RUG-IV would be implemented in fiscal year 2011. 74 Fed. 40,288 (Aug. 11, 2009). Section 10325 of the Patient Protection and Affordable Care Act (PPACA) (known as the Affordable Care Act, or ACA), Pub. L. No. 111-148, delayed the implementation date for most of RUG-IV by one year. Section 10325 was repealed by § 202 of the Medicare and Medicaid Extenders Act of 2010, Pub. L. No. 111-309, allowing full implementation of the RUG-IV system as of FY 2011. 76 Fed. Reg. 26,364, 26,367–68 (May 6, 2011).

[146] 63 Fed. Reg. 26,251 (May 12, 1998); 64 Fed. Reg. 41,643 (July 30, 1999); 65 Fed. Reg. 46,769 (July 31, 2000); 66 Fed. Reg. 39,561 (July 31, 2001); 67 Fed. Reg. 49,797 (July 31, 2002); 68 Fed. Reg. 46,035 (Aug. 4, 2003), 68 Fed. Reg. 55,882 (Sept. 29, 2003) (correction notice), 69 Fed. Reg. 45,775 (July 30, 2004); 70 Fed. Reg. 45,026 (Aug. 4, 2005); 71 Fed. Reg. 43,158 (July 31, 2006); 71 Fed. Reg. 57,519 (Sept. 29, 2006) (correction notice); 72 Fed. Reg. 43,411 (Aug. 3, 2007); 73 Fed. Reg. 46,415 (Aug. 8, 2008); 74 Fed. Reg. 40,288 (Aug. 11, 2009); 75 Fed. Reg. 42,885 (July 22, 2010 (notice); 76 Fed. Reg. 48,486 (Aug. 8, 2011); 77 Fed. Reg. 46,213 (Aug. 2, 2012); 78 Fed. Reg. 47,936 (Aug. 6, 2013); 79 Fed. Reg. 45,627 (Aug. 5, 2014); 80 Fed. Reg. 46,389, 46,405 (Aug. 4, 2015); 81 Fed. Reg. 51,969, 51,976 (Aug. 5, 2016); 82 Fed. Reg. 36530, 36536 (Aug. 4, 2017).

[147] 83 Fed. Reg. 39,163, 39,183–39,265 (Aug. 8, 2018).

3. Very High Rehabilitation
4. High Rehabilitation
5. Medium Rehabilitation
6. Low Rehabilitation
7. Extensive Services
8. Special Care High
9. Special Care Low
10. Clinically Complex

A patient classified into one of the upper 52 RUG-IV classifications following a qualifying hospital stay is presumed to meet a Medicare level of care during the first five-day assessment period.[148] A patient classified into one of the remaining 14 categories qualifies for Medicare coverage based upon the statutory and regulatory criteria for the SNF level of care.[149]

[D] Impact on Medicare Coverage: A Presumption of Medicare Coverage for "Upper 52"

A Medicare beneficiary who is classified into one of the top 52 RUG-IV categories may nevertheless experience barriers to SNF admission. These barriers are often caused by the high cost to SNFs of caring for certain groups of individuals seeking admission.

When the RUGs system was first implemented, patients who met the SNF coverage criteria experienced difficulty gaining admission to a SNF if they required complex nursing care and expensive medications or if they had high transportation costs, often related to dialysis. Hospital discharge planners reported that they were having more difficulty placing some Medicare patients and that facilities were changing their admissions practices in response to the new reimbursement system.[150] Since virtually all costs of providing services needed by patients are covered by the SNF's Medicare prospective per diem rate under consolidated billing, many SNFs were reluctant to admit individuals needing the services described above, when Medicare was the apparent payment source, because of the costs involved.

---

[148] MBP Manual, Ch. 8: § 30.1; 83 Fed. 39,162, 39,178 (Aug. 8, 2018).

[149] These Medicare-covered groups may be redesignated on an annual basis, 63 Fed. Reg. 26,251, 26,283 (May 12, 1998) (citing 42 C.F.R. §§ 409.31–35 and Medicare manuals). *See also* 83 Fed. Reg. 39,162, 39,179 (Aug. 8, 2018).

[150] Office of Inspector General (OIG), *Early Effects of the Prospective Payment System on Access to Skilled Nursing Facilities*, OEI-02-99-00400 (Aug. 1999).

In the Medicare, Medicaid, and SCHIP Balanced Budget Refinement Act of 1999 (BBRA),[151] Congress amended the Medicare statute in an effort to address these access problems. Effective April 1, 2000, the cost of an ambulance ride to a hospital for the purpose of obtaining kidney dialysis or radiation therapy for cancer treatment was "unbundled" from the SNF's Medicare payment. As a result, the per diem RUG reimbursement for SNF patients needing ambulance transportation for these purposes was no longer required to pay for the ambulance in addition to the services provided in the SNF. Instead, ambulance costs are billed separately.

The BBRA also excluded certain "high-cost, low probability" services from consolidated billing: certain chemotherapy items, chemotherapy administration services, radioisotope services, and customized prosthetic devices.[152] Despite these exclusions from consolidated billing, beneficiaries needing chemotherapy are often denied admission by SNFs that do not know that some of these drugs are excluded from the daily SNF rate. CMS has declined to exclude additional "high cost, low probability services" from consolidated billing unless they fall within one of the four categories specified in the BBRA.[153]

In September 2001, the HHS Office of Inspector General (OIG) reported that Medicare beneficiaries were difficult to place in SNFs if they needed IV antibiotics or expensive drugs or if they were medically complex, needed a ventilator, had an infectious disease or needed isolation, had renal failure or needed dialysis, had behavior problems, or needed total parental feedings.[154]

Later statutory and regulatory revisions to the SNF PPS excluded additional services from the PPS rates. At present, services excluded from the SNF rate,[155] and separately billed to Medicare,[156] include:

- Certain cardiac catheterizations;
- Certain computerized axial topography (CT) scans;
- Certain magnetic resonance imaging (MRIs);
- Certain ambulatory surgeries involving the use of a hospital operating room;

---

[151] Medicare, Medicaid, and SCHIP Balanced Budget Refinement Act of 1999 (BBRA), Pub. L. No. 106-113 (Nov. 29, 1999).

[152] BBRA § 103, 42 U.S.C. § 1395yy(e)(2)(A)(iii)(II), (III), (IV), (V); 79 Fed. Reg. 45,627, 45,641-644 (Aug. 5, 2014); 80 Fed. Reg. 46,389, 46,406–407 (Aug. 4, 2015).

[153] *See. e.g.,* 83 Fed. Reg. 39,162, 39,179–39,182 (Aug. 8, 2018).

[154] OIG, *Medicare Beneficiary Access to Skilled Nursing Facilities*, OEI-02-0330, p. 7 (Sept. 2000). In July 2001, the OIG found similar difficulties and also identified residents as difficult to place if they had decubitus ulcers and needed wound care. OIG, *Medicare Beneficiary Access to Skilled Nursing Facilities*, OEI-02-01-00160, p. 7 (July 2001).

[155] MCP Manual, Ch. 6: § 20.1.2.

[156] MBP Manual, Ch. 8: § 10.2.

- Certain radiation therapies;
- Certain angiographies, and lymphatic and venous procedures;
- Emergency services;
- Ambulance services when related to an excluded service within this list; and
- Ambulance transportation related to dialysis services.

CMS annually updates and lists the codes for exclusions from consolidated billing.[157]

The Medicare Prescription Drug, Improvement, and Modernization Act of 2003 (MMA) provided for a temporary 128 percent increase in the PPS per diem for any SNF patient with Acquired Immune Deficiency Syndrome (AIDS).[158] CMS has continued this add-on each year.[159]

Payment issues may be important when benefits are sought for SNF patients, especially for those who are not classified into one of the 52 RUG-IV categories that carry a presumption of Medicare coverage.

[E] Patient-Driven Payment System

Effective October 1, 2019, CMS will replace the RUG-IV prospective payment system with a new prospective payment system called the Patient-Driven Payment Model (PDPM).[160] The new system, which is budget-neutral, bases payment on resident characteristics, rather than on services provided. CMS cites its own research showing that, under RUGs, SNFs classify residents into the highest RUG categories and provide them with just enough therapy to meet RUG thresholds.[161] In Fiscal Year 2017, for example, more than 60 percent of Medicare-covered SNF stays were billed for one of three Ultra-High Rehabilitation categories (out of 66 total RUG-IV categories).[162] CMS cites studies by the HHS Inspector General and by the Medicare Payment Advisory Commission that similarly criticize the RUG system for encouraging excessive therapy and not paying adequately for non-therapy ancillaries (chiefly drugs).[163]

PDPM dramatically changes the financial incentives for SNFs. Under RUG-IV, a patient's Medicare rate is based on the higher of nursing or rehabilitation

---

[157] *See* CMS, "SNF Consolidated Billing," *available at* http://www.cms.gov/Medicare/Billing/SNFConsolidatedBilling/index.html (site visited Aug. 6, 2018).

[158] The Medicare Prescription Drug, Improvement, and Modernization Act (MMA), Pub. L. No. 108-173 (Dec. 8, 2003), § 511, 42 U.S.C. § 1395yy(e)(12). The increase remains in effect.

[159] 83 Fed. Reg. 39,162, 39,169 (Aug. 8, 2018).

[160] 83 Fed. Reg. 39,162, 39,183–39,265 (Aug. 8, 2018).

[161] 83 Fed. Reg. 39,162, 39,183–39,184 (Aug. 8, 2018).

[162] 83 Fed. Reg. 39,162, 39,194 (Aug. 8, 2018).

[163] 83 Fed. Reg. 39,162, 39,184–39,185 (Aug. 8, 2018).

needs, as determined by the 66 RUG-IV categories. PDPM uses more factors, with complex calculations for each.

To identify a single rate for each patient, PDPM first classifies residents into five case-mix adjusted components (physical therapy, occupational therapy, speech language pathology, nursing, and nontherapy ancillaries).[164] Physical and occupational therapy each have 16 case-mix groups (based on clinical category and functional score);[165] speech language pathology has 18 payment groups (based on clinical category, presence of a swallowing disorder or mechanically-altered diet, and cognitive status);[166] nursing has 25 case-mix groups (based on CMS's 2006 time-motion study and more recent patient assessment data);[167] and non-therapy ancillary has six case-mix groups.).[168]

CMS next calculates the rate for each case-mix adjusted component by applying the relevant variable per day adjustment schedule, which reduces the daily payment on a sliding scale.[169] For PT and OT, a 2 percent adjustment is made, beginning on day 21; by day 98, the daily rate is reduced to 76 percent of the initial payment.[170] The non-therapy ancillary case-mix component begins on day 4, reducing the component by two-thirds from the first three days of the SNF stay.[171] The nursing and speech language pathology components are not adjusted downwards over the course of a patient's stay.

Finally, these five components, as adjusted, are added together with the non-case-mix adjusted component to create the rate for the patient.[172]

Another major change from RUG-IV is that PDPM uses the five-day resident assessment for determining the Medicare rate for the patient's entire Part A stay, eliminating the RUG requirement for additional assessments on days 14, 30, 60, and 90.[173] A SNF can reclassify a patient after the five-day assessment under an optional Interim Payment Assessment (IPA), but CMS did not include criteria for triggering an IPA in the final rules.[174]

CMS notes that more than 99 percent of therapy is now provided on an individual basis and that individual therapy "should be considered the primary therapy mode and standard of care in therapy services provided to SNF residents."[175] Nevertheless, PDPM allows up to 25 percent of therapy services to be

---

[164] 83 Fed. Reg. 39,162, 39,225 (Aug. 8, 2018).

[165] 83 Fed. Reg. 39,162, 39,209 (Aug. 8, 2018).

[166] 83 Fed. Reg. 39,162, 39,210–39,214 (Aug. 8, 2018).

[167] 83 Fed. Reg. 39,162, 39,214–39,219 (Aug. 8, 2018).

[168] 83 Fed. Reg. 39,162, 39,223 (Aug. 8, 2018).

[169] 83 Fed. Reg. 39,162, 39,225, 39,226–39,229 (Aug. 8, 2018).

[170] 83 Fed. Reg. 39,162, 39,228 (Table 30) (Aug. 8, 2018).

[171] 83 Fed. Reg. 39,162, 39,227 (Aug. 8, 2018).

[172] 83 Fed. Reg. 39,162, 39,225 (Aug. 8, 2018).

[173] 83 Fed. Reg. 39,162, 3,9229

[174] 83 Fed. Reg. 39,162, 39,233 (Aug. 8, 2018).

[175] 83 Fed. Reg. 39,162, 39,238 (Aug. 8, 2018).

provided in group or concurrent settings, rather than individually.[176] A SNF exceeding the 25 percent limit will receive "a non-fatal warning edit,"—a "reminder" that it is out of compliance[177]—but "no penalty."[178]

Effective October 1, 2019, CMS adds new items to the PPS Discharge Assessment to identify minutes for each therapy discipline and the mode of therapy (that is, whether the therapy is individual, group, or concurrent), in recognition of concerns by commenters on the proposed rules and CMS itself that PDPM may lead to a considerable decline in therapy services.[179] The new items will allow CMS to monitor the total number of minutes a patient received as well as the mode of therapy.[180]

Certain groups will qualify a patient for an administrative presumption of coverage if the patient is classified into one of four specified nursing case-mix classifiers; one of 11 specified PT or OT groups; one of eight specified SLP groups; or the NTA's uppermost comorbidity group.[181] Patients not qualifying for an administrative presumption of coverage instead receive an individual determination.[182]

PDPM eliminates the AIDS add-on payment.[183]

The final rules include two tables describing the impact of PDPM's changes on a resident[184] and on facilities[185] and summarize some of the most significant changes in payments. Rates will be higher under PDPM for patients "who have high NTA costs, receive extensive services, are dually enrolled in Medicare and Medicaid, use IV medication, have ESRD, diabetes, or a wound infection, receive amputation/prosthesis care, and/or have longer prior inpatient stays."[186] Facilities will receive higher reimbursement if they have "high proportions of non-rehabilitation residents" and if they "are small facilities, non-profit facilities, government-owned facilities, and hospital-based and swing-bed facilities."[187]

§ 3.05 PROBLEM AREAS OF CONCERN FOR THE ADVOCATE

Frequent problems that stand in the way of Medicare SNF coverage are addressed below.

---

[176] 83 Fed. Reg. 39,162, 39,237–39,243 (Aug. 8, 2018).
[177] 83 Fed. Reg. 39,162, 39,239 (Aug. 8, 2018).
[178] 83 Fed. Reg. 39,162, 39,250 (Aug. 8, 2018).
[179] 83 Fed. Reg. 39,162, 39,235–39,236 (Aug. 8, 2018).
[180] 83 Fed. Reg. 39,162, 39,237 (Aug. 8, 2018).
[181] 83 Fed. Reg. 39,162, 39,253 (Aug. 8, 2018).
[182] 83 Fed. Reg. 39,162, 39,251 (Aug. 8, 2018).
[183] 83 Fed. Reg. 39,162, 39,253–39,255 (Aug. 8, 2018).
[184] 83 Fed. Reg. 39,162, 39,257–39,259 (Table 37) (Aug. 8, 2018).
[185] 83 Fed. Reg. 39,162, 39,260–39,261 (Table 38) (Aug. 8, 2018).
[186] 83 Fed. Reg. 39,162, 39,257 (Aug. 8, 2018).
[187] 83 Fed. Reg. 39,162, 39,259 (Aug. 8, 2018).

[A] Skilled Versus Custodial Care

The critical question in every Medicare SNF coverage determination is whether the patient was receiving a skilled level of care on a daily basis. The type of skilled care may be either nursing or rehabilitation services, or a combination of the two. Rehabilitation services include physical therapy, occupational therapy, and speech therapy. Rehabilitation services need only be provided five days per week to qualify as "daily," while nursing services, or a combination of nursing and therapy, must be provided seven days per week to meet the "daily" test.[188]

For example, a patient who receives physical therapy three days per week and occupational therapy two other days would be eligible for coverage. This patient has received skilled rehabilitation services five days per week. Similarly, a patient who receives physical therapy three days per week and skilled nursing care the other four days would be eligible for coverage. The key is that the patient is receiving skilled care each day of the week.

Most Medicare SNF patients require custodial care in addition to daily skilled care. Frequently these patients are nonambulatory or semiambulatory. For example, a stroke patient will require physical therapy to learn how to walk again and to rebuild muscle strength. In meeting the practical-matter requirement for inpatient coverage, it is often necessary to establish that the needed custodial care can only be provided, as a practical matter, on an inpatient basis.[189]

An assessment of whether care is skilled focuses on the inherent complexity of the service. This line of analysis has been adopted by courts in making level of care determinations.[190] Courts have also noted that a commonsense, nontechnical consideration of the patient's condition as a whole must be made in determining the level of care.[191]

There is no definition of custodial care in the law. The regulations merely state that custodial care is care that does not meet the definition of SNF care.[192] As a general rule, custodial care is interpreted to be care that a layperson without any special skills or training can safely and effectively perform.[193]

A systematic assessment of which services have actually been provided to the patient and careful review of the medical record can help determine whether the patient received a Medicare-covered level of care. A checklist may be a useful tool in evaluating level of care:

---

[188] 42 C.F.R. § 409.34. *See also* MBP Manual, Ch. 8: § 30.6.

[189] The "practical matter" criterion for coverage requires that the beneficiary need care on an inpatient basis. 42 C.F.R. § 409.35; MBP Manual, Ch. 8: § 30.7.

[190] Hurley v. Bowen, 857 F.2d 907, 911 (2d Cir. 1988); Hirsch v. Bowen, 655 F. Supp. 342, 344 (S.D.N.Y. 1987).

[191] Friedman v. Secretary of HHS, 819 F.2d 42, 45 (2d Cir. 1987); *Papciak*, 742 F. Supp. 2d 765, 769; Pfalzgraf v. Shalala, 997 F. Supp. 360, 365 (W.D.N.Y. 1998); Landa v. Shalala, 900 F. Supp. 628, 635 (E.D.N.Y. 1995); Walsh v. Secretary of HHS, 636 F. Supp. 358, 360 (E.D.N.Y. 1986).

[192] 42 C.F.R. § 411.15(g).

[193] *Hirsch*, 655 F. Supp. 342.

- Is this a rehabilitation or nursing patient (or both)?
- Which rehabilitation services have been provided (i.e., physical, occupational, or speech therapy)?
- Check the list of *per se* skilled therapy services.
- Is skilled development, management, and evaluation of the patient care plan required?
- Is skilled observation and assessment of the patient's changing or unstable condition required?
- Which specific nursing services have been provided (e.g., injections, decubitus ulcer care, dressing changes)?
- Are there any special medical complications that require the services of skilled personnel (e.g., multiple medications with potential adverse reactions, psychiatric components)?[194]
- Have the services been provided by or under the supervision of certified skilled personnel?
- Is there sufficient medical evidence to support a claim for Medicare coverage?

[B] Total Condition of the Patient

Courts have consistently taken the position that a patient's total condition must be taken into consideration, not merely each individual service provided.[195] In assessing the Medicare patient's total condition, the records should be examined to determine the need for management and evaluation of the patient's care plan or observation or monitoring, or both, of the patient's medical condition. As part of the "total condition" analysis, a federal district court recognized the need to consider whether situational depression and anxiety were temporarily limiting a patient's ability to progress in her functional capacity.[196]

---

[194] 42 C.F.R. § 409.33(a)(2); MBP Manual, Ch. 8: § 30.2.2.

[195] *Papciak*, 742 F. Supp. 2d 765; *Pfalzgraf*, 997 F. Supp. 360, 365; Yuknat v. Bowen, 1989 WL 265508 (D. Conn. Mar. 31, 1989); Stearns v. Sullivan, 1989 WL 141736 (D. Mass. Nov. 6, 1989); Perales v. Sullivan, 1989 WL 111087 (S.D.N.Y. Sept. 19, 1989); Scotto v. Bowen, 1989 WL 32805 (E.D.N.Y. Mar. 30 1989); Olson v. Bowen, 1988 WL 235560 (W.D. Wis. May 31, 1988); Babula v. Secretary of HHS, 655 F. Supp. 1117 (W.D.N.Y. 1987); *Hirsch*, 655 F. Supp. 342; Israel v. Bowen, 669 F. Supp. 61 (W.D.N.Y. 1987); Gartmann v. Secretary of HHS, 633 F. Supp. 671, 679 (E.D.N.Y. 1986); Howard v. Heckler, 618 F. Supp. 1333 (E.D.N.Y. 1985); Roth v. Secretary of HHS, 606 F. Supp. 636 (W.D.N.Y. 1985); Kuebler v. Secretary of HHS, 579 F. Supp. 1436 (E.D.N.Y. 1984).

[196] *Papciak*, 742 F. Supp. 2d 765.

[C] Management and Evaluation of the Patient Care Plan

SNF patients are entitled to Medicare coverage if they need and receive skilled observation, assessment, management of care plan, or patient education services, even if they do not require or receive specific nursing services, such as injections or catheter irrigation, and even if they do not fall within the top 52 RUG-IV categories.[197] Documentation to support coverage on these bases must be kept by the facility and should be found in the medical record, including the doctor's order, nurses' notes, and any medical assessment data that the SNF is required to keep for transmittal to the Medicare contractors for payment.[198]

Overall management and evaluation of a patient's care plan may involve skilled services, even when the individual services are not skilled. The need for skilled care may be inferred from the services provided, even when the skilled planning and management activities are not specifically identified in the patient's clinical record.[199] One or more of the following nursing services may qualify a patient for Medicare coverage of his or her SNF stay:

- Involvement of skilled nursing personnel to develop, manage, and evaluate a care plan formulated through physician orders;
- Involvement of skilled nursing personnel to meet the patient's needs, promote recovery, and ensure medical safety when considering the patient's physical and mental condition;
- Management by skilled nursing personnel of personal care services when the patient's condition and aggregate of services require technical or professional intervention;
- Involvement of skilled nursing personnel to understand the relationship between services and evaluate the ultimate effect of one service on another;
- Involvement of skilled nursing personnel required, even though each individual service is not considered skilled by itself;
- Skilled planning and management services not specifically articulated as such in the clinical record, if the patient's overall condition is documented as justifying the need for technical or professional services.[200]

Cases that rest solely on management and evaluation of the skilled service are among the most difficult to win because the standard is ambiguous and the qualifying factors are not easy to define. Certain factors are important in this type

---

[197] 42 C.F.R. § 409.33(a)(1) and (3); MBP Manual, Ch. 8: § 30.1.

[198] *See generally* 42 C.F.R. §§ 413.343 and 483.20.

[199] 42 C.F.R. § 409.33(a)(1)(ii); MBP Manual, Ch. 8: § 30.2.3.1.

[200] 42 C.F.R. § 409.33(a)(1)(ii); MBP Manual, Ch. 8: § 30.2.3.1.

of case: age, number of medical conditions, mental impairment, patient safety, and actual professional staff involvement. An individual with medical problems involving vital organs and systems is more likely to require skilled management and evaluation. Very often a case rests on the fact that skilled nursing personnel are involved in the development, management, and evaluation of the patient's care plan.

The MBP Manual provides as an example "an aged patient with a history of diabetes mellitus and angina pectoris who is recovering from an open reduction of the neck of the femur."[201] He requires "skin care, appropriate oral medications, a diabetic diet, a therapeutic exercise program to preserve muscle tone and body condition, and observation to notice signs of deterioration . . . or complications. . . ."[202] Although the individual services could be provided by nonskilled personnel, the patient's condition, age, and immobility "create a high potential for serious complications" and justify skilled care until the patient's treatment regimen is stabilized.[203]

Every aspect of the patient's condition, including the variety and intensity of services being performed by nursing personnel, should be carefully evaluated. The review should include the following steps:

- Checking the written care plan[204] and how plan elements are reflected in the ongoing medical assessment data.
- Checking whether the patient manifested behavioral symptoms of psychological or mental impairments and whether the patient had such a condition in addition to physical problems.
- Checking whether nursing intervention was necessary to ensure patient safety and promote recovery.
- Carefully assessing the aggregate of services in light of the patient's total condition. A patient may need assessment, observation, and other interventions related to a refusal of medication and nutrition, and at the same time, may require occupational therapy twice weekly as well as a variety of personal care services.
- Checking the interrelationship of services. One example is the frequent need for a nurse to assess the interaction of various medications taken simultaneously for different conditions.

---

[201] 42 C.F.R. § 409.33(a)(1)(ii); MBP Manual, Ch. 8: § 30.2.3.1, Example 1.

[202] MBP Manual, Ch. 8: § 30.2.3.1, Example 1.

[203] MBP Manual, Ch. 8: § 30.2.3.1, Example 1

[204] 42 C.F.R. § 483.20(k). Often the plan of care alone will not have sufficient information to be helpful. Physician's orders, medical treatment records, and nursing or therapy notes, or both, may contain additional and more specific proof that daily skilled care was needed and provided.

Several *per se* nonskilled services may require skilled management even if each service is nonskilled. Multiple medical diagnoses and a great deal of professional nursing services may support the need for skilled management. A need for skilled management services may also be established, even without explicit clinical references to skilled planning and management services, "if the record as a whole clearly establishes that there was a likely potential for serious complications without skilled management."[205]

Management and evaluation services are closely related to observation and assessment services.[206] Often a patient will require a combination of management and observation services. Medicare coverage is more likely to be granted when a patient requires skilled observation in addition to management of the care plan.

[D] Observation and Assessment of the Patient's Changing or Unstable Condition

Many SNF patients require skilled nursing monitoring of their overall medical condition.[207] An individual's condition may change, necessitating a change in the plan of care or additional medical interventions. Medicare covers such nursing care if the care is required and performed on a daily basis.

The Medicare statute and regulations do not require that frail or chronically ill persons deteriorate or suffer a medical setback in order to invoke Medicare coverage for skilled nursing observation and assessment. The risk of potential instability is sufficient to cover services that are needed to maintain a fragile person at the maximum medical and functional status.

The regulation and MBP Manual provide six examples of skilled observation and assessment and include stabilizing a patient's treatment regimen, observing a patient in an unstabilized post-operative period, and monitoring post-hospital heart attack and pneumonia patients.[208]

An analysis of the record to determine the need for observation and assessment should demonstrate the following:

- Medical necessity was documented by physician orders and nursing or therapy notes;
- Skilled personnel were utilized to identify and evaluate the patient's needs;
- Modification of treatment was needed for additional medical procedures;

[205] MBP Manual, Ch. 8: § 30.2.3.1.
[206] MBP Manual, Ch. 8: § 30.2.3.2.
[207] 42 C.F.R. § 409.33(a)(2); MBP Manual, Ch. 8: § 30.2.3.2.
[208] 42 C.F.R. § 409.33(a)(2); MBP Manual, Ch. 8: § 30.2.3.2.

- Care was necessary until the patient's condition stabilized or to ensure the patient remained stable;
- There was a reasonable probability of a potential complication or a new acute episode that required monitoring by skilled personnel (even if such complication or episode did not occur);
- Where applicable, acute psychological symptoms were present in addition to physical problems.

A SNF patient with acute psychological symptoms may not have the ability to cooperate with SNF personnel in the same way as patients without such symptoms. For example, a patient may have an order for pain medication, as needed. Due to psychological factors, the patient may not be able to express the need clearly. The patient's nonverbal expressions or behaviors may require skilled interpretation and interventions. Similarly, for a patient with an "as needed" order for medication for agitation or anxiety, the skill of a nurse may be needed to determine, after careful observation and assessment, when to administer such medications. These cases require careful and comprehensive development of the facts to support Medicare coverage.[209]

[E] Patient Education

Patient education services may be skilled services if technical or professional personnel are needed to teach a patient self-maintenance and how to manage his or her treatment regimen.[210] Illustrative examples include:

- Teaching self-administration of injectable medications;
- Teaching self-administration of a complex range of medications;
- "Teaching a newly diagnosed diabetic to administer insulin injections, to prepare and follow a diabetic diet, and to observe foot-care precautions;"
- "Teaching self-administration of medical gases;"
- "Gait training and teaching of prosthesis care for a patient who has had a recent leg amputation;"

---

[209] *Compare* Gregorace v. Bowen, 1988 WL 95306 (E.D.N.Y. Sept. 1, 1988) [1989-1 Transfer Binder] Medicare & Medicaid Guide (CCH) ¶ 37,444 (Medicare coverage was appropriate, based on observation and assessment, where three of the patient's medications could be administered only under certain circumstances and medications needed to be modified within 24 hours of the patient's admission because of the patient's changing condition) *and* Frohnhoefer v. Leavitt, No. 06-CV-1236 (SJF) (E.D.N.Y. Mar. 19, 2007) (Medicare coverage denied; monitoring and nursing notes, required by state law, did not mean skilled observation and assessment services were provided).

[210] 42 C.F.R. § 409.33(a)(3); MBP Manual, Ch. 8: § 30.2.3.3.

- Teaching colostomy or ileostomy care;
- "Teaching patients how to perform self-catheterization and self-administration of gastrostomy feedings;"
- "Teaching patients how to care for and maintain central venous lines, such as Hickman catheters;"
- "Teaching patients the use and care of braces, splints and orthotics, and any associated skin care;" and
- "Teaching patients the proper care of any specialized dressings or skin treatments."[211]

[F] Opinion of the Attending Physician

A critical question is how much weight should be given to various types of evidence. The concept or rule of law that the opinion of an attending or treating physician should be given special consideration was first developed in the context of Social Security disability cases.[212]

Although most courts have held that the opinion of a Medicare attending physician is not binding, the preponderance of judicial authority is that the opinion of an attending physician must be given great weight when there is no directly conflicting evidence.[213]

The U.S. Court of Appeals for the Second Circuit has twice addressed the treating physician rule in the context of Medicare.[214] In response, the Health Care Financing Administration (HCFA, now CMS) issued a formal administrative ruling concerning the weight to be given a treating physician's opinion in determining hospital and SNF coverage.[215]

---

[211] MBP Manual, Ch. 8: § 30.2.3.3.

[212] Schisler v. Heckler, 787 F.2d 76, 81–85 (2d Cir. 1986). *See also Schisler v. Bowen*, 851 F.2d 43 (2d Cir. 1988) (*Schisler II*). In response to the first two *Schisler* decisions, the Secretary of HHS promulgated regulations establishing an administrative treating physician rule. These regulations were upheld in the *Schisler v. Sullivan*, 3 F.3d 563 (2d Cir. 1993) (*Schisler III*). *See also* Executive Dir. of Office of Vt. Health Access *ex rel.* Carey v. Sebelius, 698 F. Supp. 2d 436, 441 (D. Vt. 2010).

[213] *See, e.g.*, *Hirsch*, 655 F. Supp. 342; *Israel*, 669 F. Supp. 61; *Gartmann*, 633 F. Supp. 671; *Walsh*, 636 F. Supp. 358, *aff'd by* New York *ex rel.* Bodnar, 903 F.2d 122 (2d Cir. 1990) (determination not binding on factfinder). *See also* Bodnar v. Secretary of HHS, [1989 Transfer Binder] Medicare & Medicaid Guide (CCH) ¶ 38,274 (N.D.N.Y. Aug. 1, 1989); Mazzella v. Heckler, No. H-83-953 (PCD) (D. Conn. Aug. 18, 1985) [1986-1 Transfer Binder] Medicare & Medicaid Guide (CCH) ¶ 34,863.

[214] New York *ex rel.* Holland v. Sullivan, 927 F.2d 57 (2d Cir. 1991); New York *ex rel.* Stein v. Sullivan, 924 F.2d 431 (2d Cir. 1991).

[215] HCFA Ruling, No. HCFA R93-1, [1993 Transfer Binder] Medicare & Medicaid Guide (CCH) 41,444 (May 18, 1993).

The ruling sets out four specific points:

1. No *presumptive* weight may be given to the opinion of a treating physician in determining the medical necessity of inpatient hospital or SNF services.
2. The treating physician's opinion must be evaluated in the context of all the evidence contained in the administrative record.
3. Treating physician certification is required for Medicare *payment;* however, *coverage* decisions are not based solely on physician certification.
4. Coverage decisions are based upon objective medical information available from claims forms and, when necessary, the medical record, which includes the physician certification.

Although CMS's rule is consistent with the great weight that must be afforded to the opinion of the treating physician, the attending physician's opinion may be contradicted at the hearing by a medical adviser who has been retained as a consultant by the ALJ. Cross-examination of the medical adviser is likely to establish that the medical adviser has not treated or even examined the patient. The medical adviser's opinion is totally derived from a review of the documentary medical evidence.

Courts have recognized that the opinion of a nontreating physician, which is based only on review of medical records, should not be accorded as much evidentiary weight as the opinion of an attending physician.[216] In *Gartmann v. Secretary of HHS*,[217] the court found that the opinion of the medical adviser could not be considered substantial evidence to support a denial of coverage because it was not supported by the findings or opinions of the treating physician. If the only medical testimony is presented by the non-treating medical advisor, however, it may be persuasive to the ALJ.[218] Presenting evidence from the attending physician is important, and especially so when a medical advisor testifies.

[G] Restoration Potential of the Rehabilitation Patient

Most Medicare patients qualifying for SNF coverage are rehabilitation patients under the current RUG-IV reimbursement methodology. Most of these patients receive physical therapy. The regulations recognize rehabilitation services as skilled services, including cases in which *maintenance* therapy is

---

[216] Stenger v. Bowen, 692 F. Supp. 1474, 1476 (E.D.N.Y. 1988).

[217] 633 F. Supp. 671, 680 (E.D.N.Y. 1986).

[218] *Frohnhoefer*, No. 06-CV-1236 (SJF) (E.D.N.Y. Mar. 19, 2007) (outside medical expert's testimony was uncontradicted when treating physician did not testify and beneficiary did not present evidence contrary to outside expert; Medicare coverage denied).

required to be provided by skilled personnel.[219] Over the years, Medicare contractors often, but erroneously, required that a patient show significant rehabilitation potential and steady improvement in order to receive Medicare coverage. This was not the appropriate legal standard. The nationwide class action *Jimmo v. Sebelius* has now unequivocally confirmed that maintenance nursing and maintenance therapy are covered by Medicare.[220]

An earlier case, *Fox v. Bowen*,[221] successfully challenged Medicare's policy and practice of denying coverage of SNF physical therapy services, based upon arbitrary rules of thumb and without consideration of the patient's individual condition. The court found that Medicare intermediaries were improperly denying Medicare coverage for physical therapy for maintenance therapy, non-weight-bearing therapy to patients with fractures, and passive range-of-motion exercises. Patients who were able to ambulate 50 feet with supervision, patients with amputations who were not yet fitted with prostheses, and patients who required daily skilled physical therapy for a period longer than two weeks were also improperly denied coverage.[222]

The *Fox* ruling struck down these arbitrary rules of thumb and mandated that each patient's individual medical condition be carefully assessed to determine whether skilled physical therapy services are required. Implicit in this ruling is that coverage cannot be denied merely because an individual's restoration potential is not sufficient or because insufficient progress has been achieved. Such blanket restrictions are arbitrary and contrary to the provisions of the Medicare regulations pertaining to restoration potential, which explicitly state:

> The restoration potential of a patient is not the deciding factor in determining whether skilled services are needed. Even if full recovery or medical improvement is not possible, a patient may need skilled services to prevent further deterioration or preserve current capabilities.[223]

The MBP Manual similarly provides: "When rehabilitation services are the primary services, . . . [t]he deciding factor is not the patient's potential for recovery. . . ."[224] Despite these explicit principles, Medicare coverage over the years was often denied for beneficiaries who reached a "plateau."[225] The *Jimmo* case should, once and for all, end denials of coverage on this erroneous basis.

---

[219] 42 C.F.R. § 409.33(c)(5).

[220] *Jimmo*, Civil Action No. 5:11-CV-17-CR. *See* http://www.medicareadvocacy.org/wp-content/uploads/2012/12/Jimmo-Settlement-Agreement-00011764.pdf (site visited Sept. 8, 2017).

[221] 656 F. Supp. 1236 (D. Conn. 1987). This case was certified as a statewide class action in Connecticut; however, the ruling has affected Medicare coverage standards nationwide.

[222] *Fox*, 656 F. Supp. 1236, 1252.

[223] 42 C.F.R. § 409.32(c).

[224] MBP Manual, Ch. 8: § 30.2.2, Example 1.

[225] Bohlin v. Leavitt, 2006 WL 2360058 (D. Mass. Aug. 16, 2006).

[H] Noncertified Bed

In order for Medicare to pay for a SNF stay, the patient must be in a bed that is certified for Medicare participation. Medicare will not cover skilled care if the patient is in a noncertified bed unless it can be shown that the placement was erroneous and the patient was not aware that he or she was in a noncertified bed or did not consent to the placement.[226]

The patient may inadvertently be placed in a non-Medicare-certified bed but receive a SNF level of care. The law provides that when the sole reason for denial of Medicare coverage is an unintentional, inadvertent, or erroneous action concerning transfer to a noncertified bed, payment may be made.[227] This application of waiver of liability applies only when a patient has not consented to the transfer to a noncertified bed and the only reason for denial is the fact that the patient was in a noncertified bed.[228] The patient must still establish eligibility for, and receipt of, daily skilled care.

The bed certification issue declined in significance as a concern when the Medicare program began paying SNFs on the basis of patients' assessments, rather than on the certification status of patients' beds. Today, most SNFs and beds are certified for Medicare.

§ 3.06 PRE-APPEALS ADVOCACY

[A] Overview of Pre-Appeals Advocacy

Coverage decisions for SNF care are made at various levels, first by the provider, then by the administrative appeal system,[229] and, finally, by the federal courts. A decision by a SNF is different from a decision made by Medicare. Only a formal Medicare decision triggers the appeals process. If a patient requests that the SNF submit a claim to Medicare despite the facility's belief that Medicare will not cover the stay under Part A, the facility must submit a claim.[230] A Medicare contractor then issues a Medicare initial determination. Following the initial determination, an appeal can be taken to "redetermination" and "reconsideration," then on to an ALJ hearing, the Medicare Appeals Council (Council), and, finally, federal district court.

---

[226] 42 U.S.C. § 1395pp(e); MCP Manual, Ch. 30: §§ 20, 20.1.1; Hendry Convalescent Ctr. v. Harris, [1982 Transfer Binder] Medicare & Medicaid Guide (CCH) 31,934(A) (E.D. Mich. 1982); Wright v. Califano, [1979-1 Transfer Binder] Medicare & Medicaid Guide (CCH) 29,643.

[227] 42 U.S.C. § 1395pp(e); *Wright*, [1979-1 Transfer Binder] Medicare & Medicaid Guide (CCH) 29,643.

[228] MCP Manual, Ch. 30: §§ 30.1 and 40.

[229] *See* **§ 3.08** of this Handbook.

[230] Sarrassat v. Sullivan, 1989 WL 208444 (N.D. Cal. May 17, 1989).

[B] The Importance of No-Payment or Demand Bill

SNFs submit consolidated bills to the Medicare contractor for payment in accordance with CMS requirements.[231] They must submit claims to the Medicare contractor, *even when* they believe that the patient's stay will not be covered, in order for Medicare to make a determination about coverage. This procedure, referred to as "no-payment" or "demand" billing, was not changed by the consolidated billing process. SNFs are required to submit demand bills at the request of a patient.[232] Furthermore, SNFs cannot bill the patient until the Medicare contractor issues a formal claim determination.[233] If the SNF does not submit a bill to the Medicare contractor, however, the patient's right to appeal is lost, because the Medicare contractor will never have made an initial Medicare determination from which an appeal may be taken.

Although Medicare contractors perform the first official assessment of a patient's level of care, the experience of beneficiaries is that contractors often rubber-stamp the SNF's denial.

Beneficiaries have the right to demand that Medicare be billed for services already provided to them, even when they request expedited review.[234] Submission of a demand bill is necessary because the two appeals processes have different functions. The expedited review, which seeks to keep services in place, determines eligibility or entitlement to continued coverage; the demand bill determines whether the ongoing services the beneficiary already received are coverable by Medicare. Consequently, if a beneficiary prevails on expedited review at a later stage, such as an ALJ hearing, Medicare would still not have determined whether the ongoing services provided to the beneficiary met the Medicare coverage criteria unless a demand bill had been submitted for an official determination. A Medicare beneficiary may request that a demand bill be submitted to Medicare for an official determination by checking the appropriate box on the SNFABN, the notice that SNFs must provide to beneficiaries in advance of furnishing what the SNF believes to be noncovered care. However, a demand bill may be requested at any point in a beneficiary's stay.[235]

---

[231] BBA § 4432(b); HCFA, Program Memorandum A-98-18 (Apr. 1998); MCP Manual, Ch. 6: § 10, *available at* https://www.cms.gov/Regulations-and-Guidance/Guidance/Manuals/Downloads/clm104c06.pdf (site visited Sept. 22, 2018).

[232] MCP Manual, Ch. 30: § 70; *Sarrassat*, 1989 WL 208444.

[233] MCP Manual, Ch. 30: § 70.6.1.3.

[234] *See* § **3.07[C]**.

[235] MCP Manual, Ch. 30: § 70.6.2.

[C] Waiver of Liability

A related issue involves the "waiver of liability" provision in the Medicare statute.[236] Pursuant to this provision, a patient's responsibility for the cost of care not covered by Medicare (known as "financial liability") may be waived under certain circumstances. In general, liability will be waived when it is found that the patient did not know, or have reason to know, that Medicare would not cover the services.[237]

In order for liability to be waived, there must be a determination that Medicare will not cover the services, based upon a finding that the care was not medically reasonable and necessary or that it was custodial.[238] If both the patient and provider did not know or could not be reasonably expected to know that services would not be covered, liability will rest with the Medicare program.[239]

In some instances, the patient is relieved of liability but the provider is not. Such a situation occurs, for example, when a provider has reason to know that Medicare will not cover the services because the provider has received denial notices for patients with similar medical conditions. In this situation, Medicare will indemnify the patient and reimburse him or her for any amounts he or she paid to the provider during the period for which liability was waived. Medicare will then treat the payment to the provider as an overpayment and recoup the difference from later billings.[240]

[D] Notice Issues

[1] Function of the Notice

Notice plays a key role in determining waiver of liability issues, that is, whether a patient knew or could be expected to know that Medicare would not cover the service. Medicare patients are not medical experts and cannot be expected to know whether a service is medically necessary or the difference between skilled and custodial care. Accordingly, the patient must be notified in advance that Medicare will not cover the SNF services. Notice also informs a patient of his or her right to request a demand bill so that the Medicare contractor will issue an initial determination from which the beneficiary can file an appeal, if necessary. CMS uses one notice to inform the beneficiary of both the potential liability if a claim is submitted to Medicare and Medicare determines noncoverage and the right to request a demand bill to initiate an appeal.

---

[236] 42 U.S.C. § 1395pp.

[237] 42 U.S.C. § 1395pp; *see also* MCP Manual, Ch. 30: § 70.

[238] 42 U.S.C. § 1395y(a)(1)(A) and (9).

[239] 42 U.S.C. § 1395pp(a)(2); 42 C.F.R. § 411.400.

[240] 42 U.S.C. § 1395pp(b); 42 C.F.R. § 411.402.

A SNF must give a beneficiary a notice if it intends to deny, reduce, or terminate Medicare Part A–covered services.[241]

[2] Form of Notice

Although the statute is not specific about what notice is appropriate, the regulations require that notice of noncoverage be given to the patient in writing.[242] Generally, oral notice is not legally sufficient.[243] Someone who is admitted as a Medicare patient will receive a written denial notice when the SNF believes Medicare will not pay for the care. If the reason for the noncoverage is statutory—either "medical necessity" (the services are "not reasonable and necessary") or level of care (the care is custodial, rather than skilled)—the SNF must use the revised SNF Advance Beneficiary Notice (SNFABN).[244] As of May 7, 2018, CMS discontinued use of the five denial letters.

The notice must include an explanation in lay language[245] that the patient and his or her authorized representative "can comprehend"[246] and must be given to the patient or the patient's authorized representative.[247] If the patient "is not capable of receiving the notice," the patient has not received "proper notice" and the facility may be financially responsible.[248]

A SNF using the model SNFABN form must give specific reasons in the "Because" section explaining why it believes that Medicare payment will be denied.[249] The SNF's refusal to respond to inquiries from the patient or authorized

[241] MCP Manual, Ch. 30: § 70.2.3.1.

[242] 42 C.F.R. § 411.404; MCP Manual, Ch. 30: §§ 40.3, 70.1, *available at* https://www.cms.gov/Regulations-and-Guidance/Guidance/Manuals/Downloads/clm104c30.pdf (site visited Sept. 8, 2017).

[243] *See Sarrassat*, 1989 WL 208444, establishing that a beneficiary must receive a notice of noncoverage, including notice of the opportunity to request an appeal of the SNF's noncoverage determination and establishing that where the beneficiary requests an appeal, services continue through the issuance of the formal Medicare finding of noncoverage. *But see* HCFA Ruling 95-1 (Dec. 22, 1995); MCP Manual, Ch. 30: § 30.1 (establishing when beneficiary is on notice of noncoverage; presumption that beneficiary did not know services were not covered unless there is evidence of written notice to beneficiary). Often SNF staff will note on the written notice, included in the patient's record, that oral notice was provided over the telephone. These cases require close scrutiny.

[244] For the downloadable CMS-10055 form, *see* CMS, "FFS Form SNFABN," *available at* https://www.cms.gov/Medicare/Medicare-General-Information/BNI/FFS-SNFABN-.html (site visited Aug. 6, 2018).

[245] MCP Manual, Ch. 30: § 70.3.1.

[246] MCP Manual, Ch. 30: §§ 70.3.4, 70.3.5.

[247] MCP Manual, Ch. 30: § 70.3.1.

[248] MCP Manual, Ch. 30: § 70.3.4.

[249] MCP Manual, Ch. 30: § 70.4.3.3.

representative about the notice and its meaning may result in the notice's invalidation.[250]

The MCP Manual states that the SNFABN must meet its standards for cultural competency, clearly identify the particular item or service, and include the reasons the SNF believes Medicare will not pay for the SNF stay.[251] The notice should not include abbreviations, diagnosis codes, or technical language. A SNFABN that a beneficiary cannot understand is defective and will not protect the SNF from financial liability.[252]

Effective May 7, 2018, CMS discontinued use of another notice—the Notice of Exclusion from Medicare Benefits (SNF-NEMB)—that facilities were allowed to use with "technical" denials, such as failure to meet the three-day qualifying inpatient hospital stay or absence of days left in the benefit period. CMS encourages facilities to use the SNFABN under these circumstances as well, if they choose.

Another CMS form—the Notice of Medicare Provider Non-Coverage—is used for expedited appeals, discussed below.[253]

In guidance to state survey agencies, CMS clarifies that beneficiaries have two separate types of appeals—standard claim appeals (the SNFABN or Denial Letters) and expedited appeals (Notice of Medicare Provider Non-Coverage)—each with its own notice.[254]

[3] SNF Billing Notices

CMS has established a standard process requiring SNFs to submit bills to Medicare contractors for beneficiaries who "started a spell of illness under a SNF Part A benefit for every month of the related stay even though no benefits may be payable."[255] The bills are required when a patient has exhausted his or her 100-day SNF benefit (*benefits exhaust*) and when a patient no longer needs a Medicare-covered level of care but continues to reside in a Medicare-certified part of the SNF (*no payment*). When a SNF patient dropped to nonskilled care in a

---

[250] MCP Manual, Ch. 30: § 70.4.3.4.

[251] MCP Manual, Ch. 30: § 70.3.2.

[252] MCP Manual, Ch. 30: § 70.3.5.

[253] For the downloadable form, *see* CMS, Notice of Medicare Provider Non-Coverage, OMB No. 0938-0953, *available at* https://www.cms.gov/Medicare/Medicare-General-Information/BNI/FFS-Expedited-Determination-Notices.html (site visited Aug. 6, 2018). *See* **§ 3.07[C]** of this Handbook for discussion of expedited appeals.

[254] CMS, "Survey and Certification Issues Related to Liability Notices and Beneficiary Appeal Rights in Nursing Homes," S&C-09-20 (Jan. 9, 2009), *available at* https://www.cms.gov/Medicare/Provider-Enrollment-and-Certification/SurveyCertificationGenInfo/Downloads/SCLetter09-20.pdf (site visited Aug. 6, 2018).

[255] MCP Manual, Ch. 6: § 40.8.

previous month, the SNF is allowed to submit a final discharge bill spanning multiple months through the month of discharge. CMS intends to use *benefits exhaust* and *no payment* bills to track patients' benefit periods and for purposes of national health care planning.

[4] Notice Issues for Advocates

In considering waiver of the patient's liability, review:

- Whether Medicare coverage was denied upon admission or at a later date.
- Whether the denial was because the services were not skilled or because they were not reasonable and necessary.
- Whether written notice was given by the SNF.
- Who received the notice.
- Whether the patient was capable of understanding the notice (e.g., are there language barriers?).
- Whether the notice was mailed to a family member.
- When the notice was received.

When Medicare coverage is denied at admission, the Medicare denial notice is one of many documents presented to the patient's representative on the day of admission. Consequently, people often do not remember receiving this notice. The advocate should request a copy from the provider even if a family member does not remember receiving a notice. A copy might be found in the patient's file that is signed by the patient or family member. Review the notice to determine whether it complies with the forms approved by CMS.

§ 3.07 APPEALS

[A] Medicare Advantage

If the beneficiary has enrolled in a Medicare Advantage plan, Medicare Advantage appeal rights apply.[256]

---

[256] *See* § **7.03[E]**; Giesse v. Secretary of the Dep't of HHS, 476 F. Supp. 2d 734 (N.D. Ohio 2006).

[B] Appeals Process for Traditional Medicare

[1] Initial Determinations

The claims process begins when the Medicare contractor issues an initial determination of a claim submitted by the SNF or with respect to a demand bill requested by the beneficiary.[257] The initial determination, which is issued as the Medicare Summary Notice (MSN), goes only to the beneficiary, even when the contractor is aware that the beneficiary has an appointed representative.[258] An appeal from the initial determination requires submission of a written, signed request for a redetermination within 120 days of the initial determination;[259] the regulations assume the notice is received five days after the date of the notice. Requests for redeterminations must be filed with the office indicated on the MSN.[260]

The regulations also allow SNFs to request appeal of a denial of an initial determination,[261] raising the possibility that both the beneficiary and the SNF will initiate the appeals process. In such a case, the contractor must consolidate the appeals. The contractor has 60 days from receipt of the redetermination request to issue a decision.[262] If more than one party files a request, the time period runs from the date the last request is received.[263] For example, if a beneficiary files a redetermination request on day 1, but the SNF files on day 50, the 60-day time period for the contractor to act starts on day 50.

[2] Redeterminations

Unlike the MSN, the notice of the redetermination is sent to a patient's appointed representative. The notice explains the facts, policies, and law relied on in making the redetermination decision; the right to request a reconsideration and the process for doing so; and a statement of specific missing documents that must be submitted. The notice states that SNFs, but not patients (unless they are represented by a SNF), must submit all their evidence at the next level of review in order for the evidence to be considered at any further stage of the appeals process.[264] Contractors are not required to send redetermination notices to multiple patients in overpayment cases brought by SNFs if the patient allegedly has no

---

[257] 42 C.F.R. §§ 405.920 and 405.921.
[258] 42 C.F.R. § 405.921(a).
[259] 42 C.F.R. § 405.942(a).
[260] 42 C.F.R. § 405.944(a).
[261] 42 C.F.R. § 405.906(a)(3).
[262] 42 C.F.R. § 405.950(a).
[263] 42 C.F.R. § 405.950(b)(2).
[264] 42 C.F.R. § 405.956.

liability for the claim. It is unclear how the contractor determines in such cases whether the patient has already paid for the service in question.

A reopening process may be used instead of the redetermination process to correct minor errors or omissions in initial determinations.[265] Reopenings can also be used at subsequent levels of review. Questions remain concerning the relationship of the reopening process and the process for deciding remanded cases, as well as the ability of a contractor to reopen a decision in favor of the beneficiary.

[3] Reconsiderations

A third level of review, reconsideration,[266] is conducted by Medicare contractors called Qualified Independent Contractors (QICs). Patients and other parties to the redetermination have 180 days to request a reconsideration by filing a request at the location indicated on the redetermination notice.[267] Again, reconsiderations filed by patients and the SNF are consolidated, and the time for issuing a decision runs from receipt of the last-filed appeal.

Appeals of redeterminations by the Medicare contractors concerning SNF care go through the QIC reconsideration. The reconsideration level of review is a paper review;[268] CMS states in the preamble to the final regulations that QICs will not conduct hearings. However, the QIC is supposed to solicit the view of the patient. Patients may submit additional evidence at subsequent levels of review.[269] SNFs are required to submit all the evidence they want considered in the claim to the QIC.

The QIC is required to complete its reconsideration within 60 days of the reconsideration request.[270] Again, the time runs from the last request filed if more than one party seeks reconsideration; the QIC must so notify a party who filed an earlier request. The regulations do not indicate how QICs will document receipt or how patients will know when the 60-day period ends. Although the statute allows a party to the reconsideration to ask for an extension of not more than 14 days for the QIC to conclude the reconsideration, the regulations add 14 days to the reconsideration time frame each time additional evidence is submitted.[271]

If a QIC does not issue a timely decision, a party may request that the appeal be escalated to the next level of review, the ALJ level. The regulations give the QIC five days to either issue a decision or acknowledge the escalation request and send the appeal to the ALJ level of review.[272] The regulations indicate that an

[265] 42 C.F.R. § 405.980.

[266] 42 C.F.R. §§ 405.960–978.

[267] 42 C.F.R. § 405.962(a).

[268] 42 C.F.R. § 405.968(a)(1).

[269] 42 C.F.R. § 405.966(c).

[270] 42 C.F.R. § 405.970(a).

[271] 42 C.F.R. § 405.970(b)(3).

[272] 42 C.F.R. § 405.970(e)(2).

appeal escalated to the ALJ level will be completed within 180 days of receipt, rather than the statutorily mandated 90 days for ALJ decisions.

[4] ALJ Hearing and Beyond

If the reconsideration decision by the QIC is unsatisfactory and at least $160 (in 2019) remains in controversy, the beneficiary has 60 days in which to request an ALJ hearing.[273] The hearing request should be made in writing and should be filed with the entity identified in the reconsideration notice.[274] If the hearing decision is unsatisfactory, a beneficiary may request a review from the Council.[275] The request must be made within 60 days of receipt of the hearing decision.[276] If $1,630 (in 2019) remains in controversy after the hearing, the case may proceed to a federal district court.[277]

In *Chamberlain v. Leavitt*,[278] the federal district court applied "a heightened standard of review" when a beneficiary was not represented by counsel at the administrative hearing. Heightened review required the ALJ "to ensure that the claimant secures all of the relevant medical testimony; the duty to call the claimant's physicians to testify; and the duty to instruct the claimant of his right to subpoena and cross-examine physicians." Among the key issues not considered by the ALJ were "the identity of the patient's attending physicians, therapists or nurses; the patient's daily activities, care and medications; the monitoring of the patient's nutrition and eating; and the number of times plaintiff received intramuscular injections." The court remanded the case to the ALJ for further development of the administrative hearing record.

Unrepresented beneficiaries may submit evidence without violating requirements that evidence be submitted "with the request for hearing, by the date specified in the request for hearing . . . or within ten days calendar days of receiving the notice of hearing."[279] Unrepresented beneficiaries and beneficiaries represented by someone other than a provider or supplier may also submit new evidence after a reconsideration determination without "a statement explaining why the evidence was not previously submitted. . . ."[280]

---

[273] 42 C.F.R. § 405.1014(b)(1). Section 940 of the MMA required that, starting in 2005, the amount in controversy for ALJ hearings and for judicial review be adjusted annually by the percentage increase in the medical care component of the consumer price index for urban consumers and be rounded to the nearest multiple of $10.

[274] 42 C.F.R. § 405.1014.

[275] 42 C.F.R. §§ 405.1100–1130.

[276] 42 C.F.R. § 405.1102(a).

[277] 42 C.F.R. § 405.1136(a)(1).

[278] No. 06-CV-0646 (N.D.N.Y. Feb. 10, 2009), Medicare & Medicaid Guide (CCH) 302,759.

[279] 42 C.F.R. § 405.1018(a).

[280] 42 C.F.R. § 405.1018(d).

ALJs lack authority to address breach of contract, negligence, or other claims for damages in the administrative appeal.[281]

[C] Expedited Appeals Process in Traditional Medicare

Patients in traditional Medicare may seek expedited review of a SNF's discharge from care under Part A in order to continue covered care without interruption.[282] The SNF must give the patient a general, standardized notice at least two days in advance of the proposed end of the service. If the service is to end in fewer than two days, notice must be given by the next-to-last day of service. The notice describes the service, the date coverage ends, the patient's financial liability for continued services, and how to file an appeal.

A patient must request expedited review, orally or in writing, by noon of the next calendar day after receiving notice. At that time, the patient is given a Detailed Explanation of Non-coverage (DENC),[283] a more specific notice that includes a detailed explanation of why services are being terminated, a description of any applicable Medicare coverage rules and information on how to obtain them, and other facts specific to the patient's case. The patient is not financially liable for continued services until the later of two days after receiving the notice or the termination date specified in the notice.

A reduction in service where Medicare coverage continues is not considered a termination or discharge for purposes of triggering expedited review. If the reduction in service results in a loss of Medicare coverage (e.g., the patient no longer receives seven days per week of skilled nursing care or five days per week of rehabilitation services), expedited review may be available.[284] In addition, if the SNF proposes to transfer the patient to a non-Medicare certified part of the SNF, the patient is entitled to notice and opportunity for a hearing under the Nursing Home Reform Law's transfer and discharge rules.[285]

Expedited review will be conducted by the Beneficiary and Family Centered Care Quality Improvement Organization (BFCC-QIO), which has 72 hours in which to make a decision.[286] When the BFCC-QIO receives the request for review, it must contact the provider, which then must supply the BFCC-QIO with information supporting its determination by the close of the same business day.[287] The BFCC-QIO must solicit the views of the patient and review the notice to

---

[281] Matthews v. Leavitt, 452 F.3d 145 (2d Cir. 2006).

[282] 42 C.F.R. §§ 405.1200–.1204.

[283] CMS, "FFS Expedited Determination Notices," *available at* https://www.cms.gov/Medicare/Medicare-General-Information/BNI/downloads/CMS10095B.pdf (site visited Aug. 6, 2018).

[284] 42 C.F.R. § 405.1202(a)(2).

[285] 42 U.S.C. § 1395i-3(c)(2); 42 C.F.R. § 483.12.

[286] 42 C.F.R. § 405.1202(e)(6).

[287] 42 C.F.R. §§ 405.1202(e)(1), 405.1202(f), BFCC-QIOs and SNFs, respectively.

determine whether it meets CMS requirements.[288] The patient may not incur liability if the BFCC-QIO decision is delayed because the provider did not get the necessary information to the reviewer in a timely manner.[289]

If the BFCC-QIO sustains the decision to terminate/discharge services, the patient may request expedited reconsideration, orally or in writing, by noon of the calendar day following initial notification.[290] The reconsideration will be conducted by the QIC, which must issue a decision within 72 hours of the request.[291] If the QIC does not comply with the time frame, the beneficiary may escalate the case to the ALJ level.[292]

A BFCC-QIO may review an appeal from a patient whose request is not timely filed, but the BFCC-QIO does not have to adhere to the time frame for issuing a decision, and the limitation on liability does not apply.[293]

Patients retain the right to utilize the standard appeals process as well as the new expedited process in all situations. Moreover, even if a beneficiary requests an expedited review, the beneficiary should also request that a demand bill be submitted, unless the beneficiary prevails at expedited review and Medicare-covered services are continued without interruption. The importance of invoking both the expedited appeals process as well as the demand bill process is illustrated by the fact that some Medicare contractors and ALJs, in an expedited appeal, have limited their decisions solely to a review of whether the beneficiary was entitled to continued coverage of the services in question and have refused to look at any care that was given after the decision was made to end coverage. Using the demand bill process ensures that an appealable decision will be made for all of the services a patient continues to receive.

[D] Which Cases to Appeal

The success of an appeal will be determined by the strength of the nursing and medical evidence, particularly the statements of treating physicians. Favorable decisions are more likely at higher levels of the appeals process.

When assessing a case for appeal, review whether there are technical problems with the case (e.g., whether the patient had a qualifying hospital stay and was transferred to the SNF in a timely fashion). Next, determine whether the case involves rehabilitation or skilled nursing care, or a combination of both. Cases with daily rehabilitation services are generally good cases for appeal. The services must be provided by, or under the supervision of, a professional physical therapist.

---

[288] 42 C.F.R. § 405.1202(e)(4), (2), respectively.

[289] 42 C.F.R. § 405.1202(e)(7).

[290] 42 C.F.R. § 405.1204.

[291] 42 C.F.R. § 405.1204(c)(3).

[292] 42 C.F.R. § 405.1202(c)(5).

[293] 42 C.F.R. § 405.1202(b)(2).

When assessing a skilled nursing claim, determine whether the patient received daily *per se* nursing services as listed in the regulation. If not, take a closer look at the patient's total condition. A "total condition" case should be documented by sufficient daily nursing notes. If the nursing notes are sparse or skip days, it will be more difficult to establish daily monitoring or management.

It is common for a patient to receive physical therapy three times per week. A claim for Part A coverage may be worth appealing if skilled nursing services can be documented during the other four days. Unless skilled rehabilitation therapy was provided five days per week, the skilled nursing care must be provided seven *days* per week, not seven *times* each week (five days per week in rehabilitation therapy cases).

APPENDIX 3-1 REVIEWING SKILLED NURSING FACILITY MEDICAL RECORDS

Introduction

Medicare skilled nursing facility (SNF) case files contain several types of medical records. Common medical records include hospital discharge summaries, SNF admission notes, physical examinations, physician orders, physician progress notes, daily nursing notes, medication charts, wound care charts, therapy evaluations, and therapy flow sheets (which could include physical, occupational, and speech therapy).

Hospital Discharge Summary

The hospital discharge summary contains a great deal of valuable information, including the patient's diagnoses and treatment received in the hospital. The discharge summary also lists all diagnostic procedures and a brief medical history. The patient's age and a brief statement of the events that preceded hospitalization are usually included. Look for any reference to future treatments to be performed at the SNF and for a listing of all discharge medications.

SNF Admission Notes

SNF admission notes or physical examination forms are generally completed by nursing staff. Sometimes a full physical examination is done by the patient's treating physician. These records provide assessments related to the patient's functional status upon admission, including vital sign data. Any functional or perceptual deficits are noted. Many forms include a body chart with specific references to skin problems or decubitus ulcers.

Physicians' Orders

The initial admission orders may be handwritten. It is important to make every effort to decipher these orders because of the important information they contain. If necessary, a call to the doctor's office or review by another physician or a nurse may help in reading the writing or interpreting the abbreviations, or both. The initial orders include the patient's primary and secondary diagnoses. Medications are listed with instructions for administration. For example, an order written "Inderal, PO, q.i.d." means the patient is taking Inderal, an antihypertensive medication, orally, four times daily. Some physicians will use the brand name (e.g., Inderal), while others may use the generic name (propranolol). An order for a drug "prn" means the patient is given the drug on an as-needed basis. The *Physicians' Desk Reference* and *Mosby's Nursing Drug Reference* are useful reference materials for prescription drugs.

Physician's orders include the physician certification for the required level of care. Most physician order sheets indicate whether the patient is certified for a SNF level of care. Orders are usually renewed every calendar month or 30 days and are signed by the treating physician.

The physician's orders also include all other treatments and services provided to the patient. The orders indicate skilled services, such as physical therapy treatments, as well as orders for services that may not necessarily be considered skilled services, such as the administration of over-the-counter (OTC) artificial tear drops. References such as the *Lippincott Manual of Nursing Practice* can help the advocate determine whether the level of care performed is skilled nursing care. The orders may also include quality of life information, such as whether a patient is allowed any alcoholic beverages or a leave of absence from the facility.

The file contains physician progress notes and notations from other specialists that see the patient (e.g., a consultation with an ear, nose, and throat physician or a dietitian). Often the treating physician goes to the facility only once per month to see the patient. An increase in frequency of visits may indicate that the patient needs more skilled care or that the patient's medical condition is deteriorating. The notes are helpful to define the medical issues and to indicate the frequency with which the patient's medical condition required physician intervention.

Nurses' Notes and Other Treatment Records

Other areas of the medical file may identify information about the patient's specific treatments. These areas include flow sheets and drug and treatment records. The daily nursing notes are also important. These clinical records reveal the day-to-day treatments as well as the patient's status. Some facilities keep better records than others and some nurses document patient care more thoroughly than others. First determine whether there are daily entries. Each entry is signed by the nurse on duty for the particular shift. Sometimes there may several days with no entry at all. A pattern of missing daily entries may indicate that the SNF felt the level of care was no longer skilled, which may or may not actually be the case. Unfortunately, it is difficult to document observation and assessment or management of a care plan without detailed daily nursing notes. Examining other documentation, such as wound care or medication sheets, may help substantiate daily skilled care.

A patient in a SNF may suffer from pressure sores, or decubitus ulcers. These indicate the general debility, loss of mobility, and compromised nutritional status of the patient. Specific treatments for pressure sores should be documented in the physician orders and nursing notes. A wound care chart or treatment record has a diagram of the body showing the location of the ulcers or wounds. Entries in these records indicate the location, size, and depth of the wound. They also reveal whether there is any drainage from the wound and the "stage" of the wound. Skin ulcers are classified as stages I to IV, with stages indicating progressive degeneration of the wound. Stage I is inflammation or reddening of the skin. Stage IV is skin breakdown with deep tissue involvement and the presence of necrotic or dead tissue. Treatment progress is noted in these records.

Medication Charts

Medication charts document the daily administration of prescribed medications. These records reveal the drug, dose, mode, and frequency of administration. The original date of prescription, renewal date, and administration dates are noted. The administration of other treatments may also be noted. For example, daily decubitus ulcer care may be documented in the medication chart as opposed to a separate wound care chart, or a patient's bowel movements may be monitored through entries in the medication chart. There is usually a separate chart to document medication that is administered on an as-needed basis or medication that is withheld for any reason. Nurses' initials usually appear each time a medication is administered.

Therapy Records

Patients receiving therapy have therapy evaluations and progress flow sheets. These are the most important records in cases that rely on daily physical therapy as the qualifying skilled service. The evaluation portion assesses the patient's functional problems and need for rehabilitative physical therapy. The care plan addresses the patient's specific treatments and their frequency and identifies both short-term and long-term rehabilitation goals and their frequency. Therapy records may be signed by both the registered physical therapist and the treating physician. Daily progress notes or flow sheets document the treatments actually received by the patient. These records include the dates of services, mobility status, specific rehabilitation modalities, and patient endurance. Some records also have brief narrative notes concerning each treatment. These are signed or initialed by the treating physical therapist.

Nonskilled Services

Documentation of nonskilled services, such as care provided by certified nurse aides (CNAs), may be present in the record. The records may contain valuable information regarding the total condition of the patient, for example, input and output (I&O), pattern of bowel elimination, urinary incontinence, and mobility patterns. Their value should not be overlooked in supplementing the licensed nurses' notes.

Conclusion

A careful review and understanding of the beneficiary's medical records is key to a successful Medicare appeal. Once significant portions of the medical record are identified, be certain they are available to the ALJ or other decision-makers and that they become part of the formal Medicare appeal record.

APPENDIX 3-2 WORKSHEETS

1. Reviewing Skilled Nursing Facility Records

Documents Contained in a Skilled Nursing Facility Record:

- Hospital Discharge Summary (W-10)
- Skilled Nursing Facility Admission Notes
- Physician Orders
- Nurses' Notes & Other Treatment Records
- Medication Charts
- Therapy Records
- Nonskilled Services

2. Establishing Medical Necessity

- Review patient's demographics, e.g., age, gender
- Compare assistive devices, functional limitations, and activities permitted with patient's age, disability, and diagnoses
- Note complexity of diagnoses and conditions that interact with each other
- Group medications by classification, noting multiple drugs for the same diagnosis
- Look for new medications or changes in doses of existing medications
- New physician orders may indicate a change in patient's condition
- Note changes in vital signs
- Look for increases in frequency of visits by skilled staff, which may indicate deterioration of the patient or need for skilled observation
- Examine visit documentation for evidence of observation and assessment, management of a care plan, and patient education
- Review therapy narratives, ventilator settings, wound care charts, gastric tube feedings, and medical social worker records for changes in patient condition
- Review wound care charts and diagrams, which show healing and treatment changes
- Compare therapeutic diets and fluid restrictions with patient's diagnoses, nutritional status, height, and weight
- Review nonskilled records for evidence of changes in patient's condition

3. Skilled Nursing Facility Review

Center Case No:

Date Reviewed:

Advocate:

Patient:

HIC#:

Provider:

Period at Issue:

Services at Issue/Delivered:

☐ SN ☐ PT ☐ OT ☐ ST ☐ Other

Age:

Diagnoses:

1.

2.

3.

4.

Surgical Procedures:

1.

2.

Functional Limitations:

Activities Permitted:

Mental Status:

Therapeutic Diet:

Case No.:

Reasonableness and Necessity:

- ☐ Obs. & Assess:
- ☐ Mgmt. of Care Plan:
- ☐ PT Teaching:

Skilled Nursing Services:

- ☐ IV or IM injections or IV feedings
- ☐ Enteral feedings (at least 26% of caloric requirements and at least 501 ml of fluid)
- ☐ Nasopharyngeal or tracheostomy aspiration
- ☐ Sterile insertion, irrigation, and replacement of catheters
- ☐ Dressings involving medications and aseptic technique
- ☐ Treatment of decubitus ulcers or widespread skin disorders
- ☐ Heat treatments ordered by MD
- ☐ Administration of medical gases
- ☐ Rehabilitation nursing

Therapy Services:

- ☐ Therapeutic exercises
- ☐ Gait evaluation & training
- ☐ ROM/Exercise
- ☐ Maintenance therapy
- ☐ Ultrasound, shortwave, and microwave therapy
- ☐ Hot pack, hydrocollator, infrared treatment, paraffin baths, and whirlpool
- ☐ Speech pathologist

Number of Days Used:
Dates of Discontinuation of Therapy Services:

- ☐ PT ___________ ___________
- ☐ OT ___________ ___________
- ☐ ST ___________ ___________

SNF Level of Care Required ☐ Yes ☐ No

Notice Issues:

Notice Adequate ☐ Yes ☐ No

- ☐ Unsigned Notice
- ☐ Telephone Notification Only
- ☐ No Evidence Notice Mailed/Received

Perceived issue for which claim may have been denied:

- ☐ No three-day qualifying hospital stay
- ☐ Not Reasonable and Necessary
- ☐ Non-Medicare-Certified Bed

Is documentation adequate to succeed on coverage appeal to ALJ?

- ☐ Yes
- ☐ No

If no, specify:

APPENDIX 3-3 IMPORTANT SELECTIONS FROM THE MEDICARE BENEFIT POLICY MANUAL

Chapter 8—Coverage of Extended Care (SNF) Services Under Hospital Insurance

Skilled Nursing and Rehabilitation Definitions

30. Skilled Nursing Facility Level of Care—General

(Rev. 179, Issued: 01-14-14, Effective: 01-07-14, Implementation: 01-07-14) A3-3132, SNF-214

Care in a SNF is covered if all of the following four factors are met:

- The patient requires skilled nursing services or skilled rehabilitation services, i.e., services that must be performed by or under the supervision of professional or technical personnel (see §§ 30.2–30.4); are ordered by a physician and the services are rendered for a condition for which the patient received inpatient hospital services or for a condition that arose while receiving care in a SNF for a condition for which he received inpatient hospital services;
- The patient requires these skilled services on a daily basis (see § 30.6); and
- As a practical matter, considering economy and efficiency, the daily skilled services can be provided only on an inpatient basis in a SNF. (See § 30.7.)
- The services delivered are reasonable and necessary for the treatment of a patient's illness or injury, i.e., are consistent with the nature and severity of the individual's illness or injury, the individual's particular medical needs, and accepted standards of medical practice. The services must also be reasonable in terms of duration and quantity.

If any one of these four factors is not met, a stay in a SNF, even though it might include the delivery of some skilled services, is not covered. For example, payment for a SNF level of care could not be made if a patient needs an intermittent rather than daily skilled service.

In reviewing claims for SNF services to determine whether the level of care requirements are met, the intermediary of Medicare Administrative Contractor (MAC) first considers whether a patient needs skilled care. If a need for a skilled service does not exist, then the "daily" and "practical matter" requirements are not addressed. See section 30.2.2.1 for a discussion of the role of appropriate documentation in facilitating accurate coverage determinations for claims involving skilled care. Additional material on documentation appears in the various clinical scenarios that are presented throughout these level of care guidelines.

Coverage of nursing care and/or therapy to perform a maintenance program does not turn on the presence or absence of an individual's potential for improvement from the nursing care and/or therapy, but rather on the beneficiary's need for skilled care.

Eligibility for SNF Medicare A coverage has not changed with the inception of PPS. However, the skilled criteria and the medical review process have changed slightly. For Medicare to render payment for skilled services provided to a beneficiary during a SNF Part A stay, the facility must complete and MDS.

■ **EXAMPLE:** Even though the irrigation of a suprapubic catheter may be a skilled nursing service, daily irrigation may not be "reasonable and necessary" for the treatment of a patient's illness or injury.

30.1 Administrative Level of Care Presumption

(Rev. 57, Issued: 11-08-06, Effective: 07-27-06, Implementation: 12-14-06)

Under the SNF PPS, beneficiaries who are admitted (or readmitted) directly to a SNF after a qualifying hospital stay are considered to meet the level of care requirements of 42 CFR 409.31 up to and including the assessment reference date (ARD) for the 5-day assessment prescribed in 42 CFR 413.343(b), when correctly assigned to one of the Resource Utilization Groups (RUGs) that is designated (in the annual publication of Federal prospective payment rates described in 42 CFR 413.345) as representing the required level of care. If the beneficiary is not admitted (or readmitted) directly to a SNF after a qualifying hospital Stay, the administrative level of care presumption does not apply.

For purposes of this presumption, the assessment reference date is defined in accordance with 42 CFR 483.315(d), and must occur no later than the eighth day of posthospital SNF care. Consequently, of the ARD for the 5-day assessment* prescribed in 42 CFR 413.343(b) is set on day 9, or later, the administrative level of care presumption does not apply. The coverage that arises from this presumption remains in effect for as long thereafter as it continues to be supported by the facts of the beneficiary's condition and care needs. However, this administrative presumption does not apply to any of the subsequent assessments.

To be correctly assigned, the data coded on the Resident Assessment Instrument (RAI) must be accurate and meet the definitions described in the Long Term Care Facility RAI User's Manual. The beneficiary must receive services in the SNF that are reasonable and necessary. Services provided to the beneficiary during the hospital stay are reviewed to ensure proper coding of the most recent version of the RAI. The two examples illustrated below demonstrate a correct assignment and an incorrect assignment.

---

* Includes Medicare Readmission/Return Assessment.

Incorrect Assignment:	IV med provided in hospital coded on MDS, but IV was for a surgical procedure only—as a consequence, the MDS is on accurate and the presumption does not apply (see Chapter 3, Section P of the RAI).
Correct Assignment:	Beneficiary is receiving oxygen therapy as well as rehab service. The respiratory therapy services are found reasonable and necessary; however, the rehab services are found not reasonable and necessary, resulting in a revised RUG. Beneficiary was and is now correctly assigned—presumption applies.

A beneficiary who groups into other than one of the RUGs designated as representing the required level of care on the 5-day assessment prescribed in 42 CFR 413.343(b) is not automatically classified as meeting or not meeting the SNF level of care definition. Instead, the beneficiary must receive an individual level of care determination using existing administrative criteria and procedures.

The following scenarios further clarify that a beneficiary's correct classification to one of the RUGs that is designated (in the annual publication of Federal prospective payment rates described in 42 CFR 413.345) as representing the required level of care triggers the coverage presumption under the initial 5-day, Medicare-required assessment only when that assessment occurs directly following the beneficiary's hospital discharge.

1. Routine SNF Admission Directly From Qualifying Hospital Stay. If the beneficiary is admitted to the SNF immediately following a 3-day qualifying hospital stay, there is a presumption that he or she meets the Medicare level of care criteria when correctly assigned to one of the RUGs that is designated (in the annual publication of Federal prospective payment rates described in 42 CFR 413.345) as representing the required level of care. The presumption lasts through the assessment reference date of the 5-day assessment, which must occur no later than the eighth day of the stay.
2. Admission to SNF does not immediately follow discharge from the qualifying hospital stay, but occurs within 30 days (as required under the "30 day transfer rule). If the beneficiary is discharged from the hospital to a setting other than the SNF, the presumption of coverage does not apply, even if the beneficiary's SNF admission occurs within 30 days of discharge from the qualifying hospital stay. Accordingly, coverage would be determined based on a review of the medical evidence in the file.
3. SNF Resident is Re-Hospitalized and Then Returns Directly to the SNF. If a beneficiary who has been in a covered Part A stay required readmission to a hospital, and subsequently returns directly to the SNF for

continuing care, there is a presumption that he or she meets the level of care criteria upon readmission to the SNF when correctly assigned to one of the RUGs that is designated (in the annual publication of Federal prospective payment rates described in 42 CFR 413.345) as representing the required level of care. A new Medicare 5-day assessment is required and the presumption of coverage lasts through the assessment reference date of that assessment, which must occur no later than the eighth day of the stay.

4. Routine SNF Admission Directly From Qualifying Hospital Stay, but Initial Portion of SNF Stay Covered by Another Insurer (Medicare as Secondary Payer). When a beneficiary goes directly from a qualifying hospital stay to the SNF, but the initial portion of the SNF stay is covered by another insurer that is primary to Medicare, Medicare coverage would not start until coverage by the primary insurer ends. Accordingly, the Medicare required schedule of the assessment is not required to begin until the first day of Medicare coverage. If a beneficiary met the level of care criteria for Medicare coverage during the first 8 days of the stay following a qualifying hospital stay, and the other insurer covered this part of the stay, there is no presumption. If Medicare becomes primary before the eighth day of the stay following a qualifying hospital stay, the presumption would apply through the assessment reference date on the 5-day assessment or, if earlier, the eighth day of the stay.

5. Readmission to SNF Within 30 Days After Discharge From Initial SNF Stay—No Intervening Hospitalization. As noted in scenario 1, if a beneficiary is initially admitted to the SNF directly from the hospital for a covered Part A stay, the presumption for that stay is applicable when the

6. Initial, Non-Medicare SNF Stay Followed by Qualifying Hospitalization and Readmission to SNF for Medicare Stay. Dually eligible (Medicare/Medicaid) Beneficiaries whose initial stay in the SNF is either Medicaid-covered or private pay, are eligible for the Medicare presumption of coverage when readmitted to the SNF following a qualifying hospitalization, when correctly assigned to one of the RUGs that is designated (in the annual publication of Federal prospective payment rates described in 42 CFR 413.234) are representing the required level of care. (Of course, in order to qualify for Medicare coverage upon readmission, the beneficiary must be placed in the portion of the institution that is actually certified by Medicare as a SNF.)

   No presumption of coverage applies when Medicare is the secondary payer for days 1 through 8 of the covered stay where Medicare becomes primary after day 8 due to a reversal or denial by the secondary insurer.

7. Transfer From One SNF to Another. There is no presumption of coverage in cases involving the transfer of a beneficiary from one SNF to another or from SNF-level care in a swing bed to a SNF. The presumption only applies to the SNF stay that immediately follows the qualifying hospital stay when the beneficiary is correctly assigned to one of the RUGs that is designated (in the annual publication of Federal prospective payment rates described in 2 CFR 413.345) as representing the required level of care. Therefore, in cases involving transfer of a beneficiary from a swing-bed hospital to a SNF, the presumption only applies if the beneficiary was receiving acute care (rather than SNF-level care) immediately prior to discharge from the swing-bed hospital.

30.2 Skilled Nursing and Skilled Rehabilitation Services

(Rev. 1, 10-01-03)

30.2.1 Skilled Services Defined

(Rev. 179, Issued: 01-14-14, Effective: 01-07-14, Implementation: 01-07-14)

Skilled nursing and/or skilled rehabilitation services are those services, furnished pursuant to physician orders, that:

- Require the skills of qualified technical or professional health personnel such as registered nurses, licensed practical (vocational) nurses, physical therapists, occupational therapists, and speech pathologists or audiologists; and
- Must be provided directly by or under the general supervision of these skilled nursing or skilled rehabilitation personnel to assure the safety of the patient and to achieve the medically desired result.

■ **NOTE:** "General supervision" requires initial direction and periodic inspection of the actual activity. However, the supervisor need not always be physically present or on the premises when the assistant is performing services.

Skilled care may be necessary to improve a patient's current condition, to maintain the patient's current condition, or to prevent or slow further deterioration of the patient's condition.

30.2.2 Principles for Determining Whether a Service is Skilled

(Rev. 179, Issued: 01-14-14, Effective, 01-07-14, Implementation: 01-07-14) A3-3132.1B, SNF-214.1.B

- If the inherent complexity of a service prescribed for a patient is such that it can be performed safely and/or effectively only by or under the general supervision of skilled nursing or skilled rehabilitation personnel, the service is a skilled service; e.g., the administration of intravenous feedings and intramuscular injections; the insertion of suprapubic catheters; and ultrasound, shortwave, and microwave therapy treatments.
- The intermediary or MAC considers the nature of the service and the skills required for safe and effective delivery of that service in deciding whether a service is a skilled service. While a patient's particular medical condition is a valid factor in deciding if skilled services are needed, a patient's diagnosis or prognosis should never be the sole factor in deciding that a service is not skilled.

  ■ **EXAMPLE:** When rehabilitation services are the primary services, the key issue is whether the skills of a therapist are needed. The deciding factor is not the patient's potential for recovery, but whether the services needed require the skills of a therapist or whether they can be provided by nonskilled personnel. (See § 30.5.)

- A service that is ordinarily considered nonskilled could be considered a skilled service in cases in which, because of special medical complications, skilled nursing or skilled rehabilitation personnel are required to perform or supervise it or to observe the patient. In these cases, the complications and special services involved must be documented by physicians' orders and nursing or therapy notes.

  ■ **EXAMPLE:** Whirlpool baths do not ordinarily require the skills of a qualified physical therapist. However, the skills, knowledge, and judgment of a qualified physical therapist might be required where the patient's condition is complicated by circulatory deficiency, areas of desensitization, or open wounds. The documentation needs to support the severity of the circulatory condition that requires skilled care (see section 30.2.2.1).

- In determining whether services rendered in a SNF constitute covered care, it is necessary to determine whether individual services are skilled, and whether, in light of the patient's total condition, skilled management of the services provided is needed even though many or all of the specific services were unskilled.

■ **EXAMPLE:** An 81-year-old woman who is aphasic and confused, suffers from hemiplegia, congestive heart failure, and atrial fibrillation, has suffered a cerebrovascular accident, is incontinent, has a Stage 1 decubitus ulcer, and is unable to communicate and make her needs known. Even though no specific service provided is skilled, the patient's condition requires daily skilled nursing involvement to manage a plan for the total care needed, to observe the patient's progress, and to evaluate the need for changes in the treatment plan. As discussed in section 30.2.2.1 below, the medical condition of the patient must be described and documented to support the goals for the patient and the need for skilled nursing services.

- The importance of a particular service to an individual patient, or the frequency with which it must be performed, does not, by itself, make it a skilled service.

■ **EXAMPLE:** A primary need of a nonambulatory patient may be frequent changes of position in order to avoid development of decubitus ulcers. However, since such changing of position does not ordinarily require skilled nursing or skilled rehabilitation personnel, it would not constitute a skilled service, even though such services are obviously necessary.

- The possibility of adverse effects from the improper performance of an otherwise unskilled service does not make it a skilled service unless there is documentation to support the need for skilled nursing or skilled rehabilitation personnel. Although the act of turning a patient normally is not a skilled service, for some patients the skills of a nurse may be necessary to assure proper body alignment in order to avoid contractures and deformities. In all such cases, the reasons why skilled nursing or skilled rehabilitation personnel are essential must be documented in the patient's record.

30.2.2.1 Documentation to Support Skilled Care Determinations

(Rev. 179, Issued: 01-14-14, Effective: 01-07-14, Implementation: 01-07-14) A3-3132.1.C, SNF-214.1.C

Claims for skilled care coverage need to include sufficient documentation to enable a reviewer to determine whether—

- Skilled involvement is required in order for the services in question to be furnished safely and effectively; and
- The services themselves are, in fact, reasonable and necessary for the treatment of a patient's illness or injury, i.e., are consistent with the nature and severity of the individual's illness or injury, the individual's

particular medical needs, and accepted standards of medical practice. The documentation must also show that the services are appropriate in terms of duration and quantity, and that the services promote the documented therapeutic goals.

Such determinations would be made from the perspective of the patient's condition when the services were ordered and what was, at that time, reasonably expected to be appropriate treatment for the illness or injury. Thus, when a service appears reasonable and necessary from that perspective, it would not then be appropriate to deny the service retrospectively merely because the goals of treatment have not yet been achieved. However, if it becomes apparent at some point that the goal set for the patient is no longer a reasonable one, then the treatment goal itself should be promptly and appropriately modified to reflect this, and the patient should then be reassessed to determine whether the treatment goal as revised continues to require the provision of skilled services. By the same token, the **treatment goal itself** cannot be modified retrospectively, e.g., when it becomes apparent that the initial treatment goal of restoration is no longer a reasonable one, the provider cannot retroactively alter the initial goal of treatment from restoration to maintenance. Instead, it would make such a change on a prospective basis only.

Although the presence of appropriate documentation is not, in and of itself, an element of the definition of a "skilled" service, such documentation serves as the means by which a provider would be able to establish and a contractor would be able to confirm that skilled care is, in fact, needed and received in a given case.

It is expected that the documentation in the patient's medical record will reflect the need for the skilled services provided. The patient's medical record is also expected to provide important communication among all members of the care team regarding the development, course, and outcomes of the skilled observations, assessments, treatment, and training performed. Taken as a whole, then, the documentation in the patient's medical record should illustrate the degree to which the patient is accomplishing the goals as outlined in the care plan. In this way, the documentation will serve to demonstrate why a skilled service is needed.

Thorough and timely documentation with respect to treatment goals can help clearly demonstrate a beneficiary's need for skilled care in situations where such need might not otherwise be readily apparent, as when the treatment's purpose changes (for example, from restoration to maintenance), as well as in establishing the efficacy of care that serves to prevent or slow decline—where, by definition, there would be no "improvement" to evaluate. For example, when skilled services are necessary to maintain the patient's current condition, the documentation would need to substantiate that the services of skilled personnel are, in fact, required to achieve this goal. Similarly, establishing that a maintenance program's services are reasonable and necessary would involve regularly documenting the degree to which the program's treatment goals are being accomplished. In situations where the maintenance program is performed to maintain the patient's current condition, such documentation would serve to demonstrate the program's effectiveness in achieving this goal. When the maintenance program is intended to slow further deterioration of the patient's condition, the efficacy of the services could be established by documenting that the natural progression of the patient's medical or functional decline has been interrupted. Assessments of all goals must be performed in a frequent and regular manner so that the resulting documentation provides a sufficient basis for determining the appropriateness of coverage.

Therefore the patient's medical record must document as appropriate:

- The history and physical exam pertinent to the patient's care, (including the response or changes in behavior to previously administered skilled services);
- The skilled services provided;
- The patient's response to the skilled services provided during the current visit;
- The plan for future care based on the rationale of prior results.
- A detailed rationale that explains the need for the skilled service in light of the patient's overall medical condition and experiences;
- The complexity of the service to be performed;
- Any other pertinent characteristics of the beneficiary.

The documentation in the patient's medical record must be accurate, and avoid vague or subjective descriptions of the patient's care that would not be sufficient to indicate the need for skilled care. For example, the following terminology does not sufficiently describe the reaction of the patient to his/her skilled care:

- Patient tolerated treatment well
- Continue with POC
- Patient remains stable

Such phraseology does not provide a clear picture of the results of the treatment, nor the "next steps" that are planned. Objective measurements of physical outcomes of treatment should be provided and/or a clear description of the changed behaviors due to education programs should be recorded so that all concerned can follow the results of the provided services.

30.2.3 Specific Examples of Some Skilled Nursing or Skilled Rehabilitation Services

(Rev. 179, Issued: 01-14-14, Effective: 01-07-14, Implementation: 01-07-14) A3-3132.1.C, SNF-214.1.C

30.2.3.1 Management and Evaluation of a Patient Care Plan

(Rev. 179, Issued: 01-14-14, Effective: 01-07-14, Implementation: 01-07-14) A3-3132.1.C.1, SNF-214.1.C.1

The development, management, and evaluation of a patient care plan, based on the physician's orders and supporting documentation, constitute skilled nursing services when, in terms of the patient's physical or mental condition, these services require the involvement of skilled nursing personnel to meet the patient's medical needs, promote recovery, and ensure medical safety. However, the planning and management of a treatment plan that does not involve the furnishing of skilled services may not require skilled nursing personnel; e.g., a care plan for a patient with organic brain syndrome who requires only oral medication and a protective environment. The sum total of nonskilled services would only add up to the need for skilled management and evaluation when the condition of the beneficiary is such that there is an expectation that a change in condition is likely without that intervention.

The patient's clinical record may not always specifically identify "skilled planning and management activities" as such. Therefore, in this limited context, if the documentation of the patient's overall condition substantiates a finding that the patient's medical needs and safety can be addressed only if the total care, skilled or not, is planned and managed by skilled nursing personnel, it is appropriate to infer that skilled management is being provided, but only if the record as a whole clearly establishes that there was a likely potential for serious complications without skilled management, as illustrated in the following Examples.

■ **EXAMPLE 1:** An aged patient with a history of diabetes mellitus and angina pectoris is recovering from an open reduction of the neck of the femur. He requires, among other services, careful skin care, appropriate oral medications, a diabetic diet, a therapeutic exercise program to preserve muscle tone and body condition, and observation to notice signs of deterioration in his condition or complications resulting from his restricted (but increasing) mobility. Although any of the required services could be performed by a properly instructed person, that person would not have the capability to understand the relationship among the services and their effect on each other. Since the nature of the patient's condition, his age, and his immobility create a high potential for serious complications, such an understanding is essential to assure the patient's recovery and safety. The management of this plan of care requires skilled nursing personnel until such time as skilled care is no longer required in coordinating the patient's treatment regimen, even though the individual services involved are supportive in nature and do not require skilled nursing personnel. The documentation in the medical record as a whole is essential for this determination and must illustrate the complexity of the unskilled services that are a necessary part of the medical treatment and which require the involvement of skilled nursing personnel to promote the stabilization of the patient's medical condition and safety.

■ **EXAMPLE 2:** An aged patient is recovering from pneumonia, is lethargic, is disoriented, has residual chest congestion, is confined to bed as a result of his debilitated condition, and requires restraints at times. To decrease the chest congestion, the physician has prescribed frequent changes in position, coughing, and deep breathing. While the residual chest congestion alone would not represent a high risk factor, the patient's immobility and confusion represent complicating factors which, when coupled with the chest congestion, could create high probability of a relapse. In this situation, skilled overseeing of the nonskilled services would be reasonable and necessary, pending the elimination of the chest congestion, to assure the patient's medical safety. The documentation in the medical record as a whole is essential for this determination and must illustrate the complexity of the unskilled services that are a necessary part of the medical treatment and which require the involvement of skilled nursing personnel to promote the patient's recovery and medical safety in view of the patient's overall condition.

30.2.3.2 Observation and Assessment of Patient's Condition

(Rev. 179, Issued: 01-14-14, Effective: 01-07-14, Implementation: 01-07-14) A3-3132.1.C.2, SNF-214.1.C.2

Observation and assessment are skilled services when the likelihood of change in a patient's condition requires skilled nursing or skilled rehabilitation personnel to identify and evaluate the patient's need for possible modification of treatment or initiation of additional medical procedures, until the patient's treatment regimen is essentially stabilized.

■ **EXAMPLE 1:** A patient with arteriosclerotic heart disease with congestive heart failure requires close observation by skilled nursing personnel for signs of decompensation, abnormal fluid balance, or adverse effects resulting from prescribed medication. Skilled observation is needed to determine whether the digitalis dosage should be reviewed or whether other therapeutic measures should be considered, until the patient's treatment regimen is essentially stabilized. The medical documentation must describe the skilled services that require the involvement of nursing personnel to promote the stabilization of the patient's medical condition and safety.

■ **EXAMPLE 2:** A patient has undergone peripheral vascular disease treatment including revascularization procedures (bypass) with open or necrotic areas of skin on the involved extremity. Skilled observation and monitoring of the vascular supply of the legs is required. The medical documentation must describe the skilled services that require the involvement of nursing personnel to promote the patient's recovery and medical safety in view of the patient's overall condition.

■ **EXAMPLE 3:** A patient has undergone hip surgery and has been transferred to a SNF. Skilled observation and monitoring of the patient for possible adverse reaction to the operative procedure, development of phlebitis, or skin breakdown is both reasonable and necessary. The medical documentation must describe the skilled services that require the involvement of nursing personnel to promote the patient's recovery and medical safety in view of the patient's overall condition.

■ **EXAMPLE 4:** A patient has been hospitalized following a heart attack, and following treatment but before mobilization, is transferred to the SNF. Because it is unknown whether exertion will exacerbate the heart disease, skilled observation is reasonable and necessary as mobilization is initiated, until the patient's treatment regimen is essentially stabilized. The medical documentation must describe the skilled services that require the involvement of nursing personnel to promote the stabilization of the patient's medical condition and safety.

■ **EXAMPLE 5:** A frail 85-year-old man was hospitalized for pneumonia. The infection was resolved, but the patient, who had previously maintained adequate nutrition, will not eat or eats poorly. The patient is transferred to a SNF for monitoring of fluid and nutrient intake, assessment of the need for tube feeding and forced feeding if required. Observation and monitoring by skilled nursing personnel of the patient's oral intake is required to prevent dehydration. The medical documentation must describe the skilled services that require the involvement of nursing personnel to promote the patient's recovery and medical safety in view of the patient's overall condition.

■ **EXAMPLE 6:** A patient with congestive heart failure may require continuous close observation to detect signs of decompensation, abnormal fluid balance, or adverse effects resulting from prescribed medication(s) that serve as indicators for adjusting therapeutic measures. The medical documentation must describe the skilled services that require the involvement of nursing personnel to promote the patient's recovery and medical safety in view of the patient's overall condition, to maintain the patient's current condition, or to prevent or slow further deterioration in the patient's condition.

If a patient was admitted for skilled observation but did not develop a further acute episode or complication, the skilled observation services still are covered so long as there was a reasonable probability for such a complication or further acute episode. "Reasonable probability" means that a potential complication or further acute episode was a likely possibility.

Information from the patient's medical record must document that there is a reasonable potential for a future complication or acute episode sufficient to justify the need for continued skilled observation and assessment.

Such signs and symptoms as abnormal/fluctuating vital signs, weight changes, edema, symptoms of drug toxicity, abnormal/fluctuating lab values, and respiratory changes on auscultation may justify skilled observation and assessment. Where these signs and symptoms are such that there is a reasonable potential that skilled observation and assessment by a licensed nurse will result in changes to the treatment of the patient, then the services are reasonable and necessary. However, observation and assessment by a nurse is not reasonable and necessary to the treatment of the illness or injury where these characteristics are part of a longstanding pattern of the patient's waxing and waning condition which by themselves do not require skilled services and there is no attempt to change the treatment to resolve them.

Skilled observation and assessment may also be required for patients whose primary condition and needs are psychiatric in nature or for patients who, in addition to their physical problems, have a secondary psychiatric diagnosis. These patients may exhibit acute psychological symptoms such as depression, anxiety or agitation, which require skilled observation and assessment such as observing for indications of suicidal or hostile behavior. However, these conditions often require considerably more specialized, sophisticated nursing techniques and physician attention than is available in most participating SNFs. (SNFs that are primarily engaged in treating psychiatric disorders are precluded by law from participating in Medicare.) Therefore, these cases must be carefully documented.

30.2.3.3 Teaching and Training Activities

(Rev. 179, Issued: 01-14-14, Effective: 01-07-14, Implementation: 01-07-14) A3-3132.1.C.3, SNF-214.1.C.3

Teaching and training activities, which require skilled nursing or skilled rehabilitation personnel to teach a patient how to manage their treatment regimen, would constitute skilled services. Some examples are:

- Teaching self-administration of injectable medications or a complex range of medications;
- Teaching a newly diagnosed diabetic to administer insulin injections, to prepare and follow a diabetic diet, and to observe foot-care precautions;

- Teaching self-administration of medical gases to a patient;
- Gait training and teaching of prosthesis care for a patient who has had a recent leg amputation;
- Teaching patients how to care for a recent colostomy or ileostomy;
- Teaching patients how to perform self-catheterization and self-administration of gastrostomy feedings;
- Teaching patients how to care for and maintain central venous lines, such as Hickman catheters;
- Teaching patients the use and care of braces, splints and orthotics, and any associated skin care; and
- Teaching patients the proper care of any specialized dressings or skin treatments.

The documentation must thoroughly describe all efforts that have been made to educate the patient/caregiver, and their responses to the training. The medical record should also describe the reason for the failure of any educational attempts, if applicable.

■ **EXAMPLE:** A newly diagnosed diabetic patient is seen in order to learn to self-administer insulin injections, to prepare and follow a diabetic diet, and to observe foot-care precautions. Even though the patient voices understanding of the nutritional principles of his diabetic diet, he expresses dissatisfaction with his food choices and refuses to comply with the education he is receiving. This refusal continues, notwithstanding efforts to counsel the patient on the potentially adverse consequences of the refusal and to suggest alternative dietary choices that could help to avoid or alleviate those consequences. The patient's response to the recommended treatment plan as well as to all educational attempts is documented in the medical record.

30.2.4 Questionable Situations

(Rev. 1, 10-01-03)
A3-3132.1.D, SNF-214.1.D

There must be specific evidence that daily skilled nursing or skilled rehabilitation services are required and received if:

- The primary service needed is oral medication; or
- The patient is capable of independent ambulation, dressing, feeding, and hygiene.

30.3 Direct Skilled Nursing Services to Patients

(Rev. 179, Issued: 01-14-14, Effective: 01-07-14, Implementation: 01-07-14) A3-3132.2, SNF-214.2

Nursing services are considered skilled when they are so inherently complex that they can be safely and effectively performed only by, or under the supervision of, a registered nurse or, when provided by regulation, a licensed practical (vocational) nurse. (See 42 CFR § 409.32.) If all other requirements for coverage under the SNF benefit are met, skilled nursing services are covered when an individualized assessment of the patient's clinical condition demonstrates that the specialized judgment, knowledge, and skills of a registered nurse or, when provided by regulation, a licensed practical (vocational) nurse are necessary. Skilled nursing services would be covered where such skilled nursing services are necessary to maintain the patient's current condition or prevent or slow further deterioration so long as the beneficiary requires skilled care for the services to be safely and effectively provided, and all other requirements for coverage under the SNF benefit are met. Coverage does not turn on the presence or absence of an individual's potential for improvement from nursing care, but rather on the beneficiary's need for skilled care.

A condition that would not ordinarily require skilled nursing services may nevertheless require them under certain circumstances. In such instances, skilled nursing care is necessary only when (a) the particular patient's special medical complications require the skills of a registered nurse or, when provided by regulation, a licensed practical nurse to perform a type of service that would otherwise be considered nonskilled; or (b) the needed services are of such complexity that the skills of a registered nurse or, when provided by regulation, a licensed practical nurse are required to furnish the services.

A service is not considered a skilled nursing service merely because it is performed by or under the direct supervision of a nurse. If a service can be safely and effectively performed (or self-administered) by an unskilled person, the service cannot be regarded as a skilled nursing service although a nurse actually provides the service. Similarly, the unavailability of a competent person to provide a nonskilled service, regardless of the importance of the service to the patient, does not make it a skilled service when a nurse provides the service.

Some examples of direct skilled nursing services are:

- Intravenous or intramuscular injections and intravenous feedings;
- Enteral feeding that comprises at least 26 percent of daily caloric requirements and provides at least 501 milliliters of fluid per day;
- Naso-pharyngeal and tracheotomy aspiration;
- Insertion, sterile irrigation, and replacement of suprapubic catheters;

- Application of dressings involving prescription medications and aseptic techniques (see § 30.5 for exception);
- Treatment of decubitus ulcers, of a severity rated at Stage 3 or worse, or a widespread skin disorder (see § 30.5 for exception);
- Heat treatments which have been specifically ordered by a physician as part of active treatment and which require observation by skilled nursing personnel to evaluate the patient's progress adequately (see § 30.5 for exception);
- Rehabilitation nursing procedures, including the related teaching and adaptive aspects of nursing, that are part of active treatment and require the presence of skilled nursing personnel; e.g., the institution and supervision of bowel and bladder training programs;
- Initial phases of a regimen involving administration of medical gases such as bronchodilator therapy; and
- Care of a colostomy during the early postoperative period in the presence of associated complications. The need for skilled nursing care during this period must be justified and documented in the patient's medical record.

30.4 Direct Skilled Rehabilitation Services to Patients

(Rev. 179, Issued: 01-14-14, Effective: 01-07-14, Implementation: 01-07-14) A3-3132.1.C, SNF-214.1.C

The following sections contain examples and guidelines concerning direct skilled therapy services to patients, including skilled physical therapy, occupational therapy, and speech/language pathology therapy.

Coverage for such skilled therapy services does not turn on the presence or absence of a beneficiary's potential for improvement from therapy services, but rather on the beneficiary's need for skilled care. Therapy services are considered skilled when they are so inherently complex that they can be safely and effectively performed only by, or under the supervision of, a qualified therapist. (See 42 CFR § 409.32.) These skilled services may be necessary to improve the patient's current condition, to maintain the patient's current condition, or to prevent or slow further deterioration of the patient's condition.

If all other requirements for coverage under the SNF benefit are met, such skilled therapy services are covered when an individualized assessment of the patient's clinical condition demonstrates that the specialized judgment, knowledge, and skills of a qualified therapist are necessary for the performance of the rehabilitation services.

30.4.1 Skilled Physical Therapy

(Rev. 1, 10-01-03)
A3-3132.3.A, SNF-214.3.A

30.4.1.1 General

(Rev. 179, Issued: 01-04-14, Effective: 01-07-14, Implementation: 01-07-14)

Skilled physical therapy services must meet all of the following conditions:

- The services must be directly and specifically related to an active written treatment plan that is based upon an initial evaluation performed by a qualified physical therapist after admission to the SNF and prior to the start of physical therapy services in the SNF that is approved by the physician after any needed consultation with the qualified physical therapist. In those cases where a beneficiary is discharged during the SNF stay and later readmitted, an initial evaluation must be performed upon readmission to the SNF, prior to the start of physical therapy services in the SNF;
- The services must be of a level of complexity and sophistication, or the condition of the patient must be of a nature that requires the judgment, knowledge, and skills of a qualified physical therapist;
- The services must be provided with the expectation, based on the assessment made by the physician of the patient's restoration potential, that the condition of the patient will improve materially in a reasonable and generally predictable period of time; or, the services must be necessary for the **establishment** of a safe and effective maintenance program; or, the services must require the skills of a qualified therapist for the **performance** of a safe and effective maintenance program. **NOTE:** See Section E. Maintenance Therapy for more guidance regarding when skilled therapy services are necessary for the performance of a safe and effective maintenance program.
- The services must be considered under accepted standards of medical practice to be specific and effective treatment for the patient's condition; and
- The services must be reasonable and necessary for the treatment of the patient's condition; this includes the requirement that the amount, frequency, and duration of the services must be reasonable.

■ **EXAMPLE 1:** An 80-year-old, previously ambulatory, post-surgical patient has been bedbound for one week and, as a result, has developed muscle atrophy, orthostatic hypotension, joint stiffness, and lower extremity edema. To the extent that the patient requires a brief period of daily skilled physical therapy services to restore lost functions, those services are reasonable and necessary and must be documented in the medical record (see § 30.2.2.1).

■ **EXAMPLE 2:** A patient with congestive heart failure also has diabetes and previously had both legs amputated above the knees. Consequently, the patient does not have a reasonable potential to achieve ambulation, but still requires daily skilled physical therapy to learn bed mobility and transferring skills, as well as functional activities at the wheelchair level. If the patient has a reasonable potential for achieving those functions in a reasonable period of time in view of the patient's total condition, the physical therapy services are reasonable and necessary and must be documented in the medical record (see § 30.2.2.1).

Physical therapy services are not reasonable and necessary and would not be covered if the expected results are insignificant in relation to the extent and duration of physical therapy services that would be required to achieve those results.

Some SNF inpatients do not require skilled physical therapy services but do require services, which are routine in nature. When services can be safely and effectively performed by supportive personnel, such as aides or nursing personnel, without the supervision of a physical therapist, they do not constitute skilled physical therapy. Additionally, services involving activities for the general good and welfare of the patient (e.g., general exercises to promote overall fitness and flexibility and activities to provide diversion or general motivation) do not constitute skilled physical therapy.

30.4.1.2 Application of Guidelines

(Rev. 179, Issued: 01-14-14, Effective: 01-07-14, Implementation: 01-07-14) A3-3132.3.A.2, SNF-214.3.A.2

Some of the more common skilled physical therapy modalities and procedures are:

A. Assessment

The skills of a physical therapist are required for the ongoing assessment of a patient's rehabilitation needs and potential. Skilled rehabilitation services concurrent with the management of a patient's care plan include tests and measurements of range of motion, strength, balance, coordination, endurance, and functional ability.

B. Therapeutic Exercises

Therapeutic exercises, which must be performed by or under the supervision of the qualified physical therapist, due either to the type of exercise employed or to the condition of the patient.

C. Gait Training

Gait evaluation and training furnished to a patient whose ability to walk has been impaired by neurological, muscular, or skeletal abnormality often require the skills of a qualified physical therapist.

Repetitious exercises to improve gait, or to maintain strength and endurance, and assistive walking can be appropriately provided by supportive personnel, e.g., aides or nursing personnel, and would not necessarily require the skills of a physical therapist. Thus, such services are not inherently skilled. However, see § 30.2.2 for the specific circumstances in which an ordinarily nonskilled service can nevertheless be considered skilled. Documentation of the patient's condition in the medical record must describe the circumstances which delineate the need for skilled rather than unskilled services during gait training.

D. Range of Motion

Only the qualified physical therapist may perform range of motion tests and, therefore, such **tests** are skilled physical therapy. Range of motion **exercises** constitute skilled physical therapy only if they are part of active treatment for a specific disease state which has resulted in a loss or restriction of mobility (as evidenced by physical therapy notes showing the degree of motion lost, the degree to be restored and the impact on mobility and/or function).

Range of motion exercises which are not related to the restoration of a specific loss of function may be provided safely by supportive personnel, such as aides or nursing personnel, and as such would not necessarily require the skills of a physical therapist. Passive exercises to maintain range of motion in paralyzed extremities that can be carried out by aides or nursing personnel would not be considered skilled care. However, see § 30.2.2. for the specific circumstances in which an ordinarily nonskilled service can nevertheless be considered skilled. Documentation of the patient's condition in the medical record must describe the circumstances which delineate the need for skilled rather than unskilled services during range of motion training.

E. Maintenance Therapy

Therapy services in connection with a maintenance program are considered skilled when they are so inherently complex that they can be safely and effectively performed only by, or under the supervision of, a qualified therapist. (See 42 CFR § 409.32.) If all other requirements for coverage under the SNF benefit are met, skilled therapy services are covered when an individualized assessment of the patient's clinical condition demonstrates that the specialized judgment, knowledge, and skills of a qualified therapist are necessary for the performance of a safe and effective maintenance program. Such a maintenance program to maintain the patient's current condition or to prevent or slow further deterioration is covered so long as the beneficiary requires skilled care for the safe and effective performance of the program. When, however, the individualized assessment does not demonstrate such a necessity for skilled care, including when the performance of a maintenance program does not require the skills of a therapist because it could safely and effectively be accomplished by the patient or with the assistance of non-therapists, including unskilled caregivers, such maintenance services do not constitute a covered level of care.

A service is not considered a skilled therapy service merely because it is furnished by a therapist or by a therapist/therapy assistant under the direct supervision of a therapist. If a service can be self-administered or safely and effectively furnished by an unskilled person, without the direct supervision of a therapist, the service cannot be regarded as a skilled therapy service even when a therapist actually furnishes the service. Similarly, the unavailability of a competent person to provide a non-skilled service, regardless of the importance of the service to the patient, does not make it a skilled service when a therapist furnishes the service.

However, even though it would not otherwise require the skills of a therapist, the performance of a maintenance program may nevertheless require such skills under certain circumstances. Specifically, skilled therapy services are necessary for the performance of a safe and effective maintenance program only when (a) the particular patient's special medical complications require the skills of a qualified therapist to perform a therapy service that would otherwise be considered nonskilled; or (b) the needed therapy procedures are of such complexity that the skills of a qualified therapist are required to perform the procedure.

If the specialized knowledge and judgment of a qualified therapist are required, the establishment or design of a maintenance program by a qualified therapist, the instruction of the beneficiary or appropriate caregiver by a qualified therapist regarding a maintenance program, and the necessary periodic reevaluations by a qualified therapist of the beneficiary and maintenance program are considered skilled therapy services, to the extent provided by regulation.

■ **EXAMPLE:** A patient with Parkinson's disease may require the services of a physical therapist to determine the type of exercises that are required to maintain his present level of function. The initial evaluation of the patient's needs, the designing of a maintenance program which is appropriate to the capacity and tolerance of the patient and the treatment objectives of the physician, the instruction of the patient or supportive personnel (e.g., aides or nursing personnel) in the carrying out of the program, would constitute skilled physical therapy and must be documented in the medical record (see § 30.2.2.1).

While a patient is receiving a skilled physical therapy program, the physical therapist should regularly reevaluate the patient's condition and adjust any exercise program the patient is expected to carry out independently or with the aid of supportive personnel to maintain the function being restored. Consequently, by the time it is determined that no further skilled therapy services are needed, i.e., by the end of the last skilled session, the physical therapist will have already designed any maintenance program required and instructed the patient or supportive personnel in the carrying out of the program.

F. Ultrasound, Shortwave, and Microwave Diathermy Treatments

These modalities must always be performed by or under the supervision of a qualified physical therapist.

G. Hot Packs, Infra-Red Treatments, Paraffin Baths, and Whirlpool Baths

Heat treatments and baths of this type ordinarily do not require the skills of a qualified physical therapist. However, the skills, knowledge, and judgment of a qualified physical therapist might be required in the giving of such treatments or baths in a particular case, e.g., where the patient's condition is complicated by circulatory deficiency, areas of desensitization, open wounds, fractures, or other complications. There must be clear documentation in the medical record of the special medical complications that describe the need for the skilled therapy provided by the therapist.

30.4.2 Speech Pathology

(Rev. 179, Issued: 01-14-14, Effective: 01-07-14, Implementation: 01-07-14)

See Pub. 100-02, Medicare Benefit Policy Manual, Chapter 1, "Inpatient Hospital Services."

See § 30.4.1.2.E Maintenance Therapy for the specific circumstances in which speech-language pathology therapy is appropriate in connection with a maintenance program.

30.4.3 Occupational Therapy—

(Rev. 179, Issued: 01-14-14, Effective: 01-07-14, Implementation: 01-07-14) A3-3132.3.C, SNF-214.3.C

See Pub. 100-02, Medicare Benefit Policy Manual, Chapter 1, "Inpatient Hospital Services."

See § 30.4.1.2.E Maintenance Therapy for the specific circumstances in which occupational therapy is appropriate in connection with a maintenance program.

30.5 Nonskilled Supportive or Personal Care Services—

(Rev. 1, 10-01-03) A3-332.4, SNF-214.4

The following services are not skilled services unless rendered under circumstances detailed in § 30.2:

- Administration of routine oral medications, eye drops, and ointments (the fact that patients cannot be relied upon to take such medications themselves or that State law requires all medications to be dispensed by a nurse to institutional patients would not change this service to a skilled service);
- General maintenance care of colostomy and ileostomy;
- Routine services to maintain satisfactory functioning of indwelling bladder catheters (this would include emptying and cleaning containers and clamping the tubing);
- Changes of dressings for uninfected post-operative or chronic conditions;
- Prophylactic and palliative skin care, including bathing and application of creams, or treatment of minor skin problems;
- Routine care of the incontinent patient, including use of diapers and protective sheets;
- General maintenance care in connection with a plaster cast (skilled supervision or observation may be required where the patient has a preexisting skin or circulatory condition or requires adjustment of traction);
- Routine care in connection with braces and similar devices;
- Use of heat as a palliative and comfort measure, such as whirlpool or steam pack;

- Routine administration of medical gases after a regimen of therapy has been established (i.e., administration of medical gases after the patient has been taught how to institute therapy);
- Assistance in dressing, eating, and going to the toilet;
- Periodic turning and positioning in bed; and
- General supervision of exercises, which have been taught to the patient and the performance of repetitious exercises that do not require skilled rehabilitation personnel for their performance. (This includes the actual carrying out of maintenance programs where the performances of repetitive exercises that may be required to maintain function do not necessitate a need for the involvement and services of skilled rehabilitation personnel. It also includes the carrying out of repetitive exercises to improve gait, maintain strength or endurance; passive exercises to maintain range of motion in paralyzed extremities which are not related to a specific loss of function; and assistive walking.) (See Medicare Benefit Policy Manual, Chapter 1, "Inpatient Hospital Services.")

30.6 Daily Skilled Services Defined

(Rev. 179, Issued: 01-14-14, Effective: 01-07-14, Implementation: 01-07-14)

Skilled nursing services or skilled rehabilitation services (or a combination of these services) must be needed and provided on a "daily basis," i.e., on essentially a 7-days-a-week basis. A patient whose inpatient stay is based solely on the need for skilled rehabilitation services would meet the "daily basis" requirement when they need and receive those services on at least 5 days a week. (If therapy services are provided less than 5 days a week, though, the "daily" requirement would not be met.)

This requirement should not be applied so strictly that it would not be met merely because there is an isolated break of a day or two during which no skilled rehabilitation services are furnished and discharge from the facility would not be practical.

■ **EXAMPLE:** A patient who normally requires skilled rehabilitation services on a daily basis may exhibit extreme fatigue, which results in suspending therapy sessions for a day or two. Coverage may continue for these days since discharge in such a case would not be practical.

In instances when a patient requires a skilled restorative nursing program to positively affect his functional well-being, the expectation is that the program be rendered at least 6 days a week. (Note that when a patient's skilled status is based on a restorative program, medical evidence must be documented to justify the services. In most instances, it is expected that a skilled restorative program will be, at most, only a few weeks in duration.)

The daily basis requirement can be met by furnishing a single type of skilled service every day, or by furnishing various types of skilled services on different days of the week that collectively add up to "daily" skilled services. However, arbitrarily staggering the timing of various therapy modalities through the week, merely in order to have some type of therapy session occur each day, would not satisfy the SNF coverage requirement for skilled care to be needed on a "daily basis." To meet this requirement, the patient must actually **need** skilled rehabilitation services to be furnished on each of the days that the facility makes such services available.

It is not sufficient for the scheduling of therapy sessions to be arranged so that some therapy is **furnished** each day, unless the patient's medical needs indicate that daily therapy is required. For example, if physical therapy is furnished on 3 days each week and occupational therapy is furnished on 2 other days each week, the "daily basis" requirement would be satisfied only if there is a valid medical reason why both cannot be furnished on the same day. The basic issue here is not whether the services are needed, but **when** they are needed. Unless there is a legitimate medical need for scheduling a therapy session each day, the "daily basis" requirement for SNF coverage would not be met.

30.7 Services Provided on an Inpatient Basis as a "Practical Matter"

(Rev. 179, Issued: 01-14-14, Effective: 01-07-14, Implementation: 01-07-14) A-3132.6, SNF-214.6

In determining whether the daily skilled care needed by an individual can, as a "practical matter," only be provided in a SNF on an inpatient basis, the intermediary or MAC considers the individual's physical condition and the availability and feasibility of using more economical alternative facilities or services.

As a "practical matter," daily skilled services can be provided only in a SNF if they are not available on an outpatient basis in the area in which the individual resides or transportation to the closest facility would be:

- An excessive physical hardship;
- Less economical; or
- Less efficient or effective than an inpatient institutional setting.

The availability of capable and willing family or the feasibility of obtaining other assistance for the patient at home should be considered. Even though needed daily skilled services might be available on an outpatient or home care basis, as a practical matter, the care can be furnished only in the SNF if home care would be ineffective because the patient would have insufficient assistance at home to reside there safely.

■ **EXAMPLE:** A patient undergoing skilled physical therapy can walk only with supervision but has a reasonable potential to learn to walk independently with further training. Further daily skilled therapy is available on an outpatient or home care basis, but the patient would be at risk for further injury from falling, because insufficient supervision and assistance could not be arranged for the patient in his home. In these circumstances, the physical therapy services as a practical matter can be provided effectively only in the inpatient setting.

30.7.1 The Availability of Alternative Facilities or Services

(Rev. 1, 10-01-03)
A-3132.6.A, SNF-214.6.A

Alternative facilities or services may be available to a patient when health care providers such as home health agencies are utilized. These alternatives are not always available in all communities and even where they exist they may not be available when needed.

■ **EXAMPLE:** Where the residents of a rural community generally utilize the outpatient facilities of a hospital located some distance from the area, the hospital outpatient department constitutes an alternative source of care that is available to the community. Roads in winter, however, may be impassable for some periods of time and in special situations institutionalization might be needed.

In determining the availability of more economical care alternatives, the coverage or non-coverage of that alternative care is not a factor to be considered. Home health care for a patient who is not homebound, for example, may be an appropriate alternative in some cases. The fact that Medicare cannot cover such care is irrelevant.

The issue is feasibility and not whether coverage is provided in one setting and not provided in another. For instance, an individual in need of daily skilled physical therapy might be able to receive the services needed on a more economical basis from an independently practicing physical therapist. However, the fact that Medicare payment could not be made for the services because the $500 expense limitation applicable to the services of an independent physical therapist had been exceeded or because the patient was not enrolled in Part B, would not be a basis for determining that, as a practical matter, the needed care could only be provided in a SNF.

In determining the availability of alternate facilities or services, whether the patient or another resource can pay for the alternate services is not a factor to be considered.

30.7.2 Whether Available Alternatives Are More Economical in the Individual Case

(Rev. 1, 10-01-03)
A3-3132.6.B, SNF-214.6.B

If the intermediary determines that an alternative setting is available to provide the needed care, it considers whether the use of the alternative setting would actually be more economical in the individual case.

■ **EXAMPLE 1:** If a patient's condition requires daily transportation to the alternative source of care (e.g., a hospital outpatient department) by ambulance, it might be more economical from a health care delivery viewpoint to provide the needed care in the SNF setting.

■ **EXAMPLE 2:** If needed care could be provided in the home, but the patient's residence is so isolated that daily visits would entail inordinate travel costs, care in a SNF might be a more economical alternative.

30.7.3 Whether the Patient's Physical Condition Would Permit Utilization of an Available, More Economical Care Alternative

(Rev. 1, 10-01-03)
A3-3132.6.C, SNF-214.6.C

In determining the practicality of using more economical care alternatives, the intermediary considers the patient's medical condition. If the use of those alternatives would adversely affect the patient's medical condition, the intermediary concludes that as a practical matter the daily skilled services can only be provided by a SNF on an inpatient basis.

If the use of a care alternative involves transportation of the individual on a daily basis, the intermediary considers whether daily transportation would cause excessive physical hardship. Determinations on whether a patient's condition would be adversely affected if an available, more economical care alternative were utilized should not be based solely on the fact that the patient is nonambulatory. There are individuals confined to wheelchairs who, though nonambulatory, could be transported daily by automobile from their homes to alternative care sources without any adverse impact. Conversely, there are instances where an individual's condition would be adversely affected by daily transportation to a care facility, even though the individual is able to ambulate to some extent.

■ **EXAMPLE:** A 75-year-old woman has suffered a cerebrovascular accident and cannot climb stairs safely. The patient lives alone in a second-floor apartment accessible only by climbing a flight of stairs. She requires physical therapy and occupational therapy on alternate days, and they are available in a CORF one mile away from her apartment. However, because of her inability to negotiate the stairs, the daily skilled services she requires cannot, as a practical matter, be provided to the patient outside the SNF.

The "practical matter" criterion should never be interpreted so strictly that it results in the automatic denial of coverage for patients who have been meeting all of the SNF level of care requirements, but who have occasion to be away from the SNF for a brief period of time. While most beneficiaries requiring a SNF level of care find that they are unable to leave the facility, the fact that a patient is granted an outside pass or short leave of absence for the purpose of attending a special religious service, holiday meal, family occasion, going on a car ride, or for a trial visit home, is not, by itself evidence that the individual no longer needs to be in a SNF for the receipt of required skilled care. Where frequent or prolonged periods away from the SNF become possible, the intermediary may question whether the patient's care can, as a practical matter, only be furnished on an inpatient basis in a SNF. Decisions in these cases should be based on information reflecting the care needed and received by the patient while in the SNF and on the arrangements needed for the provision, if any, of this care during any absences. (*See* the Medicare Benefit Policy Manual, Chapter 3, "Duration of Covered Inpatient Services," § 20.1.2, for counting inpatient days during a leave of absence.)

A conservative approach to retain the presumption for limitation of liability may lead a facility to notify patients that leaving the facility will result in denial of coverage. Such a notice is not appropriate. If a SNF determines that covered care is no longer needed, the situation does not change whether the patient actually leaves the facility or not.

CHAPTER 4

HOME HEALTH COVERAGE

§ 4.01 INTRODUCTION

The Medicare home health benefit is a crucial source of health care financing for Medicare beneficiaries who reside in their homes. When properly implemented, the Medicare home health benefit can provide coverage for necessary services, even if the patient has a chronic condition and even if the services are expected to extend over a long period of time. Increasingly, these services are the central component of long-term care, and are not one service, but a constellation of skilled and nonskilled services that allows a Medicare beneficiary to remain at home.

When Medicare coverage is unfairly denied, beneficiaries may be unable to afford the home health care they need. Unable to live safely in the community, they may be forced to enter a nursing home. Vigorous advocacy can protect these patients' rights to coverage and care.[1] Starting in 1998, with the implementation of the Balanced Budget Act of 1997 (BBA '97),[2] Medicare beneficiaries began experiencing increased uncertainty about the nature and extent of covered services under the Medicare home health benefit, due in large part to significant changes in the Medicare reimbursement system for home care providers that were introduced.

Even though the Medicare home health care benefit was thrown into turmoil with the passage of the BBA '97, leading to inappropriate terminations, denials, and reductions of necessary home health services,[3] other aspects of the home health benefit, such as services covered and approaches to advocacy, remain unchanged. Thoughtful, informed advocacy continues to help beneficiaries obtain the Medicare coverage to which they are entitled.

§ 4.02 COST & COVERAGE

[A] Cost

Under the law, an individual can receive the home health care benefit for as long as they continue to qualify for home health care. There is no limit on the number of visits for which Medicare will pay. With the exception of durable medical equipment (DME) and osteoporosis drugs, there is no coinsurance,

---

[1] *See* Center for Medicare Advocacy (CMA), "Self Help Packet for Home Health Care Appeals Including "Improvement Standard" Denials" & "Toolkit: Medicare Home Health Coverage & *Jimmo v. Sebelius*," *available at* http://www.medicareadvocacy.org/take-action/self-help-packets-for-medicare-appeals/ (site visited Aug. 6, 2018).

[2] *See* The Balanced Budget Act of 1997 (BBA '97), Pub. L. No. 105-33 (Aug. 5, 1997), Title IV, Subtitle G, §§ 4601–4616 (Medicare Home Health Benefit), which significantly limited home health care access. *See* **§ 4.05** of this Handbook.

[3] *See* BBA '97, Title IV, Subtitle G, §§ 4601–4616. *See* **§ 4.05** of this Handbook.

copayment, or deductible for home health services and supplies.[4] The coinsurance for DME osteoporosis drugs furnished as a home health service is 20 percent of the cost for the service. It is important to note that the Part B outpatient therapy cap that limits the amount Medicare will pay for medically necessary outpatient therapy services does not apply to therapy covered under the Part A home health benefit.

With a few exceptions, Medicare Advantage (MA) plans must provide enrollees in that plan with all Part A and Part B traditional Medicare services.[5] The MA plan can impose different cost-sharing for care provided.[6] While there is no copayment required for home health services provided under the traditional Medicare benefit, MA plans may impose cost-sharing and other restrictions such as the requirement that prior approval be obtained before the receipt of home health services.[7] It is important to review the Medicare Advantage's Evidence of Coverage to determine what the plan covers and how much an individual will be required to pay.

[B] Coverage Criteria

Medicare provides for coverage of home health services under Parts A and B when the services are medically "reasonable and necessary," and when:[8]

1. The individual is confined to his or her home (or "homebound");
2. The individual needs skilled nursing care on an intermittent basis, or physical or speech therapy or, in the case of an individual who has been furnished home health services based on such a need but no longer requires skilled nursing care or therapy, the individual continues to need occupational therapy;

---

[4] Medicare Benefit Policy (MBP) Manual, Pub. 100-02, Ch. 7: § 60.4, *available at* https://www.cms.gov/Regulations-and-Guidance/Guidance/Manuals/Downloads/bp102c07.pdf (site visited Aug. 6, 2018).

[5] 42 C.F.R. § 422.100(a).

[6] 42 C.F.R. § 422.100(f)(6).

[7] For an example regarding what MA plans can charge for home health services, *see* Center for Medicaid & Medicare Servs. (CMS), Announcement of Calendar Year (CY) 2019 Medicare Advantage Capitation Rates and Medicare Advantage and Part D Payment Policies and Final Call Letter, pp. 201 (Table 25), *available at* https://www.cms.gov/Medicare/Health-Plans/MedicareAdvtgSpecRateStats/Downloads/Announcement2019.pdf (site visited Aug. 6, 2018) (stating that MA plans that use voluntary maximum out-of-pocket amounts can charge 20 percent coinsurance or $35 for home health services). *See* **§ 7.01[A]** of this Handbook for a discussion regarding maximum out-of-pocket limits for those enrolled in an MA plan.

[8] 42 U.S.C. § 1395f(a)(2)(C); 42 C.F.R. §§ 409.42 *et seq.*

3. A plan for furnishing the services has been established and is periodically reviewed by a physician; and
4. Such services are furnished by, or under arrangement with, a Medicare-certified home health agency (HHA).[9]

[C] How Medicare Pays

It is important to note that home health coverage is often erroneously described as a short-term, acute care benefit. This is not true. Under the law, people who meet the threshold qualifying criteria are eligible for Medicare home health coverage so long as they need skilled care.[10] In 1997 Congress specifically recognized that Medicare home care was not a short term, acute care benefit and addressed payment methodologies under Parts A and B to meet the costs of longer-term home care.

The Balanced Budget Act of 1997, signed into law on August 5, 1997, made some major changes to the Medicare Act. One of those changes was to shift costs from Part A to Part B for certain home health costs. The law explicitly recognized that Medicare can cover home care for individuals who do not have a prior hospital or nursing home stay and for people who need longer term home care. In order to reduce costs for the Medicare Part A Trust Fund, however, Congress shifted the payment for this care to Medicare Part B for beneficiaries who have both Parts A and B. Importantly, by addressing this issue, Congress decided to arrange for longer term Medicare home care (over 100 visits) and care without a prior acute institutional stay.[11] Thus, in 1997 Congress reviewed Medicare home health coverage and chose not to limit it to a short-term, acute care benefit.

The Medicare home health benefit is available under Parts A and B. The substantive coverage criteria are identical under both parts. How Medicare finances home health services depends on whether a beneficiary is enrolled in Part A and Part B or is enrolled in only Part A or only Part B.

[1] Beneficiaries Enrolled in Part A and Part B

BBA '97 shifted payment for longer term home health care from Part A to Part B for individuals who are enrolled in both Part A and Part B. The 1997 law

[9] 42 U.S.C. § 1395x(m).

[10] 42 C.F.R. § 409.48 (a)-(b) (if criteria met, "payment may be . . . made for an unlimited number of covered home health visits"); MBP Manual, Ch. 7: §§ 40.1.1 (coverage is available "so long as" skilled care is needed) & § 70.1 (coverage available for "unlimited number of covered home health visits").

[11] 42 U.S.C. § 1395d.

fashioned a "post institutional home health service" benefit, which provides coverage under Part A for the first 100 visits per "spell of illness" and then shifts all other coverage during the same spell of illness to Part B.

[a] Home Health Benefit Under Medicare Part A

For individuals enrolled in both Parts A and B, Part A became the payment source for post-institutional home care, paying only following a Medicare-covered three day hospital stay or discharge from a skilled nursing facility (SNF), in which the beneficiary received extended care services.[12] In either case, in order to be paid under Part A, the home health services must commence within 14 days of discharge.

Part A home health services also became subject to a "spell of illness" or benefit period requirement.[13] Part A will pay for up to a maximum of 100 home health visits per spell of illness. Since the provision of each type of home health service counts as a visit, patients can receive more than one visit each day, for example, when both a nurse and a home health aide attend to the patient on the same day. A "spell of illness" begins on the first day on which a beneficiary receives a post-institutional home health visit. Thereafter, a new "spell of illness" cannot start (with another 100 covered visits) until the patient has gone 60 consecutive days without receiving inpatient hospital, skilled nursing facility, or home health services.[14]

[b] Home Health Benefits Under Medicare Part B

All Medicare home health services for which a beneficiary qualifies, but which are not covered under Part A due to the imposition of the new post institution "spell of illness" requirement, or the need for care after 100 visits, are covered under Medicare Part B. The monthly Medicare Part B premium was adjusted to account for the costs of shifting these home health services from Part A to Part B.[15]

---

[12] 42 U.S.C. § 1395x. *See* **§ 4.05** of this Handbook.

[13] The home health spell of illness concept is similar to that which exists for hospital and SNF care. The *home health spell of illness* is defined as a period of consecutive days beginning with the first day (not included in a previous home health spell of illness) on which the individual is furnished post-institutional home health services; and which occurs in a month for which the individual is entitled to benefits under Part A, and ending with the close of the first period of 60 consecutive days thereafter on each of which the individual is neither an inpatient of a hospital or rural primary care hospital, nor an inpatient of a skilled nursing facility, nor provided home health services. MBP Manual, Ch. 7: § 60.1.

[14] 42 U.S.C. § 1395x(tt)(1).

[15] MBP Manual, Ch. 7: § 70.1.

[2] Beneficiaries Enrolled in Part A Only or Part B Only

If a beneficiary is enrolled only in Part A and meets the Medicare home health coverage criteria then all of the home health services will be paid for under Part A and the 100 day visit limit will not apply. If a beneficiary is enrolled only in Part B and meets the Medicare home health coverage criteria then all of the home health services will be paid for under Part B. There is no 100-visit limit under Part B.[16]

[D] Coverable Home Health Services Described

If the triggering conditions described above in § **4.02[B]** of this Handbook are satisfied, the beneficiary qualifies for Medicare coverage of home health services. Home health services include:[17]

1. Part-time or intermittent nursing care provided by or under the supervision of a registered professional nurse;
2. Physical, occupational, or speech therapy;
3. Medical social services under the direction of a physician;
4. Part-time or intermittent services of a home health aide; and
5. Medical supplies.

Note that skilled nursing, physical therapy, or speech therapy services, and continuing occupational therapy services are "qualifying skilled services" for the purpose of establishing initial eligibility for the Medicare home health benefit.[18] A beneficiary has a continued need for occupational therapy when the services which the beneficiary requires meets the definition of occupational therapy services and the beneficiary's eligibility for home health services has been established by virtue of a prior need for skilled nursing care, speech-language

---

[16] 42 U.S.C. § 1395d.

[17] 42 U.S.C. § 1395x(m)(1)–(4). *See also* CMS, Revisions to Requirements for Discharge Planning for Hospitals, Critical Access Hospitals, and Home Health Agencies, 80 Fed. Reg. 68,126 (Nov. 3, 2015) (proposing revisions to requirements for discharge planning for hospitals, CAHs, and HHAs), *available at* http://www.gpo.gov/fdsys/pkg/FR-2015-11-03/pdf/2015-27840.pdf (site visited Aug. 6, 2018). The proposed rule is designed to reduce avoidable hospital readmissions and improve patient care with a focus on improvements for psychiatric and behavioral health patients, including those with substance abuse disorders. The proposed rule calls for coordination, consultation, and using information from community-based service providers as recognized by the Improving Medicare Post-Acute Care Transformation Act of 2014 (Impact Act), Pub. L. No. 113-185 (Oct. 6, 2014). The proposed rule fits within the framework of existing discharge planning regulations that are found at 42 C.F.R. § 482.43, applicable to all inpatients. *See also* Social Security Act § 1861(e), 42 U.S.C. § 1395x(ee).

[18] 42 C.F.R. § 409.42.

pathology services, or physical therapy in the current or prior certification period.[19] A patient must initially require one of these skilled services in order to receive other covered home health services.[20] Home health aide, medical social worker, and occupational therapy services[21] are "dependent services," along with durable medical equipment and medical supplies.[22]

In practice, the requirements that a patient be confined to the home (the "homebound" rule) and need a qualifying skilled service are of fundamental importance. Generally, if these preconditions are met, the beneficiary will qualify for the home health benefit and, thus, any dependent services and items they may need.

There are some important notable gaps in what the home health benefit will cover. A frequently asked question is whether home infusion therapy is a covered service under the home health benefit. On July 25, 2017, the House of Representatives passed a bill that will align policies to ensure access to home infusion. The Medicare Part B Improvement Act of 2017 (H.R. 3178) makes several improvements to the Medicare program, including the delivery of home infusion therapy.[23] The legislation includes a provision that accelerates the implementation of The Cures Act which requires Medicare to pay for services associated with providing Part B home infusion drugs, but not until 2021. If passed by the Senate, H.R. 3178, will result in Medicare payment for home infusion services beginning in January 2019. Importantly, most private insurance and Medicare Advantage plans do cover both the medication and professional services in the home for some time.

§ 4.03 REQUIREMENTS FOR COVERAGE

[A] The Homebound Rule

The requirement that a patient is homebound (confined to home) is described in detail in the Medicare statute as follows:

> an individual shall be considered to be "confined to his home" if the individual has a condition, due to an illness or injury, that restricts the ability of the individual to leave his or her home except with the assistance of another

---

[19] 42 C.F.R. § 409.42(c)(4); MBP Manual, Ch. 7: § 30.4.

[20] 42 C.F.R. § 409.44.

[21] Occupational therapy services can be either a qualifying service or a dependent service. Occupational therapy services that are not qualifying services under 42 C.F.R. § 409.44(c) can be covered as dependent services if the requirements of reasonableness and necessity are met. 42 C.F.R. § 409.45.

[22] 42 C.F.R. § 409.45.

[23] Medicare Part B Improvement Act of 2017, H.R. 3178, 115th Congress, *available at* https://www.congress.gov/bill/115th-congress/house-bill/3178 (site visited Aug. 6, 2018).

> individual or the aid of a supportive device (such as crutches, a cane, a wheelchair, or a walker), or if the individual has a condition such that leaving his or her home is medically contraindicated. While an individual does not have to be bedridden to be considered "confined to his home," the condition of the individual should be such that there exists a normal inability to leave home, that leaving home requires a considerable and taxing effort by the individual. Any absence of an individual from the home attributable to the need to receive healthcare treatment, including regular absences for the purpose of participating in therapeutic, psychosocial, or medical treatment in an adult day-care program that is licensed or certified by a State, or accredited, to furnish adult day-care services in the State shall not disqualify an individual from being considered to be "confined to his home." Any other absence of an individual from the home shall not so disqualify an individual if the absence is of infrequent or of relatively short duration. For purposes of the preceding sentence, any absence for the purpose of attending a religious service shall be deemed to be an absence of infrequent or short duration.[24]

As a careful reading will disclose, the statutory definition of homebound status is ambiguous. While the statute states, for example, that a patient is considered homebound if unable to leave home "except with the assistance of another individual or the aid of a supportive device," it also states that the "condition of the individual should be such that there exists a normal inability to leave home." The question often arises whether a patient in a wheelchair is homebound if he or she leaves home in a wheelchair on a regular basis.[25] Advocates often find themselves quoting one section of the statute to support such a patient's homebound status, while Medicare decision makers attempt to justify denials with different language.

---

[24] *See* 42 U.S.C. §§ 1395f(a)(2)(C) (Part A), 1395n(a)(2)(A)(i) (Part B), & 1395n(a)(2)(F) (further discussion of homebound criteria), as amended by the Medicare, Medicaid, & SCHIP Benefits Improvement and Protection Act of 2000 (BIPA), Pub. L. No. 106-554 (Dec. 21, 2000).

[25] *See* CMA, "Home Health," *available at* http://www.medicareadvocacy.org/medicare-info/home-health-care/ & "Improvement Standard and *Jimmo* News," *available at* http://www.medicareadvocacy.org/medicare-info/improvement-standard/ (sites visited Aug. 6, 2018); MBP Manual, Trans. 179 (Jan. 14, 2014), *available at* http://www.cms.gov/Regulations-and-Guidance/Guidance/Transmittals/Downloads/R179BP.pdf (site visited Aug. 6, 2018). *See also* Morris v. N. Haw. Cmty. Hosp., 37 F. Supp. 2d 1181 (D. Haw. 1999) (denying home health to a quadriplegic who could not leave his home without considerable assistance and effort would cause irreparable harm and violate the public interest in providing benefits to those who qualify for them); Dennis v. Shalala, 1994 WL 708166 (D. Vt. 1994) (infrequent trips to an adult day care program and to local supermarket held within the definition of homebound); Burgess v. Shalala, 1993 WL 327764 (D. Vt. 1993) (must consider both physical and mental effort of leaving home in determining homebound status); Labossiere v. Secretary of HHS, 1991 WL 531922 (D. Vt. 1991) (must show considerable and taxing effort in leaving the home, also must have strong evidentiary support of the nature of the assistance needed, including assistive devices); Pope v. Secretary of HHS, 1991 WL 236173 (D. Vt. 1991) (merely using a walker or wheelchair is not enough to trigger homebound status).

Effective November 19, 2013, CMS changed its standards for determining whether an individual meets the definition of "homebound." The new, more restrictive, policy states:[26]

> For purposes of the statute, an individual shall be considered "confined to the home" (homebound) if the following two criteria are met:
>
> 1. *Criterion One*:
>
> The patient must either:
>
> - Because of illness or injury, need the aid of supportive devices such as crutches, canes, wheelchairs, and walkers; the use of special transportation; or the assistance of another person in order to leave their place of residence
>
> OR
>
> - Have a condition such that leaving his or her home is medically contraindicated.
>
> If the patient meets one of the *criterion one* conditions, then the patient must ALSO meet two additional requirements defined in *criterion two* below.
>
> 2. *Criterion Two*:
>
> - There must exist a normal inability to leave home;
>
> AND
>
> - Leaving home must require a considerable and taxing effort.

In spite of the agency's restrictive interpretation of the law, the intent of the Medicare statute is to provide home health care to beneficiaries who lack an ordinary ability to leave home. Beneficiaries who need the assistance of another person, an assistive device, or special transportation to leave home are examples of people who lack an ordinary ability to leave and thus need health services to come to them. However, they are not the *only* beneficiaries who are homebound for purposes of Medicare coverage of home health care. Coverage also includes beneficiaries for whom leaving home is medically contraindicated. For example, an individual with chronic obstructive pulmonary disease may not require an assistive device, the assistance of another person, or specialized transportation in order to leave home, however his or her condition might be so severe that leaving home is contraindicated because his health and safety might be compromised if he or she were to leave.

[26] MBP Manual, Ch. 7: § 30.1.1, *available at* http://www.cms.gov/Regulations-and-Guidance/Guidance/Manuals/downloads/bp102c07.pdf (site visited Aug. 6, 2018).

The Medicare Benefit Policy Manual (MBPM) provides examples of homebound patients that may be useful to advocates attempting to establish homebound status, including:[27]

- A beneficiary paralyzed from a stroke who is confined to a wheelchair or requires the aid of crutches in order to walk;
- A beneficiary who is blind or senile and requires the assistance of another person in leaving their place of residence;
- A beneficiary who has lost the use of their upper extremities and, therefore, is unable to open doors, use handrails on stairways, etc., and requires the assistance of another individual in leaving their place of residence;
- A patient in the late stages of ALS or neurodegenerative disabilities;
- A beneficiary who has just returned from a hospital stay involving surgery, who may be suffering from resultant weakness and pain because of the surgery and, therefore, their actions may be restricted by their physician to certain specified and limited activities (such as getting out of bed only for a specified period of time, walking stairs only once a day, etc.);
- A beneficiary with arteriosclerotic heart disease of such severity that they must avoid all stress and physical activity; and
- A beneficiary with a psychiatric illness that is manifested in part by a refusal to leave home or is of such a nature that it would not be considered safe for the beneficiary to leave home unattended, even if they have no physical limitations.

In determining whether someone is homebound the MBPM states that it is necessary to look at the individual's overall condition over a period of time rather than looking at an isolated period.[28] It is also important to note that for purposes of determining someone's homebound status an individual may have more than one "home," and an individual who resides in more than one place of residence will not be disqualified from meeting the homebound criteria. The MBPM states "[f]or example, a person may reside in a principal home and also a second vacation home, mobile home, or the home of a caretaker relative. The fact that the patient resides in more than one home and, as a result, must transit from one to the other, is not in itself, an indication that the patient is not homebound. The requirements of homebound must be met at each location. . . ."[29]

---

[27] MBP Manual, Ch. 7: § 30.1.1.

[28] MBP Manual, Ch. 7: § 30.1.1.

[29] MBP Manual, Ch. 7: § 30.1.2.

[B] Skilled Nursing Care on an Intermittent Basis, or Physical or Speech Therapy or Occupational Therapy

[1] Generally

The second principal criterion to be met to qualify for the Medicare home health benefit is that the patient needs skilled nursing care on an intermittent basis, or physical or speech therapy, or have a continuing need for occupational therapy services.[30]

For nursing visits to be qualifying services, they must be skilled and furnished on an intermittent basis. "Intermittent" means skilled nursing care that is either provided or needed on fewer than seven days each week, or less than eight hours each day for periods of 21 days or less (with extensions in exceptional circumstances when the need for additional care is finite and predictable).[31]

There is no intermittency requirement for therapy services. Thus, if a patient meets the requirement for skilled physical or speech therapy, the criterion is met. It is important to note that occupational therapy services cannot establish *initial* eligibility for Medicare home health coverage. Occupational therapy services may be covered when initial eligibility is established on another basis, such as the need for skilled nursing or skilled physical or speech therapy. After that, however, a continued need for occupational therapy can qualify a Medicare patient for extended home health eligibility when occupational therapy is the *only* continuing skilled service needed by a patient.[32]

[2] Defining Skilled Care

The Medicare home health regulations define coverable skilled nursing services as services that must, under state law, be performed by a registered nurse or a licensed practical (vocational) nurse, be provided on a part-time or intermittent basis, be reasonable and necessary for the treatment of the illness or injury, and meet the criteria for SNFs. CMS has adopted, for purposes of defining skilled

---

[30] 42 U.S.C. § 1395f(a)(2)(C); CMS, Medicare General Information, Eligibility and Entitlement (MGIEE) Manual, Pub. 100-01, Ch. 4: § 30.3, *available at* https://www.cms.gov/Regulations-and-Guidance/Guidance/Manuals/Downloads/ge101c04.pdf (site visited Aug. 6, 2018); MBP Manual, Ch. 7: § 30.4, *available at* http://www.cms.gov/Regulations-and-Guidance/Guidance/Manuals/downloads/bp102c07.pdf (site visited Aug. 6, 2018). For paper-based manuals and internet-only manuals (IOMs), *see* CMS, "Manuals," *available at* http://www.cms.hhs.gov/manuals/ (site visited Aug. 6, 2018).

[31] 42 U.S.C. §§ 1814(a)(2)(C) & 1835(a)(2)(A).

[32] 42 C.F.R. § 409.42(c)(4) ("Subsequent to an initial covered occupational therapy service, continuing occupational therapy services which meet the requirements of § 409.44(c) are considered to be qualifying services"). *See also* MBP Manual, Ch. 7: § 40.2.4, *available at* http://www.cms.gov/Regulations-and-Guidance/Guidance/Manuals/downloads/bp102c07.pdf (site visited Aug. 6, 2018).

nursing in the home health care context, the skilled nursing examples and definitions contained in 42 C.F.R. § 409.33, applicable to Medicare certified skilled nursing facilities.[33] These regulations contain critical examples of skilled nursing services and are relied upon extensively by home health care providers and beneficiaries. The regulations provide that the service must be so inherently complex that it can be safely and effectively performed only by, or under the supervision of, professional or technical personnel.[34]

The skilled services listed in the SNF regulations include overall management and evaluation of the patient's care plan, observation and assessment of the patient's changing condition, and patient education services, as well as specific skilled treatments including, but not limited to, intravenous or intramuscular injections, tube feedings, insertion and sterile irrigation and replacement of a suprapubic catheter, wound care involving prescription medications and aseptic techniques, and suctioning a tracheotomy.[35]

The home health regulations define coverable skilled physical and occupational therapy and speech-language pathology services as services relating directly and specifically to a treatment regimen (established by the physician, after any needed consultation with the qualified therapist) that is designed to treat the beneficiary's illness or injury. The services must be reasonable and necessary and must be considered, under accepted standards of professional clinical practice, to be a specific, safe, and effective treatment for the beneficiary's condition.[36]

[3] CMS Medicare Benefit Policy Manual, Home Health Services, Chapter 7

[a] Skilled Home Care

The MBPM defines skilled home health care in a way that parallels the SNF regulations, and includes several clinical examples to illustrate when care would or would not be covered. Some principles and guidelines from the manual follow:

1. A service that, by its nature, requires the skill of a licensed nurse to be provided safely and effectively continues to be a skilled service even if it is taught to the patient, the patient's family, or other caregivers. For

[33] 42 C.F.R. § 409.44(b)(1) (amended by 82 Fed. Reg. 4578) (Jan. 13, 2017), *available at* https://www.ecfr.gov/cgi-bin/text-idx?SID=ce688615a5d6c05afffeddf6a0930c51&mc=true&node=20170113y1.36) (site visited Aug. 6, 2018). *See also* MBP Manual, Ch. 7: § 40.1 (skilled nursing care).

[34] 42 C.F.R. § 409.32(a) (SNF regulations). *See also* 42 C.F.R. § 409.44(b)(1)(i).

[35] 42 C.F.R. § 409.33(a) & (b).

[36] 42 C.F.R. § 409.44(c).

instance, wound care may continue to be covered skilled nursing care, notwithstanding that the patient's family provides it part of the time.[37]

2. A beneficiary's diagnosis should never be the sole factor in deciding that a service the beneficiary needs is either skilled or non-skilled.[38]

3. Skilled care may, depending on the unique condition of the patient, continue to be necessary for patients whose condition is stable. For example, periodic visits to change a catheter as needed, treat the symptoms of catheter malfunction, and teach proper catheter care would be covered as long as they are reasonable and necessary, even if the patient is stable and the care is expected to be needed for a long and indefinite period.[39]

4. Observation and assessment of the patient's condition by a nurse are reasonable and necessary skilled services where there is a reasonable potential for change in a patient's condition that requires skilled nursing personnel to identify and evaluate the patient's need for possible modification of treatment or initiation of additional medical procedures until the patient's clinical condition and/or treatment regimen has stabilized.[40]

5. Skilled management and evaluation of the patient's care plan are also reasonable and necessary nursing services where underlying conditions or complications require that only a registered nurse can ensure that essential non-skilled care is achieving its purpose. To be covered, the complexity of the necessary unskilled services that are a necessary part of the medical treatment must require the involvement of skilled nursing personnel to promote the patient's recovery and medical safety in view of the patient's overall condition.[41]

---

[37] MBP Manual, Ch. 7: § 40.1.1(Example 5).

[38] MBP Manual, Ch. 7: § 40.1.1.

[39] MBP Manual, Ch. 7: § 40.1.1 (Example 8).

[40] MBP Manual, Ch. 7: § 40.1.2.1.

[41] MBP Manual, Ch. 7: § 40.1.2.2. In 2009, CMS tightened the criteria for determining whether the evaluation and management of non-skilled services by a skilled nurse are considered to be a coverable skilled service. *See* CMS, Beneficiary Qualifications for Coverage of Services, 74 Fed. Reg. 58,133 (Nov. 10, 2009) (codified at 42 C.F.R. § 409.42(c)(1)(i)). The final rule allows that "[i]n some cases, the condition of the patient may cause a service that would originally be considered unskilled to be considered a skilled nursing service." However, "[w]here nursing visits are not needed to observe and assess the effects of the non-skilled services being provided to treat the illness or injury," and "[w]here a service can be safely and effectively performed (or self-administered) by non-licensed staff without the direct supervision of a nurse, the service cannot be regarded as a skilled service even if a nurse actually provides the service."

6. Teaching or training activities constitute coverable skilled nursing services when it is reasonable and necessary to teach the family or caregivers how to manage the treatment regimen of the patient's illness, injury, or functional loss. The test of whether a nursing service is skilled relates to the skill required to teach and not to the nature of what is being taught. Therefore, where skilled nursing services are necessary to teach an unskilled service, the teaching may be covered. Where it becomes apparent after a reasonable period of time that the patient, family, or caregiver will not or is not able to be trained, then further teaching and training would cease to be reasonable and necessary.[42]

[b] Intermittent Skilled Nursing Care

Although a need for skilled nursing care may be identified, the question remains whether the patient needs *intermittent* skilled nursing care as required and defined by the statute. For many years, Medicare claims were routinely denied on the basis that the patient needed *more* than intermittent skilled nursing care. The meaning of the term "intermittent" was nowhere adequately described.

On August 1, 1988, the United States District Court for the District of Columbia issued a decision clarifying this point, establishing that "intermittent" means "less than daily."[43] A patient will need intermittent skilled care if he or she needs skilled care visits on six or fewer days per week. If the patient requires daily skilled care on a seven-day-per-week basis, however, the patient will be found to have violated the intermittent rule and will be considered ineligible for continued home health coverage unless the certifying physician attests on the plan of care that the patient will require daily skilled care for only a relatively short time (three weeks, for example) or that the need for daily skilled care will end at a certain predictable time in the future.[44]

Congress, in BBA '97, amended the Medicare statute for purposes of Section 1861(m) of the Social Security Act to define "part-time or intermittent services" as:

> Skilled nursing and home health aide services furnished any number of days per week as long as they are furnished (combined) less than 8 hours each day and 28

---

[42] MBP Manual, Ch. 7: § 40.1.2.3. In 2009, CMS elaborated on the extent to which patient education services were coverable. *See* 74 Fed. Reg. 58,133 (providing that "[s]killed education services are no longer needed if it becomes apparent, after a reasonable period of time, that the patient, family, or caregiver could not or would not be trained.").

[43] Duggan v. Bowen, 691 F. Supp. 1487, 1511 (D.D.C. 1988). *See also* Rizzi v. Shalala, 1994 WL 686630 (D. Conn. 1994) (mooting the plaintiff's claim that the Secretary arbitrarily presumes that patients with a "chronic" or "stable" condition are ineligible for home health coverage. The court recognized that after *Duggan*, the HHA Manual was revised to clarify the standards that determine whether the skilled care requirement has been met).

[44] MBP Manual, Ch. 7: § 50.7.

> or fewer hours each week (or, subject to review on a case-by-case basis as to the need for care, less than 8 hours each day and 35 or fewer hours per week).[45]

In this amendment, Congress went on to define "intermittent" for purposes of Sections 1814(a)(2)(C)[46] and 1835(a)(2)(A)[47] of the Social Security Act as:

> skilled nursing care that is either provided or needed on fewer than 7 days each week, or less than 8 hours of each day for periods of 21 days or less (with extensions in exceptional circumstances when the need for additional care is finite and predictable).[48]

Together, these BBA '97 amendments codified CMS manual standards and other internal guidelines, which have been used by providers and Medicare Administrative Contractors (MACs)[49] for years to define the amount and frequency of home health nursing and aide services that are covered by Medicare.

[4] Skilled Therapy

There is no intermittency requirement for physical or speech therapy or for continuing occupational therapy. A patient's need for physical or speech therapy or for continuing occupational therapy services will, assuming the patient is homebound, trigger home health coverage even where the patient does not require skilled nursing services. In order to qualify, therapy must be skilled. The MBPM provides that the service of a physical, speech, or occupational therapist is a skilled therapy service if the inherent complexity of the service is such that it can be performed safely and/or effectively only by or under the supervision of a skilled therapist.[50]

To be covered, assuming all other eligibility and coverage criteria have been met, the skilled services must also be reasonable and necessary to the treatment of the patient's illness or injury or to the restoration or maintenance of function affected by the patient's illness or injury, within the context of the patient's unique medical condition. To be considered reasonable and necessary, the therapy must be consistent with the nature and severity of the illness or injury and the beneficiary's particular needs. The amount, frequency, and duration of the services must be

---

[45] 42 U.S.C. § 1395x(m)(7)(B).

[46] *See* 42 U.S.C. § 1395f(a)(2)(C) (conditions of and limitations on payment for services).

[47] *See* 42 U.S.C. § 1395n(a)(2)(A)(i) (procedure for payment of claims of providers of services).

[48] 42 U.S.C. § 1395x(m)(7)(B). CMS policy carves out a specific exception to the intermittent requirement for insulin-dependent diabetics who cannot self-administer insulin injections and for whom there is no willing caregiver to inject the insulin. In this circumstance, there is no need to demonstrate a predictable and finite end to daily nursing visits to administer insulin. *See* MBP Manual, Ch. 7: §§ 40.1.2.4(A.2) & 40.1.3.

[49] "Medicare Administrative Contractors" (MACs) are private health care insurers that have been awarded a geographic jurisdiction by CMS to process claims for Medicare Fee-For-Service beneficiaries.

[50] MBP Manual, Ch. 7: § 40.2.1.

reasonable, and the services must be considered, under accepted standards of medical practice, to be specific and effective treatment for the patient's condition.[51]

The issue of "improvement" and access to skilled therapy and nursing services is a significant problem and is the subject of litigation in *Jimmo v Sebelius*.[52] CMS has taken the position that there has never been an "improvement standard" but, in forging a settlement with plaintiffs, agreed to review and change language in its several manuals to clarify that improvement is not the standard for determining whether on-going skilled therapy and nursing services are necessary. The updated manuals and other CMS guidance became available in January 2014.[53]

In spite of *Jimmo*, MACs continue to deny coverage based on the lack of expectation of a significant improvement in the patient's condition within a reasonable and predictable period of time. Beneficiaries and advocates should bear in mind that "restoration potential" is not required by law, that a patient's diagnosis or prognosis should never be the sole factor in deciding whether or not a service is skilled, and that a maintenance program *can* be covered if skilled services are necessary to prevent further deterioration or preserve current capabilities. This *includes* visits by the therapist to design, establish, teach, perform, or supervise a maintenance program.[54]

Pursuant to the MBPM, the following types of skilled therapy[55] are covered by the Medicare home health benefit:

1. Assessment by a physical therapist to determine a beneficiary's rehabilitation needs and potential, or to develop and implement a physical therapy program;
2. Therapeutic exercises that must be taught by or under the supervision of a qualified physical therapist to ensure the safety of the beneficiary and the effectiveness of the treatment;

---

[51] MBP Manual, Ch. 7: § 40.2.1.

[52] *See* Jimmo v. Sebelius, 2011 WL 5104355 (D. Vt. 2011), *available at* http://www.clearinghouse.net/chDocs/public/PB-VT-0002-0002.pdf. *See also* CMS, "*Jimmo v. Sebelius* Settlement Agreement Fact Sheet," *available at* http://www.cms.gov/Medicare/Medicare-Fee-for-Service-Payment/SNFPPS/Downloads/Jimmo-FactSheet.pdf (sites visited Aug. 6, 2018).

[53] MBP Manual, Ch. 7: § 40.2.1. *See also* CMA, "Improvement Standard and *Jimmo* News," *available at* http://www.medicareadvocacy.org/medicare-info/improvement-standard/ (site visited Aug. 6, 2018). Plaintiffs remain concerned that CMS's implementation and education campaigns are inadequate.

[54] 42 C.F.R. § 409.44(c)(2)(iii); MBP Manual, Ch. 7: §§ 40.2.1 & 40.2.2.E. Note that the parties in Jimmo v. Sebelius, 5:11-CV-17 (D. Vt. Jan. 18, 2011), entered into a settlement agreement affirming that improvement is an inappropriate standard in determining whether care for chronic conditions should be continued. Problems have arisen with implementation of *Jimmo*, particularly as many HHA providers do not know about the settlement, find the documentation requirements difficult, or continue to receive improper denials from Medicare contractors. *See* **Appendix 1-9** of this Handbook.

[55] MBP Manual, Ch. 7: § 40.2.2.

3. Gait training furnished a beneficiary whose ability to walk has been impaired by neurological, muscular, or skeletal abnormality;
4. Range of motion tests, and range of motion exercises, if they are part of an active treatment for a specific disease, illness, or injury that has resulted in a loss or restriction of mobility;
5. Maintenance therapy required to maintain the patient's current function or to prevent or slow further deterioration;
6. Ultrasound, shortwave, and microwave diathermy treatments;
7. Hot packs, infra-red treatments, paraffin, and whirlpool baths may, depending on the special medical circumstances or complications of the particular patient, require the skills, knowledge, and judgment of a qualified physical therapist; and
8. Wound care that falls within the auspices of the physical therapist's State Practice Act.

[C] Part-Time or Intermittent Services

Once a patient has satisfied the definition of being homebound and established a need for skilled nursing care on an intermittent basis, or physical or speech therapy or occupational therapy, then home health coverage under Medicare is available for the therapy *and* for part-time or intermittent services of a home health aide or nurse. As discussed above, intermittent services are services delivered less than daily, that is, fewer than seven days per week. Part-time services are services delivered fewer than eight hours per day.[56]

Reading the part-time and intermittent standards together, a patient *should* be able to obtain coverage for home health aide or nursing service seven days a week but fewer than eight hours each day (part-time services), or six or fewer times a week for as many as 24 hours per day (intermittent services). In practice, however, do not assume the availability of this heavy degree of coverage on an ongoing basis. Current law and Medicare guidelines provide that coverage may be available for up to 28 hours of aide and nurse services combined each week without the necessity of special documentation. Coverage is available for aide and nurse services totaling as many as 35 hours per week if additional medical justification is shown.[57]

---

[56] *Duggan*, 691 F. Supp. 1487, 1511. 42 U.S.C. § 1395x(m)(1),(4), & (7)(B); MBP Manual, Ch. 7: §§ 40.1.3 & 50.7-50.7.2.

[57] MBP Manual, Ch. 7: § 50.7.

§ 4.04 CHRONIC, STABLE, AND MAINTENANCE-LEVEL PATIENTS

Advocates should be aware that although Medicare home health coverage *should* be available for extended periods of care, the Medicare reimbursement system works to discourage the actual delivery of long periods of care. Fearing inadequate reimbursement, HHAs may resist serving patients who require long-term care or numerous or extended visits. Excuses used may include that the patient is "chronic" or staff shortages exist. MACs routinely deny home health coverage to patients deemed chronic, stable, or in need of care to "maintain" or "prevent deterioration"[58] of their conditions, or who otherwise are not getting better or worse at a rapid pace.

It is, therefore, particularly important to note that the federal regulation states that "[t]he determination of whether skilled nursing care is reasonable and necessary must be based solely upon the beneficiary's unique condition and individual needs, without regard to whether the illness or injury is acute, chronic, terminal, or expected to last a long time."[59] The MBPM also makes it clear that:

> A patient's overall medical condition, without regard to whether the illness or injury is acute, chronic, terminal, or expected to extend over a long period of time, should be considered in deciding whether skilled services are needed. A patient's diagnosis should never be the sole factor in deciding that a service the patient needs is either skilled or not skilled. Skilled care may, depending on the unique condition of the patient, continue to be necessary for patients whose condition is stable.[60]

As enunciated by these provisions, individuals with chronic conditions can be entitled to Medicare coverage, even if the care they need will continue for long periods of time. Restoration should not be the decisive factor in determining entitlement to coverage.[61]

Furthermore, the United States District Court for the District of Connecticut ruled in *Fox v. Thompson (sub nom. Fox v. Bowen)*,[62] a federal class action concerning Medicare coverage for skilled nursing facility care, that the Secretary of Department of Health and Human Services (HHS) shall not deny Medicare coverage on the basis of "arbitrary rules of thumb." Instead, as the court ruled in

---

[58] 42 C.F.R. § 409.32.

[59] 42 C.F.R. § 409.44(b)(3)(iii).

[60] MBP Manual, Ch. 7: § 40.1.1. In the preamble to the final home health prospective payment regulations, CMS stated, "In order to address the needs of longer stay patients, we are not limiting the number of 60-day episode recertifications permitted in a given fiscal year assuming a patient remains eligible for the Medicare home health benefit." Health Care Financing Administration (HCFA), 65 Fed. Reg. 41,128, 41,140 (July 3, 2000), *available at* https://www.federalregister.gov/documents/2000/07/03/00-16432/medicare-program-prospective-payment-system-for-home-health-agencies. *See* **§ 4.05[D]** of this Handbook.

[61] 42 C.F.R. § 409.32 (incorporated into the home health regulations at 42 C.F.R. § 409.44(b)).

[62] Fox v. Bowen, 656 F. Supp. 1236 (D. Conn. 1986).

Fox, each claimant should receive an individualized assessment of his or her need for care based on the facts and circumstances of the claimant's particular case. A particular patient with multiple sclerosis, for example, may well be homebound, require intermittent skilled nursing and/or therapy, and qualify for Medicare coverage, even though the underlying medical condition will remain.[63]

Unfortunately, HHAs are often convinced that Medicare coverage is unavailable for patients who will not recover and for those in need of maintenance physical therapy. In order to avoid the financial penalties associated with a claim submission that will be denied by the MAC, many agencies deny coverage in these cases themselves and decline to submit a claim unless the patient insists. Since agencies usually rely upon the CMS manual, it is particularly important to note supportive sections of the manual and to instruct the provider that the federal regulations are clear that coverage is available even if the patient is unlikely to improve and even when the care is needed to maintain his or her condition.

In November 2010, CMS revised its regulations to clarify Medicare coverage principles for home health services, including physical therapy, occupational therapy, and speech-language pathology services.[64] Most importantly for people with long-term conditions, the revisions "clarified" that skilled care does include services that are intended to maintain a person's condition and that no "rules of thumb" should be used to deny care, including rules that require restoration potential.[65] CMS also clarified that:

> "Rules of thumb" in the Medicare medical review process are prohibited. . . . Any "rules of thumb" that would declare a claim not covered solely on the basis of elements, such as, lack of restoration potential, . . . or degree of stability, is [sic] unacceptable without individual review of all pertinent facts to determine if coverage may be justified.[66]

---

[63] Smith v. Shalala, 855 F. Supp. 658 (D. Vt. 1994); Bergeron v. Shalala, 855 F. Supp. 665 (D. Vt. 1994). *See also* Prendergast v. Leavitt, No. 08-cv-1148 (D. Conn. Aug. 1, 2008) (holding it inappropriate for a Managed Care plan to terminate services for a chronically ill patient who is not likely to improve but needs services to maintain or to slow the deterioration of her chronic condition; Anderson v. Leavitt, 2010 WL 4273238 (D. Vt. Oct. 25, 2010). The Center for Medicare Advocacy continues to pursue the revision of CMS and contractor policies that require improvement. *See* Gill Deford, Margaret Murphy, & Judith Stein, *How the "Improvement Standard" Improperly Denies Coverage to Medicare Patients with Chronic Conditions*, Clearinghouse Rev., Vol. 43, No. 9-10 (Jan-Feb. 2010), *available at* http://www.medicareadvocacy.org/how-the-improvement-standard-improperly-denies-coverage-to-medicare-patients-with-chronic-conditions-%E2%80%93-text-of-article-printed-in-clearinghouse-review-vol-43-no-9-10-jan-feb-2010/ (site visited Aug. 6, 2018).

[64] CMS, Home Health Servs. Under Hosp. Insurance, 75 Fed. Reg. 70,461 (Nov. 17, 2010) (amending 42 C.F. R. § 409.44(c)), *available at* https://www.gpo.gov/fdsys/pkg/FR-2010-11-17/pdf/2010-27778.pdf (site visited Aug. 6, 2018).

[65] CMS, Home Health Prospective Payment System Rate Update for Calendar Year 2011; Changes in Certification Requirements for Home Health Agencies and Hospices, 75 Fed. Reg. 70,395 (Nov. 17, 2010); 42 C.F.R. § 409.44(c)(2)(iii)(C).

[66] 75 Fed. Reg. 70,395.

To determine whether a service is skilled, and therefore coverable, the regulations direct decision-makers to review accepted standards of clinical practice and to consider whether a professional is needed for the service to be safe and effective for the particular beneficiary.[67]

One of the most important aspects of the revised home health coverage regulations includes a more detailed explanation of when Medicare covers establishment or performance of therapy in the context of a maintenance program. The regulation states:

> The unique clinical condition of a patient may require the specialized skills of a qualified therapist to perform a safe and effective maintenance program required in connection with the patient's specific illness or injury. Where the clinical condition of the patient is such that the complexity of the therapy services required to maintain function involve the use of complex and sophisticated therapy procedures . . . by the therapist . . . **or** the clinical condition of the patient is such that the complexity of the therapy services required to maintain function must be delivered by the therapist . . . to ensure the patient's safety and to provide an effective maintenance program, then those reasonable and necessary services shall be covered.[68]

In 2011, the Center for Medicare Advocacy, with Vermont Legal Aid and others, filed *Jimmo,* a class action lawsuit, against the Secretary of HHS to assure the broadest possible application of the rule that improvement is not required to receive care for one's chronic condition. Following plaintiffs' successful efforts in defeating defendant's motion to dismiss, the parties entered into a settlement agreement in which the defendant agreed to revise its various manuals to clarify that Medicare coverage determinations turn on the need for skilled care—not on the ability of an individual to improve. The settlement agreement applies to skilled maintenance services provided under the Medicare home health, outpatient therapy, and skilled nursing facility benefits. The settlement applies to both Medicare Part A and B and also applies equally to Medicare Advantage as to the traditional Medicare program. The settlement agreement is not limited to particular conditions or diseases. It applies to patients who require skilled services to maintain their condition or slow deterioration regardless of their underlying illness, disability, or injury.

The manual revisions were published on December 6, 2013. As CMS states in the Transmittal announcing the manual revisions:

> **No "Improvement Standard" is to be applied in determining Medicare coverage for maintenance claims that require skilled care.** Medicare has long recognized that even in situations where no improvement is possible, skilled care may nevertheless be needed for maintenance purposes (i.e., to

[67] 42 C.F.R. § 409.44(c)(2)(i).

[68] 42 C.F.R. § 409.44(c)(2)(iii)(C) (emphasis added).

> prevent or slow a decline in condition). The Medicare statute and regulations have never supported the imposition of an "Improvement Standard" rule-of-thumb in determining whether skilled care is required to prevent or slow deterioration in a patient's condition. Thus, such coverage depends not on the beneficiary's restoration potential, but on whether skilled care is required, along with the underlying reasonableness and necessity of the services themselves. The manual revisions now being issued will serve to reflect and articulate this basic principle more clearly.[69] (emphasis in original)

In spite of the agency's clarifications in manual provisions and other guidance, claims for maintenance services continue to be denied by the MACs. Consequently, HHAs remain hesitant to provide services to patients who require maintenance care and to bill those services to Medicare. This continued loss of skilled care based on an improvement requirement is occurring despite CMS's assertion that it has completed the education campaign required by the settlement. That campaign, however, has clearly failed to educate key components of the provider community and Medicare decision-making system. As such, vigorous advocacy on behalf of beneficiaries is still required in this area to ensure access to crucial home care.[70]

On March 1, 2016, the Center for Medicare Advocacy, along with Vermont Legal Aid, filed a Motion for Resolution of Non-Compliance with the *Jimmo v. Sebelius* settlement agreement. The filing comes after three years of urging CMS to fulfill its obligation to end the continued application of the "Improvement Standard" by Medicare providers, contractors, and adjudicators to deny Medicare coverage for skilled maintenance nursing and therapy. On August 17, 2016, the judge granted, in part, the plaintiff's motion for enforcement of the settlement.[71] The judge concluded in part that some of the information provided by the Secretary in

---

[69] CMS, Transmittal 179 (Jan. 14, 2014), *available at* http://www.cms.gov/Regulations-and-Guidance/Guidance/Transmittals/Downloads/R179BP.pdf (site visited Aug. 6, 2018). Pursuant to the settlement, *see* CMS, "*Jimmo v. Sebelius* Settlement Agreement Fact Sheet," *available at* http://www.cms.gov/Medicare/Medicare-Fee-for-Service-Payment/SNFPPS/Downloads/Jimmo-FactSheet.pdf (site visited Aug. 6, 2018); CMS, MLN Number MM8458 Revised, "Manual Updates to Clarify Skilled Nursing Facility (SNF), Inpatient Rehabilitation Facility (IRF), Home Health (HH), and Outpatient (OPT) Coverage Pursuant to *Jimmo v. Sebelius*," *available at* http://www.cms.gov/Outreach-and-Education/Medicare-Learning-Network-MLN/MLNMattersArticles/Downloads/MM8458.pdf (site visited Aug. 6, 2018); and CMS, "*Jimmo v. Sebelius* Settlement Agreement Program Manual Clarifications Fact Sheet," *available at* http://www.cms.gov/Medicare/Medicare-Fee-for-Service-Payment/SNFPPS/Downloads/jimmo_fact_sheet2_022014_final.pdf (site visited Aug. 6, 2018).

[70] *See* CMA, "Self Help Packet for Home Health Care Appeals Including 'Improvement Standard' Denials," *available at* http://www.medicareadvocacy.org/self-help-packet-for-expedited-home-health-care-appeals-including-improvement-standard-denials/ (site visited Aug. 6, 2018); CMA, "*Jimmo v. Sebelius*, the Improvement Standard Case FAQs," *available at* http://www.medicareadvocacy.org/jimmo-v-sebelius-the-improvement-standard-case-faqs/ (site visited Aug. 6, 2018).

[71] *See* Jimmo v. Burwell, 2016 WL 4401371 (D. Vt. Aug. 17, 2016), *available at* http://www.medicareadvocacy.org/wp-content/uploads/2016/08/Jimmo-2.pdf (site visited Aug. 6, 2018).

the Educational Campaign was "inaccurate, nonresponsive, and failed to reflect the maintenance standard" and ordered CMS to develop corrective action.

On February 2, 2017, the court released a decision ordering CMS to carry out a Corrective Action Plan to remedy noncompliance with the Settlement. The plan included a new webpage by CMS dedicated to the Jimmo settlement with frequently asked questions and a statement that affirmatively disavows the Improvement Standard; new training for Medicare contractors making coverage decisions; and a new National Call for Medicare contractors and adjudicators to correct erroneous statements that had been made on a previous call.

In late August 2017, the government published the new Jimmo-webpage on the CMS website to comply with the Corrective Action Plan.[72] The webpage includes the court-approved affirmative disavowal of the Improvement Standard in a blue box titled "Important Message About the Jimmo Settlement." Importantly, the statement notes that the "Jimmo Settlement may reflect a change in practice for those providers, adjudicators, and contractors who may have erroneously believed that the Medicare program covers nursing and therapy services under these benefits only when a beneficiary is expected to improve."[73] The webpage also contains links to Jimmo-related documents, such as the transmittals of the revised Manual provisions, and a new set of Frequently Asked Questions. The imprimatur of CMS on these materials will help beneficiaries and their advocates who are arguing against inappropriate coverage denials or service termination.

The court case has now concluded, but class counsel continues to work on ensuring that access to skilled maintenance nursing and therapy for older adults and people with disabilities is not inappropriately denied or terminated because their conditions are "chronic," "not improving," "plateaued," or "stable."

§ 4.05 PROSPECTIVE PAYMENT SYSTEM FOR HOME HEALTH SERVICES

BBA '97 added a requirement to the Medicare statute that all costs for Medicare home health services be reimbursed under a prospective payment system (PPS).[74] Final regulations to implement home health PPS were published in the *Federal Register* on July 3, 2000,[75] and CMS began paying HHAs under PPS on October 1, 2000.

---

[72] CMA, "*Jimmo* Settlement," *available at* https://www.cms.gov/Center/Special-Topic/Jimmo-Center.html (site visited Aug. 6, 2018).

[73] CMA, "Improvement Standard & *Jimmo* News," http://www.medicareadvocacy.org/medicare-info/improvement-standard/ (site visited Aug. 6, 2018).

[74] *See* 42 U.S.C. § 1395fff.

[75] HCFA, Prospective Payment System for Home Agencies, 65 Fed. Reg. 41,128 (July 3, 2000), *available at* https://www.federalregister.gov/documents/2000/07/03/00-16432/medicare-program-prospective-payment-system-for-home-health-agencies (site visited Aug. 6, 2018).

[A] What Is PPS?

PPS is a payment system. It does not change eligibility and coverage criteria for Medicare home health benefits. Under PPS, Medicare pays a fixed rate to HHAs for the services they provide a beneficiary during a 60-day episode of care.[76] PPS covers all home health services and non-routine medical supplies including outpatient physical therapy. PPS does not cover the cost of durable medical equipment (DME) or certain osteoporosis drugs, which are reimbursed separately.[77]

[B] Determining the Amount of Payment

HHAs must use the Outcome and Assessment Information Set (OASIS) to perform a comprehensive assessment of each new patient before care is provided.[78] The OASIS identifies the patient's medical, nursing, rehabilitation, social, and discharge planning needs. Information from the new assessment helps determine the appropriate payment amount under PPS for each patient. First, CMS determines a national prospective 60-day episode payment rate. The rate is then adjusted by two factors: (1) a wage index appropriate for the area in which the beneficiary receives the services, and (2) a case-mix adjuster consisting of selected data elements from OASIS plus an additional data element measuring therapy services.[79] The PPS rate varies, depending upon the patient's clinical condition, functional status, and service needs.

---

[76] 42 C.F.R. §§ 409.43(f), 424.22(b), 484.205(a). For ongoing updates on home health PPS, *see* CMS, "Home Health PPS," *available at* http://www.cms.gov/Medicare/Medicare-Fee-for-Service-Payment/HomeHealthPPS/index.html?redirect=/homehealthpps/ (site visited Aug. 6, 2018).

[77] 42 C.F.R. §§ 409.100(a)(2), 410.150(b)(19), & 413.1(h). Most durable medical equipment (DME) is now subject to cost limitations associated with Medicare's competitive bidding program for durable medical equipment, prosthetics, orthotics, and supplies (DMEPOS). *See* CMS, "DMEPOS Competitive Bidding—Home," *available at* http://www.cms.gov/Medicare/Medicare-Fee-for-Service-Payment/DMEPOSCompetitiveBid/index.html?redirect=/dmeposcompetitivebid/ (site visited Aug. 6, 2018). In order to allow the new administration an opportunity to review the program, CMS decided to temporarily delay moving forward with the next steps of the Round 2019 Durable Medical Equipment, Prosthetics, Orthotics, and Supplies (DMEPOS) Competitive Bidding Program.

[78] HCFA, Mandatory Use, Collection, Encoding, and Transmission of Outcome and Assessment Information Set (OASIS) for Home Health Agencies, 64 Fed. Reg. 32,984 (June 18, 1999), *available at* https://www.gpo.gov/fdsys/pkg/FR-1999-06-18/pdf/99-15529.pdf. OASIS is a group of data elements for CMS to assess each home health care patient and to measure patient outcomes. *See also* 42 C.F.R. § 484.20 (requiring HHAs to electronically report data from the OASIS as a Condition of Participation). For updates on OASIS, *see* CMS, "Home Health Quality Reporting Program," *available at* www.cms.gov/Medicare/Quality-Initiatives-Patient-Assessment-Instruments/HomeHealthQualityInits/index.html?redirect=/homehealthqualityinits/ (site visited Aug. 6, 2018).

[79] 42 C.F.R. §§ 484.210, 484.215, 484.220, & 484.250. The PPS rate is generally more for a beneficiary who needs at least eight hours, or ten visits, of therapy services.

A patient is reassessed at the end of each 60-day episode of care to ensure proper payment. The reassessment also helps determine the proper payment amount for the next episode of care if more services are needed.

If a patient's care needs change substantially during the 60-day episode of care, or if the patient's care plan is completed earlier than expected,[80] CMS may change the amount of payment. CMS may also make an additional payment if the actual costs of providing services are much greater than anticipated.[81] If the patient requires four or fewer home health visits, CMS makes a low-utilization payment adjustment (LUPA), and the agency is paid on a per visit amount that changes depending on the service provided.[82]

[C] The Claims Process

The claim submission process differs under PPS from the old fee-for-service process. PPS provides for split percentage payments.[83] At the beginning of an episode of care, the HHA submits to the MAC a request for anticipated payment (RAP) for the initial percentage payment. The initial payment is 60 percent of the total PPS amount for new patients and 50 percent for ongoing patients.[84] The initial request for payment does not constitute a Medicare claim.[85] At the end of the episode the agency submits a request for the residual final payment and is paid the remaining amount.

Under PPS, the RAP may be submitted without a care plan signed by a doctor. The request for payment may be based on a signed doctor's referral prescribing detailed orders or on verbal doctor's orders that are recorded in the plan of care that include a description of the patient's condition and services to be provided, that are attested to by the nurse or therapist responsible for the care, and that are included in a plan of care that is submitted to the doctor.[86] The care plan must be signed and dated by the doctor before the claim for each episode is submitted for the final percentage PPS payment.[87]

---

[80] If a beneficiary changes agencies in the middle of a 60-day episode, or if a beneficiary is discharged after reaching his or her goals and then returns to the same agency during the 60-day period, the agency will receive a partial episode payment (PEP) adjustment. The agency will be paid the prorated PPS amount based on the number of days services were provided during the 60-day episode. 42 C.F.R. §§ 484.205(d) (partial episode adjustment) & 484.235 (methodology for calculating partial episode adjustment).

[81] An agency may receive an outlier payment in addition to the PPS amount if the imputed cost of the 60-day episode exceeds a threshold amount. 42 C.F.R. § 484.205(e).

[82] 42 C.F.R. §§ 484.205(c) & 484.230.

[83] 42 C.F.R. § 484.205(b)(1), (2).

[84] 42 C.F.R. § 484.205(b).

[85] Although the initial request for payment is not a claim for Medicare purposes, it is a claim for enforcement purposes. 42 C.F.R. § 409.43(c)(2).

[86] 42 C.F.R. § 409.43(c)(1).

[87] 42 C.F.R. § 409.43(c)(3).

[1] Physician Certification

As a condition for payment, a physician must certify a patient's eligibility for the Medicare home health benefit.[88] CMS does not mandate a particular format for the certification, which is commonly included as a section on the plan of care. Specifically, a physician must certify (attest) that the patient is confined to the home and needs or needed intermittent skilled nursing care or physical or speech therapy, or continuing occupational therapy. The physician must also certify (attest) that the patient is under the care of a doctor of medicine, osteopathy, or podiatric medicine and that the services are being furnished under a plan of care that has been established and will be periodically reviewed by that doctor. The physician must recertify the patient for each subsequent 60-day episode of care in the same manner and, additionally, include an estimate of how much longer the skilled services will be required.[89]

Note that in 2009, CMS added a requirement for home health patients who require skilled management and evaluation of their care plan. If a patient's underlying condition or complication requires a registered nurse to ensure that essential non-skilled care is achieving its purpose and necessitates a registered nurse be involved in the development, management, and evaluation of a patient's care plan, the physician must include a brief narrative describing the clinical justification of this need, which is required for both certification and recertification.[90]

[a] Face-to-Face Encounter Requirement

The Affordable Care Act (ACA) added a new element to the certification requirement, mandating that the certifying physician document the occurrence of a face-to-face encounter with the patient seeking home health care.[91] The intent is to reduce fraud, waste, and abuse by assuring that a physician or other health care provider actually meet with patients to ascertain their specific care needs before ordering home health care. Implementation of the requirement began April 1, 2011.

The regulations establish that a face-to-face encounter must occur no more than 90 days prior to or within 30 days after the home health care start of care date.[92] The encounter must be performed by the certifying physician or the physician who cared for the patient in an acute or post-acute care facility. The following non-physician practitioners (NPPs) may also perform the encounter: a nurse practitioner or clinical nurse specialist working in collaboration with the certifying or facility

---

[88] 42 C.F.R. § 424.22(a); MBP Manual, Ch. 7: § 30.5.1. The certification must be complete prior to when an HHA bills Medicare for reimbursement; however, physicians should complete the certification when the plan of care is established, or as soon as possible thereafter.

[89] 42 C.F.R. § 424.22(b)(2); MBP Manual, Ch. 7: § 30.5.2.

[90] 42 C.F.R. §§ 424.22(a) (Certification), 424.22(b) (Recertification).

[91] Patient Protection and Affordable Care Act (PPACA or ACA), Pub. L. No. 111-148 (Mar. 23, 2010) § 6407; 42 U.S.C. § 1395f(a)(2)(C).

[92] 42 C.F.R. § 424.22(a)(1)(v); MBP Manual, Ch. 7: § 30.5.1.1(2).

physician and a certified nurse midwife or physician assistant working under the supervision of the certifying or facility physician.[93] Face-to-face patient encounters may occur via telehealth.[94] If the orders for home care are based on a new condition that was not evident during the encounter, then another face-to-face examination would be required within 30 days after the start of care.[95]

A face-to-face patient encounter is required only for initial certifications (i.e., any time that a Start of Care OASIS is completed to initiate home care).[96] Recertification for subsequent 60-day episodes do not require a new face-to-face encounter. However, without a complete initial certification, there cannot be payment for subsequent episodes.

From 2011 through 2014, CMS required a separate and distinct section of, or an addendum to, the certification documenting the face-to-face encounter which was clearly titled, dated, and signed by the certifying physician. CMS further required that the physician include a brief narrative statement describing how the clinical findings from the encounter supported the patient's homebound status and need for skilled services. This created a major impediment for Medicare patients' access to services and for participating HHAs' being paid. During this period, MACs denied a large percentage of home health claims on technical grounds without ever reviewing the medical record, finding that the face-to-face encounter documentation was insufficient to substantiate eligibility. Physicians were perplexed as to what was expected of them in these brief narrative statements, which never seemed to satisfy the contractors.

Effective January 1, 2015, CMS eliminated the narrative statement from the face-to-face encounter documentation requirement.[97] The current guidelines still require a physician to certify that a patient encounter was performed by a physician or allowed NPP during the prescribed time frame (and to document the date of the encounter) and was related to the primary reason for the home health services.

Although certifying physicians no longer need to compose a narrative statement describing the patient's homebound status and need for skilled care, CMS

---

[93] 42 C.F.R. § 424.22(a)(1)(v); MBP Manual, Ch. 7: § 30.5.1.1(1). The home health services may not be certified or recertified by a physician who has a financial relationship with the HHA providing the services. An NPP who has a financial relationship with the HHA may not perform the face-to-face encounter. *See* 42 C.F.R. § 424.22(d).

[94] 42 C.F.R. § 424.22(a)(1)(v)(B); MBP Manual, Ch. 7: § 30.5.1.1(4).

[95] MBP Manual, Ch. 7: § 30.5.1.1(2).

[96] MBP Manual, Ch. 7: § 30.5.1. CMS has clarified that if a home health patient is admitted to an inpatient facility and returns home from the inpatient stay after day 61 (after the first day of what would have been the next episode of care), then care would have to be initiated under a new start of care OASIS and initial certification, with a new face-to-face encounter.

[97] 76 Fed. Reg. 66,031, 66,043 (Nov. 6, 2014). *See also* CMS, MLN Number SE1436, "Certifying Patients for the Medicare Home Health Benefit," *available at* https://www.cms.gov/Outreach-and-Education/Medicare-Learning-Network-MLN/MLNMattersArticles/Downloads/SE1436.pdf (site visited Aug. 6, 2018).

has imposed a new "supporting documentation" requirement.[98] At the request of CMS and/or its review entities, an HHA must produce the actual clinical note from the face-to-face encounter, as well as any other supporting documentation from the certifying physician's and/or the acute/post-acute care facility's medical records needed to support the patient's eligibility for Medicare home health coverage.[99] CMS policy allows physicians and facilities to incorporate (by signature) clinical records from the HHA that substantiate a patient's homebound status and need for skilled care, so long as the clinical records are corroborated by their own records.[100] As a practical matter, it could make sense for an HHA to gather this documentation when working with the physician/facility on the patient's certification and plan of care. It remains to be seen whether this new requirement will be less challenging to comply with and how much of an administrative burden it will impose.

[2] Demonstrations For Home Health Services

In 2016, CMS implemented a three-year Pre-Claim Review Demonstration for Home Health Services. The Pre-Claim Review Demonstration was described as a "process through which a request for provisional affirmation of coverage is submitted for review before a final claim is submitted for payment."[101] The process was meant to assure that all relevant coverage and clinical documentation requirements were met before the final claim was submitted for payment which was meant to "decrease improper payments because of insufficient documentation, as well as reduce the need for HHAs to appeal claims."[102] The Pre-Claim review began in Illinois in August 2016 and was scheduled to begin in Florida, Texas, Michigan, and Massachusetts over the following months. However, on April 1, 2017, CMS paused the Pre-Claim Review Demonstration for Home Health Services to consider a number of changes.

During this "pause," CMS revised the process to include more flexibility and choice for providers, as well as risk-based changes to reward providers who

[98] MBP Manual, Ch. 7: § 30.5.1.2.

[99] MBP Manual, Ch. 7: § 30.5.1.2.

[100] MBP Manual, Ch. 7: § 30.5.1.2.

[101] CMS, Pre-claim Review Demonstration for Home Health Services Frequently Asked Quest ions (Update: 10/18/2016), *available at* https://www.cms.gov/Research-Statistics-Data-and-Systems/Monitoring-Programs/Medicare-FFS-Compliance-Programs/Pre-Claim-Review-Initiatives/Downloads/FAQ.pdf (site visited Aug. 6, 2018).

[102] CMS, Fact Sheet: Pre-Claim Review Demonstration of Home Health Services (June 8, 2016), *available at* https://www.cms.gov/Research-Statistics-Data-and-Systems/Monitoring-Programs/Medicare-FFS-Compliance-Programs/Pre-Claim-Review-Initiatives/Downloads/Pre_Claim_Review_Fact_Sheet.pdf (site visited Aug. 6, 2018).

show compliance with Medicare home health policies.[103] The proposed Review Choice Demonstration for Home Health Services gives providers in the demonstration states an initial choice of three options – pre-claim review, post-payment review, or minimal post-payment review with a 25% payment reduction for all home health services. A provider's compliance with Medicare billing, coding, and coverage requirements determines the provider's next steps under the demonstration. CMS will stagger implementation of the revised demonstration, beginning with the state of Illinois, then expanding to Ohio and North Carolina, and later to Texas and Florida[104] with the option to expand to other states in the Palmetto/JM Home Health and Hospice Medicare Administrative Contractor jurisdiction.[105]

According to CMS, the intent of the demonstration is to help protect the Medicare Trust Funds and taxpayer funds from fraud and improper payments, to improve provider compliance with Medicare rules and requirements, and to reduce Medicare appeals. The Review Choice Demonstration for Home Health Services does not change eligibility standards or Medicare's documentation requirements. CMS believes that the revised demonstration will have minimal effect on beneficiaries as it does not alter the Medicare home health benefit. However, concerns remain regarding whether the revised demonstration will just add administrative hurdles for providers which will lead to Medicare beneficiaries losing access to necessary care.

Unlike with the Pre-Claim Review Demonstration for Home Health Services, for the Review Choice Demonstration for Home Health Services CMS has posted a 60-day *Federal Register* Notice to give the public an opportunity to review and comment on CMS' intention to collect information from the public for the revised demonstration as part of the Paperwork Reduction Act (PRA) approval process.[106] The revised demonstration is for five years and it is expected that it

---

[103] CMS, "Pre-Claim Review Demonstration of Home Health Services," *available at* CMS, https://www.cms.gov/Research-Statistics-Data-and-Systems/Monitoring-Programs/Medicare-FFS-Compliance-Programs/Pre-Claim-Review-Initiatives/Overview.html (site visited Aug. 6, 2018).

[104] These states include known areas of fraudulent behavior and had either a high home health improper payment rate or a high denial rate during the Home Health Probe and Educate reviews. *See* CMS, Review Choice Demonstration for Home Health Services Frequently Asked Questions for the Proposed Collection of Information (Update: 05/31/2018), *available at* https://www.cms.gov/Research-Statistics-Data-and-Systems/Monitoring-Programs/Medicare-FFS-Compliance-Programs/Review-Choice-Demonstration/Downloads/RCD-FAQs-for-the-Proposed-Collection-of-Information-05-31-2018.pdf (site visited Aug. 6, 2018).

[105] CMS, "Review Choice Demonstration for Home Health Services," *available at* https://www.cms.gov/Research-Statistics-Data-and-Systems/Monitoring-Programs/Medicare-FFS-Compliance-Programs/Review-Choice-Demonstration/Review-Choice-Demonstration-for-Home-Health-Services.html (site visited Aug. 6, 2018).

[106] CMS, Agency Information Collection Activities: Proposed Collection; Comment Request (May 31, 2018), *available at* https://www.federalregister.gov/documents/2018/05/31/2018-11492/agency-information-collection-activities-proposed-collection-comment-request (site visited Aug. 6, 2018). Public comments on the proposed action must be received by July 30, 2018.

will begin no earlier than October 1, 2018. Additional details on the demonstration and start dates will be published following PRA approval.[107]

[D] Issues Under PPS

Under PPS, HHAs are paid based on the medical and service needs (home health resource utilization groups, or HHRUGs) of a particular beneficiary. Nevertheless, some beneficiaries who otherwise meet the eligibility criteria for Medicare home health benefits report problems in getting services or in getting the level of services prescribed by their doctors. Beneficiaries reporting problems include people with chronic conditions and those who use a large amount of nonroutine medical supplies. Problems in getting services or supplies may arise where the agency does not believe the PPS rate adequately covers its costs. Thus, although PPS is ostensibly only a payment system, it may deter some HHAs from serving certain beneficiaries. Advocates should continue to watch PPS closely to ensure it does not generate the same adverse consequences prompted by the interim payment system (IPS) in effect from 1998 through September 2000, when caps on reimbursement caused HHAs to reduce care, terminate services, or deny admission to patients because of their diagnosis or care needs.[108]

Recent policy changes have been made to the Home Health Prospective Payment System (HH PPS) that advocates should be aware of. CMS issued a final rule (CMS-1648-F) that updated the Medicare HH PPS rates and wage index for calendar year 2017.[109] In the final rule, CMS updated the payment rates and the case-mix weights for 2017. Areas of significant change and concern to advocates are as follows:

- Payment for high-cost outlier episodes of care will be based on visit length rather than the current cost-per-visit calculation, thus making it more difficult for individuals who need brief encounters at home to obtain care.

---

[107] CMS, Review Choice Demonstration for Home Health Services Frequently Asked Questions for the Proposed Collection of Information (Update: 05/31/2018).

[108] *See, e.g.*, Winkler v. Interim Healthcare, Inc., 36 F. Supp. 2d 1026 (D. Tenn. 1999). This problem has taken on renewed urgency in several recent Connecticut cases, particularly where services for a chronic care patient are needed on an ongoing basis. In these situations, but for the home health care services, the patient's chronic condition would deteriorate. Note that CMS has been using its PPS rate announcement as a vehicle to introduce proposed changes to home health regulations and policies on payment, eligibility, and coverage. For the 2017 rates, *see* CY 2017 Home Health Prospective Payment System Rate Update; Home Health Value-Based Purchasing Model; and Home Health Quality Reporting Requirements, (Nov. 3, 2016), *available at* https://www.gpo.gov/fdsys/pkg/FR-2016-11-03/pdf/2016-26290.pdf (site visited Aug. 6, 2018).

[109] CMS, "Home Health Agency (HHA) Center," *available at* https://www.cms.gov/center/provider-Type/home-Health-Agency-HHA-Center.html (site visited Aug. 6, 2018); CMS, CY 2017 Home Health Prospective Payment System Rate Update; Home Health Value-Based Purchasing Model; and Home Health Quality Reporting Requirements, 6 Fed. Reg. 56,767 (Nov. 7, 2014), *available at* https://www.gpo.gov/fdsys/pkg/FR-2016-11-03/pdf/2016-26290.pdf (site visited Aug. 6, 2018).

- Payment for Negative Pressure Wound Therapy (NPWT) using a disposable device may be obtained outside of the HH PPS bundled payment.
- Home Health Value Based Purchasing (HHVBP) continues to move forward since its implementation in January 2016. Increases (or decreases) in payments to providers based on HHVBP will continue gradually until 2022, when they cap at up to an 8 percent increase (or up to an 8 percent penalty). HHVBP creates incentives for increased home health payments based on narrowly defined achievements of "quality care" which are based on improvements in ambulation, bed transferring, bathing, pain interfering with activity, and shortness of breath. There are currently no HHVBP achievements that characterize functional maintenance, but comments to the final rules, addressing the Quality Reporting Program, state, "We wish to clarify that "improvement" on a measure means an improved agency performance score and that better patient outcomes can encompass both functional stabilization and improvement." (CMS-1648-F page 188).
- Home Health Quality Reporting Program adopted new Discharge to Community measures that will create further impediments to access home health coverage for those most at risk for unplanned hospitalization or death. If either an unplanned hospitalization or death occurs within 31 days of a beneficiary being discharged from home health care to independence in the community, this will be measured and count against a home health agency.

HHS released a proposed rule on July 25, 2017 that would update the home health prospective payment system payment rates, including the national, standardized 60-day episode payment rates, the national per-visit rates, and the non-routine medical supply conversion factor, effective for home health episodes of care ending on or after January 1, 2018. The rule updates payment rates and the wage index for home health agencies serving Medicare beneficiaries in 2018 and proposes to redesign the payment system in 2019. This rule proposes case-mix methodology refinements, as well as a change in the unit of payment from 60-day episodes of care to 30-day periods of care, to be implemented for home health services beginning on or after January 1, 2019. Further admittance to home health care from an institution (hospital, SNF, IRF, or LTCH) would result in a higher payment rate for all episodes of care than admittance from the community. The rule also proposes changes to the Home Health Value-Based Purchasing (HHVBP) Model and to the Home Health Quality Reporting Program (HH QRP).[110]

---

[110] The Center responded to the proposed rules with an in-depth analysis of the devastating impact their adoption would have on vulnerable Medicare beneficiaries. The Center urged CMS not to adopt the proposed rules and, instead, to engage beneficiaries, advocates, and other stakeholders in meaningful discussions to develop a system that encourages home health agencies to offer care

CMS published the 2018 Home Health Prospective Payment System final rule on November 7, 2017.[111] A broadly challenged proposed new payment system (Home Health Groupings Model, or HHGM) was not finalized. The HHGM would have provided home health agencies further disincentives to service people with longer-term chronic conditions. The proposed payment system would have paid agencies more money for a brief amount of care, and paid less after 30 days. In addition, it would have paid agencies more money when a patient started home health care within 14 days of discharge from an institution, such as a hospital, and paid less if a patient was not first an inpatient prior to starting home health care. However, some provisions of the HHGM were recently passed into law by Congress.[112] Most notably, under the law Medicare home health episodes of care were reduced from a 60-day period to a 30-day period, effective January 1, 2020. Unfortunately, discriminatory Value Based Purchasing Models and Quality Reporting Requirements were advanced in the final rule. Such measures promote disparity and create barriers against fair access to home care benefits for the most vulnerable Medicare beneficiaries. CMS also published Draft Interpretive Guidelines for new Home Health Conditions of Participation in the Medicare and Medicaid programs.

New Conditions of Participation rules and guidelines became effective January 13, 2018.[113] They provide expanded beneficiary protections and a more patient-centered focus of care. The revised regulations include: A new patient bill of rights that must be clear and accessible to patients and staff; additional patient assessment requirements to include psychosocial, functional and cognitive components; more significant consideration of patient preferences; greater patient involvement in care planning; coordination and integration with all of a patient's physicians; inclusion of patients, their representatives, and home health aides on the interdisciplinary care team; and, very significantly, greater protections for patients from arbitrary transfer or discharge from home health care.[114]

---

to all Medicare beneficiaries who qualify for coverage. CMA, "Center Comments on Proposed Home Health Payment Rules," *available at* http://www.medicareadvocacy.org/center-comments-on-proposed-home-health-payment-rules/ (site visited Aug. 6, 2018).

[111] CMA, CY 2018 Home Health Prospective Payment System Rate Update and CY 2019 Case-Mix Adjustment Methodology Refinements; Home Health Value-Based Purchasing Model; and Home Health Quality Reporting Requirements, 82 Fed. Reg. 51,676 (Nov. 7, 2017), *available at* https://www.gpo.gov/fdsys/pkg/FR-2017-11-07/pdf/2017-23935.pdf (site visited Aug. 6, 2018).

[112] Bipartisan Budget Act of 2018, H.R. 1892, 115th Congress, *available at* https://www.congress.gov/bill/115th-congress/house-bill/1892/text (site visited Aug. 6, 2018).

[113] CMS, CMS-3819-F Medicare and Medicaid Program: Conditions of Participation for Home Health Agencies Interpretive Guidelines—DRAFT, *available at* http://2whl0l41faj52syvna3ew4zl-wpengine.netdna-ssl.com/wp-content/uploads/2017/10/3819-F.HomeHealthAgency.CoPs_IGs.pdf (site visited Aug. 6, 2018); CMS, Conditions of Participation for Home Health Agencies, 85 Fed. Reg. 4,504 (Jan, 13, 2017), *available at* https://www.gpo.gov/fdsys/pkg/FR-2017-01-13/pdf/2017-00283.pdf (site visited Aug. 6, 2018).

[114] *See* CMA, "Beneficiary Protections Expanded in Revised Home Health Conditions of Participation," *available at* http://www.medicareadvocacy.org/beneficiary-protections-expanded-in-revised-home-health-conditions-of-participation/#_edn2 (site visited Aug. 6, 2018).

On July 2, 2018, CMS issued a proposed rule that outlined calendar year 2019 Medicare payment updates, quality reporting changes for home health agencies, case-mix methodology refinements and a change in the home health unit of payment from six days to 30 days for calendar year 2020. The proposed rule also discussed the implementation of temporary transitional payments for home infusion therapy services to begin on January 1, 2019 and included proposals related to the full implementation of the new home infusion therapy benefit in calendar year 2021.[115] The proposed rule was published in the *Federal Register* on July 12, 2018. CMS, CY 2019 Home Health Prospective Payment System Rate Update and CY 2020 Case-Mix Adjustment Methodology Refinements; Home Health Value-Based Purchasing Model; Home Health Quality Reporting Requirements; Home Infusion Therapy Requirements; and Training Requirements for Surveyors of National Accrediting Organizations, 83 Fed. Reg. 32, 340 (July 12, 2018), *available at* https://www.gpo.gov/fdsys/pkg/FR-2018-07-12/pdf/2018-14443.pdf (site visited August 6, 2018). CMA commented on these proposed rules.

On October 31, 2018, CMS finalized the changes to the Home Health Prospective Payment System. There are concerns that the new payment rules will further reduce access to care for people with longer term and chronic conditions. Medicare will pay agencies significantly more for services provided to beneficiaries within the first 30 days following inpatient institutional care (hospital or skilled nursing facility), than for those who begin home care without an inpatient stay. Further agencies that provide ongoing care for people with longer term and chronic conditions will receive significantly lower payments for those services.[116]

§ 4.06 CLAIMS SUBMISSION, DETERMINATION, AND APPEAL

The home health claims submission process is complex and its reimbursement system seriously impedes the granting of appropriate coverage. The sections that follow describe the procedure in detail.[117]

---

[115] CMS, CY 2019 Home Health Prospective Payment System Rate Update and CY 2020 Case-Mix Adjustment Methodology Refinements; Home Health Value-Based Purchasing Model; Home Health Quality Reporting Requirements; Home Infusion Therapy Requirements; and Training Requirements for Surveyors of National Accrediting Organizations, 83 Fed. Reg. 32,340 (July 12, 2018), *available at* https://www.gpo.gov/fdsys/pkg/FR-2018-07-12/pdf/2018-14443.pdf (site visited Aug. 6, 2018). CMA intends to comment on these proposed rules.

[116] "The final rule can be found at https://www.federalregister.gov/public-inspection/current (site visited November 12, 2018). It is expected to be published in the Federal Register on November 13, 2018. The Center for Medicare Advocacy will provide further analysis of the impact of the final rule.").

[117] *See* CMA, "Self Help Packet for Home Health Care Appeals Including "Improvement Standard" Denials" & "Toolkit: Medicare Home Health Coverage & *Jimmo v. Sebelius*," *available at* http://www.medicareadvocacy.org/take-action/self-help-packets-for-medicare-appeals/ (site visited Aug. 6, 2018).

[A] Medicare Advantage

In the event that the home health beneficiary has enrolled in a Medicare Advantage plan, then the beneficiary will be afforded the Medicare Advantage appeal rights.[118]

[B] Appeals Arising Under Parts A and B of Medicare

Rules regarding Medicare appeals were published in the *Federal Register* on March 8, 2005, and codified at Subpart G of Part 405.[119] The rules establish a combined Part A and Part B appeals process. CMS's regulations implement the changes to the appeals process for Medicare Part A and Part B claims and implement changes to the administrative law judge (ALJ) hearing process for all Medicare claims, including managed care claims and prescription drug claims.[120] Since this time the Medicare claims appeals process has undergone many changes.

[1] Regulatory Changes to Medicare Appeals

CMS recently finalized significant changes affecting Medicare appeals, particularly at the ALJ level of review. These changes apply to appeals of payment and coverage determinations for items and services furnished to Medicare beneficiaries, enrollees in Medicare Advantage (MA) and other Medicare competitive health plans, and enrollees in Medicare prescription drug plans, as well as to appeals of enrollment and entitlement determinations, and certain premium appeals.[121] HHS took administrative actions designed to reduce the number of pending appeals and to encourage resolution of cases earlier in the Medicare appeals process by implementing the regulatory changes in the final rule that became effective on March 20, 2017. The goals of the new/revised regulations

---

[118] *See* 42 C.F.R. Pt. 422 (Subpart M); Medicare Managed Care (MMC) Manual, Pub. 100-16, Ch. 13, *available at* https://www.cms.gov/Regulations-and-Guidance/Guidance/Manuals/Downloads/mc86c13.pdf (site visited Aug. 6, 2018). *See* **§ 7.04** of this Handbook for a discussion of the Medicare Advantage appeal system.

[119] *See* 42 C.F.R. §§ 405.701 *et seq.*

[120] CMS, Changes to the Medicare Claims Appeals Procedures, 70 Fed. Reg. 11,420 (Mar. 8, 2005), *available at* https://www.cms.gov/Regulations-and-Guidance/Regulations-and-Policies/QuarterlyProviderUpdates/downloads/CMS4064ifc.PDF (site visited Aug. 6, 2018). For final regulations (non-expedited appeals), *see* 42 C.F.R. §§ 405.900 *et seq.* (Subpart I—Determinations, Redeterminations, Reconsiderations, and Appeals Under Original Medicare [Part A and Part B]) (authorized by 42 U.S.C. §§ 1395ff), *available at* http://www.gpo.gov/fdsys/pkg/CFR-2011-title42-vol2/pdf/CFR-2011-title42-vol2-part405-subpartI.pdf (site visited Aug. 6, 2018).

[121] CMS, Changes to the Medicare Claims and Entitlement, Medicare Advantage Organization Determination, and Medicare Prescription Drug Coverage Determination Appeals Procedures, 82 Fed. Reg. 4974 (Jan. 17, 2017), *available at* https://www.federalregister.gov/documents/2017/01/17/2016-32058/medicare-program-changes-to-the-medicare-claims-and-entitlement-medicare-advantage-organization (site visited Aug. 6, 2018).

were to address "recent workload challenges" as the number of ALJ hearing requests continues to exceed OMHA's adjudication capacity.[122] The changes in the final rule are primarily focused on the ALJ level of review and will do a number of things including the following: permitting designation of Medicare Appeals Council (Council) decisions as precedential; expanding OMHA's available adjudicator pool by allowing attorney adjudicators to decide certain appeals; simplifying proceedings when CMS or CMS contractors are involved; clarifying areas of the regulations; and creating process efficiencies.[123] Many of the revisions do not, however, reach the heart of the problem and, if implemented, could further restrict beneficiary access to meaningful reviews.[124]

[2] Medicare Appeals Litigation

There continues to be great concern over the low success rate for appeals at the first two levels (redetermination and reconsideration) of appeal and the enormous backlog of appeals at the ALJ level.[125] The Center for Medicare Advocacy has addressed both of these issues through litigation.[126]

On February 26, 2018, a federal court preliminarily approved a settlement agreement in *Sherman v. Azar*, 3:15-cv-1468 (JAM) (D. Conn.). The lawsuit alleged that Medicare was denying beneficiaries meaningful review of their home health claims until they reached the third level of appeal, a hearing with an Administrative Law Judge. The beneficiary bringing the lawsuit on behalf of a nationwide class cited statistics in support of his claim showing that it was virtually impossible to be successful at the first two levels of appeal (called "redetermination" and "reconsideration" for appeals with standard timeframes). Under the settlement agreement, the Medicare agency transmitted four memoranda containing important principles for deciding home health appeals to the Medicare contractors that handle those decisions at the first and second levels of review.[127]

---

[122] 82 Fed. Reg. 4974, 4976.

[123] 82 Fed. Reg. 4974.

[124] CMA, "Issue Brief: CMS Issues New Rules Governing Medicare Appeals," *available at* http://www.medicareadvocacy.org/issue-brief-cms-issues-new-rules-governing-medicare-appeals/ (site visited Aug. 6, 2018).

[125] *See* CMA, "Senate Finance Committee Holds Hearing on Medicare Appeals Backlog—Proposed Solutions Are of Great Concern," *available at* http://www.medicareadvocacy.org/senate-finance-committee-holds-hearing-on-medicare-appeals-backlog-proposed-solutions-are-of-great-concern/ (site visited Aug. 6, 2018).

[126] CMA, "Center for Medicare Advocacy Sues to Fix Broken Medicare Appeals System," *available at* http://www.medicareadvocacy.org/center-for-medicare-advocacy-sues-to-fix-broken-medicare-appeals-system-2/.

[127] For the settlement agreement, *see* CMA, "Sherman Proposed Settlement Agreement," *available at* http://www.medicareadvocacy.org/wp-content/uploads/2017/12/Sherman-Proposed-Settlement-Agreement.pdf (site visited Aug. 6, 2018).

Since FY 2010, when Medicare Recovery Audit Contractors (RACs) began actively trying to identify and correct improper payments under the National Recovery Audit program, there has been a dramatic increase in the volume of appeals, leading to huge backlogs and long delays to obtain decisions for beneficiaries and providers alike. On August 1, 2016, the Center settled a nationwide class action lawsuit in federal court that challenged the long wait times for ALJ decisions faced by beneficiaries.[128] The settlement incorporates a policy of prioritizing beneficiary appeals to ensure timely processing, as well as certain reforms to make the ALJ appeals system easier for beneficiaries to use.[129] As of November 1, 2016, CMS updated scripts for 1-800-Medicare to highlight the OMHA beneficiary prioritization policy for beneficiary callers and to refer them to the toll-free OMHA Beneficiary Help Line if they have questions about filing appeals with OMHA or about ALJ appeals that are pending with OMHA.[130] OMHA also posted beneficiary appeals data required by the settlement on their website.[131] In late January 2017, OMHA issued a new ALJ request form that allows beneficiaries and enrollees to self-identify, making it easier for these claims to be classified as beneficiary appeals and given priority for processing.[132]

[3] Settlement Initiatives

Beginning February 5, 2018, CMS made available a Low Volume Appeals (LVA) Settlement Option for appellants including Medicare Fee-For-Service providers, physicians, and suppliers with fewer than 500 appeals pending at the Office of Medicare Hearings and Appeals and the Medicare Appeals Council.[133] The Office of Medicare Hearings and Appeals also recently expanded their Settlement Conference Facilitation (SCF) program. The original Settlement Conference Facilitation program was designed to be an alternative dispute resolution that

[128] Exley v. Burwell, No. 3:14-CV-1230 (D. Conn. May 24, 2016). For the settlement agreement, *see* CMA, "Approved Settlement Agreement," *available at* http://www.medicareadvocacy.org/wp-content/uploads/2016/08/Approved-Settlement-Agreement-00201898xC6348.pdf (site visited Aug. 6, 2018).

[129] *Exley*, No. 3:14-CV-1230.

[130] Dep't of Health & Human Services (HHS), Medicare Beneficiary and Medicare Advantage Part C Plan Enrollee or Part D Plan Enrollee Appeals and Assistance (OMHA Beneficiary Help Line is (844) 419–3358), *available at* https://www.hhs.gov/about/agencies/omha/filing-an-appeal/coverage-and-claims-appeals/medicare-beneficiary-and-medicare-advantage-part-c-plan-enrollee-part-d-plan-enrollee-appeals-assistance/index.html (site visited Aug. 6, 2018).

[131] HHS, Beneficiary Appeals Data, *available at* https://www.hhs.gov/about/agencies/omha/about/current-workload/beneficiary-appeals-data/index.html (site visited Aug. 6, 2018).

[132] HHS, Request for Administrative Law Judge: Hearing or Review of Dismissal, *available at* https://www.hhs.gov/sites/default/files/OMHA-100.pdf (site visited Aug. 6, 2018).

[133] CMS, "Low Volume Appeals Initiative," *available at* https://www.cms.gov/Medicare/Appeals-and-Grievances/OrgMedFFSAppeals/Appeals-Settlement-Initiatives/Low-Volume-Appeals-Initiative.html (site visited Aug. 6, 2018).

gives certain providers and suppliers an opportunity to resolve their eligible Part A and Part B appeals.[134]

[C] Medicare Home Health Claims Submission and Appeals Process

[1] Initial Determinations and Redeterminations

The claims process begins when the MAC issues an initial determination of a claim submitted by the home health provider or, occasionally, by the beneficiary. The regulations make clear that the initial determination, which is issued as the Medicare Summary Notice (MSN), goes only to the beneficiary, even when the contractor is aware that the beneficiary has an appointed representative.[135] Someone who wants to appeal from the initial determination must submit a written, signed request for a redetermination within 120 days of the initial determination; the regulations assume the notice is received five days after the date of the notice.[136] An extension to file a request after the deadline may be granted if good cause is shown.[137] Redetermination requests must be filed with the office indicated on the MSN.[138]

The regulations also allow home health providers to request appeal of a denial of an initial determination. In such a case, the contractor, an entity that contracts with the federal government to review and/or adjudicate claims, determinations, and/or decisions, must consolidate the appeals. The contractor has 60 days from receipt of the redetermination request to issue a decision. If more than one party files a request, the time period runs from the date the last request is received. If, for example, a beneficiary files a redetermination request on day 1, but the home health provider files on day 50, the 60-day time period for the contractor to act starts on day 50.[139]

Unlike the MSN (now given quarterly when there is no payment due), the notice of the redetermination is sent to the appellant, and copies are mailed to each party to the initial determination and to the party's authorized representative and/or appointed representative, if applicable.[140] The notice explains the facts, policies, and law relied upon in making the redetermination decision; the right to request a reconsideration and the process for doing so; and a statement of specific

---

[134] HHS, Settlement Conference Facilitation, *available at* https://www.hhs.gov/about/agencies/omha/about/special-initiatives/settlement-conference-facilitation/index.html (site visited Aug. 6, 2018).

[135] 42 C.F.R. § 405.921(a).

[136] 42 C.F.R. § 405.942(a).

[137] 42 C.F.R. § 405.942(b).

[138] 42 C.F.R. § 405.944(a).

[139] 42 C.F.R. §§ 405.906, 405.940, 405.944(c), and 405.950. *See* "definitions" at 42 C.F.R. § 405.902.

[140] Medicare Claims Processing (MCP) Manual, Ch. 29: § 310.5, *available at* https://www.cms.gov/Regulations-and-Guidance/Guidance/Manuals/downloads/clm104c29.pdf (site visited Aug. 6, 2018).

missing documents that must be submitted.[141] The notice states that home health providers, but not beneficiaries (unless they are represented by a provider), must submit all their evidence at the next level of review in order for the evidence to be considered at any further stage of the appeals process.[142] In addition, contractors are not required to send redetermination notices to multiple beneficiaries in overpayment cases brought by home health providers if the beneficiary allegedly has no liability for the claim.

The regulations include a reopening process to be used instead of the redetermination process to correct minor errors or omissions in initial determinations.[143] This process responds to a section of the Medicare law that allows home health providers to correct minor mistakes without going through the appeals process.[144] Reopenings can also be used at subsequent levels of review.

[2] Reconsideration

A third level of review, the reconsideration, is conducted by a separate group of Medicare contractors called Qualified Independent Contractors (QICs). Beneficiaries and other parties to the redetermination have 180 days to request a reconsideration determination by filing a request at the location indicated on the redetermination notice.[145] An extension to file a request after the deadline may be granted if good cause is shown.[146]

The reconsideration level of review is a paper review. However, the QIC is to solicit the beneficiary's position. As noted above, home health providers are required to submit all the evidence they want considered in the claim to the QIC. Evidence not submitted may be excluded at subsequent levels of review. Beneficiaries may submit additional evidence at subsequent levels of review.

The QIC is to issue a determination within 60 days of the reconsideration request.[147] Again, the time frame runs from receipt of the last request filed; the QIC must so notify a party who filed an earlier request. The regulations do not

---

[141] For examples of CMS's revised MSNs, *see* CMS, MSN Changes (Part B), *available at* http://www.cms.gov/apps/files/msn_changes.pdf (site visited Aug. 6, 2018); CMS, Part A: What is New on Your Redesigned "Medicare Summary Notice?," *available at* http://www.medicare.gov/pubs/pdf/SummaryNoticeA.pdf (site visited Aug. 6, 2018); CMS, Part B: What is New on Your Redesigned "Medicare Summary Notice?," *available at* http://www.medicare.gov/pubs/pdf/SummaryNoticeB.pdf (site visited Aug. 6, 2018); CMS, DME: What is New on Your Redesigned "Medicare Summary Notice?," *available at* http://www.medicare.gov/pubs/pdf/SummaryNoticeDME.pdf (site visited Aug. 6, 2018).

[142] 42 C.F.R. § 405.956.

[143] 42 C.F.R. §§ 405.927 and 405.980.

[144] Section 937 of the Medicare Prescription Drug Improvement and Modernization Act of 2003 (codified at 42 U.S.C. § 1395ff(b)(1)(G)).

[145] 42 C.F.R. § 405.962(a).

[146] 42 C.F.R. § 405.962(b).

[147] 42 C.F.R. § 405.970(a).

indicate how QICs are to document receipt or how beneficiaries are to know when the 60-day period ends. Although the statute allows a party to the reconsideration to ask for an extension of not more than 14 days for the QIC to conclude the reconsideration, the regulations add 14 days to the reconsideration time frame each time that additional evidence is submitted.[148]

If a QIC does not issue a timely decision, the regulations allow a party to request that the appeal be escalated to the next level of review, the ALJ level.[149] The regulations give the QIC five days to either issue a decision or acknowledge the escalation request and send it to the ALJ level of review.[150] Under the regulations, an appeal escalated to the ALJ level will be completed within 180 days of receipt, rather than the statutorily mandated 90 days for ALJ decisions.

In practice, however, Medicare contractors at the two lower levels tend to issue timely decisions. It is not until Medicare beneficiaries reach the ALJ level of review that they begin to experience significant delays in receiving decisions.[151]

[3] ALJ Hearings and Beyond

If the reconsideration decision by the QIC is unfavorable and at least $160 (in 2019) remains in controversy, the beneficiary has 60 days in which to request an ALJ hearing.[152] The hearing request should be made in writing and should be filed with the entity identified in the reconsideration notice.[153] An extension to file a request after the deadline may be granted if good cause is shown.[154] At this level of appeal a Medicare beneficiary who is dissatisfied with the previous decisions has the right to a hearing in front of an ALJ. The Office of Medicare Hearings and Appeals (OMHA) is responsible for conducting ALJ hearings.

The revised regulations authorize "Attorney Adjudicators," rather than ALJs to perform a portion of OMHA's workload that does not require a hearing.[155] Attorney adjudicators can issue decisions when a decision can be issued without an ALJ conducting a hearing under the regulations, dismissals when an appellant withdraws his or her request for an ALJ hearing, certain remands, and reviews of QIC and IRE dismissals. The revised regulations also make telephone hearings

---

[148] 42 C.F.R. § 405.970(b)(3).

[149] 42 C.F.R. § 405.970(c)(2).

[150] 42 C.F.R. § 405.970(e)(2).

[151] The current backlog of ALJ appeals has led to untimely delays in scheduling hearings and issuing decisions. Under CMS's stated policy to prioritize appeals filed by beneficiaries, it has designated a mail stop to identify when a Request for Hearing is submitted by a Beneficiary seeking an appeal or an appointed representative filing on behalf of a Beneficiary. These individuals should add: "ATTN: Beneficiary Mail Stop" above the address line in order to ensure priority processing of their ALJ appeal request.

[152] 42 C.F.R. § 405.1014(c)(1).

[153] 42 C.F.R. § 405.1014(c)(2).

[154] 42 C.F.R. § 405.1014(e).

[155] 42 C.F.R. § 405.902.

the default hearing method for individuals other than unrepresented beneficiaries.[156] Video-teleconferencing (VTC) will be retained as the default method of conducting hearings for unrepresented beneficiaries, unless good cause for an in-person appearance is shown or the beneficiary requests a phone hearing.[157]

If the ALJ hearing decision is unfavorable, a beneficiary may request a review from the Council.[158] The request must be made within 60 days of receipt of the hearing decision.[159] If at least $1,630 (in 2019) remain in controversy after the Council issues its review determination, the case may proceed to a federal district court.[160]

[D] Summary of Expedited Appeals Process

Expedited review is available in cases involving a discharge from the provider of services or a termination of services where "a physician certifies that failure to continue the provision of such services is likely to place the individual's health at significant risk."[161] Home health services are treated as a termination of services for which a doctor's certificate of significant health risk must be provided.[162] A reduction in service is not considered a termination or discharge for purposes of triggering expedited review.

Beneficiaries may seek expedited review of a home health service appeal.[163] The provider must give the beneficiary a general, standardized notice at least two days in advance of the proposed end of the service. If the service is fewer than two days, or if the time between services is more than two days, then notice must be given by the next-to-last service. The notice describes the service,

---

[156] 42 C.F.R. § 405.1020(b).

[157] 42 C.F.R. § 405.1020(b).

[158] 42 C.F.R. §§ 405.1100–1130. Previously, the Medicare Appeals Council has been referenced in a number of different ways: Departmental Appeals Board (DAB); Medicare Appeals Council (MAC); and Medicare Appeals Council (Board). CMS hosted a National Provider Call regarding changes to the Medicare claims and entitlement appeals process and indicated that all references are now to the Medicare Appeals Council (Council), *see* CMS, MLN, Changes to Medicare Claims & Entitlement Appeals Process, *available at* https://www.cms.gov/Outreach-and-Education/Outreach/NPC/Downloads/2017-06-29-Appeals-Presentation.pdf (site visited Aug. 6, 2018).

[159] 42 C.F.R. § 405.1102(a).

[160] 42 C.F.R. § 1136(a)(1).

[161] 42 U.S.C. § 1395ff(b)(1)(F).

[162] 42 C.F.R. § 405.1202(a).

[163] 42 C.F.R. §§ 405.1200-405.1204, implementing 42 U.S.C. § 1395ff(b)(1)(F). Notice of expedited review is not given in benefit situations (1) when the termination of covered services is the result of a beneficiary's, not a provider's, decision to end coverage; (2) when termination is for reasons other than medical necessity under Medicare coverage policy; and (3) when the beneficiary requires treatment at a higher level of care, such as transfer to an acute-care hospital. 42 C.F.R. §§ 405.1200–405.1204. For CMS's instructions, *see* CMS, Notice of Medicare Provider Non-Coverage: Form Number CMS-10123, *available at* https://www.cms.gov/Medicare/Medicare-General-Information/BNI/Downloads/Instructions-for-Notice-of-Medicare-Non-Coverage-NOMNC.pdf (site visited Aug. 6, 2018) & CMS, Detailed Explanation of Non-Coverage: Form Number CMS-10124, *available at* https://www.cms.gov/Medicare/Appeals-and-Grievances/MMCAG/downloads/DENCInstructions.pdf (sites visited Aug. 6, 2018).

the date coverage ends, the beneficiary's financial liability for continued services, and how to file an appeal.

A beneficiary must request expedited review, orally or in writing, by noon of the next calendar day after receiving notice. At that time, the beneficiary is given a more specific notice that includes a detailed explanation of why services are being terminated, a description of any applicable Medicare coverage rules and information on how to obtain them, and other facts specific to the beneficiary's case. The beneficiary is not financially liable for continued services until the later of two days after receiving the notice or the termination date specified on the notice.

Expedited review is conducted by the Beneficiary and Family Centered Care Quality Improvement Organization (BFCC-QIO), which has 72 hours in which to make a decision. When the BFCC-QIO receives the request for review, it must contact the provider, which then must supply the BFCC-QIO with information supporting its determination by the close of the same business day. The BFCC-QIO must solicit the views of the beneficiary and review the notice to determine whether it meets CMS requirements. The beneficiary does not incur liability if the BFCC-QIO decision is delayed because the provider did not get the necessary information to the reviewer in a timely manner.

If the BFCC-QIO sustains the decision to terminate or discharge services, the beneficiary may request expedited reconsideration, orally or in writing, by noon of the calendar day following initial notification. The reconsideration will be conducted by the QIC, which must issue a decision within 72 hours of the request. If the QIC does not comply with the time frame, the beneficiary may escalate the case to the ALJ level.

A BFCC-QIO may review an appeal from a beneficiary when the request is not timely filed, but the BFCC-QIO does not have to adhere to the time frame for issuing an expedited decision, and the limitation on liability does not apply.

It is important to note that when appealing a termination of service or item the only issue that may be addressed is whether the provider's termination of the service/item was appropriate. A contractor or ALJ may find that they lack jurisdiction to rule on whether Medicare payment should be made for these items/services that the beneficiary *did* continue to receive and pay for, because a claim was never submitted for those items/services. In other words, the scope of review is different for expedited appeals vs. regular appeals. By appealing the expedited decision a beneficiary is only appealing the termination of services decision. In order to obtain an appealable Medicare determination for any services a beneficiary continues to receive they must simultaneously request a demand bill to initiate an appeal for those services. Beneficiaries retain the right to utilize the standard (non-expedited) appeals process in all situations.

[E] Claims Development and Submission

When a beneficiary desires Medicare home health coverage, he or she must contact an HHA certified by Medicare, present a physician's order for care, and request Medicare-covered services. Typically, the agency will evaluate the patient, determine whether coverage will be available for the needed care (including developing the plan of care that must be approved and certified by the patient's physician) and determine the home health resource utilization group (HHRUG) to which the patient will be assigned under PPS. If the HHA believes coverage will be granted by the MAC, it will submit a request for anticipated payment (RAP) for the first part of its payment under PPS. The HHA will deliver the services and then submit a claim for coverage to the MAC at the end of the 60-day episode to receive the final PPS payment.[164] The claims are usually submitted at two-month intervals.

[F] Notice and Appeal Rights in Home Health Care

The Medicare statute requires HHAs, as a condition of participation, to protect and promote the following for each individual under its care:[165]

> (A) The right to be fully informed in advance about the care and treatment to be provided by the agency, to be fully informed in advance of any changes in the care or treatment to be provided by the agency that may affect the individual's well-being, and (except with respect to an individual adjudged incompetent) to participate in planning care and treatment or changes in care or treatment;
>
> (E) The right to be fully informed orally and in writing (in advance of coming under the care of the agency) of—
>
> "(iv) any change in the charges or items described in clause (i), (ii), or (iii) [services not covered by Medicare]; and
>
> (F) The right to be fully informed in writing (in advance of coming under the care of the agency) of the individual's rights and obligations under this subchapter.

Medicare regulations also require HHAs to give their patients written and oral notice concerning when Medicare will pay for services initially as well as when there is a change in expectations of Medicare payment for services.[166] In addition, the Medicare Claims Processing Manual (MCPM) requires HHAs to

---

164 42 C.F.R. §§ 409.43, 424.33.

165 42 U.S.C. § 1395bbb(a)(1). On July 7, 2017, CMS delayed the implementation of new home health Conditions of Participation (CoPs) that were to take effect on July 13, 2017, by six months–to January 13, 2018. CMS, Conditions of Participation for Home Health Agencies; Delay of Effective Date (July 10, 2017), *available at* https://www.federalregister.gov/documents/2017/07/10/2017-14347/medicare-and-medicaid-programs-conditions-of-participation-for-home-health-agencies-delay-of (site visited Aug. 6, 2018). The new CoPs include provisions that would improve care coordination, training of staff and administrators, and beneficiary protections.

166 42 C.F.R. § 484.10(e)(1), (2).

give their patients an Advance Beneficiary Notice of Non-coverage (ABN) prior to delivering an item or a service that they don't believe Medicare will cover.[167] The key notion behind the ABN is that it enables the beneficiary to make an informed decision on whether to receive the service or item in question and accept potential financial liability.

Note that while the MCPM does not require HHAs to inform patients that they can demand that a claim be submitted to Medicare, it does require HHAs to submit claims if the patients learn on their own about the demand bill process.[168] HHAs are also required to issue a Home Health Change of Care Notice (HHCCN) to notify beneficiaries of care changes involving reductions or terminations of items and/or services.[169] Expedited review is available when all Medicare-covered services are ending.[170]

Unfortunately, these notice provisions are not monitored and enforced by CMS as extensively as needed, and consequently HHAs often fail to provide patients with notice of denials, reductions, or terminations of care. As a result, beneficiaries often lack information about appeal rights, including where to file, what to file, or how best to supplement one's record in support of a claim for coverage.[171] HHAs are required to use a model notice whenever a triggering event defined by CMS occurs. Note that *Lutwin (Healey) v. Thompson* requires notice in all situations where services are denied, reduced, or terminated. Issues involving CMS's monitoring and enforcement of the notice requirement are being

---

[167] CMS, Fee for Service Advance Beneficiary Notice, Form CMS-R-131, *available at* http://www.cms.gov/Medicare/Medicare-General-Information/BNI/ABN.html (site visited Aug. 6, 2018). *See also* MCP Manual, Ch. 30: § 50 *et seq.*, *available at* https://www.cms.gov/Regulations-and-Guidance/Guidance/Manuals/downloads/clm104c30.pdf (site visited Aug. 6, 2018).

[168] MCP Manual, Ch. 10: § 50, *available at* http://www.cms.gov/Regulations-and-Guidance/Guidance/Manuals/downloads/clm104c10.pdf (site visited Aug. 6, 2018). *See also* Lutwin v. Thompson, 361 F.3d 146 (2d Cir. 2004) (requiring notice to beneficiaries whenever home health care is denied, reduced, or terminated). For the latest developments, *see* CMS, "Beneficiary Notices Initiative (BNI)," *available at* http://www.cms.gov/Medicare/Medicare-General-Information/BNI/ (site visited Aug. 6, 2018). *See also* 69 Fed. Reg. 69,264 (Nov. 26, 2004) (adding 42 C.F.R. §§ 405.1200–405.1204, to implement 42 U.S.C. § 1395ff(b)(1)(F)).

[169] CMS, Home Health Change of Care Notice (HHCCN), Form CMS-10280, *available at* http://www.cms.gov/Medicare/Medicare-General-Information/BNI/HHCCN.html (site visited Aug. 6, 2018). *See also* MCP Manual, Ch. 30: § 60, *et seq.*, *available at* https://www.cms.gov/Regulations-and-Guidance/Guidance/Manuals/downloads/clm104c30.pdf (site visited Aug. 6, 2018).

[170] HHAs must continue to issue an expedited determination notice called the Notice of Medicare Provider Non-Coverage (NOMNC), Form CMS-10123, if applicable, when all covered services are being terminated. For more information, *see* CMS, FFS Expedited Determination Notices, *available at* https://www.cms.gov/Medicare/Medicare-General-Information/BNI/FFS-Expedited-Determination-Notices.html (site visited Aug. 6, 2018).

[171] Program Memorandum (PM) A-01-30 (Feb. 28, 2001), reissued as PM A-02-017 (Feb. 26, 2002); PM A-01-05 (Jan. 16, 2001), reissued as PM A-02-018 (Feb. 26, 2002); Healey v. Thompson, 186 F. Supp. 2d 105 (D. Conn. 2001).

resolved in large part through CMS Transmittal No. 1025 (Medicare Claims Processing).[172]

Although theoretically there is a procedure for appealing Medicare home health terminations and reductions, several characteristics of its design render it useless for most beneficiaries. First, standard appeals are permitted only with respect to services actually received; second, most HHAs will not provide services after a reduction or termination; third, agencies that agree to provide services only do so if the beneficiary pays for the services pending appeal, which most beneficiaries cannot afford; and fourth, the appeal process is slow and cumbersome and decisions often come far too long after a crisis point.[173]

[G] Liability Protections

The liability of the patient for the cost of care is waived until he or she is informed in writing, by issuance of the ABN, that coverage is not available.[174] Situations exist where PPS payment has been made for the full episode. Should additional coverage be granted, for example, additional home health aide hours, but care does not increase to outlier criteria, the HHA would not receive additional payment. But it cannot charge the beneficiary for the additional cost of care.

Whenever the HHA submits a claim to the MAC, it risks a financial penalty. If the MAC determines that the services involved should not be covered, it issues an initial determination denying the claim. The HHA may not begin to charge the patient for the cost of services until the patient is informed in writing that Medicare coverage will be denied.[175] Thus, the agency is forced to absorb the cost of the care already furnished.

If the HHA believes that coverage will be denied by the contractor, or when the agency is unsure whether coverage will be granted, it will generally seek to avoid submitting a claim in order to escape any possible financial penalty. The agency may be found liable if it failed to issue a notice or issued a defective notice. Although the beneficiary has a right to insist that a claim be submitted even where the HHA believes coverage will be denied (called a "demand bill"),

---

[172] Lutwin (Healey), 361 F.3d 146. Note, too, that if an HHA decides to stop providing service for a reason not related to Medicare coverage (e.g., for its own financial and business reasons), such a cessation of service is not subject to appeal. *See* **Appendix 4-6** of this Handbook, including the discussion of "option box 2" in § 60-4. The issuance of an ABN in this circumstance is voluntary.

[173] For information on developing and pursuing an appeal of a home health care denial, *see* CMA, "Self Help Packet for Home Health Care Appeals Including 'Improvement Standard' Denials," *available at* http://www.medicareadvocacy.org/self-help-packet-for-expedited-home-health-care-appeals-including-improvement-standard-denials/ (site visited Aug. 6, 2018).

[174] See MCP Manual, Ch. 30: §§ 30.1 (beneficiary liability) & 30.2 (provider liability), *available at* http://www.cms.gov/Regulations-and-Guidance/Guidance/Manuals/downloads/clm104c30.pdf (site visited Aug. 6, 2018).

[175] 42 C.F.R. §§ 411.400–411.406.

often the agency will seek to discourage the patient from requiring such a no-payment claim submission because, under some circumstances, the agency may be penalized if the contractor determines that a claim should have been deemed covered initially by the agency.[176]

In many cases, this system results in a complete loss of care as well as the loss of the right to appeal. When the agency is afraid to claim coverage from the contractor, the agency usually will not deliver home health services unless the patient agrees to pay for them. If the patient is unable to afford the expensive home health care involved, the care will not be delivered even though Medicare coverage should have been granted, and could have been won on appeal had the care been delivered and a claim submitted. (Remember, the contractor will not make an initial determination on a claim until after the services involved have been rendered.)

Inappropriate restrictions on Medicare coverage can result in the complete loss of home health care or can mean that the patient will receive less care than he or she actually needs. Ultimately, the Medicare program may pay less home health coverage, but at the cost of increased disability, patient indigence, and unnecessary institutionalization.

§ 4.07 THE ROLE OF ADVOCACY

Advocacy in the home health arena, as in other Medicare areas, is often the key to the individual's ability to "access" services. Good advocacy allows people to be heard. It focuses on the important questions of whether the circumstances of a particular individual have been given full consideration with respect to coverage and services.

Effective advocates can include Medicare beneficiaries themselves as well as lawyers, paralegals, family members, friends, and treating physicians acting on the beneficiary's behalf. Effectiveness is grounded in good information about the Medicare program and in a keen appreciation of, and insistence upon, the right to be heard when services are denied, reduced, or terminated.

Advocates should develop a working knowledge of the Medicare benefit, as well as a good and supportive relationship with health care providers. This will ensure a broad knowledge base for advocates about the law and the relevant medical facts that must be demonstrated in order to prove eligibility for coverage and services. At the same time, this activity on behalf of a beneficiary will often educate medical providers about the basic legal requirements for Medicare coverage. This synergy is essential to effective advocacy.

---

[176] *See* Appendix **4-6** for CMS's treatment of "notice triggering" events. For CMS's revised ABN and HHCCN, *see* CMS, "FFS HHCCN," *available at* http://www.cms.gov/Medicare/Medicare-General-Information/BNI/HHCCN.html (site visited Aug. 6, 2018).

§ 4.08 HOW TO DEVELOP A WINNING APPEAL

[A] Sequential Approach to Case Development

Advocacy can make a crucial difference to your client's chance of success on appeal. The following approach is suggested:

1. Ascertain whether the HHA involved is certified to participate in the Medicare program.
2. Determine whether your client is homebound and whether he or she requires intermittent skilled nursing services or physical or speech therapy or continuing occupational therapy.
3. Ascertain whether the care billed to the Medicare program qualifies as part-time or intermittent nursing, or aide services.
4. Ensure that the home health care your client needs is delivered. The MAC will not issue an initial determination except where a claim for payment is submitted by a certified HHA for the cost of home health services already rendered. Unfortunately, unfair Medicare coverage denials often have an un-appealable prospective effect. The agency decides that services will henceforth not be covered by the MAC and declines to deliver the care unless payment is forthcoming. If the patient cannot pay for the care, the care will not be delivered, and a claim will not be submitted. The patient will not be able to challenge the unfair coverage denial. Accordingly, it is the advocate's first duty to make sure that care is rendered.

   Three ways to make sure that care is rendered in order to obtain an appealable initial determination are:

   a. If your client has funds sufficient to cover the cost involved, or if other public or private funds are available, urge him or her to consider paying for the care and then to file an appeal for Medicare coverage. This approach is often fruitful where there is a strong medical basis for coverage.

   b. If your client is unable to afford the care involved, attempt to convince the HHA to "carry" the case. That is, try to persuade the agency to deliver the care without receiving payment in advance while the claim and appeals process proceed. Your client may be required to assume liability for the cost of services in writing should Medicare coverage be denied.

   c. Finally, you may be able to persuade the HHA to take a chance on the claim. Especially if you can demonstrate a successful record in appeals of similar cases, the HHA may be willing to deliver the care without assurance of payment in expectation that your appeal will prove successful.

5. Provide the HHA with copies of relevant, supporting language from the federal regulations and CMS manual. If your client requires maintenance nursing or rehabilitation services, provide a copy of the *Jimmo* settlement agreement and Fact Sheet.[177]
6. Request *in writing* that the HHA submit a claim to Medicare for all the services ordered by the patient's physician that are potentially coverable by Medicare.
7. Solicit the written opinion of the attending physician. For care already initiated by the agency, the attending physician will have been required to sign a certification and plan-of-treatment form. You should obtain a copy of this document for review and for submission with your appeal if it is helpful.

A more detailed letter from the physician emphasizing the patient's homebound status, the need for skilled care, and the medical necessity of both the skilled care and the home health aide is often helpful. A persuasive attending physician's letter often encourages the contractor to grant the claim at the initial determination level, thereby avoiding the need for further appeal. If an appeal to the reconsideration or ALJ hearing levels is necessary, a strong and detailed attending physician's letter will often be the key to coverage in most cases.

[B] The Patient's Plan of Care as an Advocacy Tool

[1] Plan-of-Care Requirements

A plan of care is a prerequisite for Medicare coverage for home health services. The plan of care must include physician's orders as well as drug treatments and frequency and should explain the interrelationship of other medical/social services that the particular patient might receive, including physical therapy or speech therapy.[178] It must be signed and dated by a physician.[179]

---

[177] For *Jimmo* settlement agreement, *see* CMA, Settlement Agreement & Stipulation of Dismissal, http://www.medicareadvocacy.org/wp-content/uploads/2014/10/Jimmo-II-Settlement-FINAL.pdf (site visited Aug. 6, 2018). *See also* CMS, "*Jimmo v. Sebelius* Settlement Agreement Fact Sheet," *available at* http://www.cms.gov/Medicare/Medicare-Fee-for-Service-Payment/SNFPPS/Downloads/Jimmo-FactSheet.pdf (site visited Aug. 6, 2018).

[178] 42 C.F.R. §§ 409.43 *et seq.*

[179] *See* 42 C.F.R. § 424.22(d) (the certifying physician may not have a significant ownership interest in the HHA as defined in § 424.22(d), a 5 percent or more ownership interest, or financial or contractual relationship).

[2] Physician Attestation Required

The plan of care must be signed by the physician before the bill for services is submitted, and any changes in the plan must be signed and dated by the physician.[180] Orders for "as needed" services or "PRN" services must be accompanied by a description of the medical signs and symptoms that would occasion such visits and a specific number of visits that can be made under that order before an additional physician's order would have to be obtained,[181] including oral orders.[182]

[3] Plan of Care as an Advocacy Tool

In some instances, HHAs, without consulting with attending physicians and obtaining their consent, are notifying patients at the end of a plan-of-care period that home health services will no longer be provided. Advocates should therefore pay particular attention to both the plan-of-care document *and* the process of its development to ensure that the physician is responsible for the plan and supports its contents. This approach may be helpful in avoiding a termination of services initiated by the HHA. Such terminations are particularly prevalent when the patient needs costly care or care that will be required for a long period of time.

[4] Continuing Need for Care

Advocates must demonstrate that the beneficiary continues to meet Medicare home health criteria, including the need for skilled care services. The plan of care should include as much detail as possible, supporting the need for the specific services to be continued.

[5] Termination of the Plan of Care

Federal regulations provide that a plan of care is considered terminated if the beneficiary does not receive at least one covered skilled nursing, physical therapy, speech-language pathology service, or occupational therapy visit in a 60-day period, unless the physician documents that the interval without such care is appropriate.[183] Medicare regulation and manual provisions anticipate at least a minimal process for recertification, to the extent that the physician is given an opportunity to review the plan of care, every 60 days, and sign a new care plan if services are needed.[184]

---

[180] 42 C.F.R. § 409.43(c). Under PPS, a signed plan of care is submitted at the end of the 60-day episode of care and not with the initial request for anticipated payment.

[181] 42 C.F.R. § 409.43(b).

[182] 42 C.F.R. § 409.43(d).

[183] 42 C.F.R. § 409.43(f).

[184] 42 C.F.R. § 424.22(b) (recertification).

[6] Cycle for Plan Review

The plan of care should be reviewed by the physician in consultation with the professional staff of the HHA at least every 60 days under PPS. Each such review is to be signed and dated by the physician.[185] As discussed above, termination of a plan of care is often a tricky issue, especially as HHAs seek to divest themselves of their heavy care patients. Again, be sure that the patient's attending physician is in charge of the plan of care, supports its contents, and approves of any discharge from home care.

[C] Identifying Coverable Home Health Cases

The lists provided in the following sections can be used as a quick reference aid to help identify coverable home health claims.

[1] Coverage Criteria

Home health claims are suitable for Medicare coverage, and appeal if they have been denied, if they meet the following criteria:

1. A physician has signed or will sign a plan of care.
2. The patient is or will be homebound. This criterion can be met if: the person has a normal inability to leave the home and leaving home requires a considerable and taxing effort; and the person either requires assistance to leave the home which may be shown by the patient needing personal assistance or the help of a wheelchair or crutches, etc., or it is medically contraindicated for the person to leave home. Occasional but infrequent non-medical absences from home are allowable.
3. The patient needs or will need skilled nursing care on an intermittent basis (from as much as every day for recurring periods of 21 days—if there is a predictable end to the need for daily care—to as little as once every 60 days) or physical or speech therapy or ongoing occupational therapy services.
4. The care must be provided by, or under arrangements with, a Medicare-certified provider.

[185] 42 C.F.R. § 409.43(e). For ongoing updates to notices in the home health arena, *see* CMS, "Beneficiary Notices Initiative."

[2] Coverable Home Health Services

If the triggering conditions described above are met, the beneficiary is entitled to Medicare coverage for home health services. There is no coinsurance or deductible under traditional Medicare. Home health services include:

1. Part-time or intermittent nursing care provided by or under the supervision of a registered professional nurse;
2. Physical, occupational, or speech therapy;
3. Medical social services under the direction of a physician; and
4. To the extent permitted in regulations, part-time or intermittent services of a home health aide.

[3] Additional Hints for Coverage

1. Medicare coverage should not be denied simply because the patient's condition is "chronic" or "stable." "Restorative potential" is not necessary.
2. Resist arbitrary caps on coverage imposed by the MAC. For example, do not accept provider or MAC assertions that aide services in excess of one visit per day are not covered or that daily nursing visits can never be covered.
3. There is no legal limit to the duration of the Medicare home health benefit. Medicare coverage is available for necessary home care even if it is to extend over a long period of time.
4. The doctor is the patient's most important ally. If it appears that Medicare coverage will be denied, ask the doctor to help demonstrate that the standards above are met. Home care services should not be ended or reduced unless this has been ordered by the doctor.
5. In order to be able to appeal a Medicare denial, the HHA must have filed a Medicare claim for the patient's care. Request in writing that the HHA file a Medicare claim even if the agency claims that Medicare will deny coverage.

APPENDIX 4-1 HOME HEALTH CARE HEARING CHECKLIST

(Compiled by the Center for Medicare Advocacy)*

This checklist will help you make sure that the evidence you have gathered is sufficient to demonstrate that the patient involved is entitled to Medicare home health coverage. Each of the essential points you must prove is listed. Underneath each point you will find a description of the documents or other evidence which will help you meet the legal requirement involved.

		YES	NO
1.	The claimant is enrolled in the Medicare program. Look for the claimant's Medicare number, which can be found on the Medicare enrollment card.	[ ]	[ ]
2.	The patient is confined to his or her home. Look for documentation or testimony that the patient has a normal inability to leave his or her home without difficulty.	[ ]	[ ]
3.	The patient is under the care of a physician. Look for: (a) physician's order for home health services; and (b) physician's statement or Attending Physician Report.	[ ]	[ ]
4.	The beneficiary needs skilled nursing care on an intermittent basis or physical or speech therapy. Look for: (a) documentation or testimony that it is medically necessary that the patient receive a skilled service at least once every 60 days; (b) physician's testimony or written statement that skilled care is medically necessary is the best evidence of this requirement (Attending Physician's Report, etc.); and (c) nurse or therapist notes.	[ ]	[ ]
5.	The beneficiary needs home health aide care, occupational therapy, or other home medical services (if you are seeking Medicare coverage for these dependent services.)	[ ]	[ ]

* For additional information on home health care, *see* CMA, "Home Health," *available at* http://www.medicareadvocacy.org/medicare-info/home-health-care/ (site visited Aug. 6, 2018).

Look for:

(a) physician's order for the dependent services; and

(b) home health aide notes, therapist, medical social service provider notes.

APPENDIX 4-2 ATTENDING PHYSICIAN REPORT— HOME HEALTH CARE

(Compiled by the Center for Medicare Advocacy)

Patient: HIC#

Provider: Period At Issue:

Physician:

PLEASE RESPOND TO THE FOLLOWING QUESTIONS BY CHECKING THE APPROPRIATE RESPONSES AND ELABORATING WHERE INDICATED. BE SURE YOUR RESPONSES REFER TO THE TIME PERIOD ENTERED ABOVE.

1. Were you an attending physician to this patient during the period at issue described above? _____Yes _____No

2. Please indicate whether the patient required any of the following services during the period at issue: _____Yes _____No

   (a) Skilled Nursing

   If yes, please specify type(s): ________________________________

   ____

   ____

   (b) Skilled Physical Therapy _____Yes _____No

   If yes, please specify type(s): ________________________________

   ____

   ____

   (c) Skilled Speech Therapy _____Yes _____No

   If yes, please specify type(s): ________________________________

   ____

   ____

(d) Occupational Therapy ______Yes ______ No

(e) Home Health Aides ______Yes ______ No

(f) Medical Social Services ______Yes ______ No

(g) Durable Medical Equipment ______Yes ______ No

(h) Medical Supplies ______Yes ______ No

(i) Other (please specify): ____________________

3. During the time period at issue, was the patient confined to his/her home? (The individual had a condition that restricted the ability of the individual to leave his or her home except with the assistance of another individual or the aid of a supportive device, or the individual had a condition such that leaving his or her home was contraindicated.) ______Yes ______ No

   Comment: ____________________

4. Was the skilled nursing which the patient required, needed on an "intermittent" basis (from once a day for a predictable period of time to once every 60 days) ______Yes ______ No

   Comment: ____________________

5. Did the patient require the services of a "part-time" (less than 8 hours per day) or "intermittent" home health aide in addition to the skilled nursing and/or rehabilitative services? ______Yes ______ No

   Comment: ____________________

6. Please respond to the following:

(a) Did the patient have special medical complications that required the professional or technical administration of services which are generally considered nonskilled? ______Yes ______No

If yes, please elaborate: ____

____

____

(b) Did the patient's overall management and care plan require technical or professional personnel to assure recovery and/or safety? ______Yes ______No

(c) Was the patient's condition such that technical or professional personnel were needed to properly *observe* and possibly *modify* treatment? ______Yes ______No

(d) Was the use of technical or professional personnel necessary to teach the patient self-maintenance? ______Yes ______No

FURTHER REMARKS: ____

____

____

____

____

____

____

________________ ________________________
Date Signature of Physician

THANK YOU FOR YOUR TIME AND CONSIDERATION IN COMPLETING THIS REPORT.

APPENDIX 4-3 IMPORTANT SELECTIONS FROM THE MEDICARE BENEFIT POLICY MANUAL

CHAPTER 7 § 20—Conditions for Coverage

CMS PUB. 100-02*

(Compiled by the Center for Medicare Advocacy)

A finding that care is not reasonable and necessary must be based on information provided on the forms and in the medical record with respect to the unique medical condition of the individual beneficiary. *That is, a coverage denial may not be based solely on the reviewer's general inferences about patients with similar diagnoses or on data related to utilization generally, but must be based upon objective clinical evidence regarding the patient's individual need for care.*

20. Conditions To Be Met for Coverage of Home Health Services
(Rev. 1, 10-01-03)
A3-3116, HHA-203

Medicare covers HHA services when the following criteria are met:

1. The person to whom the services are provided is an eligible Medicare beneficiary;
2. The HHA that is providing the services to the beneficiary has in effect a valid agreement to participate in the Medicare program;
3. The beneficiary qualifies for coverage of home health services as described in § 30;
4. The services for which payment is claimed are covered as described in §§ 40 and 50;
5. Medicare is the appropriate payer; and
6. The services for which payment is claimed are not otherwise excluded from payment.

20.1. Reasonable and Necessary Services
(Rev. 1, 10-01-03)
A3-3116.1. HHA-203.1

20.1.1. Background
(Rev. 1, 10-01-03)
A3-3116.1A, HHA-203.1A

* *See* MBP Manual, Ch. 7, *available at* https://www.cms.gov/Regulations-and-Guidance/Guidance/Manuals/Downloads/bp102c07.pdf (site visited Aug. 6, 2018).

In enacting the Medicare program, Congress recognized that the physician would play an important role in determining utilization of services. The law requires that payment can be made only if a physician certifies the need for services and establishes a plan of care. The Secretary is responsible for ensuring that Medicare covers the claimed services, including determining whether they are "reasonable and necessary."

20.1.2. Determination of Coverage
(Rev. 208, Issued: 04-22-15, Effective: 01-01-15, Implementation: 05-11-15)

The *Medicare contractor's* decision on whether care is reasonable and necessary is based on information reflected in the home health plan of care, the OASIS as required by 42 CFR 484.55 or a medical record of the individual patient. Medicare does not deny coverage solely on the basis of the reviewer's general inferences about patients with similar diagnoses or on data related to utilization generally, but bases it upon objective clinical evidence regarding the patient's individual need for care. Coverage of skilled nursing care or therapy to perform a maintenance program does not turn on the presence or absence of a patient's potential for improvement from the nursing care or therapy, but rather on the patient's need for skilled care. Skilled care may be necessary to improve a patient's current condition, to maintain the patient's current condition, to prevent or slow further deterioration of the patient's condition.

20.2. Impact of Other Available Caregivers and Other Available Coverage on Medicare Coverage of Home Health Services
(Rev. 208, Issued: 04-22-15, Effective: 01-01-15, Implementation: 05-11-15)

Where the Medicare criteria for coverage of home health services are met, patients are entitled by law to coverage of reasonable and necessary home health services. Therefore, a patient is entitled to have the costs of reasonable and necessary services reimbursed by Medicare without regard to whether there is someone available to furnish the services. However, where a family member or other person is or will be providing services that adequately meet the patient's needs, it would not be reasonable and necessary for HHA personnel to furnish such services. Ordinarily it can be presumed that there is no able and willing person in the home to provide the services being rendered by the HHA unless the patient or family indicates otherwise and objects to the provision of the services by the HHA, or unless the HHA has first hand knowledge to the contrary.

Similarly, a patient is entitled to reasonable and necessary *Medicare* home health services even if the patient would qualify for institutional care (e.g., hospital care or skilled nursing facility care) *and Medicare payment should be made for reasonable and necessary home health services where the patient is also receiving supplemental services that do not meet Medicare's definition of skilled nursing care or home health aide services.*

■ **EXAMPLE 1:** A patient who lives with an adult daughter and otherwise qualifies for Medicare coverage of home health services, requires the assistance of a home health aide for bathing and assistance with an exercise program to improve endurance. The daughter is unwilling to bathe her elderly father and assist him with the exercise program. Home health aide services would be reasonable and necessary.

■ **EXAMPLE 2:** A patient who is being discharged from a hospital with a diagnosis of osteomyelitis and requires continuation of the I.V. antibiotic therapy that was begun in the hospital was found to meet the criteria for Medicare coverage of skilled nursing facility services. If the patient also meets the qualifying criteria for coverage of home health services, payment may be made for the reasonable and necessary home health services the patient needs, notwithstanding the availability of coverage in a skilled nursing facility.

■ **EXAMPLE 3:** A patient who needs skilled nursing care on an intermittent basis also hires a licensed practical (vocational) nurse to provide nighttime assistance while family members sleep. The care provided by the nurse, as respite to the family members, does not require the skills of a licensed nurse (as defined in § 40.1) and therefore has no impact on the beneficiary's eligibility for Medicare payment of home health services even though another third party insurer may pay for that nursing care.

20.3. Use of Utilization Screens and "Rules of Thumb"
(Rev. 1, 10-01-03)
A3-3116.3, HHA-203.3

Medicare recognizes that determinations of whether home health services are reasonable and necessary must be based on an assessment of each beneficiary's individual care needs. Therefore, denial of services based on numerical utilization screens, diagnostic screens, diagnosis or specific treatment norms is not appropriate.

APPENDIX 4-4 IMPORTANT SELECTIONS FROM THE MEDICARE BENEFIT POLICY MANUAL

CHAPTER 7 § 30—Conditions for Coverage

CMS PUB. 100-02*

(Compiled by the Center for Medicare Advocacy)

30. Conditions Patient Must Meet to Qualify for Coverage of Home Health Services (Rev. 1, 10-01-03)
A3-3117, HHA-204, A-98-49

To qualify for the Medicare home health benefit, under §§ 1814(a)(2)(C) and 1835(a)(2)(A) of the Act, a Medicare beneficiary must meet the following requirements:

- Be confined to the home;
- Under the care of a physician;
- Receiving services under a plan of care established and periodically reviewed by a physician;
- Be in need of skilled nursing care on an intermittent basis or physical therapy or speech-language pathology; or
- Have a continuing need for occupational therapy.

For purposes of benefit eligibility, under §§ 1814(a)(2)(C) and 1835(a)(2)(A) of the Act, "intermittent" means skilled nursing care that is either provided or needed on fewer than 7 days each week or less than 8 hours of each day for periods of 21 days or less (with extensions in exceptional circumstances when the need for additional care is finite and predictable).

A patient must meet each of the criteria specified in this section. Patients who meet each of these criteria are eligible to have payment made on their behalf for services discussed in §§ 40 and 50.

30.1. Confined to the Home
(Rev. 1, 10-01-03)
A3-3117.1, HHA-204.1
30.1.1 - Patient Confined to the Home
(Rev. 233, Issued: 02-24-17, Effective: 01-01-17, Implementation: 03-27-17)

For a patient to be eligible to receive covered home health services under both Part A and Part B, the law requires that a physician certify in all cases that the

* *See* MBP Manual, Ch. 7.

patient is confined to his/her home. For purposes of the statute, an individual shall be considered "confined to the home" (homebound) if the following two criteria are met:

1. *Criterion One*:

The patient must either:

> Because of illness or injury, need the aid of supportive devices such as crutches, canes, wheelchairs, and walkers; the use of special transportation; or the assistance of another person in order to leave their place of residence
>
> OR
>
> Have a condition such that leaving his or her home is medically contraindicated.

If the patient meets one of the *criterion one* conditions, then the patient must ALSO meet two additional requirements defined in *criterion two* below.

2. *Criterion Two*:

> There must exist a normal inability to leave home;
>
> AND
>
> Leaving home must require a considerable and taxing effort.

To clarify, in determining whether the patient meets criterion two of the homebound definition, the clinician needs to take into account the illness or injury for which the patient met criterion one and consider the illness or injury in the context of the patient's overall condition. The clinician is not required to include standardized phrases reflecting the patient's condition (e.g., repeating the words "taxing effort to leave the home") in the patient's chart, nor are such phrases sufficient, by themselves, to demonstrate that criterion two has been met. For example, longitudinal clinical information about the patient's health status is typically needed to sufficiently demonstrate a normal inability to leave the home and that leaving home requires a considerable and taxing effort. Such clinical information about the patient's overall health status may include, but is not limited to, such factors as the patient's diagnosis, duration of the patient's condition, clinical course (worsening or improvement), prognosis, nature and extent of functional limitations, other therapeutic interventions and results, etc.

If the patient does in fact leave the home, the patient may nevertheless be considered homebound if the absences from the home are infrequent or for periods of relatively short duration, or are attributable to the need to receive health care treatment. Absences attributable to the need to receive health care treatment include, but are not limited to:

- Attendance at adult day centers to receive medical care;
- Ongoing receipt of outpatient kidney dialysis; or
- The receipt of outpatient chemotherapy or radiation therapy.

Any absence of an individual from the home attributable to the need to receive health care treatment, including regular absences for the purpose of participating in therapeutic, psychosocial, or medical treatment in an adult day-care program that is licensed or certified by a state, or accredited to furnish adult day-care services in a state, shall not disqualify an individual from being considered to be confined to his home. Any other absence of an individual from the home shall not so disqualify an individual if the absence is of an infrequent or of relatively short duration. For purposes of the preceding sentence, any absence for the purpose of attending a religious service shall be deemed to be an absence of infrequent or short duration. It is expected that in most instances, absences from the home that occur will be for the purpose of receiving health care treatment. However, occasional absences from the home for nonmedical purposes, e.g., an occasional trip to the barber, a walk around the block or a drive, attendance at a family reunion, funeral, graduation, or other infrequent or unique event would not necessitate a finding that the patient is not homebound if the absences are undertaken on an infrequent basis or are of relatively short duration and do not indicate that the patient has the capacity to obtain the health care provided outside rather than in the home.

Some examples of homebound patients that illustrate the factors used to determine whether a homebound condition exists are listed below.

- A patient paralyzed from a stroke who is confined to a wheelchair or requires the aid of crutches in order to walk.
- A patient who is blind or senile and requires the assistance of another person in leaving their place of residence.
- A patient who has lost the use of their upper extremities and, therefore, is unable to open doors, use handrails on stairways, etc., and requires the assistance of another individual to leave their place of residence.
- A patient in the late stages of ALS or neurodegenerative disabilities. In determining whether the patient has the general inability to leave the home and leaves the home only infrequently or for periods of short duration, it is necessary (as is the case in determining whether skilled nursing services are intermittent) to look at the patient's condition over a period of time rather than for short periods within the home health stay. For example, a patient may leave the home (meeting both criteria listed above) more frequently during a short period when the patient has multiple appointments with health care professionals and medical tests in 1 week. So long as the patient's overall condition and experience is such

that he or she meets these qualifications, he or she should be considered confined to the home.

- A patient who has just returned from a hospital stay involving surgery, who may be suffering from resultant weakness and pain because of the surgery and; therefore, their actions may be restricted by their physician to certain specified and limited activities (such as getting out of bed only for a specified period of time, walking stairs only once a day, etc.).
- A patient with arteriosclerotic heart disease of such severity that they must avoid all stress and physical activity.
- A patient with a psychiatric illness that is manifested in part by a refusal to leave home or is of such a nature that it would not be considered safe for the patient to leave home unattended, even if they have no physical limitations.

The aged person who does not often travel from home because of feebleness and insecurity brought on by advanced age would not be considered confined to the home for purposes of receiving home health services unless they meet one of the above conditions.

Although a patient must be confined to the home to be eligible for covered home health services, some services cannot be provided at the patient's residence because equipment is required that cannot be made available there. If the services required by an individual involve the use of such equipment, the HHA may make arrangements with a hospital, SNF, or a rehabilitation center to provide these services on an outpatient basis. (See § 50.6.) However, even in these situations, for the services to be covered as home health services the patient must be considered confined to home and meet both criteria listed above.

If a question is raised as to whether a patient is confined to the home, the HHA will be requested to furnish the Medicare contractor with the information necessary to establish that the patient is homebound as defined above.

30.1.2. Patient's Place of Residence (Rev. 208, Issued: 04-22-15, Effective: 01-01-15, Implementation: 05-11-15)

A patient's residence is wherever he or she makes his or her home. This may be his or her own dwelling, an apartment, a relative's home, a home for the aged, or some other type of institution. However, an institution may not be considered a patient's residence if the institution meets the requirements of §§ 1861(e)(1) or 1819(a)(1) of the Act. Included in this group are hospitals and skilled nursing facilities, as well as most nursing facilities under Medicaid. (See the Medicare State Operations Manual, § 2166.)

Thus, if a patient is in an institution or distinct part of an institution identified above, the patient is not entitled to have payment made for home health services under either Part A or Part B since such an institution may not be considered their residence. When a patient remains in a participating SNF following their discharge from active care, the facility may not be considered their residence for purposes of home health coverage.

A patient may have more than one home and the Medicare rules do not prohibit a patient from having one or more places of residence. A patient, under a Medicare home health plan of care, who resides in more than one place of residence during an episode of Medicare covered home health services will not disqualify the patient's homebound status for purposes of eligibility. For example, a person may reside in a principal home and also a second vacation home, mobile home, or the home of a caretaker relative. The fact that the patient resides in more than one home and, as a result, must transit from one to the other, is not in itself, an indication that the patient is not homebound. The requirements of homebound must be met at each location (i.e., the patient must meet both criteria listed in section 30.1.1 above).

A. Assisted Living Facilities, Group Homes, and Personal Care Homes

An individual may be "confined to the home" for purposes of Medicare coverage of home health services if he or she resides in an institution that is not primarily engaged in providing to inpatients:

- Diagnostic and therapeutic services for medical diagnosis;
- Treatment;
- Care of injured, disabled or sick persons;
- Rehabilitation services or other skilled services needed to maintain a patient's current condition or to prevent or slow further deterioration; or
- Skilled nursing care or related services for patients who require medical or nursing care.

If it is determined that the assisted living facility (also called personal care homes, group homes, etc.) in which the individuals reside are not primarily engaged in providing the above services, then Medicare will cover reasonable and necessary home health care furnished to these individuals.

If it is determined that the services furnished by the home health agency are duplicative of services furnished by an assisted living facility when provision of such care is required of the facility under State licensure requirements, claims for such services should be denied under § 1862(a)(1)(A) of the Act. Section 1862(a)(1)(A) excludes services that are not necessary for the diagnosis or treatment of illness or injury or to improve the functioning of a malformed body member from Medicare coverage. Services to people who already have access to appropriate care from a willing caregiver would not be considered reasonable and necessary to the treatment of the individual's illness or injury.

Medicare coverage would not be an optional substitute for the services that a facility is required to provide by law to its patients or where the services are included in the base contract of the facility. An individual's choice to reside in such a facility is also a choice to accept the services it holds itself out as offering to its patients.

B. Day Care Centers and Patient's Place of Residence

The current statutory definition of homebound or confined does not imply that Medicare coverage has been expanded to include adult day care services. The law does not permit an HHA to furnish a Medicare covered billable visit to a patient under a home health plan of care outside his or her home, except in those limited circumstances where the patient needs to use medical equipment that is too cumbersome to bring to the home. Section 1861(m) of the Act stipulates that home health services provided to a patient be provided to the patient on a visiting basis in a place of residence used as the individual's home. A licensed/certified day care center does not meet the definition of a place of residence.

C. State Licensure/Certification of Day Care Facilities

Per Section 1861(m) of the Act, an adult day care center must be either licensed or certified by the State or accredited by a private accrediting body. State licensure or certification as an adult day care facility must be based on State interpretations of its process. For example, several States do not license adult day care facilities as a whole, but do certify some entities as Medicaid certified centers for purposes of providing adult day care under the Medicaid home and community based waiver program. It is the responsibility of the State to determine the necessary criteria for "State certification" in such a situation. A State could determine that Medicaid certification is an acceptable standard and consider its Medicaid certified adult day care facilities to be 'State certified." On the other hand, a State could determine Medicaid certification to be insufficient and require other conditions to be met before the adult day care facility is considered "State certified".

D. Determination of the Therapeutic, Medical or Psychosocial Treatment of the Patient at the Day Care Facility

It is not the obligation of the HHA to determine whether the adult day care facility is providing psychosocial treatment, but only to assure that the adult day care center is licensed/certified by the State or accrediting body. The intent of the law, in extending the homebound exception status to attendance at such adult day care facilities, recognizes that they ordinarily furnish psychosocial services.

30.2. Services Are Provided Under a Plan of Care Established and Approved by a Physician
(Rev. 1, 10-01-03)
A3-3117.2, HHA-204.2

30.2.1. Content of the Plan of Care
(Rev. 208, Issued: 04-22-15, Effective: 01-01-15, Implementation: 05-11-15)

The HHA must be acting upon a physician plan of care that meets the requirements of this section for HHA services to be covered.

The plan of care must contain all pertinent diagnoses, including:

- The patient's mental status;
- The types of services, supplies, and equipment required;
- The frequency of the visits to be made;
- Prognosis;
- Rehabilitation potential;
- Functional limitations;
- Activities permitted;
- Nutritional requirements;
- All medications and treatments;
- Safety measures to protect against injury;
- Instructions for timely discharge or referral; and
- Any additional items the HHA or physician chooses to include.

If the plan of care includes a course of treatment for therapy services:

- The course of therapy treatment must be established by the physician after any needed consultation with the qualified therapist;
- The plan must include measurable therapy treatment goals which pertain directly to the patient's illness or injury, and the patient's resultant impairments;
- The plan must include the expected duration of therapy services; and
- The plan must describe a course of treatment which is consistent with the qualified therapist's assessment of the patient's function.

30.2.2. Specificity of Orders
(Rev. 1, 10-01-03)
A3-3117.2.B, HHA-204.2.B

The orders on the plan of care must indicate the type of services to be provided to the patient, both with respect to the professional who will provide them and the nature of the individual services, as well as the frequency of the services.

■ **EXAMPLE 1:** SN x 7/wk x 1 wk; 3/wk x 4 wk; 2/wk x 3 wk, (skilled nursing visits 7 times per week for 1 week; 3 times per week for 4 weeks; and 2 times per week for 3 weeks) for skilled observation and evaluation of the surgical site, for teaching sterile dressing changes and to perform sterile dressing changes. The sterile change consists of (detail of procedure).

Orders for care may indicate a specific range in the frequency of visits to ensure that the most appropriate level of services is provided during the 60-day episode to home health patients. When a range of visits is ordered, the upper limit of the range is considered the specific frequency.

> ■ **EXAMPLE 2:** SN x 2-4/wk x 4 wk; 1-2/wk x 4 wk for skilled observation and evaluation of the surgical site.
>
> Orders for services to be furnished "as needed" or "PRN" must be accompanied by a description of the patient's medical signs and symptoms that would occasion a visit and a specific limit on the number of those visits to be made under the order before an additional physician order would have to be obtained.

30.2.3. Who Signs the Plan of Care (Rev. 1, 10-01-03) A3-3117.2.C, HHA-204-2.C

The physician who signs the plan of care must be qualified to sign the physician certification as described in 42 CFR 424.22.

30.2.4. Timeliness of Signature (Rev. 1, 10-01-03) A3-3117.2.D, HHA-204-2.D

A. Initial Percentage Payment

If a physician signed plan of care is not available at the beginning of the episode, the HHA may submit a RAP for the initial percentage payment based on physician verbal orders OR a referral prescribing detailed orders for the services to be rendered that is signed and dated by the physician. If the RAP submission is based on physician verbal orders, the verbal order must be recorded in the plan of care, include a description of the patient's condition and the services to be provided by the home health agency, include an attestation (relating to the physician's orders and the date received per 42 CFR 409.43), and the plan of care is copied and immediately submitted to the physician. A billable visit must be rendered prior to the submission of a RAP.

B. Final Percentage Payment

The plan of care must be signed and dated by a physician as described who meets the certification and recertification requirements of 42 CFR 424.22 and before the claim for each episode for services is submitted for the final percentage payment. Any changes in the plan of care must be signed and dated by a physician.

30.2.5. Use of Oral (Verbal) Orders
(Rev. 208, Issued: 04-22-15, Effective: 01-01-15, Implementation: 05-11-15)

When services are furnished based on a physician's oral order, the orders may be accepted and put in writing by personnel authorized to do so by applicable State and Federal laws and regulations as well as by the HHA's internal policies. The orders must be signed and dated with the date of receipt by the registered nurse or qualified therapist (i.e., physical therapist, speech-language pathologist, occupational therapist, or medical social worker) responsible for furnishing or supervising the ordered services. The orders may be signed by the supervising registered nurse or qualified therapist after the services have been rendered, as long as HHA personnel who receive the oral orders notify that nurse or therapist before the service is rendered. Thus, the rendering of a service that is based on an oral order would not be delayed pending signature of the supervising nurse or therapist. Oral orders must be countersigned and dated by the physician before the HHA bills for the care in the same way as the plan of care.

Services which are provided from the beginning of the 60-day episode certification period based on a request for anticipated payment and before the physician signs the plan of care are considered to be provided under a plan of care established and approved by the physician where there is an oral order for the care prior to rendering the services which is documented in the medical record and where the services are included in a signed plan of care.

Services that are provided in the subsequent 60-day episode certification period are considered provided under the plan of care of the subsequent 60-day episode where there is an oral order before the services provided in the subsequent period are furnished and the order is reflected in the medical record. However, services that are provided after the expiration of the plan of care, but before the acquisition of an oral order or a signed plan of care are not considered provided under a plan of care.

■ **EXAMPLE 1:** The HHA acquires an oral order for I.V. medication administration for a patient to be performed on August 1. The HHA provides the I.V. medication administration August 1 and evaluates the patient's need for continued care. The physician signs the plan of care for the I.V. medication administration on August 15. The visit is covered since it is considered provided under a plan of care established and approved by the physician, and the HHA had acquired an oral order prior to the delivery of services.

■ **EXAMPLE 2:** The patient is under a plan of care in which the physician orders I.V. medication administration every 2 weeks. The last day covered by the initial plan of care is July 31. The patient's next I.V. medication administration is scheduled for August 5 and the physician signs the plan of care for the new period on August 1. The I.V. medication administration on August 5 was provided under a plan of care established and approved by the physician. The episode begins on the 61 day regardless of the date of the first covered visit.

■ **EXAMPLE 3:** The patient is under a plan of care in which the physician orders I.V. medication administration every 2 weeks. The last day covered by the plan of care is July 31. The patient's next I.V. medication administration is scheduled for August 5 and the physician does not sign the plan of care until August 6. The HHA acquires an oral order for the I.V. medication administration before the August 5 visit, and therefore the visit is considered to be provided under a plan of care established and approved by the physician. The episode begins on the 61 day regardless of the date of the first covered visit.

Any increase in the frequency of services or addition of new services during a certification period must be authorized by a physician by way of a written or oral order prior to the provision of the increased or additional services.

30.2.6. Frequency of Review of the Plan of Care
(Rev. 1, 10-01-03)
A3-3117.2.F, HHA-204.2.F

The plan of care must be reviewed and signed by the physician who established the plan of care, in consultation with HHA professional personnel, at least every 60 days. Each review of a patient's plan of care must contain the signature of the physician and the date of review.

30.2.7. Facsimile Signatures
(Rev. 1, 10-01-03)
A3-3117.2.G, HHA-204.2.G

The plan of care or oral order may be transmitted by facsimile machine. The HHA is not required to have the original signature on file. However, the HHA is responsible for obtaining original signatures if an issue surfaces that would require verification of an original signature.

30.2.8. Alternative Signatures
(Rev. 1, 10-01-03)
A3-3117.2.H, HHA-204.2.H

HHAs that maintain patient records by computer rather than hard copy may use electronic signatures. However, all such entries must be appropriately authenticated and dated. Authentication must include signatures, written initials, or computer secure entry by a unique identifier of a primary author who has reviewed and approved the entry. The HHA must have safeguards to prevent unauthorized access to the records and a process for reconstruction of the records in the event of a system breakdown.

30.2.9. Termination of the Plan of Care - Qualifying Services (Rev. 1, 10-01-03) A3-3117.2.I, HHA-204.2.I

The plan of care is considered to be terminated if the patient does not receive at least one covered skilled nursing, physical therapy, speech-language pathology service, or occupational therapy visit in a 60-day period since these are qualifying services for the home health benefit. An exception is if the physician documents that the interval without such care is appropriate to the treatment of the patient's illness or injury.

30.2.10. Sequence of Qualifying Services and Other Medicare Covered Home Health Services (Rev. 233, Issued: 02-24-17, Effective: 01-01-17, Implementation: 03-27-17)

Once patient eligibility has been confirmed and the plan of care contains physician orders for the qualifying service as well as other Medicare covered home health services, the qualifying service does not have to be rendered prior to the other Medicare covered home health services ordered in the plan of care. The sequence of visits performed by the disciplines must be dictated by the individual patient's plan of care. For example, for an eligible patient in an initial 60-day episode that has both physical therapy and occupational therapy orders in the plan of care, the sequence of the delivery of the type of therapy is irrelevant as long as the need for the qualifying service is established prior to the delivery of other Medicare covered services and the qualifying discipline provides a billable visit prior to transfer or discharge in accordance with 42 CFR 409.43(f).

■ **NOTE:** Dependent services provided after the final qualifying skilled service are not covered under the home health benefit, except when the dependent service was *not* followed by a qualifying skilled service *due to* unexpected inpatient admission, death of the patient, or some other unanticipated event.

APPENDIX 4-5 IMPORTANT SELECTIONS FROM THE MEDICARE BENEFIT POLICY MANUAL

CHAPTER 7 § 40—Home Health Services

CMS PUB. 100-02*

(Compiled by the Center for Medicare Advocacy)

40. Covered Services under a Qualifying Home Health Plan of Care (Rev. 1, 10-01-03) A3-3118, HHA-205

Section 1861(m) of the Act governs the Medicare home health services that may be provided to eligible beneficiaries by or under arrangements made by a participating home health agency (HHA). Section 1861(m) describes home health services as

- Part-time or intermittent skilled nursing care (other than solely venipuncture for the purposes of obtaining a blood sample);
- Part-time or intermittent home health aide services;
- Physical therapy;
- Speech-language pathology;
- Occupational therapy;
- Medical social services;
- Medical supplies (including catheters, catheter supplies, ostomy bags, supplies related to ostomy care, and a covered osteoporosis drug (as defined in § 1861(kk) of the Act), but excluding other drugs and biologicals);
- Durable medical equipment while under the plan of care established by physician;
- Medical services provided by an intern or resident-in-training under an approved teaching program of the hospital in the case of an HHA which is affiliated or under common control with a hospital; and
- Services at hospitals, skilled nursing facilities, or rehabilitation centers when they involve equipment too cumbersome to bring to the home.

The term "part-time or intermittent" for purposes of coverage under § 1861(m) of the Act means skilled nursing and home health aide services furnished any number of days per week as long as they are furnished (combined)

* *See* MBP Manual, Ch. 7.

less than 8 hours each day and 28 or fewer hours each week (or, subject to review on a case-by-case basis as to the need for care, less than 8 hours each day and 35 or fewer hours per week). See § 50.7

For any home health services to be covered by Medicare, the patient must meet the qualifying criteria as specified in § 30, including having a need for skilled nursing care on an intermittent basis, physical therapy, speech-language pathology services, or a continuing need for occupational therapy as defined in this section.

40.1. Skilled Nursing Care
(Rev. 179, Issued: 01-14-14, Effective: 01-07-14, Implementation: 01-07-14)
A3-3118.1, HHA-205.1

To be covered as skilled nursing services, the services must require the skills of a registered nurse, or a licensed practical (vocational) nurse under the supervision of a registered nurse, must be reasonable and necessary to the treatment of the patient's illness or injury as discussed in § 40.1.1, below, and must be intermittent as discussed in § 40.1.3. Coverage of skilled nursing care does not turn on the presence or absence of a patient's potential for improvement from the nursing care, but rather on the patient's need for skilled care.

40.1.1. General Principles Governing Reasonable and Necessary Skilled Nursing Care
(Rev. 179, Issued: 01-14-14, Effective: 01-07-14, Implementation: 01-07-14)
A3-3118.1, HHA-205.1

If all other eligibility and coverage requirements under the home health benefit are met, skilled nursing services are covered when an individualized assessment of the patient's clinical condition demonstrates that the specialized judgment, knowledge, and skills of a registered nurse or, when provided by regulation, a licensed practical (vocational) nurse ("skilled care") are necessary. Skilled nursing services are covered where such skilled nursing services are necessary to maintain the patient's current condition or prevent or slow further deterioration so long as the beneficiary requires skilled care for the services to be safely and effectively provided. When, however, the individualized assessment does not demonstrate such a necessity for skilled care, including when the services needed do not require skilled nursing care because they could safely and effectively be performed by the patient or unskilled caregivers, such services will not be covered under the home health benefit.

Skilled nursing care is necessary only when (a) the particular patient's special medical complications require the skills of a registered nurse or, when provided by regulation, a licensed practical nurse to perform a type of service that would otherwise be considered non-skilled; or (b) the needed services are of such complexity that the skills of a registered nurse or, when provided by regulation, a licensed practical nurse are required to furnish the services. To be considered a skilled service, the service must be so inherently complex that it can be safely and effectively performed only by, or under the supervision of, professional or technical personnel as provided by regulation, including42 C.F.R. 409.32.

Some services may be classified as a skilled nursing service on the basis of complexity alone (e.g., intravenous and intramuscular injections or insertion of catheters) and if reasonable and necessary to the treatment of the patient's illness or injury, would be covered on that basis. If a service can be safely and effectively performed (or self-administered) by an unskilled person, without the direct supervision of a nurse, the service cannot be regarded as a skilled nursing service although a nurse actually provides the service. However, in some cases, the condition of the patient may cause a service that would ordinarily be considered unskilled to be considered a skilled nursing service. This would occur when the patient's condition is such that the service can be safely and effectively provided only by a nurse. A service is not considered a skilled nursing service merely because it is performed by or under the supervision of a nurse. The unavailability of a competent person to provide a non-skilled service, regardless of the importance of the service to the patient, does not make it a skilled service when a nurse provides the service.

A service that, by its nature, requires the skills of a nurse to be provided safely and effectively continues to be a skilled service even if it is taught to the patient, the patient's family, or other caregivers.

The skilled nursing service must be reasonable and necessary to the diagnosis and treatment of the patient's illness or injury within the context of the patient's unique medical condition. To be considered reasonable and necessary for the diagnosis or treatment of the patient's illness or injury, the services must be consistent with the nature and severity of the illness or injury, the patient's particular medical needs, and accepted standards of medical and nursing practice. The determination of whether the services are reasonable and necessary should be made in consideration that a physician has determined that the services ordered are reasonable and necessary. The services must, therefore, be viewed from the perspective of the condition of the patient when the services were ordered and what was, at that time, reasonably expected to be appropriate treatment for the illness or injury throughout the certification period.

A patient's overall medical condition, without regard to whether the illness or injury is acute, chronic, terminal, or expected to extend over a long period of time, should be considered in deciding whether skilled services are needed. A patient's diagnosis should never be the sole factor in deciding that a service the patient needs is either skilled or not skilled. Skilled care may, depending on the unique condition of the patient, continue to be necessary for patients whose condition is stable.

As is outlined in home health regulations, as part of the home health agency (HHA) Conditions of Participation (CoPs), the clinical record of the patient must contain progress and clinical notes. Additionally, in Pub. 100-04, Medicare

Claims Processing Manual, Chapter 10; "Home Health Agency Billing", instructions specify that for each claim, HHAs are required to report all services provided to the beneficiary during each episode, which includes reporting each visit in line-item detail. As such, it is expected that the home health records for every visit will reflect the need for the skilled medical care provided. These clinical notes are also expected to provide important communication among all members of the home care team regarding the development, course and outcomes of the skilled observations, assessments, treatment and training performed. Taken as a whole then, the clinical notes are expected to tell the story of the patient's achievement towards his/her goals as outlined in the Plan of Care. In this way, the notes will serve to demonstrate why a skilled service is needed.

Therefore the home health clinical notes must document as appropriate:

- the history and physical exam pertinent to the day's visit, (including the response or changes in behavior to previously administered skilled services) and the skilled services applied on the current visit, and
- the patient/caregiver's response to the skilled services provided, and
- the plan for the next visit based on the rationale of prior results,
- a detailed rationale that explains the need for the skilled service in light of the patient's overall medical condition and experiences,
- the complexity of the service to be performed, and any other pertinent characteristics of the beneficiary or home

Clinical notes should be written so that they adequately describe the reaction of a patient to his/her skilled care. Clinical notes should also provide a clear picture of the treatment, as well as "next steps" to be taken. Vague or subjective descriptions of the patient's care should not be used. For example terminology such as the following would not adequately describe the need for skilled care:

- Patient tolerated treatment well
- Caregiver instructed in medication management
- Continue with POC

Objective measurements of physical outcomes of treatment should be provided and/or a clear description of the changed behaviors due to education programs should be recorded in order that all concerned can follow the results of the applied services.

■ **EXAMPLE 1:** The presence of a plaster cast on an extremity generally does not indicate a need for skilled nursing care. However, the patient with a preexisting peripheral vascular or circulatory condition might need skilled nursing care to observe for complications, monitor medication administration for pain control, and teach proper skin care to preserve skin integrity and prevent breakdown. The documentation must support the severity of the circulatory condition that requires skilled care. The clinical notes for each home health visit should document the patient's skin and circulatory examination as well as the patient and/or care giver application of the educational principles taught since the last visit. The plan for the next visit should describe the skilled services continuing to be required.

■ **EXAMPLE 2:** The condition of a patient, who has irritable bowel syndrome or is recovering from rectal surgery, may be such that he or she can be given an enema safely and effectively only by a nurse. If the enema were necessary to treat the illness or injury, then the visit would be covered as a skilled nursing visit. The documentation must support the skilled need for the enema, and the plan for future visits based on this information.

■ **EXAMPLE 3:** Giving a bath does not ordinarily require the skills of a nurse and, therefore, would not be covered as a skilled nursing service unless the patient's condition is such that the bath could be given safely and effectively only by a nurse (as discussed in § 30.1 above).

■ **EXAMPLE 4:** A patient with a well-established colostomy absent complications may require assistance changing the colostomy bag because they cannot do it themselves and there is no one else to change the bag. Notwithstanding the need for the routine colostomy care, changing the colostomy bag does not become a skilled nursing service when the nurse provides it.

■ **EXAMPLE 5:** A patient was discharged from the hospital with an open draining wound that requires irrigation, packing, and dressing twice each day. The HHA has taught the family to perform the dressing changes. The HHA continues to see the patient for the wound care that is needed during the time that the family is not available and willing to provide the dressing changes. The wound care continues to be skilled nursing care, notwithstanding that the family provides it part of the time, and may be covered as long as the patient requires it.

■ **EXAMPLE 6:** A physician has ordered skilled nursing visits for a patient with a hairline fracture of the hip. The home health record must document the reason skilled services are required and why the nursing visits are reasonable and necessary for treatment of the patient's hip injury.

■ **EXAMPLE 7:** A physician has ordered skilled nursing visits for teaching of self-administration and self-management of the medication regimen for a patient, newly diagnosed, with diabetes mellitus in the home health plan of care. Each visit's documentation must describe the patient's progress in this activity.

■ **EXAMPLE 8:** Following a cerebrovascular accident (CVA), a patient has an in-dwelling Foley catheter because of urinary incontinence, and is expected to require the catheter for a long and indefinite period. The medical condition of the patient must be described and documented to support the need for nursing skilled services in the home health plan of care. Periodic visits to change the catheter as needed, treat the symptoms of catheter malfunction, and teach proper catheter care would be covered as long as they are reasonable and necessary, although the patient is stable, even if there is an expectation that the care will be needed for a long and indefinite period. However, at every home health visit, the patient's current medical condition must be described and there must be documentation to support the need for continued skilled nursing services.

■ **EXAMPLE 9:** A patient with advanced multiple sclerosis undergoing an exacerbation of the illness needs skilled teaching of medications, measures to overcome urinary retention, and the establishment of a program designed to minimize the adverse impact of the exacerbation. The clinical notes for each home health visit must describe why skilled nursing services were required. The skilled nursing care received by the patient would be covered despite the chronic nature of the illness.

■ **EXAMPLE 10:** A patient with malignant melanoma is terminally ill, and requires skilled observation, assessment, teaching, and treatment. The patient has not elected coverage under Medicare's hospice benefit. The documentation should describe the goal of the skilled nursing intervention, and at each visit the services provided should support that goal. The skilled nursing care that the patient requires would be covered, notwithstanding that the condition is terminal, because the documentation and description must support that the needed services required the skills of a nurse.

* * *

40.1.2. Application of the Principles to Skilled Nursing Services (Rev. 1, 10-01-03) A3-3118.1.B, HHA-205.1.B

The following discussion of skilled nursing services applies the foregoing principles to specific skilled nursing services about which questions are most frequently raised.

40.1.2.1 Observation and Assessment of the Patient's Condition When Only the Specialized Skills of a Medical Professional Can Determine Patient's Status
(Rev. 179, Issued: 01-14-14, Effective: 01-07-14, Implementation: 01-07-14)

Observation and assessment of the patient's condition by a nurse are reasonable and necessary skilled services where there is a reasonable potential for change in a patient's condition that requires skilled nursing personnel to identify and evaluate the patient's need for possible modification of treatment or initiation of additional medical procedures until the patient's clinical condition and/or treatment regimen has stabilized. Where a patient was admitted to home health care for skilled observation because there was a reasonable potential of a complication or further acute episode, but did not develop a further acute episode or complication, the skilled observation services are still covered for 3 weeks or so long as there remains a reasonable potential for such a complication or further acute episode.

Information from the patient's home health record must document the rationale that demonstrates that there is a reasonable potential for a future complication or acute episode and, therefore, may justify the need for continued skilled observation and assessment beyond the 3-week period. Such signs and symptoms as abnormal/fluctuating vital signs, weight changes, edema, symptoms of drug toxicity, abnormal/fluctuating laboratory values, and respiratory changes on auscultation may justify skilled observation and assessment. Where these signs and symptoms are such that there is a reasonable potential that skilled observation and assessment by a nurse will result in changes to the treatment of the patient, then the services would be covered. However, observation and assessment by a nurse is not reasonable and necessary for the treatment of the illness or injury where fluctuating signs and symptoms are part of a longstanding pattern of the patient's condition which has not previously required a change in the prescribed treatment.

■ **EXAMPLE 1:** A patient with atherosclerotic heart disease with congestive heart failure requires close observation by skilled nursing personnel for signs of decompensation or adverse effects resulting from prescribed medication. Skilled observation is needed to determine whether the drug regimen should be modified or whether other therapeutic measures should be considered until the patient's treatment regimen is essentially stabilized. The clinical notes for each home health visit should reflect the deliberations and their outcome.

■ **EXAMPLE 2:** A patient has undergone peripheral vascular disease treatment including a revascularization procedure (bypass). The incision area is showing signs of potential infection (e.g., heat, redness, swelling, drainage) and the patient has elevated body temperature. For each home health visit the clinical notes must demonstrate that the skilled observation and monitoring is required.

■ **EXAMPLE 3:** A patient was hospitalized following a heart attack. Following treatment he was discharged home. Because it is not known whether increasing exertion will exacerbate the heart disease, skilled observation is reasonable and necessary as mobilization is initiated in the patient's home. The patient's necessity for skilled observation must be documented at each home health visit until the patient's clinical condition and/or treatment regimen has stabilized.

■ **EXAMPLE 4:** A frail 85-year-old man was hospitalized for pneumonia. The infection was resolved, but the patient, who had previously maintained adequate nutrition, will not eat or eats poorly. The patient is discharged to the HHA for monitoring of fluid and nutrient intake, and assessment of the need for tube feeding. Observation and monitoring by licensed nurses of the patient's oral intake, output and hydration status is required to determine what further treatment or other intervention is needed. The patient's necessity for skilled observation and treatment must be documented at each home health visit, until the patient's clinical condition and/or treatment regimen has stabilized.

■ **EXAMPLE 5:** A patient with glaucoma and a cardiac condition has a cataract extraction. Because of the interaction between the eye drops for the glaucoma and cataracts and the beta blocker for the cardiac condition, the patient is at risk for serious cardiac arrhythmias. Skilled observation and monitoring of the drug actions is reasonable and necessary until the patient's condition is stabilized. The patient's necessity for skilled observation and treatment must be documented at each home health visit, until the patient's clinical condition and/or treatment regimen has stabilized.

■ **EXAMPLE 6:** A patient with hypertension suffered dizziness and weakness. The physician found that the blood pressure was too low and discontinued the hypertension medication. Skilled observation and monitoring of the patient's blood pressure and medication regimen is required until the blood pressure remains stable and in a safe range. The patient's necessity for skilled observation and treatment must be documented at each home health visit, until the patient's clinical condition and/or treatment regimen has stabilized.

■ **EXAMPLE 7:** A patient has chronic non-healing skin ulcers, Diabetes Mellitus Type I, and spinal muscular atrophy. In the past, the patient's wounds have deteriorated, requiring the patient to be hospitalized. Previously, a skilled nurse has trained the patient's wife to perform would care. The treating physician orders a new episode of skilled care, at a frequency of one visit every 2 weeks to perform observation and assessment of the patient's skin ulcers to make certain that they are not worsening. This order is reasonable and necessary because, although the unskilled family caregiver has learned to care for the wounds, the skilled nurse can use observation and assessment to determine if the condition is worsening.

40.1.2.2. Management and Evaluation of a Patient Care Plan
(Rev. 179, Issued: 01-14-14, Effective: 01-07-14, Implementation: 01-07-14)
A3-3118.1.B.2, HHA-205.1.B.2

Skilled nursing visits for management and evaluation of the patient's care plan are also reasonable and necessary where underlying conditions or complications require that only a registered nurse can ensure that essential unskilled care is achieving its purpose. For skilled nursing care to be reasonable and necessary for management and evaluation of the patient's plan of care, the complexity of the necessary unskilled services that are a necessary part of the medical treatment must require the involvement of licensed nurses to promote the patient's recovery and medical safety in view of the patient's overall condition.

* * *

40.2. Skilled Therapy Services
(Rev. 179, Issued: 01-14-14, Effective: 01-07-14, Implementation: 01-07-14)
A3-3118.2, HHA-205.2

To be covered as skilled therapy, the services must require the skills of a qualified therapist and must be reasonable and necessary for the treatment of the patient's illness or injury as discussed below. Coverage does not turn on the presence or absence of an individual's potential for improvement, but rather on the beneficiary's need for skilled care.

40.2.1. General Principles Governing Reasonable and Necessary Physical Therapy, Speech-Language Pathology Services, and Occupational Therapy
(Rev. 208, Issued: 04-22-15, Effective: 01-01-15, Implementation: 05-11-15)

The service of a physical therapist, speech-language pathologist, or occupational therapist is a skilled therapy service if the inherent complexity of the service is such that it can be performed safely and/or effectively only by or under the general supervision of a skilled therapist. To be covered, assuming all other eligibility and coverage criteria have been met, the skilled services must also be reasonable and necessary to the treatment of the patient's illness or injury or to the restoration or maintenance of function affected by the patient's illness or injury. It is necessary to determine whether individual therapy services are skilled and whether, in view of the patient's overall condition, skilled management of the services provided is needed.

The development, implementation, management, and evaluation of a patient care plan based on the physician's orders constitute skilled therapy services when, because of the patient's clinical condition, those activities require the specialized skills, knowledge, and judgment of a qualified therapist to ensure the effectiveness of the treatment goals and ensure medical safety. Where the specialized skills, knowledge, and judgment of a therapist are needed to manage and periodically reevaluate the appropriateness of a maintenance program, such services would be covered, even if the skills of a therapist were not needed to carry out the activities performed as part of the maintenance program.

While a patient's particular medical condition is a valid factor in deciding if skilled therapy services are needed, a patient's diagnosis or prognosis should never be the sole factor in deciding that a service is or is not skilled. The key issue is whether the skills of a therapist are needed to treat the illness or injury, or whether the services can be carried out by unskilled personnel.

A service that is ordinarily considered unskilled could be considered a skilled therapy service in cases where there is clear documentation that, because of special medical complications, skilled rehabilitation personnel are required to perform the service. However, the importance of a particular service to a patient or the frequency with which it must be performed does not, by itself, make an unskilled service into a skilled service.

Assuming all other eligibility and coverage criteria have been met, the skilled therapy services must be reasonable and necessary to the treatment of the patient's illness or injury within the context of the patient's unique medical condition. To be considered reasonable and necessary for the treatment of the illness or injury:

a. The services must be consistent with the nature and severity of the illness or injury, the patient's particular medical needs, including the requirement that the amount, frequency, and duration of the services must be reasonable; and

b. The services must be considered, under accepted standards of medical practice, to be specific, safe, and effective treatment for the patient's condition, meeting the standards noted below. The home health record must specify the purpose of the skilled service provided.

   To ensure therapy services are effective, at defined points during a course of treatment, for each therapy discipline for which services are provided, a qualified therapist (instead of an assistant) must perform the ordered therapy service. During this visit, the therapist must assess the patient using a method which allows for objective measurement of function and successive comparison of measurements. The therapist must document the measurement results in the clinical record. Specifically:

   i. **Initial Therapy Assessment**

   - For each therapy discipline for which services are provided, a qualified therapist (instead of an assistant) must assess the patient's function using a method which objectively measures activities of daily living such as, but not limited to, eating, swallowing, bathing, dressing, toileting, walking, climbing stairs, using assistive devices, and mental and cognitive factors. The measurement results must be documented in the clinical record.

- Where more than one discipline of therapy is being provided, a qualified therapist from each of the disciplines must functionally assess the patient. The therapist must document the measurement results which correspond to the therapist's discipline and care plan goals in the clinical record.

ii. **Reassessment at least every 30 days (performed in conjunction with an ordered therapy service)**

- At least once every 30 days, for each therapy discipline for which services are provided, a qualified therapist (instead of an assistant) must provide the ordered therapy service, functionally reassess the patient, and compare the resultant measurement to prior assessment measurements. The therapist must document in the clinical record the measurement results along with the therapist's determination of the effectiveness of therapy, or lack thereof.
- For multi-discipline therapy cases, a qualified therapist from each of the disciplines must functionally reassess the patient. The therapist must document the measurement results which correspond to the therapist's discipline and care plan goals in the clinical record.
- The 30-day clock begins with the first therapy service (of that discipline) and the clock resets with each therapist's visit/assessment/measurement/documentation (of that discipline).

c. Services involving activities for the general welfare of any patient, e.g., general exercises to promote overall fitness or flexibility and activities to provide diversion or general motivation do not constitute skilled therapy. Unskilled individuals without the supervision of a therapist can perform those services.

d. Assuming all other eligibility and coverage requirements have been met, in order for therapy services to be covered, one of the following three conditions must be met:

i. **The skills of a qualified therapist are needed to restore patient function:**

- To meet this coverage condition, therapy services must be provided with the expectation, based on the assessment made by the physician of the patient's restorative potential that the condition of the patient will improve materially in a reasonable and generally predictable period of time. Improvement is evidenced by objective successive measurements.

- Therapy is not considered reasonable and necessary under this condition if the patient's expected restorative potential would be insignificant in relation to the extent and duration of therapy services required to reach such potential.
- Therapy is not required to effect improvement or restoration of function where a patient suffers a transient or easily reversible loss of function (such as temporary weakness following surgery) which could reasonably be expected to improve spontaneously as the patient gradually resumes normal activities. Therapy in such cases is not considered reasonable and necessary to treat the patient's illness or injury, under this condition. However, if the criteria for maintenance therapy described in (3) below is met, therapy could be covered under that condition.

ii. The patient's clinical condition requires the specialized skills, knowledge, and judgment of a qualified therapist to establish or design a maintenance program, related to the patient's illness or injury, in order to ensure the safety of the patient and the effectiveness of the program, to the extent provided by regulation,

- For patients receiving rehabilitative/restorative therapy services, if the specialized skills, knowledge, and judgment of a qualified therapist are required to develop a maintenance program, the expectation is that the development of that maintenance program would occur during the last visit(s) for rehabilitative/restorative treatment. The goals of a maintenance program would be to maintain the patient's current functional status or to prevent or slow further deterioration.
- Necessary periodic reevaluations by a qualified therapist of the beneficiary and maintenance program are covered if the specialized skills, knowledge, and judgment of a qualified therapist are required.
- Where a maintenance program is not established until after the rehabilitative/restorative therapy program has been completed, or where there was no rehabilitative/restorative therapy program, and the specialized skills, knowledge, and judgment of a qualified therapist are required to develop a maintenance program, such services would be considered reasonable and necessary for the treatment of the patient's condition in order to ensure the effectiveness of the treatment goals and ensure medical safety. When the development of a maintenance program could not be accomplished during the last visits(s) of rehabilitative/

restorative treatment, the therapist must document why the maintenance program could not be developed during those last rehabilitative/restorative treatment visit(s).

- When designing or establishing a maintenance program, the qualified therapist must teach the patient or the patient's family or caregiver's necessary techniques, exercises or precautions as necessary to treat the illness or injury. The instruction of the beneficiary or appropriate caregiver by a qualified therapist regarding a maintenance program is covered if the specialized skills, knowledge, and judgment of a qualified therapist are required. However, visits made by skilled therapists to a patient's home solely to train other HHA staff (e.g., home health aides) are not billable as visits since the HHA is responsible for ensuring that its staff is properly trained to perform any service it furnishes. The cost of a skilled therapist's visit for the purpose of training HHA staff is an administrative cost to the agency.

iii. The skills of a qualified therapist (not an assistant) are needed to perform maintenance therapy:

- Coverage of therapy services to perform a maintenance program is not determined solely on the presence or absence of a beneficiary's potential for improvement from the therapy, but rather on the beneficiary's need for skilled care. Assuming all other eligibility and coverage requirements are met, skilled therapy services are covered when an individualized assessment of the patient's clinical condition demonstrates that the specialized judgment, knowledge, and skills of a qualified therapist ("skilled care") are necessary for the performance of a safe and effective maintenance program. Such a maintenance program to maintain the patient's current condition or to prevent or slow further deterioration is covered so long as the beneficiary requires skilled care for the safe and effective performance of the program. When, however, the individualized assessment does not demonstrate such a necessity for skilled care, including when the performance of a maintenance program does not require the skills of a therapist because it could safely and effectively be accomplished by the patient or with the assistance of non-therapists, including unskilled caregivers, such maintenance services will not be covered.
- Further, under the standard set forth in the previous paragraph, skilled care is necessary for the performance of a safe and effective maintenance program only when (a) the particular patient's special medical complications require the skills of a qualified

therapist to perform a therapy service that would otherwise be considered non-skilled; or (b) the needed therapy procedures are of such complexity that the skills of a qualified therapist are required to perform the procedure.

e. The amount, frequency, and duration of the services must be reasonable.

* * *

40.2.2. Application of the Principles to Physical Therapy Services (Rev. 179, Issued: 01-14-14, Effective: 01-07-14, Implementation: 01-07-14)

The following discussion of skilled physical therapy services applies the principles in § 40.2.1 to specific physical therapy services about which questions are most frequently raised.

A. Assessment

Assuming all other eligibility and coverage requirements have been met, the skills of a physical therapist to assess a patient's rehabilitation needs and potential or to develop and/or implement a physical therapy program are covered when they are reasonable and necessary because of the patient's condition. Skilled rehabilitation services concurrent with the management of a patient's care plan include objective tests and measurements such as, but not limited to, range of motion, strength, balance, coordination, endurance or functional ability.

As described in section 40.2.1(b), at defined points during a course of therapy, the qualified physical therapist (instead of an assistant) must perform the ordered therapy service visit, assess the patient's function using a method which allows for objective measurement of function and comparison of successive measurements, and document the results of the assessments, corresponding measurements, and effectiveness of the therapy in the patient's clinical record. Refer to § 40.2.1(b) for specific timing and documentation requirements associated with these requirements.

B. Therapeutic Exercises

Therapeutic exercises which require the skills of a qualified physical therapist to ensure the safety of the beneficiary and the effectiveness of the treatment constitute skilled physical therapy, when the criteria in § 40.2.1(d) above are met.

C. Gait Training

Gait evaluation and training furnished to a patient whose ability to walk has been impaired by neurological, muscular or skeletal abnormality require the skills of a qualified physical therapist and constitute skilled physical therapy and are considered reasonable and necessary if training can be expected to materially improve or maintain the patient's ability to walk or prevent or slow further deterioration of the patient's ability to walk. Gait evaluation and training that is furnished to a patient whose ability to walk has been impaired by a condition other than a neurological, muscular or skeletal abnormality would nevertheless be covered where physical therapy is reasonable and necessary to restore or maintain function or to prevent or slow further deterioration. Refer to § 40.2.1(d)(1) for the reasonable and necessary coverage criteria associated with restoring patient function.

■ **EXAMPLE 1:** A physician has ordered gait evaluation and training for a patient whose gait has been materially impaired by scar tissue resulting from burns. Physical therapy services to evaluate the patient's gait, establish a gait training program, and provide the skilled services necessary to implement the program would be covered. The patient's response to therapy must be documented. At appropriate intervals (see above), the qualified therapist must assess the patient with objective measurements of function.

■ **EXAMPLE 2:** A patient who has had a total hip replacement is ambulatory but demonstrates weakness and is unable to climb stairs safely. Physical therapy would be reasonable and necessary to teach the patient to safely climb and descend stairs. Once the patient has reached the goal of climbing and descending stairs safely, additional therapy services are no longer required, and this would not be covered.

■ **EXAMPLE 3:** A patient who has received gait training has reached his maximum restoration potential and the physical therapist is teaching the patient and family how to perform safely the activities that are a part of a maintenance program. The visits by the physical therapist to demonstrate and teach the activities (which by themselves do not require the skills of a therapist) would be covered since they are needed to establish the program (refer to § 40.2.1(d)(2)). The patient's and caregiver's understanding and implementation of the maintenance program must be documented. After the establishment of the maintenance program, any further visits would need to document why the skilled services of a physical therapist are still required.

D. Range of Motion

Only a qualified physical therapist may perform range of motion tests and, therefore, such tests are skilled physical therapy.

Range of motion exercises constitute skilled physical therapy only if they are part of an active treatment for a specific disease state, illness, or injury that has resulted in a loss or restriction of mobility (as evidenced by physical therapy notes showing the degree of motion lost and the degree to be restored). Unskilled individuals may provide range of motion exercises unrelated to the restoration of a specific loss of function often safely and effectively. Passive exercises to maintain range of motion in paralyzed extremities that can be carried out by unskilled persons do not constitute skilled physical therapy.

However, if the criteria in § 40.2.1(d)(3) are met, where there is clear documentation that, because of special medical complications (e.g., susceptible to pathological bone fractures), the skills of a therapist are needed to provide services that ordinarily do not need the skills of a therapist, then the services would be covered.

E. Maintenance Therapy

Where services that are required to maintain the patient's current function or to prevent or slow further deterioration are of such complexity and sophistication that the skills of a qualified therapist are required to perform the procedure safely and effectively, the services would be covered physical therapy services. Further, where the particular patient's special medical complications require the skills of a qualified therapist to perform a therapy service safely and effectively that would otherwise be considered unskilled, such services would be covered physical therapy services. Refer to § 40.2.1(d)(3).

■ **EXAMPLE 4:** Where there is an unhealed, unstable fracture that requires regular exercise to maintain function until the fracture heals, the skills of a physical therapist would be needed to ensure that the fractured extremity is maintained in proper position and alignment during maintenance range of motion exercises.

■ **EXAMPLE 5:** A Parkinson's patient or a patient with rheumatoid arthritis who has not been under a restorative physical therapy program may require the services of a physical therapist to determine what type of exercises are required to maintain the patient's present level of function or to prevent or slow further deterioration. The initial evaluation of the patient's needs, the designing of a maintenance program appropriate to the patient's capacity and tolerance and to the treatment objectives of the physician, the instruction of the patient, family or caregivers to carry out the program safely and effectively, and such reevaluations as may be required by the patient's condition, would constitute skilled physical therapy. Each component of this process must be documented in the home health record.

While a patient is under a restorative physical therapy program, the physical therapist should regularly reevaluate the patient's condition and adjust any exercise program the patient is expected to carry out alone or with the aid of supportive personnel to maintain the function being restored. Consequently, by the time it is determined that no further restoration is possible (i.e., by the end of the last restorative session) the physical therapist will already have designed the maintenance program required and instructed the patient or caregivers in carrying out the program.

APPENDIX 4-6 HOME HEALTH ADVANCE BENEFICIARY NOTICE (ABN)

Form Instructions—Advance Beneficiary Notice of Noncoverage (ABN) OMB Approval Number: 0938-0566*

Overview

The ABN is a notice given to beneficiaries in Original Medicare to convey that Medicare is not likely to provide coverage in a specific case. "Notifiers" include physicians, providers (including institutional providers like outpatient hospitals), practitioners and suppliers paid under Part B (including independent laboratories), as well as hospice providers and religious non-medical health care institutions (RNHCIs) paid exclusively under Part A. Since 2013, home health agencies (HHAs) providing care under Part A or Part B issue the ABN instead of the Home Health Advance Beneficiary Notice (HHABN) Option Box 1 to inform beneficiaries of potential liability. The HHABN has been discontinued.

All of the aforementioned physicians, suppliers, practitioners, and providers must complete the ABN as described below, and deliver the notice to affected beneficiaries or their representative before providing the items or services that are the subject of the notice. Medicare inpatient hospitals and skilled nursing facilities (SNFs) use other approved notices for Part A items and services when notice is required; however, these facilities must use the ABN for Part B items and services.

The ABN must be reviewed with the beneficiary or his/her representative and any questions raised during that review must be answered before it is signed. The ABN must be delivered far enough in advance that the beneficiary or representative has time to consider the options and make an informed choice. Employees or subcontractors of the notifier may deliver the ABN. ABNs are never required in emergency or urgent care situations. Once all blanks are completed and the form is signed, a copy is given to the beneficiary or representative. In all cases, the notifier must *retain a copy of the ABN delivered to the beneficiary* on file.

The ABN may also be used to provide voluntary notification of financial liability for items or services that Medicare never covers. When the ABN is used as a voluntary notice, the beneficiary doesn't choose an option box or sign the notice. CMS has issued detailed instructions on the use of the ABN in its on-line Medicare Claims Processing Manual (MCPM), Publication 100-04, Chapter 30, § 50. Related policies on billing and coding of claims, as well as coverage

* For further information, *see* CMS "Beneficiary Notices Initiative (BNI)," *available at* https://www.cms.gov/Medicare/Medicare-General-Information/BNI/index.html?redirect=/BNI (site visited Aug. 6, 2018). For ABN Form Instructions, *see* CMS, Form Instructions: Advance Beneficiary Notice of Noncoverage (ABN), *available at* https://www.cms.gov/Medicare/Medicare-General-Information/BNI/Downloads/ABN-Form-Instructions.pdf (site visited Aug. 6, 2018).

determinations, are found elsewhere in the CMS manual system or website: *http://www.cms.gov*.

ABN Changes

The ABN is a formal information collection subject to approval by the Executive Office of Management and Budget (OMB) under the Paperwork Reduction Act of 1995 (PRA). As part of this process, the notice is subject to public comment and re-approval every 3 years. With the 2016 PRA submission, a non-substantive change has been made to the ABN. In accordance with Section 504 of the Rehabilitation Act of 1973 (Section 504), the form has been revised to include language informing beneficiaries of their rights to CMS nondiscrimination practices and how to request the ABN in an alternative format if needed.

Completing the Notice

ABNs may be downloaded from the CMS website at *http://www.cms.gov/Medicare/Medicare-General-Information/BNI/ABN.html*. Notices should be used as is since the ABN is a standardized OMB-approved notice. However, some allowance for customization of format is allowed as mentioned in these instructions and the on-line manual instructions for those choosing to integrate the ABN into other automated business processes. Instructions for completion of the form are set forth below:

ABNs must be reproduced on a single page. The page may be either letter or legal-size, with additional space allowed for each blank needing completion when a legal-size page is used.

Sections and Blanks:

There are 10 blanks for completion in this notice, labeled from (A) through (J), with accompanying instructions for each blank below. We recommend that notifiers remove the lettering labels from the blanks before issuing the ABN to beneficiaries. Blanks (A)-(F) and blank (H) may be completed prior to delivering the notice, as appropriate. Entries in the blanks may be typed or hand-written, but should be large enough (i.e., approximately 12-point font) to allow ease in reading. (Note that 10 point font can be used in blanks when detailed information must be given and is otherwise difficult to fit in the allowed space.) The notifier must also insert the blank (D) header information into all of the blanks labeled (D) within the Option Box section, Blank (G). One of the check boxes in the Option Box section, Blank (G), must be selected by the beneficiary or his/her representative. Blank (I) should be a cursive signature, with printed annotation if needed in order to be understood.

Header

Blanks A-C, the header of the notice, must be completed by the notifier prior to delivering the ABN.

Blank (A) Notifier(s): Notifiers must place their name, address, and telephone number (including TTY number when needed) at the top of the notice. This information may be incorporated into a notifier's logo at the top of the notice by typing, hand-writing, pre-printing, using a label or other means.

If the billing and notifying entities are not the same, the name of more than one entity may be given in the Header as long as it is specified in the Additional Information (H) section who should be contacted for billing questions.

Blank (B) Patient Name: Notifiers must enter the first and last name of the beneficiary receiving the notice, and a middle initial should also be used if there is one on the beneficiary's Medicare (HICN) card. The ABN will not be invalidated by a misspelling or missing initial, as long as the beneficiary or representative recognizes the name listed on the notice as that of the beneficiary.

Blank (C) Identification Number: Use of this field is optional. Notifiers may enter an identification number for the beneficiary that helps to link the notice with a related claim. The absence of an identification number does not invalidate the ABN. An internal filing number created by the notifier, such as a medical record number, may be used. Medicare numbers (HICNs) or Social Security numbers **must not** appear on the notice.

Body

Blank (D): The following descriptors may be used in the header of Blank (D) fields:

- Item
- Service
- Laboratory test
- Test
- Procedure
- Care
- Equipment
- The notifier must list the specific names of the items or services believed to be noncovered in the column directly under the header of Blank (D).
- In the case of partial denials, notifiers must list in the column under Blank (D) the excess component(s) of the item or service for which denial is expected.
- For repetitive or continuous noncovered care, notifiers must specify the frequency and/or duration of the item or service. See § 50.7.1 *(b) of the MCPM, Chapter 30* for additional information.

- General descriptions of specifically grouped supplies are permitted in this column. For example, "wound care supplies" would be a sufficient description of a group of items used to provide this care. An itemized list of each supply is generally not required.
- When a reduction in service occurs, notifiers must provide enough additional information so that the beneficiary understands the nature of the reduction. For example, entering "wound care supplies decreased from weekly to monthly" would be appropriate to describe a decrease in frequency for this category of supplies; just writing "wound care supplies decreased" is insufficient.
- Please note that there are a total of 7 Blank (D) fields that the notifier must complete on the ABN. Notifiers are encouraged to populate all of the Blank (D) fields in advance when a general descriptor such as "Item(s)/Service(s)" is used. All Blank (D) fields must be completed on the ABN in order for the notice to be considered valid.

Blank (E) Reason Medicare May Not Pay: In the column under this header, notifiers must explain, in beneficiary friendly language, why they believe the items or services listed in the column under Blank (D) may not be covered by Medicare. Three commonly used reasons for noncoverage are:

- "Medicare does not pay for this test for your condition."
- "Medicare does not pay for this test as often as this (denied as too frequent)."
- "Medicare does not pay for experimental or research use tests."

To be a valid ABN, there must be at least one reason applicable to each item or service listed in the column under Blank (D). The same reason for noncoverage may be applied to multiple items in Blank (D) when appropriate.

Blank (F) Estimated Cost: Notifiers must complete the column under Blank (F) to ensure the beneficiary has all available information to make an informed decision about whether or not to obtain potentially noncovered services.

Notifiers must make a good faith effort to insert a reasonable estimate for all of the items or services listed under Blank (D). In general, we would expect that the estimate should be within $100 or 25% of the actual costs, whichever is greater; however, an estimate that exceeds the actual cost substantially would generally still be acceptable, since the beneficiary would not be harmed if the actual costs were less than predicted. Thus, examples of acceptable estimates would include, but not be limited to, the following:

For a service that costs $250:

- Any dollar estimate equal to or greater than $150
- "Between $150-300"
- "No more than $500"

For a service that costs $500:

- Any dollar estimate equal to or greater than $375
- "Between $400-600"
- "No more than $700"

Multiple items or services that are routinely grouped can be bundled into a single cost estimate. For example, a single cost estimate can be given for a group of laboratory tests, such as a basic metabolic panel (BMP). An average daily cost estimate is also permissible for long term or complex projections. As noted above, providers may also pre-print a menu of items or services in the column under Blank (D) and include a cost estimate alongside each item or service. If a situation involves the possibility of additional tests or procedures (such as in laboratory reflex testing), and the costs associated with such tests cannot be reasonably estimated by the notifier at the time of ABN delivery, the notifier may enter the initial cost estimate and indicate the possibility of further testing. Finally, if for some reason the notifier is unable to provide a good faith estimate of projected costs at the time of ABN delivery, the notifier may indicate in the cost estimate area that no cost estimate is available. We would not expect either of these last two scenarios to be routine or frequent practices, but the beneficiary would have the option of signing the ABN and accepting liability in these situations.

CMS will work with its contractors to ensure consistency when evaluating cost estimates and determining validity of the ABN in general. In addition, contractors will provide ongoing education to notifiers as needed to ensure proper notice delivery. Notifiers should contact the appropriate CMS regional office if they believe that a contractor inappropriately invalidated an ABN.

Options

Blank (G) Options: Blank (G) contains the following three options:

☐ **OPTION 1.** I want the (D) listed above. You may ask to be paid now, but I also want Medicare billed for an official decision on payment, which is sent to me on a Medicare Summary Notice (MSN). I understand that if Medicare doesn't pay, I am responsible for payment, but **I can appeal to Medicare** by following the directions on the MSN. If Medicare does pay, you will refund any payments I made to you, less co-pays or deductibles.

This option allows the beneficiary to receive the items and/or services at issue and requires the notifier to submit a claim to Medicare. This will result in a payment decision that can be appealed. *See Ch. 30, § 50.15.1 of the online Medicare Claims Processing Manual* for instructions on the notifier's obligation to bill Medicare. Suppliers and providers who don't accept Medicare assignment may make modifications to Option 1 only as specified below under "**D. Additional Information.**"

Note: Beneficiaries who need to obtain an official Medicare decision in order to file a claim with a secondary insurance should choose Option 1.

☐ **OPTION 2.** I want the (D)___listed above, but do not bill Medicare. You may ask to be paid now as I am responsible for payment. **I cannot appeal if Medicare is not billed.**

This option allows the beneficiary to receive the noncovered items and/or services and pay for them out of pocket. No claim will be filed and Medicare will not be billed. Thus, there are no appeal rights associated with this option.

☐ **OPTION 3.** I don't want the (D) ___ listed above. I understand with this choice I am not responsible for payment, and I cannot appeal to see if Medicare would pay.

This option means the beneficiary does not want the care in question. By checking this box, the beneficiary understands that no additional care will be provided; thus, there are no appeal rights associated with this option.

The beneficiary or his or her representative must choose only one of the three options listed in Blank (G). Under no circumstances can the notifier decide for the beneficiary which of the 3 checkboxes to select. Pre-selection of an option by the notifier invalidates the notice. However, at the beneficiary's request, notifiers may enter the beneficiary's selection if he or she is physically unable to do so. In such cases, notifiers must annotate the notice accordingly.

If there are multiple items or services listed in Blank (D) and the beneficiary wants to receive some, but not all of the items or services, the notifier can accommodate this request by using more than one ABN. The notifier can furnish an additional ABN listing the items/services the beneficiary wishes to receive with the corresponding option.

If the beneficiary cannot or will not make a choice, the notice should be annotated, for example: "beneficiary refused to choose an option."

Additional Information

Blank (H) Additional Information: Notifiers may use this space to provide additional clarification that they believe will be of use to beneficiaries. For example, notifiers may use this space to include:

- A statement advising the beneficiary to notify his or her provider about certain tests that were ordered, but not received;
- Information on other insurance coverage for beneficiaries, such as a Medigap policy, if applicable;
- An additional dated witness signature; or
- Other necessary annotations.

Annotations will be assumed to have been made on the same date as that appearing in Blank J, accompanying the signature. If annotations are made on different dates, those dates should be part of the annotations.

Special guidance ONLY for non-participating suppliers and providers (those who don't accept Medicare assignment):

> Strike the last sentence in the Option 1 paragraph with a single line so that it appears like this: ~~If Medicare does pay, you will refund any payments I made to you, less co- pays or deductibles~~.
>
> This single line strike can be included on ABNs printed specifically for issuance when unassigned items and services are furnished. Alternatively, the line can be hand-penned on an already printed ABN.
>
> The sentence must be stricken and can't be entirely concealed or deleted. There is no CMS requirement for suppliers or the beneficiary to place initials next to the stricken sentence or date the annotations when the notifier makes the changes to the ABN before issuing the notice to the beneficiary.

When this sentence is stricken, the supplier shall include the following CMS-approved unassigned claim statement in the (H) Additional Information section.

> "This supplier doesn't accept payment from Medicare for the item(s) listed in the table above. If I checked Option 1 above, I am responsible for paying the supplier's charge for the item(s) directly to the supplier. If Medicare does pay, Medicare will pay me the Medicare-approved amount for the item(s), and this payment to me may be less than the supplier's charge."

- This statement can be included on ABNs printed for unassigned items and services, or it can be handwritten in a legible 10 point or larger font.
- An ABN with the Option 1 sentence stricken must contain the CMS-approved unassigned claim statement as written above to be considered valid notice. Similarly, when the unassigned claim statement is included in the "Additional Information" section, the last sentence in Option 1 should be stricken.

Signature Box

Once the beneficiary reviews and understands the information contained in the ABN, the Signature Box is to be completed by the beneficiary (or representative). This box cannot be completed in advance of the rest of the notice.

Blank (I) Signature: The beneficiary (or representative) must sign the notice to indicate that he or she has received the notice and understands its contents. If a representative signs on behalf of a beneficiary, he or she should write out "representative" in parentheses after his or her signature. The representative's name should be clearly legible or noted in print.

Blank (J) Date: The beneficiary (or representative) must write the date he or she signed the ABN. If the beneficiary has physical difficulty with writing and requests assistance in completing this blank, the date may be inserted by the notifier.

Disclosure Statement: The disclosure statements in the footer of the notice is required to be included on the document.

CHAPTER 5

HOSPICE COVERAGE

§ 5.01 INTRODUCTION HOSPICE COVERAGE

Medicare covers hospice care[1] for beneficiaries diagnosed as terminally ill. Terminally ill means the individual has a medical prognosis that his or her life expectancy is six months or less if the illness runs its normal course.[2] Hospice care is a comprehensive set of services identified and coordinated by an interdisciplinary group to provide for the physical, psychosocial, spiritual, and emotional needs of a terminally ill patient and the patient's family members.[3]

The hospice benefit is different from all other Medicare benefits in that it does not provide for the curative treatment of illness or injury;[4] rather, it is designed for the palliation and management of terminal illness.[5] Palliative care is defined as patient and family centered care that optimizes quality of life by anticipating, preventing, and treating suffering. Throughout the continuum of illness, it involves addressing physical, intellectual, emotional, social, and spiritual needs and facilitates patient autonomy, access to information, and choice.[6]

Medicare-covered hospice care must be provided by a Medicare-certified hospice provider.[7] The hospice provider must comply with Medicare's conditions of participation.[8] Hospice care should "allow the patient to remain at home as long as possible by providing support to the patient and family, and by keeping the patient as comfortable as possible while maintaining his or her dignity and quality of life."[9]

One can receive covered hospice care under Medicare only after specifically opting into the hospice benefit, thereby opting out of eligibility for Medicare coverage for other medical care and services related to the terminal illness. Electing hospice care, however, does *not* mean that all curative treatment is waived. Beneficiaries who elect the Medicare hospice benefit may still receive

---

[1] 42 U.S.C. § 1395x(dd) (2012).

[2] 42 C.F.R. § 418.3.

[3] 42 U.S.C. § 1395x(dd)(1); 42 C.F.R. § 418.3.

[4] 42 U.S.C. § 1395y(a)(1)(A).

[5] 42 U.S.C. § 1395y(a)(1)(C).

[6] 42 C.F.R. § 418.3.

[7] In 2017, pursuant to the Hospice Quality Reporting Program [Sec. 1814(i)(5) of the Social Security Act], the Centers for Medicaid & Medicare Services (CMS) launched the Hospice Compare website for consumers to compare hospice providers' performance on certain quality measures relating to patient care. Hospices can be compared based on results from a national survey that asks a primary informal caregiver of a hospice patient about their hospice care experience. Consumers can also compare provider performance on select quality measures (i.e., consideration of patients' beliefs/values and treatment preferences, pain screening and assessment, dyspnea screening and treatment, and bowel regime administration to patients treated with opioids) derived from the standardized Hospice Item Set (HIS) which hospices must complete and report for all patients. The Center for Medicare Advocacy does not know yet the value of this online tool for beneficiaries.

[8] 42 C.F.R. §§ 418.52–418.116.

[9] CMS; Hospice Conditions of Participation, 73 Fed. Reg. 32,088 (June 5, 2008) (codified at 42 C.F.R. § 418).

Medicare coverage for medically reasonable and necessary treatment for diagnoses unrelated to their terminal illness.

§ 5.02 ELIGIBILITY FOR HOSPICE COVERAGE

The Medicare hospice benefit is provided under Part A of the Medicare program. Therefore, in order to be eligible for this benefit, one must be enrolled in Medicare Part A. In addition, the individual must be initially certified as terminally ill by the hospice medical director or physician member of the hospice interdisciplinary group, as well as his or her attending physician (if the individual has one).[10] A certification is based on the physician's clinical judgment regarding the normal course of the individual's illness.[11] The certification must specify that the individual's prognosis is for a life expectancy of six months or less if the terminal illness runs its normal course.[12] Nurse practitioners can act as attending physicians but they cannot certify or recertify terminal diagnosis and prognosis. Beginning in 2019, the law will recognize physician assistants as attending physicians to their patients in hospice.[13] In the event that a nurse practitioner or physician assistant is the beneficiary's attending physician, the hospice medical director or physician designee must certify or recertify the beneficiary's limited life expectancy.[14]

---

[10] 42 C.F.R. § 418.22(c):

> *Sources of certification.* (1) For the initial 90-day period, the hospice must obtain written certification statements . . . from (i) The medical director of the hospice or the physician member of the hospice interdisciplinary group; and (ii) The individual's attending physician if the individual has an attending physician. . . . (2) For subsequent periods, the only requirement is certification by one of the physicians listed in paragraph(c)(1)(i) of this section.

[11] If a Medicare beneficiary is terminally ill and has not yet elected the hospice benefit, Medicare will pay for a consultation visit with the hospice medical director or physicians who are employees of a hospice program. During this visit, the physician may evaluate the individual's need for pain and symptom management, counsel the individual with respect to end-of-life issues and care options, and advise the individual regarding advanced care planning. Hospices receive payment for this service that is equal to the amount established for an office or other outpatient visit for evaluation and management associated with presenting problems of moderate severity under the established Medicare physician fee schedule other than the portion of the amount attributable to the practice expense component. The physician, if not a volunteer, will be paid by the hospice. CMS, Medicare Benefit Policy (MBP) Manual, Ch. 9: §§ 80–80.2, *available at* http://www.cms.gov/Regulations-and-Guidance/Guidance/Manuals/Downloads/bp102c09.pdf (site visited Aug. 6, 2018).

[12] 42 C.F.R. § 418.22(b)(1). *See also* MBP Manual, Ch. 9: §§ 10-20.1, *available at* http://www.cms.gov/Regulations-and-Guidance/Guidance/Manuals/Downloads/bp102c09.pdf (site visited Aug. 6, 2018).

[13] The Medicare Patient Access to Hospice Act, H.R. 1284, 115th Cong. (2017), signed into law in February 2018, establishes that physician assistants may serve as attending physicians to patients in hospice effective January 1, 2019.

[14] MBP Manual, Ch. 9: § 40.1.3.2.

The certifying physician must include a brief narrative explanation of the clinical findings that support a life expectancy of six months or less as part of the certification and recertification forms or as an addendum to the certification and recertification forms.[15] Clinical information and other documentation that support the medical prognosis must be filed in the medical record with the written certification.[16] The clinical information will be part of the hospice provider's eligibility assessment for the patient.[17] The certification is filed with the hospice provider.[18]

§ 5.03 ELECTION OF THE HOSPICE BENEFIT

An election to receive hospice care is made by filing an election statement with a hospice provider of choice.[19] An election statement may be filed by either the beneficiary or his or her legal representative.[20] Once a beneficiary elects the hospice benefit, he or she waives all rights to Medicare payment for services that are *related to the treatment of the terminal condition* or a related condition, except for services provided by the designated hospice or by another provider under arrangements made by the designated hospice, or by the individual's attending physician.[21]

The election statement itself must:

- Identify the designated hospice provider and the individual's designated attending physician (if any);[22]
- Contain an acknowledgement that:
  — the attending physician is his or her chosen physician;

[15] 42 C.F.R. § 418.22(b)(3).

[16] 42 C.F.R. § 418.22(b)(2).

[17] 42 C.F.R. § 418.22(b)(2).

[18] 42 C.F.R. § 418.22.

[19] 42 C.F.R. § 418.24.

[20] 42 C.F.R. § 418.24.

[21] This is only the case if the attending physician is not an employee of the designated hospice or receiving compensation from the hospice for the provided services. 42 C.F.R. § 418.24(d)(2)(iii). Furthermore, the Medicare Hospice Manual limits such services to the personal professional services of the attending physician. In other words, the costs for services such as labs or X-rays must be provided under arrangements with the hospice and will not be reimbursed by Medicare if independently ordered by the attending physician. CMS, Pub. 100-04, Medicare Claims Processing (MCP) Manual, Ch. 11: § 40.1.3, *available at* https://www.cms.gov/Regulations-and-Guidance/Guidance/Manuals/Downloads/clm104c11crosswalk.pdf (site visited Aug. 6, 2018).

[22] This information should include, but is not limited to, the attending physician's full name, office address, NPI number, or any other detailed information to clearly identify the attending physician. MBP Manual, Ch. 9: § 20.2.1, *available at* http://www.cms.gov/Regulations-and-Guidance/Guidance/Manuals/Downloads/bp102c09.pdf (site visited Aug. 6, 2018).

— he or she has a full understanding of the palliative rather than the curative nature of hospice care as it relates to the individual's terminal illness;

— he or she is waiving Medicare coverage for: hospice care provided by another hospice provider and for any services related to the treatment of the terminal condition for which hospice care was elected or a related condition except for care and services provided by or under arrangement with the designated hospice or provided by the beneficiary's attending physician;[23]

- State the effective date of the election;[24] and
- Be signed by the beneficiary or his or her representative.[25]

An individual may elect to receive hospice care during one or more of the following election periods: an initial 90-day period, a subsequent 90-day period, or an unlimited number of subsequent 60-day periods.[26] At the start of the first period, a hospice physician and the beneficiary's attending physician (if he or she has one) must certify that the beneficiary is terminally ill.[27] For subsequent periods, only a hospice physician must certify the beneficiary is terminally ill.[28]

A hospice election will continue through the initial election period and through the subsequent election periods without a break in care, as long as the individual remains in the care of the hospice program, does not revoke the election, and is not discharged from the hospice.[29] Prior to each subsequent election period, a hospice physician[30] must review the patient's clinical information[31] and,

---

[23] Prompt filing of the hospice Notice of Election (NOE) with the Medicare contractor is required to properly enforce this waiver and prevent inappropriate payments to non-hospice providers. The effective date of hospice election is the same as the hospice admission date. A timely filed NOE is one that is submitted to and accepted by the Medicare contractor within five calendar days after the hospice election. MBP Manual, Ch. 9: § 20.2.1.1.

[24] 42 C.F.R. § 418.24(b)(4).

[25] 42 C.F.R. § 418.24(b)(5).

[26] 42 C.F.R. § 418.21.

[27] 42 C.F.R. § 418.22(c)(1). *See also* MBP Manual, Ch. 9: § 20.1, *available at* http://www.cms.gov/Regulations-and-Guidance/Guidance/Manuals/Downloads/bp102c09.pdf (site visited Aug. 6, 2018).

[28] 42 C.F.R. § 418.22(c):

> *Sources of certification.* (1) For the initial 90-day period, the hospice must obtain written certification statements . . . from (i) The medical director of the hospice or the physician member of the hospice interdisciplinary group; and (ii) The individual's attending physician if the individual has an attending physician. (2) For subsequent periods, the only requirement is certification by one of the physicians listed in paragraph(c)(1)(i) of this section.

[29] 42 C.F.R. § 418.24(c).

[30] 42 C.F.R. § 418.22(c)(2).

[31] 42 C.F.R. § 418.102(c).

if hospice care remains appropriate, recertify in writing that the beneficiary continues to be terminally ill.[32] Hospice election periods are also called benefit periods.

Prior to the third benefit period, and for all subsequent benefit periods, a hospice physician or nurse practitioner must have a face-to-face encounter with the hospice patient to determine continued eligibility for Medicare coverage of hospice care.[33] Additionally, if a hospice provider is deemed to have a high percentage of patients who remain on hospice care longer than 180 days (the exact percentage is to be specified by the Secretary), the Secretary will review the medical merits of all care exceeding 180 days.[34]

Because exceptional circumstances will sometimes make it impossible for providers to have face-to-face encounters prior to hospice admissions, the Centers for Medicare & Medicaid Services (CMS) has appropriately created the following policy:

> In cases where a hospice newly admits a patient who is in the third or later benefit period, exceptional circumstances may prevent a face-to-face encounter prior to the start of the benefit period. For example, if the patient is an emergency weekend admission, it may be impossible for a hospice physician or [nurse practitioner] to see the patient until the following Monday. Or, if CMS data systems are unavailable, the hospice may be unaware that the patient is in the third benefit period. In such documented cases, a face-to-face encounter which occurs within 2 days after admission will be considered to be timely. Additionally, for such documented exceptional cases, if the patient dies within 2 days of admission without a face-to-face encounter, a face-to-face encounter can be deemed as complete.[35]

§ 5.04 WHO MAY MAKE AN ELECTION FOR HOSPICE CARE

Medicare beneficiaries may elect hospice care for palliative treatment of a terminal illness.[36] Problems may arise when a person lacks the mental capacity to make an election. Under this circumstance, a representative may make the election. A representative is an individual who has the authority under state law (whether by statute or pursuant to an appointment by the courts of the state) to authorize or terminate medical care or to elect or revoke the election of hospice

---

[32] 42 C.F.R. § 418.22(c)(2). *See also* **§ 5.02** of this Handbook.

[33] 42 C.F.R. § 418.22(a)(4). *See also* MBP Manual, Ch. 9: §§ 20.1.5 & 40.1.3.2 ("Hospice nurse practitioners [employed by the hospice] may conduct face-to-face encounters . . . as part of the certification process, but are still prohibited by statute from certifying the terminal illness.").

[34] Section 3132 of the Affordable Care Act; 42 U.S.C. § 1395f(a)(7) (2012).

[35] MBP Manual, Ch. 9: § 20.1.5.d (Face-to-face encounter), *available at* http://www.cms.gov/Regulations-and-Guidance/Guidance/Manuals/Downloads/bp102c09.pdf (site visited Aug. 6, 2018).

[36] 42 C.F.R. § 418.24(b)(2).

care on behalf of a terminally ill patient who is mentally or physically incapacitated. This may include a legal guardian.[37]

§ 5.05 HOSPICE ADMISSION

The hospice provider admits a patient only on the recommendation of the hospice medical director in consultation with, or with input from, the patient's attending physician.[38] In reaching a decision to certify that the patient is terminally ill, the hospice medical director must consider at least the following information: diagnosis of the patient's terminal condition; other health conditions, whether related or unrelated to the terminal condition; and current clinically relevant information supporting all diagnoses.[39]

The hospice admission date is the first day of the benefit period, except in the case of transfers. The admission date may not precede the physician's certification date by more than two calendar days. If a new hospice admission occurs following a hospice discharge or revocation that resulted in the termination of the hospice benefit, the admission date cannot be the same as the revocation or discharge date.[40]

§ 5.06 MEDICARE ADVANTAGE

Medicare Advantage organizations must inform enrollees who are eligible for hospice care about the available Medicare hospice providers in their community.[41] Once the beneficiary elects the hospice benefit, the hospice provider will bill Medicare Part A (Medicare fee-for-service) for the beneficiary's hospice care. In other words, traditional Medicare, rather than the Medicare Advantage plan, will pay the provider for the hospice care. Also of note, if during a hospice benefit period, the beneficiary receives care from providers for care unrelated to the terminal illness, those providers will also bill traditional Medicare (Part A or B) for the care in question. While the beneficiary is on hospice, he or she is responsible for Part A and Part B cost-sharing. If the beneficiary revokes the hospice election or is discharged from hospice care, the Medicare Advantage organization

---

[37] 42 C.F.R. § 418.3.

[38] 42 C.F.R. § 418.25(a).

[39] 42 C.F.R. § 418.25(b).

[40] MCP Manual, Ch. 11: § 20.1.2 ("Completing the Uniform [Institutional Provider] Bill [Form CMS-1450] for Hospice Election, Rev. 3326," *available at* https://www.cms.gov/Regulations-and-Guidance/Guidance/Transmittals/Downloads/R3326CP.pdf (site visited Aug. 6, 2018).

[41] 42 C.F.R. § 422.320.

will become responsible for the beneficiary's health care costs on the first day of the month after the revocation or discharge.[42]

§ 5.07 PATIENT RIGHTS

During the initial assessment visit in advance of furnishing care, the hospice provider must give the patient or representative oral and written notice of the patient's rights and responsibilities in a language and manner that the patient understands.[43] Additionally, the hospice provider must inform and distribute information concerning its policies on advance directives, including a description of applicable state law.[44] Hospice providers cannot deny care because a beneficiary has not formulated an advance directive.[45] The hospice provider must obtain the patient's or representative's signature confirming that he or she received a copy of the notice of rights and responsibilities.[46]

[A] Hospice Patient Rights

Each hospice patient has the following rights:[47]

- To exercise his or her rights as a patient of the hospice;
- To have his or her property and person treated with respect;
- To voice grievances regarding treatment or care that is (or fails to be) furnished and the lack of respect for property by anyone who is furnishing services on behalf of the hospice;
- To be free from discrimination or reprisal for exercising his or her rights;[48]

[42] 42 C.F.R. §§ 417.585 & 417.531. *See also* MCP Manual, Ch. 11: § 30.4 & MBP Manual, Ch. 9: § 20.4. Since Medicare Advantage enrollees will not have a Medigap or equivalent policy, they may incur significant out-of-pocket expense for non-hospice care.

[43] 42 C.F.R. § 418.52(a)(1).

[44] 42 C.F.R. § 418.52(a)(2).

[45] *Id. See also* 73 Fed. Reg. 32,088, 32,097 (June 5, 2008) ("Under this final rule, hospices are required to comply with 42 C.F.R. part 489 Subpart I, 'Advance directives.' Patients may choose to develop advance directives in accordance with applicable State requirements. Likewise, they may choose to not formulate advance directives.").

[46] 42 C.F.R. § 418.52(b)(1).

[47] If a patient has been adjudicated incompetent under state law by a court of proper jurisdiction, the rights of the patient are exercised by the person appointed pursuant to state law to act on the patient's behalf. If a state court has not adjudged a patient incompetent, any legal representative designated by the patient in accordance with state law may exercise the patient's rights to the extent allowed by state law. 42 C.F.R. § 418.52(b)(2)-(3).

[48] 42 C.F.R. § 418.52(b)(1).

- To receive effective pain management and symptom control from the hospice for conditions related to the terminal illness;
- To be involved in developing his or her hospice plan of care;
- To refuse care or treatment;
- To choose his or her attending physician;[49]
- To have a confidential clinical record (and access to that record);
- To be free from mistreatment, neglect, or verbal, mental, sexual, and physical abuse, including injuries of unknown source, and misappropriation of patient property;
- To receive information about the services covered under the hospice benefit; and
- To receive information about the scope of services that the hospice will provide and specific limitations on those services.[50]

[B] Hospice Requirements

Each hospice must:[51]

- Ensure that all alleged violations involving mistreatment, neglect, or verbal, mental, sexual, and physical abuse, including injuries of unknown source, and misappropriation of patient property, are reported immediately by hospice employees and contracted staff to the hospice administrator;
- Immediately investigate all alleged violations involving anyone furnishing services on behalf of the hospice and immediately take action to prevent further potential violations while the alleged violation is being verified. Investigations and/or documentation of all alleged violations must be conducted in accordance with established procedures;
- Take appropriate corrective action in accordance with state law if the alleged violation is verified by the hospice administrator or an outside

---

[49] Medicare Prescription Drug, Improvement, and Modernization Act of 2003, Pub. L. No. 108-173 (Dec. 8, 2003), *available at* http://www.gpo.gov/fdsys/pkg/PLAW-108publ173/pdf/PLAW-108publ173.pdf (site visited Aug. 6, 2018). Section 408 authorized Medicare payments for the services of a nurse practitioner chosen by the beneficiary instead of a physician as having the most significant role in the determination and delivery of the beneficiary's medical care. The nurse is not authorized to certify the beneficiary as terminally ill but is able to review hospice plans of care. *See* MBP Manual, Ch. 9: § 40.1.3.2, *available at* http://www.cms.gov/Regulations-and-Guidance/Guidance/Manuals/Downloads/bp102c09.pdf (site visited Aug. 6, 2018).

[50] 42 C.F.R. § 418.52(c).

[51] 42 C.F.R. § 418.52(b)(4).

body having jurisdiction, such as the state survey agency or local law enforcement agency; and

- Ensure that the verified violations are reported to state and local bodies having jurisdiction (including to the state survey and certification agency) within five working days of becoming aware of the violation.

§ 5.08 HOSPICE REVOCATION

An individual or legal representative may revoke the election of hospice care at any time during an election period.[52] To revoke the election, the individual or legal representative must file a statement with the hospice provider that includes the following information:[53]

- The signature of the beneficiary or legal representative; and
- The date of revocation (which cannot be earlier than the date upon which the revocation is made).

Upon revocation, the beneficiary is no longer covered under Medicare for hospice care,[54] resumes Medicare coverage for benefits previously waived,[55] and may, at any time, elect to receive hospice coverage for any other hospice election periods that he or she is eligible to receive.[56]

§ 5.09 HOSPICE DISCHARGE

A hospice provider may discharge a patient if the patient moves out of the provider's service area or transfers to another provider,[57] the hospice provider determines that the patient is no longer terminally ill, or for cause if the hospice provider determines that the behavior of the patient or another person in the patient's home is disruptive, abusive, or uncooperative to the extent that delivery of care to the patient or the ability of the hospice provider to operate effectively is seriously impaired.[58]

---

[52] 42 C.F.R. § 418.28(a).

[53] 42 C.F.R. § 418.28(b)(2).

[54] 42 C.F.R. § 418.28(c)(1).

[55] 42 C.F.R. § 418.28(c)(2).

[56] 42 C.F.R. § 418.28(c)(3).

[57] A change of ownership of a hospice is not considered a change in the patient's designation of a hospice and requires no action on the patient's part. MBP Manual, Ch. 9: § 20.2.1.

[58] 42 C.F.R. § 418.26(a).

There are no appeal rights available to beneficiaries who are discharged from hospice for cause. However, pursuant to the regulations, prior to such a discharge, the hospice provider must:[59]

- Advise the patient that a discharge for cause is being considered;
- Make a serious effort to resolve the problem(s) presented by the patient's behavior or situation;
- Ascertain that the patient's proposed discharge is not due to the patient's use of necessary hospice services;
- Document the problem(s) and efforts made to resolve the problem(s) and enter this documentation into its medical record; and
- Notify the Medicare contractor and State Survey Agency of the circumstances surrounding the impending discharge. The hospice provider may need to make referrals to other relevant state or community agencies (i.e., adult protective services) as appropriate.

Prior to discharging a patient for reasons other than revocation or transfer, the hospice must obtain a written physician's discharge order from the hospice medical director.[60] If a patient has an attending physician involved in his or her care, this physician should be consulted before discharge and his or her review and decision included in the discharge note.[61]

An individual, upon discharge from the hospice during a particular election period for reasons other than immediate transfer to another hospice, is no longer covered under Medicare for hospice care, resumes previously waived Medicare coverage[62] and may at any time elect to receive hospice care if he or she is again eligible to receive the benefit.[63]

Hospice providers must have in place a discharge planning process that takes into account the prospect that a patient's condition might stabilize or otherwise change such that the patient cannot continue to be certified as terminally ill.[64] The discharge planning process must include planning for any necessary family counseling, patient education, or other services before the patient is discharged.[65]

---

[59] 42 C.F.R. § 418.26(a). *See also* MBP Manual, Ch. 9: § 20.2.1 & § 20.2.3, *available at* http://www.cms.gov/Regulations-and-Guidance/Guidance/Manuals/Downloads/bp102c09.pdf (site visited Aug. 6, 2018).

[60] 42 C.F.R. § 418.26(b).

[61] 42 C.F.R. § 418.26(b).

[62] *See* **§ 5.01** of this Handbook.

[63] 42 C.F.R. § 418.26(c).

[64] 42 C.F.R. § 418.26(d)(1).

[65] 42 C.F.R. § 418.26(d)(2).

If the hospice provider is discharging the patient because the medical director no longer believes the patient is terminally ill, the provider must deliver valid written notice to the beneficiary of this decision.[66] The standardized termination notice must indicate that Medicare coverage for hospice care is ending, the date coverage ends, the beneficiary's financial liability for continued service, and how to appeal the discharge.[67] This standardized termination notice is the first step in the expedited appeals process, which guarantees Medicare beneficiaries review of their cases within 72 hours of request.[68]

§ 5.10 CHANGING HOSPICE PROVIDERS

A beneficiary may change, once each election period, the designation of the particular hospice provider. The change of the designated hospice provider is not a revocation of the election of hospice benefits. In order to change the designated provider, the beneficiary or representative must file, with both the provider from which the beneficiary has been receiving care, and the new provider from which the beneficiary will be receiving care, a signed statement indicating the name of each provider and the effective date of the change.[69]

Note that such a change may be made only once during each election period. If an additional change were desired, the beneficiary would have to revoke the hospice coverage and then reelect hospice coverage using a new election period.

§ 5.11 HOSPICE SERVICES

[A] Interdisciplinary Group

Any hospice services that are to be provided to a Medicare beneficiary must be included in a written plan of care established by the hospice interdisciplinary group.[70] The hospice provider must designate a registered nurse who is a member of the interdisciplinary group to coordinate care and to ensure continuous assessment of each patient's and family's needs and implementation of the interdisciplinary plan of care. The interdisciplinary group must include, but is not limited

---

[66] 42 C.F.R. § 405.1200.

[67] 42 C.F.R. § 405.1200.

[68] CMS, Changes to the Medicare Claims Appeals Procedures, 70 Fed. Reg. 11,419 (codified at 42 C.F.R. §§ 401 & 405) (Mar. 8, 2005); 42 C.F.R. § 405.1202. *See also* **§ 1.07[A][5]** and **§ 5.15[D]** of this Handbook.

[69] 42 C.F.R. § 418.30.

[70] 42 C.F.R. §§ 418.56, 418.58 & 418.68 ("The hospice must designate an interdisciplinary group . . . which, in consultation with the patient's attending physician, must prepare a written plan of care. The plan of care must specify the hospice care and services necessary to meet the patient and family-specific needs identified in the comprehensive assessment as such needs relate to the terminal illness and related conditions.").

to, individuals who are qualified and competent to practice in the following professional roles:[71]

- Doctor of medicine or osteopathy (who is an employee or under contract with the hospice);
- Registered nurse;
- Social worker; and
- Pastoral or other counselor.

[B] Hospice Plan of Care

The plan of care must be created in collaboration with the beneficiary's attending physician (if any), the patient or representative, and the primary caregiver in accordance with the patient's needs.[72] The plan of care must account for all services necessary for the palliation and management of the terminal illness and related conditions, including the following:[73]

- Interventions to manage pain and symptoms;
- A detailed statement of the scope and frequency of services necessary to meet the specific patient and family needs;
- Measurable outcomes anticipated from implementing and coordinating the plan of care;
- Drugs and treatment necessary to meet the needs of the patient;
- Medical supplies and appliances necessary to meet the needs of the patient; and
- The interdisciplinary group's documentation of the patient's or representative's level of understanding, involvement, and agreement with the plan of care, in accordance with the hospice's own policies.

The plan of care must be reviewed and/or revised as the patient's condition requires, but no less frequently than every 15 calendar days.[74]

[C] Physician Services

The hospice medical director, physician employees, and contracted physician(s) of the hospice provider, in conjunction with the patient's attending

[71] 42 C.F.R. § 418.56(a)(1).
[72] 42 C.F.R. § 418.56(b).
[73] 42 C.F.R. § 418.56(c).
[74] 42 C.F.R. § 418.56(d).

physician, are responsible for the palliation and management of the terminal illness and conditions related to the terminal illness.[75]

[D] Nursing Care

The hospice provider must render nursing care and services by or under the supervision of a registered nurse. Nursing services must ensure that the nursing needs of the patient are met as identified in the patient's initial assessment,[76] comprehensive assessment,[77] and updated assessments.[78] Nursing care may be provided on a continuous basis for as much as 24 hours a day *during periods of crisis* as necessary to maintain an individual at home. A period of crisis is one in which the patient requires continuous care to achieve palliation or management of acute medical symptoms.[79]

[E] Medical Social Services

Medical social services must be provided by a qualified social worker, under the direction of a physician. Social work services must be based on the patient's psychosocial assessment and the patient's family's needs and acceptance of these services.[80]

[F] Counseling Services

Counseling services must be available to the patient and family to assist the patient and family in minimizing stress and problems that arise from the terminal

---

[75] 42 C.F.R. § 418.64(a). *See also* MBP Manual, Ch. 9: § 40.1.3.

[76] Initial assessment is an evaluation of the patient's physical, psychosocial, and emotional status related to the terminal illness and related conditions to determine the patient's immediate care and support needs. 42 C.F.R. § 418.3. The hospice registered nurse must complete an initial assessment within 48 hours after the election of hospice care. 42 C.F.R. § 418.54(a).

[77] The comprehensive assessment "must identify the physical, psychosocial, emotional, and spiritual needs related to the terminal illness that must be addressed in order to promote the hospice patient's well-being, comfort, and dignity throughout the dying process." 42 C.F.R. § 418.54(c). It must take into consideration: the nature and condition causing admission; complications and risk factors that affect care planning; functional status, including the patient's ability to understand and participate in his or her own care; imminence of death; severity of symptoms; drug profile; bereavement; and the need for referrals and further evaluation by appropriate health professionals. *Id.* The assessment includes a thorough evaluation of the caregiver's and family's willingness and capability to take care of the patient. 42 C.F.R. § 418.3. The comprehensive assessment must be completed no later than five days after the election of hospice care. 42 C.F.R. § 418.54(b).

[78] 42 C.F.R. §§ 418.54(c) & 418.64(b)(1). *See also* MBP Manual, Ch. 9: § 40.1.1.

[79] 42 C.F.R. § 418.204(a). *See also* MBP Manual, Ch. 9: § 40.2.1.

[80] 42 C.F.R. § 418.64(c).

illness, related conditions, and the dying process.[81] Counseling services must include, but are not limited to, bereavement counseling, dietary counseling, and spiritual counseling.[82]

[1] Bereavement Counseling

Bereavement counseling is emotional, psychosocial, and spiritual support and services provided before and after the death of a patient to assist with issues related to grief, loss, and adjustment.[83] Though not reimbursed by Medicare, bereavement counseling is a required hospice service.[84] Each Medicare-certified hospice provider must have an organized program for the provision of bereavement services under the supervision of a qualified professional with experience or education in grief or loss counseling.[85] Bereavement services should be made available to family and other affected individuals[86] for up to one year after the death of the patient.[87]

[2] Dietary Counseling

Dietary counseling should be provided when identified in the plan of care as a needed service. When provided, it must be performed by a qualified individual, which might be a dietitian, nurse, or other individual who is able to address and assure that the dietary needs of the patient are met.[88]

[3] Spiritual Counseling

Regarding spiritual counseling the hospice must:[89]

- Provide an assessment of the patient's and family's spiritual needs;
- Provide spiritual counseling to meet these needs in accordance with the patient's and family's acceptance of this service, and in a manner consistent with patient and family beliefs and desires;

---

[81] 42 C.F.R. § 418.64(d).

[82] 42 C.F.R. § 418.64(d). *See also* MBP Manual, Ch. 9: § 40.1.4.

[83] 42 C.F.R. § 418.3.

[84] 42 C.F.R. § 418.204(c).

[85] 42 C.F.R. § 418.64(d)(1)(i).

[86] Bereavement counseling extends to residents of a residential care center when appropriate and identified in the bereavement plan of care. 42 C.F.R. § 418.64(d)(1)(ii).

[87] 42 C.F.R. § 418.64(d)(1)(ii). *See also* MBP Manual, Ch. 9: § 40.2.3.

[88] 42 C.F.R. §§ 418.64(d)(2) & 418.74. *See also* MBP Manual, Ch. 9: § 40.5. Under certain conditions, CMS may waive the requirements for non-urban hospices to make dietary counseling available (as needed) on a 24-hour basis and to provide dietary counseling directly.

[89] 42 C.F.R. § 418.64(d)(3).

- Make all reasonable efforts to facilitate visits by local clergy, pastoral counselors, or other individuals who can support the patient's spiritual needs; and
- Advise the patient and family of this service.

[G] Physical Therapy, Occupational Therapy, and Speech-Language Pathology

Physical therapy, occupational therapy, and speech-language pathology services must be available to hospice patients and, when provided, offered in a manner consistent with accepted standards of practice.[90]

[H] Hospice Aide and Homemaker Services

[1] Hospice Aides

Hospice aide training and supervision requirements are extensive and are described in the conditions of participation.[91] Hospice aides are assigned to a specific patient by a registered nurse who is a member of the interdisciplinary group.[92] The hospice aide provides services that are:[93]

- Ordered by the interdisciplinary group;
- Included in the plan of care;
- Permitted to be performed under state law by such hospice aide; and
- Consistent with the hospice aide training.

The duties of the hospice aide include, but are not limited to:[94]

- Provision of hands-on personal care;
- Performance of simple procedures as an extension of therapy or nursing services;
- Assistance in ambulation or exercises; and

---

[90] 42 C.F.R. §§ 418.72 & 418.74. *See also* MBP Manual, Ch. 9: §§ 40.1.8 & 40.5. Physical therapy, occupational therapy, and speech-language pathology services may be provided for purposes of symptom control or to enable the individual to maintain activities of daily living and basic functional skills. Section 1861(dd)(5) of the Act allows CMS to waive, under certain conditions, provision of therapy services by hospices in non-urban areas.

[91] 42 C.F.R. § 418.76.

[92] 42 C.F.R. § 418.76(g).

[93] 42 C.F.R. § 418.76(g)(2).

[94] 42 C.F.R. § 418.76(g)(3).

- Assistance in administering medications that are ordinarily self-administered.

Hospice aides must report changes in the patient's medical, nursing, rehabilitative, and social needs to a registered nurse, as the changes relate to the plan of care and quality assessment and improvement activities. Hospice aides must also complete the appropriate records in compliance with the hospice's policies and procedures.[95]

[2] Hospice Homemakers

Homemaker services must be provided by individuals who have successfully completed a hospice orientation addressing the needs and concerns of patients and families coping with a terminal illness.[96] Homemaker services must be coordinated and supervised by a member of the interdisciplinary group.[97] Instructions for homemaker duties must be prepared by a member of the interdisciplinary group.[98] Homemakers must report all concerns about the patient or family to the member of the interdisciplinary group who is coordinating homemaker services.[99]

[3] Hospice Interface with Medicaid Waiver Program

Section 1915(c) of the Social Security Act permits the Secretary of Health and Human Services (HHS) to waive Medicaid requirements in order to allow states to use Medicaid money to pay for the delivery of long-term services within community settings. The provisions waived are Section 1902(a)(1) (requirement that provisions be statewide), Section 1902(a)(10)(B) (requirement that services be comparable), and Section 1902(a)(10)(C)(i)(III) (regarding income and resource applicable in the community). Thus, Section 1915(c) waivers permit states to target waivers to particular areas of the state, for instance, where the need is greatest. States are also able to make waiver services available only to certain people, such as those at risk of institutionalization, or to people with particular diseases. And finally, states are permitted to provide Medicaid to individuals in the community who otherwise would have been eligible had they been institutionalized.

Medicare beneficiaries who receive personal care services under a Medicaid Waiver Program may continue to receive those benefits after they have elected the

---

[95] 42 C.F.R. § 418.76(g)(4). *See also* MBP Manual, Ch. 9: § 40.1.7.

[96] 42 C.F.R. § 418.76(j)(1).

[97] 42 C.F.R. § 418.76(k)(1).

[98] 42 C.F.R. § 418.76(k)(2).

[99] 42 C.F.R. § 418.76(k)(3). *See also* MBP Manual, Ch. 9: § 40.1.7.

hospice benefit.[100] Services under the Medicaid personal care benefit may be used to the extent that the hospice provider would routinely use the services of a hospice patient's family in implementing a patient's plan of care.[101] The hospice must coordinate its hospice aide and homemaker services with the Medicaid personal care benefit to ensure the patient receives the hospice aide and homemaker services he or she needs.[102]

[I] Volunteer Services

For each Medicare certified hospice program, volunteers must provide day-to-day administrative and/or direct patient care services in an amount that, at a minimum, equals 5 percent of all paid hospice employees and contract staff.[103]

[J] Medical Supplies and Durable Medical Equipment

Medical supplies and appliances and durable medical equipment (DME) related to the palliation and management of the terminal illness and related conditions must be provided by the hospice while the patient is under hospice care.[104] Medical supplies and appliances include things such as colostomy bags and supplies directly related to colostomy care.[105] DME includes items such as hospital beds and wheelchairs.[106]

[K] Drugs and Biologicals

Drugs and biologicals related to the palliation and management of the terminal condition and related conditions, as identified in the hospice plan of care, must be provided by the hospice while the patient is under hospice care.[107] A hospice provider may use chemotherapy, radiation therapy, and other modalities for palliative purposes if it determines that these services are needed.[108]

---

[100] 42 C.F.R. § 418.76(i).
[101] 42 C.F.R. § 418.76(i)(2).
[102] 42 C.F.R. § 418.76(i)(3).
[103] 42 C.F.R. § 418.78.
[104] 42 C.F.R. § 418.106.
[105] 42 C.F.R. § 410.36.
[106] 42 C.F.R. § 410.38.
[107] 42 C.F.R. § 418.106.
[108] MBP Manual, Ch. 9: § 40.2.4 (the determination is "based on the patient's condition and the individual hospice's care-giving philosophy. No additional Medicare payment may be made regardless of the cost of the services.").

For each medication provided while the beneficiary is not an inpatient (general inpatient or respite care), the hospice program may charge the beneficiary a coinsurance payment.[109] This coinsurance cannot exceed $5.00.[110]

The hospice provider must ensure that the interdisciplinary group confers with an individual with education and training in drug management as defined in hospice policies and procedures and state law, who is an employee of or under contract with the hospice, to ensure that drugs and biologicals meet each patient's needs.[111]

The Medicare Prescription Drug,[112] Improvement, and Modernization Act of 2003[113] added prescription drug coverage as a Medicare benefit. If a hospice patient signed up for a Part D plan,[114] then whether the hospice, Medicare Part B, the beneficiary's Part D plan, or the beneficiary is responsible for paying for the hospice patient's medications will depend on the medication's purpose.

Palliative medications related to the hospice patient's terminal illness should be paid for by the beneficiary's hospice provider.[115] Curative medications related to the patient's terminal illness will not be paid for by the hospice provider, Medicare Part B, or the beneficiary's Medicare Part D plan.[116] Medications prescribed for the treatment of illness not related to the patient's terminal illness should be billed to Part B, when they are Part B medications (incident to a physician's visit);[117] when they are not Part B medications, they should be billed to the patient's Part D plan.[118] If the patient receives Medicare covered inpatient care for a condition not related to his or her terminal illness, then the medications that he or she receives in the inpatient facility that are not related to the terminal illness will be covered under the Medicare Part A benefit for hospital[119] or SNF care.[120] The medications that are related to the terminal illness should continue to be paid for by the hospice provider.

---

[109] 42 C.F.R. § 418.400.

[110] 42 C.F.R. § 418.400(a).

[111] 42 C.F.R. § 418.106.

[112] *See* **Chapter 11** of this Handbook.

[113] Medicare Prescription Drug, Improvement, and Modernization Act of 2003.

[114] *See* **§ 11.01** of this Handbook.

[115] *See* **§ 5.11[B]** of this Handbook.

[116] *See* **§ 5.01** of this Handbook.

[117] *See* **§ 6.03[A]** of this Handbook.

[118] *See* **§ 11.04** of this Handbook.

[119] *See* **§ 2.06[C]** of this Handbook.

[120] *See* **Chapter 3** of this Handbook. *See also* CMS, "SNF Consolidating Billing: Overview on Skilled Nursing Facility (SNF) Consolidated Billing (CB)," *available at* https://www.cms.gov/Medicare/Billing/SNFConsolidatedBilling/index.html?redirect=/SNFConsolidatedBilling/ (site visited Aug. 6, 2018).

In June 2012, the Health and Human Services Office of Inspector General (OIG) issued a report suggesting that Part D plans were frequently paying for hospice medications.[121] In 2014, CMS issued a memorandum directing Part D plans to seek prior authorization after a beneficiary elects hospice care, for analgesics, antiemetics, laxatives, and anxiolytics (used to treat anxiety), because these medications are usually related to an individual's terminal condition.[122]

[L] Short-Term General Inpatient Care

Short-term general inpatient care must be made available by the hospice provider for pain control and symptom management.[123] The care must be provided in a Medicare certified inpatient hospice facility, or hospital or skilled nursing facility.[124] While an individual is receiving general inpatient care for pain control or symptom management, each shift at the facility must include a registered nurse who provides direct patient care.[125] Hospices that provide inpatient care directly in their own facilities must provide rooms that have a home-like atmosphere and are designed to preserve the dignity, comfort, and privacy of hospice patients.[126]

On August 31, 2007, CMS issued the following policy "clarification":

> To receive payment for general inpatient care under the Medicare hospice benefit, beneficiaries *must* require an intensity of care directed towards pain control and symptom management that cannot be managed in any other settings. It is the level of care provided to meet the individual's needs and not the location of where the individual resides, or caregiver breakdown, that determines payment rates for Medicare services (*Emphasis in original*).[127]

When an individual's hospice care is billed to Medicare at a general inpatient level of care, the per diem rate pays for both the beneficiary's hospice care and the beneficiary's room and board.[128] On the other hand, if a hospice patient

---

[121] *See* Office of the Inspector General: Department of Health & Human Services, "Medicare Could Be Paying Twice for Prescription Drugs for Beneficiaries in Hospice" (June28, 2012), *available at* https://oig.hhs.gov/oas/reports/region6/61000059.asp (site visited Aug. 6, 2018).

[122] *See* CMS, Part D Payment for Drugs for Beneficiaries Enrolled in Medicare Hospice (July 18, 2014), *available at* http://www.cms.gov/Medicare/Medicare-Fee-for-Service-Payment/Hospice/Downloads/2014-PartD-Hospice-Guidance-Revised-Memo.pdf (site visited Aug. 6, 2018).

[123] 42 C.F.R. § 418.108.

[124] 42 C.F.R. § 418.108.

[125] 42 C.F.R. §§ 418.108 & 418.110(b).

[126] 42 C.F.R. § 418.110(e)-(f).

[127] CMS, Hospice Wage Index for Fiscal Year 2008, 72 Fed. Reg. 50,214, 50,220 (Aug. 31, 2007), *available at* https://www.federalregister.gov/documents/2007/08/31/07-4292/medicare-program-hospice-wage-index-for-fiscal-year-2008 (site visited on Aug. 6, 2018).

[128] 42 C.F.R. § 418.302.

receives general inpatient care for three or more days and then revokes the hospice benefit, then the three day stay in the inpatient facility (although not necessarily the same as a hospital level of care in terms of kind of care provided) qualifies the beneficiary for covered SNF services.[129] In other words, the three day general inpatient hospice stay is considered, for purposes of obtaining Medicare coverage of SNF care, to be the equivalent of a three day qualifying hospital stay.

When a beneficiary has been receiving Medicare covered general inpatient care and the hospice provider determines that continued general inpatient care is no longer medically reasonable and necessary, the provider must issue an Advance Beneficiary Notice (ABN) if the beneficiary or his or her authorized representative believe the beneficiary should continue to receive that level of care.[130] If the beneficiary or the beneficiary's authorized representative indicate on the ABN that the beneficiary would like the care billed to Medicare (demand bill), the hospice provider must bill Medicare for an appealable determination.[131]

[M] Inpatient Care for Respite Purposes

Inpatient care for respite purposes is provided to the hospice patient when necessary to relieve the beneficiary's caregiver(s).[132] Respite care may be provided only on an occasional basis and is limited to no more than five consecutive days at a time.[133] The respite care must be provided in a Medicare certified hospice, a Medicare certified hospital, a Medicare certified SNF, or a Medicare or Medicaid certified nursing facility (NF).[134] Rooms must be designed to ensure the dignity, comfort, and privacy of patients.[135] The facility providing respite care must provide 24-hour nursing services that meet the nursing needs of all patients and are furnished in accordance with each patient's plan of care. Each patient must receive all nursing services as prescribed and must be kept comfortable, clean, well-groomed, and protected from accident, injury, and infection.[136]

While the beneficiary is at a respite level of care, the hospice benefit pays for both the beneficiary's medical care and the beneficiary's room and board. There is a coinsurance amount that the hospice provider may require the patient to pay if respite services are received. The daily coinsurance amount for respite care can be no more than 5 percent of the payment made by CMS for a respite

[129] MBP Manual, Ch. 9: § 40.1.5. *See also* **§ 3.03[E]** of this Handbook regarding calculating benefit periods for skilled nursing facility (SNF) care.

[130] MCP Manual, Ch. 11: § 100.2.

[131] MCP Manual, Ch. 11: § 100.2.

[132] 42 C.F.R. § 418.204(b)(1). *See also* MBP Manual, Ch. 9: § 40.2.2.

[133] 42 C.F.R. § 418.204(b)(2).

[134] 42 C.F.R. §§ 418.108(b) & 418.110(e)-(f).

[135] 42 C.F.R. §§ 418.108(b)(2) & 418.110(f).

[136] 42 C.F.R. § 418.108(b)(2).

day. The actual amount will vary depending on the provider. However, in no event may the total amount of the coinsurance exceed the inpatient hospital deductible in effect in the year in which the hospice benefit was elected. In 2019, this amount is $1,364. The coinsurance is payable for each coinsurance period. A coinsurance period begins on the first day an election is effective and ends with the close of the first period of 14 consecutive days on each of which an election is not in effect for the beneficiary.[137] So, for example, if the patient elected 210 consecutive days of hospice coverage, the patient would be required to pay the respite coinsurance up to the maximum only once.

§ 5.12 HOSPICE INPATIENT FACILITY RULES

The conditions of participation are extensive for hospice providers that provide inpatient care directly in their own facilities.[138] The provider must provide a home like atmosphere and ensure that patient areas are designed to preserve the dignity, comfort, and privacy of patients.[139] There must be physical space for private patient and family visiting, accommodations for family members to remain with the patient throughout the night, and physical space for family privacy after a patient's death.[140] There must be opportunity for patients to receive visitors at any hour, including infants and small children.[141]

The patient rooms must be designed and equipped for nursing care, as well as the dignity, comfort, and privacy of patients.[142] The hospice provider must accommodate a patient and family request for a single room whenever possible.[143] Each patient's room must be at or above grade level; contain a suitable bed and other appropriate furniture for each patient; have closet space that provides security and privacy for clothing and personal belongings; accommodate no more than two patients and their family members; provide at least 80 square feet for each residing patient in a double room and at least 100 square feet for each patient residing in a single room; and be equipped with an easily activated, functioning device accessible to the patient that is used for calling for assistance.[144] A recent rule adds a condition of participation that hospices must comply with all

[137] 42 C.F.R. § 418.400(b).

[138] 42 C.F.R. § 418.110.

[139] 42 C.F.R. § 418.110(f).

[140] 42 C.F.R. § 418.110(f)(1).

[141] 42 C.F.R. § 418.110(f)(2).

[142] 42 C.F.R. § 418.110(g)(1).

[143] 42 C.F.R. § 418.110(g)(2).

[144] 42 C.F.R. § 418.110(g)(3). Waivers for some of these requirements are available for hospices operating prior to December 2, 2008. 42 C.F.R. § 418.110(g)(4).

applicable federal, state, and local emergency preparedness requirements, with additional requirements for hospice inpatient facilities.[145]

§ 5.13 HOSPICE CARE FOR RESIDENTS OF FACILITIES

Medicare beneficiaries who reside in SNF/NF or intermediate care facilities for persons with mental retardation (ICF/MR) can receive Medicare covered hospice care if the hospice provider and facility have a contract.[146] Under these circumstances, the hospice provider must assume professional management of the resident's hospice services in accordance with the hospice plan of care and the hospice conditions of participation.[147] The conditions of participation mandate that the contracts include very specific information.[148] They must include, but are not limited to:

- The manner in which the facility and the hospice are to communicate with each other and document such communications to ensure that the needs of the patient are addressed and met 24 hours a day;
- A provision stating that the hospice assumes responsibility for determining the appropriate course of hospice care, including the determination to change the level of services if needed;
- An agreement that it is the hospice's responsibility to provide services at the same level and to the same extent as those services would be provided if the resident were in his or her own home; and
- A provision that the hospice may use the facility staff where permitted by state law and as specified by the facility to assist in the administration of prescribed therapies included in the plan of care only to the extent that the hospice would routinely use the services of a hospice patient's family in implementing the plan of care.[149]

It is important to understand that when a Medicare beneficiary has elected hospice care, is at a routine level of care, and is residing in a nursing home, the Medicare hospice benefit will pay for the beneficiary's hospice care but **not** for the beneficiary's room and board.

---

[145] CMS, Hospice Care, 81 Fed. Reg. 64024 (Sept. 16, 2016), *available at* https://www.gpo.gov/fdsys/pkg/FR-2016-09-16/pdf/2016-21404.pdf#page=166 (site visited Aug. 6, 2018); 42 C.F.R. § 418.113.

[146] 42 C.F.R. § 418.112. *See also* MBP Manual, Ch. 9: § 20.3.

[147] 42 C.F.R. § 418.112(b).

[148] 42 C.F.R. § 418.112(c).

[149] 42 C.F.R. § 418.112(c).

Alternatively, it is possible for an individual to receive both Medicare covered SNF care and Medicare covered hospice care.[150] For this to occur, the Medicare SNF care must be for a condition unrelated to the terminal condition. For instance, if a Medicare beneficiary who has elected hospice falls and breaks a hip, has a three day qualifying hospital stay,[151] and then is transferred to a SNF, so long as the broken hip is not related to the beneficiary's underlying terminal illness, then the beneficiary may continue to receive Medicare covered hospice care for the terminal illness while also receiving Medicare covered SNF care for the broken hip. This is significant because Medicare covered SNF inpatient care includes payment for room and board.

§ 5.14 DEDUCTIBLES AND COINSURANCE FOR NONHOSPICE CARE

The hospice patient is liable for coinsurance amounts only for drugs and biologicals and respite care (*see* **§ 5.11[K]** and **§ 5.11[M]**). No other services *provided by the hospice* for the palliation and management of the patient's terminal illness may be billed to the patient.

If, while on hospice, the patient receives medical care for conditions not related to his or her terminal condition, then he or she will be liable for the standard Medicare deductibles and coinsurance payments related to that care. Also, if he or she receives care from his or her attending physician, the beneficiary will be financially responsible for any Part B cost-sharing associated with the care.[152]

§ 5.15 HOSPICE DENIALS AND APPEALS

Hospice patients are afforded the same appeal rights as those granted to other recipients of medical care under Part A of Medicare.[153]

[A] Coding Problems

Sometimes Medicare beneficiaries who elected the hospice benefit inappropriately receive coverage denials for care they received that was not related to the terminal illness. For instance, a hospice patient may have outpatient physical therapy for chronic back pain not related to the terminal illness. She might receive a denial for the physical therapy because the billing department at the therapist's office failed to code the bill correctly. Generally this problem can be solved by asking the billing department to re-bill Medicare using the code (GW Modifier) indicating that the individual is a hospice patient but that the provided care was

---

150 42 C.F.R. § 418.112(c).

151 42 U.S.C. § 1395x(i). *See also* **§ 3.03** of this Handbook.

152 42 C.F.R. § 418.402.

153 *See* **§ 1.07** of this Handbook.

not related to the terminal illness. In the event that the provider's billing office is not cooperative or if Medicare continues to deny the claim despite the fact that the provider has billed correctly, these claims should be appealed. As was discussed above, upon electing hospice, one does not waive all rights to Medicare coverage, only some of those rights related to the terminal illness.[154]

[B] Billing Errors

Another source of inappropriate denials also occurs through billing error. Hospice providers frequently have contractual relationships with other entities for the provision of care related to the terminal illness.[155] For instance, a provider may have a contractual relationship with a DME provider for the provision of items such as wheelchairs and hospital beds. These contracts specify that the providers of services and goods are to bill the hospice provider for the rendered services and goods. In other words, they are not to bill Medicare and they are not to bill the beneficiary. However, sometimes, through billing error, the contracted provider will bill Medicare rather than the hospice provider. This will result in a Medicare denial. Should this occur, contact the hospice provider. If the provider is unwilling or unable to remedy the problem, then the denial should be appealed.

Beneficiaries must remember that upon electing hospice, they waive their rights to Medicare coverage for treatment of the terminal illness that is not provided by their attending physician, the hospice, or under arrangement with the hospice.[156] Should beneficiaries seek out care for their terminal illness from other providers, their care will not be covered by Medicare.

[C] Terminal Status

Because Medicare coverage of hospice care hinges almost exclusively on whether the beneficiary has a life expectancy of six months or less,[157] denials of hospice coverage are most likely made based on a finding that the beneficiary's life expectancy was not six months or less. In pursuing a hospice appeal, the advocate should attempt to obtain an explicit and detailed letter from the patient's attending physician, listing specific clinical findings supporting the beneficiary's limited life expectancy. Moreover, the advocate should ask the physician to provide clinical documentation (medical records) that supports his or her clinical findings. This letter and documentation often can be the pivotal factors in achieving a successful result. In addition, the advocate should closely examine the medical record for notations indicating that the beneficiary was terminally ill with a

[154] *See* § **5.01** of this Handbook.
[155] MBP Manual, Ch. 9: § 40.4.
[156] *See* § **5.01** of this Handbook.
[157] *See* § **5.02** of this Handbook.

limited life expectancy. Doctors' orders, nurses' notes, and the written care plan[158] established for the patient will often be useful sources of evidence to support a claim for Medicare coverage. Any notes of the hospice's interdisciplinary group regarding the patient's care will also prove helpful.[159]

Advocates should be especially wary of hospice discharges when the beneficiary's health status has not changed and the only apparent reason for the discharge is that the beneficiary has lived "too long."[160] These discharges may be motivated by the "hospice cap." Since its inception, the Medicare regulations have included a cap limiting the average annual payment per patient a hospice can receive.[161] When the cap was first implemented, due to the structure of the election periods, few beneficiaries received more than six months of Medicare-covered hospice care. However, in 1998, the regulations were changed to increase access to hospice care. Beneficiaries became eligible for an unlimited number of 60-day certification periods so long as they have a life expectancy of 6 months or less if the terminal illness runs its course.

Since the change in the benefit structure, many hospices have exceeded the hospice cap. Consequently, they were asked to pay significant sums of money back to Medicare. As a result, to avoid this sanction in the future, hospices may inappropriately discharge patients who live beyond six months. Should this occur, the beneficiary's right to appeal should be exercised immediately.

Another problem could arise if a hospice provider fails to timely obtain the required face-to-face documentation. Affected Medicare beneficiaries would become ineligible for Medicare payment for their continued hospice care.[162]

---

[158] 42 C.F.R. § 418.56 ("The hospice must designate an interdisciplinary group . . . which, in consultation with the patient's attending physician, must prepare a written plan of care for each patient. The plan of care must specify the hospice care and services necessary to meet the patient and family-specific needs identified in the comprehensive assessment as such needs relate to the terminal illness and related conditions.").

[159] 42 C.F.R. § 418.56(a) ("The hospice must designate an interdisciplinary group or groups composed of individuals who work together to meet the physical, medical, psychosocial, emotional, and spiritual needs of the hospice patients and families facing terminal illness and bereavement. Interdisciplinary group members must provide the care and services offered by the hospice, and the group, in its entirety, must supervise the care and services.")

[160] MBP Manual, Ch. 9: § 20.2.3 reads as follows:

> Once a hospice chooses to admit a Medicare beneficiary, it may not automatically or routinely discharge the beneficiary at its discretion, even if the care promises to be costly or inconvenient, or the State allows for discharge under State requirements. The election of the hospice benefit is the beneficiary's choice rather than the hospice's choice, and the hospice cannot revoke the beneficiary's election. Neither should the hospice request or demand that the patient revoke his/her election.

[161] 42 C.F.R. § 418.309.

[162] MBP Manual, Ch. 9: § 20.1 reads as follows:

> For recertifications on or after January 1, 2011, a hospice physician or hospice nurse practitioner must have a face-to-face encounter with each hospice patient prior to the beginning of the patient's third benefit period, and prior to each subsequent benefit

However, this should not permit hospices to shift financial liability for this care to the beneficiaries. Pursuant to the regulations, the provider should be financially responsible for any uncovered care.[163] If hospice beneficiaries are held financially responsible for this care, they should certainly appeal.

[D] Expedited Appeals

In the event that the hospice provider intends to discharge a beneficiary because the medical director no longer believes he or she is terminally ill, it must first give the beneficiary a standardized termination notice.[164] The standardized termination notices are designed to inform beneficiaries that they are being discharged from hospice care and that they have a right to an expedited appeal.[165] A beneficiary who wishes to exercise the right to an expedited appeal must call the Beneficiary and Family Center Care Quality Improvement Organization (BFCC-QIO) (number supplied on the notice) by no later than noon of the calendar day following receipt of the provider's notice of termination.[166] No later than 72 hours after receipt of the request for an expedited review, the BFCC-QIO must notify the beneficiary, beneficiary's physician, and the hospice program of its determination.[167]

[E] Waiver of Liability

Section 1879 of the Social Security Act provides protections from liability for charges for claims denied by Medicare for services provided to beneficiaries who were not aware that the services would not be covered by Medicare. On August 5, 1997, the limitation of liability was extended to Medicare hospice coverage via Section 1879(g) of the Act.[168]

> period. Failure to meet the face-to-face encounter requirements . . . results in a failure by the hospice to meet the patient's recertification of terminal illness eligibility requirement. The patient would cease to be eligible for the benefit.

[163] 42 C.F.R. § 489.21 (stating that if a beneficiary "would be entitled to have payment made if the provider [h]ad in its files the required certification and recertification by a physician related to the services furnished to the beneficiary," the provider "agrees not to charge [the] beneficiary."). *See also* MCP Manual, Ch. 30: § 50.15.3.1 ("The ABN must not be issued when the face to face requirement is not met within the required time frame. Failure to meet the face to face requirement should not be misrepresented as a determination that the beneficiary is no longer terminally ill.").

[164] 42 C.F.R. § 411.404.

[165] 42 C.F.R. § 411.404. *See also* **§ 1.07** of this Handbook for a full discussion of expedited appeals.

[166] 42 C.F.R. § 405.1202(b).

[167] 42 C.F.R. § 405.1202(e)(6).

[168] 42 U.S.C. § 1395pp(g); *see also* MBP Manual, Ch. 9: § 50.

[F] Standard Appeals

Not only do Medicare beneficiaries have a right to an expedited appeal, but they also have a right to a standard appeal. To exercise the right to a standard appeal, the beneficiary must ask the hospice provider to bill Medicare for rendered hospice care (demand bill). Once the hospice receives the request, it should submit the claim to the Medicare contractor for an initial determination.[169] The Medicare contractor, upon receiving the claim, will review the medical evidence and issue an initial determination indicating whether the hospice care is covered by Medicare.[170] After this determination, a notice of initial determination will be sent to the beneficiary's last known address.[171] The notice must be written in a manner calculated to be understood by the beneficiary.[172] It must contain:[173]

- The reasons for the determination, including whether a local medical review policy, a local coverage determination, or a national coverage determination was applied;
- Procedures for obtaining additional information concerning the contractor's determination, such as a specific provision of a policy, manual, law, or regulation used in making the determination;
- Information on the right to a redetermination if the beneficiary is dissatisfied with the outcome of the initial determination and instructions on how to request a redetermination; and
- Any other requirements specified by CMS.

If the beneficiary receives a full denial, a partial denial, or a denial, but his or her liability is waived, the patient may wish to appeal.[174]

§ 5.16 ADVANCE CARE PLANNING

In November 2015, CMS issued final rules that addressed payment for advance care planning (ACP) provided to Medicare beneficiaries by physicians and other health care professionals.[175] The ACP billing codes went into effect for services to the Physician Fee Schedule (PFS) under CPT codes 99497 and 99498

---

[169] MCP Manual, Ch. 11: § 30.3.

[170] 42 C.F.R. § 405.921.

[171] 42 C.F.R. § 405.921(a)(1).

[172] 42 C.F.R. § 405.921(a)(1).

[173] 42 C.F.R. § 405.921(a)(2).

[174] *See* **§ 1.07[A]** of this Handbook for a description of the appeal process.

[175] CMS, Revisions to Payment Policies Under the Physician Fee Schedule and Other Revisions to Part B for CY 2016, 80 Fed. Reg. 70,885 (Nov. 16, 2015), *available at* https://www.federalregister.gov/articles/2015/11/16/2015-28005/medicare-program-revisions-to-payment-policies-under-

beginning January 1, 2016. These included explanation and discussion of advance directives and standard forms. Completion of an advance directive is not a requirement for billing the service.[176]

Through these codes, providers can now bill for discussions about long-term treatment options and planning, including advance care directives that outline considerations like patient preference in the event that the patient has a health event that adversely affects decision-making capacity.[177]

There are no place of service limitations on the ACP codes; ACP services may be appropriately furnished in a variety of settings depending on the needs and condition of the beneficiary. The codes are separately payable to the billing physician or practitioner in both facility and non-facility settings, and are not limited to particular physician specialties.[178]

The conversations are voluntary, and can be an optional element of the Annual Wellness Visit (AWV); ACP services furnished on the same day and by the same provider as an AWV are considered a preventive service. Therefore, the deductible and coinsurance are not applied to the codes used to report ACP services when performed as part of an AWV.[179]

---

the-physician-fee-schedule-and-other-revisions?utm_campaign=pi+subscription+mailing+list&utm_medium=email&utm_source=federalregister.gov (site visited Aug. 6, 2018).

[176] CMS, "Frequently Asked Questions about Billing the Physician Fee Schedule for Advance Care Planning Services," *available at* https://www.cms.gov/Medicare/Medicare-Fee-for-Service-Payment/PhysicianFeeSched/Downloads/FAQ-Advance-Care-Planning.pdf (site visited Aug. 6, 2018).

[177] *See* 80 Fed. Reg. 70,885.

[178] *See* CMS, "Frequently Asked Questions about Billing the Physician Fee Schedule for Advance Care Planning Services," *available at* https://www.cms.gov/Medicare/Medicare-Fee-for-Service-Payment/PhysicianFeeSched/Downloads/FAQ-Advance-Care-Planning.pdf (site visited Aug. 6, 2018).

[179] CMS, MLN Matter Number MM9271, "Advance Care Planning (ACP) as an Optional Element of an Annual Wellness Visit (AWV)," *available at* https://www.cms.gov/Outreach-and-Education/Medicare-Learning-Network-MLN/MLNMattersArticles/downloads/MM9271.pdf (site visited Aug. 6, 2018).

CHAPTER 6

MEDICARE PART B: SUPPLEMENTARY MEDICAL INSURANCE BENEFITS FOR THE AGED AND DISABLED

§ 6.03 Covered Medical and Other Health Care Services
- [A] Covered Services
  - [1] Medically Reasonable and Necessary Medical and Other Health Services
  - [2] Annual Wellness Visit Added by the Patient Protection and Affordable Care Act
  - [3] Elimination of Cost-Sharing for Preventive Services
  - [4] Implications for Medicare Advantage Plans
  - [5] Medicare Caps for Physical Therapy/Speech Pathology Services and Occupational Therapy
    - [a] Repeal of Medicare Outpatient Therapy Caps
    - [b] Historical Context
- [B] Excluded Services
- [C] Waiver of Liability Payment for Certain Excluded Items and Services
- [D] Special Coverage Areas
  - [1] Ambulance Service
  - [2] Durable Medical Equipment
    - [a] General
    - [b] Competitive Acquisition of Certain Durable Medical Equipment, Prosthetics, Orthotics, and Supplies
      - [i] Competitive Bidding Areas
      - [ii] Terms to Remember
      - [iii] Competitive Bidding Implementation Contractor
      - [iv] Product Categories
      - [v] Grandfathering Certain Contractors
      - [vi] Repair and Replacement of Beneficiary-Owned Items
      - [vii] Mail Order Diabetic Supplies Under the Program
      - [viii] Competitive Bidding and Advance Beneficiary Notice Information
      - [ix] No Administrative or Judicial Review of Process
    - [c] Medicare Coverage of Power Mobility Devices
    - [d] Medicare Payment for and Maintenance of Oxygen Equipment
      - [i] CMS's Consumer Alert on Oxygen Equipment and Supplies
      - [ii] Payment Rules for Oxygen and Supplies
      - [iii] No Separate Payment for Maintenance and Repairs

§ 6.01 INTRODUCTION TO MEDICARE PART B

[A] Medicare Part B Services

Part B of the Medicare program, Supplementary Medical Insurance (SMI) Benefits for the Aged and Disabled,[1] provides coverage for a host of services for beneficiaries, including:

- Physician services;
- Services and supplies incident to a physician's professional services, including drugs and biologicals that cannot be self-administered, including chemotherapy;
- Outpatient hospital services;
- Physical and occupational therapy services;
- Speech language pathology services;
- X-ray, laboratory, and other diagnostic tests;
- Some preventive services;
- Surgical dressings and devices for reduction of fractures;
- Durable medical equipment (DME); and
- Prosthetic devices, orthotics, and supplies.

Definitions of Medicare-covered services, along with critical Medicare terms, are found at 42 U.S.C. § 1395x.[2]

---

[1] 42 U.S.C. §§ 1395k, x.

[2] 42 U.S.C. § 1395k (scope of benefits), *available at* http://www.gpo.gov/fdsys/pkg/USCODE-2010-title42/pdf/USCODE-2010-title42-chap7-subchapXVIII-partB.pdf (site visited Aug. 6, 2018), and § 1395x (definitions), *available at* http://www.gpo.gov/fdsys/pkg/USCODE-2010-title42/pdf/USCODE-2010-title42-chap7-subchapXVIII-partE-sec1395x.pdf (site visited Aug. 6, 2018). Definitions include § 1395x(a) (spell of illness), § 1395x(b) (inpatient hospital services), § 1395x(c) (inpatient psychiatric hospital services), § 1395x(e) (definition of hospital), § 1395x(f) (psychiatric hospital), § 1395x(g) (outpatient occupational therapy services), § 1395x(h) (extended care services), § 1395x(i) (post hospital extended care services), § 1395x(j) (skilled nursing facility), § 1395x(m) (home health services), § 1395x(o) (home health agency), § 1395x(p) (outpatient physical therapy services), § 1395x(q) (physician services), § 1395x(r) (physician), and § 1395x(s) (medical and other services, including durable medical equipment (DME), prosthetic devices, and ambulance services). *See* Centers for Medicare & Medicaid Services (CMS), "2018 Medicare & You," *available at* https://www.medicare.gov/pubs/pdf/10050-Medicare-and-You.pdf (site visited June 27, 2018); *see also* CMS, "What Medicare Covers," *available at* https://www.medicare.gov/what-medicare-covers/index.html (site visited Aug. 6, 2018).

[B] Administration of Medicare Part B

Part B is financed by premiums paid by individuals enrolled in the program and by general revenues from the federal government. Since 1993, individuals receiving Social Security retirement benefits, individuals receiving Social Security disability benefits for 24 months, and individuals otherwise entitled to Medicare Part A are automatically enrolled in Part B unless they decline coverage.[3] Persons with amyotrophic lateral sclerosis (ALS) are entitled to Part A the first month that they are entitled to Social Security disability cash benefits.[4] There are also special eligibility rules for persons with end-stage renal disease (ESRD).[5]

Section 911 of the Medicare Prescription Drug, Improvement, and Modernization Act of 2003 (MMA), as part of the government's regulatory reform initiative, created a new Section 1874A of the Social Security Act that modifies and consolidates the administration of the Medicare program.[6] In particular, the Secretary of Health and Human Services (HHS) now has the authority to contract with an eligible entity known as a Medicare Administrative Contractor (MAC). These entities perform certain functions previously performed by insurance companies and other entities known as carriers (Part B) and intermediaries (Part A). Functions include determining payment amounts, local medical coverage decisions, beneficiary education, technical assistance, and other functions.[7]

The MMA also created the office of the Medicare Beneficiary Ombudsman, located in HHS. The Ombudsman is to assist beneficiaries with appeals and related matters in fee-for-service and Medicare Advantage (MA)—formerly called Medicare+Choice—settings.[8]

---

[3] 42 U.S.C. § 1395o; *see also* 42 C.F.R. § 407.10(a)(1).

[4] *See* CMS, "Original Medicare (Part A and B) Eligibility and Enrollment," *available at* http://www.cms.gov/Medicare/Eligibility-and-Enrollment/OrigMedicarePartABEligEnrol/ (site visited Aug. 6, 2018).

[5] CMS, "Original Medicare (Part A and B) Eligibility and Enrollment."

[6] *See* 42 U.S.C. § 1395kk-1 (contracts with Medicare Administrative Contractors, or MACs).

[7] Sections 911 & 912 of the Medicare Prescription Drug, Improvement, and Modernization Act of 2003 (MMA), Pub. L. No. 108-173 (Dec. 8, 2003), and conforming modifications to 42 U.S.C. § 1395h and u removing references to fiscal intermediaries and carriers. CMS has consolidated the functions of intermediaries and carriers into the new MACs. *See* CMS, "Medicare Administrative Contractors" (July 2013), *available at* http://www.cms.gov/Medicare/Medicare-Contracting/Medicare-Administrative-Contractors/MedicareAdministrativeContractors.html (site visited Aug. 6, 2018).

[8] Provision is effective one year from date of enactment of MMA. *See* Section 923 of MMA (amending § 1808 of the Social Security Act). *See* CMS, "Ombudsman Center," *available at* http://www.cms.hhs.gov/center/ombudsman.asp (site visited Aug. 6, 2018). There is also an ombudsman for the competitive acquisition of durable medical equipment. *See* CMS, "Filing a Complaint About Durable Medical Equipment," *available at* http://www.medicare.gov/claims-and-appeals/file-a-complaint/durable-medical-equipment/complaints-about-dme.html (site visited Aug. 6, 2018).

§ 6.02 MEDICARE PART B ENROLLMENT AND PAYMENT REQUIREMENTS

[A] Eligibility

Medicare Part B, the SMI program, is a voluntary program for eligible enrollees who enroll and pay a monthly premium.[9] An eligible enrollee is a person who is either entitled to Part A[10] or age 65 or older who is a citizen or who

---

[9] *See* 42 U.S.C. § 1395j–w. The Part B monthly premium in 2019 is $135.50 for an individual whose modified adjusted gross income (MAGI) is less than $85,000. *See* 2019 is 135.50 CMS, Medicare Part B

Monthly Actuarial Rates, Premium Rate, and Annual Deductible Beginning January 1, 2016, 80 Fed. Reg. 70,811-820 (Nov. 16, 2015), *available at* https://www.gpo.gov/fdsys/pkg/FR-2015-11-16/pdf/2015-29181.pdf (site visited Aug. 6, 2018). See **Appendix 1-3** for the premium for individuals not "held harmless." Premiums for a subsequent year are usually announced in the *Federal Register* prior to November of the preceding year. In subsequent years, it will be increased by the same percentage as the Part B premium (monthly actuarial value of benefits payable under Part B), rounded up to the nearest dollar. *See* MMA § 629 (amending § 1833(b) of the Social Security Act, 42 U.S.C. § 1395l(b)). *See* § **6.02[C][2]** of this Handbook for discussion of the Part B Income-Related Premium. *See* 77 Fed. Reg. 69,850 (Nov. 21, 2012). The program was set to expire in 2002 but has been continually extended.

[10] 42 U.S.C. § 1395o; 42 C.F.R. § 407.10(a)(1). *See* the June 26, 2015, favorable Supreme Court ruling in Obergefell v. Hodges, Dir., Ohio Dep't of Health, Nos. 14-556, 14-562, 14-571 and 14-574, 576 U.S. ____ (2015), *available at* http://www.supremecourt.gov/opinions/14pdf/14-556_3204.pdf (site visited Aug. 6, 2018). In *Obergefell,* the Court found that the failure to grant same-sex couples a marriage license is a violation of equal protection under the United States Constitution. Advocates should pay close attention to implementation issues as they arise.

For background on the tortuous history of the recognition of same-sex marriages at the federal level and access to benefits, see United States v. Windsor, *available at* http://www.supremecourt.gov/opinions/12pdf/12-307_6j37.pdf (site visited Aug. 6, 2018). *Windsor* holds Section 3 of the Defense of Marriage Act (DOMA) unconstitutional because DOMA limits a valid marriage as only between a man and a woman. With respect to *Windsor*, persons in state-recognized same-sex marriages should consider filing for spousal benefits as appropriate.

Same-sex spouses of Medicare beneficiaries who are in valid marriages may be eligible for benefits as a spouse and should apply for benefits as appropriate. *See* Center for Medicare Advocacy (CMA), "Demise of DOMA: Implementing Federal Benefits for Same-Sex Spouses," *available at* http://www.medicareadvocacy.org/demise-of-doma-implementing-federal-benefits-for-same-sex-spouses/ (site visited Aug. 6, 2018); *see also* Attorney General Holder's Memorandum to the President, "Implementation of *United States v. Windsor*" (June 20, 2014), *available at* http://www.justice.gov/iso/opa/resources/9722014620103930904785.pdf (site visited Aug. 6, 2018). The Holder Memorandum summarizes various agencies' practices with respect to following the law of celebration or the law of domicile in determining a valid same-sex marriage.

On August 23, 2013, the Social Security Administration (SSA) added two Program Operation Manual Systems (POMS) provisions: GN 00210.005, "Processing Cases Involving Same-Sex Marriages and Non-Marital Legal Relationships that were Previously on Hold," (updated Jan. 24, 2017) *available at* https://secure.ssa.gov/apps10/poms.nsf/lnx/0200210005 (site visited Aug. 6, 2018), & GN 00210.010, "Interviewing and Handling Inquiries for Individuals with Claims Involving Same-Sex Relationships," (updated June 20, 2014) *available at* https://secure.ssa.gov/apps10/poms.nsf/lnx/0200210010 (site visited Aug. 6, 2018). *See also* Section 1557 of the Affordable Care Act

has been a lawful permanent resident for five years preceding the month of application.[11] Persons not entitled to Part A benefits may request enrollment in Part B.[12] Persons convicted of crimes against national security (subversive activity) may not enroll.[13]

An individual must enroll for SMI or must be enrolled by a state under a buy-in agreement.[14] The SMI program pays only for covered expenses incurred during an individual's period of entitlement.[15]

Persons younger than 65 may enroll in Medicare if they have been found disabled under Title II of the Social Security Act and are entitled to social security or railroad retirement disability benefits.[16] However, such persons must satisfy a 24-month waiting period (benefits begin in the 25th month after they have been entitled to Social Security cash disability benefits). An individual is entitled or deemed entitled to social security disability benefits as an insured individual, child, widow, or widower who is "under a disability" or is a disabled qualified beneficiary certified under Section 7(d) of the Railroad Retirement Act.[17]

Disabled persons[18]

> Disabled persons who are not insured for monthly social security disability benefits, but would be insured for such benefits if their QCs [quarters of coverage] from government employment were social security QCs, are

---

(ACA) which prohibits discrimination on the basis of race, color, national origin, sex, age, or disability in certain health programs and activities. For a summary of the final rule, *see* Dep't of Health & Human Servs. (HHS), Summary: Final Rule Implementing Section 1557 of the Affordable Care Act, *available at* http://www.hhs.gov/sites/default/files/2016-06-07-section-1557-final-rule-summary-508.pdf (site visited Aug. 6, 2018). *See also* HHS, Nondiscrimination in Health Programs and Activities, 81 Fed. Reg. 31,375 (May 18, 2016), *available at* https://www.federalregister.gov/articles/2016/05/18/2016-11458/nondiscrimination-in-health-programs-and-activities?utm_campaign=subscription+mailing+list&utm_medium=email&utm_source=federalregister.gov (site visited Aug. 6, 2018); *see also* Health Affairs, "LGBT Protections In Affordable Care Act Section 1557," *available at* http://healthaffairs.org/blog/2016/06/06/lgbt-protections-in-affordable-care-act-section-1557/ (site visited Aug. 6, 2018).

[11] 42 U.S.C. § 1395i-2; 42 C.F.R. § 407.10(a)(2)(i)–(iii).

[12] 42 C.F.R. § 407.22(a)(1).

[13] 42 C.F.R. § 407.10(b).

[14] 42 C.F.R. §§ 407.4(a)(2) and 407.40.

[15] 42 C.F.R. § 407.4(b). *See also* CMS, Medicare General Information, Eligibility, and Entitlement (MGIEE), Chapter 1, *available at* http://www.cms.gov/Regulations-and-Guidance/Guidance/Manuals/Downloads/ge101c01.pdf (site visited Aug. 6, 2018) & Chapter 2, *available at* https://www.cms.gov/Regulations-and-Guidance/Guidance/Manuals/downloads/ge101c02.pdf (site visited Aug. 6, 2018).

[16] 42 C.F.R. § 406.12.

[17] 42 C.F.R. § 406.12.

[18] *See* CMS, "Original Medicare (Part A and B) Eligibility and Enrollment." *See also* CMS, Medicare Coverage of Kidney Dialysis and Kidney Transplant Services (revised July 2017), *available at* https://www.medicare.gov/Pubs/pdf/10128-Medicare-Coverage-ESRD.pdf (site visited Aug. 6, 2018).

deemed to be entitled to disability benefits and automatically entitled to Part A after being disabled for 29 months.

Part A entitlement on the basis of disability is available, not only to the worker, but also to the widow, widower, or child of a deceased, disabled, or retired worker if any of them become disabled within the meaning of the Social Security or Railroad Retirement Acts. Beginning July 1, 2001, individuals whose disability is Amyotrophic Lateral Sclerosis (ALS) are entitled to Part A the first month they are entitled to Social Security disability cash benefits.

End-stage renal disease (ESRD)[19]

Individuals are eligible for Part A if they receive regular dialysis treatments or a kidney transplant, have filed an application, and meet one of the following conditions:

- have worked the required amount of time under Social Security, the Railroad Retirement Board, or as a government employee; or
- are getting or are eligible for Social Security or Railroad Retirement benefits; or
- are the spouse or dependent child of a person who has worked the required amount of time under Social Security, the Railroad Retirement Board, or as a government employee; or
- are getting Social Security or Railroad Retirement benefits.

Part A ESRD coverage begins:[20]

- the 3rd month after the month in which a regular course of dialysis begins; or
- the first month in which a regular course of dialysis begins if the individual engages in self-dialysis training; or
- the month of kidney transplant; or
- two (2) months prior to the month of transplant if the individual was hospitalized during those earlier months in preparation for the transplant.

[B] Medicare Part B Enrollment

[1] Enrollment Periods

Persons enrolled in Part A are presumed to want Part B. An individual can, however, opt out of Part B before coverage begins or within a specified period (not less than two months) beginning after notice that Part B coverage has started.[21]

---

[19] *See* CMS, "Original Medicare (Part A and B) Eligibility and Enrollment."

[20] CMS, "Original Medicare (Part A and B) Eligibility and Enrollment." *See also* CMS, Medicare Coverage of Kidney Dialysis and Kidney Transplant Services (revised July 2017).

[21] 42 C.F.R. § 407.17(b).

Enrollment in Part B, and Medicare generally, is automatic for most persons who qualify for Medicare Part A. For others, it is usually handled through the local office of the Social Security Administration (SSA). An application for benefits can be submitted by mail, in person, or online at socialsecurity.org. If one wishes to decline Part B, a signed statement to that effect should be sent to the local SSA office.[22]

Most beneficiaries enroll during their initial enrollment period, which includes the seven-month period beginning on the first day of the third month before the month when all eligibility requirements are met and extends for seven months from that date.[23] Generally, early application is recommended so as to avoid gaps in coverage.[24] For example, if an individual enrolls in the first three months of the initial enrollment period, entitlement begins with the first month of eligibility.[25] If the individual enrolls during the fourth month of the initial enrollment period, entitlement begins with the following month.[26] If the individual enrolls in the fifth month of the initial enrollment period, entitlement begins the second month after the month of enrollment.[27] If the individual waits until the last two months of the initial enrollment period to enroll, entitlement begins the third month after the month of enrollment.[28]

Beneficiaries age 65 or older who continue to be covered by an employer group health plan that covers any number of employees (except plans that cover only self-employed individuals and no employees) through their own active employment or the active employment of their spouse[29] may delay their enrollment in Medicare Part B without incurring a penalty.[30] Such beneficiaries will be entitled to a "special enrollment period" (SEP) when the earlier of two things

---

[22] 42 C.F.R. § 407.17(b).

[23] 42 U.S.C. § 1395p(d); 42 C.F.R. § 407.14(a)(1). Under the Medicare Advantage (MA) program, enrollees must make an election whether to participate in an MA managed care option. *See* 42 C.F.R. §§ 422.62 *et seq.*

[24] *See* 42 U.S.C. § 1395q; 42 C.F.R. § 407.25.

[25] 42 C.F.R. § 407.25(a)(1).

[26] 42 C.F.R. § 407.25(a)(2).

[27] 42 C.F.R. § 407.25(a)(3).

[28] 42 C.F.R. § 407.25(a)(4).

[29] 42 U.S.C. § 1395p(i). Individuals entitled to Medicare on the basis of disability (except end-stage renal disease) may also qualify for a special enrollment period (SEP) if they are covered by a large group health plan (100 employees) through their own employment or the employment of a family member. 42 C.F.R. § 407.20(d)(2). *See also* CMS, "Special Circumstances (Special Enrollment Periods)," *available at* http://www.medicare.gov/sign-up-change-plans/when-can-i-join-a-health-or-drug-plan/special-circumstances/join-plan-special-circumstances.html (site visited Aug. 6, 2018).

[30] Beneficiaries age 65 or older who are covered through active employment by an Employer Group Health Plan (EGHP) that covers fewer than 20 employees may need to enroll in Part B in spite of Medicare's SEP provisions, however, because the EGHP is a secondary payer. Under these circumstances, beneficiaries are advised to check with the EGHP's administrator to determine whether enrollment in Medicare Part B is required.

occurs: the employment through which they have the insurance ends or the insurance terminates. The special enrollment period runs for a period of eight months.[31] Advocates should explore the consequences of delaying enrollment in Part B at age 65 and obtaining access to Medigap insurance and its pre-existing condition exclusions and limitations.[32]

Persons enrolling late, because they missed their initial enrollment period and were not eligible for a special enrollment period, must wait for a general enrollment period to apply.[33] There is a general enrollment period each year from January 1st through March 31st.[34] There may be penalties attached to enrollment during a general enrollment period, however, as explained in detail below.

[2] Penalty for Late Enrollment

As a general matter, persons eligible for Part B should consider filing an application for benefits at the earliest possible time.[35] There is a ten percent penalty added to the premium for each full year of late enrollment.[36] The penalty has no durational limit.[37] There is no increase in premium if the late enrollment gap is less than 12 months.[38] Late enrollment is allowed only during the first three months of each calendar year (coverage becomes effective July 1 of that calendar year).[39]

---

[31] 42 U.S.C. § 1395p(i); 42 C.F.R. § 406.24(b)(2). *See generally* 42 C.F.R. § 406.24 for a discussion of SEPs; *see also* CMS, "Getting Health Coverage Outside Open Enrollment," *available at* https://www.healthcare.gov/coverage-outside-open-enrollment/special-enrollment-period/ (site visited Aug. 6, 2018).

[32] *See* **Chapter 8** (Medigap Services) & **Chapter 9** (Medicare's Relationship with Private Insurance) of this Handbook.

[33] 42 C.F.R. §§ 406.24 & 407.25.

[34] 42 U.S.C. § 1395p(e).

[35] Advocates should advise their low-income clients of Medicaid provisions that require states to pay the premiums for Medicare beneficiaries with incomes at or below the federal poverty level and resources at or below twice the Supplemental Security Income (SSI) limit. *See* 42 U.S.C. §§ 1396a and 1396d(p) of the Medicaid statute, *available at* https://www.gpo.gov/fdsys/pkg/USCODE-2010-title42/pdf/USCODE-2010-title42-chap7-subchapXIX.pdf (site visited Aug. 6, 2018). Medicaid buy-in for low-income Medicare beneficiaries and other Medicare Savings Programs (MSPs) are discussed in **Chapter 10** of this Handbook. In addition, **Chapter 11** discusses access to the low-income subsidy (LIS) for assistance in paying for prescription drugs under the Medicare Part D program.

[36] 42 U.S.C. § 1395(r); 42 C.F.R. § 408.22. The standard monthly premium is determined under 42 C.F.R. § 408.20.

[37] *See* §§ 408.24 and 408.25. For disabled beneficiaries under age 65, the penalty will end when they turn 65.

[38] 42 C.F.R. § 408.22. The 10 percent penalty is implemented for full 12-month periods of late enrollment.

[39] 42 C.F.R. §§ 407.15(a) and 407.25.

There is no late enrollment penalty if the delay is the result of error, fault, or delay by a federal government official or agent of the government.[40] The enrollee must establish that he or she with good cause relied on erroneous information provided by such an official, for example, an SSA or Medicare official.[41]

[C] Medicare Part B Premiums

[1] Standard Monthly Premium

Persons enrolled in Medicare Part B are required to pay a monthly premium, the amount of which is established annually by HHS.[42] Payments are either deducted from government benefits or by direct payment or remittance as provided in the law.[43]

Premiums are deducted from Social Security, Railroad Retirement, or federal civil service retirement benefits.[44] Part B premiums submitted by direct payment are generally billed quarterly but can be billed monthly where the beneficiary is unwilling or unable to pay quarterly.[45]

If the beneficiary receives only a civil service annuity and has a spouse who is eligible for Medicare SMI, the beneficiary may authorize the deduction of the spouse's premium from the beneficiary's check.[46]

If benefits are suspended for excess earnings and are to be resumed before the close of the taxable year, the individual is not billed for Part B premiums but can continue to pay such premiums to keep his or her coverage.[47] If payment of

---

[40] 42 C.F.R. § 407.32. For disabled beneficiaries, the SSA's Program Operations Manual System (POMS) provides for equitable relief when the delay in enrollment was caused by incorrect information provided by their employer or group health plan. *See* SSA, POMS, HI 00805.320, *available at* https://secure.ssa.gov/poms.nsf/lnx/0600805320 (site visited Aug. 6, 2018).

[41] 42 C.F.R. § 407.32. For disabled beneficiaries, the POMS provides for equitable relief when the delay in enrollment was caused by incorrect information provided by their employer or group health plan. *See* SSA, POMS, HI 00805.320, *available at* https://secure.ssa.gov/poms.nsf/lnx/0600805320 (site visited Aug. 6, 2018).

[42] 42 U.S.C. § 1395r; *see also* 42 C.F.R. §§ 408.4(a) and 407.17(b) (automatic enrollment). (*See* discussion of special provisions for payment of Medicare premiums, copayments, and deductibles for persons with low incomes and resources found in **Chapter 10** of this Handbook). *See also* Medicare Access and CHIP Reauthorization Act, Pub. L. No.114-10 (Apr. 16, 2015), and § 402, Income Related Premium, *available at* https://www.congress.gov/114/plaws/publ10/PLAW-114publ10.pdf (site visited Aug. 6, 2018).

[43] 42 U.S.C. § 1395r; 42 C.F.R. § 408.20 (monthly premiums); 42 C.F.R. § 408.40 (deduction from monthly benefits).

[44] 42 C.F.R. §§ 408.42, 408.43, and 408.44.

[45] 42 C.F.R. § 408.60(b).

[46] 42 C.F.R. § 408.44. The authorization is through the Office of Personnel Management (OPM).

[47] 42 C.F.R. § 408.46(a).

premiums is not to be resumed before the end of the taxable year, the individual is billed directly for premiums.[48]

The grace period for failing to pay the initial premium or subsequent monthly premium ends with the last day of the third month after the billing month; termination of coverage for nonpayment is effective with the first month following the end of the grace period.[49] Overdue payments remain an obligation and can be deducted from future Social Security or Railroad Retirement or offset against any Part B payments otherwise due, or can be collected directly from the enrollee or the enrollee's estate.[50]

In general, Medicare beneficiaries pay approximately 25 percent of Medicare Part B program costs, with some beneficiaries paying slightly more if they have incurred an increased enrollment premium for late enrollment or re-enrollment.[51] Approximately 75 percent of the Medicare Part B premium is subsidized by the federal government through contributions to the SMI trust fund.[52]

[2] "Hold Harmless" Part B Premiums

Medicare has a "hold harmless" provision that is used to protect beneficiaries from a decrease in the monthly amount of their Social Security checks from the previous year that would otherwise apply in order to cover an increase in the standard Medicare Part B premium amount.[53]

[3] Part B Income-Related Premium (Above the Standard Premium Amount)

While representing savings to the SMI trust fund, the Part B income-related premium implements a public policy shift, requiring Medicare beneficiaries to pay more in premiums depending on income. Under this provision, the

---

[48] 42 C.F.R. § 408.46(b).

[49] 42 C.F.R. § 408.8.

[50] 42 C.F.R. § 408.4(b).

[51] 42 C.F.R. § 408.20(c)(1). Note, too, that MA plans can provide a reduction in the Medicare Part B premium as an additional benefit. *See* 42 C.F.R. § 408.21.

[52] 42 U.S.C. § 1395r. Note that since January 2003, an MA plan may elect to receive a reduction in its payments if 80 percent of the reduction is applied to reduce the standard Medicare Part B premiums of its Medicare enrollees, and the Medicare Part B premium is reduced monthly and is offered to all Medicare enrollees in a specific plan benefit package. 42 C.F.R. § 408.21(a). In addition, the reduction cannot be greater than the standard premium amount determined for the year; however, it can be less. 42 C.F.R. § 408.21(b).

[53] *See* Social Security Act § 1839(f), 42 U.S.C. § 1395r(f). *See* SSA Cost-of-Living Adjustment, *available at* http://www.ssa.gov/cola/ (site visited Aug. 6, 2018). *See also* CMA, "Information about Part B," *available at* http://www.medicareadvocacy.org/medicare-info/medicare-part-b/ (site visited Aug. 6, 2018). Check website periodically for updates.

responsibility for determining the income-related portion of the Part B premium resides with SSA, using individual federal income tax data from the Internal Revenue Service (IRS). In resolving administrative disputes about the amount of an income-related Part B premium, SSA must use its administrative review process for the determination of rights regarding non-medical issues.

January 2007 marked the beginning of the application of the Medicare Part B income-related premium whereby Medicare beneficiaries with higher incomes are required to pay a greater portion of the Part B premium costs.[54] This higher premium is added to the Medicare Part B standard monthly premium, plus any applicable premium increase for late enrollment or re-enrollment.[55]

The higher premium amount applies to beneficiaries with federal modified adjusted gross taxable income (as defined by the IRS) over the threshold income amount of $85,000 per individual or $170,000 for a couple.[56] The new approach was phased in from calendar year 2007 through calendar year 2009.[57] At or above this threshold amount, the beneficiary will pay an income-related monthly adjustment amount.[58] For 2011 through 2019, the monthly adjustment amounts are unchanged.[59]

The purpose of the income-related monthly adjustment amount is to reduce the federal subsidy of the Medicare Part B program for beneficiaries with modified adjusted gross income above an established threshold.[60] The Centers for Medicare & Medicaid Services (CMS) must publish the threshold amounts annually in September in the *Federal Register*. Published threshold amounts will be effective January 1 of the next calendar year for the full calendar year.[61]

---

[54] The income-related premium is a requirement of the MMA, § 811. For final regulations implementing the Part B income-related premium, *see* SSA, Medicare Part B Income-Related

Monthly Adjustment Amount, 71 Fed. Reg. 62,923 (Oct. 27, 2006) (codified at 20 C.F.R. § 418.1001 *et seq.*), *available at* https://www.ssa.gov/legislation/medicare/E6-17690MedicarePartBReg.pdf (site visited Aug. 6, 2018).

[55] 20 C.F.R. § 418.1001 *et seq.* The income-related premium provision amends § 1839 of the Social Security Act, 42 U.S.C. § 1395r. The Deficit Reduction Act of 2005 (DRA), Pub. L. No. 109-171 (Feb. 8, 2006), § 5111, further amended § 1839(i) of the Social Security Act to provide that the payment of the full amount of the income-related monthly adjustment amount was phased in starting in 2007 and was completed in 2009, with a 33 percent phase-in in 2007, 67 percent in 2008, and 100 percent in 2009. Before the DRA, there was a five-year phase-in period. 42 U.S.C. § 1395r(i)(3)(B).

[56] *See* 20 C.F.R. § 418.1105(b). *See also* SSA, "Social Security: Medicare Premiums: Rules for Higher-Income Beneficiaries" (2018) *available at* https://www.ssa.gov/pubs/EN-05-10536.pdf (site visited Aug. 6, 2018). Check the SSA.gov website periodically for updates.

[57] 20 C.F.R. §§ 418.1001(b) and 418.1130.

[58] 20 C.F.R. §§ 418.1001(b) and 418.1130.

[59] *See* 20 C.F.R. § 418.1120, *available at* http://www.socialsecurity.gov/OP_Home/cfr20/418/418-1120.htm (site visited Aug. 6, 2018).

[60] *See* 20 C.F.R. § 418.1005.

[61] The SSA is the agency responsible for the administration of the Part B Income-related premium process in conjunction with the Internal Revenue Service of the U.S. Department of the

[a] Higher Income Medicare Beneficiary Payment Amount Elements

A beneficiary with income above the threshold amount must pay:[62]

1. The Medicare Part B standard monthly premium; plus
2. Any applicable increase in the standard monthly premium for late enrollment or re-enrollment; plus
3. An income-related monthly adjustment amount.

The federal premium subsidy is the portion of the full cost of providing Medicare Part B coverage that is paid by the federal government through transfers into the SMI trust fund, and the income-related monthly adjustment amount is an additional amount of premium that beneficiaries will pay for Medicare Part B coverage if they have income above the threshold. A person's income-related monthly adjustment amount is based on his or her modified adjusted gross income (MAGI).[63]

Medicare beneficiaries required to pay an income-related monthly adjustment amount are not eligible for the limitation on a Medicare Part B standard monthly premium increase beyond the amount of their Social Security (or tier 1 railroad retirement) cost-of-living adjustments.[64]

Those who enroll in Medicare after January 1, 2007, and who are determined to be responsible for an income-related Part B premium will be notified shortly after enrolling in Medicare Part B.[65] Persons who became Medicare beneficiaries during 2007 or thereafter are notified by the SSA prior to the start of each year if required to pay an income-related Part B premium.[66]

CMS publishes the Medicare Part B standard monthly premium each year.[67] CMS also establishes rules for entitlement to a non-standard premium as well as premium penalties for late enrollment or re-enrollment.[68]

Treasury and CMS of the Department of Health and Human Services (HHS). *See* 20 C.F.R. § 418.1005. The modified adjusted gross income (MAGI) ranges will be adjusted annually as described in 20 C.F.R. § 418.1115(e). CMS publishes in the *Federal Register* the dollar amounts for the income-related monthly adjustment amount.

[62] 20 C.F.R. § 418.1005.

[63] *See* 20 C.F.R. § 418.1001. MAGI is defined in **§ 6.02[C][3][c]** of this Handbook.

[64] 20 C.F.R. §§ 418.1001, 418.1010 (definitions), and 418.1125 (effect on an individual's total Medicare Part B premium).

[65] 20 C.F.R. §§ 418.1001, 418.1010, and 418.1125.

[66] 20 C.F.R. §§ 418.1001, 418.1010, and 418.1125.

[67] 42 C.F.R. § 408.20.

[68] 42 C.F.R. § 408.20(e)(6).x

PART B
INCOME-RELATED PREMIUM IN 2019

*Beneficiaries who file an individual tax return with income:**	*Beneficiaries who file a joint tax return with income:*	*Beneficiaries who are married, but file a separate tax return with income:*	*Income-related monthly adjustment amount*	*Total monthly Part B premium amount*
Less than or equal to $85,000	Less than or equal to $170,000	Less than or equal to $85,000	$0.00	$135.50
Greater than $85,000 and less than or equal to $107,000	Greater than $170,000 and less than or equal to $214,000	—	$54.10	$189.60
Greater than $107,000 and less than or equal to $133,500	Greater than $214,000 and less than or equal to $267,000	—	$135.40	$270.90
Greater than $133,500 and less than or equal to $160,000	Greater than $267,000 and less than or equal to $320,000		$216.70	$352.20
Greater than $160,000	Greater than $320,000	Greater than $85,000 and less than $415,000	$297.90	$433.40
Greater than $500,000	Greater than $750,000	Greater than $415,000	$325.00	$460.50

* MAGI ranges are adjusted annually and published in the *Federal Register* in September of each year. *See* 20 C.F.R. § 418.1115(e). For 2019, *see* CMS, Medicare Part B Monthly Actuarial Rates, Premium Rate, and Annual Deductible Beginning January 1, 2017, 81 Fed. Reg. 80,063 (Nov. 11, 2016), *available at* https://www.federalregister.gov/documents/2016/11/15/2016-27425/medicare-program-medicare-part-b-monthly-actuarial-rates-premium-rate-and-annual-deductible (site visited Aug. 6, 2018).

The SSA modified and clarified its definition of major life-changing events that allow a beneficiary to request a review of a determination that states the beneficiary must pay an income-related premium. A beneficiary may request that the SSA use more recent tax information to make the calculation if:

1. A beneficiary receives a settlement payment from a former employer in lieu of periodic pension payments and/or health insurance coverage as a result of the former employer's closure, bankruptcy, or reorganization;

2. A beneficiary experiences a loss of investment property as a result of fraud or theft due to a criminal act by a third party; and
3. A beneficiary experiences a reduction in or loss of income from an employer's pension plan due to termination or reorganization of the pension plan or a scheduled cessation of pension, regardless of whether the pension is insured.[69]

A non-standard premium may be established in individual cases only if the individual is entitled to old age or disability benefits for the months of November and December, and actually receives the corresponding benefit checks in December and January.[70] For calendar years after 1988, beginning with calendar year 1989, a premium increase greater than the cost-of-living increase is still a prerequisite for a non-standard premium.[71] A non-standard premium, however, is not precluded solely because the cash benefit is further reduced as a result of government pension offset or workers' compensation payment.[72] The non-standard premium is the greater of the following: the premium paid for December; the standard premium promulgated for January, reduced as necessary to compensate for (1) the fact that the cost-of-living increase was less than the increase in the standard premium; or (2) the further reduction in benefit because of government pension offset of workers' compensation payments.[73]

[b] Determining the Amount to Be Paid

SSA uses information that it gets from the IRS to determine whether beneficiaries who are enrolled in Medicare Part B are required to pay an income-related monthly adjustment amount. SSA changes income-related monthly adjustment amount determinations using information provided by a beneficiary under certain circumstances. SSA also notifies beneficiaries when the Social Security benefit amounts they receive will change based on its income-related monthly adjustment amount determination.[74]

SSA determines a beneficiary's income-related monthly adjustment amount using the beneficiary's tax filing status and MAGI.[75] A beneficiary's

[69] SSA, Amendments to Regulations Regarding Major Life-Changing Events Affecting Income-Related Monthly Adjustment Amounts to Medicare Part B Premiums, 75 Fed. Reg. 41,084 (July 15, 2010) (amending 20 C.F.R. §§ 418.1205, 418.1210, 418.1230, 418.1255, and 418.1265).

[70] 42 C.F.R. § 408.20(e)(1) (basic rule).

[71] 42 C.F.R. § 408.20(e)(3(i).

[72] 42 C.F.R. § 408.20(e)(3)(ii).

[73] 42 C.F.R. § 408.20(e)(4).

[74] 20 C.F.R. § 418.1005(c). *See* 20 C.F.R. § 418.1120, *available at* http://www.ssa.gov/OP_Home/cfr20/418/418-1120.htm (site visited Aug. 6, 2018). MAGI ranges are adjusted annually and generally published in the *Federal Register* in September for the following year. *See* 20 C.F.R. § 418.1115(e).

[75] 20 C.F.R. § 418.1120.

income-related premium amount is determined using a set of tables reflecting MAGI ranges. For each range, an unsubsidized Medicare Part B premium percentage is assigned. The remainder is subsidized from the SMI trust fund. The first year in which affected Part B enrollees had to pay the full amount of the income-related premiums was 2009. In 2008, if a beneficiary had to pay a Part B income-related monthly adjustment amount, he or she was responsible for 67 percent of any applicable income-related monthly adjustment amount.[76] In 2007, the beneficiary was responsible for 33 percent of the applicable amount.[77] Legislation passed in 2015 made changes to the income thresholds for 2018 and 2019; in 2020 and after, the thresholds will be adjusted annually for inflation.[78]

[c] Subpart B Income-Related Monthly Adjustment Amount

The Medicare Part B income-related monthly adjustment amount is codified in the Code of Federal Regulations at 20 C.F.R. Part 418. It contains the rules that SSA uses to determine when one will be required to pay an income-related monthly adjustment amount, in addition to one's Medicare Part B standard monthly premium, plus any applicable premium increase for late enrollment or reenrollment.[79]

Section 811 of the MMA amended the Social Security Act to provide that the limitation on increases in the Medicare Part B standard monthly premium for some beneficiaries will not apply to beneficiaries who are responsible for an income-related premium.[80] The standard Part B Medicare premium is set to cover approximately 25 percent of the Medicare Part B program costs. The other 75 percent is subsidized in large part by the federal government by contributions to the SMI trust fund.[81]

In determining whether one is required to pay an income-related premium, SSA requests information about a beneficiary's MAGI from IRS for the tax year two years prior to the effective year of the income-related monthly adjustment amount determination.[82] If IRS does not provide information about a beneficiary's MAGI for two years prior to the effective year, then SSA will use a beneficiary's MAGI for the tax year three years prior to the effective year of the income-related monthly adjustment amount determination.[83] If the beneficiary must pay

---

[76] 72 Fed. Reg. 57,039 (Oct. 5, 2007).

[77] *Id.* Check the tables at 72 Fed. Reg. 57,041–47 (Oct. 5, 2007) for the listings of income-related premium ranges, income-related monthly adjustment amounts, and total monthly premium amounts.

[78] Section 402 of the Medicare Access and CHIP Reauthorization Act of 2015 (MACRA; Pub. L. No. 114-10).

[79] *See* Table at 20 C.F.R. § 418.1120(b)(1).

[80] *See* Table at 20 C.F.R. § 418.1120(b)(1).

[81] 20 C.F.R. §§ 418.1115 and 418.1120.

[82] 20 C.F.R. § 418.1135(a).

[83] 20 C.F.R. § 418.1135(b).

an income-related monthly adjustment amount, the beneficiary will not be eligible for the limitation on Medicare Part B standard monthly premium increase beyond the amount of his or her Social Security (or tier 1 railroad retirement) cost-of-living adjustments.[84]

MAGI is defined at 26 U.S.C. Section 62 and in related regulations and includes certain other forms of income that may be excluded from adjusted gross income for purposes of determining the amount of federal income tax that one must pay.[85] The definition includes the beneficiary's adjusted gross income as defined by the IRS, plus the following forms of tax-exempt income:[86]

1. Tax-exempt interest income;
2. Income from United States savings bonds used to pay higher education tuition and fees;
3. Foreign earned income;
4. Income derived from sources within Guam, American Samoa, or the Northern Mariana islands; and
5. Income from sources within Puerto Rico.

SSA will use three years of tax information only until information for two years prior becomes available.[87]

If three years of IRS information is used, the beneficiary may request that SSA use information provided by the beneficiary for the tax year two years before that year. SSA will use this information if it will result in a lower income-related monthly adjustment amount. In order to make an initial determination based on beneficiary-supplied information, the beneficiary must provide a retained copy of his or her signed federal income tax return for that year, a copy that the beneficiary has requested for that year from IRS, or an IRS transcript of the beneficiary's return. If the beneficiary supplies a copy of his or her retained IRS return, SSA will verify this information with IRS.[88]

In some cases, IRS will not have data to provide SSA regarding an individual's MAGI because the amount of the individual's income is below the level for which an income tax return must be filed. SSA will not be making income-related

---

[84] 71 Fed. Reg. 10,926 (Mar. 3, 2006); 42 C.F.R. Pt. 418, *available at* http://www.ecfr.gov/cgi-bin/retrieveECFR?gp=1&SID=2176b8f0721322be2e8bfd80a8a2881f&ty=HTML&h=L&r=PART&n=20y2.0.1.1.10#20:2.0.1.1.10.2 (site visited Aug. 6, 2018).

[85] 71 Fed. Reg. 10,926 (Mar. 3, 2006). *See* 42 C.F.R. Pt. 418, *available at* http://www.ecfr.gov/cgi-bin/retrieveECFR?gp=1&SID=2176b8f0721322be2e8bfd80a8a2881f&ty=HTML&h=L&r=PART&n=20y2.0.1.1.10#20:2.0.1.1.10.2 (site visited Aug. 6, 2018).

[86] *See* 20 C.F.R. § 418.1010(b)(6).

[87] *See* 20 C.F.R. §§ 418.1135–418.1150.

[88] *See* 20 C.F.R. § 418.1240.

monthly adjustment amount determinations in such situations because this individual's income would also be below the MAGI threshold. If, however, SSA receives information which indicates that an individual who has not filed a tax return has income which exceeds the established threshold for an income-related monthly adjustment amount, SSA will make such a determination.[89] The statute requires that the Secretary of HHS, in conjunction with the Secretary of the Treasury, issue regulations that provide for the treatment of the premium adjustment with respect to such individuals.[90]

[d] The Sliding Scale Formula and How It Applies

Section 1839(i) of the Social Security Act, 42 U.S.C. Section 1395r, prescribes a sliding scale formula that SSA will use to establish annually four income-related monthly adjustment amounts beginning in 2007.[91] The calculation of the income-related monthly adjustment amount reduces a beneficiary's Medicare Part B premium subsidy using specified percentages, and the amount of this premium subsidy reduction is the income-related monthly adjustment amount.[92]

To determine each income-related monthly adjustment amount, CMS will use the unsubsidized Medicare Part B premium (approximately four times the Medicare Part B standard monthly premium) and multiply it by a specified percentage.[93] The percentage used in the calculation increases as the amount of MAGI increases.[94] The premium subsidy is the amount of the Part B premium paid by the SMI trust fund.[95] Currently, beneficiaries not subject to the Part B income-related premium pay 25 percent of monthly premium costs.[96]

The income thresholds applicable to the **increased** Part B premiums were the same for the period January 1, 2011, through December 31, 2017.[97]

Legislation passed in 2015 made changes to the income thresholds for 2018 and 2019; in 2020 and after, the thresholds will be adjusted annually for inflation.[98] In 2019 the thresholds are:

[89] *See* 20 C.F.R. § 418.1135(f).

[90] 42 U.S.C. § 1395r(i)(4)(B)(iii).

[91] *See* 20 C.F.R. § 418.1115.

[92] 20 C.F.R. § 418.1120.

[93] *Id.*

[94] 20 C.F.R. § 418.1120.

[95] *Id.*

[96] *Id.*

[97] *See* ACA § 3402 (amending § 1839(i) of the Social Security Act).

[98] Section 402 of the Medicare Access and CHIP Reauthorization Act of 2015 (MACRA; Pub. L. No. 114-10).

1. Greater than $85,000 and less than or equal to $107,000;
2. Greater than $107,000 and less than or equal to $133,500;
3. Greater than $133,500 and less than or equal to $160,000;
4. Greater than $160,000 and less than $500,000;
5. Greater than or equal to $500,000.

In 2019, the MAGI ranges for individuals who are married and file a joint tax return for the tax year used by SSA to make its income-related monthly adjustment amount determinations are as follows:[99]

1. Greater than $170,000 and less than or equal to $214,000;
2. Greater than $214,000 and less than or equal to $267,000;
3. Greater than $267,000 and less than or equal to $320,000;
4. Greater than $320,000 and less than $750,000;
5. Greater than or equal to $750,000.

In 2019 the MAGI ranges for married individuals who file a separate return and have lived with their spouse at any time during the tax year used by SSA to make the income-related monthly adjustment amount determinations are as follows:[100]

1. Greater than $85,000 and less than $415,000.
2. Greater than or equal to $415,000.

Section 1839(i)(3)(C)(iii) (42 U.S.C. § 1395r) provides for the MAGI ranges for individuals who file their federal income tax return with a filing status of married filing separately and who also have lived with their spouse at any time during the year to be reduced by the threshold amount established for that calendar year which may result in a higher income-related monthly adjustment amount for these individuals.[101]

SSA will use this information to determine which amount applies to a beneficiary based on the beneficiary's tax filing status in the tax year SSA is using to determine the beneficiary's income-related monthly adjustment amount.[102]

[e] Applicable Modified Adjusted Gross Income Ranges

The range amounts for individuals who are married filing jointly are double the range amounts for single income tax filers, with IRS recognizing three

[99] 20 C.F.R. § 418.1120.
[100] 20 C.F.R. § 418.1120(b)(3).
[101] 20 C.F.R. § 418.1120(b)(3).
[102] 20 C.F.R. § 418.1120(c).

additional filing statuses: head of household, qualifying widow(er), and married filing separately.[103]

If a beneficiary files an amended tax return for the tax year SSA used to make a determination of his or her income-related monthly adjustment amount, the beneficiary may request that SSA use his or her amended tax return for that year; the beneficiary must provide to SSA proof that he or she filed an amended tax return with IRS, including the beneficiary's retained copy of the amended tax return, and a letter from IRS verifying receipt of the return, or an IRS transcript of his or her amended tax return. If the beneficiary believes that IRS provided incorrect modified adjusted gross income information and SSA used that information to determine the beneficiary's income-related monthly adjustment amount, the beneficiary may request that SSA make a new income-related monthly adjustment amount determination.[104]

[f] Applicable Modified Adjusted Gross Income Adjustment Amount

Section 1839(i)(3)(B) requires the amount of the full income-related monthly adjustment to be phased in over a three-year period beginning in 2007. The percentage changed each year so that the income-related monthly adjustment amount was phased in starting in 2009.[105]

[g] When the Social Security Administration Will Use a More Recent Tax Year (Major Life Changing Events)

The Secretary of HHS is to establish procedures in conjunction with the Secretary of the Treasury for determining a person's MAGI for a tax year more recent than the information ordinarily provided by IRS when:[106]

- The beneficiary experiences a major life-changing event;[107]
- The major life-changing event in question results in a significant reduction in the beneficiary's MAGI;
- The beneficiary requests that SSA use a more recent tax year's MAGI; and

---

[103] *See* 20 C.F.R. § 418.1120.

[104] 20 C.F.R. § 418.1150.

[105] 20 C.F.R. § 418.1120.

[106] 20 C.F.R. §§ 418.1201 and 418.1225.

[107] For applying for a change based on a life-changing event, *see* SSA, Medicare Income-Related Monthly Adjustment Amount—Life-Changing Event: Form SSA-44 (12-2017), *available at* http://www.ssa.gov/online/ssa-44.pdf (site visited Aug. 6, 2018).

- The beneficiary provides evidence of the event and evidence of the reduction in MAGI.

Such events include marriage, divorce, death of a spouse; partial or full work stoppage; and loss of income from income-producing property (when the loss is not at the beneficiary's direction, for example, loss of income from real property due to a natural disaster declared by the President of the United States or by a state governor or arson, or destruction of livestock or crops).[108]

Life-changing events also include a reduction or loss of certain forms of pension income due to termination or reorganization of the pension plan, or a scheduled cessation of one's pension benefits.[109] For reductions made in income-related monthly adjustment amount determination based on one's request due to a qualifying major life-changing event, the determination will generally be effective on January 1 of the calendar year for which SSA makes the determination; and if the beneficiary enrolled in Medicare Part B after January 1 of the year for which SSA makes an income-related monthly adjustment amount determination based on the beneficiary's request due to a major life-changing event, the determination will be effective the month of the beneficiary's Medicare Part B enrollment.[110]

A life-changing event does not include events that affect expenses but not income; in addition, a life-changing event does not include events that result in the loss of dividend income.[111]

When a beneficiary asks SSA to use a more recent tax year because of a life-changing event, SSA will ask the beneficiary to provide evidence of the major life-changing event and evidence as to how the event significantly reduced the beneficiary's MAGI.[112] Unless SSA has information in its records that raises a doubt about the evidence presented, additional evidence documenting the life-changing event will not be necessary.[113]

The effective date of an income-related monthly adjustment amount initial determination based on a more recent tax year for requests made during or after 2007 and the beneficiary's MAGI for the more recent tax year can be significantly reduced as a result of a major life-changing event. SSA's initial determination is generally effective on January 1 of the year in which the beneficiary makes his or her request.[114] If the beneficiary's first month of enrollment or

---

[108] 20 C.F.R. §§ 418.1205 and 418.1225.

[109] 20 C.F.R. § 418.1205(f).

[110] 20 C.F.R. § 418.1230. For a useful SSA form for requesting a reduction in one's income-related monthly adjustment amount based on a recognized life-changing event, *see* SSA, Medicare Income-Related Monthly Adjustment Amount - Life-Changing Event: Form SSA-44 (12-2017).

[111] 20 C.F.R. § 418.1210.

[112] 20 C.F.R. §§ 418.1255 and 418.1265.

[113] 20 C.F.R. § 418.1250.

[114] 20 C.F.R. § 418.1230.

re-enrollment in Medicare Part B is after January of the year for which he or she makes a request for use of a more recent tax year, SSA's initial determination is effective on the first day of the beneficiary's entitlement to Medicare Part B enrollment or re-enrollment.[115]

If a beneficiary knows of changes in the information provided to SSA that will result in the use of a more recent tax year, the beneficiary is to inform SSA, allowing SSA to ascertain whether the beneficiary's income-related monthly adjustment amount should be eliminated or adjusted.[116] SSA will accept new MAGI information at any time after the beneficiary's request until the end of the calendar year following the more recent tax year(s) SSA used.[117]

[h] Appealing an Income-Related Monthly Adjustment (IRMA)

[i] General Provisions. When SSA decides that a beneficiary must pay an income-related monthly adjustment (IRMA), that decision and the amount of any adjustment, based on information SSA receives from IRS or the beneficiary, will be communicated to the beneficiary through a notice of an initial determination from SSA, explaining that if the beneficiary disagrees, he or she may request that SSA reconsider the determination.[118] This notice will also explain the beneficiary's right to reconsideration or a new determination.[119] The notice will explain that the beneficiary may request a new initial determination, rather than reconsideration, if he or she believes the information SSA used in its initial determination was correct, but the beneficiary wants SSA to use different information about his or her modified adjusted gross income.[120]

In making initial determinations and reconsiderations, SSA will use the rules for the administrative review process that it uses for determinations of beneficiary rights regarding non-medical issues under Title II of the Act.[121] SSA will use its rules for determinations and decisions about a beneficiary's rights regarding non-medical issues under Title II of the Social Security Act, as described in 42 C.F.R. Part 404, Subpart J.[122] If dissatisfied with SSA's reconsideration, the beneficiary may request further review, including a hearing before an administrative law judge (ALJ) from the Office of Medicare Hearings and Appeals (OMHA) at HHS, review by the Medicare Appeals Council (Council), and judicial review,

[115] 20 C.F.R. § 418.1230.
[116] 20 C.F.R. § 418.1240.
[117] 20 C.F.R. §§ 418.1240 and 418.1245.
[118] 20 C.F.R. § 418.1315.
[119] 20 C.F.R. § 418.1315.
[120] 20 C.F.R. §§ 418.1315, 418.1325, 418.1330, and 418.1335.
[121] 20 C.F.R. § 418.1340.
[122] 20 C.F.R. § 418.1340.

consistent with 42 C.F.R. Part 405, subpart I.[123] As part of the request, the beneficiary will be required to provide consent to HHS for the agency to release relevant tax return information to OMHA or the Council for the purposes of adjudicating any appeal of the amount of an income-related adjustment to the Part B premium subsidy and for any judicial review of that appeal.[124] An initial determination is the determination SSA will make about a beneficiary's income-related monthly adjustment amount that is subject to administrative review.[125] For the purposes of administering the income-related monthly adjustment amount, initial determinations include but are not limited to determinations about (1) the amount of the beneficiary's income-related monthly adjustment amount based on information provided by IRS and (2) any change in the beneficiary's income-related monthly adjustment amount based on a request for a new determination.[126]

[ii] New Initial Determination. SSA regulations provide for requesting a "new initial determination" that a beneficiary may use when he or she does not dispute the accuracy of the IRS modified adjusted gross income information SSA used, or the determination SSA made based on that information, but the beneficiary wants SSA to use different information.[127] The beneficiary may provide evidence of his or her modified adjusted gross income for a more recent tax year than the information provided by IRS when the beneficiary has experienced a major life-changing event that significantly reduces his or her income or when IRS has provided modified adjusted gross income information from three years prior to the premium effective year and the beneficiary supplies a retained copy of his or her federal income tax return for the tax year two years prior.[128]

[D] Copayments and Deductibles

Under Part B, a beneficiary is responsible for an annual deductible and copayment (or coinsurance amount) for covered items and services,[129] which is based on the Medicare-approved amount (not the actual charge) for incurred expenses.[130]

---

[123] 20 C.F.R. § 418.1350.

[124] 20 C.F.R. § 418.1350.

[125] 20 C.F.R. §§ 418.1301–418.1310.

[126] 20 C.F.R. § 418.1310.

[127] 20 C.F.R. § 418.1310.

[128] 20 C.F.R. § 418.1310.

[129] 42 U.S.C. § 1395l.

[130] 42 U.S.C. § 1395l(b); 42 C.F.R. § 410.160. *See* 42 U.S.C. § 1395u(b)(3). The Medicare-approved charge is sometimes referred to as the Medicare reasonable charge amount. The reasonable charge amount is a complicated calculation. It is generally the (1) lowest of the physician's actual charge; (2) the physician's customary charge to other Medicare beneficiaries for similar services as determined by the contractor according to its profile of that physician's charges; and

The annual deductible is offset against first incurred expenses in a given calendar year.[131]

Generally, Medicare requires beneficiaries to pay a 20 percent copayment amount based on the Medicare-approved amount for most Part B services.[132] Medicare then reimburses the Part B provider or supplier 80 percent of the Medicare-approved amount.[133]

Under the Outpatient Prospective Payment System (OPPS), a beneficiary's coinsurance with respect to outpatient hospital services is calculated for each ambulatory payment classification (APC), based on 20 percent of the national median APC calculation.[134] This is a different calculation from the usual 20 percent copayment amount calculation under Medicare Part B. Under OPPS, the 20 percent copayment amount could be quite large. Section 204 of the Balanced Budget Refinement Act of 1999 (BBRA) provides that no *single* APC coinsurance amount can be greater than the hospital inpatient deductible in a given year.[135] However, hospitals may charge more than one APC per beneficiary outpatient department encounter, depending on the services provided.[136]

---

(3) the local or geographic prevailing charge recognized by the contractor for similar services provided by physicians to Medicare patients. *See also* 42 C.F.R. § 405.501.

[131] *See* 42 C.F.R. § 408.40 *et seq.*

[132] 42 U.S.C. § 1395l(a); 42 C.F.R. § 410.152(b). (Exceptions include clinical diagnostic laboratory tests provided by laboratories and physicians who participate in the Medicare assignment program; home health care; used durable medical equipment that is purchased at a price that is at least 25 percent less than the reasonable charge for comparable new equipment; outpatient and ambulatory surgical services; pneumococcal vaccine; donation of a kidney for transplant surgery.) *See also* list of covered services found below. Note, too, that with respect to outpatient hospital services reimbursed under Part B, the beneficiary copayment amount was being based on actual charges rather than the Medicare-approved amount. *See* Stephenson v. Shalala, 87 F.3d 350 (9th Cir. 1996). Also, the Balanced Budget Act of 1997 (BBA '97), Pub. L. No. 105-33 (Aug. 5, 1997), required the establishment of a Prospective Payment System for Hospital Outpatient Department Services, including fee schedules and coinsurance amounts, effective for services on or after January 1, 1999. (§ 4523(a), amending § 1833(t) of the Social Security Act, 42 U.S.C. § 1395l(t).) This payment system has resulted in beneficiaries sometimes paying substantially more than 20 percent for some outpatient services. The Middle Class Tax Relief and Job Creation Act of 2012 (Pub. L. No. 112-96, 126 Stat. 156, § 3002 (Feb. 22, 2012), *available at* http://www.gpo.gov/fdsys/pkg/PLAW-112publ96/pdf/PLAW-112publ96.pdf (site visited Aug. 6, 2018) made changes to the time periods that rural hospitals are able to bill for services.

[133] 42 U.S.C. § 1395l(a); 42 C.F.R. § 410.152(b). Persons using non-participating physicians may be charged 15 percent above the Medicare approved amount where the actual charge is greater than Medicare's approved amount.

[134] *See* BBA '97, § 4523, amending 42 U.S.C. § 1395l.

[135] *See* BBRA 1999, Pub. L. No. 106-113, amending 42 U.S.C. § 1395l(t)(8)(C).

[136] *See* Medicare Claims Processing (MCP)Manual, Ch. 4: § 10.2 (APC Payment Groups), *available at* http://www.cms.gov/Regulations-and-Guidance/Guidance/Manuals/downloads/clm104c04.pdf (site visited Aug. 6, 2018).

§ 6.03 COVERED MEDICAL AND OTHER HEALTH CARE SERVICES

[A] Covered Services

[1] Medically Reasonable and Necessary Medical and Other Health Services

Medicare Part B provides coverage for expenses incurred by beneficiaries for medically reasonable and necessary medical and other health services.[137] Advocates should consult the Medicare National Coverage Determinations (NCD) Manual for updates and modifications to Medicare coverage policy.[138] Medicare provides coverage for categories of services as follows:[139]

- Physician services, including surgery, consultation, and office and institutional calls (visits), and services and supplies, including drugs and biologicals that cannot be self-administered, furnished incident to a physician's professional service;[140]
- Outpatient rehabilitation services;[141]
- Outpatient hospital services furnished incident to physician services;[142]
- Outpatient physical therapy; outpatient speech language pathology services; and diagnostic X-ray tests, laboratory tests,[143] and other diagnostic tests;[144]

---

[137] 42 U.S.C. § 1395y(a)(1)(A). The reasonable and necessary determination, while informed by physician and other health care provider opinion, is ultimately a determination of the Secretary. *See, e.g.*, MedPac, "Appendix B: An Introduction to How Medicare Makes Coverage Decisions," *available at* http://67.59.137.244/publications/congressional_reports/Mar03_AppB.pdf (site visited Aug. 6, 2018); *see also* Erringer v. Thompson, 371 F.3d 625 (9th Cir. 2004), *available at* http://openjurist.org/371/f3d/625/erringer-v-thompson (site visited Aug. 6, 2018).

[138] Medicare National Coverage Determinations (NCD) Manual, CMS Pub. 100-03, *available at* http://www.cms.gov/medicare-coverage-database/overview-and-quick-search.aspx (site visited Aug. 6, 2018). *See also* CMS, "Medicare Coverage Database Archive site," https://localcoverage.cms.gov/mcd_archive/overview.aspx (site visited Aug. 6, 2018).

[139] 42 U.S.C. §§ 1395k(a) and 1395x.

[140] *See also* 42 C.F.R. §§ 410.20(b) and 410.22–410.25.

[141] *See also* 42 C.F.R. §§ 410.61 and 410.100.

[142] 42 U.S.C. § 1395k(a)(2)(B)(i), 42 C.F.R. § 410.27; CMS, Medicare Benefit Policy (MBP) Manual, CMS Pub. 100-02, Ch. 6, § 10, *available at* http://www.cms.hhs.gov/manuals/Downloads/bp102c06.pdf (site visited Aug. 6, 2018).

[143] Note, too, that the Medicare Improvements for Patients and Providers Act of 2008 (MIPPA), Pub. L. No. 110-275, (July 15, 2008), § 145 (clinical laboratory tests) repealed the Medicare Competitive Bidding Demonstration Project for Clinical Laboratory Services, effective on enactment of MIPPA.

[144] *See also* 42 C.F.R. §§ 410.61 and 410.100; MIPPA § 143 (Speech-language pathology services), which states that the term "out-patient speech-language pathology services" has the meaning given the term "outpatient physical therapy services" in § 1661(ll) of the Social Security Act, 42

- X-ray, radium, and radioactive isotope therapy;[145]
- Surgical dressings, and splints, casts, and other devices used for reduction of fractures and dislocations;[146]
- Rental or purchase of DME for use in the patient's home;[147]
- Ambulance service;[148]

U.S.C. § 1395x(ll) and that "speech-language pathology" shall be substituted for "physical therapy" each place it occurs, and that the term "speech-language pathologist" shall be substituted for "physical therapist" each place it appears. Medicare has been making decisions with respect to speech generating devices (SGDs) that are causing controversy, including limiting access to certain devices that also have smartphone technologies. *See, e.g.*, CMA, "Medicare's Reluctance to Embrace Technology: Effects on the Coverage of Speech Generating Devices," *available at* http://www.medicareadvocacy.org/medicares-reluctance-to-embrace-technology-effects-on-the-coverage-of-speech-generating-devices/ (site visited Aug. 6, 2018); CMA, "CMS Rescinds Restrictive Policy and Will Reconsider Technological Advances," *available at* http://www.medicareadvocacy.org/welcome-reprieve-for-people-who-need-speech-generating-devices-sgds-to-communicate/ (site visited Aug. 6, 2018). A final SGD NCD was published by CMS on July 29, 2015. It authorizes Medicare coverage for SGDs for other types of communication e-mail, text and phone messages- in addition to speech. Further, Congress passed, and the President signed, the Steve Gleason Act, which moves the coverage of SGDs from the rental category to the purchase category for three years, allowing SGD users to take their personalized devices into any care setting. The Steve Gleason Act also allows better access to accessories necessary to operate SGDs. *See* CMA, "Better Medicare Coverage of Speech Generating Devices, *available at* http://www.medicareadvocacy.org/better-medicare-coverage-of-speech-generating-devices/ (site visited Aug. 6, 2018). For extended coverage of LGBT issues, *see also* HHS, Section 1557 of the Patient Protection and Affordable Care Act, http://www.hhs.gov/civil-rights/for-individuals/section-1557/index.html (site visited Aug. 6, 2018); HHS, Summary: Final Rule Implementing Section 1557 of the Affordable Care Act, *available at* http://www.hhs.gov/sites/default/files/2016-06-07-section-1557-final-rule-summary-508.pdf (site visited Aug. 6, 2018).

[145] 42 C.F.R. § 410.35; MBP Manual, Ch. 6: § 10.

[146] 42 C.F.R. § 410.36(a)(1); MBP Manual, Ch. 6: § 10.

[147] Rules for customized items of DME are located at 42 C.F.R. § 414.224. Note that ACA § 6407 requires a face-to-face encounter with the patient and physician for certification of the need for DME or for home health care services. This requirement is applicable to all certifications on or after January 1, 2010. Certifications via telehealth (subject to certain limitations) are permitted. 42 C.F.R. § 414.224.

[148] *See* 42 C.F.R. § 410.40. As an additional fraud and abuse protection, the ACA states that only Medicare-enrolled physicians or other "eligible professionals" can prescribe DME and home health care. Section 6407(d) *See* 42 C.F.R. § 424.506 *et seq.* (May 5, 2010), effective July 6, 2010. CMS is using its Provider Enrollment, Chain, and Ownership System (PECOS), described in the above interim final regulations, as the vehicle through which it is an eligible professional, defined in the ACA, as one who has enrolled under Medicare's Quality Care Reporting System for providers. *See* § 6405(a), and its reference to § 1866(j) of the Social Security Act, 42 U.S.C. § 1395cc(j) (Enrollment Process for Providers of Services and Suppliers). An "enrolled physician" is defined as one who has registered with Medicare in accordance with rules established by the Secretary. *See* § 6505(a) and its reference to § 1848(k)(3)(B) of the Social Security Act, 42 U.S.C. § 1395w-4 (Payment Based on Fee Schedule). 42 U.S.C. § 1395w-4(k)(3)(B) (Covered Professional Services and Eligible Professionals Defined) describes an "eligible professional" as a physician, a practitioner (including a certified nurse anesthetist, a certified midwife, a clinical social worker, a clinical

- Prosthetic devices that replace all or part of an internal body organ;[149]
- Preventive benefits (discussed below);[150]
- Leg, arm, back, and neck braces and artificial legs, arms, and eyes;[151]
- Certain medical supplies used in connection with home dialysis delivery systems;[152]
- Rural health clinic (RHC) services;[153]
- Ambulatory surgical center (ASC) services;[154]
- Antigens and blood-clotting factors;[155]
- Influenza, pneumococcal, and hepatitis B vaccines;[156]
- Some health maintenance organization (HMO) services;[157]
- Some Pap smear screenings;[158]
- Some mammography screenings;[159]
- Qualified psychologist services; and[160]
- Therapeutic shoes for patients with severe diabetic foot disease.[161]

---

psychologist (*see* 42 U.S.C. § 1395u)), and a physical or occupational therapist or a qualified speech-language pathologist. Requests for payments need to include the national provider identifier for the physician who periodically reviews the plan for services. *See* Middle Class Tax Relief and Job Creation Act of 2012, Pub. L. No. 112-96 (Feb. 22, 2012), 126 Stat. 156.

[149] 42 C.F.R. § 410.36(a)(2); MBP Manual, Ch. 6: § 10.

[150] 42 C.F.R. § 410.16; MBP Manual, Ch. 15: § 280, *available at* http://www.cms.gov/Regulations-and-Guidance/Guidance/Manuals/downloads/bp102c15.pdf (site visited Aug. 6, 2018). It should be noted that ACA, § 4001 *et seq.* (Pub. L. No. 111-148 (Mar. 23, 2010)), puts a major emphasis on preventive services and education about the value of preventive services through the creation of interagency task forces and community-based initiatives. One should look for the steady addition over time of new preventive services to Medicare's array of benefits.

[151] 42 C.F.R. § 410.36(a)(3); MBP Manual, Ch. 6: § 10.

[152] Special rules governing payment for suppliers of home dialysis supplies and equipment are found at 42 C.F.R. § 414.330.

[153] *See also* 42 C.F.R. §§ 405.2401–405.2417.

[154] 42 U.S.C. § 1395k(a)(2)(F)(i), 42 C.F.R. §§ 410.3 and 410.165, and MBP Manual, Ch. 15: § 280.

[155] 42 C.F.R. § 410.63; MBP Manual, Ch. 15: § 50.

[156] 42 C.F.R. § 410.57; MBP Manual, Ch. 15: § 50.

[157] 42 C.F.R. § 410.58.

[158] 42 C.F.R. § 410.56; MBP Manual, CMS Pub. 100-02, Ch. 15: § 250.

[159] 42 U.S.C. § 1395m(c)(2). Medicare will pay for one mammogram for female beneficiaries between the ages of 35 to 39 and Medicare will pay for annual mammograms for female beneficiaries age 40 and over. The Part B annual deductible is waived for these services.

[160] 42 U.S.C. § 1395k(2)(B)(iii), 42 C.F.R. § 410.71, and MBP Manual, Ch. 15: § 250.

[161] 42 U.S.C. § 1395l(o) and MBP Manual, Ch. 15: § 290.

Medicare Part B also covers home health visits not covered under Part A and outpatient hospital services not reimbursed by a contractor (an entity under contract with CMS for the administration of Part A services).

It should also be noted that some medical services may be considered for coverage under more than one of the categories of services mentioned above, for example, EKG services. In those instances, if the requirements for one category of service are met, payment is available.[162]

The Balanced Budget Act of 1997 (BBA '97)[163] added a set of "preventive services" to the Medicare program. They include:

- An annual mammogram for women age 40 and over (deductible does not apply).[164]
- Annual Pap smears and pelvic exams for beneficiaries considered at high risk or following an abnormal Pap smear; for women not in these groups, coverage is for Pap smears and pelvic exams once every two years (deductible does not apply).[165]
- Prostate cancer screening annually for men over age 50.[166]
- Colorectal cancer screening tests for beneficiaries age 50 and older except there is no minimum age for having a screening colonoscopy. Fecal occult blood tests are covered annually; flexible sigmoidoscopy is generally covered every 48 months (or every 120 months when used instead of a colonoscopy for those not at high risk); screening colonoscopy is covered every 120 months or every 24 months for those at high risk; and barium enemas are covered every 48 months (or every 24 months for those at high risk) when used instead of sigmoidoscopy or colonoscopy. The Part B related deductible for colorectal screenings was eliminated by the Deficit Reduction Act of 2005 (DRA), effective January 1, 2007.[167]

---

[162] MBP Manual, Ch. 15: § 10.

[163] *See* §§ 4101(a)–(b), 4103(a), 4104(a), 4105(a), 4106(a), and 4107 of BIPA, amending §§ 1834, 1861 of the Social Security Act.

[164] 42 U.S.C. §§ 1395l(b) and 1395m(c)(2)(A).

[165] 42 U.S.C. §§ 1395l(b) and 1395x(nn).

[166] 42 U.S.C. §§ 1395l(h)(1)(A) and 1395x(oo).

[167] DRA § 5113, amending 42 U.S.C. §§ 1395l and 1395m. In May 2009, Medicare decided that it would not cover virtual colonoscopies. *See* CMS, "Decision Memo for Screening Computed Tomography Colonography (CTC) for Colorectal Cancer (CAG-00396N)," *available at* https://www.cms.gov/medicare-coverage-database/details/nca-decision-memo.aspx?NCAId=220&ver=14&NcaName=Screening+Computed+Tomography+Colonography+(CTC)+for+Colorectal+Cancer&bc=BEAAAAAAEAAA&&fromdb=true (site visited Aug. 6, 2018).

- Outpatient diabetes self-management training services, blood testing strips, and monitors.[168]
- Medical nutrition therapy services for beneficiaries who have diabetes or renal disease who have not received diabetes outpatient self-management training services within a time period determined by the Secretary, are not receiving maintenance dialysis for which Medicare payment is being made, and who meet such other criteria determined by the Secretary.
- Bone mass measurements once every two years for qualified high-risk individuals.[169]
- Glaucoma screening for individuals determined to be at high risk for glaucoma, individuals with a family history of glaucoma, and individuals with diabetes.[170]
- Telehealth services when a beneficiary resides in a rural county designated as a health professional shortage area and where other criteria are met.[171]
- Other services not otherwise described that identify medical conditions or risk factors as the Secretary determines.[172]

Advocates should be aware that in making coverage decisions, Medicare uses screens and norms of treatment. These norms and screens generally go to the issue of frequency of use of certain services and procedures. They are not to be used to deny services outright but can be used as a tool for identifying certain usage patterns and trends. When norms and screens are used, beneficiaries are to

[168] 42 U.S.C. § 1395x.

[169] *Id.* High-risk persons include an estrogen-deficient woman at clinical risk for osteoporosis; an individual with vertebral abnormalities; an individual receiving long-term glucocorticoid steroid therapy; an individual with primary hyperparathyroidism; or an individual being monitored to assess the response to or efficacy of an approved osteoporosis drug therapy.

[170] 42 U.S.C. § 1395x(s)(2)(u).

[171] 42 U.S.C. § 1395m(m); 42 C.F.R. § 410.78. *See also* CMA, "Medicare and Telemedicine (or Telehealth)," *available at* http://www.medicareadvocacy.org/medicare-and-telemedicine-or-telehealth/ (site visited Aug. 6, 2018).

[172] *See* MIPPA, Pt. I (Prevention, Mental health, and Marketing), § 101 (improvements to coverage of preventive services). The Secretary has authority to add preventive services that he or she determines are reasonable and necessary for the prevention or early detection of an illness or a disability, recommended with a grade of A or B by the U.S. Preventive Services Task Force, and appropriate for individuals entitled to benefits under Part A or enrolled under Part B. In the case of additional preventive services, the Medicare agency will pay 80 percent of the lesser of the actual charge for the service or the amount determined under a fee schedule established by the Secretary.

be provided an opportunity to rebut any unfavorable coverage assumptions made on the basis of such screens and norms.[173]

The MMA added more preventive services. These new services include:

- *Preventive Physical Exams.* When initially enacted, the law stated that this exam was for an initial physical exam performed no later than six months after the individual's initial date of coverage under Part B.[174] The Medicare Improvements for Patients and Providers Act of 2008 (MIPPA), however, changed the time period for this exam to 12 months after the initial date of coverage under Part B, effective January 1, 2009.[175] The term "initial preventive physical examination" means physicians' services consisting of a physical examination (including measurement of height, weight, and blood pressure, and an electrocardiograph) with the goal of health promotion and disease detection and includes education, counseling, and referral with respect to screening and other preventive services described in MIPPA Section 611(b)(2) but does not include clinical laboratory tests.[176]
- *Cardiovascular Screening Blood Tests.* This is a blood test for the early detection of cardiovascular disease. The tests can only be performed once every two years. The provision was effective on January 1, 2005.[177]
- *Diabetes Laboratory Diagnostic Tests.* The tests include fasting plasma glucose tests as well as other tests and modifications. It applies to individuals at risk of diabetes or who have any combination of the following: hypertension; dyslipidemia; obesity (body mass index greater than or equal to 30kg/m2); previous identification of an elevated impaired glucose tolerance; a risk factor consisting of at least two of the following characteristics: overweight, defined as body mass index greater than 25, but less than 30, kg/m2; a family history of diabetes; a history of gestational diabetes mellitus or delivery of a baby weighing greater than 9 pounds; 65 years of age or older.[178]

---

[173] *See* Vorster v. Bowen, 709 F. Supp. 934 (C.D. Cal. 1989) (Part B—frequency of service screens); Fox v. Bowen, 656 F. Supp. 1236 (D. Conn. 1987) (Part A—access to physical therapy services in a skilled nursing facility).

[174] MMA § 611, adding § 1861(ww) and amending §§ 1861(s)(2), 1833(a)(1), and 1848(j)(3) of the Social Security Act. Effective Jan. 1, 2005, 42 U.S.C. §§ 1395x(s)(2), 1395l(a)(1), and 1395w-4(j).

[175] *See* MIPPA § 101(b)(3), Pub. L. No. 110-275 (July 15, 2008).

[176] *See* MMA § 611(b)(1).

[177] *See* MMA § 612, amending §§ 1861(s)(2) and 1862(a)(1) and adding § 1861(xx)(1) to the Social Security Act, 42 U.S.C. §§ 1395x(s)(2), 1395l(a)(1), and 1395w-4(j).

[178] *See* MMA § 613.

- *Abdominal Aortic Aneurysm Screening.* In addition, note that the DRA adds coverage for this screening test as part of the "Welcome to Medicare" physical exam discussed above for certain Medicare beneficiaries as of January 1, 2007, and eliminates the Medicare Part B Premium for this screening test.[179]
- *Screening for Depression in Adults.* Coverage is available in primary care settings (defined in the Social Security Act at Sections 1833(u)(6), 1833(x)(2)(A)(i)(I), and 1833(x)(2)(A)(i)(II)) that have staff-assisted depression care supports in place to assure accurate diagnosis, effective treatment, and follow-up.[180]
- *Screening and Behavioral Counseling Interventions in Primary Care to Reduce Alcohol Misuse.* CMS will cover up to four brief, face-to-face, behavioral counseling interventions per year for Medicare beneficiaries, including pregnant women. Covered are those beneficiaries who misuse alcohol, but whose levels or patterns of alcohol consumption do not meet criteria for alcohol dependence (defined as at least three of the following: tolerance; withdrawal symptoms; impaired control; preoccupation with acquisition and/or use; persistent desire or unsuccessful efforts to quit; sustains social, occupational, or recreational disability; use continues despite adverse consequences); who are competent and alert at the time that counseling is provided; and whose counseling is furnished by qualified primary care physicians or other primary care practitioners in a primary care setting.[181]

[2] Annual Wellness Visit Added by the Patient Protection and Affordable Care Act

Medicare beneficiaries are entitled to an annual wellness visit that includes a personalized prevention plan.[182] The personalized prevention plan is based on a health risk assessment made prior to, or as part of, a visit with a health care

[179] DRA § 5112, amending 42 U.S.C. § 1395x.

[180] NCD Manual, § 210.9, *available at* http://www.cms.gov/Regulations-and-Guidance/Guidance/Manuals/downloads/ncd103c1_part4.pdf (site visited Aug. 6, 2018).

[181] CMS, "Decision Memo for Screening for Depression in Adults" (CAG-00425N) (Oct. 14, 2011), *available at* http://www.cms.gov/medicare-coverage-database/details/nca-decision-memo.aspx?NCAId=251 (site visited Aug. 6, 2018).

[182] ACA § 4103, *see* http://www.cdc.gov/policy/hst/hra/4103.html (site visited Aug. 6, 2018) amending 42 U.S.C. § 1395x(s)(2), *see* https://www.gpo.gov/fdsys/pkg/USCODE-2010-title42/pdf/USCODE-2010-title42-chap7-subchapXVIII-partE-sec1395x.pdf (site visited Aug. 6, 2018). The annual wellness visit became available on January 1, 2011.

professional (physician, health educator, registered dietician, or nutrition professional or a team of professionals).[183]

The assessment establishes or updates medical and family history; lists current providers and suppliers that are regularly involved in providing medical care to the individual (including a list of prescribed medications); lists height, weight, body mass index (or waist circumference, if appropriate), blood pressure, and other routine measurements; and indicates any cognitive impairment.[184] In addition, the health professional is to establish a screening schedule for the next five to ten years, as appropriate, based on recommendations of the United States Preventive Services Task Force and the Advisory Committee on Immunization Practices, and the individual's health status, screening history, and age-appropriate preventive services.[185]

The annual wellness visit builds on the current "Welcome to Medicare" check-up or "initial physical examination" that is available to beneficiaries within 12 months of their becoming covered under Medicare Part B. The initial preventive physical examination consists of a physical examination, including measurement of height, weight, and blood pressure, and an electrocardiograph, with the goal of health promotion and disease detection. As discussed above, the initial preventive physical examination also includes education, counseling, and referral with respect to screening and other preventive services, although it does not include clinical laboratory tests.[186] A beneficiary is entitled to only a "Welcome to Medicare" check-up, not an annual wellness visit exam, during the 12-month period after coverage begins under Part B as described above.[187]

[3] Elimination of Cost-Sharing for Preventive Services

The Patient Protection and Affordable Care Act (PPACA, also known as the Affordable Care Act, or ACA) also eliminated cost-sharing for most of the preventive services covered under Medicare, effective January 1, 2011.[188] The services for which there is no cost-sharing (deductible and/or copayment) are:

---

[183] 42 U.S.C. § 1395x(s)(2)(hhh) ACA § 4103.

[184] ACA § 4103(a)(2)(A)–(D).

[185] ACA § 4103(a)(2)(E).

[186] *See* 42 U.S.C. § 1395x(ww).

[187] *See* CMS, Quick Reference Information: The ABCs of the Initial Preventive Physical Examination (Apr. 2017), *available at* http://www.cms.gov/Outreach-and-Education/Medicare-Learning-Network-MLN/MLNProducts/downloads/MPS_QRI_IPPE001a.pdf (site visited Aug. 6, 2018). *See also* CMS, Your Guide to Medicare's Preventive Services (revised Mar. 2015), *available at* http://www.medicare.gov/Pubs/pdf/10110.pdf (site visited Aug. 6, 2018)

[188] *See* CMS, "Preventive Services," *available at* http://www.cms.gov/Medicare/Prevention/PrevntionGenInfo/ (site visited Aug. 6, 2018). Because there is no cost-sharing for these services, providers are not required to issue an Advance Beneficiary Notice (ABN) to beneficiaries. If, however,

1. Mammograms every 12 months for eligible beneficiaries age 40 and older;
2. Colorectal cancer screening, including flexible sigmoidoscopy or colonoscopy;
3. Cervical cancer screening, including a Pap smear test and pelvic exam;
4. Cholesterol and other cardiovascular screenings;
5. Diabetes screening;
6. Medical nutrition therapy to help people manage diabetes or kidney disease;
7. Prostate cancer screening (for most codes);
8. Annual flu shot, pneumonia vaccine, and the hepatitis B vaccine;
9. Bone mass measurement;
10. Abdominal aortic aneurysm screening to check for a bulging blood vessel;
11. HIV screening for people who are at increased risk or who ask for the test; and
12. Smoking cessation counseling.[189]

Cost-sharing is also eliminated for the Wellness Visit and Personal Prevention Plan.

CMS indicates that the following preventive services covered by Medicare are not recommended by USPSTF with a grade of A or B for any populations or indications and will therefore *continue to be subject to cost-sharing:*[190]

1. Digital rectal examination furnished as a prostate cancer screening service;
2. Glaucoma screening;

---

the frequency of the services covered by Medicare is surpassed and the patient still wants to continue treatment, the provider must issue an ABN before providing the additional services in order to transfer liability to the beneficiary for the services received. *See* CMA, "CMS Clarifies When the Advance Beneficiary Notice of Non-Coverage (ABN) Must be Issued," (Aug. 16, 2012), *available at* http://www.medicareadvocacy.org/cms-clarifies-when-the-advance-beneficiary-notice-of-non-coverage-abn-must-be-issued/ (site visited Aug. 6, 2018). *See also* MCP Manual.

[189] On August 25, 2010, CMS announced that it was extending coverage for smoking cessation counseling. *See* CMS, "HHS Announces Medicare Expands Coverage of Tobacco Cessation Counseling" (Aug. 25, 2010), *available at* http://cms.hhs.gov/Newsroom/MediaReleaseDatabase/Press-Releases/2010-Press-Releases-Items/2010-08-25.html (site visited Aug. 6, 2018).

[190] 75 Fed. Reg. 73,169 *et seq.* (Nov. 29, 2010), amending 42 C.F.R. §§ 410.152 and 410.160, *see* http://www.ecfr.gov/cgi-bin/text-idx?SID=e13f94c394a8bf2b77a7cd15ecc417d0&mc=true&node=se42.2.410_1152&rgn=div8 (site visited Aug. 6, 2018).

3. Diabetes self-management training services; and
4. Barium enema furnished as a colorectal cancer screening.

Note that, for all services, current coverage policies continue to apply. For example, Medicare covers bone mass measurements only once every two years for qualified high-risk individuals.[191] Testing within that time frame for people who meet the eligibility criteria will not be subject to a deductible or copayment. Bone mass measurement will not be covered for someone who is not a high-risk individual, however, regardless of the change in cost-sharing requirements.

[4] Implications for Medicare Advantage Plans

With the exception of hospice care, MA plans are required to provide all items and services that are covered under Medicare Part A and Part B.[192] Since January 1, 2011, MA plans are required to offer an Annual Wellness Visit to their enrollees.[193]

Medicare Advantage plans have more leeway with regard to elimination of cost-sharing for preventive services. Medicare Advantage plans have always been allowed to impose different cost-sharing than Part A and Part B, as long as the cost-sharing is actuarially equivalent to cost-sharing under traditional Medicare.[194] By placing limits on Medicare Advantage cost-sharing for certain costly services, ACA expands that authority by allowing plans to impose cost-sharing for services for which Part A and Part B do not have cost-sharing.[195]

While many Medicare Advantage plans have traditionally eliminated cost-sharing for preventive benefits under their authority to offer an actuarially equivalent benefit package, some have not. CMS issued regulations, effective January 2012, that prohibit plans from charging deductibles, copayments, or coinsurance for *in-network* Medicare-covered preventive services, as specified by CMS on an annual basis.[196]

---

[191] 42 U.S.C. § 1395x.

[192] 42 U.S.C. § 1395w-22(a); 42 C.F.R. § 422.101.

[193] For information on no cost-sharing services and an analysis of their use, *see* HHS, "The Affordable Care Act: Strengthening Medicare in 2011," *available at* http://www.cms.gov/apps/files/Medicarereport2011.pdf (site visited Aug. 6, 2018).

[194] 42 U.S.C. § 1395w-24.

[195] PPACA § 3202, amending 42 U.S.C. § 1395w-24. Cost-sharing for chemotherapy, skilled nursing facility stays, and kidney dialysis charged by MA plans can be no greater than cost-sharing for these services in traditional Medicare. However, MA plans may, for example, charge cost-sharing for home health services for which there is no cost-sharing in traditional Medicare.

[196] CMS, Proposed Changes to the Medicare Advantage and the Medicare Prescription Drug Benefit Programs for Contract Year 2012 and Other Proposed Changes, 75 Fed. Reg. 71,189 (Nov. 22, 2010), amending 42 C.F.R. § 422.100(k), *available at* https://www.federalregister.gov/documents/2010/11/22/2010-28774/medicare-program-proposed-changes-to-the-medicare-advantage-and-the-medicare-prescription-drug (site visited Aug. 6, 2018).

[5] Medicare Caps for Physical Therapy/Speech Pathology Services and Occupational Therapy

[a] Repeal of Medicare Outpatient Therapy Caps

Pursuant to the Balanced Budget Act of 1997, Medicare Part B outpatient therapy was subject to payment caps that required therapists to seek exceptions in order to continue providing care once those caps were reached. The Bipartisan Budget Act of 2018 (BBA) permanently repealed annual Medicare payment caps on outpatient physical, speech, and occupational therapy services.[197] The repeal was a welcome relief for Medicare beneficiaries who were often left with uncertainty as Congress wrestled with the exceptions process over the last 20 years.

Although the BBA repealed outpatient therapy caps, it still requires providers to use a modifier code when submitting claims for therapy services above $2,100 annually for the purpose of "[I]ndicating that such services are medically necessary as justified by appropriate documentation in the medical record involved."[198] The BBA also provides CMS with $5 million a year for nationwide targeted medical review of claims that surpass $3,000.[199]

[b] Historical Context

The BBA '97 placed limitations on the amount of financial coverage available to Medicare beneficiaries receiving outpatient rehabilitation therapy services (except those provided under arrangements with a hospital[200]), including physical therapy, speech-language pathology services, and occupational therapy. Two categories were defined, one covering physical therapy services and speech-language pathology services combined, and the other covering occupational therapy services. These so-called therapy caps are indexed each year by the Medicare Economic Index (MEI), per the BBA '97. The caps were intended to become effective in 1999.

---

[197] Bipartisan Budget Act of 2018, Pub. L. No. 115-123, § 50202 (2018)

[198] *Id.* In 2018, the modifier must be added when services total over $2,010 for physical therapy and speech-language pathology combined, and, $2,010 for occupational therapy; *see* CMS, "Your Medicare Coverage: Physical Therapy/Occupational Therapy/Speech-Language Pathology Services," *available at* https://www.medicare.gov/coverage/pt-and-ot-and-speech-language-pathology.html (site visited Aug. 6, 2018).

[199] Bipartisan Budget Act of 2018, Pub. L. No. 115-123. § 50202 (2018). Targeted review may apply when services total over $3,000 for physical therapy and speech-language pathology combined, and $3,000 for occupational therapy; *see* CMS, "Your Medicare Coverage: Physical Therapy/Occupational Therapy/Speech-Language Pathology Services," *available at* https://www.medicare.gov/coverage/pt-and-ot-and-speech-language-pathology.html (site visited Aug. 6, 2018).

[200] *See* MCP Manual, Ch. 5: § 10.2, *available at* https://www.cms.gov/manuals/downloads/clm104c05.pdf (site visited Aug. 6, 2018).

In 1999, Congress passed a Balanced Budget Refinement Act[201] that placed a moratorium on the "therapy caps." For calendar year 2009, CMS established a combined therapy cap per beneficiary for outpatient physical therapy and speech language pathology services and a separate cap for outpatient occupational therapy services.[202] The therapy caps exceptions process for PT, OT, and SLP services was extended through CY 2017.[203] A beneficiary was required to cover the deductible and pay 20 percent coinsurance. Medicare would then cover the remaining 80 percent up to the annual cap. Either a provider or the beneficiary could submit a request for an exception. All services that required exceptions to caps were processed using the automatic exceptions process.[204]

[B] Excluded Services

Medicare Part B, as described above, is fairly comprehensive but not complete. Certain categories of services and procedures are excluded from its purview.[205]

Services are also denied on the basis of Local Coverage Determinations (LCDs). These policies are often hidden and not explicitly discussed in denial motions. Currently, CMS has a website for searching for NCDs and LCDs.[206] Advocates should ask contractors and hearing officers whether an LCD is the basis of a denial of coverage and ask that the LCD be made available.

Among the categories of services and procedures that are excluded are the following:

---

[201] Medicare, Medicaid, and SCHIP Balanced Budget Refinement Act of 1999, Pub. L. No. 106-113 (Nov. 29, 1999).

[202] *See* 72 Fed. Reg. 66,356 (Nov. 27, 2007). For updated information on therapy cap changes, *see* CMS, "Therapy Services," *available at* https://www.cms.gov/Medicare/Billing/TherapyServices/index.html?redirect=/TherapyServices (site visited Aug. 6, 2018).

[203] *See* CMS, "Therapy Services." *See also* the Medicare Access and CHIP Reauthorization Act of 2015 (MACRA) § 202. It also extended the therapy caps exceptions process through December 31, 2017, and modified the requirement for manual review of services over the $3,700 therapy thresholds. MACRA extended the application of the therapy caps, and related provisions, to outpatient hospitals until January 1, 2018.

[204] *See* CMS, "Therapy Services."

[205] *See generally* 42 U.S.C. § 1395y(a).

[206] *See* CMS, "The Medicare Coverage Database (MCD)," *available at* http://www.cms.gov/medicare-coverage-database/overview-and-quick-search.aspx (site visited Aug. 6, 2018). *See also* CMS, Review of National Coverage Determinations and Local Coverage Determinations, 68 Fed. Reg. 63,692 (Nov. 7, 2003), *available at* https://www.cms.gov/DeterminationProcess/Downloads/FR11072003.pdf (site visited Aug. 6, 2018). The definitions of an NCD and an LCD are included in regulations at 42 C.F.R. § 400.202. An LCD must conform to § 1862(a)(1)(A) of the Social Security Act (reasonable and necessary criteria); it is an intermediary-wide or carrier-wide decision; and it has not gone through the full review process of an NCD and is not a decision of CMS.

- Services that are not medically reasonable or necessary;
- Custodial care;
- Personal comfort items and services;
- Care that does not meaningfully contribute to the treatment of illness, injury, or a malformed body member;
- Prescription drugs that do not require administration by a physician;
- Routine physical checkups;
- Eyeglasses or contact lenses in most cases;
- Eye examinations for purpose of prescribing, fitting, or changing eyeglasses or contact lenses;
- Hearing aids and examinations for hearing aids;
- Immunizations except for pneumococcal and hepatitis B vaccine;
- Orthopedic shoes and other supportive devices for the foot unless intended as an instrumental part of a leg brace;
- Cosmetic surgery;
- Most dental services; and
- Routine foot care.

[C] Waiver of Liability Payment for Certain Excluded Items and Services

As described above, Medicare pays for covered services that are deemed reasonable and necessary, and not otherwise excluded. There are circumstances, however, in which Medicare will pay for excluded services. The general rule is that neither the beneficiary nor the provider knew or should have known that the service at issue was excluded.[207] Further, if Medicare determines that the beneficiary was unaware of the exclusion, but the provider knew or should have known, Medicare will indemnify the beneficiary or release the beneficiary from liability for payment.[208]

---

[207] 42 U.S.C. § 1395pp; 42 C.F.R. § 411.400. Provider knowledge of Medicare rules is presumed through written notices of non-coverage from Medicare contractors to providers, utilization review committees, and other communications; beneficiary knowledge is imputed through having received denials of coverage under comparable circumstances. *See* 42 C.F.R. §§ 411.404 and 411.406.

[208] 42 U.S.C. § 1395pp; 42 C.F.R. §§ 411.400 *et seq. See* New CMS Manual Issuance: Transmittal 2480 (June 1, 2012), Change Request 6136, Pub. 100-04 Medicare Claims Processing (Revised Form CMS-R-131 Advance Beneficiary Notice of Non-coverage), *available at* http://www.cms.gov/Regulations-and-Guidance/Guidance/Transmittals/Downloads/R2480CP.pdf (site

Under these circumstances, the provider is not entitled to payment for the excluded service either from the beneficiary or from Medicare.[209] Providers with persistent problems in this regard, or with poor track records, lose the presumption of lack of knowledge of whether an item or a service is covered, and their requests for payment for excluded items and services will be denied.[210]

[D] Special Coverage Areas

[1] Ambulance Service

Ambulance service is covered under Part B of the Medicare Program if certain conditions are met.[211] Generally, the ambulance supplier must meet the ambulance vehicle, staff, billing, and reporting standards established by CMS in regulations,[212] and no payment is made directly or indirectly for ambulance services under Part A,[213] including a national fee schedule.[214]

Ambulance regulations clarify rules defining medical necessity for ambulance transport, amending 42 C.F.R. § 410.40 to state that for non-emergency transport, bed confinement is not the sole criterion in determining medical necessity of ambulance transport.[215] In addition, on April 1, 2002, CMS established a

---

visited Aug. 6, 2018), which also includes CMS's further update to the ABN and its usages. *See also* CMA, "CMS Clarifies When the Advance Beneficiary Notice of Non-Coverage (ABN) Must be Issued" (Aug. 16, 2012) (discussing changes that became effective on September 4, 2012), *available at* http://www.medicareadvocacy.org/cms-clarifies-when-the-advance-beneficiary-notice-of-non-coverage-abn-must-be-issued/ (site visited Aug. 6, 2018).

[209] 42 U.S.C. § 1395pp; 42 C.F.R. §§ 411.400 *et seq.*

[210] 42 C.F.R. § 411.406.

[211] 42 C.F.R. § 410.40. CMS provides for separate reasonable charge rates for ambulance reimbursement. Rates are dependent on the level of service provided. 42 C.F.R. § 410.40 provides for seven different levels of service. *See* MCP Manual, Ch. 15: §§ 20.2–20.6; *see also* CMS, "Ambulance Fee Schedule Public Use Files," *available at* http://www.cms.gov/Medicare/Medicare-Fee-for-Service-Payment/AmbulanceFeeSchedule/afspuf.html (site visited Aug. 6, 2018); *see also* MMA, § 415, amending 42 U.S.C. § 1395m(l), with respect to rural air ambulance.

[212] 42 C.F.R. §§ 410.40 and 410.41. Note that MIPPA § 146(b) makes improvements to air ambulance fees. Section 146(a) extends current increases for Medicare payments for ground ambulances through 2010. *See* CMS, "Ambulance Fee Schedule Public Use Files," *available at* http://www.cms.gov/Medicare/Medicare-Fee-for-Service-Payment/AmbulanceFeeSchedule/afspuf.html (site visited Aug. 6, 2018).

[213] 42 C.F.R. § 410.40(a)(2).

[214] *See* 42 C.F.R. § 414.615. For on-going updates, *see* CMS, "Ambulances Services Center," *available at* http://www.cms.gov/Center/Provider-Type/Ambulances-Services-Center.html?redirect=/center/ambulance.asp (site visited Aug. 6, 2018)

[215] Amending 42 C.F.R. § 410.40(d). *See also* CMS, "Ambulance Fee Schedule Public Use Files." For further background, *see* 42 C.F.R. Pt. 414 subpt. H, ambulance services. *See* 42 C.F.R. § 414.610 (basis of payment, which requires ambulance service providers to accept Medicare assignment, including air ambulance providers). 42 C.F.R. § 414.620 requires the publication of an

fee schedule for the payment of ambulance services, including requiring ambulance service providers to accept assignment, thus limiting patient liability.[216] Medical necessity, origin, and destination requirements must be met.

Payment for ambulance services under Part B is available for ambulance trips within the United States for basic life support (BLS) services and advanced life support (ALS) services, and for paramedic ALS intercept services.[217] All payments for ambulance services are made on an assignment-only basis, and providers can collect from beneficiaries only the unmet Part B deductible and Part B coinsurance amounts.[218]

With respect to medical necessity, ambulance service is available under Medicare only if the services are furnished to a beneficiary with a medical condition such that other modes of transportation are contraindicated.[219] If the ambulance trip is necessary for non-emergency services, the beneficiary must be unable

---

ambulance fee schedule. 42 C.F.R. § 414.625 provides that there is no administrative or judicial review of the amounts established under the ambulance fee schedule.

[216] 42 C.F.R. § 414.610(a)–(g). Section 414.610(b) addresses mandatory assignment for claims filed on or after April 1, 2002. *See* § 414.610(c)(5), rural adjustment factor (RAF), adding interim final rules on payment increases for rural and urban ambulance services. This notice implements MMA, § 414.

[217] 42 C.F.R. § 410.40(a)(2)(b)(1)–(3). Paramedic ALS intercept services must be furnished in a rural area as defined in 42 C.F.R. § 412.62(f) and must be furnished under contract with one or more volunteer ambulance services that are certified to furnish ambulance service; that furnish services only at the BLS level; and that are prohibited by state law from billing for any service. They can also be furnished by a paramedic ALS intercept supplier certified to furnish ALS services as provided in 42 C.F.R. § 410.41(b)(2) and that bills all the recipients who receive ALS intercept services for the entity, regardless of whether those recipients are Medicare beneficiaries. For purposes of payment for paramedic intercept ambulance services, a rural area is an area designated as a rural area by any law or regulation of the state or if it is located in a rural census tract of a metropolitan statistical area (MSA) (as determined under the most recent Goldsmith Modification). CMS defines a rural area to mean "an area located outside an urban area, or a rural census tract within an MSA as determined under the most recent version of the Goldsmith modification as determined by the Office of Rural Health Policy of the Health Resources and Services Administration." Definitions applicable to ambulance services, both land and water (referred to as "ground") are found at 42 C.F.R. § 414.605. Specialty care transport (SCT) means the hospital-to-hospital transportation of a critically injured or ill beneficiary by a ground ambulance vehicle, including medically necessary supplies and services, at a level of service beyond the scope of the EMT-Paramedic. SCT is necessary when a beneficiary's condition requires ongoing care that must be furnished by one or more health professionals in an appropriate specialty area, for example, nursing, emergency medicine, respiratory care, cardiovascular care, or a paramedic with additional training. An urban area means an MSA, as defined by the Executive Office of Management and Budget.

[218] CMS, Fee Schedule for Payment of Ambulance Services and Revisions to the Physician Certification Requirements for Coverage of Nonemergency Ambulance Services, 67 Fed. Reg. 9099, 9134, amending 42 C.F.R. § 414.610(a)–(g) by adding new § 414.610(b), *available at* https://www.gpo.gov/fdsys/pkg/FR-2002-02-27/pdf/02-4548.pdf (site visited Aug. 6, 2018).

[219] 42 U.S.C. § 1395x(s)(7); 42 C.F.R. § 410.40(d).

to get up from bed without assistance; the beneficiary must be unable to ambulate; and the beneficiary must be unable to sit in a chair or wheelchair.[220] If the ambulance ride is not medically necessary and the provider has reason to know that Medicare will not cover the cost, the provider may shift liability for the cost to the beneficiary only by providing the beneficiary with an ABN. Issuance of an ABN is mandatory in such a situation if three conditions are met: (1) the service being provided is a Medicare covered ambulance ride; (2) the provider believes that the service may be denied in part or in full because it is not medically necessary; and (3) the ambulance service is being provided in a *non-emergency* situation.[221]

Medicare covers scheduled non-emergency ambulance services if the ambulance supplier, in advance of the service, obtains a written order from the treating physician certifying that the medical necessity requirements of the coverage regulations are met. The order must be dated no earlier than 60 days before the ambulance service is provided.[222]

For ambulance service for a resident of a facility who is under the care of a physician, the physician must certify that the trip meets the above-described medical necessity requirements within 48 hours after the trip.[223] If the trip is for

---

[220] 42 C.F.R. § 410.40(d)(1)(i)–(iii).

[221] *See* New CMS Manual Issuance: Transmittal 2480 (June 1, 2012), Change Request 6136, Pub. 100-04 Medicare Claims Processing (Revised Form CMS-R-131 Advance Beneficiary Notice of Non-coverage), *available at* http://www.cms.gov/Regulations-and-Guidance/Guidance/Transmittals/Downloads/R2480CP.pdf (site visited Aug. 6, 2018).

[222] 42 C.F.R. § 410.40(d)(2).

[223] 42 C.F.R. § 410.40(d)(3)(i). CMS is interpreting its rules such that physician certification can be signed by a physician's assistant, a nurse practitioner, or a clinical nurse specialist, acting under the supervision of the physician, as recognized under state law. Further, for purposes of certification with respect to unscheduled, non-emergency ambulance transports, a registered nurse who is employed by the attending physician or who is an employee of the hospital or facility where the patient is being treated may sign a physician certification statement on oral orders from the physician or other qualified practitioner.

On October 23, 2015, CMS announced an expansion of the "3-year Medicare Prior Authorization Model for Repetitive Scheduled Non-Emergent Ambulance Transport" in accordance with § 515(a) of the Medicare Access and CHIP Reauthorization Act of 2015. ([CMS-6063-N2] http://www.gpo.gov/fdsys/pkg/FR-2015-10-23/pdf/2015-27030.pdf (site visited Aug. 6, 2018)) The model is being expanded to the states of Maryland, Delaware, North Carolina, West Virginia, and Virginia and the District of Columbia. The expansion began on January 1, 2016. *See* CMS, "Prior Authorization of Repetitive, Scheduled Non-Emergent Ambulance Transport," *available at* https://www.cms.gov/Research-Statistics-Data-and-Systems/Monitoring-Programs/Medicare-FFS-Compliance-Programs/Prior-Authorization-Initiatives/Prior-Authorization-of-Repetitive-Scheduled-Non-Emergent-Ambulance-Transport-.html (site visited Aug. 6, 2018).

Medicare may cover ambulance services, including air ambulance (fixed-wing and rotary-wing) services, if the ambulance service is furnished to a beneficiary whose medical condition is such that other means of transportation are contraindicated. The beneficiary's condition must require both the ambulance transportation itself and the level of service provided in order for the billed service to be considered medically necessary. A repetitive ambulance service is defined as medically necessary

a beneficiary residing at home or in a facility and is not under the direct care of a physician, no certification is required.[224]

Origin and destination requirements for ambulance service coverage are as follows:[225]

- From any point of origin to the nearest hospital, critical access hospital (CAH), or SNF that is capable of furnishing the required level and type of care for the beneficiary's illness or injury, including the necessary physician specialists needed to treat the beneficiary's condition;
- From a hospital, CAH, or SNF to the beneficiary's home;
- From a SNF to the nearest supplier of medically necessary services not available at the SNF where the beneficiary is a resident, including the return trip;
- For a beneficiary who is receiving renal dialysis for treatment of ESRD, from the beneficiary's home to the nearest facility that furnishes renal dialysis, including the return trip.

[2] Durable Medical Equipment

[a] General

Coverage is available under Part B for the rental, purchase, or lease of DME for use in the home.[226] Generally, items of DME include such things as wheelchairs, hospital beds, walkers, canes, oxygen systems, and dialysis systems. A physician's order is generally necessary to obtain DME.[227] Under the DME rules,

---

ambulance transportation that is furnished in three or more round trips during a ten-day period, or at least 1 round trip per week for at least three weeks (42 C.F.R. § 410.40(d)(l)). Repetitive ambulance services are often needed by beneficiaries receiving dialysis or cancer treatment. Medicare may cover repetitive, scheduled, non-emergent transportation by ambulance if (1) the medical necessity requirements are met; and (2) the ambulance provider/supplier, before furnishing the service to the beneficiary, obtains a written order from the beneficiary's attending physician certifying that the medical necessity requirements are met. *See* 42 C.F.R. § 410.40(d)(l), (2). *See also* 42 C.F.R. §§ 410.40, 410.41, and MBP Manual, Ch. 10, *available at* https://www.cms.gov/Regulations-and-Guidance/Guidance/Manuals/Downloads/bp102c10.pdf (site visited Aug. 6, 2018).

[224] 42 C.F.R. § 410.40(d)(3)(ii).

[225] 42 C.F.R. § 410.40(e)(1)–(4).

[226] 42 U.S.C. § 1395m(a); 42 C.F.R. § 410.38. Advocates should consult the Medicare NCD Manual to identify the sections covering the issues in question for the most up-to-date DME coverage listings. *See* http://www.cms.gov/Regulations-and-Guidance/Guidance/Manuals/Internet-Only-Manuals-IOMs-Items/CMS014961.html (site visited Aug. 6, 2018). This listing is generally given great weight in the administrative review process and in federal court review. It is particularly helpful in understanding the specific coverage criteria, including the necessary medical factors for coverage.

[227] 42 U.S.C. § 1395m(a)(11)(B).

the Medicare program pays 80 percent of the payment basis and schedules established by the Secretary's exclusive authority to set payment amounts under the program.[228] Note that Section 6407 of ACA requires a face-to-face encounter with the patient and physician (or other recognized certifier) for certification of the need for DME or for home health care services. This requirement is applicable to all certifications on or after January 1, 2010. Certifications via telehealth (subject to certain limitations) are permitted.[229] In addition, ACA gives the Secretary the authority to apply this face-to-face requirement to other services for which payment under the Medicare program is available based upon a finding that such a decision would reduce the risk of waste, fraud, or abuse.[230] Further, the ACA gives the Secretary the authority to apply the face-to-face requirement to similar services paid for under the Medicaid program if the Secretary deems such an approach would reduce waste, fraud, and abuse.[231]

The issue of whether to rent, purchase, or lease DME is often a problem. The best approach is to work closely with the contractor and physician to determine the appropriate DME for the individual and the coverage rationale for its use. It is also important to understand that Medicare, under guidelines established by the Secretary, makes the determination of whether DME should be rented, purchased, or leased, and how much Medicare will pay for such equipment.[232]

Where customized items of DME are involved, it is important to show how the item is uniquely designed to meet the needs of the particular beneficiary,

---

[228] 42 U.S.C. § 1395m(a)(1)(A), (B), (C).

[229] Amending 42 U.S.C. § 1395m(a)(11)(2)(B). *See* CMS, "Face to Face Encounter Requirement for Certain Durable Medical Equipment (updated Sept. 9, 2015)," *available at* https://www.cms.gov/Research-Statistics-Data-and-Systems/Monitoring-Programs/Medicare-FFS-Compliance-Programs/Medical-Review/FacetoFaceEncounterRequirementforCertainDurableMedicalEquipment.html (site visited Aug. 6, 2018).

[230] ACA § 6407(c).

[231] ACA § 6407(d). On November 16, 2012, CMS published a final rule to implement ACA, 6407. *See* CMS, Justification of Estimates for Appropriations Committees, Fiscal Year 2015, *available at* http://www.cms.gov/About-CMS/Agency-Information/PerformanceBudget/Downloads/FY2015-CJ-Final.pdf (site visited Aug. 6, 2018).

[232] 42 U.S.C. § 1395m(a)(1)(C), 1395m(a)(1)(A)–(C); 42 C.F.R. § 421.210. Also, note that CMS has a system of DMERCs. *See* 42 U.S.C. § 1395m(a)(12). These contractors have established protocols and coverage criteria that they employ in making DME coverage decisions. In many instances, the protocols reflect Medicare national coverage determinations and thus a uniform coverage policy. In other instances, from region to region, DMERCs may employ differing approaches to coverage of the same item or category of DME. *See* CMS, Durable Medical Equipment (DME) Center, *available at* http://www.cms.hhs.gov/center/dme.asp (site visited Aug. 6, 2018); For a discussion of speech generating devices (SGDs), *see* CMS, "Speech Generating Devices," *available at* http://www.cms.gov/medicare-coverage-database/details/medicare-coverage-document-details.aspx?MCDId=26&ExpandComments=n&mcdtypename=National+Benefit+Category+Analyses&MCDIndexType=3&bc=AgAEAAAAACAAAA%3d%3d& (site visited Aug. 6, 2018).

consistent with Medicare's requirements of medical necessity, and not merely an item of convenience.[233]

Additions or modifications of DME that are not considered to be medically necessary will not be covered by Medicare. In order for the supplier to shield itself from liability for the cost of the improvements or modifications when it knows the modifications will not be covered by Medicare, the supplier must issue an ABN.[234] Since issuing an ABN is mandatory in this case, liability for the cost of the equipment modifications or improvements cannot be shifted to the beneficiary if the beneficiary is not provided with notice of his or her liability.

[b] Competitive Acquisition of Certain Durable Medical Equipment, Prosthetics, Orthotics, and Supplies

The implementation of CMS's competitive acquisition program is currently underway, in some regional areas. Rules describing the program and its roll out in 2009 provided important information about the structure and function of the program and are described throughout this section, including relevant citation.[235] Expansion of "Round 2" bidding of the DME competitive bidding program proceeded and expanded to additional metropolitan statistical areas (MSAs).[236] Regulations implementing aspects of the program are in place.[237]

---

[233] *See* 42 C.F.R. § 414.224.

[234] *See* New CMS Manual Issuance: Transmittal 2480 (June 1, 2012), Change Request 6136, Pub. 100-04 Medicare Claims Processing (Revised Form CMS-R-131 Advance Beneficiary Notice of Non-coverage), *available at* http://www.cms.gov/Regulations-and-Guidance/Guidance/Transmittals/Downloads/R2480CP.pdf (site visited Aug. 6, 2018).

[235] *See* MIPPA § 154(A)(1)(D). *See also* CMS, "DMEPOS Competitive Bidding—Home," *available at* http://www.cms.gov/Medicare/Medicare-Fee-for-Service-Payment/DMEPOSCompetitiveBid/index.html?redirect=/DMEPOSCompetitiveBid/%20(Rules%20for%20DME%20competitive%20bidding%20project? (site visited Aug. 6, 2018).

[236] *See* ACA § 6410, amending 42 U.S.C. § 1395w-3(a)(1). See discussion of MSAs and other aspects of the program throughout this section. Under ACA, the Secretary is to expand the program to the next 21 largest MSAs. The current list of MSAs is described in **§ 6.03[D][2][b][i]** of this Handbook. The DMEPOS program remains controversial, and there are efforts to repeal the program and replace it with a market pricing program at the manufacturer level for DMEPOS under Medicare Part B. *See* H.R. 1717, 113th Congress (Apr. 24, 2013), *available at* http://www.gpo.gov/fdsys/pkg/BILLS-113hr1717ih/pdf/BILLS-113hr1717ih.pdf (site visited Aug. 6, 2018); *see also* CMA, "Medicare's National Mail Order Program for Diabetic Testing Supplies," *available at* http://www.medicareadvocacy.org/medicares-national-mail-order-program-for-diabetic-testing-supplies/ (site visited Aug. 6, 2018).

[237] *See* CMS, Establishing Additional Medicare Durable Medical Equipment, Prosthetics, Orthotics, and Supplies (DMEPOS) Supplier Enrollment Safeguards, 74 Fed. Reg. 61,737– 62,206 (Nov. 25, 2009) (*see* material starting at 61,887), *available at* https://www.gpo.gov/fdsys/pkg/FR-2010-08-27/pdf/2010-21354.pdf (site visited Aug. 6, 2018). *See also* CMS, Establishing Additional Medicare Durable Medical Equipment, Prosthetics, Orthotics, and Supplies (DMEPOS) Supplier Enrollment Safeguards, 75 Fed. Reg. 52,629 (Aug. 27, 2010) (setting out final regulations that

As required by Section 302 of the MMA, Medicare published final regulations establishing the requirements for a new competitive bidding program for certain durable medical equipment, prosthetics, orthotics, and supplies (DMEPOS). As required by the MMA, the competitive bidding program is being phased in with high-cost and high-volume items or those with the largest savings potential based on the following factors: total Medical expenditures (allowable charges) for the item; growth in Medicare expenditures; number of suppliers of the item; savings potential; and findings and reports and studies by the Office of Inspector General (OIG) or the Government Accountability Office (GAO).[238]

The basic structure of the program described below remains intact. Note, however, that all contracts issued under the first phase of the DMEPOS program were terminated by MIPPA.[239] As the program has rolled out, it has been resisted by provider and supplier associations and their members. In some instances, the authors have observed that suppliers are winning bids and then refusing to provide the required services and equipment, saying that they cannot honor their commitments because the bid prices are too low. Suppliers are obligated to deliver set up, and train a beneficiary on use of an item.[240] In general, suppliers and

---

DMEPOS suppliers must meet). For a useful overview of the Competitive Bidding program for DMEPOS and its implementation problems, potential for savings, and related issues, *see* Government Accountability Office (GAO), GAO-10-1057T, CMS Has Addressed Some Implementation Problems from Round 1 of the Durable Medical Equipment Competitive Bidding Program for the Round 1 Rebid (Sept. 15, 2010), *available at* http://www.gao.gov/new.items/d101057t.pdf (site visited Aug. 6, 2018).

[238] *See* § 1847B of the Social Security Act, 42 U.S.C. 1395w–3b; *see also* § 1847(a)(1) of the Social Security Act, 42 U.S.C. § 1395w-3(a)(1); 72 Fed. Reg. 17,992 *et seq.* (Apr. 10, 2007). Rules were effective June 11, 2007. Ongoing standards for DMEPOS providers with respect to payment rules for items furnished by DMEPOS suppliers and issuance of DMEPOS supplier billing privileges are set out at 42 C.F.R. § 424.57. Advocates should continue to watch for emerging developments. *See also* CMS, Marketing Rules Reminders for DME Suppliers Including Contract Suppliers under the Durable Medical Equipment, Prosthetics, Orthotics and Supplies (DMEPOS) Competitive Bidding Program, *available at* http://www.cms.hhs.gov/MLNMattersArticles/downloads/SE0820.pdf (site visited Aug. 6, 2018) & CMS, Durable Medical Equipment, Prosthetics, Orthotics and Supplies (DMEPOS) Competitive Bidding Program, *available at* http://www.cms.gov/Outreach-and-Education/Medicare-Learning-Network-MLN/MLNProducts/downloads/dme_ref_agt_factsheet_icn900927.pdf (site visited Aug. 6, 2018). For more information about the accreditation and bonding requirement, *see* CMS, "Medicare Provider-Supplier Enrollment," *available at* http://www.cms.hhs.gov/MedicareProviderSupEnroll (site visited Aug. 6, 2018). For ongoing updates on the competitive bidding process, *see* CMS, "DMEPOS Competitive Bidding – Home."

[239] MIPPA § 154(A)(1)(D)(ii).

[240] *See* CMS, "Supplier Directory Results," *available at* https://www.medicare.gov/supplierdirectory/results.html?loc=ZIP0647041.382137173.30012330&filters=catg1143$mpart0&sort=15ASC&paging=110&prtlname=&rnd=4false&mftrname=&mdlname=&viewmap=0 (site visited Aug. 6, 2018).

providers are to honor their bid obligations.[241] Even as beneficiaries are bearing the brunt of provider resistance, the Office of the Inspector General (OIG) for HHS and the General Accountability Office (GAO) have issued reports stating that beneficiary access to necessary items of DMEPOS has not been compromised.[242] These reports belie beneficiary experience, particularly since January 2014.[243] Moreover, providers are continuing to push for legislation that would replace the current competitive bidding system with an auction system.[244] Beneficiary advocates are concerned that such an approach leaves too much control of the costs of and access to DMEPOS in the hands of the supplier industry.[245]

In December 2015, CMS issued a final rule establishing a prior authorization for certain durable medical equipment, prosthetics, orthotics, and supplies (CMS-6050-F).[246] A major focus of the proposal is reigning in costs of certain expensive items and services.

---

[241] *See* CMA, "Delivery and Set-Up Guidelines for Durable Medical Equipment, Prosthetics, Orthotics, and Supplies (DMEPOS)," *available at* http://www.medicareadvocacy.org/delivery-and-set-up-guidelines-for-durable-medical-equipment-prosthetics-orthotics-and-supplies-dmepos/ (site visited Aug. 6, 2018). 42 C.F.R. § 424.57(c)(12)(delivery), *available at* http://www.ecfr.gov/cgi-bin/text-idx?SID=50cc231bebd54e92b9479bb2d43b852b&mc=true&node=se42.3.424_157&rgn=div8 (site visited Aug. 6, 2018). Contract terms for suppliers are provided in 42 C.F.R. §§ 414.422(e) (furnishing items) and 414.422(g) (breach of contract), *available at* http://www.gpo.gov/fdsys/pkg/CFR-2011-title42-vol3/pdf/CFR-2011-title42-vol3-sec414-422.pdf (site visited Aug. 6, 2018). For other important regulatory guidance, *see* CMS's Outreach and Education/MedLearn Series.

[242] For the Center's analysis of the problem, *see* CMA, "Memorandum: GAO and OIG Reports Note No Problems in Beneficiary Access to DMEPOS. Beneficiary Advocates Disagree," *available at* http://www.medicareadvocacy.org/memorandum-gao-and-oig-reports-note-no-problems-in-beneficiary-access-to-dmepos-beneficiary-advocates-disagree/ (site visited Aug. 6, 2018). *See also* CMA, "The DMEPOS Competitive Bidding Process: Is It Working?" (June 26, 2014), *available at* http://www.medicareadvocacy.org/the-dmepos-competitive-bidding-process-is-it-working/ (site visited Aug. 6, 2018).

[243] *See* CMA, "Memorandum: GAO and OIG Reports Note No Problems in Beneficiary Access to DMEPOS. Beneficiary Advocates Disagree."

[244] *See* Medicare DMEPOS Competitive Bidding Improvement Act of 2014, H.R. 4920, 113th Congress (June 19, 2014), *available at* https://www.congress.gov/bill/113th-congress/house-bill/4920 (site visited Aug. 6, 2018); American Association for Homecare, "Support Medicare DMEPOS Competitive Bidding Improvement Act—H.R. 4920," *available at* https://www.aahomecare.org/pages/take-action-support-binding-bid-legislation (site visited Aug. 6, 2018).

[245] For an analysis of the earlier version of the auction approach (H.R. 1717), *see* CMA, "Let DMEPOS Competitive Bidding Proceed While Addressing Identified Problems and Concerns," *available at* http://www.medicareadvocacy.org/let-dmepos-competitive-bidding-proceed-while-addressing-identified-problems-and-concerns/ (site visited Aug. 6, 2018). The same concerns are applicable to the industry's newest proposal, H.R. 4920.

[246] CMS, "Prior Authorization Process for Certain Durable Medical Equipment, Prosthetics, Orthotics, and Supplies" (Dec. 30, 2015), *available at* https://www.gpo.gov/fdsys/pkg/FR-2015-12-30/pdf/2015-32506.pdf (site visited Aug. 6 2018).

[i] Competitive Bidding Areas. For a list of the existing competitive bidding areas across the country, see the following link: https://www.medicare.gov/what-medicare-covers/part-b/competitive-bidding-program-areas.html#collapse-4770 (site visited Aug. 6, 2018).

[ii] Terms to Remember. The competitive acquisition program for DMEPOS has introduced new terms, including:[247]

- *contract supplier*—an entity that is awarded a contract by CMS to furnish items under a competitive bidding program;
- *non-contract supplier*—a supplier that is not awarded a contract by CMS to furnish items included in a competitive bidding program;
- *referral agents*—applies to the range of physicians, practitioners, or providers who prescribe DMEPOS (in essence, "order" or "refer") for their patients;
- *grandfathered supplier*—a non-contract supplier that chooses to continue to furnish grandfathered items to a beneficiary in a CBA;
- *grandfathered item*—means all rented items within a product category for which payment was made prior to the implementation of a competitive bidding program to a grandfathered supplier that chooses to continue to furnish the items in accordance with 42 C.F.R. § 414.408(j) of this subpart and that fall within the following payment categories for competitive bidding:
    1. An inexpensive or routinely purchased item described in 42 C.F.R. § 414.220 of this part.
    2. An item requiring frequent and substantial servicing, as described in 42 C.F.R. § 414.222 of this part.
    3. Oxygen and oxygen equipment described in 42 C.F.R. § 414.226 of this part.
    4. Other DME described in 42 C.F.R. § 414.229 of this part.
- *Single payment amount*—allowed payment for an item furnished under a competitive bidding program.
- *competitive bidding ombudsman*—The Secretary has provided for a competitive acquisition ombudsman within the CMS in order to respond to complaints and inquiries made by suppliers and individuals relating to the application of the competitive acquisition program under this section. The ombudsman may be within the office of the Medicare Beneficiary

[247] 42 C.F.R. § 414.402.

Ombudsman appointed under section 1808(c). The ombudsman shall submit to Congress an annual report on the activities under this subsection, which report shall be coordinated with the report provided under section 1808(c)(2)(C).[248]

[iii] Competitive Bidding Implementation Contractor. CMS has established a DMEPOS Competitive Bidding Implementation Contractor (CBIC) website and has contracted with Palmetto GBA to conduct certain functions in relation to the administration of the DMEPOS competitive bidding program.[249] The functions of the CBIC are to prepare the request for bids (RFB), perform bid evaluations, and ensure that suppliers meet all applicable financial and quality standards. The contractor is also to conduct an education program for beneficiaries, suppliers, and referral agents.

In general, competitively bid items that are related and are used to treat a similar medical condition will be grouped into product categories, for example, hospital beds and accessories. Suppliers do not have to bid on all product categories, but for those product categories for which they bid, the supplier must bid on every item in the product category. In addition, contract suppliers will be required to furnish all items within a product category.

[iv] Product Categories. For a list of the current product categories, see the following link: https://www.medicare.gov/what-medicare-covers/part-b/competitive-bidding-program-areas.html#collapse-4770 (site visited Aug. 6, 2108).

[v] Grandfathering Certain Contractors. The competitive bidding rules provide for "grandfathering" the provision of certain rental items for which payment is made on a rental basis prior to the implementation of a competitive bidding program and for which payment is made after implementation of a competitive bidding program to a grandfathered supplier that continues to furnish the items as provided under the payment regulations.[250] These items include certain

---

[248] MIPPA § 154(f).

[249] *See* CMS, "DMEPOS Competitive Bidding Program: About the Program," *available at* http://www.dmecompetitivebid.com (site visited Aug. 6, 2018) (this site has information for beneficiaries who must use suppliers that participate in the competitive bidding process); for competitive bidding rules, *see* CMS, Competitive Acquisition for Certain Durable Medical Equipment, Prosthetics, Orthotics, and Supplies (DMEPOS) and Other Issues, 72 Fed. Reg. 17,991 (Apr. 10, 2007), amending 42 C.F.R. Pts. 411 and 414, *available at* http://www.cms.hhs.gov/quarterlyproviderupdates/downloads/cms1270f.pdf (site visited Aug. 6, 2018). In addition, CMS is amending Chapter 36 of its online MCP Manual to reflect its implementation policies with respect to its DMEPOS competitive bidding program. For updates, *see* MCP Manual, Ch. 36, *available at* http://www.cms.gov/Regulations-and-Guidance/Guidance/Manuals/downloads/clm104c36.pdf (site visited Aug. 6, 2018). *See also* CMS, "DMEPOS Competitive Bidding—Home."

[250] CMS has published several Tip Sheets for providers affected by the DMEPOS competitive bidding program. "Grandfathered" DMEPOS suppliers are non-contract suppliers that elect to continue to provide certain rented DME or oxygen and oxygen equipment at the time the DMEPOS

inexpensive or routinely purchased items (brand name items); an item requiring frequent and substantial servicing; oxygen and oxygen equipment and other DME described in the regulations.[251] It also allows for the grandfathering of certain special physician/practitioners—nurses, physician assistants, clinical nurse specialists, physical therapists, and occupational therapists in private practice to receive payment for certain competitively bid items furnished to their own patients as part of the professional service even though they have not submitted a bid and have not been selected as a contract supplier.[252]

With respect to choice of providers, beneficiaries who are renting an item of DME or oxygen and oxygen equipment that meets the definition of a grandfathered item may elect to obtain the item from a grandfathered supplier.[253] The rules also contain special provisions for small suppliers, including the forming of networks of small suppliers.[254]

[vi] Repair and Replacement of Beneficiary-Owned Items.

Repair Only

A beneficiary who owns a competitively bid item that needs to be repaired may have the repairs performed by either a contract supplier or by a non-contract supplier.[255] Medicare will pay for reasonable and necessary labor that is not otherwise covered under a manufacturer's or supplier's warranty.

---

competitive bidding program begins in a given competitive bidding area (CBA). The grandfathering exception may also apply to beneficiaries who transition from an MA plan. "Referral agents" are to assist beneficiaries to determine whether they are seeking and using suppliers who are in the CBAs in which they reside, and with referrals to appropriate providers. In addition, CMS has issued a "Tip Sheet" to explain how certain physicians and other treating practitioners can provide certain types of competitively bid items in a CBA to their patients without submitting a bid and being selected as a contract-provider. *See* CMS, MLN Numbers SE0805 Revised, "Overview of New Medicare Competitive Bidding Program for Durable Medical Equipment, Prosthetics, Orthotics, and Supplies (DMEPOS)," *available at* http://www.cms.gov/Outreach-and-Education/Medicare-Learning-Network-MLN/MLNMattersArticles/downloads/SE0805.pdf (site visited Aug. 6, 2018); CMS, MLN Matters Number SE0806 Revised, "Durable Medical Equipment, Prosthetics, Orthotics, and Supplies (DMEPOS) Competitive Bidding Program: Grandfathering, Repair and Replacement, Mail Order Diabetic Supplies and Advance Beneficiary Notices (ABNs)," https://www.cms.gov/Medicare/Medicare-Contracting/ContractorLearningResources/Downloads/JA0806.pdf (site visited Aug. 6, 2018).

[251] *See* 42 C.F.R. § 414.402 (definitions).

[252] *Id. See also* 42 C.F.R. §§ 414.226–414.229.

[253] *See* 42 C.F.R. § 414.408(e)(2). *See also* 42 C.F.R. § 414.408(j)(4).

[254] *See* 42 C.F.R. § 414.418.

[255] *See* 42 C.F.R. § 414.408(k).

Repair and Replacement

If a part needs to be replaced to make the beneficiary-owned equipment serviceable, and the replacement part is also a competitively bid item for the CBA in which the beneficiary maintains a permanent residence, the part may be obtained from either a contract supplier or a non-contract supplier. In these situations, Medicare pays the single payment amount provided under the competitive bidding program for the replacement part.

Replacement Only

Beneficiaries who are permanent residents within a CBA are required to obtain replacement of all items subject to competitive bidding from a contract supplier—including replacement of base equipment and replacement of parts or accessories for base equipment that are being replaced for reasons other than servicing of the base equipment.

Beneficiaries who are not permanent residents of a CBA but require a replacement of a competitively bid item while visiting in a different CBA must obtain the replacement item from a contract supplier. The supplier will be paid the fee schedule amount for the state in which the beneficiary is a permanent resident.

[vii] Mail Order Diabetic Supplies Under the Program. Medicare beneficiaries who are permanent residents in a CBA may purchase their diabetic testing supplies from a mail order contract supplier for the area in which the beneficiary is a permanent resident or from a non-contract supplier in cases where the supplies are not furnished on a mail order basis.[256] These supplies will be reimbursed at the single payment amount for the CBA where the beneficiary maintains a permanent residence. For diabetic supplies that are not furnished through mail order, suppliers will be paid the fee schedule amount.

[viii] Competitive Bidding and Advance Beneficiary Notice Information. In general, if a non-contract supplier in a CBA furnishes a competitively bid item to any Medicare beneficiary regardless of whether that beneficiary maintains a permanent residence in the CBA or another area, and no applicable exceptions

---

[256] *See* § 636 of the American Taxpayer Relief Act of 2012, Pub. L. No. 112-240, H.R. 8, 126 Stat. 2313 (Jan. 2, 2013), amending Social Security Act, § 1834(a)(1), 42 U.S.C. 1395m(a)(1), *available at* http://www.gpo.gov/fdsys/pkg/BILLS-112hr8eas/pdf/BILLS-112hr8eas.pdf (site visited Aug. 6, 2018). The DMEPOS program for mail-order diabetic supplies went into effect July 1, 2013. *See* CMA, "Medicare's National Mail Order Program for Diabetic Testing Supplies," *available at* http://www.medicareadvocacy.org/medicares-national-mail-order-program-for-diabetic-testing-supplies/ (site visited Aug. 6, 2018); *see also* CMS, The Durable Medical Equipment, Prosthetics, Orthotics, and Supplies (DMEPOS) Competitive Bidding Program, *available at* http://www.cms.gov/Outreach-and-Education/Medicare-Learning-Network-MLN/MLNProducts/downloads/DME_Mail_Order_Factsheet_ICN900924.pdf (site visited Aug. 6, 2018).

apply, Medicare will not make payment. In these circumstances, the beneficiary is not liable for payment unless the non-contract supplier in a CBA obtains an ABN signed by the beneficiary.[257]

A signed ABN indicates that the beneficiary was informed in writing prior to receiving the item that there would be no Medicare coverage due to the supplier's contract status and that the beneficiary understands that he or she will be liable for all costs that the non-contract supplier may charge for the item.[258]

[ix] No Administrative or Judicial Review of Process. There is no administrative or judicial review under the DMEPOS competitive bidding process for the following: establishment of payment amounts; awarding of contracts; designation of CBAs; phase-in of the competitive bidding program; selection of items for competitive bidding; and the bidding structure and number of contract suppliers selected for a competitive bidding program.[259] In addition, a denied claim is not appealable if the denial is based on a determination by CMS that a competitively bid item was furnished in a CBA in a manner not authorized under the competitive bidding program.[260]

[c] Medicare Coverage of Power Mobility Devices

[i] As originally announced in the *Federal Register*, published on December 21, 2016,[261] CMS imposed a prior authorization process for two items of durable medical equipment to be subject to required prior authorization beginning on July 17, 2017:

- K0856: Power Wheelchair, group 3 std., single power option, sling/solid seat/back, patient weight capacity up to and including 300 pounds

---

[257] CMS has available a series of Fact Sheets that may help beneficiaries understand the importance of an ABN in the context of Medicare's competitive bidding program. *See* http://www.cms.gov.

[258] The beneficiary must also understand that he or she can get the supplies from a Medicare-approved contractor. Although the non-contract supplier does not have to refer the beneficiary to the Medicare-approved contractor, it must at least direct the beneficiary to the 1-800-MEDICARE number. *See* CMS Transmittal 2480 Advanced Beneficiary Notice of Non-Coverage § 50.12, *available at* http://www.cms.gov/Regulations-and-Guidance/Guidance/Transmittals/Downloads/R2480CP.pdf (site visited Aug. 6, 2018).

[259] 42 C.F.R. § 414.424.

[260] 42 C.F.R. § 414.424. Note, too, that MIPPA § 154(a)(1)(D) provides that nothing in the subsection terminating contracts awarded under the initial competition round shall be construed to provide an independent cause of action or right to administrative or judicial review with regard to the termination of the initially awarded contracts under round one.

[261] *See* https://www.gpo.gov/fdsys/pkg/FR-2016-12-21/pdf/FR-2016-12-21.pdf (site visited Sept. 28, 2017).

K0861: Power Wheelchair, group 3 std., multiple power option, sling/solid seat/back, patient weight capacity up to and including 300 pounds. Effective September 1, 2018, 31 new items were added to the prior authorization requirement. The items are all types of power wheelchairs. They can be found at https://federalregister.gov/d/2018-11953. Suppliers or beneficiaries submitting the first claims in the series for these items must receive prior authorization before the item is furnished or a claim is submitted, as a condition for payment. DME MACs began accepting prior authorization requests for this expansion beginning July 3, 2017.[262]

[ii] On May 5, 2005, CMS issued an NCD defining access to Medicare-covered mobility assistive equipment (MAE) such as power wheelchairs and scooters (three-wheel devices). These devices are under the broad umbrella of power mobility devices (PMDs).[263] In making its coverage determination with respect to the appropriateness of such equipment for a particular beneficiary, CMS has moved away from a chair- or bed-confined standard and is now basing coverage determinations on an evaluation of a beneficiary's ability to engage in certain mobility-related activities of daily living (MRADLs) such as toileting, feeding, and bathing in customary locations in the home. Where such criteria are met, and properly documented, CMS will consider the item of DME at issue reasonable and necessary as defined in the Medicare law.[264]

---

[262] *See* CMS, Prior Authorization Process for Certain Durable Medical Equipment, Prosthetic, Orthotics, Supplies (DMEPOS) Items, *available at* https://www.cms.gov/Research-Statistics-Data-and-Systems/Monitoring-Programs/Medicare-FFS-Compliance-Programs/DMEPOS/Prior-Authorization-Process-for-Certain-Durable-Medical-Equipment-Prosthetic-Orthotics-Supplies-Items.html (site visited Aug. 6, 2018).

[263] NCD, 280.3, *available at* http://www.cms.gov/medicare-coverage-database/details/ncd-details.aspx?NCDId=219&ncdver=2 (site visited Aug. 6, 2018). *Also see* CMS, Decision Memo for Mobility Assistive Equipment (CAG-00274N), *available at* http://www.cms.gov/medicare-coverage-database/details/nca-decision-memo.aspx?NCAId=143&fromdb=true (site visited Aug. 6, 2018). For other important sources pertaining to access to power mobility devices (PMDs) under Medicare, *see* CMS, Power Mobility Devices (PMDs): Documentation & Coverage Requirements, (Oct. 2017), *available at* http://www.cms.gov/Outreach-and-Education/Medicare-Learning-Network-MLN/MLNProducts/downloads/pmd_DocCvg_FactSheet_ICN905063.pdf (site visited Aug. 6, 2018); CMS, Medicare Coverage Database (Advocates should check this website frequently for updates).

[264] *See* § 1862(a)(1)(A) of the Social Security Act, 42 U.S.C. § 1395y(a)(1)(A). For rules pertaining to an advance determination of Medicare coverage (ADMC) for customized DME, *see also* HHS, Medicare Program Integrity (MPI) Manual, Transmittal 5, *available at* http://www.cms.gov/Regulations-and-Guidance/Guidance/Transmittals/downloads/R5PIM.pdf (site visited Aug. 6, 2018). It is important to note that ADMCs are not initial determinations as defined at 42 C.F.R. § 405.801(a).

In April 2007, CMS issued, through its Medicare Learning Network, a detailed treatment of access to PMDs, including power wheelchairs and power operated vehicles (POVs).[265] It provides the following useful definitions:[266]

> **Power Mobility Devices:** PMDs are defined as covered items of Durable Medical Equipment (DME) that are in a class of wheelchairs that includes power wheelchairs (four-wheeled motorized vehicles whose steering is operated by an electronic device or joystick to control direction and turning) or POVs (three- or four-wheeled motorized scooters that are operated by a tiller) that a beneficiary uses in the home.
>
> **Power (Motorized) Wheelchairs:** Most beneficiaries who require power wheelchairs are non-ambulatory and have severe weakness of the upper extremities due to a neurologic or muscular condition. Under the MAE national coverage policy, power wheelchairs may be medically necessary for beneficiaries who cannot effectively perform Mobility-Related Activities of Daily Living (MRADLs) in the home using a cane, walker, manually operated wheelchair, or a POV/scooter. In addition, the beneficiary must demonstrate the ability to safely and effectively operate the power wheelchair in the home environment.
>
> **Power Operated Vehicles (POVs or scooters):** These vehicles have been appropriately used in the home environment to improve the ability of chronically disabled persons to cope with normal domestic, vocational, and social activities. Under the MAE national coverage policy, POVs may be medically necessary for beneficiaries who cannot effectively perform MRADLs in the home using a cane, walker, or manually operated wheelchair. In addition, the beneficiary must demonstrate sufficient strength and postural stability to safely and effectively operate the POV in the home environment.

In its NCD issuance, CMS set forth new function-based criteria for PMD, setting out an algorithmic process called the "Clinical Criteria for MAE Coverage." It replaces the older "bed or chair-confined" standard.[267] It is felt that this new approach gives greater consideration to the beneficiary's abilities to engage mobility activities within the home. Moreover, the issuance does not preclude use of the PMD outside the home. The chief concern is to establish that the beneficiary has a mobility limitation such that a PMD is medically necessary and that the beneficiary has the physical and mental ability to use the equipment in the home and is willing to do so. When these factors are appropriately documented by physicians and treating practitioners, the beneficiary is free to use the MOE

[265] *See* CMS, "Medicare Coverage of Power Mobility Devices (PMDs): Power Wheelchairs and Power Operated Vehicles (POVs)," (Mar. 2009), *available at* http://www.cms.hhs.gov/MLNProducts/downloads/PMDFactSheet07_Quark19.pdf (site visited Aug. 6, 2018).

[266] CMS, "Medicare Coverage of Power Mobility Devices (PMDs): Power Wheelchairs and Power Operated Vehicles (POVs)," (Mar. 2009).

[267] CMS, "Medicare Coverage of Power Mobility Devices (PMDs): Power Wheelchairs and Power Operated Vehicles (POVs)," (Mar. 2009).

both in the home, and out in the community (but not primarily for the pursuit of leisure or recreational activities).

In making an assessment whether an item of PMD is appropriate the physician or treating practitioner must conduct a face-to-face evaluation of the beneficiary before writing a prescription. The decision memorandum provides the additional clarification that Medicare no longer restricts the type of physician able to prescribe a PMD. Also, a physician assistant, nurse practitioner, or clinical nurse specialist may prescribe a PMD. In addition the prescription for the PMD must be writing and signed and dated by the physician or treating practitioner who performed the face-to-face examination, and must be received by the PMD supplier within 30 days of the face-to-face examination.[268]

Other supporting information that the physician or treating practitioner must provide the supplier of the PMD includes:[269]

- The medical necessity for the use of the PMD in the home,
- Relevant information from the beneficiary's medical record, and
- Information establishing that the beneficiary or caregiver is capable of operating the PMD.

With respect to prior documentation, CMS clarifies that the information in the record at the face-to-face evaluation will be sufficient to support medical necessity. It notes, however, that prior documentation may be necessary when the information from the face-to-face examination refers to previous notes in the medical record.[270]

[d] Medicare Payment for and Maintenance of Oxygen Equipment

Medicare provides for coverage of home oxygen therapy under the Part B DME benefit if certain medical pre-conditions are met.[271] This coverage includes the rental of oxygen delivery systems.[272]

In regulations issued November 25, 2009, and effective January 1, 2010,[273] CMS clarified that the oxygen suppler that furnishes oxygen equipment during the

---

[268] *See* CMS, "Medicare Coverage of Power Mobility Devices (PMDs): Power Wheelchairs and Power Operated Vehicles (POVs)," (Mar. 2009)

[269] CMS, "Medicare Coverage of Power Mobility Devices (PMDs): Power Wheelchairs and Power Operated Vehicles (POVs)," (Mar. 2009).

[270] CMS, "Medicare Coverage of Power Mobility Devices (PMDs): Power Wheelchairs and Power Operated Vehicles (POVs)," (Mar. 2009).

[271] *See* § 1834 of the Social Security Act, 42 U.S.C. § 1395m(a)(5)(A)–(F); *see also* 42 C.F.R. § 414.226 (oxygen and oxygen equipment).

[272] *See* § 1834 of the Social Security Act, 42 U.S.C. § 1395m(a)(5)(A)–(F); *see also* 42 C.F.R. § 414.226 (oxygen and oxygen equipment).

[273] *See* 74 Fed. Reg. 61,888 (Nov. 25, 2009), discussing 42 C.F.R. § 414.226.

36-month rental period (described below) must continue to furnish the oxygen equipment after the 36-month rental period. The supplier is required to continue to furnish the equipment during any period of medical need for the remainder of the reasonable useful life of the equipment as provided in Section 144(b) of MIPPA (discussed below).[274]

Providers are paid a monthly payment amount for furnishing medically necessary stationary oxygen equipment of a particular class—including stationary oxygen concentrators, stationary liquid oxygen systems, and gaseous oxygen systems.[275] Medicare also pays a monthly add-on payment to suppliers furnishing medically necessary portable oxygen equipment, including traditional portable liquid oxygen systems and portable gaseous oxygen systems and oxygen generating portable equipment, as well as oxygen transfilling equipment. Both the liquid and gaseous oxygen systems (stationary and portable) require ongoing delivery of oxygen contents.[276]

CMS further clarified that under no circumstance will a new period of continuous use begin following the 36-month rental period and before the end of the equipment's reasonable useful lifetime; and that the supplier is responsible for furnishing the equipment after the 36-month rental period and before the end of the equipment's reasonable useful lifetime.[277] Further, regardless of any break in the medical need that occurs following the 36-month rental period, the regulations provide that once the break ends and medical need for the oxygen equipment resumes, the supplier is obligated to continue furnishing the item for no additional rental payments until the end of the equipment's reasonable useful life.[278]

Effective January 1, 2006, Medicare pays for stationary and portable oxygen equipment for a 36-month capped rental period. Under the Deficit Reduction Act (DRA) of 2005, ownership of the oxygen equipment was transferred to the beneficiary at the end of the 36-month period.[279] Section 144(b) of MIPPA repealed the transfer of ownership provision applicable to oxygen equipment created by the DRA.[280] Under MIPPA, the supplier continues to own the equipment after the 36-month capped rental period.[281]

---

[274] 74 Fed. Reg. 61,888 (Nov. 25, 2009).

[275] 42 C.F.R. § 414.226(c)(1)(ii) and (iii).

[276] *See* 42 C.F.R. § 414.226.

[277] *See* 42 C.F.R. § 414.230(h).

[278] 42 C.F.R. § 414.230.

[279] The Deficit Reduction Act (DRA) of 2005, §§ 5101(a)–(b), Pub. L. No. 109-171. *See also* Government Accountability Office (GAO), Medicare Home Oxygen: Refining Payment Methodology Has Potential to Lower Program and Beneficiary Spending (Jan. 2011), *available at* http://www.gao.gov/assets/320/315094.pdf (site visited Aug. 6, 2018).

[280] MIPPA § 144(b).

[281] *See* CMS, Transmittal Number 497 (May 22, 2009), *available at* http://www.cms.hhs.gov/transmittals/downloads/R497OTN.pdf (site visited Aug. 6, 2018).

Suppliers participating in the Medicare program are paid over a 36-month period for furnishing a beneficiary's oxygen and oxygen equipment needs for up to five years. The supplier is required to continue to maintain the oxygen equipment and is to furnish the equipment and any necessary supplies and accessories during this five-year period. For beneficiaries who use oxygen tanks or cylinders that need delivery of gaseous or liquid oxygen contents, Medicare will continue to pay each month for the delivery after the 36-month capped rental period.[282]

At the end of the five-year period, the obligation of the supplier to furnish the oxygen and oxygen equipment ends. The beneficiary may elect to obtain replacement equipment from any Medicare-certified contract supplier serving the area in which the beneficiary resides. A new 36-month payment period and five-year supplier obligation period starts at the end of the initial five-year period.

[i] CMS's Consumer Alert on Oxygen Equipment and Supplies. CMS, through its Office of Public Affairs, announced that beneficiaries should continue to receive the oxygen and oxygen supplies that they need; that Medicare is required to make 36 monthly payments to oxygen equipment suppliers; that suppliers must continue to provide beneficiaries with properly functioning oxygen equipment and associated supplies after the 36th month (three-year) payment period; that the supplier is required to perform any repairs or to provide replacements at no cost to beneficiaries until the beneficiary has used the equipment for five years; and that after five years, the supplier may replace the equipment, but a new 36-month rental period will begin at that time; that if a supplier refuses to comply with these rules, the beneficiary should notify CMS *immediately* by calling 1-800-Medicare (1-800-633-4227) or, for users of TTY, 1-877-486-2048.[283]

[ii] Payment Rules for Oxygen and Supplies. Medicare's monthly rental rate covers the beneficiary's oxygen equipment and necessary supplies and accessories such as tubing or a mouth piece, oxygen contents, maintenance, servicing, and repairs. Medicare pays 80 percent of the rental amount, and the Medicare beneficiary is responsible for any unpaid Part B deductible and the remaining 20 percent of the rental amount.[284] Medigap policies A–G and K–N pay the 20 percent

---

[282] CMS, Transmittal Number 497 (May 22, 2009).

[283] *See* CMS, "Medicare Consumer Alert for Beneficiaries Who Use Oxygen Equipment and Supplies" (Dec. 17, 2008), *available at* https://www.cms.gov/newsroom/press-releases/medicare-consumer-alert-beneficiaries-who-use-oxygen-equipment-and-supplies (site visited Aug. 6, 2018). *See also* CMA, "Medicare Coverage of Home Oxygen Therapy," *available at* http://www.medicareadvocacy.org/medicare-info/medicare-part-b/#OXYGEN%20THERAPY (site visited Aug. 6, 2018).

[284] *See* CMS, "Medicare Coverage of Durable Medical Equipment and Other Devices," *available at* http://www.medicare.gov/Pubs/pdf/11045-Medicare-Coverage-of-DME.pdf (site visited Aug. 6, 2018).

cost-sharing.[285] Note that these payment rules apply to traditional Medicare. Medicare Advantage plans have their own rules concerning payment and cost-sharing for oxygen and supplies. Some plans require beneficiaries to pay more than 20 percent cost-sharing; some plans continue to impose a 20 percent cost-sharing even after the 36-month capped rental period under traditional Medicare.

[iii] No Separate Payment for Maintenance and Repairs. Under MIPPA, ownership of the oxygen equipment is retained by the supplier after the rental payments stop. The MIPPA law requires the suppliers to provide all necessary maintenance of the equipment without charge. A beneficiary may not be charged for repairing or replacing the equipment or parts necessary to make the equipment function properly. If the equipment has to be replaced because it no longer functions properly, the supplier must replace the equipment with the same or similar make and model of equipment at no charge.[286]

[iv] Service for Oxygen Equipment for Persons Outside Their Home Geographic Area. Persons who travel outside their home geographic areas for extensive periods of time (several weeks or more at a time) or who relocate should ask their current supplier for assistance in finding a supplier in the area where they visit extensively or in the area in which they have relocated. This can get tricky as the initial supplier has been paid for furnishing the necessary equipment and for servicing it for five years. Beneficiaries may find that some suppliers are unwilling or slow to meet their maintenance and service responsibility when the beneficiary is no longer in the area in which the supplier does business. The supplier may choose to make arrangements with a supplier in the beneficiary's new area to provide necessary maintenance and service but otherwise remains responsible for the maintenance and service functions for which it has been paid. Beneficiaries who encounter problems with their suppliers in making such arrangements should call 1-800-MEDICARE (1-800-633-4227). TTY users should call 1-877-486-2048.[287]

[v] Competitive Bidding. It is important to mention that competitive bidding (discussed in **§ 6.03[D][2][b]**) is part of the concern of many suppliers of durable medical equipment, including oxygen equipment. CMS is continuing the cost-containment steps and provisions that have been enacted over the years.

---

[285] *See* CMS, 2018 Choosing a Medigap Policy: A Guide to Health Insurance for People with Medicare," *available at* https://www.medicare.gov/Pubs/pdf/02110-Medicare-Medigap.guide.pdf (site visited Aug. 6, 2018).

[286] *See* CMS, "Medicare Consumer Alert for Beneficiaries Who Use Oxygen Equipment and Supplies."

[287] *See* CMS, "Medicare Consumer Alert for Beneficiaries Who Use Oxygen Equipment and Supplies." Note that suppliers are working with members of the United States Congress to change this rule. Many suppliers feel that this requirement is burdensome. *See* https://www.gainesvilletimes.com/news/health-companies-complain-as-medicare-reduces-payments-for-oxygen-therapy/ (site visited July 3, 2017).

Containment of costs for oxygen and oxygen equipment is part of that overall containment effort. Specifically, oxygen and oxygen equipment are included in the ten categories of items and services that are part of the constellation of services and supplies on which suppliers must bid in order to become Medicare-certified contract suppliers of durable medical equipment.[288]

[3] National Coverage Determinations

The Medicare statute gives the Secretary the obligation and authority to make determinations about what specific items and services are covered under the Medicare program.[289] CMS uses its NCD process to discharge this responsibility.[290]

Advocates should visit Medicare's Coverage Determinations web page.[291] Medicare's database of national and local coverage decisions should be consulted for updates.[292] When seeking to petition for a new coverage decision or to set aside an old one, it is important to have extensive medical support for the coverage of the item, service, or procedure at issue. In addition to one's treating physician, local and national medical societies can be helpful in such endeavors. Also, it is important to keep in mind that the removal of a negative NCD may only pave the way to assert that a more favorable NCD should be established. In any event, the removal of a negative NCD opens the way for local Medicare Administrative Contractors (MACs) to issue local coverage decisions LCDs on the matter at issue, pending the development of an NCD on the particular matter.

An NCD does not include a determination of what code, if any, is assigned to a service nor is it a determination with respect to the amount of payment to be made for the service.[293] NCDs are binding on all Medicare contractors, Quality Improvement Organizations (QIOs), HMOs, competitive medical plans, health care prepayment plans, and the MAC when published in the *Federal Register*.[294]

---

[288] CMS, "Your Medicare Coverage: Oxygen Equipment & Accessories," *available at* https://www.medicare.gov/coverage/oxygen-equipment-and-accessories.html (site visited Aug. 6, 2018).

[289] 42 U.S.C. §§ 1395y(a)(1)(A), 1395ff(b)(3), 1395hh. *See also* 42 C.F.R. § 405.205. *See also* NCD Manual.

[290] *See* current Medicare authority to make NCDs without the requirement of notice-and-comment rule-making procedures, §§ 1871(a)(2), 1869(c)(3)(B) of the Social Security Act, 42 U.S.C. §§ 1395hh(a)(2) and 1395ff(b)(3)(B); procedures for maintaining code lists in the Negotiated NCDs for Clinical Diagnostic Services *and* CMS, "Medicare Coverage Database."

[291] *See* CMS, "Medicare Coverage Determination Process," *available at* http://www.cms.gov/Medicare/Coverage/DeterminationProcess/ (site visited Aug. 6, 2018).

[292] *See* CMS, "Medicare Coverage Database."

[293] 42 C.F.R. § 400.202 (definitions specific to Medicare); *see also* CMS, Medicare Managed Care (MMC) Manual, Ch. 4: § 90 (national and local coverage determinations), *available at* http://www.cms.gov/Regulations-and-Guidance/Guidance/Manuals/downloads/mc86c04.pdf (site visited Aug. 6, 2018).

[294] 42 C.F.R. § 405.1060(a).

An ALJ may not disregard, set aside, or otherwise review an NCD.[295] An ALJ may review the facts of a particular case to determine whether an NCD applies to a specific claim for benefits and, if so, whether the NCD was applied correctly to the claim.[296] A provider of services or a supplier may not introduce evidence in any appeal under Section 1395ff of the Social Security Act that was not presented at the reconsideration unless there is good cause that precluded the introduction of such evidence at or before that reconsideration.[297] The federal courts may set aside an NCD only after it has received and considered the Secretary's rationale for the coverage determination.[298] Advocates encounter problems with the NCD process when they seek coverage for new procedures. Problem areas usually revolve around getting access to the national coverage process itself; the lack of the ability to participate in the process in a meaningful way such that information in support of coverage is fairly and fully heard and utilized in making NCDs; and the extremely slow nature of the process itself. The current process, and relevant definitions, effective December 8, 2003, are set out in the final regulations.[299]

An LCD is a decision by a contractor under Medicare Part A or Part B whether to cover a particular service on a contractor-wide basis in accordance with Medicare's reasonable and necessary criteria; it may provide that a service is not reasonable and necessary for certain diagnoses and/or for certain diagnosis codes; but it does not include a determination of which procedure code, if any, is assigned to a service or a determination with respect to the amount of payment to be made for the service.[300]

With respect to LCD and NCD reviews and individual claim appeals, an aggrieved party (a Medicare beneficiary or the estate of a Medicare beneficiary)[301] must notify the ALJ or the Departmental Appeals Board (DAB), as appropriate, regarding the submission and disposition of any pending claim or appeal relating to the subject of the aggrieved party's LCD and NCD complaint;

---

[295] 42 C.F.R. § 405.1060(b)(1).

[296] 42 C.F.R. § 1060(b)(2).

[297] 42 U.S.C. § 1395ff(b)(3); 42 C.F.R. § 405.1050; Section 522 of the Medicare, Medicaid, and SCHIP Benefits Improvement and Protection Act of 2000 provides for Departmental Appeals Board (DAB) review of NCDs. *See also* 42 U.S.C. § 1395ff(f)(1)(a)(v). A DAB decision would constitute final HHS action and would be subject to limited judicial review. 42 C.F.R. §§ 405.732 and 405.860.

[298] 42 U.S.C. § 1395ff(b)(3). *See also* 42 C.F.R. § 426.100–426.587 (review of LCDs and NCDs, including the process and timelines for review).

[299] *See* 68 Fed. Reg. 63,692 (preamble), 42 C.F.R. § 405.902 (definitions), and 42 C.F.R. § 405.1050 (applicability of national coverage determinations). For further background discussion, *see* HHS, Procedures for Making National Coverage Decisions, 64 Fed. Reg. 22,619–25 (Apr. 27, 1999). Information about the application of NCDs or LCDs in the denial of coverage should be included in Medicare Summary Notices (MSNs). For the redesigned MSN, *see* CMS, "MSN Changes," *available at* http://www.cms.gov/apps/files/msn_changes.pdf (site visited Aug. 6, 2018).

[300] 42 C.F.R. § 400.202 (definitions specific to Medicare).

[301] 42 C.F.R. § 426.110. *See* CMS, "Local Coverage Database," *available at* http://www.cms.gov/medicare-coverage-database/indexes/national-and-local-indexes.aspx (site visited Aug. 6, 2018).

this reporting obligation continues through the entire LCD and NCD review process.[302] Only an aggrieved party may initiate a review of an LCD and NCD and must do so through filing an acceptable complaint.[303] Only currently effective (no drafts or other predecisional material) LCDs or NCDs (or deemed NCDs) may be challenged.[304] During the review of an NCD or LCD, the aggrieved party bears the burden of proof and the burden of persuasion for the issue(s) raised in a complaint; the burden of proof is judged by a preponderance of the evidence.[305]

§ 6.04 MEDICARE PART B AND PAYMENT

[A] Medicare Assignment Program

The Medicare assignment program was established in 1984 and initially focused on physicians.[306] The program now includes both physicians and suppliers.[307] Under this program, physicians and suppliers agree to accept the Medicare reasonable charge amount (the Medicare-approved amount) as payment in full (no balance billing) with the beneficiary being responsible for a 20 percent copayment.[308]

In order to participate, physicians and suppliers must make an annual election whether to participate and sign a participation agreement. Physicians and

---

[302] 42 C.F.R. § 426.310.

[303] 42 C.F.R. § 426.320; *see also* Hays v. Leavitt, 583 F. Supp. 2d 62 (D.D.C. 2008), in which the federal district court confirmed that only the beneficiary can challenge an LCD and that the term "reasonable and necessary" refers to coverage and not to cost. The opinion is presently *available at* https://ecf.dcd.uscourts.gov/cgi-bin/show_public_doc?2008cv1032-22 (site visited Aug. 6, 2018).

[304] 42 C.F.R. § 426.325.

[305] 42 C.F.R. § 426.330. For further discussion of the NCD process, *see* CMS, "Medicare Coverage Determination Process," *available at* https://www.cms.gov/Medicare/Coverage/DeterminationProcess/ (site visited Aug. 6, 2018); *see also* CMS, Revised Process for Making Medicare National Coverage Determinations, 68 Fed. Reg. 55,634 (Sept. 26, 2003), *available at* http://www.cms.gov/Medicare/Coverage/DeterminationProcess/Downloads/FR09262003.pdf (site visited Aug. 6, 2018) & CMS, Meeting of the Medicare Coverage Advisory Committee—November 4, 2004, 69 Fed. Reg. 57,325 (Sept. 24, 2004), *available at* http://www.cms.gov/Medicare/Coverage/DeterminationProcess/Downloads/guidance.pdf (site visited Aug. 6, 2018). *See also* Medicare Payment Advisory Commission (MedPac), "Appendix B: An Introduction to How Medicare Makes Coverage Decisions," *available at* http://67.59.137.244/publications/congressional_reports/Mar03_AppB.pdf (site visited Aug. 6, 2018). For *Federal Register* material on challenging an NCD/LCD, *see* 68 Fed. Reg. 63,692.

[306] 42 U.S.C. § 1395u(b)(4). *See also* MCP Manual, Ch. 1: §§ 30.3 *et seq.* For the physician assignment form, *see* CMS, Medicare Participating Physician or Supplier Agreement, *available at* https://www.cms.gov/cmsforms/downloads/cms460.pdf (site visited Aug. 6, 2018).

[307] *See* 42 C.F.R. §§ 424.55 (payment to supplier), 414.48 (limits on actual charges of nonparticipating suppliers), and 400.202 (definition specific to Medicare, including payment on an assignment-related basis).

[308] 42 U.S.C. § 1395u(b)(3)(B)(ii); 42 C.F.R. § 410.152. *See also* 42 U.S.C. § 1395n; 42 C.F.R. § 424.55(b).

suppliers who do not elect to participate may participate on a case-by-case basis.[309] Physicians and suppliers who participate are designated as participating physicians and suppliers, are listed in directories of Medicare participating physicians and suppliers, and receive certain insignia they can use in their offices to identify themselves as participants in the Medicare assignment program. Participating physicians and suppliers also receive a five percent higher Medicare fee schedule amount.[310]

[B] Fee Schedules and Limiting Charge Amounts

Beginning in November 1989, Congress enacted additional physician payment reforms that limited what physicians who do not participate in the Medicare assignment program can charge their Medicare patients, effective January 1, 1991.[311] The limiting charge amount for non-participating physicians for their Medicare patients is no more than 115 percent above the Medicare fee schedule amount, which is the recognized payment amount or limiting charge.[312] For example, if Medicare sets the recognized payment amount for a service at $100, even though the non-participating physician might bill non-Medicare patients at $175, the physician can bill his or her Medicare patient for the service no more than $115.

Physicians who treat patients eligible for Medicaid, including qualified Medicare beneficiaries (QMBs), must bill on an assignment-only basis.[313] Moreover, if the services of a non-participating physician to Medicare beneficiaries are determined not to be medically necessary, the physician must return the billed amount to the beneficiary.[314] With respect to elective surgery costing $500 or

---

[309] 42 U.S.C. § 1395u(h)(2)–(6).

[310] 42 U.S.C. §§ 1395w-4(g), 1395u(b)(4)(A)(iv). *See also* Whitney v. Heckler, 780 F.2d 963, 970-72 (11th Cir. 1986) (upholding the five percent cost differential).

[311] *See* Omnibus Budget Reconciliation Act of 1989 (OBRA '89), Pub. L. No. 101-239, 6102 (adding § 1848(g) to the Social Security Act, 42 U.S.C. § 1395w-4(g) (limitation on beneficiary liability)); 42 C.F.R. § 414.48.

[312] 42 U.S.C. § 1395w-4(g)(2)(B), (C). It should be noted that states can establish more stringent balance billing limits, given that Congress has not totally preempted the field. *See* Pennsylvania Med. Soc'y v. Marconis, 942 F.2d 842 (3d Cir 1991); Massachusetts Med. Soc'y v. Dukakis, 815 F.2d 790 (1st Cir. 1987); Medical Soc'y of N.Y. State v. Cuomo, 777 F. Supp. 1157 (S.D.N.Y. 1991); Downhour v. Somani, 85 F.3d 261 (6th Cir.), *cert. denied*, 519 U.S. 965 (1996). In addition, New York Medicare beneficiaries have been found to have a private right of action against hospit2als to seek repayment against a hospital for physician overcharges under Medicare and state law that limits charge laws. *See* Medicare Beneficiaries Def. Fund v. Memorial Sloan-Kettering Cancer Ctr., 603 N.Y.S.2d 1016 (Sup. Ct. 1993).

[313] 42 U.S.C. § 1395w-4(g)(3) (applies to services furnished on or after April 1, 1990).

[314] 42 C.F.R. § 411.408.

more, nonparticipating physicians must provide the beneficiary with written information that sets out the difference in the Medicare reimbursement and the physician's full charge.[315] In addition, physicians must submit all claims, both assigned and unassigned, for their Medicare beneficiaries; they cannot charge extra for this service, and claims have to be submitted within one year of the date of providing services(s) for which reimbursement is sought.[316] All payments for ambulance services are made on an assignment-only basis. Providers can collect from beneficiaries only the unmet Part B deductible and Part B coinsurance amounts.[317]

[C] Limited Prior Determination Process

Section 938 amends the MMA[318] to create a limited prior determination process regarding physician services determined by the Secretary to be subject to the process.[319] Under the process, a participating physician who has permission from the patient or an individual who has received an ABN may ask the appropriate Medicare contractor for a determination of whether Medicare will pay for a service before actually receiving the service.[320]

The Secretary may require that the request be accompanied by a description of the physician's service, supporting medical necessity documentation, the ABN if the requester is the individual, and other appropriate documents. The contractor must then provide a written notice, within 45 days of receipt of the request, as to whether the service is covered, is not covered, or the contractor lacks sufficient information to make a coverage determination. The contractor must inform the beneficiary of the decision if the request was made by the physician.

A determination that a service is covered is binding on the contractor in the absence of fraud or misrepresentation of the facts. If the determination is not favorable, the individual has no appeal rights. However, the individual may still receive the service and have a claim submitted to the contractor. If the claim for services received is denied, the individual may then pursue an appeal through the regular appeals process. Similarly, an individual who decides not to go through the prior determination process, but who chooses instead to receive the service and seek reimbursement, retains current appeals rights.

---

[315] 42 U.S.C. § 1395w-4(g).

[316] 42 U.S.C. § 1395w-4(g)(4).

[317] 67 Fed. Reg. 9099, 9134, amending 42 C.F.R. § 414.610(a)–(g) by adding new § 414.610(b).

[318] 42 U.S.C. § 1395ff(h).

[319] 42 U.S.C. § 1395ff(h).

[320] 42 U.S.C. § 1395ff(h).

[D] Advance Determination of Medicare Coverage

The current Advance Determination of Medicare Coverage (ADMC) is an optional process[321] that takes the place of the old "prior approval" process, but it is only for certain wheelchairs (manual or power-driven), related options, and accessories.[322] It is used to obtain a coverage decision from a DME MAC prior to delivery and payment for DME that is subject to the ADMC process. Requests for an ADMC are submitted to the relevant DME MAC, which will have on its web page, or will otherwise make available, a statement of the information that is required for review of an ADMC request. A negative ADMC determination is not subject to an appeal because it does not meet the definition of an initial determination, as no request for payment is being made. ADMC requests may be resubmitted only once during the six-month period following a negative determination. Likewise, if the wheelchair base is approved, but one or more accessories are denied, an ADMC request may not be resubmitted for those accessories.

[E] Private Physician Contracts

BBA '97 established an option allowing Medicare beneficiaries to enter into private contracts with their physicians (either a provider group, a network of providers, or an individual provider) to pay privately for services otherwise covered by the Medicare program.[323] Medicare limitations on actual charges and the physician requirement to submit claims do not apply.[324] For purposes of this provision, a Medicare beneficiary is an individual who is entitled to benefits under Part A or enrolled under Part B.[325]

Contracts under this provision are outside the Medicare program and physicians must agree not to bill Medicare for Medicare-covered service for a period of two years and submit a written affidavit to the Secretary of HHS to that

---

[321] *See* § 1834a (15) of the Social Security Act, 42 U.S.C. § 1395m(a)(15) (Advance Determinations of Coverage for Certain Items). *See also* MPI Manual, Ch. 5, *available at* http://www.cms.gov/Regulations-and-Guidance/Guidance/Manuals/downloads/pim83c05.pdf (site visited Aug. 6, 2018).

[322] *See* MPI Manual, Ch. 5: § 5.16. Relevant Wheelchair HCPCS codes are E1161, E1231–E1234, K0005, K0009, K0835–K0843, K0848–K0855 (only if an alternative drive control interface will be provided at the time of initial issue), K0856–K0864, K0868–K0871 (only if an alternative drive control interface will be provided at the time of initial issue), and K0877–K0891. When the base code is eligible, all options and accessories ordered by the physician for the chair are eligible for an ADMC. For information on the DME MAC covering your jurisdiction, *see* CMS, DME MAC Jurisdiction Map (Jan. 2016), *available at* https://www.cms.gov/Medicare/Medicare-Contracting/Medicare-Administrative-Contractors/Downloads/DME-MAC-Jurisdiction-Map-Jan-2016.pdf (site visited Aug. 6, 2018).

[323] 42 U.S.C. § 1395a(b)(1)–(4); 42 C.F.R. §§ 405.400–405.450.

[324] 42 U.S.C. § 1395a(b)(4).

[325] 42 U.S.C. § 1395a(b)(4).

effect.[326] A copy of the affidavit of the physician showing that the physician has advised the beneficiary of his or her rights under this provision must be filed with the Secretary of HHS within ten days after the first such contract has been signed.[327]

Moreover, the provider of service must warn the beneficiary that Medicare balance billing limits do not apply and that Medicare Supplemental Insurance (Medigap) may not provide coverage under these circumstances.[328] In addition, the provision stipulates that a Medicare beneficiary who has entered such a contract is free to use his or her Medicare card with other physicians who have not signed such a contract.[329] The law also provides that such contracts cannot be entered when the beneficiary is facing the need for emergency or urgently needed care.[330]

Contracts must clearly indicate that the beneficiary:[331]

- Agrees not to submit a claim (or request that a physician or practitioner submit a claim) to Medicare for covered services;
- Agrees to be responsible, whether through insurance or otherwise, for payment for services provided and that no reimbursement will be provided from Medicare;
- Acknowledges that no fee schedule or balance billing limits will apply to physician or provider charges;
- Acknowledges that Medigap plans do not, and that other supplemental insurance plans may not, elect to make payments for such services because payment is not made under Medicare; and
- Acknowledges that the Medicare beneficiary has the right to use other physicians who have not entered into such contracts.

[F] Accountable Care Organizations

On November 1, 2011, the final rule establishing a Medicare Shared Savings Program (MSSP) was released.[332] An MSSP promotes accountability for a defined patient population, coordinates items and services under traditional Medicare Parts A and B, and encourages investment in infrastructure and redesigned

---

[326] 42 U.S.C. § 1395a(b)(3).

[327] 42 U.S.C. § 1395a(b)(3); 42 C.F.R. § 405.420 (requirements of the opt-out affidavit).

[328] 42 U.S.C. § 1395a(b)(2).

[329] 42 U.S.C. § 1395a(b)(2).

[330] 42 U.S.C. § 1395a(b)(2); 42 C.F.R. § 405.420(j).

[331] 42 U.S.C. § 1395a(b)(2)(B); 42 C.F.R. § 405.420.

[332] 42 Fed. Reg. 67,802.

care processes for high quality and efficient service delivery.[333] Under the MSSP, groups of providers of services and suppliers that meet criteria established by the Secretary may work together to manage and coordinate care for Medicare fee-for-service beneficiaries through an accountable care organization (ACO). An ACO that meets quality performance standards established by the Secretary is eligible to receive payments for shared savings.

The provisions for the MSSP outlined below bring many of the features that are associated with MA coordinated care plans into the traditional Medicare program. Because the MSSP operates only in the traditional Medicare program, beneficiaries enrolled in an MA plan under Medicare Part C, a competitive medical plan, or in a Program of All-Inclusive Care for the Elderly (PACE) cannot receive services through an ACO under the MSSP.

On June 9, 2015, CMS published in the *Federal Register* a final rule concerning the workings of its ACO program.[334] With the exception of the amendments to Sections 425.312, 425.704, and 425.708, the provisions of the final rule are effective on August 3, 2015. The amendments to Sections 425.312 and 425.708 became effective November 1, 2015. The amendments to Section 425.704 became effective January 1, 2016. The rule concerns the workings of CMS's ACOs, established by Section 3022 of the Affordable Care Act.[335] ACOs, part of the Medicare Shared Savings Program, are part of Medicare's fee-for-service offerings and are designed to improve health care delivery and patient experience and to reduce costs. As discussed below, it is a voluntary program. Applications from ACOs are accepted on an annual basis for contracts of three years' duration.[336]

[1] Eligible Providers and Suppliers

As determined by the Secretary, the following groups of suppliers and providers of services, who have established a mechanism for shared governance, are eligible to participate as ACOs under the program:

---

[333] See ACA § 3022, creating the Medicare Shared Savings Program (MSSP), effective March 23, 2010. Section 3022 amends the Social Security Act to add a new § 1899, 42 U.S.C. 1395jjj. For regulations implementing the accountable care organization (ACO) program, *see* 42 C.F.R. Pt. 425 (Nov. 2, 2011).

[334] *See* CMS, Medicare Shared Savings Program: Accountable Care Organizations, *available at* http://www.gpo.gov/fdsys/pkg/FR-2015-06-09/pdf/2015-14005.pdf (site visited Aug. 6, 2018). *See also* 42 C.F.R. Pt. 425.

[335] *See* CMS, "Shared Savings Program," *available at* http://www.cms.gov/Medicare/Medicare-Fee-for-Service-Payment/sharedsavingsprogram/index.html (site visited Aug. 6, 2018).

[336] For a description of the program, *see* CMS, "Accountable Care Organization (ACO) Investment Model," *available at* https://www.cms.gov/newsroom/fact-sheets/accountable-care-organization-aco-investment-model (site visited Aug. 6, 2018).

- ACO professionals (physicians and other professionals recognized under the Medicare program) in group practice arrangements; networks of individual practices of ACO professionals;
- Partnerships or joint venture arrangements between hospitals and ACO professionals;
- Hospitals employing ACO professionals; and
- Such other groups of suppliers or providers of services as the Secretary determines appropriate.

[2] Ineligible Providers and Suppliers

Under the MSSP, a supplier or provider of services who participates in any of the following is *not* eligible to participate in an ACO:

- A model tested or expanded under the demonstration projects authority of the Secretary that involves shared savings under this title;
- Any other program or demonstration project that involves such shared savings; and
- The independence at home medical practice pilot program.

[3] Accountable Care Organization Contractual Requirements

An ACO must: be willing to become accountable for the quality, cost, and overall care of the Medicare fee-for-service beneficiaries assigned to it; enter into an agreement with the Secretary to participate in the program for not less than a three-year period (the agreement period); have a formal legal structure that would allow the organization to receive and distribute payments for shared savings to participating suppliers and providers of services; include primary care ACO professionals that are sufficient for the number of Medicare fee-for-service beneficiaries assigned to the ACO (at a minimum, the ACO shall have at least 5,000 beneficiaries assigned to it); provide the Secretary with information regarding professionals participating in the ACO as the Secretary determines necessary to support the assignment of Medicare fee-for-service beneficiaries to an ACO, the implementation of quality and other reporting requirements, and the determination of payments for shared savings; have in place a leadership and management structure that includes clinical and administrative systems; have a defined process to promote evidence-based medicine and patient engagement, report on quality and cost measures, and coordinate care, such as through the use of telehealth, remote patient monitoring, and other such enabling technologies; and demonstrate to the Secretary that it meets patient-centeredness criteria specified by the

Secretary, such as the use of patient and caregiver assessments or the use of individualized care plans.[337]

[4] Quality Measures Reporting

The Secretary is to determine appropriate measures to assess the quality of care furnished by the ACO, including such measures as clinical processes and outcomes; patient and (where practicable) caregiver experiences; and utilization, such as rates of hospital admissions for conditions for which good outpatient care could potentially prevent the need for hospitalization, or for which early intervention could prevent complications or more severe disease ("ambulatory care sensitive conditions"). The Secretary may, as she determines appropriate, incorporate reporting requirements and incentive payments related to the physician quality reporting initiative, including electronic prescribing, electronic health records, and other similar initiatives, and may use alternative criteria that would otherwise apply under for determining whether to make such payments. Incentive payments shall not be taken into consideration when calculating payments otherwise made under the ACO provision.[338]

[5] Assignment of Traditional Medicare Beneficiaries to Accountable Care Organizations

The Secretary shall determine an appropriate method to assign traditional Medicare beneficiaries to an ACO, based on their utilization of primary care services provided by an ACO professional. Under the program, payments shall continue to be made to suppliers and providers of services participating in an ACO in the same manner as they would otherwise be made except that a participating ACO is eligible to receive payment for shared savings if the ACO meets quality performance standards established by the Secretary and meets the contracting requirements above.[339]

[6] Savings Requirement and Benchmark

An ACO shall be eligible to receive payment for shared savings only if the estimated average per capita Medicare expenditures for traditional Medicare

---

[337] *See also* Office of Inspector General (OIG), "Accountable Care Organizations," *available at* http://oig.hhs.gov/compliance/accountable-care-organizations/index.asp (site visited Aug. 6, 2018).

[338] *See also* CMS, "Quality Measures," *available at* https://www.cms.gov/Medicare/Quality-Initiatives-Patient-Assessment-Instruments/QualityMeasures/index.html (site visited Aug. 6, 2018).

[339] For a review of ongoing developments with respect to ACOs, *see* CMS, "Accountable Care Organizations (ACOs)," *available at* http://www.medicare.gov/manage-your-health/coordinating-your-care/accountable-care-organizations.html (site visited Aug. 6, 2018).

beneficiaries for Part A and Part B services under the ACO (adjusted for beneficiary characteristics), is below the applicable benchmark by at least the percentage specified by the Secretary for a given year.[340] The Secretary shall determine the appropriate percentage to account for normal variation in expenditures, based on the number of Medicare fee-for-service beneficiaries assigned to an ACO. The Secretary will estimate a benchmark for each agreement period for each ACO. The benchmark will be based on the most recent data available for three years of per-beneficiary expenditures for Medicare Parts A and B services for fee-for-service beneficiaries assigned to the ACO. The benchmark will be adjusted for beneficiary characteristics and other factors the Secretary determines appropriate and will be updated by the projected absolute amount of growth in national per capita expenditures for Medicare Parts A and B services under the original fee-for-service program, as estimated by the Secretary. The benchmark will be reset at the start of each agreement period.[341]

[7] Payments for Shared Savings

The Secretary will establish limits on the total amount of shared savings that may be paid to an ACO. If the Secretary determines that an ACO has taken steps to avoid more costly patients to reduce the likelihood of increasing expenses to the ACO, the Secretary may impose an appropriate sanction on the ACO, including termination from the program. Payment of shared savings to ACOs, based on meeting quality performance measures established by the Secretary, will be a percentage (as determined by the Secretary) of the difference between the estimated average per capita Medicare expenditures in a year (adjusted for beneficiary characteristics) under the ACO and the benchmark established for the ACO. The remainder of the difference will be retained by the MSSP.[342]

[8] Termination, Administration, and Waiver Authority

The Secretary may terminate an agreement with an ACO if it does not meet the Secretary's quality performance standards. Rules concerning the coordination of federal information policy and security (printing and documents) will not apply to the ACO program. In addition, the Secretary may waive civil money penalties

---

[340] *See* CMA, "Accountable Care Organizations Should Increase Coordinated Care in Traditional Medicare," *available at* http://www.medicareadvocacy.org/accountable-care-organizations-should-increase-care-coordination-in-traditional-medicare/ (site visited Aug. 6, 2018).

[341] *See also* CMS, Medicare Shared Savings Program Quality Measure Benchmarks for the 2016 and 2017 Reporting Years, *available at* https://www.cms.gov/Medicare/Medicare-Fee-for-Service-Payment/sharedsavingsprogram/Downloads/MSSP-QM-Benchmarks-2016.pdf (site visited Aug. 6, 2018).

[342] *See also* CMS, "Shared Savings Programs."

requirements for false claims and the criminal penalties for fraud under the Medicare program as necessary to carry out the MSSP.[343]

[9] Limitations on Review

There will be no administrative or judicial review of the specific criteria for establishing an ACO; the assessment of the quality of care furnished by an ACO and the establishment of performance standards; the assignment of Medicare fee-for-service beneficiaries to an ACO; the determination of whether an ACO is eligible for shared savings and the amount of such shared savings, including the determination of the estimated average per capita Medicare expenditures under the ACO for Medicare fee-for-service beneficiaries and the average benchmark for the ACO; the percent of shared savings specified by the Secretary and any limit on the total amount of shared savings established by the Secretary; and the termination of an ACO.

[10] Bipartisan Budget Act of 2018

The Bipartisan Budget Act (BBA) of 2018 incorporated provisions of the 2017 Creating High-Quality Results and Outcomes Necessary to Improve Chronic Care Act (CHRONIC Care Act) intended to provide ACOs with increased flexibility.[344] The BBA expands ACO use of telehealth services by allowing the beneficiary's home to be used as an eligible originating site beginning in 2020.[345] In addition, the BBA allows MSSP ACO models to prospectively assign beneficiaries at the beginning of a performance year, and permits some ACOs to make incentive payments to beneficiaries for qualifying primary care services.[346]

§ 6.05 FILING MEDICARE PART B CLAIMS

Claims for Part B services, including physician services and other services reimbursable on a charge basis or fee schedule basis, must be filed no later than the end of the calendar year following the year in which the services were furnished. The time limit on filing claims for services is the period ending one

---

[343] *See also* CMA, "Accountable Care Organizations Should Increase Care Coordination in Traditional Medicare."

[344] Bipartisan Budget Act of 2018, Pub. L. No. 115-123 (2018); S. 870, 115th Cong. §§ 304, 401, 501 (2017).

[345] Bipartisan Budget Act of 2018, Pub. L. No. 115-123, § 50324, 140 (2018).

[346] Bipartisan Budget Act of 2018, Pub. L. No. 115-123. §§ 50331, 50341, 142-146 (2018); *see also* National Association of ACOs, "Provisions in the Bipartisan Budget Act of 2018 Pertaining to Accountable Care Organizations," *available at* https://www.naacos.com/provisions-in-the-bipartisan-budget-act-of-2018-pertaining-to-accountable-care-organizations (site visited Aug. 6 2018).

calendar year after the date of the service (the Secretary may create exceptions).[347]

For services furnished on or after September 1, 1990, physicians and suppliers are required to complete and submit both assigned and non-assigned Part B claims for their Medicare patients within 12 months of the date of the services received.[348] Physicians and suppliers who submit claims beyond this time period will have their claims reduced by 10 percent of the amount that would otherwise be paid; physicians who submit non-assigned claims late are subject to monetary penalties.[349]

With respect to the submission of claims, a claim is any writing submitted by or on behalf of the claimant, indicating a request or claim for payment from Medicare in connection with the receipt of medical services. No particular claim form is required, although a variety of Medicare billing forms are prepared and recognized by CMS. Claims should identify the beneficiary and the services received, although the identification of services does not have to be complete. Claims are considered filed when mailed or delivered to CMS or any contractor (entity under contract with CMS to administer Part A and Part B claims).[350]

Contractor jurisdiction for the submission and processing of claims is generally the geographic area in which the physician's or supplier's office is located. If the physician or supplier maintains offices in more than one contractor service area, each office is serviced for that area. If the physician does not maintain an office but uses his or her home address, that address determines the contractor jurisdiction. If the office where the service is rendered is in another contractor's jurisdiction, the claim must be transferred to that contractor.[351]

---

[347] 42 C.F.R. § 424.44(1); MCP Manual, Ch. 1: § 70. ACA § 6404(a)(2)(A) (Part B) (in the case of services furnished before January 1, 2010, a bill or request for payment under § 1814(a)(1) (conditions and limitations for payment for services), § 1842(b)(3)(B) (provisions related to the administration of Part B), or § 1835(a) (procedures for the payment of claims for providers of services) shall be filed not later than December 31, 2010). *See* ACA § 6404(b)(2). For a list of exceptions, *see* 42 C.F.R. § 424.44(2).

[348] 42 U.S.C. § 1395w-4(g)(4). *See* https://www.gpo.gov/fdsys/pkg/USCODE-2011-title42/html/USCODE-2011-title42-chap7-subchapXVIII.htm (site visited Aug. 6, 2018). MCP Manual, Ch. 1, §§ 70 *et seq.* Claims submitted for Part B services received from a non-participating hospital or for services received out of the United States must be submitted in accordance with the rules described above. *See* 42 C.F.R. §§ 424.100 *et seq. See* MCP Manual, Ch. 1: § 10.2.1. *See also* 42 U.S.C. § 1395u(b)(6) (who can receive payment).

[349] 42 U.S.C. § 1395w-4(g)(4)(B).

[350] MCP Manual, Ch. 1: § 70.7.1.

[351] MCP Manual, Ch. 1: § 10.1.1

§ 6.06 INFORMATION ABOUT COVERAGE

[A] Annual Notice to Beneficiaries

The BBA '97 required the Secretary to provide Medicare beneficiaries with an Annual Notice to Beneficiaries, instructing beneficiaries to check carefully their explanations of benefits or itemized statements for accuracy, along with a toll-free telephone number for reporting errors and questionable charges, including fraud and abuse reporting.[352] The annual notice to beneficiaries also must tell them that they have a right to request of their physician, provider, supplier, or other entity providing services, an itemized statement of Medicare-covered items and services provided.

The requested itemization is to be provided no later than 30 days from the date of the request.[353] Failure to provide the requested itemization can result in civil money penalties of $100 for each such failure.[354] The beneficiary has 90 days from the date of receipt of the itemization to submit a written request to the Secretary for review of the itemization.[355]

[B] Medicare Summary Notices

Generally, official notice from Medicare must be obtained before a beneficiary has a right to file an appeal.[356] The Medicare Summary Notice (MSN) constitutes the "initial determination" or written notice that briefly explains what Medicare will pay on a claim. The MSN is prepared by the Medicare contractor that reviews the claim. Many claims are denied in whole or in part on the MSN due to insufficient information and mistakes. Determinations finding that the medical service was not medically necessary and is, therefore, not covered under Medicare should be closely examined. Errors are often made. If the claimant does not think Medicare is allowing a sufficient reimbursement amount, the claimant should also question the MSN.[357]

---

[352] 42 U.S.C. § 1395b-2. The annual notice requirement became effective on the date of the enactment of BBA '97, Aug. 5, 1997.

[353] 42 U.S.C. § 1395b-7(2)(A).

[354] 42 U.S.C. § 1395b-7(2)(B). The effective date of the itemization requirement was January 1999.

[355] 42 U.S.C. § 1395b-7(3).

[356] *See* MCP Manual, Ch. 21. *See also* HHS, Office of Medicare Hearings and Appeals (OMHA), "The Appeals Process," *available at* http://www.hhs.gov/omha/process/index.html (site visited Aug. 6, 2018).

[357] For a discussion of CMS's updates to its MSN, *see* CMA, "New Medicare Summary Notice," *available at* http://www.medicareadvocacy.org/new-medicare-summary-notice/ (site visited Aug. 6, 2018). Note that CMS has reduced the frequency of Medicare Summary Notice (MSN) deliveries. They are sent quarterly when beneficiaries are not due a payment from Medicare. *See* CMS, Transmittal 1347, *available at* http://www.cms.hhs.gov/transmittals/downloads/R1347CP.pdf (site visited

It is important to note that for most Part B claims, the first notice beneficiaries should receive informing them that care will not be covered by Medicare is from the health care provider. Before they can charge a beneficiary, providers who participate in the Medicare program must first issue a written notice to the patient informing him or her that Medicare coverage will not be available. Providers have a financial incentive to issue denial notices because they may have to absorb the cost of the care they provide if they erroneously inform the beneficiary that the care will be covered but not if they erroneously deny coverage.

Notices from providers, however, do not form the basis for an appeal. The beneficiary must obtain a formal Medicare coverage determination or "initial determination" from the appropriate Medicare contractor.[358]

§ 6.07 APPEALS

[A] Appeals Arising Under Parts A and B of Medicare

Rules regarding Medicare appeals are codified at Subpart G of Part 405.[359] For Part B claims, the rules were phased in over the course of 2005 and fully in place by January 1, 2006. The rules establish a combined Part A and Part B appeals process.[360] CMS's regulations, referred to above, implement the changes to the appeals process for Medicare Part A and Part B claims and implement changes to the ALJ hearing process for all Medicare claims, including managed care claims and prescription drug claims.[361] For Part B claims that are currently decided by a Medicare carrier (or contractor), these appeal procedures are effective for redeterminations issued on or after January 1, 2006.[362]

Aug. 6, 2018). Beneficiaries may receive bills from providers that need to be paid before they have received an MSN. Under this circumstance, the beneficiary will not be able to verify in advance of payment whether the amount billed agrees with CMS's calculation, thus possibly increasing the number of disputes about payments. This has proved problematic, and there is an effort to return to a monthly MSN. For the redesigned MSN, along with the previous version, *see* CMS, "MSN Changes," For downloadable MSN files, *see* CMS, "Medicare Summary Notice," *available at* http://www.cms.gov/Medicare/Medicare-General-Information/MSN/index.html (site visited Aug. 6, 2018).

[358] *See* CMS, "First Level of Appeal: Redetermination by a Medicare Contractor," *available at* http://www.cms.gov/Medicare/Appeals-and-Grievances/OrgMedFFSAppeals/RedeterminationbyaMedicareContractor.html (site visited Aug. 6, 2018).

[359] *See* 42 C.F.R. §§ 405.900 *et seq.*

[360] The chart in **Appendix 6-3** outlines the basic structure of the Parts A & B appeals process. *See also* https://www.cms.gov/MLNProducts/downloads/MedicareAppealsprocess.pdf (site visited Aug. 6, 2018).

[361] *See* 42 C.F.R. §§ 405.900 *et seq.* (Subpart I—Determinations, Redeterminations, Reconsiderations, and Appeals under Original Medicare (Part A and Part B)), *available at* http://www.ecfr.gov/cgi-bin/text-idx?rgn=div6&node=42:2.0.1.2.5.8 (site visited Aug. 6, 2018).

[362] *See* 42 C.F.R. §§ 405.900 *et seq.*

CMS issued a final rule on March 20, 2017 that finalized significant changes affecting Medicare appeals, particularly at the ALJ level of review. These changes apply to appeals of payment and coverage determinations for items and services furnished to Medicare beneficiaries, enrollees in MA and other Medicare competitive health plans, and enrollees in Medicare prescription drug plans, as well as to appeals of enrollment and entitlement determinations, and certain premium appeals.[363]

There remains great concern over the low success rate for appeals at the first two levels (redetermination and reconsideration) of appeals and the enormous backlog of appeals at the ALJ level.[364] As discussed in the sections below, the Center for Medicare Advocacy has addressed both of these issues through litigation.

CMS issued final regulations for the Medicare Claims Appeals Process (Parts A & B combined). The rules were effective as of January 8, 2010. Regulations governing the combined appeals process for Medicare Parts A and B, authorized by 42 U.S.C. § 1395ff, are codified at 42 C.F.R. § 405.900 *et seq.* (Subpart I—Determinations, Redeterminations, Reconsiderations, and Appeals under Original Medicare process).[365]

Highlights of the changes and clarifications for Parts A and B appeals are as follows:

- *Definition of a Contractor.* CMS has clarified the term contractor for purposes of Subpart I as an entity that has a contract with the federal government to review and/or adjudicate claims, determinations and/or decisions. This includes, but is not limited to, Medicare Administrative Contractors (MACs), Qualified Independent Contractors (QICs), and Quality Improvement Organizations (QIOs).
- *State Medicaid Agency as Party.* A Medicaid state agency cannot be a party to an initial determination. Rather, it can only be a party to a redetermination, reconsideration, hearing, or Council review. Only after

---

[363] CMS, Changes to the Medicare Claims and Entitlement, Medicare Advantage Organization Determination, and Medicare Prescription Drug Coverage Determination Appeals Procedures, 82 Fed. Reg. 4974 (Jan. 17, 2017), *available at* https://www.federalregister.gov/documents/2017/01/17/2016-32058/medicare-program-changes-to-the-medicare-claims-and-entitlement-medicare-advantage-organization (site visited Aug. 6, 2018).

[364] *See* CMA, "Senate Finance Committee Holds Hearing on Medicare Appeals Backlog—Proposed Solutions Are of Great Concern," *available at* http://www.medicareadvocacy.org/senate-finance-committee-holds-hearing-on-medicare-appeals-backlog-proposed-solutions-are-of-great-concern/ (site visited Aug. 6, 2018).

[365] For the final regulations, *see* 74 Fed. Reg. 65,296 *et seq.* (Dec. 9, 2009). *See* CMS, Changes to the Medicare Claims Appeal Procedures, *available at* http://edocket.access.gpo.gov/2009/pdf/E9-28707.pdf (site visited Aug. 6, 2018). *See also* CMS, Medicare Parts A & B Appeals Process (Feb. 2015), *available at* https://www.cms.gov/Outreach-and-Education/Medicare-Learning-Network-MLN/MLNProducts/downloads/MedicareAppealsProcess.pdf (site visited Aug. 6, 2018).

Medicare has issued its initial determination on a claim for items or services provided to a dually eligible beneficiary can a determination be made about a state agency's potential liability for all or part of the associated charges.

- *Appointment of Representative.* If an appeal request is filed by an individual attempting to represent a party, but the submission contains a defective Appointment of Representative (AOR) form, the adjudicator will give the party notice of the defect and time to correct it. A representative must submit, with each appeal request, a copy of the valid, effective AOR or other conforming written instrument in order to request a redetermination or other appeal on behalf of the party. A valid, executed AOR will be honored for the duration of the initial appeal request for which it is filed, and for any subsequent appeal requests with which it is submitted, provided the initial appeal request is filed within one year of the effective date of the AOR. With respect to Medicare Secondary Payer recovery claims, the AOR is deemed valid for longer than one year because liability, no-fault, and worker's compensation claims often take more than one year to resolve.
- *Proof of Authority to Represent Where Beneficiary Has Died.* In order to prevent unauthorized disclosures, CMS contractors must obtain documentation of the status of any person attempting to appeal on behalf of a deceased beneficiary, that is, authority to administer the estate by probate or intestate provisions of the relevant state probate law.
- *Approval of Fees before Charging Beneficiary.* In these final regulations, CMS reiterates its position, as in Social Security cases, that persons, including attorneys, wishing to charge a fee for representation services before the Secretary, must obtain approval of fees before charging a beneficiary. The requirement applies to proceedings at the Administrative Law Judge (ALJ) level and beyond. CMS also clarifies that the requirement does not apply to non-beneficiary appellants.
- *Medicare Summary Notice (MSN).* This notice and a remittance advice (RA) are only sent to parties of an initial determination. They are not sent to appointed representatives. The MSN covers the entire range of health care services and items billed to Medicare within a 90 calendar day period. An RA contains comprehensive claims information for all claims processed for a provider or supplier during a specific period.
- *Assignment of Appeal Rights.* CMS has clarified that appointing a representative and assigning appeal rights are two different and unrelated actions. Beneficiaries have the option of either (1) assigning (transferring), by a signed agreement, their appeal rights to the provider or supplier that provided the item or service at issue, if such person or entity is

not a party to the initial determination, or (2) appointing a representative (by a signed writing) to act on their behalf during the appeal.

- *Clean Claims.* Claims for services that cannot be timely adjudicated at the initial determination level because they lack sufficient documentation and/or require special handling do not come within the definition of clean claims.
- *Notice of Non-coverage.* A provider's notice of non-coverage does not constitute an initial determination because it is not a determination made by the Medicare program.
- *Effect of Claim Suspended for Medical Review by Contractor Staff.* A claim suspended for medical staff review is not considered a claim that is invalid or incomplete and would not preclude review. Rather, a claim that is suspended for development is one that appears technically sufficient on its face, but requires additional information in order to make a coverage and payment decision.
- *Calendar Days.* Throughout Subpart I, unless otherwise specified, CMS is now using the term "calendar day" to define what it means when it uses the word "day."
- *Final or Binding Decisions.* CMS is reserving the term "final" decision of the Secretary to describe those actions or decisions for which judicial review may be immediately sought. The term "binding" describes situations in which the parties are obligated to abide by the adjudicator's action or decision, unless further recourse to challenge the action or decision is available and a party exercises that right. In its comments, CMS notes that a binding decision is not a final decision of the Secretary for the purposes of exhausting administrative remedies prior to judicial review.
- *ALJ Subpoena Power.* An ALJ may not issue a subpoena to CMS or its contractors, on his or her own initiative or at the request of a party, to compel an appearance, testimony, or the production of evidence. Parties to an ALJ hearing who wish to subpoena documents or witnesses must file a written request for the issuance of a subpoena within the time period required (within ten calendar days of the receipt of the notice of the hearing).
- *Limits of ALJ and Medicare Administrative Contractors.* All laws and regulations pertaining to the Medicare and Medicaid programs, including but not limited to Titles XI, XVIII, and XIX of the Social Security Act and applicable implementing regulations, are binding on ALJs and Council.

- *Escalation to Council from the ALJ.* With respect to escalation, language says "if the ALJ does not issue a decision, dismissal order, or remand order within the later of 5 calendar days of receiving the request for escalation or 5 calendar days from the end of the applicable adjudication period as prescribed in the regulations at 42 C.F.R. § 405.1016,"[366] the appellant may request Council review. In addition, the appellant must send a copy of the request for review to the other parties to the ALJ decision or dismissal who received a copy of the hearing decision or a copy of the notice of dismissal.

With respect to QIO review, the Medicare agency has now separated out the review entities that will respond to beneficiary complaints from those that are to handle quality improvement matters for providers. On May 9, 2014, CMS announced the first phase of its restructuring of the QIO functions. In the first phase, CMS has contracted with Livanta LLC (for geographic areas 1 and 5), located in Annapolis Junction, Maryland, and KePRO (for geographic areas 2, 3, and 4), located in Seven Hills, Ohio. These contractors will be responsible for ensuring consistency in the review process with respect to beneficiary complaints. CMS describes these two contractors as its Beneficiary and Family-Centered Care (BFCC) QIO contractors.[367]

The states in the designated geographic areas are Area 1: Connecticut, Maine, Massachusetts, New Hampshire, New Jersey, New York, Pennsylvania, Puerto Rico, Rhode Island, Vermont, and Virgin Islands; Area 2: District of Columbia, Delaware, Florida, Georgia, Maryland, North Carolina, South Carolina, Virginia, and West Virginia; Area 3: Alabama, Arkansas, Colorado, Kentucky, Louisiana, Mississippi, Montana, North Dakota, New Mexico, Oklahoma, South Dakota, Tennessee, Texas, Utah, and Wyoming; Area 4: Iowa, Illinois, Indiana, Kansas, Michigan, Minnesota, Missouri, Nebraska, Ohio, Wisconsin; and Area 5: Alaska, Arizona, California, Hawaii, Idaho, Nevada, Oregon, and Washington.[368]

On July 18, 2014, as part of the restructuring of the QIO program—separating the beneficiary quality of care complaint review process from provider quality improvement functions—CMS awarded additional contracts to assist providers with quality improvement matters. The new contracts represent the second

---

[366] 42 C.F.R. § 405.1104(b).

[367] *See* CMS, "CMS Launches Next Phase of New Quality Improvement Program" (July 18, 2014), *available at* https://www.cms.gov/newsroom/press-releases/cms-launches-next-phase-new-quality-improvement-program (site visited Aug. 6, 2018).

[368] CMS, "CMS Launches Next Phase of New Quality Improvement Program" (July 18, 2014). *See also* CMS, Beneficiary and Family Centered Care Quality Improvement Organization Provider/Practitioner Frequently Asked Questions, *available at* http://qioprogram.org/sites/default/files/BFCC-QIO%20Provider%20and%20Practitioner%20FAQs%2011.17.15_508.pdf (site visited Aug. 6, 2018).

phase of QIO restructuring. These QIOs are known as the Quality Innovation Network (QIN)-QIOs.[369]

[B] Initial Determinations, Redeterminations, and Appeals

The claims process begins when the Medicare contractor issues an initial determination of a claim submitted by a provider.[370] The notice of the initial determination is sent to the beneficiary.[371] This happens even when the contractor is aware that the beneficiary has an appointed representative. An initial determination is made by the appropriate contractor with respect to coverage or reimbursement under the Medicare Act, including any amounts payable.[372] An initial determination is binding unless it is revised or reconsidered or revised as a result of a reopening.[373] The contractor must make an initial decision on clean claims (generally electronically submitted and about which there are no obvious computer/clerical errors) within 30 days of receipt; otherwise, interest must be paid as specified in the regulation.[374]

Notice of the initial determination must contain the reasons for the determination, including whether a local medical review policy, a local coverage determination, or a national coverage determination was applied.[375] The notice should also contain additional information about the determination, such as specific policies, manuals, laws, or regulations used in making the determination.[376] In addition, the notice should provide information about the right to a redetermination if the beneficiary is dissatisfied with the outcome of the initial determination[377] and instructions on how to request a redetermination.

Parties to the initial determination include the beneficiary, supplier, and provider.[378] Parties to the redetermination, reconsideration, hearing, and Council are the parties to the initial determination as provided in Section 409.906(a), except where the beneficiary has assigned his or her appeal rights to a provider or supplier under Section 409.912.[379] Parties to the redetermination, reconsideration, hearing, and Council also can include a state agency; a provider or supplier that has accepted an assignment of appeal rights; or a non-participating physician or

---

[369] *See* CMS, "CMS Launches Next Phase of New Quality Improvement Program" (July 18, 2014). Each QIN-QIO will work on strategic quality improvement initiatives.

[370] 42 C.F.R. § 405.904.

[371] 42 C.F.R. § 405.921(a)(2)(i).

[372] 42 C.F.R. § 405.920.

[373] 42 C.F.R. § 405.928. *See also* 20 C.F.R. §§ 404.907 and 404.988.

[374] 42 C.F.R. § 405.922.

[375] 42 C.F.R. § 405.921(a)(2)(ii).

[376] 42 C.F.R. § 405.921(b).

[377] 42 C.F.R. § 405.921(a)(2)(iii).

[378] 42 C.F.R. § 405.906(a).

[379] 42 C.F.R. § 409.906(b)(1).

supplier not billing on an assignment basis who may be liable to refund monies collected for services furnished to the beneficiary that were deemed not reasonable and necessary.[380]

Someone who wants to appeal from the initial determination must submit a written, signed request for a redetermination within 120 days of the initial determination; the regulations assume the notice is received five days after the date of the notice. Requests for redeterminations must be filed with the contractor.[381] A request is considered as filed on the date it is received by the contractor.[382]

The regulations allow providers and suppliers to request appeal of a denial of an initial determination,[383] raising the possibility that both the beneficiary and the provider or supplier will initiate the appeals process. In such a case the Medicare contractor must consolidate the appeals. The contractor has 60 days from receipt of the redetermination request to issue a decision.[384] If more than one party files a request, the time period runs from the date the last request is received.[385] For example, if a beneficiary files a redetermination request on day 1, but the provider files on day 50, the 60 calendar day time period for the contractor to act starts on day 50.

The regulations create a reopening process to be used instead of the redetermination process to correct minor errors or omissions in initial determinations, including at subsequent levels of review.[386]

It has been the experience of the Center for Medicare Advocacy (the Center) that virtually all appeals are denied at the first two levels of the administrative review process, with Medicare contractors performing only cursory reviews of the medical record and low-quality analysis. Consequently, the Center filed litigation[387] to address the problem. A critical issue is whether the Secretary of HHS's denial rate of about 98 percent at the lowest two levels of appeal in Medicare's system of administrative review (redetermination and reconsideration) violates the Medicare statute and the Due Process Clause. The plaintiff sought declaratory and injunctive relief for a nationwide class of Medicare beneficiaries who have received or will receive adverse redetermination and reconsideration decisions on their claims for coverage of home health care services. The court denied the government's motion to dismiss the due process claim, granted the motion to dismiss the statutory claim, and certified a nationwide class action on

---

[380] 42 C.F.R. § 409.906(b)(2).

[381] 42 C.F.R. § 405.942.

[382] 42 C.F.R. § 405.942(a)(2).

[383] *See* 42 C.F.R. § 405.906(c).

[384] 42 C.F.R. § 405.950.

[385] 42 C.F.R. § 405.950(b)(2).

[386] 42 C.F.R. § 405.980(a)(3). *See also* 42 C.F.R. § 405.980(a)(l)(i)-(iv).

[387] *Sherman v. Burwell*, (formerly *Olsen-Ecker v. Burwell*), No. 3:15-CV-01468 (D. Conn., Complaint filed Oct. 9, 2015).

August 8, 2016.[388] On December 12, 2017, the parties filed a joint motion for preliminary approval of a settlement agreement and notice to the class. The proposed settlement applies to all beneficiaries whose appeals for coverage of home health services have been or will be denied at the first two levels of review and who received an initial determination or notice of termination of coverage for those services dated on or after January 1, 2012. Under the agreement, the Medicare agency will transmit four memoranda containing important principles for deciding home health appeals to the Medicare contractors that handle those decisions at the first and second levels of review. A final fairness hearing was held on February 26, 2018, and the court approved the settlement, finding it fair, reasonable, and adequate.[389]

[C] The Qualified Independent Contractors—Reconsideration Determinations

The 2000 law created a third level of review, the reconsideration. Reconsiderations are conducted by a group of Medicare contractors called Qualified Independent Contractors (QICs).[390] The use of the QICs became effective for Part B claims currently handled by Medicare contractors with respect to redeterminations issued on or after January 1, 2006. Beneficiaries and other parties to the redetermination have 180 days to request reconsideration by filing a request at the location indicated on the redetermination notice.[391] Reconsiderations filed by both a beneficiary and a provider or supplier will be consolidated, and the time for the QIC to issue a decision runs from receipt of the last-filed appeal.[392]

The reconsideration level of review is a paper review; CMS states clearly in the preamble to the final regulations that QICs will not be conducting hearings. However, the QIC may solicit the view of the beneficiary.[393] As noted above, if providers or suppliers appeal from the QIO to the QIC, they are required to submit all of the evidence they want considered in the claim to the QIC. Evidence

---

[388] *Sherman*, No. 3:15-CV-01468 (ruling denying motion to dismiss and granting motion for class certification issued Aug. 8, 2016). For updates, *see* CMA, "Active Cases," *available at* http://www.medicareadvocacy.org/litigation/active-cases/ (site visited Aug. 6, 2018).

[389] *See* CMA, "CMA Alert – Tax Cuts will Hurt, Not Help; Sherman Fairness Hearing Set; 'Homebound' Settlement Objections Due; More," *available at* http://www.medicareadvocacy.org/tax-cuts-will-hurt-not-help-sherman-fairness-hearing-set-homebound-settlement-objections-due-more/ (site visited Aug. 6, 2018).

[390] 42 C.F.R. § 405.960. The QIC's jurisdiction over reconsideration determinations commenced on May 1, 2005, for all Part A determinations and those Part B determinations made by a QIO or fiscal intermediary (or contractor). The QIC's jurisdiction over Part B reconsideration determinations for all determination currently made by a Medicare Part B carrier (or contractor) commenced January 1, 2006. *See* 70 Fed. Reg. 11,424–26 (Mar. 8, 2005).

[391] 42 C.F.R. § 405.962.

[392] 42 C.F.R. § 405.964(c).

[393] 70 Fed. Reg. 11,447–78 (Mar. 8, 2005).

not submitted by providers or suppliers to the QIC may be excluded at subsequent levels of review.[394] However, beneficiaries who appeal (except those who are represented by a provider) may present evidence at further levels of appeal.[395]

The QIC must complete its reconsideration within 60 days of the reconsideration request.[396] Again, the time frame runs from the last request filed if more than one party seeks reconsideration; the QIC must so notify a party who filed an earlier request.[397] Although the statute allows a party to the reconsideration to ask for an extension of not more than 14 days for the QIC to conclude the reconsideration, the regulations add 14 days to the reconsideration time frame each time that additional evidence is submitted.[398]

In making its reconsideration determination, the QIC is bound by the NCDs promulgated by Medicare and CMS Rulings, as well as statute and regulations.[399] It is not bound by LCDs made by Medicare contractors nor by Medicare policy issued by CMS itself; however, the QIC must give "substantial deference" to these determinations and policy in making its decision.[400] If the QIC declines to apply them, the QIC's decision must state the reason why they were not followed.[401]

[D] Escalation

The MMA introduced the concept of "escalation" into the Medicare appeals process. Commencing at the reconsideration level of appeal, if a decision is not rendered within a set time frame,[402] a party to the appeal may "escalate" the appeal to the next level. For Part B claims currently processed by a Medicare contractor, the escalation process will not be in effect with respect to reconsiderations after January 1, 2006. If a QIC does not issue a timely reconsideration decision (60 days from the date of its receipt of the request for reconsideration),

---

[394] 42 C.F.R. § 405.966(a).

[395] 42 C.F.R. § 405.966(c).

[396] 42 C.F.R. § 405.970(a).

[397] 42 C.F.R. § 405.970(b)(2).

[398] 42 C.F.R. § 405.970(b)(3).

[399] 42 C.F.R. § 405.968(b).

[400] 42 C.F.R. § 405.968(b)(1), (2).

[401] 42 C.F.R. § 405.968(b)(3).

[402] The time frames are 60 days for the QIC to render a reconsideration determination (42 C.F.R. § 405.970); 90 days for an ALJ to issue a hearing decision (42 C.F.R. § 405.1016); 180 days for the Medicare Appeals Council (Council) to issue its decision (42 C.F.R. § 405.1100). *See* HHS, "Departmental Appeals Board (DAB)," *available at* http://www.hhs.gov/dab/index.html (site visited Aug. 6, 2018); *see* HHS, "Appeals to the Medicare Appeals Council (Council)," *available at* http://www.hhs.gov/dab/divisions/medicareoperations/index.html (site visited Aug. 6, 2018); To search MAC decisions, *see* HHS, "Medicare Appeals Council (Council) Decisions," *available at* http://www.hhs.gov/dab/divisions/medicareoperations/macdecisions/mac_decisions.html (site visited Aug. 6, 2018).

the statute and regulations allow a party to request that the appeal be escalated to the next level of review, the ALJ level. The regulations give the QIC five days to either issue a decision or acknowledge the escalation request and send it to the ALJ level of review. The regulations indicate that an appeal escalated to the ALJ level must be completed within 180 days of receipt, rather than the statutorily mandated 90 days for ALJ decisions. Even at the ALJ level, however, additional extensions of the time frame for issuing a decision can occur.[403]

[E] Administrative Law Judge Hearings

Beneficiaries and other parties have 60 days from receipt of the reconsideration determination to file a request for an ALJ hearing and if the amount in controversy is $160 or more in 2019.[404] The request for hearing must be filed at the address indicated on the reconsideration determination.[405] In addition, a party may escalate to the ALJ hearing from the QIC, when the QIC fails to issue a timely decision.[406] However, if an appeal is escalated to the ALJ, the 90 calendar day time frame for deciding an ALJ appeal is automatically extended to 180 days, with the possibility for additional extensions beyond the 180 days.[407]

The ALJ appeal level (transferred from the SSA) is under the administration of the Office of Hearings and Appeals (OMHA) at HHS, a change which was mandated by the MMA.[408] ALJs operate out of four locations: Miami, Florida; Cleveland, Ohio; Irvine, California; and Falls Church, Virginia. These are the only hearing offices in which Medicare ALJs are housed, effective on or after July 1, 2005.[409]

The revised regulations, pursuant to a final rule issued in January 2017,[410] authorize "Attorney Adjudicators," rather than ALJs to perform a portion of

---

[403] 42 C.F.R. §§ 405.970(b) and 405.1002(a) (reconsideration level); 42 C.F.R. §§ 405.1016(a)–(d) and 405.1104 (ALJ level); 42 C.F.R. §§ 405.1106(b) and 405.1132 (MAC level).

[404] Extension of this 60-day time frame may be granted upon a showing of good cause. 42 C.F.R. § 405.1014(c). *See also* 42 C.F.R. § 405.1108(a), (d)(3) and 80 Fed. Reg. 57,827–828 (Sept. 25, 2015).

[405] 42 C.F.R. § 405.1014(b)(2).

[406] 42 C.F.R. § 405.1002.

[407] 42 C.F.R. § 405.1016(c). Among the bases for an extension are if CMS is a party and a party requests discovery against another party (42 C.F.R. § 405.1016(d)); submission of additional evidence by a party later than 10 days after receiving a notice of hearing (42 C.F.R. § 405.1018(b)); a party's request for a copy of all or part of the administrative record [42 C.F.R. § 405.1042(b)(2)]; and a granted request for postponement of the hearing (42 C.F.R. § 405.1020(h)).

[408] 42 C.F.R. §§ 405.1004 *et seq.*

[409] *See* 70 Fed. Reg. 11,425 (Mar. 8, 2005).

[410] 82 Fed. Reg. 4974 (Jan. 17, 2017). For a summary of some of the provisions in the final rule, *see* CMA, "CMS Issues New Rules Governing Medicare Appeals" (Feb. 8, 2017) *available at* http://www.medicareadvocacy.org/issue-brief-cms-issues-new-rules-governing-medicare-appeals/ (site visited Aug. 6, 2018).

OMHA's workload that does not require a hearing.[411] Attorney adjudicators can issue decisions when a decision can be issued without an ALJ conducting a hearing under the regulations, dismissals when an appellant withdraws his or her request for an ALJ hearing, certain remands, and reviews of QIC and IRE dismissals. The revised regulations also make telephone hearings the default hearing method for individuals other than unrepresented beneficiaries.[412] Video-teleconferencing (VTC) will be retained as the default method of conducting hearings for unrepresented beneficiaries, unless good cause for an in-person appearance is shown or the beneficiary requests a phone hearing.[413]

CMS or its contractors may participate in or be made a party to the ALJ hearings, with rights to submit "position papers" and present witnesses (if they are "participants") and the right to cross-examine the other party's witnesses (if they are "parties").[414] An ALJ may seek to have CMS or its contractors participate or joined as parties, and CMS itself can request that it be a participant or party.[415] Under the regulations, an ALJ must permit CMS or its contractors to participate or be joined as parties, if they so request.

A notice of the hearing must be given to all parties, the Medicare contractor, and the QIC, advising them of the time and date for the hearing at least 20 days prior to the date of its scheduled date.[416] All of those receiving a notice of hearing are required to acknowledge whether they plan to attend the hearing or object to the proposed time and/or place of the hearing.[417] An objection to the time and/or place must be in writing and state the reasons for the objection.[418] If a party objects to the issues as stated in the notice of hearing, that party must notify the ALJ in writing no later than five days prior to the hearing of the objections, and send a copy of the objections to all other parties to the appeal.[419] The ALJ will make a decision with respect to the objections either in writing or at the hearing.[420]

Any new written evidence which a beneficiary wishes to submit must be submitted with the request for hearing or within ten days prior to the scheduled date of the hearing.[421] Evidence may be submitted later than ten days prior to the hearing, but the time frame for the ALJ's issuance of his or her decision is tolled for the period between when the evidence was required to be submitted and when

---

[411] 42 C.F.R. § 405.902.

[412] 42 C.F.R. § 405.1020(b).

[413] *Id.*

[414] 42 C.F.R. §§ 405.1010 (participants) and 405.1012 (parties).

[415] 42 C.F.R. §§ 405.1010 (participants), 405.1010(a), and 405.1012 (parties).

[416] 42 C.F.R. §§ 405.1020(c) and 405.1022(a).

[417] 42 C.F.R. § 405.1020(c)(2).

[418] 42 C.F.R. § 405.1020(e).

[419] 42 C.F.R. § 405.1024(a), (b).

[420] 42 C.F.R. § 405.1024(c).

[421] 42 C.F.R. § 405.1018(a). This provision does not apply to unrepresented beneficiaries or oral testimony given. 42 C.F.R. § 405.1018(d).

it was actually received.[422] Although providers are generally required to submit all relevant evidence at the QIC level of appeal, they may submit additional evidence if they establish "good cause" for failing to do so earlier.[423] The ALJ must review the new evidence submitted by the provider and notify all parties whether it is excluded.[424]

Generally, the issues at an ALJ hearing include all issues brought out at any prior level of appeal and not decided in a party's favor; even so, the ALJ may also include as an issue any portion of any prior determination that was decided favorably.[425] New issues may be raised at any time prior to the start of the hearing, if those new issues could have a material impact on the claims that are the subject of the request for hearing.[426]

Discovery at the ALJ level of appeal is permissible only when CMS elects to be made a party to the hearing.[427] Discovery is permissible with respect to any matter that is relevant to the subject matter of the hearing, although the party from whom discovery is sought may raise objections based on the assertion that the material sought is privileged or otherwise protected.[428] Additionally, an ALJ may deny a request for discovery if he or she concludes that the discovery request is unreasonable, unduly burdensome or expensive, or otherwise inappropriate.[429] Discovery is limited. A party may request reasonable production of documents for inspection and copying, but depositions may not be taken unless the deponent agrees or the ALJ finds the proposed deposition is appropriate and necessary.[430] Similarly, requests for admissions and interrogatories are generally not permitted.[431]

The ALJ may hold a pre-hearing or a post-hearing conference, either at his or her own initiative or at the request of a party.[432] The ALJ must inform the parties of the time, place, and purpose of the conference at least seven calendar days prior to the conference date.[433] The ALJ or an OMHA attorney designated by the ALJ conducts the conference, but only the ALJ conducting a conference may consider matters in addition to those stated in the conference notice if the parties consent to consideration of the additional matters in writing.[434] A record of the

---

[422] 42 C.F.R. § 405.1018(b).
[423] 42 C.F.R. § 405.1018(c).
[424] 42 C.F.R. § 405.1028(a)–(d).
[425] 42 C.F.R. § 405.1032(a).
[426] 42 C.F.R. § 405.1032(b). Certain limitations apply. *See* 42 C.F.R. § 405.980.
[427] 42 C.F.R. § 405.1037(a).
[428] 42 C.F.R. § 405.1037(a)(2).
[429] 42 C.F.R. § 405.1037(a)(2).
[430] 42 C.F.R. § 405.1037(b)(1), (2).
[431] 42 C.F.R. § 405.1037(b)(3).
[432] 42 C.F.R. § 405.1040.
[433] 42 C.F.R. § 405.1040(b).
[434] 42 C.F.R. § 405.1040(c).

hearing will be made, and the ALJ must issue an order stating all agreements and actions resulting from the conference.[435]

An administrative record, including marked exhibits, will be made.[436] A party may request to review the record prior to or at the hearing or, if a hearing is not held, at any time prior to the issuance of an ALJ decision.[437] However, given that hearings will most often not be held in person, the regulations offer no explanation as to how such a review can be accomplished. A party may request and receive a copy of all or part of the record; however, the party can be asked to pay the costs of providing the requested items.[438]

Once a hearing has been held,[439] the ALJ must issue a written decision that sets out findings of fact, conclusions of law, and the reasons for the decision.[440] The decision must be mailed or otherwise transmitted to each party, the Medicare contractors, and the QIC.[441]

If an ALJ decision is not rendered within the appropriate time frame for the circumstances of the case, a party may escalate the appeal to the Council.[442] If an appellant files a request to escalate an appeal to the Council level because the ALJ or attorney adjudicator has not completed his or her action on the request for hearing within an applicable adjudication period, the request for escalation must be filed with OMHA and the appellant must also send a copy of the request for escalation to the other parties who were sent a copy of the QIC reconsideration.[443] In a case that has been escalated from OMHA, the Council's 180-calendar-day period to issue a final decision, dismissal order, or remand order begins on the date the request for escalation is received by the Council.[444] In addition, the Council may, on its own initiative, remove a case from the ALJ and assume responsibility for holding a hearing and adjudicating the case itself.[445]

Currently, there is a considerable backlog of appeals at the ALJ level. Since FY 2010, when Medicare Recovery Audit Contractors (RACs) began actively trying to identify and correct improper payments under the National Recovery Audit program, there has been a dramatic increase in the volume of appeals, leading to huge backlogs and long delays to obtain decisions for beneficiaries and providers

---

[435] 42 C.F.R. §§ 405.1040(c) and 405.100(d).

[436] 42 C.F.R. § 405.1042.

[437] 42 C.F.R. § 405.1042(a)(3).

[438] 42 C.F.R. § 405.1042(b)(1).

[439] Parties are free to waive the right to a hearing, and have a decision issued solely on the administrative record. 42 C.F.R. §§ 405.1020(d) and 405.1038(b). In addition, an ALJ or OMHA attorney adjudicator may, without holding a hearing, issue a decision that is fully favorable to the appellant(s) if the hearing record supports such a finding. 42 C.F.R. § 405.1038(a).

[440] 42 C.F.R. § 405.1046(a).

[441] 42 C.F.R. § 405.1046(a).

[442] 42 C.F.R. § 405.1106(b).

[443] 42 C.F.R. § 405.1046(a).

[444] 2 C.F.R. § 405.1046(a).

[445] 42 C.F.R. § 405.1050.

alike. On August 1, 2016, the Center of Medicare Advocacy settled a nationwide class action lawsuit in federal court that challenged the long wait times for ALJ decisions faced by beneficiaries.[446] The settlement incorporates a policy of prioritizing beneficiary appeals to ensure timely processing, as well as certain reforms to make the ALJ appeals system easier for beneficiaries to use.[447] As of November 1, 2016, CMS updated scripts for 1-800-Medicare to highlight the OMHA beneficiary prioritization policy for beneficiary callers and to refer them to the toll-free OMHA Beneficiary Help Line if they have questions about filing appeals with OMHA or about ALJ appeals that are pending with OMHA. OMHA also posted beneficiary appeals data required by the settlement on their website.[448] In late January 2017, OMHA issued a new ALJ request form which allows beneficiaries and enrollees to self-identify, making it easier for these claims to be classified as beneficiary appeals and given priority for processing.[449]

HHS took administrative actions designed to reduce the number of pending appeals and to encourage resolution of cases earlier in the Medicare appeals process by implementing the regulatory changes in the final rule that became effective on March 20, 2017. The goals of the new/revised regulations were to address "recent workload challenges" as the number of ALJ hearing requests continues to exceed OMHA's adjudication capacity.[450] The changes in the final rule are primarily focused on the ALJ level of review and include the following modifications to the appeals process: permitting designation of Council decisions as precedential; expanding OMHA's available adjudicator pool by allowing attorney adjudicators to decide certain appeals; simplifying proceedings when CMS or CMS contractors are involved; clarifying areas of the regulations; and creating process efficiencies.[451] Many of the revisions do not, however, reach the heart of the problem and, if implemented, could further restrict beneficiary access to meaningful reviews.[452]

---

[446] *Exley v. Burwell*, No. 3:14-CV-1230 (D. Conn. May 24, 2016). The settlement is *available at* http://www.medicareadvocacy.org/exley-v-burwell-settlement-in-medicare-appeals-delay-case-granted-final-approval/ (site visited Aug. 6, 2018).

[447] *Exley*, No. 3:14-CV-1230.

[448] HHS, "Beneficiary Appeals Data," *available at* https://www.hhs.gov/about/agencies/omha/about/current-workload/beneficiary-appeals-data/index.html (site visited Aug. 6, 2018).

[449] https://www.hhs.gov/sites/default/files/OMHA-100%20Request%20for%20Hearing%20or%20Review%20of%20Dismissal%200329.pdf (site visited Aug. 10, 2017).

[450] 82 Fed. Reg. 4976 (Jan. 17, 2017).

[451] 82 Fed. Reg. 4974.

[452] CMA, "Issue Brief: CMS Issues New Rules Governing Medicare Appeals," *available at* http://www.medicareadvocacy.org/issue-brief-cms-issues-new-rules-governing-medicare-appeals/ (site visited Aug. 6, 2018).

[F] Medicare Appeals Council (Council) Review

A party who is dissatisfied with an ALJ decision may request review by the Council.[453] A written request for Council review must be filed with the Council or the appropriate ALJ office.[454] The request must identify those parts of the ALJ decision (or other determination being appealed, if the case is before the Council due to escalation) to which the party objects, and state the reasons for those objections.[455] Unless the appellant is an unrepresented beneficiary, the Council will limit its review to those parts of the decision below specifically identified as objectionable in the request for review.

If a party has requested review because he or she is dissatisfied with an ALJ decision, or has escalated an appeal from the ALJ to the Council, the Council will review *de novo* the decision below.[456] A party seeking Council review does not have a right to a new hearing; however, the Council, in its discretion, may conduct any additional proceedings, including holding a hearing.[457]

Generally, absent good cause,[458] no additional evidence may be introduced at the Council level of appeal, unless the ALJ decision being reviewed decides a new issue about which the parties were not afforded an opportunity to address before the ALJ.[459] However, a party to the Council review which is before the Council because of escalation may file a request for a subpoena of specified documents within 10 days of the request for escalation.[460]

The parties have the right to file briefs or other written statements with the Council.[461] In addition, the Council may request (but cannot require) CMS or its contractors to file a brief or position paper, if the Council determines that it is

---

[453] The Council may also exercise its "own motion" review. 42 C.F.R. § 405.1110. This review can occur upon the initiative of the Council or when CMS (or any of its contractors) refers a case to the Council that it thinks has been erroneously decided or the decision presents a broad policy or procedural issue that may affect the public interest. Note that previously, the Medicare Appeals Council has been referenced in a number of different ways: Departmental Appeals Board (DAB); Medicare Appeals Council (MAC); and Medicare Appeals Council (Board). CMS has indicated that all references are now to the Medicare Appeals Council (Council). *See, e.g.*, CMS, Changes to the Medicare Claims and Entitlement Appeals Process, *available at* https://www.cms.gov/Outreach-and-Education/Outreach/NPC/Downloads/2017-06-29-Appeals-Presentation.pdf (site visited Aug. 6, 2018).

[454] 42 C.F.R. § 405.1112(a).

[455] 42 C.F.R. § 405.1112(b).

[456] 42 C.F.R. § 405.1108.

[457] 42 C.F.R. § 405.1108(a), (d)(3).

[458] 42 C.F.R. § 405.1122(c).

[459] 42 C.F.R. § 405.1122(a).

[460] 42 C.F.R. § 405.1122(d)(1)–(4).

[461] 42 C.F.R. § 405.1120.

necessary to resolve the issues in the case.[462] In some instances, the Council may permit, or seek, oral argument on the appeal.[463]

The Council may dispose of the case in a number of ways: it may remand the case to the ALJ;[464] it may dismiss the request for Council review;[465] or it may issue a decision.[466] If the Council fails to issue its decision within the required 90-calendar-day time frame from its receipt of the request for Council review,[467] the appellant may request escalation to federal court.[468] If, upon filing of the escalation request and the lapse of the permissible time plus five additional days, the Council is unable to issue a decision, remand, or dismissal, it must notify the appellant informing him or her that it is not able to do so.[469] A party may file an action in federal district court within 60 days after the date it receives this notification from the Council.[470]

[G] Judicial Review

A party to a Council decision who is dissatisfied with that decision may obtain judicial review if the amount in controversy meets established requirements.[471]

The civil action must be filed within 60 days after receipt of notice of the Council decision.[472] Provisions exist in the regulations for applying to the Council for extension of the filing time.[473] The civil action must be filed in the district court for the judicial district in which the beneficiary resides or, if filed by a provider, in the judicial district where it has its principal place of business.[474] The Secretary of HHS in his or her official capacity is the proper defendant.[475] The

---

[462] 42 C.F.R. § 405.1120.

[463] 42 C.F.R. § 405.1124.

[464] 42 C.F.R. § 405.1108(d)(3).

[465] 42 C.F.R. § 405.1108(c), (d)(4)–(5).

[466] 42 C.F.R. § 405.1108(a), (d)(1).

[467] 42 C.F.R. § 405.1132. As with the other levels of appeal, the time frame for issuing a determination is subject to various extensions. *See, e.g.,* 42 C.F.R. § 405.1114 (extension when party seeks evidence from the Council), § 405.1120 (extension when briefs are filed), and § 405.1122(e)(2)(ii) (stay upon issuance of subpoena).

[468] 42 C.F.R. § 405.1132.

[469] 42 C.F.R. § 405.1132(a)(2).

[470] 42 C.F.R. § 405.1132(b).

[471] 42 C.F.R. § 405.1136. The calculation for the amount in controversy requirement is increased by the percentage increase in the medical care component of the consumer price index for all urban consumers (U.S. city average) as measured from July 2003 to the July preceding the current year involved. 42 C.F.R. § 405.1006. For calendar year (CY) 2019, the amount in controversy requirement for ALJ review is $160 or more; for judicial review, $1,600 or more.

[472] 42 C.F.R. § 405.1130.

[473] 42 C.F.R. § 405.1134.

[474] 42 C.F.R. § 405.1136(b).

[475] 42 C.F.R. § 405.1136(d).

standard of review for the court is whether the Secretary's decision is supported by substantial evidence.[476]

In addition, Section 932 of the MMA modified 42 U.S.C. § 1395ff(b) to create expedited access to the judicial review process whereby beneficiaries, providers, and suppliers can have expedited access to judicial review in certain appeals of Medicare Part A or Part B claims.[477] The expedited appeals process also applies to provider contract disputes—primarily nursing home enforcement cases.[478] Expedited review is available when it is determined both that the Council lacks authority to decide a question of law or regulation relevant to the case and that there is no material issue of fact in dispute.[479]

A beneficiary may file a request for expedited access to judicial review at the same time as, or after, filing a request for an ALJ hearing.[480] A review entity made up of three reviewers who are ALJs or members of the Council has 60 days after receipt of the request to issue a written decision.[481] The review entity may request appropriate documents and materials from the beneficiary to support his or her contention that (1) no material issues of fact exist and (2) the Council lacks authority to decide the relevant question of law or regulations.[482] If the review entity agrees with the beneficiary's request for expedited review, or if the review entity fails to act within 60 days of receipt of the request, the beneficiary skips ALJ and Council review and may go directly to district court.[483] If the review entity finds against the beneficiary, he or she has no further recourse and may not make another request for expedited review regarding the matter in dispute.[484]

§ 6.08 APPOINTMENTS OF REPRESENTATIVES AND ATTORNEYS' FEES

The regulations also specify the elements of a proper appointment of representative, its duration, and rules about collection of fees for representing Medicare beneficiaries in an appeal of a Medicare denial.[485] These rules are applicable to all Medicare appeals, including Part B appeals currently being handled by a Medicare contractor, effective May 1, 2005.[486]

A valid appointment of representation (AOR) form must:[487]

---

[476] 42 C.F.R. § 405.1136(f).
[477] 42 C.F.R. § 405.990.
[478] 42 C.F.R. §§ 405.906(a)–(c) and 405.990(e).
[479] 42 C.F.R. § 405.990(a)(2).
[480] 42 C.F.R. § 405.990(d)(2).
[481] 42 C.F.R. § 405.990(a)(1).
[482] 42 C.F.R. § 405.990(c).
[483] 42 C.F.R. § 405.990(f)(4).
[484] 42 C.F.R. § 405.990(h)(3)(i).
[485] 42 C.F.R. §§ 405.910 and 405.912.
[486] 70 Fed. Reg. 11,425 (Mar. 8, 2005).
[487] 42 C.F.R. § 405.910(c).

- Be in writing and signed and dated by both the beneficiary and the representative.
- Authorize the representative to act on behalf of the beneficiary and authorize the adjudicator to release identifiable health information to the representative.
- Include an explanation of the purpose and scope of the representation.
- Include the name, phone number, and address for the beneficiary and the representative.
- Include the beneficiary's Medicare health insurance claim number.
- Include the representative's professional status or relationship to the beneficiary.
- Be filed with the entity processing the party's initial determination or appeal.

If a form is defective, the representative will be given an opportunity to correct the defect. Otherwise, the representative will not have the authority to act on behalf of the beneficiary or to receive health information.[488] In addition, a representative must submit, with each appeal request, a copy of the valid, effective AOR or other conforming written instrument in order to request a redetermination or other appeal on behalf of the party. A valid, executed AOR will be honored for the duration of the initial appeal request for which it is filed, and for any subsequent appeal requests with which it is submitted, provided the initial appeal request is filed within one year of the effective date of the AOR. With respect to Medicare Secondary Payer recovery claims, the AOR is deemed valid for longer than one year because liability, no-fault, and worker's compensation claims often take more than one year to resolve.[489]

The regulations limit the duration of the appointment of representation form to one year. A duly appointed representative may file multiple appeals on behalf of an individual beneficiary during the course of that year, but must submit a copy of the original appointment form with each additional appeal filed. Once an appointment of representation form has been filed in a case, the appointment lasts for the duration of the appeal, even upon the death of the assignor, unless it is revoked.[490]

The regulations prohibit an appointed representative from delegating the appointment to another person without the beneficiary's consent. Thus, a family member who already serves as an appointed representative cannot delegate that

[488] 42 C.F.R. § 405.910(d)(2); *see also* material at **§ 6.07[A]**; For the final regulations, *see* CMS, Changes to the Medicare Claims Appeal Procedures, 74 Fed. Reg. 65,296 *et seq.* (Dec. 9, 2009), *available at* http://edocket.access.gpo.gov/2009/pdf/E9-28707.pdf (site visited Aug. 6, 2018).

[489] 74 Fed. Reg. 65,296 *et seq.*

[490] 42 C.F.R. §§ 405.910(e) and 405.912(e).

appointment to an advocate for purposes of pursing an appeal unless the beneficiary signs a written notice. A signed statement is not required where both the appointed and new representatives are attorneys (but not paralegals) in the same law firm or organization. When a beneficiary lacks the capacity to sign an appointment of representation form or form acknowledging delegation of the appointment, state law determines who has authority to authorize representation on his or her behalf.[491]

Under the regulations, a beneficiary's appointed representative (but not a provider or supplier's representative) who wishes to charge a fee for services at the ALJ and Council levels of review must obtain approval of the fee from the Secretary. The regulations also say that no award of fees or costs may be made against the Medicare trust fund, and that limitations on the amount of fees that apply in Social Security and Supplemental Security Income disability cases do not apply to Medicare appeals.[492]

The regulations do not contain a standard by which fee requests will be judged. However, attorneys are requested to submit the application for a fee form used in Social Security cases for review. The "Appointment of Representative in Medicare Appeals" form refers to the SSA "Petition to Obtain Representative Fee" as the form to use to provide information in support of a petition for fees (no standard form) in Medicare appeals. It should accompany the fee petition.[493]

In appeals brought to federal district court, attorneys' fees are generally available for cases under the Social Security Act, either through the Social Security Act Title II provisions[494] or under the EAJA.[495]

Under EAJA, fees are available to prevailing parties against the government in civil cases where the government's position is deemed not "substantially justified" or where there are special circumstances that would make an award unjust.[496] Proving entitlement to benefits is generally regarded as meeting the prevailing party status.[497] Having established prevailing party status, the burden shifts to the government to prove that its position was substantially justified.[498]

---

[491] 42 C.F.R. § 405.910(l).

[492] 42 C.F.R. § 405.910(f).

[493] Attorneys should review the material at these links: SSA, "The Fee Petition Process," (petition to obtain approval of a fee for representing a claimant—SSA), *available at* http://www.ssa.gov/representation/fee_petitions.htm (site visited Aug. 6, 2018) & CMS, "Appointment of Representative," (appointment of representative in Medicare appeals), *available at* http://cms.gov/Medicare/CMS-Forms/CMS-Forms/downloads/cms1696.pdf (site visited Aug. 6, 2018).

[494] *See* 42 U.S.C. § 406(b).

[495] *See* 28 U.S.C. § 2412.

[496] 28 U.S.C. § 2412(d)(1)(A).

[497] *See* McGill v. Secretary of HHS, 712 F.2d 28, 32 (2d Cir. 1983), *cert. denied*, 465 U.S. 1068 (1984).

[498] 28 U.S.C. § 2412(d)(1)(A).

The government must meet a strong burden of showing that its position was substantially justified.[499] Fees are awarded in accordance with the statute's fee provisions.[500]

[499] Pierce v. Underwood, 487 U.S. 552 (1988).
[500] *See* 28 U.S.C. § 2412(d)(2).

APPENDIX 6-1 SELECTED TITLE 42—PUBLIC HEALTH AND TITLE 20—EMPLOYEES' BENEFITS (CODE OF FEDERAL REGULATIONS) PROVISIONS

Below is a list of important provisions related to supplementary medical insurance:

- Title 42—Public Health:

  Part 405—Federal Health Insurance for the Aged and Disabled (Subpart I—Determinations, Redeterminations, and Appeals Under Original Medicare (Part A and Part B))[501]

  Part 406—Hospital Insurance Eligibility and Entitlement (Subpart C—Premium Hospital Insurance)[502]

  Part 407—Supplementary Medical Insurance (SMI) Enrollment and Entitlement (Subpart B—Individual Enrollment and Entitlement of SMI)[503]

  Part 408—Premiums for Supplementary Medical Insurance (Subpart B—Amount of Monthly Premiums)[504]

  Part 410—Supplementary Medical Insurance (SMI) Benefits (Subpart B—Medical and Other Health Services)[505]

  Part 411—Exclusions from Medicare and Limitations on Medicare Payment (Subpart K—Payment for Certain Excluded Services)[506]

- Title 20—Employees' Benefits: Part 418—Medicare Subsidies[507]

---

[501] *See* https://www.ecfr.gov/cgi-bin/text-idx?rgn=div5&node=42:2.0.1.2.5 (site visited Aug. 6, 2018).

[502] *See* https://www.ecfr.gov/cgi-bin/text-idx?SID=2c616ae62c37176ac2e8bd5dbdec0de8&mc=true&node=pt42.2.406&rgn=div5#sp42.2.406.c (site visited Aug. 6, 2018).

[503] *See* https://www.ecfr.gov/cgi-bin/text-idx?SID=2c616ae62c37176ac2e8bd5dbdec0de8&mc=true&node=pt42.2.407&rgn=div5 (site visited Aug. 6, 2018).

[504] *See* https://www.ecfr.gov/cgi-bin/text-idx?SID=de405e4a31a35eeb1a7be4ab9fef74c3&mc=true&node=pt42.2.408&rgn=div5 tpl (site visited Aug. 6, 2018).

[505] *See* https://www.ecfr.gov/cgi-bin/text-idx?SID=de405e4a31a35eeb1a7be4ab9fef74c3&mc=true&node=pt42.2.410&rgn=div5 (site visited Aug. 6, 2018).

[506] *See* https://www.ecfr.gov/cgi-bin/text-idx?SID=de405e4a31a35eeb1a7be4ab9fef74c3&mc=true&node=pt42.2.411&rgn=div5 (site visited Aug. 6, 2018).

[507] *See* https://www.ecfr.gov/cgi-bin/text-idx?SID=de405e4a31a35eeb1a7be4ab9fef74c3&mc=true&node=pt20.2.418&rgn=div5 (site visited Aug. 6, 2018).

APPENDIX 6-2 COMPARISON OF REDESIGNED MEDICARE SUMMARY NOTICE WITH ITS PREDECESSOR

For a discussion of the MSN, see Center for Medicare Advocacy, "New Medicare Summary Notice," *available at* http://www.medicareadvocacy.org/new-medicare-summary-notice/ (site visited Aug. 6, 2018).

APPENDIX 6-3 ORIGINAL MEDICARE (PARTS A & B) APPEALS PROCESS

The following chart provides an overview of the appeals process for Original Medicare (Parts A&B). For more information on each level, click on the level name on the left hand side of this document or visit http://www.hhs.gov/omha/

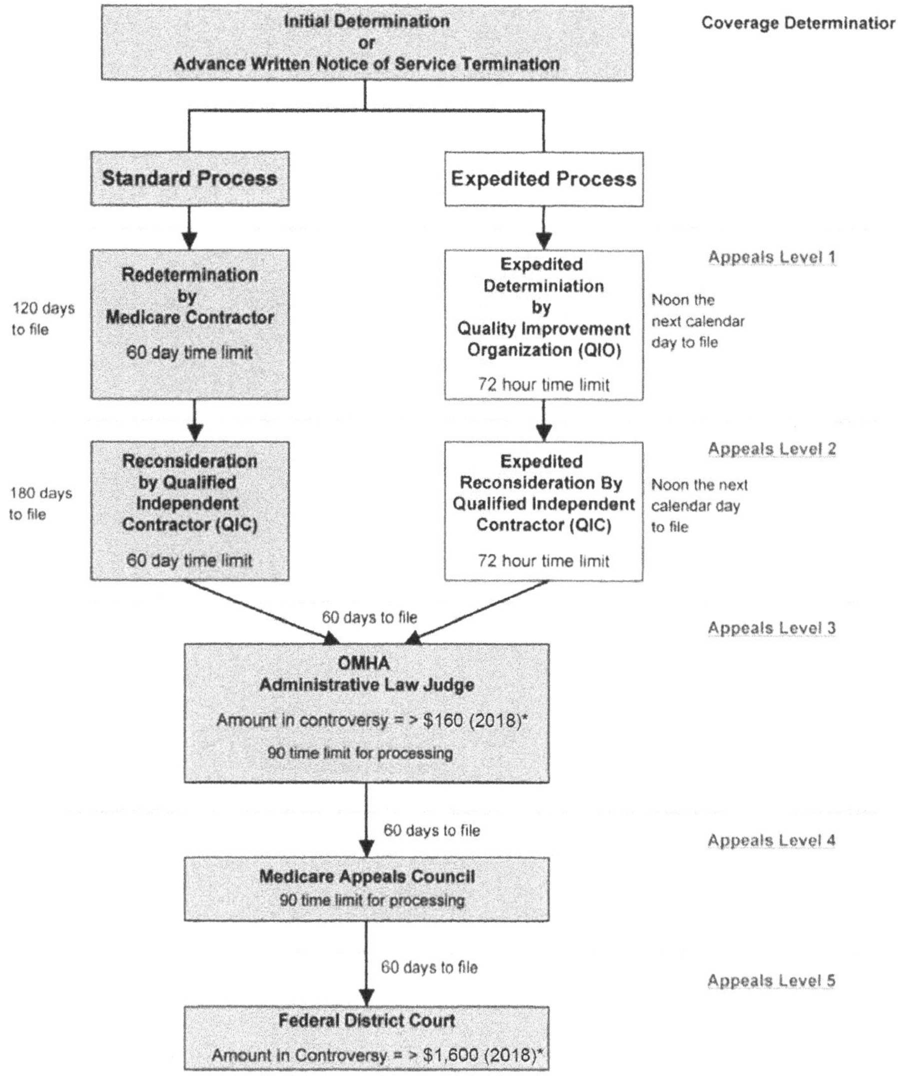

*The AIC requirements for an ALJ hearing and Federal District Court are annually in accordance with the medical care component of the Consumer Price Index.

CHAPTER 7

MEDICARE ADVANTAGE: COORDINATED CARE PLANS, PRIVATE FEE-FOR-SERVICE, AND OTHER DELIVERY OF SERVICES OPTIONS

Some helpful resources often referred to when discussing Medicare are:

- **The Medicare Statute**, Title XVIII of the Social Security Act (with parallel citations to the United States Code), can be found at http://ssa.gov/OP_Home/ssact/title18/1800.htm (site visited June 4, 2018).
- **Code of Federal Regulations, Title 42** (most Medicare regulations are in Parts 405–426), can be found at http://www.ecfr.gov/cgi-bin/text-idx?c=ecfr&tpl=/ecfrbrowse/Title42/42tab_02.tpl. The Medicare Advantage regulations (in Part 422) can be found at http://www.ecfr.gov/cgi-bin/text-idx?SID=8d866696bbaf69e90e0557482ce3c33&mc=true&node=pt42.3.422&rgn=div5 (sites visited June 4 9, 2018).
- **Medicare Manuals** can be found at https://www.cms.gov/Regulations-and-Guidance/Guidance/Manuals/Internet-Only-Manuals-IOMS.html (site visited June 4, 2018).
  - — The Medicare Managed Care Manual (CMS Pub. No. 100-16) is at https://www.cms.gov/Regulations-and-Guidance/Guidance/Manuals/Internet-Only-Manuals-IOMs-Items/CMS019326.html (site visited June 4, 2018), and
  - — Chapter 2 (enrollment and disenrollment guidance, 2017 updates) of the Medicare Managed Care Manual is at https://www.cms.gov/Medicare/Eligibility-and-Enrollment/MedicareMangCareEligEnrol/Downloads/CY_2017_MA_Enrollment_and_Disenrollment_Guidance_06-03-2016.pdf (site visited Aug. 9, 2017).

§ 7.01 INTRODUCTION TO MEDICARE ADVANTAGE

[A] What Is Medicare Advantage?

Medicare provides for a variety of delivery of care options for the receipt of Medicare-covered services, including managed care.[1] These services are found in Part C of the Medicare Statute, formerly known as the Medicare+Choice (M+C)

---

[1] 42 U.S.C. § 1395w-21 (2016); The Balanced Budget Act of 1997 (BBA '97), Pub. L. No. 105-33, § 4001 (Aug. 5, 1997); *see also* The Medicare Prescription Drug, Improvement, and Modernization Act of 2003 (MMA), Pub. L. No. 108-173, § 201(c) (Dec. 8, 2003). Managed care is used generally in this chapter to refer to all Medicare Part C plans. Manual provisions concerning Medicare managed care are found in the Centers for Medicare & Medicaid Services online manuals which are available on the CMS website at http://cms.hhs.gov/Regulations-and-Guidance/Guidance/Manuals/Internet-Only-Manuals-IOMs.html (site visited Feb. 19, 2018). *See* Centers for Medicare & Medicaid Services, Medicare Managed Care (MMC) Manual,CMS Pub. 100-16, *available at* https://www.cms.gov/Regulations-and-Guidance/Guidance/Manuals/Internet-Only-Manuals-IOMs-Items/CMS019326.html?DLPage=2&DLEntries=10&DLSort=0&DLSortDir=ascending (site visited Feb. 19, 2018).

Program[2] and now known as Medicare Advantage (MA). Medicare Advantage plans are a type of Medicare health plan that are administered and run by private insurers that contract with Medicare to provide an individual with all of their Part A and Part B benefits. The private MA health plans are approved by Medicare and regulated by the federal government. Someone who joins an MA plan is still in the Medicare program and still has Medicare rights and protections. An MA enrollee will get his or her Medicare Part A, Part B, and sometimes Part D benefits covered through the private MA plan and not traditional Medicare.

The Secretary of the Department of Health and Human Services (HHS) is required to establish standards, regulations, and rules for Medicare Part C that are consistent with existing standards and regulations governing health maintenance organizations (HMOs) and competitive medical plans (CMPs).[3]

Each MA organization must provide the benefits currently available under Medicare Parts A and B, except hospice.[4] The MA organization, through its MA plan[5] or plans, however, may impose copayments and deductibles different from those under Parts A and B of traditional Medicare, as long as the monthly premium and cost-sharing are actuarially equivalent to cost-sharing under traditional Medicare.[6] Since 2011, local MA plans (and, since 2012 regional preferred provider plans, or PPOs) must establish a yearly maximum out-of-pocket (MOOP) liability amount for enrollees for all Part A and B services that does not exceed the maximum set yearly by CMS.[7] MA plans must also pass on to beneficiaries a percentage of any cost savings in the form of additional health benefits or reduced premiums.[8] Plans may offer supplemental benefits for which a separate

---

[2] 42 U.S.C. § 1395w-21 (2016).

[3] 42 U.S.C. § 1395w-26(b)(1)–(2) (2003); *see also* 42 U.S.C. § 1395mm (2015) (payments to health plan organizations and competitive medical plans); 42 C.F.R. § 422.312 (2005).

[4] *See* **§ 7.03[C][1]** for a discussion of hospice coverage. 42 U.S.C. § 1395w-22(a) (2016);42 C.F.R. § 422.100(c)(1) (2015); 42 C.F.R. § 422.101 (2012). Note that 42 C.F.R. § 422.2 (2014) (MA definitions) and 42 C.F.R. § 423.4 (2011) (Voluntary Prescription Drug Benefit, Medicare Part D, definitions) contain an important explanatory list of terms of importance in discussing and understanding the MA program.

[5] An MA plan means health benefits coverage offered through a policy or contract with an MA organization that includes a specific set of health benefits offered at a uniform premium and uniform level of cost-sharing to all Medicare beneficiaries residing in the service area of the MA plan (or individual segments of a service area). 42 C.F.R. § 422.2 (2014) (definitions). Though different in meaning, "MA organization" and "MA plan" are often used interchangeably. In general, an MA organization is the overarching structure that may comprise one or more MA plans.

[6] 42 U.S.C. § 1395w-24(e)(4).

[7] 42 C.F.R. §§ 422.100 (2015) & 422.101 (2012). In 2019, the mandatory MOOP is $ 6,700. Plans that use a lower, voluntary MOOP of $3,400 have greater flexibility in establishing cost-sharing amounts.

[8] 42 C.F.R. § 422.266 (2011).

premium may be charged, but the separate premium may not vary among individuals within the plan and must not exceed certain actuarial and community rating requirements.[9]

With respect to Medicare Part D drug coverage, MA sponsors must offer drug coverage unless the sponsor offers plans with and without drug coverage. Private fee-for-service (PFFS) plans do not have to offer drug coverage.[10] The type of MA plan an individual is enrolled in determines whether the individual can also enroll in a stand-alone Part D plan if his or her MA plan does not offer Part D coverage.[11]

Although there are some benefits to enrolling in an MA plan, those who do enroll in a plan have additional issues to consider than those who remain in the traditional Medicare program. MA enrollees must understand the various rules and guidelines associated with enrollment in an MA plan that might involve network restrictions and other rules for getting coverage for certain services like referrals to see specialists. Enrollees must also review MA plan material with a vigilant eye toward changes to plan premiums, benefits, and copayments that can change each year. MA enrollees should also be aware of the various enrollment periods that occur during the year and when they can make changes to their coverage.

[B] Background and History of Medicare Advantage Program

Although some form of managed care has existed in Medicare since the program's inception, the Balanced Budget Act of 1997 (BBA '97) formalized private plan contracting in Medicare by adding "Part C" to the Medicare statute and creating the Medicare+Choice (M+C) program.[12] Between 1999 and 2003, the early years of the introduction of a broader array of private plan offerings, almost half of all M+C plans stopped offering services completely or cut back on the counties served, affecting about 2.4 million beneficiaries.[13] To address this instability, the Medicare Prescription Drug, Improvement, and Modernization Act of 2003 (MMA) made significant changes to the M+C program, including substantial

---

[9] 42 U.S.C. § 1395w-22 (2016); 42 C.F.R. § 422.102 (2012).

[10] 42 C.F.R. § 422.4(c)(3) (2011).

[11] *See* 42 C.F.R. § 423.30(b) (2015). Individuals enrolled in an MA coordinated care plan (HMO, PPO, Provider Service Organization (PSO)) cannot also be enrolled in a stand-alone Part D plan, even if the MA plan does not provide Part D coverage. If a private fee-for-service (PFFS) plan does not offer Part D coverage, enrollees can enroll in a separate Part D plan. Medical Savings Accounts (MSAs) cannot offer Part D coverage, so enrollees can also enroll in a Part D plan.

[12] Balanced Budget Act (BBA '97) of 1997, Pub. L. No. 105-33 (1997). For a history of private managed care plans in the Medicare program, *see e.g.* Carlos Zarabozo, "Milestones in Medicare Managed Care," 22 Health Care Financing Rev. 61 (2000), *available at* https://www.cms.gov/Research-Statistics-Data-and-Systems/Research/HealthCareFinancingReview/downloads/00fallpg61.pdf (site visited Feb. 21, 2018).

[13] "Private Insurance Plans & Medicare: The Disappointing History," Public Citizen (2003), *available at* www.citizen.org/documents/privatemedicare.pdf (site visited Feb. 21, 2018).

increases to plan payment rates and a change in the program's name from M+C to Medicare Advantage (MA).[14] The number of MA plan offerings grew tremendously in the years following passage of the MMA, and while the average number of plans available to enrollees nationwide has declined since 2009, overall enrollment in MA plans has increased.[15] As of June 2017, one in three (33 percent) people on Medicare were enrolled in an MA plan.[16] Payment rates for MA plans currently remain higher than those for traditional Medicare (sometimes referred to as "original Fee-for-Service [FFS] Medicare"), even while, as discussed in the **§ 7.01[C]**, MA payment reform pursuant to the Affordable Care Act of 2010 is phased in.[17] There is, however, widespread concern that MA plans, despite increased rates, may not provide sufficient services even though they have been significantly overpaid.[18] The Affordable Care Act provides steps toward

---

[14] 42 U.S.C. § 1395w-23(k)(2)(B)(iv)(III) (2016); *see also* MMA, § 211 (amending 42 U.S.C. § 1395w-23 [Payment to Medicare+Choice Organizations]). 42 C.F.R. §§ 422.304–422.311. Rates and related data are posted on the CMS website at http://www.cms.gov/Medicare/Health-Plans/MedicareAdvtgSpecRateStats/index.html?redirect=/MedicareAdvtgSpecRateStats/ (site visited Feb. 21, 2018); *see also* Congressional Budget Office (CBO), Medicare Advantage: Private Health Plans In Medicare, 3 (2007), *available at* http://www.cbo.gov/sites/default/files/cbofiles/ftpdocs/82xx/doc8268/06-28-medicare_advantage.pdf (site visited Feb. 21, 2018).

[15] *See e.g.* "Medicare Advantage 2017 Spotlight: Enrollment Market Update," Kaiser Family Foundation (2017), *available at* http://www.kff.org/medicare/issue-brief/medicare-advantage-2017-spotlight-enrollment-market-update/ (site visited Feb. 21, 2018).

[16] "Medicare Advantage 2017 Spotlight: Enrollment Market Update," Kaiser Family Foundation (2017), *available at* http://www.kff.org/medicare/issue-brief/medicare-advantage-2017-spotlight-enrollment-market-update/ (site visited Feb. 21, 2018).

[17] The Medicare Payment Advisory Commission (MedPAC), an independent federal body established by the BBA '97 to advise Congress, releases annual reports to Congress and other publications. MedPAC projected that 2018 MA payments would be 98 percent of fee-for-service spending, however, including other factors such as quality bonuses and "higher coding intensity" MA payments average 103 percent of fee-for-service spending. *See* "Report to the Congress: Medicare Payment Policy," MedPAC (2018), *available at* http://medpac.gov/docs/default-source/reports/mar18_medpac_ch13_sec.pdf?sfvrsn=0 (site visited June 5, 2018). This is down from, for example, 113 percent in 2009. *See* "March 2009 Report to Congress: Medicare Payment Policy," MedPAC (2009), *available at* http://medpac.gov/ documents /reports?op=OR&SortBy=YEAR&SortDircction=DESC&FilterByYear=2009# (site visited Feb. 21, 2018).

[18] *See, e.g.* David J. Meyers *et. al.*, Medicare Advantage Enrollees More Likely to Enter Lower-Quality Nursing Homes Compared to Fee-For-Service Enrollees, Health Affairs (Jan. 2018), https://doi.org/10.1377/hlthaff.2017.0714; General Accounting Office (GAO), GAO-17-393, Medicare Advantage: CMS Should Use Data on Disenrollment and Beneficiary Health Status to Strengthen Oversight (2017), *available at* http://www.gao.gov/products/GAO-17-393 (site visited Feb. 21, 2018); Austin Frakt, "Sicker Patients Seen at a Disadvantage with Medicare Advantage," NY Times (Apr. 4, 2016), *available at* http://www.nytimes.com/2016/04/05/upshot/sicker-patients-signal-a-drawback-of-medicare-advantage.html?emc=eta1 (site visited Feb. 21, 2018); Momotazur Rahman et al., "High-Cost Patients Had Substantial Rates of Leaving Medicare Advantage and Joining Traditional Medicare," Health Affairs 34(10):1676-82 (2015), *available at* https://www.healthaffairs.org/doi/full/10.1377/hlthaff.2015.0272 (site visited Feb. 21, 2018); Gerald F. Riley, CMS, Impact of Continued Biased Disenrollment from the Medicare Advantage Program to Fee-for-Services, 2

addressing overpayment issues.[19] While controversial, their impact over time has brought about more payment equity.

Advocates should watch closely the growth of enrollment in and use of MA options, paying particular attention to plan structure and benefits, scope of coverage, and beneficiary appeal rights, particularly in an environment of increased copayments for services and the push toward premium support ("vouchers") and other defined contribution approaches.[20]

Medicare & Medicaid Research Rev. 1 (2012), *available at* http://www.cms.gov/mmrr/Articles/A2012/mmrr-2012-002-04-a08.html (site visited Feb. 21, 2018). *See also* "What Do We Know About Health Care Access and Quality in Medicare Advantage Versus the Traditional Medicare Program?" Kaiser Family Foundation (Nov. 2014), *available at* http://kff.org/medicare/report/what-do-we-know-about-health-care-access-and-quality-in-medicare-advantage-versus-the-traditional-medicare-program/ (site visited Feb. 21, 2018) (noting that "beneficiaries continue to rate traditional Medicare more favorably than Medicare Advantage plans in terms of quality and access. . . . [and] Among beneficiaries who are sick, the differential between traditional Medicare and Medicare Advantage is particularly large [relative to those who are healthy], favoring traditional Medicare"). *See also* GAO, GAO-11-247R, Medicare Advantage: Comparison of Plan Bids to Fee-for-Service Spending by Plan and Market Characteristics (2011), *available at* http://www.gao.gov/new.items/d11247r.pdf (site visited Feb. 21, 2018). *See also* GAO, GAO-08-522T, Medicare Advantage: Higher SpendingRelative to Medicare Fee-for-Service May Not Ensure Lower Out-of-Pocket Costs for Beneficiaries (2008), *available at* http://www.gao.gov/products/GAO-08-522T (site visited Feb. 21, 2018). *See also* GAO, GAO-08-359, Medicare Advantage: Increased Spending Relative to Medicare Fee-for-Service May Not Always Reduce Beneficiary Out-of-Pocket Costs (2008), *available at* http://www.gao.gov/products/GAO-08-359 (site visited Feb. 21, 2018); Kathleen M. King & Mark Schlesinger (eds.), "Final Report of the Study Panel on Medicare and Markets—The Role of Private Health Plans in Medicare: Lessons from the Past, Looking to the Future," National Academy of Social Insurance (2003), *available at* https://www.nasi.org/research/2003/role-private-health-plans-medicare-lessons-past-looking. *See also* "The Continuing Cost of Privatization: Extra Payments to Medicare Advantage," The Commonwealth Fund (2008), *available at* http://www.commonwealthfund.org/Publications/Issue-Briefs/2008/Sep/The-Continuing-Cost-of-Privatization--Extra-Payments-to-Medicare-Advantage.aspx (site visited Feb. 21, 2018).

[19] Patient Protection and Affordable Care Act of 2010 (PPACA or ACA), Pub. L. No. 111-148, Mar. 23, 2010, §§ 3201 *et seq.* and Health Care and Education Reconciliation Act of 2010 (HCERA), Pub. L. No. 111-152, Mar. 30, 2010, §§ 1102 *et seq.*

[20] *See* "Medicare Premium Support Proposals Could Increase Costs for Today's Seniors, Despite Assurances," Health Affairs Blog, March 9, 2017. DOI: 10.1377/hblog20170309.059109; Marilyn Moon & Judy Feder, "Proceed with Caution: Renewed Calls to End Medicare as We Know It Because We Can't Afford It Misunderstand the Facts" (May 2011), Center for American Progress, *available at* http://www.americanprogress.org/issues/healthcare/report/2011/05/13/9679/proceed-with-caution/ (site visited Aug. 3, 2018); Marilyn Moon, "Restructuring Medicare: Impacts on Beneficiaries" (Urban Inst., Jan. 1999); *see also* Marilyn Moon, Stephanie Maxwell, & Matthew Storeygard, "Reforming Medicare's Benefit Package: Impact on Beneficiary Expenditures" (Urban Inst., May 1, 2001), *available at* http://www.urban.org/publications/1000313.html (site visited Aug. 3, 2018); and Marilyn Moon et al., "Medicare Extra: A Comprehensive Benefit Option for Medicare Beneficiaries" (Health Affairs, Oct. 4, 2005), *available at* https://www.commonwealthfund.org/publications/journal-article/2005/oct/medicare-extra-comprehensive-benefit-option-medicare (site visited Aug. 3, 2018). Benefit package issues remain key factors in plan utilization and plan satisfaction. Plan flexibility in benefit design, plus favorable reimbursement rates, will continue to be a

[C] Medicare Advantage Plans and Health Care Reform

In March 2010, President Obama signed into law the Patient Protection and Affordable Care Act (PPACA) and the Health Care and Education Reconciliation Act of 2010 (HCERA) (together, the Affordable Care Act, or ACA).[21] A great deal of the discussion surrounding the implications of health care reform for older people and people with disabilities centered on changes in funding for MA plans. Some of the changes have been under consideration for many years.

In order to address payment to MA plans that has been disproportionately higher relative to what traditional Medicare spends on a given beneficiary (or, put more simply, MA overpayments), Section 1102 of HCERA phased in changes to the MA plan payment structure, starting with a freeze in payments to MA plans for 2011. Since being fully phased in by 2017, payments are based on national county benchmarks, with plans being paid a fixed percentage of traditional Medicare costs. As a result of the payment scheme, plans in some lower-paid counties, generally rural and suburban areas, continue to receive payments that exceed the traditional Medicare amount, while plans in higher-paid counties, many of them large cities, see substantial reductions. The new payment structure also provides for an increase in payments by up to 5 percent for plans that receive four or more stars on the CMS star rating system.[22] Rebates (an amount plans receive if they bid less than the county benchmark) have also been reduced. In an effort to counter some of these payment reductions, there is evidence indicating that some MA plans have sought to improperly inflate payments to plans through

driver with respect to beneficiary utilization. An important caution is to look carefully at one's overall health status, drug needs, and other factors before making a decision to elect an MA plan. With respect to benefit plan design, costs, and health status, see "Medicare Advantage: Relationship between Benefit Package Designs and Plans' Average Beneficiary Health Status" (Apr. 2010), GAO Study, GAO-10-403, *available at* http://www.gao.gov/new.items/d10403.pdf (site visited Aug. 3, 2018). As has been seen in other studies, this April 2010 study shows that plans with lower premiums tend to have higher cost-sharing requirements and tend to attract healthier beneficiaries.

[21] ACA, Pub. L. No.111-148 (Mar. 23, 2010); Health Care and Education Reconciliation Act of 2010 (HCERA), Pub. L. No. 111-152 (Mar. 30, 2010).

[22] Each year CMS issues performance quality ratings, using a five-star system where five stars indicate the highest quality, of Part C and D plan sponsors. CMS adopts the authority to terminate the contracts of Part C and D sponsors that fail for three consecutive years to achieve at least a three-star rating. 42 C.F.R. §§ 422.504, 422.510, 423.505, and 423.509. CMS also adopts the authority to deny applications submitted by MA organizations and Part D sponsors that have performed so poorly that CMS terminated or did not renew a contract with the organization in the past. 42 C.F.R. §§ 422.502 and 423.503. Section 17001 of the 21st Century Cures Act (Pub. L. No. 114-255), signed into law by President Obama on December 13, 2016, delays CMS's authority to terminate consistently poor performing plans (solely on the basis that plans have failed to achieve minimum quality ratings) through the end of plan year 2018.

overstatements of enrollees' health risks, a practice sometimes referred to as "upcoding."[23]

In addition to attempting to achieve more payment parity between traditional Medicare and MA plans, the ACA also sets limits on how much MA plans can spend on administrative costs. As of 2014, if the Secretary of HHS determines that an MA plan does not maintain a medical loss ratio (MLR) of 85 percent (meaning that 85 percent of its revenues does not go toward benefits), the plan must remit a specified sum to the Secretary.[24]

Note that the provisions of the ACA that apply to stand-alone Part D plans, discussed in **Chapter 11**, also apply to MA plans that offer Part D prescription drug coverage, which are referred to as Medicare Advantage-Prescription Drug (MA-PD) plans. Other changes to the MA program pursuant to the ACA are incorporated into this chapter.[25]

[D] Policy and Technical Changes for 2019

Medicare implements MA plans through a series of regulations[26] and other issuances, particularly its call letters.[27]

---

[23] *See, e.g.*, Kronick. R., "Projected Coding Intensity In Medicare Advantage Could Increase Medicare Spending By $200 Billion Over Ten Years," Health Affairs (Feb. 2017), *available at* https://www.healthaffairs.org/doi/abs/10.1377/hlthaff.2016.0768 (site visited Aug. 3, 2018); GAO report entitled "Medicare Advantage:
Fundamental Improvements Needed in CMS's Effort to Recover Substantial Amounts of Improper Payments" (Apr. 2016), *available at* http://www.gao.gov/assets/680/676441.pdf (site visited Aug. 3, 2018); *see also* Center for Public Integrity's investigative series entitled "Medicare Advantage Money Grab" *available at* https://www.publicintegrity.org/health/medicare/medicare-advantage-money-grab (site visited Aug. 3, 2018). *See* "Report to the Congress: Medicare Payment Policy," MedPAC (2018), *available at*: http://medpac.gov/docs/default-source/reports/mar18_medpac_ch13_sec.pdf?sfvrsn=0 (site visited June 5, 2018).

[24] HCERA § 1103. CMS published a final rule on Medicare Advantage and Part D medical loss ratio (MLR) requirements on May 23, 2013. *See* 78 Fed. Reg. 31,284. Note that if a plan fails to have an MLR of 85 percent for three consecutive years, the Secretary must preclude new enrollment in that plan. The plan's contract must be terminated if the plan fails to have an MLR of 85 percent for five consecutive years.

[25] For a summary of changes the ACA made to the Medicare program, see, e.g., Kaiser Family Foundation, "Summary of Key Changes to Medicare in 2010 Health Reform Law" (Apr. 2010), *available at* http://kff.org/health-reform/issue-brief/summary-of-key-changes-to-medicare-in/ (site visited June 7, 2018).

[26] *See generally* 42 C.F.R. Pt. 422, which contains the rules pertaining to Part C (Medicare Advantage).

[27] *See* Medicare's system of call letters used by CMS in setting out its goals and objectives and the operating parameters that plans must use in preparing to offer a plan under programs operated by Medicare. *See generally* 42 C.F.R. Pt. 422 subpt. F and Pt. 423 subpt. F, for the bid submission and plan approval processes. 42 C.F.R. Part 422 contains the rules pertaining to Part C, and 42 C.F.R. Pt. 423 contains the rules pertaining to Part D. It contains information for MA plans and MA-PD plans as well as Part D prescription drug plans. The 2019 "Call Letter," formally known as

[1] Final Regulations

On April 16, 2018, CMS issued final regulations to provide policy and technical changes to the Medicare Part C (Medicare Advantage) and Part D programs for contract year 2019.[28] In addition to being the first final rule addressing Part C in three years, the rule includes a number of significant policy changes related to MA plan benefits effective in 2019.[29] The 2019 rule includes, among other things, provisions that:

- reinterpret the uniformity requirement at 42 C.F.R. § 422.100(d) to allow plans to reduce cost-sharing for certain covered benefits, and/or offer lower deductibles for enrollees that meet specific medical criteria as designated by the plan, provided that similarly situated enrollees are treated the same; see **§ 7.03[C][1]** of this chapter;
- Eliminate the "meaningful difference" requirement at 42 C.F.R. §§ 422.254 and 422.256 that required MA plan sponsors offering more than one plan in a given service area to ensure the plan benefit packages were substantially different from one another with respect to key plan characteristics such premiums, cost sharing, or benefits offered so that beneficiaries had an easier time comparing plans;
- Revise the timing and default delivery method of certain beneficiary documents: the Annual Notice of Change (ANOC) must be delivered 15 days before first day of ACEP (10/1), whereas Evidence of Coverage (EOC) must by delivered by the first day of ACEP (10/15), and MA and Part D sponsors can now provide certain materials, such as the EOC, electronically, with provision of hard copy upon request; see **§ 7.03[D]** of this chapter.
- Limit the Part D Special Enrollment Period for Dual and Other LIS-Eligible Beneficiaries (also applicable to MA plans with Part D coverage): the Special Election Period (SEP) for dual-eligible and LIS beneficiaries has been revised from an open-ended monthly SEP to one that may be used only <u>once</u> per calendar quarter during the first nine

the Announcement of Calendar Year (CY) 2019 Medicare Advantage Capitation Rates and Medicare Advantage and Part D Payment Policies and Final Call Letter, is *available at* https://www.cms.gov/Medicare/Health-Plans/MedicareAdvtgSpecRateStats/Downloads/Announcement2019.pdf (site visited June 7, 2018).

[28] 83 Fed. Reg. 16,440 (Apr. 16, 2018), amending 42 C.F.R. Pts. 405, 417, 422, 423, 460 and 498.

[29] *See, e.g.*, the Center's "Special Report: Recent Changes in Law, Regulations and Guidance Relating to Medicare Advantage and Medicare Part D" (September 2018), *available at* http://www.medicareadvocacy.org/wp-content/uploads/2018/09/Report.-Summary-2019-Call-letter-and-C-D-Rule-1.pdf (site visited Oct. 15, 2018).

months of the year (January through September); see **§ 7.03[D][6]** of this chapter.

- Eliminate the requirement that an MA provider be enrolled in Medicare. Instead, CMS will compile a preclusion list of providers that will be made available to MA organizations that must deny payment for claims submitted by providers on the list.

Note that the Bipartisan Budget Act of 2018 (BBA), signed into law on February 9, 2018, included provisions related to Part C, including permanently reauthorizing MA Special Needs Plans (SNPs), discussed in this chapter at **§ 7.03[B][6]**, and, starting in 2020, allowing MA plans to offer expanded supplemental benefits to plan enrollees deemed to be chronically ill. [30]

[2] Annual Notice of Payment Rates and Capitation Policies

On April 2, 2018, CMS released its annual Call Letter: "Announcement of Calendar Year (CY) 2019 Medicare Advantage Capitation Rates and Medicare Advantage and Part D Payment Policies and Final Call Letter."[31] This document includes various policy and technical updates, including Part C and Part D payment rates, Part D benefit parameters, and fees and liabilities for vaccine administration, drug dispensing, and negotiated drug pricing. Many of the new polices discussed in the Call Letter relate to provisions included in the final rule, discussed above, and elsewhere in this chapter.

[3] MA, MA-PD, and PDP Calendar for 2019

CMS's calendar contains dates of importance to beneficiaries and their advocates:

The annual coordinated election period (ACEP) begins on October 15 and ends on December 7.[32]

As discussed below in **§ 7.03[D][1]**, the Medicare Advantage disenrollment period (MADP) ended in 2018 and, effective 2019, has been replaced with the reinstated Medicare Advantage Open Enrollment Period (OEP) which allows for certain changes in MA coverage between January and the end of March each calendar year.

---

[30] Pub. L. No. 115-123. Section 50311 permanently reauthorizes Medicare Advantage Special Needs Plans (SNPs). Note that the benefit expansion provided for in Section 50322, which allows MA plans to provide supplemental benefits to chronically ill enrollees beginning in 2020, is distinct from the regulatory changes to supplemental benefits effective 2019 discussed in this chapter at **§ 7.03[C][1]**.

[31] Available on the CMS website at https://www.cms.gov/Medicare/Health-Plans/MedicareAdvtgSpecRateStats/Downloads/Announcement2019.pdf (site visited June 7, 2018).

[32] 42 U.S.C. § 1395w-21(e)(3); 42 C.F.R. § 422.62(a)(2). .

§ 7.02 CHOOSING BETWEEN TRADITIONAL MEDICARE AND MEDICARE ADVANTAGE

[A] Advantages and Disadvantages of Medicare Advantage Options

There are many advantages and disadvantages that should be taken in to consideration before choosing a Medicare Advantage plan.

[1] Advantages of Medicare Advantage

Some advantages in choosing an MA option include:

- *No claims.* Generally, a beneficiary need not submit claims unless emergency or urgent care is received while outside the service area.
- *Emphasis on preventive care.* Preventive health care, including annual physical exams, as well as health care screening services not covered under traditional Medicare.
- *Coverage of comprehensive services.* These services, which are not covered under traditional Medicare, often include some level of vision care, prescription drugs (but see **Chapter 11**, Medicare Prescription Drug Benefit, Medicare Part D), dental care, and hearing exams.
- *No need for Medigap insurance.* Managed care plans should provide beneficiaries with all or most of the benefits offered by a Medigap policy.
- *Easier to budget health care expenses.* Beneficiaries should know the amount of any premiums and copayments for doctor services in advance. In addition, unlike traditional Medicare, MA plans have beneficiary out-of-pocket spending caps.
- *Avoid unnecessary surgeries.* Plans are interested in avoiding unnecessary risks and have no financial incentive to perform unnecessary procedures. Consequently, if a plan recommends surgery, a beneficiary can be relatively certain that it is necessary.

[2] Disadvantages of Medicare Advantage

Some disadvantages in choosing an MA option include:

- *Plan terminations.* Plans may decide to terminate services and make elections whether to participate in a given market annually.
  — *Utilization management and cost containment.* As a general matter, MA options by design focus on at least some level of utilization management and cost containment, the savings from which are supposed

to be passed on to beneficiaries in the form of reduced costs or additional services. For example, many plans require a beneficiary to have the prior approval of his or her primary care physician in order to see a specialist. Because of financial incentives and pressures from plan administrators, some primary care physicians resist making referrals. Prior authorization may also be required for non-emergency in-network or out-of-network care.

- *Financial incentives to limit service.* Plans receive a capitated rate per beneficiary member. The Center for Medicare Advocacy has heard from a number of providers who report that MA enrollees have shorter periods of covered hospital, skilled nursing facility, and home health care than Medicare beneficiaries in traditional Medicare receive. Waiting time may be longer, fewer tests may be performed, or services may be limited. Limiting services based on financial considerations may result in questionable quality of care.
- *Requirement to use plan providers.* In most plans, a beneficiary is not free to go to any physician or hospital he or she may choose. Beneficiaries are often "locked in" and must use the plan's providers and facilities or must pay higher premiums for the privilege of going outside the network. In other plans, a beneficiary must pay more to see "non-network" providers. In addition, plans can terminate providers from their networks mid-year, while a beneficiary's corresponding rights to change plans mid-year are limited.
- *Out-of-area care limitations.* If a beneficiary lives outside the plan service area for more than a specified period of time, the plan may not sell a beneficiary a plan or may disenroll a beneficiary. Plans cover emergency and urgent care if a beneficiary is out of the service area for a brief time, but a beneficiary must return to the area for routine care. The plan may offer a separate option that covers out-of-area care, but the beneficiary will have to pay an additional premium.
- *Service locations.* In most plans, there are limited locations where a beneficiary can receive care.
- *Higher copayments and deductibles.* Provided that services and costs are actuarially equivalent, some plans charge higher copayments and deductibles than traditional Medicare, including larger copayments for hospital, skilled nursing facility (SNF),[33] and home health services, and for durable medical equipment (DME), including oxygen. This has been criticized as a way of cherry picking (e.g., forcing heavy care patients out of the managed care plan).

[33] See the discussion of cost-sharing in § **7.03[C][2]** of this Handbook.

- *Disenrollment.* Most enrollees are locked in to their plan for most of the year. When an individual has a right to leave the plan, it can take up to 30 days to disenroll or other rules may apply, and a beneficiary must continue to use the health plan during this time. Even after the disenrollment becomes effective, Medicare's computers may not be updated, and some traditional Medicare claims will be erroneously rejected.

[B] Guidelines for Considering Medicare Advantage Options

Beneficiaries should make informed decisions before enrolling in an MA plan. Following some general guidelines before enrolling in a plan, beneficiaries can avoid problems and disappointment later. These guidelines will help ensure that beneficiaries make wise decisions about MA options. After careful evaluation, some Medicare beneficiaries will choose managed care, while others may determine that the traditional Medicare program better suits their needs. Beneficiaries should consider the following:

1. Review coverage provided by the traditional Medicare program and by Medigap insurance policies. Beneficiaries should understand the coverage and costs available through the traditional Medicare system combined with an appropriate Medigap policy. Assess whether or not someone is entitled to other insurance coverage that might supplement Medicare, such as retiree coverage, and how such coverage might coordinate (or not) with an MA plan. **Chapter 8** provides more information on Medigap plans. Note that many retiree health insurance is offered in the form of MA plans, which could limit individuals' choices.
2. Read each plan's literature to understand the type of plan being considered, what it provides, and what copayments are required for different kinds of services.
3. Find out if services outside of the plan's service area will be covered and if so how they will be covered. Some Medicare Advantage plans may cover out-of-network services but with higher cost-sharing. Some Medicare Advantage plans may also cover emergency services when you are traveling outside of the United States.
4. Determine what plan services are provided at additional cost and how much they cost. In addition, determine the preventive services available under the plan, as well as any limitations associated with visits or services. The beneficiary should fully understand where to go for emergency, urgently needed, and routine care.

5. Review carefully the nature and extent of any offered prescription drug coverage. Identify whether the plan is a stand-alone MA plan or a combined Medicare Advantage-Prescription Drug (MA-PD) plan. If the plan is a stand-alone MA plan, beneficiaries should be aware that they may want a stand-alone prescription drug plan (PDP). For combined MA-PD plans, beneficiaries should scrutinize the prescription drug coverage as if it were a stand-alone PDP. Consideration should be given to whether the plan covers brand names or only generics, imposes different copayments based on the type of drug, or provides coverage on a monthly, quarterly, or yearly basis. In addition, beneficiaries should compare drug coverage with other available PDPs. **Chapter 11** provides more information on PDPs; see in particular **§ 11.03[B]** for rules concerning when an individual can have both an MA plan and a PDP.
6. If plan materials do not provide answers to all questions, contact the plan for additional information. Beneficiaries should make a note of how the plan's staff responds to such inquiries and use that information in evaluating the plan.
7. Ask about plan physicians, determine whether the physicians you use or wish to use are in the plan, and find out how to change physicians if a satisfactory relationship with a plan physician cannot be established. In addition, beneficiaries should inquire as to which hospitals, SNFs, and home care agencies have contracts with the plans under consideration and whether those facilities represent satisfactory choices. Note, though, that current rules allow MA plans to terminate network providers and facilities mid-year without cause.
8. Know how to use the plan's complaint system and how appeals and grievances are handled.
9. Inquire among friends and relatives to determine whether any are currently enrolled in managed care plans or have been enrolled in the past and ascertain whether and to what degree they were satisfied with the services received through those plans. Ask plan representatives whether member satisfaction surveys are conducted and whether the results are available for review.

Contact the Centers for Medicare & Medicaid Services (CMS) Regional Office of Beneficiary Services to determine whether a plan has failed to comply with CMS regulations.[34]

[34] For online information about enforcement and compliance actions CMS has taken against individual Part C and D plans, see CMS, "Part C and D Enforcement Actions," *available at* http://www.cms.gov/Medicare/Compliance-and-Audits/Part-C-and-Part-D-Compliance-and-Audits/PartCandPartDEnforcementActions-.html (site visited June 7, 2018).

[C] How to Learn More About Your Options

In order to find Medicare Advantage plans available to a beneficiary in their area they can go to Medicare's Plan Finder tool.[35] The plan finder tool allows a beneficiary to complete a general or personalized plan search to compare costs and benefits of Medicare Advantage plans available to them. In addition, a Medicare beneficiary can speak to a volunteer at their State Health Insurance Assistance Program, or SHIP. SHIP volunteers are trained to provide one-on-one insurance counseling and assistance to Medicare beneficiaries.[36]

§ 7.03 MEDICARE ADVANTAGE BASICS

[A] Medicare Advantage Eligibility

[1] Eligible Persons

To be eligible for an MA plan, an individual must be entitled to benefits under Part A and enrolled in Medicare Part B.[37] To enroll in an MA plan, an individual must complete and sign an election form or complete a CMS-approved election method offered by the MA organization.[38]

An individual cannot be denied enrollment in an MA plan due to a preexisting condition, unless that individual has end-stage renal disease (ESRD).[39] Individuals with ESRD are excluded, except that an individual who develops ESRD while enrolled in an MA plan may continue to be enrolled in that plan.[40] Such an individual may also enroll in another MA plan if the ESRD beneficiary loses MA plan coverage when his or her plan terminates its contract with CMS or reduces its service area. Note, however, that an individual with ESRD may elect an MA special needs plan as long as that plan has opted to enroll ESRD

---

[35] https://www.medicare.gov/find-a-plan/questions/home.aspx (site visited July 11, 2018).

[36] To locate the SHIP in your state, use the "Contact your state SHIP" search tool on the home page of this website: https://www.shiptacenter.org/ (site visited July 11, 2018).

[37] 42 U.S.C. § 1395w-21; 42 C.F.R. § 422.50(a)(1).

[38] 42 C.F.R. § 422.50(a)(5). *But see* discussion of seamless conversion enrollment at **§ 7.03[D][9]**.

[39] 42 U.S.C. § 1395w-21(g); 42 C.F.R. § 422.60(a)(1)and (2). For further discussion regarding anti-discrimination and review for discrimination and steering, see Medicare Managed Care (MMC) Manual, CMS Pub. No. 100-16, Ch. 4, §§ 10.5.2 and 10.5.3, *available at* http://www.cms.gov/Regulations-and-Guidance/Guidance/Manuals/downloads/mc86c04.pdf (site visited Aug. 3, 2018).

[40] 42 C.F.R. § 422.50(a)(2)(i). For additional exceptions to the general exclusion of individuals with ESRD, see, e.g., MMC Manual, CMS Pub. No. 100-16, Ch. 2, § 20.2.2 and 20.2.3, *available at* https://www.cms.gov/Medicare/Eligibility-and-Enrollment/MedicareMangCareEligEnrol/Downloads/CY_2019_MA_Enrollment_and_Disenrollment_Guidance.pdf (site visited Aug. 3, 2018).

individuals.[41] Note that Section 17006 of the 21st Century Cures Act[42], signed into law by President Obama on December 13, 2016, removes the barrier for people with ESRD to enroll in MA plans beginning in 2021.[43]

An individual is eligible to enroll in a particular MA plan if the plan serves the geographic area in which the individual resides.[44] If, after enrolling in a plan, the individual leaves the geographic area, the plan can offer the individual the option of staying in the plan if the plan provides the individual with reasonable geographic access to all basic plan benefits.

[2] Persons Ineligible to Enroll

An individual who is a Qualified Medicare Beneficiary (QMB), a Specified Low-Income Medicare Beneficiary (SLMB), a Qualified Disabled and Working Individual (QDWI), or otherwise eligible for Medicaid and entitled to Medicare cost-sharing under a state Medicaid program may not enroll in an MA Medical Savings Accounts (MSA) plan.[45]

Federal Employee Health Benefit Plan (FEHBP) members must make sure that plan choices under consideration are those that have been certified by the Director of the Office of Management and Budget (OMB) to the Secretary that the Office of Personnel Management (OPM) has adopted policies that ensure that the enrollment of FEHBP individuals in such plans will not result in increased expenditures for health benefits under FEHBP.[46] Similar rules may be applied to individuals eligible for health care from either the Veterans Administration (VA) or the Department of Defense (DOD).[47]

[B] Medicare Advantage Options

There are many different options available under MA.[48] Each MA organization could offer multiple types of plans. Even among similar types of

---

[41] *See* 42 C.F.R. § 422.50(a)(2)(iii). A Medicare Advantage Special Needs Plan (MS-SNP) is defined in 42 C.F.R. § 422.2.

[42] Pub. L. No. 114-255.

[43] Note that on its own, this provision significantly improves coverage options for people with ESRD, however, their options still remain limited. Congress failed to extend Medigap rights to people with ESRD at the same time it removed prohibitions on enrollment in MA. For more information about Medigap plans, see **Chapter 8**.

[44] 42 C.F.R. § 422.50(a)(3).

[45] 42 U.S.C. § 1395w-21(b)(3).

[46] 42 U.S.C. § 1395w-21(b)(2)(A).

[47] 42 U.S.C. § 1395w-21(b)(2)(B).

[48] The types of plans described in this section are available to Medicare beneficiaries through the MA program. Note that the MMA also created Health Savings Accounts (HSAs) outside the Medicare program and under the Internal Revenue Code. MMA § 1201, amending the Internal Revenue Code (Title 26) at § 223. *See also* https://www.irs.gov/publications/p969 (site visited Aug. 3,

plans benefits and cost-sharing can differ so it is important to read the literature for each plan closely.[49]

[1] Coordinated Care Plans

In order to offer an MA coordinated care plan in an area,[50] the MA organization offering the plan must offer qualified Part D coverage that includes the requirements related to qualified prescription drug coverage.[51] These plans include the following:[52]

- *Health Maintenance Organizations.* A type of managed care plan that can take a variety of forms such as a staff-based facility of service providers and/or a group of independent practice associations that acts as both insurer and provider of services to its members; services and benefits usually financed through a capitated payment; copayments may apply;

2018). Under this provision, an individual opens an HSA in connection with the purchase of high-deductible private health insurance. The individual can carry over unspent balances from year to year. Funds deposited in the HSA trust account are to be used for the sole purpose of paying qualified medical expenses of beneficiaries. An individual will be able to withdraw sums from his or her HSA trust account to cover deductibles and other health care expenses in connection with a related high-deductible health insurance policy. Deposits into the trust account each year will be excluded from taxable income; earnings on the accounts are not taxed, nor are amounts withdrawn from the trust account to pay health expenses. MMA § 1201, amending the Internal Revenue Code at § 223. Note that according to an IRS publication, only an "eligible individual" can establish an HSA. An "eligible individual" means, with respect to any month, any individual who (1) is covered under a high-deductible health plan (HDHP) on the first day of such month; (2) is not also covered by any other health plan that is not an HDHP (with certain exceptions for plans providing certain limited types of coverage); (3) is not enrolled in Medicare (generally, has not yet reached age 65); and (4) may not be claimed as a dependent on another person's tax return [emphasis added]. See IRS Publication, Part III-Administrative, Procedural, and Miscellaneous, Section 1, Q2, *available at* http://www.irs.gov/pub/irs-drop/n-04-2.pdf (site visited Aug. 3, 2018).

[49] In order to provide context for the following descriptions of MA plan types, here is a breakdown of plan type by enrollment as of March 2017. Approximately two-thirds (63%) of MA enrollees are in HMOs; one-third are in PPOs (26% in local PPOs, 7% in regional PPOs); and the balance are in Private Fee-For Service (PFFS) plans (1%) and other types of MA plans (3%), including cost plans and Medicare Medical Savings Accounts (MSAs). Kaiser Family Foundation, "Medicare Advantage 2017 Spotlight: Enrollment Market Update" (June 6, 2017), *available at* http://www.kff.org/medicare/issue-brief/medicare-advantage-2017-spotlight-enrollment-market-update/ (site visited Oct. 1, 2018).

[50] 42 U.S.C. § 1395w-21; 42 C.F.R. § 422.4.

[51] 42 C.F.R. § 422.4(c)(1); 42 C.F.R. § 422.104. *See* **Chapter 11** of this Handbook. Note that if an MA organization offers multiple coordinated care plans in a given area, some might not offer Part D prescription drug coverage (e.g., some HMOs might not offer Part D benefits).

[52] 42 C.F.R. § 422.4(a).

- *Provider Sponsored Organizations.* An organization created by health care providers to act as insurer for a defined group of enrollees, including physician-based models, hospital-based models, or a combination of service delivery models; and
- *Preferred Provider Organizations.* Managed care entities that contract with networks or panels of providers for serving the PPOs' enrolled population(s) and are paid on the basis of a contractually specified reimbursement for covered benefits with the organization offering the plan and provide reimbursement for all covered benefits regardless of whether the benefits are provided within the network of providers. A PPO organization does not permit prior notification for out-of-network services (out-of-network services can be obtained without prior notification and without a reduction in the plan's standard cost-sharing levels).[53]

[2] Medicare Medical Savings Accounts

MA organizations offering MSAs are not permitted to offer prescription drug coverage, other than that required under Parts A and B of the Medicare statute.[54] The MMA makes the MA MSA demonstration a permanent Medicare option, starting with contract years beginning January 1, 2006; removes the capacity limits and the deadline for enrollment; and eliminates the requirement for a quality assurance program because MSAs are bank accounts and not plans.[55]

As with the old MSA demonstration, the new option combines the use of a health care savings account with a high deductible catastrophic health plan. To participate in an MA MSA, the beneficiary has to enroll in an MA MSA health plan.[56]

Under rules established by the Secretary, an individual is not eligible to enroll (or continue enrollment) in an MA MSA plan for a year unless the individual provides assurances satisfactory to the Secretary that the individual will reside in the United States for at least 183 days during the year.[57] Individuals must enroll during an initial enrollment period or an annual coordinated election period.[58]

---

[53] 42 C.F.R. § 422.4(a)(1)(v)(A)–(D) (applies to PPOs, MSA plans, and PFFS plans) (Apr. 15, 2010).

[54] 42 C.F.R. § 422.4(c)(2).

[55] MMA § 233, amending §§ 1851(b)(4), 1851(e)(5)(A), 1852, 1852(e)(1), and 1852(k) of the Social Security Act, 42 U.S.C. §§ 1395w-21(b)(4), 1395w-21(e)(5)(A), 1395w-22, 1395w-22(e)(1), and 1395w-22(k); *see also* CMS's guidance document for MA MSAs, *available at* http://www.cms.gov/Medicare/Medicare-Advantage/MedicareAdvantageApps/downloads/2007_MSA_Useful_Information.pdf (site visited Aug. 3, 2018).

[56] 42 C.F.R. § 422.4(a)(2) (types of plans).

[57] 42 C.F.R. § 422.56 (types of plans).

[58] 42 C.F.R. § 422.4(a)(2) (types of plans). Note that there are very few Medicare MSA plans offered across the country.

[3] Private Fee-for-Service Plans

MA organizations offering PFFS plans may choose to offer qualified Part D coverage that meets the requirement for that coverage.[59] A PFFS plan is an MA plan that:

- Reimburses hospitals, physicians, and other providers at a rate determined by the plan on an FFS basis without placing the provider at financial risk;
- Does not vary such rates for such a provider based on utilization relating to such provider; and
- Does not restrict the selection of providers among those who are lawfully authorized to provide the covered services and who agree to accept the terms and conditions of payment established by the plan. However, effective 2011, PFFS plans in certain areas have an obligation to establish provider networks.[60]

The Medicare program will make a capitated payment to the PFFS plan just as it would to an HMO or a PSO.[61] A physician, provider of service, or other entity that has a contract for Medicare services furnished to Medicare enrollees must accept as payment in full for covered services an amount not to exceed (including any permitted deductibles, coinsurance, copayments, or balance billing) 115 percent of its contracted rate.[62] The plan must establish procedures to enforce its billing limits. If the plan fails to adhere to its billing limits, the plan may be subject to sanctions. Beneficiaries must be provided with an appropriate explanation of benefits, consistent with current beneficiary information requirements for Medicare Parts A and B, and for applicable Medicare Supplemental

---

[59] 42 C.F.R. § 422.4(c)(3). See the discussion of Part D drug plan requirements in **Chapter 11** of this Handbook. *See also* CMS, "Private Fee-for-Service: Beneficiary Questions and Answers" (Feb. 10, 2006), *available at* http://www.cms.gov/Medicare/Health-Plans/PrivateFeeforServicePlans/downloads/benqa.pdf (site visited Aug. 3, 2018); CMS website at https://www.cms.gov/Medicare/Health-Plans/PrivateFeeforServicePlans/index.html, (site visited Aug. 3, 2018).

[60] 42 U.S.C. § 1395w-28(b)(2); 42 C.F.R. § 422.4(a)(3). PFFS market penetration in both rural and urban areas from 2006 through 2009 was robust, but since the implementation of this MIPPA provision, enrollment in such plans has dramatically decreased and some plans have pulled out of certain markets. Advocates and beneficiaries continue to raise cautions about the scope of services actually available under PFFS when compared to traditional Medicare. Some advocates have reported marketing abuses, particularly with respect to not being clear about the nature of PFFS and its limitations. Reimbursement rates to physicians have been an issue, leading some physicians to decline participation in PFFS plans and thus frustrating patient access to service. These rules also apply to employer-based plans.

[61] 42 U.S.C. § 1395w-23.

[62] 42 U.S.C. §§ 1395w-22(k), 1395w-24.

policies.[63] The explanation must include a clear statement of the amount of the enrollee's liability, including any allowable balance billing.

The PFFS plan must provide the Medicare beneficiary with advance balance billing information before incurring inpatient hospital services (and certain other services to be identified by the Secretary) for which balance billing amounts could be substantial.[64]

[4] Religious Fraternal Benefit Society Plans

MA allows a religious fraternal benefit (RFB) society to establish a plan that limits enrollment to members of the church, convention, or group with which it is affiliated.[65] Such plans must be exempt from taxation as provided under the Internal Revenue Code of 1986[66] and be affiliated with, carry out the tenets of, and share a religious bond with a church or convention or association of churches or an affiliated group of churches.[67] In addition, the society must meet certain requirements, and the Secretary can adjust the payment amounts.[68]

[5] Local and Regional Medicare Advantage Plans

An MA local plan is defined as an MA plan that is not an MA regional plan.[69] Regional MA plans are structured as PPOs.[70] An MA Regional PPO is an MA plan that has a network of providers that has a contractual agreement with CMS for a specified reimbursement to provide covered benefits regardless of whether such benefits are provided within the network of providers, and the regional PPO service area covers one or more entire MA regions.[71]

---

[63] 42 U.S.C. § 1395w-22(k); 42 C.F.R. § 422.111 (disclosure requirements), § 422.112 (access to services), § 422.113 (special rules for ambulance services, emergency and urgently needed services, and maintenance and post-stabilization care services), § 422.114 (access to services under an MA private fee-for-service plan), § 422.133 (return to home skill nursing facility).

[64] Check the websites of specific plans and Medicare.gov or MyMedicare.gov for plan details and locations.

[65] 42 U.S.C. § 1395w-28(e); 42 C.F.R. § 422.57.

[66] 42 C.F.R. § 422.2.

[67] 42 U.S.C. § 1395w-28(e).

[68] 42 U.S.C. § 1395w-28(e).

[69] 42 U.S.C. § 1395w-28(b)(5).

[70] *See* CMS, "Medicare Managed Care" (Transmittal 81, CMS Pub. No. 100-16, Apr. 25, 2007), *available at* http://www.cms.gov/Regulations-and-Guidance/Guidance/Transmittals/downloads/R81MCM.pdf (site visited Aug. 3, 2018), for CMS's information on the Regional PPO program; *see also* http://www.cms.gov/Medicare/Prescription-Drug-Coverage/PrescriptionDrugCovGenIn/downloads/MAPDRegions.pdf (site visited Aug. 3, 2018) for a chart of the 26 Medicare Advantage Regional PPO regions. 42 U.S.C. § 1395w-28(b)(5).

[71] 42 C.F.R. § 422.4(a)(1)(v).

There are special cost-sharing rules for MA regional plans. To the extent such plans apply a deductible, they are only permitted to have a single deductible related to Medicare Part A and Part B services.[72] The applicability of the single deductible may be different for specific in-network services and may also be waived for preventative services or other items and services.[73]

MA regional plans are required to provide for a catastrophic limit on beneficiary out-of-pocket expenditures for in-network and out-of-network benefits under the traditional Medicare program.[74] The total out-of-pocket catastrophic limit may be higher than the in-network catastrophic limit but may not increase the total catastrophic limit.[75] MA regional plans are required to track the deductibles and catastrophic limits and are to notify members and health care providers when the limits have been reached.[76] Starting with the January 2012 plan year, regional PPO plans are subject to the mandatory MOOP and catastrophic limit requirements that apply to local MA plans.[77]

MA regional plans are required to provide reimbursement for all covered benefits, regardless of whether those benefits are provided within or outside of the network of contracted providers.[78] In applying the actuarially equivalent level of cost-sharing on MA bids related to benefits under the traditional Medicare program option, only the catastrophic limit on out-of-pocket expenses for in-network benefits will be taken into account.[79]

[6] Specialized Medicare Advantage Plans for Special Needs Individuals

The MMA adds specialized MA plans for special needs individuals. A SNP is defined as an MA plan that exclusively serves people who are institutionalized; are entitled to medical assistance under a state plan under Title 19 (Medicaid) of the Social Security Act (i.e., those dually eligible for Medicare and Medicaid); or meet such requirements as the Secretary may determine would benefit from enrollment in a specialized MA plan for individuals with severe or disabling chronic conditions.[80]

---

[72] 42 C.F.R. § 422.101(d)(1).

[73] 42 C.F.R. § 422.101(d)(1).

[74] 42 C.F.R. § 422.101(d)(2).

[75] 42 C.F.R. § 422.101(d)(3).

[76] 42 C.F.R. § 422.101(d)(4).

[77] 42 C.F.R. §§ 422.100 and 422.101.

[78] 42 C.F.R. § 422.101(e)(1).

[79] 42 C.F.R. § 422.101(e)(2); *see also* § 422.256(b)(3).

[80] 42 U.S.C. § 1395w-28(b)(6). MIPPA, Pub. L. No. 110-275, provides that each type of SNP—Institutional (I-SNP), Dual Eligible (D-SNP), and Disabling Chronic Condition (C-SNP)—must, effective January 1, 2010, enroll only individuals who meet the statutory definition of special needs individual for its SNP type. Nothing in the provisions affects benefits to which dual eligible individuals are entitled through their state Medicaid programs. Note that these provisions, taken

Special rules for SNP enrollment and eligibility have been established by the Secretary.[81]

As set out in MIPPA, there are several types of SNPs.[82] Previously set to expire in 2018, Section 50311 of the Bipartisan Budget Act of 2018 permanently reauthorizes SNPs.[83] In addition, Section 165 of MIPPA prohibits Dual Eligible SNPs from imposing cost-sharing requirements on persons dually eligible for Medicare and Medicaid or Qualified Medicare Beneficiaries (QMB) that would exceed the amounts permitted under the state Medicaid plan if the individual were not enrolled in the Dual Eligible SNP. The provision was effective January 1, 2010. Each type of SNP—Institutional, Dual Eligible, and Disabling Chronic Condition—must enroll only individuals who meet the statutory definition of special needs individual for its SNP type.[84]

- *Institutional SNPs* (I-SNPs) seeking to enroll individuals living in the community but requiring an institutional level of care must use a state assessment tool to determine the need for institutional level of care and must have the assessment performed by an entity other than the organization offering the plan.
- *Dual-Eligible SNPs* (D-SNPs) must provide each prospective enrollee, prior to enrollment, with a comprehensive written statement of benefits and cost-sharing protections under the relevant state Medicaid plan and an explanation of which such benefits and cost-sharing protections are available under the plan.[85] D-SNPs must also have a contract with the

together, suggest that Congress is inclined to have dual eligible beneficiaries receive all their Medicare and Medicaid services through MA-SNPs. While plans that fully integrate Medicare and Medicaid services have worked well in some situations, these situations have generally evolved with impetus from and a great deal of planning by the states, rather than from private plans.

[81] 42 C.F.R. § 422.52(e). Note that the Secretary may designate certain MA plans that disproportionately serve special needs individuals as SNPs. *See* 42 C.F.R. § 422.52(f). *See also* Halperin, Nemore, & Gottlich, *What's So Special About Special Needs Plans? Assessing Medicare Special Needs Plans for "Dual Eligibles,"* Marquette Elder's Advisor, Vol. 8, No. 2 (Spring 2007). This article discusses the limits of SNPs as a health care delivery vehicle in meeting the needs of low-income people and those with multiple chronic conditions.

[82] MIPPA § 164, Pub. L. No. 110-275.

[83] The Bipartisan Budget Act of 2018 (BBA) was signed into law on February 9, 2018 (Pub. L. No. 115-123).

[84] MIPPA § 164 (effective Jan. 1, 2010).

[85] Note that this provision presumably would allow a prospective dual enrollee to determine whether he or she will receive any value from a dual SNP that is not already available under his or her state Medicaid program. One challenge for those helping individuals make choices is to determine whether the plan has accurately presented state Medicaid coverage, which is not an easy undertaking. Note, too, that the Secretary of the Department of Health and Human Services (HHS) is directed to designate staff and resources to assist states that are inquiring about coordination with SNPs. However, states are not required to enter into contracts with SNPs.

state Medicaid agency to provide, or arrange for the provision of, benefits to which the individual is entitled under Medicaid. Such benefits may, but apparently are not required to, include long-term care services. Those D-SNPs that do not have such a contract, which had to be in effect by January 1, 2010, may continue to operate but cannot expand their service areas. Also note that beginning in CY 2013, all MA organizations that offer D-SNPs (existing, new, and expanding) are required to have contracts with the state Medicaid agencies in the states in which they operate. D-SNPs that fail to secure a State Medicaid agency contract will not be permitted to operate. The Bipartisan Budget Act of 2018 included provisions requiring enhanced coordination between states and the federal government, including with respect to appeals and grievances.[86]

- *Severe or Disabling Chronic Condition SNPs* (C-SNPs). The definition for persons eligible for the services of C-SNPs is amended to include having "one or more [co-morbid] and medically complex chronic conditions that are substantially disabling or life threatening, have a high risk of hospitalization or other significant adverse health outcomes, and require specialized delivery systems across domains of care." The Secretary is directed to convene a panel including the Director of the Agency for Healthcare Research and Quality to determine conditions that meet this new definition.[87]

All SNPs, regardless of type, must meet new requirements for care management. They must have in place an evidence-based model of care with appropriate networks of providers and specialists; conduct an initial assessment and annual reassessment of each individual's physical, psychosocial, and functional needs; develop a care plan, in consultation with the individual, as feasible, that identifies goals and objectives and specific services and benefits to be provided; and use an interdisciplinary team in the management of care. The Secretary is directed to review each plan's care management compliance as part of a periodic audit.

All SNPs, regardless of type, must meet data collection and reporting requirements relating to their compliance with the plan requirements introduced by MIPPA. Such data "may be based on claims data" and must be reported at the plan, rather than sponsor, level. Nothing in the provisions affects benefits to which dual eligible individuals are entitled through their state Medicaid programs.

For more information about managed care issues for dual eligible individuals, see **§ 10.07** in this Handbook.

---

[86] *See* § 50311 of the Bipartisan Budget Act of 2018 (BBA), signed into law on February 9, 2018 (Pub. L. No. 115-123).

[87] For a list of SNP-specific chronic conditions, see CMS website at: https://www.cms.gov/Medicare/Health-Plans/SpecialNeedsPlans/C-SNPs.html (site visited Oct. 15, 2018).

[7] Cost Plans

Cost plus plans should not be confused with MA plans. Note that "Section 1876 cost plans" are a health plan option for some Medicare beneficiaries that are sometimes confused with MA plans. Cost plans, though, are not MA plans and are authorized under a different section of the Social Security Act than are MA plans. As noted in the MMC Manual:

> Section 1876 cost plans are plans operated by an HMO or Competitive Medical Plan (CMP) in accordance with a cost reimbursement contract under section 1876 of the Act and Title 42, Part 417 of the Code of Federal Regulations. Medicare cost plan enrollees are not restricted to the HMO or CMP network for receipt of covered Medicare services (i.e., Original Medicare services may be received through non-HMO/CMP sources and are reimbursed separately by Medicare intermediaries and carriers). Medicare payment to the HMO/CMP is based on the reasonable costs of providing services to the Medicare beneficiaries.[88]

Note that cost contracts were authorized through 2018. Section 209 of the Medicare Access and CHIP Reauthorization Act of 2015, Pub. L. No. 114-10, signed into law by President Obama on April 16, 2015, required that cost contract plans transition to MA plans by 2019. Note that sponsors of cost plans were authorized to deem enrollees into an affiliated MA plan offered by the same sponsor. CMS has indicated that it will non-renew cost plans beginning contract year (CY) 2019 in service areas where two or more competing local or regional MA coordinated care plans meet minimum enrollment requirements over the course of the entire prior contract year.[89]

[C] Medicare Advantage Coverage, Costs, and Access to Care

At the time of enrollment and every year thereafter, MA plans must disclose to enrollees their service area emergency service options and procedures for obtaining emergency services; out-of-state service coverage; optional supplemental coverage and costs; prior authorization rules; grievance and appeals procedures; quality assurance mechanisms; the number of grievances and appeals and their disposition; and a summary of the method of compensating doctors.[90]

---

[88] MMC Manual, Ch. 1: § 40, *available at* http://www.cms.gov/Regulations-and-Guidance/Guidance/Manuals/Downloads/mc86c01.pdf (site visited Aug. 3, 2018).

[89] For more information about cost plans, see the CMS website at https://www.cms.gov/Medicare/Health-Plans/MedicareCostPlans/index.html (site visited June 12, 2018).

[90] 42 U.S.C. § 1395w-22(c); 42 C.F.R. § 422.111.

An MA plan is required to clearly communicate to enrollees through the Evidence of Coverage (EOC) and Summary of Benefits (SB) the MA plan's service area, benefits offered under the plan including premiums and cost-sharing, and information related to access to services.[91] This must be done at the time of enrollment and at least annually thereafter.[92] An MA enrollee will receive an Annual Notice of Change (ANOC) each fall that will include any changes to the MA's rules.[93] Note that a rule finalized in 2018 changes both the timing of and default delivery mode of certain beneficiary documents.[94] Effective the 2019 plan year, the ANOC must be delivered 15 days before the first day of the ACEP (by October 1), whereas the EOC must be delivered by the first day of the ACEP (by October 15). MA and Part D sponsors can now provide certain materials, such as the EOC, electronically, with provision of hard copy upon request. Upon receipt, an enrollee should review the changes for the following year and decide whether the plan's terms continue to meet their needs.

[1] Coverage of Benefits

MA plans offer a specific set of health benefits at a uniform premium and uniform level of cost-sharing to all Medicare beneficiaries residing in the service area of the MA plan.[95] Each MA organization must provide the benefits currently available under Medicare Parts A and B, except for hospice, as discussed below.[96] As a practical matter, most of the rules that apply to coverage under Parts A and B as discussed in other chapters of this Handbook also apply to MA plans. MA plans generally impose the same coverage limits set in traditional Medicare (e.g., limit on number of consecutive covered days in hospitals and skilled nursing facilities, outpatient therapy caps), but plans have some discretion to ease such restrictions (e.g., most MA plans waive the three-day prior hospitalization requirement for subsequent coverage of a SNF stay, as is required under Part A). MA plans are required to provide in-network Medicare-covered preventive benefits at zero cost-sharing.[97]

MA plans may not deny, limit, or condition the coverage or provision of benefits based on any health status-related factor; similarly, MA plans cannot

---

[91] 42 C.F.R. § 422.111(a) and (b).

[92] 42 C.F.R. § 422.111(a)(3).

[93] 42 C.F.R. § 422.111(d).

[94] Final rule CMS-4182-F at 82 Fed. Reg. 16,440 (Apr. 16, 2018), amending 42 C.F.R. § 422.111.

[95] 42 C.F.R. § 422.2. *But see* **§ 7.03[C][1]** for discussion of "uniformity requirements."

[96] 42 U.S.C. § 1395w-22(a); 42 C.F.R. § 422.101. Note that 42 C.F.R. § 422.2 (MA definitions) and 42 C.F.R. § 423.4 (Voluntary Prescription Drug Benefit, Medicare Part D, definitions) contain an important explanatory list of terms important in discussing and understanding the MA program.

[97] 42 C.F.R. §§ 417.454 and 422.100. *See also* ACA § 4103 (annual wellness visit and personalized prevention plan).

design plan benefits in such a way that is likely to substantially discourage enrollment by certain individuals.[98]

Pursuant to a final rule issued in 2018, MA plans have significant new flexibilities in the management of benefits offered to enrollees starting in 2019.[99] Previously, the MA uniformity standard outlined at 42 C.F.R. § 422.100(d) was interpreted to mean that plan sponsors had to offer all enrollees in a plan in a given service area access to the same benefits at the same level of cost-sharing. CMS is reinterpreting this uniformity requirement to allow plans to "reduce cost-sharing for certain covered benefits, offer lower deductibles for enrollees that meet specific medical criteria, provided that similarly situated enrollees (that is, all enrollees who meet the medical criteria identified by the MA plan for the benefits) are treated the same. In addition, there must be a nexus between the health status or disease state and the specific benefit package designed for enrollees meeting that health status or disease state."[100] In other words, starting in 2019, MA plans can offer targeted benefits and/or reduced cost-sharing, at their discretion, based upon enrollees' particular health condition(s). CMS has also expanded the interpretation of what items and services can be covered as "primarily health-related" supplemental benefits as part of the new benefits targeted by health condition described above. Pursuant to the Bipartisan Budget Act of 2018, starting in plan year 2020, MA plans can also provide supplemental benefits to chronically ill enrollees.[101] While the change in uniformity standards and supplemental benefits will potentially give beneficiary's access to more covered services targeted to their health care needs it will also likely make informed decision-making more difficult. The Center for Medicare Advocacy drafted a summary of the Part C and Part D revised regulations in which we highlighted some of our concerns regarding these changes.[102]

With respect to Medicare Part D prescription drug coverage, MA sponsors may not offer an MA plan in an area unless either that plan (or another MA plan offered by the organization in that same service area) includes required prescription drug coverage.[103] MA plans offering Part D prescription drug coverage are

---

[98] 42 U.S.C. § 1395w-22(b).

[99] Final rule CMS-4182-F at 82 Fed. Reg. 16,440 (Apr. 16, 2018). For a summary of the final rule, *see, e.g.*, the Center's "Special Report: Recent Changes in Law, Regulations and Guidance Relating to Medicare Advantage and Medicare Part D" (September 2018), *available at* http://www.medicareadvocacy.org/wp-content/uploads/2018/09/Report.-Summary-2019-Call-letter-and-C-D-Rule-1.pdf (site visited Oct. 15, 2018).

[100] 83 Fed. Reg. 16,480.

[101] Section 50322 of the Bipartisan Budget Act of 2018 (BBA), signed into law on February 9, 2018 (Pub. L. No. 115-123).

[102] *See, e.g.*, the Center's "Special Report: Recent Changes in Law, Regulations and Guidance Relating to Medicare Advantage and Medicare Part D" (September 2018), *available at* http://www.medicareadvocacy.org/wp-content/uploads/2018/09/Report.-Summary-2019-Call-letter-and-C-D-Rule-1.pdf (site visited Oct. 15, 2018).

[103] 42 U.S.C.§ 1395w-131(a).

known as MA-PD plans and must follow Part D rules concerning drug coverage, as outlined in **Chapter 11.**[104] If an MA plan does not offer Part D coverage, then the type of MA plan an individual is enrolled in determines whether the individual can also enroll in a stand-alone Part D plan.[105] Individuals enrolled in an MA coordinated care plan (HMO, PPO, PSO) cannot also be enrolled in a stand-alone Part D plan, even if the MA plan does not provide Part D coverage. Private fee-for-service (PFFS) plans are not required to offer Part D coverage. If PFFS plan does not offer Part D coverage, enrollees can enroll in a separate Part D plan. MSAs cannot offer Part D coverage, so enrollees can also enroll in a Part D plan.

On an annual basis, insurance companies that wish to offer MA coverage in the following calendar year submit bids to CMS, which are compared to a CMS-established local benchmark rate. Whether a plan's bid is below or above the benchmark determines, in part, a plan's premiums and supplemental benefits it may offer.[106] If a plan's bid is below the CMS-established benchmark, the plan receives a rebate payment from Medicare, a percentage of which must be passed along to plan enrollees in the form of either lower premiums or supplemental benefits.[107] Plans may offer supplemental benefits for which a separate premium may be charged, but the separate premium may not vary among individuals within the plan and must not exceed certain actuarial and community rating requirements.[108] It is largely due to these rebates that many MA plans offer supplemental benefits—things not covered under Part A or B—such as limited vision, hearing, and dental services.

MA plans are not required to cover hospice services, which is a benefit available under Part A of Medicare.[109] MA plans must tell an enrollee about hospice care, if a hospice program is located within the MA organization's service area, or, if not located within the service area, if it is common to refer patients to hospice programs outside the service area.[110] Medicare fee-for-service contractors are required by federal regulations to maintain payment responsibility for MA

[104] Note that in 2017 the vast majority of MA enrollees (89 percent) are in MA-PDs. Kaiser Family Foundation, "Medicare Advantage 2017 Spotlight: Enrollment Market Update" (June 2017), *available at* http://www.kff.org/medicare/issue-brief/medicare-advantage-2017-spotlight-enrollment-market-update (site visited Aug. 9, 2017).

[105] *See* 42 C.F.R. § 423.30(b).

[106] *See, e.g.*, Medicare Payment Advisory Commission (MedPAC), "Medicare Advantage Program Payment System" (Oct. 2016) *available at* http://www.medpac.gov/docs/default-source/payment-basics/medpac_payment_basics_16_ma_final.pdf (site visited Aug. 3, 2018).

[107] 42 C.F.R. § 422.266.

[108] 42 U.S.C. § 1395w-22; 42 C.F.R. § 422.102.

[109] 42 C.F.R. § 422.100(c)(1). See **Chapter 5** of this Handbook regarding Medicare coverage of hospice services.

[110] 42 U.S.C. § 1395w-23(h); 42 C.F.R. § 422.320; *see also* **Chapter 5** of this Handbook for discussion of the Medicare hospice program.

enrollees who elect hospice.[111] If the patient elects hospice care, CMS makes payments directly to the hospice program and makes monthly payments to the MA organization for additional benefits not provided by hospice care.[112]

[2] Premiums and Cost-Sharing

Out-of-pocket costs in an MA plan depend on whether the plan charges a monthly premium, whether the plan has a yearly deductible, how much an individual pays for each visit or service (copayments or coinsurance), the type of health care services needed and how often and whether network providers are used. MA plans can differ with respect to expected costs so it is imperative to read each plan's literature to see what kind of plan it is and what it pays for.

As noted in the previous section, MA premiums are based on the difference between Medicare payments to the plan and the plan's bid submitted to Medicare. These amounts vary by county.[113] MA plan enrollees must continue to pay their Part B premium regardless of any additional premium amount charged by the MA plan, however MA plans are allowed to offer reduced Medicare Part B premiums as an additional benefit to their enrollees. Information about Part B premium reductions would be included with the information beneficiaries receive about plans during the annual open enrollment period.[114]

The MA organization, through its MA plan or plans, may impose copayments and deductibles different from those under Parts A and B, as long as the monthly premium and cost-sharing are actuarially equivalent to cost-sharing under traditional Medicare.[115] However, cost-sharing under MA plans cannot exceed the cost-sharing imposed under traditional Medicare for three specific services—chemotherapy administration, renal dialysis services, and skilled nursing

---

[111] 42 C.F.R. §§ 417.585 and 417.531.

[112] 42 U.S.C. § 1395w-23(h); 42 C.F.R. § 422.320(c). Note that when an MA enrollee elects hospice care and requires nonterminal care or treatment, the individual might have to pay cost-sharing rates under traditional Medicare, which might be greater than cost-sharing through the MA plan; additionally, if an individual opts out of hospice care and wishes to return to the MA plan, MA coverage might not begin until the following month. *See* MMC Manual, Ch. 4: § 10.4, *available at* http://www.cms.gov/Regulations-and-Guidance/Guidance/Manuals/Downloads/mc86c04.pdf, and Medicare Claims Processing (MCP) Manual, Ch. 11: § 30. 4, *available at* http://www.cms.gov/Regulations-and-Guidance/Guidance/Manuals/Downloads/clm104c11.pdf (sites visited Aug. 3, 2018).

[113] In 2017, the average MA-PD enrollee pays a monthly premium of about $36; however, 50 percent of MA-PD enrollees are in zero-premium plans. Kaiser Family Foundation, "Medicare Advantage 2017 Spotlight: Enrollment Market Update" (June 2017), *available at* http://www.kff.org/medicare/issue-brief/medicare-advantage-2017-spotlight-enrollment-market-update (site visited Aug. 9, 2017).

[114] Medicare, Medicaid, and SCHIP Benefits Improvement and Protection Act of 2000 (BIPA), Pub. L. No. 106-554, § 606 (Dec. 21, 2000).

[115] 42 U.S.C. § 1395w-24(e).

care.[116] Cost-sharing can vary depending on what type of plan an individual is enrolled in and whether in-network or out-of-network providers are used.[117] In addition, as discussed in the previous section, MA plans can offer targeted benefits, including reduced cost-sharing for certain services, based upon certain health conditions designated by the plan.

Since 2011, local MA plans (and since 2012 regional PPOs) must establish a maximum out-of-pocket (MOOP) liability amount for enrollees for all Part A and B services to be set yearly by CMS.[118] In 2019, the mandatory MOOP is $6,700. Plans that use a lower, voluntary MOOP of $3,400 have greater flexibility in establishing cost-sharing amounts.[119]

Note that low-income MA enrollees, similar to other low-income Medicare beneficiaries, may be entitled to assistance with certain premiums and cost-sharing. See **§ 10.04[B]** of this Handbook for information concerning MA plans and the QMB benefit; also see **§ 11.06** of this Handbook concerning the Part D low-income subsidy.

[3] Access to Care

By virtue of their design, most MA plans impose restrictions on enrollees' access to Medicare-covered services. Coordinated care plans (e.g., HMOs) can use mechanisms to control use of services, such as referrals from a gatekeeper for an enrollee to receive services within the plan.[120] While such plans may specify

---

[116] ACA § 3202; 42 C.F.R. §§ 417.454, and 422.100 (effective Jan. 2011). Note that the Secretary of HHS has discretion to require that cost-sharing for other services also not exceed traditional Medicare cost-sharing but, to date, has not exercised this discretion. In the preamble to the final rules, CMS clarified that this limitation to MA cost-sharing applies only to in-network services. Under traditional Medicare, beneficiaries are not charged any cost-sharing for a covered SNF stay for the first 20 days. MA plans that establish a lower, voluntary maximum out-of-pocket amount (MOOP) may have cost sharing for the first 20 days of a SNF stay. The per-day cost sharing for days 21 through 100 must not be greater than the Original Medicare SNF amount and total cost sharing for the overall SNF benefit must be no higher than the actuarially equivalent cost sharing in Original Medicare.

[117] Note that in the final 2016 Parts C and D rule issued on February 12, 2015, CMS revises 42 C.F.R. § 422.100 to codify and further clarify an MA plan's obligations when plan services are affected by public health emergencies or disasters. The clarification includes a requirement that MA plans "ensure access, at in-network cost-sharing, to covered services even when furnished by non-contracted providers when disruption in the service area impedes enrollees' ability to access contracted providers and/or contracted providers' ability to provide needed services." 80 Fed. Reg. 7912-58, 7953 (Feb. 12, 2015).

[118] 42 C.F.R. §§ 422.100 and 422.101.

[119] *See* CMS, "Announcement of Calendar Year (CY) 2019 Medicare Advantage Capitation Rates and Medicare Advantage and Part D Payment Policies and Final Call Letter," (Apr. 2, 2018), *available at* https://www.cms.gov/Medicare/Health-Plans/MedicareAdvtgSpecRateStats/Downloads/Announcement2019.pdf (site visited June 12, 2018).

[120] 42 C.F.R. § 422.4(a)(1)(ii).

the networks of providers from whom enrollees may obtain services, such networks must be sufficient to provide adequate access to covered services to meet the needs of the population served.[121]

Specialist referral policies are set by plans, however plans must provide or arrange for necessary specialist care, and in particular give female enrollees the option of direct access to a women's health specialist within the network for women's routine and preventive health care services. In addition, the plan must arrange for specialty care outside of the plan provider network when network providers are unavailable or inadequate to meet a member's medical needs.[122]

The distinction between "in-network" vs. "out-of-network" providers is relevant to the type of MA plan, coverage of services and enrollees' out-of-pocket liabilities. PPOs have networks of contracting providers but, unlike HMOs, also provide for reimbursement for all covered benefits regardless of whether the benefits are provided within the network of providers (i.e., out-of-network care).[123] PFFS plans in non-network areas and MSAs do not need to establish networks.

MA plans generally have a prior-authorization process: if an enrollee wishes to receive a service from an in-network provider, the provider must seek prior authorization from the plan and inform the enrollee if the plan makes an adverse determination, triggering appeal rights; if, however, the provider furnishes the service and without seeking prior authorization from the plan and the service is not covered, the provider cannot bill the enrollee for more than standard in-plan cost-sharing.[124] Similarly, plan enrollees are protected against balance billing (meaning they generally pay only plan-allowed cost-sharing) when they obtain services that are covered by the plan (either by a plan decision or through an appeal), including from noncontracted providers.[125]

---

[121] 42 C.F.R. § 422.112(a). Ongoing concerns have been raised regarding both the scope of MA network adequacy rules and regulatory oversight. *See, e.g.,* General Accounting Office (GAO), "Medicare Advantage: Actions Needed to Enhance CMS Oversight of Provider Network Adequacy," GAO-15-710 (Aug. 31, 2015), *available at* http://www.gao.gov/products/GAO-15-710 (site visited Aug. 3, 2018). For analysis of the robustness of MA physician networks, see Kaiser Family Foundation, "Medicare Advantage: How Robust Are Plans' Physician Networks?" (Oct 2017), *available at* https://www.kff.org/medicare/report/medicare-advantage-how-robust-are-plans-physician-networks/ (site visited Aug. 3, 2018). For an analysis of network adequacy relating to hospitals, see Kaiser Family Foundation, "Medicare Advantage Hospital Networks: How Much Do They Vary?" (June 2016), *available at* http://kff.org/medicare/report/medicare-advantage-hospital-networks-how-much-do-they-vary/ (site visited Aug. 3, 2018).

[122] 42 C.F.R. § 422.112(a)(3); *see also* MMC Manual, Ch. 4: § 110.1, *available at* http://www.cms.gov/Regulations-and-Guidance/Guidance/Manuals/Downloads/mc86c04.pdf (site visited Aug. 3, 2018).

[123] 42 C.F.R. § 422.4(a)(1)(v).

[124] 42 C.F.R. § 422.105(a); *see also* MMC Manual, Ch. 4: §§ 170-180.2, *available at* http://www.cms.gov/Regulations-and-Guidance/Guidance/Manuals/Downloads/mc86c04.pdf (site visited Aug. 3, 2018).

[125] MMC Manual, Ch. 4: § 170, *available at* http://www.cms.gov/Regulations-and-Guidance/Guidance/Manuals/Downloads/mc86c04.pdf (site visited Aug. 6, 2018).

MA plans can change their provider networks any time during the year, as long as they continue to meet network adequacy standards, provide timely notice (at least 30 days advance notice to affected enrollees), and ensure continuity of care for enrollees.[126] In response to significant mid-year network provider terminations by certain MA plan sponsors starting in the fall of 2013, CMS created a new, but limited, special enrollment period (SEP) right to change MA plans available to certain plan enrollees affected by mid-year provider terminations, effective in 2015.[127]

Emergency services obtained out-of-network are covered by plans with a limit on charges to enrollees to an amount determined by CMS annually ($90 for plans using mandatory MOOP and $120 for plans using voluntary MOOP in 2019), or what the plan would charge the enrollee if he or she obtained the services through the MA organization, whichever is less).[128] Urgently needed services that are medically necessary and immediately required can also be covered if provided when an enrollee is temporarily absent from the MA plan's service area, or provided when the enrollee is in the service area but the organization's provider network is temporarily unavailable or inaccessible.[129]

With respect to drug coverage, MA-PD plans are required to establish and maintain a process to ensure that appropriate payment is assigned at the point of sale (POS) so that claims for drugs that may be covered under Part A or B, rather than Part D, are properly adjudicated. If a denial under Part D is based on the existence of coverage under Parts A or B, the MA-PD plan should authorize or provide the drug under that other benefit without requiring the enrollee to make a subsequent request for coverage under that other benefit.[130]

---

[126] *See generally* MMC Manual, Ch. 4 (Part II), *available at* http://www.cms.gov/Regulations-and-Guidance/Guidance/Manuals/Downloads/mc86c04.pdf (site visited Aug. 6, 2018).

[127] *See* MMC Manual, Ch. 2: § 30.4.6, *available at* https://www.cms.gov/Medicare/Eligibility-and-Enrollment/MedicareMangCareEligEnrol/Downloads/CY_2019_MA_Enrollment_and_Disenrollment Guidance.pdf (site visited Aug. 6, 2018).

[128] 42 C.F.R. § 422.113(b). For both MA plan and enrollee responsibilities concerning post-stabilization care related to an emergency medical condition, see 42 C.F.R. § 422.113(c).

[129] 42 C.F.R. § 422.113(b). Note that in the final 2016 Parts C and D rule issued on February 12, 2015, CMS finalized a proposal to improve MA enrollees' access to out-of-network facilities in non-extraordinary circumstances by revising 42 C.F.R. § 422.113 to remove the phrase "under extraordinary and unusual circumstances." As noted in the preamble, this revision is meant to encourage plans to cover care provided in clinics that operate on weekends and outside of normal business hours when the plan network is not available. 80 Fed. Reg. 7912-58, 7949 (Feb. 12, 2015).

[130] 42 C.F.R. § 422.112(b)(7). According to the preamble of the final 2016 rule for Medicare Part C, CMS amended 42 C.F.R. § 422.112(b)(7) to "require MA-PDs to coordinate with their network pharmacies and prescribers to improve existing processes and develop new ones in order to ensure that enrollees receive their Medicare-covered prescription medications, without delay, when they present at the network pharmacy." 80 Fed. Reg. 7912-58, 7941 (Feb. 12, 2015).

[D] Process for Exercising Choice

The Secretary of HHS must establish a process through which Medicare beneficiaries can elect how they wish to obtain their Medicare covered services. Elections are made or changed only during coverage election periods.[131]

[1] Medicare Advantage Disenrollment Period Ended in 2018

Between 2011 and 2018, beneficiaries who were in an MA plan had a 45-day MA disenrollment period (MADP).[132] During this period, they could only drop the MA plan and return to traditional Medicare and enroll in a PDP; they were not able to enroll in a different MA plan. Pursuant to federal legislation enacted in December 2016, the MADP ended in 2018, and the open enrollment period (OEP), similar to the OEP that was in effect before 2011, has been reinstated effective 2019.[133]

[2] Open Enrollment Period—2019 and Beyond

Effective 2019, for the first three months of the calendar year there is a continuous open enrollment and disenrollment period for those individuals enrolled in an MA plan. Unlike the "old OEP" which was in effect from 2007 to 2010, the "new OEP" permits changes to Part D coverage for those who, prior to the change in election during the new OEP, were enrolled in an MA plan. Therefore, during this three-month period an MA eligible beneficiary can make a one-time change as follows: an individual enrolled in an MA-PD plan may use the new OEP to switch to: (1) Another MA-PD plan; (2) an MA-only plan; or (3) Original Medicare with or without a PDP. The new OEP would also allow an individual enrolled in an MA-only plan to switch to—(1) another MA-only plan; (2) an MA-PD plan; or (3) Original Medicare with or without a PDP. Also unsolicited marketing is prohibited by statute during this period.[134]

[131] 42 U.S.C. § 1395w-21(c); 42 C.F.R. §§ 422.60 (election process), 422.62 (election of coverage under an MA plan), 422.66 (coordination of enrollment and disenrollment through MA organizations), 422.74 (disenrollment by the MA organization). *But see* **§ 7.03[D][6]** of this Handbook for a discussion of special enrollment periods (SEPs).

[132] 42 C.F.R. § 422.62(a)(7).

[133] Section 17005, 21st Century Cures Act, Pub. L. No 114-255, signed into law by President Obama on December 13, 2016.

[134] *See* final rule CMS-4182-F at 82 Fed. Reg. 16,440 (Apr. 16, 2018), amending 42 C.F.R. §§ 422.60, 422.62, 422.68, 423.38 and 423.40.

[3] Initial Coverage Election Period

If there are one or more MA plans offered in an individual's service area at the time the individual first becomes entitled to benefits under Part A and enrolled under Part B, the individual must make the election during a defined election period beginning three months before the individual is entitled to both Parts A and B and ending the last month preceding the month of entitlement.[135] An election is considered to have been made on the date the election form is received by the MA plan.[136] An election made during an initial coverage election period (ICEP) is effective as of the first day of the month of entitlement to both Part A and Part B.[137]

Individuals who do not make an election during the initial coverage election period will remain in the traditional Medicare program.[138] If an individual is in a non-Medicare health plan the month before enrolling in Part B, that individual will be entitled to remain in the health plan if the plan sponsor also offers an MA plan.[139]

[4] Annual Coordinated Election Period

Starting in the fall of 2011, the annual coordinated election period (ACEP) was changed from November 15 through December 31 every year so that it begins on October 15 and ends on December 7.[140] Each October, the Secretary of HHS must conduct an ACEP during which time a beneficiary may choose to enroll in an MA plan, change to a different MA plan, or return to traditional Medicare.[141] An election made during this time period becomes effective on January 1 of the following year.[142] A beneficiary who makes no election will remain in traditional Medicare or in the MA plan in which she or he is enrolled. The Secretary of HHS must mail written comparative information about plan choices to all beneficiaries

---

[135] 42 U.S.C. § 1395w-22(c); 42 C.F.R. §§ 422.60 (election process), 422.62(a) (election of coverage under an MA plan).

[136] 42 C.F.R. § 422.60 (election process).

[137] 42 C.F.R. § 422.68(a).

[138] 42 C.F.R. § 422.66(c). The MMC Manual defines "passive" election as when the beneficiary has been informed by the MA plan that he or she may make an election of a different plan but takes no action. *See* MMC Manual, Ch. 2: § 20.4.2.

[139] 42 U.S.C. § 1395w-21(c)(3) (default); 42 C.F.R. § 422.66(d). However, persons who fail to make an election during the initial coverage election period (have not joined an MA plan) are deemed to have elected traditional Medicare. 42 C.F.R. § 422.66(c). *See also* **§ 7.03[D][9]** of this Handbook.

[140] 42 C.F.R. § 422.62(a)(2).

[141] 42 U.S.C. § 1395w-21(c)(1)–(3).

[142] 42 C.F.R. § 422.68(b).

who live in an area in which at least one MA plan is offered at least 15 days before the annual coordinated enrollment period.[143]

During the ACEP, an individual eligible to enroll in an MA plan may change his or her election from an MA plan to traditional Medicare or to a different MA plan, or from traditional Medicare to an MA plan; and if an individual changes his or her election from an MA plan that offers prescription drug coverage to traditional Medicare, he or she may also elect a PDP.[144]

[5] Open Enrollment Period for Institutionalized Individuals

An individual who is eligible to elect an MA plan and who is institutionalized is not limited, except as provided for in special rules for MA MSA plans, in the number of elections or changes he or she may make.[145] Subject to the MA plan being open to enrollees, an MA eligible institutionalized individual may at any time elect an MA plan or change his or her election from an MA plan, or from traditional Medicare to an MA plan.[146] A beneficiary is considered institutionalized if they continuously reside or are expected to continuously reside for 90 days or longer in a long-term care facility, which is a skilled nursing facility or nursing facility; an intermediate care facility for individuals with intellectual disabilities; or an inpatient psychiatric facility.[147]

[6] Special Election Periods

An individual may also change his or her election in the form and manner specified by CMS, from an MA plan to traditional Medicare or to a different MA plan under several special circumstances during a special election period (SEP), including the following:[148]

---

[143] 42 U.S.C. § 1395w-21(d)(1)–(7). It is important to note that there has been some concern recently about the neutrality of the information disseminated by CMS. *See, e.g.*, the Center's Weekly Alert "Advocates Raise Concerns About Inaccuracies and Bias in Draft MEDICARE & YOU Handbook" (May 31, 2018), *available at* http://www.medicareadvocacy.org/advocates-raise-concerns-about-comparisons-between-traditional-medicare-and-medicare-advantage-in-draft-2019-medicare-you-handbook/ (site visited Oct. 1, 2018).

[144] *See* 42 C.F.R. § 422.62(a)(2).

[145] 42 C.F.R. § 422.62(a)(6).

[146] *See* 42 C.F.R. § 422.62(a)(6). *See also* MMC Manual, Ch. 2: § 30.3, *available at* https://www.cms.gov/Medicare/Eligibility-and-Enrollment/MedicareMangCareEligEnrol/Downloads/CY_2019_MA_Enrollment_and_Disenrollment_Guidance.pdf (site visited Aug. 6, 2018).

[147] 42 C.F.R. § 422.2.

[148] 42 C.F.R. § 422.62(b). Note that CMS has exercised its discretion to SEPs in a number of additional situations; for a complete list of SEPs, see CMS MMC Manual, CMS Pub. 100-16, Ch. 2, §§ 30.4, *et seq.*, *available at* https://www.cms.gov/Medicare/Eligibility-and-Enrollment/MedicareMangCareEligEnrol/Downloads/CY_2019_MA_Enrollment_and_Disenrollment_Guidance.pdf (site visited Aug. 6, 2018).

(1) CMS or the organization has terminated the organization's contract for the plan, discontinued the plan, discontinued the plan in the area in which the individual resides, or the organization has notified the individual of the impending termination of the plan, or the impending discontinuation of the plan in the area in which the individual resides;
(2) The individual is not eligible to remain enrolled in the plan because of a change in his or her place of residence to a location out of the service area or continuation area or other change in circumstances as determined by CMS but not including terminations resulting from a failure to make timely payment of an MA plan monthly or supplemental beneficiary premium, or from disruptive behavior;
(3) The individual demonstrates to CMS, that—

   (i) the organization offering the plan substantially violated a material provision of its contract in relation to the individual, such as (a) failing to provide the beneficiary on a timely basis medically necessary services for which benefits are available under the plan; (b) failing to provide medical services in accordance with applicable quality standards; or the organization (or its agent, representative, or plan provider) materially misrepresented the plan's provisions in marketing the plan to the individual,
   (ii) the organization (or its agent, representative, or plan provider) materially misrepresents the plan's provisions in marketing the plan to an individual.

(4) The individual meets such other exceptional conditions as CMS may provide.
(5) There is an SEP for individuals with Medicare who receive any type of assistance from the Medicaid program, including through one of the

---

As of 2015 there is a new SEP, which occurs when an MA plan terminates providers from its network. In its 2015 Call Letter, CMS describes the SEP:

> CMS will [. . .] find that an enrollee meets exceptional conditions sufficient to justify a special enrollment period (SEP) when the enrollee is affected by substantial mid-year provider network terminations initiated by an [MA plan] without cause. CMS will determine whether the terminations are substantial and require the granting of an SEP. CMS will use a variety of criteria for determining whether or not the network terminations are substantial, such as: (1) the number of enrollees affected; (2) the size of the service area affected; (3) the timing of the termination; (4) whether adequate and timely notice is provided to enrollees, (5) and any other information that may be relevant to the particular circumstance(s). In addition, the enrollee must demonstrate that the enrollee has been affected by this change. SEPs will not be granted when [MA plans] make changes to their network that are effective on January 1 of the following contract year, as long as affected enrollees are notified of the changes prior to the start of the AEP.

2015 Call Letter, p. 104, *available at* http://www.cms.gov/Medicare/Health-Plans/MedicareAdvtgSpecRateStats/Downloads/Announcement2015.pdf (site visited Oct. 1, 2018). This SEP is incorporated in the MMC Manual, Ch. 2, at § 30.4.6, *available at* https://www.cms.gov/Medicare/Eligibility-and-Enrollment/MedicareMangCareEligEnrol/Downloads/CY_2019_MA_Enrollment_and_Disenrollment_Guidance.pdf (site visited , Aug. 62018).

Medicare Savings Programs (QMB, SLMB, or QI) and/or the Part D low-income subsidy (LIS).[149] A final rule issued in 2018 revised this SEP from an open-ended monthly SEP to one that may be used only once per calendar quarter during the first nine months of the year (January through September). Separate SEPs can be used in the following circumstances: (1) within a certain period of time after a CMS or state-initiated enrollment; and (2) within a certain period of time after a change to an individual's LIS or Medicaid status.[150]

[7] Retroactive Disenrollments

CMS may grant a request for disenrollment when an enrollment was never legally valid or if a valid request for disenrollment was properly made, but not processed or acted upon which includes both system error and plan error.[151] A retroactive disenrollment may also be allowed if the reason for disenrollment is related to a permanent move out of the plan service area, a contract violation or other limited exceptional conditions established by CMS which may include fraudulent enrollment or misleading marketing practices.[152] The beneficiary or an MA organization can submit a retroactive disenrollment request to CMS.[153] If a request for retroactive disenrollment is approved by CMS the MA organization must return any premium paid by the enrollee for any month for which CMS processed a retroactive disenrollment.[154]

[8] Coordination of Enrollment and Disenrollment Through Medicare Advantage Organizations

The enrollment and disenrollment of an individual in an MA plan of an MA organization is governed by the election of coverage under MA plans.[155] An individual may elect a different MA plan by filing the appropriate election with the MA organization;[156] or submit a request for disenrollment to the MA in the form and manner prescribed by CMS, or file the appropriate disenrollment form through other mechanisms as determined by CMS.[157] A disenrollment request is

---

[149] Medicare Managed Care Manual, Ch. 2: §§ 30.4.4.5 and .12, *available at* https://www.cms.gov/Medicare/Eligibility-and-Enrollment/MedicareMangCareEligEnrol/Downloads/CY_2019_MA_Enrollment_and_Disenrollment_Guidance.pdf (site visited Aug. 6, 2018).

[150] *See* final rule CMS-4182-F at 82 Fed. Reg. 16,440 (Apr. 16, 2018), amending 42 C.F.R. § 423.38(c).

[151] 42 C.F.R. § 422.66(b)(5) and Medicare Managed Care Manual, Ch. 2: § 60.5.

[152] 42 C.F.R. § 422.66(b)(5) and Medicare Managed Care Manual, Ch. 2: § 60.5.

[153] 42 C.F.R. § 422.66(b)(5) and Medicare Managed Care Manual, Ch. 2: § 60.5.

[154] 42 C.F.R. § 422.66(b)(5) and Medicare Managed Care Manual, Ch. 2: § 60.5.

[155] 42 C.F.R. § 422.66(a)–(b).

[156] 42 C.F.R. § 422.66(b)(1)(i).

[157] 42 C.F.R. § 422.66(b)(1)(ii).

considered to have been made on the date the disenrollment request is received by the MA organization.[158]

The MA organization or plan must submit a disenrollment notice to CMS within time frames specified by CMS;[159] provide the enrollee with notice of disenrollment; include in the notice a statement explaining that the enrollee remains enrolled until the effective date of disenrollment and that until that date, neither the MA organization nor CMS pays for services not provided or arranged for by the MA plan in which the enrollee is enrolled; and file and retain disenrollment request for the period specified in CMS instructions.[160]

[a] Failure to Submit Disenrollment Notice to CMS Promptly

If the MA organization fails to submit the correct and complete required notice, the MA organization must reimburse CMS for any capitation payments received after the month in which payment would have ceased if the requirement had been met timely.[161]

[9] Conversion of Enrollment (Seamless Continuation of Coverage)

The Medicare statute allows the Secretary of HHS to establish procedures under which an individual who is enrolled in a health plan (offered by an organization that also offers MA plans) at the time of the initial election period and who fails to elect to receive coverage other than through the organization to be deemed to have elected the MA plan offered by the organization.[162] Until recently, in other words, subject to CMS approval, an insurance company could enroll an individual who was covered by the company's product into the same company's MA product upon becoming eligible for Medicare unless the individual "opted out." Given the minimal notice requirements related to such enrollments, advocates found that it was possible for individuals to be enrolled in an MA plan without express consent.[163] In October 2016, CMS temporarily suspended new seamless conversion enrollments pending revision of guidelines for this process.

---

[158] 42 C.F.R. § 422.66(b)(2).

[159] 42 C.F.R. § 422.66(b)(3)(i).

[160] 42 C.F.R. § 422.66(b)(3)(i)–(iv).

[161] 42 C.F.R. § 422.66(b)(4).

[162] 42 U.S.C. § 1395w-21(c)(3)(A)(ii); *see also* 42 C.F.R. § 422.66(d) and MMC Manual, Ch. 2: § 40.1.4, *available at* https://www.cms.gov/Medicare/Eligibility-and-Enrollment/MedicareMangCareEligEnrol/Downloads/CY_2019_MA_Enrollment_and_Disenrollment_Guidance.pdf (site visited Aug. 6, 2018).

[163] *See, e.g.*, the Center Medicare Advocacy's Weekly Alert "Case Study: Enrolled in a Medicare Advantage Plan Without Her Knowledge Through 'Seamless Conversion Enrollment'" (June 1, 2016) *available at* http://www.medicareadvocacy.org/case-study-enrolled-in-a-medicare-advantage-plan-without-her-knowledge-through-seamless-conversion-enrollment/ (site visited June 13, 2018).

A final rule issued in 2018 narrows the scope of seamless conversion enrollments to individuals dually eligible for Medicare and Medicaid (dual eligibles) into MA Special Needs Plans for dual eligibles (D-SNPs) only, with several conditions, including state and CMS approval, and from affiliated Medicaid managed care plans. CMS also allows passive enrollment for full-benefit dually eligible beneficiaries from a non-renewing integrated D-SNP to another comparable plan, after certain conditions are met, including consultation with state Medicaid agency.[164]

[10] Maintenance of Enrollment

An individual who has made an election is considered to have continued that election until either (1) the individual changes the election; (2) the elected MA plan is discontinued or no longer serves the area in which the individual resides; or (3) the organization does not offer or the individual does not elect the option of continuing enrollment.[165] An individual enrolled in an MA-PD plan as of December 31 of a year is deemed to have elected to remain enrolled in that plan on January 1 of the following year.[166]

[11] Exception for Employer Group Health Plans

In cases when an MA organization has both a Medicare contract and a contract with an employer group health plan, and in which the MA organization arranges for the employer to process election forms for Medicare-entitled group members who wish to disenroll from the Medicare contract, the effective date of the election may be retroactive; a retroactive effective date may be made for up to a 90-day period.[167] Upon receipt of the election from the employer, the MA organization must submit a disenrollment notice to CMS.[168]

[12] Disenrollment by the MA Organization

[a] Basis for Disenrollment

An MA organization may not disenroll an individual from any MA plan it offers nor, by any action or inaction, request or encourage an individual to disenroll,[169] except as follows:

---

[164] *See* final rule CMS-4182-F at 82 Fed. Reg. 16,440 (Apr. 16, 2018), amending 42 C.F.R. § 422.66.

[165] 42 C.F.R. § 422.66(e)(1)(i)–(ii).

[166] 42 C.F.R. § 422.66(e)(5).

[167] 42 C.F.R. § 422.66(f)(1).

[168] 42 C.F.R. § 422.66(f)(2).

[169] 42 C.F.R. § 422.74(a)(1)–(2).

[i] Optional Disenrollment. An MA organization may disenroll an individual from an MA plan it offers in any of the following circumstances: (1) any monthly basic and supplementary beneficiary premiums are not paid on a timely basis, subject to the grace period for late payment; (2) the individual has engaged in disruptive behavior; and (3) the individual provides fraudulent information on his or her election form or permits abuse of his or her enrollment card.[170]

[ii] Required Disenrollment. An MA organization must disenroll an individual from any MA plan it offers in any of the following circumstances: (1) the individual no longer resides in the MA plan's service area as specified in the plan, is no longer eligible under the plan, and optional continued enrollment has not been offered or elected; (2) the individual loses entitlement under Part A or Part B benefits; (3) death of the individual; (4) the individual enrolled in a specialized MA plan for special needs individuals that exclusively serves and enrolls special needs individuals no longer meets the special needs status of that plan (or deemed continued eligibility, if applicable); and (5) the individual is not lawfully present in the United States.[171]

[b] Plan Termination or Reduction of Area Where Plan Is Available

General rule. An MA organization that has its MA plan terminated, or terminates an MA plan, or that discontinues offering the plan in any portion of the area where the plan had previously been available, must disenroll affected enrollees.[172]

Exception. When an MA organization discontinues offering an MA plan in a portion of its service area, the MA organization may elect to offer enrollees residing in all or portions of the affected area the option to continue enrollment in plan offered by the organization, provided that there is no other MA plan offered in the affected area at the time of the discontinuation.[173] The organization may require an enrollee who chooses to continue enrollment to agree to receive the full range of basic benefits (excluding emergency and urgently needed care) exclusively through facilities designated by the organization within the plan service area.[174]

Note, however, that if the MA plan (organization) offers a *visitor/traveler benefit*, the 2010 regulations require that when the individual is out of the service

---

[170] 42 C.F.R. § 422.74(b)(i)–(iii). Note that 42 C.F.R. § 422.74(d)(2) defines "disruptive behavior."

[171] 42 C.F.R. § 422.74(b)(2).

[172] 42 C.F.R. § 422.74(b)(3).

[173] 42 C.F.R. § 422.74(b)(3). Note that an individual who is disenrolled from a plan due to the plan's termination or area reduction has a SEP right to enroll in another plan. *See* 42 C.F.R. § 422.74(e)(2).

[174] 42 C.F.R. § 422.74(b)(3).

area but within the United States (as defined in 42 C.F.R. § 400.200) for a period of consecutive days longer than 6 months but less than 12 months, the plan may elect to offer to the individual the option of remaining enrolled in the MA plan if:[175]

> (A) The individual is disenrolled on the first day of the 13th month after the individual left the service area (or residence, if paragraph (d)(4)(i)(B) of this section applies);
>
> (B) The individual understands and accepts any restrictions imposed by the MA plan on obtaining these services while absent from the MA plan's service area for the extended period, consistent with paragraph (d)(4)(i)(C) of the section;
>
> (C) The MA organization makes this visitor/traveler option available to all Medicare enrollees who are absent for an extended period from the MA plan's service area. MA organizations may limit this visitor/traveler option to enrollees who travel to certain areas, as defined by the MA organization, and who receive services from qualified providers who directly provide, arrange for, or pay for health care; and
>
> (D) The MA organization furnishes all Medicare Parts A and B services and all mandatory and optional supplemental benefits at the same cost sharing levels as apply within the plan's service area; and
>
> (E) The MA organization furnishes the services in paragraph (d)(4)(iii)(D) of this section consistent with Medicare access and availability requirements at § 422.112 of this part.[176]

[c] Notice Requirement

If the disenrollment is for reasons such as failure to pay premiums, disruptive behavior, or provision of fraudulent information with respect to plan election (other than death or loss of entitlement to Part A or Part B), the MA organization must give the individual a written notice of the disenrollment, with an explanation of the reasons for disenrollment provided to the individual before submission of the disenrollment to CMS. Moreover, the notice must include an explanation of the individual's right to a hearing under MA organization's grievance procedures.[177]

[d] Process for Disenrollment

[i] Monthly Basic and Supplementary Premiums Are Not Paid Timely. An MA organization may disenroll an individual from the MA plan for failure to pay basic and supplemental premiums if:

---

[175] 42 C.F.R. § 422.74(d)(4)(iii)(A)–(E) (Apr. 2010 amendments).

[176] 42 C.F.R. § 422.74(d)(4)(iii)(A)–(E) (Apr. 2010 amendments).

[177] 42 C.F.R. § 422.74(c).

1. The MA organization can demonstrate to CMS that it made reasonable efforts to collect the unpaid premium amount. Such efforts include alerting the individual that the premiums are due and providing the individual with a grace period, that is, an opportunity to pay past due premiums in full; (2) the length of the grace period will be at least two months and will begin on the first day of the month for which the premium is unpaid or the first day of the month following the date on which premium payment is requested, whichever is later.[178]

2. Beneficiaries who establish good cause for failure to pay a premium that leads to disenrollment from an MA plan or a PDP and who pay the arrearage in full within three months of the disenrollment may be reinstated into the plan. The failure to pay the premiums must have been due to circumstances beyond the beneficiary's control. CMS will provide further guidance on what constitutes good cause.[179] With respect to a PDP, if a beneficiary is disenrolled from the PDP for failure to pay his or her monthly premiums, the PDP has the option to decline future enrollment until the past due premiums are paid.[180] Until now, the process of accepting, reviewing, and processing beneficiary requests for reinstatement for good cause has been carried out exclusively by CMS. Despite concerns about impartiality and the "quality of work currently performed by plans and CMS contractors" raised by beneficiary advocates, CMS will assign the responsibility to effectuate reinstatements when good cause criteria are met to a third party, which can include an MA or Part D plan sponsor.[181]

Further, the MA organization must demonstrate to CMS that it has provided the enrollee with notice of disenrollment.[182] If the enrollee fails to pay the premiums for optional services, but pays the premium for basic and mandatory supplemental services, the MA organization has the option to discontinue the optional supplemental benefits and retain the individual as an MA enrollee.[183]

[ii] Disruptive Behavior. An MA plan enrollee is disruptive if his or her behavior substantially impairs the plan's ability to arrange for or provide services to the individual or other plan members.[184] An individual cannot be considered disruptive if such behavior is related to the use of medical service or compliance (or noncompliance) with medical advice or treatment. Plans must make efforts to

---

[178] 42 C.F.R. § 422.74(d)(1)(i)(B) (Apr. 2010 amendments).

[179] 42 C.F.R. §§ 422.74(d)(1)(v) and 423.44. *See also* MMC Manual, Ch. 2: § 60.3.4.

[180] 42 C.F.R. § 423.44(d)(1)(iv).

[181] See discussion at 80 Fed. Reg. 7912-58, 7942-43 (Feb. 12, 2015).

[182] 42 C.F.R. § 422.74(c).

[183] 42 C.F.R. § 422.74(d)(1)(iii).

[184] 42 C.F.R. § 422.74(d)(2)(i)–(vi).

resolve the problems and document the enrollee's behavior and its efforts to resolve the problem. In addition, CMS will review the information on the matter as submitted by the plan and the enrollee and make a decision whether to approve or deny the disenrollment. If CMS permits the disenrollment of a disruptive individual, disenrollment is the first day of the calendar month after the month in which the MA organization gives the individual notice of its plan to disenroll the individual for disruptive behavior.[185]

[E] Appeal and Grievance in Medicare Advantage Plans

MA appeal procedures include an internal grievance process and a formal appeal process with external review. The grievance and appeal processes are intended for different kinds of complaints. MA organizations must ensure that all enrollees receive written information about the grievance and appeal procedures that are available to them.[186]

CMS has modified its regulations to clarify that a *representative* is an individual appointed by an enrollee or other party, or authorized under state or other applicable law, to act on behalf of an enrollee or other party involved in the grievance or appeal. Generally, unless otherwise stated, the representative will have all the rights and responsibilities of an enrollee or party in filing a grievance, and in obtaining an organization determination or in dealing with any of the levels of the appeals process, as provided under the regulations.[187]

[1] Grievances

[a] Generally

Each MA organization must provide meaningful procedures for timely hearing and resolving grievances between enrollees and the organization or any other entity or individual through which the organization provides health care services under any MA plan it offers.[188] Grievance procedures are separate and distinct from appeals.[189] Appeals address concerns and disagreements with organizational determinations (whether an item, service, or procedure is covered). Grievances go to issues about the quality of services received, time and location of services, and

---

[185] 42 C.F.R. § 422.74(d)(2)(i-vi).

[186] 42 C.F.R. § 422.562(a)(2)(i). *See* Transmittal 88, effective Sept. 21, 2007, through which CMS clarifies various notice and other procedures applicable to the review and appeal of a managed care (MA) claim, *available at* https://www.cms.gov/Regulations-and-Guidance/Guidance/Transmittals/downloads/R88MCM.pdf (site visited Aug. 6, 2018).

[187] 42 C.F.R. § 422.561 (Apr. 15, 2010).

[188] 42 C.F.R. § 422.564(a).

[189] 42 C.F.R. § 422.564(b); *see also* 42 C.F.R. § 422.566(a)–(b) (definition of an organization determination).

related matters.[190] In addition, the MA plan's grievance process is separate from the quality of care complaint filed with a Quality Improvement Organization (QIO), which address beneficiaries' written complaints about the quality of services received under the Medicare program. For quality of care issues, the beneficiary may file a written complaint with the MA organization or the QIO, or both.[191]

Further, the MA organization must have an established recordkeeping process for tracking records on all grievances received, both orally and in writing. The record is to contain, at a minimum, the date of receipt of the grievance, and the final disposition of the grievance, and the date that the MA organization notified the enrollee of the disposition.[192]

[b] Expedited Grievances

Expedited grievances must be responded to within 24 hours. This process is available if the complaint involves an MA organization's decision to invoke an extension relating to an organization determination or reconsideration, or the MA organization's refusal to grant an enrollee's request for an expedited organization determination.[193]

[c] Grievance Process

CMS defines a grievance as an issue that does not involve organization determinations, and that is:

> any complaint or dispute, other than one that constitutes an organization determination, expressing dissatisfaction with any aspect of an MA Organization's or provider's operations, activities, or behavior, regardless of whether remedial action is requested.[194]

The grievance process is designed to provide a remedy for MA beneficiaries who have concerns about things other than coverage of benefits. For example, a grievance might be brought concerning rudeness of staff members, inconvenience of facilities, location and hours of service, or receipt of membership materials. Every MA organization is required to provide "meaningful procedures for timely hearing and resolving grievances between enrollees and the

---

[190] 42 C.F.R. § 422.561 (definition of a grievance).

[191] 42 C.F.R. § 422.564(c); for the functions of the Quality Improvement Organization (QIO), see 42 U.S.C. 1320c-3(a)(14).

[192] 42 C.F.R. § 422.564(g).

[193] 42 C.F.R. § 422.564(f).

[194] 42 C.F.R. § 422.561.

organization."[195] Grievances also include disputes with "any other entity or individual through which the organization provides health care services."[196]

An enrollee may file a grievance with an MA plan either orally or in writing. The grievance must be filed no later than 60 days after the event or incident that precipitates the grievance.[197] The MA plan must notify the enrollee of its decision as expeditiously as possible, based on health status, but no later than 30 days of receipt of grievance.[198] The MA organization may extend the 30-day time frame by up to 14 days if the enrollee requests the extension, or if the MA organization justifies a need for additional information and documents how the delay is in the interest of the enrollee. If the MA organization extends the deadline, it must notify the enrollee in writing of the reasons for the delay.[199]

Grievances submitted in writing must be responded to in writing; grievances submitted orally may be responded to either orally or in writing, unless the enrollee requests a written response.[200] Grievances related to quality of care, regardless of how filed, must be responded to in writing and must include a description of the enrollee's right to file a written complaint with the QIO. In addition, the MA organization must cooperate with the QIO in resolving the complaint.[201]

Upon receiving a complaint, an MA organization must promptly determine and inform the enrollee whether the complaint is subject to its grievance procedures or its appeal procedures.[202]

[2] Organization Determinations

[a] Generally

Each MA organization must have a procedure for making timely organization determinations regarding the benefits to which the enrollee is entitled under the MA plan, including such things as basic benefits, mandatory and optional supplemental benefits, and the amount, if any, the beneficiary is to pay.[203]

An organization determination is any determination made by an MA organization with respect to (1) payment for temporary out of the area renal dialysis services, emergency services, post-stabilization care or urgent care; (2) payment for any other health services furnished by a provider other than the MA

---

[195] 42 C.F.R. § 422.564(a).
[196] 42 C.F.R. § 422.564(a).
[197] 42 C.F.R. § 422.564(d).
[198] 42 C.F.R. § 422.564(e)(1).
[199] 42 C.F.R. § 422.564(e)(2).
[200] 42 C.F.R. § 422.564(e)(3)(i)–(ii).
[201] 42 C.F.R. § 422.564(e)(3)(iii).
[202] 42 C.F.R. § 422.564(b).
[203] 42 C.F.R. § 422.566(a).

organization that the enrollee believes are covered under Medicare or if not covered under Medicare, should be furnished, arranged for, or reimbursed by the MA organization; (3) the MA organization's refusal to provide or pay for services, in whole or in part, including the type or level of services, that the enrollee believes should be furnished or arranged for by the MA organization; (4) reduction, or premature discontinuation, of a previously authorized ongoing course of treatment;[204] or (5) the failure of the MA organization to approve, furnish, arrange for, or provide payment for health care services in a timely manner, or to provide the enrollee with timely notice of an adverse determination, such that a delay would adversely affect the health of the enrollee.[205]

[b] Who Can Request an Organization Determination?

Individuals or entities who can request an organization determination are the enrollee (including his or her authorized representative); any provider that furnishes, or intends to furnish, services to the enrollee; or the legal representative of a deceased enrollee's estate).[206]

An expedited organization determination, as explained below, can be requested by an enrollee (including his or her authorized representative) or a physician (regardless of whether the physician is affiliated with the MA organization).[207]

[c] Standard Time Frames and Notice—Organization Determinations

An enrollee must ask for a standard organization determination by making a request with the MA organization or, if applicable, to the entity responsible for making the determination (as directed by the MA organization), in accordance with the following: (1) the request may be made orally or in writing, and (2) requests for payment must be made in writing (unless the MA organization or entity responsible for making the determination has implemented a voluntary policy of accepting verbal payment requests).[208]

---

[204] 42 C.F.R. § 422.566(b)(1-4) (Apr. 2010 amendments). The settlement in *Jimmo v. Sebelius*, Civil Action No. 5:11-cv-17-CR (D. Vt. Jan. 24, 2013), applies to MA plans. With appropriate documentation, Medicare-covered skilled nursing and skilled therapy services are available to improve, maintain, or slow deterioration of a patient's condition. *See* Center for Medicare Advocacy, "*Jimmo v. Sebelius*, the Improvement Standard Case FAQs," *available at* http://www.medicareadvocacy.org/jimmo-v-sebelius-the-improvement-standard-case-faqs/ (site visited Aug. 6, 2018). *See also* **Appendix 1-9** of this Handbook.

[205] 42 C.F.R. § 422.566(b)(5).

[206] 42 C.F.R. § 422.566(c)(1)(i)–(iii). *See also* § **7.03[C][3]**.

[207] 42 C.F.R. § 422.566(c)(2)(i)–(ii).

[208] 42 C.F.R. § 422.568(a)(1)–(2).

The MA organization must give the enrollee a written notice if (1) an MA organization decides to deny service or payment in whole or in part, or reduce or prematurely discontinue the level of care for a previously authorized ongoing course of treatment or (2) an enrollee requests an MA organization to provide an explanation of a practitioner's denial of an item or service, in whole or in part.[209] Parties to the organization determination include the enrollee (including his or her representative); an assignee of the enrollee (a physician or other provider who has furnished a service to the enrollee and formally agrees to waive any right to payment from the enrollee for that service); the legal representative of a deceased enrollee's estate; or any other provider or entity (other than the MA organization) determined to have an appealable interest in the proceeding.[210]

[i] Time Frame for Requests for Service. When a party has made a request for a service, the MA organization must notify the enrollee of its determination as expeditiously as the enrollee's health condition requires, but no later than 14 calendar days after the day the organization receives a request for a standard review.[211] The MA organization may extend the time frame by up to 14 calendar days upon request of the enrollee, if the extension is both justified and in the enrollee's interest because it is necessary to obtain additional medical evidence from a noncontract provider that might change the decision from the MA organization to deny an item or service, or if the extension is both justified due to extraordinary, exigent, or other non-routine circumstances and is also in the enrollee's interest.[212] The enrollees must be informed in writing of the MA organization's decision to extend the time frame, and its reasons, and the MA

---

[209] 42 C.F.R. § 422.568(d)(1)–(2).

[210] 42 C.F.R. § 422.574.

[211] 42 C.F.R. § 422.568(b).

[212] 42 C.F.R. § 422.568(b)(1)(i)–(iii), In the preamble to the final 2016 rules for Medicare Part C, CMS explains that some MA plans are inappropriately extending their own deadlines:

> [W]e believe the current language that permits extension of the adjudication timeframes set forth in § 422.568(b), § 422.572(b), § 422.590(a)(1), and § 422.590(d)(2) is being interpreted more broadly than we intended and that MA organizations are regularly invoking extensions of the adjudication timeframes for organization determinations and reconsiderations. Based on information ascertained during recent MA program audits, we have seen circumstances in which MA organizations are routinely and inappropriately invoking the 14-day extension in cases where the plan: (1) Lacks adequate internal controls to ensure coverage requests are reviewed and adjudicated within the required regulatory timeframe; and (2) is awaiting receipt of supporting clinical documentation from one of its contract providers. [CMS goes on to state:] Routinely invoking an extension of the applicable adjudication timeframe is counter to the intent of the statutory and regulatory requirements for timely determinations that emphasize the health needs of the beneficiary in determining the appropriate adjudication timeframe. Extensions that are not affirmatively requested by the enrollee should be permitted only in limited circumstances, and only if the extension is in the enrollee's interest.

80 Fed. Reg. 7912-58, 7943 (Feb. 12, 2015).

organization must inform the beneficiary of his or her right to file an expedited grievance if he or she disagrees with the MA organization's decision.[213]

[ii] Time Frame for Request for Payment. The MA organization must process requests for payment according to the Secretary's "prompt payment" provisions which call for paying 95 percent of clean claims (no obvious errors on the face of the claim) within 30 days, with all other claims to be paid, or denied, within 60 days from the date of the request.[214]

[iii] Written Notification of Organization Denials. If the MA organization decides to deny service or payment in whole or in part, or if an enrollee disagrees with an MA organization's decision to discontinue or reduce the level of care for an ongoing course of treatment, the organization must give the enrollee written notice of the determination.[215]

[iv] Expediting Certain Organization Determinations. An enrollee or a physician may request that an MA organization expedite an organization determination that involves the MA organization's refusal to provide or pay for services including the type or level of services, that the enrollee believes should be furnished or arranged for by the MA organization or the reduction, or premature discontinuation, of a previously authorized ongoing course of treatment. There is no right to an expedited organization determination of requests for payment of services already furnished.[216]

To ask for an expedited determination, an enrollee or a physician must submit an oral or written request directly to the MA organization; if applicable, to the entity responsible for making the determination, as directed by the MA organization.[217] A physician may provide oral or written support for a request for an expedited determination.[218]

Accordingly, CMS revised the applicable regulations to clarify that extensions should be permitted in only limited circumstances. CMS revisions included clarifying in § 422.568(b)(1)(ii), § 422.572(b)(1)(ii), and § 422.590(e)(1)(ii) that an extension may be justified and in the enrollee's interest due to the need to obtain additional medical information, which may result in changing the denial of coverage only from a non-contract provider. New sections were added at § 422.568(b)(1)(iii), § 422.572(b)(1)(iii), and § 422.590(e)(1)(iii) to clarify that the adjudication time frame extension may be permitted when the extension is both justified due to extraordinary, exigent, or other non-routine circumstances and that the extension is in the enrollee's interest. 80 Fed. Reg. 7912-58, 7943 (Feb. 12, 2015).

[213] 42 C.F.R. § 422.568(b)(2).

[214] 42 C.F.R. § 422.568(c).

[215] 42 C.F.R. § 422.568(d)(1).

[216] 42 C.F.R. § 422.570(a).

[217] 42 C.F.R. § 422.570(b)(1).

[218] 42 C.F.R. § 422.570(b)(2).

An MA plan that processes expedited requests must establish an efficient and convenient means for individuals to submit oral or written requests, and document in case files requests made by enrollees.[219] In addition, the MA organization must promptly decide whether to expedite a determination based on the following: for a request made by an enrollee, the MA organization must provide an expedited determination if it determines that applying the standard time frame for making a determination could seriously jeopardize the life or health of the enrollee or the enrollee's ability to regain maximum function; for a request made or supported by a physician, the MA organization must provide an expedited determination if the physician indicates that applying the standard time frame for making a determination could seriously jeopardize the life or health of the enrollee or the enrollee's ability to regain maximum function.[220]

[v] Actions Following a Denial. If the MA organization denies a request for an expedited determination, the MA plan is to automatically transfer a request to the standard time frame and make the determination within 14 days (from the date the MA organization received the request), give the enrollee prompt oral notice of the denial, and within 3 days, a written letter explaining that the request will be processed using the 14-day standard time frame, as well as explain that the enrollee has the right to submit an expedited grievance and a right to re-submit the request for an expedited determination with physician support.[221]

[vi] Timeline for Expedited Organization Determinations. If the MA organization approves the request for an expedited determination it must make an adverse or favorable determination as expeditiously as the enrollee's health condition requires, but not later than 72 hours after receiving the request.[222] The MA organization may extend the time frame by up to 14 calendar days upon request of the enrollee, if the extension is both justified and in the enrollee's interest because it is necessary to obtain additional medical evidence from a noncontract provider that might change the decision from the MA organization to deny an item or service, or if the extension is both justified due to extraordinary, exigent, or other nonroutine circumstances and is also in the enrollee's interest.[223] The enrollee must be informed in writing of reasons for the delay and that he or she can file an expedited grievance.[224] If notice of an adverse expedited determination is oral, the MA must confirm it in writing within three days of oral notice.[225]

---

[219] 42 C.F.R. § 422.570(c)(1).

[220] 42 C.F.R. § 422.570(c)(2)(i)and(ii).

[221] 42 C.F.R. § 422.570(d).

[222] 42 C.F.R. § 422.572(a).

[223] 42 C.F.R. § 422.572(b)(1)(i)–(iii).

[224] 42 C.F.R. § 422.572(b)(2).

[225] 42 C.F.R. § 422.572(c).

[d] Right to Reconsideration

The effect of an organization determination is binding on all parties unless it is reconsidered or reopened.[226] Any party to an organization determination may request that the determination be reconsidered under the procedures described in 42 C.F.R. § 422.582 (requests for a standard reconsideration).[227] An enrollee or a physician (acting on behalf of an enrollee) can request an expedited reconsideration.[228]

[i] Reconsideration Defined. A reconsideration is defined as consisting of a review of an adverse organization determination, the evidence and findings upon which it was based, and any other evidence the parties submit or the MA organization or CMS obtains.[229] A party to an organization determination must ask for a reconsideration of the determination by making a written request to the MA organization that made the organization determination. The MA organization may adopt a policy for accepting oral requests.[230]

[ii] Filing a Request for Reconsideration. A party must file a request for reconsideration within 60 calendar days from the date of the notice of the organization determination.[231] If a party shows good cause, the MA organization may extend the time frame for filing a request for reconsideration.[232]

If the 60-day period in which to file a request for reconsideration has expired, a party to the organization determination may file a request for a reconsideration with the MA organization. The request for reconsideration and to extend the time frame must be in writing and must state why the request for reconsideration was not filed timely.[233]

[iii] Parties to Reconsideration. The parties to the reconsideration are the parties to the organization determination, and any other provider or entity (other than the MA organization) whose rights with respect to the organization determination may be affected by the reconsideration, as determined by the entity that conducts the reconsideration.[234] The party who files a request for

---

[226] 42 C.F.R. § 422.576. *See* 42 C.F.R. § 422.578–422.596 (reconsideration), 42 C.F.R. § 422.616 (reopening).

[227] 42 C.F.R. § 422.578.

[228] 42 C.F.R. § 422.584(a).

[229] 42 C.F.R. § 422.580.

[230] 42 C.F.R. § 422.582(a).

[231] 42 C.F.R. § 422.582(b).

[232] 42 C.F.R. § 422.582(c)(1).

[233] 42 C.F.R. § 422.582(c)(2).

[234] 42 C.F.R. § 422.582(d).

reconsideration may withdraw it by filing a written request for withdrawal to the MA organization.[235]

[iv] Time Frames and Responsibilities for Reconsiderations. *Standard reconsideration: Requests for services*—determinations completely favorable to the enrollee must be issued as expeditiously as the beneficiary's health condition requires, but not later than 30 calendar days from the date the MA organization received the request for a standard review.[236]

If the MA organization affirms, in whole or in part, its adverse organization determination, it must prepare a written explanation and send the case file to the independent entity contracted by CMS as expeditiously as the enrollee's health condition requires, but no later than 30 calendar days from the date it receives the request for a standard reconsideration.[237] The organization must make reasonable and diligent efforts to assist in gathering and forwarding information to the independent entity.[238]

Standard reconsideration: Requests for payment—determinations completely favorable to the enrollee must be issued (and effectuated) no later than 60 calendar days from the date it receives the request for a standard reconsideration.[239]

If the MA organization affirms, in whole or in part, its adverse organization determination, it must prepare a written explanation and send the case file to the independent entity contracted by CMS no later than 60 calendar days from the date it receives the request for a standard reconsideration.[240] The organization must make reasonable and diligent efforts to assist in gathering and forwarding information to the independent entity.[241]

If the MA organization fails to provide a reconsideration determination within the specified time frames, the failure constitutes an affirmation of its adverse organization determination, and the organization must submit the file to the independent entity.[242]

Expedited reconsideration: The MA organization that approves a request for expedited reconsideration must complete its reconsideration and give the enrollee (and physician if involved) notice of its decision as expeditiously as the enrollee's health condition requires but no later than 72 hours after receiving the request.[243]

---

[235] 42 C.F.R. § 422.582(e).

[236] 42 C.F.R. § 422.590(a)(1).

[237] 42 C.F.R. § 422.590(a)(2).

[238] 42 C.F.R. § 422.590(a)(2).

[239] 42 C.F.R. § 422.590(b)(1).

[240] 42 C.F.R. § 422.590(b)(2).

[241] 42 C.F.R. § 422.590(b)(2).

[242] 42 C.F.R. § 422.590(c).

[243] 42 C.F.R. § 422.590(d)(1).

If the MA organization first notifies an enrollee of a completely favorable expedited reconsideration, it must mail written confirmation to the enrollee within three calendar days.[244]

If the MA organization must receive medical information from noncontract providers, the MA organization must request the necessary information from the noncontract provider within 24 hours of the initial request for an expedited reconsideration.[245] Noncontract providers must make reasonable and diligent efforts to expeditiously gather and forward all necessary information to assist the MA organization in meeting the required time frame.[246]

If, as a result of its reconsideration, the MA organization affirms, in whole or in part, its adverse expedited organization determination, the MA organization must submit a written explanation and the case file to the independent entity contracted by CMS as expeditiously as the enrollee's health condition requires, but not later than within 24 hours of its affirmation.[247] The organization must make reasonable and diligent efforts to assist in gathering and forwarding information to the independent entity.[248]

The MA organization may extend the standard or expedited reconsideration deadline time frame by up to 14 calendar days upon request of the enrollee, if the extension is both justified and in the enrollee's interest because it is necessary to obtain additional medical evidence from a noncontract provider that might change the decision from the MA organization to deny an item or service, or if the extension is both justified due to extraordinary, exigent, or other non-routine circumstances and is also in the enrollee's interest.[249] The enrollee must be informed

---

[244] 42 C.F.R. § 422.590(d)(2).

[245] 42 C.F.R. § 422.590(d)(3).

[246] 42 C.F.R. § 422.590(d)(3).

[247] 42 C.F.R. § 422.590(d)(4).

[248] 42 C.F.R. § 422.590(d)(4).

[249] 42 C.F.R. § 422.590(e)(1)(i)–(iii). In the preamble to the final 2016 rules for Medicare Part C, CMS explains that some MA plans are inappropriately extending their own deadlines:

> [W]e believe the current language that permits extension of the adjudication timeframes set forth in § 422.568(b), § 422.572(b), § 422.590(a)(1), and § 422.590(d)(2) is being interpreted more broadly than we intended and that MA organizations are regularly invoking extensions of the adjudication timeframes for organization determinations and reconsiderations. Based on information ascertained during recent MA program audits, we have seen circumstances in which MA organizations are routinely and inappropriately invoking the 14-day extension in cases where the plan: (1) Lacks adequate internal controls to ensure coverage requests are reviewed and adjudicated within the required regulatory timeframe; and (2) is awaiting receipt of supporting clinical documentation from one of its contract providers. [CMS goes on to state:] Routinely invoking an extension of the applicable adjudication timeframe is counter to the intent of the statutory and regulatory requirements for timely determinations that emphasize the health needs of the beneficiary in determining the appropriate adjudication timeframe. Extensions that are not affirmatively requested by the enrollee should be permitted only in limited circumstances, and only if the extension is in the enrollee's interest.

in writing of reasons for the delay and that he or she can file an expedited grievance.[250]

[v] Expediting Certain Reconsiderations. Excluding requests for payment for services already furnished, an enrollee or a physician (regardless of whether he or she is affiliated with the MA organization) may request an expedited reconsideration.[251] An enrollee, or a physician acting on behalf of an enrollee, must submit an oral or written request directly to the MA organization or, if applicable, to the entity responsible for making the reconsideration, as directed by the MA organization.[252] A physician may provide oral or written support for the request.[253]

The MA organization must establish and maintain efficient and convenient means to submit oral and written requests and documents and maintain the documentation in the case file, and make prompt decisions whether to expedite the reconsideration or follow the standard time frame.[254] When requested by an enrollee, the MA organization must provide an expedited reconsideration if it determines that applying the standard time frame for reconsidering a determination could seriously jeopardize the life or health of the enrollee or the enrollee's ability to regain maximum function.[255] When requested or supported by a physician, the MA organization must provide an expedited reconsideration if the physician indicates that applying the standard time frame for conducting a reconsideration could seriously jeopardize the life or health of the enrollee or the enrollee's ability to regain maximum function.[256]

If the request for expedited reconsideration is denied, the MA organization must transfer a request to the standard time frame and make the determination within the 30 days that begins the day the MA organization received the request for expedited reconsideration.[257] The MA organization also must give the enrollee

80 Fed. Reg. 7912-58, 7943 (Feb. 12, 2015).

Accordingly, CMS revised the applicable regulations to clarify that extensions should be permitted in only limited circumstances. CMS revisions included clarifying in § 422.568(b)(1)(ii), § 422.572(b)(1)(ii), and § 422.590(e)(1)(ii) that an extension may be justified and in the enrollee's interest due to the need to obtain additional medical information, which may result in changing the denial of coverage only from a noncontract provider. New sections were added at § 422.568(b)(1)(iii), § 422.572(b)(1)(iii), and § 422.590(e)(1)(iii) to clarify that the adjudication time frame extension may be permitted when the extension is both justified due to extraordinary, exigent, or other nonroutine circumstances and that the extension is in the enrollee's interest. 80 Fed. Reg. 7912-58, 7943 (Feb. 12, 2015).

[250] 42 C.F.R. § 422.590(e)(2).

[251] 42 C.F.R. § 422.584(a).

[252] 42 C.F.R. § 422.584(b)(1).

[253] 42 C.F.R. § 422.584(b)(2).

[254] 42 C.F.R. § 422.584(c).

[255] 42 C.F.R. § 422.584(c)(2)(i).

[256] 42 C.F.R. § 422.584(c)(2)(ii).

[257] 42 C.F.R. § 422.584(d)(1).

prompt oral notice, followed within three calendar days by a written letter, that explains that the MA organization will process the enrollee's request using the 30-day time frame for standard reconsiderations, informs the enrollee of the right to file a grievance if he or she disagrees with the organization's decision not to expedite, informs the enrollee of the right to resubmit a request for an expedited reconsideration with any physician's support, and provides instructions about the grievance process and its time frames.[258]

If an MA organization grants a request for expedited reconsideration, it must conduct the reconsideration and give notice as required by the regulations.[259] Moreover, if the MA organization must receive medical information from noncontract providers, the organization must request the necessary information within 24 hours of the initial request for an expedited reconsideration.[260] Noncontract providers are to make a diligent effort to supply the information, and the MA organization is still responsible for meeting the time frame and notice requirements.[261]

If the MA organization affirms in whole or in part, its adverse expedited organization determination, it must submit a written explanation and the case file to the independent review entity (IRE) contracted by CMS as expeditiously as the enrollee's health condition requires, but not later than within 24 hours of its affirmation. In addition, the organization must make a reasonable and diligent effort to gather and forward the information to the IRE.[262] Note that a final rule issued in 2018 eliminated the requirement that MA plans notify an enrollee when a reconsideration decision is deemed adverse or partially adverse to the enrollee and has been referred to the IRE. The rationale for this is that the plan notice is duplicative and nonessential because the Part C IRE is contractually responsible for notifying an enrollee that the IRE has received and will review the case. .[263]

If the MA organization fails to provide the enrollee with timely results of its reconsideration within the time frame set out above, the failure constitutes an adverse reconsidered determination, and the MA organization must submit the file to the IRE within 24 hours of expiration of the above-described time frame.[264]

[vi] Who Can Hear an Adverse Medicare Advantage Organization Determination. Persons not involved in the organization determination may hear an adverse MA organization determination.[265] Medical necessity

---

[258] 42 C.F.R. § 422.584(d)(2)(i-iv).

[259] 42 C.F.R. § 422.584(e); *see also* 42 C.F.R. § 422.590.

[260] 42 C.F.R. § 422.584(d); *see also* 42 C.F.R. § 422.590(d)(3).

[261] 42 C.F.R. § 422.584(d); *see also* 42 C.F.R. § 422.590(d)(3).

[262] 42 C.F.R. § 422.590(d)(4).

[263] *See* final rule CMS-4182-F at 82 Fed. Reg. 16,440 (Apr. 16, 2018), amending 42 C.F.R. § 422.590(f).

[264] 42 C.F.R. § 422.590(g).

[265] 42 C.F.R. § 422.590(h)(1).

determinations must be made by a physician with expertise in the field of medicine that is appropriate for the service at issue, although the physician need not in all cases be of the same specialty or subspecialty as the treating physician.[266]

[e] Reconsideration by an Independent Entity

When the MA organization affirms, in whole or part, its adverse organization determinations, the issues that remain in dispute must be reviewed and resolved by an independent, outside entity that contracts with CMS; the entity must meet contract deadlines for its decisions; the parties to a reconsideration are the same as those before the MA organization's reconsideration, with the addition of the MA organization.[267] The independent entity is responsible for mailing a notice of its reconsideration determination to the parties and for sending a copy to CMS.[268] The notice must state the specific reasons for the entity's decision in understandable language; and if the decision is adverse, it must inform the parties of their right to review by an Administrative Law Judge (ALJ) if the amount in controversy is $160 (in 2019) or more and describe the procedures for obtaining ALJ review.[269]

A reconsidered determination is final and binding on all parties unless a party other than the MA organization files a request for a hearing under the provisions for request for an ALJ review, or unless the reconsidered determination is revised.[270] If the amount remaining in controversy after reconsideration meets the threshold requirement established annually by the Secretary, any party to the reconsideration (except the MA organization) who is dissatisfied with the reconsideration determination has a right to a hearing before an ALJ.[271]

[f] Right to an Administrative Law Judge Hearing

The Office of Medicare Hearings and Appeals (OMHA), an agency of the HHS, administers the third level of appeals nationwide for the Medicare program and is responsible for conducing ALJ hearings.[272] OMHA operates separately from the other agencies involved in the Medicare claims appeals process.

---

[266] 42 C.F.R. § 422.590(h)(2).

[267] 42 C.F.R. § 422.592.

[268] 42 C.F.R. § 422.594(a).

[269] 42 C.F.R. § 422.594(b).The amount in controversy (AIC) for administrative law judge (ALJ) hearings is $160 in 2019. The AIC for federal court review increases to $1,630 in 2019. *See* 83 Fed. Reg. 47619 (Sept. 20, 2018).

[270] 42 C.F.R. § 422.596; *see* 42 C.F.R. § 422.616 (reopening and revising determinations and decisions).

[271] 42 C.F.R. § 422.600(a).

[272] https://www.hhs.gov/about/agencies/omha/index.html (site visited Aug. 6, 2018).

Any party to the reconsideration (except the MA organization) who is dissatisfied with the reconsidered determination has a right to a hearing before an ALJ, so long as the amount remaining in controversy meets the threshold requirement established annually by the Secretary.[273] The amount remaining in controversy, which can include any combination of Part A and Part B services, is computed by the Secretary.[274]

On January 17, 2017, CMS published a final rule that revised the procedures the HHS follows for Medicare Appeals. These changes became effective on March 20, 2017. The revised regulations, in part, authorize "Attorney Adjudicators," rather than ALJs to perform a portion of OMHA's workload that does not require a hearing.[275] Attorney adjudicators can issue decisions when a decision can be issued without an ALJ conducting a hearing under the regulations, dismissals when an appellant withdraws his or her request for an ALJ hearing, certain remands, and reviews of QIC and IRE dismissals. The revised regulations also make telephone hearings the default hearing method for individuals other than unrepresented beneficiaries.[276] Video-teleconferencing (VTC) will be retained as the default method of conducting hearings for unrepresented beneficiaries, unless good cause for an in-person appearance is shown or the beneficiary requests a phone hearing.[277]

[i] Request for an ALJ Hearing. A party must file a written request for a hearing with the entity specified in the IRE's reconsideration notice, and except when an ALJ extends the time frame, a party must file a request within 60 days of receipt of the notice of a reconsidered determination.[278] The parties to a hearing are the parties to the reconsideration, the MA organization, and any other person or entity whose rights with respect to the reconsideration may be affected by the hearing, as determined by the ALJ.[279]

If a request for a hearing clearly shows that the amount in controversy is less than the required jurisdictional amount, the ALJ dismisses the request; if the hearing is initiated, and the ALJ finds the amount in controversy is less than the required jurisdictional amount, the ALJ discontinues the hearing and does not rule on the substantive issues raised in the appeal.[280]

---

[273] 42 C.F.R. § 422.600(a).

[274] 42 C.F.R. § 422.600(b).

[275] 42 C.F.R. § 405.902.

[276] 42 C.F.R. § 405.1020(b).

[277] 42 C.F.R. § 405.1020(b).

[278] 42 C.F.R. §§ 422.602(a)–(b).

[279] 42 C.F.R. § 422.602(c).

[280] 42 C.F.R. § 422.602(d). This provision implements § 1869(b)(1)(E)(iii) (Amount in Controversy) (MMA) of the Social Security Act, 42 U.S.C. § 1395w-22(g)(5). The amount in controversy (AIC) requirement for ALJ hearing requests and judicial review is amended so that it will be adjusted annually by the Secretary, beginning January 1, 2005, by the percentage increase in the medical care component of the consumer price index (CPI) for all urban consumers and rounded to

[ii] When Other Regulations Apply. When an MA appeal reaches the ALJ level of review, for the most part, the appeal system merges with claims originating from traditional Medicare. At this stage, absent a regulation specific to MA appeals, the regulations governing administrative review of Part A and B claims found in Part 405 apply. The Medicare regulations specifically state that "Unless this subpart provides otherwise and subject to paragraph (d)(2) of this section, the regulations in part 405 of this chapter . . . apply under this subpart to the extent they are appropriate."[281] This reference to Part 405 (the traditional Medicare Appeals regulations) has been helpful in filling in gaps in rules for Part C appeals when there is no rule on point for those appeals. However, the revised regulations published by CMS on January 17, 2017 revised the procedures HHS follows for Medicare Appeals. The revisions changed the way Part 405 rules and protections apply to MA (Part C) appeals.

The new rule clarifies that the following provisions of Part 405 are not applicable to other parts of the Medicare regulations: Adjudication time frames for redeterminations, reconsiderations, ALJ or attorney adjudicator decisions (this includes the 90-day time frame for issuing decisions), and Council review; Escalation provisions for advancing to the next level of appeal without first receiving a decision at the current level; and Rules requiring good cause for the introduction of new evidence by a provider, supplier, or a beneficiary represented by a provider or supplier.[282] CMS's reasoning was that there are statutory differences among the procedures and provisions governing Medicare A and B, appeals of QIO determinations and appeals of MA Claims and it would not be appropriate to apply parts of 405 when there are no corresponding statutory provisions for QIO or MA appeals that apply.

It should be noted, however, that on August 1, 2016, the Center settled a nationwide class action lawsuit in federal court that challenged the long wait times for ALJ decisions faced by beneficiaries.[283] The settlement, whose terms are set to last for three years from the final approval date of August 1, 2016, incorporates a policy of prioritizing beneficiary appeals to ensure timely processing, as well as certain reforms to make the ALJ appeals system easier for beneficiaries to use.[284]

As of November 1, 2016 CMS updated scripts for 1-800-Medicare representatives to highlight the OMHA beneficiary prioritization policy for beneficiary callers and to refer them to the toll-free OMHA Beneficiary Help Line if they

---

the nearest multiple of $10. *See* 42 C.F.R. § 405.950(a), 405.970(a), and 405.1006. The 2019 AIC threshold amounts are $160 for ALJ hearings and $1,630 for judicial review.

[281] 42 C.F.R. § 422.562(d)(1).

[282] 42 C.F.R. § 422.562(d)(2).

[283] Exley v. Burwell, No. 3:14-CV-1230 (D. Conn. May 24, 2016). The settlement is *available at* http://www.medicareadvocacy.org/wp-content/uploads/2016/08/Approved-Settlement-Agreement-00201898xC6348.pdf (site visited Aug. 6, 2018).

[284] *Exley*, No. 3:14-CV-1230.

have questions about filing appeals with OMHA or about ALJ appeals that are pending with OMHA. OMHA also posted beneficiary appeals data required by the settlement on their website.[285] In late January 2017, OMHA issued a new ALJ request form which allows beneficiaries and enrollees to self-identify, making it easier for these claims to be classified as beneficiary appeals and given priority for processing.[286]

Significantly, in the final rule published on January 17, 2017, when discussing the fact that the 90-day time frame for issuing a decision did not apply to MA or QIO Appeals, CMS specifically pointed out that their current policy provides for the prioritization of appeals filed by beneficiaries or enrollees so they anticipate that the changes they are making will not take away any of the current protections or safeguards for beneficiaries.[287] Therefore, despite the changes to the regulations it appears that the protections that exist in the *Exley* settlement, including the right to a decision within 90-days, will continue to extend to those enrolled in an MA plan.

[g] Medicare Appeals Council (Council) Review

Any[288] party to the ALJ's or attorney adjudicator's decision or dismissal, including the MA organization, who is dissatisfied with the decision or dismissal may request that the Council review the decision or dismissal.[289] The regulations under Part 405 apply to matters addressed by this subpart to the extent they are appropriate with certain exceptions set forth in 42 C.F.R. § 422.562(d)(2).[290]

[h] Judicial Review

Any party, including the MA organization, may request judicial review (upon notifying the other parties) of an ALJ's or attorney adjudicator's decision if the Council denied the party's request for review and the amount in controversy meets the threshold requirement established annually by the Secretary.[291]

---

[285] https://www.hhs.gov/about/agencies/omha/about/current-workload/beneficiary-appeals-data/index.html (site visited Aug. 6, 2018).

[286] https://www.hhs.gov/sites/default/files/OMHA-100.pdf (site visited Aug. 6, 2018).

[287] 82 Fed. Reg. 4991–4992.

[288] Previously, the Medicare Appeals Council has been referenced in a number of different ways: Departmental Appeals Board (DAB); Medicare Appeals Council (MAC); and Medicare Appeals Council (Board). CMS hosted a National Provider Call regarding changes to the Medicare claims and entitlement appeals process and indicated that all references are now to the Medicare Appeals Council (Council) *available at* https://www.cms.gov/Outreach-and-Education/Outreach/NPC/Downloads/2017-06-29-Appeals-Presentation.pdf (site visited Aug. 6, 2018).

[289] 42 C.F.R. § 422.608

[290] 42 C.F.R. §§ 422.608 and 422.562(d)(2).

[291] 42 C.F.R. § 422.612(a).

With respect to a review of a Council decision, any party, including the MA organization, may request judicial review (upon notifying the other parties) of the Council decision if it is the final decision of CMS and the amount in controversy meets the threshold established by the Secretary ($1,630 in 2019).[292]

In order to request judicial review, a party must file a civil action in a district court of the United States in accordance with Section 205(g) of the Social Security Act.[293]

[i] Reopening and Revising Determinations and Decisions

An organization or reconsidered determination made by an MA organization, a reconsidered determination made by the IRE, or the decision of an ALJ or attorney adjudicator or of the Council may be reopened and revised by the entity that made the determination or decision, under the rules in Part 405 of the Code of Federal Regulations.[294]

[j] Effectuating Standard Reconsidered Determinations and Decisions

For a request for service, if on reconsideration, the MA organization completely reverses its organization determination, the MA organization must authorize or provide the service under dispute as expeditiously as the enrollee's condition requires, but no later than 30 calendar days after the date the MA organization receives the request for reconsideration (or no later than the end of an extension).[295]

For a request for payment, if on reconsideration, the MA organization completely reverses its organization determination, the organization must pay for the service no later than 60 days after the date the MA organization receives the request for reconsideration.[296]

[k] Effectuating Reversals by the Independent, Outside Review Entity

For a request for service, the IRE must authorize the service within 72 hours from the date it receives notice reversing the determination; with respect to

---

[292] 42 C.F.R. § 422.612(b).

[293] 42 C.F.R. § 422.612(c). (*See* 42 C.F.R. part 405 for a description of the procedures to follow in requesting judicial review.)

[294] 42 C.F.R. § 422.616(a).

[295] 42 C.F.R. § 422.618(a)(1).

[296] 42 C.F.R. § 422.618(a)(2).

request for payment, the IRE must authorize payment within 30 calendar days from the date it receives notice reversing the organization determination.[297]

[i] Effectuating Standard Reconsiderations. For reversals other than by the MA organization or the IRE, decisions by an ALJ or attorney adjudicator or higher level of appeal must be effectuated as expeditiously as the enrollee's health requires, but no later than 60 calendar days from the date it receives notice reversing the decision.[298] When, however, the MA organization files an appeal with the Council, the MA organization may await the outcome of the review before it pays for, authorizes, or provides the service under dispute. The MA organization must concurrently send a copy of its appeal request and any accompanying documents to the enrollee and must notify the outside entity that it has requested an appeal.[299]

[ii] Effectuating Expedited Reconsidered Determinations. If the MA organization completely reverses its determination, the service must be authorized as expeditiously as the enrollee's health condition requires, but no later than 72 hours after receipt of the request for reconsideration (or no later than upon expiration of any extension).[300]

[iii] Effectuating Reversals by the Independent Review Entity, Expedited Reconsideration. If the MA organization's decision is reversed in whole or in part, the decision must be effectuated as expeditiously as the enrollee's condition requires, but no later than 72 hours from the date it receives the notice reversing the determination.[301]

[iv] Effectuating Expedited Reversals by Other Than the MA Organization or the Independent Review Entity. If reversed in whole or in part by the ALJ or attorney adjudicator, or at a higher level of appeal, the MA organization must authorize payment as expeditiously as the enrollee's condition requires, but no later than 60 days from the date it receives the notice reversing the determination.[302] If the MA organization requests Council review, the MA organization may await the outcome of the review before it authorizes or provides the service under dispute, and if the MA organization files an appeal with the Council, it must concurrently notify the enrollee and notify the IRE.[303]

---

[297] 42 C.F.R. § 422.618(b)(1)–(2).
[298] 42 C.F.R. § 422.618(c)(1).
[299] 42 C.F.R. § 422.618(c)(2).
[300] 42 C.F.R. § 422.619(a).
[301] 42 C.F.R. § 422.619(b).
[302] 42 C.F.R. § 422.619(c)(1).
[303] 42 C.F.R. § 422.619(c)(2).

[I] Medicare Advantage Organization Enrollee Notice of Non-Covered Inpatient Hospital Care

[i] Notice Requirement. Beginning July 1, 2007, hospitals must deliver a revised version of the Important Message from Medicare (IM) (CMS-R-193) (approved July 2010) and the Detailed Notice of Discharge (CMS 10066) (approved July 2010).[304] Under 42 C.F.R. § 405.1205 (Traditional Medicare) and 42 C.F.R. § 422.620 (Medicare Advantage), Medicare participating hospitals must deliver valid, written notice (the "Important Message from Medicare" (IM)) of a patient's rights as a hospital patient, including discharge appeal rights, within 2 calendar days of admission. A follow-up copy of the signed IM is given again as far as possible in advance of discharge, but no more than 2 calendar days before discharge.[305] Follow-up notice is not required if the provision of the admission IM falls within 2 calendar days of discharge.[306]

For a hospital stay, a beneficiary must request immediate (expedited) review, orally or in writing, no later than the day of discharge.[307] The beneficiary (or his or her authorized representative), upon request by the QIO, must be prepared to discuss the case with the QIO.[308] On the date that the QIO receives the beneficiary's request, the QIO must notify the hospital that the beneficiary has filed a request for immediate review.[309] The hospital must supply any information, including medical records, that the QIO requires to conduct its review and must make the information available, by phone or in writing, by the close of business of the first full working day after the day the beneficiary receives notice of the planned discharge.[310] When the beneficiary requests an expedited determination in accordance with 42 C.F.R. § 422.622(b)(1), the QIO must make a determination and notify the enrollee, MA organization, the hospital, and the physician of its determination by close of business of the first working day after it receives all requested pertinent information.[311]

[ii] Coverage During QIO Immediate (Expedited) Review. If the beneficiary remains in the hospital after receiving the hospital-issued notice of non-coverage and the hospital and the physician who concurred in the hospital's determination of non-coverage and subsequent advanced notice of non-coverage,

---

[304] 72 Fed. Reg. 17,169 (Apr. 6, 2007); *see also* MCPM, CMS Pub. No. 100-4, Ch. 30 § 200.6.2 and 200.6.3, *available at* https://www.cms.gov/Regulations-and-Guidance/Guidance/Manuals/Downloads/clm104c30.pdf (site visited Aug. 6, 2018).

[305] 42 C.F.R. § 422.620(c)(1).

[306] 42 C.F.R. § 422.620(c)(2).

[307] 42 C.F.R. § 422.622(b)(1).

[308] 42 C.F.R. § 422.622(b)(2).

[309] 42 C.F.R. § 422.622(d)(1).

[310] 42 C.F.R. § 422.622(e)(2).

[311] 42 C.F.R. § 422.622(d)(8). Notice is by telephone, with a written follow-up notice.

or the QIO subsequently finds that the beneficiary requires an acute level of inpatient hospital care, the beneficiary is not financially responsible for continued care until the hospital once again determines that the beneficiary no longer requires inpatient care, secures concurrence from the physician responsible for the beneficiary's care or the QIO, and notifies the beneficiary.[312]

If a beneficiary files a request for an expedited determination by the QIO in accordance with 42 C.F.R. § 422.622(b)(1) and meets the "waiver of liability" provisions of Section 1879(a)(2) of the Social Security Act[313] (did not know or could not reasonably have been expected to know, that payment would not be made for such items or service under Part A or Part B), the beneficiary is not financially responsible for inpatient hospital services furnished until noon of the day after the QIO provides the beneficiary with notice (either orally or in writing) of the immediate determination of the QIO.[314] If the QIO determines that a beneficiary still requires inpatient hospital care, the hospital must provide the enrollee with a notice consistent with 42 C.F.R. § 422.620(c).[315]

When a beneficiary does not request an immediate QIO review in accordance with 42 C.F.R. § 422.622(b)(1), he or she may request expedited reconsideration by the MA organization (42 C.F.R. § 422.584), but the financial liability rules of 42 C.F.R. § 422.622(f) do not apply.[316]

A beneficiary who fails to request an expedited determination in accordance with 42 C.F.R. § 422.622(b)(1) above and who is no longer an inpatient in the hospital and is dissatisfied with the determination of the QIO may appeal to OMHA for an ALJ hearing, the Council, or a federal court, as provided under Subpart M.[317]

[m] MA Notice of Denial for Payment or Services

MA plans are required to issue a Notice of Denial of Medical Coverage (or Payment), also known as the Integrated Denial Notice (IDN) to inform enrollees of their appeals rights for payment or service denials and for discontinuation or reduction of a previously authorized course of treatment.[318] In addition to combining and replacing the Notice of Denial of Payment and Notice of Denial of Medical Coverage, the IDN integrates Medicaid appeals rights information for

---

[312] 42 C.F.R. § 422.622(f)(3).

[313] *See* 42 U.S.C. § 1395pp(a)(2).

[314] 42 C.F.R. § 422.622(f)(4).

[315] 42 C.F.R. § 422.622(f)(3) (Apr. 2010 amendments).

[316] 42 C.F.R. § 422.622(b)(5).

[317] 42 C.F.R. § 422.622(g)(2).

[318] The revised Integrated Denial Notice, Form CMS-10003-NDMCP (Notice of Denial of Medical Coverage), and form instructions can be found at https://www.cms.gov/Medicare/Medicare-General-Information/BNI/MADenialNotices.html (site visited June 13, 2018).

enrollees receiving full benefits under a State Medical Assistance (Medicaid) program. As of April 10, 2017, all MA plans should use the IDN notice.

[n] MA Notice of Termination of Services

Before terminating covered services authorized by an MA organization, Home Health Agencies (HHAs), SNFs, and Comprehensive Outpatient Rehabilitation Facilities (CORFs) are required to provide a Notice of Medicare Non-Coverage (NOMNC) to an MA enrollee.[319] This includes the cessation of coverage at the end of a course of treatment, regardless of whether the enrollee agrees with the termination.[320]

It is important to note that when appealing a termination of service or item the only issue that may be addressed is whether the provider's termination of the service/item was appropriate. A contractor or ALJ may find that they lack jurisdiction to rule on whether Medicare payment should be made for any items or services that the beneficiary continues to receive after the decision to terminate has already been made because a claim was never submitted for those items/services. In other words, the scope of review is different for expedited appeals versus regular appeals. By appealing from the NOMNC, the beneficiary is only appealing the termination of services decision. In order to obtain an appealable Medicare determination for any services a beneficiary continues to receive they must simultaneously request an organization determination to initiate an appeal for those services. Beneficiaries retain the right to utilize the standard (non-expedited) appeals process in all situations.

[i] Timing of Notice. The NOMNC is to be provided no later than two days before the proposed end of services.[321] If services are expected to be fewer than two days in duration, notify the enrollee at the time of admission to the provider; for non-institutional settings if the span of time between services exceeds two days, the notice should be given no later than the next to last time services are furnished.[322]

[ii] Content of Notice. Standardized notice should include the date that coverage ends; the date of enrollee's liability; a description of the enrollee's right

---

[319] 42 C.F.R. § 422.624(a)(1) and (2). Notice of Medicare Non-Coverage, Form CMS-10123-NOMNC and form instructions can be found at https://www.cms.gov/Medicare/Medicare-General-Information/BNI/MAEDNotices.html (site visited Oct. 2, 2018). Additional guidance for MA notices can be found at Ch. 13, § 90.2–90.9 of the Medicare Managed Care Manual, *available at* https://www.cms.gov/Regulations-and-Guidance/Guidance/Manuals/Downloads/mc86c13.pdf (site visited June 13, 2018).

[320] 42 C.F.R. § 422.624(a)(2).

[321] 42 C.F.R. § 422.624(b)(1).

[322] 42 C.F.R. § 422.624(b)(1).

to a fast-track appeal, described below, to the IRE; an enrollee's right to submit evidence that services should continue; availability of other MA appeal procedures; the right to receive detailed information about the IRE process; and other information required by the Secretary.[323]

[iii] When Delivery of Notice Is Valid. Delivery of notice is not valid unless (1) the enrollee (or authorized rep) has signed and dated the notice to indicate receipt and comprehension of content, and (2) the notice is delivered as described above and has the notice content described above in **§§ 7.03[E][2][n][i]** and **7.03[E][2][n][ii]**.[324] Moreover, with respect to notifying enrollees of termination of provider services, the MA plan is to ensure that the enrollee (or the enrollee's representative) has signed and dated the notice to indicate that he or she has received the notice and can comprehend its contents.[325]

[iv] Financial Liability for Failure to Deliver Valid Notice. An MA organization is financially liable for continued services until two days after the enrollee receives valid notice; an enrollee may waive continuation of service if he or she agrees with being discharged sooner than two days after receiving the notice.[326]

[v] Right to Fast-Track Appeal. An enrollee of an MA organization has a right to a fast-track appeal of an MA organization decision to terminate provider services, which can be requested of the IRE in writing or by telephone by noon of the first day after the day of delivery of the termination notice (or by noon of the next day that the IRE is open for business).[327] If the enrollee fails to make a timely request to the IRE, he or she may request an expedited reconsideration by the MA organization.[328] If, after delivery of the termination notice, the enrollee chooses to leave a provider or discontinue receipt of services on or before the proposed termination, the enrollee cannot later assert a right to IRE appeal for the services at issue.[329]

[vi] Continuation of Coverage. Coverage of provider services continues until the date and time designated on the termination notice, unless the enrollee appeals and the IRE reverses the MA organization decision.[330] If the decision is delayed because the provider did not submit requested information

[323] 42 C.F.R. § 422.624(b)(2).

[324] 42 C.F.R. § 422.624(c).

[325] 42 C.F.R. § 422.624(c)(1).

[326] 42 C.F.R. § 422.624(d).

[327] 42 C.F.R. § 422.626(a)(1); CMS Manual Provisions on Fast Track can be found in the MMC Manual, Ch. 13: § 90.8.

[328] 42 C.F.R. § 422.626(a)(2).

[329] 42 C.F.R. § 422.626(a) (3).

[330] 42 C.F.R. § 422.626(b).

timely, the MA organization is liable for any additional coverage required by the delayed IRE decision; if the IRE finds that enrollee did not receive valid notice, coverage continues until at least two days after valid notice is received, unless the continued coverage poses a threat to the enrollee's health and safety.[331]

[vii] Burden of Proof. The burden of proof rests with the MA organization to demonstrate that termination of coverage is the correct decision, either based on medical necessity or on other Medicare coverage policies.[332]

[viii] Procedures Independent Review Entity Must Follow. On the date of receipt of enrollee's request for an appeal, the IRE must immediately notify the MA organization and the provider of the appeal request and of its responsibility to submit documentation as requested by the IRE.[333] The IRE must make a decision and notify the enrollee, the MA organization, and the provider, by close of business of the day after it receives the necessary information for decision.[334] It can defer the decision until it receives necessary information from the MA, and until it does, coverage continues until the IRE makes its decision.[335] If an IRE reverses an MA organization's termination decision, the provider must provide the enrollee with a new notice as provided in 42 C.F.R. § 422.624(b).[336]

[ix] Responsibilities of the Medicare Advantage Organization. If the enrollee requests an expedited determination, the MA organization is to provide a Detailed Explanation of Non-Coverage (DENC) detailed notice to the enrollee about why services are either no longer reasonable and necessary or no longer covered and is to include in the notice a description of any applicable Medicare coverage rule, instruction, policy, including citation, or any applicable MA rationale or contract provision, or facts specific to the enrollee, and other information required by CMS, including cost for copying documents, as well as any information required by the IRE.[337]

[x] Reconsiderations of Independent Review Entity Decisions. An enrollee may request reconsideration no later than 60 days after notification that the IRE has upheld the decision.[338] The reconsideration must be rendered

[331] 42 C.F.R. § 422.626(b).

[332] 42 C.F.R. § 422.626(c).

[333] 42 C.F.R. § 422.626(d)(1).

[334] 42 C.F.R. § 422.626(d)(5).

[335] 42 C.F.R. § 422.626(d)(5).

[336] 42 C.F.R. § 422.626(f) (Apr. 2010 amendments).

[337] 42 C.F.R. § 422.626(e)(1). Detailed Explanation of Non-Coverage, Form CMS-10124-DENC and form instructions are *available at* https://www.cms.gov/Medicare/Medicare-General-Information/BNI/MAEDNotices.html (site visited June 13, 2018).

[338] 42 C.F.R. § 422.626(g)(1).

expeditiously, but no later than within 14 days of receipt of the enrollee's request.[339] If affirmed in whole or part, the enrollee may appeal to OMHA for an ALJ hearing, the Council, or a federal court as provided in these rules.[340]

---

[339] 42 C.F.R. § 422.626(g)(2).

[340] 42 C.F.R. § 422.626(g)(3).

APPENDIX 7-1 MEDICARE ADVANTAGE (PART C) DETERMINATION/APPEALS PROCESS

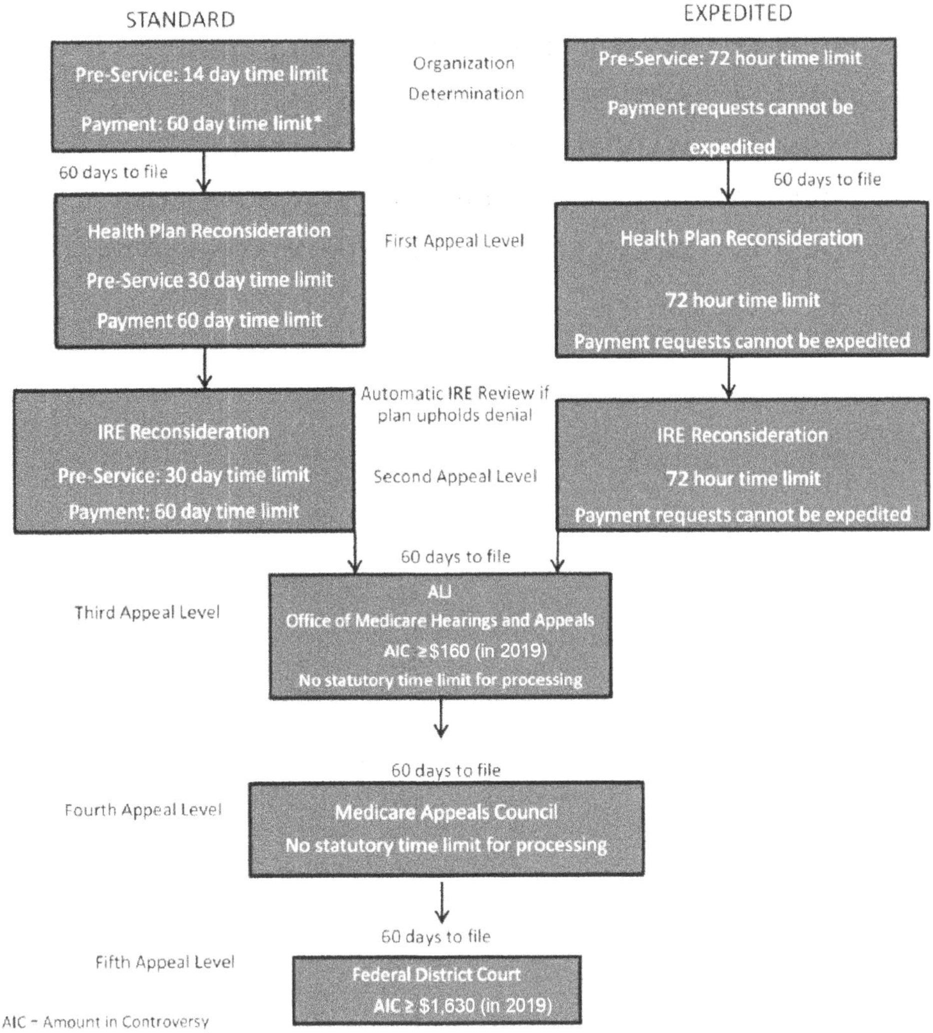

AIC – Amount in Controversy

ALJ=Administrative Law Judge

IRE=Independent Review Entity

*Plans must process 95% of all clean claims from out-of-network providers within 30 days. All other claims must be processed within 60 days.

APPENDIX 7-2

FORMS

FORM 7A	INTEGRATED DENIAL NOTICE (IDN)
FORM 7B	NOTICE OF DISCHARGE
FORM 7C	WAIVER OF LIABILITY STATEMENT
FORM 7D	NOTICE OF MEDICARE NON-COVERAGE
FORM 7E	DETAILED EXPLANATION OF NON-COVERAGE

FORM 7A INTEGRATED DENIAL NOTICE (IDN)

Important: This notice explains your right to appeal our decision. Read this notice carefully. If you need help, you can call one of the numbers listed on the last page under "Get help & more information."

Notice of Denial of Medical Coverage

{Replace *Denial of Medical Coverage* with *Denial of Payment*, if applicable}

Date: **Member number:**

Name:

[Insert other identifying information, as necessary (e.g., provider name, enrollee's Medicaid number, service subject to notice, date of service)]

Your request was denied

We've {Insert appropriate term: *denied, stopped, reduced, suspended*} the {*payment of*} medical services/items listed below requested by you or your doctor [*provider*]:

Why did we deny your request?

We {Insert appropriate term: *denied, stopped, reduced, suspended*} the {*payment of*} medical services/items listed above because {Provide specific rationale for decision and include State or Federal law and/or Evidence of Coverage provisions to support decision}:

You have the right to appeal our decision

You have the right to ask {health plan name} to review our decision by asking us for an appeal [Insert Medicaid information, if applicable: *and/or you can request a State Fair Hearing. You can ask for both types of review at the same time, as long as you meet the deadlines. If you ask us for an appeal first, you may miss the deadline for requesting a State Fair Hearing.*]:

Appeal: Ask {health plan name} for an appeal within **60 days** [Insert State Medicaid timeframe, if different] of the date of this notice. We can give you more time if you have a good reason for missing the deadline.

State Fair Hearing: *Ask for a State Fair Hearing within ( ) days of the date of this notice. You have up to ( ) days if you have a good reason for being late.*

If we're stopping or reducing a service, you can keep getting the service while your case is being reviewed. ***If you want the service to continue, you must ask for an appeal*** (Insert, if applicable: ***or a State Fair Hearing***) ***within 10 days*** *of the date of this notice or before the service is stopped or reduced, whichever is later. Your provider must agree that you should continue getting the service. If you lose your State Fair Hearing appeal, you may have to pay for these services.*

Form CMS 10003-NDMCP (Iss. 06/2013) OMB Approval 0938-0829

If you want someone else to act for you

You can name a relative, friend, attorney, doctor, or someone else to act as your representative. If you want someone else to act for you, call us at: {number(s)} to learn how to name your representative. TTY users call {number}. Both you and the person you want to act for you must sign and date a statement confirming this is what you want. You'll need to mail or fax this statement to us.

Important Information About Your Appeal Rights

There are 2 kinds of appeals

Standard Appeal – We'll give you a written decision on a standard appeal within **30 days** [Insert timeframe for standard Medicaid appeals, if different] after we get your appeal. Our decision might take longer if you ask for an extension, or if we need more information about your case. We'll tell you if we're taking extra time and will explain why more time is needed. If your appeal is for payment of a service you've already received, we'll give you a written decision within **60 days**.

Fast Appeal – We'll give you a decision on a fast appeal within **72 hours** after we get your appeal. You can ask for a fast appeal if you or your doctor believe your health could be seriously harmed by waiting up to 30 days for a decision.

We'll automatically give you a fast appeal if a doctor asks for one for you or supports your request. If you ask for a fast appeal without support from a doctor, we'll decide if your request requires a fast appeal. If we don't give you a fast appeal, we'll give you a decision within 30 days.

How to ask for an appeal with {health plan name}

Step 1: You, your representative, or your doctor [*provider*] must ask us for an appeal [*or State Fair Hearing*]. Your {*written*} request must include:

- Your name
- Address
- Member number
- Reasons for appealing
- Any evidence you want us to review, such as medical records, doctors' letters, or other information that explains why you need the item or service. Call your doctor if you need this information.

[Insert, if applicable: *You can ask to see the medical records and other documents we used to make our decision before or during the appeal. At no cost to you, you can also ask for a copy of the guidelines we used to make our decision.*]

Step 2: Mail, fax, or deliver your appeal {*or call us*}.

For a Standard Appeal: Address:
{Phone:} Fax:

{Insert, if applicable: *If you ask for a standard appeal by phone, we will send you a letter confirming what you told us.*}

For a Fast Appeal: Phone: Fax:

Form CMS 10003-NDMCP (Iss. 06/2013) OMB Approval 0938-0829

What happens next?

If you ask for an appeal and we continue to deny your request for {*payment of*} a service, we'll send you a written decision and automatically send your case to an independent reviewer. **If the independent reviewer denies your request, the written decision will explain if you have additional appeal rights.**

[Insert additional State-specific Medicaid rules, as applicable.]

How to ask for a Medicaid State Fair Hearing

[You have the right to ask for a State Fair Hearing without asking us (health plan) to review our decision first.]

Step 1: *You or your representative must ask for a State Fair Hearing (in writing) within ( ) days of the date of this notice. You have up to ( ) days if you have a good reason for your request being late.*

Your {written} request must include:

- Your name
- Address
- Member number
- Reasons for appealing
- Any evidence you want us to review, such as medical records, doctors' letters, or other information that explains why you need the item or service. Call your doctor if you need this information.

Step 2: *Send your request to:* Address:
Phone: Fax:

What happens next?

The State will hold a hearing. You may attend the hearing in person or by phone. You'll be asked to tell the State why you disagree with our decision. You can ask a friend, relative, advocate, provider, or lawyer to help you. You'll get a written decision within ( ) days. The written decision will explain if you have additional appeal rights.

[A copy of this notice has been sent to:]

Get help & more information

- {Health Plan Name} Toll Free: TTY users call:
  {Insert plan hours of operation}
- 1-800-MEDICARE (1-800-633-4227), 24 hours, 7 days a week. TTY users call: 1-877-486-2048
- Medicare Rights Center: 1-888-HMO-9050
- Elder Care Locator: 1-800-677-1116
- [Medicaid/State contact information]

Form CMS 10003-NDMCP (Iss. 06/2013) OMB Approval 0938-0829

MA plans are required (effective November 1, 2013) to issue the Integrated Denial Notice (IDN) upon denial, in whole or in part, of an enrollee's request for coverage and upon discontinuation or reduction of a previously authorized course of treatment.

FORM 7B NOTICE OF DISCHARGE

Patient Name: OMB Approval No. 0938-1019
Patient ID Number: Date Issued:
Physician:

{Insert Hospital or Plan Logo here}

Detailed Notice Of Discharge

You have asked for a review by the Quality Improvement Organization (QIO), an independent reviewer hired by Medicare to review your case. This notice gives you a detailed explanation about why your hospital and your managed care plan (if you belong to one), in agreement with your doctor, believe that your inpatient hospital services should end on ________________________________. This is based on Medicare coverage policies listed below and your medical condition.

This is not an official Medicare decision. The decision on your appeal will come from your Quality Improvement Organization (QIO).

- Medicare Coverage Policies:

  _____ Medicare does not cover inpatient hospital services that are not medically necessary or could be safely furnished in another setting. (Refer to 42 Code of Federal Regulations, 411.15 (g) and (k)).

  _____ Medicare Managed Care policies, if applicable: ______________________________ ______________________________ {insert specific managed care policies}

  _____ Other ______________________________ {insert other applicable policies}

- Specific information about your current medical condition:

- If you would like a copy of the documents sent to the QIO, or copies of the specific policies or criteria used to make this decision, please call ______________________________{insert hospital and/or plan telephone number}.

According to the Paperwork Reduction Act of 1995, no persons are required to respond to a collection of information unless it displays a valid OMB control number. The valid OMB control number for this information collection is 0938-1019. The time required to complete this information collection is estimated to average 60 minutes per response, including the time to review instructions, search existing data resources, gather the data needed, and complete and review the information collection. If you have comments concerning the accuracy of the time estimate(s) or suggestions for improving this form, please write to: CMS, 7500 Security Boulevard, Attn: PRA Reports Clearance Officer, Mail Stop C4-26-05, Baltimore, Maryland 21244-1850.

CMS 10066 (approved 07/10)

Instructions for Completing the Detailed Notice of Discharge
CMS 10066

This is a standardized notice. Hospitals may not deviate from the content of the form except where indicated. Please note that the OMB control number must be displayed on the notice. Insertions must be typed or legibly hand-written in 12-point font or the equivalent.

Hospitals or plans may modify the following sections to incorporate use of a sticker or label that includes this information:

Patient Name: Fill in the patient's full name.

Patient ID number: Fill in the patient's ID number. This should not be, nor should it contain, the patient's social security or HICN number.

Physician: Fill in the name of the patient's physician.

Date Issued: Fill in the date the notice is delivered to the patient by the hospital/plan.

Insert logo here: Hospitals/plans may elect to place their logo in this space. However, the name, address, and telephone number of the hospital/plan must be immediately under the logo, if not incorporated into the logo. If no logo is used, the name and address and telephone number (including TTY) of the hospital/plan must appear above the title of the form.

BLANK 1: "**This notice gives you a detailed explanation of why your hospital and your managed care plan (if you belong to one), in agreement with your doctor, believe that your inpatient hospital services should end on ______________________.** In the space provided, fill in planned date of discharge.

First Bullet: **"Medicare Coverage Policies:"** Place a check next to the applicable Medicare and/or managed care policies. If necessary, hospitals may also use the selection "Other" to list other applicable policies, guidelines or instructions. Hospitals or plans may also preprint frequently used coverage policies or add more space below this line, if necessary. Policies should be written in full sentences and in plain language. In addition, the hospital or plan may attach additional pages or specific policies or discharge criteria to the notice. Any attachments must be included with the copy sent to the QIO as well.

Second Bullet: **"Specific information about your current medical condition"** Fill in detailed and specific information about the patient's current medical condition and the reasons why services are no longer reasonable or necessary for this patient or are no longer covered according to Medicare or Medicare managed care coverage guidelines. Use full sentences and plain language.

Third Bullet: **"If you would like a copy of the documents sent to the QIO, or copies of the specific policies or criteria used to make this decision, please call ______________________."** The hospital/plan should also supply a telephone number for patients to call to get a copy of the relevant documents sent to the QIO. If the hospital/plan has not attached the Medicare policies and/or the Medicare managed care plan policies used to decide the discharge date, the hospital should supply a telephone number for patients to call to obtain copies of this information.

Hospitals or plans may add space below this section to insert a signature line and date, if they so choose.

FORM 7C WAIVER OF LIABILITY STATEMENT

(Rev. 105, Issued: 04-20-12, Effective Date: 04-20-12; Implementation Date: 04-20-12)

WAIVER OF LIABILITY STATEMENT

____
Medicare/HIC Number

____
Enrollee's Name

____
Provider

____
Dates of Service

____
Health Plan

I hereby waive any right to collect payment from the above-mentioned enrollee for the aforementioned services for which payment has been denied by the above-referenced health plan. I understand that the signing of this waiver does not negate my right to request further appeal under 42 CFR 422.600.

____
Signature

____
Date

FORM 7D NOTICE OF MEDICARE NON-COVERAGE

{Insert provider contact information here}
Notice of Medicare Non-Coverage

Patient name: **Patient number:**

The Effective Date Coverage of Your Current **{insert type}** Services Will End: **{insert effective date}**

- Your Medicare provider and/or health plan have determined that Medicare probably will not pay for your current {insert type} services after the effective date indicated above.
- You may have to pay for any services you receive after the above date.

Your Right to Appeal This Decision

- You have the right to an immediate, independent medical review (appeal) of the decision to end Medicare coverage of these services. Your services will continue during the appeal.
- If you choose to appeal, the independent reviewer will ask for your opinion. The reviewer also will look at your medical records and/or other relevant information. You do not have to prepare anything in writing, but you have the right to do so if you wish.
- If you choose to appeal, you and the independent reviewer will each receive a copy of the detailed explanation about why your coverage for services should not continue. You will receive this detailed notice only after you request an appeal.
- If you choose to appeal, and the independent reviewer agrees services should no longer be covered after the effective date indicated above;
  - Neither Medicare nor your plan will pay for these services after that date.
- If you stop services no later than the effective date indicated above, you will avoid financial liability.

How to Ask For an Immediate Appeal

- You must make your request to your Quality Improvement Organization (also known as a QIO). A QIO is the independent reviewer authorized by Medicare to review the decision to end these services.
- Your request for an immediate appeal should be made as soon as possible, but no later than noon of the day before the effective date indicated above.
- The QIO will notify you of its decision as soon as possible, generally no later than two days after the effective date of this notice if you are in Original Medicare. If you are in a Medicare health plan, the QIO generally will notify you of its decision by the effective date of this notice.
- Call your QIO at: {insert QIO name and toll-free number of QIO} to appeal, or if you have questions.

See page 2 of this notice for more information.

Form CMS 10123-NOMNC (Approved 12/31/2011) OMB approval 0938-0953

If You Miss The Deadline to Request An Immediate Appeal, You May Have Other Appeal Rights:

- If you have Original Medicare: Call the QIO listed on page 1.
- If you belong to a Medicare health plan: Call your plan at the number given below.

  Plan contact information ____

  ____

Additional Information (Optional):

Please sign below to indicate you received and understood this notice.

I have been notified that coverage of my services will end on the effective date indicated on this notice and that I may appeal this decision by contacting my QIO.

______________________________________ ________________

Signature of Patient or Representative Date

Form CMS 10123-NOMNC (Approved 12/31/2011) OMB approval 0938-0953

FORM 7E DETAILED EXPLANATION OF NON-COVERAGE

Insert contact information here

Detailed Explanation of Non-coverage

Date:

Patient name: Patient number:

This notice gives a detailed explanation of why your Medicare provider and/or health plan has determined Medicare coverage for your current services should end. ***This notice is not the decision on your appeal.*** The decision on your appeal will come from your Quality Improvement Organization (QIO).

We have reviewed your case and decided that Medicare coverage of your current {insert type} services should end.

- **The facts used to make this decision:**

- **Detailed explanation of why your current services are no longer covered, and the specific Medicare coverage rules and policy used to make this decision:**

- **Plan policy, provision, or rationale used in making the decision (health plans only):**

If you would like a copy of the policy or coverage guidelines used to make this decision, or a copy of the documents sent to the QIO, please call us at: {insert provider/plan toll-free telephone number}

Form CMS-10124-DENC (Approved 12/31/2011) OMB Approval No. 0938–0953

CHAPTER 8

MEDIGAP SERVICES

§ 8.01 INTRODUCTION TO MEDIGAP SERVICES

Despite the benefits provided by Medicare, beneficiaries can be faced with financial burdens in the form of deductibles, copayments, and other out-of-pocket costs. Medicare Supplement Insurance (commonly known as Medigap), is a form of supplemental insurance offered by private insurers to help pay for these gaps in costs.[1] Medigap insurance generally does not pay for gaps in services in traditional (or original) Medicare, but rather is intended to "bridge the gap" between what Medicare pays and the balance of a beneficiary's medical bills.[2]

Medigap insurance is meant to work in tandem with the fee-for-service Medicare program (also known as traditional, or original, Medicare) and typically covers only services that Medicare has already approved for payment. Generally, if Medicare denies coverage for an item or a service, the Medigap policy will also refuse to pay its portion of the bill, unless such coverage is specified in the policy.[3] Medigap coverage is a key component of health insurance protection for individuals who rely on the original Medicare program to finance their health care. In choosing a Medigap plan, consumers should carefully assess the various plans offered so as to ensure they purchase the appropriate coverage to meet their financial and coverage needs.[4]

§ 8.02 STANDARDIZED MEDIGAP POLICIES AND BENEFITS

Private insurers selling Medigap policies in most states may only sell consumers standardized policies that are identified by the letters A through N. They are standardized so that regardless of which insurance company is selling a particular plan, all benefits contained therein must be identical (i.e., all Plan A's must contain the same benefits across companies, all Plan B's must be the same across companies, and so forth). Instead, variation amongst the plans occurs in premium pricing; the only difference between Medigap policies of the same letter is that their cost may differ among insurance companies. For example, while all Plan A's must contain the same benefits, the premiums charged for those plans can vary

---

[1] *See* Center for Medicaid & Medicare Servs. (CMS), "What's Medicare Supplement Insurance (Medigap)?," *available at* http://www.medicare.gov/supplement-other-insurance/medigap/whats-medigap.html (site visited Aug. 6, 2018); *see also* CMS, "Medigap (Medicare Supplement Health Insurance)," *available at* http://www.cms.gov/Medicare/Health-Plans/Medigap/index.html (site visited Aug. 6, 2018).

[2] *See* CMS, "Medigap (Medicare Supplement Insurance)."

[3] *See* CMS, "What's Medicare Supplement Insurance (Medigap)?"

[4] For a helpful resource, *see* CMS, 2016 Choosing a Medigap Policy: A Guide to Health Insurance for People with Medicare, *available at* https://www.medicare.gov/Pubs/pdf/02110-Medicare-Medigap.guide.pdf (site visited Aug. 6, 2018).

drastically depending on which company is offering the plan. It is therefore critical that consumers be aware of all their options and choose the most cost-effective plan and insurer.

In all states except Minnesota, Massachusetts, and Wisconsin,[5] federal law requires insurers to sell Medigap policies that are one of 10 standard supplemental plans.[6] These 10 plans are labeled with the letters A through L to make it easier for consumers to compare plans.[7] Medigap policies pay most, if not all, of traditional Medicare's coinsurance amounts and some provide coverage for deductibles as well. Some of the 10 standardized plans pay for services not covered by Medicare, such as extended hospital coverage and emergency medical care while traveling outside the United States.[8] When describing the benefits of each Medigap policy, insurance companies must use the same format, language, and definitions to make it easier for consumers to compare.[9]

Plan A (not to be confused with Part A) contains the basic or "core" benefits. The other 9 policies contain the core benefits plus one or more additional benefits. The following is a list of the benefits contained in the core policy and that must be contained in all new Medigap policies sold since July 31, 1992:[10]

1. Part A hospital coinsurance for days 61 to 90 ($341 per day in the year 2018);
2. Part A lifetime reserve coinsurance for days 91 to 150 ($682 per day in 2018);
3. 365 lifetime hospital days beyond Medicare coverage;
4. Parts A and B Three Pint Blood Deductible; and
5. Part B 20 percent coinsurance.

---

[5] For information on these three states' Medigap plans for 2018 as well as the 10 standardized plans, *see* 2018: Choosing a Medigap Policy: A Guide to Health Insurance for People with Medicare, *available at* https://www.medicare.gov/Pubs/pdf/02110-Medicare-Medigap.guide.pdf (site visited Aug. 6, 2018). For additional updates, *see also* National Association of Insurance Commissioners, "Home Page," *available at* https://www.naic.org/ (site visited Aug. 6, 2018).

[6] 42 U.S.C. § 1395ss(a).

[7] Policies sold before July 31, 1992, were not standardized, and although these policies are no longer offered for sale, many beneficiaries continue to renew their existing pre-standardization policies.

[8] Some Medigap polices offered coverage for outpatient prescription drugs. Effective January 1, 2006, no new standardized Medigap policies that provide outpatient prescription drug benefits will be sold. Consumers who were enrolled in those plans as of December 1, 2005, may retain and renew those policies. 42 U.S.C. § 1395ss(v), as added by the MMA.

[9] 42 U.S.C. § 1395ss(e).

[10] 42 U.S.C. § 1395ss(o). *See* CMS, "What's Medicare Supplement Insurance (Medigap)?"

Additional benefits are offered in Policies B through N. Each plan offers a different combination of these benefits in addition to the core benefits. The Medicare website contains a chart comparing Medigap plans and their benefits (See **Appendix 8-1** at the end of this chapter).[11] The additional benefits include:

1. Part A Skilled Nursing Facility (SNF) coinsurance for days 21 to 100 ($167.50 per day in 2018);
2. Part A hospital deductible ($1,364 in 2019);
3. Part B deductible ($185 in 2019);
4. Part B charges above the Medicare approved amount (if the provider does not accept assignment);
5. Foreign travel emergency coverage;
6. At-home recovery (home health aide services);
7. Prescription drug coverage (basic or extended);[12] and
8. Preventive medical care.

§ 8.03 HIGH DEDUCTIBLE PLANS

The Medigap Plan F policy has a high deductible option, which comes with a lower monthly premium in exchange for imposing a high deductible ($2,300.00 in 2019)[13]. Plan F generally offers the most comprehensive coverage among Medigap policies and as such carries high premiums. It can thus at times be more cost effective to choose a high deductible option in lieu of the traditional Plan F. If the savings in premiums between the high deductible and traditional plan options exceeds the amount of the high deductible ($2,300.00), it may be advantageous to choose the high deductible plan. However as discussed above, premiums for Plan F and its high deductible counterpart can vary widely among companies and from year to year and therefore beneficiaries must be prudent in

---

[11] *See* CMS, "How to compare Medigap policieshttps://www.medicare.gov/supplement-other-insurance/compare-medigap/compare-medigap.html. The plans for Massachusetts, Minnesota, and Wisconsin are different. *See* http://www.medicare.gov/supplement-other-insurance/compare-medigap/massachusetts/medigap-massachusetts.html; http://www.medicare.gov/supplement-other-insurance/compare-medigap/minnesota/medigap-minnesota.html; *and* http://www.medicare.gov/supplement-other-insurance/compare-medigap/wisconsin/medigap-wisconsin.html (sites visited July 1, 2017).

[12] No new policies offering prescription drug coverage may be sold on or after January 1, 2006. 42 U.S.C. § 1395ss(v).

[13] *See* https://www.cms.gov/Medicare/Health-Plans/Medigap/FandJ.html (site visited Nov. 19, 2018). CMS, "Deductible Amount for Medigap High Deductible Options F & J for Calendar Year 2017" *available at* https://www.cms.gov/Medicare/Health-Plans/Medigap/FandJ.html (site visited Nov. 19, 2018). The deductible is increased by the percentage increase in the Consumer Price Index for all urban consumers for the 12-month period ending with August of the preceding year. *See* 42 U.S.C. § 1395ss(p)(11)(C)(ii).

their decision making. These high deductible options offer the same basic benefits as Plan F, but the beneficiary enrolled in the high deductible option must pay a deductible each year before the policy pays anything. Additional deductibles must be met, including a separate foreign travel emergency deductible per year for Plans F and J.[14] Because of these additional deductibles, the premiums for these plans may be significantly lower than for plans without the high deductible.

§ 8.04 MEDICARE CERTIFICATION OF POLICIES

All Medigap policies must abide by federal and state laws that dictate the structure of benefits and provide consumer protections. Beginning in 1990, the Health Care Financing Administration (HCFA), now the Centers for Medicare & Medicaid Services (CMS), established a program of mandatory certification of Medigap policies along with 10 standard plans.[15] Under this authority, the Secretary of Health and Human Services is required to establish a procedure whereby Medigap policies are certified as meeting minimum standards and requirements.[16] The Medicare statute deems Medigap policies offered in various states to meet the Secretary's certification requirements if they provide for the application and enforcement of regulatory standards equal to the model standards of the National Association of Insurance Commissioners (NAIC).[17] The Secretary is tasked with periodically reviewing the compliance of states with these requirements[18] and must also submit a report to Congress at least once every two years evaluating the effectiveness of the certification process.[19]

---

[14] 42 U.S.C. § 1395ss(p)(11). For updated information, check http://www.medicare.gov (site visited Aug. 6, 2018).

[15] See § 4353(a) of the Omnibus Budget Reconciliation Act of 1990 (OBRA '90), Pub. L. No. 101-508 (Nov. 5, 1990) (codified at 42 U.S.C. § 1395ss(a)), applicable to policies sold after July 1992; such policies must conform to one of the 10 standardized model policies developed by the National Association of Insurance Commissioners (NAIC). Previously, certification was voluntary as provided in § 507(a) of the Social Security Disability Amendments of 1980, Pub. L. No. 96-265 (June 9, 1980). (*See* 42 U.S.C. § 1395ss(b)–(f) for a full discussion of the state and federal certification processes and § 1395ss(i)–(n) for a full discussion and history of the effective dates for adopting and meeting the NAIC Model Regulation or federal model standards.) *See also* http://www.cms.gov/Medicare/Health-Plans/Medigap/Downloads/ModelMedigapRegulation2008.pdf (site visited Sept. 18, 2018).

[16] 42 U.S.C. § 1395ss(a)(1). The Secretary's authority to promulgate rules for the administration of its certification program for Medigap policies is found at 42 U.S.C. § 1395ss(h). The requirements for certification by the Secretary are found at 42 U.S.C. § 1395ss(c). Procedures for certification are found in the regulations at 42 C.F.R. § 403.232.

[17] *See* 42 U.S.C. § 1395ss(g)(2)(A). NAIC Model Standards are found at 42 C.F.R. § 403.210. *See* http://www.naic.org/documents/committees_models_table_of_contents.pdf (site visited Sept. 18, 2018).

[18] 42 U.S.C. § 1395ss(b).

[19] 42 U.S.C. § 1395ss(f)(2).

§ 8.05 MEDICARE SELECT

Sections 4358(a) and (b) of the Omnibus Budget Reconciliation Act of 1990 (OBRA '90)[20] authorize approval of certain Medigap policies as Medicare SELECT policies if they meet the NAIC model standards and otherwise comply with the statute.[21] Medicare SELECT is the same as standard Medigap insurance in nearly all ways, however typically have stricter network limitations. Medicare SELECT policies restrict full benefits to only those items and services furnished by a local network of providers (hospitals and other entities), except in emergency situations. The plans essentially function as supplement policy HMOs and are only offered in certain areas. Reduced coverage for gaps in coverage may be provided for items and services furnished by non-network providers and members usually require a referral from their primary care doctor in order be treated by specialists. As such, Medicare SELECT policies generally have lower premiums because of these limitations.[22]

§ 8.06 A HISTORY OF MEDIGAP'S EVOLUTION THROUGH LEGISLATION

[A] Changes to Policies Effective in 2006

The Medicare Prescription Drug, Improvement, and Modernization Act of 2003 (MMA) added two new standardized plans in 2006 and changed the benefits under three existing plans,.[23] The MMA authorized the NAIC to review and revise the model standards to incorporate the new plans and reflect these changes in the existing plans.[24] Effective January 1, 2006, insurers were prohibited from selling Medigap policies that provided prescription drug coverage. Medigap Plans

---

[20] *See* § 4353(a) of the Omnibus Budget Reconciliation Act of 1990 (OBRA '90), Pub. L. No. 101-508 (Nov. 5, 1990) (codified at 42 U.S.C. § 1395ss(a)), applicable to policies sold after July 1992; such policies must conform to one of the 10 standardized model policies developed by the National Association of Insurance Commissioners (NAIC). Previously, certification was voluntary as provided in § 507(a) of the Social Security Disability Amendments of 1980, Pub. L. No. 96-265 (June 9, 1980). (*See* 42 U.S.C. § 1395ss(b)–(f) for a full discussion of the state and federal certification processes and § 1395ss(i)–(n) for a discussion and history of the effective dates for adopting and meeting the NAIC Model Regulation or federal model standards.).

[21] *See* Medicare.gov, "How to Compare Medigap Policies," *available at* http://www.medicare.gov/supplement-other-insurance/compare-medigap/compare-medigap.html (site visited July 1, 2017). *See also* CMS, "2017 Choosing a Medigap Policy," *available at* https://www.medicare.gov/Pubs/pdf/02110-Medicare-Medigap.guide.pdf (site visited Sept. 18, 2018).

[22] 42 U.S.C. § 1395ss(t)(1).

[23] Medicare Prescription Drug, Improvement, and Modernization Act of 2003 (MMA), Pub. L. No. 108-173 (Dec. 8, 2003), amending 42 U.S.C. § 1395ss.

[24] Legislation required implementation of the modifications made by NAIC to the standard Medigap plans, which include restructuring of the current benefit packages. NAIC had until October 31, 2008, to complete its modifications; the states then had one year from the time NAIC adopted

H, I, and J were no longer able to be sold, issued, or renewed to anyone with Medicare who was enrolled in or eligible for Medicare Part D prescription drug coverage. The Act did create an exception for people with a Plan H, I, or J policy that was issued before January 1, 2006, however.[25] If the beneficiary decides to keep a Medigap prescription drug plan, the Medigap plan's coverage is modified to eliminate prescription drug coverage for expenses of drugs incurred after the effective date of coverage under Part D. Premiums are also adjusted to reflect the elimination of this coverage.

Note that the MMA did not modify the standard plans to require that any or all of them pay the cost-sharing under the new Medicare Part D prescription drug benefit. Thus, neither existing nor newer Medigap policies will cover any of the out-of-pocket costs associated with prescription drug benefits provided under Part D.

The legislation also introduced two new Medigap policies, Plan K and Plan L. Plan K covers 50 percent of cost-sharing applicable under Medicare Parts A and B, except for the Part B deductible. It covers 100 percent of cost-sharing for preventive benefits, all inpatient hospital coinsurance, and 365 extra lifetime days of coverage of inpatient hospital services. There is also a limitation on annual out-of-pocket expenses under Parts A and B.[26] The second benefit package, Plan L, is the same as Plan K except that it covers 75 percent of cost-sharing applicable under Parts A and B.[27]

[B] Changes to Policies Effective in June 2010

The Medicare Improvement for Patients and Providers Act of 2008 (MIPPA)[28] made changes to the standardized Medigap policies that may be sold on or after June 1, 2010. MIPPA authorized a reduction in the number of standardized plans offered from twelve to ten. Plans E, H, I, and J were completely eliminated, as Plans H, I, and J became duplicative of other plans after the MMA added a prescription drug benefit to Medicare.[29] Plan E became unnecessary as a result of the other MIPPA changes. MIPPA also eliminated the "at-home recovery" and "preventive care" benefits from additional benefits Medigap plans could

---

the revised model law to conform. The Medicare Improvements for Patients and Providers Act of 2008 (MIPPA), Pub. L. No. 100-275 (July 15, 2008).

[25] 42 U.S.C. § 1395ss(v).

[26] *See* CMS, "How to Compare Medigap Policies," *available at* http://www.medicare.gov/supplement-other-insurance/compare-medigap/compare-medigap.html (site visited Aug. 6, 2018).

[27] 42 U.S.C. § 1395ss(w)(2). Please check http://www.cms.gov or https://www.medicare.gov for updated information (site visited Aug. 6, 2018).

[28] MIPPA, Pub. L. No. 110-275 (July 25, 2008).

[29] MMA, Pub. L. No. 108-173 (Dec. 8, 2003).

offer. A new hospice benefit, which covers all cost-sharing for Part A eligible hospice care and respite care expenses, was added as a core benefit available with every Medigap plan offered for purchase.

Two new plans created by the Act, M and N, offer options with higher beneficiary cost-sharing and lower anticipated premiums. Plan M offers the basic core benefits required of every Medigap plan and additionally covers skilled nursing facility copayments, medically necessary emergency care in a foreign country, and 50 percent of the Medicare Part A deductible.[30]

Plan N offers the basic core benefits required of every Medigap plan and additionally covers 100 percent of the Medicare Part A deductible, skilled nursing facility copayments, and medically necessary emergency care in a foreign country. Plan N also includes copayments for covered services as follows: (1) the lesser of $20 or the Medicare Part B coinsurance or copayment for each covered health care provider office visit and (2) the lesser of $50 or the Medicare Part B coinsurance or copayment for each covered emergency room visit. However, this copayment for an emergency room visit is waived if the insured is admitted to any hospital and the emergency visit is subsequently covered as a Part A expense.[31]

In order to help define what constitutes an office visit for purposes of determining whether the beneficiary must pay the Plan N cost-sharing amount, CMS has identified the codes for services that fall within the appropriate category.[32] These are codes for office visits or evaluation and management visits. Codes for laboratory, x-ray, durable medical equipment, or other services are not subject to the cost-sharing. However, if the physician bills for multiple Medicare-covered office visits in one day, the coinsurance or copayment amount is applicable to each Medicare-covered office visit.

[C] Sales of New Policies After June 2010

After June 1, 2010, only new Medigap policies authorized under MIPPA may be sold. Beneficiaries who have Medigap policies with effective dates prior to June 1, 2010 are allowed to keep and renew their older Medigap policies after that date. These policies may become more expensive over time as the number of policyholders decreases, however.

It is up to each individual insurance company to decide whether it will offer beneficiaries who have pre-June 1, 2010 policies the opportunity to purchase one of the new policies without medical underwriting. According to the NAIC, this

---

[30] *See* CMS, "How to Compare Medigap Policies."

[31] *See* Center for Medicare Advocacy (CMA), "Medigap," *available at* http://www.medicareadvocacy.org/medicare-info/medigap/ (site visited Aug. 6, 2018).

[32] *See* CMA, "Medigap."

may depend on whether the insurance company chooses not to underwrite existing policyholders into the new standard policies.[33] If the insurance company does not exercise this option, a beneficiary may still apply for a new policy, but the application would be subject to medical underwriting (unless other protections apply).[34]

If an insurer provides a period for policyholders to change to a new plan, or sells a new policy to replace a policy of equivalent or lesser coverage, the insurer must waive pre-existing condition time periods, waiting periods, and probationary periods for people whose previous policy was in effect for at least six months. Agents are prohibited from selling duplicate Medicare policies; one of the new Medigap policies cannot be sold to someone who already has a policy unless the new policy will replace the existing policy.[35]

[D] Sales of Policies for Those Newly Eligible as of January 2020

The Medicare Access and CHIP Reauthorization Act of 2015 (MACRA) made major changes to those who will be eligible for certain Medigap policies starting in 2020.[36] Beginning in 2020, Plans C and F will be eliminated and newly eligible Medicare beneficiaries will not be able to purchase any Medigap policies that cover the Part B deductible ($185 in 2019)This includes all individuals who become eligible for Medicare, whether due to age, disability or end-stage renal disease. All persons eligible for Medicare before January 1, 2020 may however continue to be offered and to purchase policies that cover the Part B deductible up until that date. Enrollees in Plans C and F prior to 2020 will be able to keep their policies indefinitely and may also change insurance carriers. However premiums for these plans are expected to rise as the pool of enrollees shrinks in the future.

MACRA eliminates Plans C and F, which provide first-dollar coverage on all doctor and hospital visits. Given their comprehensive coverage, the plans are the most popular among enrollees, with over half of Medigap policyholders in one of these two plans.[37] Despite their popularity, Congress is eliminating the plans out of concerns for cost and moral hazard. These plans, known as the "Cadillac"

---

[33] National Association of Insurance Commissioners, Implementation Materials for Revision to Medigap Model (Oct. 7, 2008), *available at* http://www.naic.org/documents/committees_b_senior_issues_medigap_impl_guide.pdf (site visited Aug. 6, 2018).

[34] *See* CMA, "Medigap."

[35] *See* CMS, "Guaranteed Issue Rights," *available at* https://www.medicare.gov/find-a-plan/staticpages/learn/rights-and-protections.aspx (site visited Aug. 6, 2018).

[36] MACRA, § 401, Pub. L. No.114-10 (Apr.16, 2015).

[37] Modern Healthcare, "Changes loom as most-popular Medigap plans face extinction" (June 2016), *available at* http://www.modernhealthcare.com/article/20160625/MAGAZINE/306259966 (site visited Aug. 6, 2018).

policies of the supplement market, are feared to fuel the overutilization of medical services. However, others argue that without such coverage many beneficiaries will forgo care, leading to higher costs in the future. MACRA's changes are likely to change Medigap buying behaviors, perhaps pushing more beneficiaries into Medicare Advantage plans.

§ 8.07 CONSUMER PROTECTIONS

Federal law requires insurance companies that sell Medigap policies to abide by certain consumer protection requirements.[38] Insurers are required by statute to provide a one-time, six-month open enrollment period for Medigap policies that begins on the first month that a beneficiary turns 65 and elects Part B coverage. During this period, these beneficiaries must be "guaranteed issue" of Medigap plans regardless of their age, sex, or health status. While they may be subject to higher premiums, a beneficiary aged 65 or older cannot be denied Medigap enrollment by an insurance company.[39]

Pursuant to the Balanced Budget Act of 1997,[40] Medicare beneficiaries who are at least 65 years old are also guaranteed issuance of certain Medigap policies with no wait for coverage of preexisting conditions if they apply within 63 days of the following certain circumstances:[41]

- A Medicare beneficiary, who enrolled in a Medicare Advantage (MA) plan upon first becoming eligible for Medicare, and subsequently disenrolled within 12 months is guaranteed issuance of any Medigap policy offered for sale in the beneficiary's state. That period is extended for another 12 months if the MA plan terminated its contract with CMS or the beneficiary was otherwise involuntarily disenrolled within the first 12 months of enrollment and enrolled in another MA plan.[42]
- A Medicare beneficiary who dropped a Medigap policy upon enrolling for the first time in an MA plan but who subsequently disenrolled within 12 months is guaranteed issuance of the same Medigap policy from the same insurance company *if that policy* is still being offered for sale. Otherwise, such an individual is entitled to guaranteed issuance of Medigap Plans A, B, C, or F. That period is extended for an additional 12 months if the MA plan terminated its contract with CMS or the beneficiary was

[38] 42 U.S.C. § 1395ss(s).

[39] For a useful chart on guaranteed issue rules, *see* CMS, "How to Compare Medigap Policies," *available at* https://www.medicare.gov/supplement-other-insurance/compare-medigap/compare-medigap.html (site visited Aug. 6, 2018).

[40] The Balanced Budget Act of 1997 (BBA '97), Pub. L. No. 105-33 (Aug. 5, 1997).

[41] 42 U.S.C. § 1395ss(s)(3).

[42] 42 U.S.C. § 1395ss(s).

otherwise involuntarily disenrolled within the first 12 months of enrollment and enrolled in another MA plan.[43]

- A Medicare beneficiary who moved out of the area or whose plan terminated service to the beneficiary's area, became bankrupt, or violated or misrepresented a provision of the plan, or engaged in marketing violations is guaranteed issuance of Medigap Plans A, B, C, or F. These same rights apply to Medicare beneficiaries whose employer stops providing employee or retiree health insurance coverage, or when COBRA health care continuation insurance ends.[44] A Medicare beneficiary whose employer stopped providing employee retirement health benefits or whose COBRA health care continuation insurance coverage ends is guaranteed issuance of Medigap policies A, B, C, F, K, or L.
- A Medicare beneficiary who has original Medicare and a Medicare SELECT policy and moves out of the Medicare SELECT policy's service area.
- A beneficiary's Medigap insurance company goes bankrupt causing a loss of coverage, or Medigap policy coverage otherwise ends through no fault of the beneficiary.

A beneficiary that purchases a Medigap policy is also guaranteed renewal of that policy unless he or she does not pay the policy premiums or there has been some material misrepresentation of information leading to obtaining the policy. The health status of the individual is not a valid reason to cancel or to refuse to renew a policy.[45]

Each Medigap policy must provide that benefits and premiums can be suspended at the request of the policyholder for a period up to 24 months when the policyholder has applied for and is determined to be eligible for medical assistance under the Medicaid program, provided the policyholder notifies the issuer of the policy within 90 days after the entitlement to such assistance. If the beneficiary's Medicaid entitlement is suspended or terminated, the Medigap policy can be automatically reinstated effective the day of the suspension or termination.[46] There are penalties for insurers who fail to abide by these provisions.[47] The Ticket to Work and Work Incentives Improvement Act of 1999[48] provides for suspension of Medigap coverage and premiums for disabled workers entitled to

---

[43] 42 U.S.C. § 1395ss(s).

[44] 42 U.S.C. § 1395ss(s).

[45] 42 U.S.C. § 1395ss(q)(1)(A)–(B).

[46] 42 U.S.C. § 1395ss(q)(5)(A).

[47] 42 U.S.C. § 1395ss(q)(5)(C).

[48] The Ticket to Work and Work Incentives Improvement Act of 1999, Pub L. No. 106-170 (Dec. 17, 1999), *available at* http://www.gpo.gov/fdsys/pkg/PLAW-106publ170/html/PLAW-106publ170.htm (site visited Aug. 6, 2018); *see also* Social Security Legislative Bulletin, December 3, Subject:

Medicare Part A covered under certain group health plans. It also requires reinstatement of a Medigap policy if group coverage is lost provided that the policyholder gives notice of the loss of such coverage within 90 days.[49]

[A] Consumer Protections for Those Under Age 65

Federal consumer protections for Medigap policies do not apply to beneficiaries under age 65.[50] Insurance companies are not required to guarantee issuance of policies to these beneficiaries and therefore have free reign to deny coverage due to age, sex, and health status.[51] However many states have elected to voluntarily extend protections to their under-65 population. Currently, 31 states grant some degree of protection to disabled and end-stage renal disease (ESRD) Medicare beneficiaries.[52] Of the 31 states, some choose to extend the protections only to those with a disability (e.g., California and Vermont) while Massachusetts and Delaware extend it only to those with ESRD. In the 19 states without state-protections (with the exception of Arizona and Nevada), insurers still voluntarily offer Medigap policies to those with disabilities and ESRD. However, given the health conditions of under age 65 beneficiaries, insurers can often charge much higher premiums based on their health status.

[B] Prohibition Against Sale of Duplicate Policies

Another important consumer protection found in federal law is the prohibition against the sale of a second Medigap policy to a beneficiary.[53] It is also unlawful for a person to knowingly sell or issue a Medigap policy that duplicates health benefits to which the individual is entitled under Title 19 (Medicaid) or other benefit programs under a state or federal law.[54] An insurance agent is required to disclose this provision of the law to Medicare beneficiaries and must obtain a written acknowledgment of their receipt of this information. A new policy may be sold to replace an existing policy, but this fact must also be

---

1999 Congress Passes the Ticket to Work and Work Incentives Improvement Act of 1999, *available at* http://www.ssa.gov/legislation/legis_bulletin_120399.html (site visited Aug. 6, 2018).

[49] 42 U.S.C. § 1395ss(q)(6).

[50] 42 U.S.C. § 1395ss(s)(2).

[51] 42 U.S.C. § 1395ss(s)(2).

[52] Kaiser Family Foundation (KFF), "The Gap in Medigap" (Sept. 27, 2016), *available at* http://www.kff.org/medicare/perspective/the-gap-in-medigap/ (site visited Aug. 6, 2018).

[53] It is not illegal for a beneficiary to renew existing policies. For that reason, there are a few beneficiaries who do have more than one Medigap policy because the policies were purchased before this provision of the law took effect.

[54] 42 U.S.C. § 1395ss(d)(3).

acknowledged in writing. Furthermore, it is unlawful to knowingly sell a Medigap policy to a beneficiary currently enrolled in a MA plan, unless coverage under the MA plan is set to end before the effective date of the Medigap policy.[55]

In addition, since January 2006, issuers of Medigap policies are required to eliminate coverage that duplicates prescription drug benefits for individuals who have a Medigap prescription drug policy and who enroll in a Medicare Part D prescription drug plan.[56] Affected individuals could either enroll in a Medicare supplemental policy without prescription drug coverage or remain in their current plan if that plan has been modified to eliminate the drug benefit.[57]

[C] Coverage of Preexisting Conditions

In general, insurance companies are permitted to sell Medigap policies with exclusions for coverage of preexisting conditions for a period of up to six months.[58] A preexisting condition is a medical condition present prior to obtaining the health insurance coverage. Under the Health Insurance Portability and Accountability Act (HIPAA)[59] such exclusions *cannot* be imposed on an individual who applies for a Medigap policy during his or her initial open enrollment period, who had at least six months of "creditable coverage", and who has not had a break in creditable coverage of more than 63 days prior to applying for the Medigap policy.[60]

---

[55] CMS, "Illegal Medigap Practices," *available at* https://www.medicare.gov/supplement-other-insurance/medigap/illegal-practices/10-illegal-medigap.html (site visited Aug. 6, 2018).

[56] A Medigap prescription drug policy is defined as Plans H, I, and J, including a high deductible Plan J, or a policy to which the standards do not apply but which provides prescription drug benefits. 42 U.S.C. § 1395ss(v)(6)(A).

[57] 42 U.S.C. § 1395ss(v)(2)(A).

[58] GINA, Pub. L. No. 110-233 (May 21, 2008), prohibits Medigap issuers from denying or conditioning the issuance or effectiveness of a policy on the basis of a beneficiary's genetic information. Issuers are also prohibited from requesting, requiring, or purchasing a beneficiary's genetic information and from using that information in discriminating in the pricing of a policy. However, issuers may raise the premiums for beneficiaries with pre-existing conditions, except as indicated in this chapter. Note that for plan years starting on or after January 1, 2014, group health plans and health insurers that offer group or individual health insurance coverage are prohibited from imposing any preexisting condition exclusion. *See* Affordable Care Act (ACA) § 1201(2)(A). *See also* CMS, "When Can I Buy Medigap?" *available at* http://www.medicare.gov/supplement-other-insurance/when-can-i-buy-medigap/when-can-i-buy-medigap.html (site visited Aug. 6, 2018). However, the ACA's prohibitions on preexisting condition exclusions do not apply to Medigap policies.

[59] 42 U.S.C. § 300gg.

[60] 42 U.S.C. § 1395ss(s)(2)(D).

A beneficiary's initial open enrollment period occurs during the first six months the beneficiary is both age 65 or older and enrolled in Medicare Part B.[61] Creditable coverage is defined as coverage under:

- A group health plan;
- Health insurance coverage;
- Part A or Part B of Medicare;
- Medicaid;
- A medical program on the Indian Health Service or tribal organization;
- A state health benefits risk pool;
- CHAMPUS (Civilian Health and Medical Program of the Uniformed Services);
- The Federal Employees Health Benefit Plan;
- A public health plan; or
- A health plan under the Peace Corps Act.[62]

For beneficiaries who are switching from one Medigap policy to another, the issuer of the replacement Medigap policy must waive any time periods applicable to preexisting conditions, waiting periods, elimination periods, and probation periods in the new Medigap policy for similar benefits to the extent of time spent under the original policy.[63]

§ 8.08 REQUIRED RATIO OF AGGREGATE BENEFITS TO AGGREGATE PREMIUMS

Medigap policies may not be issued or renewed in any state unless the policy can be expected to provide a return to policyholders in the form of aggregate benefits provided under the policy of at least 75 percent of the aggregate amount of premiums collected in the case of group policies, and at least 65 percent in the case of individual policies.[64] Issuers of policies must provide for a proportional refund or credit against future premiums in order to ensure this required ratio of aggregate benefits provided as compared to the aggregate premiums collected, also known as

[61] State law can and does, in many instances, offer additional consumer protections to beneficiaries purchasing Medigap policies, including requiring a similar open enrollment period for individuals under age 65.

[62] 42 U.S.C. § 300gg(c)(1).

[63] 42 U.S.C. § 1395ss(s)(1).

[64] 42 U.S.C. § 1395ss(r)(1)(A). For purposes of this provision, only policies issued as a result of solicitations of individuals through the mail or by mass media advertising shall be deemed to be individual policies.

loss ratios.[65] Refunds or credits must include interest from the end of the calendar year involved until the date of the refund or credit at a rate specified by the Secretary.[66]

Since 1993 the Secretary of Health and Human Services has been required to submit an annual report each October on loss ratios under Medigap policies to the Committees on Energy and Commerce and Ways and Means of the House of Representatives and the Committee on Finance of the Senate.[67] The Comptroller General is required to perform audits to ascertain compliance with the loss ratio requirements at least once every three years and to report the results of the audits to the state involved and to the Secretary.[68] The Secretary also has independent audit authority.[69] An insurer who fails to provide the required premium refunds or credits is subject to fines of up to $25,000 for each policy issued for which such failure occurred.[70]

§ 8.09 DISSEMINATION OF INFORMATION ABOUT MEDIGAP POLICY BENEFITS

The Secretary of Health and Human Services is required to provide Medicare beneficiaries with information that will assist them in evaluating whether a Medigap policy will be of value to them and with information that will be helpful in comparing Medigap policies.[71] Pursuant to this requirement, beneficiaries are to be provided information about the actions and practices that are subject to sanctions under Medicare, the manner in which such actions and practices may be reported, and a toll-free telephone number for individuals to report suspected violations.[72] In addition, beneficiaries are to be provided a listing, including addresses and telephone numbers, of state and federal agencies and offices that provide information and assistance to individuals on selecting Medigap policies.[73] The Secretary is also to provide a toll-free telephone number for information about Medigap policies, including the relationship of state Medicaid

---

[65] 42 U.S.C. § 1395ss(r)(1)(B), *available at* http://www.ssa.gov/OP_Home/ssact/title18/1882.htm (site visited Aug. 6, 2018).

[66] 42 U.S.C. § 1395ss(r)(2)(A)–(D), *available at* http://www.ssa.gov/OP_Home/ssact/title18/1882.htm.

[67] 42 U.S.C. § 1395ss(r)(4)–(5), *available at* http://www.ssa.gov/OP_Home/ssact/title18/1882.htm. *See also* Dep't of Health & Human Servs., "Variations and Trends in Medigap Premiums" (Dec. 16, 2011), *available at* http://aspe.hhs.gov/health/reports/2011/medigappremiums/index.pdf (site visited Aug. 6, 2018).

[68] 42 U.S.C. § 1395ss(r)(5)(A).

[69] 42 U.S.C. § 1395ss(r)(5)(B).

[70] 42 U.S.C. § 1395ss(r)(6)(A).

[71] 42 U.S.C. § 1395ss(e)(1).

[72] 42 U.S.C. § 1395ss(e)(2)(A).

[73] 42 U.S.C. § 1395ss(e)(3).

programs to Medigap policies.[74] Much of this required information is found on the Medicare website.

The Medicare Modernization Act required issuers of Medicare prescription drug policies[75] to provide written notice, during the 60 days immediately before the initial Medicare Part D prescription drug enrollment period to everyone who held a Medigap prescription drug policy.[76] The standard notice, approved by the Secretary and by NAIC, advised policyholders of the effects on the new Medicare prescription drug benefit on their policies, and their rights to either retain or change Medigap coverage. The notice also explained that the coverage under the Medigap drug policy may not count as creditable coverage, raising the possibility of limited enrollment periods and a late enrollment penalty should they subsequently decide to enroll in a Part D plan.[77]

§ 8.10 CONCLUSION

Medicare Supplement Insurance continues to be a valuable source of assistance for beneficiaries in paying for coverage. Legislative changes have led to an expansion of services and protections to enrollees in pace with changes to the Medicare program. On the other hand, Medigap policies are currently under threat by policymakers, as evidenced by changes pursuant to MACRA, which prevent future Medicare beneficiaries from enrolling in Medigap plans that provide generous benefits. The future of Medigap policies and how they will evolve with legislation is uncertain, and should be watched closely in the coming years.

---

[74] 42 U.S.C. § 1395ss(f)(3).

[75] State law can and does, in many instances, offer additional consumer protections to beneficiaries purchasing Medigap policies. Medicare beneficiaries should check with their state's insurance commissioner for additional information.

[76] The initial enrollment period for Part D began November 15, 2005. MMA § 101(a), adding § 1860D-1(b)(2)(A) to the Social Security Act.

[77] 42 U.S.C. § 1395ss(v)(2)(B).

APPENDIX 8-1 COMPARE MEDIGAP PLANS SIDE-BY-SIDE

The chart below shows basic information about the different benefits Medigap policies cover.

Yes = the plan covers 100% of this benefit
No = the policy doesn't cover that benefit
% = the plan covers that percentage of this benefit
N/A = not applicable

	A	B	C	D	F*	G	K	L	M	N
Part A coinsurance and hospital costs up to an additional 365 days after Medicare benefits are used up	Yes	Yes	Yes	Yes	Yes	Yes	Yes	Yes	Yes	Yes
Part B coinsurance or copayment	Yes	Yes	Yes	Yes	Yes	Yes	50%	75%	Yes	Yes***
Blood (first 3 pints)	Yes	Yes	Yes	Yes	Yes	Yes	50%	75%	Yes	Yes
Part A hospice care coinsurance or copayment	Yes	Yes	Yes	Yes	Yes	Yes	50%	75%	Yes	Yes
Skilled nursing facility care coinsurance	No	No	Yes	Yes	Yes	Yes	50%	75%	Yes	Yes
Part A deductible	No	Yes	Yes	Yes	Yes	Yes	50%	75%	50%	Yes
Part B deductible	No	No	Yes	No	Yes	No	No	No	No	No
Part B excess charge	No	No	No	No	Yes	Yes	No	No	No	

continues

	A	B	C	D	F*	G	K	L	M	N
Foreign travel exchange (up to plan limits)	No	No	80%	80%	80%	80%	No	No	80%	80%
Out-of-pocket limit**	N/A	N/A	N/A	N/A	N/A	N/A	$5,120	$2,560	N/A	N/A

* Plan F also offers a high-deductible plan. If you choose this option, this means you must pay for Medicare-covered costs up to the deductible amount of $2,300 in 2019 before your Medigap plan pays anything.

** After you meet your out-of-pocket yearly limit and your yearly Part B deductible, the Medigap plan pays 100% of covered services for the rest of the calendar year.

*** Plan N pays 100% of the Part B coinsurance, except for a copayment of up to $20 for some office visits and up to a $50 copayment for emergency room visits that don't result in inpatient admission.

Source: CMS, "How to Compare Medigap Policies," available at https://www.medicare.gov/supplement-other-insurance/compare-medigap/compare-medigap.html.

CHAPTER 9

MEDICARE'S RELATIONSHIP WITH PRIVATE INSURANCE

§ 9.01 INTRODUCTION TO MEDICARE'S RELATIONSHIP TO PRIVATE INSURANCE

Many Medicare beneficiaries have other forms of health care coverage and therefore it is important to be aware of the rules regarding the program's relationship with other insurance. Medicare's laws and regulations facilitate the coordination of care and ultimately protect the program's resources in light of other payment sources. In 1980, Congress prohibited Medicare from paying for health services that are also covered by other insurers through its creation of the Medicare Secondary Payer (MSP; not to be confused with the acronym for "Medicare Savings Program," discussed in **Chapter 10**) program.[1] The MSP program has been subsequently modified and expanded by legislation in order to shift more health care costs from the federal government to private insurers.

The MSP law determines circumstances in which Medicare would be the "secondary payer" to other forms of insurance, meaning that payment with respect to an item or service will only be made by Medicare if payment hasn't been made, or cannot reasonably be expected to be made, by the other coverage.[2] Under the statute, Medicare is generally secondary payer to coverage provided under employer group health plans (EGHPs),[3] worker's compensation plans, liability insurance policies, and no-fault insurance.[4] MSP provisions and their payment-shifting to private insurers seek to promote the financial integrity of the Medicare program by ensuring that funds are not expended until all other primary sources of payment have been exhausted.

In addition to MSP laws, Medicare has rules for how it coordinates with other sources of private insurance, including Consolidated Omnibus Budget Reconciliation Act (COBRA), Medicare Advantage plans, health savings accounts, flexible spending accounts, and qualified health plans (QHPs) purchased through the Affordable Care Act. It is important for beneficiaries and advocates to understand how Medicare coordinates with all forms of insurance, as noncompliance can often result in lack of coverage and financial consequences.

§ 9.02 EMPLOYER GROUP HEALTH PLANS

[A] Medicare as Secondary to Employer Group Health Plans

The Medicare program's coordination of benefit (COB) rules determine circumstances in which Medicare will have secondary payment responsibility when a beneficiary has other insurance coverage, such as an EGHP. If Medicare is the

---

[1] Section 953 of the Omnibus Budget Reconciliation Act (OBRA) of 1980, Pub. L. No. 96-499 (Dec. 5, 1980).

[2] 42 U.S.C. § 1395y(b)(2)(A)(i).

[3] 42 U.S.C. § 1395y(b)(2)(A)(ii).

[4] 42 U.S.C. § 1395y(b)(2)(A)(ii).

"primary payer," health care expenses eligible for coverage will first be paid by Medicare with all or some remaining charges potentially paid by the employer's plan coverage.[5] Alternatively, if Medicare is the "secondary payer," Medicare coverage will pay for health care expenses only after the EGHP insurance has paid first.

Whether Medicare pays primary or secondary to an actively working individual's EGHP is contingent upon two factors: (1) the individual's basis for eligibility for Medicare, and (2) their employer's size.[6] If one became eligible for Medicare coverage due to their age (65 years or older), their EGHP will pay secondary to Medicare if the sponsoring employer has fewer than 20 full- or part-time employees.[7] If one is eligible for Medicare coverage due to disability rather than age, Medicare will be the primary payer if their employer has fewer than 100 employees and will be secondary payer if the employer has 100 or greater employees.[8] These same standards apply to the individual's spouse if he or she receives an EGHP through their spouse's employer.

Eligible for Medicare due to age (65+ years old) and fewer than 20 employees	*Eligible for Medicare due to age (65+ years old) and more than 20 employees*
Medicare pays <u>primary</u>	Medicare pays <u>secondary</u>
Eligible for Medicare due to disability and fewer than 100 employees	*Eligible for Medicare due to disability and 100 or more employees*
Medicare pays <u>primary</u>	Medicare pays <u>secondary</u>

Medicare can also be secondary payer in circumstances when an individual qualifies for Medicare solely due their diagnosis of end-stage renal disease (ESRD).[9] MSP provisions for Medicare beneficiaries with ESRD apply to individuals who are covered under a group health plan (GHP) based on either current employment *or* a retirement plan.[10] This is in contrast to MSP provisions for aged and disabled beneficiaries that only apply when GHP coverage is based on current employment status. Employer size is not a consideration under MSP rules for ESRD beneficiaries; even an employer that covers only a single employee would

---

[5] 42 U.S.C. § 1395y(b)(2)(A)(i); Center for Medicaid & Medicare Servs., Medicare Secondary Payer (MSP) Manual, Pub. 100-5, Ch. 1: § 10.1, *available at* https://www.cms.gov/Regulations-and-Guidance/Guidance/Manuals/downloads//msp105c01.pdf (site visited Aug. 6, 2018).

[6] Medicare sets out aggregation rules that determine the size of an employer for purposes of MSP. *See* MSP Manual, Ch. 1: § 60.

[7] 42 U.S.C. § 1395y(b)(2)(A)(i); MSP Manual, Ch. 2: § 10.3, *available at* https://www.cms.gov/Regulations-and-Guidance/Guidance/Manuals/downloads/msp105c02.pdf (site visited Aug. 6, 2018).

[8] 42 U.S.C. § 1395y(b)(1)(B)(iii); MSP Manual, Ch. 2: § 30.1.

[9] MSP Manual, Ch. 2: § 20.

[10] MSP Manual, Ch. 2: § 20.

pay primary to Medicare.[11] There is the requirement, however, that Medicare be secondary payer for only the limited coordination period of 30 months. This 30-month period begins on the date that the individual first becomes eligible to enroll in Medicare due the diagnosis of ESRD. Medicare then becomes primary payer to the GHP after the 30-month coordination period ends, assuming the individual retains Medicare eligibility based on ESRD.[12]

[B] Calculation of the MSP Amount

[1] Medicare's Payment Amount When Secondary

Medicare can pay secondary benefits to a primary EGHP when a provider, physician, supplier, or beneficiary submits a claim that is payable under Medicare's coverage requirements and the primary plan does not pay the entire charge.[13] Medicare does not make secondary payments if the health care provider is obligated to accept the primary plan payment as full satisfaction of the patient's responsibility.[14] Furthermore, when an individual is enrolled in a managed care plan (MCO) (e.g., a health maintenance organization (HMO)) EGHP, Medicare does not pay secondary for services obtained outside of the MCO's contracted network.[15] This has caused problems for beneficiaries who have gone outside of the MCO's service area or counted on Medicare's less restrictive application of coverage rules to fill in gaps in services under their EGHP.

Primary payers under Medicare as Secondary Payer (MSP) rules are expected to be billed directly by health care providers. The fact that Medicare reimbursement is limited by formulas such as DRGs, fee schedules, reasonable charges, or other rates should not affect the amount a primary payer covers.[16] If it is uncertain whether the EGHP pays primary or secondary (or it is unclear that the EGHP will pay at all), Medicare will generally make a conditional payment that may be recovered later once it is confirmed that the EGHP had primary payment responsibility.[17]

If, after the primary EGHP payments have been made there are remaining charges owed to the provider, Medicare will make payments according to a set of formulas. When the item or service provided is based on a Medicare fee schedule

---

[11] MSP Manual, Ch. 2: § 20.

[12] MSP Manual, Ch. 2: § 20.1.

[13] 42 U.S.C. § 1395y(b)(4); 42 C.F.R. § 411.33.

[14] MSP Manual, Ch. 1: § 10.8.

[15] MSP Manual, Ch. 5: § 40.1.2, *available at* https://www.cms.gov/regulations-and-guidance/guidance/manuals/downloads/msp105c05.pdf (site visited Aug. 6, 2018).

[16] 42 C.F.R. § 411.31.

[17] 42 U.S.C. § 1395y(b)(2)(B)(iii).

or reasonable charge basis, the amount that Medicare will pay is the *lowest* of the following amounts, calculated without reduction by the usual coinsurance:[18]

1. The actual charge by the provider (or the amount they are obligated to accept as payment in full) minus the amount paid by the primary payer.
2. The amount Medicare would pay if the services were not covered by a primary payer.
3. The higher of the Medicare fee schedule, Medicare reasonable charge, or other amount which would be payable under Medicare (without regard to any Medicare deductible or coinsurance amounts) or the primary payer's allowable charge (without regard to the primary plan's deductibles or coinsurance) minus the amount actually paid by the primary payer.[19]

Importantly, expenses that serve to meet a beneficiary's Medicare Part A or Part B deductibles are credited when an EGHP makes primary payment.[20] This is true even when the EGHP paid the entire bill and there is no secondary Medicare benefit payable. Primary payments made by an EGHP are also creditable to pay for Part A or Part B coinsurance amounts, though only after all deductibles have been paid.

Example: An individual has previously not met any of their $183 Part B deductible. They then receive a health care service for $183, of which their primary EGHP paid only $50. Medicare's fee schedule amount for that same service was $183. Even if no secondary Medicare benefits are payable in this situation, the Medicare beneficiary would still have $183 credited towards their $183 Part B deductible. They would then be left with a $133 in out-of-pocket costs ($183 – $50).

[2] EGHP's Payment Amount When Secondary

Employer plans have several methods available to them for determining their secondary payer coverage obligations, each with varying cost impacts to the covered individual.[21] Depending on the generosity of the EGHP, a covered individual could still face significant costs when Medicare is the primary payer. In no circumstance will an EGHP pay for benefits not covered under the plan, regardless of which payment method they employ. It is therefore critical that Medicare

---

[18] 42 U.S.C. § 1395y(b)(4); 42 C.F.R. § 411.33.

[19] 42 C.F.R. § 411.33.

[20] MSP Manual, Ch. 1: § 40.

[21] National Association of Insurance Commissioners, Coordination of Benefits Model Regulation (Oct. 2013), *available at* https://www.naic.org/store/free/MDL-120.pdf (site visited Aug. 6, 2018).

beneficiaries be aware of the both the MSP terms and benefit limitations/exclusions of their employer plan, which are typically outlined in summary plan descriptions (SPDs) required to be distributed under federal law.

1. **"Carve-Out" Method:** In what typically results in the highest cost burden to EGHP participants,[22] the carve-out payment method calculates what the plan would normally pay as primary payer and reduces this amount by the Medicare payment. In a situation where Medicare does not pay for the item or service at all, the individual would be subject to all cost-sharing imposed by their EGHP.
2. **Traditional COB:** With a "traditional" coordination of benefits method,[23] the beneficiary may receive up to full reimbursement for expenses Medicare did not cover. Under this method, reimbursement from multiple plans are combined to cover up to 100 percent of the costs, typically resulting in the least financial burden to the plan participant. However in no circumstance will a plan cover an item or service not covered by its own terms or pay more than it would in the absence of Medicare.

[C] Rights Associated with EGHPs

[1] Rights Under ERISA

Medicare beneficiaries may obtain coverage through an EGHP either by virtue of their current employment status[24] or their spouse's employment status. They may also have the opportunity to obtain coverage after their employment ends through retiree plans offered by their employers. The Consolidated Omnibus Budget Reconciliation Act (COBRA), which gives employees and their families who lose employment health benefits the opportunity to continue their coverage under certain circumstances, provides yet another avenue to obtain employer coverage. Regardless of the source, if a health plan is being offered through a private

---

[22] National Association of Insurance Commissioners, Coordination of Benefits Model Regulation at § 7.

[23] National Association of Insurance Commissioners, Coordination of Benefits Model Regulation at § 7.

[24] An individual is considered to have "current employment" status if they are actively working as an employee, are the employer (self-employed), or are associated with the employer in a business relationship. Individuals who are not actively working but are receiving disability benefits from an employer for up to six months are also considered to have current employment status. MSP Manual, Ch. 1: § 50. Individuals must be cognizant of when their employer coverage changes from being based on current employment to becoming a retiree plan, as often times coverage is identical. Failing to enroll in Part B when employment status changes can result in late enrollment penalties in the form of increased premiums.

employer or union, the benefit plan is subject to the federal statute known as the Employee Retirement Security Act of 1974 (ERISA).[25]

Despite being the exclusive source for EGHP regulation, ERISA was originally enacted in 1974 with the primary purpose of solving the pension plan crisis in the country.[26] As a result, many of the rules and protections contained in ERISA are inapplicable to health plans. Furthermore, since employers are not mandated to offer EGHPs to their employees, Congress did not want to overburden employers with regulations and in turn discourage them from offering plans voluntarily. The consequence is that employers are free, with some exceptions, to decide what benefits to offer, to change or reduce the level of benefits, and even to eliminate coverage entirely without any protection for employees or retirees.[27] The Equal Employment Opportunity Commission has also clarified through regulation that employers may reduce benefits for retirees aged 65 and older without violating the Age Discrimination in Employment Act.[28]

Because ERISA's scope is broad with respect to its regulation of employee benefits, state laws that attempt to provide further protections can be "preempted" by the federal statute.[29] Increasingly, many employers are providing EGHPs on a self-insured basis, meaning that they set aside their own funds and assume the risk of paying for health claims of their employees and dependents (as opposed to fully insured arrangements, where a third-party insurer assumes the risk of claim payments). Under ERISA's preemption doctrine, self-insured EGHPs are exempted from state laws that provide more protection, such as those that mandate plans cover certain services (e.g., home health benefits or mental health coverage).[30]

[2] Rights Under Medicare Law

While Medicare beneficiaries with EGHPs are vulnerable to uncertainties and lack of protections, employers may not discriminate against beneficiaries due to their Medicare status.[31] Employers are required to provide individuals aged 65 or older (and if their spouse is 65 or older) the same benefits under the EGHP under the same conditions as any individuals who are under the age of 65.[32] Also, an employer is prohibited from offering Medicare beneficiaries financial or other benefits as an incentive not to enroll in or terminate their EGHP that is or would

[25] 29 U.S.C. § 1003.

[26] *See* Brendan S. Maher, *The Benefits of Opt-in Federalism*, 52 B.C. L. Rev. 1733, 1754 (2011).

[27] 29 U.S.C. § 1341; *see* McGann v. H&H Music, 946 F.2d 401 (5th Cir. 1991).

[28] 29 C.F.R. § 1625.32, Appendix to § 1625.32.

[29] 29 U.S.C. § 1144(a).

[30] 29 U.S.C. § 1144(b)(2)(B); *see* FMC Corp. v. Holliday, 498 U.S. 52, 61 (1990).

[31] 42 U.S.C. § 1395y(b)(1)(A)(i)(I).

[32] 42 U.S.C. § 1395y(b)(1)(A)(i)(II).

be primary to Medicare.[33] Such incentives are a violation of Medicare law and each offense is subject to civil monetary penalties up to $5,000.[34] Employers may neither refuse to cover these individuals nor may they restrict their coverage or charge more for premiums, deductibles, and co-pays by "taking into account" their Medicare entitlement.[35] Other examples of actions by employers that constitute "taking into account" Medicare entitlement when offering benefits include:

- Failing to pay benefits when required to as primary payer;
- Terminating coverage because the individual has become entitled to Medicare (except as permitted under COBRA rules, discussed **§ 9.08** below);
- Requiring a Medicare entitled individual to wait longer for coverage to begin;
- Paying providers less for services furnished to a Medicare beneficiary than for the same services furnished to a non-Medicare beneficiary;
- Providing misleading or incomplete information that causes a Medicare entitled individual to forgo their employer plan, thereby making Medicare the primary payer;
- Including instructions on plan documents, claims, and insurance cards to bill Medicare first for services furnished to Medicare beneficiaries without specifying to only do so when Medicare is primary payer.[36]

[D] Disenrolling from Medicare While on EGHP

Medicare beneficiaries who also have coverage through an EGHP may wish to delay or discontinue their Medicare benefits in order to avoid paying monthly premiums associated with the plans. Beneficiaries may disenroll from or delay enrollment in Part B without penalty if they are covered by their current employer's (or spouse's employer's) EGHP.[37] A beneficiary who is covered under an EGHP will not incur any penalties for disenrolling or delaying enrollment and will avoid any future penalties so long as they enroll again during their special

[33] MSP Manual, Ch. 1: § 70.1.

[34] MSP Manual, Ch. 1: § 70.1.

[35] MSP Manual, Ch. 1: § 70.4.

[36] 42 C.F.R. § 411.108(a).

[37] 42 C.F.R. §§ 407.20 & 406.24(a)(3). Note that while one may disenroll in Part B without penalty, the same does not apply to Part A. Individuals who disenroll from Part A requires repayment of all Social Security payments along with any benefits paid under Part A. *See* Social Security Administration (SSA),Programs Operations Manual System (POMS)—HI 00801.002, *available at* https://secure.ssa.gov/apps10/poms.nsf/lnx/0600801002 (site visited Aug. 6, 2018).

enrollment period (SEP). The SEP for Part B plans extend up to eight months after their employment or coverage ends, whichever is sooner.[38]

A Medicare beneficiary with Part D coverage who has an EGHP may also disenroll from Part D coverage without penalty so long as the EGHP provides prescription coverage and the coverage is "creditable."[39] An employer's prescription drug plan is considered creditable by Medicare if its actuarial value is as good as or better than Medicare's Part D coverage.[40] So long as the individual's employer drug plan is creditable, he or she will be able to reenroll in a Part D SEP that extends up to 60 days after their creditable employer coverage ends without incurring any penalty.[41] When reapplying a Part D plan, the plan will check to see that the beneficiary had creditable coverage within the last 63 days. If the plan cannot find evidence of creditable drug coverage, the beneficiary must show proof of coverage from their employer in order to take advantage of the SEP and avoid late enrollment penalties. A 60-day SEP will also be granted to individuals who involuntarily lost creditable coverage (e.g., because their employer reduced prescription drug benefits) beginning on the day of termination.[42]

Notably, the addition of a Medicare prescription drug benefit has caused some employers and unions to reconsider the prescription drug coverage they provide through their retiree health plans. Because the drug coverage is not separate from the rest of the retiree health benefit package offered by an employer or a union, retirees who enroll in a Medicare Part D drug plan can lose all their retiree health coverage for themselves and for their dependents who are also covered under the retiree health plan. This has created problems for some individuals with retiree health coverage who are dually eligible for Medicare and Medicaid and who were automatically enrolled in a Part D plan.[43]

§ 9.03 MEDICARE AS SECONDARY TO LIABILITY AND NO-FAULT INSURANCE

Medicare pays secondary when a beneficiary incurs medical expenses that are also covered by a liability or no-fault insurance policy.[44] However, if

---

[38] 42 C.F.R. § 406.24(b)(2).

[39] Medicare Prescription Drug Benefit (MPDB) Manual, Pub. 100-18, Ch. 3: § 30, *available at* https://www.cms.gov/medicare/prescription-drug-coverage/prescriptiondrugcovcontra/Partdmanuals.html (site visited Aug. 6, 2018).

[40] 42 C.F.R. § 423.56(a).

[41] 42 C.F.R. § 423.38(c); MPDB Manual, Ch. 3: §§ 30.3.5 & 30.3.8.1.

[42] 42 C.F.R. § 423.38(c); MPDB Manual, Ch. 3: §§ 30.3.5 & 30.3.8.1.

[43] *See* discussion on Medicare Part D in **Chapter 11** of this Handbook.

[44] 42 U.S.C. § 1395y(b)(2)(A)(ii). The definitions of liability and no-fault insurance are broad, and include motorist coverage, homeowner's policies, malpractice insurance, Personal Injury Protection (PIP) and Med-Pay. MSP Manual, Ch. 1: § 10.7, *available at* http://www.cms.gov/Regulations-and-Guidance/Guidance/Manuals/Downloads/msp105c01.pdf (site visited Aug. 6, 2018).

"prompt" payment cannot be made by the primary liability policy, meaning payment cannot be made within 120 days of receiving medical care or filing a claim, Medicare will pay the expenses first on a conditional basis.[45] Once the liability insurance payment is made, or could reasonably have been made, Medicare is entitled to reimbursement from the primary payer or anyone who received payment from a primary payer.[46]

[A] Conditional Payments and Recovery

As soon as Centers for Medicare and Medicaid Services (CMS) learns that payment has been made, or could be made, under a primary insurance plan, the Medicare program is given broad authority by statute to seek reimbursement. Under the MSP program, CMS may recover conditional payments[47] from a broad range of entities other than just the primary payer source, including beneficiaries, providers, suppliers, attorneys, private insurers, and self-insured entities.[48] With the promulgation of the Medicare Modernization Act of 2007 (MMA), the Medicare statute was amended to expand the definition of "self-insured" entities to also include uninsured individual tortfeasors that pay their own settlements or judgments in liability suits.[49] As such, even tort liability defendants who have no formal insurance "plan" are considered insured for purposes of MSP collection. Furthermore, the Act clarified that Medicare's right to recovery of conditional payments takes priority over any other claim against settlement proceeds, including the injured party's own right to reimbursement.[50] Conditional payments may also be recovered from personal injury attorneys whose fees are paid from settlement proceeds.[51] If an attorney is not in possession of any settlement funds, he or she still has a duty to advise their clients of their obligation to repay Medicare within 60 days of receiving any funds intended to pay for medical expenses that Medicare previously covered.[52]

---

[45] 42 U.S.C. § 1395y(b)(2)(B); 42 C.F.R. § 411.20.

[46] 42 U.S.C. § 1395y(b)(2)(B); 42 C.F.R. § 411.20.

[47] CMS has contracted with a private entity, the Benefits Coordination & Recovery Center (BCRC), to handle MSP collections from beneficiaries. For more information, *see* CMS, "Coordination of Benefits & Recovery Overview," *available at* https://www.cms.gov/Medicare/Coordination-of-Benefits-and-Recovery/Coordination-of-Benefits-and-Recovery-Overview/overview.html (site visited Aug. 6, 2018).

[48] 42 U.S.C. § 1395(y)(b)(3)(A).

[49] Section 301(b)(1) of the Medicare Prescription Drug, Improvement, and Modernization Act of 2003, Pub. L. No. 108-173 (2003) (codified at 42 U.S.C. § 1395y(b)(2)(A) (2006)).

[50] 42 C.F.R. § 411.24(b).

[51] *See* United States v. Harris, No. 5:08CV102, 2009 WL 891931 (N.D. W. Va. Mar. 26, 2009) (holding that the government may recover conditional payments from any entity, including an attorney).

[52] 42 C.F.R. § 411.24(h).

When a provider receives a conditional payment from Medicare, it must accept payment at the Medicare rate and cannot seek additional payment from the liability insurance recovery.[53] However, if payment by the primary payer will be made promptly, a provider can choose not to bill Medicare but instead to bill the liability insurer or assert a lien on the beneficiary's insurance settlement or estate.[54] This is a situation that often arises when liability recovery is anticipated, leaving injured persons with liens substantially larger than the rate of Medicare reimbursement for a claim.

[B] Amount of Medicare Recovery

In general, CMS may take legal action to recover either an amount equal to Medicare payment or the full amount payable by the third-party primary payer, whichever is less.[55] The amount of the Medicare recovery for medical expenses caused by torts stops accruing at the time of settlement.[56] There is no MSP recovery for future medical expenses covered by Medicare after that time, unless the settlement includes a specific allocation for such expenses.[57] Currently, the MSP law provides little guidance on treatment of settlement agreements to Medicare that allocate an amount for future medical expenses, known as "Medicare set-aside" arrangements (which are commonly used in workers' compensation settlements; see **§ 9.04**). Statutes and regulations do not require that a settlement agreement be submitted to Medicare, but rather that a reasonable amount be allocated to future medical expenses to take Medicare interests into account.[58] The extension of a Medicare set-aside requirement in liability cases remains of subject of interest within CMS, and among federal legislators.

In cases involving liability insurers, Medicare reduces its recovery to take account of the cost of procuring the judgment or settlement.[59] Under this provision, a proportionate share of attorney's fees and costs should be subtracted from the amount recovered by Medicare. If the primary insurer's payment is less than the MSP claim, Medicare will take it all, minus the legal costs of procurement.

---

[53] 42 U.S.C. § 1395y(b)(2)(B); 42 C.F.R. § 411.20.

[54] CMS, Medicare Program: Third Party Liability Insurance Regulations, 68 Fed. Reg. 43,940 (2003) (modifying 42 C.F.R. §§ 411.54 & 489.20); *see also* Wentz v. Kindred Hosps. East, 333 F. Supp. 2d 1298 (S.D. Fla. 2004).

[55] 42 C.F.R. § 411.24(c).

[56] 42 C.F.R. § 411.24(c).

[57] See CMS, "Medicare Secondary Payer—Liability Insurance (Including Self-Insurance) Settlements, Judgments, Awards, or Other Payments and Future Medicals" (Sept. 30, 2011), *available at* http://www.cms.gov/Medicare/Coordination-of-Benefits-and-Recovery/Coordination-of-Benefits-and-Recovery-Overview/Non-Group-Health-Plan-Recovery/Downloads/Future-Medicals.pdf (site visited Aug. 6, 2018).

[58] 42 C.F.R. § 411.46.

[59] 42 C.F.R. § 411.37.

The MSP legislation allows full recovery of conditional Medicare payments even when the beneficiary's settlement is less than her total damages.[60]

> ■ **EXAMPLE:** Following her auto accident, for which liability was disputed, Vicki Victim received a settlement of $50,000. Her medical expenses were $40,000, of which Medicare paid $25,000; her pain and suffering were valued at $10,000; lost wages were $20,000; and her permanent loss of limb was valued at $30,000.
>
> Despite the fact that Vicki's settlement was only 50 percent of her $100,000 damages, Medicare would demand recovery of its entire $25,000 outlay, reduced only by its proportionate share of the legal costs. Assuming a 30 percent contingency fee arrangement, Medicare would actually take $17,500, Vicki's personal injury attorney would receive a fee of $15,000, and Vicki would receive only $17,500, leaving $82,500 in uncompensated losses.

This basic formula is limited to Medicare outlays for health services resulting from the accident or other incident that gave rise to liability. Thus, Medicare should not recover for health services to the extent that they were aggravated by, for example, a preexisting heart condition.

Beneficiaries and their representatives should carefully examine the list of conditional payments presented by Medicare and object to the inclusion of any that were not caused entirely by the incident that triggered third-party insurer liability.[61] Medicare is not immune from making mistakes in their recovery identification including seeking reimbursement for:

Claims wholly unrelated to the liability incident;

Claims incurred prior to the date of the accident;

Claims outside the scope of an agreed upon Medicare set-aside agreement; and

Claims for preexisting medical conditions that existed prior to the incident giving rise to liability.

If Medicare is improperly seeking reimbursement of payments, beneficiaries should go through the appeal process to contest the claims (described in **§ 9.07[A]**).

[C] Duties of Personal Injury Attorneys

It is critical that attorneys representing Medicare beneficiaries to be cognizant of Medicare's financial interests at the outset of a case. Attorneys

---

[60] 42 C.F.R. § 411.24(c); Zinman v. Shalala, 67 F.3d 841 (9th Cir. 1995).

[61] *See* Medicare Secondary Payer and Workers' Compensation Settlement Agreements Act of 2013, H.R. 1982, 113th Cong. (2013).

should
immediately contact the Benefits Coordination and Recovery Center (BCRC) to report a potential recovery case.[62] Information on the beneficiary including their full name, gender, date of birth, Health Insurance Claim Number (HICN), date of the incident, and description of the incident should be reported to the BCRC.[63] This information is updated in CMS's Common Working File and is used to create a potential recovery case in the system. Attorneys should also make sure to obtain the Medicare beneficiary's common working file ID number from CMS and obtain copies of all conditional payment summaries and updates. The BCRC then begins identifying payments that Medicare has made conditionally on the case.[64] Note that a personal injury attorney representing a client who is a Medicare beneficiary does not owe a fiduciary duty to the Medicare program. However, the attorney does have a legal obligation to ensure that Medicare is reimbursed for conditional payments related to the suit.[65]

When a judgment award or settlement is reached, attorneys must notify the BCRC in writing of the date and amount of the settlement or award as well as any attorney's fees or other associated procurement costs.[66] The BCRC then uses this information to calculate the amount of recovery and issue a demand letter. The recovery demand letter includes information on the beneficiary's administrative appeal rights with regards to the amount of recovery (discussed in **§ 9.07[A]**) and right to request a waiver (discussed in **§ 9.07[B]**).

To assist Medicare in its recovery efforts and ensure that the proper amount of conditional payments are recovered, attorneys should consider negotiating settlement payment terms with opposing counsel to ensure Medicare will be reimbursed (i.e., Medicare set-aside agreements, as discussed in **§ 9.03[B]** above). Potential terms in the settlement agreement could call for the settling defendant to pay the amount due to Medicare directly and pay the balance of the proceeds to the plaintiff. Alternatively, an arrangement can be made for the defendant to pay the entire settlement to plaintiff's counsel and held in escrow until the demand letter is received from the BCRC.[67]

---

[62] The BCRC may be reached at 1-855-798-2627 or by mail at: P.O Box 138897 Oklahoma City, OK 73113. For further information on the BCRC, *see* **§ 9.06**.

[63] CMS, "Reporting a Case," *available at* https://www.cms.gov/Medicare/Coordination-of-Benefits-and-Recovery/Attorney-Services/Reporting-a-Case/Reporting-a-Case.html (site visited Aug. 6, 2018).

[64] CMS, "Reporting a Case."

[65] Robert G. Trusiak, *The Medicare Secondary Payer Statute Medicare's Recovery Rights in the Context of Liability Insurance (Including Self-Insurance) and No-Fault Insurance*, N.Y. St. B.J. (Jan. 2009), at 39, 42.

[66] Trusiak, *The Medicare Secondary Payer Statute Medicare's Recovery Rights in the Context of Liability Insurance (Including Self-Insurance) and No-Fault Insurance.*

[67] Toni J. Ellington, *What Every Attorney Must Know About Medicare Reporting and Reimbursement*, 84 Okla. Bar J. 2, 139 (2013), *available at* http://www.okbar.org/Portals/13/PDF/OBJ/2013/OBJ2013January12.pdf (site visited Aug. 6, 2018).

§ 9.04 MEDICARE AS SECONDARY TO WORKERS' COMPENSATION PLANS

The MSP program also makes workers' compensation plans primary payers of medical expenses for Medicare beneficiaries receiving an award or settlement to treat an accident or illness that is work-related.[68] Not only is a workers' compensation plan responsible for reimbursing Medicare conditional payments made prior to the award or settlement, but also for accident-related future medical expenses when there has been a "commutation" of future medical expenses in the settlement agreement.[69] Typically a commutation happens when a Medicare beneficiary accepts a lump-sum payment as full and final satisfaction of the workers' compensation plan's obligation to pay future medical expenses. If the lump-sum settlement allocates certain amount for future medical expenses, Medicare will not pay for those services until all the funds in the settlement have been exhausted.[70]

■ **EXAMPLE:** Following her work-related accident, for which liability was disputed, Vicki Victim received a settlement of $100,000. Of that amount, $60,000 represents lost income and $40,000 represents future medical expenses. If CMS believes that $40,000 is too low to cover future medicals and that the settlement effectively shifts costs onto Medicare, CMS may refuse to pay for accident-related future medical expenses until the entire $100,000 fund has been exhausted on medical expenses.

[A] Medicare Set-Aside Arrangements

Beneficiaries should keep records of their expenditures for medical services from their settlement so they can establish when funds have been exhausted, triggering Medicare's primary payment responsibilities. It is recommended that this recordkeeping be done through a workers' compensation Medicare set-aside arrangement (WCMSA). While there are no laws requiring that a WCMSA proposal be submitted to CMS for review[71] a submission is recommended when (1) the Medicare beneficiary has a total settlement amount that is greater than $25,000; or (2) the claimant has a "reasonable expectation of Medicare enrollment" within 30 months of the settlement date and the anticipated settlement

---

[68] 42 U.S.C. § 1395y(b)(2)(B); MSP Manual, Ch. 7: § 40.3.

[69] 42 C.F.R. § 411.46(a).

[70] 42 C.F.R. § 411.46(d)(2).

[71] CMS, Medicare Secondary Payer—Workers' Compensation (May 11, 2011), *available at* https://www.cms.gov/Medicare/Coordination-of-Benefits-and-Recovery/Workers-Compensation-Medicare-Set-Aside-Arrangements/Downloads/May-11-2011-Memorandum.pdf (site visited Aug. 6, 2018). WCMSAs may be submitted to CMS electronically online through the WCMSA Portal or by mail.

amount for future medical expenses is expected to be greater than $250,000.[72] Without a WCMSA, Medicare may withhold payment for future medical claims until settlement funds are exhausted.[73] By obtaining Medicare's pre-approval of a workers' compensation settlement, beneficiaries can reduce the risk of future benefit denials by Medicare and ensure all expenses are adequately compensated.

§ 9.05 MSP COORDINATION AND REPORTING

The Benefits Coordination and Recovery Center (BCRC)[74] supports the collection, management, and reporting of other insurance coverage for Medicare beneficiaries. They work to ensure that COB rules are being followed and that Medicare is appropriately paying as either a primary or secondary payer when a beneficiary has other health insurance.[75] The BCRC does not process claims or handle mistaken payment recoveries from primary payers, but rather uses a variety of methods and programs to identify situations where Medicare beneficiaries have other coverage such as a GHP, liability insurance, or workers' compensation.[76] The BCRC is the sole gatekeeper in charge of ensuring accuracy of MSP information on beneficiaries. Any information on beneficiary/spouse/family changes in employment, federal program coverage changes, and other insurance coverage information is reported to the BCRC.

The Medicare, Medicaid, and SCHIP Extension Act of 2007 (MMSEA) requires that Medicare be notified of all claims and settlements involving a Medicare beneficiary where the primary payer is a GHP, liability insurer, no-fault insurer, or workers' compensation plan.[77] Section 111 of the Act imposes duties

[72] CMS, "Workers Compensation Medicare Set-aside Arrangements," *available at* https://www.cms.gov/Medicare/Coordination-of-Benefits-and-Recovery/Workers-Compensation-Medicare-Set-Aside-Arrangements/WCMSA-Overview.html (hereinafter "WCMSA"). A claimant may have a "reasonable expectation" of Medicare enrollment when the individual (1) has applied for Social Security Disability Benefits; (2) has been denied Social Security Disability Benefits but anticipates appealing that decision; (3) is in the process of appealing and/or refiling for Social Security Disability Benefits; (4) is 62 and six months old; or, (5) has an End Stage Renal Disease condition but does not yet qualify for Medicare. CMS, "Medicare Secondary Payer—Workers' Compensation (WC) Frequently Asked Questions" (Apr. 22, 2013), *available at* https://www.cms.gov/Medicare/Coordination-of-Benefits-and-Recovery/Workers-Compensation-Medicare-Set-Aside-Arrangements/WCMSA-Memorandums/Downloads/April-21-2003-Memorandum.pdf (site visited Aug. 6, 2018).

[73] 42 C.F.R. § 411.46(d)(2).

[74] Formerly known as the Coordination of Benefits Contractor (COBC).

[75] CMS, "Coordination of Benefits & Recovery Overview," *available at* https://www.cms.gov/Medicare/Coordination-of-Benefits-and-Recovery/Coordination-of-Benefits-and-Recovery-Overview/Overview.html (site visited Aug. 6, 2018).

[76] CMS, "Coordination of Benefits & Recovery Overview."

[77] 42 U.S.C. § 1395y(b)(7), (b)(8).

on these payers, called "Responsible Reporting Entities" (RREs), to report certain information on individuals who are Medicare eligible (or likely to be Medicare eligible) and report the data to Medicare on a quarterly basis.[78] RREs are required to register with the BCRC for purposes of data submission.[79] Registered RREs are then responsible for electronically reporting the identity of a Medicare beneficiary "whose illness, injury, incident, or accident was at issue" as well as any other information specified by the government to assist in the COB process.[80] With the aid of this reporting requirement, CMS more accurately makes determinations concerning COB and is alerted whenever a beneficiary receives payment from a primary payer. Failure of an applicable RRE to comply with reporting requirements may result in a civil monetary penalties of $1,000 for each day of noncompliance on each claim.[81]

§ 9.06 MSP ENFORCEMENT

The MSP statute grants CMS the right to recover conditional payments from a broad range of entities other than just primary payer plans. The government is authorized by federal law to recover payments from "any or all entities that are or were required or responsible . . . to make payment with respect to the same item or service (or any portion thereof) under a primary plan"[82] such as beneficiaries, providers, suppliers, physicians, attorneys, state agencies, private insurers, and self-insured entities.[83] This can be accomplished by method of direct recovery,[84] subrogation,[85] or independent legal action.[86] Indeed, Medicare's right to reimbursement has been described as a "super lien" due to its extensive scope and reach.[87]

---

[78] 42 U.S.C. § 1395y(b)(7), (b)(8). In the Employer Group Health Plan context, the RRE is the employer's insurer or third-party administrator (TPA), or in the case of a self-insured and self-administered plan, the plan's administrator or fiduciary.

[79] MMSEA Section 111 Medicare Secondary Payer Mandatory Reporting Liability Insurance (Including Self-Insurance), No-Fault Insurance and Workers' Compensation User Guide, Version 4 (Feb. 3, 2014), *available at* https://www.cms.gov/Medicare/Coordination-of-Benefits-and-Recovery/Mandatory-Insurer-Reporting-For-Non-Group-Health-Plans/Downloads/New-Downloads/NGHP UserGuideVer40Ch3Policy.pdf (site visited Aug. 6, 2018).

[80] 42 U.S.C. § 1395y(b)(7), (b)(8).

[81] 42 U.S.C. § 1395y(b)(7)(B)(i), (b)(8)(E).

[82] 42 U.S.C. § 1395(y)(b)(2)(B).

[83] 42 C.F.R. § 411.24(g).

[84] 42 U.S.C. § 1395(y)(b)(2)(B)(ii); 42 C.F.R. § 411.24(d).

[85] 42 U.S.C. § 1395(y)(b)(2)(B)(iv); 42 C.F.R. § 422.26.

[86] 42 U.S.C. § 1395(y)(b)(2)(B)(iii)

[87] Glenn E. Bradford & Melinda M. Ward, *The Medicare "Super Lien" Revisited*, 56 J. Mo. Bar, 44, 49 (2000). Courts have clarified, however, that Medicare has no formal "lien" rights, as the MSP statute does not give the government a claim against property. Zinman v. Shalala, 835 F. Supp. 1163, 1171 (N.D. Cal. 1993), *aff'd*, 67 F.3d 841 (9th Cir. 1995).

Beneficiaries, providers, suppliers, and other entities that have received payment from a primary payer must reimburse Medicare within 60 days of receipt of the payment.[88] In the event that Medicare is not reimbursed for conditional payments, the MSP statute authorizes recovery by (1) "direct collection or by offset against any monies [it] owes the entity responsible for refunding the conditional payment"[89]; (2) "action against any or all entities that were responsible . . . to make payment with respect to the same item or service . . . under a primary plan"[90]; and (3) subrogation.[91] Additionally, when conditional payments are made, the MSP allows CMS to recover double damages from a primary plan that has failed to make payments according to secondary payer laws and reimburse conditional payments.[92] However, the government may only recover double damages if it is forced to take legal action to recover the funds from a primary payer/insurer.[93] Other entities, such as beneficiaries, providers, attorneys, etc., who have received payment from an insurer are not subject to double damages, but are still subject to recovery.[94]

§ 9.07 BENEFICIARY RIGHTS TO SEEK WAIVER OR APPEAL THE MSP RECOVERY CLAIM

Under the Medicare statute, beneficiaries have the right to appeal the amount of MSP payment recovery if they believe the amount of a claim is not correct.[95] They also have the right to ask Medicare to waive or compromise recovery under several different provisions of the law.[96] With the implementation of Section 201 of the SMART Act, CMS has also extended a right of appeal to liability insurance (including self-insurance), no-fault insurance, and worker's compensation plans when Medicare pursues an MSP recovery claim directly from them.[97]

---

[88] 42 C.F.R. § 411.24(g), (h).

[89] 42 U.S.C. § 1395y(b)(2)(B)(iii).

[90] 42 C.F.R. § 411.24(c)(2).

[91] 42 U.S.C. § 1395y(b)(2)(B)(iv).

[92] 42 U.S.C. § 1395(y)(b)(3)(A).

[93] 42 U.S.C. § 1395y(b)(2)(B)(iii).

[94] 42 U.S.C. § 1395y(b)(2)(B)(iii).

[95] *See* 42 U.S.C. § 1395ff.

[96] 42 U.S.C. §§ 1395y(b)(2)(B)(v) (waiver provisions in the MSP statute) & 1395gg(c) (general provisions for waiver of Medicare overpayments); 31 U.S.C. § 3711 (Federal Claims Collection Act). A 2011 court decision has held that CMS should not begin collection procedures while a beneficiary's appeal of CMS's claimed amount is pending. *See* Haro v. Sebelius, 789 F. Supp. 2d 1179 (D. Ariz. 2011). *See also* Center for Medicare Advocacy (CMA), "Haro v. Johnson," *available at* http://www.medicareadvocacy.org/haro-v-johnson/ (site visited Aug. 6, 2018).

[97] CMS, Right of Appeal for Medicare Secondary Payer Determinations Relating to Liability Insurance (Including Self-Insurance), No-Fault Insurance, and Workers' Compensation Laws and Plans, 80 Fed. Reg. 10611–10618 (Feb. 27, 2015), *available at* https://www.federalregister.gov/

[A] Appeals of MSP Recovery Claims

If it appears that Medicare is demanding more of a beneficiary's award than it is entitled to under MSP rules, there is an administrative appeals process that can be pursued.[98] The appeal follows the standard Medicare Part A appeals process, consisting of a paper reconsideration by a Medicare Administrative Contractor (MAC), followed by a hearing before an Office of Medicare Hearings and Appeals administrative law judge, an appeal before the Medicare Appeals Council, and finally judicial review in federal district court if the amount in controversy is $1,630 or more in 2019.[99]

Appeal rights are generated after an initial determination is made by the MSP program. The beneficiary must be given notice of their appeals rights within the initial determination document.[100] The beneficiary may appeal:

1. The existence of the overpayment;
2. The amount of the overpayment; and
3. A less than fully favorable determination of a waiver request.[101]

[B] Waiver or Compromise of MSP Recovery Claims

In addition to the appeals process, a beneficiary can seek to reduce the amount of Medicare's recovery by requesting a waiver or compromise of the MSP claim.[102] Medicare has authority under the law to waive its recovery rights or compromise its claims if:

1. Medicare determines the waiver is "in the best interest of the program";[103]
2. The probability of recovery, or the amount of money involved, does not warrant pursuit of the claim;[104] or

articles/2015/02/27/2015-04143/medicare-program-right-of-appeal-for-medicare-secondary-payer-determinations-relating-to-liability (site visited Aug. 6, 2018).

[98] 42 U.S.C. § 1395ff; 42 C.F.R. §§ 404.900 *et seq.*

[99] CMS, Medicare Appeals; Adjustment to the Amount in Controversy Threshold Amounts for Calendar Year 2010, 83 Fed. Reg. 47,619 (Sept. 20, 2018), *available at* https://www.federalregister.gov/documents/2018/09/20/2018-20506/medicare-program-medicare-appeals-adjustment-to-the-amount-in-controversy-threshold-amounts-for (site visited Nov. 20, 2018).

[100] MSP Manual, Ch. 7: § 50.8.2.

[101] MSP Manual, Ch. 7: § 50.8.1.

[102] 42 U.S.C. § 1395y(b)(2)(B)(v).

[103] 42 U.S.C. § 1395y(b)(2)(B)(v).

[104] 42 C.F.R. § 411.28(a).

3. The beneficiary "is without fault and recovery would either defeat the purpose of the Social Security and Medicare programs or would be against equity and good conscience."[105]

The third ground for waiver is handled by Medicare contractors and is the typical avenue for beneficiaries to reduce MSP recovery claims when they have received a personal injury award that is inadequate to fully compensate their damages.[106] In order to obtain a waiver, the beneficiary must fill out a questionnaire form sent by the Medicare contractor and providing supporting documentation for procurement costs, accident-related out-of-pocket medical expenses, and income information that demonstrates financial hardship (if the beneficiary is using financial hardship as grounds for waiver).[107] Examples of financial hardship include a case where the beneficiary has already spent the insurance proceeds and would have inadequate living expenses if the beneficiary repaid Medicare; a case where the beneficiary is living at the poverty level (although preexisting poverty is not in itself enough to justify waiver); and a case where some unforeseen financial circumstance occurs, such as grandchildren becoming the financial responsibility of the beneficiary.[108] In determining whether recovery would "defeat the purpose of the Social Security or Medicare programs," the contractor assesses whether the recovery would cause the beneficiary financial hardship by depriving their income for ordinary and necessary living expenses.[109] In determining whether recovery "would be against equity and good conscience," the contractor looks to the following factors:

- The degree to which the beneficiary did not contribute to causing the overpayment;
- The degree to which Medicare did contribute to causing the overpayment;
- The degree to which repayment would cause undue hardship to the beneficiary; and
- Whether the beneficiary would be unjustly enriched by waiver, or was harmed by relying on erroneous Medicare information.[110]

The difference between a request for waiver versus a request for appeal is that while an appeal disputes the existence or amount of the recovery, a waiver does not. Instead, with a waiver the beneficiary objects to the recovery on the

---

[105] 42 U.S.C. § 1395gg(c); 42 C.F.R. § 405.358.
[106] *See* MSP Manual, Ch. 7: § 50.6.
[107] MSP Manual, Ch. 7: § 50.6.1.
[108] MSP Manual, Ch. 7: §§ 50.6.5 *et seq.*
[109] MSP Manual, Ch. 7: §§ 50.6.5 *et seq.*
[110] MSP Manual, Ch. 7: §§ 50.6.5 *et seq.*

basis of financial hardship or inequity. If a beneficiary uses an appeal form to request a waiver, the Medicare contractor will treat the appeal as a request for a waiver.[111] If the beneficiary simultaneously requests both an appeal and a waiver, the contractor will process the appeal before processing the waiver.[112]

§ 9.08 COORDINATION OF COBRA RIGHTS AND MEDICARE

[A] What Is COBRA?

The Consolidated Omnibus Budget Reconciliation Act (COBRA) grants employees the right to pay for premiums and temporarily continue the health insurance coverage offered through their employer after losing it because of certain specified events, discussed below.[113] COBRA generally applies to all EGHPs maintained by private employers with at least 20 employees and by state and local governments.[114] COBRA does not apply to plans sponsored by the federal government or by religious organizations.[115]

[B] Eligibility and Coverage

An individual eligible to purchase COBRA through an employer is referred to as a "qualified beneficiary."[116] Qualified beneficiaries include:

- Covered employees;
- Spouses;
- Dependent children; and
- Retirees, their dependents, or their surviving spouse if the retiree's former employer files a petition for bankruptcy.[117]

In order to trigger an offer of COBRA coverage, the qualified beneficiary must experience a loss of their employer health coverage as a result of one of six "qualifying events:"[118]

---

[111] MSP Manual, Ch. 7: § 50.8.3.

[112] MSP Manual, Ch. 7: § 50.8.3.

[113] 29 U.S.C. § 1161(b).

[114] 29 U.S.C. § 1161(b).

[115] 42 U.S.C. § 300bb-1(a), (b)(1). Federal employees have their own health care continuation coverage. 5 U.S.C. § 8905a.

[116] 29 U.S.C. § 1167(3).

[117] 29 U.S.C. § 1167(2), (3).

[118] 29 U.S.C. § 1167(3).

1. The death of the covered employee;[119]
2. The termination, other than for gross misconduct, or reduction in hours of the covered employee's employment;[120]
3. The divorce or legal separation of the covered employee from the employee's spouse;[121]
4. The covered employee's entitlement to Medicare;[122]
5. A dependent child's losing dependent status;[123] and
6. The filing for bankruptcy by a retiree's former employer.[124]

Employers must provide covered employees and their families notice of their COBRA rights.[125] These rights are described in the COBRA initial (or "general") notice required under law to be given to all participants within the first 90 days of coverage under the EGHP.[126] It is generally the responsibility of the employer to notify the EGHP administrator when there is a qualifying event triggering COBRA coverage.[127] However, it is the qualified beneficiary's responsibility to notify the plan if the qualifying event is due to a family event such as divorce, legal separation, or a child's loss of dependent status.[128] Once the plan is made aware of a qualifying event, the plan must deliver a COBRA election notice to the qualified beneficiary that contains information on how to elect COBRA. This notice must be provided within 14 days after the plan administrator is informed of the qualifying event. Qualified beneficiaries then have a period of 60 days in which to elect COBRA coverage.[129]

The coverage offered to qualified beneficiaries must be identical to the coverage provided to similarly situated active employees and their families who have not experienced a qualifying event.[130] The plan design should contain coverage of the same benefits and services and be subject to the same rules and limits

---

[119] 29 U.S.C. § 1163(1).
[120] 29 U.S.C. § 1163(2).
[121] 29 U.S.C. § 1163(3).
[122] 29 U.S.C. § 1163(4).
[123] 29 U.S.C. § 1163(5).
[124] 29 U.S.C. § 1163(6).
[125] 29 U.S.C. § 1166(a); 26 C.F.R. §§ 2590.606-1, 2590.606-4, and appendices.
[126] 29 C.F.R. § 2590.606-1.
[127] 29 U.S.C. § 1166(a); 26 C.F.R. §§ 2590.606-1, 2590.606-4, and appendices.
[128] 29 U.S.C. § 1166(a)(3).
[129] 29 U.S.C. § 1166(a)(3).
[130] 29 U.S.C. § 1162(1). Note that while coverage offered must be identical, employers may charge up to 102 percent of the premium offered to active employees (the COBRA premium may not exceed 102 percent of the applicable premium for the continuation period; *see* 29 U.S.C. § 1162(3)); this may come as a surprise to individuals who previously had most or all of their premiums paid by their employer.

regarding co-payments, deductibles, cost sharing.[131] If, however, coverage is expanded or reduced for current workers, it must be modified in the same manner for qualified beneficiaries.[132]

COBRA coverage lasts 18 or 36 months, depending on the qualifying event that triggered coverage.[133] A plan may, however, voluntarily offer a longer period of coverage beyond this maximum prescribed by law. There are also many state COBRA laws that grant further rights and periods of coverage. When the qualifying event is the covered employee's termination of employment or reduction in employment hours, qualified beneficiaries are entitled to 18 months of continued coverage.[134] All other qualifying events entitle the qualified beneficiary to 36 months of continued coverage. For events that have an 18-month period, coverage may be extended beyond that period, for a total of 36 months, if the qualified beneficiary experiences another qualifying event during that timeframe.[135]

[C] Coordination of COBRA and Medicare

Medicare is the primary payer for Medicare beneficiaries who are also covered under COBRA insurance.[136] Although COBRA is a continuation of existing EGHP coverage, COBRA is not considered equivalent to an EGHP for purposes of MSP laws.[137] Accordingly, COBRA is secondary payer to Medicare when a beneficiary has both forms of insurance. However, determining whether an individual may elect COBRA in addition to Medicare, and the duration of such coverage, is a function of some often confusing timing rules.

For individuals who qualify for Medicare because of ESRD and are also entitled to health coverage under an employer plan, the group plan will be the primary payer for a 30-month COB period.[138] This rule applies regardless of whether the individual is a current or former employee and regardless of whether the individual has coverage through COBRA. Also note that if an individual enrolls in Medicare after electing COBRA coverage, the employer can elect to terminate the COBRA coverage.

---

[131] 29 U.S.C. § 1162(1).

[132] 29 U.S.C. § 1162(1).

[133] 29 U.S.C. § 1162(2)(A). Coverage for retirees whose employer filed for bankruptcy extends for the lifetime of the retiree.

[134] 29 U.S.C. § 1162(2)(A)(i).

[135] 29 U.S.C. § 1162(2)(A)(iv).

[136] 42 C.F.R. § 411.162(a)(3).

[137] 42 C.F.R. § 411.162(a)(3).

[138] 42 U.S.C. § 1395y(b)(1)(C); 42 C.F.R. § 411.162.

[D] Medicare "Entitlement" as a Qualifying Event

For purposes of determining rights of Medicare beneficiaries to COBRA coverage, the law contemplates when one first became "entitled" to Medicare. The term "entitled" is synonymous with "enrolled" as opposed to "eligible."[139] A qualified beneficiary becomes entitled to Medicare on the effective date of enrollment in either Part A or Part B, whichever comes first. Thus, an individual who continues working at age 65 and does not elect to receive Social Security benefits or Medicare at that time is not entitled to Medicare for purposes of COBRA eligibility.

One's entitlement to Medicare typically should not result in a loss of employer coverage and therefore Medicare entitlement is rarely a qualifying event that triggers COBRA. This is because employers are prohibited by law from terminating an active employee's employer group health coverage due to their entitlement to Medicare (see discussion on "taking into account" Medicare entitlement in **§ 9.02[C]**).

The only narrow circumstance in which Medicare entitlement would trigger COBRA coverage is with regards to spouses and dependent children covered under a retiree employer plan. In contrast to active employee plans, employers are not prohibited from terminating retirees from their retiree plans when they become entitled to Medicare. As such, if a retiree loses their employer's retiree plan coverage upon enrolling in Medicare, and the retiree's spouses and/or dependents who are also covered under the retiree plan lose coverage as a result of that, the retiree's spouses and/or dependents are considered to have experienced a qualifying event and must be offered COBRA coverage. The retiree, however, is not considered to have experienced a qualifying event and does not have to be offered COBRA. This is due to COBRA retiree plan rules which only provide rights to spouses and dependents.

[E] Duration of COBRA Coverage

[1] Medicare Entitlement as Qualifying Event

When Medicare entitlement results in a loss of retiree plan coverage for spouses and dependent children, they are permitted to elect up to 36 months of COBRA under the plan.[140] The 36-month period begins to run on the date on which the retiree's spouse and dependents lost coverage as a result of Medicare entitlement.[141] Consider the following examples involving Medicare entitlement as a qualifying event:

[139] 29 U.S.C. §§ 1162(2)(A) & 1163.

[140] 29 U.S.C. § 1163(3).

[141] 29 U.S.C. § 1163(3).

■ **EXAMPLE 1:** Jane is an **active employee** of ABC Company who has coverage for herself and her family under ABC's employer group health plan. She becomes entitled to Medicare on May 1, 2018. Neither Jane nor her spouse/dependents lose employer coverage in this situation. Here there is no COBRA qualifying event as a result of Medicare entitlement.

■ **EXAMPLE 2:** Jane is a **retiree** of ABC Company who has coverage for herself and her family under ABC's retiree health plan. ABC's retiree plan provides that all participants will be terminated from the plan upon the retiree's entitlement to Medicare. She becomes entitled to Medicare on May 1, 2018. As a result Jane and her spouse/dependents lose retiree coverage on that day. Jane's spouse and children will therefore be entitled to COBRA until April 30, 2021, which is 36 months from the day they lost retiree coverage as a result of Medicare entitlement. Jane, however, did not experience a qualifying event and is not offered COBRA.

[2] Medicare Entitlement as an Extension of COBRA

Medicare entitlement can also have the effect of extending the COBRA duration of coverage for an active employee's spouse and dependent children. When an active employee becomes entitled to Medicare, and subsequently experiences a COBRA qualifying event (i.e., termination of employment or reduction in hours resulting in loss of employer coverage) within 18 months of Medicare entitlement, the employee's spouse and dependents are eligible for an extension of their COBRA coverage.[142] The duration of coverage is extended up to 36 months, depending on when within that 18-month period the employee experienced a qualifying event.[143] Consider the following examples:

■ **EXAMPLE 1:** Joe is an active employee of ABC Company who has coverage for himself and his family under ABC's employer group health plan. He becomes entitled to Medicare on May 1, 2018. He retires the next day on May 2, 2018 and as a result loses employer coverage for himself and his family (qualifying event) on that date, triggering an offer of COBRA coverage. Joe will be entitled to the standard 18 months of coverage ending on December 1, 2019. His family is also entitled to the standard COBRA, however their duration is extended to May 1, 2021, which is 36 months from the date of Joe's Medicare entitlement (a total of 18 extra months less one day).

■ **EXAMPLE 2:** Same scenario as above except Joe retires on the same day that he becomes entitled to Medicare, May 1, 2018. Both he and his family are entitled to the standard 18 months of COBRA coverage ending

[142] 29 U.S.C. § 1162(2)(a)(ii).

[143] 29 U.S.C. § 1162(2)(a)(ii).

on November 30, 2019. His family does not get an extension in this timeline because Joe is not considered to have retired "within 18 months" of Medicare entitlement, but rather before.

■ **EXAMPLE 3:** Joe becomes entitled to Medicare on May 1, 2018, but does not retire and lose employer coverage until January 1, 2020. Because Joe's retirement date (qualifying event) is more than 18 months after the date of his Medicare entitlement, his family is not entitled to any extension of COBRA coverage beyond the standard 18 month period.

[F] Early Termination of COBRA and Medicare

In certain circumstances, an employer is permitted to terminate COBRA prior to the full period to which the individual is entitled to coverage. Any qualified beneficiary (including the employee, spouse, and dependents) will lose their right to COBRA upon the date they become entitled to Medicare.[144] Accordingly, their employer has the right to cut short their COBRA coverage upon the date of Medicare entitlement.

On the other hand, if a qualified beneficiary elects COBRA *after* becoming entitled to Medicare, the employer may not terminate their COBRA coverage early. This is true even if the qualified beneficiary elects COBRA only one day after enrolling in Medicare. Therefore, if an individual wants COBRA in addition to Medicare, it is critical to enroll in Medicare prior to experiencing a qualifying event, if possible

To avoid a gap in health coverage before Medicare entitlement begins,[145] employees or their dependents determined to be disabled under Title II or Title XVI of the Social Security Act may receive 29 months of extended COBRA coverage if certain conditions are met.[146] The disability onset date (the date the qualified beneficiary is found disabled) must occur sometime during the first 60 days of the qualifying event.[147] The qualified beneficiary has the responsibility of informing the health plan administrator within 60 days of the determination. Individuals who do not meet these requirements because, for example, their disability onset date is past the first 60 days of the COBRA qualifying event or they fail to notify the plan administrator in a timely manner are not eligible for extended coverage. Health plans may also increase the COBRA premium for the 19th through

---

[144] *See* 29 U.S.C. § 1162(2)(D)(ii); Treas. Reg. § 54.4980B-7 (Q&A 3), *available at* https://www.conexis.org/pdfs/COBRA%20Treasury%20Regulations.pdf (site visited Aug. 6, 2018).

[145] Individuals under age 65 become eligible for Medicare only after they have been entitled to Social Security Disability Benefits for 24 months. Eligibility for Medicare begins in the 25th month. 42 C.F.R. § 406.12.

[146] 29 U.S.C. § 1162(2)(A).

[147] 29 U.S.C. § 1162(2)(A).

the 29th month of extended coverage,[148] making it difficult for some to continue purchasing coverage.

[G] COBRA and Special Enrollment

COBRA qualified beneficiaries who have delayed their enrollment in Medicare Part B do not qualify for a special enrollment period (SEP) to enroll in Part B after their COBRA coverage ends.[149] Although COBRA is a continuation of existing EGHP coverage, COBRA is not considered equivalent to an EGHP for purposes of Medicare and therefore SEPs that apply by reason of current employment will not be granted.[150] Instead, those who delay their enrollment will have to wait to enroll in Part B until the general enrollment period. Therefore those who may someday elect COBRA coverage should enroll in Medicare upon turning 65 years old or else face lifetime late enrollment penalties of 10 percent for every 12 months of delayed enrollment.

Some COBRA-qualified beneficiaries may delay enrollment in a Part D drug plan because the drug coverage they have under COBRA constitutes "creditable coverage." An employer's prescription drug plan is considered creditable by Medicare if its actuarial value is as good as or better than Medicare's Part D coverage. So long as the qualified beneficiary's drug plan is creditable, he or she will be able to enroll in a Part D plan before the next annual coordinated enrollment period. The SEP begins with the month they are advised of the loss of creditable drug coverage and ends 60 days from the loss of coverage or from the date of notice, whichever is later.[151]

§ 9.09 MSP RULES APPLICABLE TO MEDICARE ADVANTAGE PLANS

While the MSP statute grants the Medicare program explicit authority to identify and recover funds from primary payer sources, the rules concerning Medicare Advantage (MA) plans and their rights are not as clear. An MA plan may bill, or authorize a provider to bill, entities for covered Medicare services for which Medicare is not the primary payer, including GHPs, workers' compensation plans, liability, and no-fault insurance policies.[152] However, when it comes to enforcing their rights, courts have held that there is no cause of action to allow

---

[148] 29 U.S.C. § 1162(3)(B); *see* 26 C.F.R. § 54.4980B-8, Q & A-1.

[149] 42 C.F.R. §§ 407.20 & 406.24(a)(3); *see* CMA, "People with Medicare Beware: COBRA Is Not Coverage as a 'Current' Employee," *available at* http://www.medicareadvocacy.org/people-with-medicare-beware-cobra-is-not-coverage-as-a-current-employee/ (site visited Aug. 6, 2018).

[150] 42 C.F.R. § 407.20(b), (c); 42 C.F.R. § 411.104.

[151] 42 C.F.R. §§ 423.38(c) and 423.46; MPDB Manual, Ch. 3: §§ 30.3.5 & 30.3.8.1.

[152] 42 U.S.C. § 1395w-22(a)(4).

and MA plan to bring suit in federal court to recover the cost of care it provided to a beneficiary.[153]

Surprisingly, the statute and regulation do not limit the MSP amount that the MA plans and their providers can charge or recover to the rates that they receive under the Medicare program. Beneficiary advocates should keep in mind that they have the opportunity to appeal and/or request waiver of MSP recovery claims. Beneficiaries must be informed of this right at the time repayment is requested; however, MA collection notices may not advise them of this right. They should be prepared to cite the criteria for waiver and the appeal rights set out in the CMS MSP Manual.[154]

§ 9.10 MEDICAL SAVINGS ACCOUNTS: HSAs AND FSAs

[A] Medicare and Health Savings Accounts

[1] What Is an HSA?

Health Savings Accounts (HSAs) are savings accounts that allow consumers to put money aside to pay for certain "qualified medical expenses" on a tax-free basis.[155] HSAs are used in tandem with high deductible health plans (HDHPs), which are health insurance plans that require high deductibles to be paid prior to triggering insurance coverage.[156] To ease the financial burden of these high out-of-pocket costs, HSAs are used in conjunction with HDHPs to make tax-free health care purchases while spending toward the high deductible.

[2] Eligibility for HSAs

Anyone who is enrolled in an HDHP (or has coverage through a family member's HDHP) is eligible to setup an HSA. IRS rules, however, prohibit the active use of HSAs when one has a plan other than an HDHP.[157] The reasoning

[153] *See* Care Choices HMO v. Engstrom, 330 F.3d 786 (6th Cir. 2003); Nott v. Aetna U.S. Healthcare, Inc., 303 F. Supp. 2d 565, 571 (E.D. Pa. 2004). *See also In re* Avandia Mktg., Sales Practices & Prods. Liab. Litig., 11-2664, 2012 WL 2433508 (3d Cir. June 28, 2012) (holding that an MA insurance company could bring private cause of action for reimbursement under MSP Act).

[154] MSP Manual, Ch. 7: §§ 50.5.4.4–50.6.5.4, & 50.8; CMA, "CMS Revises Its Medicare Secondary Payer Collection Letters Following *Haro v. Sebelius* Decision," *available at* http://www.medicareadvocacy.org/cms-revises-its-medicare-secondary-payer-collection-letters-following-haro-v-sebelius-decision/ (site visited Aug. 6, 2018).

[155] 26 U.S.C § 223.

[156] 26 U.S.C § 223(c).

[157] *Id.*; IRS, Publication 969: Health Savings Accounts and Other Tax-Favored Health Plans, p. 3 (2015), *available at* https://www.irs.gov/pub/irs-pdf/p969.pdf (site visited Aug. 6, 2018).

is that those in non-HDHP plans do not face the same high out-of-pocket cost burdens to justify tax relief. Therefore, if one has any form of coverage other than an HDHP (including dual coverage under a non-HDHP plan), they are ineligible to setup an HSA.

Medicare Part A and B plans are not considered HDHPs and therefore individuals cannot setup an HSA after they are enrolled in Medicare. One can however continue to withdraw from an existing HSA while on Medicare (with limitations, as explained below).[158]

[3] Retaining and Using HSAs While on Medicare

While Medicare beneficiaries cannot *set up* HSAs after they are enrolled in Medicare, they may keep an HSA if it was in existence prior to Medicare enrollment.[159] For example, an individual previously covered under an employer's HSA+HDHP plan who chooses to retire may keep the HSA even after terminating the underlying HDHP coverage and enrolling in Medicare. Alternatively, an individual who chooses to keep an HSA+HDHP plan (or remain in a spouse's plan) and dually enroll in Medicare may keep the HSA. However, individuals may not continue to contribute funds to the HSA if enrolled in Medicare (or other, non-HDHP plan).[160]

If a beneficiary chooses to keep an HSA after enrolling in Medicare, he or she may continue to withdraw existing funds from the account to pay for "qualified medical expenses" on a tax-free basis.[161] Qualified medical expenses are defined by the IRS and include a large range of health care services, medications, and equipment. The definition also includes Medicare premiums and copays, a valuable way for Medicare beneficiaries to make use of their unused HSA funds. (Note, however, that premiums for Medicare supplemental policies, also known as Medigap plans, are excluded from the definition and cannot be paid from an HSA).[162]

[4] Consequences of Contributing Funds While on Medicare

Medicare beneficiaries who continue to contribute funds to an HSA may face IRS penalties including payment of back taxes on their tax-free contributions and account interest, excise taxes, and additional income taxes.[163]

[158] IRS, Publication 969, at 3.
[159] IRS, Publication 969, at 6.
[160] IRS, Publication 969, at 6.
[161] IRS, Publication 969, at 8.
[162] IRS, Publication 969, at 8.
[163] IRS, Publication 969, at 7.

Individuals receiving Social Security benefits will be automatically enrolled in Medicare Part A upon turning 65 and therefore must pay particular attention to HSA rules. The HSA trustee in charge of administering the plan may or may not be aware of the individual's new Medicare enrollment. Some HSA trustees may have the ability to lock the beneficiary's account from any additional contributions, but this is not always the case. It is therefore incumbent on the beneficiary to be aware of the consequences and immediately cease contributing to their HSA upon their date of enrollment in Medicare.

■ **Example:** Mr. K. has been receiving Social Security benefits since he turned 62 in 2014. He turns 65 in March 2017. He should stop contributing to his HSA in February 2017.

Individuals who turn 65 but are not yet receiving Social Security benefits must take affirmative steps to enroll in Medicare. They must stop making HSA contributions for up to six months before enrolling in Medicare. This is because the IRS will consider an individual to have had Medicare (non-HDHP) coverage during those retroactive benefit months for purposes of HSA contribution rules.[164] Thus, any contributions made during the retroactive period will be subject to the same IRS penalties as someone who contributed after their Medicare enrollment date. Therefore, it is critical that prospective Medicare beneficiaries stop contributing to an HSA up to six months prior to enrolling in Medicare.

■ **Example 1:** Mr. G. turns 65 in March 2017. He plans to retire in June 2017. He should stop contributing to his HSA in February 2017.

■ **Example 2:** Ms. S. turns 65 in March 2017. She plans to retire in July 2018. She should stop contributing to her HSA in December 2017.

Individuals have no recourse to contest the penalties after they have been imposed by the IRS. Steps can be taken, however, to prevent penalties for ineligible contributions. An individual beneficiary can withdraw any contributions made while ineligible for an HSA without penalty if they:

1. Withdraw the contributions by the due date of the tax return for the year the contributions were made, and
2. Withdraw any income earned on the withdrawn contributions and include the earnings on their tax return.[165]

[164] IRS, IRS Information Letter 2016-0082 (Mar. 8, 2017), *available at* https://www.irs.gov/pub/irs-wd/16-0082.pdf (site visited Aug. 6, 2018).

[165] IRS, Publication 969: Health Savings Accounts and Other Tax-Favored Health Plans, at 7.

[B] Medicare and Flexible Spending Accounts

[1] What Is an FSA?

Flexible Spending Accounts (FSAs) are another form of savings account that allows consumers to put money aside on a tax-free basis to pay for qualified medical expenses.[166] FSAs can only be set up by employers as a benefit plan for their employees.[167] Employees contribute pre-tax funds to their FSAs by instructing their employer to divert a portion of their salary from each paycheck into the FSA account.[168] An employer may also voluntarily contribute funds to the employee's account.[169] FSA contributions are exempt from federal income and employment taxes and withdrawals from the account are also tax-free so long as they are used to purchase qualified health expenses.[170]

[2] Use of FSAs While on Medicare

Unlike HSAs, there are no restrictions to contributing to and withdrawing from an FSA while enrolled in Medicare.[171] However, FSAs are not portable and will terminate on the date the employee terminates from their employer.[172] Any unused FSA funds must be forfeited and any health expenses incurred after the date of unemployment will not be reimbursed by the account.[173] Therefore, while FSAs can be used in tandem with Medicare coverage, it is only in circumstances where the Medicare beneficiary is actively working for an employer with an FSA plan.

Funds in FSAs can be used to purchase all items IRS defines as qualified medical expenses, however unlike for HSAs, Medicare premiums, deductibles, and co-pays are not included in the definition.[174] Thus, while FSAs can be used to help pay for medical expenses that Medicare does not cover, they cannot be used by beneficiaries to pay for Medicare related expenses.

---

[166] 26 U.S.C. § 106(c).

[167] 26 U.S.C. § 106(c).

[168] IRS, Publication 969: Health Savings Accounts and Other Tax-Favored Health Plans, at 15.

[169] IRS, Publication 969: Health Savings Accounts and Other Tax-Favored Health Plans, at 15.

[170] IRS, Publication 969: Health Savings Accounts and Other Tax-Favored Health Plans, at 15.

[171] IRS, Publication 969: Health Savings Accounts and Other Tax-Favored Health Plans, at 15.

[172] IRS, Publication 969: Health Savings Accounts and Other Tax-Favored Health Plans, at 15.

[173] IRS, Publication 969: Health Savings Accounts and Other Tax-Favored Health Plans, at 17.

[174] IRS, Publication 502: Medical and Dental Expenses (2016), *available at* https://www.irs.gov/pub/irs-pdf/p502.pdf (site visited Aug. 6, 2018).

§ 9.11 MEDICARE AND QUALIFIED HEALTH PLANS OFFERED THROUGH THE AFFORDABLE CARE ACT MARKETPLACE

The Affordable Care Act (ACA), signed into law in 2010, was enacted to increase the quality and affordability of health care and lower the rate of uninsured by expanding private and public health insurance.[175] One mechanism the ACA established to achieve this goal was the creation of health insurance "Exchanges"—regulated online marketplaces where individuals and small businesses can purchase QHPs that provide minimum essential coverage at specified actuarial values.[176] Depending on their income, individuals purchasing QHPs on an Exchange may qualify for reduced cost sharing and premium subsidies in the form of tax credits, making the plans affordable.

As a result of the Exchange QHP tax subsidies, some individuals may find that coverage under the ACA appears to be a more attractive option than Medicare. Those who currently have QHPs may believe they want to keep their plans rather than transition to Medicare. Others who are enrolled or otherwise eligible for Medicare may also wish to drop their coverage in favor of a QHP. Thus, given that historically most people have transitioned from employer-sponsored plans to Medicare rather than from QHPs to Medicare, the advent of Exchanges has spawned new transition of coverage issues and questions.

[A] QHP Subsidies for Those with Premium-Free Part A Medicare

While the Exchanges offer valuable premium subsidies and tax credits to many individuals purchasing QHPs, these financial benefits are not available to individuals who are entitled to premium-free Part A Medicare coverage (the majority of Medicare beneficiaries).[177] These individuals will lose their qualification for subsidies as soon as they become *eligible* for (and not necessarily enrolled in) Medicare.[178] As such, anyone looking to purchase a QHP while they are Medicare eligible will find plans on the Exchange to be less affordable. Those who currently have a QHP will also find themselves losing any subsidies applied to their plan as soon as they become eligible for Medicare.[179] It is therefore

---

[175] Patient Protection and Affordable Care Act, 42 U.S.C. §§ 18001 *et seq.* (2010).

[176] 42 U.S.C. § 18021(a).

[177] CMS, "Frequently Asked Questions Regarding Medicare and the Marketplace (Question A6)," (Aug. 1, 2014), *available at* https://www.cms.gov/Medicare/Eligibility-and-Enrollment/Medicare-and-the-Marketplace/Downloads/Medicare-Marketplace_Master_FAQ_4-28-16_v2.pdf (site visited Aug. 6, 2018).

[178] CMS, "Frequently Asked Questions Regarding Medicare and the Marketplace (Question A6)."

[179] CMS, "Frequently Asked Questions Regarding Medicare and the Marketplace (Question A8)."

important for individuals to be aware of their Medicare eligibility date so to make the appropriate financial decisions when choosing coverage.

Medicare beneficiaries who qualify for premium-free Part A and choose to drop Medicare coverage in favor of a QHP will incur steep penalties for doing so. Not only will they be ineligible for QHP subsidies, but also they must stop collecting their retiree benefits (Social Security or railroad) and pay back all benefits they have already received.[180] Furthermore if they choose to enroll in Medicare again at a future date, they may have to pay penalties in the form of higher premiums for Part A and B proportionate to the length of time enrollment was deferred.[181] These individuals will also be limited to enroll during the general enrollment period and may experience a gap in coverage. These consequences often render the QHP plan option less financially viable than their current Medicare plan.

In theory, when someone becomes eligible for premium-free Part A Medicare, the premium subsidy they receive on their QHP should automatically terminate and change the price of their plan. CMS regulations require Exchanges to redetermine the eligibility of a QHP enrollee if it receives new information about the enrollee through periodic examination of data sources and records.[182] If one becomes eligible for Medicare while enrolled in a QHP, the Exchange system is required to periodically detect this, make any adjustments (e.g., remove subsidies if entitled to free Part A), and promptly notify the enrollee of changes.[183] CMS has clarified that in the initial stages of implementing this notice requirement, only those who are dually enrolled in both Medicare and a QHP will receive notices. Those who are only eligible for Medicare will not, for the time being, receive any type of notice that their QHP subsidies will be lost.[184] Therefore, consumers must be diligent in manually terminating their QHP plans promptly upon becoming eligible for premium-free Part A, or risk having to pay back taxes at the end of the year for the subsidies that they continued to receive.

[B] QHP Subsidies for Those Who Must Pay Premium for Part A

Individuals who must pay a premium for Part A coverage (a small minority of Medicare beneficiaries, including those qualify due to ESRD) are permitted to drop both their Part A and Part B coverage and purchase a plan on the Exchange

---

[180] CMS, "Frequently Asked Questions Regarding Medicare and the Marketplace (Question A6)."

[181] CMS, "Frequently Asked Questions Regarding Medicare and the Marketplace (Question A9)"

[182] 45 C.F.R. § 155.330(d)(1)(ii).

[183] 45 C.F.R. § 155.330(d)(1)(ii).

[184] *See* CMS, "Frequently Asked Questions Regarding Medicare and the Marketplace (Question A8)."

with tax subsidies.[185] Although QHPs will be more affordable for these individuals due to their potential qualification for subsidies, there are still potential repercussions to forgoing Medicare in the form of late enrollment penalties. Choosing to enroll in Medicare at a later date could result in higher premiums for Part A and B proportionate to the length of time enrollment is deferred. A gap in coverage may also occur given that these individuals will only be able to enroll during the general enrollment period. Finally, while the ACA placed underwriting restrictions on charging higher premiums based on preexisting health conditions, insurers are still able to discriminate based on age when they price plans.[186] Consequently, enrollees who are over 65 may find QHPs to be the more expensive option. These factors can disincentivize Medicare beneficiaries from dropping Medicare in favor of a private QHP, even if they have the benefit of subsidies on the Exchange.

Individuals with ESRD may also be eligible for Medicare coverage and are able to voluntarily enroll by paying a premium for Part A and Part B coverage.

[C] Simultaneous Medicare and QHP Coverage

Under section 1882(d) of the Social Security Act, it is unlawful to sell to an individual a plan that duplicates coverage that the individual already receives under their Medicare Part A or B plan.[187] This law, referred to as the "anti-duplication statute," remains applicable in the ACA Exchange context. Therefore, unless the Medicare beneficiary drops Medicare coverage, issuers offering plans on the Exchange may not lawfully sell the beneficiary a plan.

The Social Security Act's prohibition on duplication of coverage does not apply to those who are eligible for Medicare but have not yet enrolled (i.e., those who have turned 65 but are not yet collecting Social Security or railroad retirement benefits as well as those with disabilities or ESRD).[188] Thus, an individual may choose to purchase a QHP offered on the Exchange because he or she believes it offers a better value than Medicare.

---

[185] CMS, "Frequently Asked Questions Regarding Medicare and the Marketplace (Question A6)."

[186] 45 C.F.R. § 147.102.

[187] 42 U.S.C. § 1395ss(d)(3)(A)(III).

[188] CMS, "Frequently Asked Questions Regarding Medicare and the Marketplace (Question A14)."

CHAPTER 10

DUAL ELIGIBILITY: ISSUES FOR MEDICARE BENEFICIARIES ALSO ELIGIBLE FOR MEDICAID

§ 10.01 INTRODUCTION TO DUAL ELIGIBILTY

There were approximately 11.7 million older people and people with disabilities enrolled in both Medicare and some form of Medicaid in 2016,[1] These beneficiaries are referred to as "dual eligibles" because of their simultaneous enrollment in Medicare and Medicaid. Their demographic and health utilization characteristics distinguish them from other Medicare beneficiaries. Generally speaking, they are poorer and sicker than the rest of the Medicare population. They use the emergency room more often.[2, 3]

Between 2006 and 2016, the total number of Medicare-Medicaid beneficiaries increased by 35.6 percent, from 8.6 million to 11.7 million; in comparison, the number of Medicare-only beneficiaries grew by 29.7 percent, from 37.0 million to 48.1 million. Most of the growth among Medicare-Medicaid beneficiaries was attributable to partial-benefit Medicare-Medicaid beneficiaries, a subgroup that increased by 81.7 percent over these 11 years.[4]

For those eligible for Medicare Parts A and B and for full Medicaid benefits, Medicaid provides wrap-around coverage—operating as a Medigap policy—both by paying some, or all, of the Medicare cost-sharing, and by extending coverage to services not covered by Medicare. These services include non-skilled long-term care and, in some states, vision, dental, and hearing aid coverage. Medicare and Medicaid are programs with different medical necessity definitions, coverage definitions, provider participation requirements, and reimbursement structures.[5] Ironically, entitlement to the benefits of both Medicare and Medicaid can result in less, rather than more, health care. This is due at least in

---

[1] Medicare-Medicaid Coordination Office, Medicare-Medicaid Dual Enrollment from 2006 through 2016: Data Analysis Brief, *available at* https://www.cms.gov/Medicare-Medicaid-Coordination/Medicare-and-Medicaid-Coordination/Medicare-Medicaid-Coordination-Office/Data StatisticalResources/Downloads/Eleven-YearEver-EnrolledTrendsReport_2006-2016.pdf (site visited Aug. 6, 2018).

[2] Kaiser Family Foundation, "A Primer on Medicare: Key Facts About the Medicare Program and the People it Covers," (Mar. 20, 2015) *available at* https://www.kff.org/report-section/a-primer-on-medicare-what-is-medicare/ (site visited Aug. 6, 2018).

[3] The Congressional Budget Office (CBO), "Dual-Eligible Beneficiaries of Medicare and Medicaid: Characteristics, Health Care Spending, and Evolving Policies" (June 2013), p. 2, *available at* https://www.cbo.gov/sites/default/files/113th-congress-2013-2014/reports/44308_DualEligibles2.pdf (site visited Aug. 6, 2018) (hereinafter *CBO Dual-Eligible Beneficiaries*).

[4] Medicare-Medicaid Coordination Office, Medicare-Medicaid Dual Enrollment from 2006 through 2016: Data Analysis Brief.

[5] Medicare-Medicaid Coordination Office (MMCO), created by the Patient Protection and Affordable Care Act of 2010 (PPACA, or the Affordable Care Act (ACA)), Pub. L. No. 111-148, solicited comments on a document it created identifying various aspects of Medicare and Medicaid that are misaligned such that they cause difficulties for dual eligibles seeking health care. *See* CMS, Opportunities for Alignment in Medicaid and Medicare, 76 Fed. Reg. 94, pp. 28,196 *et seq.* (May 16, 2011). For more information on the Alignment Initiative, including comments on the MMCO

part to confusion that arises, in efforts to coordinate benefits, from statutory and regulatory differences between the two programs.

For those dually eligible who are entitled to full Medicaid benefits, Medicaid is the payer of last resort. Generally, in traditional Medicare, this means that Medicare determines the allowable amount, pays its portion, and then sends the remainder of the bill to Medicaid to pay the balance. However, when the Medicare allowable amount is either more or less than the Medicaid reimbursement for the same service, when the definition of the covered service differs, or when the Medicare beneficiary is enrolled in a private Medicare plan, administrative and other complications can result in the beneficiary's being denied access to care or delays in care.

Prior to January 1, 2006, when Part D took effect, Medicaid also provided prescription drug coverage for dual eligibles since, prior to that date, Medicare provided only very limited drug coverage. Effective January 1, 2006, dually eligible beneficiaries were no longer eligible for prescription drug coverage under Medicaid.[6] They are entitled to Medicare Part D prescription drug coverage and are automatically enrolled in a Part D plan if they do not choose a plan on their own.[7] This coverage change, including automatic qualification of the federal subsidy to help pay for prescription drug costs, is discussed in detail in **Chapter 11,** Prescription Drug Coverage.

The high utilization of health care by, and high levels of spending for, dual eligibles make that population a focus for policy discussion and policy initiatives. It is essential that any policy aimed at lowering costs to public programs in providing care to dual eligibles does not come with barriers to access or threats to quality of care. Many policymakers and researchers believe, with some justification, that the quality of care for those beneficiaries who are dually eligible can be improved by greater care coordination, reduction in duplication of tests, and improved medication management, all of which may result in reduced use of hospitals, emergency rooms, and nursing facilities.[8] The Affordable Care Act (ACA) created an Office for Dual Eligibles (formally called the Medicare and Medicaid Coordination Office) and the Center for Medicare and Medicaid Innovation, both

---

document, *see* https://www.cms.gov/Medicare-Medicaid-Coordination/Medicare-and-Medicaid-Coordination/Medicare-Medicaid-Coordination-Office/AlignmentInitiative/AlignmentInitiative.html (site visited Aug. 6, 2018).

[6] 42 U.S.C. § 1396u-5(d)(1).

[7] 42 U.S.C. § 1395w-101(b)(D).

[8] The Kaiser Family Foundation, "Best Bets for Reducing Medicare Costs for Dual Eligible Beneficiaries: Assessing the Evidence" (Oct. 31, 2012), *available at* http://kff.org/health-reform/report/best-bets-for-reducing-medicare-costs-for-duals/ (site visited Aug. 6, 2018); CMS, "Cost Drivers for Dually Eligible Beneficiaries: Potentially Avoidable Hospitalizations from Nursing Facility, Skilled Nursing Facility, and Home and Community-Based Services Waiver Programs" (Aug. 2010), *available at* https://www.cms.gov/Research-Statistics-Data-and-Systems/Statistics-Trends-and-Reports/Reports/downloads/costdriverstask2.pdf (site visited Aug. 6, 2018).

of which have focused considerable attention on this population in the past several years. As a result, in many states great changes are underway in the financing and delivery of care for people with Medicare and Medicaid. These changes are discussed in greater detail in **§ 10.09** of this chapter.

This chapter discusses and analyzes issues that affect dually eligible individuals. These issues continue to affect the population in states that are not creating new delivery systems, and some persist even in states with new programs.

In addition, this chapter includes descriptions of Medicaid eligibility and services as they pertain to Medicare beneficiaries.

§ 10.02 PROFILE OF THE DUALLY ELIGIBLE

[A] Demographic Data

Those dually eligible for Medicare and Medicaid are a heterogeneous population. However, some general comparisons with Medicare only beneficiaries are illustrative. In 2016, Medicare-Medicaid beneficiaries were more likely to be younger, female, and of race/ethnic minority status, compared to other Medicare beneficiaries.[9] Compared with other Medicare beneficiaries, dually eligible beneficiaries are more likely to need help with activities of daily living (ADL), have significantly worse self-reported health status, are more likely to have chronic or serious medical conditions, and are more likely to have cognitive impairments.[10]

§ 10.03 SUMMARY OF MEDICAID ELIGIBILITY AND MEDICAID BENEFITS

Unlike Medicare, Medicaid is a needs-based program, which means all those who receive benefits do so by virtue of having very low incomes or very high medical bills. The ACA substantially changed the structure of the Medicaid program.[11] To qualify for Medicaid prior to health reform, individuals had to meet

---

[9] Medicare-Medicaid Coordination Office, Medicare-Medicaid Dual Enrollment from 2006 through 2016: Data Analysis Brief.

[10] Kaiser Family Foundation, "Medicaid's Role for Medicare Beneficiaries," (Feb. 2017) *available at* http://files.kff.org/attachment/Issue-Brief-Medicaids-Role-for-Medicare-Beneficiaries (site visited Aug. 6, 2018).

[11] Although the law as it was passed by Congress mandated all states expand Medicaid to persons below 133 percent of poverty, the Supreme Court ruled in National Federation of Independent Business v. Sebelius, 576 U.S. 1 (2012), that mandatory Medicaid expansion was unconstitutionally coercive. As a result, states have the option to expand their Medicaid program to all persons under 133 percent of FPL. As of November 7, 2018, 37 States and the District of Columbia have adopted Medicaid expansion. Fourteen states have chosen not to expand Medicaid. Maine adopted the Medicaid expansion through a ballot initiative in November 2017; the ballot measure requires submission of a state plan amendment within 90 days and implementation of expansion within 180 days

financial eligibility criteria *and* belong to one of the following specific groups: children, parents, pregnant women, people with a severe disability, seniors, and people in institutions like nursing homes.[12] Additionally, states were required to provide Medicare cost-sharing coverage for poor Medicare beneficiaries called qualified Medicare beneficiaries (QMBs) and premium payments for near-poor Medicare beneficiaries called specified low-income Medicare beneficiaries (SLMBs),[13] qualified disabled and working individuals (QDWIs),[14] and qualified individuals (QIs) under their Medicaid programs.[15] Collectively, these programs are known as the Medicare Savings Programs (MSPs) (not to be confused with the same acronym for "Medicare Secondary Payer," discussed in **Chapter 9**).

For those under 65, non-disabled adults without dependent children were generally excluded from Medicaid unless the state obtained a waiver to cover them.[16] The ACA expanded Medicaid, in the states that have adopted Medicaid expansion,[17] to nearly all people between 19 and 65 who are not eligible for Medicare and have incomes at or below 133 percent of the federal poverty level (FPL).[18] For this "newly eligible" population, income eligibility is determined based on modified adjusted gross income (MAGI).[19] Reference to MAGI replaces the system of income exclusion and income disregards based on the SSI

---

of the measure's effective date. *See generally* Kaiser Family Foundation, "Status of State Action on the Medicaid Expansion Decision," *available at* http://kff.org/health-reform/state-indicator/state-activity-around-expanding-medicaid-under-the-affordable-care-act/ (site visited Aug. 6, 2018).

[12] ACA § 2001 (amending § 1902(a)(10(A)(i) of the Social Security Act); 42 U.S.C. § 1396a(a)(10)(A)(i).

[13] *See* **§ 10.04[B]** of this Handbook.

[14] *See* **§ 10.04[D][2]** of this Handbook.

[15] *See* **§ 10.04[D][1]** of this Handbook. For this group, coverage need only be provided up to the limit of the state's block grant. Authorization for the qualified individual (QI) program was made permanent in April 2015 through the Medicare Access and CHIP Reauthorization Act of 2015 (MACRA), Pub. L. No. 114-10 (Apr. 16, 2015).

[16] States generally pursued this Medicaid through the § 1115 waiver process; § 1115 of the Social Security Act, 42 U.S.C. § 1315.

[17] Kaiser Family Foundation, "Status of State Action on the Medicaid Expansion Decision." As of November 20, 2017, 33 states and the District of Columbia had adopted Medicaid expansion. Eighteen states have chosen *not* to expand Medicaid. Maine adopted the Medicaid expansion through a ballot initiative in November 2017; the ballot measure requires submission of a state plan amendment within 90 days and implementation of expansion within 180 days of the measure's effective date.

[18] Some sources state that the new minimum Medicaid eligibility threshold is 133 percent FPL; other sources state it is 138 percent. Both are correct. The text of the ACA, ACA § 2002, amending § 1902(e) of the Social Security Act (42 U.S.C. § 1396a(e)),says 133 percent, but the law also calls for a new methodology of calculating income, which makes the effective minimum threshold 138 percent.

[19] ACA § 2002 (amending § 1902(e) of the Social Security Act (42 U.S.C. § 1396a(e))).

program.[20] Moreover, no asset test is applied to this "newly eligible" adult population.[21]

Categories of eligibility that predated the ACA remain with the old eligibility rules. For people with Medicare, eligibility for Medicaid and the MSP will still adhere to the old, SSI-based income disregard and categorical eligibility system.[22] Income thresholds will continue to be very low (generally around 100 percent of FPL), and an asset test continues to be imposed. For individuals receiving expanded ACA Medicaid who become eligible for Medicare, transitions to Medicare with Medicaid for the aged, blind, and disabled or to Medicare with an MSP can prove problematic.

The disconnect in eligibility rules for those with Medicaid and Medicare, as opposed to those receiving expanded Medicaid, can have profound effects on individuals as they become eligible for Medicare. These individuals are subject to generally lower poverty levels against which their income is measured, to different ways of measuring the income, and to asset tests that otherwise do not apply in expanded Medicaid.[23]

Most Medicare beneficiaries who qualify for Medicaid will do so under pre-ACA aged, blind, and disabled categories. The broad category of aged, blind, and disabled can be further segmented into the following subgroups:

1. Individuals who receive SSI or a mandatory state supplement to SSI;[24]

---

[20] *Id.*

[21] *Id.*

[22] Kaiser Family Foundation, "Medicaid Financial Eligibility for Seniors and People with Disabilities in 2015" (Mar. 1, 2016), *available at* http://www.kff.org/report-section/medicaid-financial-eligibility-for-seniors-and-people-with-disabilities-in-2015-report/ (site visited Aug. 6, 2018). This methodology allows a disregard of $20 per month of income from any source, as well as a disregard of the first $65 per month of earned income, plus one-half the remainder. Other disregards are available for individuals with specific circumstances, such as amounts set aside in a plan for achieving self-support. Certain resources are excluded from consideration, including the homestead, personal possessions, a car, a burial plot, a separate burial fund, and a very limited amount of life insurance. States may use methodologies for determining Medicaid and MSP eligibility that are more generous than SSI's, but not less generous.

[23] *See* discussion at **§ 10.06[A]** of this Handbook. *See also* Ilene Stein & Joe Baker, "A Bridge to Health," The Medicare Rights Center (Jan. 2013), *available at* http://www.medicarerights.org/a-bridge-to-health (site visited Aug. 6, 2018). *See also* Kaiser Family Foundation, "AHIP Proposal: Achieving Medicare/Medicaid Integration for Dually Eligible Beneficiaries" (Oct. 2011), *available at* https://kaiserhealthnews.files.wordpress.com/2011/11/dual-eligibles-proposal.pdf (site visited Aug. 6, 2018); *CBO Dual-Eligible Beneficiaries.*

[24] 42 U.S.C. § 1396a(a)(10)(A)(i)(II); 42 U.S.C. § 1396a note referring to § 13(c) of Pub. L. No. 93-233. Individuals are entitled to a mandatory state supplement if they were receiving supplemental assistance from their state prior to the start of the federal Supplemental Security Income (SSI) program. The provision was intended to ensure that such individuals did not receive less assistance under SSI than they had previously received through their state program.

2. Individuals who formerly received SSI and are qualified severely impaired individuals, as defined by law, who qualify for SSI if their earnings are not counted;[25] and

3. Individuals who formerly received SSI and are in one of several categories of people deemed to receive SSI in order to ensure continued Medicaid coverage.[26]

Generally speaking, each of these three paths to Medicaid eligibility must be included in a state's Medicaid program; individuals in these categories are referred to as mandatory categorically eligible.[27] In addition, states have the option of choosing to cover other groups of aged, blind, or disabled individuals:

1. Individuals who are eligible for, but not receiving, SSI or an optional state supplement.[28]

---

[25] 42 U.S.C. § 1396d(q).

[26] These are "Pickle people," who have received SSI in the past and who would continue to be eligible for SSI but for cost-of-living increases in Title II in 1977 and thereafter, 42 U.S.C. § 1396a note; "Kennelly Widows," who are widows and widowers between age 60 and age 65 who lose SSI due to eligibility for early widows' benefits under the Social Security survivors program and are considered to be receiving SSI for Medicaid eligibility purposes until they are entitled to Medicare at age 65, 42 U.S.C. § 1383c(d); disabled adult children (DACs) who are individuals age 18 and over who had received SSI based on a disability that began before age 22 and who subsequently became eligible for children's benefits under Title II. They are deemed eligible for SSI for Medicaid purposes. 42 U.S.C. § 1383c(c). A fourth category of "deemed SSI recipients" are children who lost SSI due to a change in eligibility rules in the 1996 welfare law. These children are unlikely to be Medicare beneficiaries and therefore are unlikely to be dually eligible.

[27] The exception to coverage of these otherwise mandatory categories is for states that have chosen the so-called 209(b) option. This option, named for the section of the public law in which it was enacted, is set out at 42 U.S.C. § 1396a(f). It permits states to use more restrictive eligibility rules, if they expressly choose to do so. When Congress enacted the all-federal SSI program, replacing federal-state programs of aid to the aged, blind, and disabled, it provided states with an option to otherwise mandatory Medicaid coverage: they may establish eligibility standards in their Medicaid program that are more restrictive than SSI's, but no more restrictive than the eligibility rules that were in effect in the state in January 1972. Congress provided this option to encourage states that would have had dramatic increases in their Medicaid populations due to the higher SSI standards not to drop out of Medicaid altogether. Ten states currently use this option: Connecticut, Hawaii, Illinois, Minnesota, Missouri, New Hampshire, North Dakota, Ohio, Oklahoma, and Virginia. According to a 2016 Kaiser Family Foundation Report, two of these states (Connecticut and Ohio) use Section 209(b) to apply more restrictive income eligibility limits than the federal SSI rules, although Connecticut also uses a more generous income disregard than the federal SSI general income disregard ($337 vs. $20). Kaiser Family Foundation, "Medicaid Financial Eligibility for Seniors and People with Disabilities in 2015," *available at* http://kff.org/report-section/medicaid-financial-eligibility-for-seniors-and-people-with-disabilities-in-2015-report/ (site visited Aug. 6, 2018).

[28] 42 U.S.C. § 1396a(a)(10)(A)(ii)(I).

2. Individuals who have been in an institution for 30 days and who meet an income standard set by the state equal to or less than 300 percent of the SSI federal benefit rate.[29]

3. Individuals who receive home- and community-based services under a waiver of certain Medicaid requirements[30] or under a State Plan Amendment as authorized by the Deficit Reduction Act of 2005 (DRA).[31]

4. Individuals who would be eligible if they were in an institution, who are terminally ill, and who receive only hospice care.[32]

5. Individuals who receive an optional state supplement to SSI.[33]

6. Individuals who are aged or disabled with income under 100 percent of the FPL.[34]

7. Individuals who are aged, blind, or disabled and are "medically needy" due to high medical bills.[35] Individuals in this group must show incurred or paid medical expenses that, when deducted from their income, reduce their income to an amount called the medically needy income level (MNIL), which is often substantially below the SSI benefit rate.[36] The

---

[29] 42 U.S.C. § 1396a(a)(10)(A)(ii)(V). Identifying states that have chosen this option is more difficult than one would think. For reasons unfathomable to the authors, every reliable source of information on this subject lists the states somewhat differently. *See* "How Does Medicaid Treat Income," *available at* http://www.elderlawanswers.com/how-does-medicaid-treat-income-12017 (site visited Aug. 6, 2018). The harsh effect of an income cap that precludes eligibility of someone even one dollar above the cap has been mitigated by amendments to federal Medicaid law that allow individuals in states with the income cap category and no medically needy program to create a trust (known as a Miller Trust) for their excess income that allows that income to be excluded in determining Medicaid eligibility. *See* 42 U.S.C. § 1396p(d)(4)(B). For additional information, *see* Kaiser Family Foundation, "Medicaid Financial Eligibility: Primary Pathways for the Elderly and People with Disabilities," *available at* https://kaiserfamilyfoundation.files.wordpress.com/2013/01/8048.pdf (site visited Aug. 6, 2018). According to the website, states with no medically needy program are Alabama, Alaska, Colorado, Delaware, Idaho, Indiana, Mississippi, Missouri, Nevada, New Mexico, Ohio, Oklahoma, Oregon, South Carolina, South Dakota, Texas, and Wyoming. Arizona has a program that is comparable to the medically needy program.

[30] 42 U.S.C. § 1396a(a)(10)(A)(ii)(VI).

[31] The Deficit Reduction Act of 2005 (DRA), Pub. L. No. 109-171 (Feb. 8, 2006), § 6086 (amending 42 U.S.C. § 1396n by adding subsection (i)).

[32] 42 U.S.C. § 1396a(a)(10)(A)(ii)(VII).

[33] 42 U.S.C. § 1396a(a)(10)(A)(ii)(XI).

[34] 42 U.S.C. § 1396a(a)(10)(A)(ii)(X), referring to § 1396a(m)(1).

[35] 42 U.S.C. § 1396a(a)(10)(C), referring to 42 U.S.C. § 1396d(a).

[36] The medically needy income level (MNIL) has been limited for years by statutory language that prohibits federal Medicaid payments for people with incomes in excess of 133 1/3 percent of the state's standard for a family receiving Aid to Families with Dependent Children (AFDC). 42 U.S.C. § 1396b(f). This standard, in most states, was substantially below federal poverty levels and even below the SSI level, which is 75 percent of the poverty level. Although AFDC was repealed in 1996 and replaced with a block grant called Temporary Assistance for Needy Families, the old

amount of incurred or paid medical expense they must document is referred to as their "spend-down."

Individuals in groups 1 through 6 are referred to as the Optional Categorically Needy; individuals in group 7 are referred to as the Medically Needy.

States are required to provide certain services to the Mandatory and Optional Categorically Needy and have the option of including other services. Required Medicaid services are:

- Inpatient hospital services;
- Outpatient hospital services;
- Laboratory and x-ray services;
- Nursing facility services for people age 21 or over;
- Early and periodic screening, diagnosis, and treatment for people under 21;
- Family planning services and supplies for individuals of child-bearing age;
- Physicians' services and some dental services;
- Midwife services;
- Services furnished by certain certified nurse practitioners; and
- Home health services for people entitled to nursing facility services.[37]

Optional services include:

- Physical therapy;
- Occupational therapy;
- Dentures;
- Prosthetic devices;
- Eyeglasses;
- Personal care;

AFDC standard, indexed for inflation, is still used. A separate statutory provision, at 42 U.S.C. § 1396a(r)(2), permits states to use methodologies for determining eligibility for Medicaid that are less restrictive than the income program they relate to, but not more restrictive. The Health Care Financing Administration (HCFA), then the name of the federal agency that administers Medicare and Medicaid (now CMS), interpreted that provision as being circumscribed by the payment limit provision. An amendment to the regulation at 42 C.F.R. § 435.1007 that became effective August 4, 2001, changes that interpretation to allow states to apply their less restrictive methodologies to income *before* measuring it against the payment limit. 66 Fed. Reg. 33,810 (June 25, 2001).

[37] 42 U.S.C. § 1396d(a)(xvii)(1-29).

- Home and community-based attendant services and supports (effective October 1, 2011);[38]
- Podiatry;
- Optometry;
- Transportation; and
- Long-term care support and services provided under a home and community-based services waiver or, with limitations, as an optional service.

Generally speaking, when a state offers an optional service to one group of Optional Categorically Needy individuals, it must offer the same service to all groups.[39] The state does not have to offer all services to the Medically Needy.

Because Medicare is the primary payer for those who are dually eligible, some Medicaid services are more important to these beneficiaries than others. For example, a significant Medicaid service for this population is non-skilled long-term care, both in an institution and in the community. It is, therefore, extremely useful to low-income Medicare beneficiaries to qualify for full Medicaid benefits in addition to assistance with Medicare cost-sharing.

§ 10.04 UNIVERSE OF DUAL ELIGIBILITY

[A] Categories of Dually Eligible Individuals[40]

The term "dually eligible" is used differently depending on the setting or situation. Dual eligibles comprise three primary subgroups of low-income Medicare beneficiaries:

1. QMBs or SLMBs with full Medicaid benefits and all or some Medicare cost-sharing (QMB-plus or SLMB-plus) or QMBs or SLMBs with all or some Medicare cost-sharing assistance but without any additional Medicaid coverage (QMB-only or SLMB-only);

---

[38] Section 2401 of the ACA (amending § 1915 of the Social Security Act (42 U.S.C. 1396n)), as amended by Health Care and Education Reconciliation Act of 2010 (HCERA), Pub. L. No. 111-152 (Mar. 30, 2010), § 1205.

[39] 42 U.S.C. § 1396a(a)(10)(B)(i) (services shall be not less in amount, duration, and scope than those available to other categorically needy groups); 42 C.F.R. § 440.240(b). *But see* DRA § 6044 that allows states to establish specific benefit packages for specific groups of people. Dual eligibles are exempt from coverage under this new option.

[40] For CMS's descriptions of dual eligible categories, *see* CMS, Dual Eligible Beneficiaries Under Medicare & Medicaid, *available at* http://www.cms.gov/MLNProducts/downloads/Medicare_Beneficiaries_Dual_Eligibles_At_a_Glance.pdf (site visited Aug. 6, 2018).

2. Individuals with full Medicaid benefits but not Medicare cost-sharing as QMBs or SLMBs;
3. Individuals entitled to Medicaid benefits only to pay for Medicare premiums, with no additional Medicaid coverage for other Medicare out-of-pocket costs, and without full Medicaid benefits. This category comprises two groups, in addition to the SLMB-only named above:
   a. QIs[41]
   b. QDWIs[42]

It is useful to understand that the Medicare Prescription Drug, Improvement, and Modernization Act of 2003 (MMA)[43] uses a different nomenclature for dual eligibles. It refers to "full benefit dual eligibles" and defines those people as Medicare beneficiaries entitled to full Medicaid benefits.[44] This definition excludes those in group 3 above, as well as those in group 1 who receive assistance only with Medicare cost-sharing. In this chapter, we will clearly label the groups or subgroups to which we are referring in the various sections.

[B] QMB or SLMB with Full Medicaid Benefits and Medicare Cost-Sharing (QMB/SLMB-Plus) or with Only Medicare Cost-Sharing Assistance (QMB/SLMB-Only)

For 2019, a QMB is an aged or disabled individual with Medicare Part A, whose countable income is at or below the federal poverty level and whose countable resources do not exceed $7,560 for one person and $11,340 for a married couple.[45] The QMB benefit relieves the beneficiary of the cost-sharing that is otherwise imposed on a Medicare beneficiary: the Medicare Part B premium, the Part

---

[41] *See* **§ 10.04[D][1]** of this Handbook. For this group, coverage need only be provided up to the limit of the state's block grant. MACRA makes the QI program permanent, rather than subject to periodic reauthorization tied to Medicare physician payment, as was the case for many years.

[42] QDWI enrollment was estimated to be fewer than 100 beneficiaries as of 2011. Medicaid and CHIP Payment and Access Commission (MACPAC), Report to the Congress on Medicaid and CHIP: Ch. 4, (Mar. 2013), *available at* https://www.macpac.gov/wp-content/uploads/2015/01/2013-03-15_MACPAC_Report.pdf (site visited Aug. 6, 2018) (hereinafter *March 2013 MACPAC Report*).

[43] The Medicare Prescription Drug, Improvement, and Modernization Act of 2003 (MMA), Pub. L. No. 108-173 (Dec. 8, 2003) (adding 42 U.S.C. § 1395w-101 *et seq.*) (2008 supplement).

[44] 42 U.S.C. § 1396u-5(c)(6); 42 C.F.R. § 423.902.

[45] The income eligibility level for 2018 is $1,032 per month for an individual in the 48 states and slightly higher for those in Alaska and Hawaii. The amount includes a $20-per-month federally mandated income disregard that is available to all applicants. In addition to the $20, states must disregard a portion of earned income and may disregard other income, effectively expanding coverage. Likewise, they may offer more generous resource exclusions than federal law requires. About 40 states have some provision for MSP populations that is more generous than the federal rules. Income

A premium for voluntary enrollees (i.e., those who do not receive premium-free Part A), and all deductibles and coinsurance imposed under Medicare Part A and Medicare Part B and copayments or other cost-sharing charged by Medicare Advantage (MA) plans. Numerous CMS transmittals over the past 10 years have affirmed this protection.[46] A provider is prohibited from billing a QMB for Medicare Part A or B deductibles or coinsurance.[47] States have the option of paying premiums or enrollment fees charged by MA plans.[48] In essence, the QMB benefit operates like a basic Medicare supplemental health insurance policy (often called a "Medigap" policy). QMB coverage can save a recipient hundreds or even thousands of dollars each year.[49] Moreover, since all forms of dual eligibility,

---

Poverty Guidelines are published each year between January and March by the Department of Health and Human Services (HHS). The asset test for QMB, SLMB, and QI was changed, effective 2010, to conform to the asset test for Part D full low-income subsidy, *see* 42 U.S.C. § 1395w-114(a)(3)(D). MIPPA § 112.

Please check the Medicare.gov site periodically for 2019 updates.

[46] 42 U.S.C. § 1396d(p)(3), 1396a(n)(2); CMS, State Medicaid (SM) Manual, Pub. 45, Ch. 3: Eligibility § 3490.12, *see* **Appendix 10-1** of this Handbook. *See also* CMS, MMCO-CMCS Informational Bulletin: Payment of Medicare Cost Sharing for Qualified Medicare Beneficiaries (QMBs) (June 7, 2013), *available at* http://www.medicaid.gov/Federal-Policy-Guidance/downloads/CIB-06-07-2013.pdf (site visited Aug. 6, 2018); CMS, MMCO-CMCS Informational Bulletin: Billing for Services Provided to Qualified Medicare Beneficiaries (QMBs) (Jan. 6, 2012), *available at* http://www.medicaid.gov/federal-policy-guidance/downloads/CIB-01-06-12.pdf (site visited Aug. 6, 2018); CMS, MLN Number SE1128 Revised, Prohibition on Balance Billing Qualified Medicare Beneficiaries (QMBs), *available at* http://www.cms.gov/Outreach-and-Education/Medicare-Learning-Network-MLN/MLNMattersArticles/downloads/SE1128.pdf (site visited Aug. 6, 2018); Memorandum of Feb. 27, 2008 from Gale P. Arden, Director, Disabled and Elderly Health Programs Group (DEHPG) to All Associate Regional Administrators, Division of Medicaid and Children's Health, Subject: Medicare Cost Sharing for Medicaid Beneficiaries (hereinafter *Feb. 2008 Memo*) and two attachments, memo *available at* http://www.medicareadvocacy.org/old-site/InfoByTopic/MedicareSavingsPrograms/MedSavProg_08_04.24.ARACostShare.pdf, Balance Billing attachment *available at* http://www.medicareadvocacy.org/old-site/InfoByTopic/MedicareSavingsPrograms/MedSavProg_08_04.24.ARABalanceBilling.pdf, and Capitation attachment *available at* http://www.medicareadvocacy.org/old-site/InfoByTopic/MedicareSavingsPrograms/MedSavProg_08_04.24.ARACapitation.pdf (sites visited Apr. 12, 2017); Memorandum of Nov. 22, 1991, from Director, Office of Medicaid Management, MB, to Deputy Chief Counsel, Office of General Counsel, Subject: State Requirement to Pay Premiums for Qualified Medicare Beneficiaries (QMB)—ACTION (hereinafter *Nov. 1991 Memo*) (**Appendix 10-2**); Memorandum of June 11, 2007, "Cost Sharing for Medicare Advantage Plans," CMS/CMSO/DEHPG/DEEO and Attachment (hereinafter *June 2007 Memo*) (**Appendix 10-3** of this Handbook); and Memorandum of Jan. 6, 2012, from Director, MMCO-CMCS Informational Bulletin Concerning Billing for Services Provided to Qualitied Medicare Beneficiaries (QMBs) (hereinafter January 6, 2012 Memo) (**Appendix 10-4** of this Handbook).

[47] *See* discussion at **§ 10.06[B]** of this Handbook.

[48] 42 U.S.C. §§ 1396d(p)(3) and 1396a(n)(2); SM Manual, Ch. 3.

[49] Out-of-pocket costs for 2013 averaged $3,020 per Medicare-only beneficiary (without supplemental coverage) who reported fair to poor health. *MedPAC June 2017 Data Book*, at 34, *available at* http://www.medpac.gov/docs/default-source/data-book/jun17_databookentirereport_sec.pdf?sfvrsn=0 (site visited Aug. 6, 2018). Because dual eligibles are three times more likely than non-dual

including receipt of only an MSP, entitle one to the full Part D low income subsidy (LIS), the value of the benefit is increased by the value of the LIS, estimated by the Social Security Administration (SSA) to be $1,234 in 2018.[50] Unlike virtually all other Medicaid benefits, QMB coverage cannot be granted for months prior to the application.[51] The benefit is available in the first month after the month eligibility is determined.[52] An individual can be eligible for both the QMB benefit and full Medicaid coverage, or for only the QMB benefit.[53] Eighty percent of QMBs qualify for full Medicaid benefits in addition to QMB (QMB-plus).[54]

A SLMB is an individual who would be a QMB but for his or her countable income, which must be between 100 and 120 percent of the federal poverty level.[55] The SLMB benefit is payment by Medicaid of the Medicare Part B premium. Thus, a SLMB does not have the Medicare Part B premium ($134.00 in 2018 for most people) deducted from his or her Social Security or Railroad Retirement check each month. However, unlike the QMB benefit, no additional Medicare cost-sharing is included in the SLMB benefit. A SLMB without full Medicaid coverage should consider the need for a Medicare supplemental (Medigap) policy to cover the costs of other Medicare out-of-pocket expenses, such as copayments and deductibles. SLMB coverage can be granted for up to three months prior to the date of application if the individual was eligible during those months.[56] An individual could be eligible for both SLMB benefits and full Medicaid benefits or for only SLMB benefits.[57]

Medicare beneficiaries to report poor health, this number seems like a reasonable proxy for what can be saved by having access to the QMB benefit.

[50] Social Security Administration (SSA), "Extra Help with Medicare Prescription Drug Plan Costs," *available at* http://www.ssa.gov/prescriptionhelp/ (site visited Aug. 6, 2018). Please check the ssa.gov site periodically for 2019 updates.

[51] 42 U.S.C. § 1396d(a).

[52] 42 U.S.C. § 1396d(a).

[53] CMS, Dual Eligible Beneficiaries Under Medicare & Medicaid (Feb. 2017), *available at* https://www.cms.gov/Outreach-and-Education/Medicare-Learning-Network-MLN/MLNProducts/downloads/Medicare_Beneficiaries_Dual_Eligibles_At_a_Glance.pdf (site visited Aug. 6, 2018).

[54] *March 2013 MACPAC Report*, at 134.

[55] 42 U.S.C. § 1396a(a)(10)(E)(iii). The income eligibility limit for SLMB for 2018 was $1,234 per month for an individual in the 48 states, slightly higher for Alaska and Hawaii. This amount includes the $20 income disregard. For updated information, *see* CMS, "Medicare Savings Programs," *available at* http://www.medicare.gov/your-medicare-costs/help-paying-costs/medicare-savings-program/medicare-savings-programs.html#slmb (site visited Aug. 6, 2018).

[56] 42 U.S.C. § 1396d(a).

[57] CMS, Dual Eligible Beneficiaries Under Medicare & Medicaid (Feb. 2017).

[C] Recipients of Full Medicaid Benefits but Not Full Medicare Cost-Sharing as a QMB

These individuals receive Medicare Part A and/or Medicare Part B, and receive full Medicaid benefits. The group comprises two slightly different populations. First, there are those whose incomes are under 100 percent of the FPL but who do not have Part A premium-free and whose state does not pay their Part A premium for them. The lack of Part A prevents them from being QMBs and thus entitled to full Medicare benefits, which may include better hospitalization, home health, or rehabilitation therapy coverage than they have under their state Medicaid program. The Centers for Medicare & Medicaid Services (CMS) has told states they must purchase Part A for their Medicaid recipients whose income is under 100 percent of the FPL to ensure their enrollment as QMBs.[58] CMS has not, however, enforced this requirement.

The second group comprises those whose income is above 100 percent of the FPL who are precluded from QMB coverage for that reason, even if they have Medicare Part A. Generally, these would be individuals entitled to Medicaid under a special income cap, or as medically needy because they are receiving costly long-term care services. If they are not entitled to payment of their Medicare Part B premium as SLMBs, the state nonetheless has the option of paying their Part B premium.[59] If the state chooses not to pay the Part B premium, it cannot receive its federal share of the Medicaid payment for a Medicaid service that is also covered by Medicare Part B if the individual could have been enrolled in Part B but was not.[60]

[D] Recipients of Medicaid Payments for Medicare Premiums Only

In addition to individuals with SLMB-only eligibility who are entitled to payment only of the Medicare Part B premium, two other groups are entitled to Medicaid payments only for Medicare premiums. To be eligible for either of these benefits, an individual cannot be eligible for full Medicaid benefits.

---

[58] SM Manual, Ch. 3: § 3490.13. *See* **Appendix 10-1** of this Handbook. *See also* Nov. 1991 Memo (**Appendix 10-2** of this Handbook).

[59] 42 U.S.C. § 1395v authorizes states to enter into "buy-in" agreements with the federal CMS through which states purchase Medicare Part B coverage for Medicaid recipients; 42 U.S.C. § 1395i-2(g) authorizes modifications of such agreements to permit the states also to purchase Part A. *See* 42 C.F.R. § 407.42 for the eligibility groups that states can include in their buy-in agreements and 42 C.F.R. § 431.625 for authorization for states to receive federal matching dollars, known as federal financial participation (FFP) for their buy-in costs.

[60] 42 U.S.C. § 1396b(b)(1), 42 C.F.R. § 431.625(d)(3).

[1] Qualified Individual

This group comprises individuals with Medicare Part A whose countable income is between 120 percent and 135 percent of poverty and whose countable resources are $7,560 for an individual and $11,340 for a couple in 2018.[61] The benefit for a QI is payment of the Part B premium ($135.50/month in 2019 for most people). Payment is made from a block grant to the state that was authorized to be available from January 1998 through December 2002.[62] After a series of short-term extensions, the benefit was permanently extended in April 2015 through the Medicare Access and CHIP Reauthorization Act of 2015 (MACRA).[63]

Although the QI benefit is the same amount as the SLMB benefit, the difference between the two programs, in addition to the higher income eligibility threshold for QI, is that SLMB is an entitlement for the individual and QI is not. Thus, all individuals who are found eligible for SLMB will receive the benefit; individuals found eligible for QI will receive the benefit only as long as the state still has funds in its block grant. States must pay the benefit on a first-come, first-served basis. While individuals must reapply each year, priority is given to those who received the benefit in the previous year.[64] Recipients are entitled to three months retroactive coverage if they were eligible in the three months prior to their application.[65]

[2] Qualified Disabled and Working Individual

A QDWI is an individual who is disabled and working under a work incentive plan, who has exhausted premium-free Part A coverage (available for a period of eight and one-half years, including a trial work period) under such plan, whose

---

[61] 42 U.S.C. § 1396a(a)(10)(E)(iv). Dep't of Health & Human Servs. (HHS), The 2018 Federal Poverty Guidelines, 83 Fed. Reg. 2642 (Jan. 18, 2018), *available at* https://aspe.hhs.gov/poverty-guidelines (site visited Aug. 6, 2018).

[62] 42 U.S.C. § 1396u-3. *See* https://www.cms.gov/newsroom/fact-sheets/2019-medicare-parts-b-premiums-and-deductibles.

[63] Pub. L. No. 114-10 (Apr. 16, 2015). HHS issued Notice of Proposed Rulemaking on May 9, 2016, as a first step in implementing certain provisions of MACRA. The proposed rule implements changes through a framework called the Quality Payment Program, which includes two paths: the Merit-based Incentive Payment System (MIPS), and Advanced Alternative Payment Models (APMs). The comment period ended on June 27, 2016. Final regulations were published in the *Federal Register* on November 4, 2016. CMS, Merit-Based Incentive Payment System (MIPS) and Alternative Payment Model (APM) Incentive Under the Physician Fee Schedule, and Criteria for Physician-Focused Payment Models, 81 Fed. Reg. 77,008, *available at* https://www.federalregister.gov/documents/2016/11/04/2016-25240/medicare-program-merit-based-incentive-payment-system-mips-and-alternative-payment-model-apm (site visited Aug. 6, 2018).

[64] 42 U.S.C. § 1396u-3(b)(2)(B).

[65] 42 U.S.C. § 1396d.

countable income is not more than 200 percent of poverty, and whose countable resources are not more than twice those allowed for SSI.[66] Resource limits for the program are $4,000 for one person and $6,000 for a married couple. The benefit for a QDWI is payment for the Medicare Part A premium, not the Part B premium. (A QDWI wanting Part B would have to pay for it him- or herself.) Like the QMB and SLMB benefit, the QDWI benefit is an entitlement, so that anyone found eligible should get the benefit. Like SLMB and QI, QDWI is available up to three months prior to application if the individual was eligible during those months. The QDWI benefit is rarely used. Although it is one of the MSPs, citations to MSPs often refer only to QMB, SLMB, and QI. These three programs are the programs that provide automatic enrollment into the Part D Low-Income Subsidy.

LOW INCOME ASSISTANCE*

Program	Income (FPL)	Assets	Benefit
QMB	Up to 100%	$7,560/$11,340	Part A and B premiums, deductibles; cost-sharing
SLMB	Up to 120%	$7,560/$11,340	Part B premium
QI	Up to 135%	$7,560/$11,340	Part B premium
QDWI	Up to 200%	$4,000/$6,000	Part A premium
LIS/Extra Help	Sliding scale up to 150%	$14,100/$28,150 (updated annually)	Most or all of Part D premium; most drug cost-sharing

* CMS, Medicare Savings Program, *available at* https://www.medicare.gov/your-medicare-costs/get-help-paying-costs/medicare-savings-programs#slmb (site visited July 24, 2017).

§ 10.05 ENROLLMENT ISSUES FOR MEDICARE SAVINGS PROGRAMS POPULATION

[A] Overview

MSPs—QMB, SLMB, QI, and QDWI—that pay all or some of the Medicare out-of-pocket costs provide critical links to the health care system for low-income Medicare beneficiaries. Yet, an estimated 67 percent of those eligible for QMB-only benefits and about 87 percent of those eligible for SLMB benefits are not participating in the programs.[67] A 2010 study estimated that 15 percent of

[66] 42 U.S.C. §§ 1396a(a)(10)(E)(ii) & 1396d(s). HHS, The 2018 Federal Poverty Guidelines, 83 Fed. Reg. 2642.

[67] CBO, "A Detailed Description of CBO's Cost Estimate for the Medicare Prescription Drug Benefit" (July 2004), *available at* http://www.cbo.gov/sites/default/files/cbofiles/ftpdocs/56xx/doc

eligible beneficiaries were enrolled in QI.[68] Barriers to program participation have been exhaustively identified in numerous reports that also include policy and practice recommendations.[69] These barriers to enrollment include:

5668/07-21-medicare.pdf (site visited Aug. 6, 2018). According to a 2013 GAO report and a 2013 MACPAC report, these 2004 numbers are the most recent available.

[68] MACPAC, "Medicare Savings Programs: New Estimates Continue to Show Many Eligible Individuals Not Enrolled" (Aug. 2017), *available at* https://www.macpac.gov/wp-content/uploads/2017/08/Medicare-Savings-Programs-New-Estimates-Continue-to-Show-Many-Eligible-Individuals-Not-Enrolled.pdf (site visited Aug. 6, 2018).

[69] Medicare Rights Center, "Streamlining Medicare and QMB Enrollment for New Yorkers: Medicare Part A Buy-in Analysis and Policy Recommendations" (Feb. 2011), *available at* http://www.medicarerights.org/pdf/Part-A-Buy-In-Analysis.pdf (site visited Oct. 15, 2018); National Center for Benefits Outreach and Enrollment, "Express Lane Eligibility: New Strategies for Increasing Enrollment," Issue Brief (June 2009), *available at* http://www.ncoa.org/assets/files/pdf/center-for-benefits/express-lane-eligibility.pdf (site visited Oct. 15, 2018); Robert Wood Johnson Foundation, "State Solutions: An Initiative to Improve Enrollment in Medicare Savings Programs" (Oct. 2009), *available at* http://www.rwjf.org/en/research-publications/find-rwjf-research/2009/10/state-solutions.html (site visited Oct. 15, 2018); MedPAC, "Report to the Congress: Medicare Payment Policy," Ch. 5, (Mar. 2008), *available at* http://www.medpac.gov/docs/default-source/reports/Mar08_Entire Report.pdf (site visited Oct. 15, 2018) (hereinafter *MedPAC Report March 2008*); Jack Ebeler, Paul N. Van de Water, & Cyanne Demchak (eds.), "Improving the Medicare Savings Programs" (2006), National Academy of Social Insurance, *available at* http://www.nasi.org/usr_doc/Improving_the_Medicare_Savings_Programs.pdf (site visited Oct. 15, 2018); P.B. Nemore, J.A. Bender, & W. Kwok, "Toward Making Medicare Work for Low-Income Beneficiaries: A Baseline Comparison of the Part D Low-Income Subsidy and Medicare Savings Programs Eligibility and Enrollment Rules" prepared for the Henry J. Kaiser Family Foundation (Apr. 2006), *available at* https://kaiserfamilyfoundation.files.wordpress.com/2013/01/7519.pdf (site visited Oct. 15, 2018); Laura L. Summer & Emily S. Ihara, "Simplifying Enrollment in Medicaid and Medicare Savings Programs for the Elderly and Individuals with Disabilities" (Dec. 2005), Georgetown University Health Policy Institute, *available at* http://assets.aarp.org/rgcenter/health/2005_10_medicaid_msp.pdf (site visited Oct. 15, 2018); Alex D. Federman, Bruce C. Vladeck, & Albert L. Siu, "Avoidance of Health Care Services Because of Cost: Impact of the Medicare Savings Program," *Health Affairs* 24(1):263-270 (2005), *available at* http://content.healthaffairs.org/cgi/content/abstract/24/1/263 (site visited Oct. 15, 2018); Amy M. Tiedemann & Kimberley Fox, "Promising Strategies for Medicare Savings Program Enrollment: Modifying Eligibility Criteria and Documentation Requirements," prepared for the State Solutions Project (Dec. 2004), *available at* http://www.cshp.rutgers.edu/Downloads/5300.pdf (site visited Oct. 15, 2018); L. Sue Andersen & William F. Benson, "Medicare Savings Programs Outreach in Housing for Elders," prepared for the State Solutions Project (Sept. 2004); GAO, "Medicare Savings Programs: Results of Social Security Administration's 2002 Outreach to Low-Income Beneficiaries," GAO-04-363 (Mar. 2004), *available at* http://www.gao.gov/new.items/d04363.pdf (site visited Oct. 15, 2018); GAO-12-871 (Sept. 2012), *available at* http://www.gao.gov/assets/650/648370.pdf (site visited Oct. 15, 2018); Dalia K. Remler & Sherry A. Glied, *What Other Programs Can Teach Us: Increasing Participation in Health Insurance Programs*, Am. J. Pub. Health (Jan. 2003), *available at* http://www.ajph.org/cgi/reprint/93/1/67.pdf (site visited Oct. 15, 2018); Susan G. Haber et al., "Evaluation of Qualified Medicare Beneficiary (QMB) and Specified Low-Income Medicare Beneficiary (SLMB) Programs" (Oct. 2003), RTI International, *available at* https://www.cms.gov/Research-Statistics-Data-and-Systems/Statistics-Trends-and-Reports/Reports/Downloads/HaberVol1.pdf (site visited Oct. 15, 2018); Kim Glaun, "Medicaid Programs to Assist Low-Income Medicare Beneficiaries: Medicare Savings Programs Case Study Findings," prepared

- Restrictive asset ceilings used in determining eligibility;
- Lack of effective outreach to program beneficiaries;
- Lack of knowledge of the programs on the part of welfare workers, Social Security employees, and community-based organizations;
- Cumbersome and obstacle-laden enrollment processes that require long waits in welfare offices, face-to-face interviews, and extensive documentation of income and assets; and
- Difficulties with language and transportation.

Some of these problems arise because MSP benefits are disconnected from the Medicare program: instead of applying for Medicare and MSP at the same time and place, an individual must go through the SSA for Medicare, and through

for the KCMU (2002), *available at* https://kaiserfamilyfoundation.files.wordpress.com/2013/01/medicaid-programs-to-assist-low-income-medicare-beneficiaries-medicare-savings-programs-case-study-findings-background-paper.pdf (site visited Oct. 15, 2018); Laura Summer & Robert Friedland, "The Role of the Asset Test in Targeting Benefits for Medicare Savings Programs" (Oct. 2002), Center on an Aging Society, Georgetown University, *available at* http://ihcrp.georgetown.edu/agingsociety/pdfs/summer_assettest_579.pdf (site visited Oct. 15, 2018); Jennifer Weiss, Joe Baker, & Diane Archer, "An Investigative Report on Medicare Savings Programs in New York City: Local Involvement in Federal Programs Impedes Access for People with Low Incomes" (Dec. 2001), Medicare Rights Center, *available at* http://www.medicarerights.org/pdf/Investigative_Report_MSPinNYC.pdf (site visited Oct. 15, 2018); CME, "Increasing Enrollment for the Medicare Savings Programs," Vol. 2, No. 7 (2001), *available at* http://ihcrp.georgetown.edu/agingsociety/pdfs/MedicareSavings.pdf (site visited Oct. 15, 2018); Patricia B. Nemore, "Variations in State Medicaid Buy-in Practices for Low-Income Medicare Beneficiaries: A 1999 Update," (Dec. 1999), Kaiser Family Foundation, available upon request from the Center for Medicare Advocacy (hereinafter *Variations in State Medicaid*); GAO, "Low-Income Medicare Beneficiaries: Further Outreach and Administrative Simplification Could Increase Enrollment," GAO/HEHS-99-61 (Apr. 1999), *available at* http://www.gao.gov/archive/1999/he99061.pdf (site visited Oct. 15, 2018); Margo L. Rosenbach & JoAnn Lamphere, *Bridging the Gaps Between Medicare and Medicaid: The Case of QMBs and SLMBs*, AARP Pub. Pol'y Inst. (Jan. 1999), *available at* http://assets.aarp.org/rgcenter/health/9902_qmbs.pdf (site visited Oct. 15, 2018); Families USA, "Shortchanged: Billions Withheld from Medicare Beneficiaries" (1998), *available at* http://research.policyarchive.org/6354.pdf (site visited Oct. 15, 2018); Patricia B. Nemore, "Variations in State Medicaid Buy-In Practices for Low-Income Medicare Beneficiaries" (Nov. 1997), Kaiser Family Foundation (available for copying from the authors); Peter J. Neumann et al., "Identifying Barriers to Elderly Participation in the Qualified Medicare Beneficiary Program," Final Report submitted to HCFA (1994); GAO, "Medicare and Medicaid—Many Eligible People Not Enrolled in Qualified Medicare Beneficiary Program," GAO/HEHS-94-52 (Jan. 1994), *available at* http://archive.gao.gov/t2pbat4/150626.pdf (site visited Oct. 15, 2018); Families USA, "The Medicare Buy-In: A Promise Unfulfilled" (Mar. 1993); Families USA, "The Medicare Buy-In: Still a Government Secret" (Mar. 1992); Families USA, "The Secret Benefit—The Failure to Provide the Medicare Buy-In to Poor Seniors" (1991) (Families USA reports available for copying from the authors).

the state Medicaid or welfare system for MSP benefits.[70] Other issues arise because MSP benefits are needs-based, requiring people both to disclose information about their income and assets, and to provide documentation to support their disclosures. One barrier was eliminated beginning in 2010: Medicaid estate recovery rules no longer apply to MSP benefits.[71] A second barrier, the application disconnect described above, was addressed in part through a provision in the Medicare Improvements for Patients and Providers Act of 2008 (MIPPA). That provision and several other of the more complex issues are discussed below.

[B] Failure of State Medicaid Systems and Workers to Identify Buy-In Eligibility When Processing Medicaid Applications

State Medicaid agencies are required to operate their programs in a manner consistent with simplicity of administration and in the best interests of recipients.[72] The agency, moreover, must consider the applicant's eligibility for *any* program for which he or she qualifies.[73] Yet, eligibility workers are often unfamiliar with the MSPs, and state Medicaid agencies have failed to institute computer prompts during screening. Because each state's Medicaid program has many paths to eligibility, it is difficult, if not impossible, for an applicant to identify with precision the particular coverage group for which he or she is applying, or should be applying. The applicant is unlikely to ask explicitly to be considered for full Medicaid, for QMB, for SLMB, or for QI, although in some states, the applicant must check off on the application all Medicaid categories for which he or she wishes to be considered. An additional complexity is that an individual can receive both full Medicaid and QMB or SLMB benefits.

Being screened for all possible categories of eligibility is essential for applicants to be considered for each one. However, if eligibility determination systems are not fully coordinated with applicants screened for eligibility for all programs, they may be erroneously denied benefits. Another potential MSP eligibility issue

---

[70] The Medicare, Medicaid, and SCHIP Benefits Improvement and Protection Act of 2000 (BIPA), Pub. L. No. 106-554 (Dec. 21, 2000), included two provisions attempting to address enrollment difficulties experienced by those eligible for MSPs. One provision requires the Secretary of HHS to create a single simplified application form for MSP benefits that states may adopt if they choose. BIPA § 709. For the application form, *see* SSA, "Social Security Medicare Savings Program," *available at* https://www.benefits.gov/benefits/benefit-details/4396 (site visited Aug. 6, 2018). The second provision requires the Commissioner of the SSA to conduct outreach to identify individuals who might be eligible for MSP benefits, to notify them of their potential eligibility, and to notify each state of the names and addresses of those whom the Commissioner had identified who are residents of that state. BIPA § 911. MIPPA § 113 requires additional action with respect to SSA data sent to the states. The MIPPA provision is discussed in **§ 10.05[D]** of this Handbook.

[71] MIPPA § 115, effective Jan. 1, 2010.

[72] 42 U.S.C. § 1396a(a)(19); 42 C.F.R. § 435.902.

[73] 42 U.S.C. § 1396a(a)(10); 42 C.F.R. § 435.902; SM Manual, Ch. 3: § 3490.3.

arises every January, when Social Security cost-of-living adjustments (COLAs) become effective. The COLAs typically increase individuals' income by a small amount. Because updated income poverty guidelines, on which MSP eligibility is based, may not become effective until a few months into the year, there can be a period of several months when an individual's income may exceed the poverty level standard for the MSP in which the individual is enrolled. Congress recognized the harm caused by the disconnect in the operation of two different annual adjusters and amended the statute to require Social Security cost-of-living increases to be disregarded in determining eligibility until the second month after the month in which new poverty guidelines are published.[74]

Such systems and screening failures often result in dually eligible applicants being found eligible for categories of Medicaid that may not be as useful to them as MSP benefits would be. For example, an individual living in the community may be found eligible for a medically needy coverage group, with an income spend-down requirement, rather than for QMB benefits. This is significant because medically needy individuals must spend precious income on medical bills before their Medicaid entitlement is effective, while remaining liable for all Medicare cost-sharing or perhaps paying for a Medigap supplemental policy to cover some of the Medicare cost-sharing obligation. If the services they use most regularly are covered by Medicare, an MSP may be a more useful benefit for them. Conversely, it may be in an applicant's interest to forgo MSP benefits and use Medicare cost-sharing, especially the monthly Part B premium payment, to meet a spend-down that would then grant access to full Medicaid benefits. Similarly, institutionalized individuals may be found eligible for a long-term care coverage group with a share of cost obligation, without having their MSP entitlement assessed. When this happens, they may incur two potential sources of liability to the nursing facility where none should be occurring: share of cost under Medicaid and a Medicare copayment charge for the 21st through the 100th day of a Medicare Part A covered stay. This issue is addressed in more detail in **§ 10.06** of this Handbook.

The implementation of the ACA provides another application pathway to Medicaid and the MSPs.[75] Many people access this application through the federal health insurance marketplace online portal (*www.healthcare.gov*) and through various state-based marketplaces. This single streamlined application, and the health insurance marketplaces more generally, serve as an entry point to all categories of Medicaid, including the MSP. If, after completing the single streamlined application, the individual is found to be potentially eligible for the MSP, the marketplace should transfer the application to the single state Medicaid

---

[74] 42 U.S.C. § 1396d(p)(2)(D).

[75] *See* **§ 10.03** of this Handbook.

agency for processing.[76] The applicant may be required to fill out a supplemental application with more detailed questions and submit documentation of income and assets. The application should be processed in 45 days. Practically, however, when counseling clients advocates should continue to encourage people to apply for MSP at the Medicaid office. While an MSP application should in theory be processed through the marketplace, in practice this adds another layer of complexity and delay to a process already fraught with complexity and delay.

[C] Complexities of Enrolling in Medicare Part A for Eligibility for Qualified Medicare Beneficiary Benefits

To be eligible as a QMB for state Medicaid payment of Medicare cost-sharing obligations, applicants must have Medicare Part A.[77] Most Medicare beneficiaries receive Part A without payment of a premium, due to receipt of Social Security income or related benefits, such as Civil Service or Railroad Retirement. Some people, however, are not entitled to premium-free Medicare Part A. For example, individuals who do not have a long enough work history under the Social Security system may not have sufficient quarters of coverage to obtain Social Security benefits. Such individuals can purchase Part A for a premium of $437 per month in 2019 (a $15 increase from 2018).[78] Enrollment in Part A by paying a premium is called "voluntary enrollment."

The cost of the Medicare Part A premium represents a significant financial burden for lower income persons: it is more than 50 percent of monthly income for a person in poverty. Although states are required to pay the Part A premium for QMBs who must voluntarily enroll,[79] an individual must have Part A to be eligible as a QMB. To circumvent this apparent "Catch-22," in about 1989 the

[76] If the Marketplace is a governmental entity, states will have the option to enable their state-based Marketplace to make MSP eligibility determinations for people with Medicare. The Federally Facilitated Exchange/Marketplace will not be making MSP eligibility determinations for non-MAGI groups; the Federally Facilitated Exchange will either do final determinations or assessments for the MAGI eligibility groups. *See* CMS, Medicaid/CHIP Affordable Care Act Implementation: Coordination Across Insurance Affordability Programs (May 22, 2012), *available at* http://www.medicaid.gov/State-Resource-Center/FAQ-Medicaid-and-CHIP-Affordable-Care-Act-Implementation/Downloads/Coordination-FAQs.pdf (site visited Aug. 6, 2018).

[77] 42 U.S.C. § 1396d(p)(1)(A).

[78] Those with at least 30 quarters of Social Security coverage pay a lower premium ($240 in 2019, a $8 increase from 2018). *See* CMS, "2019 Medicare A & B Premiums and Deductibles Announced," (Oct. 12, 2018) *available at* https://www.cms.gov/newsroom/fact-sheets/2019-medicare-parts-b-premiums-and-deductibles (site visited Aug. 6, 2018).

[79] *See, e.g.*, Notice of Hearing: Reconsideration of Disapproval of Michigan State Plan Amendment, 57 Fed. Reg. 57,469 (Dec. 4, 1992).

Health Care Financing Administration (HCFA), now CMS, created a "conditional" enrollment process, through which a potential QMB enrolls in Part A conditioned upon his or her being found eligible for QMB benefits.[80]

The conditional enrollment process is complex.[81] The individual must contact a Social Security Administration office to enroll in Part A. He or she should attach a statement to the enrollment application to the following effect:

> I wish to enroll for hospital insurance on a monthly premium basis, and I understand that the hospital insurance premium will be in addition to the monthly premium for supplementary medical insurance. I want this enrollment to be effective only if I am determined to be eligible as a qualified Medicare beneficiary (QMB) and only beginning with the month in which I am eligible as a QMB. I also understand that, if I lose my QMB status, I will have to pay my premiums in order to keep my Medicare hospital insurance.

The individual then takes proof of his or her enrollment to the state Medicaid office, where he or she applies for QMB benefits, appending a copy of the Part A enrollment application to the Medicaid application. If the individual does not already have Part B, he or she will be required to enroll in Part B at the same time.[82]

Generally, persons who fail to voluntarily enroll in Medicare Parts A and B during their initial eligibility period (the seven months surrounding their 65th birthday or, for a person with disabilities under age 65, the seven months beginning when he or she has received disability payments for 21 months) must wait for a general enrollment period to enroll. They are penalized financially for late enrollment and their Medicare coverage is not effective until July 1 of that year. A general enrollment period occurs only once each year from January through March.

States can avoid the enrollment limitations, the penalty, and even the complex conditional enrollment process by having buy-in agreements with the federal government that permit them to enroll individuals in Part A or Part B at any time

---

[80] Advocates advising clients about conditional enrollment should first check with both their state Medicaid office and their local Social Security office. Despite the legal requirement for states to pay the Part A premium, where necessary, it is not clear that all states honor conditional enrollment, nor that all Social Security offices even know about it in those states that do honor it. Advocates will want to arm their clients with a copy of SSA, Program Operations Manual System (POMS), Premium-Part A Enrollments for Qualified Medicare Beneficiaries (QMBs)—Part A Buy-In States and Group Payer States § HI 00801.140, *available at* https://secure.ssa.gov/poms.nsf/lnx/0600801140 (site visited Aug. 6, 2018).

[81] SSA, POMS § HI 00801.140.

[82] 42 U.S.C. § 1395i-2; SSA, POMS § HI 00801.138, *available at* https://secure.ssa.gov/poms.nsf/lnx/0600801138 (site visited Aug. 6, 2018).

of the year.[83] Not all states have such buy-in agreements for Part A; states without them effectively deny potential beneficiaries access to the QMB benefit during those nine months of the year when Medicare enrollment is closed and subject their applicants to the multi-step and complicated conditional enrollment process during the brief three-month general enrollment period.[84]

Even in the 37 jurisdictions (36 states and the District of Columbia) that do have Medicare Part A buy-in agreements authorizing enrollment in Medicare Part A at any time, significant barriers are sometimes placed in the way of applicants.[85] In some such states, individuals are still directed to the SSA to enroll conditionally in Medicare Part A. For individuals who have not yet enrolled in Part B, the process can be even more complex. Social Security's electronic system will not accept an enrollment for Part B outside the general enrollment period. For states with a Part A buy-in agreement, Social Security has established an emergency process, described in a Policy Instruction, to override its system.[86] Advocates are advised to arm their clients with a copy of this policy instruction when sending them off to the SSA to apply for Parts A and B.

States have the income and resource information to identify whether someone is a potential QMB (i.e., under 100 percent of poverty); if they do not already have it, states can get Medicare information about such persons from CMS. Yet, many states make little effort to identify these individuals in order to enroll them for Medicare Part A automatically. Therefore, even individuals entitled to full *Medicaid* benefits may be put through the conditional enrollment process to get Medicare Part A if they are not already enrolled in Medicare Part A. Part A benefits can be useful even to a recipient of full Medicaid benefits because they entitle the individual to hospital, skilled nursing facility (SNF), home health, and hospice benefits that are often more extensive than those offered by the state Medicaid program. They also enable the individual to reduce his or her Medicaid estate recovery liability by using fewer Medicaid services.

The myriad problems related to getting individuals actually enrolled in QMB and other MSPs and, where relevant, getting the amount of their Part B premium restored to their Social Security checks are addressed in litigation filed in

[83] 42 U.S.C. § 1395v for Part B, § 1395i-2(g) for Part A; 42 C.F.R. § 406.26. "Buy-in," used in connection with agreements between state Medicaid programs and the federal government to describe a process for paying Medicare premiums, is a term of art, used in regulations.

[84] The states that do *not* have Part A buy-in agreements are AL, AZ, CA, CO, IL, KS, KY, MO, NE, NJ, NM, SC, UT, and VA.

[85] SSA, POMS § HI 00801.140. For an excellent detailed analysis of Part A issues in a state with a Part A buy-in agreement, *see* Medicare Rights Center, "Streamlining Medicare and QMB Enrollment for New Yorkers: Medicare Part A Buy-In Analysis and Policy Recommendations" (Feb. 2011), *available at* http://www.medicarerights.org/pdf/Part-A-Buy-In-Analysis.pdf (site visited Aug. 6, 2018).

[86] *See* Social Security Administration Policy Instruction for Individuals in Part A Buy-In States Who Do Not Have Medicare Part B, EM-08071 REV effective Aug. 11, 2008 through Oct. 6, 2012, included as **Appendix 10-6** of this Handbook.

early 2009 against the State of Pennsylvania, the HHS, and the SSA.[87] Settlement was approved by the court on April 23, 2010.[88] Terms of settlement included Pennsylvania's agreement to:

- Send and receive data to and from CMS on a daily basis, instead of monthly as it had prior to the lawsuit;
- Scan its Medicaid rolls monthly to search for individuals eligible for, but not enrolled in, Medicare;
- Submit enrollments for Part B and Part A simultaneously for those individuals with Medicaid who are eligible for, but not enrolled in, either part of Medicare;
- Increase field staff training to promote better understanding of the program and the prompt resolution of data errors that can hold up enrollments; and
- Evaluate all applications for MSP benefits to determine whether the applicant is entitled to retroactive benefits.

[D] MSPs and the Medicare Part D Low-Income Subsidy

The LIS available to Medicare beneficiaries to help with Part D covered drugs[89] is closely related to the MSPs in both design and administration. Eligibility rules for the two programs are similar, though not identical, and states are required by law to make LIS eligibility determinations through their Medicaid programs. Moreover, the law requires states, when they are assisting beneficiaries with LIS applications, to screen them for eligibility for MSPs and, if eligible, offer them an opportunity to enroll.[90] Finally, individuals enrolled in QMB, SLMB, or QI programs are deemed eligible for the LIS without having to apply or separately qualify by meeting the LIS income and asset eligibility rules.

---

[87] Garcia v. Johnson, Case 2:09-cv-1747 JS (E.D. Pa. Complaint filed Apr. 24, 2009).

[88] For the joint motion for approval of the settlement agreement, *see* Citizenship & Immigration Servs. (CIS), "Notice of Proposed Settlement & Hearing Class Action Involving Detained Non-Citizens Who Are Awaiting Reasonable Fear Determination," *available at* https://www.uscis.gov/laws/legal-settlement-notices/notice-proposed-settlement-and-hearing-class-action-involving-detained-non-citizens-who-are-awaiting-reasonable-fear-determination (site visited Aug. 6, 2016); for the order approving the settlement agreement, *see* CIS, Notice of Final Settlement Involving Detained Non-Citizens Who Are Waiting a "Reasonable Fear Determination," *available at* https://www.aclusocal.org/sites/default/files/wp-content/uploads/2015/12/Alfaro-Notice-of-Final-Settlement.pdf (sites visited Aug. 6, 2018).

[89] *See* discussion of LIS in **Chapter 11** of this Handbook.

[90] 42 U.S.C. § 1396u-5(a)(3).

The screen and enroll requirement has great potential for two reasons. First, because it is piggybacked on an application for assistance with paying for prescription drugs (the LIS), it may promote a higher enrollment rate in the MSPs themselves, since drug coverage may be viewed as a more attractive and necessary benefit than premium assistance. MSP eligibility rules vary be state, so they can be more liberal in at least some respect than the nationally uniform LIS rules. Therefore, enrollment in an MSP can provide a back-door route to eligibility for the LIS for some who would not otherwise qualify.[91] Unfortunately, this potential is not much realized: staff members at the SSA reported in 2012 that only one state, Colorado, was sending LIS applications to SSA.[92]

Although the SSA does not have a screen and enroll mandate with respect to MSP benefits for those who apply through the SSA for LIS, it does, effective January 1, 2010, have an obligation to send data from the LIS application to the applicant's state.[93] This is done only with the applicant's consent. The state receiving the data must consider it an application for MSP benefits and process it accordingly. States' compliance with the requirement that they treat the data as initiating an application varies considerably throughout the country: some states automatically enroll into MSP virtually all individuals whose data they receive; others merely send a "formal" application to those individuals whose data they receive, or a formal notice requesting additional information or requiring submission of documentation to the state. In some states, community-based organizations are working with the Medicaid eligibility agency to help applicants successfully complete these applications.[94] Advocates are monitoring implementation of this important provision in the law and working with CMS to improve state performance.[95]

Advocates assisting clients with enrolling in MSPs can enhance their assistance by helping clients understand the complexities of enrollment choices for LIS. It may be more expeditious for a client to make one trip to Medicaid rather than two separate trips, one to Medicaid for MSP and one to Social Security for LIS, but clients will need to be clear about what they are seeking when they go

---

[91] For a detailed discussion of the interrelationships between MSPs and LIS, *see* The Kaiser Family Foundation, "Toward Making Medicare Work: A Baseline Comparison of the Part D Low-Income Subsidy and Medicare Savings Programs Eligibility and Enrollment Rules" (Apr. 30, 2006), *available at* http://kff.org/medicare/report/toward-making-medicare-work-for-low-income/ (site visited Aug. 6, 2018).

[92] Telephone message from Kojuan Almond, Office of External Affairs, Social Security Administration, left for Patricia Nemore, July 9, 2012.

[93] MIPPA § 113.

[94] *See* Douglas Goggin-Callahan, "Warning Signs: Preliminary Report Highlights Problems with State Implementation of MIPPA Low-Income Reforms" (Feb. 2010), Medicare Rights Center, *available at* http://www.medicarerights.org/pdf/Warning-Signs-MIPPA.pdf (site visited Aug. 6, 2018).

[95] *See* Government Accountability Office (GAO), The Medicare Savings Program: Implementation of Requirements Aimed at Increasing Enrollment (Sept. 2012), *available at* http://www.gao.gov/assets/650/648370.pdf (site visited Aug. 6, 2018).

to their Medicaid office. Those clients who have access to the Internet can be advised to make their LIS application online.[96]

§ 10.06 ACCESS ISSUES FOR THE DUALLY ELIGIBLE POPULATION

[A] Transition Issues for Certain Medicaid Enrollees upon Becoming Eligible for Medicare

The ACA's expansion and simplification of Medicaid financial eligibility rules, including the increase in Medicaid income limits to 133 percent of FPL and the elimination of asset tests, do not apply to the Medicare population.[97] For individuals receiving expanded ACA Medicaid who become eligible for Medicare, transitions to Medicare with Medicaid for the aged, blind, and disabled or to Medicare with an MSP can be problematic.[98]

When individuals on Medicaid become eligible for Medicare, the agency is required to do an automatic redetermination and reassess them for medical assistance programs for which they may be eligible.[99] Because expanded Medicaid does not have an asset test and relies on a simplified MAGI standard to determine income, new Medicare beneficiaries undergoing a redetermination will be asked for additional documentation of income and assets.[100] Some people with expanded Medicaid may find that they continue to qualify for their state Medicaid program and will become full dual eligibles.[101] Others may qualify for only an MSP and will become partial dual eligibles.[102] Finally, some individuals will lose eligibility for all medical assistance programs upon becoming Medicare eligible. This is the case for people with income below 133 percent of the FPL but assets above MSP resource limits.

---

[96] Go to https://secure.ssa.gov/i1020/start (site visited Aug. 6, 2018) and look for the button called "Apply Now."

[97] ACA § 2001.

[98] For an excellent analysis of transition issues beneficiaries moving from expanded ACA coverage to Medicare will face, *see* Ilene Stein & Joe Baker, "A Bridge to Health" (Jan. 2013), The Medicare Rights Center, *available at* http://www.medicarerights.org/pdf/A-Bridge-to-Health.pdf (site visited Aug. 6, 2018). *See also* Amber Cutler & Anna Rich, "Medicaid Expansion in California: Opportunities and Challenges for Older Adults and People with Disabilities" (Nov. 2013), The National Senior Citizens Law Center, *available at* http://nsclcarchives.org/wp-content/uploads/2013/11/1CA-Eligibility-Brief-4.pdf (site visited Aug. 6, 2018).

[99] 42 C.F.R. § 435.930; 42 C.F.R. § 435.916(c) (requires state agency to re-determine eligibility when it receives information about changes in a recipient's circumstances that may affect his/her eligibility). Individuals receiving SSI should be automatically "deemed" for an MSP without going through an ex parte redetermination requiring supplemental documentation. *See* SSA, POMS HI 00815.006.

[100] 42 C.F.R. § 435.916

[101] *See* discussion at **§ 10.04** of this Handbook.

[102] *See* discussion at **§ 10.04** of this Handbook.

[B] Prescription Drug Coverage and Medicare Part D

Prior to January 1, 2006, dually eligible beneficiaries received their prescription drug coverage exclusively from Medicaid, with the exception of drugs covered under Medicare Parts A and B, delivered in institutions or in physicians' offices.

Since January 1, 2006, any individual eligible to enroll in a Medicare Part D plan who is eligible for full Medicaid cannot receive prescription drug coverage through Medicaid.[103] This is true regardless of whether the individual has actually enrolled in a Part D plan, and regardless of whether the plan covers the specific drug needed. Concomitantly, the state cannot receive federal matching payments for such services.

[1] Definition of Dual Eligibles

For purposes of Part D, dual eligibles are defined as individuals who have coverage under a Part D plan and who are eligible for full Medicaid benefits under any category of a state Medicaid plan. Those with full coverage under a Section 1115 Research and Demonstration waiver fall within the definition. This definition is narrower than the definition of dual eligibles offered in **§ 10.04** of this Handbook.

[2] Assignment of Dual Eligibles to Drug Plans

Congress required the automatic enrollment in a drug plan of any dual eligible who does not voluntarily enroll.[104] Auto enrollment must be into Part D plans with premiums at or below the average ("benchmark") plan premium for the region. The difficulties that developed for dual eligibles during the first transition of about 7 million individuals from Medicaid to Medicare in January 2006 led to beneficiaries filing a nationwide class action lawsuit, *Situ v. Leavitt*, challenging the failure of the HHS to implement Part D to ensure drug coverage for dual eligibles.[105] Enrollment for Medicaid-eligible individuals who become eligible for Medicare after January 1, 2006, is effective on the first day of the month the individual becomes eligible for Part D. Enrollment for Part D eligibles who become newly eligible for Medicaid is effective on the first day of the month in

---

[103] 42 U.S.C. § 1396u-5(d)(1). For a more detailed discussion of the entire Medicare drug benefit, see **Chapter 11** of this Handbook.

[104] 42 U.S.C. § 1395w-101(b)(D).

[105] Situ v. Leavitt, C06-02841 TEH (N.D. Cal. Complaint filed Apr. 26, 2006); Defendants' Motion to Dismiss denied, 2000 WL 3734373 (N.D. Cal. Dec. 18, 2006); Plaintiffs' Motion for Class Certification granted, 240 F.R.D. 551 (N.D. Cal. 2007); Settlement approved Situ v. Leavitt, No. 06-2841 TEH (N.D. Cal., Order Approving Final Approval of Settlement Agreement, Oct. 22, 2008).

which the individual becomes Medicaid eligible.[106] Although coverage is effective the date the individual becomes dually eligible, significant lag times can occur in making the coverage operational, leaving the dually eligible beneficiary in the position of having to pay potentially high copayments with the hope of being reimbursed in the future.[107] Such payments are often not feasible for dual eligibles, due to their very low incomes.

Beginning January 1, 2010, CMS instituted a program called Limited Income Newly Eligible Transition program (LI NET), operated by Humana, Inc. under contract with CMS.[108] The LI NET serves essentially three purposes: it acts as the process for initial auto-enrollment of full-benefit dual eligibles and individuals with Supplemental Security Income; it acts as the point-of-sale (POS) contractor for individuals whose Part D enrollment is not evident in the system when they arrive at the pharmacy to fill a prescription; and it acts as the Part D plan for purposes of retroactive reimbursements that are due to individuals whose enrollment was actually effective before it was available in the system (due, usually, to eligibility for Medicaid benefits retroactive to a period prior to the date of application). Although the point-of-sale enrollment process is not required to be used by pharmacists, CMS did remove the financial liability of pharmacists if their use of the system was in error. This change may make use of the system more attractive to pharmacists.[109] The LI NET demonstration has been extended through the end of 2019. In its 2014 yearly report to Congress, the Medicare-Medicaid Coordination Office (MMCO)[110] recommended that the demonstration be made permanent.[111]

Related to the POS system is CMS's best available evidence (BAE) policy.[112] BAE is used when CMS records are incorrect with respect to an individual's LIS status (in contrast with the POS, which relates to whether they are

---

[106] 42 C.F.R. § 423.34(f)(2), (3), effective June 7, 2010.

[107] *See* GAO, Medicare Part D: Enrolling New Dual-Eligible Beneficiaries in Prescription Drug Plans, GAO-07-824T (May 2007), *available at* http://www.gao.gov/new.items/d07824t.pdf (site visited Aug. 6, 2018).

[108] *See* CMS, The Limited Income Newly Eligible Transition (LI NET) Program, *available at* http://www.cms.gov/LowIncSubMedicarePresCov/Downloads/LINETgeneral100909.pdf (site visited Aug. 6, 2018).

[109] Humana, "Limited Income Newly Eligible Transition (NET) Program: Four Steps for Pharmacy Providers" (Dec. 10, 2009), *available at* http://apps.humana.com/marketing/documents.asp?file=1285050 (site visited Aug. 6, 2018). *See also* CMS, Medicare's Limited Income NET Program for People at the Pharmacy Counter, *available at* http://www.cms.gov/partnerships/downloads/11328-P.pdf (site visited Aug. 6, 2018).

[110] *See* **§ 10.09** of this Handbook.

[111] CMS, Medicare-Medicaid Coordination Office Fiscal Year 2014 Report to Congress, *available at* https://www.cms.gov/Medicare-Medicaid-Coordination/Medicare-and-Medicaid-Coordination/Medicare-Medicaid-Coordination-Office/Downloads/MMCO_2014_RTC.pdf (site visited Aug. 6, 2018).

[112] *See generally* documents at CMS, "Best Available Evidence (BAE)," *available at* http://www.cms.gov/Medicare/Prescription-Drug-Coverage/PrescriptionDrugCovContra/Best_Available_

enrolled in a plan), so that they are being charged incorrect cost-sharing. Under the policy, a plan must honor an individual's stated low-income status (and apply appropriate cost-sharing levels) if the individual provides or is able to procure one of five specific types of documentation of Medicaid eligibility, or some other documentation provided by a state Medicaid agency for the relevant period. Requirements on plans with respect to BAE mandate that a plan help beneficiaries establish their LIS status. Although CMS directs plans to use the BAE, including helping beneficiaries, not all plans do so. Advocates would be well advised to have a copy of the policy in hand when they engage the plan.

Both the POS and BAE were subject to the settlement in the *Situ* case and, as such, were subject to ongoing monitoring by plaintiffs' counsel. Official monitoring ended in late 2010, but the Part D advocacy community continues to pay attention to how well these systems are working.

A final rule for Parts C & D (CMS-4182-F) was published on April 16, 2018: "Medicare Program; Contract Year 2019 Policy and Technical Changes to the Medicare Advantage, Medicare Cost Plan, Medicare Fee-for-Service, the Medicare Prescription Drug Benefit Programs, and the PACE Program."[113] The final rule states that the Special Election Period (SEP) that used to exist for dual-eligible and LIS beneficiaries will be revised from an open-ended monthly SEP to one that may be used only once per calendar quarter during the first nine months of the year (January through September). Separate SEPs can be used in the following circumstances: (1) within a certain period of time after a CMS or state-initiated enrollment; and (2) within a certain period of time after a change to an individual's LIS or Medicaid status.[114]

[3] Medicaid Wrap-Around

Medicare Part D's complete elimination of coverage for an otherwise covered Medicaid service represents a substantial departure from the historic Medicare-Medicaid relationship for dual eligibles, under which Medicaid has paid Medicare's cost-sharing and provided "wrap-around coverage" for certain services. These include home health, where Medicare coverage is more limited than Medicaid coverage; prescription drugs before January 1, 2006; and non-skilled long-term care because Medicare coverage was or is nearly non-existent. The significance of this situation cannot be overstated. Because of the design of

---

Evidence_Policy.html. For other documents relevant to Part D and low income subsidies, *see* http://www.cms.gov/PrescriptionDrugCovContra/17_Best_Available_Evidence_Policy.asp (sites visited Aug. 6, 2018).

[113] 82 Fed. Reg. 16,440 (Apr. 16, 2018).

[114] 42 C.F.R. § 423.38(c).

the Medicare drug benefit, many dual eligibles find themselves with less prescription drug coverage than they had under Medicaid and potentially fewer protections during appeals processes to challenge denials or other barriers to coverage. Further, all but those who are receiving long-term care services have to pay copayments for their prescriptions, with the copayment amounts increasing yearly. Copayments are not required under federal Medicaid law and, in the past, their use was not enforceable, although this is no longer true.[115]

Using both federal and state funding, Medicaid can continue to cover for dual eligibles those drugs that it is permitted, but not required by law, to cover for any Medicaid beneficiary and that are not, by definition, Part D covered drugs. In 2014, such drugs included weight gain and weight loss drugs (used in connection with HIV treatments), prescription vitamins, cough and cold relief drugs, and nonprescription drugs, among others. Prior to January 1, 2013, Part D did not cover benzodiazepines (used for anxiety, panic attacks, seizure disorders, and muscle spasms) or barbiturates (used in the treatment of epilepsy, cancer, or a chronic mental disorder) but has since begun covering these classes of medication.[116] As of January 1, 2014, Medicaid programs may not exclude smoking cessation drugs, barbiturates, and benzodiazepines from coverage under Medicaid.[117] The January 2006 transition from Medicaid to Medicare coverage for prescription drugs was so chaotic for dual eligibles that between 38 and 44 states initiated some sort of emergency coverage programs, some declaring a health care emergency in the state.[118] Few states provide ongoing wrap-around payments—either of Part D copayments or of non-formulary drugs—for their dually eligible residents.[119]

---

[115] *See* 42 C.F.R. § 447.53(e). The non-enforceability of copayments was changed by the DRA § 6041.

[116] MIPPA § 175.

[117] ACA § 2502, amending § 1927(d) of the Social Security Act, 42 U.S.C. § 1397r-8(d).

[118] *See* Vernon Smith, Kathleen Gifford, Sandy Kramer, & Linda Elam, "The Transition of Dual Eligibles to Medicare Part D Prescription Drug Coverage: State Actions during Implementation" (Feb. 2006), Kaiser Family Foundation, *available at* http://www.kff.org/medicaid/upload/7467.pdf (site visited Aug. 6, 2018).

[119] *See* National Conference of State Legislatures, "State Pharmaceutical Assistance Programs," *available at* http://www.ncsl.org/issues-research/health/state-pharmaceutical-assistance-programs.aspx (site visited Aug. 6, 2018). The website includes discussions of and charts listing various state efforts with respect to prescription drug coverage. It is difficult to discern from this information exactly which states, if any, still have wrap-around drug coverage for dual eligibles, especially for paying Part D copayments and for non-formulary drugs. For a 2013 chart of State Pharmaceutical Assistance Programs, *see* Medicare Rights Center, "State Pharmaceutical Assistance Programs," *available at* http://www.medicareinteractive.org/uploadedDocuments/mi_extra/SPAP-Chart.pdf (site visited Aug. 6, 2018).

[4] Nursing Facility Residents and Other Beneficiaries Receiving Long-Term Care Services

In addition to experiencing the problems of all dually eligible individuals, those who reside in nursing homes and other institutions experience problems that arise because of the setting in which they live. For example, there is no assurance that a dually eligible resident who does not choose a Part D prescription drug plan will be automatically assigned to a plan that includes the pharmacy used by his or her nursing facility, although plans are required to include long-term care pharmacies in their networks.

Dually eligible individuals who reside in a nursing facility pay no copayment for their medications.[120] Prior to 2012, this benefit had not been extended to residents of assisted living facilities and others who are receiving home and community-based services pursuant to a Section 1915 waiver, even though these individuals must meet the medical eligibility requirements for a nursing facility to qualify for community-based services. The ACA changed this. Effective January 1, 2012, individuals receiving home and community-based services under waiver or state plan provisions of the Medicaid law were relieved of all Part D copayments.[121]

[5] Transitioning into a Part D Plan

When Medicare beneficiaries transition from another source of payment for their prescriptions to a Part D plan, they may encounter difficulties caused by changes in formularies and other utilization management tools used by Part D plans to contain costs. The transition may be particularly difficult for those dual eligibles who transition from more generous Medicaid programs.

All Part D plans are required to establish a transition process for new enrollees who are already taking Medicare-covered drugs that are not on the plan's formulary.[122] The transition process is to ensure access to non-formulary drugs, including those subject to step therapy or prior authorization requirements, during the first 90 days of coverage under a new plan. The transition process is available for new enrollees following the annual coordinated enrollment period, newly eligible Medicare beneficiaries moving from other coverage, individuals who change plans mid-year, and current enrollees who are affected by formulary changes. Eligible enrollees are generally entitled to a 30-day transition fill unless the prescription is for fewer than 30 days. Residents in long-term care facilities

---

[120] 423.782(a)(2)(ii).

[121] ACA § 3309 (amending § 1860D-14(a)(1)(D)(i) of the Social Security Act); 42 U.S.C. § 1395w-114(a)(1)(D)(i).

[122] 42 C.F.R. § 423.120(b)(3)(i)(A).

are entitled to up to 98-days of transition fills, depending on the dispensing increment. Plans must send enrollees written notice explaining that the prescription has been filled on a transition basis within three business days of approving the transition fill. Plans must also ensure that reasonable notice is made to inform the prescriber of the temporary fill.[123]

[C] Payment of Medicare Cost-Sharing at Medicaid Rates

A provision in the Balanced Budget Act of 1997 (BBA '97), gave states the option to reimburse Medicare cost-sharing to providers for services provided to dually eligible beneficiaries at their lower Medicaid rate, rather than the full Medicare rate.[124] Federal law also authorizes states to pay at the Medicare rate even if that rate is higher than what the state would pay for a non-dual eligible on Medicaid.[125] Under the BBA '97 provision, if the Medicare share (80 percent of the Medicare allowable amount for most Part B services) is more than the state's Medicaid rate for the same service, the state need pay nothing. This is sometimes referred to as the "lesser-of" policy.

> ■ **EXAMPLE:** If the *Medicare* approved rate is $100, the Medicare payment would be $80 and the beneficiary coinsurance (for which Medicaid would be responsible for a QMB) would be $20. However, if the *Medicaid* rate for the service is only $75, the state would make no payment for the beneficiary's share, since Medicare has already paid above the state reimbursement rate. Thus, the provider would get $20 less than it would from a non-QMB beneficiary. The QMB is not liable for the unreimbursed state portion.

Since the enactment of BBA '97, courts have held, even in cases that predated BBA '97, that states *may* reimburse at the lower of the two reimbursement rates.[126] Thus, dually eligible beneficiaries are treated as Medicaid rather than Medicare beneficiaries, with respect to provider reimbursement. A July 2015 CMS report, *Access to Care Issues Among Qualified Medicare Beneficiaries (QMB)*, revealed several access to care problems for low-income Medicare beneficiaries enrolled in the QMB program.[127] The report found that QMB enrollees

---

[123] 42 C.F.R. § 423.120(b)(3)(iv).

[124] The Balanced Budget Act of 1997 (BBA '97), Pub. L. No. 105-33 (Aug. 5, 1997), § 4714, (amending 42 U.S.C.A. § 1396a(n) (Supp. 2009) by adding subparagraphs (2) and (3)).

[125] 42 U.S.C. § 1396a(n)(1).

[126] Beverly Cmty. Hosp. Ass'n v. Belshe, 132 F.3d 1259 (9th Cir. 1997); Stohler v. Menke, 998 F. Supp. 836 (E.D. Tenn. 1997).

[127] CMS, Access to Care Issues Among Qualified Medicare Beneficiaries (QMB) (July 2015), *available at* https://www.cms.gov/Medicare-Medicaid-Coordination/Medicare-and-Medicaid-Coordination/Medicare-Medicaid-Coordination-Office/Downloads/Access_to_Care_Issues_Among_Qualified_Medicare_Beneficiaries.pdf (site visited Aug. 6, 2018) (hereinafter *July 2015 QMB Report*).

were less likely to use office visits and hospital outpatient services compared to Medicare-only enrollees in states that employed the "lesser-of" policy for reimbursement, thereby limiting access to essential routine and preventive care for beneficiaries. The report provided troubling information regarding barriers to access to care for low-income beneficiaries, something that advocates have long asserted.[128]

A 2003 study of the effects of lesser-of policies on access to services concluded that payment reductions reduced utilization. It did not, however, evaluate the effect of reduced utilization on health outcomes.[129] In 2013, the Medicaid and CHIP Payment and Access Commission (MACPAC) undertook a study of current state payment policies in the 50 states and the District of Columbia.[130] The study found that Medicaid payment for Medicare cost-sharing varied among both states and provider types within individual states. The provider types surveyed were hospital inpatient, hospital outpatient, skilled nursing facility, and physician services. Of the 51 Medicaid programs for which researchers collected information, about half paid the lesser-of amount for all provider types. Only four states (Arkansas, Iowa, Vermont, and Wyoming) pay Medicare's full deductibles and coinsurance for every provider type researchers investigated. The remaining 18 states mix and match policies in almost every possible combination with no clear patterns emerging. The MACPAC report did not address the effect of lesser-of policies on access or health outcomes as suggested by the 2003 BBA report.

The BBA '97 provision authorizing lower payments to providers also expressly prohibits providers from billing dually eligible patients. Providers must accept the Medicare payment and the Medicaid payment, if any, as payment in full.[131]

Until 2008, CMS had interpreted these requirements to permit providers to choose whether to accept a patient as private pay, QMB-only, or, if applicable, full Medicaid.[132] This interpretation eviscerates the statutory protection, since the provider can avoid its reach by telling the beneficiary it will serve him or her only as

---

[128] Letter of July 28, 2009, from Center for Medicare Advocacy and D.C. Legal Aid Society to Ted Gallagher, CMS Region III, concerning specific client issues and general systemic issues with respect to providers billing QMBs for the cost-sharing portion of Medicare payment, available from the Center at kkertesz@medicareadvocacy.org.

[129] Tommy G. Thompson, Secretary of HHS, "Report to Congress, State Payment Limitations on Medicare Cost-Sharing: Impacts on Dually Eligible Beneficiaries and Their Providers," transmitted by letter of May 20, 2003 to Speaker of the House of Representatives, J. Dennis Hastert, *available at* http://inq.sagepub.com/content/41/4/391.full.pdf+html (site visited Aug. 6, 2018).

[130] *March 2013 MACPAC Report*, at 128; *see also March 2015 MACPAC Report* at 103, citing 2013 study.

[131] BBA '97 § 4714(a)(1)(B).

[132] SM Manual, Ch. 3: § 3490.14B, *available at* http://www.cms.gov/Regulations-and-Guidance/Guidance/Manuals/Paper-Based-Manuals-Items/CMS021927.html (site visited Aug. 6, 2018).

private pay. Moreover, it appears to violate Medicare law, to the extent the provider in question "accepts assignment" under Medicare,[133] which prohibits the provider from charging the beneficiary anything more than the coinsurance amount. For a QMB, this would be paid for by the state. CMS, in February 2008, issued a Memorandum to its Regional Administrators stating clearly that a provider of services covered by Parts A and B may not bill a QMB either for the balance of the Medicare rate (the 20%) or for the provider's customary charge in excess of the Medicare rate.[134] In January 2012, CMS reissued this guidance.[135] The July 2015 CMS Report also underscores this prohibition.

In addition, in 2010, CMS Region III issued letters to two providers in the District of Columbia informing them that their billing of their QMB patients was illegal and could result in sanctions.[136] Advocates have successfully used these letters to educate providers and persuade them to desist from billing their QMB patients. Despite the clear prohibition on balance billing, the July 2015 CMS report shows an alarming trend that low-income beneficiaries enrolled in the

---

[133] 42 U.S.C. § 1395u(b)(3)(B)(ii). *See generally* **§ 6.04** of this Handbook on the Medicare Assignment Program. While the federal protections only apply with respect to physicians who agree to take assignment, some states require Medicare participating physicians to take assignment. *See also* **§ 1.05[B][2]**.

[134] *See* 42 U.S.C. §§ 1396d(p)(3) and 1396a(n)(2); SM Manual, CMS Pub. 45, Ch. 3: Eligibility § 3490.12, *see* **Appendix 10-1** of this Handbook. *See also* Feb. 2008 Memo and two attachments, memo *available at* http://www.medicareadvocacy.org/old-site/InfoByTopic/MedicareSavingsPrograms/MedSavProg_08_04.24.ARACostShare.pdf (site visited Aug. 6, 2018); Balance Billing attachment *available at* http://www.medicareadvocacy.org/old-site/InfoByTopic/MedicareSavingsPrograms/MedSavProg_08_04.24.ARABalanceBilling.pdf (site visited Aug. 6, 2018); Capitation attachment *available at* http://www.medicareadvocacy.org/old-site/InfoByTopic/MedicareSavingsPrograms/MedSavProg_08_04.24.ARACapitation.pdf (site visited Aug. 6, 2018); Nov. 1991 Memo (**Appendix 10-2** of this Handbook); June 2007 Memo (**Appendix 10-3** of this Handbook); and Memorandum of June 30, 2000 from Director, DEHPG, Subject: Policy Memorandum on Medicaid Obligations to Pay Medicare Cost-sharing Expenses for Qualified Medicare Beneficiaries in Medicare Health Maintenance Organizations or Competitive Medical Plans or Medicare Plus Choice Organizations—Information (hereinafter June 2000 Memo) (**Appendix 10-4** of this Handbook). *See also* 42 U.S.C. § 1396a (a)(25)(C) and (D) concerning non-discrimination by providers serving Medicaid beneficiaries with third party insurance.

[135] MMCO-CMCS Informational Bulletin June 7, 2013, Subject: Payment of Medicare Cost Sharing for Qualified Medicare Beneficiaries (QMBs), *available at* http://www.medicaid.gov/Federal-Policy-Guidance/downloads/CIB-06-07-2013.pdf (site visited Aug. 6, 2018); MMCO-CMCS Informational Bulletin Jan. 6, 2012, Subject: Billing for Services Provided to Qualified Medicare Beneficiaries (QMBs), *available at* http://www.medicareadvocacy.org/wp-content/uploads/2012/01/cib-01-06-12.pdf (site visited Aug. 6, 2018); CMS, MLN Number SE1128 Revised, "Prohibition on Balance Billing Qualified Medicare Beneficiaries (QMBs)."

[136] Letter of February 4, 2010 from John David Smith, Manager, Medicare Operations Branch, Region III Division of Financial Management and FFS Operations, Centers for Medicare & Medicaid Services, Philadelphia, Pennsylvania (the names of providers and beneficiaries are redacted from these documents), *available at* http://www.medicareadvocacy.org/old-site/InfoByTopic/MedicareSavingsPrograms/10_02.04.LtrFromROtoDCproviderReCostSharing.pdf (site visited Aug. 6, 2018).

QMB program are frequently being illegally balance-billed and that although beneficiaries are not liable for the charges, many of the bills were sent on to collections if unpaid, and most beneficiaries actually paid.[137]

In October of 2017, CMS began, a change to the Medicare claims processing system that provides notifications to providers and beneficiaries alerting them the beneficiary is enrolled in the QMB and has no Medicare cost-sharing liability for all Medicare A/B claims. The trigger notifications are sent to providers (through the Provider Remittance Advice) and to beneficiaries (through the Medicare Summary Notice).[138]

[D] Skilled Nursing Facilities/Nursing Facilities: Inappropriate Transfers and Obstruction of Medicaid Services

Medicaid is the primary payer for nursing home care, $55 billion in 2015.[139] MedPAC's report notes that "spending on Medicaid-funded nursing home services (combined state and federal funds) totaled $44 billion in 2016."[140] These long-term care services are not covered by Medicare and would otherwise be unaffordable for seniors with low incomes. *Medicare* pays for *skilled* nursing or rehabilitative care, following a three- (or more) day inpatient hospitalization. The care must be provided in a certified skilled nursing facility (SNF) and coverage is available for up to 100 days. After the 20th day, the beneficiary must pay a copayment ($167.50 in 2018). See a full discussion of Medicare coverage of SNF care in **Chapter 3** of this Handbook. *Medicaid* pays for nursing or rehabilitative care that can be provided only in a nursing facility on an inpatient basis. A "nursing facility" in Medicaid is a place that provides both skilled care and "health related care and services."[141] The care must be provided in a certified nursing facility; there is no limit on the number of days of coverage as long as the services are medically necessary. Medicaid requires the individual to pay a "share of cost" that comprises the individual's whole monthly income less certain required and permitted deductions. Medicaid then pays the facility the difference between the individual's share of cost and the Medicaid rate.

---

[137] *July 2015 QMB Report, available at* https://www.cms.gov/Medicare-Medicaid-Coordination/Medicare-and-Medicaid-Coordination/Medicare-Medicaid-Coordination-Office/Downloads/Access_to_Care_Issues_Among_Qualified_Medicare_Beneficiaries.pdf (site visited Aug. 6, 2018).

[138] CMS, MLN Number MM9911 Revised, Qualified Medicare Beneficiary Indicator in the Medicare Fee-For-Service Claims Processing System, *available at* https://www.cms.gov/Outreach-and-Education/Medicare-Learning-Network-MLN/MLNMattersArticles/Downloads/MM9911.pdf (site visited Aug. 6, 2018).

[139] Kaiser Family Foundation, "Medicare's Role in Nursing Home Care" (June 20, 2017), *available at* http://www.kff.org/infographic/medicaids-role-in-nursing-home-care/ (site visited Aug. 6, 2018).

[140] *See* http://www.medpac.gov/docs/default-source/reports/mar18_medpac_entirereport_sec.pdf.

[141] 42 U.S.C. § 1396r(a).

Difficulties can arise for dually eligible beneficiaries because facilities may not be certified for both Medicare and Medicaid or may have separate wings certified for each program.[142] If such a beneficiary enters the facility with Medicaid paying for his or her stay and is subsequently hospitalized for three days, the beneficiary may then be eligible for a period of skilled nursing coverage under Medicare. The beneficiary may be told—either by the facility or by the state Medicaid program—that he or she cannot return to his or her Medicaid bed because the beneficiary must be placed in a bed in a Medicare-only certified portion of the facility. The motivation for this could be that the facility may receive higher reimbursement rates under Medicare. The state might try to force the beneficiary to get Medicare coverage because of its interpretation of its obligation under federal law to seek reimbursement from all liable third parties.

Medicare law requires that if a beneficiary's old bed is available or, if not, another bed is available, the facility must readmit the beneficiary to it, regardless of whether the facility can get higher reimbursement if the beneficiary is in a bed in a Medicare-certified portion of the facility.[143] Moreover, with respect to the state's concern about third-party liability, CMS has said that states are required to seek third-party coverage only where such coverage exists; if a resident is in a bed in a portion of a facility not certified for Medicare, there would be no Medicare coverage for that bed, and so there would be no third-party liability.[144]

Conversely, a dually eligible beneficiary might enter the facility for the first time needing skilled care after a three-day hospitalization and be entitled to Medicare coverage immediately. When that coverage ends, the beneficiary may be told by the facility that he or she must move because it needs the bed for another Medicare resident. While the law gives the beneficiary an absolute right to refuse

---

[142] Although national data report that about 87 percent of all nursing facility beds and 91 percent of all nursing facilities in the country are certified for both programs, nursing home advocates report that movement between wings separately certified continues to be an issue for dually eligible beneficiaries. *See* American Health Care Association, LTC Stats: Nursing Facility Operational Characteristics Report, March 2013 Update, Table 3: Nursing Facility Certification and Table 6: Nursing Facility Beds by Certification Type (Mar. 2013).

[143] *See* 42 U.S.C. § 1396r(c)(2)(D)(i),(ii) concerning a Medicaid resident's right to notice of state bed hold policies when he or she is being transferred to a hospital. Although states are not required to pay nursing facilities to hold beds while residents are absent, they may do so, and the resident must be informed of the state's policy and his or her right to return to the bed the state paid for, if any, or to the first available bed in the facility. In addition to this right of the nursing home resident, Medicaid provides a generic right of free choice of provider to all beneficiaries. 42 U.S.C. § 1396a(a)(23).

[144] Letter of March 31, 1999, from Associate Regional Administrator, Region I, HCFA to Center for Medicare Advocacy, Inc. (hereinafter Preston letter). *See* **Appendix 10-5** of this Handbook. Advocates are cautioned that while the principles enunciated in this letter are embodied in the law, actual state policy and practice is likely to be less favorable and the state may refuse to pay for a resident who has declined Medicare coverage. Advocates are encouraged, nonetheless, to make these arguments for clients who wish to return to a non-Medicare-certified bed.

this transfer,[145] he or she will not be able to get Medicaid to pay for continued stay unless the bed is also certified for Medicaid.

As a general matter, when a facility asks a resident to move from one part of the facility to another, an advocate or a family member should try to find out what the certification is for both parts of the facility. If they are certified differently—e.g., one is only Medicare-certified and the other is only Medicaid-certified—the resident is entitled to a notice of the reasons for the transfer and an opportunity for a fair hearing to challenge the transfer.[146] If the move is merely from one room to another within a certified portion of the facility, the resident is entitled only to notification, not to a hearing, but may nonetheless be able to prevent the relocation by invoking federal standards that promote self-determination, participation, and accommodation of the resident's need.[147]

From the resident's perspective, these problems would be eliminated by the state's requiring that all beds in facilities be certified for both Medicare and Medicaid. Data suggest that no state does this, but that the District of Columbia, Idaho, Montana, North Dakota, and Vermont come very close.[148]

[E] Medicaid Individual Share of Cost Issues During a Skilled Nursing Facility Benefit Period

If a dually eligible individual's nursing home stay is paid for by Medicaid, he or she will pay all of his or her income, less deductions allowed for personal needs, the support of family members, and a few other purposes,[149] to the facility as his or her share of cost. This payment is also called net available monthly

---

[145] 42 U.S.C. §§ 1395i-3(c)(1)(A)(x) (Medicare) and 1396r(c)(1)(A)(x) (Medicaid).

[146] Federal law limits the permissible reasons for transfers. The reasons, which apply to all nursing home residents, not just to those dually eligible, are: (1) the resident's welfare cannot be met by the facility, (2) the resident no longer needs the facility's services because of improved health, (3) safety of individuals in the facility is endangered, (4) health of individuals in the facility would be endangered, (5) resident has failed to pay, and (6) facility ceases to operate. 42 U.S.C. §§ 1396r(c)(2)(A)(i)–(vi) and 1395i-3(c)(2)(A)(i)–(vi). In addition, a resident can refuse a transfer to or from a Medicare-certified portion of the facility when the purpose is to relocate him or her from or to a non-Medicare certified portion of the facility. 42 U.S.C. §§ 1395i-3(c)(1)(A)(x) (Medicare), 1396r(c)(1)(A)(x) (Medicaid). *See also* Eric Carlson, "20 Common Nursing Home Problems and How to Solve Them" (June 2010), National Senior Citizens Law Center, *available at* http://www.elderlawanswers.com/20-common-nursing-home-problems--and-how-to-resolve-them-5166 (site visited Aug. 6, 2018).

[147] *See, e.g.*, 42 C.F.R. § 483.15(b), (e).

[148] *See* American Health Care Association, LTC Stats: Nursing Facility Operational Characteristics Report, Mar. 2013 Update, Table 6: Nursing Facility Beds by Certification Type, Mar. 2013).

[149] 42 U.S.C. §§ 1396a(r)(1) and 1396r-5(d)(1); 42 C.F.R. §§ 435.725, 435.733, and 435.832. The deductions from gross income include incurred medical expenses, a personal needs allowance of at least $30 a month, monies diverted to create a minimum monthly needs allowance for a community spouse, and/or a family allowance for other dependents, if any, and certain reparation payments. Although the above-cited regulations do, indeed, describe certain required and permissible

income (NAMI), patient pay amount, or applied income. Medicaid then pays the difference between the share of cost and the established Medicaid rate for the facility.

However, when a portion of the stay is paid for by Medicare, different rules apply. If the individual is a QMB, he or she should have no share of cost for any portion of the nursing home stay that is covered by Medicare. This is because Medicare will cover fully the first 20 days of the Medicare-covered stay, and the copayment ($170.50 in 2019) for days 21 to 100 is Medicaid's responsibility.[150] Even if Medicaid does not pay the full Medicare cost-sharing amount, the nursing home can neither charge the individual for the copayment nor receive his or her Medicaid share of cost for that period of time. Sometimes, nursing facilities and Medicaid agencies are not as clear as they could be in informing residents about their rights and obligations with respect to share of cost.[151]

[F] Wheelchairs, Supplies, and Other Durable Medical Equipment

Generally, Medicare pays for wheelchairs only if the wheelchair will improve the mobility of the beneficiary and improve his or her ability to undertake ADL. ADL include personal feeding, dressing, and bathing. Other items that might be thought of as durable medical equipment (DME), such as bathroom grab bars, are explicitly excluded from Medicare coverage. DME is covered when needed for use in the home.[152] Medicaid coverage rules may be more expansive and must include a process for a beneficiary to request coverage for a non-covered item.[153]

When a physician believes that a patient requires Medicare-covered DME, the physician refers the patient to a medical equipment supplier who then obtains a Certificate of Medical Necessity from the physician.[154] The supplier provides the equipment to the patient and then submits a claim to the regional DME carrier for a determination as to Medicare coverage. As with most Medicare coverage decisions, determinations as to whether DME will be covered are generally made

---

deductions from income before determining share of cost, advocates should not rely on them as they do not reflect changes that have been made in the law since 1987.

[150] *See* CMS, "Skilled Facility Nursing (SNF) Care," http://www.medicare.gov/coverage/skilled-nursing-facility-care.html (site visited Aug. 6, 2018). Data in the *March 2013 MACPAC Report* show that 12 states pay nursing homes the full Medicare copayment rate. The rest pay the lesser-of amount (see discussion at **§ 10.06[C]**).

[151] *See, e.g.*, Conrad v. Perales, 92 F. Supp. 2d 175 (W.D.N.Y. 2000) for discussion of a variation on this theme.

[152] 42 C.F.R. §§ 410.38 (regulations for durable medical equipment) & 414.224 (regulations governing customized durable medical equipment).

[153] *See, e.g.*, Lankford v. Sherman, 451 F.3d 496 (8th Cir. 2006); State Medicaid Director Letter, Sept. 4, 1998, *available at* http://downloads.cms.gov/cmsgov/archived-downloads/SMDL/downloads/SMD090498.pdf (site visited Aug. 6, 2018).

[154] See **Chapter 6** of this Handbook for a general discussion of Medicare's coverage of durable medical equipment (DME), including wheelchairs.

after the equipment has been provided to the patient. If Medicare coverage is denied, the patient, or a third-party payer such as Medicaid, may be liable.

Advocates have reported misalignment of coverage and payment procedures in Medicare and Medicaid that lead to denials and delays for important DME for this vulnerable population. While having both types of coverage should enhance benefits, the logistical problems created by this misalignment lead to barriers in accessing needed care.

Often these problems arise when beneficiaries transition from Medicaid-only status to dual Medicare-Medicaid status. In these instances, individuals who previously had no difficulty obtaining their DME through Medicaid, may face vendors who refuse to deliver the same DME once they become eligible for Medicare.

Advocates report that Medicaid's practice of only processing payment after issuance of a Medicare coverage decision, coupled with Medicare's lack of a coverage decision until after delivery of the DME, often creates an insurmountable barrier to an essential element of care for those individuals who are most in need. In August 2016, a group of almost 80 advocacy organizations[155] submitted a letter to CMS in response to a CMS request for information regarding DME access issues faced by individuals who are dually eligible for Medicare and Medicaid. The letter, stressed the logistical problems created by Medicare and Medicaid processing rules that lead to barriers in accessing the needed care that individuals who are on only Medicaid **or** Medicare do not have.

Several states have addressed this issue by creating, in their Medicaid programs, a three-step process that promotes better access to DME coverage for dual eligibles. First, the individual gets prior authorization from the state for the wheelchair he or she needs. Then the individual gets the wheelchair from the supplier, who bills Medicare. If Medicare denies coverage, the supplier can still bill Medicaid because the prior authorization established Medicaid coverage.[156]

---

[155] CMA, "Sign-On Letter: Access to Care Issues for Durable Medical Equipment" (Aug. 19 2016), *available at* http://www.medicareadvocacy.org/sign-on-letter-access-to-care-issues-for-durable-medical-equipment/ (site visited Aug. 6, 2018).

[156] *See, e.g.*, Connecticut law at C.G.S.A. § 17b-281a:

> (a) The Commissioner of Social Services shall extend the procedure in effect on October 1, 1998, for the preauthorization of the purchase or rental of new durable medical **equipment** and modification or repair of existing **equipment** to include services provided to **Medicaid** recipients who are also recipients of **Medicare.** The commissioner may enter into any necessary agreements with the Centers for **Medicare** and **Medicaid** Services to ensure the coordination of **authorization** and payment for durable medical **equipment** for such recipients.
>
> (b) Access to such procedure shall not be denied to a recipient on the basis that a **Medicare** coverage determination has not been made prior to the submission of a request for preauthorization to the commissioner. The commissioner shall not make payment for an item to a supplier of durable medical **equipment** on behalf of a **Medicare** recipient until the commissioner has received documentation establishing that a

On January 13, 2017, the CMS posted a State Informational Bulletin encouraging states to adopt strategies like this three-step process to improve dual eligible beneficiaries' access to DME.[157] The Bulletin addresses a serious and persistent obstacle to obtaining DME faced by people dually eligible for Medicare and Medicaid in many states because of the mismatch of processing rules in the two programs.

The CMS Bulletin addresses these serious obstacles to needed equipment and outlines strategies for states to employ in order to improve timely DME access, referencing Medicaid prior authorization processes. The CMS Bulletin states that if Medicare does not allow for prior authorization of certain items, then the state Medicaid agency should do so as the means to prevent blocked access for duals to DME covered under Medicaid. The CMS Bulletin also reminds states that a recently amended regulation, 42 C.F.R. § 440.70, codifies long-standing agency policy that Medicaid must cover appropriate medical supplies, equipment and appliances suitable for use in any setting in which normal life activities take place, other than inpatient settings. The Bulletin states that coverage cannot be limited to the home setting, as long as the other coverage requirements are met.

Advocates also report challenges due to the mismatch between Medicaid and Medicare suppliers, and how the competitive bidding process may affect availability of suppliers.[158]

In addition to limiting coverage for wheelchairs, Medicare may reimburse for wheelchairs and other mobility devices at a rate lower than that of many state Medicaid programs, whose fee structures for such items are often more generous.[159] Medical supplies may also be treated differently by the two programs: for example, a month's supply of catheters under Medicare is 30; a state Medicaid program may pay for 31 in a 31-day month. These disparities result in claims for dually eligible individuals being denied or reduced by Medicare, with complications ensuing when the individual seeks Medicaid coverage.

In the past, states told providers serving dually eligible individuals that they were required to serve them on an assignment-related basis, even though this is

---

claim has been filed with, and a coverage and reimbursement decision has been rendered, under the **Medicare** program.

[157] CMCS Informational Bulletin, "Strategies to Support Dual Eligible Beneficiaries' Access to Durable Medical Equipment, Prosthetics, Orthotics, and Supplies" (Jan. 13, 2017), *available at* https://www.medicaid.gov/federal-policy-guidance/downloads/cib011317.pdf (site visited Aug. 6, 2018).

[158] On June 30, 2016, CMS published a proposed rule seeking information about the difficulties of dually eligible people obtaining DME. CMS also seeks information about potential solutions. 81 Fed. Reg. 42,801 (June 30, 2016), Request for information (Section IX. Access to Care Issues for DME, page 42864-5), *available at* https://www.gpo.gov/fdsys/pkg/FR-2016-06-30/pdf/2016-15188.pdf (site visited Oct. 1, 2018).

[159] As a general matter, in most states, Medicaid pays less for similar services than does Medicare. Customized wheelchairs and certain medical supplies are anomalous in this regard.

only required for physicians.[160] "Assignment-related basis" means they cannot receive more than the Medicare-approved amount for the supply or service. Because this amount is often less than they would receive from Medicaid for a Medicaid-only client, and because they are prohibited from billing a dually eligible person the way they would a non-dually eligible Medicare beneficiary, providers are often reluctant to serve dually eligible individuals. These state practices can be challenged as violations of comparability requirements in the Medicaid program and possibly as violations of state medical necessity law.[161]

The BBA '97 prohibits providers from billing dually eligible beneficiaries who are QMBs more than the provider receives from Medicare and Medicaid together, regardless of what that amount is.[162] It is not as clear whether the prohibition on billing *QMBs* includes within its meaning a prohibition on the provider receiving a payment *from the state* that is higher than the Medicare rate.[163]

[G] Differing Home Care Coverage Standards in Medicare and Medicaid Programs

Medicare covers a defined package of home health services when specified coverage criteria are met.[164] It covers a finite amount (no more than 35 hours per week) of skilled nursing care and home health aide services combined. In addition, the Medicare home health benefit covers skilled physical therapy, occupational therapy, speech language, pathology services, medical social work services, and some medical equipment and supplies.

Several Medicare requirements restrict the availability of the Medicare home health benefit. To qualify for home health services, a Medicare beneficiary

---

[160] 42 U.S.C. § 1395w-4(g)(3).

[161] *See, e.g.*, Charpentier v. Belshe, 1994 WL 792591, Medicare & Medicaid Guide (CCH) 43,123 (N.D. Cal. 1994) (holding that policies resulting in no access to certain Medicaid services for categorically needy individuals who were also eligible for Medicare, where such access was not so limited for individuals not "dually eligible," violated comparability requirements). *But see* Ralabate v. Wing, 1996 WL 377204, Medicare & Medicaid Guide (CCH) 44,550 (W.D.N.Y. 1996).

[162] BBA '97 § 4714(a)(1)(B) (amending 42 U.S.C. § 1396a(n) by adding subparagraphs (2) and (3) (2009 Supp.)). Note that this provision applies explicitly to QMBs, not necessarily to other dual eligibles. This particular protection is one reason that advocates should assure that their dually eligible clients with incomes under the state's QMB qualifying level are enrolled in the QMB program even though such enrollment might otherwise seem unnecessary.

[163] An additional wrinkle in this thorny issue is raised in CMS guidance from early 2008 that states that all providers must take assignment for all dual eligibles. *See, e.g.*, Feb. 2008 Memo. While providers are, by virtue of 42 U.S.C. § 1395cc(a)(1)(A)(i), prohibited from charging any QMB more than the Medicare and Medicaid payments (if any from the latter source), other provisions of Medicare law require only that physicians, not other providers, take assignment for dual eligibles. 42 U.S.C. § 1395w-4(g)(3).

[164] 42 U.S.C. §§ 1395f(a)(2)(C), 1395x(m). *See* **Chapter 4** of this Handbook for a thorough discussion of Medicare home health coverage criteria.

must be homebound[165] and must require a skilled service.[166] The requirement that an individual be homebound is included in the statute.[167] Homebound status does not preclude infrequent absences from the home for non-medical reasons such as hair dresser appointments, religious services, weddings, an occasional dinner, etc. To meet the statutory definition there must remain a normal inability to leave home without a considerable and taxing effort, or the assistance of another.

However, interpretations by both home health providers and Medicare Administrative Contractors (formerly, and sometimes still, called Fiscal Intermediaries) are often narrower than necessary and operate to limit the availability of the Medicare home health benefit.

For example, *any* absence from the home setting may lead to a decision by the home health agency that the patient is not homebound and therefore does not qualify for Medicare coverage. As a result of such a determination, the agency will no longer bill Medicare. If the beneficiary can pay to continue the services, he or she can ask the agency to submit a "demand bill" to Medicare to get an official coverage determination by Medicare. A demand bill is submitted when the agency itself does not believe there is Medicare coverage but the beneficiary seeks an official determination, which is a condition precedent to a Medicare appeal. There is no right under Medicare, as there is in Medicaid,[168] to continued coverage pending the outcome of an appeal. Accordingly, unless another payment source exists, as a practical matter, the home health agency makes final decisions regarding Medicare coverage.

Individuals who are dually eligible may need to look to Medicaid home care benefits to meet some or all of their needs, as well as to sustain their Medicare appeals. Medicaid mandatory home health care coverage rules are similar to Medicare rules, with two significant exceptions: they require neither homebound status nor that a skilled service be needed.[169] In addition to mandatory home health, all states include in their Medicaid programs home- and community-based

---

[165] 42 U.S.C. §§ 1395f(a)(2)(C) & 1395n(a)(2)(A).

[166] 42 U.S.C. § 1395f(a)(2)(C).

[167] 42 U.S.C. §§ 1395f(a)(8) & 1395n(a)(2)(F). The statutory language is "confined to the home." Under an amendment to this section passed in 2000, beneficiaries receiving therapeutic, psychosocial, or medical treatment in an adult day care program may still be considered "homebound." Moreover, absences from home for the purpose of attending a religious service are deemed to be of infrequent or short duration, in keeping with the statutory standard.

[168] 42 U.S.C. § 1396a(a)(3); 42 C.F.R. § 431.220; Goldberg v. Kelly, 397 U.S. 254 (1970). This concept is often referred to as aid paid pending. It is a hallmark of the Medicaid program that advocates seek to have expanded to all health care recipients.

[169] 42 U.S.C. §§ 1396a(a)(10)(D), 1396d. Although neither the Medicaid statute nor the Medicaid regulations use the "homebound" standard, states have, in the past, incorporated it into their Medicaid home health programs. CMS has informed states that such a requirement is impermissible under Medicaid regulations at 42 C.F.R. §§ 440.230(c) and 440.240(b). State Medicaid Director Letter of July 25, 2000, Olmstead Update No. 3, Attachment 3-g, *available at* http://www.cms.gov/smdl/downloads/smd072500b.pdf (site visited Aug. 6, 2018). To the author's knowledge, the most recent action by CMS with respect to this issue came in a letter sent to the Director of the Missouri

services provided to limited populations through waiver of certain federal Medicaid requirements or modifications of their Medicaid State Plan.[170] These programs vary widely in their eligibility and services. They usually offer "nonmedical" services, such as companion services, chore services, or adult day care, in addition to the more traditional home health care services offered by Medicare and the Medicaid mandatory home health benefit.

While some dual eligibles may need the services of one or the other program, many could benefit from enhanced coordination of the services offered by Medicare and Medicaid. This is particularly true with respect to coordination between Medicare and the Medicaid waiver home care programs. BBA '97 imposed a statutory limit on the amount of certain key home health services for which Medicare will pay. BBA '97 explicitly defined the "part-time or intermittent" quantitative standard for Medicare home health services to mean less than 35 hours a week of a combination of skilled nursing and home health aide services. That is the maximum amount of those services that Medicare will cover. Although Medicaid home health regulations adopt the "part-time or intermittent" language from Medicare, the Medicaid statute contains no such limitation. The regulations, therefore, may be subject to challenge. Most waiver programs also limit coverage through a cap on the amount of money or hours of care available to a beneficiary. Coordination of Medicare and Medicaid benefits can thus enhance the total quantity of care that may be offered to an individual and, in doing so, can also enhance the quality of care and quality of life for the beneficiary. Indeed, it can make the difference between being able to remain in a home setting and being forced to accept a residential long-term care placement.

§ 10.07 MANAGED CARE ISSUES FOR DUALLY ELIGIBLE INDIVIDUALS

[A] Overview

Dual eligibility presents a particularly wide spectrum of complexity when enrollment in managed care is introduced into the mix of possibilities. While both Medicare and Medicaid offer managed care options, with limited exceptions, neither program requires those who are dually eligible to enroll. Changes in payment for, and structure of, MA plans made in the MMA have resulted in a surge

---

Department of Social Services in February 2010 informing the state that it was out of compliance with federal Medicaid law by requiring homebound status for the receipt of Medicaid home health services.

[170] 42 U.S.C. § 1396a(a)(10)(D). These programs are referred to as waiver programs because certain Medicaid statutory requirements are waived by the federal government for limited purposes. The DRA authorizes states to provide such services as part of their regular Medicaid program, without having to seek a waiver. DRA, § 6086, amending 42 U.S.C. § 1396n by adding subsection (i). ACA § 2401, amending § 1915 of the Social Security Act, 42 U.S.C. § 1396n, further expands home and community-based options for care.

in the number of dually eligible beneficiaries participating in such plans. According to CMS's April 2018 *Special Needs Plans Comprehensive Report*, over 2.2 million beneficiaries were enrolled in Special Needs Plans for Dual Eligibles. This number does not account for duals who are enrolled in other types of MA plans.[171] Programmatic differences between Medicare and Medicaid in requirements for beneficiaries and for participating managed care organizations have made coordination between the two programs difficult. Due to this and other coordination difficulties, few states have promoted enrollment of dually eligible individuals into Medicaid managed care; fewer states require them to enroll.[172]

Policy initiatives developing under provisions of the ACA favor an integrated approach to care for the dually eligible that blends Medicare and Medicaid dollars and covers both acute care (now primarily paid for by Medicare) and non-skilled long-term care (now primarily paid for by Medicaid).[173] Programs of All-Inclusive Care for the Elderly (PACE), which have operated for more than 20

---

[171] MMA §§ 201, 211; 42 U.S.C. § 1395w-23. For April 2018, CMS reports that 2,209,691 individuals are enrolled in Medicare Advantage (MA) Special Needs Plans (SNPs) for Dual Eligibles. CMS, "Special Needs Plans Comprehensive Report" (2018-04), *available at* https://www.cms.gov/Research-Statistics-Data-and-Systems/Statistics-Trends-and-Reports/MCRAdvPartDEnrolData/Special-Needs-Plan-SNP-Data-Items/SNP-Comprehensive-Report-2018-04.html?DLPage=1&DLEntries=10&DLSort=1&DLSortDir=descending (site visited Aug. 6, 2018). For a discussion of this, *see e.g.*, Kaiser Family Foundation, "Medicare's Role for Dual Eligible Beneficiaries" (Apr. 2012), *available at* http://www.kff.org/medicare/upload/8138-02.pdf (site visited Aug. 6, 2018). *See also* CBO, "Dual Eligible Beneficiaries of Medicare and Medicaid: Characteristics, Health Care Spending and Evolving Policies" (June 2013), *available at* http://www.cbo.gov/publication/44308 (site visited Aug. 6, 2018). In a more general discussion of dual eligibles in managed care (either Medicare, or Medicaid, or both) the March 2010 report from the Center for Health Care Strategies called *Options for Integrating Care for Dual Eligible Beneficiaries* reports that over 80 percent of dual eligibles get their care through fee-for-service delivery systems. The report does not distinguish between Medicare and Medicaid enrollments, though it is possible for a dual eligible to receive Medicare services outside a managed care plan but receive Medicaid through a plan, and vice versa. For historical experience of duals in managed care, *see e.g.*, Edith Walsh et al., "Case Studies of Managed Care Arrangements for Dually Eligible Beneficiaries," Research Triangle Institute for CMS (Sept. 26, 2003), *available at* https://www.rti.org/sites/default/files/resources/ManagedCareStudies.pdf (site visited Aug. 6, 2018) (hereinafter Case Studies). The range of participation among the states historically is remarkable: in 1998, Oregon had 36.5 percent of its dual eligibles in MA plans while Mississippi had 0.1 percent (one-tenth of one percent). To this author's knowledge, similar data do not exist for later years. With respect to Medicare Advantage Dual Eligible SNPs, in 2016, the following states had no dual eligible SNPs at all (Alaska, Nevada, New Hampshire, North Dakota, South Dakota, Vermont, Wyoming). *See* CMS, 2017 SNP Landscape, *available at* https://www.cms.gov/Medicare/Prescription-Drug-Coverage/PrescriptionDrugCovGenin/ (site visited Aug. 6, 2018).

[172] *See e.g.*, The Kaiser Family Foundation, "Dual Eligible Enrollment in Medicaid Managed Care, by Plan Type" (2011 data), *available at* http://kff.org/medicaid/state-indicator/dual-eligible-enrollment-in-medicaid-managed-care-by-plan-type/ (site visited Aug. 6, 2018).

[173] *See e.g.*, Medicare and Medicaid Coordination Office website at https://www.cms.gov/Medicare-Medicaid-Coordination/Medicare-and-Medicaid-Coordination/Medicare-Medicaid-Coordination-Office/ (site visited Aug. 6, 2018).

years, are one such model, but PACE programs are limited in their scope, currently serving less than one percent of the dually eligible population.[174] The ACA moved this agenda forward in significant ways by mandating the establishment of two new Centers within the CMS, both of which focus attention on such integrated care.[175] The MMCO and the Center for Medicare and Medicaid Innovation (Innovation Center, or CMMI) will be discussed more fully at the end of this section.

The MMA's authorization of Medicare Advantage SNPs, including such plans for dual eligibles, has changed the landscape with respect to dual eligibles in Medicare managed care.[176] In April 2018, 641 SNPs were available to "special needs" Medicare beneficiaries (down from 769 in 2008, up from 583 in 2017); 412 of those are designed to serve dually eligible beneficiaries (down from 443 in 2008, up from 377 in 2017).[177] Some are Medicaid managed care plans entering the Medicare market. In many respects these plans, with their state contracts and experience serving special needs individuals such as dual eligibles, represent the SNPs with the most promise of actually meeting the special needs of the dually eligible population. Many approved SNPs, however, do not have contracts with state Medicaid agencies and are new to serving special needs individuals. Although it is clear that the SNP option is popular with private MA health plan sponsors, little is known about what SNPs are actually providing that distinguishes them from other MA plans or from traditional Medicare, and it is not known whether fully integrated care that benefits the beneficiary will result.[178]

---

[174] Notably, in its 2013 report to Congress, the Medicare-Medicaid Coordination Office recommended a PACE pilot program for individuals between the ages of 21 and 55. Currently PACE programs are available only to those 55 and older. Recent data from the National PACE organization show 124 PACE programs operating in 31 states. National PACE Association, *available at* http://www.npaonline.org/pace-you/find-pace-program-your-neighborhood (site visited Aug. 6, 2018).

[175] ACA §§ 2602 & 3021.

[176] MMA § 231 (amending 42 U.S.C. §§ 1395w-21(a)(2)(A) & 1395w-28).

[177] *See* CMS, SNP Comprehensive Report—April 2018, *available at* https://www.cms.gov/Research-Statistics-Data-and-Systems/Statistics-Trends-and-Reports/MCRAdvPartDEnrolData/Special-Needs-Plan-SNP-Data-Items/SNP-Comprehensive-Report-2018-04.html?DLPage=1&DLEntries=10&DLSort=1&DLSortDir=descending (site visited Aug. 6, 2018) *and*, for 2017 data, SNP Comprehensive Report—December 2017, *available at* https://www.cms.gov/Research-Statistics-Data-and-Systems/Statistics-Trends-and-Reports/MCRAdvPartDEnrolData/Special-Needs-Plan-SNP-Data-Items/SNP-Comprehensive-Report-2017-12.html?DLPage=1&DLEntries=10&DLSort=1&DLSortDir=descending (site visited Aug. 6, 2018); for 2008 data, SNP Comprehensive Report—June 2008, *available at* http://www.cms.gov/Research-Statistics-Data-and-Systems/Statistics-Trends-and-Reports/MCRAdvPartDEnrolData/Special-Needs-Plan-SNP-Data-Items/CMS1211836.html (site visited Aug. 6, 2018).

[178] *See e.g.*, Alissa Halperin, Patricia Nemore & Vicki Gottlich, *What's So Special About Medicare Advantage Special Needs Plans? Assessing Medicare Special Needs Plans for Dual Eligibles*, 8 Marquette Elder's Advisor 2 (Spring 2007), *available at* http://scholarship.law.marquette.edu/cgi/viewcontent.cgi?article=1077&context=elders (site visited Aug. 6, 2018); Christie Provost Peters, "Medicare Advantage SNPs: A New Opportunity for Integrated Care?" National Health Policy

MIPPA included new requirements for SNPs, effective beginning the 2010 plan year.[179] All SNPs must exclusively enroll individuals who meet the definition of the population for which they are designated. All plans must have in place an evidence-based model of care with appropriate networks of providers and specialists and must provide care management that includes an annual assessment of the enrollee's needs, a plan of care, and the provision of care by an interdisciplinary team. Dual Eligible SNPs (D-SNPs) must provide each enrollee a comprehensive statement about his or her coverage under Medicaid and cost-sharing requirements/protections. Any D-SNP wishing to start up or expand its existing coverage area must have a contract with the state Medicaid agency under which the plan will provide or arrange for the provision of benefits to which the enrollee is entitled under the state Medicaid plan. Contracts with the state may, but are not required to, include coverage for long-term care services.[180] Beyond the state contract issue for D-SNPs, the fate of SNPs, especially D-SNPs, may be partially linked to the success or lack of success of initiatives being proposed by some states to integrate financing and care delivery systems for the dually eligible, discussed in **§ 10.09**. Some states propose to rely on D-SNPs in the design of their delivery systems. To the extent states are permitted to enroll all their dually eligible beneficiaries into their new systems, SNPs may gain or lose enrollees.

The MMA required ongoing Congressional reauthorization of SNPs. The SNPs were reauthorized through 2018 by MACRA.[181]

The Bipartisan Budget Act of 2018 (BBA)[182] permanently authorized SNPs, which include D-SNPs, Chronic Condition SNPs (C-SNPs), and Institutional SNPs (I-SNPs). Section 50311(b) of the BBA creates a new § 1859(f)(8) of the Social Security Act (the Act) in order to increase integration of Dual Eligible Special Needs Plans (D-SNPs). In particular, the statute directs CMS to: (1) develop unified grievance and appeals processes for D-SNPs; and (2) establish new standards for integration of Medicare and Medicaid benefits for D-SNPs.

The Duals office must establish uniform grievances and appeals procedures, to the extent feasible, for D-SNPs by April 1, 2020. They are to align procedures such as single notifications, unified time frames, and simplified reporting. Unified procedures must be used by D-SNPs with contracts with state Medicaid agencies for 2021 and subsequent years.

Forum, Issue Brief #808 (Nov. 11, 2005), *available at* http://www.nhpf.org/library/details.cfm/2503 (site visited Aug. 6, 2018); Memo from Danielle Moon, Director, Medicare Drug and Health Plan Contract Administration Group to Medicare Advantage Organizations offering Special Needs Plans, "CMS Expectations of Special Needs Plans for 2010," *available at* http://www.medicareadvocacy.org/old-site/InfoByTopic/MedicareAdvantageAndHMOs/10_01.11.SNPMemo.pdf (site visited Aug. 6, 2018).

[179] MIPPA §§ 164 and 165 (amending § 1859 of the Social Security Act, 42 U.S.C. § 139w-28(f)).

[180] 42 C.F.R. §§ 422.2, 422.4, 422.52, 422.107, and 422.504 for new requirements on SNPs.

[181] MACRA § 206.

[182] Pub. L. No. 115-123.

The Duals office serves as the dedicated point of contact for states to address misalignments that arise with the integration of specialized MA plans for special needs individuals. The Duals office is working with stakeholders in 2018 to implement these provisions.[183]

[B] Managed Care/Fee-for-Service Matrix

At least four combinations of health care coverage for dually eligible individuals are possible when managed care is offered in the mix. A dually eligible individual can be in:

1. Medicaid fee-for-service/traditional Medicare
2. Medicaid fee-for-service/Medicare Advantage
3. Medicaid managed care/traditional Medicare
4. Medicaid managed care/Medicare Advantage

In the last case, the individual could be enrolled in two different managed care plans and become very confused as to which plan he or she should look to for coverage. Dually eligible individuals may increasingly find themselves in this situation as more states move their Medicaid, and especially Medicaid Long Term Services and Supports (LTSS) programs into managed care.[184] Managed care issues arise concerning state obligations to pay Medicare managed care cost-sharing for QMBs, as well as concerning MA organizations' efforts to limit their liability for providing care by trying to shift coverage to the Medicaid program. Additional issues arise with respect to a dually eligible individual's right to choose a nursing facility if he or she is in an MA plan that has a network of nursing facilities. These issues are discussed below.

---

[183] CMS Request for Stakeholder Input: Implementing the Dual Eligible Special Needs Plans (D-SNPs) Provisions of the Bipartisan Budget Act of 2018 (Mar. 13, 2018), *available at* https://www.cms.gov/Medicare-Medicaid-Coordination/Medicare-and-Medicaid-Coordination/Medicare-Medicaid-Coordination-Office/Downloads/RequestForStakeholderInputBBADSNPProvisions03132018.pdf (site visited Aug. 6, 2018).

[184] *See generally* National Senior Citizens Law Center, "LTSS in Managed Care," *available at* http://nsclcarchives.org/index.php/mltss/#.VipV6H6rTct (site visited Aug. 6, 2018). Traditionally, Medicaid beneficiaries in need of Long Term Services and Supports were exempt from state mandatory Medicaid managed care. Increasingly, this exemption is being lifted as states transition their entire Medicaid populations into managed care.

[C] State Medicaid Payment of Cost-Sharing for Medicare Managed Care Enrollees

Dual eligibles who are enrolled in MA plans and who are QMBs are entitled to have their states pay MA plan copayments and are excused from liability for such payments; other dual eligibles are entitled to have at least some copayments paid.[185] Little is known, however, about whether, and how, states actually make such copayments.[186] Information is available from CMS to identify MA plan enrollees.[187] Until a state has a formal system in place, advocates should advise clients to inform their state of their MA plan enrollment and have the MA plan providers bill the state for any copayments for which the individual is responsible.[188] Recent regulations governing Medicare Advantage plans should

---

[185] 42 U.S.C. § 1396d(p)(3); SM Manual, Chap. 3: § 3490.12; MMCO-CMCS Informational Bulletin June 7, 2013, Subject: Payment of Medicare Cost Sharing for Qualified Medicare Beneficiaries (QMBs), *available at* http://www.medicaid.gov/Federal-Policy-Guidance/downloads/CIB-06-07-2013.pdf (site visited Aug. 6, 2018); MMCO-CMCS Informational Bulletin Jan. 6, 2012, Subject: Billing for Services Provided to Qualified Medicare Beneficiaries (QMBs), *available at* http://www.medicareadvocacy.org/wp-content/uploads/2012/01/cib-01-06-12.pdf (site visited Aug. 6, 2018); CMS MLN Matters, "Prohibition on Balance Billing Qualified Medicare Beneficiaries (QMBs); Feb. 2008 Memo and two attachments, memo *available at* http://www.medicareadvocacy.org/old-site/InfoByTopic/MedicareSavingsPrograms/MedSavProg_08_04.24.ARACostShare.pdf (site visited Aug. 6, 2018); Balance Billing attachment *available at* http://www.medicareadvocacy.org/old-site/InfoByTopic/MedicareSavingsPrograms/MedSavProg_08_04.24.ARABalanceBilling.pdf (site visited Aug. 6, 2018); and Capitation attachment *available at* http://www.medicareadvocacy.org/old-site/InfoByTopic/MedicareSavingsPrograms/MedSavProg_08_04.24.ARACapitation.pdf (site visited Aug. 6, 2018); June 2007 Memo (**Appendix 10-3** of this Handbook); January 2012 Memo (**Appendix 10-4** of this Handbook).

[186] *See Variations in State Medicaid.* Only 19 states responded affirmatively to a 1999 survey question asking whether the state pays copayments in Medicare managed care. Eighteen states reported that they did not; the remaining states either did not answer or do not have Medicare managed care in their state. The author is not aware of more recent data on this subject.

[187] According to one CMS official, "States still do get that information on their MMA response file. If they'd like, they can also query our system on an ad hoc basis (i.e., when they need it, not just when MMA response file is returned)." E-mail of July 3, 2012, from Sharon Donovan, Medicare-Medicaid Coordination Office CMS, to Patricia B. Nemore, Center for Medicare Advocacy, *available from* kkertesz@medicareadvocacy.org. CMS now accepts MMA files from states on a daily basis.

[188] Guidance from CMS issued in February 2008 discusses potential complexities associated with paying cost-sharing for services delivered through MA plans. *See* 42 U.S.C. §§ 1396d(p)(3), 1396a(n)(2); SM Manual, Pub. 45, Ch. 3: Eligibility § 3490.12, *see* **Appendix 10-1** of this Handbook. *See also* Feb. 2008 Memo and two attachments, memo *available at* http://www.medicareadvocacy.org/old-site/InfoByTopic/MedicareSavingsPrograms/MedSavProg_08_04.24.ARACostShare.pdf , Balance Billing attachment *available at* http://www.medicareadvocacy.org/old-site/InfoByTopic/MedicareSavingsPrograms/MedSavProg_08_04.24.ARABalanceBilling.pdf, and Capitation attachment *available at* http://www.medicareadvocacy.org/old-site/InfoByTopic/MedicareSavingsPrograms/MedSavProg_08_04.24.ARACapitation.pdf (sites visited Aug. 6, 2018); Nov. 1991 Memo (**Appendix 10-2** of this Handbook); June 2007 Memo (**Appendix 10-3** of this Handbook);

improve this situation as well because plans must include provisions in contracts with all providers in their networks prohibiting providers from charging dual eligibles cost-sharing that is not due under their state Medicaid program.[189]

[D] Managed Long-Term Care

Several problematic scenarios can arise if an individual enrolled in an MA plan needs or is receiving nursing home care.

> ■ **SCENARIO ONE:** A dually eligible beneficiary living at home and enrolled in an MA plan needs skilled nursing home care. The MA plan waives the Medicare three-day prior hospitalization requirement. The beneficiary wants to move to an out-of-network nursing home. The MA plan says it will not cover such care. The state Medicaid agency refuses to pay for Medicaid coverage since the individual could have received Medicare coverage through the MA plan in which she chose to enroll.

A solution to this problem is to disenroll from the MA plan. Disenrollment is effective the month following the individual's notice to disenroll; the beneficiary is then free to choose a nursing facility and have Medicaid pay, since she would not have met the three-day prior hospitalization requirement for Medicare coverage. This solution will not work for most Medicare beneficiaries because they are generally "locked" into MA plans for most of the plan year, but dual eligibles are able to change enrollment monthly.[190]

> ■ **SCENARIO TWO:** The same beneficiary needs a nursing home placement but does not need skilled care. There is no possibility of Medicare coverage for the nursing home stay.

---

and Memorandum of June 30, 2000 from Director, DEHPG, Subject: Policy Memorandum on Medicaid Obligations to Pay Medicare Cost-sharing Expenses for Qualified Medicare Beneficiaries in Medicare Health Maintenance Organizations or Competitive Medical Plans or Medicare Plus Choice Organizations—Information (hereinafter Jan. 6, 2000 Memo) (**Appendix 10-4** of this Handbook).

[189] 42 C.F.R. § 422.504(g)(1)(iii).

[190] 42 C.F.R. § 422.62(b)(4) authorizes CMS to establish a special enrollment period for an individual who meets "such other exceptional conditions" as CMS may provide. Through informal guidance, CMS has established a permanent special enrollment period for dual eligibles. *See* Medicare Managed Care (MMM) Manual, Chapter 2: § 30.4.4 #5, *available at* https://www.cms.gov/MedicareMangCareEligEnrol/Downloads/FINALMAEnrollmentandDisenrollmentGuidanceUpdatefor CY2011.pdf (site visited Aug. 6, 2018).

Even though she chooses an out-of-network nursing facility, Medicaid will pay because the MA plan has no liability for non-Medicare-covered nursing facility care.[191] But, note that this outcome assumes the beneficiary is not also enrolled in a Medicaid managed care plan that has its own network of facilities, which may exclude this facility. This is unlikely, however, as few states include nursing facility care in their Medicaid managed care coverage, and few dual eligibles are enrolled in Medicaid managed care. However, this scenario is rapidly changing as states look to managed care to provide long-term care.

■ **SCENARIO THREE:** A dually eligible individual enrolled in an MA plan resides in a non-Medicare-certified bed in a nursing facility. She becomes eligible for the Medicare SNF benefit after a three-day hospitalization. Would she be required to move to an in-network Medicare certified bed or would she be allowed to waive her right to Medicare coverage and remain in the non-Medicare-certified bed, with Medicaid as the payer?

The Medicaid law requires states to allow beneficiaries to receive services from any certified provider who chooses to serve them.[192] While there is legal support for the view that if the individual chooses to remain in a bed in which she could not receive Medicare services, there is no Medicare liability and Medicaid must pay, it is unlikely that many states interpret their obligations that way, so advocates should be cautious about advising their clients in this regard.[193]

Legislation enacted in December 2000 addressed a fourth variation of the nursing home musical bed game for dually eligible beneficiaries enrolled in an MA plan: the situation where an MA plan enrollee in a non-network SNF is transferred to a hospital and seeks to return to his or her former SNF instead of going to an in-network facility.[194] The legislation permits the enrollee to choose to return to the former (out-of-network) facility if the facility agrees to accept the MA plan payment for services. This provision appears to actually undermine existing rights of dually eligible individuals, although the situation it addresses seems unlikely to arise very often.

---

[191] *See, e.g.*, Preston letter. Advocates are cautioned that while the principles enunciated in this letter are embodied in the law, actual state policy and practice is likely to be less favorable and the state may refuse to pay for a resident who has declined Medicare coverage. Advocates are encouraged, nonetheless, to make these arguments for clients who wish to return to a non-Medicare-certified bed. A copy of the letter can be found in **Appendix 10-5** of this Handbook.

[192] 42 U.S.C. § 1396a(a)(23).

[193] *But see* Preston letter at **Appendix 10-5** of this Handbook. Advocates are cautioned that while the principles enunciated in this letter are embodied in the law, actual state policy and practice is likely to be less favorable and the state may refuse to pay for a resident who has declined Medicare coverage.

[194] BIPA § 621.

Historically, enrollment of dually eligible beneficiaries in Medicare and Medicaid managed care has been considerably more limited than such enrollment of non-dual populations in both programs. Even states that have used managed care for this population may "carve out" long-term care for different treatment. As noted above, this situation appears to be shifting, bolstered by the MMA provision for MA plans for special populations, including plans for institutionalized individuals (I-SNPs), and by state Medicaid programs' increased interest in using managed care for this population in need of long-term services and supports. Current enrollment in I-SNPs is relatively low: 74,452 (up from 68,888 in 2017 but down from 138,097 in 2008) individuals were enrolled in 97 (up from 83 in 2017) plans as of April 2018.[195] This author has no data on how many of these individuals are dually eligible. More importantly, little is known about what I-SNPs offer by way of extra or "special" benefits that would not be required either through the Medicaid program of the state in which they operate or by the federal nursing home reform law.[196]

§ 10.08 PROGRAMS OF ALL-INCLUSIVE CARE FOR THE ELDERLY

As noted briefly earlier, PACE programs are operated under both the Medicare and Medicaid programs[197] to replicate the comprehensive services delivery and financing model for acute and long-term care created by On Lok Senior Health Services in San Francisco in the late 1970s. Until the BBA '97, PACE programs were operated under waivers of both Medicare and Medicaid requirements. The BBA '97 amended both Medicare and Medicaid to establish PACE as a non-waiver program, with states having the option to include PACE in their Medicaid program. PACE is the embodiment of the "integrated" approach to serving dually eligible older people, putting Medicare and Medicaid dollars and acute and long-term care services together and thus avoiding many of the confusions and complexities described elsewhere in this chapter. A goal of PACE is to provide a full range of long-term care services to frail older people in a community-based setting.

---

[195] *See* https://www.cms.gov/Research-Statistics-Data-and-Systems/Statistics-Trends-and-Reports/MCRAdvPartDEnrolData/Special-Needs-Plan-SNP-Data-Items/SNP-Comprehensive-Report-2018-04.html?DLPage=1&DLEntries=10&DLSort=1&DLSortDir=descending.

[196] *See, e.g.*, Alissa Eden Halperin, Patricia Nemore, Vicki Gottlich & Toby Edelman, *Medicare Advantage Special Needs Plans for "Institutionalized Individuals": What Advantage to Enrollment?*, 1 St. Louis U.J. Health L. & Pol'y 175 (2007).

[197] The principal statutory provisions governing PACE, 42 U.S.C. § 1395eee (Medicare) and 42 U.S.C. § 1396u-4 (Medicaid), are substantially the same. Final regulations are at 42 C.F.R. Pt. 460, 71 Fed. Reg. 71,334 (Dec. 8, 2006). While most enrollees in PACE programs will be dually eligible, such dual enrollment is not a requirement for the program. However, for those who are enrolled in either Medicare or Medicaid or both, regulations for those programs will govern beneficiaries' rights and entitlements, in addition to the provisions of the PACE regulations.

To be eligible for PACE services, enrollees must need the level of health care required from a nursing facility under Medicaid.[198] But PACE programs are not merely long-term care programs; generally speaking, they must provide the full array of both acute and long-term care services required under Medicare and Medicaid as well as any services determined necessary for the individual enrollee by his or her interdisciplinary team.[199]

Based on a study released in May 2015, HHS can no longer limit PACE programs to nonprofit entities. The CMS study found "no statistically significant difference" between seniors enrolled in PACE through Senior LIFE and those in other PACE programs in regard to frailty, access to care, and quality of care received. Expenditures for both the nonprofit and for-profit programs also were similar.[200]

As noted above, PACE is a paradigm of integrated care for dual eligibles. However it has been very slow to develop. The National PACE Association's website in 2018 lists 124 PACE programs (up from 116 in 2016) in 31 states enrolling over 45,000 current participants (an increase from 38,284 in 2016).[201]

§ 10.09 MEDICARE-MEDICAID COORDINATION OFFICE AND CENTER FOR MEDICARE AND MEDICAID INNOVATION

The ACA created two new centers within CMS, both of which have an impact on the care for dual eligibles.[202]

The purpose of the MMCO (originally called the Federal Coordinated Health Care Officer) is to integrate benefits under Medicare and Medicaid and to improve coordination between the federal government and the states on behalf of individuals dually eligible for Medicare and Medicaid. The Office has eight statutory goals:

1. Provide dual eligibles full access to all benefits of both programs;
2. Simplify access to services;
3. Improve quality;
4. Eliminate regulatory conflicts;

---

[198] 42 C.F.R. § 460.150(b)(2).

[199] *See generally* 42 C.F.R. § 460.92.

[200] CMS, "Report to Congress: The Centers for Medicare & Medicaid Services' Evaluation of For-Profit PACE Programs under Section 4804(b) of the Balanced Budget Act of 1997," (May 19, 2015), *available at* http://innovation.cms.gov/Files/reports/RTC_For-Profit_PACE_Report_to_Congress_051915_Clean.pdf (site visited Aug. 6, 2018).

[201] National PACE Association, *available at* http://www.npaonline.org/pace-you/find-pace-program-your-neighborhood.

[202] ACA § 2602 (Federal Coordinated Health Care Office) & 3021 (Center for Medicare and Medicaid Innovation). The latter section amends the Social Security Act by adding, after § 1115, a new § 1115A.

5. Improve continuity of care and safe transitions;
6. Increase dual eligibles' understanding of the programs;
7. Eliminate cost-shifting between the two programs and among providers; and
8. Improve performance of providers.

Specific responsibilities are to:

- Provide states, Medicare Advantage SNPs, plan sponsors, and others with the tools to develop programs that align Medicare and Medicaid benefits;
- Support state efforts to align acute and long-term care services for duals with Medicare service;
- Support coordination of contracting and oversight with respect to Medicare and Medicaid to promote the statutory goals;
- Consult and coordinate with the Medicare Payment Advisory Commission (MedPac); and
- Study drug coverage for new full-benefit dual eligibles.

The Secretary is directed to report annually to Congress on recommendations for legislation to improve care for dual eligibles.[203]

The MMCO has no authority, per se, with respect to Medicare or Medicaid. The authority rests with the Secretary of HHS, but on a practical basis, with CMS, which has jurisdiction over Medicare and Medicaid within HHS.

The purpose of the Innovation Center "is to test innovative payment and service delivery models to reduce program expenditures under the applicable titles while preserving or enhancing the quality of care furnished to individuals under such titles."[204] Among the 18 models to be tested by the new Center is one that allows states "to test and evaluate fully integrating care for dual eligible individuals in the state, including the management and oversight of all funds under the applicable titles with respect to such individuals."[205] Through the section of the law that created the Innovation Center, the Secretary of HHS is given broad authority to waive provisions of the Medicare law to advance the specific models identified in the legislation.

In July 2011, the MMCO, in partnership with the Innovation Center, launched a demonstration initiative intended to better serve dual eligibles by

[203] Medicare-Medicaid Coordination Office Fiscal Year 2012 Report to Congress; Medicare-Medicaid Coordination Office Fiscal Year 2013 Report to Congress, *available at* http://www.cms.gov/Medicare-Medicaid-Coordination/Medicare-and-Medicaid-Coordination/Medicare-Medicaid-Coordination-Office/Downloads/MMCO_2013_RTC.pdf (site visited Aug. 6, 2018).

[204] ACA § 3021(a)(1).

[205] ACA § 3021(b)(2)(B)(x).

increasing coordination and integration between Medicare and Medicaid.[206] The MMCO has also shown willingness to explore alternative demonstration models with states.

It is an ambitious initiative: MMCO aims to have as many as 2 million of the roughly 7 million full dual eligibles enrolled in demonstrations once all are fully operational. The demonstrations are jointly managed by CMS and the participating states. The centerpiece of the capitated model is the Medicare–Medicaid Plan (MMP), a health plan that provides all Medicare-covered and all or most Medicaid-covered services to dual eligibles. MMPs receive a blended capitation rate that combines Medicare Part A, Part B, and Part D and Medicaid payments. The aim is that the integration of Medicare and Medicaid financing, combined with extensive requirements for care coordination, will lead to better care for this vulnerable population, while maintaining or reducing Medicare and Medicaid spending.[207]

Though the initiative is in its early stages, it has gotten off to a rough start with delays in enrollment, high costs, and withdrawals of states and plans from the program.[208] The demonstrations were initially set to run for three years, but CMS announced in July 2015 that states may extend their demonstrations by two years.[209]

As of June 2017, about 400,000 beneficiaries were enrolled and receiving services from health plans in 10 states with capitated financial alignment demonstrations.[210] The capitated financial alignment demonstrations are in 10 states as of June 2017. These states include California, Illinois, Massachusetts, Michigan, New York, Ohio, Rhode Island, South Carolina, Texas, and Virginia.[211]

All states that currently have demonstrations approved by CMS have now started to enroll beneficiaries, and enrollment will continue. In addition, Colorado and Washington are enrolling beneficiaries in managed fee-for-service (FFS) demonstrations, and Minnesota is implementing an administrative alignment demonstration using Medicare Advantage Special Needs Plans for Dual Eligible Beneficiaries.[212]

---

[206] For updates on states with innovation models, see CMS, "The CMS Innovation Center," http://innovation.cms.gov/ (site visited Aug. 6, 2018).

[207] *MedPAC June 2016 Report* at 264-5.

[208] Virgil Dickson, "Future of Dual-Eligible Demonstrations Questioned Due to Low Enrollment," Modern Healthcare (Apr. 21, 2015), *available at* http://www.modernhealthcare.com/article/20150421/NEWS/150429978 (site visited Aug.6, 2018).

[209] CMS letter July 16, *available at* http://www.modernhealthcare.com/assets/pdf/CH10117592.PDF (site visited Aug. 6, 2018).

[210] Kaiser Family Foundation, "Health Plan Enrollment in the Capitated Financial Alignment Demonstrations for Dual Eligible Beneficiaries," *available at* https://www.kff.org/medicaid/fact-sheet/health-plan-enrollment-in-the-capitated-financial-alignment-demonstrations-for-dual-eligible-beneficiaries/ (site visited Nov. 20, 2017).

[211] 26 U.S.C § 223(c).

[212] *Id.*

As of June 2017, California's demonstration had the largest enrollment, with nearly 118,000 beneficiaries, followed by Ohio, Illinois, Texas, Michigan, Virginia, Massachusetts, Rhode Island, New York, and South Carolina. These states' demonstrations have been in effect for different lengths of time, with Massachusetts first enrolling beneficiaries in October, 2013 and Michigan beginning voluntary enrollment in April 2015. At least two states (Colorado and Virginia) are planning to discontinue their demonstrations at the end of 2017.

In all states, beneficiaries can opt out of the demonstration.[213]

[213] CMS letter July 16, *available at* http://www.modernhealthcare.com/assets/pdf/CH10117592.PDF (site visited Aug. 6, 2018).

APPENDIX 10-1 CMS PUB. 45: STATE MEDICAID MANUAL, CHAPTER 3 ELIGIBILITY

Sec. 3490.12 Medicare Cost-Sharing Expenses and Federal Financial Participation

Sec. 3490.13 Payment of Monthly Premiums for Medicare Part B and for Premium Hospital Insurance Under Medicare Part A

3490.12 Medicare Cost Sharing Expenses and Federal Financial Participation.—FFP is available for medical assistance for Medicare cost sharing expenses. These expenses are defined as:

- Monthly premiums for Medicare Part B and, where applicable, for Premium Hospital Insurance under Medicare Part A;
- Medicare Part A and Part B deductibles and coinsurance, including deductibles and coinsurance that HMOs and CMPs charge their Medicare enrollees in lieu of the Medicare deductibles and coinsurance that the beneficiaries would pay if they were not enrolled in an HMO or CMP; and
- At your option, premiums for enrollment with a Health Maintenance Organization (HMO) or a Competitive Medical Plan (CMP) under § 1876 of the Act.

Note that FFP is available for Medicare cost sharing expenses at the beginning of the month after the month in which you determine an individual is eligible for Medicaid as a QMB.

3490.13 Payment of Monthly Premiums for Medicare Part B and for Premium Hospital Insurance Under Medicare Part A.—You are required to pay the full amount of monthly premiums for Medicare Part B and, where applicable, for Premium Hospital Insurance under Medicare Part A. You may enroll QMBs and pay the Medicare Part B premiums under the State buy-in process under § 1843 of the Act. Effective January 1, 1990, a State may request and obtain a buy-in agreement modification to include payment of Part A premiums on behalf of QMBs. Payment of premiums through buy-in is advantageous because premiums paid through this method are not subject to the increases otherwise applicable in the case of late enrollment or re-enrollment. States without a buy-in agreement for Part B and/or Part A, are billed for the premiums (which may include any penalty applicable to the QMB for late enrollment) when the State seeks to enroll the QMB in Part A or Part B.

APPENDIX 10-2 NOVEMBER 22, 1991, MEMORANDUM FROM DIRECTOR OF OFFICE OF MEDICAID MANAGEMENT, MB, TO DEPUTY CHIEF COUNSEL, OFFICE OF THE GENERAL COUNSEL, RE: STATE REQUIREMENT TO PAY MEDICARE PREMIUMS FOR QUALIFIED MEDICARE BENEFICIARIES (QMB)—ACTION

DEPARTMENT OF HEALTH & HUMAN SERVICES

Health Care Financing Administration

Memorandum

Refer to: FMC-33

Date NOV 22 1991

From Director
Office of Medicaid Management, MB

Subject State Requirement to Pay Medicare Premiums for Qualified Medicare Beneficiaries (QMB)--ACTION

To Deputy Chief Counsel
Office of the General Counsel

ISSUE

It has come to our attention that as many as 3 million Medicare beneficiaries may not be receiving the benefits to which they are entitled under section 1902(a)(10)(E) of the Social Security Act (the QMB provision).

We seek to confirm that the Federal Government has the authority necessary to compel States to: (a) enroll these individuals as QMBs, and (b) provide such individuals with all the benefits to which they are entitled under the QMB provision. Can the Health Care Financing Administration (HCFA) unilaterally accrete likely QMBs in Part A buy-in States and all other States without any State approval up front?

BACKGROUND

The Medicare Catastrophic Coverage Act of 1988 amended the Social Security Act to make coverage of certain Medicare beneficiaries for Medicare cost sharing expenses a mandatory Medicaid coverage group.

The State Medicaid Manual (SMM), Part 3, Eligibility, was revised to instruct the States as to their obligations under this section. A QMB is defined as an individual who:

- is entitled to Medicare hospital insurance benefits under Part A, with or without payment of premiums;
- has income (as determined for Supplemental Security Income (SSI) purposes) that does not exceed 100 percent of the Federal poverty level; and
- has resources (as determined for SSI purposes) that do not exceed twice the maximum amount established for SSI eligibility.

Page 2 - Deputy Chief Counsel, OGC

Potential QMBs Currently Without Part A

Part A Buy-in States

As a result of the Omnibus Budget Reconciliation Act of 1989, States are permitted, at their option, to modify their Part B buy-in agreement (copy attached) to include paying Part A premiums for QMBs. On February 7, 1990, we sent a letter to all State Medicaid Directors informing States of this option.

Thirty-Four States currently participate in Part A buy-in. The buy-in process allows States to accrete individuals as QMBs and to automatically enroll them in Part A. States are required (SMM section 3490.5) to conduct a review of all recipients currently eligible under the State plan and who also are entitled under Part A of Medicare to determine whether they meet the eligibility requirements for QMB status.

At the time the buy-in process became effective, there were 270,000 individuals in the 34 buy-in States for whom the States were purchasing Part B coverage on their behalf but who lacked Part A coverage and should have been accreted as QMBs through the Part A buy-in process. Of these, only 124,458 individuals have been accreted as QMBs. These States have had more than 15 months to perform the required review of their records, and accrete the remaining 145,000 individuals as QMBs, but have failed to do so.

We have sent a letter to the 18 most egregious States asking that they review the records of the remaining individuals in order to make the QMB determination and accrete them as QMBs. We have asked that they let us know what they plan to do in this regard.

It is our intention that after a period of 6 weeks from the date of our letter (October 10) HCFA will accrete the remaining individuals as QMBs and bill the State for the Part A premium. The State will then have an opportunity to delete any individuals they have determined do not meet the QMB eligibility criteria.

Page 3 - Deputy Chief Counsel, OGC

Non-Part A Buy-in States

In the 16 States which did not modify their buy-in agreement, there were 250,000 individuals who could have been QMBs except for their lack of enrollment in Part A. In these States the individual must enroll in Part A. In 1989 we made available an easy method for the States to have these individuals enroll in Part A. An SSA-795 contact form was modified permitting the individual to sign a preprinted statement asking to be enrolled in Part A with the understanding that the State would be billed for the premium. To date, only 34,962 individuals have enrolled using this process. This is due, we believe, to State failure to inform the individual of this process.

It is our intention to mail the form directly to the remaining individuals, explaining the benefit to them, and instructing them to sign and return the form to us. Having thus established their enrollment in Part A, we intend to accrete these individuals as QMBs in a manner similar to that described earlier for the Part A buy-in States.

Potential QMBs Already Entitled to Part A

Finally, approximately 3.2 million Medicaid recipients are currently covered under Part A and have their Part B coverage purchased by States on their behalf. The vast majority of these individuals are SSI recipients. Of these, only 845,000 have been identified as QMBs.

Although States are paying the $358.80 annual Part B premium, the beneficiary is not guaranteed the financial protection afforded under the statute for other costs; e.g., the $100 annual Part B deductible and 20-percent copayment for physician charges in excess of the deductible.

It is our intention to insert the required QMB identifier in the records of these 3.2 million individuals, and to inform the State of the QMB status of these individuals.

We are writing seeking your concurrence with these intended actions. Your prompt reply is appreciated. Should you have any questions please contact Mike Sparacino on extension 6-5918.

/S/
David McNally

Attachment

FMC-33:MSparacino:SGullick:MPSMISC DISK:A:OGCNOTE:11-12-91

APPENDIX 10-3 JUNE 11, 2007, MEMORANDUM FROM GALE P. ARDEN, DIRECTOR, DISABLED AND ELDERLY HEALTH PROGRAMS GROUP, TO ALL ASSOCIATE REGIONAL ADMINISTRATORS, DIVISION OF MEDICAID AND CHILDREN'S HEALTH, RE: MEDICAID OBLIGATIONS FOR COST-SHARING IN MEDICARE PART C PLANS

DEPARTMENT OF HEALTH & HUMAN SERVICES
Centers for Medicare & Medicaid Services
7500 Security Boulevard, Mail Stop S2-14-26
Baltimore, Maryland 21244-1850

CMS
CENTERS for MEDICARE & MEDICAID SERVICES

Center for Medicaid and State Operations
Disabled and Elderly Health Programs Group (DEHPG)

DATE: JUN 1 1 2007

FROM: Gale P. Arden, Director
Disabled and Elderly Health Programs Group

SUBJECT: Medicaid Obligations for Cost-Sharing in Medicare Part C Plans

TO: All Associate Regional Administrators
Division of Medicaid and Children's Health

Many questions have been raised by States, providers and Medicare Part C plans regarding Medicaid's obligation to pay cost-sharing for individuals who are eligible for both Medicare and Medicaid (dual eligibles) and who are enrolled in Medicare Part C, i.e. Medicare Advantage (MA) plans. Over the years CMS has issued guidance on various aspects of this question; however there has been no single document that brings this guidance together. The purpose of this memorandum is to provide a compilation of pertinent information found in statute, regulation and guidance in a concise format.

Dual eligibles are individuals enrolled in Medicare and eligible for Medicaid coverage, whether that Medicaid coverage is limited to certain costs, such as Medicare premiums, or the full benefits covered under the State Plan. Dual eligibles whose benefits are limited include Qualified Medicare Beneficiaries (QMB), Specified Low-income Medicare Beneficiaries (SLMB), Qualifying Individuals (QI), and Qualified Disabled Working Individuals (QDWI). Those eligible for full Medicaid benefits are called Full Benefit Dual Eligibles (FBDE). At times individuals may qualify for both limited coverage of Medicare cost sharing as well as full Medicaid benefits.

MA plans are health plan options approved by Medicare and run by private companies. These plans must provide all Part A and Part B services, and may offer additional services including Part D drug coverage. MA plans include Medicare Preferred Provider Organizations (PPO), Medicare Health Maintenance Organizations (HMO), Medicare Private Fee-for-Service (PFFS) plans, Medicare Medical Savings Account (MSA) plans and Medicare Special Needs Plans (SNP).

Medicare cost-sharing includes Part A and B premiums and Part C premiums for those enrolled in an MA plan. Medicare cost sharing also includes deductibles, co-insurance and, for MA plans, may include co-pays. Deductibles are fixed dollar amounts that an individual must pay out-of-pocket before the costs of services are covered. Co-insurance is a percentage of the cost of services. Co-payments are fixed dollar amounts that an individual must pay each time a service is received.

Page 2- All Associate Regional Administrators

Several factors determine whether or not Medicaid is liable for coverage of cost-sharing in MA plans. These factors include the dual eligible's coverage category, the type of cost-sharing, the options elected by the State, and payment limitations specified in the State Plan. The attached chart is intended to clarify how these factors affect whether or not the State Medicaid program has a liability for cost-sharing for dual eligibles in MA plans.

The information presented in this policy clarification is not intended to address all issues related to Part C cost-sharing for dual eligibles. This clarification is limited to State Medicaid program cost-sharing obligations, and does not address issues related to provider billing practices or beneficiary obligations.

Please share this information with the States in your regions. If you have any questions regarding this memorandum, please contact Christine Gerhardt at 410-786-0693, or christine.gerhardt@cms.hhs.gov.

Attachment

CMS/CMSO/DEHPG/DEEO: 5/9/07

Cost Sharing for Medicare Advantage Plans

Questions have been raised by States, providers and Medicare Advantage plans regarding the obligations of State Medicaid programs, and the availability of Federal Financial Participation (FFP), for dual-eligibles enrolled in Medicare Advantage plans.[1] In the past, guidance has been issued in the State Medicaid Manual, letters to CMS Associate Regional Administrators and other correspondence that addressed various aspects of this issue. To properly determine Medicaid liability for Part C cost sharing for a dual-eligible it is necessary to determine the individual's Medicaid coverage group and the type of Part C cost-sharing. Below is a description of the various coverage groups in which a dual-eligible could be certified. The chart that follows identifies the Medicaid liability by coverage group and type of Part C cost-sharing. The purpose of the chart is to clarify existing Centers for Medicare and Medicaid Services (CMS) policy by combining material from previously issued guidance, statute and regulation into a concise format, addressing all categories of dual-eligibles and all forms of Medicare Part C cost-sharing.

Description of Coverage Groups

Qualified Medicare Beneficiary (QMB Only)

A "QMB" is an individual who is entitled to Medicare Part A, has income that does not exceed 100% of the Federal Poverty Level (FPL), and whose resources do not exceed twice the Supplemental Security Income (SSI) limit. A QMB is eligible for Medicaid payment of Medicare premiums, deductibles, co-insurance and co-pays (except for Part D). QMBs who do not qualify for any additional Medicaid Benefits are called "QMB Only."

QMB Plus

A "QMB Plus" is an individual who meets all of the standards for QMB eligibility as described above, but who also meets the financial criteria for full Medicaid coverage. Such individuals are entitled to all benefits available to a QMB, as well as all benefits available under the State Plan to a fully eligible Medicaid recipient. These individuals often qualify for full Medicaid benefits by meeting the Medically Needy standards, or through spending down excess income to the Medically Needy level.

Specified Low-income Medicare Beneficiary (SLMB Only)

A "SLMB" is an individual who is entitled to Medicare Part A, has income that exceeds 100% FPL but is less than 120% FPL, and whose resources do not exceed twice the SSI limit. The only Medicaid benefit a SLMB is eligible for is payment of Medicare Part B premiums. SLMBs who do not qualify for any additional Medicaid benefits are called "SLMB Only".

[1] Sec. 201 of P. L. 108-173 established the Medicare Advantage program, consisting of the program under part C of Medicare. Any references to part C or "Medicare + Choice" were deemed to be references to "Medicare Advantage" or "MA". Thus, any references in past policy documents to "Medicare + Choice" plans are applicable to Medicare Advantage plans.

SLMB Plus

A "SLMB Plus" is an individual who meets the standards for SLMB eligibility, but who also meets the financial criteria for full Medicaid coverage. Such individuals are entitled to payment of Medicare Part B premiums, as well as all benefits available under the State Plan to a fully eligible Medicaid recipient. These individuals often qualify for Medicaid by meeting the Medically Needy standards, or though spending down excess income to the Medically Needy level.

Qualifying Individual (QI)

A "QI" is an individual who is entitled to Part A, has income that is at least 120% FPL but less than 135% FPL, resources that do not exceed twice the SSI limit, and who is not otherwise eligible for Medicaid. A QI is similar to a SLMB, in that the only benefit available is Medicaid payment of the Medicare Part B premium, however expenditures for QIs are 100% federally funded and the total expenditures are limited by statute.

Other Full Benefit Dual Eligibles (FBDE)

An individual who is eligible for Medicaid either categorically or through optional coverage groups such as medically needy or special income levels for institutionalized or home and community-based waivers, but who does not meet the income or resource criteria for QMB or SLMB.

Qualified Disabled and Working Individual (QDWI)

A QDWI is an individual who lost Medicare Part A benefits due to returning to work, but who is eligible to enroll in and purchase Medicare Part A. The individual's income may not exceed 200% FPL and resources may not exceed twice the SSI limit. The individual may not be otherwise eligible for Medicaid. QDWIs are eligible only for Medicaid payment of Part A premiums.

Description of Medicare Part C Benefits

Mandatory Supplemental Benefits

Mandatory supplemental benefits are non-drug benefits that are not covered by Medicare, but are covered by the plan for every enrollee of the plan. Mandatory supplemental benefits are paid for in full, directly by (or on behalf of) Medicare enrollees, in the form of premiums, cost sharing or through application of rebate dollars.

Optional Supplemental Benefits

Optional supplemental benefits are non-drug benefits that are not covered by Medicare. However, plan enrollees may choose whether to elect and pay for optional supplemental benefits. These services may be grouped or offered individually.

Deductibles, Coinsurance and Co-payments

Deductibles are fixed dollar amounts that an individual must pay out-of-pocket before the cost of services are covered by the MA organization. Coinsurance charges are a percentage of the costs for services. Co-payments are fixed dollar amounts that a beneficiary must pay when he or she uses a particular service. For purposes of this memorandum, co-payments charged by a Part C plan are considered to be coinsurance.

Medicare Part C Cost Sharing Chart

	Part C Premium for Basic Medicare Part A and Part B Benefits and Mandatory Supplemental Benefits	Part C Premium for Optional Supplemental Benefits	Medicare Deductibles, Coinsurance & Co-pays* (except Part D) **
QMB Only	Optional [1]	Not allowed [2]	Required [3]
QMB Plus	Optional [4]	Optional [5]	Required [6]
SLMB Only	Not allowed [7]	Not allowed [8]	Not allowed [9]
SLMB Plus	Not allowed [10]	Optional [11]	Conditional [12]
QI	Not allowed [13]	Not allowed [14]	Not allowed [15]
Other FBDEs	Not allowed [16]	Optional [17]	Conditional [18]
QDWI	Not allowed [19]	Not allowed [20]	Not allowed [21]

*Section 1902(n)(2) of the Social Security Act provides that a State is not required to provide any payment for any expenses incurred relating to payment for deductibles, coinsurance, or co-payment for Medicare cost-sharing to the extent that payment under Medicare for the service would exceed the payment amount that otherwise would be made under the State Medicaid plan. In any case where Medicare deductibles, coinsurance or co-payments are required to be paid or may be paid conditionally, the State may limit Medicaid payment as specified in Supplement 1 to Attachment 4.19-B of the State Plan, including nominal cost sharing amounts as permitted under Section 1916 of the Social Security Act and specified in attachment 4.18 of the State Plan. These payment limitations may result in a Medicaid payment of zero.

** Section 1935(d)(1) of the Social Security Act specifies that FFP is not available for the coverage of Part D drugs for Part D eligible individuals.

Notes to Cost Sharing Chart

1. Section 1905(p)(3) of the Social Security Act (the Act) provides that the State may opt to cover premiums for enrollment of QMBs in organizations under §1876. In a June 30, 2000 Policy Memorandum, from the Director of the Disabled and Elderly Health Programs Group, Thomas E. Hamilton, to Associate Regional Administrators (Hamilton Memo), CMS affirmed that §1905(p)(3) may be read to permit Medicare + Choice (now known as Medicare Advantage) to be included, at State option, under the same terms as §1876 contracts. States may make this election on page 29, 3.2(a)(1) of their Medicaid State Plan.

2. Section 1902(a)(10)(E)(i) specifies that QMB coverage is limited to the cost sharing described in §1905(p)(3) of the Act, and does not include coverage of additional services.

3. Coverage of Medicare deductibles and coinsurance are required for QMBs under §1902(a)(10)(E)(i) and §1905(p)(3) of the Act. Hamilton Memo, page 3, Medicare Cost Sharing, "... coinsurance includes the co-payments that M+C organizations charge when beneficiaries use services."

4. See note #1.

5. Section 1905(a) of the Act permits coverage of health insurance premiums, other than Medicare Part B, for medical or remedial care, except for individuals who could be enrolled in Part B but are not. Hamilton Memo, page 3, Monthly premiums in Medicare +Choice Organizations, "...since QMB Plus is also eligible for full Medicaid benefits, Medicaid may also pay premiums for supplemental benefits not covered by Medicare, but which are covered by Medicaid, if so elected in the State Plan (page 29b, 3.2(a)(2))."

6. See note #3.

7. Section 1902(a)(10)(E)(iii) and §1905(p)(3)(A)(ii) limit SLMB coverage to Part B premiums.

8. See note #7.

9. See note #7.

10. See note #7. For non-QMB dual-eligibles, FFP is not available for Medicaid coverage of Medicare Advantage premiums for basic Medicare services.

11. Section 1905(a) of the Act permits payment of health insurance premiums, other than Medicare Part B, for coverage of medical or remedial services, except for individuals who could be enrolled in Part B but are not. States may elect this option in their State Plan, page 29b, 3.2(a)(2).

12. For non-QMB eligibles, there is no Medicaid liability for cost sharing in a Medicare Advantage plan, however, States are liable for payment for Medicaid covered services rendered by Medicaid providers to Medicaid eligible individuals in excess of any third party (including Medicare Part C) liability. When the following conditions are met, there may be a liability for a specific service received through a Medicare Advantage plan:

- The Medicare service is also a covered service under the State Plan;
- The Medicare provider is also a Medicaid provider; and
- The amount specified in the State plan is greater than the Medicare payment amount.

13. Sections 1902(a)(10)(E)(iv) and §1905(p)(3)(A)(ii) of the Act limit QI coverage to Part B premiums.

14. See note #13.

15. See note #13.

16. For non-QMB dual-eligibles, there is no FFP available for Medicaid coverage of Medicare Advantage premiums for basic Medicare services.

17. See note #11.

18. See note #12.

19. Section 1902(a)(10)(E)(ii) and §1905(p)(3)(A)(i) limit QDWI coverage to Part A premiums.

20. See note #19.

21. See note #19.

APPENDIX 10-4 JANUARY 6, 2012, MEMORANDUM FROM DIRECTOR, MMCO-CMCS INFORMATIONAL BULLETIN CONCERNING BILLING FOR SERVICES PROVIDED TO QUALIFIED MEDICARE BENEFICIARIES (QMBs)

DEPARTMENT OF HEALTH AND HUMAN SERVICES
Centers for Medicare & Medicaid Services
7500 Security Boulevard, Mail Stop S2-26-12
Baltimore, MD 21244-1850

Center for Medicaid and CHIP Services

MMCO - CMCS Informational Bulletin

DATE: January 6, 2012

FROM: Melanie Bella, Director
Medicare-Medicaid Coordination Office

Cindy Mann, Director
Center for Medicaid and CHIP Services (CMCS)

SUBJECT: Billing for Services Provided to Qualified Medicare Beneficiaries (QMBs)

This Informational Bulletin provides information for State Medicaid Agencies and other interested parties regarding the prohibition on "balance-billing" Qualified Medicare Beneficiaries (QMB) for Medicare cost-sharing, including deductible, coinsurance, and copayments. This Bulletin is provided as a companion to a communication on this topic to Medicare providers in the form of a recently published Medicare Learning Network Matters article which is available at: http://www.cms.gov/MLNMattersArticles/Downloads/SE1128.pdf

Background on QMBs and Benefits
QMBs are persons who are entitled to Medicare Part A and are eligible for Medicare Part B; have incomes below 100 percent of the Federal Poverty Level; and have been determined to be eligible for QMB status by their State Medicaid Agency. Medicaid pays the Medicare Part A and B premiums, deductibles, co-insurance and co-payments for QMBs. At the State's discretion, Medicaid may also pay Part C Medicare Advantage premiums for those who join a Medicare Advantage plan that covers Medicare Part A and B benefits and Mandatory Supplemental Benefits. Regardless of whether the State Medicaid Agency opts to pay the Part C premium, the QMB is not liable for any co-insurance or deductibles for Part C benefits. States also have the authority to pay cost-sharing for QMBs for either the Medicare cost-sharing amount, the Medicaid State plan rate for the same service, or a rate between those amounts that is established by the State and approved by CMS.

Balance-billing Is Prohibited by Federal Law
Section 1902(n)(3)(B) of the Social Security Act (the Act), as modified by section 4714 of the Balanced Budget Act of 1997, prohibits Medicare providers from balance-billing QMBs for Medicare cost-sharing. All Medicare physicians, providers, and suppliers who offer services and supplies to QMBs are prohibited from billing QMBs for Medicare cost-sharing, including deductible, coinsurance, and copayments. This section of the Act is available at:

CMCS Informational Bulletin
January 6, 2012
Page 2

http://www.ssa.gov/OP_Home/ssact/title19/1902.htm. QMBs have no legal obligation to make further payment to a provider or Medicare managed care plan for Part A or Part B cost sharing. Providers who inappropriately bill QMBs for Medicare cost-sharing are subject to sanctions. Please note that the statute referenced above supersedes Section 3490.14 of the State Medicaid Manual, which is no longer in effect, but may be causing confusion about QMB billing.

How State Medicaid Agencies Process QMB Claims

Providers who serve QMBs are responsible for billing the State Medicaid Agency for any Medicare cost-sharing amounts the State is responsible for covering. When the State receives the claim, the Medicaid processing system determines whether the QMB is eligible and to which services they are entitled. Next, the system determines whether the provider is registered as a Medicaid-participating provider for the service. Particularly for QMB claims, the provider might only be a participating Medicare provider, and not a Medicaid-enrolled provider. The process for a Medicare provider to become enrolled as a Medicaid provider varies by State, and providers must follow each State's specific rules for provider enrollment to receive payment. Once the provider's registration is confirmed, the system uses the State's Medicaid payment policy to determine the State's cost-sharing contribution.

Ways to Improve the Claims Process

Effective communications between State Medicaid Agencies and QMB providers can improve the claims process for beneficiaries, States, and providers.

Below are strategies State Medicaid Agencies can consider to both improve communication with QMB providers and reinforce the provider prohibition on QMB balance-billing:

1. Offer separate enrollment forms for QMB-only providers, or allow providers to identify as "QMB-only" on provider enrollment applications.

2. Include guidance in all communications with QMB providers to emphasize that balance-billing of QMBs is a violation of the provider's Medicare agreement.

3. Provide clear guidelines for QMB providers on Medicaid provider enrollment and billing processes.

Additionally, CMS suggests the following for providers to improve communications with State Medicaid Agencies and better understand the billing process for services provided to QMBs:

1. Recognize that you must complete the State's provider enrollment process to be entered into the State payment system.

2. Contact the State Medicaid Agency directly to determine the process you need to follow to begin submitting claims and receiving payment.

CMCS Informational Bulletin
January 6, 2012
Page 3

Additional Information
More information about QMBs and other people dually eligible for Medicare and Medicaid is available through the Medicare Learning Network:
http://www.cms.gov/mlnproducts/downloads/medicare_beneficiaries_dual_eligibles_at_a_glance.pd

For more information about Medicare cost-sharing, see the "Get Help with Your Medicare Costs" publication:
http://www.medicare.gov/Publications/Pubs/pdf/10126.pdf

We hope this information is helpful. Please address any questions to Nancy Dieter at nancy.dieter@cms.hhs.gov or Edo Banach at edo.banach@cms.hhs.gov.

APPENDIX 10-5 LETTER OF MARCH 31, 1999, FROM THE ASSOCIATE REGIONAL ADMINISTRATOR, REGION 1, HEALTH CARE FINANCING ADMINISTRATION, TO HILARY S. DALIN, STAFF ATTORNEY, CENTER FOR MEDICARE ADVOCACY, INC., CONCERNING DUALLY ELIGIBLE INDIVIDUALS IN NURSING FACILITIES

Region I
J.F.K. Federal Building Government Center
Boston, MA 02203

March 31, 1999

Hilary S. Dalin
Staff Attorney
Center for Medicare Advocacy, Inc.
P.O. Box 350
Willimantic, Connecticut 06226

Dear Ms. Dalin:

This letter is the response to the questions you asked us by letter, dated February 10, 1999. Your questions and our responses follow below.

1. If a dually eligible individual who is enrolled in a Medicare HMO sought nursing home admission due solely to a need for custodial care and the Medicare HMO denied Medicare coverage on the grounds that the nursing facility was out-of-network, would Medicaid reimbursement also be precluded?

Neither Medicaid nor Medicare cover custodial care. However, if the individual met the nursing facility (NF) level of care requirements for Medicaid, then coverage by Medicaid would not be precluded. Medicare only covers skilled nursing facility (SNF) services, so Medicare or the Medicare HMO would not be a liable third party in this situation.

2. If a dually eligible individual who was enrolled in a Medicare HMO and resided in a non-Medicare-certified bed in a NF became eligible for the Medicare SNF benefit, would the resident be compelled to move to an in-network Medicare-certified bed or would such an individual be allowed to waive her right to Medicare coverage and remain in the non-Medicare-certified bed, with Medicaid as the payor?

Our answer is that the individual would not have to move, and thus Medicare would not be an available third party resource. A State may not, as a condition of eligibility, require an individual entitled to Medicare to obtain a "Medicare bed" in order to utilize her Medicare benefits. A liable third party resource exists for Medicaid purposes only to the extent that the services the individual receives from the provider of her choice are covered by the third party entity. According to section 1902(a)(23) of the Social Security Act (the Act), a Medicaid eligible individual may obtain Medicaid covered services from any qualified provider who undertakes to provide her the services.

In general, if the individual is in a "Medicaid bed" that is not also a "Medicare bed," then Medicare is not a liable third party and the Medicaid agency must pay the full amount allowed under the Medicaid payment schedule (42 CFR 433.139(c)). However, if a Medicaid/Medicare bed is available *at no cost* to the individual, *at the time of placement in a facility*, then the State may deny or reduce payment for a Medicaid only bed in an amount corresponding to the value of the available resource (section 1902(a)(17)(B) of the Act). In other words, Medicaid would only be liable for that amount of the Medicaid rate which exceeded the amount the third party would have paid, if any, had the individual been placed in an available Medicare covered bed.

I trust I have answered your questions fully. Should you have further questions, do not hesitate to contact me.

Sincerely

Ronald Preston
Associate Regional Administrator

APPENDIX 10-6 SOCIAL SECURITY ADMINISTRATION POLICY INSTRUCTION FOR INDIVIDUALS IN PART A BUY-IN STATES WHO DO NOT HAVE MEDICARE PART B

Identification Number:	**EM-08071 REV**	**Effective Date: 08/11/2008**
Intended Audience:	**All RCs/ARCs/ADs/FOs/TSCs/PSCs/ OCO//OCO-STs/ODARHQ/CMS**	
Originating Office:	**ORDP OISP**	
Title:	**Processing Instructions—Premium HI for Individuals in Part A Buy-In States Who Do Not Have Medicare Part B—Instructions Will Follow Shortly**	
Type:	**EM—Emergency Messages**	
Program:	**Medicare**	
Link To Reference:	**HI 00801.134, HI 00801.138, HI 00801.139, HI 00801.140, HI 00815.023, SM 00850.355, SM 00850.700, SM 03040.025**	

Retention Date: November 8, 2013

In Part A buy-in states, some low income individuals that appear eligible for Medicare Part A and Part B buy-in as qualified Medicare beneficiaries (QMB) are experiencing difficulty enrolling in Part B at their local Social Security offices. QMB's are individuals who are eligible for Medicaid payment of their Medicare premiums, deductibles, and coinsurance. The confusion seems to occur with individuals who want to file for Premium Part A, do not have Part B, and are outside of an enrollment period.

If an individual contacts the field office (FO) and appears to meet the QMB eligibility requirements, resides in a Part A buy-in State, wishes to file for Premium Part A, and does not have Part B, the individual may file an application for Part B and conditional enrollment in Premium Part A. Since the individual resides in a Part A buy-in State, the application does not have to be filed in an enrollment period; it may be filed at any time.

Currently, MCS will not accept a Part B and conditional Part A enrollment filed outside of an enrollment period for an individual who resides in a Part A Buy-in State. MCS will generate exception message number 20604—Check BIC M Decision Status—SMI Application Not in Enrollment Period. To address this exception, the FO needs to input the claim into MCS and then prepare an A101/ EF101 for the Part B and conditional Part A award when the exception is received.

POMS instructions are being updated. Until national instructions are published, follow these processing instructions:

FO Processing Instructions:

- Take an initial claim for Part B and conditional Part A through MCS (i.e. select claim type 5 = UNINS MED ONLY on APPL screen)
- Develop proofs of age, citizenship or LAPR, and residency.
- Review the earnings record for accuracy. A reduced Hospital Insurance Premium (HI) may apply if the individual or spouse has 30–39 quarters of coverage (see HI 01005.007, Reduced Hospital Insurance (HI) Premium).
- Prepare an A101. If problems occur with the A101 prepare an EF101. Instructions for screen completion for the A101 are in MCS 014.000 and EF101 are in T2PE 009.000.

Include the following entries:

➢ Part A entitlement on the HI Data screen (HIDA or EFHIDA);

- START equal to the current operating month (COM)
- BASIS of 'A'
- TYPE of 'P'
- PERIOD of 'Q'
- FILING date;

➢ HI THIRD PARTY DATA (HITP or EFHITP);

- START equal to PREMIUM HI START
- CODE of Z99
- CATEGORY of 'Q'

➢ HI Premium/Reduction (HIPR or EFHIPR)

- START equal to PREMIUM HI START
- PENALTY PERCENTAGE OF 00
- Complete the following fields if applicable:
  - HAS 30 QTR
  - STOP
  - 30 QTR SSN

➢ Part B entitlement on the SMI Data screen (SMID or EFSMID);

- START equal to COM
- BASIS of 'A'
- PERIOD of 'Q'

- FILING date
- MED-RET-US, if applicable

➢ SMI THIRD PARTY DATA (SMTP or EFSMTP);

- Do not code THIRD PARTY DATA for Part B. See NOTE below.

➢ SMI PREMIUM HISTORY/VARIABLE SMI (SMPR or EFSMPR);

- START equal to SMI START
- PENALTY PERCENTAGE of 000

NOTE:
Refer the individual to the appropriate State office to file for QMB benefits. Emphasize the importance of promptly contacting the State. The individual may be billed for Part B premiums until state buy-in begins.

PSC Processing Instructions:

- Propagate A101/EF101 into MACADE.
- NOTE: Technicians should ensure that all coding referred to above are included on the screens of their MACADE action (see SM 00850.700).

If the enrollee does not contact the State and does not pay the Part B premiums when billed, Part B will terminate for nonpayment of premiums (HI 00820.035). Conditional Premium Part A will not generate a bill.

Direct all program-related and technical questions to your RO support staff or PSC OA staff. RO support staff or PSC OA staff may refer questions or problems to their Central Office contacts.

CHAPTER 11

PRESCRIPTION DRUG COVERAGE

§ 11.01 INTRODUCTION TO PRESCRIPTION DRUG COVERAGE

On January 1, 2006, Medicare began providing limited assistance in paying for prescription drugs through Medicare Part D. The drug benefit, added by the Medicare Prescription Drug, Improvement, and Modernization Act of 2003 (MMA),[1] is not part of the traditional Medicare program but rather is offered through private insurance plans.

The Part D benefit is premised on the notion that individual Medicare beneficiaries should have a choice of private drug plans in order to select a drug benefit that best meets their needs. The statute creates three categories of drug plans: (1) stand-alone plans that offer only prescription drug coverage, (2) Medicare Advantage (MA) plans with a drug benefit, and (3) fallback plans. The categories of drug plans are discussed below.

Most significantly, the MMA established a low-income subsidy (LIS) for beneficiaries with incomes up to 150 percent of the federal poverty level (FPL) and with limited resources. The Act also eliminated, beginning January 1, 2006, all Medicaid drug coverage for the more than 11 million individuals who are dually eligible for Medicare and some form of Medicaid (dual eligibles). Moreover, it required states to pay back to the federal government (also known as the "claw back" provision) much of the savings they would otherwise realize from their reduced Medicaid obligation to dual eligible individuals. The Act also included other provisions that affect state budgets.

In 2019, private companies continue to offer a wide array of Part D plans throughout the country.[2] The average Part D premium (weighted by 2019 plan enrollment) is projected to decrease by 9 percent from 2018 to 2019, down to $32.50 per month.[3]

§ 11.02 ELIGIBILITY FOR PART D COVERAGE

Prescription drug coverage under Part D is voluntary. A beneficiary may purchase Part D coverage if he or she has Part A or Part B. Beneficiaries do not

---

[1] Medicare Prescription Drug, Improvement, and Modernization Act of 2003 (MMA), Pub. L. No. 108-73 (Dec. 8, 2003); 42 U.S.C. §§ 1395w-101 *et seq.* (2004 Supp.); 42 C.F.R. § 423.506.

[2] For detailed information about Part D plans available in 2019, *see* CMS, "Medicare Plan Finder," *available at* https://www.medicare.gov/find-a-plan/questions/home.aspx (site visited Aug. 6, 2018) & CMS, "Prescription Drug Coverage—General Information," *available at* https://www.cms.gov/PrescriptionDrugCovGenIn/ (site visited Aug. 6, 2018). Note that rules may change as CMS issues additional program guidance to clarify how the Part D program operates. *See, e.g.*, CMS, "Prescription Drug Coverage Contracting," *available at* http://www.cms.gov/Medicare/Prescription-Drug-Coverage/PrescriptionDrugCovContra/index.html?redirect=/prescriptiondrugcovcontra/ (site visited Aug. 6, 2018).

[3] *See* CMS, "Medicare Part D premiums continue to decline in 2019" (July 31, 2018), *available at* https://www.cms.gov/newsroom/press-releases/medicare-part-d-premiums-continue-decline-2019 (site visited Aug. 6, 2018).

have to have both Part A and Part B coverage to choose prescription drug coverage, unless they choose to enroll in an MA plan, in which case they must be in both Parts A and B.[4] The beneficiary must enroll in a Part D plan that serves the geographic region in which he or she resides.[5] Beneficiaries who are incarcerated are not eligible to participate in Part D, nor are beneficiaries who live outside the United States.[6]

§ 11.03 CHOICE OF DRUG PLANS

[A] Prescription Drug Plans

Medicare beneficiaries who remain in the traditional Medicare program will be able to purchase drug coverage through prescription drug plans (PDPs) that offer only prescription drug coverage. PDPs are offered by sponsoring organizations pursuant to a one-year contract with the Centers for Medicare & Medicaid Services (CMS).[7]

[B] Medicare Advantage Plans

Individuals who are enrolled in an MA plan established under Medicare Part C must receive their prescription drug coverage through their MA plan, known as a Medicare Advantage-Prescription Drug (MA-PD) plan. They may not purchase a separate PDP. However, individuals who are enrolled in a Medicare Medical Savings Account (MSA) or an MA Private Fee-for-Service (PFFS) plan that does not include a prescription drug option may purchase a PDP for their Part D coverage. Individuals who want to join an MA-PD must have both Medicare Part A and Part B.[8]

[C] Fallback Plans

The MMA authorized the creation of a fallback PDP in any prescription drug region[9] in which beneficiaries did not have a choice of enrollment in at least two

---

[4] 42 C.F.R. § 423.30(a)(1)(i).

[5] 42 U.S.C. § 1395w-101(b)(1)(B)(i).

[6] 42 C.F.R. §§ 423.4 and 423.30(a)(1).

[7] 42 U.S.C. §§ 1395w-101(a)(1)(A), 1395w-112(b)(1), and 1395w-151(a)(14).

[8] 42 U.S.C. § 1395w-101(a)(1)(B). Note that individuals enrolled in a Medicare Part C Medical Savings Account (MSA) may also purchase a prescription drug plan (PDP) to obtain drug coverage, as may individuals who are enrolled in "cost plans" that do not offer drug coverage.

[9] 42 C.F.R. § 423.112. CMS has established 34 PDP regions, several of which include more than one state. Each PDP must offer coverage to all beneficiaries in the region that it serves. A PDP may also offer a plan that serves more than one region or that is national in scope. 42 U.S.C. § 1395w-111(a).

plans.[10] However, since the beginning of the Part D program, there have been substantially more than two drug plans in each PDP region and CMS has not needed to contract with fallback plans. CMS anticipates that sufficient drug plans will be available for the foreseeable future.

§ 11.04 THE PART D DRUG BENEFIT

[A] Covered Part D Drugs

The MMA defines the drugs that are covered under Part D and therefore the drugs for which payment will be made under Part D in relationship to their coverage under Medicaid and under other parts of Medicare. A Part D drug is a drug that is approved by the Food and Drug Administration, for which a prescription is required, which is medically necessary and for a medically accepted indication, and for which payment is required under Medicaid.[11] Only compounds that contain at least one ingredient that is a Part D covered drug may be covered under Part D.[12] Biological products, including insulin and insulin supplies and smoking cessation drugs, are also covered under Part D.[13]

The MMA excludes from coverage those categories of drugs for which Medicaid payment is optional.[14] Excluded drugs may include drugs for erectile dysfunction (ED), drugs for weight gain or loss,[15] vitamins, and over-the-counter medications. Note that benzodiazepines and barbiturates, classes of drugs previously excluded from Part D coverage, are now considered Part D covered drugs.[16] Also note that some of the excluded drugs may be covered if prescribed

[10] 42 U.S.C. §§ 1395w-103(a)(1) and 1395w-111(g)(4). At least one of the available plans must be a PDP.

[11] 42 U.S.C. §§ 1395w-102(e)(1) and 1396r-8(d), (k).

[12] For low-income subsidy (LIS)-eligible individuals (*see* **§ 11.06** of this Handbook), the copayment amount is based on whether the most expensive Part D covered component of the compound drug is a generic or brand name drug. 42 C.F.R. § 423.120(d)(2)(i).

[13] 42 U.S.C. § 1395w-102(e)(1)(B), (2)(A).

[14] Congress added an exclusion for drugs used to treat sexual or erectile dysfunction unless prescribed for a different use approved by the Food and Drug Administration. QI, TMA, and Abstinence Programs Extension and Hurricane Katrina Unemployment Relief Act of 2005, Pub. L. No. 109-91 (Oct. 20, 2005), § 103; 42 U.S.C. §§ 1395w-102(e)(2)(A) and 1396r-8(d)(2).

[15] Drugs for weight gain will be covered to treat wasting diseases for people with HIV/AIDS, but weight loss drugs are not covered for treatment of obesity. CMS, Policy and Technical Changes to the Medicare Prescription Drug Benefit, 73 Fed. Reg. 20,486 (Apr. 15, 2008), *available at* https://www.gpo.gov/fdsys/pkg/FR-2008-04-15/pdf/08-1120.pdf (site visited Aug. 6, 2018).

[16] Effective January 1, 2013, benzodiazepines and barbiturates (used for treating epilepsy, cancer, or a chronic mental health disorder) are included as Part D covered drugs. Medicare Improvements for Patients and Providers Act of 2008 (MIPPA), Pub. L. No. 110-275 (July 15, 2008), § 175. Effective January 1, 2014, all barbiturates are covered by Medicaid and therefore are covered by Medicare Part D. Patient Protection and Affordable Care Act of 2010 (PPACA; also known as the Affordable Care Act, or ACA), Pub. L. No. 111-148 (Mar. 23, 2010), § 2502.

for a purpose other than those prohibited by the MMA. For example, Viagra is an excluded drug if it is prescribed for ED, but it may be coverable if it is prescribed for pulmonary hypertension. The MMA also excludes from Part D coverage those drugs for which payment could be made under Medicare Part A or Part B. CMS has determined that such drugs are excluded from Part D coverage even if the beneficiary does not have coverage under the part of Medicare (either Part A or Part B) that would generally pay for the drug.[17]

When certain conditions are met, Part D plans can cover drugs that are FDA-approved but prescribed in a manner not specifically approved by the FDA (in other words, for a diagnosis or condition that is not approved for that specific drug), sometimes called "off-label" use. Peer-reviewed medical journals that are identified by Medicare may be used to establish a medically accepted indication for off-label drugs, but only for those used in an anticancer chemotherapeutic regimen covered under Medicare Part D. For other uses, Part D covers drugs prescribed for off-label use only if the drugs are identified as safe and effective for that use in an officially recognized drug compendia.[18] "Compendia" are encyclopedias of drug chemicals, with information on dosage and usage. Part D rules concerning peer-reviewed medical journals differ from Part B rules, which allow reliance on such peer-reviewed medical journals for all categories and classes of drugs.[19]

Part D plans are not required to pay for all covered Part D drugs. They may establish their own formularies, or list of covered drugs for which they will make payment, as long as their formularies and benefit structures are not found by CMS to discourage enrollment by certain Medicare beneficiaries.[20] Part D plans that follow the formulary classes and categories established by the United States Pharmacopoeia will pass the first discrimination test. However, CMS indicates it will still review formularies to determine whether the placement of specific drugs in each category or class, as well as other benefit design issues, discriminates against particular individuals. Plans also have the flexibility to change the drugs on their formulary during the course of the year, provided the change is approved by CMS.

---

[17] 42 C.F.R. § 423.100. *See also* CMS, Medicare Prescription Drug Benefit (PDB) Manual, Ch. 6: § 20.2, *available at* https://www.cms.gov/Medicare/Prescription-Drug-Coverage/PrescriptionDrugCovContra/downloads/chapter6.pdf (site visited Aug. 6, 2018).

[18] 42 U.S.C. § 1395w-102(e)(4)(A)(i)(II); 42 C.F.R. § 423.100 (see definition of "Part D drug"); PDB) Manual, Ch. 6: § 10.6. *See also* CMA, "CMA Report: Medicare Coverage for Off-Label Drug Use" (Sept. 2010), *available at* http://www.medicareadvocacy.org/cma-report-medicare-coverage-for-off-label-drug-use/ (site visited Aug. 6, 2018); CMA, "Federal Court Issues Favorable Off-label Part D Drug Coverage Decision" (May 18, 2016), *available at* http://www.medicareadvocacy.org/federal-court-issues-favorable-off-label-part-d-drug-coverage-decision/ (site visited Aug. 6, 2018); CMS, "Medicare Part D and Off-Label Rx Denials" (June 29, 2016), *available at* http://www.medicareadvocacy.org/medicare-part-d-and-off-label-rx-denials/ (site visited Aug. 6, 2018).

[19] 42 U.S.C. § 1395(t)(2)(B).

[20] 42 C.F.R. §§ 423.120(b) and 423.272(b).

Additionally, drug plan sponsors must include in their plans' formularies substantially all covered Part D drugs in a category or class identified by CMS. CMS has discretion to establish exceptions that allow a plan sponsor to exclude or attach utilization management requirements to a drug within a protected category or class.[21] The current six protected classes of drugs remain protected until such time as CMS establishes new criteria. They are:

1. antidepressant,
2. antipsychotic,
3. anticonvulsant,
4. anticancer,
5. immunosuppressant, and
6. anti-retroviral drugs.[22]

In response to the national issue of opioid abuse, Congress passed a bill in 2016 that allows Part D plan sponsors to establish drug management programs for enrollees who are deemed to be at-risk of prescription drug abuse that can limit access to coverage for frequently abused drugs, in part, by limiting the number of prescribers and pharmacies from which such drugs can be obtained.[23] In 2018, CMS published a final rule that establishes such drug utilization control, or management programs, beginning with the 2019 plan year.[24] Part D sponsors may not implement such limitations unless they have engaged in case management with the prescribers of these drugs, and followed proper notice requirements.[25]

[B] Structure of the Drug Benefit

[1] Introduction

PDPs are given a great deal of flexibility to design their own benefit structure.[26] Thus, the majority of plans have chosen not to offer the statutory

[21] ACA § 3307.

[22] PDB Manual, Ch. 6: § 30.2.5.

[23] Title VII, § 704, Comprehensive Addiction and Recovery Act of 2016 (CARA), Pub. L. No. 114-198 (signed into law by President Obama on July 22, 2016).

[24] CMS, Contract Year 2019 Policy and Technical Changes to the Medicare Advantage, Medicare Cost Plan, Medicare Fee-for-Service, the Medicare Prescription Drug Benefit Programs, and the PACE Program (CMS-4182-F), 82 Fed. Reg. 16,440 (Apr. 16, 2018), *available at* https://www.federalregister.gov/documents/2018/04/16/2018-07179/medicare-program-contract-year-2019-policy-and-technical-changes-to-the-medicare-advantage-medicare (site visited Aug. 6, 2018).

[25] For the requirements for drug management programs, including beneficiary notice and appeal rights, *see* 42 C.F.R. § 423.153(f).

[26] All prescription drug plans, regardless of their benefit design, are supposed to provide beneficiaries with access to negotiated prices for the covered Part D drugs they include in their

"standard" benefit and instead offer an alternative benefit structure.[27] Variations in plan benefit structure, along with the substantial number of plans available, have adversely affected the ability of Medicare beneficiaries to compare plans that may best meets their needs. Beneficiaries are encouraged to use CMS's Plan finder tool (www.medicare.gov/find-a-plan/questions/home.aspx [site visited May 17, 2018]) or to avail themselves of the counseling services of their local State Health Insurance Assistance (SHIP) agencies.

[2] The Standard Drug Benefit

The MMA establishes a standard drug benefit that Part D plans may offer. The standard benefit is defined in terms of the financial structure of the cost-sharing and not in terms of the drugs that must be covered. In 2019, this standard benefit requires payment of a $415 deductible (an increase of $10 from 2018). The beneficiary then pays 25 percent of the cost of a covered Part D prescription drug up to the initial coverage limit of $3,820.[28] The initial coverage limit is calculated based on the total cost of the drugs used by the beneficiary.

Prior to 2019, once the initial coverage limit was reached, the beneficiary entered a second deductible period known as the "donut hole" or coverage gap during which he or she was required to pay a percentage of the full cost of his or her medicine.[29] The Health Care and Education Reconciliation Act of 2010 (HCERA)[30] provided for the gradual phasing down of the donut hole until 2020. The Bipartisan Budget Act of 2018 (BBA) accelerated the closure of the donut

formulary, even if the beneficiary is required to pay the full cost of the prescription. 42 C.F.R. § 423.104(g)(1). Note that CMS revised the definition of "negotiated price" at 42 C.F.R. § 423.100 to reflect pharmacy price concessions. CMS, Contract Year 2015 Policy and Technical Changes to the Medicare Advantage and the Medicare Prescription Drug Benefit Programs, 79 Fed. Reg. 29,844, 29876 (May 23, 2014), *available at* https://www.gpo.gov/fdsys/pkg/FR-2014-05-23/pdf/2014-11734.pdf (site visited Aug. 6, 2018).

[27] Kaiser Family Foundation, "The Medicare Part D Prescription Drug Benefit" (Oct. 2, 2017) https://www.kff.org/medicare/fact-sheet/the-medicare-prescription-drug-benefit-fact-sheet/ (site visited Aug. 6, 2018).

[28] The beneficiary's share of cost is $851.25, or 25 percent of the difference between $3,820 and $415. When added to the deductible, the beneficiary's total cost-sharing for formulary drugs up to the initial coverage limit is $1,266.25.

[29] CMS estimates that the total spending (both plan and beneficiary) needed to reach catastrophic coverage will decrease from $8,417.60 (the 2018 figure) to $8,139.54. CMS, "Announcement of Calendar Year (CY) 2019 Medicare Advantage Capitation Rates and Medicare Advantage and Part D Payment Policies and Final Call Letter" (Apr. 2, 2018), *available at* https://www.cms.gov/Medicare/Health-Plans/MedicareAdvtgSpecRateStats/Downloads/Announcement2019.pdf (site visited Aug. 6, 2018).

[30] HCERA § 1101. On April 15, 2011, CMS issued final regulations implementing the Act's provisions that close the Part D coverage gap between 2011 and 2019. 42 C.F.R. §§ 423.104, 423.884(d)(4).

hole by one year, to 2019, for brand name drugs (but not generics).[31] Thus, beginning in 2019, beneficiaries in the standard drug plan who have met their deductible will then pay 25 percent coinsurance for brand name prescriptions until they reach the catastrophic level. Also in 2019, the coinsurance for generic drugs in the donut hole will be reduced from 44 percent to 37 percent. In order to cover the costs in the coverage gap, drug manufacturers are required to offer discounts and Part D plans are obligated to cover the balance up to the beneficiary coinsurance amount (25 percent for brand name drugs). Note that even though the beneficiary is paying a discounted price, 95 percent of the cost of brand name drugs counts toward meeting the annual out-of-pocket threshold. Starting in 2020, beneficiaries will pay a 25 percent cost share for both generic and name brand drugs during the initial phase until they enter the catastrophic phase, thus eliminating the coverage gap all together.

When the beneficiary's true out-of-pocket expenses for the year, including the deductible and initial coinsurance, reach $5,100, the beneficiary enters the catastrophic coverage period. The beneficiary then pays $3.40 for a generic or preferred drug and $8.50 for other drugs, or 5 percent coinsurance, whichever is greater.[32] Note that the $5,100 amount is calculated on a calendar year basis; a beneficiary who amasses $5,100 in out-of-pocket costs on December 31 will have to start all over again on January 1. The deductible and annual out-of-pocket threshold have usually increased each year by the increase in expenditures for Part D drugs.

The MMA does not mandate a set premium amount. Premiums are determined by a bidding process and vary from plan to plan and from region to region. Private insurance companies that want to continue participating in the Part D drug benefit must submit new bids each year. Thus, the premiums they charge are likely to change on a yearly basis. Premium amounts are especially critical for individuals with low incomes, as they receive full LIS premium assistance only for plans that offer the standard benefit and that charge the lowest premiums.[33]

Beneficiaries with higher incomes who pay the Part B income-related premium are also subject to a Part D income-related premium. The increased premium amount is based on a percentage of the base beneficiary premium for that year as determined by CMS.[34]

---

[31] The Bipartisan Budget Act of 2018 (BBA) was signed into law on February 9, 2018 (Pub. L. No. 115-123); see § 53116.

[32] 42 U.S.C. § 1395w-102(b)(4)(A)(i)(II). *See also* CMS, "Announcement of Calendar Year (CY) 2019 Medicare Advantage Capitation Rates and Medicare Advantage and Part D Payment Policies and Final Call Letter."

[33] *See* **§ 11.06[B][1]** in this Handbook.

[34] ACA § 3308. *See* **Appendix 1-4** of this Handbook for the 2019 income-related adjustment amounts.

[3] Alternative Coverage and Enhanced Alternative Coverage

Part D drug plans are not required to offer the standard benefit, but they can offer alternative prescription drug coverage. Alternative coverage must be "actuarially equivalent" to the standard benefit. In other words, the value of the benefit package must be equal to the value of the standard benefit package.[35] In an actuarially equivalent plan, the cost-sharing varies through the use of such mechanisms as tiered copayments.[36] For example, a beneficiary's share of cost may be less for a generic or preferred brand name drug than for a non-preferred brand name drug. However, a plan that offers an alternative benefit package cannot impose a higher deductible ($415 in 2019) or require a higher out-of-pocket limit ($5,100 in 2019) than required by the standard benefit.

Plans can also offer enhanced alternative coverage that might include changes to the deductible and the initial coverage limit, although the deductible cannot be higher than the amount set in the statute ($415 in 2019). Enhanced alternative coverage might also include coverage of drugs that are excluded under Part D or coverage of some drugs in the coverage gap or donut hole. If supplemental coverage includes payment or discounted prices for brand name drugs in the donut hole, the supplemental coverage will pay first, before the manufacturer discount, and will include the dispensing fee. The beneficiary would then be responsible for any remainder of the negotiated price after the supplemental coverage, dispensing fee, and discounted price have been calculated.[37]

A PDP that wants to offer a drug plan with enhanced alternative coverage in a region must also offer a PDP with the basic benefit package in that region.[38]

[4] Calculating Beneficiary Expenses

As indicated above, only the costs of Part D covered drugs that are included on a plan's formulary (or that are approved through a formulary exception or appeal) count toward the deductible and out-of-pocket threshold[39] For example, a beneficiary whose only drug expense in January 2019 is $500 for a Part D drug that is not on his or her plan's formulary will not meet the deductible, and the

[35] 42 C.F.R. §§ 423.4, 423.100 and 423.104(e).

[36] Tiered cost-sharing above an amount set annually by CMS will be considered to be discriminatory. 42 C.F.R. § 423.104(d)(2)(iii).

[37] As discussed above the coverage gap (or donut hole) will be closed for brand name drugs in 2019 and generic drugs in 2020.). Note that CMS revised the definition of "negotiated price" at 42 C.F.R. § 423.100 to reflect pharmacy price concessions. 79 Fed. Reg. 29,844, 29,876.

[38] 42 C.F.R. § 423.104(f)(2).

[39] The regulations discuss beneficiary cost-sharing in terms of "covered Part D drugs." 42 C.F.R. § 423.104(g)(1). CMS uses the term to describe Part D drugs that are on a plan's formulary. CMS, Medicare Prescription Drug Benefit, 70 Fed. Reg. 4228 (Jan. 28, 2005), *available at* https://www.gpo.gov/fdsys/pkg/FR-2005-01-28/pdf/05-1321.pdf (site visited Aug. 6, 2018).

$5,100 in out-of-pocket expenses he or she will incur for the year for the non-formulary drug do not qualify for the reduced cost-sharing for high out-of-pocket costs.

Payments that count toward the yearly out-of-pocket threshold are referred to as true out-of-pocket expenses, or TrOOP. Only out-of-pocket costs for formulary drugs that are paid for by the beneficiary; by a family member or other person acting on the beneficiary's behalf; or by a State Pharmaceutical Assistance Program (SPAP), AIDS Drug Assistance Programs (ADAPs), and the Indian Health Service are considered TrOOP and are counted toward the out-of-pocket threshold.[40] Payments made by other insurance, including employer-sponsored plans, do not count toward the limit. Such uncounted payments increase the amount the beneficiary must spend before the reduced cost-sharing for high drug expenses begins. In sum, the beneficiary is responsible for paying premiums and the full costs of non-formulary prescriptions and gets no credit for these payments toward the out-of-pocket threshold.

Calculating TrOOP gets more complicated as the donut hole is being phased down. The 70 percent manufacturer rebate for brand name drugs in the donut hole counts toward TrOOP. This is because the beneficiary is still responsible for the full cost of the drug. The manufacturer's rebate is treated the same as a payment by an SPAP or ADAP. However, the additional subsidy paid by the plan (5 percent in 2019) does not count toward TrOOP. In addition, the 63 percent reduction in the cost of a generic drug in the donut hole does not count toward TrOOP. This is because the beneficiary is responsible for only 37 percent of the drug's cost, not 100 percent.[41]

[C] Access to Pharmacies

A drug plan may establish a network of retail pharmacies with which it enters into contracts in its service area as long as the pharmacies are conveniently located for all enrollees in the drug plan. The network must include access to long-term care (LTC) pharmacies that serve residents of nursing facilities.[42] A plan that does not offer the standard benefit can offer reduced copayments to

[40] 42 U.S.C. § 1395w-102(b)(4)(C)(ii), as amended by ACA § 3314; 42 C.F.R. §§ 423.100 and 423.464. Note that a final rule issued in 2015 amends § 423.464 to codify the requirement that Part D plans transfer and apply TrOOP-related data when an individual changes Part D plans mid-year. CMS, Contract Year 2016 Policy and Technical Changes to the Medicare Advantage and the Medicare Prescription Drug Benefit Programs, 80 Fed. Reg. 7912, 7934 (Feb. 12, 2015), *available at* https://www.gpo.gov/fdsys/pkg/FR-2015-02-12/pdf/2015-02671.pdf (site visited Aug. 6, 2018).

[41] *See, e.g.*, CMS, "Announcement of Calendar Year (CY) 2019 Medicare Advantage Capitation Rates and Medicare Advantage and Part D Payment Policies and Final Call Letter."

[42] *See* 73 Fed. Reg. 20,486.

enrollees who use its preferred pharmacies. A plan may also offer access to formulary drugs through a mail-order pharmacy.[43]

A Part D plan must provide coverage for formulary drugs purchased at an out-of-network pharmacy if a beneficiary cannot reasonably be expected to obtain the drugs through a network pharmacy. A beneficiary may not use an out-of-network pharmacy on a routine basis. A beneficiary may also have to pay a larger copayment or coinsurance for using an out-of-network pharmacy.[44] Plans may establish policies and procedures, including contracting with pharmacies that are outside of their service areas, to accommodate seasonal residents, often known as "snowbirds," and travelers.[45]

In an effort to reduce the amount of unused prescription drugs in LTC facilities, a rule effective in January 2013 requires all Part D plan sponsors to contract with network pharmacies servicing LTC facilities to dispense nonexempt brand name medications in 14-day-or-less increments, rather than in 30-day supplies.[46]

§ 11.05 ENROLLING IN A PART D PLAN

[A] Introduction to Enrolling in a Part D Plan

Enrollment in Medicare Part D differs dramatically from enrollment in Medicare Part B, which is also voluntary. A beneficiary who becomes entitled to Part A is automatically enrolled in Part B unless he or she takes steps to notify the Social Security Administration (SSA) that he or she does not want Part B coverage. Enrollment in Part D requires the beneficiary to take affirmative steps to enroll and get Part D coverage. The beneficiary must first choose a drug plan from the options available in his or her area. Then, the beneficiary must enroll through the plan he or she chooses. If the beneficiary may be eligible for the LIS, he or she must file a separate application for the subsidy either with his or her state Medicaid agency or with SSA.

---

[43] 42 C.F.R. § 423.120(a)(9).

[44] 42 C.F.R. § 423.124(1).

[45] CMS, Medicare Prescription Drug Benefit, 70 Fed. Reg. 4193, 4249 (Jan. 28, 2005), *available at* https://www.gpo.gov/fdsys/pkg/FR-2005-01-28/pdf/05-1321.pdf (site visited Aug. 6, 2018).

[46] 76 Fed. Reg. 21,573 (Apr. 15, 2011) (adding 42 C.F.R. § 423.154). In response to comments from advocates and others, CMS clarified that regardless of the number of incremental dispensing events, the total cost-sharing for a Part D drug to which the 14-day-or-less dispensing requirements apply shall be no greater than the total cost-sharing that would be imposed for such Part D drug if the 14-day-or-less requirements did not apply.

[B] Enrollment Periods

[1] Initial Enrollment Period

The initial enrollment period (IEP) for Part D for individuals who are newly eligible for Medicare corresponds to the IEP for Part B, that is, the seven-month period running from three months before the month the individual first becomes eligible and ending three months after the first month of eligibility.[47] Individuals who are not eligible to enroll in Part D during their IEP, generally because they were living out of the country or were incarcerated, have an IEP that begins three months before they meet the eligibility criteria for Part D, the month of Part D eligibility, and three months afterward.[48]

There are two exceptions to the IEP that apply to people whose Medicare entitlement is based on disability, not age. People who become entitled to Medicare retroactively, generally because of a determination of retroactive entitlement to Social Security disability benefits, have a Part D IEP that begins with the month of receipt of notice of Medicare entitlement and continues for three months afterward. Additionally, people whose entitlement to Medicare is based on disability have a second Part D IEP when they turn age 65.[49]

[2] Annual Coordinated Election Period

The annual coordinated election period (ACEP) corresponds to the ACEP for Part C. Starting in 2011, that period runs from October 15 through December 7.[50]

[3] Special Enrollment Periods

Individuals may be eligible for a special enrollment period (SEP)[51] in certain situations, including, but not limited to:

- They did not enroll in Part D during their initial enrollment because they had other prescription drug coverage deemed to be "creditable coverage," and they lose the creditable coverage;

---

[47] 42 C.F.R. §§ 423.38 and 407.14.

[48] PDB Manual, Ch. 3: § 30.1, *available at* https://www.cms.gov/Medicare/Eligibility-and-Enrollment/MedicarePresDrugEligEnrol/Downloads/CY_2018_PDP_Enrollment_and_Disenrollment_Guidance_6-15-17.pdf (site visited Aug. 6, 2018).

[49] PDB Manual, Ch. 3: § 30.1.

[50] ACA § 3204 (amending 42 U.S.C. §§ 1395w-21(e)(2)(C) and 1395w-101(b)(1)(iii)).

[51] 42 C.F.R. § 423.38(c). For a complete list of available SEPs, *see* PDB Manual, Ch. 3. Note that effective December 2011, there is a SEP to join a PDP or MA plan with a 5 star performance rating (*see* PDB Manual, Ch. 3: § 30.3.8.8.H).

- They were given incorrect information concerning the status of their other prescription drug coverage as creditable coverage;
- They were given incorrect information about enrollment by a federal employee;
- They have Medicare and full Medicaid coverage or a Medicare Savings Program (MSP) or are otherwise eligible for the Part D LIS;[52]
- They move out of a plan's service area;
- Their PDP's or Medicare Advantage plan's contract with Medicare is terminated;
- They enrolled in an MA-PD during the first year of eligibility and want to return to traditional Medicare and a PDP;
- Their eligibility for an SPAP changes; and
- They move into, reside in, or move out of a nursing home.

[4] Effective Date of Enrollment

Part D coverage becomes effective:[53]

- For an enrollment made prior to the month of eligibility, the first month of Part D eligibility;
- For an enrollment made subsequently, the month after the election of the Part D plan;
- For an enrollment made during the Annual Enrollment Period, January 1 of the following year; and
- The effective date of an enrollment made during a SEP, including a SEP for someone who becomes eligible for the LIS, depends on the SEP.[54]

[52] Note that CMS issued a final rule in 2018 (CMS-4182-F), 82 Fed. Reg. 16,440 (Apr. 16, 2018), which amended 42 C.F.R. § 423.38(c) to limit the SEP for dual-eligible and LIS beneficiaries from an open-ended monthly SEP to one that may be used only once per calendar quarter during the first nine months of the year (January through September). Separate SEPs can be used in the following circumstances: (1) within a certain period of time after a CMS or state-initiated enrollment; and (2) within a certain period of time after a change to an individual's LIS or Medicaid status.

[53] 42 C.F.R. § 423.40.

[54] CMS, Policy and Technical Changes to the Medicare Advantage and the Medicare Prescription Drug Benefit Programs, 75 Fed. Reg. 19,677 (Apr. 15, 2010) (amending 42 C.F.R. § 423.34); PDB Manual, Ch. 3: § 30.3.

[5] Involuntary Disenrollment

An individual may be involuntarily disenrolled from a drug plan for reasons similar to the grounds for disenrollment from an MA plan.[55] These include no longer living in the plan's service area, loss of eligibility for Part D, death of the individual, termination of the PDP, failure to pay premiums on a timely basis, and engaging in disruptive behavior that substantially impairs the ability of the plan to arrange for or provide services.[56] Note that a PDP may neither disenroll someone for failure to pay a premium if the enrollee is having premiums withheld from a monthly cash benefit check nor bill the enrollee directly for the premium. As of January 2011, there is a two-month grace period before a beneficiary can be involuntarily disenrolled from a Part D plan for failure to pay premiums. The grace period begins only after the beneficiary is notified that payment is due. It runs from the later of the first day of the month for which the premium is unpaid or the first day of the month after the date on which payment is requested.[57] Note that beneficiaries who establish good cause for failure to pay a premium that leads to disenrollment from a PDP and who pay the arrearage in full within three months of the disenrollment may be reinstated into the plan.[58] To the extent that an individual fails to pay only the Part D Income-Related Monthly Adjusted Amount (IRMAA), if applicable (the additional premium amount based on income, discussed at **§ 11.04[B][2]**), there will be an initial three-month grace period to pay this amount before the individual is disenrolled from the Part D plan.[59]

---

[55] 75 Fed. Reg. 19,677 (Apr. 15, 2010) (amending 42 C.F.R. § 423.44). *See* discussion on enrollment and disenrollment in **Chapter 7**, Medicare Advantage, of this Handbook.

[56] 42 C.F.R. § 423.44.

[57] CMS, Medicare Advantage and Prescription Drug Benefit Programs: Negotiated Pricing and Remaining Revisions, 74 Fed. Reg. 1494 (Jan. 12, 2009) (amending 42 C.F.R. §§ 423.44 and 423.293), *available at* https://www.gpo.gov/fdsys/pkg/FR-2009-01-12/pdf/E9-148.pdf (site visited Aug. 6, 2018).

[58] 76 Fed. Reg. 21,570 (Apr. 15, 2011), amending 42 C.F.R. § 423.44. Note that the failure to pay premiums must have been due to circumstances beyond the beneficiary's control. For further guidance on what constitutes good cause, *see* PDB Manual, Ch. 3: § 60.2.4.

[59] 76 Fed. Reg. 21,456 (Apr. 15, 2011), amending 42 C.F.R. § 423.44. Note that this is similar to the three-month grace period for individuals who fail to pay their Part B IRMAA. If payment is not made during the grace period, an individual will have an additional three months to establish "good cause" for failure to pay the Part D IRMAA and make payment to be reinstated into the Part D plan. The failure to pay the premiums must have been due to circumstances beyond the beneficiary's control. For further guidance, *see* Ch. 3: § 60.2.4.

[6] Ability to Change Plan Mid-Year

[a] Changes During the Annual Coordinated Enrollment Period

All beneficiaries may switch plans during the ACEP, which runs from October 15th through December 7th each year.[60] Enrollment becomes effective on January 1 of the next year.

In each year, most individuals who enroll in a PDP are "locked in" to their plan for the remainder of the calendar year, even though the plan in which they enroll may change the formulary or cost-sharing arrangements during the year. Enrollees in PDPs must wait until the next ACEP to switch plans, with enrollment in the new plan becoming effective on January 1 of the following year.

[b] Medicare Advantage Open Enrollment Period—2019

Pursuant to federal legislation enacted in December 2016, the annual 45-day Medicare Advantage Disenrollment Period (MADP) ended in 2018, and the Medicare Advantage Open Enrollment Period (OEP) that was in effect before 2011 has been reinstated effective 2019.[61] Effective 2019, for the first three months of the calendar year there will be a continuous open enrollment and disenrollment period relating to MA plans. During this three-month period an MA eligible beneficiary can make a one-time change to another MA plan, they can elect traditional Medicare, or they can elect coverage under Part D. The statute specifically limits the enrollment period's application to Part D coverage in that changes to prescription drug coverage can only be made during this period "in the case of an individual who, previous to such change in enrollment, is enrolled in a Medicare Advantage plan." In other words, someone in traditional Medicare with a stand-alone Part D plan may not use this enrollment period to switch from one Part D plan to another, whereas, if someone starts the year in an MA-PD, such person can switch to another MA-PD.[62]

---

[60] 42 C.F.R. § 423.38(b). Note that an individual has one choice or "election" during this period. In practice, an individual can make several changes between plans during this period, with the last election made prior to the end of the period the one that takes effect on the following January 1.

[61] Section 17005, 21st Century Cures Act (Pub. L. No. 114-255), signed into law by President Obama on December 13, 2016.

[62] Note that the plain language of the reinstated enrollment period in the 21st Century Cures Act seems to add limitations that did not exist in the previous OEP. *See* CMA, "'Cures' Act Tips the Scales Even Further in Favor of Medicare Advantage Over Traditional Medicare" (Dec. 28, 2016), *available at* http://www.medicareadvocacy.org/cures-act-tips-the-scales-even-further-in-favor-of-medicare-advantage-over-traditional-medicare/ (site visited Aug. 6, 2018).

[c] *Special Enrollment Periods*

Beneficiaries may also be eligible to change plans mid-year if they qualify for a SEP described above.

[7] Enrollment Process for Individuals Who Are Eligible for Medicare and Medicaid

The MMA established an enrollment process that provides for automatic assignment into drug plans for individuals who are dually eligible for Medicare and Medicaid (dual eligibles) and who do not choose their own PDP or MA-PD during their IEP. In addition, dual eligibles are eligible for a limited SEP during the first nine months of the calendar year.[63] A similar process provides for the enrollment into a drug plan for individuals who have applied and been found eligible for the LIS and who did not choose their own drug coverage.[64] Every year since the start of Medicare Part D, a large number of dual eligible beneficiaries have had to be reassigned to a new PDP because the plan to which they were originally assigned did not qualify in the following year as a plan eligible for the LIS and a plan to which dual eligibles may be automatically enrolled. The Affordable Care Act (ACA) modified the method for determining which plans qualify as LIS plans in order to reduce the number of LIS-eligible individuals who must be reassigned to a new drug plan each year.[65]

[8] Failure to Enroll on a Timely Basis

[a] *Late Enrollment Penalty*

A beneficiary who does not enroll in a Part D plan within 63 days of his or her IEP and has no other "creditable" prescription drug coverage must pay a late penalty if he or she subsequently enrolls in a Part D plan. The penalty is assessed at 1 percent of the national base beneficiary premium for each month of delayed

---

[63] 42 U.S.C. § 1395w-101(b)(3)(D); 42 C.F.R. § 423.38(c)(4). As noted in footnote [X] above, CMS issued a final rule in 2018 (CMS-4182-F), 82 Fed. Reg. 16,440 (Apr. 16, 2018), which amended 42 C.F.R. § 423.38(c) to limit the SEP for dual-eligible and LIS beneficiaries from an open-ended monthly SEP to one that may be used only once per calendar quarter during the first nine months of the year (January through September).

[64] 75 Fed. Reg. 19,677 (amending 42 C.F.R. § 423.34). *See also* PDB Manual, Ch. 3: § 40.1.4.

[65] ACA §§ 3302 and 3303. Note that this provision codifies existing CMS policy whereby the Secretary may permit a plan whose premium exceeds the benchmark amount by a de minimis amount to waive payment of that portion of the Part D premium that is above the benchmark for LIS-eligible individuals. To the extent that plans choose to waive such increases, the individuals affected would not need to be reassigned to benchmark plans. 76 Fed. Reg. 21,451 (Apr. 15, 2011) (amending 42 C.F.R. § 423.34).

enrollment, for the remainder of the time in which the beneficiary is enrolled in a Part D plan.[66] Thus, a beneficiary who becomes eligible for Part D at age 65 but who delays enrolling until age 70 may be assessed a 60 percent penalty on his or her premium (5 years × 12 months × 1%). Since the penalty is based on a percentage of the average premium each year, the dollar value of the penalty changes as the national base beneficiary premium changes.

A beneficiary who becomes eligible for Medicare based on disability has a new IEP for Part D upon turning age 65. As a result, any late enrollment penalty assessed against such a beneficiary ends with the new IEP.[67]

The Medicare Improvements for Patients and Providers Act of 2008 (MIPPA) permanently waived the late enrollment penalty for LIS-eligible individuals, effective January 1, 2009.[68]

Beneficiaries who are assessed a late enrollment penalty may file an appeal with their drug plan.[69]

[b] Creditable Coverage

Someone who delays enrollment because he or she has creditable coverage, that is, coverage through another insurance plan deemed comparable to Part D coverage, will not be assessed a penalty for late enrollment if he or she later decides to enroll in Part D. A determination of whether coverage is creditable involves an actuarial assessment of whether the other insurance provides coverage of the costs of prescription drugs that equals or exceeds the actuarial value of the prescription drug benefit.[70]

Coverage offered through an employer or union-sponsored health plan, the federal employee health benefits program (FEHBP), Medicaid, an SPAP, programs for veterans, and TRICARE may constitute creditable coverage. The entity sponsoring the coverage must inform beneficiaries whether the coverage provided meets the definition of creditable coverage by September 30 of each year.[71]

Coverage offered through some pre-standardized Medicare Supplemental (Medigap) policies may qualify as creditable, as may coverage through some policies sold in Michigan, Minnesota, and Wisconsin, which are not required to sell the standard policies. The standard Medigap policies H, I, and J that offered drug coverage to beneficiaries who purchased them before January 1, 2006, do not

---

[66] 42 C.F.R. §§ 423.46 and 423.286(d)(3).

[67] PDB Manual, Ch. 4: § 10.1.3, *available at* https://www.cms.gov/Medicare/Eligibility-and-Enrollment/MedicarePresDrugEligEnrol/Downloads/FINAL_CY2010_MedicarePrescriptionDrugBenefitManualChapter4_Dec2009.pdf (site visited Aug. 6, 2018).

[68] MIPPA § 114. The section codifies a CMS policy that had waived the late enrollment penalty for this population.

[69] PDB Manual, Ch. 4.

[70] 42 U.S.C. § 1395w-113(b)(5).

[71] 42 U.S.C. § 1395w-113(b)(4), 42 C.F.R. § 423.56.

meet the definition of creditable coverage. Insurers that offer Medigap policies were required to notify their insured persons concerning the status of their policies. Beneficiaries are advised to check with their insurers about the status of their policies.[72]

[C] Choosing a Part D Plan

CMS is supposed to provide information to all Medicare beneficiaries to help them choose a Part D PDP. Information is made available through the Medicare & You handbook, through the Medicare toll-free number, and through the Medicare website (*www.medicare.gov*). In addition, Part D plan sponsors are required to make available to all individuals eligible to enroll in Part D information about all beneficiary cost-sharing, their formulary and cost control mechanisms, their pharmacy network, and their exceptions and appeals process.[73] Beneficiaries who want this information have to check with each drug plan.

Beneficiaries who have retiree health coverage also must contact their former employers or unions to determine the effect of enrollment in a Part D plan on their retiree health benefits. Some employers and unions will terminate all retiree health coverage, not just the drug benefit, for retirees and their dependents if the retiree enrolls in a Part D plan. Dual eligible beneficiaries who have employer coverage for which a Part D retiree drug subsidy is being paid will be presumed to have declined auto enrollment in a Part D plan.[74] CMS will send such beneficiaries a notice informing them of the option to receive Part D and advising them to contact their plan to discuss the impact of Medicare Part D coverage on their retiree plan.[75]

---

[72] Note that when an individual issued such a policy prior to 2006 chooses to join a Part D plan, the Medigap issuer must remove any prescription drug coverage under such policies and adjust the premiums accordingly. 42 U.S.C. § 1395ss(v).

[73] 42 C.F.R. § 423.128. Note that a final rule issued in 2018 revised the timing and default delivery method of certain beneficiary documents: the Annual Notice of Change (ANOC) must be delivered 15 days before first day of ACEP (10/1), whereas Evidence of Coverage (EOC) must by delivered by first day of ACEP (10/15), and MA and Part D sponsors can now provide certain materials, such as the EOC, electronically, with provision of hard copy upon request. 83 Fed. Reg. 16,440 (Apr. 16, 2018)

[74] 42 C.F.R. § 423.34.

[75] For a copy of the model notice, *see* CMS, Introduction to the FBDE RDS Notice, *available at* http://www.cms.gov/Medicare/Prescription-Drug-Coverage/LimitedIncomeandResources/downloads/11334.pdf (site visited Aug. 6, 2018).

§ 11.06 PREMIUM AND COST-SHARING SUBSIDIES FOR PART D PRESCRIPTION DRUGS FOR LOW-INCOME INDIVIDUALS

[A] Introduction to Premium and Cost-Sharing Subsidies

For the first time in program history, Medicare has a low-income benefit for people with limited incomes and resources. While the Medicaid program has also played a role in paying Medicare's cost-sharing for beneficiaries dually eligible for both programs, Medicare has never provided direct low-income subsidies. In its design of the benefit, Congress adopted aspects of the federal Supplemental Security Income program (SSI) and of Medicaid's MSPs. Similarly, to administer the benefit, Congress looks to SSA and to state Medicaid agencies.

[B] The Subsidies

To help pay the costs of Medicare Part D, some form of the low-income subsidy (LIS) is available to Medicare beneficiaries with incomes up to 150 percent of the FPL for a family of the size involved.[76] Subsidies vary according to income, Medicaid status, and institutional status. So-called full subsidy eligible individuals are those with full Medicaid status (full-benefit dual eligibles), those with SSI but no Medicaid, those enrolled in one of three MSPs, and individuals with incomes below 135 percent of FPL and countable resources in 2019 of not more than $9,060 for an individual and $14,340 for a couple (including $1,500 per person for burial).[77] Partial subsidy individuals can have incomes up to 150 percent of FPL and resources in 2019 of not more than $14,100 per individual and $28,150 per couple (including $1,500 per person for burial).[78] Resource levels will increase each year based on increases in the consumer price index. Income and resource levels are generally announced in January of each year.

Note that CMS systems do not always reflect a beneficiary's correct subsidy status. In response, CMS created a best available evidence (BAE) policy that

[76] 42 U.S.C. § 1395w-114.

[77] 42 C.F.R. § 423.773(b); CMS, "2018 Resource and Cost-Sharing Limits for Low-Income Subsidy (LIS)," *available at* https://www.medicaid.gov/state-resource-center/state-operations-and-technical-assistance/downloads/sota-update-20171213.pdf (site visited Aug. 6, 2018). New numbers for 2019 were not available at the time of publication. *See* CMS, "Medicare Savings Programs," *available at* http://www.medicare.gov/your-medicare-costs/help-paying-costs/medicare-savings-program/medicare-savings-programs.html#slmb for updated information (site visited Aug. 6, 2018).

[78] 42 C.F.R. § 423.773(a); CMS, "2018 Resource and Cost-Sharing Limits for Low-Income Subsidy (LIS)." For the 2018 Federal Poverty Guidelines, *see* HHS, "Poverty Guidelines," *available at* https://aspe.hhs.gov/poverty-guidelines (site visited on Aug. 6, 2018). The 2019 Federal Poverty Guidelines were not available at the time of publication.

requires Part D plans to establish appropriate cost-sharing when presented with evidence that information about the beneficiary is not accurate.[79]

[1] Full Subsidy Eligible Individuals

All full subsidy individuals are entitled to a 100 percent subsidy for the "low-income benchmark premium"[80] for a plan offering the standard Part D benefit, or partial subsidy for enhanced plans with premiums above the benchmark, elimination of the deductible, continuation of coverage through the donut hole, and elimination of all cost-sharing after they meet the annual out-of-pocket threshold. In addition, their cost-sharing is reduced as follows:

- Full-benefit dual eligibles who are institutionalized, or who participate in a Home and Community-Based Waiver Program, have no cost-sharing at all.[81]
- Full-benefit dual eligibles with incomes up to 100 percent of FPL initially pay no more than $1.25/generic or preferred brand or $3.80/non-preferred brand, in 2019.[82]
- All other full subsidy individuals initially pay copayments of no more than $3.40/generic or preferred brand or $8.50/non-preferred brand, with copayments indexed annually to the cost of Part D drugs in 2019.[83]

[2] Partial Subsidy Eligible Individuals

In 2019, partial subsidy individuals pay a sliding scale premium; a $85 deductible; coinsurance of 15 percent instead of the full 25 percent, including continued coverage through the donut hole; and a copayment of no more than

---

[79] For more information about the BAE, *see* CMS, "Best Available Evidence (BAE)," *available at* http://www.cms.gov/Medicare/Prescription-Drug-Coverage/PrescriptionDrugCovContra/Best_Available_Evidence_Policy.html (site visited on Aug. 6, 2018).

[80] The "low-income benchmark premium" is the weighted average of plan premiums for the basic benefit package in the region in which the individual lives. As of January 2011, CMS is required to calculate the LIS benchmarks using basic Part D premiums before the application of Part C rebates each year. 42 C.F.R. § 423.780. This provision prevents the artificial lowering of the overall average (benchmark) amount of all Part D plans, which in turn should reduce the number of annual Part D plan reassignments of LIS enrollees.

[81] 42 C.F.R. § 423.782(a).

[82] 42 C.F.R. § 423.782(a); CMS, "Announcement of Calendar Year (CY) 2019 Medicare Advantage Capitation Rates and Medicare Advantage and Part D Payment Policies and Final Call Letter."

[83] 42 C.F.R. § 423.782(a); CMS, "Announcement of Calendar Year (CY) 2019 Medicare Advantage Capitation Rates and Medicare Advantage and Part D Payment Policies and Final Call Letter."

$3.40/generic or preferred brand or $8.50/non-preferred brand for all drugs after the out-of-pocket threshold is met.[84]

[3] Deemed Subsidy Eligible Individuals

Certain individuals are treated as full subsidy eligible individuals regardless of their actual income and resources. These are full-benefit dual eligibles, recipients of SSI benefits, and beneficiaries of the three MSPs: Qualified Medicare Beneficiaries (QMBs), Specified Low-income Medicare Beneficiaries (SLMBs), and Qualified Individuals (QIs).[85]

[4] Length of Eligibility Determination

An initial determination that someone qualifies for the LIS remains in effect for a full year. SSA selects a portion of subsidy-eligible individuals for cyclical redeterminations in August of each year. Individuals are chosen for redetermination based on criteria SSA believes indicate that they are more likely to have had a change in subsidy amount.[86]

An individual who is deemed eligible for LIS between January 1 and June 30 of a given year is deemed LIS-eligible for the rest of the year. An individual who is deemed eligible between July 1 and December 31 of a given year is deemed eligible for the remainder of that calendar year and for the next calendar year.[87] An individual who loses deemed LIS-eligibility will be notified in the fall of the year before LIS-eligibility ends and given the opportunity to apply for LIS. Many people who lose deemed status are "re-deemed" later in the year or are found eligible for LIS based on filing an application.

[C] Eligibility Determinations

[1] Where to Apply

Beneficiaries who are not "deemed eligible" have the choice of filing an application for the LIS either at their state Medicaid office or through SSA.[88] Because of strong encouragement by SSA and CMS, the overwhelming majority

---

[84] 42 C.F.R. § 423.782(b); CMS, "Announcement of Calendar Year (CY) 2019 Medicare Advantage Capitation Rates and Medicare Advantage and Part D Payment Policies and Final Call Letter."

[85] 42 C.F.R. § 423.773(c). *See* **Chapter 10** of this Handbook for a full discussion of the MSPs.

[86] 20 C.F.R. §§ 418.3600 *et seq.*; Social Security Administration (SSA), Program Operations Manual System (POMS), Section HI 03050.015, *available at* https://secure.ssa.gov/poms.nsf/lnx/0603050015 (site visited Aug. 6, 2018).

[87] 75 Fed. Reg. 19,677 (Apr. 15, 2010) (amending 42 C.F.R. § 423.773(c)(2)).

[88] 42 C.F.R. § 423.774(a).

of beneficiaries apply through SSA. Applying at Medicaid may have offered some advantages, however, as Medicaid offices screen for other benefits as well as LIS.[89] In a state with more generous income and/or resource limits for its MSP than applicable for LIS, someone found ineligible for the LIS might still qualify for MSP benefits. By qualifying for MSP benefits, that individual is deemed eligible for the LIS. Additionally, Medicaid may have speedier determination time frames and more user-friendly appeals systems than SSA.[90] Unlike the Medicaid regulations, the Social Security regulations impose no time restrictions by which SSA must act on applications and appeals.[91]

The choice of location may have less relevance due to changes in LIS eligibility calculation and in information exchanges between SSA and the states. SSA is now required to transmit LIS applications of consenting beneficiaries to the states for purposes of determining eligibility for one of the MSPs.[92] As discussed below, MIPPA modified what counts toward income and resources for LIS eligibility but not for MSP eligibility. Thus, in some states MSP eligibility criteria may not be more generous than LIS criteria.

[2] Eligibility Criteria

In determining eligibility for the LIS, income is to be determined according to MSP rules, which in turn refer to SSI rules. One improvement over both SSI and MSP rules is the definition of "family size," which requires using a standard that reflects the actual number of dependents in an applicant's household. "Dependent" is defined as one who relies on the applicant or spouse for at least one-half of his or her support. "Resources" is defined as liquid resources "such as checking and savings accounts, stocks, bonds, and other resources that can be readily converted to cash within 20 days," and real estate that is neither the primary residence of the applicant nor the land on which the residence is located.[93]

MIPPA also added exemptions from income and resources for determinations of LIS eligibility but not for determinations of MSP eligibility. For applications filed on or after January 1, 2010, non-financial support (in-kind support and maintenance) provided to an LIS applicant will no longer be considered as income, and the cash surrender value of a life insurance policy will no longer be considered as a resource.[94]

---

[89] 42 U.S.C. § 1396a(a)(10); 42 C.F.R. § 435.902.

[90] Eligibility regulations proposed by SSA do not include time frames for making eligibility determinations and include a very limited appeals process. 20 C.F.R. §§ 418.3600 *et seq.*

[91] 20 C.F.R. §§ 418.3110, 418.3220, and 418.3230.

[92] MIPPA § 113 (amending 42 U.S.C. § 1396u-5(a)(4)).

[93] 42 C.F.R. § 423.772.

[94] 42 U.S.C. § 1395w-114(a)(3)(C), (D), (G).

[3] Appeals Process

The appeals process for someone who is denied the LIS depends on where the application is filed. When the Medicaid agency makes the decision, any appeal must follow the procedures used for Medicaid appeals. SSA will use its redeterminations and appeals procedures for the determinations it makes.[95] SSA regulations provide for a telephone hearing or a case review. The preamble indicates that the hearings will not be conducted by administrative law judges (ALJs) who hear other Social Security appeals.[96] An individual whose application for LIS has been denied is entitled to judicial review of the final decision to the same extent as other decisions made by SSA.[97]

[D] Effect of Eligibility Determination for Low-Income Subsidy

CMS will enroll into a Part D plan those individuals who are either deemed or found eligible for the LIS and who have not chosen a Part D plan on their own. These individuals are randomly assigned to a Part D plan in their region that meets the criteria to be a LIS plan, that is, a plan for which an individual eligible for the full LIS pays no premium.[98] Full-benefit dual eligible individuals who are enrolled in certain retiree health plans may decline automatic enrollment by CMS in a PDP; CMS will not automatically assign to a PDP other LIS-eligible individuals who are enrolled in certain retiree health plans.[99]

§ 11.07 DUAL ELIGIBLES

[A] Introduction to Dual Eligibles to Drug Plans

Among the most dramatic aspects of the Medicare drug benefit legislation is its complete elimination of Medicaid prescription drug coverage for all individuals who are dually eligible for both Medicare and Medicaid. Beginning January 1, 2006, any individual eligible to enroll in a Part D plan who is receiving full Medicaid services cannot receive prescription drug coverage through Medicaid.[100] This is true regardless of whether the individual has actually enrolled in a

[95] 42 C.F.R. § 423.774(c).

[96] 70 Fed. Reg. 77,664, 77,674 (Dec. 30, 2005).

[97] 42 U.S.C. § 1395w-114(a)(3)(B)(iv).

[98] 75 Fed. Reg. 1967 (Apr. 15, 2010) (amending 42 C.F.R. § 423.34(d)). Such plans are sometimes referred to as "benchmark plans."

[99] 75 Fed. Reg. 1967 (Apr. 15, 2010) (amending 42 C.F.R. § 423.34(d)(3)). The retiree health plans to which this section applies receive a subsidy from CMS to continue offering drug coverage. Enrollment in a Part D plan terminates the retiree drug benefit and, in most cases, the full retiree health benefit.

[100] 42 U.S.C. § 1396u-5(d)(1).

Part D plan and regardless of whether the plan covers the specific drug needed. Concomitantly, the state cannot receive federal matching payments for such services.

[B] Definition of Dual Eligibles

Dual eligibles are defined as individuals who have coverage under a Part D plan and who are eligible for full Medicaid benefits under any category of a state Medicaid plan. Those with full coverage under a so-called Section 1115 research and demonstration waiver fall within the definition.[101]

[C] Assignment of Dual Eligibles to Drug Plans

Presumably because of dual eligibles' loss of Medicaid drug coverage, Congress requires the automatic enrollment in a PDP of any dual eligible who has not voluntarily enrolled.[102] Dual eligible beneficiaries are randomly assigned to Part D plans with premiums at or below the average premium for their region (sometimes referred to as a "benchmark plan"). The effective date of auto-enrollment into a Part D plan for individuals with Medicare who become eligible for Medicaid will be the same as the effective date of Medicaid eligibility. The effective date of auto-enrollment for individuals who become eligible for Medicare and Medicaid in the same month will also be the date of Medicaid eligibility. New dual eligible individuals who have Medicaid first will be auto-enrolled retroactively to the date of their Medicare eligibility. In all situations, retroactive enrollment raises the possibility that dual eligibles may be required to pay for their drugs out of their own pockets and then be reimbursed.[103]

The ACA requires the Office of the Inspector General (OIG) of the Department of Health and Human Services (HHS) to conduct an annual study of the extent to which Part D plan formularies include drugs most commonly used by full-benefit dual eligibles.[104] In its 2018 report, OIG found that the "rate of Part D plan formularies' inclusion of the 197 drugs commonly used by dual eligibles is high, with some variation. On average, Part D plan formularies include 96 percent of the 197 commonly used drugs. In addition, 68 percent of the commonly used drugs are included by all Part D plan formularies. These results are largely

---

[101] 42 C.F.R. § 423.772.

[102] 42 U.S.C. § 1396u-5(c)(6).

[103] 75 Fed. Reg. 1967 (Apr. 15, 2010) (amending 42 C.F.R. § 423.34(f)). Effective January 1, 2010, CMS has implemented a new process for retroactive and temporary drug coverage for all LIS-eligible individuals entitled the Limited Income Newly Eligible Transition (NET) Program. For more information, *see* CMS, "Medicare Limited Income NET Program," *available at* http://www.cms.gov/Medicare/Eligibility-and-Enrollment/LowIncSubMedicarePresCov/MedicareLimitedIncomeNET.html (site visited Aug. 6, 2018).

[104] ACA § 3313.

unchanged from OIG's findings for formularies reported in the mandated annual report from 2017, as well as our findings from 2011 through 2016." OIG also notes that "the percentage of drugs to which plan formularies applied utilization management tools increased slightly between 2017 and 2018. On average, formularies applied utilization management tools to 29 percent of the unique drugs we reviewed in 2018, an increase of 1 percentage point from 2017."[105] Unlike other Medicare beneficiaries, however, dual eligible beneficiaries have several opportunities to switch plans during the first nine months of the calendar year.[106] Thus, individuals assigned to a plan whose formulary does not include the prescriptions they use may have an opportunity to switch to a more appropriate plan. Note that due to prior problems surrounding changing plans, CMS has instituted an enrollment reconciliation process to address multiple plan enrollments and/or discrepancies in CMS records of enrollment.

[D] Medicaid Wrap-Around

The elimination of coverage for an otherwise covered Medicaid service represents a substantial departure from the historic Medicare-Medicaid relationship for dual eligibles, under which Medicaid has paid Medicare's cost-sharing and provided "wrap-around coverage" for services where, as with home health, Medicare coverage is more limited than Medicaid's or where, as with LTC, Medicare coverage is nearly nonexistent.[107] The significance of this situation cannot be overstated. Because of the design of the Medicare drug benefit, many dual eligibles who were on Medicaid before becoming eligible for Medicare have less prescription drug coverage than they had under Medicaid and potentially less protection during appeals processes to challenge denials or other barriers to coverage. Further, they may have to make copayments for their prescriptions, with the copayment amounts increasing yearly.

Medicaid can continue to cover for dual eligibles, using both federal and state funding, those drugs that it is permitted but not required by law to cover for any Medicaid beneficiary and that are not, by definition, Part D covered drugs.

---

[105] OIG, "Part D Plans Generally Include Drugs Commonly Used by Dual Eligibles: 2018 Report (OEI-05-17-00160) (June 2018), *available at* https://oig.hhs.gov/oei/reports/oei-05-18-00240.pdf (site visited Aug. 6, 2018).

[106] 42 C.F.R. § 423.38(c). Note that CMS issued a final rule in 2018 (CMS-4182-F), 82 Fed. Reg. 16,440 (Apr. 16, 2018), which amended 42 C.F.R. § 423.38(c) to limit the SEP for dual-eligible and LIS beneficiaries from an open-ended monthly SEP to one that may be used only once per calendar quarter during the first nine months of the year (January through September). Separate SEPs can be used in the following circumstances: (1) within a certain period of time after a CMS or state-initiated enrollment; and (2) within a certain period of time after a change to an individual's LIS or Medicaid status.

[107] For a full discussion of dual eligibility, see **Chapter 10** of this Handbook.

Such drugs include prescription vitamins, cough and cold relief drugs, and non-prescription drugs, among others.[108] States also have the option of paying copayments for dual eligibles and/or for drugs that are not on a plan's formulary. However, they will receive no federal matching payments and must use only state funds if they assist dual eligibles with these costs. Many states continue to cover at least some of the excluded Part D drugs.[109] Few, if any, states also cover Part D cost-sharing.

[E] Nursing Facility Residents

In addition to the problems that may be experienced by other dually eligible individuals, those who reside in nursing and other LTC facilities experience problems that arise because of the setting in which they live. For example, there is no assurance that a dually eligible resident who does not choose a plan for himself or herself will be automatically assigned to a plan that includes the pharmacy used by his or her nursing facility, although all plans are required to include LTC pharmacies in their networks. Drug plans are not required to provide covered medications in the packaging utilized by nursing facilities or formats utilized by residents, though CMS expects that plan sponsors will do so. CMS also expects plans to allow for at least a 31-day fill for residents in accordance with industry best practices.[110] If access to medically necessary drugs and drug formats is not provided, a beneficiary may need to file an appeal in order to get the prescription ordered by the treating physician. Also, as noted in **§ 11.05[B][3]** of this Handbook, individuals who move into, reside in, or move out of an institution have a SEP right to change Part D plans.[111]

Dually eligible individuals who reside in a nursing facility pay no copayment for their medications. As of January 2012, cost-sharing for covered Part D drugs is also eliminated for full-benefit dually eligible individuals who are receiving home and community-based services (HCBS) under certain home and community-based waivers or a state plan amendment, or if enrolled in certain Medicaid managed care organizations.[112]

---

[108] As noted above, effective January 1, 2013, benzodiazepines and barbiturates (used for treating epilepsy, cancer, or a chronic mental health disorder) are included as Part D covered drugs. MIPPA § 175. Effective January 1, 2014, all barbiturates are covered by Medicaid and therefore by Medicare Part D. ACA § 2502.

[109] For a list of Medicaid coverage of Medicare Part D excluded drugs, by state, *see* CMS, "Excluded Drug Coverage," *available at* https://www.medicaid.gov/medicaid/prescription-drugs/excluded-drug-coverage/index.html (site visited Aug. 6, 2018).

[110] PDB Manual, Ch. 6: § 30.2.3.

[111] *See, e.g.*, PDB Manual, Ch. 3: § 30.3.8.5.

[112] This applies to individuals receiving home and community-based services (HCBS) under § 1115 or § 1915(c) or (d) of the Social Security Act, or under a State Plan Amendment under § 1915(i) of the Act, or if such services are provided through enrollment in a Medicaid managed

[F] Transitioning into a Part D Plan

When Medicare beneficiaries move from another source of payment for their prescriptions to a Part D plan or change to a different Part D plan, they may encounter difficulties caused by changes in formularies and other utilization management tools used by Part D plans to contain costs. The transition may be particularly difficult for nursing home residents and other dual eligibles, and for beneficiaries with chronic conditions who are stabilized on their current treatments.

All Part D plans are required to establish a transition process to ensure access to non-formulary drugs, including those subject to step therapy or prior authorization requirements, during the first 90 days of coverage under a new plan. The transition process is available for new enrollees following the annual coordinated enrollment period; newly eligible Medicare beneficiaries from other coverage; individuals who change plans mid-year; and current enrollees who are affected by formulary changes. Eligible enrollees are generally entitled to a 30-day transition fill, unless the prescription is for fewer than 30 days. Residents in LTC facilities were previously entitled to up to 93 days of transition fills, however as of 2019 they are entitled only to a 30-day transition fill.[113] Plans must also send enrollees written notice explaining that the prescription has been filled on a transition basis within three business days of approving the transition fill. They are also to ensure that reasonable notice is made to inform the prescriber of the temporary fill.[114]

Cost-sharing requirements for transition fills has been modified as follows:

- For LIS enrollees, a plan cannot charge higher cost-sharing for transition supplies than the statutory maximum copayment amounts.
- For non-LIS enrollees, a plan must charge the same cost-sharing for non-formulary Part D drugs provided during the transition that would apply for non-formulary drugs approved through a formulary exception in accordance with 42 C.F.R. § 423.578(b), and the same cost-sharing for formulary drugs subject to utilization management edits provided during the transition that would apply once the utilization management criteria are met.[115]

---

care organization with a contract under § 1903(m) or § 1932 of the Act. Individuals residing in assisted living facilities are included in the definition of an "individual receiving [HCBS]" if they satisfy the inclusion criteria listed in the previous sentence. 76 Fed. Reg. 21,458–59 (Apr. 15, 2011) (amending 42 C.F.R. §§ 423.772 and 423.782(a)(2)(ii)).

[113] For final rule issued in 2018 (CMS-4182-F), *see* 82 Fed. Reg. 16,440, 16601 (Apr. 16, 2018).

[114] 75 Fed. Reg. 19,678 (Apr. 15, 2010) (amending 42 C.F.R. § 423.120(b)(3)).

[115] 79 Fed. Reg. 29,962 (May 23, 2014) (amending 42 C.F.R. § 423.120(b)(3)).

§ 11.08 STATE PHARMACEUTICAL ASSISTANCE PROGRAMS

States may choose to provide cost-sharing and wrap-around drug coverage for dual eligibles and other low-income residents through an SPAP.[116] Any payments made by the SPAP on behalf of a Part D enrollee will count toward the enrollee's true out-of-pocket costs. In other words, SPAP payments for cost-sharing and for a plan's covered drugs while the beneficiary is in the "donut hole" count toward meeting the $5,100 out-of-pocket limit (in 2019) which, in turn, leads to reduced enrollee cost-sharing. State Medicaid programs, including Pharmacy Plus waivers under Section 1115 of the Social Security Act, and any other programs where the majority of the funding is from federal sources, cannot be SPAPs.[117]

SPAPs must not discriminate among drug plans with respect to their supplemental coverage;[118] this requirement prevents an SPAP from automatically enrolling subsidy-eligible individuals into one particular drug plan. Plans must coordinate with SPAPs concerning certain basic elements of the drug benefit they offer.

§ 11.09 GRIEVANCE, APPEALS, AND EXCEPTIONS PROCESSES

[A] Grievance Procedures

All drug plans must establish processes for hearing and resolving grievances similar to the process utilized by MA plans under Medicare Part C.[119] Grievances are separate and distinct from appeals and from quality of service complaints filed with a Quality Improvement Organization (QIO). Grievances may be filed with the drug plan orally or in writing within 60 days after the incident; plans generally must resolve grievances within 30 days. However, plans must resolve within 24 hours a grievance arising from the plan's decision not to expedite a coverage determination or redetermination under the appeals process.[120]

Since January 2012, Part D plans must address complaints received by CMS against the plan by addressing and resolving complaints in the CMS complaint tracking system and displaying a link to the electronic complaint form on the *www.medicare.gov* website on the plan's main web page.[121] Complaints about

---

[116] 42 C.F.R. §§ 423.454 and 423.464(e)(1).

[117] 42 C.F.R. § 423.464(e)(1)(iv).

[118] 42 C.F.R. §§ 423.464(e)(1)(ii) and 423.464(e)(1)(ii).

[119] 42 U.S.C. § 1395w-104(f). *See* **§ 7.04[E]** of this Handbook.

[120] 42 C.F.R. § 423.564.

[121] 76 Fed. Reg. 21,470 (Apr. 15, 2011) (amending 42 C.F.R. § 423.505).

plans may be filed on the *www.medicare.gov* website or by contacting the local State Health Insurance Assistance Program (SHIP) to access the complaint tracking module (CTM).

[B] Coverage Determinations and Appeals

[1] The Coverage and Appeals Process

As directed by Congress, the coverage determination and appeals process for Part D also mirrors closely the process utilized by MA plans.[122] The process begins when the beneficiary or prescriber requests a coverage determination, either orally or in writing,[123] and the drug plan issues the formal coverage determination. For appeals filed on or after January 1, 2012, PDP sponsors must make available uniform model forms for requesting coverage determinations and redeterminations, establish a toll-free telephone number and website for accepting requests for coverage determinations and redeterminations, and arrange with their network providers to distribute written notices at the pharmacy instructing enrollees how to contact their plans to obtain a coverage determination or request an exception if they disagree with the information provided by the pharmacist.[124] The plan may provide oral notice to the beneficiary of a completely favorable coverage determination as long as it sends a written follow-up notice within three calendar days of the oral notification. Notices must meet regulatory requirements. Favorable coverage determination notices must describe in readable and understandable form the conditions of the approval. Unfavorable decisions must use approved notice language that is readable and understandable, that states the specific reason for the denial, and that describes the redetermination process.[125] If the

[122] 42 U.S.C. § 1395w-104(g)–(h).

[123] Plans must establish and maintain a method of documenting all oral requests. 75 Fed. Reg. 19,677 (Apr. 15, 2010) (amending 42 C.F.R. § 423.568(a)(3)). See discussion about notice at **§ 11.09[D]** of this Handbook.

[124] 76 Fed. Reg. 21,573 (Apr. 15, 2011) (amending 42 C.F.R. § 423.128); 76 Fed. Reg. 21,575 (Apr. 15, 2011) (amending 42 C.F.R. § 423.562). In the final rule, CMS noted its intention to develop separate model forms for coverage determinations and redeterminations, and will continue to allow plan sponsors to develop and make available drug-specific coverage determination request forms to supplement the model forms. In addition, instead of requiring an interactive web-based application for coverage determinations and appeals, CMS will simply require plan enrollees to have the ability to send a secure e-mail via the plan's website in order to initiate a request. Note that as of October 2017, Part D plan sponsors are required to use an updated Notice of Denial of Medicare Prescription Drug Coverage (Form CMS-10146). For the notice and corresponding form instructions, *see* CMS, "Plan Sponsor Notices and Other Documents," *available at* http://www.cms.gov/Medicare/Appeals-and-Grievances/MedPrescriptDrugApplGriev/PlanNoticesAndDocuments.html (site visited Aug. 6, 2018).

[125] 75 Fed. Reg. 19,677 (Apr. 15, 2010) (amending 42 C.F.R. §§ 423.568(d)–(g) and 423.572(b)–(c)).

plan intends to issue a partially or fully unfavorable decision, a physician or other appropriate health care professional must be involved in the review.[126]

The beneficiary or prescriber[127] may make an oral or written request for a redetermination, performed by the drug plans, of an unfavorable coverage determination.[128] Individuals or their prescribers who remain dissatisfied after the redetermination can request a further review known as reconsideration; the reconsideration will be performed by the Independent Review Entity (IRE). Following an IRE review, the enrollee may appeal to an ALJ, then to the Medicare Appeals Council (Council), and finally to federal court. An expedited review is available if the standards set out in Medicare Part C are met.[129]

Plans must notify enrollees of initial coverage determinations involving requests for drug benefits as expeditiously as the enrollee's health condition requires, but no later than 72 hours after receipt of the request. They have seven calendar days in which to notify enrollees of a redetermination decision. Plans must act on requests for expedited coverage determination no later than 24 hours after receiving the request or the physician's supporting statement, and on expedited redeterminations within 72 hours.[130] Note that beneficiaries who file a coverage determination request after paying out of pocket for a needed prescription are not eligible for expedited consideration. Plans in payment cases must notify the beneficiary and make payment no later than 14 calendar days after receipt of the request.[131]

Unlike under Medicare Part C, unfavorable redeterminations on Part D claims are not automatically forwarded to the IRE. The beneficiary must file a request for reconsideration with the drug plan within 60 calendar days of the redetermination decision.[132] The plan must forward the beneficiary's request to

---

[126] This is required even when the plan uses a claims specialist who is not a physician to conduct the initial review of a Part D coverage determination. 42 C.F.R. §§ 423.562, 423.566, and 423.4.

[127] The prescribing physician or other professional may request a redetermination without having an appointment of representative form filed with the drug plan. An appointment of representative form is still necessary, however, if the prescriber wants to appeal beyond the plan level. 42 C.F.R. § 423.582.

[128] A plan may provide oral notification of either a favorable or an unfavorable expedited redetermination, provided that written confirmation is sent within three calendar days. As with coverage determination notices, redetermination notices must meet regulatory requirements. 75 Fed. Reg. 19,677 (Apr. 15, 2010) (amending 42 C.F.R. § 423.590). Note that effective January 1, 2013, prescribers can request a reconsideration on an enrollee's behalf without obtaining an appointed representative form. CMS, Changes to the Medicare Advantage and the Medicare Prescription Drug Benefit Programs for Contract Year 2013 and Other Changes, 77 Fed. Reg. 22,071 (Apr. 12, 2012) (amending 42 C.F.R. §§ 600 and 602).

[129] 42 C.F.R. §§ 423.560–423.2140.

[130] 42 C.F.R. §§ 423.568, 423.572, 423.582, and 423.590.

[131] 75 Fed. Reg. 19,677 (Apr. 15, 2010) (amending 42 C.F.R. § 423.568(c)). CMS encourages plan sponsors to issue unfavorable payment determinations in fewer than 14 days.

[132] 42 C.F.R. § 423.600.

the IRE within 24 hours if it does not act in a timely manner on a coverage determination or redetermination request.[133] The IRE must issue its reconsideration decision within the same time frames noted above for issuing a redetermination.[134]

A beneficiary may file a written request for an ALJ hearing with the entity specified in the IRE reconsideration notice within 60 calendar days of receiving an unfavorable reconsideration determination, provided the amount remaining in controversy meets the threshold requirement.[135] In determining whether the jurisdictional amount is met in a claim involving the refusal to provide a covered drug, CMS projects the costs of the drug based on the number of refills prescribed for the disputed drug during the calendar year. The ALJ hearing is conducted pursuant to the procedures for hearings of Part A and B appeals, with some modifications.[136] A beneficiary may appeal further to the Council and then to federal court, following procedures for MA plans.[137]

Rules that went into effect in 2010 require ALJs and the Council to issue decisions within the 90-day time frame that applies to Part A and Part B claims. The new rules also add a process for expedited review of all Part D coverage determinations except for those that solely involve a request for payment of drugs already furnished. To qualify for expedited review, the prescriber must indicate, or the ALJ or Council must determine, that applying the standard 90-day time frame may seriously jeopardize the beneficiary's life, health, or ability to regain

---

[133] 42 C.F.R. §§ 423.568(h) and 423.590(c), (e). In 2016, CMS noted that due to many Part D plans' failure to act in a timely manner, "the volume of cases auto-forwarded to the IRE has been significant and sustained over the past several years." *See* CMS, Announcement of Calendar Year (CY) 2017 Medicare Advantage Capitation Rates and Medicare Advantage and Part D Payment Policies and Final Call Letter, pp. 153, (Apr. 4, 2016), *available at* https://www.cms.gov/Medicare/Health-Plans/MedicareAdvtgSpecRateStats/Downloads/Announcement2017.pdf (site visited Aug. 6, 2018).

[134] 42 C.F.R. § 423.600. Note that in a final rule issued in 2018 (CMS-4182-F), 82 Fed. Reg. 16,440 (Apr. 16, 2018), CMS lengthened existing timeframes for adjudicating enrollee payment appeal requests at the redetermination and independent review entity (IRE) reconsideration levels from a maximum of 7 calendar days to a maximum of 14 calendar days.

[135] The amount in controversy, $160 for ALJ in 2019, may increase yearly based on increases in health costs. 83 Fed. Reg. 47,619 (Sept. 20, 2018).

[136] 74 Fed. Reg. 65,340 (Dec. 9, 2009) (adding 42 C.F.R. §§ 423.1968–423.2063). CMS and the IRE cannot be parties at the hearing. They may be participants at the hearing, however, if their request to participate is granted by the ALJ or if the ALJ requests their participation. The limitation on the submission of new evidence at the ALJ hearing in Part A and Part B appeals filed by providers and suppliers also does not apply, although the Part D rules contain some limitations on the submission of new evidence by the beneficiary.

[137] 74 Fed. Reg. 65,340 (Dec. 9, 2009), adding 42 C.F.R. §§ 423.2100–423.2140. The amount in controversy for federal court review in 2019 is $1,630. 83 Fed. Reg. 47,619 (Sept. 20, 2018).

maximum function. The ALJ or Council may consider the standard as having been met if a lower-level adjudicator has granted a request for an expedited hearing.

A beneficiary may make an oral request for an expedited ALJ hearing or Council review, but only after first receiving the written decision from the IRE, in the case of a request for an ALJ hearing, or the written ALJ decision, in the case of Council review. The ALJ/Council must inform the beneficiary, within five days of receipt of the request, as to whether the request for expedited review has been granted. If the request is granted, then the decision must be issued within ten days of receipt of the request for the appeal.[138]

CMS recently finalized significant changes affecting Medicare appeals, particularly at the ALJ level of review. These changes apply to appeals of payment and coverage determinations for items and services furnished to Medicare beneficiaries, enrollees in MA and other Medicare competitive health plans, and enrollees in Medicare PDPs, as well as to appeals of enrollment and entitlement determinations, and certain premium appeals. The final rule became effective on March 20, 2017.[139]

[2] What Constitutes a Coverage Determination

Coverage determinations that trigger appeal rights include a drug plan's decision not to pay for or provide a medication because the drug is not on the plan's formulary, is not considered medically necessary, is furnished by an out-of-network pharmacy, or is not a drug for which Medicare will pay under Part D. Starting in 2011, a dispute involving the availability and amount of the manufacturer discount for brand name drugs in the coverage gap constitutes a coverage determination. An individual may also appeal when a coverage determination is not provided in a timely manner and delay would adversely affect the health of the beneficiary; a request for an exception is rejected; and the individual is dissatisfied with a decision regarding the copayment required for a drug. A coverage determination may be requested by the beneficiary, the beneficiary's appointed representative, the prescribing physician, or another health care professional authorized under state law to write prescriptions.[140]

---

[138] 74 Fed. Reg. 65,340 (Dec. 9, 2009) (adding 42 C.F.R. § 423.2016).

[139] 82 Fed. Reg. 4974 (Jan. 17, 2017). *See* CMS, Changes to the Medicare Claims and Entitlement, Medicare Advantage Organization Determination, and Medicare Prescription Drug Coverage Determination Appeals Procedures, *available at* https://www.federalregister.gov/documents/2017/01/17/2016-32058/medicare-program-changes-to-the-medicare-claims-and-entitlement-medicare-advantage-organization (site visited Aug. 6, 2018).

[140] 42 C.F.R. §§ 423.560 and 423.566.

[C] The Exceptions Process

Part D plans that use formularies to manage drug utilization must also have an exceptions process whereby plan enrollees can seek coverage for a non-formulary drug or request that a formulary drug be provided at a lower tier for cost-sharing (thereby reducing the copayment or coinsurance).[141] As noted above, denial of an exception request constitutes an unfavorable coverage determination from which appeal rights flow. The importance of the exceptions process cannot be overstated; the exceptions process should be used to give beneficiaries access to the medically necessary drugs prescribed for them.

In order to get an exception to require the plan to cover a non-formulary drug, the prescribing doctor or other prescribing professional must show that all of the drugs on any tier of the plan's formulary for treatment of the same condition would not be as effective or would have adverse consequences, or both, for the individual requesting the exception. For this purpose formulary includes the application of cost-savings tools, such as dose restrictions, quantity limits, prior authorization, step therapy, and therapeutic substitution requirements, all of which would result in non-coverage for an otherwise coverable Part D drug. If the plan approves the exception request, the drug will be treated as other drugs on the formulary, so that the beneficiary's cost-sharing counts toward the deductible and the annual out-of-pocket limit. A beneficiary will not have to file a new exception request each time the prescription is refilled. If the beneficiary renews her membership in the plan after the plan year, the plan has the option of continuing coverage of the medicine.[142] If the plan does not adopt this option, the beneficiary would have to reapply for an exception the next year.

Plan enrollees may also use the exceptions process to ask that a drug they require be assigned to a lower tier to reduce their cost-sharing for the drug when the preferred drug would not be as effective or would have adverse consequences; such requests are called tiering exceptions. The exceptions process must address situations where a formulary's tiered copayment structure changes during the year and an enrollee is using a drug affected by the change. However, a plan does not have to cover non-preferred drugs at the lower, generic drug copay level if the plan maintains a separate tier dedicated to generic drugs. Further, if the plan maintains a specialty tier, that is, a formulary copay tier in which it places very high cost and unique items such as genomic and biotech products, it may exclude these very high costs or unique drugs from its exceptions process.[143]

---

[141] 42 U.S.C. § 1395w-104(g), (h); 42 C.F.R. § 423.578.

[142] 42 C.F.R. § 423.578(c)(4).

[143] 42 C.F.R. § 423.578(a)(6), (7). Note that CMS issued a final rule in 2018 (CMS-4182-F), 82 Fed. Reg. 16,440 (Apr. 16, 2018) which somewhat loosens the restrictions on tiering exceptions by basing eligibility for tiering exceptions on the lowest applicable cost-sharing for the tier containing the preferred alternative for treatment. CMS also stated that plans may not exclude a dedicated generic tier from the tiering exceptions process. *See* CMS, Announcement of Calendar Year (CY)

Because exceptions requests are coverage determinations and are governed by the rules for coverage determinations, the plan must act within the time frames for standard coverage determinations (72 hours) or expedited coverage determinations (24 hours), depending on which standards are met. A beneficiary may appeal the denial of an exception request through the appeals process.

Despite its importance, the exceptions process has proven to be both burdensome and lengthy to use. Drug plans may require a doctor's or other prescriber's certificate explaining why the plan enrollee needs the non-formulary drug. Each plan has its own criteria for what should be included in the certificate; many plans have different forms a doctor must use depending on the drug in question. CMS has approved a standard exceptions request form developed by the American Medical Association, the Center for Medicare Advocacy, and other groups but has not required that plans honor the standard form. Each plan determines how it will evaluate the doctor's determination that the enrollee requires a non-formulary drug, including establishing a process to compare the medical and scientific evidence about the safety and effectiveness of the non-formulary and formulary drugs. Most plans require extensive documentation, sometimes asking for both the beneficiary's own medical records and medical journals. Because the Part D appeals process follows the appeals process for MA plans, it involves the exhaustion of multiple layers in order to get a face-to-face hearing.

[D] Notice and Other Due Process Issues

The PDP has the responsibility for giving its plan enrollees notice of a change in the formulary or notice that coverage for a requested drug has been denied. The plan must provide written notice of a formulary change, including a change in tiered cost-sharing, 60 days in advance of the change to those enrollees who use the prescription, as well as to CMS, prescribing physicians, and pharmacies. The notice must include the change, other available drugs, and a description of the exceptions process. Alternatively, a plan can choose to give an enrollee the 60 days' notice and a 60-day supply of the drug when a refill request is presented to the plan.[144] When the formulary change is a non-maintenance change—that is, it does not involve changes based on the availability of a new generic drug, new

2018 Medicare Advantage Capitation Rates and Medicare Advantage and Part D Payment Policies and Final Call Letter (Apr. 3, 2017) (providing several policy clarifications concerning tiering exceptions), *available at* https://www.cms.gov/Medicare/Health-Plans/MedicareAdvtgSpecRateStats/Downloads/Announcement2018.pdf (site visited Aug. 6, 2018). These clarifications include, e.g., that "approval of a tiering exception is to the lowest applicable tier when alternative drugs are in multiple lower tiers." *See* CMS, "Announcement of Calendar Year (CY) 2018 Medicare Advantage Capitation Rates and Medicare Advantage and Part D Payment Policies and Final Call Letter" at p. 143–146.

[144] 42 C.F.R. § 423.120(b)(5).

clinical guidelines, or FDA approval—plan enrollees who are currently taking the affected drug are exempt from the change for the plan year.[145]

How enrollees learn of their rights when coverage of or payment for a prescription is denied at the pharmacy has been problematic. The regulations place the burden on the plan to provide notice of appeal rights for coverage determinations. CMS states that the pharmacy is not required to provide notice of the reasons for the denial or of the appeals process.[146] Until 2012, each drug plan had to arrange with its network pharmacies to either post at the pharmacy or distribute a generic notice that tells enrollees to contact the plan if they disagree with the information provided by the pharmacist; most pharmacies satisfied this obligation by merely posting a written notice about appeal rights. As noted above, though, for appeals filed on or after January 1, 2012, PDP sponsors must arrange with their network providers to distribute written notices at the pharmacy instructing enrollees how to contact their plans to obtain a coverage determination or request an exception if they disagree with the information provided by the pharmacist.[147]

Although the requirement that pharmacies distribute a generic notice at the point of sale is an improvement for enrollees, this approach does not consider the extra burden placed on the enrollee, who must still act on the notice, or the practicalities of providing notice when an enrollee uses a non-network pharmacy.

The appeals process also does not provide adequate protection to someone who must appeal to continue receiving coverage of a drug he or she has been using. Unlike under Medicaid, Part D does not provide for continued access to the medication if an appeal is filed on a timely basis. Thus, dually eligible individuals whose prescription drug coverage will be paid for under Medicare instead of Medicaid may lose an important protection. CMS has indicated in sub-regulatory guidance that Part D plans must provide a continued supply of a medicine to nursing home residents through the exceptions process.

In response to some of these appeals challenges faced by Part D enrollees, CMS announced in its 2016 Call Letter that it plans to move forward with efforts to improve the Medicare Advantage and Part D appeals process for Medicare beneficiaries, including improving Part D denial notices, clarifying plan sponsors' obligations, expanding data collection regarding Part D appeals, and exploring a

---

[145] PDB Manual, Ch. 6: § 30.3.3.3.

[146] 70 Fed. Reg. 4194, 4349–50 (Jan. 28, 2005).

[147] 76 Fed. Reg. 21,573 (Apr. 15, 2011) (amending 42 C.F.R. § 423.128); 76 Fed. Reg. 21,575 (Apr. 15, 2011) (amending 42 C.F.R. § 423.562). Note that as of October 2017, Part D plan sponsors are required to use an updated Notice of Denial of Medicare Prescription Drug Coverage (Form CMS-10146). The notice and corresponding form instructions are *available at* http://www.cms.gov/Medicare/Appeals-and-Grievances/MedPrescriptDrugApplGriev/PlanNoticesAndDocuments.html (site visited Aug. 6, 2018).

Note that a final Part D rule issued in 2015 revises 42 C.F.R. § 423.562(a)(3) to remove reference of an enrollee's "disagreement with information provided by the pharmacist" as a condition requiring delivery of the pharmacy notice. 80 Fed. Reg. 7912, 7952 (Feb. 12, 2015).

streamlined Part D appeals process that is initiated when a request for coverage of a prescription drug is denied at the pharmacy counter. Among other things, the Final Call Letter announced a pilot program to help identify options for resolving certain point-of-sale claims rejections without an enrollee having to request a coverage determination from a plan. In addition, CMS indicated that it planned to move forward with improved data collection concerning Part D appeals data, with an implementation target of 2018.[148]

§ 11.10 CONCLUSION

The Medicare Part D prescription drug program continues to evolve. Advocates should monitor plan changes to their premiums, formularies, and/or cost-sharing structures. Each year a substantial number of LIS-eligible individuals must choose a different plan because their plan no longer qualifies for a subsidy to pay the entire premium; those who are in the drug plans to which they were assigned by CMS are automatically reassigned to a new plan by CMS. All enrollees may need to change plans or pursue exceptions if the plan they chose eliminates drugs from its formulary or adds utilization management tools.

---

[148] CMS, "Announcement of Calendar Year (CY) 2016 Medicare Advantage Capitation Rates and Medicare Advantage and Part D Payment Policies and Final Call Letter" (Apr. 6, 2015), *available at* http://www.cms.gov/Medicare/Health-Plans/MedicareAdvtgSpecRateStats/Downloads/Announcement2016.pdf (site visited Aug. 6, 2018). CMS noted in its 2017 Call Letter that after analyzing the results of the pilot, it is not imposing any operational requirements for the 2017 plan year. *See* CMS, Announcement of Calendar Year (CY) 2017 Medicare Advantage Capitation Rates and Medicare Advantage and Part D Payment Policies and Final Call Letter (Apr. 4, 2016). Neither the 2018 or 2019 call letters included additional significant operational guidance.

APPENDIX 11-1 MEDICARE PRESCRIPTION DRUG PLAN (PART D) APPEALS PROCESS*

The following chart provides an overview of the appeals process for the Medicare Prescription Drug Plan (Plan D). For more information on each level, click on the level name on the left hand side of this document or visit http://www.hhs.gov/omha/

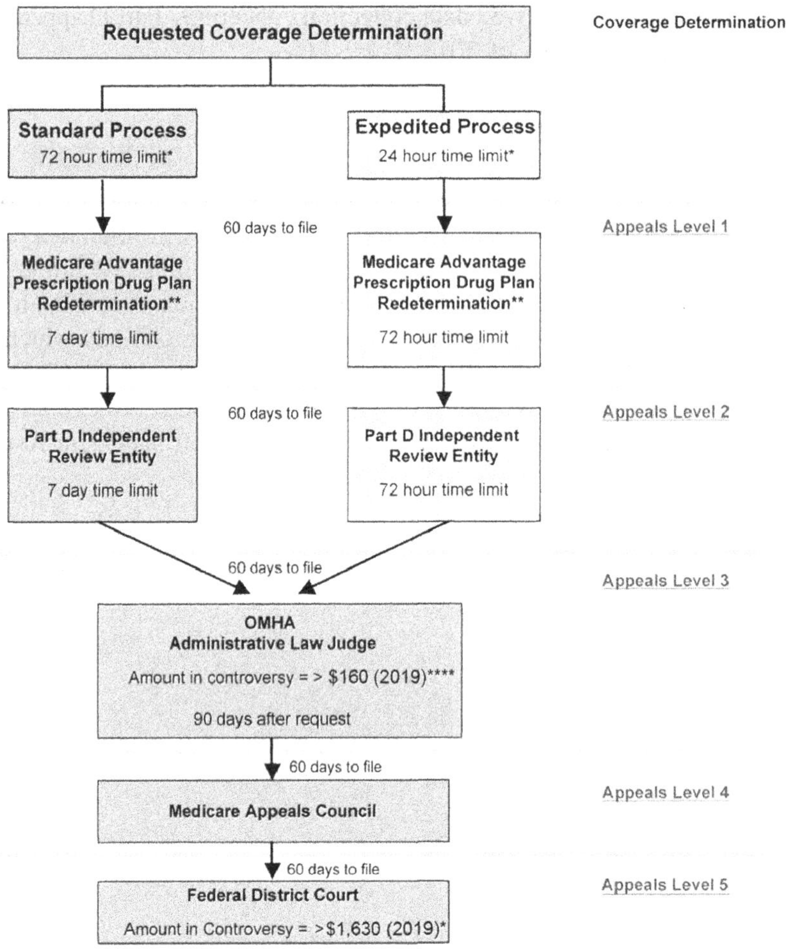

* The adjudication timeframes generally begin when the request is received by the plan sponsor. However, if the request involves an exception request, the adjudication timeframe begins when the plan sponsor receives the physician's supporting statement.

** A request for a coverage determination includes a request for a tiering exception or a formulary exception. A request for a coverage determination may be filed by the enrollee, the enrollee's appointed representative, or the enrollee's physician.

*** Starting in 2005, the AIC requirements for an ALJ hearing and Federal District Court are adjusted in accordance with the medical care component of the consumer price index.

****See 83 FR 47,619 (Sept. 20, 2018)

* On January 1, 2011, for the standard process in coverage determination level, Part D plan sponsors shall notify an enrollee of a payment decision no later than 14 calendar-days after receiving a reimbursement request instead of within a 72-hour time period. In addition, if the decision is partially or fully favorable, the plan sponsor must also make a payment within the same 14 calendar-day period. 75 Fed. Reg. 19,780 (Apr. 15, 2010), revising 42 C.F.R. § 423.568(b).

TABLE OF CASES

References are to sections.

H

I

J

K

L

M

N

O

P

TABLE OF AUTHORITIES

A complete table of contents for each chapter is included at the beginning of the chapter.

CODE OF FEDERAL REGULATIONS

BALANCED BUDGET ACT OF 1997 (BBA)

BIPARTISAN BUDGET ACT OF 2015

CONSOLIDATED OMNIBUS BUDGET RECONCILIATION ACT OF 1985

DEFICIT REDUCTION ACT OF 2005 (DRA)

EXTENSION ACT OF 2010

GENETIC INFORMATION NONDISCRIMINATION ACT OF 2008

HEALTH CARE AND EDUCATION RECONCILIATION ACT OF 2010 (HCERA)

MEDICARE ACCESS AND CHIP REAUTHORIZATION ACT OF 2015

MEDICARE CATASTROPHIC COVERAGE ACT OF 1988

MEDICARE IMPROVEMENTS FOR PATIENTS AND PROVIDERS ACT OF 2008 (MIPPA)

MEDICARE,MEDICAID, AND SCHIP BALANCED BUDGET REFINEMENT ACT OF 1999 (BBRA)

MEDICARE,MEDICAID, AND SCHIP BENEFITS IMPROVEMENT AND PROTECTION ACT OF 2000 (BIPA)

MEDICARE,MEDICAID, AND SCHIP EXTENSION ACT OF 2007

MEDICARE PRESCRIPTION DRUG, IMPROVEMENT, AND MODERNIZATION ACT OF 2003 (MMA)

MEDICARE POST-ACUTE CARE TRANSFORMATION ACT OF 2014 (IMPACT ACT)

NOTICE OF OBSERVATION TREATMENT AND IMPLICATION FOR CARE ELIGIBILITY ACT (NOTICE ACT)

NURSING HOME REFORM LAW

OMNIBUS BUDGET RECONCILIATION ACT OF 1980

OMNIBUS BUDGET RECONCILIATION ACT OF 1987

OMNI BUS BUDGET RECONCILIATION ACT OF 1989

OMNIBUS BUDGET RECONCILIATION ACT OF 1990

PAPERWORK REDUCTION ACT (PRA)

PATIENT PROTECTION AND AFFORDABLE CARE ACT OF 2010 (PPACA)

PROTECTING ACCESS TO MEDICARE ACT OF 2014 (PAMA)

QI,TMA, AND ABSTINENCE PROGRAMS EXTENSION AND HURRICANE KATRINA UNEMPLOYMENT RELIEF ACT OF 2005

REHABILITATION ACT OF 1973

SOCIAL SECURITY ACT

SOCIAL SECURITY AMENDMENTS OF 1972

SOCIAL SECURITY DISABILITY AMENDMENTS OF 1980

TAX RELIEF AND HEALTH CARE ACT OF 2006

TICKET TO WORK AND WORK INCENTIVES IMPROVEMENT ACT OF 1999

21ST CENTURY CURES ACT

INDEX

References are to sections.

B

C

I

J

L

M

N

O

P

Q

T

U

V